How to get the most from this textbook

1 PREPARING FOR CLASS: Read the Book

FEATURE	DESCRIPTION	BENEFIT	PAGE
■ Chapter Opener	Provides a colorful photo and a mathematical context to make the subject of each chapter more exciting and relevant for the students.	Students are immediately motivated and engaged to learn how calculus applies to real-world settings.	58
■ Chapter Overview	Chapters begin with an overview to give students a sense of what they are going to learn.	This roadmap of the chapter also describes how the different topics are connected under one big idea.	59
■ Objectives and Topics	The objectives of the section are summarized, and the topics are briefly listed.	Teachers and students will see how learning objectives are achieved through studying particular topics to gain essential knowledge as the course unfolds.	59
■ Vocabulary and Properties	Vocabulary is highlighted in yellow, and Properties are boxed in green.	Allows for easy reference and review when preparing for exams.	74, 79
■ Margin Notes and Tips	*Margin Notes* and *Tips* appear throughout the text on various topics.	*Tips* offer practical advice; *Margin Notes* include historical information, hints about examples, and provide additional insight to help students avoid common pitfalls.	46, 121, 219

2 PRACTICE: Work the Problems

FEATURE	DESCRIPTION	BENEFIT	PAGE
■ Now Try *Now Try Exercise 1*	Each example ends with a suggestion to *Now Try* a related exercise.	This is an easy way for students to check their essential knowledge of the material while reading each section, instead of waiting until the end of the section or chapter. (MPACs 2, 3, 4, 5, 6)	89, 90
■ Quick Review	Each exercise set begins with *Quick Review* exercises and includes section references from earlier chapters where relevant skills were covered.	Helps students to review the skills needed in the exercise set and make connections among concepts, reminding them again that mathematics is not modular. (MPACs 2, 4)	93
■ Exercises	Carefully graded exercises, from routine to challenging, follow the *Quick Review* exercises.	Allow students to apply what they have learned in the section and engage in the recommended Mathematical Practices for AP Calculus (MPACs).	93, 95
■ Standardized Test Questions	These include two true-false problems with justifications and four multiple-choice questions.	Students can use these test questions to find out whether they have mastered the material that they have just covered. (MPACs 1, 2, 3, 4, 5)	95

2 PRACTICE: Work the Problems (continued)

FEATURE	DESCRIPTION	BENEFIT	PAGE
▪ Quick Quiz for AP Preparation	A cumulative quiz appears after every two or three sections and includes three multiple-choice questions and one AP-type free-response question.	Provides another apportunity for students to review their understanding as they progress through each chapter. (MPACs 1, 2, 3, 4, 5, 6)	96
▪ Explorations	*Explorations* exercises appear throughout the text. Some of these are technology-based, and others involve exploring mathematical ideas and connections.	Students are provided with the perfect opportunity to become active learners and to discover mathematics on their own. (MPACs 1, 2, 4, 5)	72, 95
▪ Writing to Learn	Students are asked to write out solutions in prose.	These questions provide a good way to fulfill writing across the curriculum requirements. (MPACs 5, 6)	94
▪ Group Activity	Students can work on these problems individually or as group projects. Worksheets are available in the Teacher's Resource Manual.	Allows for collaborative learning. (MPACs 1, 2, 4, 6)	96
▪ Extending the Ideas Exercises	These questions go beyond what is presented in the textbook.	They offer more challenging exercise options and extend the scope of the book's material. (MPACs 1, 2, 3, 4, 5, 6)	96

3 REVIEW: Study for Quizzes and Tests

FEATURE	DESCRIPTION	BENEFIT	PAGE
▪ Key Terms	Each chapter concludes with a list of *Key Terms* with references back to where they are covered in the chapter.	This allows students to both quickly see which terms they need know and to review the definitions with ease. (MPACs 1, 2)	96–97
▪ Review Exercises	Represent the full range of exercises covered in the chapter.	By covering all the ideas developed in the chapter, students are given more opportunity to practice and review the material. (MPACs 1, 2, 3, 4, 5, 6)	97–99
▪ AP Examination Preparation	Appears at the end of each set of chapter review exercises and includes three free-response questions of the AP* type.	Gives students the additional opportunity to practice skills and problem-solving techniques needed for the AP Calculus Exam. (MPACs 2, 3, 4, 5, 6)	99

Calculus

Graphical, Numerical, Algebraic

FIFTH EDITION

AP® Edition

Calculus

Graphical, Numerical, Algebraic

FIFTH EDITION

AP® Edition

Ross L. Finney

Franklin D. Demana
THE OHIO STATE UNIVERSITY

Bert K. Waits
THE OHIO STATE UNIVERSITY

Daniel Kennedy
BAYLOR SCHOOL

David M. Bressoud
MACALESTER COLLEGE

PEARSON

Boston Columbus Hoboken Indianapolis New York San Francisco Amsterdam
Cape Town Dubai London Madrid Milan Munich Paris Montreal Toronto Delhi
Mexico City São Paulo Sydney Hong Kong Seoul Singapore Taipei Tokyo

Editor in Chief	Anne Kelly
Manager, Product Management and Marketing	Jackie Flynn
Assistant Editor	Judith Garber
Program Manager	Danielle Miller
Project Manager	Mary Sanger
Program Management Team Lead	Marianne Stepanian
Project Management Team Lead	Christina Lepre
Media Producer	Jean Choe
MathXL Content Developer	Kristina Evans
Senior Author Support/ Technology Specialist	Joe Vetere
Rights and Permissions Project Manager	Maureen Griffin
Procurement Specialist	Carol Melville
Associate Director of Design	Andrea Nix
Program Design Lead	Beth Paquin
Text Design, Composition, Illustrations, Production Coordination	Cenveo® Publisher Services
Cover Design	Cenveo® Publisher Services
Cover Image	Jule Berlin/Shutterstock

Library of Congress Cataloging-in-Publication Data
Finney, Ross L., author.
  Calculus : graphical, numerical, algebraic / Ross L. Finney, Franklin D. Demana, The Ohio State University, Bert K. Waits, The Ohio State University, Daniel Kennedy, Baylor School, David M. Bressoud. – 5th edition.
    pages cm
  ISBN 0-13-331161-9 – ISBN 0-13-331162-7
  1. Calculus–Textbooks. I. Demana, Franklin D., 1938- author. II. Waits, Bert K., author. III. Kennedy, Daniel, 1946- author. IV. Title.
    QA303.2.F547 2016
    515–dc23
                                                                                      2014031803
    13   20

www.pearsonschool.com/advanced

ISBN 13: 978-0-13-331161-7
(high school binding)
ISBN 10: 0-13-331161-9
(high school binding)

Dedication

This fifth edition of our calculus book is dedicated to the memory of our friend and coauthor, Bert K. (Hank) Waits, whose larger-than-life personality and infectious enthusiasm for mathematics education inspired two generations of teachers and, through them, millions of mathematics students.

Foreword

If you could wave a magic wand and assemble your dream team of authors for an AP Calculus textbook, you would be very pleased if the group included the likes of Ross Finney, Frank Demana, Bert Waits, Dan Kennedy, and David Bressoud. I feel blessed to have known and worked closely with every one of them from as far back as 1989. With a pedigree that includes George Thomas in the storied authorship bloodline, this book represents the finest combination of excellent writing, creative insight, terrific problems, and captivating explorations. A dream team indeed!

Any teacher in search of a textbook for use in an AP Calculus class should look critically at whether or not the book is faithful to the philosophy and goals of the course, as well as the topic outline, each described in the AP Calculus Course Description. On both accounts, the FDWKB text shines brightly. True to its title, care is taken to attend to a genuine multirepresentational approach. You'll find problems and discourse involving graphs, tables, symbolic definitions, and verbal descriptions. And the text covers every topic that is tested on the AP exams. Dan Kennedy, who joined the author team with the 2003 publication, and David Bressoud, its most recent addition, both contribute an intimate knowledge of the AP Calculus course. The two share a familiarity with the program borne from years of service. Back in the mid 1990s, when I saw Dan describe how to teach series with an approach that ultimately became an integral part of Chapter 10 of the current edition, I knew it was the way to go. My students have used this text, and that approach, for many years with great success. David's presence on the team brings his passion both for the history of calculus and for its careful and precise presentation. He describes the contributions to the development of calculus by great thinkers that preceded Newton and Leibniz. He also illuminates the idea of using the derivative as a measure of sensitivity.

This text is a proven winner that just keeps getting better. With the new course framework rolling out, it is a perfect fit for any AP Calculus class today, and promises to be for years to come.

Mark Howell
Gonzaga College High School
Washington, DC

Mark Howell has taught AP Calculus at Gonzaga High School for more than thirty years. He has served the AP Calculus community at the AP Reading as a reader, table leader, and question leader for eighteen years, and for four years he served as a member of the AP Calculus Development Committee. A College Board consultant for more than twenty years, Mark has led workshops and summer institutes throughout the United States and around the world. In 1993 he won a state Presidential Award in the District of Columbia, and in 1999 he won a Tandy Technology Scholars Award and the Siemens Foundation Award for Advanced Placement Teachers. He is the author of the current AP Teacher's Guide for AP Calculus, *and is co-author with Martha Montgomery of the popular AP Calculus review book* Be Prepared for the AP Calculus Exam *from Skylight Publishing.*

About the Authors

Ross L. Finney

Ross Finney received his undergraduate degree and Ph.D. from the University of Michigan at Ann Arbor. He taught at the University of Illinois at Urbana–Champaign from 1966 to 1980 and at the Massachusetts Institute of Technology (MIT) from 1980 to 1990. Dr. Finney worked as a consultant for the Educational Development Center in Newton, Massachusetts. He directed the Undergraduate Mathematics and its Applications Project (U MAP) from 1977 to 1984 and was founding editor of the *UMAP Journal*. In 1984, he traveled with a Mathematical Association of America (MAA) delegation to China on a teacher education project through People to People International.

Dr. Finney co-authored a number of Addison-Wesley textbooks, including *Calculus; Calculus and Analytic Geometry; Elementary Differential Equations with Linear Algebra;* and *Calculus for Engineers and Scientists*. Dr. Finney's co-authors were deeply saddened by the death of their colleague and friend on August 4, 2000.

Franklin D. Demana

Frank Demana received his master's degree in mathematics and his Ph.D. from Michigan State University. Currently, he is Professor Emeritus of Mathematics at The Ohio State University. As an active supporter of the use of technology to teach and learn mathematics, he is co-founder of the international Teachers Teaching with Technology (T^3) professional development program. He has been the director and co-director of more than $10 million of National Science Foundation (NSF) and foundational grant activities, including a $3 million grant from the U.S. Department of Education Mathematics and Science Educational Research program awarded to The Ohio State University. Along with frequent presentations at professional meetings, he has published a variety of articles in the areas of computer- and calculator-enhanced mathematics instruction. Dr. Demana is also co-founder (with Bert Waits) of the annual International Conference on Technology in Collegiate Mathematics (ICTCM). He is co-recipient of the 1997 Glenn Gilbert National Leadership Award presented by the National Council of Supervisors of Mathematics, and co-recipient of the 1998 Christofferson-Fawcett Mathematics Education Award presented by the Ohio Council of Teachers of Mathematics.

Dr. Demana co-authored *Precalculus: Graphical, Numerical, Algebraic; Essential Algebra: A Calculator Approach; Transition to College Mathematics; College Algebra and Trigonometry: A Graphing Approach; College Algebra: A Graphing Approach; Precalculus: Functions and Graphs*; and *Intermediate Algebra: A Graphing Approach*.

Bert K. Waits

Bert Waits received his Ph.D. from The Ohio State University and taught Ohio State students for many years before retiring as Professor Emeritus of Mathematics. Dr. Waits co-founded the international Teachers Teaching with Technology (T^3) professional development program and was co-director or principal investigator on several large projects funded by the National Science Foundation. Active in both the Mathematical Association of America and the National Council of Teachers of Mathematics, he published more than 70 articles in professional journals and conducted countless lectures, workshops, and minicourses on how to use computer technology to enhance the teaching and learning of mathematics. Dr. Waits was co-recipient of the 1997 Glenn Gilbert National Leadership Award presented by the National Council of Supervisors of Mathematics and of the 1998 Christofferson-Fawcett Mathematics Education Award presented by the Ohio Council of Teachers of Mathematics. He was the co-founder (with Frank Demana) of the ICTCM and was one of six authors of the high school portion of the groundbreaking 1989 *NCTM Standards*. Dr. Waits was hard at work on revisions for the fifth edition of this calculus textbook when he died prematurely on July 27, 2014, leaving behind a powerful legacy in the legions of teachers whom he inspired.

Dr. Waits coauthored *Precalculus: Graphical, Numerical, Algebraic; College Algebra and Trigonometry: A Graphing Approach; College Algebra: A Graphing Approach; Precalculus: Functions and Graphs*; and *Intermediate Algebra: A Graphing Approach*.

Daniel Kennedy

Dan Kennedy received his undergraduate degree from the College of the Holy Cross and his master's degree and Ph.D. in mathematics from the University of North Carolina at Chapel Hill. Since 1973 he has taught mathematics at the Baylor School in Chattanooga, Tennessee, where he holds the Cartter Lupton Distinguished Professorship. Dr. Kennedy joined the Advanced Placement® Calculus Test Development Committee in 1986, then in 1990 became the first high school teacher in 35 years to chair that committee. It was during his tenure as chair that the program moved to require graphing calculators and laid the early groundwork for the 1998 reform of the Advanced Placement Calculus curriculum. The author of the 1997 *Teacher's Guide—AP® Calculus*, Dr. Kennedy has conducted more than 50 workshops and institutes for high school calculus teachers. His articles on mathematics teaching have appeared in the *Mathematics Teacher* and the *American Mathematical Monthly*, and he is a frequent speaker on education reform at professional and civic meetings. Dr. Kennedy was named a Tandy Technology Scholar in 1992 and a Presidential Award winner in 1995.

Dr. Kennedy coauthored *Precalculus: Graphical, Numerical, Algebraic; Prentice Hall Algebra I; Prentice Hall Geometry;* and *Prentice Hall Algebra 2.*

David M. Bressoud

David Bressoud received his undergraduate degree from Swarthmore College and Ph.D. from Temple University. He taught at Penn State from 1977 to 1994, is currently DeWitt Wallace Professor of Mathematics at Macalester College, and is a former president of the Mathematical Association of America. He is the author of several textbooks on number theory, combinatorics, vector calculus, and real analysis, all with a strong historical emphasis. He taught AP Calculus at the State College Area High School in 1990–91, began as an AP Reader in 1993, and served on the AP Calculus Test Development Committee for six years and as its chair for three of those years. He currently serves on the College Board Mathematical Sciences Academic Advisory Committee. He has been Principal Investigator for numerous grants, including two large National Science Foundation grants to study Characteristics of Successful Programs in College Calculus and Progress Through Calculus. He also writes *Launchings,* a monthly blog on issues of undergraduate mathematics education.

Contents

CHAPTER 1

Prerequisites for Calculus   2

1.1 Linear Functions   3

Increments and Slope • Point-Slope Equation of a Linear Function • Other Linear Equation Forms • Parallel and Perpendicular Lines • Applications of Linear Functions • Solving Two Linear Equations Simultaneously

1.2 Functions and Graphs   13

Functions • Domains and Ranges • Viewing and Interpreting Graphs • Even Functions and Odd Functions—Symmetry • Piecewise-Defined Functions • Absolute Value Function • Composite Functions

1.3 Exponential Functions   23

Exponential Growth • Exponential Decay • Compound Interest • The Number e

1.4 Parametric Equations   29

Relations • Circles • Ellipses • Lines and Other Curves

1.5 Inverse Functions and Logarithms   36

One-to-One Functions • Inverses • Finding Inverses • Logarithmic Functions • Properties of Logarithms • Applications

1.6 Trigonometric Functions   45

Radian Measure • Graphs of Trigonometric Functions • Periodicity • Even and Odd Trigonometric Functions • Transformations of Trigonometric Graphs • Inverse Trigonometric Functions

Key Terms   53

Review Exercises   54

CHAPTER 2

Limits and Continuity   58

2.1 Rates of Change and Limits   59

Average and Instantaneous Speed • Definition of Limit • Properties of Limits • One-Sided and Two-Sided Limits • Squeeze Theorem

2.2 Limits Involving Infinity   70

Finite Limits as $x \to \pm\infty$ • Squeeze Theorem Revisited • Infinite Limits as $x \to a$ • End Behavior Models • "Seeing" Limits as $x \to \pm\infty$

2.3 Continuity   78

Continuity at a Point • Continuous Functions • Algebraic Combinations • Composites • Intermediate Value Theorem for Continuous Functions

2.4 Rates of Change, Tangent Lines, and Sensitivity   87

Average Rates of Change • Tangent to a Curve • Slope of a Curve • Normal to a Curve • Speed Revisited • Sensitivity

Key Terms   96

Review Exercises   97

CHAPTER 3

Derivatives   100

3.1 **Derivative of a Function**   101

Definition of Derivative • Notation • Relationships Between the Graphs of f and f' • Graphing the Derivative from Data • One-Sided Derivatives

3.2 **Differentiability**   111

How $f'(a)$ Might Fail to Exist • Differentiability Implies Local Linearity • Numerical Derivatives on a Calculator • Differentiability Implies Continuity • Intermediate Value Theorem for Derivatives

3.3 **Rules for Differentiation**   118

Positive Integer Powers, Multiples, Sums, and Differences • Products and Quotients • Negative Integer Powers of x • Second and Higher Order Derivatives

3.4 **Velocity and Other Rates of Change**   129

Instantaneous Rates of Change • Motion Along a Line • Sensitivity to Change • Derivatives in Economics

3.5 **Derivatives of Trigonometric Functions**   143

Derivative of the Sine Function • Derivative of the Cosine Function • Simple Harmonic Motion • Jerk • Derivatives of the Other Basic Trigonometric Functions

Key Terms   150

Review Exercises   150

CHAPTER 4

More Derivatives   154

4.1 **Chain Rule**   155

Derivative of a Composite Function • "Outside-Inside" Rule • Repeated Use of the Chain Rule • Slopes of Parametrized Curves • Power Chain Rule

4.2 **Implicit Differentiation**   164

Implicitly Defined Functions • Lenses, Tangents, and Normal Lines • Derivatives of Higher Order • Rational Powers of Differentiable Functions

4.3 **Derivatives of Inverse Trigonometric Functions**   173

Derivatives of Inverse Functions • Derivative of the Arcsine • Derivative of the Arctangent • Derivative of the Arcsecant • Derivatives of the Other Three

4.4 **Derivatives of Exponential and Logarithmic Functions**   180

Derivative of e^x • Derivative of a^x • Derivative of $\ln x$ • Derivative of $\log_a x$ • Power Rule for Arbitrary Real Powers

Key Terms   189

Review Exercises   189

CHAPTER 5

Applications of Derivatives   192

5.1 **Extreme Values of Functions**   193

Absolute (Global) Extreme Values • Local (Relative) Extreme Values • Finding Extreme Values

5.2 **Mean Value Theorem**   202

Mean Value Theorem • Physical Interpretation • Increasing and Decreasing Functions • Other Consequences

5.3   Connecting f' and f'' with the Graph of f   211

First Derivative Test for Local Extrema • Concavity • Points of Inflection • Second Derivative Test for Local Extrema • Learning About Functions from Derivatives

5.4   Modeling and Optimization   224

A Strategy for Optimization • Examples from Mathematics • Examples from Business and Industry • Examples from Economics • Modeling Discrete Phenomena with Differentiable Functions

5.5   Linearization, Sensitivity, and Differentials   238

Linear Approximation • Differentials • Sensitivity Analysis • Absolute, Relative, and Percentage Change • Sensitivity to Change • Newton's Method • Newton's Method May Fail

5.6   Related Rates   252

Related Rate Equations • Solution Strategy • Simulating Related Motion

Key Terms   261

Review Exercises   262

CHAPTER 6

The Definite Integral   268

6.1   Estimating with Finite Sums   269

Accumulation Problems as Area • Rectangular Approximation Method (RAM) • Volume of a Sphere • Cardiac Output

6.2   Definite Integrals   281

Riemann Sums • Terminology and Notation of Integration • Definite Integral and Area • Constant Functions • Definite Integral as an Accumulator Function • Integrals on a Calculator • Discontinuous Integrable Functions

6.3   Definite Integrals and Antiderivatives   293

Properties of Definite Integrals • Average Value of a Function • Mean Value Theorem for Definite Integrals • Connecting Differential and Integral Calculus

6.4   Fundamental Theorem of Calculus   302

Fundamental Theorem, Antiderivative Part • Graphing the Function $\int_a^x f(t)\, dt$ • Fundamental Theorem, Evaluation Part • Area Connection • Analyzing Antiderivatives Graphically

6.5   Trapezoidal Rule   314

Trapezoidal Approximations • Other Algorithms • Error Analysis

Key Terms   323

Review Exercises   323

CHAPTER 7

Differential Equations and Mathematical Modeling   328

7.1   Slope Fields and Euler's Method   329

Differential Equations • Slope Fields • Euler's Method

7.2   Antidifferentiation by Substitution   340

Indefinite Integrals • Leibniz Notation and Antiderivatives • Substitution in Indefinite Integrals • Substitution in Definite Integrals

7.3   Antidifferentiation by Parts   349

Product Rule in Integral Form • Solving for the Unknown Integral • Tabular Integration
• Inverse Trigonometric and Logarithmic Functions

7.4   Exponential Growth and Decay   358

Separable Differential Equations • Law of Exponential Change • Continuously
Compounded Interest • Radioactivity • Modeling Growth with Other Bases
• Newton's Law of Cooling

7.5   Logistic Growth   369

How Populations Grow • Partial Fractions • The Logistic Differential Equation
• Logistic Growth Models

Key Terms   378

Review Exercises   379

CHAPTER 8

Applications of Definite Integrals   384

8.1   Accumulation and Net Change   385

Linear Motion Revisited • General Strategy • Consumption over Time • Coming and
Going • Net Change from Data • Density • Work

8.2   Areas in the Plane   397

Area Between Curves • Area Enclosed by Intersecting Curves • Boundaries with
Changing Functions • Integrating with Respect to y • Saving Time with Geometry
Formulas

8.3   Volumes   406

Volume as an Integral • Square Cross Sections • Circular Cross Sections • Cylindrical
Shells • Other Cross Sections

8.4   Lengths of Curves   420

A Sine Wave • Length of a Smooth Curve • Vertical Tangents, Corners, and Cusps

8.5   Applications from Science and Statistics   427

Work Revisited • Fluid Force and Fluid Pressure • Normal Probabilities

Key Terms   438

Review Exercises   438

CHAPTER 9

Sequences, L'Hospital's Rule, and Improper Integrals   442

9.1   Sequences   443

Defining a Sequence • Arithmetic and Geometric Sequences • Graphing a Sequence
• Limit of a Sequence

9.2   L'Hospital's Rule   452

Indeterminate Form $0/0$ • Indeterminate Forms ∞/∞, $\infty \cdot 0$, and $\infty - \infty$
• Indeterminate Forms 1^∞, 0^0, ∞^0

9.3   Relative Rates of Growth   461

Comparing Rates of Growth • Using L'Hospital's Rule to Compare Growth Rates
• Sequential Versus Binary Search

9.4 **Improper Integrals**   467

Infinite Limits of Integration • Integrands with Infinite Discontinuities • Test for Convergence and Divergence • Applications

Key Terms   477

Review Exercises   478

CHAPTER 10

Infinite Series   480

10.1 **Power Series**   481

Geometric Series • Representing Functions by Series • Differentiation and Integration • Identifying a Series

10.2 **Taylor Series**   492

Constructing a Series • Series for sin x and cos x • Beauty Bare • Maclaurin and Taylor Series • Combining Taylor Series • Table of Maclaurin Series

10.3 **Taylor's Theorem**   503

Taylor Polynomials • The Remainder • Bounding the Remainder • Analyzing Truncation Error • Euler's Formula

10.4 **Radius of Convergence**   513

Convergence • nth-Term Test • Comparing Nonnegative Series • Ratio Test • Endpoint Convergence

10.5 **Testing Convergence at Endpoints**   523

Integral Test • Harmonic Series and p-series • Comparison Tests • Alternating Series • Absolute and Conditional Convergence • Intervals of Convergence • A Word of Caution

Key Terms   537

Review Exercises   537

CHAPTER 11

Parametric, Vector, and Polar Functions   542

11.1 **Parametric Functions**   543

Parametric Curves in the Plane • Slope and Concavity • Arc Length • Cycloids

11.2 **Vectors in the Plane**   550

Two-Dimensional Vectors • Vector Operations • Modeling Planar Motion • Velocity, Acceleration, and Speed • Displacement and Distance Traveled

11.3 **Polar Functions**   561

Polar Coordinates • Polar Curves • Slopes of Polar Curves • Areas Enclosed by Polar Curves • A Small Polar Gallery

Key Terms   574

Review Exercises   575

APPENDICES

A1 Formulas from Precalculus Mathematics 577

A2 A Formal Definition of Limit 583

A3 A Proof of the Chain Rule 591

A4 Hyperbolic Functions 592

A5 A Very Brief Table of Integrals 601

Glossary 604

Selected Answers 615

Applications Index 672

Subject Index 676

To the Teacher

The fifth edition of *Calculus: Graphical, Numerical, Algebraic*, AP* Edition, by Finney, Demana, Waits, Kennedy, and Bressoud completely supports the content, philosophy, and goals of the Advanced Placement (AP*) Calculus courses (AB and BC).

The College Board has recently finished a lengthy and thorough review of the AP* Calculus courses to ensure that they continue to keep pace with the best college and university courses that are taught with similar educational goals. This review has resulted in a repackaging of the course descriptions in terms of big ideas, enduring understandings, learning objectives, and essential knowledge, but the learning goals remain essentially the same. That has allowed us to retain the overall flow of our previous edition and concentrate our attention on how we might be more helpful to you and your students in certain parts of the course.

A very broad look at the overall goals of this textbook is given in the following bulleted summary. Although these are not explicit goals of the AP program and do not include all of the learning objectives in the new AP Curriculum Framework, they do reflect the intentions of the AP Calculus program. (Note that the asterisked goals are aligned with the BC course and are not required in AB Calculus.)

- Students will be able to work with functions represented graphically, numerically, analytically, or verbally, and will understand the connections among these representations; graphing calculators will be used as a tool to facilitate such understanding.

- Students will, in the process of solving problems, be able to use graphing calculators to graph functions, solve equations, evaluate numerical derivatives, and evaluate numerical integrals.

- Students will understand the meaning of the derivative as a limit of a difference quotient and will understand its connection to local linearity and instantaneous rates of change.

- Students will understand the meaning of the definite integral as a limit of Riemann sums and as a net accumulation of change over an interval, and they will understand and appreciate the connection between derivatives and integrals.

- Students will be able to model real-world behavior and solve a variety of problems using functions, derivatives, and integrals; they will also be able to communicate solutions effectively, using proper mathematical language and syntax.

- Students will be able to represent and interpret differential equations geometrically with slope fields and (*) numerically with Euler's method; they will be able to model dynamic situations with differential equations and solve initial value problems analytically.

- (*) Students will understand the convergence and divergence of infinite series and will be able to represent functions with Maclaurin and Taylor series; they will be able to approximate or bound truncation errors in various ways.

- (*) Students will be able to extend some calculus results to the context of motion in the plane (through vectors) and to the analysis of polar curves.

The incorporation of graphing calculator technology throughout the course continues to be a defining feature of this textbook, but we urge teachers to read the next section, Philosophy on Technology Usage, to see how our philosophy has changed over time (again, in harmony with our AP* Calculus colleagues). Whether you are concerned about how to use calculators enough or how not to use calculators too much, we believe you can trust this author team to address your concerns with the perspective that only long experience can provide.

Whether you are a veteran user of our textbooks or are coming on board for this fifth edition, we thank you for letting us join you in the important adventure of educating your students. Some of the best suggestions for improving our book over the years have come from students and teachers, so we urge you to contact us through Pearson if you have any questions or concerns. To paraphrase Isaac Newton, if this textbook enables your students to see further down the road of mathematics, it is because we have stood on the shoulders of dedicated teachers like you.

Philosophy on Technology Usage

When the AP Calculus committee, after consultation with leaders in mathematics and mathematics education, made the decision to require graphing calculators on the AP examinations, their intent was to enhance the teaching and learning of calculus in AP classrooms. In fact, that decision probably had an impact on the entire secondary mathematics curriculum, as teachers discovered that graphing utilities could make a deeper understanding of function behavior possible in earlier courses. The authors of this textbook have supported the use of this technology from its inception and, well aware of its potential for either facilitating or circumventing true understanding, have employed it carefully in our approach to problem solving. Indeed, longtime users of this textbook are well acquainted with our insistence on the distinction between **solving** the problem and **supporting** or **confirming** the solution, and how technology figures into each of those processes.

As hand-held graphing technology enters its fourth decade, we have come to realize that advances in technology and increased familiarity with calculators have gradually blurred some of the distinctions between solving and supporting that we had once assumed to be apparent. Textbook exercises that we had designed for a particular pedagogical purpose are now being solved with technology in ways that either side-step or obscure the learning we had hoped might take place. For example, students might find an equation of the line through two points by using linear regression, or they might match a set of differential equations with their slope fields by simply graphing each slope field. Now that calculators with computer algebra systems have arrived on the scene, exercises meant for practicing algebraic manipulations are being solved without the benefit of the practice. We do not want to retreat in any way from our support of modern technology, but we feel that the time has come to provide more guidance about the intent of the various exercises in our textbook.

Therefore, as a service to teachers and students alike, exercises in this textbook that **should be solved without calculators** will be identified with gray ovals around the exercise numbers. These will usually be exercises that demonstrate how various functions behave algebraically or how algebraic representations reflect graphical behavior and vice versa. Application problems will usually have no restrictions, in keeping with our emphasis on **modeling** and on bringing **all representations** to bear when confronting real-world problems. We are pleased to note that this all meshes well with the Mathematical Practices for AP Calculus (MPACs).

When the AP Calculus committee decided to change the number of noncalculator problems on the free-response portions of the AP examinations from three to four (out of six), their concern was related to test development rather than pedagogy. Still, their decision, like ours, was informed by years of experience with the teachers, the students, and the technology. The goal today is the same as it was thirty years ago: to enhance the teaching and learning of mathematics.

Incidentally, we continue to encourage the use of calculators to **support** answers graphically or numerically after the problems have been solved with pencil and paper. Any time students can make those connections among the graphical, analytical, and numerical representations, they are doing good mathematics. We just don't want them to miss something along the way because they brought in their calculators too soon.

As a final note, we will freely admit that different teachers use our textbook in different ways, and some will probably override our no-calculator recommendations to fit with their pedagogical strategies. In the end, the teachers know what is best for their students, and we are just here to help.

Changes for This Edition

The big change in this new edition, of course, is that we welcome David M. Bressoud to the author team. As a college mathematician with years of experience with the Advanced Placement (AP) program, he is well acquainted with the scope and the goals of the course, and he is well versed in the mathematics that calculus students should know. As an experienced writer with a particular passion for the history of mathematics, he can provide contexts that make calculus topics more interesting for students and teachers alike. Teachers who have used our previous editions will have no trouble identifying (and, we hope, enjoying) the ways that David has enriched what was already a gratifyingly popular book.

A Few Global Changes

As with previous editions, we have kept our focus on high school students taking one of the College Board's AP courses, Calculus AB or Calculus BC. The topics in the book reflect both the curriculum and the pedagogy of an AP course, and we do what we can to prepare students for the AP examinations throughout the book. As the College Board has moved toward objective-based course descriptions, we have replaced our "What You Will Learn . . . and Why" feature in each section opener by learning objectives and bulleted context topics. Also, as free-response questions on the AP examinations have evolved in focus and style, we have added or amended our exercises to reflect those changes. Although the role of graphing calculators in the course has not changed significantly since the fourth edition, we have made a few changes based on calculator evolution. We have also removed some of the gray "no calculator" ovals from the fourth edition to reflect an emerging consensus among calculus teachers that *not every* problem that can be solved without a calculator *ought to* be solved without a calculator.

We have expanded the treatment of the derivative as a measure of *sensitivity*, which now appears as an ongoing topic in several different sections of the book. We have also made a more consistent commitment to *point-slope form* for linear equations throughout the book, as that is the form that emphasizes the concept of local linearity, critical for understanding differential calculus.

We decided in this edition to eliminate all references to calculator regression functionality and all solutions that involved fitting curves to data points. There are still plenty of examples and exercises based on numerical data and tables, but the solutions do not involve first finding functions to fit the points to allow for an analytic solution. Calculator regression has never been permissible on AP calculus examinations, precisely because it changes the intent of the problem. We therefore felt that our regression references might be doing more harm than good.

Most of the motivational "Chapter Opener" problems are new and improved in this edition, and (thanks to David) many more historical nuggets have been sprinkled throughout the book. We also confess that some of the nuggets that were already there were in need of refinement. For example, the name of one of the key players has been restored to its original spelling: Guillaume de l'Hospital.

Finally, be assured that we have looked carefully at the content of the new AP Calculus Curriculum Framework, and there is nothing therein that is not covered in this book. Moreover, the emphases are in harmony with the objectives of the AP course, as they have always been.

Some Specific Chapter Changes

Chapter 1, which is really a review of precalculus topics, has been altered in several places to be less of a "here is a summary of what you have learned" experience and more of a "here are some things you have learned that you will need for studying calculus" experience. For example, the section on lines is now about linear *functions* and makes references to their importance in calculus—despite the fact that it appears before the section that reviews functions. We have also added a subsection on solving simultaneous linear equations (including by matrices with a calculator).

The Chapter 2 opener has been changed to introduce the topic of sensitivity, the measurement of how change in the input variable affects change in the output variable, and a subsection with examples about sensitivity has been added. The epsilon-delta definition of limit (not an AP topic, and no longer assumed in many first-year college courses) has been entirely moved to the appendices, while the intuitive definition has been strengthened and clarified. In line with the AP course descriptions, the Sandwich Theorem has been renamed the Squeeze Theorem.

In most cases, linear equations appearing as answers in examples and exercises in Chapter 3 have been converted to point-slope form to reinforce the idea of local linearity. Additional attention is now paid to the "MathPrint" version of the numerical derivative, while retaining references to what is now called the "classic" syntax.

A new example has been added to the end of Chapter 4 to illustrate (in multiple-choice form) the most common errors students make when applying, or failing to apply, the Chain Rule.

In Chapter 5, examples and exercises have been added to illustrate sensitivity as an application of the derivative. A proof of the Mean Value Theorem and an exploration of Lagrange's bound on the difference between a function and its tangent line approximation have been added as exercises in *Extending the Ideas*.

Chapter 6 now contains more coverage of *accumulation* as a fundamental interpretation of integration, and more attention is paid to the *accumulator function* $\int_a^x f(t)\,dt$ and its applications. The two parts of the Fundamental Theorem of Calculus have been helpfully distinguished as the Antiderivative Part and the Evaluation Part.

In Chapter 7, the example showing how to handle discontinuity in an initial value problem has been modified to show more clearly why the domain of the solution must be restricted. Exercises involving exponential and logistic regression have been replaced with additional exercises involving separation of variables and the solution to the general logistic equation. More free-response questions involving slope fields and separation of variables have been added to the chapter review.

More exercises and examples on accumulation have been added to Chapter 8. Another example and some exercises have been added to give students more familiarity with solids of revolution around lines that are not the coordinate axes.

In Chapter 9, more material has been added on the Fibonacci sequence and the golden ratio φ. Graphing calculator screens have been updated to reflect the newer sequence format and to show how the TRACE feature can be used to explore limits of sequences.

In Chapter 10, a margin note has been added to make term-by-term differentiation of power series simpler for students. Section 3 (Taylor's Theorem) has been extensively revised to make truncation error analysis easier for BC students. The alternating series error bound is now introduced in this section so it can be compared with the Lagrange error bound in examples and exercises, and more AP-style problems involving truncation error analysis have been added. The Remainder Estimation Theorem has been renamed the Remainder Bounding Theorem to reflect how the theorem is actually used.

Chapter 11 now includes a discussion of how polar equations can be used to describe conic sections. There is also a brief introduction to the use of conic sections in orbital mechanics, along with several new exercises in that context. Some interesting new historical references have been added to explain how certain polar curves acquired their names.

Finally, we have performed some appendectomies on the material in the back of the book that has been accruing over the years. We removed the appendices on Mathematical Induction and Conic Sections, as those are really precalculus topics. We also removed nearly half of the formulas in the Brief Table of Integrals, retaining only those that were within the scope of the course, or interesting, or both.

Continuing Features

Mathematical Practices for AP Calculus (MPACs)

The Mathematical Practices highlighted in the *AP Calculus Curriculum Framework* always have been and continue to be represented in the text, examples, and exercises.

MPAC 1, Reasoning with definitions and theorems is one of the dominant themes in the development of each new idea and of the exercises. Definitions and theorems are highlighted in each section and summarized at the end of each chapter for reference and review.

MPAC 2, Connecting concepts runs throughout this book, introducing new concepts by connecting them to what has come before and in the reliance of many exercises that draw on applications or build on student knowledge. *Quick Review* exercises at the start of each Exercise set review concepts from previous sections (or previous courses) that will be needed for the solutions.

MPAC 3, Implementing algebraic/computational processes is well represented in the foundational exercises with which each exercise set begins and in the thoughtful use of technology.

MPAC 4, Connecting multiple representations has always been present in the emphasis on the connections among graphical, numerical, and algebraic representations of the key concepts of calculus. The title of this book speaks for itself in that regard.

MPAC 5, Building notational fluency is represented in the intentional use of a variety of notational forms and in their explicit connection to graphical, numerical, and algebraic representations. Many margin notes explicitly address notational concerns.

MPAC 6, Communicating is a critical component of the Explorations that appear in each section. Communication is also essential to the *Writing to Learn* exercises as well as the *Group Activities*. Many of the exercises and examples in the book have "justify your answer" components in the spirit of the AP exams.

Balanced Approach

A principal feature of this edition is the balance attained among the rule of four: analytic/algebraic, numerical, graphical, and verbal methods of representing problems. We believe that students must value all of these methods of representation, understand how they are connected in a given problem, and learn how to choose the one(s) most appropriate for solving a particular problem. **(MPACs 2 and 4)**

The Rule of Four

In support of the rule of four, we use a variety of techniques to solve problems. For instance, we obtain solutions algebraically or analytically, support our results graphically or numerically with technology, and then interpret the result in the original problem context. We have written exercises in which students are asked to solve problems by one method and then support or confirm their solutions by using another method. We want students to understand that technology can be used to support (but not prove) results, and that algebraic or analytic techniques are needed to prove results. We want students to understand that mathematics provides the foundation that allows us to use technology to solve problems. **(MPACs 1, 3, 4, and 5)**

Applications

The text includes a rich array of interesting applications from biology, business, chemistry, economics, engineering, finance, physics, the social sciences, and statistics. Some applications are based on real data from cited sources. Students are exposed to functions as mechanisms for modeling data and learn about how various functions can model real-life problems. They learn to analyze and model data, represent data graphically, interpret from graphs, and fit curves. Additionally, the tabular representations of data presented in the text highlight the concept that a function is a correspondence between numerical variables, helping students to build the connection between the numbers and the graphs. **(MPACs 2, 4, and 6)**

Explorations

Students are expected to be actively involved in understanding calculus concepts and solving problems. Often the explorations provide a guided investigation of a concept. The explorations help build problem-solving ability by guiding students to develop a mathematical model of a problem, solve the mathematical model, support or confirm the solution, and interpret the solution. The ability to communicate their understanding is just as important to the learning process as reading or studying, not only in mathematics but also in every academic pursuit. Students can gain an entirely new perspective on their knowledge when they explain what they know, either orally or in writing. **(MPACs 1, 2, 4, and 6)**

Graphing Utilities

The book assumes familiarity with a graphing utility that will produce the graph of a function within an arbitrary viewing window, find the zeros of a function, compute the derivative of a function numerically, and compute definite integrals numerically. Students are expected to recognize that a given graph is reasonable, identify all the important characteristics of a graph, interpret those characteristics, and confirm them using analytic methods. Toward that end, most graphs appearing in this book resemble students' actual grapher output or suggest hand-drawn sketches. This is one of the first calculus textbooks to take full advantage of graphing calculators, philosophically restructuring the course to teach new things in new ways to achieve new understanding, while (courageously) abandoning some old things and old ways that are no longer serving a purpose. **(MPACs 3. 4 and 5)**

Exercise Sets

The exercise sets were updated for this edition, including many new ones. There are nearly 4000 exercises, with more than 80 Quick Quiz exercises and 560 Quick Review exercises. The different types of exercises included are Algebraic and analytic manipulation, Interpretation of graphs, Graphical representations, Numerical representations, Explorations, Writing to learn, Group activities, Data analyses, Descriptively titled applications, Extending the ideas.

Each exercise set begins with the Quick Review feature, which can be used to introduce lessons, support Examples, and review prerequisite skills. The exercises that follow are graded from routine to challenging. Some exercises are also designed to be solved *without a calculator*; these exercises have numbers printed within a gray oval. Students are urged to **support** the answers to these (and all) exercises graphically or numerically, but only after they have solved them with pencil and paper. An additional block of exercises, Extending the Ideas, may be used in a variety of ways, including group work. We also provide Review Exercises and AP Examination Preparation at the end of each chapter.

Print Supplements and Resources

For the Student

The following supplements are available for purchase:

AP* Test Prep Series: AP* Calculus (ISBN: 0133314588)

- Introduction to the AP AB and BC Calculus Exams
- Precalculus Review of Calculus Prerequisites
- Review of AP Calculus AB and Calculus BC Topics
- Practice Exams
- Answers and Solutions

For the Teacher

The following supplements are available to qualified adopters:

Annotated Teacher's Edition

- Answers included on the same page as the problem appears, for most exercises. All answers included in the back of the book.
- Solutions to Chapter Opening Problems, Teaching Notes, Common Errors, Notes on Examples and Exploration Extensions, and Assignment Guide included at the beginning of the book.

Solutions Manual

- Complete solutions for Quick Reviews, Exercises, Explorations, and Chapter Reviews

Technology Resources

The Fifth Edition of Finney, Demana, Waits, Kennedy, Bressoud *Calculus* is accompanied by an extensive range of technology resources designed to support students in practicing and learning the material, and to assist teachers in managing and delivering their courses.

MathXL® for School (optional, for purchase only)—access code required, www.mathxlforschool.com

MathXL for School is a powerful online homework, tutorial, and assessment supplement that aligns to Pearson Education's textbooks in mathematics or statistics. With MathXL for School, teachers can:

- Create, edit, and assign auto-graded online homework and tests correlated at the objective level to the textbook
- Utilize automatic grading to rapidly assess student understanding
- Track both student and group performance in an online gradebook
- Prepare students for high-stakes testing, including aligning assignments to state and Common Core State Standards, where available
- Deliver quality, effective instruction regardless of experience level

With MathXL for School, students can:

- Do their homework and receive immediate feedback
- Get self-paced assistance on problems in a variety of ways (guided solutions, step-by-step examples, video clips, animations)
- Have a large number of practice problems to choose from, helping them master a topic
- Receive personalized study plans and homework based on test results

For more information and to purchase student access codes after the first year, visit our Web site at www.mathxlforschool.com, or contact your Pearson Account General Manager.

MyMathLab® Online Course (optional, for purchase only)—access code required, www.mymathlab.com

MyMathLab is a text-specific, easily customizable, online course that integrates interactive multimedia instruction with textbook content. MyMathLab gives you the tools you need to deliver all or a portion of your course online.

MyMathLab features include:

- Interactive eText, including highlighting and note taking tools, and links to videos and exercises
- Rich and flexible course management, communication, and teacher support tools
- Online homework and assessment, and personalized study plans
- Complete multimedia library to enhance learning
- All teacher resources in one convenient location

For more information, visit www.mymathlabforschool.com or contact your Pearson Account General Manager.

Video Resources

These video lessons feature an engaging team of mathematics teachers who present comprehensive coverage of each section of the text. The lecturers' presentations include examples and exercises from the text and support an approach that emphasizes visualization and problem solving. Available in MyMathLab for School.

Additional Support for Teachers

Most of the teacher supplements and resources for this book are available electronically upon adoption or to preview. For more information, please contact your Pearson School sales representative.

Downloadable Teacher's Resources

- **Texas Instruments Graphing Calculator Manual** is an introduction to Texas Instruments' graphing calculators, as they are used for calculus. Featured are the TI-84 Plus Silver Edition with MathPrint, the TI-83 Plus Silver Edition, and the TI-89 Titanium. The keystrokes, menus, and screens for the TI-84 Plus are similar to the TI-84 Plus Silver Edition; those for the TI-83 Plus are similar to the TI-83 Plus Silver Edition; and the TI-89, TI-92 Plus, and Voyage™ 200 are similar to the TI-89 Titanium.

- **Resources for AP* Exam Preparation and Practice** includes many resources to help prepare students for the AP* Calculus exam, including concepts worksheets, sample AB and BC exams, and answers to those exams.

- **AP* Calculus Implementation Guide** is a tool to help teachers manage class time and ensure the complete Advanced Placement* Calculus Curriculum Framework is covered. It includes pacing guides (for AB and BC Calculus), assignment guides, topic correlations, and lesson plans.

- **PowerPoint® Lecture Presentation** This time-saving resource includes classroom presentation slides that align to the topic sequence of the textbook.

- **Assessment Resources** include chapter quizzes, chapter tests, semester test, final tests, and alternate assessments.

TestGen®

TestGen enables teachers to build, edit, print, and administer tests using a computerized bank of questions developed to cover all the objectives of the text. TestGen is algorithmically based, allowing teachers to create multiple but equivalent versions of the same question or test with the click of a button. Teachers can also modify test bank questions or add new questions. Tests can be printed or administered online.

To the AP Student

We know that as you study for your AP course, you're preparing along the way for the AP exam. By tying the material in this book directly to AP course goals and exam topics, we help you to focus your time most efficiently. And that's a good thing!

The AP exam is an important milestone in your education. A high score will position you optimally for college acceptance—and possibly will give you college credits that put you a step ahead. Our primary commitment is to provide you with the tools you need to excel on the exam . . . the rest is up to you!

Test-Taking Strategies for an Advanced Placement Calculus Examination

You should approach the AP Calculus Examination the same way you would any major test in your academic career. Just remember that it is a one-shot deal—you should be at your peak performance level on the day of the test. For that reason you should do everything that your "coach" tells you to do. In most cases your coach is your classroom teacher. It is very likely that your teacher has some experience, based on workshop information or previous students' performance, to share with you.

You should also analyze your own test-taking abilities. At this stage in your education, you probably know your strengths and weaknesses in test-taking situations. You may be very good at multiple choice questions but weaker in essays, or perhaps it is the other way around. Whatever your particular abilities are, evaluate them and respond accordingly. Spend more time on your weaker points. In other words, rather than spending time in your comfort zone where you need less work, try to improve your soft spots. In all cases, concentrate on clear communication of your strategies, techniques, and conclusions.

The following table presents some ideas in a quick and easy form.

General Strategies for AP Examination Preparation

Time	Dos
Through the Year	• Register with your teacher/coordinator • Pay your fee (if applicable) on time • Take good notes • Work with others in study groups • Review on a regular basis • Evaluate your test-taking strengths and weaknesses
Several Weeks Before	• Combine independent and group review • Get tips from your teacher • Do lots of mixed review problems • Check your exam date, time, and location • Review the appropriate AP Calculus syllabus (AB or BC) • Make sure your calculator is on the approved list
The Night Before	• Put new batteries in your calculator or make sure it is charged • Set your calculator in Radian Mode • Lay out your clothes and supplies so that you are ready to go out the door • Do a short review • Go to bed at a reasonable hour
Exam Day	• Get up a little earlier than usual • Eat a good breakfast/lunch • Get to your exam location 15 minutes early
Exam Night	• Relax—you have earned it

Topics from the Advanced Placement Curriculum for Calculus AB, Calculus BC

As an AP student, you are probably well aware of the good study habits that are needed to be a successful student in high school and college:

- attend all the classes

- ask questions (either during class or after)

- take clear and understandable notes

- make sure you are understanding the concepts rather than memorizing formulas

- do your homework; extend your test-prep time over several days or weeks, instead of cramming

- use all the resources—text and people—that are available to you.

No doubt this list of "good study habits" is one that you have seen or heard before. You should know that there is powerful research that suggests a few habits or routines will enable you to go beyond "knowing about" calculus, to more deeply "understanding" calculus. Here are three concrete actions for you to consider:

- Review your notes at least once a week and rewrite them in summary form.

- Verbally explain concepts (theorems, etc.) to a classmate.

- Form a study group that meets regularly to do homework and discuss reading and lecture notes.

Most of these tips boil down to one mantra, which all mathematicians believe in:

Mathematics is not a spectator sport.

The AP Calculus Examination is based on the following Topic Outline. For your convenience, we have noted all Calculus AB and Calculus BC objectives with clear indications of topics required only by the Calculus BC Exam. The outline cross-references each AP Calculus objective with the appropriate section(s) of this textbook: *Calculus: Graphical, Numerical, Algebraic,* AP* Edition, Fifth Edition, by Finney, Demana, Waits, Kennedy, and Bressoud.

Use this outline to track your progress through the AP exam topics. Be sure to cover every topic associated with the exam you are taking. Check it off when you have studied and/or reviewed the topic.

Even as you prepare for your exam, I hope this book helps you map—and enjoy—your calculus journey!

—*John Brunsting*
Hinsdale Central High School

Concept Outline for AP Calculus AB and AP Calculus BC

(excerpted from the College Board's Curriculum Framework—AP Calculus AB and AP Calculus BC, Fall 2014)

EU = Enduring Understanding,   LO = Learning Objective, BC only topics

Big Idea 1: Limits	Sections
EU 1.1: The concept of a limit can be used to understand the behavior of functions.	
LO 1.1A(a): Express limits symbolically using correct notation.	2.1, 2.2
LO 1.1A(b): Interpret limits expressed symbolically.	2.1, 2.2
LO 1.1B: Estimate limits of functions.	2.1, 2.2
LO 1.1C: Determine limits of functions.	2.1, 2.2, 9.2, 9.3
LO 1.1D: Deduce and interpret behavior of functions using limits.	2.1, 2.2, 9.3
EU 1.2: Continuity is a key property of functions that is defined using limits.	
LO 1.2A: Analyze functions for intervals of continuity or points of discontinuity.	2.3
LO 1.2B: Determine the applicability of important calculus theorems using continuity.	2.3, 5.1, 5.2, 6.2–4

Big Idea 2: Derivatives	Sections
EU 2.1: The derivative of a function is defined as the limit of a difference quotient and can be determined using a variety of strategies.	
LO 2.1A: Identify the derivative of a function as the limit of a difference quotient.	3.1
LO 2.1B: Estimate the derivative.	3.1, 3.2
LO 2.1C: Calculate derivatives.	3.3, 3.5, 4.1–4, 11.1–3
LO 2.1D: Determine higher order derivatives.	3.3, 4.2
EU 2.2: A function's derivative, which is itself a function, can be used to understand the behavior of the function.	2.4
LO 2.2A: Use derivatives to analyze properties of a function.	5.1–3, 11.1–3
LO 2.2B: Recognize the connection between differentiability and continuity.	3.2
EU 2.3: The derivative has multiple interpretations and applications including those that involve instantaneous rates of change.	
LO 2.3A: Interpret the meaning of a derivative within a problem.	2.4, 3.1, 3.4, 5.5
LO 2.3B: Solve problems involving the slope of a tangent line.	2.4, 3.4, 5.5
LO 2.3C: Solve problems involving related rates, optimization, rectilinear motion, (BC) and planar motion.	3.4, 5.1, 5.3, 5.4, 5.6, 11.1–3
LO 2.3D: Solve problems involving rates of change in applied contexts.	5.5, 5.6
LO 2.3E: Verify solutions to differential equations.	7.1
LO 2.3F: Estimate solutions to differential equations.	7.1
EU 2.4: The Mean Value Theorem connects the behavior of a differentiable function over an interval to the behavior of the derivative of that function at a particular point in the interval.	
LO 2.4A: Apply the Mean Value Theorem to describe the behavior of a function over an interval.	5.2

Big Idea 3: Integrals and the Fundamental Theorem of Calculus	Sections
EU 3.1: Antidifferentiation is the inverse process of differentiation.	
LO 3.1A: Recognize antiderivatives of basic functions.	6.3

EU 3.2: The definite integral of a function over an interval is the limit of a Riemann sum over that interval and can be calculated using a variety of strategies.

    LO 3.2A(a): Interpret the definite integral as the limit of a Riemann sum.   6.1, 6.2

    LO 3.2A(b): Express the limit of a Riemann sum in integral notation.   6.2

    LO 3.2B: Approximate a definite integral.   6.1, 6.2, 6.5

    LO 3.2C: Calculate a definite integral using areas and properties of definite integrals.   6.2, 6.3

    LO 3.2D: (BC) Evaluate an improper integral or show that an improper integral diverges.   9.4

EU 3.3: The Fundamental Theorem of Calculus, which has two distinct formulations, connects differentiation and integration.

    LO 3.3A: Analyze functions defined by an integral.   6.1–4, 8.1

    LO 3.3B(a): Calculate antiderivatives.   6.3, 6.4, 7.2, 7.3, 7.5

    LO 3.3B(b): Evaluate definite integrals.   6.3, 6.4, 7.2, 7.3, 7.5

EU 3.4: The definite integral of a function over an interval is a mathematical tool with many interpretations and applications involving accumulation.

    LO 3.4A: Interpret the meaning of a definite integral within a problem.   6.1, 6.2, 8.1, 8.5

    LO 3.4B: Apply definite integrals to problems involving the average value of a function.   6.3

    LO 3.4C: Apply definite integrals to problems involving motion.   6.1, 8.1, 11.1–3

    LO 3.4D: Apply definite integrals to problems involving area, volume, (BC) and length of a curve.   8.2, 8.3, 8.4

    LO 3.4E: Use the definite integral to solve problems in various contexts.   6.1, 8.1, 8.5

EU 3.5: Antidifferentiation is an underlying concept involved in solving separable differential equations. Solving separable differential equations involves determining a function or relation given its rate of change.

    LO 3.5A: Analyze differential equations to obtain general solutions.   7.1, 7.4, 7.5

    LO 3.5B: Interpret, create, and solve differential equations from problems in context.   7.1, 7.4, 7.5

Big Idea 4: Series (BC)   *Sections*

EU 4.1: The sum of an infinite number of real numbers may converge.

    LO 4.1A Determine whether a series converges or diverges.   9.1, 10.1, 10.4, 10.5

    LO 4.1B: Determine or estimate the sum of a series.   10.1

EU 4.2: A function can be represented by an associated power series over the interval of convergence for the power series.

    LO 4.2A: Construct and use Taylor polynomials.   10.2, 10.3

    LO 4.2B: Write a power series representing a given function.   10.1–3

    LO 4.2C: Determine the radius and interval of convergence of a power series.   10.4, 10.5

For the most current AP* Exam Topic correlation for this textbook, visit PearsonSchool.com/AdvancedCorrelations.

Using the Book for Maximum Effectiveness

So, how can this book help you to join in the game of mathematics for a winning future? Let us show you some unique tools that we have included in the text to help prepare you not only for the AP Calculus exam, but also for success beyond this course.

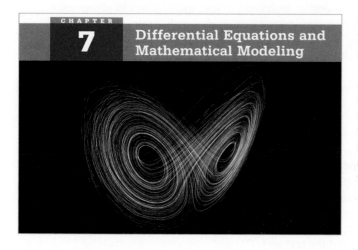

CHAPTER 7
Differential Equations and Mathematical Modeling

Chapter Openers provide a photograph and application to show you an example that illustrates the relevance of what you'll be learning in the chapter.

A **Chapter Overview** then follows to give you a sense of what you are going to learn. This overview provides a roadmap of the chapter as well as tells how the different topics in the chapter are connected under one big idea. It is always helpful to remember that mathematics isn't modular, but interconnected, and that the different skills you are learning throughout the course build on one another to help you understand more complex concepts.

CHAPTER 7 Overview

One of the early accomplishments of calculus was predicting the future position of a planet from its present position and velocity. Today this is just one of many situations in which we deduce everything we need to know about a function from one of its known values and its rate of change. From this kind of information, we can tell how long a sample of radioactive polonium will last; whether, given current trends, a population will grow or become extinct; and how large major league baseball salaries are likely to be in the year 2020. In this chapter, we examine the analytic, graphical, and numerical techniques on which such predictions are based.

You will be able to use slope fields to analyze solution curves to differential equations, and you will be able to use Euler's method to construct solutions numerically.

- Differential equations
- General and particular solutions of differential equations
- Solving exact differential equations
- Slope fields
- Euler's Method

Similarly, the **Objectives and Topics** feature gives you the big ideas in each section and explains their purpose. You should read this as you begin the section and always review it after you have completed the section to make sure you understand all of the key topics that you have just studied.

Margin Notes appear throughout the book on various topics. Some notes provide more information on a key concept or an example. Other notes offer practical advice on using your graphing calculator to obtain the most accurate results.

Differential Equation Mode

If your calculator has a *differential equation mode* for graphing, it is intended for graphing slope fields. The usual "Y=" turns into a "*dy/dx* = " screen, and you can enter a function of *x* and/or *y*. The grapher draws a slope field for the differential equation when you press the GRAPH button.

Brief **Historical Notes** present the stories of people and the research that they have done to advance the study of mathematics. Reading these notes will often provide you with a deeper appreciation for calculus as a human achievement and may inspire you to do great things yourself some day.

J. Ernest Wilkins, Jr. (1923–2011)

By the age of nineteen, J. Ernest Wilkins had earned a Ph.D. degree in Mathematics from the University of Chicago. He then taught, served on the Manhattan project (the goal of which was to build the first atomic bomb), and worked as a mathematician and physicist for several corporations. In 1970, Dr. Wilkins joined the faculty at Howard University and served as head of the electrical engineering, physics, chemistry, and mathematics departments before retiring. He was also Distinguished Professor of Applied Mathematics and Mathematical Physics at Clark Atlanta University.

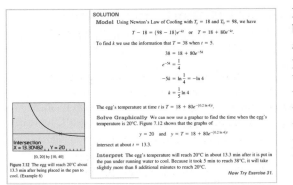

SOLUTION

Model Using Newton's Law of Cooling with $T_s = 18$ and $T_0 = 98$, we have

$$T - 18 = (98 - 18)e^{-kt} \quad \text{or} \quad T = 18 + 80e^{-kt}.$$

To find k we use the information that $T = 38$ when $t = 5$.

$$38 = 18 + 80e^{-5k}$$
$$e^{-5k} = \frac{1}{4}$$
$$-5k = \ln\frac{1}{4} = -\ln 4$$
$$k = \frac{1}{5}\ln 4$$

The egg's temperature at time t is $T = 18 + 80e^{-(0.2\ln 4)t}$.

Solve Graphically We can now use a grapher to find the time when the egg's temperature is 20°C. Figure 7.12 shows that the graphs of

$$y = 20 \quad \text{and} \quad y = T = 18 + 80e^{-(0.2\ln 4)t}$$

intersect at about $t = 13.3$.

Interpret The egg's temperature will reach 20°C in about 13.3 min after it is put in the pan under running water to cool. Because it took 5 min to reach 38°C, it will take slightly more than 8 additional minutes to reach 20°C.

Now Try Exercise 31.

Intersection
X = 13.30482 , Y = 20
[0, 20] by [10, 40]
Figure 7.12 The egg will reach 20°C about 13.3 min after being placed in the pan to cool. (Example 6)

Many examples make use of multiple representations of functions (algebraic, graphical, and numerical) to highlight the different ways of looking at a problem and to highlight the insights that different representations can provide. You should be able to use different approaches for finding solutions to problems. For instance, you would obtain a solution algebraically when that is the most appropriate technique to use, and you would obtain solutions graphically or numerically when algebra is difficult or impossible to use. We urge you to solve problems by one method, then support or confirm your solution by using another method, and finally, interpret the results in the context of the problem. Doing so reinforces the idea that to understand a problem fully, you need to understand it algebraically, graphically, and numerically whenever possible.

Each example ends with a suggestion to **Now Try** a related exercise. Working the suggested exercise is an easy way for you to check your comprehension of the material while reading each section, instead of waiting until the end of each section or chapter to see if you "got it." True comprehension of the textbook is essential for your success on the AP Exam.

Explorations appear throughout the text and provide you with the perfect opportunity to become an active learner and discover mathematics on your own. Honing your critical thinking and problem-solving skills will ultimately benefit you on all of your AP Exams.

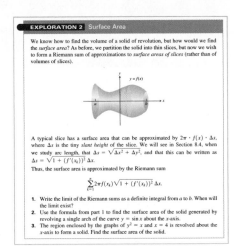

EXPLORATION 2 Surface Area

We know how to find the volume of a solid of revolution, but how would we find the *surface area*? As before, we partition the solid into thin slices, but now we wish to form a Riemann sum of approximations to *surface areas of slices* (rather than of volumes of slices).

$y = f(x)$

A typical slice has a surface area that can be approximated by $2\pi \cdot f(x) \cdot \Delta s$, where Δs is the tiny *slant height* of the slice. We will see in Section 8.4, when we study *arc length*, that $\Delta s = \sqrt{\Delta x^2 + \Delta y^2}$, and that this can be written as $\Delta s = \sqrt{1 + (f'(x_k))^2}\,\Delta x$.

Thus, the surface area is approximated by the Riemann sum

$$\sum_{k=1}^{n} 2\pi f(x_k)\sqrt{1 + (f'(x_k))^2}\,\Delta x.$$

1. Write the limit of the Riemann sums as a definite integral from a to b. When will the limit exist?
2. Use the formula from part 1 to find the surface area of the solid generated by revolving a single arch of the curve $y = \sin x$ about the x-axis.
3. The region enclosed by the graphs of $y^2 = x$ and $x = 4$ is revolved about the x-axis to form a solid. Find the surface area of the solid.

Each exercise set begins with a **Quick Review** to help you review skills needed in the exercise set, reminding you again that mathematics is not modular. Each Quick Review includes section references to show where these skills were covered earlier in the text. If you find these problems overly challenging, you should go back through the book and your notes to review the material covered in previous chapters. Remember, you need to *understand* the material from the *entire* calculus course for the AP Calculus Exam, not just memorize the concepts from the last part of the course.

Quick Review 7.3   *(For help, go to Sections 4.3 and 4.4.)*

Exercise numbers with a gray background indicate problems that the authors have designed to be solved *without a calculator*.

In Exercises 1–4, find dy/dx.

1. $y = x^3 \sin 2x$
2. $y = e^{2x}\ln(3x + 1)$
3. $y = \tan^{-1} 2x$
4. $y = \sin^{-1}(x + 3)$

In Exercises 5 and 6, solve for x in terms of y.

5. $y = \tan^{-1} 3x$
6. $y = \cos^{-1}(x + 1)$

7. Find the area under the arch of the curve $y = \sin \pi x$ from $x = 0$ to $x = 1$.
8. Solve the differential equation $dy/dx = e^{2x}$.
9. Solve the initial value problem $dy/dx = x + \sin x$, $y(0) = 2$.
10. Use differentiation to confirm the integration formula

$$\int e^x \sin x \, dx = \frac{1}{2}e^x(\sin x - \cos x).$$

For exercises designed to be solved *without a calculator* the numbers of these exercises are printed in a grey oval. We encourage you to *support* the answers to exercises graphically or numerically when you can, but only after you have solved them with pencil and paper.

Along with the standard types of exercises, including skill-based, application, writing, exploration, and extension questions, each exercise set includes a group of **Standardized Test Questions.** Each group includes two true-false with justifications and four multiple-choice questions, with instructions about the permitted use of your graphing calculator.

Standardized Test Questions

You may use a graphing calculator to solve the following problems.

47. **True or False** If $dy/dx = ky$, then $y = e^{kx} + C$. Justify your answer.

48. **True or False** The general solution to $dy/dt = 2y$ can be written in the form $y = C(3^{kt})$ for some constants C and k. Justify your answer.

49. **Multiple Choice** A bank account earning continuously compounded interest doubles in value in 7.0 years. At the same interest rate, how long would it take the value of the account to triple?

(A) 4.4 years   (B) 9.8 years   (C) 10.5 years
(D) 11.1 years   (E) 21.0 years

50. **Multiple Choice** A sample of Ce-143 (an isotope of cerium) loses 99% of its radioactive matter in 199 hours. What is the half-life of Ce-143?

(A) 4 hours   (B) 6 hours   (C) 30 hours
(D) 100.5 hours   (E) 143 hours

CHAPTER 6   Key Terms

accumulator function (p. 288)
area under a curve (p. 285)
average value (p. 295)
bounded function (p. 289)
cardiac output (p. 275)
characteristic function of the rationals
  (p. 290)
definite integral (p. 283)
differential calculus (p. 269)
dummy variable (p. 284)
error bounds (p. 319)
Fundamental Theorem of Calculus,
  Antiderivative Part (p. 302)
Fundamental Theorem of Calculus,
  Evaluation Part (p. 307)
integrable function (p. 283)

integral calculus (p. 269)
Integral Evaluation Theorem (p. 307)
integral of f from a to b (p. 284)
integral sign (p. 284)
integrand (p. 284)
lower bound (p. 294)
lower limit of integration (p. 284)
LRAM (p. 272)
mean value (p. 295)
Mean Value Theorem for Definite Integrals
  (p. 296)
MRAM (p. 272)
net area (p. 286)
NINT (p. 289)
norm of a partition (p. 282)
partition (p. 281)

Rectangular Approximation Method
  (RAM) (p. 272)
regular partition (p. 283)
Riemann sum (p. 281)
Riemann sum for f on the interval $[a, b]$
  (p. 282)
RRAM (p. 272)
sigma notation (p. 281)
Simpson's Rule (p. 317)
subinterval (p. 282)
total area (p. 308)
Trapezoidal Rule (p. 315)
upper bound (p. 294)
upper limit of integration (p. 284)
variable of integration (p. 284)

CHAPTER 6   Review Exercises

Exercise numbers with a gray background indicate problems that the authors have designed to be solved *without a calculator.*

The collection of exercises marked in red could be used as a chapter test.

Exercises 1–6 refer to the region R in the first quadrant enclosed by the x-axis and the graph of the function $y = 4x - x^3$.

1. Sketch R and partition it into four subregions, each with a base

5. Sketch the trapezoids and compute (by hand) the area for the T_4 approximation.

6. Find the exact area of R by using the Fundamental Theorem of Calculus.

7. Use a calculator program to compute the RAM approximations in the following table for the area under the graph of $y = 1/x$ from $x = 1$ to $x = 5$.

Each chapter concludes with a list of **Key Terms,** with references back to where they are covered in the chapter, as well as **Chapter Review Exercises** to check your comprehension of the chapter material.

The **Quick Quiz for AP* Preparation** provides another opportunity to review your understanding as you progress through each chapter. A quiz appears after every two or three sections and asks you to answer questions about topics covered in those sections. Each quiz contains three multiple-choice questions and one free-response question of the AP* type. This continual reinforcement of ideas steers you away from rote memorization and toward the conceptual understanding needed for the AP* Calculus Exam.

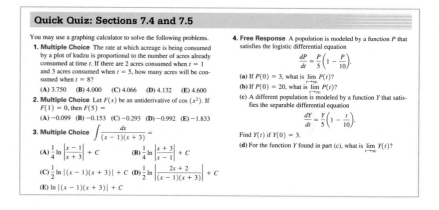

Quick Quiz: Sections 7.4 and 7.5

You may use a graphing calculator to solve the following problems.

1. Multiple Choice The rate at which acreage is being consumed by a plot of kudzu is proportional to the number of acres already consumed at time t. If there are 2 acres consumed when $t = 1$ and 3 acres consumed when $t = 5$, how many acres will be consumed when $t = 8$?

(A) 3.750   (B) 4.000   (C) 4.066   (D) 4.132   (E) 4.600

2. Multiple Choice Let $F(x)$ be an antiderivative of $\cos(x^2)$. If $F(1) = 0$, then $F(5) =$

(A) −0.099   (B) −0.153   (C) −0.293   (D) −0.992   (E) −1.833

3. Multiple Choice $\int \dfrac{dx}{(x-1)(x+3)} =$

(A) $\dfrac{1}{4}\ln\left|\dfrac{x-1}{x+3}\right| + C$ (B) $\dfrac{1}{4}\ln\left|\dfrac{x+3}{x-1}\right| + C$

(C) $\dfrac{1}{2}\ln|(x-1)(x+3)| + C$ (D) $\dfrac{1}{2}\ln\left|\dfrac{2x+2}{(x-1)(x+3)}\right| + C$

(E) $\ln|(x-1)(x+3)| + C$

4. Free Response A population is modeled by a function P that satisfies the logistic differential equation

$$\frac{dP}{dt} = \frac{P}{5}\left(1 - \frac{P}{10}\right).$$

(a) If $P(0) = 3$, what is $\lim_{t\to\infty} P(t)$?

(b) If $P(0) = 20$, what is $\lim_{t\to\infty} P(t)$?

(c) A different population is modeled by a function Y that satisfies the separable differential equation

$$\frac{dY}{dt} = \frac{Y}{5}\left(1 - \frac{t}{10}\right).$$

Find $Y(t)$ if $Y(0) = 3$.

(d) For the function Y found in part (c), what is $\lim_{t\to\infty} Y(t)$?

AP* Examination Preparation

56. Consider the infinite region R in the first quadrant under the curve $y = xe^{-x/2}$.

(a) Write the area of R as an improper integral.

(b) Express the integral in part (a) as a limit of a definite integral.

(c) Find the area of R.

57. The infinite region in the first quadrant bounded by the coordinate axes and the curve $y = \dfrac{1}{x} - 1$ is revolved about the y-axis to generate a solid.

(a) Write the volume of the solid as an improper integral.

(b) Express the integral in part (a) as a limit of a definite integral.

(c) Find the volume of the solid.

58. Determine whether or not $\int_0^\infty xe^{-x}\,dx$ converges. If it converges, give its value. Show your reasoning.

An **AP* Examination Preparation** section appears at the end of each set of Chapter Review Exercises and includes three free-response questions of the AP type. This set of questions, which also may or may not permit the use of your graphing calculator, gives you additional opportunity to practice skills and problem-solving techniques needed for the AP Calculus Exam.

In addition to this text, *Pearson Education AP* Test Prep Series: AP* Calculus,* written by experienced AP teachers, is also available to help you prepare for the AP Calculus Exam. What does it include?

- **Text-specific correlations** between key AP test topics and *Calculus: Graphical, Numerical, Algebraic*

- Reinforcement of the important **connections** between what you'll learn and what you'll be tested on in May

- 2 full **sample AB exams** & 2 **sample BC exams**, including answers and explanation

- Test-taking **strategies**

You can order *Pearson Education AP* Test Prep Series: AP* Calculus* by going online to PearsonSchool.com or calling 1-800-848-9500 and requesting ISBN 0-13-331458-8.

Calculus

Graphical, Numerical, Algebraic

FIFTH EDITION

AP® Edition

Prerequisites for Calculus

1.1 Linear Functions

1.2 Functions and Graphs

1.3 Exponential Functions

1.4 Parametric Equations

1.5 Inverse Functions and Logarithms

1.6 Trigonometric Functions

Willard Libby won the 1960 Nobel Prize in Chemistry for his 1949 discovery of the method of **radiocarbon dating** for estimating the age of organic substances that were once living tissue. The method relies on the slow decay of carbon-14, a radioactive isotope of carbon with a half-life of approximately 5730 years. Using exponential functions and the properties reviewed in Section 1.3, researchers have used radiocarbon dating to study the carefully preserved remains of early Egyptian dynasties and thus reconstruct the history of an important ancient civilization.

CHAPTER 1 Overview

The main prerequisite for a student who wants to undertake the study of calculus is an understanding of functions. It is the context of functions that brings coherence to the study of algebra and provides the connection between algebra and geometry, especially through the graphical representations of algebraic expressions. Students who have taken a modern precalculus course (emphasizing algebraic, numerical, and graphical representations of functions) will probably have already seen everything in this first chapter, but we offer it here mainly in the spirit of review. Since calculus is basically a tool for understanding how functions of various kinds model real-world behavior, a solid understanding of the basic functions makes the applications of calculus considerably easier. Any time you spend in this chapter strengthening your understanding of functions and graphs will pay off later in the course.

We begin by reviewing the easiest type of function, surely the most familiar to most students. Happily, it is also the most important (by far) for understanding how calculus works.

1.1 | Linear Functions

You will be able to analyze linear functions in their algebraic, numerical, and graphical representations.

- Increments and slope
- Linear models
- Point-slope form of linear equations
- Other forms of linear equations
- Parallel and perpendicular lines
- Simultaneous linear equations

Increments and Slope

Calculus is the mathematics of change. It explores the fundamental question: When two quantities are linked, how does change in one affect change in the other?

Calculus is written in the language of functions, $y = f(x)$, because functions describe how one quantity or variable depends on another. The distance a person has walked can be a function of time. The pressure that an underwater diver feels is a function of depth below the surface. Calculus asks: If we know how much time has passed, can we determine how far the person has walked? If we know how far the diver has descended, do we also know how much the pressure has increased? These changes in time, distance, or pressure are known as *increments*.

DEFINITION **Increments**

The change in a variable, such as t from t_1 to t_2, x from x_1 to x_2, or y from y_1 to y_2, is called an **increment** in that variable, denoted by

$$\Delta t = t_2 - t_1, \quad \Delta x = x_2 - x_1, \quad \Delta y = y_2 - y_1.$$

The symbols Δt, Δx, and Δy are read "delta t," "delta x," and "delta y." The letter Δ is a Greek capital D for "difference." Neither Δt, Δx, nor Δy denotes multiplication; Δx is not "delta times x." Increments can be positive, negative, or zero.

EXAMPLE 1 **Finding Increments**

(a) Find the increments Δx and Δy from the point $(1, -3)$ to the point $(4, 5)$. Find the increments Δx and Δy from the point $(5, 6)$ to the point $(5, 1)$.

(b) As a diver descends below sea level from a depth of $d_1 = 20$ meters to $d_2 = 25$ meters, the pressure increases from $p_1 = 2.988$ to $p_2 = 3.485$ atmospheres. What are the increments in depth, Δd, and pressure, Δp?

continued

SOLUTIONS

(a) From the point $(1, -3)$ to the point $(4, 5)$, the increments in x and y are

$$\Delta x = 4 - 1 = 3, \quad \Delta y = 5 - (-3) = 8.$$

From the point $(5, 6)$ to the point $(5, 1)$, the increments in x and y are

$$\Delta x = 5 - 5 = 0, \quad \Delta y = 1 - 6 = -5.$$

(b) The increments in depth and pressure are

$$\Delta d = 25 - 20 = 5 \text{ meters}, \quad \Delta p = 3.485 - 2.988 = 0.497 \text{ atmosphere}.$$

Now Try Exercise 1.

Among all functions, *linear functions* are special. They are the functions in which an increment of one unit in one variable always produces exactly the same increment in the other variable. Another way of saying this is that the *ratio of the increments* is constant.

Why Sensitivity?

Sensitivity is a useful way of thinking about the response of one variable to a small change in another variable. The sensitivity to change is measured by the ratio of the increments.

> **DEFINITION   Linear Function**
>
> The variable y is a **linear function** of x if the ratio of the increment of y to the increment of x is constant; that is,
>
> $$\frac{\Delta y}{\Delta x} = \text{constant}.$$

In a linear function, the constant ratio of the increments is known as the *rate of change* or the *sensitivity*. The graph of a linear function is a straight line. The constant ratio of the increments is the *slope* of this line.

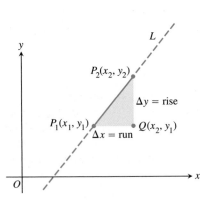

Figure 1.1 The slope of line L is

$$m = \frac{\text{rise}}{\text{run}} = \frac{\Delta y}{\Delta x}.$$

> **DEFINITION   Slope**
>
> Let (x_1, y_1) and (x_2, y_2) be two points on the graph of a linear function. The **slope** m of this line is the ratio of the increments; that is, $m = \dfrac{\text{rise}}{\text{run}} = \dfrac{\Delta y}{\Delta x} = \dfrac{y_2 - y_1}{x_2 - x_1}$.

A line with positive slope goes uphill as x increases (Figure 1.1). A line with negative slope goes downhill as x increases. A line with slope zero is horizontal, since $\Delta y = 0$ implies that all of the points have the same y-coordinate. If $\Delta x = 0$, then the x-coordinate never changes and the line is vertical. In this case, we say that the line *has no slope*.

EXAMPLE 2 Using the Slope to Find Coordinates.

Given a line through the point $(2, 3)$ with slope $m = -2$, find the y-coordinate of the point on this line that has x-coordinate 3.6.

SOLUTION

The increment in x is $\Delta x = 3.6 - 2 = 1.6$. Since the ratio of the increments is -2, $\Delta y = -2 \cdot \Delta x = -3.2$.

The y-coordinate is $3 + (-3.2) = -0.2$.

Now Try Exercise 9.

EXAMPLE 3 **Finding Additional Values of a Linear Function**

The pressure, p, on a diver is a linear function of the depth, d. We know that the pressure at 20 meters is 2.988 atmospheres, and an increase of 5 meters in depth corresponds to an increase of 0.497 atmosphere. Find the pressure at 23 meters, 42 meters, and 16 meters.

SOLUTION

Because this is a linear function, the ratio of the increments is constant:

$$\frac{\Delta p}{\Delta d} = \frac{0.497}{5} = 0.0994 \text{ atmosphere per meter}$$

From $d = 20$ to 23, the change in depth is $\Delta d = 3$, so $\Delta p = 3(0.0994) = 0.2982$. The pressure at 23 m is $2.988 + 0.2982 = 3.2862$ atmospheres.

From $d = 20$ to 42, the change in depth is $\Delta d = 22$, so $\Delta p = 22(0.0994) = 2.1868$. The pressure at 42 m is $2.988 + 2.1868 = 5.1748$ atmospheres.

From $d = 20$ to 16, the change in depth is $\Delta d = -4$, so $\Delta p = -4(0.0994) = -0.3976$. The pressure at 16 m is $2.988 - 0.3976 = 2.5904$ atmospheres. ***Now Try Exercise 13.***

EXAMPLE 4 **Modeling a Linear Equation**

Using the information given in Example 3, find the linear equation that describes pressure, p, as a linear function of depth, d.

SOLUTION

If p is the pressure at depth d, we get the same constant ratio of increments as the pressure changes from 2.988 to p and the depth changes from 20 to d. We can replace Δp by $p - 2.988$ and Δd by $d - 20$ and solve for p:

$$\frac{p - 2.988}{d - 20} = 0.0994$$

$$p - 2.988 = 0.0994(d - 20) \text{ or } p = 0.0994d + 1$$

Now Try Exercise 17.

Point-Slope Equation of a Linear Function

There are many ways to represent a linear relationship between two variables, and each has a role to play in calculus. The most useful representation will be the *point-slope equation*, built from knowledge of some point on the graph of the function and the value of the constant slope.

If we know some ordered pair (x_1, y_1) that satisfies a linear equation, then the slope m between (x_1, y_1) and any *other* point (x, y) must satisfy the equation $\frac{y - y_1}{x - x_1} = m$.

If we multiply this equation by the denominator, we get an equivalent equation that is also valid when (x, y) equals the point (x_1, y_1) itself. This leads to the following definition.

DEFINITION   **Point-Slope Equation of a Line**

The equation

$$y - y_1 = m(x - x_1)$$

is the **point-slope equation** of the line through the point (x_1, y_1) with slope m. We will sometimes find it useful to write this equation in the "calculator-ready" form

$$y = m(x - x_1) + y_1.$$

Notice that the equation $\dfrac{y - 3}{x - 2} = 5$ does *not* work as an answer in Example 5. Significantly, the graph does not pass through the point $(2, 3)$!

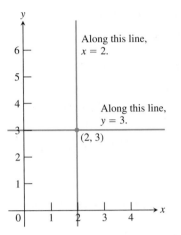

Figure 1.2 The standard equations for the vertical and horizontal lines through the point $(2, 3)$ are $x = 2$ and $y = 3$. (Example 5)

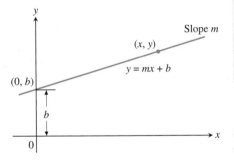

Figure 1.3 A line with slope m and y-intercept b.

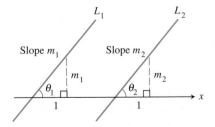

Figure 1.4 If $L_1 \| L_2$, then $\theta_1 = \theta_2$ and $m_1 = m_2$. Conversely, if $m_1 = m_2$, then $\theta_1 = \theta_2$ and $L_1 \| L_2$.

EXAMPLE 5 Using the Point-Slope Equation

Find the point-slope equation of the line with slope 5 that passes through the point $(2, 3)$.

SOLUTION

Letting $m = 5$ and $(x_1, y_1) = (2, 3)$, the point-slope equation is $y - 3 = 5(x - 2)$.

Now Try Exercise 19.

As previously noted, a horizontal line has slope 0. Therefore, the equation of a horizontal line through the point (a, b) has equation $y - b = 0(x - a)$, which simplifies to $y = b$. A vertical line through (a, b) has no slope, and its equation is $x = a$. Horizontal and vertical lines through the point $(2, 3)$ are shown, along with their equations, in Figure 1.2.

Other Linear Equation Forms

The idea of "slope at a point" is a central theme in calculus, and the point-slope equation of a line conveys the information so perfectly that we will rarely have need in this book for the two other common forms that you may have studied. We list them here under their usual names.

DEFINITION   Slope-Intercept Equation and General Linear Equation

The **slope-intercept equation** of a line with slope m that passes through the point $(0, b)$ is

$$y = mx + b.$$

(The number b is called the **y-intercept.** See Figure 1.3.)

A **general linear equation** in x and y has the form

$$Ax + By = C \quad \text{(assuming } A \text{ and } B \text{ are not both } 0\text{).}$$

Slope-intercept form is useful in modeling real-world problems that have a fixed part and a (proportionately) varying part. For example, $y = mx + b$ could represent the salary of a salesman who earns a base salary of b dollars and a fixed percentage m of his sales of x dollars. It also has the advantage of being *unique* (there is only one possible slope-intercept form for any nonvertical line). The latter quality is quite helpful for authors of multiple-choice tests and textbooks with answer keys, which probably accounts for its dominance in algebra classrooms.

The general linear form is useful in linear algebra. You used it in earlier courses when solving simultaneous linear equations, especially if you used matrices. It is also the only form that accommodates vertical lines, as the other forms require a numerical slope m. We will have very little use for the equations of vertical lines, as they do not represent linear *functions*.

Parallel and Perpendicular Lines

Parallel lines form equal angles with the x-axis (Figure 1.4). Hence, nonvertical parallel lines have the same slope. Conversely, lines with equal slopes form equal angles with the x-axis and are therefore parallel.

If two nonvertical lines L_1 and L_2 are perpendicular, their slopes m_1 and m_2 satisfy $m_1 m_2 = -1$, so each slope is the *negative reciprocal* of the other: If $m_1 = a/b$, then $m_2 = -b/a$.

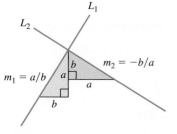

Figure 1.5 A little geometry shows why the slopes of perpendicular lines are negative reciprocals of each other.

In Figure 1.5, the two triangles are congruent right triangles with perpendicular legs of lengths a and b. The angle where lines L_1 and L_2 meet is the sum of the acute angles in this triangle, which is 90°.

EXAMPLE 6 Finding Equations of Lines

Find an equation for:

(a) the line through $(3, 5)$ parallel to the line with equation $y = 2x - 8$;

(b) the line with x-intercept 6 and perpendicular to the line with equation $2x + y = 7$;

(c) the perpendicular bisector of the segment with endpoints $(2, 3)$ and $(6, 17)$.

SOLUTION

(a) The line $y = 2x - 8$ has slope 2, so the line through $(3, 5)$ with the same slope has equation $y - 5 = 2(x - 3)$.

(b) The line $2x + y = 7$ has slope -2, so the line through $(6, 0)$ with negative reciprocal slope has equation $y - 0 = \dfrac{1}{2}(x - 6)$.

(c) The midpoint of the segment is found by averaging the endpoint coordinates: $\left(\dfrac{2 + 6}{2}, \dfrac{3 + 17}{2}\right) = (4, 10)$. The slope of the segment is $\dfrac{17 - 3}{6 - 2} = \dfrac{7}{2}$, so the line through the midpoint and perpendicular to the segment has equation

$$y - 10 = -\frac{2}{7}(x - 4).$$

Now Try Exercise 29.

Note that we gave the answers in Example 6 in point-slope form, not only because it was easiest, but also because the equation is self-identified as "*the* line through *this* point with *this* slope." It is exactly this interpretation of lines that you will be using in calculus.

If you need to convert from point-slope form to some other form (for example, to select an answer on a multiple-choice test), just do the algebra.

EXAMPLE 7 Doing the Algebra

Match each linear equation below with one of the answers in Example 6.

(a) $x - 2y = 6$ **(b)** $7y + 2x = 78$

(c) $y = 0.5x - 3$ **(d)** $y + 1 = 2x$

SOLUTION

(a) (b)   **(b)** (c)

(c) (b)   **(d)** (a)

Now Try Exercise 46.

Applications of Linear Functions

When we use variables to represent quantities in the real world, it is not at all unusual for the relationship between them to be linear. As we have seen, the defining characteristic for a linear function is that equal increments in the independent variable must result in equal increments of the dependent variable. In calculus, we will be more interested in extending the slope concept to other functions than in exploring linear functions themselves, but we want to include at least one well-known linear model.

EXAMPLE 8 Temperature Conversion

The relationship between the temperatures on the Celsius and Fahrenheit scales is linear.

(a) Find the linear equations for converting Celsius temperatures to Fahrenheit and Fahrenheit temperatures to Celsius.

(b) Convert 20°C to Fahrenheit and 95°F to Celsius.

(c) Find the unique temperature that is the same in both scales.

SOLUTION

(a) Let C be the Celsius temperature and F the Fahrenheit temperature. Using the freezing point of water and the boiling point of water gives us two reference points in the linear (C, F) relationship: $(0, 32)$ and $(100, 212)$. The slope is $\dfrac{212 - 32}{100 - 0} = \dfrac{9}{5}$, and the point-slope equation through $(0, 32)$ is $F - 32 = \dfrac{9}{5}(C - 0)$. This simplifies to $F = \dfrac{9}{5}C + 32$.

If we solve this equation for C, we get $C = \dfrac{5}{9}(F - 32)$, which converts Fahrenheit to Celsius.

(b) When $C = 20$, $F = \dfrac{9}{5}(20) + 32 = 68$, so 20°C = 68°F.

When $F = 95$, $C = \dfrac{5}{9}(95 - 32) = 35$, so 95°F = 35°C.

(c) If $F = C$, then $C = \dfrac{9}{5}C + 32$. Solving for C, we get $C = -40$. When the wind chill is "forty below," it does not matter what scale is being used!

Now Try Exercise 41.

Solving Two Linear Equations Simultaneously

Some exercises in this book will require you to find a unique ordered pair (x, y) that solves two different linear equations simultaneously. There are many ways to do this, and we will review a few of them in Example 9 below. If you need further review, you can consult an algebra textbook.

EXAMPLE 9 Solving Two Linear Equations Simultaneously

Find the unique pair (x, y) that satisfies both of these equations simultaneously:

$$3x - 5y = 39$$
$$2x + 3y = 7$$

SOLUTION 1 (Substitution)

Solve the first equation for x to find that $x = \dfrac{5}{3}y + 13$. Substitute the expression into the second equation to get $2\left(\dfrac{5}{3}y + 13\right) + 3y = 7$. Solve this equation to get $y = -3$. Finally, plug $y = -3$ into either original equation to get $x = 8$. The answer is $(8, -3)$.

continued

SOLUTION 2 (Elimination)

$$3x - 5y = 39 \qquad 6x - 10y = 78$$
$$\Rightarrow$$
$$2x + 3y = 7 \qquad 6x + 9y = 21$$

Subtract the bottom equation from the top to "eliminate" the x variable and get $-19y = 57$. Solve this equation to get $y = -3$ and proceed as in Solution 1.

SOLUTION 3 (Graphical)

Graph the two lines and use the "intersect" command on your graphing calculator:

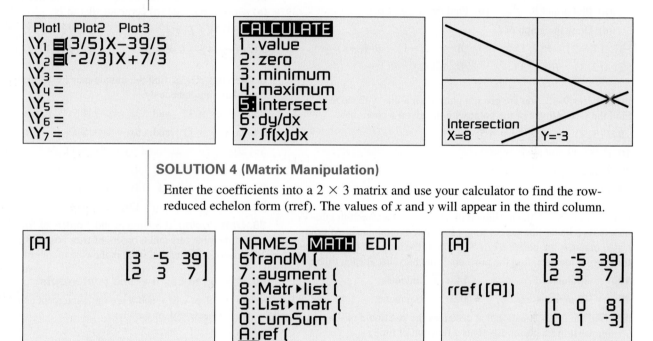

SOLUTION 4 (Matrix Manipulation)

Enter the coefficients into a 2×3 matrix and use your calculator to find the row-reduced echelon form (rref). The values of x and y will appear in the third column.

Now Try Exercise 33.

There is much more that could be said about solving simultaneous linear equations, but that is for another course. If you can use one or more of these methods to solve two linear equations in two variables, that will suffice for now.

Quick Review 1.1   *(For help, go to Section 1.1.)*

Exercise numbers with a gray background indicate problems that the authors have designed to be solved *without a calculator.*

1. Find the value of y that corresponds to $x = 3$ in
$y = -2 + 4(x - 3)$.

2. Find the value of x that corresponds to $y = 3$ in
$y = 3 - 2(x + 1)$.

In Exercises 3 and 4, find the value of m that corresponds to the values of x and y.

3. $x = 5, \quad y = 2, \quad m = \dfrac{y - 3}{x - 4}$

4. $x = -1, \quad y = -3, \quad m = \dfrac{2 - y}{3 - x}$

In Exercises 5 and 6, determine whether the ordered pair is a solution to the equation.

5. $3x - 4y = 5$
   (a) $(2, 1/4)$ **(b)** $(3, -1)$

6. $y = -2x + 5$
   (a) $(-1, 7)$ **(b)** $(-2, 1)$

In Exercises 7 and 8, find the distance between the points.

7. $(1, 0), \quad (0, 1)$

8. $(2, 1), \quad (1, -1/3)$

In Exercises 9 and 10, solve for y in terms of x.

9. $4x - 3y = 7$

10. $-2x + 5y = -3$

Section 1.1 Exercises

Exercise numbers with a gray background indicate problems that the authors have designed to be solved *without a calculator*.

In Exercises 1–4, find the coordinate increments from A to B.

1. $A(1, 2)$, $B(-1, -1)$ **2.** $A(-3, 2)$, $B(-1, -2)$

3. $A(-3, 1)$, $B(-8, 1)$ **4.** $A(0, 4)$, $B(0, -2)$

In Exercises 5–8, let L be the line determined by points A and B.

   (a) Plot A and B.   **(b)** Find the slope of L.

   (c) Draw the graph of L.

5. $A(1, -2)$, $B(2, 1)$ **6.** $A(-2, -1)$, $B(1, -2)$

7. $A(2, 3)$, $B(-1, 3)$ **8.** $A(1, 2)$, $B(1, -3)$

In Exercises 9–12, you are given a point P on a line with slope m. Find the y-coordinate of the point with the given x-coordinate.

9. $P(3, 5)$ $m = 2$ $x = 4.5$

10. $P(-2, 1)$ $m = 3$ $x = 2$

11. $P(3, 2)$ $m = -3$ $x = 5$

12. $P(-1, -2)$ $m = 0.8$ $x = 1$

In Exercises 13–17, the position d of a bicyclist (measured in kilometers) is a linear function of time t (measured in minutes). At time $t = 6$ minutes, the position is $d = 5$ km. If the bicyclist travels 2 km for every 5 minutes, find the position of the bicyclist at each time t.

13. $t = 8$ minutes   **14.** $t = 3$ minutes

15. $t = 12$ minutes   **16.** $t = 20$ minutes

17. Find the linear equation that describes the position d of the bicyclist in Exercises 13–16 as a function of time t.

18. *Club Fees* A tennis club charges a monthly fee of $65 and a rate of $20 for each half-hour of court time. Find the linear equation that gives the total monthly fee F for a club member who accumulates t hours of court time during the month.

In Exercises 19–22, write the point-slope equation for the line through the point P with slope m.

19. $P(1, 1)$, $m = 1$ **20.** $P(-1, 1)$, $m = -1$

21. $P(0, 3)$, $m = 2$ **22.** $P(-4, 0)$, $m = -2$

In Exercises 23 and 24, the line contains the origin and the point in the upper right corner of the grapher screen. Write an equation for the line.

23.   **24.**

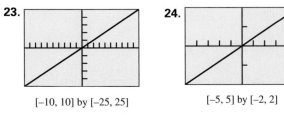

$[-10, 10]$ by $[-25, 25]$ $[-5, 5]$ by $[-2, 2]$

In Exercises 25–28, find the **(a)** slope and **(b)** y-intercept, and **(c)** graph the line.

25. $3x + 4y = 12$ **26.** $x + y = 2$

27. $\dfrac{x}{3} + \dfrac{y}{4} = 1$ **28.** $y = 2x + 4$

In Exercises 29–32, write an equation for the line through P that is **(a)** parallel to L, and **(b)** perpendicular to L.

29. $P(0, 0)$, $L: y = -x + 2$ **30.** $P(-2, 2)$, $L: 2x + y = 4$

31. $P(-2, 4)$, $L: x = 5$ **32.** $P(-1, 1/2)$, $L: y = 3$

In Exercises 33–38, find the unique pair (x, y) that satisfies both equations simultaneously.

33. $x - 2y = 13$ and $3x + y = 4$

34. $2x + y = 11$ and $6x - y = 5$

35. $20x + 7y = 22$ and $y - 5x = 11$

36. $2y - 5x = 0$ and $4x + y = 26$

37. $4x - y = 4$ and $14x + 3y = 1$

38. $3x + 2y = 4$ and $12x - 5y = 3$

39. *Unit Pricing* If 5 burgers and 4 orders of fries cost $30.76, while 8 burgers and 6 orders of fries cost $48.28, what is the cost of a burger and what is the cost of an order of fries?

40. **Writing to Learn** *x- and y-intercepts*

   (a) Explain why c and d are the x-intercept and y-intercept, respectively, of the line

   $$\frac{x}{c} + \frac{y}{d} = 1.$$

   (b) How are the x-intercept and y-intercept related to c and d in the line

   $$\frac{x}{c} + \frac{y}{d} = 2?$$

41. *Parallel and Perpendicular Lines* For what value of k are the two lines $2x + ky = 3$ and $x + y = 1$ **(a)** parallel? **(b)** perpendicular?

Group Activity In Exercises 42–44, work in groups of two or three to solve the problem.

42. *Insulation* By measuring slopes in the figure below, find the temperature change in degrees per inch for the following materials.

   (a) gypsum wallboard

   (b) fiberglass insulation

   (c) wood sheathing

(d) Writing to Learn Which of the materials in (a)–(c) is the best insulator? the poorest? Explain.

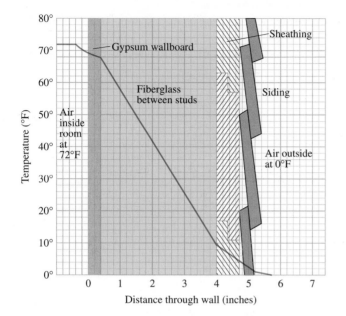

Distance through wall (inches)

43. For the Birds The level of seed in Bruce's bird feeder declines linearly over time. If the feeder is filled to the 12-inch level at 10:00 AM and is at the 7-inch level at 2:00 PM the same day, at approximately what time will the seed be completely gone?

44. Modeling Distance Traveled A car starts from point P at time $t = 0$ and travels at 45 mph.

(a) Write an expression $d(t)$ for the distance the car travels from P.

(b) Graph $y = d(t)$.

(c) What is the slope of the graph in (b)? What does it have to do with the car?

(d) Writing to Learn Create a scenario in which t could have negative values.

(e) Writing to Learn Create a scenario in which the y-intercept of $y = d(t)$ could be 30.

Standardized Test Questions

45. True or False The slope of a vertical line is zero. Justify your answer.

46. True or False The slope of a line perpendicular to the line $y = mx + b$ is $1/m$. Justify your answer.

47. Multiple Choice Which of the following is an equation of the line through $(-3, 4)$ with slope $1/2$?

(A) $y - 4 = \dfrac{1}{2}(x + 3)$ **(B)** $y + 3 = \dfrac{1}{2}(x - 4)$

(C) $y - 4 = -2(x + 3)$ **(D)** $y - 4 = 2(x + 3)$

(E) $y + 3 = 2(x - 4)$

48. Multiple Choice Which of the following is an equation of the vertical line through $(-2, 4)$?

(A) $y = 4$ **(B)** $x = 2$ **(C)** $y = -4$

(D) $x = 0$ **(E)** $x = -2$

49. Multiple Choice Which of the following is the x-intercept of the line $y = 2x - 5$?

(A) $x = -5$ **(B)** $x = 5$ **(C)** $x = 0$

(D) $x = 5/2$ **(E)** $x = -5/2$

50. Multiple Choice Which of the following is an equation of the line through $(-2, -1)$ parallel to the line $y = -3x + 1$?

(A) $y = -3x + 5$ **(B)** $y = -3x - 7$ **(C)** $y = \dfrac{1}{3}x - \dfrac{1}{3}$

(D) $y = -3x + 1$ **(E)** $y = -3x - 4$

Extending the Ideas

51. Tangent to a Circle A circle with radius 5 centered at the origin passes through the point $(3, 4)$. Find an equation for the line that is tangent to the circle at that point.

52. Knowing Your Rights The vertices of triangle ABC have coordinates $A(-3, 10)$, $B(1, 3)$, and $C(15, 11)$. Prove that it is a right triangle. Which side is the hypotenuse?

53. Simultaneous Linear Equations Revisited The two linear equations shown below are said to be *dependent and inconsistent*:

$$3x - 5y = 3$$
$$-9x + 15y = 8$$

(a) Solve the equations simultaneously by an algebraic method, either substitution or elimination. What is your conclusion?

(b) What happens if you use a graphical method?

(c) Writing to Learn Explain in algebraic and graphical terms what happens when two linear equations are dependent and inconsistent.

54. Simultaneous Linear Equations Revisited Again The two linear equations shown below are said to be *dependent and consistent*:

$$2x - 5y = 3$$
$$6x - 15y = 9$$

(a) Solve the equations simultaneously by an algebraic method, either substitution or elimination. What is your conclusion?

(b) What happens if you use a graphical method?

(c) Writing to Learn Explain in algebraic and graphical terms what happens when two linear equations are dependent and consistent.

55. ***Parallelogram*** Three different parallelograms have vertices at $(-1, 1)$, $(2, 0)$, and $(2, 3)$. Draw the three and give the coordinates of the missing vertices.

56. ***Parallelogram*** Show that if the midpoints of consecutive sides of any quadrilateral are connected, the result is a parallelogram.

57. ***Tangent Line*** Consider the circle of radius 5 centered at $(1, 2)$. Find an equation of the line tangent to the circle at the point $(-2, 6)$.

58. **Group Activity** ***Distance from a Point to a Line*** This activity investigates how to find the distance from a point $P(a, b)$ to a line $L: Ax + By = C$.

(a) Write an equation for the line M through P perpendicular to L.

(b) Find the coordinates of the point Q in which M and L intersect.

(c) Find the distance from P to Q.

1.2 | Functions and Graphs

You will be able to use the language, notation, and graphical representation of functions to express relationships between variable quantities.

- Function, domain, and range
- Interval notation
- Graphs in the coordinate plane
- Odd and even symmetry
- Piecewise-defined functions, including absolute value
- Composite functions

Functions

We assumed some familiarity with the language of functions and graphs in Section 1.1, where we connected lines in the coordinate plane with their algebraic representations, called linear functions. In this section we will review some of the other terminology associated with functions and graphs so that you will be comfortable with them in the chapters to come.

DEFINITION   Function (and Related Terms)

A **function** from a set D to a set R is a rule that assigns to every element in D a unique element in R. The set of all input values in D is the **domain** of the function, and the set of all output values in R is the **range** of the function. In **function notation,** we use $f(x)$ to denote the range value that f assigns to the domain value x. The set of all points (x, y) in the coordinate plane determined by the rule $y = f(x)$ is the **graph of the function f.** The variable x is the **independent variable** and the variable y is the **dependent variable.**

Most of the functions in this course will be from the real numbers to the real numbers. Indeed, this course might be more fully described as "the calculus of real functions of a real variable." In this context, the domain is a subset (not always the whole set) of the real numbers, as is the range.

The uniqueness in the definition of $f(x)$ is essential. It might be helpful to think of f as a machine that assigns a unique range value to every domain value (Figure 1.6). If the same x were put into the same machine, the same $f(x)$ would result. On the other hand, two (or more) different domain values could be assigned the same range value (Figure 1.7).

Figure 1.6 A "machine" diagram for a function.

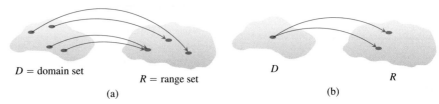

Figure 1.7 (a) A function from a set D to a set R. (b) *Not* a function. The assignment is not unique.

Euler invented a symbolic way to say "y is a function of x":

$$y = f(x),$$

which we read as "y equals f of x." This notation enables us to give different functions different names by changing the letters we use. To say that the boiling point of water is a function of elevation, we can write $b = f(e)$. To say that the area of a circle is a function of the circle's radius, we can write $A = A(r)$, giving the function the same name as the dependent variable.

Leonhard Euler (1707–1783)

Leonhard Euler, the dominant mathematical figure of his century and the most prolific mathematician ever, was also an astronomer, physicist, botanist, and chemist, and an expert in oriental languages. His work was the first to give the function concept the prominence that it has in mathematics today. Euler's collected books and papers fill 72 volumes. This does not count his enormous correspondence to approximately 300 addresses. His introductory algebra text, written originally in German (Euler was Swiss), is still available in English translation.

The notation $y = f(x)$ gives a way to denote specific values of a function. The value of f at a can be written as $f(a)$, read "f of a."

EXAMPLE 1 The Circle-Area Function

Write a formula that expresses the area of a circle as a function of its radius. Use the formula to find the area of a circle of radius 2 in.

SOLUTION

If the radius of the circle is r, then the area $A(r)$ of the circle can be expressed as $A(r) = \pi r^2$. The area of a circle of radius 2 can be found by evaluating the function $A(r)$ at $r = 2$.

$$A(2) = \pi(2)^2 = 4\pi$$

The area of a circle of radius 2 in is 4π in^2.   *Now Try Exercise 3.*

Domains and Ranges

When we define a function $y = f(x)$ with a formula and the domain is not stated or restricted by context, the domain is assumed to be the largest set of x values for which the formula gives real y values. This is the **implied domain.** In Example 1, the domain of the function is restricted by context, since the independent variable is a radius and must be nonnegative. The restricted domain is called the **relevant domain.** The domain of a function can also be restricted as part of its definition, as in the function $v(t) = 32t + 25$ for $t \geq 0$.

The domains and ranges of many real-valued functions of a real variable are intervals or combinations of intervals. The intervals may be open, closed, or half-open (Figures 1.8 and 1.9) and finite or infinite (Figure 1.10).

Name: The set of all real numbers
Notation: $-\infty < x < \infty$ or $(-\infty, \infty)$

Name: The set of numbers greater than a
Notation: $a < x$ or (a, ∞)

Name: The set of numbers greater than or equal to a
Notation: $a \leq x$ or $[a, \infty)$

Name: The set of numbers less than b
Notation: $x < b$ or $(-\infty, b)$

Name: The set of numbers less than or equal to b
Notation: $x \leq b$ or $(-\infty, b]$

Figure 1.10 Infinite intervals—rays on the number line and the number line itself. The symbol ∞ (infinity) is used merely for convenience; it does not mean there is a number ∞.

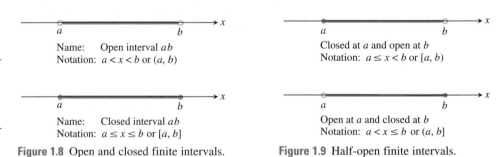

Name: Open interval ab
Notation: $a < x < b$ or (a, b)

Name: Closed interval ab
Notation: $a \leq x \leq b$ or $[a, b]$

Figure 1.8 Open and closed finite intervals.

Closed at a and open at b
Notation: $a \leq x < b$ or $[a, b)$

Open at a and closed at b
Notation: $a < x \leq b$ or $(a, b]$

Figure 1.9 Half-open finite intervals.

The endpoints of an interval make up the interval's **boundary** and are called **boundary points.** The remaining points make up the interval's **interior** and are called **interior points. Closed intervals** contain their boundary points. **Open intervals** contain no boundary points. Every point of an open interval is an interior point of the interval.

Viewing and Interpreting Graphs

The points (x, y) in the plane whose coordinates are the input-output pairs of a function $y = f(x)$ make up the function's graph. The graph of the function $y = x + 2$, for example, is the set of points with coordinates (x, y) for which y equals $x + 2$.

EXAMPLE 2 Identifying Domain and Range of a Function

Identify the domain and range, and then sketch a graph of the function.

(a) $y = \dfrac{1}{x}$ **(b)** $y = \sqrt{x}$

SOLUTION

(a) The formula gives a real y value for every real x value except $x = 0$. (*We cannot divide any number by* 0.) The domain is $(-\infty, 0) \cup (0, \infty)$. The value y takes on every real number except $y = 0$. ($y = c \neq 0$ if $x = 1/c$). The range is also $(-\infty, 0) \cup (0, \infty)$. A sketch is shown in Figure 1.11a.

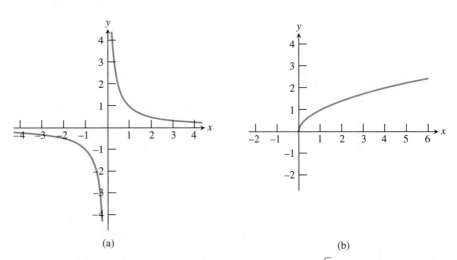

(a) (b)

Figure 1.11 A sketch of the graph of (a) $y = 1/x$ and (b) $y = \sqrt{x}$. (Example 2)

(b) The formula gives a real number only when x is positive or zero. The domain is $[0, \infty)$. Because $\sqrt{x}$ denotes the principal square root of x, y is greater than or equal to zero. The range is also $[0, \infty)$. A sketch is shown in Figure 1.11b.

Now Try Exercise 9.

Graphing with pencil and paper requires that you develop graph *drawing* skills. Graphing with a grapher (graphing calculator) requires that you develop graph *viewing* skills.

Power Function

Any function that can be written in the form $f(x) = kx^a$, where k and a are nonzero constants, is a **power function.**

Graph Viewing Skills

1. Recognize that the graph is reasonable.
2. See all the important characteristics of the graph.
3. Interpret those characteristics.
4. Recognize grapher failure.

Being able to recognize that a graph is reasonable comes with experience. You need to know the basic functions, their graphs, and how changes in their equations affect the graphs.

Grapher failure occurs when the graph produced by a grapher is less than precise—or even incorrect—usually due to the limitations of the screen resolution of the grapher.

EXAMPLE 3 Identifying Domain and Range of a Function

Use a grapher to identify the domain and range, and then draw a graph of the function.

(a) $y = \sqrt{4 - x^2}$ **(b)** $y = x^{2/3}$

SOLUTION

(a) Figure 1.12a shows a graph of the function for $-4.7 \le x \le 4.7$ and $-3.1 \le y \le 3.1$, that is, the viewing window $[-4.7, 4.7]$ by $[-3.1, 3.1]$, with x-scale = y-scale = 1. The graph appears to be the upper half of a circle. The domain appears to be $[-2, 2]$. This observation is correct because we must have $4 - x^2 \ge 0$, or equivalently, $-2 \le x \le 2$. The range appears to be $[0, 2]$, which can also be verified algebraically.

Graphing $y = x^{2/3}$—Possible Grapher Failure

On some graphing calculators you need to enter this function as $y = (x^2)^{1/3}$ or $y = (x^{1/3})^2$ to obtain a correct graph. Try graphing this function on your grapher.

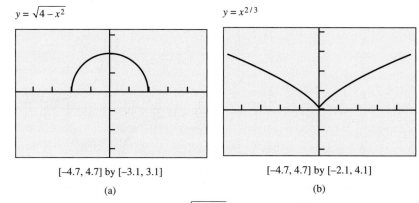

Figure 1.12 The graph of (a) $y = \sqrt{4 - x^2}$ and (b) $y = x^{2/3}$. (Example 3)

(b) Figure 1.12b shows a graph of the function in the viewing window $[-4.7, 4.7]$ by $[-2.1, 4.1]$, with x-scale = y-scale = 1. The domain appears to be $(-\infty, \infty)$, which we can verify by observing that $x^{2/3} = (\sqrt[3]{x})^2$. Also the range is $[0, \infty)$ by the same observation. ***Now Try Exercise 15.***

Even Functions and Odd Functions—Symmetry

The graphs of *even* and *odd* functions have important symmetry properties.

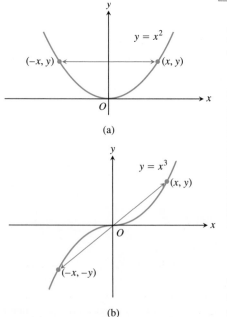

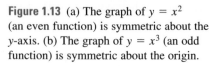

Figure 1.13 (a) The graph of $y = x^2$ (an even function) is symmetric about the y-axis. (b) The graph of $y = x^3$ (an odd function) is symmetric about the origin.

DEFINITIONS Even Function, Odd Function

A function $y = f(x)$ is an

even function of x if $f(-x) = (x)$,

odd function of x if $f(-x) = -(x)$,

for every x in the function's domain.

The names even and odd come from powers of x. If y is an even power of x, as in $y = x^2$ or $y = x^4$, it is an even function of x (because $(-x)^2 = x^2$ and $(-x)^4 = x^4$). If y is an odd power of x, as in $y = x$ or $y = x^3$, it is an odd function of x (because $(-x)^1 = -x$ and $(-x)^3 = -x^3$).

The graph of an even function is **symmetric about the y-axis.** Since $f(-x) = f(x)$, a point (x, y) lies on the graph if and only if the point $(-x, y)$ lies on the graph (Figure 1.13a).

The graph of an odd function is **symmetric about the origin.** Since $f(-x) = -f(x)$, a point (x, y) lies on the graph if and only if the point $(-x, -y)$ lies on the graph (Figure 1.13b).

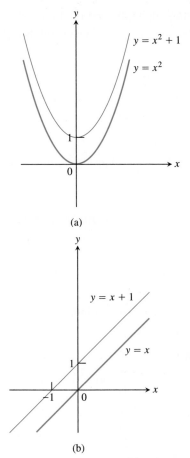

(a)

(b)

Figure 1.14 (a) When we add the constant term 1 to the function $y = x^2$, the resulting function $y = x^2 + 1$ is still even and its graph is still symmetric about the y-axis. (b) When we add the constant term 1 to the function $y = x$, the resulting function $y = x + 1$ is no longer odd. The symmetry about the origin is lost. (Example 4)

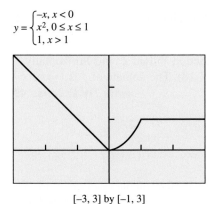

$[-3, 3]$ by $[-1, 3]$

Figure 1.15 The graph of a piecewise-defined function. (Example 5)

Equivalently, a graph is symmetric about the origin if a rotation of 180° about the origin leaves the graph unchanged.

EXAMPLE 4 Recognizing Even and Odd Functions

$f(x) = x^2$ Even function: $(-x)^2 = x^2$ for all x; symmetry about y-axis.

$f(x) = x^2 + 1$ Even function: $(-x)^2 + 1 = x^2 + 1$ for all x; symmetry about y-axis (Figure 1.14a).

$f(x) = x$ Odd function: $(-x) = -x$ for all x; symmetry about the origin.

$f(x) = x + 1$ Not odd: $f(-x) = -x + 1$, but $-f(x) = -x - 1$. The two are not equal.

                    Not even: $(-x) + 1 \neq x + 1$ for all $x \neq 0$ (Figure 1.14b).

Now Try Exercises 21 and 23.

It is useful in graphing to recognize even and odd functions. Once we know the graph of either type of function on one side of the y-axis, we know its graph on both sides.

Piecewise-Defined Functions

While some functions are defined by single formulas, others are defined by applying different formulas to different parts of their domains.

EXAMPLE 5 Graphing Piecewise-Defined Functions

Graph $y = f(x) = \begin{cases} -x, & x < 0 \\ x^2, & 0 \leq x \leq 1 \\ 1, & x > 1. \end{cases}$

SOLUTION

The values of f are given by three separate formulas: $y = -x$ when $x < 0$, $y = x^2$ when $0 \leq x \leq 1$, and $y = 1$ when $x > 1$. However, the function is *just one function*, whose domain is the entire set of real numbers (Figure 1.15).

Now Try Exercise 33.

EXAMPLE 6 Writing Formulas for Piecewise Functions

Write a formula for the function $y = f(x)$ whose graph consists of the two line segments in Figure 1.16.

SOLUTION

We find formulas for the segments from $(0, 0)$ to $(1, 1)$ and from $(1, 0)$ to $(2, 1)$ and piece them together in the manner of Example 5.

Segment from $(0, 0)$ to $(1, 1)$ The line through $(0, 0)$ and $(1, 1)$ has slope $m = (1 - 0)/(1 - 0) = 1$ and y-intercept $b = 0$. Its slope-intercept equation is $y = x$. The segment from $(0, 0)$ to $(1, 1)$ that includes the point $(0, 0)$ but not the point $(1, 1)$ is the graph of the function $y = x$ restricted to the half-open interval $0 \leq x < 1$, namely,

$$y = x, \quad 0 \leq x < 1.$$

continued

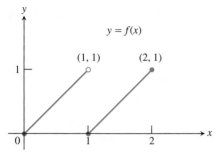

Figure 1.16 The segment on the left contains $(0, 0)$ but not $(1, 1)$. The segment on the right contains both of its endpoints. (Example 6)

Segment from $(1, 0)$ to $(2, 1)$ The line through $(1, 0)$ and $(2, 1)$ has slope $m = (1 - 0)/(2 - 1) = 1$ and passes through the point $(1, 0)$. The corresponding point-slope equation for the line is

$$y = 1(x - 1) + 0, \quad \text{or} \quad y = x - 1.$$

The segment from $(1, 0)$ to $(2, 1)$ that includes both endpoints is the graph of $y = x - 1$ restricted to the closed interval $1 \le x \le 2$, namely,

$$y = x - 1, \quad 1 \le x \le 2.$$

Piecewise Formula Combining the formulas for the two pieces of the graph, we obtain

$$f(x) = \begin{cases} x, & 0 \le x < 1 \\ x - 1, & 1 \le x \le 2. \end{cases} \qquad \textbf{\textit{Now Try Exercise 43.}}$$

Absolute Value Function

The **absolute value function** $y = |x|$ is defined piecewise by the formula

$$|x| = \begin{cases} -x, & x < 0 \\ x, & x \ge 0. \end{cases}$$

The function is even, and its graph (Figure 1.17) is symmetric about the y-axis.

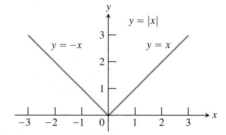

Figure 1.17 The absolute value function has domain $(-\infty, \infty)$ and range $[0, \infty)$.

$y = |x - 2| - 1$

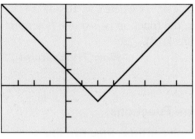

[-4, 8] by [-3, 5]

Figure 1.18 The lowest point of the graph of $f(x) = |x - 2| - 1$ is $(2, -1)$. (Example 7)

EXAMPLE 7 Using Transformations

Draw the graph of $f(x) = |x - 2| - 1$. Then find the domain and range.

SOLUTION

The graph of f is the graph of the absolute value function shifted 2 units horizontally to the right and 1 unit vertically downward (Figure 1.18). The domain of f is $(-\infty, \infty)$ and the range is $[-1, \infty)$. **_Now Try Exercise 49._**

Figure 1.19 Two functions can be composed when a portion of the range of the first lies in the domain of the second.

Composite Functions

Suppose that some of the outputs of a function g can be used as inputs of a function f. We can then link g and f to form a new function whose inputs x are inputs of g and whose outputs are the numbers $f(g(x))$, as in Figure 1.19. We say that the function $f(g(x))$

(read "f of g of x") is the **composite of g and f.** It is made by *composing* g and f in the order of first g, then f. The usual "stand-alone" notation for this composite is $f \circ g$, which is read as "f of g." Thus, the value of $f \circ g$ at x is $(f \circ g)(x) = f(g(x))$.

Composition Is Not Commutative

Function composition is *not* a commutative operation. In Example 8, $(f \circ g)(x) = x^2 - 7$, but $(g \circ f)(x) = (x - 7)^2$. For most functions, $f \circ g \neq g \circ f$.

EXAMPLE 8 Composing Functions

Find a formula for $f(g(x))$ if $g(x) = x^2$ and $f(x) = x - 7$. Then find $f(g(2))$.

SOLUTION

To find $f(g(x))$, we replace x in the formula $f(x) = x - 7$ by the expression given for $g(x)$.

$$f(x) = x - 7$$
$$f(g(x)) = g(x) - 7 = x^2 - 7$$

We then find the value of $f(g(2))$ by substituting 2 for x.

$$f(g(2)) = (2)^2 - 7 = -3$$

Now Try Exercise 51.

EXPLORATION 1 Composing Functions

Some graphers allow a function such as y_1 to be used as the independent variable of another function. With such a grapher, we can compose functions.

1. Enter the functions $y_1 = f(x) = 4 - x^2$, $y_2 = g(x) = \sqrt{x}$, $y_3 = y_2(y_1(x))$, and $y_4 = y_1(y_2(x))$. Which of y_3 and y_4 corresponds to $f \circ g$? to $g \circ f$?
2. Graph y_1, y_2, and y_3 and make conjectures about the domain and range of y_3.
3. Graph y_1, y_2, and y_4 and make conjectures about the domain and range of y_4.
4. Confirm your conjectures algebraically by finding formulas for y_3 and y_4.

Quick Review 1.2 *(For help, go to Appendix A1 and Section 1.2.)*

Exercise numbers with a gray background indicate problems that the authors have designed to be solved *without a calculator*.

In Exercises 1–6, solve for x.

1. $3x - 1 \leq 5x + 3$
2. $x(x - 2) > 0$
3. $|x - 3| \leq 4$
4. $|x - 2| \geq 5$
5. $x^2 < 16$
6. $9 - x^2 \geq 0$

In Exercises 7 and 8, describe how the graph of f can be transformed to the graph of g.

7. $f(x) = x^2$, $g(x) = (x + 2)^2 - 3$
8. $f(x) = |x|$, $g(x) = |x - 5| + 2$

In Exercises 9–12, find all real solutions to the equations.

9. $f(x) = x^2 - 5$
  (a) $f(x) = 4$ (b) $f(x) = -6$
10. $f(x) = 1/x$
  (a) $f(x) = -5$ (b) $f(x) = 0$
11. $f(x) = \sqrt{x + 7}$
  (a) $f(x) = 4$ (b) $f(x) = 1$
12. $f(x) = \sqrt[3]{x - 1}$
  (a) $f(x) = -2$ (b) $f(x) = 3$

Section 1.2 Exercises

Exercise numbers with a gray background indicate problems that the authors have designed to be solved *without a calculator*.

In Exercises 1–4, (a) write a formula for the function and (b) use the formula to find the indicated value of the function.

1. the area A of a circle as a function of its diameter d; the area of a circle of diameter 4 in.

2. the height h of an equilateral triangle as a function of its side length s; the height of an equilateral triangle of side length 3 m

3. the surface area S of a cube as a function of the length of the cube's edge e; the surface area of a cube of edge length 5 ft

4. the volume V of a sphere as a function of the sphere's radius r; the volume of a sphere of radius 3 cm

In Exercises 5–12, (a) identify the domain and range and (b) sketch the graph of the function.

5. $y = 4 - x^2$
6. $y = x^2 - 9$
7. $y = 2 + \sqrt{x - 1}$
8. $y = -\sqrt{-x}$
9. $y = \dfrac{1}{x - 2}$
10. $y = \sqrt[4]{-x}$
11. $y = 1 + \dfrac{1}{x}$
12. $y = 1 + \dfrac{1}{x^2}$

In Exercises 13–20, use a grapher to (a) identify the domain and range and (b) draw the graph of the function.

13. $y = \sqrt[3]{x}$
14. $y = 2\sqrt{3 - x}$
15. $y = \sqrt[3]{1 - x^2}$
16. $y = \sqrt{9 - x^2}$
17. $y = x^{2/5}$
18. $y = x^{3/2}$
19. $y = \sqrt[3]{x - 3}$
20. $y = \dfrac{1}{\sqrt{4 - x^2}}$

In Exercises 21–30, determine whether the function is even, odd, or neither.

21. $y = x^4$
22. $y = x + x^2$
23. $y = x + 2$
24. $y = x^2 - 3$
25. $y = \sqrt{x^2 + 2}$
26. $y = x + x^3$
27. $y = \dfrac{x^3}{x^2 - 1}$
28. $y = \sqrt[3]{2 - x}$
29. $y = \dfrac{1}{x - 1}$
30. $y = \dfrac{1}{x^2 - 1}$

In Exercises 31–34, graph the piecewise-defined functions.

31. $f(x) = \begin{cases} 3 - x, & x \le 1 \\ 2x, & 1 < x \end{cases}$

32. $f(x) = \begin{cases} 1, & x < 0 \\ \sqrt{x}, & x \ge 0 \end{cases}$

33. $f(x) = \begin{cases} 4 - x^2, & x < 1 \\ (3/2)x + 3/2, & 1 \le x \le 3 \\ x + 3, & x > 3 \end{cases}$

34. $f(x) = \begin{cases} x^2, & x < 0 \\ x^3, & 0 \le x \le 1 \\ 2x - 1, & x > 1 \end{cases}$

35. **Writing to Learn** The *vertical line test* to determine whether a curve is the graph of a function states: If every vertical line in the xy-plane intersects a given curve in at most one point, then the curve is the graph of a function. Explain why this is true.

36. **Writing to Learn** For a curve to be *symmetric about the x-axis*, the point (x, y) must lie on the curve if and only if the point $(x, -y)$ lies on the curve. Explain why a curve that is symmetric about the x-axis is not the graph of a function, unless the function is $y = 0$.

In Exercises 37–40, use the vertical line test (see Exercise 35) to determine whether the curve is the graph of a function.

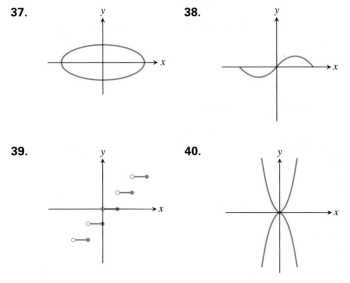

37. 38.

39. 40.

In Exercises 41–48, write a piecewise formula for the function.

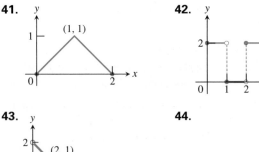

41. 42.

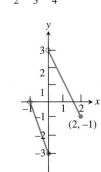

43. 44.

45.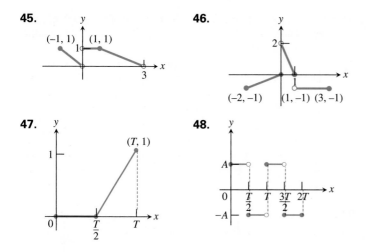

46.

47.

48.

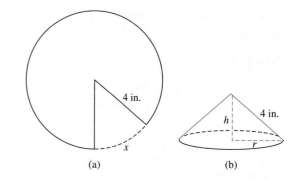

(a)   (b)

In Exercises 49 and 50, **(a)** draw the graph of the function. Then find its **(b)** domain and **(c)** range.

49. $f(x) = -|3 - x| + 2$ **50.** $f(x) = 2|x + 4| - 3$

In Exercises 51 and 52, find

   (a) $f(g(x))$ **(b)** $g(f(x))$ **(c)** $f(g(0))$
   (d) $g(f(0))$ **(e)** $g(g(-2))$ **(f)** $f(f(x))$

51. $f(x) = x + 5$, $g(x) = x^2 - 3$
52. $f(x) = x + 1$, $g(x) = x - 1$

53. Copy and complete the following table.

	$g(x)$	$f(x)$	$(f \circ g)(x)$
(a)	?	$\sqrt{x - 5}$	$\sqrt{x^2 - 5}$
(b)	?	$1 + 1/x$	x
(c)	$1/x$	?	x
(d)	$\sqrt{x}$	?	$|x|, x \geq 0$

54. *The Cylindrical Can Problem* A cylindrical can is to be constructed so that its height h is equal to its diameter.

   (a) Write the volume of the cylinder as a function of its height h.

   (b) Write the total surface area of the cylindrical can (including the top and bottom) as a function of its height h.

   (c) Find the volume of the can if its total surface area is 54π square inches.

55. *The Cone Problem* Begin with a circular piece of paper with a 4-in. radius as shown in (a). Cut out a sector with an arc length of x. Join the two edges of the remaining portion to form a cone with radius r and height h, as shown in (b).

   (a) Explain why the circumference of the base of the cone is $8\pi - x$.

   (b) Express the radius r as a function of x.

   (c) Express the height h as a function of x.

   (d) Express the volume V of the cone as a function of x.

56. *Industrial Costs* Dayton Power and Light, Inc., has a power plant on the Miami River where the river is 800 ft wide. To lay a new cable from the plant to a location in the city 2 mi downstream on the opposite side costs $180 per foot across the river and $100 per foot along the land.

   (a) Suppose that the cable goes from the plant to a point Q on the opposite side that is x ft from the point P directly opposite the plant. Write a function $C(x)$ that gives the cost of laying the cable in terms of the distance x.

   (b) Generate a table of values to determine if the least expensive location for point Q is less than 2000 ft or greater than 2000 ft from point P.

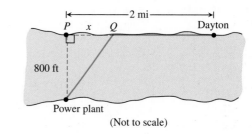

(Not to scale)

Standardized Test Questions

57. **True or False** The function $f(x) = x^4 + x^2 + x$ is an even function. Justify your answer.

58. **True or False** The function $f(x) = x^{-3}$ is an odd function. Justify your answer.

59. Multiple Choice Which of the following gives the domain of

$$f(x) = \frac{x}{\sqrt{9 - x^2}}?$$

(A) $x \neq \pm 3$ (B) $(-3, 3)$ (C) $[-3, 3]$

(D) $(-\infty, -3) \cup (3, \infty)$ (E) $(3, \infty)$

60. Multiple Choice Which of the following gives the range of

$$f(x) = 1 + \frac{1}{x - 1}?$$

(A) $(-\infty, 1) \cup (1, \infty)$ (B) $x \neq 1$ (C) all real numbers

(D) $(-\infty, 0) \cup (0, \infty)$ (E) $x \neq 0$

61. Multiple Choice If $f(x) = 2x - 1$ and $g(x) = x + 3$, which of the following gives $(f \circ g)(2)$?

(A) 2   (B) 6   (C) 7   (D) 9   (E) 10

62. Multiple Choice The length L of a rectangle is twice as long as its width W. Which of the following gives the area A of the rectangle as a function of its width?

(A) $A(W) = 3W$ (B) $A(W) = \frac{1}{2}W^2$

(C) $A(W) = 2W^2$ (D) $A(W) = W^2 + 2W$

(E) $A(W) = W^2 - 2W$

Explorations

In Exercises 63–66, **(a)** graph $f \circ g$ and $g \circ f$ and make a conjecture about the domain and range of each function. **(b)** Then confirm your conjectures by finding formulas for $f \circ g$ and $g \circ f$.

63. $f(x) = x - 7$, $g(x) = \sqrt{x}$

64. $f(x) = 1 - x^2$, $g(x) = \sqrt{x}$

65. $f(x) = x^2 - 3$, $g(x) = \sqrt{x + 2}$

66. $f(x) = \dfrac{2x - 1}{x + 3}$, $g(x) = \dfrac{3x + 1}{2 - x}$

Group Activity In Exercises 67–70, a portion of the graph of a function defined on $[-2, 2]$ is shown. Complete each graph assuming that the graph is **(a)** even, **(b)** odd.

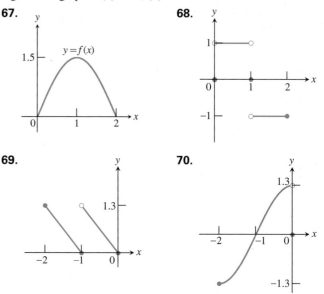

67.

68.

69.

70.

Extending the Ideas

71. Enter $y_1 = \sqrt{x}$, $y_2 = \sqrt{1 - x}$ and $y_3 = y_1 + y_2$ on your grapher.

    (a) Graph y_3 in $[-3, 3]$ by $[-1, 3]$.

    (b) Compare the domain of the graph of y_3 with the domains of the graphs of y_1 and y_2.

    (c) Replace y_3 by

$$y_1 - y_2, \quad y_2 - y_1, \quad y_1 \cdot y_2, \quad y_1/y_2, \quad \text{and} \quad y_2/y_1,$$

    in turn, and repeat the comparison of part (b).

    (d) Based on your observations in (b) and (c), what would you conjecture about the domains of sums, differences, products, and quotients of functions?

72. *Even and Odd Functions*

    (a) Must the product of two even functions always be even? Give reasons for your answer.

    (b) Can anything be said about the product of two odd functions? Give reasons for your answer.

1.3 | Exponential Functions

You will be able to model exponential growth and decay with functions of the form $y = k \cdot a^x$ and recognize exponential growth and decay in algebraic, numerical, and graphical representations.

- Exponential functions
- Rules of exponents
- Applications of exponential functions (growth and decay)
- Compound interest
- The number e

Exponential Growth

Table 1.1 shows the growth of $100 invested in 1996 at an interest rate of 5.5%, compounded annually.

TABLE 1.1 Savings Account Growth		
Year	Amount (dollars)	Increase (dollars)
1996	100	
1997	$100(1.055) = 105.50$	5.50
1998	$100(1.055)^2 = 111.30$	5.80
1999	$100(1.055)^3 = 117.42$	6.12
2000	$100(1.055)^4 = 123.88$	6.46

After the first year, the value of the account is always 1.055 times its value in the previous year. After n years, the value is $y = 100 \cdot (1.055)^n$.

Compound interest provides an example of *exponential growth* and is modeled by a function of the form $y = P \cdot a^x$, where P is the initial investment (called the *principal*) and a is equal to 1 plus the interest rate expressed as a decimal.

The equation $y = P \cdot a^x$, $a > 0$, $a \neq 1$, identifies a family of functions called *exponential functions*. Notice that the ratio of consecutive amounts in Table 1.1 is always the same: $111.30/105.30 = 117.42/111.30 = 123.88/117.42 \approx 1.055$. This fact is an important feature of exponential curves that has widespread application, as we will see.

$y = 2^x$

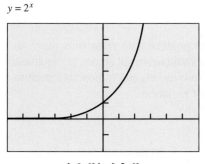

[–6, 6] by [–2, 6]

(a)

$y = 2^{-x}$

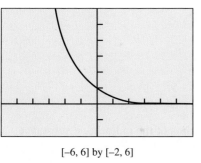

[–6, 6] by [–2, 6]

(b)

Figure 1.20 A graph of (a) $y = 2^x$ and (b) $y = 2^{-x}$.

EXPLORATION 1   Exponential Functions

1. Graph the function $y = a^x$ for $a = 2, 3, 5$, in a $[-5, 5]$ by $[-2, 5]$ viewing window.
2. For what values of x is it true that $2^x < 3^x < 5^x$?
3. For what values of x is it true that $2^x > 3^x > 5^x$?
4. For what values of x is it true that $2^x = 3^x = 5^x$?
5. Graph the function $y = (1/a)^x = a^{-x}$ for $a = 2, 3, 5$.
6. Repeat parts 2–4 for the functions in part 5.

DEFINITION   Exponential Function

Let a be a positive real number other than 1. The function

$$f(x) = a^x$$

is the **exponential function with base a.**

The domain of $f(x) = a^x$ is $(-\infty, \infty)$ and the range is $(0, \infty)$. If $a > 1$, the graph of f looks like the graph of $y = 2^x$ in Figure 1.20a. If $0 < a < 1$, the graph of f looks like the graph of $y = 2^{-x}$ in Figure 1.20b.

$y = 2(3^x) - 4$

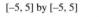

[–5, 5] by [–5, 5]

Figure 1.21 The graph of $y = 2(3^x) - 4$. (Example 1)

$y = 5 - 2.5^x$

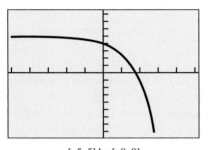

[–5, 5] by [–8, 8]

(a)

$y = 5 - 2.5^x$

Zero
X=1.7564708 Y=0

[–5, 5] by [–8, 8]

(b)

Figure 1.22 (a) A graph of $f(x) = 5 - 2.5^x$. (b) Showing the use of the ZERO feature to approximate the zero of f. (Example 2)

$y = 5\left(\frac{1}{2}\right)^{t/20}, y = 1$

Intersection
X=46.438562 Y=1

[0, 80] by [–3, 5]

Figure 1.23 (Example 3)

EXAMPLE 1 Graphing an Exponential Function

Graph the function $y = 2(3^x) - 4$. State its domain and range.

SOLUTION

Figure 1.21 shows the graph of the function y. It appears that the domain is $(-\infty, \infty)$. The range is $(-4, \infty)$ because $2(3^x) > 0$ for all x. **Now Try Exercise 1.**

EXAMPLE 2 Finding Zeros

Find the zeros of $f(x) = 5 - 2.5^x$ graphically.

SOLUTION

Figure 1.22a suggests that f has a zero between $x = 1$ and $x = 2$, closer to 2. We can use our grapher to find that the zero is approximately 1.756 (Figure 1.22b).
Now Try Exercise 9.

Exponential functions obey the rules for exponents.

Rules for Exponents

If $a > 0$ and $b > 0$, the following hold for all real numbers x and y.

1. $a^x \cdot a^y = a^{x+y}$ **2.** $\dfrac{a^x}{a^y} = a^{x-y}$ **3.** $(a^x)^y = (a^y)^x = a^{xy}$

4. $a^x \cdot b^x = (ab)^x$ **5.** $\left(\dfrac{a}{b}\right)^x = \dfrac{a^x}{b^x}$

Exponential Decay

Exponential functions can also model phenomena that produce a decrease over time, such as happens with radioactive decay. The **half-life** of a radioactive substance is the amount of time it takes for half of the substance to change from its original radioactive state to a nonradioactive state by emitting energy in the form of radiation.

EXAMPLE 3 Modeling Radioactive Decay

Suppose the half-life of a certain radioactive substance is 20 days and that there are 5 grams present initially. When will there be only 1 gram of the substance remaining?

SOLUTION

The number of grams remaining after 20 days is

$$5\left(\frac{1}{2}\right) = \frac{5}{2}.$$

The number of grams remaining after 40 days is

$$5\left(\frac{1}{2}\right)\left(\frac{1}{2}\right) = 5\left(\frac{1}{2}\right)^2 = \frac{5}{4}.$$

The function $y = 5(1/2)^{t/20}$ models the mass in grams of the radioactive substance after t days. Figure 1.23 shows that the graphs of $y_1 = 5(1/2)^{t/20}$ and $y_2 = 1$ (for 1 gram) intersect when t is approximately 46.44.

There will be 1 gram of the radioactive substance left after approximately 46.44 days, or about 46 days 10.5 hours. **Now Try Exercise 23.**

Compound interest investments, population growth, and radioactive decay are all examples of *exponential growth and decay.*

DEFINITIONS **Exponential Growth, Exponential Decay**

The function $y = k \cdot a^x$, $k > 0$ is a model for **exponential growth** if $a > 1$, and a model for **exponential decay** if $0 < a < 1$.

Compound Interest

One common application of exponential growth in the financial world is the compounding effect of accrued interest in a savings account. We saw at the beginning of this section that an account paying 5.5% annual interest would multiply by a factor of 1.055 every year, so an account starting with principal P would be worth $P(1.055)^t$ after t years.

Some accounts pay interest multiple times per year, which increases the compounding effect. An account earning 6% annual interest compounded monthly would pay one-twelfth of the interest each month, effectively a monthly interest rate of 0.5%. Thus, after t years, the account would be worth $P(1.005)^{12t}$. The general formula is given below.

Compound Interest Formula

If an account begins with principal P and earns an annual interest rate r compounded n times per year, then the value of the account in t years is

$$P\left(1 + \frac{r}{n}\right)^{nt}.$$

EXAMPLE 4 **Compound Interest**

Bernie deposits $2500 in an account earning 5.4% annual interest. Find the value of the account in 10 years if the interest is compounded

(a) annually; **(b)** quarterly; **(c)** monthly.

SOLUTION

(a) $2500(1 + 0.054)^{10} \approx 4230.06$, so the account is worth $4230.06.

(b) $2500\left(1 + \dfrac{0.054}{4}\right)^{4(10)} \approx 4274.55$, so the account is worth $4274.55.

(c) $2500\left(1 + \dfrac{0.054}{12}\right)^{12(10)} \approx 4284.82$, so the account is worth $4284.82.

Now Try Exercises 25 and 26.

The Number e

You may have noticed in Example 4 that the value of the account becomes greater as the number of interest payments per year increases, but the value does not appear to be increasing without bound. In fact, a bank can even offer to compound the interest *continuously* without paying that much more per year. This is because the number that serves as the base of the exponential function in the compound interest formula has a finite limit as n approaches infinity:

$$\left(1 + \frac{r}{n}\right)^n \to e^r \quad \text{as} \quad n \to \infty$$

$y = (1 + 1/x)^x$

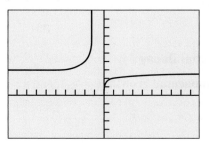

[–10, 10] by [–5, 10]

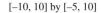

X	Y1	
1000	2.7169	
2000	2.7176	
3000	2.7178	
4000	2.7179	
5000	2.718	
6000	2.7181	
7000	2.7181	

Y1 = (1+1/X)^X

Figure 1.24 A graph and table of values for $f(x) = (1 + 1/x)^x$ both suggest that as $x \rightarrow \infty$, $f(x) \rightarrow e \approx 2.718$.

You can get an estimate of the number e by looking at values of $\left(1 + \dfrac{1}{x}\right)^x$ for increasing values of x, as shown graphically and numerically in Figure 1.24. This number e, which is approximately 2.71828, is one of the most important numbers in mathematics. Like π, it is an irrational number that shows up in many different contexts, some of them quite surprising. You will encounter several of them in this course.

One place that e appears is in the formula for continuously compounded interest.

Continuously Compounded Interest Formula

If an account begins with principal P and earns an annual interest rate r compounded continuously, then the value of the account in t years is

$$P(e^r)^t = Pe^{rt}.$$

EXAMPLE 5 Continuously Compounded Interest

Bernice deposits $2500 in an account earning 5.4% annual interest. Find the value of the account in 10 years if the interest is compounded

(a) daily;   **(b)** continuously.

SOLUTION

(a) $2500\left(1 + \dfrac{0.054}{365}\right)^{365(10)} \approx 4289.85$, so the account is worth $4289.85.

(b) $2500e^{0.054(10)} \approx 4290.02$, so the account is worth $4290.02.

Notice that the difference between "daily" and "continuously" for Bernice is 17 cents!

Now Try Exercise 27.

Quick Review 1.3   *(For help, go to Section 1.3.)*

Exercise numbers with a gray background indicate problems that the authors have designed to be solved *without a calculator*.

In Exercises 1–3, evaluate the expression. Round your answers to 3 decimal places.

1. $5^{2/3}$ **2.** $3^{\sqrt{2}}$

3. $3^{-1.5}$

In Exercises 4–6, solve the equation. Round your answers to 4 decimal places.

4. $x^3 = 17$ **5.** $x^5 = 24$

6. $x^{10} = 1.4567$

In Exercises 7 and 8, find the value of investing P dollars for n years with the interest rate r compounded annually.

7. $P = \$500$, $r = 4.75\%$, $n = 5$ years

8. $P = \$1000$, $r = 6.3\%$, $n = 3$ years

In Exercises 9 and 10, simplify the exponential expression.

9. $\dfrac{(x^{-3}y^2)^2}{(x^4y^3)^3}$

10. $\left(\dfrac{a^3b^{-2}}{c^4}\right)^2\left(\dfrac{a^4c^{-2}}{b^3}\right)^{-1}$

Section 1.3 Exercises

Exercise numbers with a gray background indicate problems that the authors have designed to be solved *without a calculator*.

In Exercises 1–4, graph the function. State its domain and range.

1. $y = -2^x + 3$ **2.** $y = e^x + 3$

3. $y = 3 \cdot e^{-x} - 2$ **4.** $y = -2^{-x} - 1$

In Exercises 5–8, rewrite the exponential expression to have the indicated base.

5. 9^{2x},   base 3   **6.** 16^{3x},   base 2

7. $(1/8)^{2x}$,   base 2   **8.** $(1/27)^x$,   base 3

In Exercises 9–12, use a graph to find the zeros of the function.

9. $f(x) = 2^x - 5$

10. $f(x) = e^x - 4$

11. $f(x) = 3^x - 0.5$

12. $f(x) = 3 - 2^x$

In Exercises 13–18, match the function with its graph. Try to do it without using your grapher.

13. $y = 2^x$

14. $y = 3^{-x}$

15. $y = -3^{-x}$

16. $y = -0.5^{-x}$

17. $y = 2^{-x} - 2$

18. $y = 1.5^x - 2$

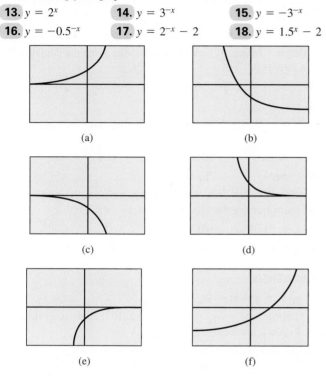

(a) (b)

(c) (d)

(e) (f)

In Exercises 19–32, use an exponential model to solve the problem.

19. *Population Growth* The population of Knoxville is 500,000 and is increasing at the rate of 3.75% each year. Approximately when will the population reach 1 million?

20. *Population Growth* The population of Silver Run in the year 1890 was 6250. Assume the population increased at a rate of 2.75% per year.

(a) Estimate the population in 1915 and 1940.

(b) Approximately when did the population reach 50,000?

21. *Half-life* The approximate half-life of titanium-44 is 63 years. How long will it take a sample to lose

(a) 50% of its titanium-44?

(b) 75% of its titanium-44?

22. *Half-life* The amount of silicon-32 in a sample will decay from 28 grams to 7 grams in approximately 340 years. What is the approximate half-life of silicon-32?

23. *Radioactive Decay* The half-life of phosphorus-32 is about 14 days. There are 6.6 grams present initially.

(a) Express the amount of phosphorus-32 remaining as a function of time t.

(b) When will there be 1 gram remaining?

24. *Finding Time* If John invests $2300 in a savings account with a 6% interest rate compounded annually, how long will it take until John's account has a balance of $4150?

25. *Doubling Your Money* Determine how much time is required for an investment to double in value if interest is earned at the rate of 6.25% compounded annually.

26. *Doubling Your Money* Determine how much time is required for an investment to double in value if interest is earned at the rate of 6.25% compounded monthly.

27. *Doubling Your Money* Determine how much time is required for an investment to double in value if interest is earned at the rate of 6.25% compounded continuously.

28. *Tripling Your Money* Determine how much time is required for an investment to triple in value if interest is earned at the rate of 5.75% compounded annually.

29. *Tripling Your Money* Determine how much time is required for an investment to triple in value if interest is earned at the rate of 5.75% compounded daily.

30. *Tripling Your Money* Determine how much time is required for an investment to triple in value if interest is earned at the rate of 5.75% compounded continuously.

31. *Cholera Bacteria* Suppose that a colony of bacteria starts with 1 bacterium and doubles in number every half hour. How many bacteria will the colony contain at the end of 24 h?

32. *Eliminating a Disease* Suppose that in any given year, the number of cases of a disease is reduced by 20%. If there are 10,000 cases today, how many years will it take

(a) to reduce the number of cases to 1000?

(b) to eliminate the disease; that is, to reduce the number of cases to less than 1?

Group Activity In Exercises 33–36, copy and complete the table for the function.

33. $y = 2x - 3$

x	y	Change (Δy)
1	?	
		?
2	?	
		?
3	?	
		?
4	?	

34. $y = -3x + 4$

x	y	Change (Δy)
1	?	
		?
2	?	
		?
3	?	
		?
4	?	

35. $y = x^2$

x	y	Change (Δy)
1	?	
		?
2	?	
		?
3	?	
		?
4	?	

36. $y = 3e^x$

x	y	Ratio (y_i/y_{i-1})
1	?	
		?
2	?	
		?
3	?	
		?
4	?	

37. Writing to Learn Explain how the change Δy is related to the slopes of the lines in Exercises 33 and 34. If the changes in x are constant for a linear function, what would you conclude about the corresponding changes in y?

38. Bacteria Growth The number of bacteria in a petri dish culture after t hours is

$$B = 100e^{0.693t}.$$

(a) What was the initial number of bacteria present?

(b) How many bacteria are present after 6 hours?

(c) Approximately when will the number of bacteria be 200? Estimate the doubling time of the bacteria.

39. The graph of the exponential function $y = a \cdot b^x$ is shown below. Find a and b.

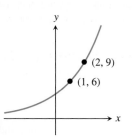

40. The graph of the exponential function $y = a \cdot b^x$ is shown below. Find a and b.

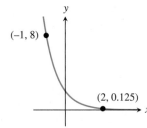

Standardized Test Questions

You may use a graphing calculator to solve the following problems.

41. True or False The number 3^{-2} is negative. Justify your answer.

42. True or False If $4^3 = 2^a$, then $a = 6$. Justify your answer.

43. Multiple Choice John invests \$200 at 4.5% compounded annually. About how long will it take for John's investment to double in value?

(A) 6 yr   **(B)** 9 yr   **(C)** 12 yr   **(D)** 16 yr   **(E)** 20 yr

44. Multiple Choice Which of the following gives the domain of $y = 2e^{-x} - 3$?

(A) $(-\infty, \infty)$ **(B)** $[-3, \infty)$ **(C)** $[-1, \infty)$ **(D)** $(-\infty, 3]$

(E) $x \neq 0$

45. Multiple Choice Which of the following gives the range of $y = 4 - 2^{2x}$?

(A) $(-\infty, \infty)$ **(B)** $(-\infty, 4)$ **(C)** $[-4, \infty)$

(D) $(-\infty, 4]$ **(E)** all reals

46. Multiple Choice Which of the following gives the best approximation for the zero of $f(x) = 4 - e^x$?

(A) $x = -1.386$ **(B)** $x = 0.386$ **(C)** $x = 1.386$

(D) $x = 3$ **(E)** There are no zeros.

Exploration

47. Let $y_1 = x^2$ and $y_2 = 2^x$.

(a) Graph y_1 and y_2 in $[-5, 5]$ by $[-2, 10]$. How many times do you think the two graphs cross?

(b) Compare the corresponding changes in y_1 and y_2 as x changes from 1 to 2, 2 to 3, and so on. How large must x be for the changes in y_2 to overtake the changes in y_1?

(c) Solve for x: $x^2 = 2^x$.

(d) Solve for x: $x^2 < 2^x$.

Extending the Ideas

In Exercises 48 and 49, assume that the graph of the exponential function $f(x) = k \cdot a^x$ passes through the two points. Find the values of a and k.

48. $(1, 4.5), (-1, 0.5)$

49. $(1, 1.5), (-1, 6)$

Quick Quiz for AP* Preparation: Sections 1.1–1.3

You may use a graphing calculator to solve the following problems.

1. Multiple Choice Which of the following gives an equation for the line through $(3, -1)$ and parallel to the line $y = -2x + 1$?

(A) $= \frac{1}{2}x + \frac{7}{2}$ **(B)** $y = \frac{1}{2}x - \frac{5}{2}$ **(C)** $y = -2x + 5$

(D) $y = -2x - 7$ **(E)** $y = -2x + 1$

2. Multiple Choice If $f(x) = x^2 + 1$ and $g(x) = 2x - 1$, which of the following gives $(f \circ g)(2)$?

(A) 2   **(B)** 5   **(C)** 9   **(D)** 10   **(E)** 15

3. Multiple Choice The half-life of a certain radioactive substance is 8 hr. There are 5 grams present initially. Which of the following gives the best approximation when there will be 1 gram remaining?

(A) 2   **(B)** 10   **(C)** 15   **(D)** 16   **(E)** 19

4. Free Response Let $f(x) = e^{-x} - 2$.

(a) Find the domain of f.

(b) Find the range of f.

(c) Find the zeros of f.

1.4 | Parametric Equations

You will be able to analyze functions and relations defined parametrically and know how to determine their graphs; in particular, you will be able to analyze inverse relations algebraically and graphically by switching parametrizations of *x* and *y*.

- Parametrically defined curves
- Parametrizations of simple curves (lines and segments, circles, ellipses)
- The witch of Agnesi

$x = \sqrt{t}, y = t$

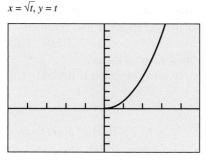

[–5, 5] by [–5, 10]

Figure 1.25 You must choose a *smallest* and *largest* value for *t* in parametric mode. Here we used 0 and 10, respectively. (Example 1)

Relations

A **relation** is a set of ordered pairs (x, y) of real numbers. The **graph of a relation** is the set of points in the plane that correspond to the ordered pairs of the relation. If *x* and *y* are *functions* of a third variable *t*, called a *parameter*, then we can use the *parametric mode* of a grapher to obtain a graph of the relation.

EXAMPLE 1 Graphing Half a Parabola

Describe the graph of the relation determined by

$$x = \sqrt{t}, \quad y = t, \quad t \geq 0.$$

Indicate the direction in which the curve is traced. Find a Cartesian equation for a curve that contains the parametrized curve.

SOLUTION

Set $x_1 = \sqrt{t}$, $y_1 = t$, and use the parametric mode of the grapher to draw the graph in Figure 1.25. The graph appears to be the right half of the parabola $y = x^2$. Notice that there is no information about *t* on the graph itself. The curve appears to be traced to the upper right with starting point $(0, 0)$.

Both *x* and *y* will be greater than or equal to zero because $t \geq 0$. Eliminating *t* we find that for every value of *t*,

$$y = t = \left(\sqrt{t}\right)^2 = x^2.$$

Thus, the relation is the function $y = x^2, x \geq 0$. ***Now Try Exercise 5.***

DEFINITIONS Parametric Curve, Parametric Equations

If *x* and *y* are given as functions

$$x = f(t), \quad y = g(t)$$

over an interval of *t* values, then the set of points $(x, y) = (f(t), g(t))$ defined by these equations is a **parametric curve**. The equations are **parametric equations** for the curve.

The variable *t* is a **parameter** for the curve and its domain *I* is the **parameter interval.** If *I* is a closed interval, $a \leq t \leq b$, the point $(f(a), g(a))$ is the **initial point of the curve** and the point $(f(b), g(b))$ is the **terminal point of the curve.** When we give parametric equations and a parameter interval for a curve, we say that we have **parametrized** the curve. The equations and interval constitute a **parametrization of the curve.**

In Example 1, the parameter interval is $[0, \infty)$, so $(0, 0)$ is the initial point and there is no terminal point.

A grapher can draw a parametrized curve only over a closed interval, so the portion it draws has endpoints even when the curve being graphed does not. Keep this in mind when you graph.

Circles

In applications, t often denotes time, an angle, or the distance a particle has traveled along its path from its starting point. In fact, parametric graphing can be used to simulate the motion of the particle.

EXPLORATION 1 Parametrizing Circles

Let $x = a \cos t$ and $y = a \sin t$.

1. Let $a = 1, 2,$ or 3 and graph the parametric equations in a *square viewing window* using the parameter interval $[0, 2\pi]$. How does changing a affect this graph?
2. Let $a = 2$ and graph the parametric equations using the following parameter intervals: $[0, \pi/2]$, $[0, \pi]$, $[0, 3\pi/2]$, $[2\pi, 4\pi]$, and $[0, 4\pi]$. Describe the role of the length of the parameter interval.
3. Let $a = 3$ and graph the parametric equations using the intervals $[\pi/2, 3\pi/2]$, $[\pi, 2\pi]$, $[3\pi/2, 3\pi]$, and $[\pi, 5\pi]$. What are the initial point and terminal point in each case?
4. Graph $x = 2 \cos(-t)$ and $y = 2 \sin(-t)$ using the parameter intervals $[0, 2\pi]$, $[\pi, 3\pi]$, and $[\pi/2, 3\pi/2]$. In each case, describe how the graph is traced.

For $x = a \cos t$ and $y = a \sin t$, we have

$$x^2 + y^2 = a^2 \cos^2 t + a^2 \sin^2 t = a^2(\cos^2 t + \sin^2 t) = a^2(1) = a^2,$$

using the identity $\cos^2 t + \sin^2 t = 1$. Thus, the curves in Exploration 1 were either circles or portions of circles, each with center at the origin.

EXAMPLE 2 Graphing a Circle

Describe the graph of the relation determined by

$$x = 2 \cos t, \quad y = 2 \sin t, \quad 0 \le t \le 2\pi.$$

Find the initial and terminal points, if any, and indicate the direction in which the curve is traced. Find a Cartesian equation for a curve that contains the parametrized curve.

SOLUTION

Figure 1.26 shows that the graph appears to be a circle with radius 2. By watching the graph develop we can see that the curve is traced exactly once counterclockwise. The initial point at $t = 0$ is $(2, 0)$, and the terminal point at $t = 2\pi$ is also $(2, 0)$.

Next we eliminate the variable t.

$$x^2 + y^2 = 4 \cos^2 t + 4 \sin^2 t$$
$$= 4 (\cos^2 t + \sin^2 t)$$
$$= 4 \qquad \text{Because } \cos^2 t + \sin^2 t = 1$$

The parametrized curve is a circle centered at the origin of radius 2.

Now Try Exercise 9.

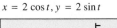

$x = 2 \cos t, y = 2 \sin t$

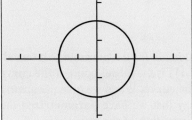

[−4.7, 4.7] by [−3.1, 3.1]

Figure 1.26 A graph of the parametric curve $x = 2 \cos t$, $y = 2 \sin t$, with Tmin $= 0$, Tmax $= 2\pi$, and Tstep $= \pi/24 \approx 0.131$. (Example 2)

Ellipses

Parametrizations of ellipses are similar to parametrizations of circles. Recall that the standard form of an ellipse centered at $(0, 0)$ is

$$\frac{x^2}{a^2} + \frac{y^2}{b^2} = 1.$$

$x = 3 \cos t, y = 4 \sin t$

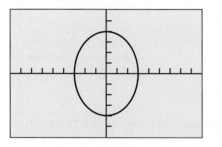

[–9, 9] by [–6, 6]

Figure 1.27 A graph of the parametric equations $x = 3 \cos t$, $y = 4 \sin t$ for $0 \leq t \leq 2\pi$. (Example 3)

EXAMPLE 3 Graphing an Ellipse

Graph the parametric curve $x = 3 \cos t$, $y = 4 \sin t$, $0 \leq t \leq 2\pi$.

Find a Cartesian equation for a curve that contains the parametric curve. What portion of the graph of the Cartesian equation is traced by the parametric curve? Indicate the direction in which the curve is traced and the initial and terminal points, if any.

SOLUTION

Figure 1.27 suggests that the curve is an ellipse. The Cartesian equation is

$$\left(\frac{x}{3}\right)^2 + \left(\frac{y}{4}\right)^2 = \cos^2 t + \sin^2 t = 1,$$

so the parametrized curve lies along an ellipse with major axis endpoints $(0, \pm 4)$ and minor axis endpoints $(\pm 3, 0)$. As t increases from 0 to 2π, the point $(x, y) = (3 \cos t, 4 \sin t)$ starts at $(3, 0)$ and traces the entire ellipse once counterclockwise. Thus, $(3, 0)$ is both the initial point and the terminal point. **Now Try Exercise 13.**

EXPLORATION 2 Parametrizing Ellipses

Let $x = a \cos t$ and $y = b \sin t$.

1. Let $a = 2$ and $b = 3$. Then graph using the parameter interval $[0, 2\pi]$. Repeat, changing b to 4, 5, and 6.
2. Let $a = 3$ and $b = 4$. Then graph using the parameter interval $[0, 2\pi]$. Repeat, changing a to 5, 6, and 7.
3. Based on parts 1 and 2, how do you identify the axis that contains the major axis of the ellipse? the minor axis?
4. Let $a = 4$ and $b = 3$. Then graph using the parameter intervals $[0, \pi/2]$, $[0, \pi]$, $[0, 3\pi/2]$, and $[0, 4\pi]$. Describe the role of the length of the parameter interval.
5. Graph $x = 5 \cos (-t)$ and $y = 2 \sin (-t)$ using the parameter intervals $(0, 2\pi]$, $[\pi, 3\pi]$, and $[\pi/2, 3\pi/2]$. Describe how the graph is traced. What are the initial point and terminal point in each case?

For $x = a \cos t$ and $y = b \sin t$, we have $(x/a)^2 + (y/b)^2 = \cos^2 t + \sin^2 t = 1$. Thus, the curves in Exploration 2 were either ellipses or portions of ellipses, each with center at the origin.

In the exercises you will see how to graph hyperbolas parametrically.

Lines and Other Curves

Lines, line segments, and many other curves can be defined parametrically.

$x = 3t, y = 2 - 2t$

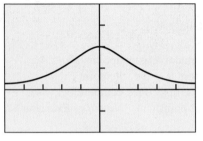

[−4, 4] by [−2, 4]

Figure 1.28 The graph of the line segment $x = 3t$, $y = 2 - 2t$, $0 \le t \le 1$, with trace on the initial point $(0, 2)$. (Example 4)

$x = 2 \cot t, y = 2 \sin^2 t$

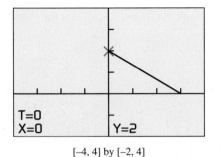

[−5, 5] by [−2, 4]

Figure 1.29 The witch of Agnesi. (Exploration 3)

Maria Agnesi (1718–1799)

Analytical Institutions, the most complete treatment of calculus of its time, was written in Italian by Maria Agnesi and quickly translated into many other languages. Agnesi started writing it when she was 20, the same year she published her *Philosophical Propositions,* a series of essays on natural science and philosophy. At the age of 32 she was offered the position of Professor of Mathematics at the University of Bologna, the first woman to be offered such a position in Europe. She declined it, but remained an honorary faculty member.

Today, Agnesi is remembered chiefly for a bell-shaped curve called *the witch of Agnesi.* This name, found only in English texts, is the result of a mistranslation. Agnesi's own name for the curve was *versiera* or "turning curve." John Colson, a noted Cambridge mathematician, probably confused *versiera* with *avversiera,* which means "wife of the devil" and translated it into "witch."

EXAMPLE 4 Graphing a Line Segment

Draw and identify the graph of the parametric curve determined by

$$x = 3t, \quad y = 2 - 2t, \quad 0 \le t \le 1.$$

SOLUTION

The graph (Figure 1.28) appears to be a line segment with endpoints $(0, 2)$ and $(3, 0)$. When $t = 0$, the equations give $x = 0$ and $y = 2$. When $t = 1$, they give $x = 3$ and $y = 0$. When we substitute $t = x/3$ into the y equation, we obtain

$$y = 2 - 2\left(\frac{x}{3}\right) = -\frac{2}{3}x + 2.$$

Thus, the parametric curve traces the segment of the line $y = -(2/3)x + 2$ from the point $(0, 2)$ to $(3, 0)$. *Now Try Exercise 17.*

If we change the parameter interval $[0, 1]$ in Example 4 to $(-\infty, \infty)$, the parametrization will trace the entire line $y = -(2/3)x + 2$.

The bell-shaped curve in Exploration 3 is the famous witch of Agnesi. You will find more information about this curve in Exercise 47.

EXPLORATION 3 Graphing the Witch of Agnesi

The witch of Agnesi is the curve

$$x = 2 \cot t, \quad y = 2 \sin^2 t, \quad 0 < t < \pi.$$

1. Draw the curve using the window in Figure 1.29. What did you choose as a closed parameter interval for your grapher? In what direction is the curve traced? How far to the left and right of the origin do you think the curve extends?
2. Graph the same parametric equations using the parameter intervals $(-\pi/2, \pi/2)$, $(0, \pi/2)$, and $(\pi/2, \pi)$. In each case, describe the curve you see and the direction in which it is traced by your grapher.
3. What happens if you replace $x = 2 \cot t$ by $x = -2 \cot t$ in the original parametrization? What happens if you use $x = 2 \cot(\pi - t)$?

EXAMPLE 5 Parametrizing a Line Segment

Find a parametrization for the line segment with endpoints $(-2, 1)$ and $(3, 5)$.

SOLUTION

Using $(-2, 1)$ we create the parametric equations

$$x = -2 + at, \quad y = 1 + bt.$$

These represent a line, as we can see by solving each equation for t and equating to obtain

$$\frac{x + 2}{a} = \frac{y - 1}{b}.$$

continued

This line goes through the point $(-2, 1)$ when $t = 0$. We determine a and b so that the line goes through $(3, 5)$ when $t = 1$.

$$3 = -2 + a \quad \Rightarrow \quad a = 5 \quad \text{\small x = 3 when t = 1.}$$

$$5 = 1 + b \quad \Rightarrow \quad b = 4 \quad \text{\small y = 5 when t = 1.}$$

Therefore,

$$x = -2 + 5t, \quad y = 1 + 4t, \quad 0 \le t \le 1$$

is a parametrization of the line segment with initial point $(-2, 1)$ and terminal point $(3, 5)$.

Now Try Exercise 23.

Quick Review 1.4   *(For help, go to Section 1.1 and Appendix A1.)*

Exercise numbers with a gray background indicate problems that the authors have designed to be solved *without a calculator.*

In Exercises 1–3, write an equation for the line.

1. the line through the points $(1, 8)$ and $(4, 3)$

2. the horizontal line through the point $(3, -4)$

3. the vertical line through the point $(2, -3)$

In Exercises 4–6, find the *x*- and *y*-intercepts of the graph of the relation.

4. $\dfrac{x^2}{9} + \dfrac{y^2}{16} = 1$ **5.** $\dfrac{x^2}{16} - \dfrac{y^2}{9} = 1$

6. $2y^2 = x + 1$

In Exercises 7 and 8, determine whether the given points lie on the graph of the relation.

7. $2x^2y + y^2 = 3$

   (a) $(1, 1)$ **(b)** $(-1, -1)$ **(c)** $(1/2, -2)$

8. $9x^2 - 18x + 4y^2 = 27$

   (a) $(1, 3)$ **(b)** $(1, -3)$ **(c)** $(-1, 3)$

9. Solve for t.

   (a) $2x + 3t = -5$ **(b)** $3y - 2t = -1$

10. For what values of a is each equation true?

   (a) $\sqrt{a^2} = a$ **(b)** $\sqrt{a^2} = \pm a$

   (c) $\sqrt{4a^2} = 2|a|$

Section 1.4 Exercises

In Exercises 1–4, match the parametric equations with their graph. State the approximate dimensions of the viewing window. Give a parameter interval that traces the curve exactly once.

1. $x = 3 \sin(2t), \quad y = 1.5 \cos t$

2. $x = \sin^3 t, \quad y = \cos^3 t$

3. $x = 7 \sin t - \sin(7t), \quad y = 7 \cos t - \cos(7t)$

4. $x = 12 \sin t - 3 \sin(6t), \quad y = 12 \cos t + 3 \cos(6t)$

(a)   (b)

(c)   (d)

In Exercises 5–22, a parametrization is given for a curve.

   (a) Graph the curve. What are the initial and terminal points, if any? Indicate the direction in which the curve is traced.

   (b) Find a Cartesian equation for a curve that contains the parametrized curve. What portion of the graph of the Cartesian equation is traced by the parametrized curve?

5. $x = 3t, \quad y = 9t^2, \quad -\infty < t < \infty$

6. $x = -\sqrt{t}, \quad y = t, \quad t \ge 0$

7. $x = t, \quad y = \sqrt{t}, \quad t \ge 0$

8. $x = (\sec^2 t) - 1, \quad y = \tan t, \quad -\pi/2 < t < \pi/2$

9. $x = \cos t, \quad y = \sin t, \quad 0 \le t \le \pi$

10. $x = \sin(2\pi t), \quad y = \cos(2\pi t), \quad 0 \le t \le 1$

11. $x = \cos(\pi - t), \quad y = \sin(\pi - t), \quad 0 \le t \le \pi$

12. $x = 4 \cos t, \quad y = 2 \sin t, \quad 0 \le t \le 2\pi$

13. $x = 4 \sin t, \quad y = 2 \cos t, \quad 0 \le t \le \pi$

14. $x = 4 \sin t, \quad y = 5 \cos t, \quad 0 \le t \le 2\pi$

15. $x = 2t - 5, \quad y = 4t - 7, \quad -\infty < t < \infty$

16. $x = 1 - t, \quad y = 1 + t, \quad -\infty < t < \infty$

17. $x = t, \quad y = 1 - t, \quad 0 \le t \le 1$

18. $x = 3 - 3t, \quad y = 2t, \quad 0 \le t \le 1$

19. $x = 4 - \sqrt{t}, \quad y = \sqrt{t}, \quad 0 \le t$

20. $x = t^2, \quad y = \sqrt{4 - t^2}, \quad 0 \le t \le 2$

21. $x = \sin t, \quad y = \cos 2t, \quad -\infty < t < \infty$

22. $x = t^2 - 3, \quad y = t, \quad t \le 0$

In Exercises 23–28, find a parametrization for the curve.

23. the line segment with endpoints $(-1, -3)$ and $(4, 1)$

24. the line segment with endpoints $(-1, 3)$ and $(3, -2)$

25. the lower half of the parabola $x - 1 = y^2$

26. the left half of the parabola $y = x^2 + 2x$

27. the ray (half line) with initial point $(2, 3)$ that passes through the point $(-1, -1)$

28. the ray (half line) with initial point $(-1, 2)$ that passes through the point $(0, 0)$

Group Activity In Exercises 29–32, refer to the graph of

$$x = 3 - |t|, \quad y = t - 1, \quad -5 \le t \le 5,$$

shown in the figure. Find the values of t that produce the graph in the given quadrant.

29. Quadrant I

30. Quadrant II

31. Quadrant III

32. Quadrant IV

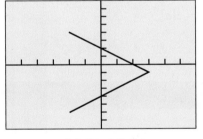

[–6, 6] by [–8, 8]

In Exercises 33 and 34, find a parametrization for the part of the graph that lies in Quadrant I.

33. $y = x^2 + 2x + 2$ **34.** $y = \sqrt{x + 3}$

35. *Circles* Find parametrizations to model the motion of a particle that starts at $(a, 0)$ and traces the circle $x^2 + y^2 = a^2, a > 0$, as indicated.

(a) once clockwise   **(b)** once counterclockwise

(c) twice clockwise   **(d)** twice counterclockwise

36. *Ellipses* Find parametrizations to model the motion of a particle that starts at $(-a, 0)$ and traces the ellipse

$$\left(\frac{x}{a}\right)^2 + \left(\frac{y}{b}\right)^2 = 1, \quad a > 0, b > 0,$$

as indicated.

(a) once clockwise   **(b)** once counterclockwise

(c) twice clockwise   **(d)** twice counterclockwise

Standardized Test Questions

You may use a graphing calculator to solve the following problems.

37. True or False The graph of the parametric curve $x = 3 \cos t$, $y = 4 \sin t$ is a circle. Justify your answer.

38. True or False The parametric curve $x = 2 \cos (-t)$, $y = 2 \sin (-t), 0 \le t \le 2\pi$ is traced clockwise. Justify your answer.

In Exercises 39 and 40, use the parametric curve $x = 5t, y = 3 - 3t$, $0 \le t \le 1$.

39. Multiple Choice Which of the following describes its graph?

(A) circle   **(B)** parabola   **(C)** ellipse

(D) line segment   **(E)** line

40. Multiple Choice Which of the following is the initial point of the curve?

(A) $(-5, 6)$ **(B)** $(0, -3)$ **(C)** $(0, 3)$ **(D)** $(5, 0)$

(E) $(10, -3)$

41. Multiple Choice Which of the following describes the graph of the parametric curve $x = -3 \sin t, y = -3 \cos t$?

(A) circle   **(B)** parabola   **(C)** ellipse

(D) hyperbola   **(E)** line

42. Multiple Choice Which of the following describes the graph of the parametric curve $x = 3t, y = 2t, t \ge 1$?

(A) circle   **(B)** parabola   **(C)** line segment

(D) line   **(E)** ray

Explorations

43. *Hyperbolas* Let $x = a \sec t$ and $y = b \tan t$.

(a) Writing to Learn Let $a = 1, 2$, or 3, $b = 1, 2$, or 3, and graph using the parameter interval $(-\pi/2, \pi/2)$. Explain what you see, and describe the role of a and b in these parametric equations. [*Hint:* Recall that $\sec t = 1/\cos t$.]

(b) Let $a = 2, b = 3$, and graph in the parameter interval $(\pi/2, 3\pi/2)$. Explain what you see.

(c) Writing to Learn Let $a = 2, b = 3$, and graph using the parameter interval $(-\pi/2, 3\pi/2)$. The two lines that look like asymptotes are not really part of the graph; they show up because the grapher is in CONNECTED mode while drawing a disconnected curve. Give a more complete explanation for the appearance of these lines based on the parameter t.

(d) Use algebra to explain why

$$\left(\frac{x}{a}\right)^2 - \left(\frac{y}{b}\right)^2 = 1.$$

(e) Let $x = a \tan t$ and $y = b \sec t$. Repeat (a), (b), and (d) using an appropriate version of (d).

44. *Transformations* Let $x = (2 \cos t) + h$ and $y = (2 \sin t) + k$.

(a) Writing to Learn Let $k = 0$ and $h = -2, -1, 1$, and 2, in turn. Graph using the parameter interval $[0, 2\pi]$. Describe the role of h.

(b) Writing to Learn Let $h = 0$ and $k = -2, -1, 1$, and 2, in turn. Graph using the parameter interval $[0, 2\pi]$. Describe the role of k.

(c) Find a parametrization for the circle with radius 5 and center at $(2, -3)$.

(d) Find a parametrization for the ellipse centered at $(-3, 4)$ with semimajor axis of length 5 parallel to the x-axis and semiminor axis of length 2 parallel to the y-axis.

In Exercises 45 and 46, a parametrization is given for a curve.

(a) Graph the curve. What are the initial and terminal points, if any? Indicate the direction in which the curve is traced.

(b) Find a Cartesian equation for a curve that contains the parametrized curve. What portion of the graph of the Cartesian equation is traced by the parametrized curve?

45. $x = -\sec t, \quad y = \tan t, \quad -\pi/2 < t < \pi/2$

46. $x = \tan t, \quad y = -2 \sec t, \quad -\pi/2 < t < \pi/2$

Extending the Ideas

47. *The Witch of Agnesi* The bell-shaped witch of Agnesi can be constructed as follows. Start with the circle of radius 1, centered at the point $(0, 1)$ as shown in the figure.

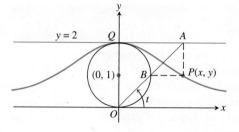

Choose a point A on the line $y = 2$, and connect it to the origin with a line segment. Call the point where the segment crosses the circle B. Let P be the point where the vertical line through A crosses the horizontal line through B. The witch is the curve traced by P as A moves along the line $y = 2$.

Find a parametrization for the witch by expressing the coordinates of P in terms of t, the radian measure of the angle that segment OA makes with the positive x-axis. The following equalities (which you may assume) will help:

(i) $x = AQ$ **(ii)** $y = 2 - AB \sin t$ **(iii)** $AB \cdot AO = (AQ)^2$

48. *Parametrizing Lines and Segments*

(a) Show that $x = x_1 + (x_2 - x_1)t, \quad y = y_1 + (y_2 - y_1)t$, $-\infty < t < \infty$ is a parametrization for the line through the points (x_1, y_1) and (x_2, y_2).

(b) Find a parametrization for the line segment with endpoints (x_1, y_1) and (x_2, y_2).

1.5 Inverse Functions and Logarithms

You will be able to find inverses of one-to-one functions and will be able to analyze logarithmic functions algebraically, graphically, and numerically as inverses of exponential functions.

- One-to-one functions and the horizontal line test
- Finding inverse functions graphically and algebraically
- Base *a* logarithm functions
- Properties of logarithms
- Changing bases
- Using logarithms to solve exponential equations algebraically

One-to-One Functions

As you know, a function is a rule that assigns a single value in its range to each point in its domain. Some functions assign the same output to more than one input. For example, $f(x) = x^2$ assigns the output 4 to both 2 and -2. Other functions never output a given value more than once. For example, the cubes of different numbers are always different.

If each output value of a function is associated with exactly one input value, the function is *one-to-one*.

DEFINITION **One-to-One Function**

A function $f(x)$ is **one-to-one** on a domain D if $f(a) \neq f(b)$ whenever $a \neq b$.

The graph of a one-to-one function $y = f(x)$ can intersect any horizontal line at most once (the *horizontal line test*). If it intersects such a line more than once it assumes the same *y* value more than once, and is therefore not one-to-one (Figure 1.30).

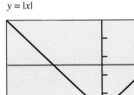
$y = |x|$

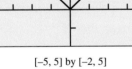
$y = \sqrt{x}$

[–5, 5] by [–2, 5]

(a)

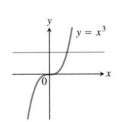

One-to-one: Graph meets each horizontal line once.

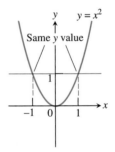

Not one-to-one: Graph meets some horizontal lines more than once.

Figure 1.30 Using the horizontal line test, we see that $y = x^3$ is one-to-one and $y = x^2$ is not.

EXAMPLE 1 Using the Horizontal Line Test

Determine whether the functions are one-to-one.

(a) $f(x) = |x|$ **(b)** $g(x) = \sqrt{x}$

SOLUTION

(a) As Figure 1.31a suggests, each horizontal line $y = c, c > 0$, intersects the graph of $f(x) = |x|$ twice. So f is not one-to-one.

(b) As Figure 1.31b suggests, each horizontal line intersects the graph of $g(x) = \sqrt{x}$ either once or not at all. The function g is one-to-one. **Now Try Exercise 1.**

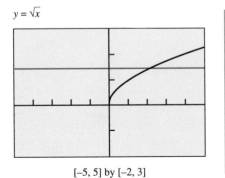

[–5, 5] by [–2, 3]

(b)

Figure 1.31 (a) The graph of $f(x) = |x|$ and a horizontal line. (b) The graph of $g(x) = \sqrt{x}$ and a horizontal line. (Example 1)

Inverses

Since each output of a one-to-one function comes from just one input, a one-to-one function can be reversed to send outputs back to the inputs from which they came. The function defined by reversing a one-to-one function f is the **inverse of** f. The functions in Tables 1.2 and 1.3 are inverses of one another. The symbol for the inverse of f is f^{-1}, read "f inverse." The -1 in f^{-1} is not an exponent; $f^{-1}(x)$ does not mean $1/f(x)$.

TABLE 1.2 Rental Charge versus Time	
Time x (hours)	Charge y (dollars)
1	5.00
2	7.50
3	10.00
4	12.50
5	15.00
6	17.50

TABLE 1.3 Time versus Rental Charge	
Charge x (dollars)	Time y (hours)
5.00	1
7.50	2
10.00	3
12.50	4
15.00	5
17.50	6

As Tables 1.2 and 1.3 suggest, composing a function with its inverse in either order sends each output back to the input from which it came. In other words, the result of composing a function and its inverse in either order is the **identity function,** the function that assigns each number to itself. This gives a way to test whether two functions f and g are inverses of one another. Compute $f \circ g$ and $g \circ f$. If $(f \circ g)(x) = (g \circ f)(x) = x$, then f and g are inverses of one another; otherwise they are not. The functions $f(x) = x^3$ and $g(x) = x^{1/3}$ are inverses of one another because $(x^3)^{1/3} = x$ and $(x^{1/3})^3 = x$ for every number x.

EXPLORATION 1 Testing for Inverses Graphically

For each of the function pairs below,

(a) Graph f and g together in a square window.

(b) Graph $f \circ g$.   **(c)** Graph $g \circ f$.

What can you conclude from the graphs?

1. $f(x) = x^3$, $g(x) = x^{1/3}$ **2.** $f(x) = x$, $g(x) = 1/x$

3. $f(x) = 3x$, $g(x) = x/3$ **4.** $f(x) = e^x$, $g(x) = \ln x$

Finding Inverses

How do we find the graph of the inverse of a function? Suppose, for example, that the function is the one pictured in Figure 1.32a. To read the graph, we start at the point x on the x-axis, go up to the graph, and then move over to the y-axis to read the value of y. If we start with y and want to find the x from which it came, we reverse the process (Figure 1.32b).

The graph of f is already the graph of f^{-1}, although the latter graph is not drawn in the usual way with the domain axis horizontal and the range axis vertical. For f^{-1}, the input-output pairs are reversed. To display the graph of f^{-1} in the usual way, we have to reverse the pairs by reflecting the graph across the $45°$ line $y = x$ (Figure 1.32c) and interchanging the letters x and y (Figure 1.32d). This puts the independent variable, now called x, on the horizontal axis and the dependent variable, now called y, on the vertical axis.

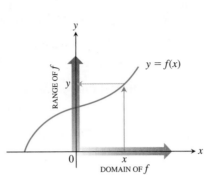

(a) To find the value of f at x, we start at x, go up to the curve, and then over to the y-axis.

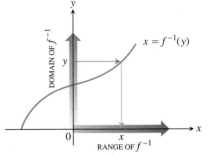

(b) The graph of f is also the graph of f^{-1}. To find the x that gave y, we start at y and go over to the curve and down to the x-axis. The domain of f^{-1} is the range of f. The range of f^{-1} is the domain of f.

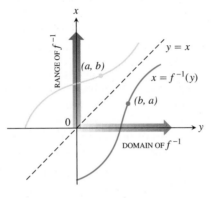

(c) To draw the graph of f^{-1} in the usual way, we reflect the system across the line $y = x$.

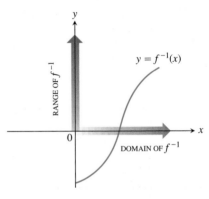

(d) Then we interchange the letters x and y. We now have a normal-looking graph of f^{-1} as a function of x.

Figure 1.32 The graph of $y = f^{-1}(x)$.

The fact that the graphs of f and f^{-1} are reflections of each other across the line $y = x$ is to be expected because the input-output pairs (a, b) of f have been reversed to produce the input-output pairs (b, a) of f^{-1}.

The pictures in Figure 1.32 tell us how to express f^{-1} as a function of x algebraically.

Writing f^{-1} as a Function of x

1. Solve the equation $y = f(x)$ for x in terms of y.
2. Interchange x and y. The resulting formula will be $y = f^{-1}(x)$.

EXAMPLE 2 Finding the Inverse Function

Show that the function $y = f(x) = -2x + 4$ is one-to-one and find its inverse function.

SOLUTION

Every horizontal line intersects the graph of f exactly once, so f is one-to-one and has an inverse.

Step 1:

Solve for x in terms of y: $\quad y = -2x + 4$

$$x = -\frac{1}{2}y + 2$$

continued

Step 2:

Interchange x and y: $y = -\dfrac{1}{2}x + 2$

The inverse of the function $f(x) = -2x + 4$ is the function $f^{-1}(x) = -(1/2)x + 2$. We can verify that both composites are the identity function.

$$f^{-1}(f(x)) = -\frac{1}{2}(-2x + 4) + 2 = x - 2 + 2 = x$$

$$f(f^{-1}(x)) = -2\left(-\frac{1}{2}x + 2\right) + 4 = x - 4 + 4 = x$$

Now Try Exercise 13.

Graphing $y = f(x)$ and $y = f^{-1}(x)$ Parametrically

We can graph any function $y = f(x)$ as

$$x_1 = t, \quad y_1 = f(t).$$

Interchanging t and $f(t)$ produces parametric equations for the inverse:

$$x_2 = f(t), \quad y_2 = t$$

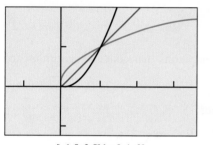

[−1.5, 3.5] by [−1, 2]

Figure 1.33 The graphs of f and f^{-1} are reflections of each other across the line $y = x$. (Example 3)

We can use parametric graphing to graph the inverse of a function without finding an explicit rule for the inverse, as illustrated in Example 3.

EXAMPLE 3 Graphing the Inverse Parametrically

(a) Graph the one-to-one function $f(x) = x^2$, $x \geq 0$, together with its inverse and the line $y = x$, $x \geq 0$.

(b) Express the inverse of f as a function of x.

SOLUTION

(a) We can graph the three functions parametrically as follows:

Graph of f: $x_1 = t, \quad y_1 = t^2, \quad t \geq 0$

Graph of f^{-1}: $x_2 = t^2, \quad y_2 = t$

Graph of $y = x$: $x_3 = t, \quad y_3 = t$

Figure 1.33 shows the three graphs.

(b) Next we find a formula for $f^{-1}(x)$.

Step 1:
Solve for x in terms of y.

$$y = x^2$$
$$\sqrt{y} = \sqrt{x^2}$$
$$\sqrt{y} = x \qquad \text{Because } x \geq 0$$

Step 2:
Interchange x and y.

$$\sqrt{x} = y$$

Thus, $f^{-1}(x) = \sqrt{x}$.

Now Try Exercise 27.

Logarithmic Functions

If a is any positive real number other than 1, the base a exponential function $f(x) = a^x$ is one-to-one. It therefore has an inverse. Its inverse is called the *base a logarithm function*.

> **DEFINITION   Base a Logarithm Function**
>
> The **base a logarithm function** $y = \log_a x$ is the inverse of the base a exponential function $y = a^x (a > 0, a \neq 1)$.

The domain of $\log_a x$ is $(0, \infty)$, the range of a^x. The range of $\log_a x$ is $(-\infty, \infty)$, the domain of a^x.

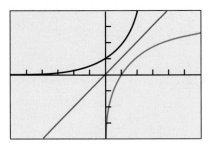

[-6, 6] by [-4, 4]

Figure 1.34 The graphs of $y = 2^x (x_1 = t,$ $y_1 = 2^t)$, its inverse $y = \log_2 x (x_2 = 2^t,$ $y_2 = t)$, and $y = x (x_3 = t, y_3 = t)$.

Because we have no technique for solving for x in terms of y in the equation $y = a^x$, we do not have an explicit formula for the logarithm function as a function of x. However, the graph of $y = \log_a x$ can be obtained by reflecting the graph of $y = a^x$ across the line $y = x$, or by using parametric graphing (Figure 1.34).

Logarithms with base e and base 10 are so important in applications that calculators have special keys for them. They also have their own special notation and names:

$$\log_e x = \ln x,$$

$$\log_{10} x = \log x$$

The function $y = \ln x$ is called the **natural logarithm function** and $y = \log x$ is often called the **common logarithm function.**

Properties of Logarithms

Because a^x and $\log_a x$ are inverses of each other, composing them in either order gives the identity function. This gives two useful properties.

Inverse Properties for a^x and $\log_a x$

1. Base $a > 0$ and $a \neq 1$: $a^{\log_a x} = x$ for $x > 0$; $\log_a a^x = x$ for all x
2. Base e: $e^{\ln x} = x$ for $x > 0$; $\ln e^x = x$ for all x

---

These properties help us with the solution of equations that contain logarithms and exponential functions.

EXAMPLE 4 Using the Inverse Properties

Solve for x: (a) $\ln x = 3t + 5$ (b) $e^{2x} = 10$

SOLUTION

(a) $\ln x = 3t + 5$

$e^{\ln x} = e^{3t+5}$ Exponentiate both sides.

$x = e^{3t+5}$ Inverse Property

(b) $e^{2x} = 10$

$\ln e^{2x} = \ln 10$ Take logarithms of both sides.

$2x = \ln 10$ Inverse Property

$x = \dfrac{1}{2} \ln 10 \approx 1.15$ ***Now Try Exercises 33 and 37.***

The logarithm function has the following useful arithmetic properties.

Properties of Logarithms

For any real numbers $x > 0$ and $y > 0$,

1. *Product Rule:* $\log_a xy = \log_a x + \log_a y$
2. *Quotient Rule:* $\log_a \dfrac{x}{y} = \log_a x - \log_a y$
3. *Power Rule:* $\log_a x^y = y \log_a x$

EXPLORATION 2 Supporting the Product Rule

Let $y_1 = \ln(ax)$, $y_2 = \ln x$, and $y_3 = y_1 - y_2$.

1. Graph y_1 and y_2 for $a = 2, 3, 4,$ and 5. How do the graphs of y_1 and y_2 appear to be related?
2. Support your finding by graphing y_3.
3. Confirm your finding algebraically.

The following formula allows us to evaluate $\log_a x$ for any base $a > 0$, $a \neq 1$, and to obtain its graph using the natural logarithm function on our grapher.

Changing the Base for Changing the Base

The log button on your calculator works just as well as the ln button in the change of base formula:

$$\log_a x = \frac{\log x}{\log a}$$

Change of Base Formula

$$\log_a x = \frac{\ln x}{\ln a}$$

EXAMPLE 5 Graphing a Base *a* Logarithm Function

Graph $f(x) = \log_2 x$.

SOLUTION

We use the change of base formula to rewrite $f(x)$.

$$f(x) = \log_2 x = \frac{\ln x}{\ln 2}$$

Figure 1.35 gives the graph of f.

Now Try Exercise 41.

$y = \dfrac{\ln x}{\ln 2}$

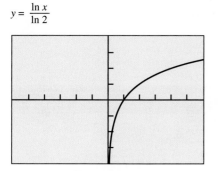

[–6, 6] by [–4, 4]

Figure 1.35 The graph of $f(x) = \log_2 x$ using $f(x) = (\ln x)/(\ln 2)$. (Example 5)

Applications

In Section 1.3 we used graphical methods to solve exponential growth and decay problems. Now we can use the properties of logarithms to solve the same problems algebraically.

EXAMPLE 6 Finding Time

Sarah invests $1000 in an account that earns 5.25% interest compounded annually. How long will it take the account to reach $2500?

SOLUTION

The amount in the account at any time t in years is $1000(1.0525)^t$, so we need to solve the equation

$$1000(1.0525)^t = 2500.$$

continued

$$(1.0525)^t = 2.5 \qquad \text{Divide by 1000.}$$

$$\ln (1.0525)^t = \ln 2.5 \qquad \text{Take logarithms of both sides.}$$

$$t \ln 1.0525 = \ln 2.5 \qquad \text{Power Rule}$$

$$t = \frac{\ln 2.5}{\ln 1.0525} \approx 17.9$$

The amount in Sarah's account will be $2500 in about 17.9 years, or about 17 years and 11 months.   ***Now Try Exercise 47.***

Quick Review 1.5   *(For help, go to Sections 1.2, 1.3, and 1.4.)*

Exercise numbers with a gray background indicate problems that the authors have designed to be solved *without a calculator*.

In Exercises 1–4, let $f(x) = \sqrt[3]{x - 1}$, $g(x) = x^2 + 1$, and evaluate the expression.

1. $(f \circ g)(1)$

2. $(g \circ f)(-7)$

3. $(f \circ g)(x)$

4. $(g \circ f)(x)$

In Exercises 5 and 6, choose parametric equations and a parameter interval to represent the function on the interval specified.

5. $y = \dfrac{1}{x - 1}$, $x \geq 2$

6. $y = x$, $x < -3$

In Exercises 7–10, find the points of intersection of the two curves. Round your answers to 2 decimal places.

7. $y = 2x - 3$, $y = 5$

8. $y = -3x + 5$, $y = -3$

9. (a) $y = 2^x$, $y = 3$

(b) $y = 2^x$, $y = -1$

10. (a) $y = e^{-x}$, $y = 4$

(b) $y = e^{-x}$, $y = -1$

Section 1.5 Exercises

In Exercises 1–6, determine whether the function is one-to-one.

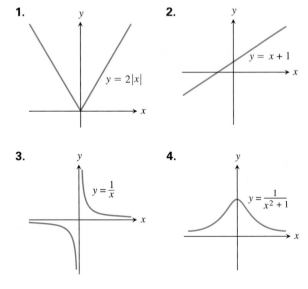

1. $y = 2|x|$

2. $y = x + 1$

3. $y = \dfrac{1}{x}$

4. $y = \dfrac{1}{x^2 + 1}$

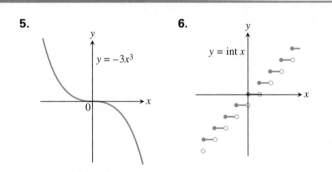

5. $y = -3x^3$

6. $y = \text{int } x$

In Exercises 7–12, determine whether the function has an inverse function.

7. $y = \dfrac{3}{x - 2} - 1$

8. $y = x^2 + 5x$

9. $y = x^3 - 4x + 6$

10. $y = x^3 + x$

11. $y = \ln x^2$

12. $y = 2^{3-x}$

In Exercises 13–24, find f^{-1} and verify that
$$(f \circ f^{-1})(x) = (f^{-1} \circ f)(x) = x.$$

13. $f(x) = 2x + 3$
14. $f(x) = 5 - 4x$
15. $f(x) = x^3 - 1$
16. $f(x) = x^2 + 1, \quad x \geq 0$
17. $f(x) = x^2, \quad x \leq 0$
18. $f(x) = x^{2/3}, \quad x \geq 0$
19. $f(x) = -(x - 2)^2, \quad x \leq 2$
20. $f(x) = x^2 + 2x + 1, \quad x \geq -1$
21. $f(x) = \dfrac{1}{x^2}, \quad x > 0$
22. $f(x) = \dfrac{1}{x^3}$
23. $f(x) = \dfrac{2x + 1}{x + 3}$
24. $f(x) = \dfrac{x + 3}{x - 2}$

In Exercises 25–32, use parametric graphing to graph f, f^{-1}, and $y = x$.

25. $f(x) = e^x$
26. $f(x) = 3^x$
27. $f(x) = 2^{-x}$
28. $f(x) = 3^{-x}$
29. $f(x) = \ln x$
30. $f(x) = \log x$
31. $f(x) = \sin^{-1} x$
32. $f(x) = \tan^{-1} x$

In Exercises 33–36, solve the equation algebraically. You can check your solution graphically.

33. $(1.045)^t = 2$
34. $e^{0.05t} = 3$
35. $e^x + e^{-x} = 3$
36. $2^x + 2^{-x} = 5$

In Exercises 37 and 38, solve for y.

37. $\ln y = 2t + 4$
38. $\ln(y - 1) - \ln 2 = x + \ln x$

In Exercises 39–42, draw the graph and determine the domain and range of the function.

39. $y = 2 \ln(3 - x) - 4$
40. $y = -3 \log(x + 2) + 1$
41. $y = \log_2(x + 1)$
42. $y = \log_3(x - 4)$

In Exercises 43 and 44, find a formula for f^{-1} and verify that $(f \circ f^{-1})(x) = (f^{-1} \circ f)(x) = x$.

43. $f(x) = \dfrac{100}{1 + 2^{-x}}$
44. $f(x) = \dfrac{50}{1 + 1.1^{-x}}$

45. Self-inverse Prove that the function f is its own inverse.

  (a) $f(x) = \sqrt{1 - x^2}, \quad x \geq 0$
  (b) $f(x) = 1/x$

46. Radioactive Decay The half-life of a certain radioactive substance is 12 hours. There are 8 grams present initially.

  (a) Express the amount of substance remaining as a function of time t.

  (b) When will there be 1 gram remaining?

47. Doubling Your Money Determine how much time is required for a \$500 investment to double in value if interest is earned at the rate of 4.75% compounded annually.

48. Population Growth The population of Glenbrook is 375,000 and is increasing at the rate of 2.25% per year. Predict when the population will be 1 million.

49. Guess the Curve A curve is defined parametrically as the set of points $\left(\sqrt{2 - t}, \sqrt{2 + t}\right)$ for $-2 \leq t \leq 2$. Answer parts (a) through (d) before using your grapher.

  (a) Explain why this parametrization cannot be used for other values of t.

  (b) If a point is on this curve, what is its distance from the origin?

  (c) Find the endpoints of the curve (determined by $t = -2$ and $t = 2$, respectively).

  (d) Explain why all other points on this curve must lie in the first quadrant.

  (e) Based on what you know from (a) through (d), give a complete geometric description of the curve. Then verify your answer with your grapher.

50. Logarithmic Equations For an algebraic challenge, solve these equations *without a calculator* by using the Laws of Logarithms.

  (a) $4 \ln \sqrt{e^x} = 26$

  (b) $x - \log(100) = \ln(e^3)$

  (c) $\log_x(7x - 10) = 2$

  (d) $2 \log_3 x - \log_3(x - 2) = 2$

51. Group Activity Inverse Functions Let $y = f(x) = mx + b$, $m \neq 0$.

  (a) **Writing to Learn** Give a convincing argument that f is a one-to-one function.

  (b) Find a formula for the inverse of f. How are the slopes of f and f^{-1} related?

  (c) If the graphs of two functions are parallel lines with a non-zero slope, what can you say about the graphs of the inverses of the functions?

  (d) If the graphs of two functions are perpendicular lines with a nonzero slope, what can you say about the graphs of the inverses of the functions?

Standardized Test Questions

52. True or False The function displayed in the graph below is one-to-one. Justify your answer.

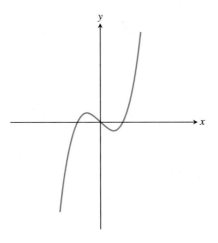

53. True or False If $(f \circ g)(x) = x$, then g is the inverse function of f. Justify your answer.

In Exercises 54 and 55, use the function $f(x) = 3 - \ln (x + 2)$.

54. Multiple Choice Which of the following is the domain of f?

(A) $x \neq -2$ **(B)** $(-\infty, \infty)$ **(C)** $(-2, \infty)$

(D) $[-1.9, \infty)$ **(E)** $(0, \infty)$

55. Multiple Choice Which of the following is the range of f?

(A) $(-\infty, \infty)$ **(B)** $(-\infty, 0)$ **(C)** $(-2, \infty)$

(D) $(0, \infty)$ **(E)** $(0, 5.3)$

56. Multiple Choice Which of the following is the inverse of $f(x) = 3x - 2$?

(A) $g(x) = \dfrac{1}{3x - 2}$ **(B)** $g(x) = x$ **(C)** $g(x) = 3x - 2$

(D) $g(x) = \dfrac{x - 2}{3}$ **(E)** $g(x) = \dfrac{x + 2}{3}$

57. Multiple Choice Which of the following is a solution of the equation $2 - 3^{-x} = -1$?

(A) $x = -2$ **(B)** $x = -1$ **(C)** $x = 0$

(D) $x = 1$ **(E)** There are no solutions.

Exploration

58. Supporting the Quotient Rule Let $y_1 = \ln (x/a)$, $y_2 = \ln x$, $y_3 = y_2 - y_1$, and $y_4 = e^{y_3}$.

  (a) Graph y_1 and y_2 for $a = 2, 3, 4,$ and 5. How are the graphs of y_1 and y_2 related?

  (b) Graph y_3 for $a = 2, 3, 4,$ and 5. Describe the graphs.

  (c) Graph y_4 for $a = 2, 3, 4,$ and 5. Compare the graphs to the graph of $y = a$.

  (d) Use $e^{y_3} = e^{y_2 - y_1} = a$ to solve for y_1.

Extending the Ideas

59. One-to-One Functions If f is a one-to-one function, prove that $g(x) = -f(x)$ is also one-to-one.

60. One-to-One Functions If f is a one-to-one function and $f(x)$ is never zero, prove that $g(x) = 1/f(x)$ is also one-to-one.

61. Domain and Range Suppose that $a \neq 0$, $b \neq 1$, and $b > 0$. Determine the domain and range of the function.

  (a) $y = a(b^{c-x}) + d$

  (b) $y = a \log_b (x - c) + d$

62. Group Activity *Inverse Functions*

Let $f(x) = \dfrac{ax + b}{cx + d}$, $c \neq 0$, $ad - bc \neq 0$.

  (a) **Writing to Learn** Give a convincing argument that f is one-to-one.

  (b) Find a formula for the inverse of f.

  (c) Find the horizontal and vertical asymptotes of f.

  (d) Find the horizontal and vertical asymptotes of f^{-1}. How are they related to those of f?

1.6 | Trigonometric Functions

You will be able to analyze trigonometric functions and their inverses
algebraically, graphically, and
numerically and will be able to model
periodic behavior with sinusoids.

- Radian measure
- The six basic trigonometric
  functions
- Periodicity
- Properties of trigonometric
  functions (symmetry, period)
- Transformations of trigonometric
  functions
- Sinusoids and their properties
  (amplitude, period, frequency, shifts)
- Inverse trigonometric functions and
  their graphs

Radian Measure

The **radian measure** of the angle ACB at the center of the unit circle (Figure 1.36) equals
the length of the arc that ACB cuts from the unit circle.

EXAMPLE 1 Finding Arc Length

Find the length of an arc subtended on a circle of radius 3 by a central angle of measure $2\pi/3$.

SOLUTION

According to Figure 1.36, if s is the length of the arc, then

$$s = r\theta = 3(2\pi/3) = 2\pi. \qquad \textit{Now Try Exercise 1.}$$

When an angle of measure θ is placed in *standard position* at the center of a circle of
radius r (Figure 1.37), the six basic trigonometric functions of θ are defined as follows:

sine: $\sin \theta = \dfrac{y}{r}$ **cosecant:** $\csc \theta = \dfrac{r}{y}$

cosine: $\cos \theta = \dfrac{x}{r}$ **secant:** $\sec \theta = \dfrac{r}{x}$

tangent: $\tan \theta = \dfrac{y}{x}$ **cotangent:** $\cot \theta = \dfrac{x}{y}$

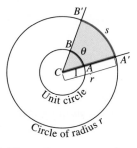

Figure 1.36 The radian measure of angle
ACB is the length θ of arc AB on the unit
circle centered at C. The value of θ can be
found from any other circle, however, as
the ratio s/r.

Graphs of Trigonometric Functions

When we graph trigonometric functions in the coordinate plane, we usually denote the
independent variable (radians) by x instead of θ. Figure 1.38 on the next page shows
sketches of the six trigonometric functions. It is a good exercise for you to compare these
with what you see in a grapher viewing window. (Some graphers have a "trig viewing
window.")

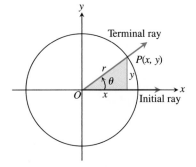

Figure 1.37 An angle θ in standard
position.

EXPLORATION 1 Unwrapping Trigonometric Functions

Set your grapher in *radian mode*, parametric mode, and *simultaneous mode* (all
three). Enter the parametric equations

$$x_1 = \cos t, \quad y_1 = \sin t \quad \text{and} \quad x_2 = t, \quad y_2 = \sin t.$$

1. Graph for $0 \le t \le 2\pi$ in the window $[-1.5, 2\pi]$ by $[-2.5, 2.5]$. Describe the
   two curves. (You may wish to make the viewing window square.)
2. Use TRACE to compare the y values of the two curves.
3. Repeat part 2 in the window $[-1.5, 4\pi]$ by $[-5, 5]$, using the parameter interval $0 \le t \le 4\pi$.
4. Let $y_2 = \cos t$. Use TRACE to compare the x values of curve 1 (the unit circle)
   with the y values of curve 2 using the parameter intervals $[0, 2\pi]$ and $[0, 4\pi]$.
5. Set $y_2 = \tan t, \csc t, \sec t$, and $\cot t$. Graph each in the window $[-1.5, 2\pi]$ by
   $[-2.5, 2.5]$ using the interval $0 \le t \le 2\pi$. How is a y value of curve 2 related
   to the corresponding point on curve 1? (Use TRACE to explore the curves.)

Angle Convention: Use Radians

From now on in this book it is assumed that all angles are measured in radians unless degrees or some other unit is stated explicitly. When we talk about the angle $\pi/3$, we mean $\pi/3$ radians (which is 60°), not $\pi/3$ degrees. When you do calculus, keep your calculator in radian mode.

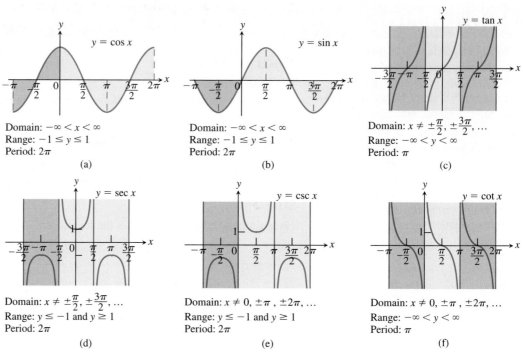

Domain: $-\infty < x < \infty$
Range: $-1 \leq y \leq 1$
Period: 2π
(a)

Domain: $-\infty < x < \infty$
Range: $-1 \leq y \leq 1$
Period: 2π
(b)

Domain: $x \neq \pm\frac{\pi}{2}, \pm\frac{3\pi}{2}, \ldots$
Range: $-\infty < y < \infty$
Period: π
(c)

Domain: $x \neq \pm\frac{\pi}{2}, \pm\frac{3\pi}{2}, \ldots$
Range: $y \leq -1$ and $y \geq 1$
Period: 2π
(d)

Domain: $x \neq 0, \pm\pi, \pm2\pi, \ldots$
Range: $y \leq -1$ and $y \geq 1$
Period: 2π
(e)

Domain: $x \neq 0, \pm\pi, \pm2\pi, \ldots$
Range: $-\infty < y < \infty$
Period: π
(f)

Figure 1.38 Graphs of the (a) cosine, (b) sine, (c) tangent, (d) secant, (e) cosecant, and (f) cotangent functions using radian measure.

Periods of Trigonometric Functions

Period π: $\tan(x + \pi) = \tan x$
                    $\cot(x + \pi) = \cot x$
Period 2π: $\sin(x + 2\pi) = \sin x$
                    $\cos(x + 2\pi) = \cos x$
                    $\sec(x + 2\pi) = \sec x$
                    $\csc(x + 2\pi) = \csc x$

Periodicity

When an angle of measure θ and an angle of measure $\theta + 2\pi$ are in standard position, their terminal rays coincide. The two angles therefore have the same trigonometric function values:

$$\cos(\theta + 2\pi) = \cos\theta \quad \sin(\theta + 2\pi) = \sin\theta \quad \tan(\theta + 2\pi) = \tan\theta$$
$$\sec(\theta + 2\pi) = \sec\theta \quad \csc(\theta + 2\pi) = \csc\theta \quad \cot(\theta + 2\pi) = \cot\theta \tag{1}$$

Similarly, $\cos(\theta - 2\pi) = \cos\theta$, $\sin(\theta - 2\pi) = \sin\theta$, and so on.

We see the values of the trigonometric functions repeat at regular intervals. We describe this behavior by saying that the six basic trigonometric functions are *periodic*.

DEFINITION   **Periodic Function, Period**

A function $f(x)$ is **periodic** if there is a positive number p such that $f(x + p) = f(x)$ for every value of x. The smallest such value of p is the **period** of f.

As we can see in Figure 1.38, the functions $\cos x$, $\sin x$, $\sec x$, and $\csc x$ are periodic with period 2π. The functions $\tan x$ and $\cot x$ are periodic with period π.

Even and Odd Trigonometric Functions

The graphs in Figure 1.38 suggest that $\cos x$ and $\sec x$ are even functions because their graphs are symmetric about the y-axis. The other four basic trigonometric functions are odd.

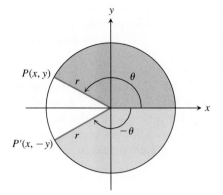

Figure 1.39 Angles of opposite sign. (Example 2)

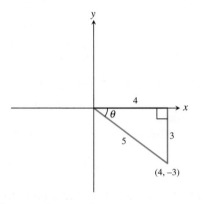

Figure 1.40 The angle θ in standard position. (Example 3)

EXAMPLE 2 Confirming Even and Odd

Show that cosine is an even function and sine is odd.

SOLUTION

From Figure 1.39 it follows that

$$\cos(-\theta) = \frac{x}{r} = \cos\theta, \quad \sin(-\theta) = \frac{-y}{r} = -\sin\theta,$$

so cosine is an even function and sine is odd. ***Now Try Exercise 5.***

EXAMPLE 3 Finding Trigonometric Values

Find all the trigonometric values of θ if $\sin\theta = -3/5$ and $\tan\theta < 0$.

SOLUTION

The angle θ is in the fourth quadrant, as shown in Figure 1.40, because its sine and tangent are negative. From this figure we can read that $\cos\theta = 4/5$, $\tan\theta = -3/4$, $\csc\theta = -5/3$, $\sec\theta = 5/4$, and $\cot\theta = -4/3$. ***Now Try Exercise 9.***

Transformations of Trigonometric Graphs

The rules for shifting, stretching, shrinking, and reflecting the graph of a function apply to the trigonometric functions. The following diagram will remind you of the controlling parameters.

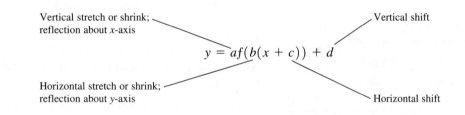

The general sine function, or **sinusoid,** can be written in the form

$$f(x) = A \sin[B(x - C)] + D,$$

where $|A|$ is the *amplitude,* $|2\pi/B|$ is the *period,* C is the *horizontal shift,* and D is the *vertical shift.*

EXAMPLE 4 Graphing a Trigonometric Function

Determine the **(a)** period, **(b)** domain, **(c)** range, and **(d)** draw the graph of the function $y = 3\cos(2x - \pi) + 1$.

SOLUTION

We can rewrite the function in the form

$$y = 3\cos\left[2\left(x - \frac{\pi}{2}\right)\right] + 1.$$

(a) The period is given by $|2\pi/B|$, where $B = 2$. The period is π.

(b) The domain is $(-\infty, \infty)$.

(c) The graph is a basic cosine curve with amplitude 3 that has been shifted up 1 unit. Thus, the range is $[-2, 4]$.

continued

$y = 3 \cos (2x - \pi) + 1, y = \cos x$

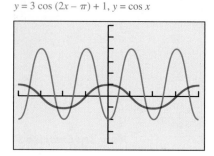

[−2π, 2π] by [−4, 6]

Figure 1.41 The graph of
$y = 3 \cos (2x - \pi) + 1$ (blue) and the
graph of $y = \cos x$ (red). (Example 4)

(d) The graph has been shifted to the right $\pi/2$ units. The graph is shown in
Figure 1.41 together with the graph of $y = \cos x$. Notice that four periods of
$y = 3 \cos (2x - \pi) + 1$ are drawn in this window. *Now Try Exercise 13.*

Musical notes are produced by pressure waves in the air. The wave behavior can be
modeled by sinusoids in which the amplitude affects the loudness and the period affects
the tone we hear. In this context, it is the reciprocal of the period, called the *frequency,*
that is used to describe the tone. We measure frequency in cycles per second, or hertz
(1 Hz = 1 cycle per second), so in this context we would measure period in seconds per
cycle.

EXAMPLE 5 Finding the Frequency of a Musical Note

A computer analyzes the pressure displacement versus time for the wave produced
by a tuning fork and gives its equation as $y = 0.6 \sin (2488.6x - 2.832) + 0.266$.
Estimate the frequency of the note produced by the tuning fork.

SOLUTION

The period is $\dfrac{2\pi}{2488.6}$, so the frequency is $\dfrac{2488.6}{2\pi}$, which is about 396 Hz. (Notice that
the amplitude, horizontal shift, and vertical shift are not important for determining the
frequency of the note.)

A tuning fork vibrating at a frequency of 396 Hz produces the note G above middle C
on the "pure tone" scale. It is a few cycles per second different from the frequency of
the G we hear on a piano's "tempered" scale, which is 392 Hz.

Now Try Exercise 23.

Inverse Trigonometric Functions

None of the six basic trigonometric functions graphed in Figure 1.38 is one-to-one. These
functions do not have inverses. However, in each case the domain can be restricted to
produce a new function that does have an inverse, as illustrated in Example 6.

$x = t, y = \sin t, -\dfrac{\pi}{2} \le t \le \dfrac{\pi}{2}$

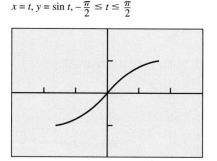

[−3, 3] by [−2, 2]

(a)

$x = \sin t, y = t, -\dfrac{\pi}{2} \le t \le \dfrac{\pi}{2}$

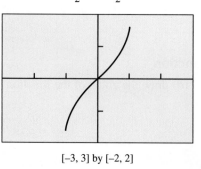

[−3, 3] by [−2, 2]

(b)

Figure 1.42 (a) A restricted sine function
and (b) its inverse. (Example 6)

EXAMPLE 6 Restricting the Domain of the Sine Function

Show that the function $y = \sin x, -\pi/2 \le x \le \pi/2$, is one-to-one, and graph its
inverse.

SOLUTION

Figure 1.42a shows the graph of this restricted sine function using the parametric
equations

$$x_1 = t, \quad y_1 = \sin t, \quad -\frac{\pi}{2} \le t \le \frac{\pi}{2}.$$

This restricted sine function is one-to-one because it does not repeat any output values. It therefore has an inverse, which we graph in Figure 1.42b by interchanging the
ordered pairs using the parametric equations

$$x_2 = \sin t, \quad y_2 = t, \quad -\frac{\pi}{2} \le t \le \frac{\pi}{2}. \quad \textit{Now Try Exercise 25.}$$

The inverse of the restricted sine function of Example 6 is called the *inverse sine function.*
The inverse sine of x is the angle whose sine is x. It is denoted by $\sin^{-1} x$ or arcsin x. Either
notation is read "arcsine of x" or "the inverse sine of x."

The domains of the other basic trigonometric functions can also be restricted to produce a function with an inverse. The domains and ranges of the resulting inverse functions become parts of their definitions.

DEFINITIONS **Inverse Trigonometric Functions**

Function	Domain	Range
$y = \cos^{-1} x$	$-1 \le x \le 1$	$0 \le y \le \pi$
$y = \sin^{-1} x$	$-1 \le x \le 1$	$-\dfrac{\pi}{2} \le y \le \dfrac{\pi}{2}$
$y = \tan^{-1} x$	$-\infty < x < \infty$	$-\dfrac{\pi}{2} < y < \dfrac{\pi}{2}$
$y = \sec^{-1} x$	$\lvert x \rvert \ge 1$	$0 \le y \le \pi,\, y \ne \dfrac{\pi}{2}$
$y = \csc^{-1} x$	$\lvert x \rvert \ge 1$	$-\dfrac{\pi}{2} \le y \le \dfrac{\pi}{2},\, y \ne 0$
$y = \cot^{-1} x$	$-\infty < x < \infty$	$0 < y < \pi$

The graphs of the six inverse trigonometric functions are shown in Figure 1.43.

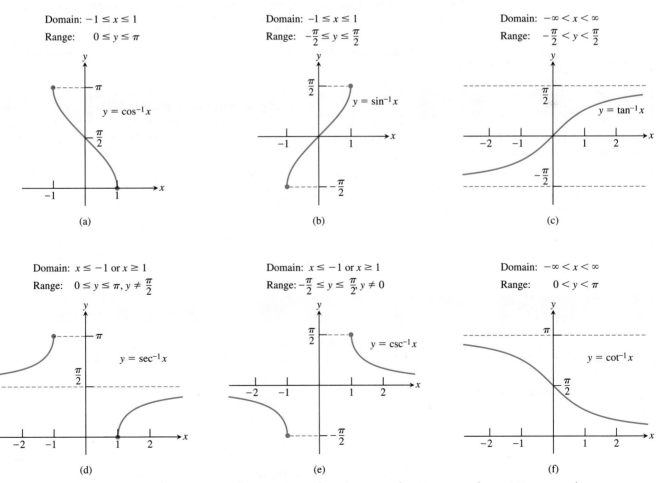

Figure 1.43 Graphs of (a) $y = \cos^{-1} x$, (b) $y = \sin^{-1} x$, (c) $y = \tan^{-1} x$, (d) $y = \sec^{-1} x$, (e) $y = \csc^{-1} x$, and (f) $y = \cot^{-1} x$.

EXAMPLE 7 Finding Angles in Degrees and Radians

Find the measure of $\cos^{-1}(-0.5)$ in degrees and radians.

SOLUTION

Put the calculator in degree mode and enter $\cos^{-1}(-0.5)$. The calculator returns 120, which means 120 degrees. Now put the calculator in radian mode and enter $\cos^{-1}(-0.5)$. The calculator returns 2.094395102, which is the measure of the angle in radians. You can check that $2\pi/3 \approx 2.094395102$.   ***Now Try Exercise 27.***

EXAMPLE 8 Using the Inverse Trigonometric Functions

Solve for x.

(a) $\sin x = 0.7$ in $0 \leq x < 2\pi$

(b) $\tan x = -2$ in $-\infty < x < \infty$

SOLUTION

(a) Notice that $x = \sin^{-1}(0.7) \approx 0.775$ is in the first quadrant, so 0.775 is one solution of this equation. The angle $\pi - x$ is in the second quadrant and has sine equal to 0.7. Thus two solutions in this interval are

$$\sin^{-1}(0.7) \approx 0.775 \quad \text{and} \quad \pi - \sin^{-1}(0.7) \approx 2.366.$$

(b) The angle $x = \tan^{-1}(-2) \approx -1.107$ is in the fourth quadrant and is the only solution to this equation in the interval $-\pi/2 < x < \pi/2$ where $\tan x$ is one-to-one. Since $\tan x$ is periodic with period π, the solutions to this equation are of the form

$$\tan^{-1}(-2) + k\pi \approx -1.107 + k\pi$$

where k is any integer.   ***Now Try Exercise 31.***

Quick Review 1.6   *(For help, go to Sections 1.2 and 1.6.)*

Exercise numbers with a gray background indicate problems that the authors have designed to be solved without a calculator.

In Exercises 1–4, convert from radians to degrees or degrees to radians.

1. $\pi/3$ **2.** -2.5 **3.** $-40°$ **4.** $45°$

In Exercises 5–7, solve the equation graphically in the given interval.

5. $\sin x = 0.6, \quad 0 \leq x \leq 2\pi$ **6.** $\cos x = -0.4, \quad 0 \leq x \leq 2\pi$

7. $\tan x = 1, \quad -\dfrac{\pi}{2} \leq x < \dfrac{3\pi}{2}$

8. Show that $f(x) = 2x^2 - 3$ is an even function. Explain why its graph is symmetric about the y-axis.

9. Show that $f(x) = x^3 - 3x$ is an odd function. Explain why its graph is symmetric about the origin.

10. Give one way to restrict the domain of the function $f(x) = x^4 - 2$ to make the resulting function one-to-one.

Section 1.6 Exercises

In Exercises 1–4, the angle lies at the center of a circle and subtends an arc of the circle. Find the missing angle measure, circle radius, or arc length.

Angle	Radius	Arc Length
1. $5\pi/8$	2	?
2. $175°$	?	10
3. ?	14	7
4. ?	6	$3\pi/2$

In Exercises 5–8, determine if the function is even or odd.

5. secant   **6.** tangent

7. cosecant   **8.** cotangent

In Exercises 9 and 10, find all the trigonometric values of θ with the given conditions.

9. $\cos \theta = -\dfrac{15}{17}, \quad \sin \theta > 0$

10. $\tan \theta = -1, \quad \sin \theta < 0$

In Exercises 11–14, determine **(a)** the period, **(b)** the domain, **(c)** the range, and **(d)** draw the graph of the function.

11. $y = 3 \csc(3x + \pi) - 2$ **12.** $y = 2 \sin(4x + \pi) + 3$

13. $y = -3 \tan(3x + \pi) + 2$

14. $y = 2 \sin\left(2x + \dfrac{\pi}{3}\right)$

In Exercises 15 and 16, choose an appropriate viewing window to display two complete periods of each trigonometric function in radian mode.

15. (a) $y = \sec x$ **(b)** $y = \csc x$ **(c)** $y = \cot x$

16. (a) $y = \sin x$ **(b)** $y = \cos x$ **(c)** $y = \tan x$

In Exercises 17–22, specify **(a)** the period, **(b)** the amplitude, and **(c)** identify the viewing window that is shown. [Caution: Do not assume that the tick marks on both axes are at integer values.]

17. $y = 1.5 \sin 2x$

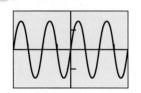

18. $y = 2 \cos 3x$

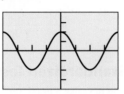

19. $y = -3 \cos 2x$

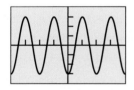

20. $y = 5 \sin \dfrac{x}{2}$

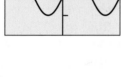

21. $y = -4 \sin \dfrac{\pi}{3}x$

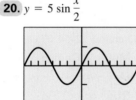

22. $y = \cos \pi x$

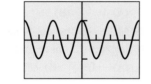

23. The frequencies for the seven "white key" notes produced on the tempered scale of a piano (starting with middle C) are shown in Table 1.4. A computer analyzes the pressure displacement versus time for the wave produced by a tuning fork and gives its equation as $y = 1.23 \sin(2073.55x - 0.49) + 0.44$.

  (a) Estimate the frequency of the note produced by the tuning fork.

  (b) Identify the note produced by the tuning fork.

TABLE 1.4 Frequencies of Musical Notes

C	D	E	F	G	A	B
262	294	330	349	392	440	494

24. *Temperature Data* Table 1.5 gives the average monthly temperatures for St. Louis for a 12-month period starting with January. Model the monthly temperature with an equation of the form

$$y = a \sin[b(t - h)] + k,$$

with y in degrees Fahrenheit, t in months, as follows:

TABLE 1.5
Temperature Data for St. Louis

Time (months)	Temperature (°F)
1	34
2	30
3	39
4	44
5	58
6	67
7	78
8	80
9	72
10	63
11	51
12	40

  (a) Find the value of b, assuming that the period is 12 months.

  (b) How is the amplitude a related to the difference $80° - 30°$?

  (c) Use the information in (b) to find k.

  (d) Find h, and write an equation for y.

  (e) Superimpose a graph of y on a scatter plot of the data.

In Exercises 25–26, show that the function is one-to-one, and graph its inverse.

25. $y = \cos x, \quad 0 \le x \le \pi$ **26.** $y = \tan x, \quad -\dfrac{\pi}{2} < x < \dfrac{\pi}{2}$

In Exercises 27–30, give the measure of the angle in radians and degrees. Give exact answers whenever possible.

27. $\sin^{-1}(0.5)$ **28.** $\sin^{-1}\left(-\dfrac{\sqrt{2}}{2}\right)$

29. $\tan^{-1}(-5)$ **30.** $\cos^{-1}(0.7)$

In Exercises 31–36, solve the equation in the specified interval.

31. $\tan x = 2.5, \quad 0 \le x \le 2\pi$

32. $\cos x = -0.7, \quad 2\pi \le x < 4\pi$

33. $\csc x = 2, \quad 0 < x < 2\pi$ **34.** $\sec x = -3, \quad -\pi \le x < \pi$

35. $\sin x = -0.5, \quad -\infty < x < \infty$

36. $\cot x = -1, \quad -\infty < x < \infty$

In Exercises 37–40, use the given information to find the values of the six trigonometric functions at the angle θ. Give exact answers.

37. $\theta = \sin^{-1}\left(\dfrac{8}{17}\right)$ **38.** $\theta = \tan^{-1}\left(-\dfrac{5}{12}\right)$

39. The point $P(-3, 4)$ is on the terminal side of θ.

40. The point $P(-2, 2)$ is on the terminal side of θ.

In Exercises 41 and 42, evaluate the expression.

41. $\sin\left(\cos^{-1}\left(\dfrac{7}{11}\right)\right)$

42. $\tan\left(\sin^{-1}\left(\dfrac{9}{13}\right)\right)$

43. *Chattanooga Temperatures* The average monthly temperatures in Chattanooga, TN, range from a low of 40.5°F in January to a high of 80.0°F in July. Setting January as month 0 and December as month 11, the temperature cycle can be nicely modeled by a sinusoid with equation $y = A\cos(Bx) + C$, as shown in the graph below. Find the values of A, B, and C. [*Source: www.weatherbase.com*]

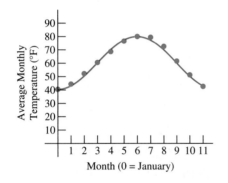

Month (0 = January)

44. *Rocky Mountain Highs* The average monthly high temperatures in Steamboat Springs, CO, are shown in Table 1.6 below. Setting January as month 0 and December as month 11, construct a sinusoid with equation $y = A\cos(Bx) + C$ that models the temperature cycle in Steamboat Springs. Support your answer with a graph and a scatter plot on your calculator. [*Source: www.weatherbase.com*]

TABLE 1.6
Average Monthly Highs in Steamboat Springs, CO

JAN	FEB	MAR	APR	MAY	JUN
28.9	33.8	42.0	53.6	65.4	75.5
JUL	AUG	SEP	OCT	NOV	DEC
82.6	80.3	72.5	60.4	43.3	30.7

45. *Even-Odd*

(a) Show that cot x is an odd function of x.

(b) Show that the quotient of an even function and an odd function is an odd function.

46. *Even-Odd*

(a) Show that csc x is an odd function of x.

(b) Show that the reciprocal of an odd function is odd.

47. *Even-Odd* Show that the product of an even function and an odd function is an odd function.

48. *Finding the Period* Give a convincing argument that the period of tan x is π.

49. *Is the Product of Sinusoids a Sinusoid?* Make a conjecture, and then use your graphing calculator to support your answers to the following questions.

(a) Is the product $y = (\sin x)(\sin 2x)$ a sinusoid? What is the period of the function?

(b) Is the product $y = (\sin x)(\cos x)$ a sinusoid? What is the period of the function?

(c) One of the functions in (a) or (b) above can be written in the form $y = A\sin(Bx)$. Identify the function and find A and B.

Standardized Test Questions

You may use a graphing calculator to solve the following problems.

50. **True or False** The period of $y = \sin(x/2)$ is π. Justify your answer.

51. **True or False** The amplitude of $y = \frac{1}{2}\cos x$ is 1. Justify your answer.

In Exercises 52–54, $f(x) = 2\cos(4x + \pi) - 1$.

52. **Multiple Choice** Which of the following is the domain of f?

(A) $[-\pi, \pi]$ (B) $[-3, 1]$ (C) $[-1, 4]$

(D) $(-\infty, \infty)$ (E) $x \neq 0$

53. **Multiple Choice** Which of the following is the range of f?

(A) $(-3, 1)$ (B) $[-3, 1]$ (C) $(-1, 4)$

(D) $[-1, 4]$ (E) $(-\infty, \infty)$

54. **Multiple Choice** Which of the following is the period of f?

(A) 4π (B) 3π (C) 2π (D) π (E) $\pi/2$

55. **Multiple Choice** Which of the following is the measure of $\tan^{-1}\left(-\sqrt{3}\right)$ in degrees?

(A) $-60°$ (B) $-30°$ (C) $30°$ (D) $60°$ (E) $120°$

Exploration

56. *Trigonometric Identities* Let $f(x) = \sin x + \cos x$.

(a) Graph $y = f(x)$. Describe the graph.

(b) Use the graph to identify the amplitude, period, horizontal shift, and vertical shift.

(c) Use the formula

$$\sin \alpha \cos \beta + \cos \alpha \sin \beta = \sin(\alpha + \beta)$$

for the sine of the sum of two angles to confirm your answers.

Extending the Ideas

57. Exploration Let $y = \sin(ax) + \cos(ax)$.

Use the symbolic manipulator of a computer algebra system (CAS) to help you with the following:

(a) Express y as a sinusoid for $a = 2, 3, 4$, and 5.

(b) Conjecture another formula for y for a equal to any positive integer n.

(c) Check your conjecture with a CAS.

(d) Use the formula for the sine of the sum of two angles (see Exercise 56c) to confirm your conjecture.

58. Exploration Let $y = a \sin x + b \cos x$.

Use the symbolic manipulator of a computer algebra system (CAS) to help you with the following:

(a) Express y as a sinusoid for the following pairs of values:
$a = 2, b = 1$; $a = 1, b = 2$; $a = 5, b = 2$;
$a = 2, b = 5$; $a = 3, b = 4$.

(b) Conjecture another formula for y for any pair of positive integers. Try other values if necessary.

(c) Check your conjecture with a CAS.

(d) Use the following formulas for the sine or cosine of a sum or difference of two angles to confirm your conjecture.

$$\sin \alpha \cos \beta \pm \cos \alpha \sin \beta = \sin(\alpha \pm \beta)$$
$$\cos \alpha \cos \beta \pm \sin \alpha \sin \beta = \cos(\alpha \mp \beta)$$

In Exercises 59 and 60, show that the function is periodic and find its period.

59. $y = \sin^3 x$ **60.** $y = |\tan x|$

In Exercises 61 and 62, graph one period of the function.

61. $f(x) = \sin(60x)$ **62.** $f(x) = \cos(60\pi x)$

Quick Quiz for AP* Preparation: Sections 1.4–1.6

1. Multiple Choice Which of the following is the domain of $f(x) = -\log_2(x + 3)$?

(A) $(-\infty, \infty)$ **(B)** $(-\infty, 3)$ **(C)** $(-3, \infty)$

(D) $[-3, \infty)$ **(E)** $(-\infty, 3]$

2. Multiple Choice Which of the following is the range of $f(x) = 5 \cos(x + \pi) + 3$?

(A) $(-\infty, \infty)$ **(B)** $[2, 4]$ **(C)** $[-8, 2]$

(D) $[-2, 8]$ **(E)** $\left[-\dfrac{2}{5}, \dfrac{8}{5}\right]$

3. Multiple Choice Which of the following gives the solution of $\tan x = -1$ in $\pi < x < \dfrac{3\pi}{2}$?

(A) $-\dfrac{\pi}{4}$ **(B)** $\dfrac{\pi}{4}$ **(C)** $\dfrac{\pi}{3}$ **(D)** $\dfrac{3\pi}{4}$ **(E)** $\dfrac{5\pi}{4}$

4. Free Response Let $f(x) = 5x - 3$.

(a) Find the inverse g of f.

(b) Compute $(f \circ g)(x)$. Show your work.

(c) Compute $(g \circ f)(x)$. Show your work.

CHAPTER 1   Key Terms

absolute value function (p. 18)
base a logarithm function (p. 39)
boundary of an interval (p. 14)
boundary points (p. 14)
change of base formula (p. 41)
closed interval (p. 14)
common logarithm function (p. 40)

composing (p. 19)
composite function (p. 19)
compounded continuously (p. 26)
cosecant function (p. 45)
cosine function (p. 45)
cotangent function (p. 45)
dependent variable (p. 13)

domain (p. 13)
even function (p. 16)
exponential decay (p. 25)
exponential function with base a (p. 23)
exponential growth (p. 25)
function (p. 13)
function notation (p. 13)

general linear equation (p. 6)

graph of a function (p. 13)

graph of a relation (p. 29)

grapher failure (p. 15)

half-life (p. 24)

half-open interval (p. 14)

identity function (p. 37)

implied domain (p. 14)

increments (p. 3)

independent variable (p. 13)

initial point of parametrized curve (p. 29)

interior of an interval (p. 14)

interior points of an interval (p. 14)

inverse cosecant function (p. 49)

inverse cosine function (p. 49)

inverse cotangent function (p. 49)

inverse function (p. 37)

inverse properties for a^x and $\log_a x$ (p. 40)

inverse secant function (p. 49)

inverse sine function (p. 49)

inverse tangent function (p. 49)

linear function (p. 4)

natural logarithm function (p. 40)

odd function (p. 16)

one-to-one function (p. 36)

open interval (p. 14)

parallel lines (p. 6)

parameter (p. 29)

parameter interval (p. 29)

parametric curve (p. 29)

parametric equations (p. 29)

parametrization of a curve (p. 29)

parametrize (p. 29)

period of a function (p. 46)

periodic function (p. 46)

perpendicular lines (p. 6)

piecewise-defined function (p. 17)

point-slope equation (p. 5)

power function (p. 15)

power rule for logarithms (p. 40)

product rule for logarithms (p. 40)

quotient rule for logarithms (p. 40)

radian measure (p. 45)

range (p. 13)

relation (p. 29)

relevant domain (p. 14)

rules for exponents (p. 24)

secant function (p. 45)

sine function (p. 45)

sinusoid (p. 47)

slope (p. 4)

slope-intercept equation (p. 6)

symmetry about the origin (p. 16)

symmetry about the y-axis (p. 16)

tangent function (p. 45)

terminal point of parametrized curve (p. 29)

witch of Agnesi (p. 32)

x-intercept (p. 6)

y-intercept (p. 6)

CHAPTER 1   Review Exercises

Exercise numbers with a gray background indicate problems that the authors have designed to be solved without a calculator.

The collection of exercises marked in red could be used as a chapter test.

In Exercises 1–14, write an equation for the specified line.

1. through $(1, -6)$ with slope 3

2. through $(-1, 2)$ with slope $-1/2$

3. the vertical line through $(0, -3)$

4. through $(-3, 6)$ and $(1, -2)$

5. the horizontal line through $(0, 2)$

6. through $(3, 3)$ and $(-2, 5)$

7. with slope -3 and y-intercept 3

8. through $(3, 1)$ and parallel to $2x - y = -2$

9. through $(4, -12)$ and parallel to $4x + 3y = 12$

10. through $(-2, -3)$ and perpendicular to $3x - 5y = 1$

11. through $(-1, 2)$ and perpendicular to $\dfrac{1}{2}x + \dfrac{1}{3}y = 1$

12. with x-intercept 3 and y-intercept -5

13. the line $y = f(x)$, where f has the following values:

x	-2	2	4
$f(x)$	4	2	1

14. through $(4, -2)$ with x-intercept -3

In Exercises 15–18, determine whether the graph of the function is symmetric about the y-axis, the origin, or neither.

15. $y = x^{1/5}$

16. $y = x^{2/5}$

17. $y = x^2 - 2x - 1$

18. $y = e^{-x^2}$

In Exercises 19–26, determine whether the function is even, odd, or neither.

19. $y = x^2 + 1$

20. $y = x^5 - x^3 - x$

21. $y = 1 - \cos x$

22. $y = \sec x \tan x$

23. $y = \dfrac{x^4 + 1}{x^3 - 2x}$

24. $y = 1 - \sin x$

25. $y = x + \cos x$

26. $y = \sqrt{x^4 - 1}$

In Exercises 27–38, find the **(a)** domain and **(b)** range, and **(c)** graph the function.

27. $y = |x| - 2$

28. $y = -2 + \sqrt{1 - x}$

29. $y = \sqrt{16 - x^2}$

30. $y = 3^{2-x} + 1$

31. $y = 2e^{-x} - 3$

32. $y = \tan(2x - \pi)$

33. $y = 2\sin(3x + \pi) - 1$

34. $y = x^{2/5}$

35. $y = \ln(x - 3) + 1$

36. $y = -1 + \sqrt[3]{2 - x}$

37. $y = \begin{cases} \sqrt{-x}, & -4 \le x \le 0 \\ \sqrt{x}, & 0 < x \le 4 \end{cases}$

38. $y = \begin{cases} -x - 2, & -2 \le x \le -1 \\ x, & -1 < x \le 1 \\ -x + 2, & 1 < x \le 2 \end{cases}$

In Exercises 39 and 40, write a piecewise formula for the function.

39.

40.

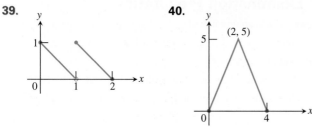

In Exercises 41 and 42, find

(a) $(f \circ g)(-1)$ (b) $(g \circ f)(2)$ (c) $(f \circ f)(x)$ (d) $(g \circ g)(x)$

41. $f(x) = \dfrac{1}{x}, \quad g(x) = \dfrac{1}{\sqrt{x + 2}}$

42. $f(x) = 2 - x, \quad g(x) = \sqrt[3]{x + 1}$

In Exercises 43 and 44, (a) write a formula for $f \circ g$ and $g \circ f$ and find the (b) domain and (c) range of each.

43. $f(x) = 2 - x^2, \quad g(x) = \sqrt{x + 2}$

44. $f(x) = \sqrt{x}, \quad g(x) = \sqrt{1 - x}$

In Exercises 45–48, a parametrization is given for a curve.

(a) Graph the curve. Identify the initial and terminal points, if any. Indicate the direction in which the curve is traced.

(b) Find a Cartesian equation for a curve that contains the parametrized curve. What portion of the graph of the Cartesian equation is traced by the parametrized curve?

45. $x = 5 \cos t, \quad y = 2 \sin t, \quad 0 \le t \le 2\pi$

46. $x = 4 \cos t, \quad y = 4 \sin t, \quad \pi/2 \le t < 3\pi/2$

47. $x = 2 - t, \quad y = 11 - 2t, \quad -2 \le t \le 4$

48. $x = 1 + t, \quad y = \sqrt{4 - 2t}, \quad t \le 2$

In Exercises 49–52, give a parametrization for the curve.

49. the line segment with endpoints $(-2, 5)$ and $(4, 3)$

50. the line through $(-3, -2)$ and $(4, -1)$

51. the ray with initial point $(2, 5)$ that passes through $(-1, 0)$

52. $y = x(x - 4), \quad x \le 2$

Group Activity In Exercises 53 and 54, do the following.

(a) Find f^{-1} and show that $(f \circ f^{-1})(x) = (f^{-1} \circ f)(x) = x$.

(b) Graph f and f^{-1} in the same viewing window.

53. $f(x) = 2 - 3x$ **54.** $f(x) = (x + 2)^2, \quad x \ge -2$

In Exercises 55 and 56, find the measure of the angle in radians and degrees.

55. $\sin^{-1}(0.6)$ **56.** $\tan^{-1}(-2.3)$

57. Find the six trigonometric function values of $\theta = \cos^{-1}(3/7)$. Give exact answers.

58. Solve the equation $\sin x = -0.2$ in the following intervals.

(a) $0 \le x < 2\pi$ (b) $-\infty < x < \infty$

59. Solve for x: $e^{-0.2x} = 4$

60. The graph of f is shown. Draw the graph of each function.

(a) $y = f(-x)$

(b) $y = -f(x)$

(c) $y = -2f(x + 1) + 1$

(d) $y = 3f(x - 2) - 2$

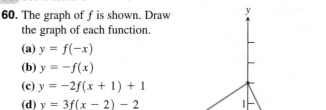

61. A portion of the graph of a function defined on $[-3, 3]$ is shown. Complete the graph assuming that the function is

(a) even.

(b) odd.

62. *Depreciation* Smith Hauling purchased an 18-wheel truck for $100,000. The truck depreciates at the constant rate of $10,000 per year for 10 years.

(a) Write an expression that gives the value y after x years.

(b) When is the value of the truck $55,000?

63. *Drug Absorption* A drug is administered intravenously for pain. The function

$$f(t) = 90 - 52 \ln (1 + t), \quad 0 \le t \le 4$$

gives the number of units of the drug in the body after t hours.

(a) What was the initial number of units of the drug administered?

(b) How much is present after 2 hours?

(c) Draw the graph of f.

64. *Finding Time* If Joenita invests $1500 in a retirement account that earns 8% compounded annually, how long will it take this single payment to grow to $5000?

65. *Guppy Population* The number of guppies in Susan's aquarium doubles every day. There are four guppies initially.

(a) Write the number of guppies as a function of time t.

(b) How many guppies were present after 4 days? after 1 week?

(c) When will there be 2000 guppies?

(d) **Writing to Learn** Give reasons why this might not be a good model for the growth of Susan's guppy population.

66. ***The Rule of 70*** A well-known rule in the world of finance is that an annual interest rate of $R\%$ will double an investment in approximately $70/R$ years. Assume that the money is compounded continuously so that you can use the Pe^{rt} formula.

(a) Solve the equation $Pe^{rt} = 2P$ to find t as a function of r.

(b) If $r = R\%$, write t as a function of R.

(c) If the money is not compounded continuously, the doubling time will be a little longer than the answer in (b). Approximate the typical doubling time by increasing the numerator by 1. This should explain the Rule of 70!

67. Writing to Learn Many people refer to the Rule of 70 (see Exercise 66) as the ***Rule of 72.*** Since this is usually less accurate, why do you suppose some people prefer it?

AP* Examination Preparation

You may use a graphing calculator to solve the following problems.

68. Consider the point $P(-2, 1)$ and the line $L: x + y = 2$.

(a) Find the slope of L.

(b) Write an equation for the line through P and parallel to L.

(c) Write an equation for the line through P and perpendicular to L.

(d) What is the x-intercept of L?

69. Let $f(x) = 1 - \ln(x - 2)$.

(a) What is the domain of f?

(b) What is the range of f?

(c) What are the x-intercepts of the graph of f?

(d) Find f^{-1}.

(e) Confirm your answer algebraically in part (d).

70. Let $f(x) = 1 - 3\cos(2x)$.

(a) What is the domain of f?

(b) What is the range of f?

(c) What is the period of f?

(d) Is f an even function, odd function, or neither?

(e) Find all the zeros of f in $\pi/2 \leq x \leq \pi$.

CHAPTER 2

Limits and Continuity

2.1 Rates of Change and Limits

2.2 Limits Involving Infinity

2.3 Continuity

2.4 Rates of Change, Tangent Lines, and Sensitivity

The yield on the June to August rice crop in Laos depends on the amount of rainfall, which is usually between 0.5 and 0.8 meter over this three-month growing season. More rain produces a higher yield, but the benefits diminish as the amount of rain increases. Crop yield in normal years can be approximated by

$$C(r) = -2.1 + 8.7r - 3.7r^2$$

metric tons per hectare, where r is the total rainfall, measured in meters. When the total rainfall is about 0.7 meter, how sensitive is the crop yield to a small increase in the amount of rain? Section 2.4 can help answer this question.

CHAPTER 2 Overview

The concept of limit is one of the fundamental building blocks of calculus, enabling us to describe with precision how change in one variable affects change in another variable.

In this chapter, we show how to define and calculate limits of function values. The calculation rules are straightforward, and most of the limits we need can be found by substitution, graphical investigation, numerical approximation, algebra, or some combination of these.

One of the uses of limits lies in building a careful definition of continuity. Continuous functions arise frequently in scientific work because they model such an enormous range of natural behavior and because they have special mathematical properties.

2.1 | Rates of Change and Limits

You will be able to interpret, estimate, and determine limits of function values.

- Interpretation and expression of limits using correct notation
- Estimation of limits using numerical and graphical information
- Limits of sums, differences, products, quotients, and composite functions
- Interpretation and expression of one-sided limits
- The Squeeze Theorem

Average and Instantaneous Speed

The average speed of a moving body during an interval of time is found by dividing the change in distance or position by the change in time. More precisely, if $y = f(t)$ is a distance or position function of a moving body at time t, then the **average rate of change** (or **average speed**) is the ratio

$$\frac{\Delta y}{\Delta t} = \frac{f(t + \Delta t) - f(t)}{\Delta t},$$

where the elapsed time is the interval from t to $t + \Delta t$, or simply Δt, and the distance traveled during this time interval is $f(t + \Delta t) - f(t)$. It is also common to use the letter h instead of Δt to denote the elapsed time, in which case the average rate of change can be written

$$\frac{\Delta y}{\Delta t} = \frac{f(t + h) - f(t)}{h}.$$

Free Fall

Near the surface of the earth, all bodies fall with the same constant acceleration. The distance a body falls after it is released from rest is a constant multiple of the square of the time fallen. At least, that is what happens when a body falls in a vacuum, where there is no air to slow it down. The square-of-time rule also holds for dense, heavy objects like rocks, ball bearings, and steel tools during the first few seconds of fall through air, before the velocity builds up to where air resistance begins to matter. When air resistance is absent or insignificant and the only force acting on a falling body is the force of gravity, we call the way the body falls *free fall*.

EXAMPLE 1 Finding an Average Speed

A rock breaks loose from the top of a tall cliff. What is its average speed during the first 2 seconds of fall?

SOLUTION

Experiments show that a dense solid object dropped from rest to fall freely near the surface of the earth will fall

$$y = 16t^2$$

feet in the first t seconds. The average speed of the rock over any given time interval is the distance traveled, Δy, divided by the length of the interval Δt. For the first 2 seconds of fall, from $t = 0$ to $t = 2$, we have

$$\frac{\Delta y}{\Delta t} = \frac{16(2)^2 - 16(0)^2}{2 - 0} = 32 \,\frac{\text{ft}}{\text{sec}}. \qquad \textbf{\textit{Now Try Exercise 1.}}$$

The speed of a falling rock is always increasing. If we know the position as a function of time, we can calculate average speed over any given interval of time. But we can also talk about its **instantaneous speed** or **instantaneous rate of change,** the speed at one instant of time. As we will see after the next example, we need the idea of *limit* to make precise what we mean by instantaneous rate of change.

TABLE 2.1	
Average Speeds over Short Time Intervals Starting at $t = 2$	
$$\frac{\Delta y}{\Delta t} = \frac{16(2 + h)^2 - 16(2)^2}{h}$$	
Length of Time Interval, h (sec)	Average Speed for Interval $\Delta y / \Delta t$ (ft/sec)
1	80
0.1	65.6
0.01	64.16
0.001	64.016
0.0001	64.0016
0.00001	64.00016

Formal Definition of Limit

The formal definition of a limit is given in Appendix A, pp. 583–589. This appendix also illustrates how the formal definition is applied and how it leads to the *Properties of Limits* given in Theorem 1.

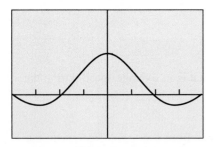

[−2π, 2π] by [−1, 2]

(a)

X	Y1
−.3	.98507
−.2	.99335
−.1	.99833
0	ERROR
.1	.99833
.2	.99335
.3	.98507

Y1 ≣ sin(X)/X

(b)

Figure 2.1 (a) A graph and (b) table of values for $f(x) = (\sin x)/x$ that suggest the limit of f as x approaches 0 is 1.

EXAMPLE 2 Finding an Instantaneous Speed

Find the speed of the rock in Example 1 at the instant $t = 2$.

SOLUTION

We can calculate the average speed of the rock over the interval from time $t = 2$ to any slightly later time $t = 2 + h$ as

$$\frac{\Delta y}{\Delta t} = \frac{16(2 + h)^2 - 16(2)^2}{h}. \tag{1}$$

We cannot use this formula to calculate the speed at the exact instant $t = 2$ because that would require taking $h = 0$, and $0/0$ is undefined. However, we can get a good idea of what is happening at $t = 2$ by evaluating the formula at values of h *close* to 0. When we do, we see a clear pattern (Table 2.1). As h approaches 0, the average speed approaches the limiting value 64 ft/sec.

If we expand the numerator of Equation 1 and simplify, we find that

$$\frac{\Delta y}{\Delta t} = \frac{16(2 + h)^2 - 16(2)^2}{h} = \frac{16(4 + 4h + h^2) - 64}{h}$$

$$= \frac{64h + 16h^2}{h} = 64 + 16h$$

For values of h different from 0, the expressions on the right and left are equivalent and the average speed is $64 + 16h$ ft/sec. We can now see why the average speed has the limiting value $64 + 16(0) = 64$ ft/sec as h approaches 0. ***Now Try Exercise 3.***

Definition of Limit

As in the preceding example, most limits of interest in the real world can be viewed as numerical limits of values of functions. And this is where a graphing utility and calculus come in. A calculator can suggest the limits, and calculus can give the mathematics for confirming the limits analytically.

Limits give us a language for describing how the outputs of a function behave as the inputs approach some particular value. In Example 2, the average speed was not defined at $h = 0$ but approached the limit 64 as h approached 0. We were able to see this numerically and to confirm it algebraically by eliminating h from the denominator. But we cannot always do that. For instance, we can see both graphically and numerically (Figure 2.1) that the values of $f(x) = (\sin x)/x$ approach 1 as x approaches 0.

We cannot eliminate the x from the denominator of $(\sin x)/x$ to confirm the observation algebraically. We need to use a theorem about limits to make that confirmation, as you will see in Exercise 77.

The sentence $\lim_{x \to c} f(x) = L$ is read, "The limit of f of x as x approaches c equals L." The notation means that we can force $f(x)$ to be as close to L as we wish simply by restricting the distance between x and c, *but not allowing x to equal c.*

We saw in Example 2 that $\lim_{h \to 0}(64 + 16h) = 64$.

As suggested in Figure 2.1,

$$\lim_{x \to 0} \frac{\sin x}{x} = 1.$$

Because we need to distinguish between what happens at c and what happens near c, the value or existence of the limit as $x \to c$ never depends on how the function may or may not be defined at c. This is illustrated in Figure 2.2. The function f has limit 2 as $x \to 1$ even though f is not defined at 1. The function g has limit 2 as $x \to 1$ even though $g(1) \neq 2$. The function h is the only one whose limit as $x \to 1$ equals its value at $x = 1$.

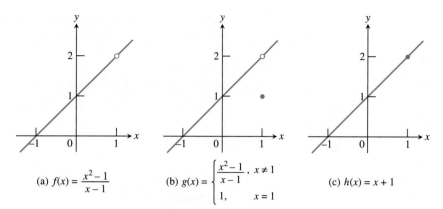

(a) $f(x) = \dfrac{x^2 - 1}{x - 1}$

(b) $g(x) = \begin{cases} \dfrac{x^2 - 1}{x - 1}, & x \neq 1 \\ 1, & x = 1 \end{cases}$

(c) $h(x) = x + 1$

Figure 2.2 $\lim\limits_{x \to 1} f(x) = \lim\limits_{x \to 1} g(x) = \lim\limits_{x \to 1} h(x) = 2.$

Properties of Limits

By applying six basic facts about limits, we can calculate many unfamiliar limits from limits we already know. For instance, from knowing that

$$\lim_{x \to c} (k) = k \qquad \text{Limit of the function with constant value } k$$

and

$$\lim_{x \to c} (x) = c, \qquad \text{Limit of the identity function at } x = c$$

we can calculate the limits of all polynomial and rational functions. The facts are listed in Theorem 1.

THEOREM 1   Properties of Limits

If L, M, c, and k are real numbers and

$$\lim_{x \to c} f(x) = L \quad \text{and} \quad \lim_{x \to c} g(x) = M, \text{ then}$$

1. *Sum Rule:* $\qquad\qquad\qquad\qquad\qquad \lim\limits_{x \to c} (f(x) + g(x)) = L + M$

   The limit of the sum of two functions is the sum of their limits.

2. *Difference Rule:* $\qquad\qquad\qquad\quad \lim\limits_{x \to c} (f(x) - g(x)) = L - M$

   The limit of the difference of two functions is the difference of their limits.

3. *Product Rule:* $\qquad\qquad\qquad\qquad \lim\limits_{x \to c} (f(x) \cdot g(x)) = L \cdot M$

   The limit of a product of two functions is the product of their limits.

4. *Constant Multiple Rule:* $\qquad\qquad \lim\limits_{x \to c} (k \cdot f(x)) = k \cdot L$

   The limit of a constant times a function is the constant times the limit of the function.

5. *Quotient Rule:* $\qquad\qquad\qquad\quad \lim\limits_{x \to c} \dfrac{f(x)}{g(x)} = \dfrac{L}{M}, \; M \neq 0$

   The limit of a quotient of two functions is the quotient of their limits, provided the limit of the denominator is not zero.

   continued

6. *Power Rule:* If r and s are integers, $s \neq 0$, then

$$\lim_{x \to c} (f(x))^{r/s} = L^{r/s}$$

provided that $L^{r/s}$ is a real number and $L > 0$ if s is even.

The limit of a rational power of a function is that power of the limit of the function, provided the latter is a real number and $L > 0$ if s is even.

Here are some examples of how Theorem 1 can be used to find limits of polynomial and rational functions.

Using Analytic Methods

We remind the student that *unless otherwise stated* all examples and exercises are to be done using analytic algebraic methods *without* the use of graphing calculators or computer algebra systems.

EXAMPLE 3 Using Properties of Limits

Use the observations $\lim_{x \to c} k = k$ and $\lim_{x \to c} x = c$, and the properties of limits to find the following limits.

(a) $\lim_{x \to c} (x^3 + 4x^2 - 3)$ **(b)** $\lim_{x \to c} \dfrac{x^4 + x^2 - 1}{x^2 + 5}$

SOLUTION

(a) $\lim_{x \to c} (x^3 + 4x^2 - 3) = \lim_{x \to c} x^3 + \lim_{x \to c} 4x^2 - \lim_{x \to c} 3$ Sum and Difference Rules

$$= c^3 + 4c^2 - 3 \qquad \text{Product and Constant Multiple Rules}$$

(b) $\lim_{x \to c} \dfrac{x^4 + x^2 - 1}{x^2 + 5} = \dfrac{\lim_{x \to c} (x^4 + x^2 - 1)}{\lim_{x \to c} (x^2 + 5)}$ Quotient Rule

$$= \dfrac{\lim_{x \to c} x^4 + \lim_{x \to c} x^2 - \lim_{x \to c} 1}{\lim_{x \to c} x^2 + \lim_{x \to c} 5} \qquad \text{Sum and Difference Rules}$$

$$= \dfrac{c^4 + c^2 - 1}{c^2 + 5} \qquad \text{Product Rule}$$

Now Try Exercises 5 and 6.

Example 3 shows the remarkable strength of Theorem 1. From the two simple observations that $\lim_{x \to c} k = k$ and $\lim_{x \to c} x = c$, we can immediately work our way to limits of polynomial functions and most rational functions using substitution.

THEOREM 2   Polynomial and Rational Functions

1. If $f(x) = a_n x^n + a_{n-1} x^{n-1} + \cdots + a_0$ is any polynomial function and c is any real number, then

$$\lim_{x \to c} f(x) = f(c) = a_n c^n + a_{n-1} c^{n-1} + \cdots + a_0.$$

2. If $f(x)$ and $g(x)$ are polynomials and c is any real number, then

$$\lim_{x \to c} \frac{f(x)}{g(x)} = \frac{f(c)}{g(c)}, \quad \text{provided that } g(c) \neq 0.$$

EXAMPLE 4 Using Theorem 2

(a) $\lim\limits_{x \to 3} \left[x^2(2 - x) \right] = (3)^2(2 - 3) = -9$

(b) $\lim\limits_{x \to 2} \dfrac{x^2 + 2x + 4}{x + 2} = \dfrac{(2)^2 + 2(2) + 4}{2 + 2} = \dfrac{12}{4} = 3$

Now Try Exercises 9 and 11.

As with polynomials, limits of many familiar functions can be found by substitution at points where they are defined. This includes trigonometric functions, exponential and logarithmic functions, and composites of these functions. Feel free to use these properties.

EXAMPLE 5 Using the Product Rule

Determine $\lim\limits_{x \to 0} \dfrac{\tan x}{x}$.

SOLUTION

The graph of $f(x) = (\tan x)/x$ in Figure 2.3 suggests that the limit exists and is about 1. Using the analytic result of Exercise 77, we have

$$\lim\limits_{x \to 0} \frac{\tan x}{x} = \lim\limits_{x \to 0} \left(\frac{\sin x}{x} \cdot \frac{1}{\cos x} \right) \qquad \tan x = \frac{\sin x}{\cos x}$$

$$= \lim\limits_{x \to 0} \frac{\sin x}{x} \cdot \lim\limits_{x \to 0} \frac{1}{\cos x} \qquad \text{Product Rule}$$

$$= 1 \cdot \frac{1}{\cos 0} = 1 \cdot \frac{1}{1} = 1$$

Now Try Exercise 33.

Sometimes we can use a graph to discover that limits do not exist, as illustrated by Example 6.

EXAMPLE 6 Exploring a Nonexistent Limit

Use a graph to explore whether

$$\lim\limits_{x \to 2} \frac{x^3 - 1}{x - 2}$$

exists.

SOLUTION

Notice that the denominator is 0 when x is replaced by 2, so we cannot use substitution to determine the limit. The graph in Figure 2.4 of $f(x) = (x^3 - 1)/(x - 2)$ strongly suggests that as $x \to 2$ from either side, the absolute values of the function values get very large. This, in turn, suggests that the limit does not exist.

Now Try Exercise 35.

One-Sided and Two-Sided Limits

Sometimes we need to distinguish between what happens to the function just to the right of c and just to the left. To do this, we call the limit of f as x approaches c from the right the **right-hand limit** of f at c and the limit as x approaches c from the left the **left-hand limit** of f at c. Here is the notation we use:

right-hand: $\qquad \lim\limits_{x \to c^+} f(x) \qquad$ *The limit of f as x approaches c from the right.*

left-hand: $\qquad \lim\limits_{x \to c^-} f(x) \qquad$ *The limit of f as x approaches c from the left.*

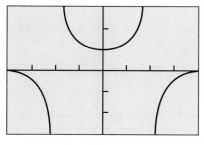

$[-\pi, \pi]$ by $[-3, 3]$

Figure 2.3 The graph of

$$f(x) = (\tan x)/x$$

suggests that $f(x) \to 1$ as $x \to 0$. (Example 5)

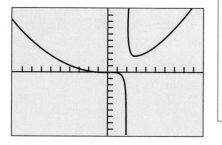

$[-10, 10]$ by $[-100, 100]$

Figure 2.4 The graph of

$$f(x) = (x^3 - 1)/(x - 2).$$

(Example 6)

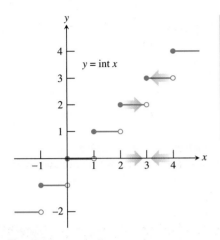

Figure 2.5 At each integer, the greatest integer function $y = \text{int } x$ has different right-hand and left-hand limits. (Example 7)

On the Far Side

If *f* is not defined to the left of $x = c$, then *f* does not have a left-hand limit at *c*. Similarly, if *f* is not defined to the right of $x = c$, then *f* does not have a right-hand limit at *c*.

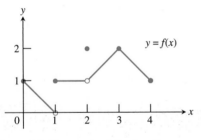

Figure 2.6 The graph of the function

$$f(x) = \begin{cases} -x + 1, & 0 \leq x < 1 \\ 1, & 1 \leq x < 2 \\ 2, & x = 2 \\ x - 1, & 2 < x \leq 3 \\ -x + 5, & 3 < x \leq 4. \end{cases}$$

(Example 8)

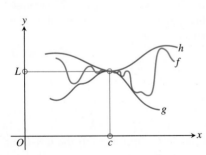

Figure 2.7 Squeezing *f* between *g* and *h* creates a bottleneck around the point (c, L). If we keep *x* close to *c*, the bottleneck forces $f(x)$ to be close to *L*.

EXAMPLE 7 Function Values Approach Two Numbers

The greatest integer function $f(x) = \text{int } x$ has different right-hand and left-hand limits at each integer, as we can see in Figure 2.5. For example,

$$\lim_{x \to 3^+} \text{int } x = 3 \quad \text{and} \quad \lim_{x \to 3^-} \text{int } x = 2.$$

The limit of int *x* as *x* approaches an integer *n* from the right is *n*, while the limit as *x* approaches *n* from the left is $n - 1$.   ***Now Try Exercises 37 and 38.***

The greatest integer function, which appears as int *x* on most calculators, is known to mathematicians as the **floor function,** written $\lfloor x \rfloor$, where we use only the bottom horizontal parts of the brackets to indicate that we go *down* until we reach an integer. You should be able to recognize and use either notation.

We sometimes call $\lim_{x \to c} f(x)$ the **two-sided limit** of *f* at *c* to distinguish it from the *one-sided* right-hand and left-hand limits of *f* at *c*. Theorem 3 shows how these limits are related.

THEOREM 3 One-Sided and Two-Sided Limits

A function $f(x)$ has a limit as *x* approaches *c* if and only if the right-hand and left-hand limits at *c* exist and are equal. In symbols,

$$\lim_{x \to c} f(x) = L \Longleftrightarrow \lim_{x \to c^+} f(x) = L \quad \text{and} \quad \lim_{x \to c^-} f(x) = L.$$

Thus, the greatest integer function $f(x) = \text{int } x$ of Example 7 does not have a limit as $x \to 3$ even though each one-sided limit exists.

EXAMPLE 8 Exploring Right- and Left-Hand Limits

All the following statements about the function $y = f(x)$ graphed in Figure 2.6 are true.

At $x = 0$: $\lim_{x \to 0^+} f(x) = 1.$

At $x = 1$: $\lim_{x \to 1^-} f(x) = 0$ even though $f(1) = 1$,

$\qquad\qquad \lim_{x \to 1^+} f(x) = 1$,

$\qquad$ *f* has no limit as $x \to 1$. (The right- and left-hand limits at 1 are not equal, so $\lim_{x \to 1} f(x)$ does not exist.)

At $x = 2$: $\lim_{x \to 2^-} f(x) = 1$,

$\qquad\qquad \lim_{x \to 2^+} f(x) = 1$,

$\qquad\qquad \lim_{x \to 2} f(x) = 1$ even though $f(2) = 2$.

At $x = 3$: $\lim_{x \to 3^-} f(x) = \lim_{x \to 3^+} f(x) = 2 = f(3) = \lim_{x \to 3} f(x).$

At $x = 4$: $\lim_{x \to 4^-} f(x) = 1.$

At noninteger values of *c* between 0 and 4, *f* has a limit as $x \to c$.

Now Try Exercise 43.

Squeeze Theorem

If we cannot find a limit directly, we may be able to find it indirectly with the Squeeze Theorem. The theorem refers to a function *f* whose values are squeezed between the values of two other functions, *g* and *h*. If *g* and *h* have the same limit as $x \to c$, then *f* has that limit too, as suggested by Figure 2.7.

THEOREM 4   The Squeeze Theorem

If $g(x) \le f(x) \le h(x)$ for all $x \ne c$ in some interval about c, and

$$\lim_{x \to c} g(x) = \lim_{x \to c} h(x) = L,$$

then

$$\lim_{x \to c} f(x) = L.$$

EXAMPLE 9 Using the Squeeze Theorem

Show that $\lim_{x \to 0} \left[x^2 \sin(1/x) \right] = 0$.

SOLUTION

We know that the values of the sine function lie between -1 and 1. So, it follows that

$$\left| x^2 \sin \frac{1}{x} \right| = |x^2| \cdot \left| \sin \frac{1}{x} \right| \le |x^2| \cdot 1 = x^2$$

and

$$-x^2 \le x^2 \sin \frac{1}{x} \le x^2.$$

Because $\lim_{x \to 0} (-x^2) = \lim_{x \to 0} x^2 = 0$, the Squeeze Theorem gives

$$\lim_{x \to 0} \left(x^2 \sin \frac{1}{x} \right) = 0.$$

The graphs in Figure 2.8 support this result.   ***Now Try Exercise 65.***

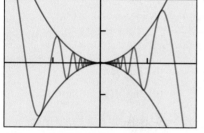

[−0.2, 0.2] by [−0.02, 0.02]

Figure 2.8 The graphs of $y_1 = x^2$, $y_2 = x^2 \sin(1/x)$, and $y_3 = -x^2$. Notice that $y_3 \le y_2 \le y_1$. (Example 9)

Quick Review 2.1   *(For help, go to Section 1.2.)*

Exercise numbers with a gray background indicate problems that the authors have designed to be solved *without a calculator.*

In Exercises 1–4, find $f(2)$.

1. $f(x) = 2x^3 - 5x^2 + 4$

2. $f(x) = \dfrac{4x^2 - 5}{x^3 + 4}$

3. $f(x) = \sin\left(\pi \dfrac{x}{2}\right)$

4. $f(x) = \begin{cases} 3x - 1, & x < 2 \\ \dfrac{1}{x^2 - 1}, & x \ge 2 \end{cases}$

In Exercises 5–8, write the inequality in the form $a < x < b$.

5. $|x| < 4$

6. $|x| < c^2$

7. $|x - 2| < 3$

8. $|x - c| < d^2$

In Exercises 9 and 10, write the fraction in reduced form.

9. $\dfrac{x^2 - 3x - 18}{x + 3}$

10. $\dfrac{2x^2 - x}{2x^2 + x - 1}$

Section 2.1 Exercises

In Exercises 1–4, an object dropped from rest from the top of a tall building falls $y = 16t^2$ feet in the first t seconds.

1. Find the average speed during the first 3 seconds of fall.

2. Find the average speed during the first 4 seconds of fall.

3. Find the speed of the object at $t = 3$ seconds and confirm your answer algebraically.

4. Find the speed of the object at $t = 4$ seconds and confirm your answer algebraically.

In Exercises 5 and 6, use $\lim_{x \to c} k = k$, $\lim_{x \to c} x = c$, and the properties of limits to find the limit.

5. $\lim\limits_{x \to c} (2x^3 - 3x^2 + x - 1)$

6. $\lim\limits_{x \to c} \dfrac{x^4 - x^3 + 1}{x^2 + 9}$

In Exercises 7–14, determine the limit by substitution.

7. $\lim\limits_{x \to -1/2} 3x^2 (2x - 1)$

8. $\lim\limits_{x \to -4} (x + 3)^{2016}$

9. $\lim\limits_{x \to 1} (x^3 + 3x^2 - 2x - 17)$

10. $\lim\limits_{y \to 2} \dfrac{y^2 + 5y + 6}{y + 2}$

11. $\lim\limits_{y \to -3} \dfrac{y^2 + 4y + 3}{y^2 - 3}$

12. $\lim\limits_{x \to 1/2} \text{int } x$

13. $\lim\limits_{x \to -2} (x - 6)^{2/3}$

14. $\lim\limits_{x \to 2} \sqrt{x + 3}$

In Exercises 15–20, complete the following tables and state what you believe $\lim_{x \to 0} f(x)$ to be.

(a)

x	-0.1	-0.01	-0.001	-0.0001	$\ldots$
$f(x)$	?	?	?	?	

(b)

x	0.1	0.01	0.001	0.0001	$\ldots$
$f(x)$	?	?	?	?	

15. $f(x) = \dfrac{x^2 + 6x + 2}{x + 1}$

16. $f(x) = \dfrac{x^2 - x}{x}$

17. $f(x) = x \sin \dfrac{1}{x}$

18. $f(x) = \sin \dfrac{1}{x}$

19. $f(x) = \dfrac{10^x - 1}{x}$

20. $f(x) = x \sin (\ln |x|)$

In Exercises 21–24, explain why you cannot use substitution to determine the limit. Find the limit if it exists.

21. $\lim\limits_{x \to -2} \sqrt{x - 2}$

22. $\lim\limits_{x \to 0} \dfrac{1}{x^2}$

23. $\lim\limits_{x \to 0} \dfrac{|x|}{x}$

24. $\lim\limits_{x \to 0} \dfrac{(4 + x)^2 - 16}{x}$

In Exercises 25–34, explore the limit graphically. Confirm algebraically.

25. $\lim\limits_{x \to 1} \dfrac{x - 1}{x^2 - 1}$

26. $\lim\limits_{t \to 2} \dfrac{t^2 - 3t + 2}{t^2 - 4}$

27. $\lim\limits_{x \to 0} \dfrac{5x^3 + 8x^2}{3x^4 - 16x^2}$

28. $\lim\limits_{x \to 0} \dfrac{\frac{1}{2 + x} - \frac{1}{2}}{x}$

29. $\lim\limits_{x \to 0} \dfrac{(2 + x)^3 - 8}{x}$

30. $\lim\limits_{x \to 0} \dfrac{\sin 2x}{x}$

31. $\lim\limits_{x \to 0} \dfrac{\sin x}{2x^2 - x}$

32. $\lim\limits_{x \to 0} \dfrac{x + \sin x}{x}$

33. $\lim\limits_{x \to 0} \dfrac{\sin^2 x}{x}$

34. $\lim\limits_{x \to 5} \dfrac{x^3 - 125}{x - 5}$

In Exercises 35 and 36, use a graph to explore whether the limit exists.

35. $\lim\limits_{x \to 1} \dfrac{x^2 - 4}{x - 1}$

36. $\lim\limits_{x \to 2} \dfrac{x + 1}{x^2 - 4}$

In Exercises 37–42, determine the limit.

37. $\lim\limits_{x \to 0^+} \text{int } x$

38. $\lim\limits_{x \to 0^-} \text{int } x$

39. $\lim\limits_{x \to 0.01} \text{int } x$

40. $\lim\limits_{x \to 2^-} \text{int } x$

41. $\lim\limits_{x \to 0^+} \dfrac{x}{|x|}$

42. $\lim\limits_{x \to 0^-} \dfrac{x}{|x|}$

In Exercises 43 and 44, which of the statements are true about the function $y = f(x)$ graphed there, and which are false?

43.

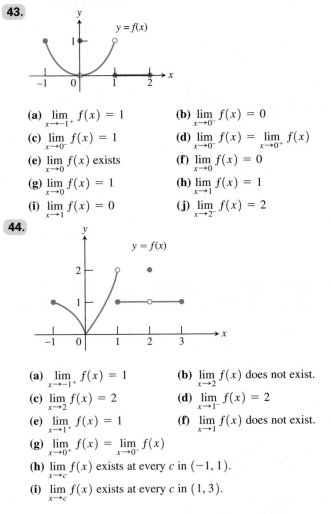

(a) $\lim\limits_{x \to -1^+} f(x) = 1$

(b) $\lim\limits_{x \to 0^-} f(x) = 0$

(c) $\lim\limits_{x \to 0^-} f(x) = 1$

(d) $\lim\limits_{x \to 0^-} f(x) = \lim\limits_{x \to 0^+} f(x)$

(e) $\lim\limits_{x \to 0} f(x)$ exists

(f) $\lim\limits_{x \to 0} f(x) = 0$

(g) $\lim\limits_{x \to 0} f(x) = 1$

(h) $\lim\limits_{x \to 1} f(x) = 1$

(i) $\lim\limits_{x \to 1} f(x) = 0$

(j) $\lim\limits_{x \to 2^-} f(x) = 2$

44.

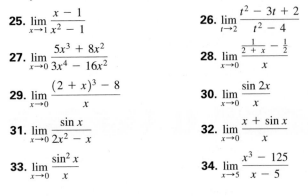

(a) $\lim\limits_{x \to -1^+} f(x) = 1$

(b) $\lim\limits_{x \to 2} f(x)$ does not exist.

(c) $\lim\limits_{x \to 2} f(x) = 2$

(d) $\lim\limits_{x \to 1^-} f(x) = 2$

(e) $\lim\limits_{x \to 1^+} f(x) = 1$

(f) $\lim\limits_{x \to 1} f(x)$ does not exist.

(g) $\lim\limits_{x \to 0^+} f(x) = \lim\limits_{x \to 0^-} f(x)$

(h) $\lim\limits_{x \to c} f(x)$ exists at every c in $(-1, 1)$.

(i) $\lim\limits_{x \to c} f(x)$ exists at every c in $(1, 3)$.

In Exercises 45–50, use the graph to estimate the limits and value of the function, or explain why the limits do not exist.

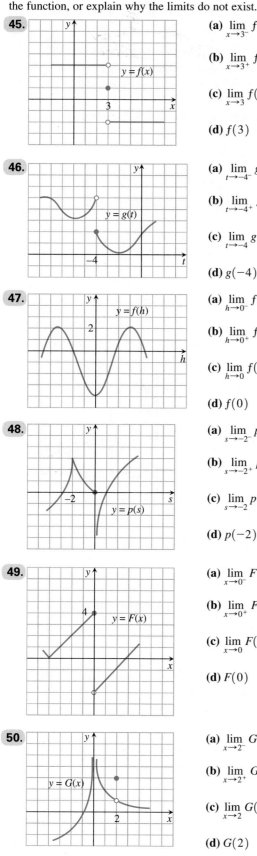

45.
(a) $\lim\limits_{x \to 3^-} f(x)$

(b) $\lim\limits_{x \to 3^+} f(x)$

(c) $\lim\limits_{x \to 3} f(x)$

(d) $f(3)$

46.
(a) $\lim\limits_{t \to -4^-} g(t)$

(b) $\lim\limits_{t \to -4^+} g(t)$

(c) $\lim\limits_{t \to -4} g(t)$

(d) $g(-4)$

47.
(a) $\lim\limits_{h \to 0^-} f(h)$

(b) $\lim\limits_{h \to 0^+} f(h)$

(c) $\lim\limits_{h \to 0} f(h)$

(d) $f(0)$

48.
(a) $\lim\limits_{s \to -2^-} p(s)$

(b) $\lim\limits_{s \to -2^+} p(s)$

(c) $\lim\limits_{s \to -2} p(s)$

(d) $p(-2)$

49.
(a) $\lim\limits_{x \to 0^-} F(x)$

(b) $\lim\limits_{x \to 0^+} F(x)$

(c) $\lim\limits_{x \to 0} F(x)$

(d) $F(0)$

50.
(a) $\lim\limits_{x \to 2^-} G(x)$

(b) $\lim\limits_{x \to 2^+} G(x)$

(c) $\lim\limits_{x \to 2} G(x)$

(d) $G(2)$

In Exercises 51–54, match the function with the table.

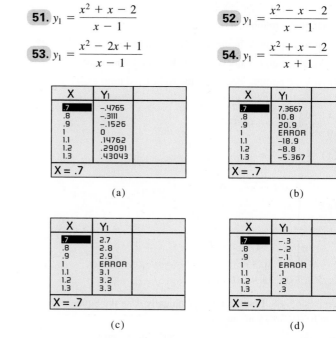

51. $y_1 = \dfrac{x^2 + x - 2}{x - 1}$

52. $y_1 = \dfrac{x^2 - x - 2}{x - 1}$

53. $y_1 = \dfrac{x^2 - 2x + 1}{x - 1}$

54. $y_1 = \dfrac{x^2 + x - 2}{x + 1}$

X	Y₁	
.7	-.4765	
.8	-.3111	
.9	-.1526	
1	0	
1.1	.14762	
1.2	.29091	
1.3	.43043	

X = .7

(a)

X	Y₁	
.7	7.3667	
.8	10.8	
.9	20.9	
1	ERROR	
1.1	-18.9	
1.2	-8.8	
1.3	-5.367	

X = .7

(b)

X	Y₁	
.7	2.7	
.8	2.8	
.9	2.9	
1	ERROR	
1.1	3.1	
1.2	3.2	
1.3	3.3	

X = .7

(c)

X	Y₁	
.7	-.3	
.8	-.2	
.9	-.1	
1	ERROR	
1.1	.1	
1.2	.2	
1.3	.3	

X = .7

(d)

In Exercises 55 and 56, determine the limit.

55. Assume that $\lim\limits_{x \to 4} f(x) = 0$ and $\lim\limits_{x \to 4} g(x) = 3$.

(a) $\lim\limits_{x \to 4} (g(x) + 3)$ (b) $\lim\limits_{x \to 4} x\,f(x)$

(c) $\lim\limits_{x \to 4} g^2(x)$ (d) $\lim\limits_{x \to 4} \dfrac{g(x)}{f(x) - 1}$

56. Assume that $\lim\limits_{x \to b} f(x) = 7$ and $\lim\limits_{x \to b} g(x) = -3$.

(a) $\lim\limits_{x \to b} (f(x) + g(x))$ (b) $\lim\limits_{x \to b} (f(x) \cdot g(x))$

(c) $\lim\limits_{x \to b} 4\,g(x)$ (d) $\lim\limits_{x \to b} \dfrac{f(x)}{g(x)}$

In Exercises 57–60, complete parts (a), (b), and (c) for the piecewise-defined function.

(a) Draw the graph of f.

(b) Determine $\lim\limits_{x \to c^+} f(x)$ and $\lim\limits_{x \to c^-} f(x)$.

(c) **Writing to Learn** Does $\lim\limits_{x \to c} f(x)$ exist? If so, what is it? If not, explain.

57. $c = 2,\ f(x) = \begin{cases} 3 - x, & x < 2 \\ \dfrac{x}{2} + 1, & x > 2 \end{cases}$

58. $c = 2,\ f(x) = \begin{cases} 3 - x, & x < 2 \\ 2, & x = 2 \\ x/2, & x > 2 \end{cases}$

59. $c = 1,\ f(x) = \begin{cases} \dfrac{1}{x - 1}, & x < 1 \\ x^3 - 2x + 5, & x \geq 1 \end{cases}$

60. $c = -1,\ f(x) = \begin{cases} 1 - x^2, & x \neq -1 \\ 2, & x = -1 \end{cases}$

In Exercises 61–64, complete parts (a)–(d) for the piecewise-defined function.

(a) Draw the graph of f.

(b) At what points c in the domain of f does $\lim_{x \to c} f(x)$ exist?

(c) At what points c does only the left-hand limit exist?

(d) At what points c does only the right-hand limit exist?

61. $f(x) = \begin{cases} \sin x, & -2\pi \le x < 0 \\ \cos x, & 0 \le x \le 2\pi \end{cases}$

62. $f(x) = \begin{cases} \cos x, & -\pi \le x < 0 \\ \sec x, & 0 \le x \le \pi \end{cases}$

63. $f(x) = \begin{cases} \sqrt{1 - x^2}, & 0 \le x < 1 \\ 1, & 1 \le x < 2 \\ 2, & x = 2 \end{cases}$

64. $f(x) = \begin{cases} x, & -1 \le x < 0, \text{ or } 0 < x \le 1 \\ 1, & x = 0 \\ 0, & x < -1, \text{ or } x > 1 \end{cases}$

In Exercises 65–68, find the limit graphically. Use the Squeeze Theorem to confirm your answer.

65. $\lim_{x \to 0} x \sin x$

66. $\lim_{x \to 0} x^2 \sin x$

67. $\lim_{x \to 0} x^2 \sin \dfrac{1}{x^2}$

68. $\lim_{x \to 0} x^2 \cos \dfrac{1}{x^2}$

69. *Free Fall* A water balloon dropped from a window high above the ground falls $y = 4.9t^2$ m in t sec. Find the balloon's

(a) average speed during the first 3 sec of fall.

(b) speed at the instant $t = 3$.

70. *Free Fall on a Small Airless Planet* A rock released from rest to fall on a small airless planet falls $y = gt^2$ m in t sec, g a constant. Suppose that the rock falls to the bottom of a crevasse 20 m below and reaches the bottom in 4 sec.

(a) Find the value of g.

(b) Find the average speed for the fall.

(c) With what speed did the rock hit the bottom?

Standardized Test Questions

71. True or False If $\lim_{x \to c^-} f(x) = 2$ and $\lim_{x \to c^+} f(x) = 2$, then $\lim_{x \to c} f(x) = 2$. Justify your answer.

72. True or False $\lim_{x \to 0} \dfrac{x + \sin x}{x} = 2$. Justify your answer.

In Exercises 73–76, use the following function.

$$f(x) = \begin{cases} 2 - x, & x \le 1 \\ \dfrac{x}{2} + 1, & x > 1 \end{cases}$$

73. Multiple Choice What is the value of $\lim_{x \to 1^-} f(x)$?

(A) 5/2 (B) 3/2 (C) 1 (D) 0 (E) does not exist

74. Multiple Choice What is the value of $\lim_{x \to 1^+} f(x)$?

(A) 5/2 (B) 3/2 (C) 1 (D) 0 (E) does not exist

75. Multiple Choice What is the value of $\lim_{x \to 1} f(x)$?

(A) 5/2 (B) 3/2 (C) 1 (D) 0 (E) does not exist

76. Multiple Choice What is the value of $f(1)$?

(A) 5/2 (B) 3/2 (C) 1 (D) 0 (E) does not exist

77. Group Activity To prove that $\lim_{\theta \to 0} (\sin \theta)/\theta = 1$ when θ is measured in radians, the plan is to show that the right- and left-hand limits are both 1.

(a) To show that the right-hand limit is 1, explain why we can restrict our attention to $0 < \theta < \pi/2$.

(b) Use the figure to show that

$$\text{area of } \triangle OAP = \frac{1}{2} \sin \theta,$$

$$\text{area of sector } OAP = \frac{\theta}{2},$$

$$\text{area of } \triangle OAT = \frac{1}{2} \tan \theta.$$

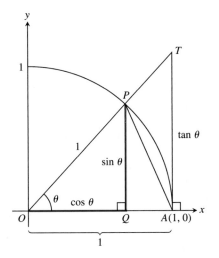

(c) Use part (b) and the figure to show that for $0 < \theta < \pi/2$,

$$\frac{1}{2} \sin \theta < \frac{1}{2} \theta < \frac{1}{2} \tan \theta.$$

(d) Show that for $0 < \theta < \pi/2$ the inequality of part (c) can be written in the form

$$1 < \frac{\theta}{\sin \theta} < \frac{1}{\cos \theta}.$$

(e) Show that for $0 < \theta < \pi/2$ the inequality of part (d) can be written in the form

$$\cos \theta < \frac{\sin \theta}{\theta} < 1.$$

(f) Use the Squeeze Theorem to show that

$$\lim_{\theta \to 0^+} \frac{\sin \theta}{\theta} = 1.$$

(g) Show that $(\sin \theta)/\theta$ is an even function.

(h) Use part (g) to show that

$$\lim_{\theta \to 0^-} \frac{\sin \theta}{\theta} = 1.$$

(i) Finally, show that

$$\lim_{\theta \to 0^+} \frac{\sin \theta}{\theta} = 1.$$

Extending the Ideas

78. *Controlling Outputs* Let $f(x) = \sqrt{3x - 2}$.

(a) Show that $\lim_{x \to 2} f(x) = 2 = f(2)$.

(b) Use a graph to estimate values for a and b so that $1.8 < f(x) < 2.2$ provided $a < x < b$.

(c) Use a graph to estimate values for a and b so that $1.99 < f(x) < 2.01$ provided $a < x < b$.

79. *Controlling Outputs* Let $f(x) = \sin x$.

(a) Find $f(\pi/6)$.

(b) Use a graph to estimate an interval (a, b) about $x = \pi/6$ so that $0.3 < f(x) < 0.7$ provided $a < x < b$.

(c) Use a graph to estimate an interval (a, b) about $x = \pi/6$ so that $0.49 < f(x) < 0.51$ provided $a < x < b$.

80. *Limits and Geometry* Let $P(a, a^2)$ be a point on the parabola $y = x^2$, $a > 0$. Let O be the origin and $(0, b)$ the y-intercept of the perpendicular bisector of line segment OP. Find $\lim_{P \to O} b$.

2.2 Limits Involving Infinity

You will be able to interpret, estimate, and determine infinite limits and limits at infinity.

- The Squeeze Theorem for limits at infinity
- Asymptotic and unbounded behavior of functions
- End behavior of functions

Finite Limits as $x \to \pm\infty$

The symbol for infinity (∞) does not represent a real number. We use ∞ to describe the behavior of a function when the values in its domain or range outgrow all finite bounds. For example, when we say, "the limit of f as x approaches infinity is L," we mean that we can force the value of the function to be as close as we wish to L by taking values of x that are sufficiently far to the right on the number line. When we say, "the limit of f as x approaches negative infinity ($-\infty$) is L," we mean that we can force the value of the function to be as close as we wish to L by taking values of x that are sufficiently far to the left. (The limit in each case may or may not exist.)

Looking at $f(x) = 1/x$ (Figure 2.9), we observe

(a) as $x \to \infty$, $(1/x) \to 0$ and we write

$$\lim_{x \to \infty} (1/x) = 0,$$

(b) as $x \to -\infty$, $(1/x) \to 0$ and we write

$$\lim_{x \to -\infty} (1/x) = 0.$$

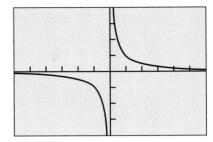

[−6, 6] by [−4, 4]

Figure 2.9 The graph of $f(x) = 1/x$.

We say that the line $y = 0$ is a *horizontal asymptote* of the graph of f.

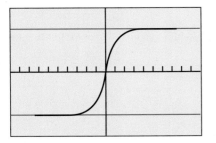

X	Y1	
0	0	
1	.7071	
2	.8944	
3	.9487	
4	.9701	
5	.9806	
6	.9864	
Y1 ▤ X/√ (X² + 1)		

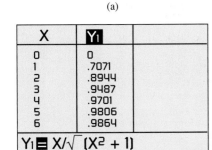

X	Y1	
-6	-.9864	
-5	-.9806	
-4	-.9701	
-3	-.9487	
-2	-.8944	
-1	-.7071	
0	0	
Y1 ▤ X/√ (X² + 1)		

(b)

Figure 2.10 (a) The graph of $f(x) = x/\sqrt{x^2 + 1}$ has two horizontal asymptotes, $y = -1$ and $y = 1$. (b) Selected values of f. (Example 1)

[−10, 10] by [−1.5, 1.5]

(a)

> **DEFINITION** **Horizontal Asymptote**
>
> The line $y = b$ is a **horizontal asymptote** of the graph of a function $y = f(x)$ if either
>
> $$\lim_{x \to \infty} f(x) = b \quad \text{or} \quad \lim_{x \to -\infty} f(x) = b.$$

The graph of $f(x) = 2 + (1/x)$ has the single horizontal asymptote $y = 2$ because

$$\lim_{x \to \infty} \left(2 + \frac{1}{x} \right) = 2 \quad \text{and} \quad \lim_{x \to -\infty} \left(2 + \frac{1}{x} \right) = 2.$$

A function can have more than one horizontal asymptote, as Example 1 demonstrates.

EXAMPLE 1 Looking for Horizontal Asymptotes

Use graphs and tables to find $\lim_{x \to \infty} f(x)$, $\lim_{x \to -\infty} f(x)$, and identify all horizontal asymptotes of $f(x) = x/\sqrt{x^2 + 1}$.

SOLUTION

Figure 2.10a shows the graph for $-10 \le x \le 10$. The graph climbs rapidly toward the line $y = 1$ as x moves away from the origin to the right. On our calculator screen, the graph soon becomes indistinguishable from the line. Thus $\lim_{x \to \infty} f(x) = 1$. Similarly, as x moves away from the origin to the left, the graph drops rapidly toward the line $y = -1$ and soon appears to overlap the line. Thus $\lim_{x \to -\infty} f(x) = -1$. The horizontal asymptotes are $y = 1$ and $y = -1$.

continued

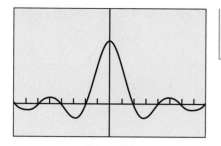

[−4π, 4π] by [−0.5, 1.5]

(a)

X	Y₁	
100	−.0051	
200	−.0044	
300	−.0033	
400	−.0021	
500	−9E−4	
600	7.4E−5	
700	7.8E−4	

Y₁ ▤ sin(X)/X

(b)

Figure 2.11 (a) The graph of $f(x) = (\sin x)/x$ oscillates about the *x*-axis. The amplitude of the oscillations decreases toward zero as $x \to \pm\infty$. (b) A table of values for *f* that suggests $f(x) \to 0$ as $x \to \infty$. (Example 2)

The table in Figure 2.10b confirms the rapid approach of $f(x)$ toward 1 as $x \to \infty$. Since *f* is an odd function of *x*, we can expect its values to approach -1 in a similar way as $x \to -\infty$.

Now Try Exercise 5.

Squeeze Theorem Revisited

The Squeeze Theorem also holds for limits as $x \to \pm\infty$.

EXAMPLE 2 Finding a Limit as *x* Approaches ∞

Find $\lim\limits_{x\to\infty} f(x)$ for $f(x) = \dfrac{\sin x}{x}$.

SOLUTION

The graph and table of values in Figure 2.11 suggest that $y = 0$ is the horizontal asymptote of *f*.

We know that $-1 \le \sin x \le 1$. So, for $x > 0$ we have

$$-\frac{1}{x} \le \frac{\sin x}{x} \le \frac{1}{x}.$$

Therefore, by the Squeeze Theorem,

$$0 = \lim_{x\to\infty}\left(-\frac{1}{x}\right) = \lim_{x\to\infty}\frac{\sin x}{x} = \lim_{x\to\infty}\frac{1}{x} = 0.$$

Since $(\sin x)/x$ is an even function of *x*, we can also conclude that

$$\lim_{x\to-\infty}\frac{\sin x}{x} = 0.$$

Now Try Exercise 9.

Limits at infinity have properties similar to those of finite limits.

THEOREM 5   Properties of Limits as $x \to \pm\infty$

If *L*, *M*, and *k* are real numbers and

$$\lim_{x\to\pm\infty} f(x) = L \quad \text{and} \quad \lim_{x\to\pm\infty} g(x) = M, \text{ then}$$

1. *Sum Rule:* $\quad\quad\quad\quad\quad \lim\limits_{x\to\pm\infty}(f(x) + g(x)) = L + M$

2. *Difference Rule:* $\quad\quad\quad \lim\limits_{x\to\pm\infty}(f(x) - g(x)) = L - M$

3. *Product Rule:* $\quad\quad\quad\quad \lim\limits_{x\to\pm\infty}(f(x) \cdot g(x)) = L \cdot M$

4. *Constant Multiple Rule:* $\quad \lim\limits_{x\to\pm\infty}(k \cdot f(x)) = k \cdot L$

5. *Quotient Rule:* $\quad\quad\quad\quad \lim\limits_{x\to\pm\infty}\dfrac{f(x)}{g(x)} = \dfrac{L}{M}, \; M \ne 0$

6. *Power Rule:* If *r* and *s* are integers, $s \ne 0$, then

$$\lim_{x\to\pm\infty}(f(x))^{r/s} = L^{r/s}$$

provided that $L^{r/s}$ is a real number and $L > 0$ if *s* is even.

We can use Theorem 5 to find limits at infinity of functions with complicated expressions, as illustrated in Example 3.

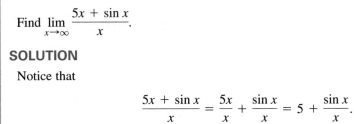

EXAMPLE 3 **Using Theorem 5**

Find $\lim\limits_{x \to \infty} \dfrac{5x + \sin x}{x}$.

SOLUTION

Notice that

$$\frac{5x + \sin x}{x} = \frac{5x}{x} + \frac{\sin x}{x} = 5 + \frac{\sin x}{x}.$$

So,

$$\lim_{x \to \infty} \frac{5x + \sin x}{x} = \lim_{x \to \infty} 5 + \lim_{x \to \infty} \frac{\sin x}{x} \qquad \text{Sum Rule}$$

$$= 5 + 0 = 5 \qquad\qquad \text{Known values}$$

Now Try Exercise 25.

EXPLORATION 1 Exploring Theorem 5

We must be careful how we apply Theorem 5.

1. (Example 3 again) Let $f(x) = 5x + \sin x$ and $g(x) = x$. Do the limits as $x \to \infty$ of f and g exist? Can we apply the Quotient Rule to $\lim_{x \to \infty} f(x)/g(x)$? Explain. Does the limit of the quotient exist?
2. Let $f(x) = \sin^2 x$ and $g(x) = \cos^2 x$. Describe the behavior of f and g as $x \to \infty$. Can we apply the Sum Rule to $\lim_{x \to \infty}(f(x) + g(x))$? Explain. Does the limit of the sum exist?
3. Let $f(x) = \ln(2x)$ and $g(x) = \ln(x + 1)$. Find the limits as $x \to \infty$ of f and g. Can we apply the Difference Rule to $\lim_{x \to \infty}(f(x) - g(x))$? Explain. Does the limit of the difference exist?
4. Based on parts 1–3, what advice might you give about applying Theorem 5?

Infinite Limits as $x \to a$

If the values of a function $f(x)$ outgrow all positive bounds as x approaches a finite number a, we say that $\lim_{x \to a} f(x) = \infty$. If the values of f become large and negative, exceeding all negative bounds as $x \to a$, we say that $\lim_{x \to a} f(x) = -\infty$.

Looking at $f(x) = 1/x$ (Figure 2.9, page 70), we observe that

$$\lim_{x \to 0^+} 1/x = \infty \quad \text{and} \quad \lim_{x \to 0^-} 1/x = -\infty.$$

We say that the line $x = 0$ is a *vertical asymptote* of the graph of f.

DEFINITION **Vertical Asymptote**

The line $x = a$ is a **vertical asymptote** of the graph of a function $y = f(x)$ if either

$$\lim_{x \to a^+} f(x) = \pm\infty \quad \text{or} \quad \lim_{x \to a^-} f(x) = \pm\infty.$$

EXAMPLE 4 Finding Vertical Asymptotes

Find the vertical asymptotes of $f(x) = \dfrac{1}{x^2}$. Describe the behavior to the left and right of each vertical asymptote.

SOLUTION

The values of the function approach ∞ on either side of $x = 0$.

$$\lim_{x \to 0^+} \frac{1}{x^2} = \infty \quad \text{and} \quad \lim_{x \to 0^-} \frac{1}{x^2} = \infty.$$

The line $x = 0$ is the only vertical asymptote. *Now Try Exercise 27.*

We can also say that $\lim_{x \to 0}\left(1/x^2\right) = \infty$. We can make no such statement about $1/x$.

EXAMPLE 5 Finding Vertical Asymptotes

The graph of $f(x) = \tan x = (\sin x)/(\cos x)$ has infinitely many vertical asymptotes, one at each point where the cosine is zero. If a is an odd multiple of $\pi/2$, then

$$\lim_{x \to a^+} \tan x = -\infty \quad \text{and} \quad \lim_{x \to a^-} \tan x = \infty,$$

as suggested by Figure 2.12. *Now Try Exercise 31.*

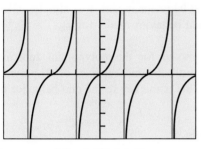

[$-2\pi, 2\pi$] by [$-5, 5$]

Figure 2.12 The graph of $f(x) = \tan x$ has a vertical asymptote at

$$\dots, -\frac{3\pi}{2}, -\frac{\pi}{2}, \frac{\pi}{2}, \frac{3\pi}{2}, \dots \text{(Example 5)}$$

You might think that the graph of a quotient always has a vertical asymptote where the denominator is zero, but that need not be the case. For example, we observed in Section 2.1 that $\lim_{x \to 0}(\sin x)/x = 1$.

End Behavior Models

For numerically large values of x, we can sometimes model the behavior of a complicated function by a simpler one that acts virtually in the same way.

EXAMPLE 6 Modeling Functions for $|x|$ Large

Let $f(x) = 3x^4 - 2x^3 + 3x^2 - 5x + 6$ and $g(x) = 3x^4$. Show that while f and g are quite different for numerically small values of x, they are virtually identical for $|x|$ large.

SOLUTION

The graphs of f and g (Figure 2.13a), quite different near the origin, are virtually identical on a larger scale (Figure 2.13b).

We can test the claim that g models f for numerically large values of x by examining the ratio of the two functions as $x \to \pm\infty$. We find that

$$\lim_{x \to \pm\infty} \frac{f(x)}{g(x)} = \lim_{x \to \pm\infty} \frac{3x^4 - 2x^3 + 3x^2 - 5x + 6}{3x^4}$$

$$= \lim_{x \to \pm\infty}\left(1 - \frac{2}{3x} + \frac{1}{x^2} - \frac{5}{3x^3} + \frac{2}{x^4}\right)$$

$$= 1,$$

convincing evidence that f and g behave alike for $|x|$ large. *Now Try Exercise 39.*

$y = 3x^4 - 2x^3 + 3x^2 - 5x + 6$

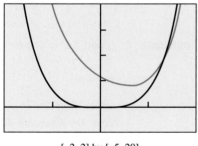

[$-2, 2$] by [$-5, 20$]

(a)

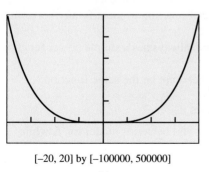

[$-20, 20$] by [$-100000, 500000$]

(b)

Figure 2.13 The graphs of f and g, (a) distinct for $|x|$ small, are (b) nearly identical for $|x|$ large. (Example 6)

> **DEFINITION** **End Behavior Model**
>
> The function g is
>
> **(a)** a **right end behavior model** for f if and only if $\lim\limits_{x \to \infty} \dfrac{f(x)}{g(x)} = 1$.
>
> **(b)** a **left end behavior model** for f if and only if $\lim\limits_{x \to -\infty} \dfrac{f(x)}{g(x)} = 1$.

If one function provides both a left and right end behavior model, it is simply called an **end behavior model.** Thus, $g(x) = 3x^4$ is an end behavior model for $f(x) = 3x^4 - 2x^3 + 3x^2 - 5x + 6$ (Example 6).

In general, $g(x) = a_n x^n$ is an end behavior model for the polynomial function $f(x) = a_n x^n + a_{n-1} x^{n-1} + \cdots + a_0, a_n \neq 0$. Overall, the end behavior of all polynomials behave like the end behavior of monomials. This is the key to the end behavior of rational functions, as illustrated in Example 7.

EXAMPLE 7 Finding End Behavior Models

Find an end behavior model for

(a) $f(x) = \dfrac{2x^5 + x^4 - x^2 + 1}{3x^2 - 5x + 7}$ **(b)** $g(x) = \dfrac{2x^3 - x^2 + x - 1}{5x^3 + x^2 + x - 5}$

SOLUTION

(a) Notice that $2x^5$ is an end behavior model for the numerator of f, and $3x^2$ is one for the denominator. This makes

$$\frac{2x^5}{3x^2} = \frac{2}{3} x^3$$

an end behavior model for f.

(b) Similarly, $2x^3$ is an end behavior model for the numerator of g, and $5x^3$ is one for the denominator of g. This makes

$$\frac{2x^3}{5x^3} = \frac{2}{5}$$

an end behavior model for g. *Now Try Exercise 43.*

Notice in Example 7b that the end behavior model for g, $y = 2/5$, is also a horizontal asymptote of the graph of g, while in 7a, the graph of f does not have a horizontal asymptote. We can use the end behavior model of a rational function to identify any horizontal asymptote.

We can see from Example 7 that a rational function always has a simple power function as an end behavior model.

A function's right and left end behavior models need not be the same function.

EXAMPLE 8 Finding End Behavior Models

Let $f(x) = x + e^{-x}$. Show that $g(x) = x$ is a right end behavior model for f, while $h(x) = e^{-x}$ is a left end behavior model for f.

SOLUTION

On the right,

$$\lim_{x \to \infty} \frac{f(x)}{g(x)} = \lim_{x \to \infty} \frac{x + e^{-x}}{x} = \lim_{x \to \infty} \left(1 + \frac{e^{-x}}{x} \right) = 1 \text{ because } \lim_{x \to \infty} \frac{e^{-x}}{x} = 0.$$

continued

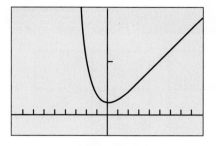

[−9, 9] by [−2, 10]

Figure 2.14 The graph of $f(x) = x + e^{-x}$ looks like the graph of $g(x) = x$ to the right of the y-axis, and like the graph of $h(x) = e^{-x}$ to the left of the y-axis. (Example 8)

On the left,

$$\lim_{x \to -\infty} \frac{f(x)}{h(x)} = \lim_{x \to -\infty} \frac{x + e^{-x}}{e^{-x}} = \lim_{x \to -\infty} \left(\frac{x}{e^{-x}} + 1 \right) = 1 \text{ because } \lim_{x \to -\infty} \frac{x}{e^{-x}} = 0.$$

The graph of f in Figure 2.14 supports these end behavior conclusions.

Now Try Exercise 45.

"Seeing" Limits as $x \to \pm\infty$

We can investigate the graph of $y = f(x)$ as $x \to \pm\infty$ by investigating the graph of $y = f(1/x)$ as $x \to 0$.

EXAMPLE 9 Using Substitution

Find $\lim_{x \to \infty} \sin (1/x)$.

SOLUTION

Figure 2.15a suggests that the limit is 0. Indeed, replacing $\lim_{x \to \infty} \sin (1/x)$ by the equivalent $\lim_{x \to 0^+} \sin x = 0$ (Figure 2.15b), we find

$$\lim_{x \to \infty} \sin 1/x = \lim_{x \to 0^+} \sin x = 0.$$

Now Try Exercise 49.

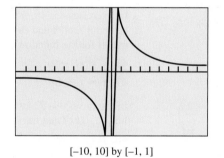

[−10, 10] by [−1, 1]

(a)

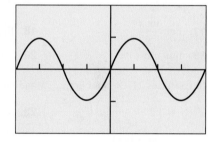

[−2π, 2π] by [−2, 2]

(b)

Figure 2.15 The graphs of (a) $f(x) = \sin (1/x)$ and (b) $g(x) = f(1/x) = \sin x$. (Example 9)

Quick Review 2.2   *(For help, go to Sections 1.2 and 1.5.)*

Exercise numbers with a gray background indicate problems that the authors have designed to be solved *without a calculator*.

In Exercises 1–4, find f^{-1} and graph f, f^{-1}, and $y = x$ in the same square viewing window.

1. $f(x) = 2x - 3$ **2.** $f(x) = e^x$

3. $f(x) = \tan^{-1} x$ **4.** $f(x) = \cot^{-1} x$

In Exercises 5 and 6, find the quotient $q(x)$ and remainder $r(x)$ when $f(x)$ is divided by $g(x)$.

5. $f(x) = 2x^3 - 3x^2 + x - 1$, $g(x) = 3x^3 + 4x - 5$

6. $f(x) = 2x^5 - x^3 + x - 1$, $g(x) = x^3 - x^2 + 1$

In Exercises 7–10, write a formula for **(a)** $f(-x)$ and **(b)** $f(1/x)$. Simplify where possible.

7. $f(x) = \cos x$

8. $f(x) = e^{-x}$

9. $f(x) = \dfrac{\ln |x|}{x}$

10. $f(x) = \left(x + \dfrac{1}{x} \right) \sin x$

Section 2.2 Exercises

In Exercises 1–8, use graphs and tables to find (a) $\lim_{x \to \infty} f(x)$ and (b) $\lim_{x \to -\infty} f(x)$. (c) Identify all horizontal asymptotes.

1. $f(x) = \cos\left(\dfrac{1}{x}\right)$

2. $f(x) = \dfrac{\sin 2x}{x}$

3. $f(x) = \dfrac{e^{-x}}{x}$

4. $f(x) = \dfrac{3x^3 - x + 1}{x + 3}$

5. $f(x) = \dfrac{3x + 1}{|x| + 2}$

6. $f(x) = \dfrac{2x - 1}{|x| - 3}$

7. $f(x) = \dfrac{x}{|x|}$

8. $f(x) = \dfrac{|x|}{|x| + 1}$

In Exercises 9–12, find the limit and confirm your answer using the Squeeze Theorem.

9. $\lim_{x \to \infty} \dfrac{1 - \cos x}{x^2}$

10. $\lim_{x \to -\infty} \dfrac{1 - \cos x}{x^2}$

11. $\lim_{x \to -\infty} \dfrac{\sin x}{x}$

12. $\lim_{x \to \infty} \dfrac{\sin(x^2)}{x}$

In Exercises 13–20, use graphs and tables to find the limits.

13. $\lim_{x \to 2^+} \dfrac{1}{x - 2}$

14. $\lim_{x \to 2^-} \dfrac{x}{x - 2}$

15. $\lim_{x \to -3^-} \dfrac{1}{x + 3}$

16. $\lim_{x \to -3^+} \dfrac{x}{x + 3}$

17. $\lim_{x \to 0^+} \dfrac{\text{int } x}{x}$

18. $\lim_{x \to 0^-} \dfrac{\text{int } x}{x}$

19. $\lim_{x \to 0^+} \csc x$

20. $\lim_{x \to (\pi/2)^+} \sec x$

In Exercises 21–26, find $\lim_{x \to \infty} y$ and $\lim_{x \to -\infty} y$.

21. $y = \left(2 - \dfrac{x}{x + 1}\right)\left(\dfrac{x^2}{5 + x^2}\right)$

22. $y = \left(\dfrac{2}{x} + 1\right)\left(\dfrac{5x^2 - 1}{x^2}\right)$

23. $y = \dfrac{\cos(1/x)}{1 + (1/x)}$

24. $y = \dfrac{2x + \sin x}{x}$

25. $y = \dfrac{\cos x - 2x^3}{x^3}$

26. $y = \dfrac{x \sin x + 2 \cos x}{2x^2}$

In Exercises 27–34, (a) find the vertical asymptotes of the graph of $f(x)$. (b) Describe the behavior of $f(x)$ to the left and right of each vertical asymptote.

27. $f(x) = \dfrac{1}{x^2 - 4}$

28. $f(x) = \dfrac{x^2 - 1}{2x + 4}$

29. $f(x) = \dfrac{x^2 - 2x}{x + 1}$

30. $f(x) = \dfrac{1 - x}{2x^2 - 5x - 3}$

31. $f(x) = \cot x$

32. $f(x) = \sec x$

33. $f(x) = \dfrac{\tan x}{\sin x}$

34. $f(x) = \dfrac{\cot x}{\cos x}$

In Exercises 35–38, match the function with the graph of its end behavior model.

35. $y = \dfrac{2x^3 - 3x^2 + 1}{x + 3}$

36. $y = \dfrac{x^5 - x^4 + x + 1}{2x^2 + x - 3}$

37. $y = \dfrac{2x^4 - x^3 + x^2 - 1}{2 - x}$

38. $y = \dfrac{x^4 - 3x^3 + x^2 - 1}{1 - x^2}$

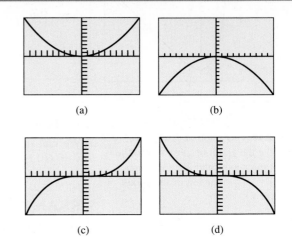

(a)   (b)

(c)   (d)

In Exercises 39–44, (a) find a power function end behavior model for f. (b) Identify any horizontal asymptotes.

39. $f(x) = 3x^2 - 2x + 1$

40. $f(x) = -4x^3 + x^2 - 2x - 1$

41. $f(x) = \dfrac{x - 2}{2x^2 + 3x - 5}$

42. $f(x) = \dfrac{3x^2 - x + 5}{x^2 - 4}$

43. $f(x) = \dfrac{4x^3 - 2x + 1}{x - 2}$

44. $f(x) = \dfrac{-x^4 + 2x^2 + x - 3}{x^2 - 4}$

In Exercises 45–48, find (a) a simple basic function as a right end behavior model and (b) a simple basic function as a left end behavior model for the function.

45. $y = e^x - 2x$

46. $y = x^2 + e^{-x}$

47. $y = x + \ln |x|$

48. $y = x^2 + \sin x$

In Exercises 49–52, use the graph of $y = f(1/x)$ to find $\lim_{x \to \infty} f(x)$ and $\lim_{x \to -\infty} f(x)$.

49. $f(x) = xe^x$

50. $f(x) = x^2 e^{-x}$

51. $f(x) = \dfrac{\ln |x|}{x}$

52. $f(x) = x \sin \dfrac{1}{x}$

In Exercises 53 and 54, find the limit of $f(x)$ as (a) $x \to -\infty$, (b) $x \to \infty$, (c) $x \to 0^-$, and (d) $x \to 0^+$.

53. $f(x) = \begin{cases} 1/x, & x < 0 \\ -1, & x \geq 0 \end{cases}$

54. $f(x) = \begin{cases} \dfrac{x - 2}{x - 1}, & x \leq 0 \\ 1/x^2, & x > 0 \end{cases}$

Group Activity In Exercises 55 and 56, sketch a graph of a function $y = f(x)$ that satisfies the stated conditions. Include any asymptotes.

55. $\lim_{x \to 1} f(x) = 2$, $\quad \lim_{x \to 5^-} f(x) = \infty$, $\quad \lim_{x \to 5^+} f(x) = \infty$,

$\lim_{x \to \infty} f(x) = -1$, $\quad \lim_{x \to -2^+} f(x) = -\infty$,

$\lim_{x \to -2^-} f(x) = \infty$, $\quad \lim_{x \to -\infty} f(x) = 0$

56. $\lim_{x \to 2} f(x) = -1$, $\quad \lim_{x \to 4^+} f(x) = -\infty$, $\quad \lim_{x \to 4^-} f(x) = \infty$,

$\lim_{x \to \infty} f(x) = \infty$, $\quad \lim_{x \to -\infty} f(x) = 2$

57. Group Activity *End Behavior Models* Suppose that $g_1(x)$ is a right end behavior model for $f_1(x)$ and that $g_2(x)$ is a right end behavior model for $f_2(x)$. Explain why this makes $g_1(x)/g_2(x)$ a right end behavior model for $f_1(x)/f_2(x)$.

58. Writing to Learn Let L be a real number, $\lim_{x \to c} f(x) = L$, and $\lim_{x \to c} g(x) = \infty$ or $-\infty$. Can $\lim_{x \to c} (f(x) + g(x))$ be determined? Explain.

Standardized Test Questions

59. True or False It is possible for a function to have more than one horizontal asymptote. Justify your answer.

60. True or False If $f(x)$ has a vertical asymptote at $x = c$, then either $\lim_{x \to c^-} f(x) = \lim_{x \to c^+} f(x) = \infty$ or $\lim_{x \to c^-} f(x) = \lim_{x \to c^+} f(x) = -\infty$. Justify your answer.

61. Multiple Choice $\lim_{x \to 2^-} \dfrac{x}{x - 2} =$

(A) $-\infty$ (B) ∞ (C) 1 (D) $-1/2$ (E) -1

You may use a graphing calculator to solve the following problems.

62. Multiple Choice $\lim_{x \to 0} \dfrac{\cos (2x)}{x} =$

(A) 1/2 (B) 1 (C) 2 (D) cos 2 (E) does not exist

63. Multiple Choice $\lim_{x \to 0} \dfrac{\sin (3x)}{x} =$

(A) 1/3 (B) 1 (C) 3 (D) sin 3 (E) does not exist

64. Multiple Choice Which of the following is an end behavior for
$$f(x) = \frac{2x^3 - x^2 + x + 1}{x^3 - 1}?$$

(A) x^3 (B) $2x^3$ (C) $1/x^3$ (D) 2 (E) 1/2

Exploration

65. *Exploring Properties of Limits* Find the limits of f, g, and fg as $x \to c$.

(a) $f(x) = \dfrac{1}{x}$, $g(x) = x$, $c = 0$

(b) $f(x) = -\dfrac{2}{x^3}$, $g(x) = 4x^3$, $c = 0$

(c) $f(x) = \dfrac{3}{x - 2}$, $g(x) = (x - 2)^3$, $c = 2$

(d) $f(x) = \dfrac{5}{(3 - x)^4}$, $g(x) = (x - 3)^2$, $c = 3$

(e) **Writing to Learn** Suppose that $\lim_{x \to c} f(x) = 0$ and $\lim_{x \to c} g(x) = \infty$. Based on your observations in parts (a)–(d), what can you say about $\lim_{x \to c} (f(x) \cdot g(x))$?

Extending the Ideas

66. *The Greatest Integer Function*

(a) Show that
$$\frac{x - 1}{x} < \frac{\text{int } x}{x} \le 1 \ (x > 0) \text{ and } \frac{x - 1}{x} > \frac{\text{int } x}{x} \ge 1 \ (x < 0).$$

(b) Determine $\lim_{x \to \infty} \dfrac{\text{int } x}{x}$.

(c) Determine $\lim_{x \to -\infty} \dfrac{\text{int } x}{x}$.

67. *Squeeze Theorem* Use the Squeeze Theorem to confirm the limit as $x \to \infty$ found in Exercise 3.

68. Writing to Learn Explain why there is no value L for which $\lim_{x \to \infty} \sin x = L$.

In Exercises 69–71, find the limit. Give a convincing argument that the value is correct.

69. $\lim_{x \to \infty} \dfrac{\ln x^2}{\ln x}$

70. $\lim_{x \to \infty} \dfrac{\ln x}{\log x}$

71. $\lim_{x \to \infty} \dfrac{\ln (x + 1)}{\ln x}$

Quick Quiz for AP* Preparation: Sections 2.1 and 2.2

1. Multiple Choice Find $\lim_{x \to 3} \dfrac{x^2 - x - 6}{x - 3}$, if it exists.

(A) -1 (B) 1 (C) 2 (D) 5 (E) does not exist

2. Multiple Choice Find $\lim_{x \to 2^+} f(x)$, if it exists, where
$$f(x) = \begin{cases} 3x + 1, & x < 2 \\ \dfrac{5}{x + 1}, & x \ge 2 \end{cases}$$

(A) 5/3 (B) 13/3 (C) 7 (D) ∞ (E) does not exist

3. Multiple Choice Which of the following lines is a horizontal asymptote for
$$f(x) = \frac{3x^3 - x^2 + x - 7}{2x^3 + 4x - 5}?$$

(A) $y = \dfrac{3}{2}x$ (B) $y = 0$ (C) $y = 2/3$ (D) $y = 7/5$ (E) $y = 3/2$

4. Free Response Let $f(x) = \dfrac{\cos x}{x}$.

(a) Find the domain and range of f.

(b) Is f even, odd, or neither? Justify your answer.

(c) Find $\lim_{x \to \infty} f(x)$.

(d) Use the Squeeze Theorem to justify your answer to part (c).

2.3 | Continuity

You will be able to analyze functions to find intervals of continuity and points of discontinuity and to determine the applicability of the Intermediate Value Theorem.

- Definition of continuity at a point
- Types of discontinuities
- Sums, differences, products, quotients, and compositions of continuous functions
- Common continuous functions
- Continuity and the Intermediate Value Theorem

Continuity at a Point

When we plot function values generated in the laboratory or collected in the field, we often connect the plotted points with an unbroken curve to show what the function's values are likely to have been at the times we did not measure (Figure 2.16). In doing so, we are assuming that we are working with a *continuous function*, a function whose outputs vary continuously with the inputs and do not jump from one value to another without taking on the values in between. Any function $y = f(x)$ whose graph can be sketched in one continuous motion without lifting the pencil is an example of a continuous function.

Continuous functions are those we use to find a planet's closest point of approach to the sun or the peak concentration of antibodies in blood plasma. They are also the functions we use to describe how a body moves through space or how the speed of a chemical reaction changes with time. In fact, so many physical processes proceed continuously that throughout the 18th and 19th centuries it rarely occurred to anyone to look for any other kind of behavior. It came as a surprise when the physicists of the 1920s discovered that light comes in particles and that heated atoms emit light at discrete frequencies (Figure 2.17). As a result of these and other discoveries, and because of the heavy use of discontinuous functions in computer science, statistics, and mathematical modeling, the issue of continuity has become one of practical as well as theoretical importance.

To understand continuity, we need to consider a function like the one in Figure 2.18, whose limits we investigated in Example 8, Section 2.1.

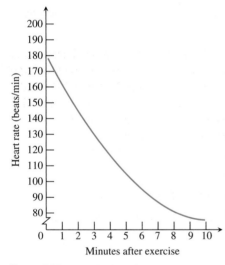

Figure 2.16 How the heartbeat returns to a normal rate after running.

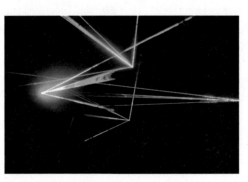

Figure 2.17 The laser was developed as a result of an understanding of the nature of the atom.

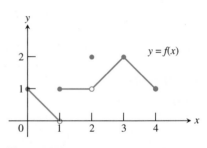

Figure 2.18 The function is continuous on $[0, 4]$ except at $x = 1$ and $x = 2$. (Example 1)

EXAMPLE 1 Investigating Continuity

Find the points at which the function f in Figure 2.18 is continuous, and the points at which f is discontinuous.

SOLUTION

The function f is continuous at every point in its domain $[0, 4]$ except at $x = 1$ and $x = 2$. At these points there are breaks in the graph. Note the relationship between the limit of f and the value of f at each point of the function's domain.

Points at which f is continuous:

At $x = 0$, $\qquad\qquad \lim_{x \to 0^+} f(x) = f(0)$.

At $x = 4$, $\qquad\qquad \lim_{x \to 4^-} f(x) = f(4)$.

At $0 < c < 4, c \neq 1, 2$, $\quad \lim_{x \to c} f(x) = f(c)$.

continued

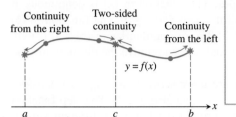

Figure 2.19 Continuity at points a, b, and c for a function $y = f(x)$ that is continuous on the interval $[a, b]$.

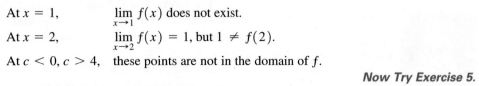

Points at which f is discontinuous:

At $x = 1$, $\lim\limits_{x \to 1} f(x)$ does not exist.

At $x = 2$, $\lim\limits_{x \to 2} f(x) = 1$, but $1 \neq f(2)$.

At $c < 0, c > 4$, these points are not in the domain of f.

Now Try Exercise 5.

To define continuity at a point in a function's domain, we need to define continuity at an interior point (which involves a two-sided limit) and continuity at an endpoint (which involves a one-sided limit) (Figure 2.19).

DEFINITION   Continuity at a Point

Interior Point: A function $y = f(x)$ is **continuous at an interior point c** of its domain if

$$\lim_{x \to c} f(x) = f(c).$$

Endpoint: A function $y = f(x)$ is **continuous at a left endpoint a** or is **continuous at a right endpoint b** of its domain if

$$\lim_{x \to a^+} f(x) = f(a) \quad \text{or} \quad \lim_{x \to b^-} f(x) = f(b), \quad \text{respectively.}$$

The assumption that exponential functions such as 2^x are continuous makes it possible to define a number raised to an irrational exponent such as 2^π. Fractional exponents come from combining integer roots and powers: $2^{2/3} = \left(\sqrt[3]{2}\right)^2$. This means that $2^{3.14} = 2^{314/100}$ is the 314th power of the 100th root of 2. As we add more decimal digits, we get closer to the value of 2^π, which is *defined* to be the limit of 2^x as x approaches π through rational numbers.

If a function f is not continuous at a point c, we say that f is **discontinuous** at c and c is a **point of discontinuity** of f. Note that c need not be in the domain of f.

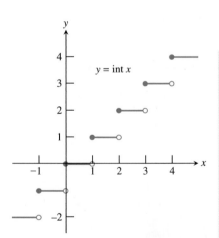

Figure 2.20 The function int x is continuous at every noninteger point. (Example 2)

EXAMPLE 2 Finding Points of Continuity and Discontinuity

Find the points of continuity and the points of discontinuity of the greatest integer function (Figure 2.20).

SOLUTION

For the function to be continuous at $x = c$, the limit as $x \to c$ must exist and must equal the value of the function at $x = c$. The greatest integer function is discontinuous at every integer. For example,

$$\lim_{x \to 3^-} \text{int } x = 2 \quad \text{and} \quad \lim_{x \to 3^+} \text{int } x = 3$$

so the limit as $x \to 3$ does not exist. Notice that int $3 = 3$. In general, if n is any integer,

$$\lim_{x \to n^-} \text{int } x = n - 1 \quad \text{and} \quad \lim_{x \to n^+} \text{int } x = n,$$

so the limit as $x \to n$ does not exist.

The greatest integer function is continuous at every other real number. For example,

$$\lim_{x \to 1.5} \text{int } x = 1 = \text{int } 1.5.$$

In general, if $n - 1 < c < n$, n an integer, then

$$\lim_{x \to c} \text{int } x = n - 1 = \text{int } c.$$

Now Try Exercise 7.

Figure 2.21 is a catalog of discontinuity types. The function in (a) is continuous at $x = 0$. The function in (b) would be continuous if it had $f(0) = 1$. The function in (c) would be continuous if $f(0)$ were 1 instead of 2. The discontinuities in (b) and (c) are **removable.** Each function has a limit as $x \to 0$, and we can remove the discontinuity by setting $f(0)$ equal to this limit.

The discontinuities in (d)–(f) of Figure 2.21 are more serious: $\lim_{x \to 0} f(x)$ does not exist and there is no way to improve the situation by changing f at 0. The step function in (d) has a **jump discontinuity:** The one-sided limits exist but have different values. The function $f(x) = 1/x^2$ in (e) has an **infinite discontinuity.** The function in (f) has an **oscillating discontinuity:** It oscillates and has no limit as $x \to 0$.

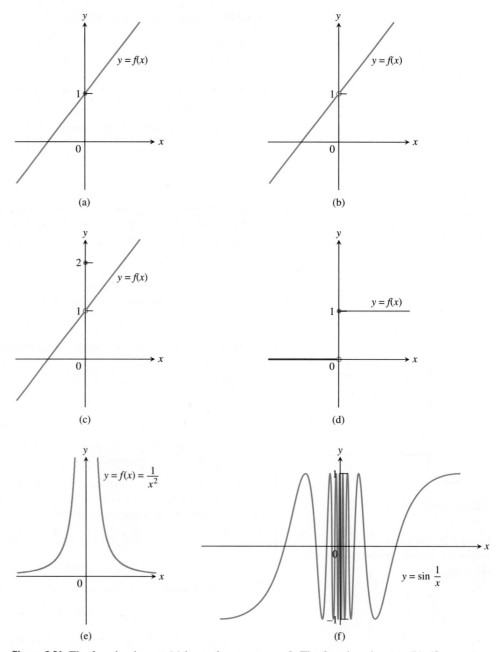

Figure 2.21 The function in part (a) is continuous at $x = 0$. The functions in parts (b)–(f) are not.

EXPLORATION 1 Removing a Discontinuity

Let $f(x) = \dfrac{x^3 - 7x - 6}{x^2 - 9}$.

1. Factor the denominator. What is the domain of f?
2. Investigate the graph of f around $x = 3$ to see that f has a removable discontinuity at $x = 3$.
3. How should f be defined at $x = 3$ to remove the discontinuity? Use ZOOM-IN and tables as necessary.
4. Show that $(x - 3)$ is a factor of the numerator of f, and remove all common factors. Now compute the limit as $x \to 3$ of the reduced form for f.
5. Show that the *extended function*

$$g(x) = \begin{cases} \dfrac{x^3 - 7x - 6}{x^2 - 9}, & x \neq 3 \\ 10/3, & x = 3 \end{cases}$$

is continuous at $x = 3$. The function g is the **continuous extension** of the original function f to include $x = 3$.

Now Try Exercise 25.

Continuous Functions

A function is **continuous on an interval** if and only if it is continuous at every point of the interval. A **continuous function** is one that is continuous at every point of its domain. A continuous function need not be continuous on every interval. For example, $y = 1/x$ is not continuous on $[-1, 1]$.

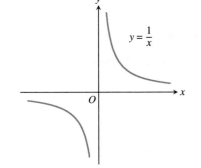

Figure 2.22 The function $y = 1/x$ is continuous at every value of x except $x = 0$. It has a point of discontinuity at $x = 0$. (Example 3)

EXAMPLE 3 Identifying Continuous Functions

The reciprocal function $y = 1/x$ (Figure 2.22) is a continuous function because it is continuous at every point of its domain. However, it has a point of discontinuity at $x = 0$ because it is not defined there. *Now Try Exercise 31.*

Polynomial functions f are continuous at every real number c because $\lim_{x \to c} f(x) = f(c)$. Rational functions are continuous at every point of their domains. They have points of discontinuity at the zeros of their denominators. The absolute value function $y = |x|$ is continuous at every real number. The exponential functions, logarithmic functions, trigonometric functions, and radical functions like $y = \sqrt[n]{x}$ (n a positive integer greater than 1) are continuous at every point of their domains. All of these functions are continuous functions.

Algebraic Combinations

As you may have guessed, algebraic combinations of continuous functions are continuous wherever they are defined.

THEOREM 6   Properties of Continuous Functions

If the functions f and g are continuous at $x = c$, then the following combinations are continuous at $x = c$.

1. *Sums:* $f + g$
2. *Differences:* $f - g$
3. *Products:* $f \cdot g$
4. *Constant multiples:* $k \cdot f$, for any number k
5. *Quotients:* f/g, provided $g(c) \neq 0$

Composites

All composites of continuous functions are continuous. This means composites like

$$y = \sin (x^2) \quad \text{and} \quad y = |\cos x|$$

are continuous at every point at which they are defined. The idea is that if $f(x)$ is continuous at $x = c$ and $g(x)$ is continuous at $x = f(c)$, then $g \circ f$ is continuous at $x = c$ (Figure 2.23). In this case, the limit as $x \to c$ is $g(f(c))$.

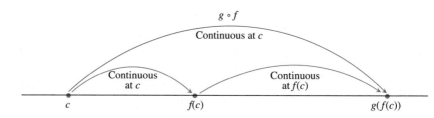

$g \circ f$
Continuous at c

Continuous at c Continuous at $f(c)$

c $f(c)$ $g(f(c))$

Figure 2.23 Composites of continuous functions are continuous.

THEOREM 7   Composite of Continuous Functions

If f is continuous at c and g is continuous at $f(c)$, then the composite $g \circ f$ is continuous at c.

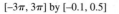

$[-3\pi, 3\pi]$ by $[-0.1, 0.5]$

Figure 2.24 The graph suggests that $y = |(x \sin x)/(x^2 + 2)|$ is continuous. (Example 4)

EXAMPLE 4 Using Theorem 7

Show that $y = \left| \dfrac{x \sin x}{x^2 + 2} \right|$ is continuous.

SOLUTION

The graph (Figure 2.24) of $y = |(x \sin x)/(x^2 + 2)|$ suggests that the function is continuous at every value of x. By letting

$$g(x) = |x| \quad \text{and} \quad f(x) = \frac{x \sin x}{x^2 + 2},$$

we see that y is the composite $g \circ f$.

We know that the absolute value function g is continuous. The function f is continuous by Theorem 6. Their composite is continuous by Theorem 7.   ***Now Try Exercise 33.***

Intermediate Value Theorem for Continuous Functions

Functions that are continuous on intervals have properties that make them particularly useful in mathematics and its applications. One of these is the *intermediate value property*. A function is said to have the **intermediate value property** if it never takes on two values without taking on all the values in between.

THEOREM 8   The Intermediate Value Theorem for Continuous Functions

A function $y = f(x)$ that is continuous on a closed interval $[a, b]$ takes on every value between $f(a)$ and $f(b)$. In other words, if y_0 is between $f(a)$ and $f(b)$, then $y_0 = f(c)$ for some c in $[a, b]$.

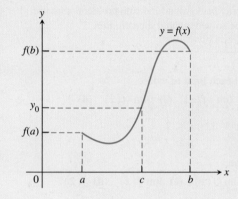

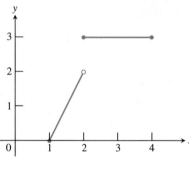

Figure 2.25 The function

$$f(x) = \begin{cases} 2x - 2, & 1 \le x < 2 \\ 3, & 2 \le x \le 4 \end{cases}$$

does not take on all values between $f(1) = 0$ and $f(4) = 3$; it misses all the values between 2 and 3.

Grapher Failure

In connected mode, a grapher may conceal a function's discontinuities by portraying the graph as a connected curve when it is not. To see what we mean, graph $y =$ int (x) in a $[-10, 10]$ by $[-10, 10]$ window in both connected and dot modes. A knowledge of where to expect discontinuities will help you recognize this form of grapher failure.

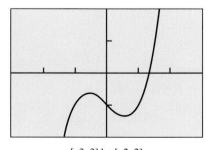

[–3, 3] by [–2, 2]

Figure 2.26 The graph of $f(x) = x^3 - x - 1$. (Example 5)

This theorem may seem so obvious that it does not need to be singled out for special attention. However, it is important because it provides a foundation for the fundamental theorems on which calculus is built. The continuity of f on the interval is essential to Theorem 8. If f is discontinuous at even one point of the interval, the theorem's conclusion may fail, as it does for the function graphed in Figure 2.25.

A Consequence for Graphing: Connectivity Theorem 8 is the reason why the graph of a function continuous on an interval cannot have any breaks. The graph will be **connected,** a single, unbroken curve, like the graph of sin x. It will not have jumps like those in the graph of the greatest integer function int x, or separate branches like we see in the graph of $1/x$.

Most graphers can plot points (*dot mode*). Some can turn on pixels between plotted points to suggest an unbroken curve (*connected mode*). For functions, the connected format basically assumes that outputs *vary continuously* with inputs and do not jump from one value to another without taking on all values in between.

EXAMPLE 5   Using Theorem 8

Is any real number exactly 1 less than its cube? Compute any such value accurate to three decimal places.

SOLUTION

We answer this question by applying the Intermediate Value Theorem in the following way. Any such number must satisfy the equation $x = x^3 - 1$ or, equivalently, $x^3 - x - 1 = 0$. Hence, we are looking for a zero value of the continuous function $f(x) = x^3 - x - 1$ (Figure 2.26). The function changes sign between 1 and 2, so there must be a point c between 1 and 2 where $f(c) = 0$.

continued

There are a variety of methods for numerically computing the value of c to be accurate to as many decimal places as your technology allows. For example, a simple application of ZOOM (box) and TRACE using a graphing calculator will quickly give the result of $c \approx 1.324$ accurate to three decimal places. Most calculators have a numerical zero finder that will give an immediate solution as well. **Now Try Exercise 46.**

Can you find the *exact* value of c such that $f(c) = c^3 - c - 1 = 0$ and that you know exists by the application of the Intermediate Value Theorem? Discuss your answer with your classmates and your teacher.

Quick Review 2.3 (For help, go to Sections 1.2 and 2.1.)

Exercise numbers with a gray background indicate problems that the authors have designed to be solved *without a calculator*.

1. Find $\lim\limits_{x \to -1} \dfrac{3x^2 - 2x + 1}{x^3 + 4}$.

2. Let $f(x) = \text{int } x$. Find each limit or value.

(a) $\lim\limits_{x \to -1^-} f(x)$ (b) $\lim\limits_{x \to -1^+} f(x)$ (c) $\lim\limits_{x \to -1} f(x)$ (d) $f(-1)$

3. Let $f(x) = \begin{cases} x^2 - 4x + 5, & x < 2 \\ 4 - x, & x \geq 2. \end{cases}$

Find each limit or value.

(a) $\lim\limits_{x \to 2^-} f(x)$ (b) $\lim\limits_{x \to 2^+} f(x)$ (c) $\lim\limits_{x \to 2} f(x)$ (d) $f(2)$

In Exercises 4–6, find the remaining functions in the list of functions: $f, g, f \circ g, g \circ f$.

4. $f(x) = \dfrac{2x - 1}{x + 5}$, $g(x) = \dfrac{1}{x} + 1$

5. $f(x) = x^2$, $(g \circ f)(x) = \sin x^2$, domain of $g = [0, \infty)$

6. $g(x) = \sqrt{x - 1}$, $(g \circ f)(x) = 1/x$, $x > 0$

7. Use factoring to solve $2x^2 + 9x - 5 = 0$.

8. Use graphing to solve $x^3 + 2x - 1 = 0$.

In Exercises 9 and 10, let

$$f(x) = \begin{cases} 5 - x, & x \leq 3 \\ -x^2 + 6x - 8, & x > 3. \end{cases}$$

9. Solve the equation $f(x) = 4$.

10. Find a value of c for which the equation $f(x) = c$ has no solution.

Section 2.3 Exercises

In Exercises 1–10, find the points of continuity and the points of discontinuity of the function. Identify each type of discontinuity.

1. $y = \dfrac{1}{(x + 2)^2}$

2. $y = \dfrac{x + 1}{x^2 - 4x + 3}$

3. $y = \dfrac{1}{x^2 + 1}$

4. $y = |x - 1|$

5. $y = \sqrt{2x + 3}$

6. $y = \sqrt[3]{2x - 1}$

7. $y = |x|/x$

8. $y = \cot x$

9. $y = e^{1/x}$

10. $y = \ln(x + 1)$

In Exercises 11–18, use the function f defined and graphed below to answer the questions.

$$f(x) = \begin{cases} x^2 - 1, & -1 \leq x < 0 \\ 2x, & 0 < x < 1 \\ 1, & x = 1 \\ -2x + 4, & 1 < x < 2 \\ 0, & 2 < x < 3 \end{cases}$$

11. (a) Does $f(-1)$ exist?

(b) Does $\lim\limits_{x \to -1^+} f(x)$ exist?

(c) Does $\lim\limits_{x \to -1^+} f(x) = f(-1)$?

(d) Is f continuous at $x = -1$?

12. (a) Does $f(1)$ exist?

(b) Does $\lim\limits_{x \to 1} f(x)$ exist?

(c) Does $\lim\limits_{x \to 1} f(x) = f(1)$?

(d) Is f continuous at $x = 1$?

13. (a) Is f defined at $x = 2$? (Look at the definition of f.)

(b) Is f continuous at $x = 2$?

14. At what values of x is f continuous?

15. What value should be assigned to $f(2)$ to make the extended function continuous at $x = 2$?

16. What new value should be assigned to $f(1)$ to make the new function continuous at $x = 1$?

17. Writing to Learn Is it possible to extend f to be continuous at $x = 0$? If so, what value should the extended function have there? If not, why not?

18. Writing to Learn Is it possible to extend f to be continuous at $x = 3$? If so, what value should the extended function have there? If not, why not?

In Exercises 19–24, **(a)** find each point of discontinuity. **(b)** Which of the discontinuities are removable? not removable? Give reasons for your answers.

19. $f(x) = \begin{cases} 3 - x, & x < 2 \\ \dfrac{x}{2} + 1, & x > 2 \end{cases}$

20. $f(x) = \begin{cases} 3 - x, & x < 2 \\ 2, & x = 2 \\ x/2, & x > 2 \end{cases}$

21. $f(x) = \begin{cases} \dfrac{1}{x - 1}, & x < 1 \\ x^3 - 2x + 5, & x \geq 1 \end{cases}$

22. $f(x) = \begin{cases} 1 - x^2, & x \neq -1 \\ 2, & x = -1 \end{cases}$

23.

24.

In Exercises 25–30, give a formula for the extended function that is continuous at the indicated point.

25. $f(x) = \dfrac{x^2 - 9}{x + 3}, \quad x = -3$

26. $f(x) = \dfrac{x^3 - 1}{x^2 - 1}, \quad x = 1$

27. $f(x) = \dfrac{\sin x}{x}, \quad x = 0$

28. $f(x) = \dfrac{\sin 4x}{x}, \quad x = 0$

29. $f(x) = \dfrac{x - 4}{\sqrt{x} - 2}, \quad x = 4$

30. $f(x) = \dfrac{x^3 - 4x^2 - 11x + 30}{x^2 - 4}, \quad x = 2$

In Exercises 31 and 32, explain why the given function is continuous.

31. $f(x) = \dfrac{1}{x - 3}$

32. $g(x) = \dfrac{1}{\sqrt{x - 1}}$

In Exercises 33–36, use Theorem 7 to show that the given function is continuous.

33. $f(x) = \sqrt{\left(\dfrac{x}{x + 1}\right)}$

34. $f(x) = \sin(x^2 + 1)$

35. $f(x) = \cos\left(\sqrt[3]{1 - x}\right)$

36. $f(x) = \tan\left(\dfrac{x^2}{x^2 + 4}\right)$

Group Activity In Exercises 37–40, verify that the function is continuous and state its domain. Indicate which theorems you are using, and which functions you are assuming to be continuous.

37. $y = \dfrac{1}{\sqrt{x + 2}}$

38. $y = x^2 + \sqrt[3]{4 - x}$

39. $y = |x^2 - 4x|$

40. $y = \begin{cases} \dfrac{x^2 - 1}{x - 1}, & x \neq 1 \\ 2, & x = 1 \end{cases}$

In Exercises 41–44, sketch a possible graph for a function f that has the stated properties.

41. $f(3)$ exists but $\lim_{x \to 3} f(x)$ does not.

42. $f(-2)$ exists, $\lim_{x \to -2^+} f(x) = f(-2)$, but $\lim_{x \to -2} f(x)$ does not exist.

43. $f(4)$ exists, $\lim_{x \to 4} f(x)$ exists, but f is not continuous at $x = 4$.

44. $f(x)$ is continuous for all x except $x = 1$, where f has a nonremovable discontinuity.

45. Solving Equations Is any real number exactly 1 less than its fourth power? Give any such values accurate to 3 decimal places.

46. Solving Equations Is any real number exactly 2 more than its cube? Give any such values accurate to 3 decimal places.

47. Continuous Function Find a value for a so that the function

$$f(x) = \begin{cases} x^2 - 1, & x < 3 \\ 2ax, & x \geq 3 \end{cases}$$

is continuous.

48. Continuous Function Find a value for a so that the function

$$f(x) = \begin{cases} 2x + 3, & x \leq 2 \\ ax + 1, & x > 2 \end{cases}$$

is continuous.

49. *Continuous Function* Find a value for a so that the function

$$f(x) = \begin{cases} 4 - x^2, & x < -1 \\ ax^2 - 1, & x \geq -1 \end{cases}$$

is continuous.

50. *Continuous Function* Find a value for a so that the function

$$f(x) = \begin{cases} x^2 + x + a, & x < 1 \\ x^3, & x \geq 1 \end{cases}$$

is continuous.

51. **Writing to Learn** Explain why the equation $e^{-x} = x$ has at least one solution.

52. *Salary Negotiation* A welder's contract promises a 3.5% salary increase each year for 4 years and Luisa has an initial salary of $36,500.

(a) Show that Luisa's salary is given by

$$y = 36,500(1.035)^{\text{int } t},$$

where t is the time, measured in years, since Luisa signed the contract.

(b) Graph Luisa's salary function. At what values of t is it continuous?

53. *Airport Parking* Valuepark charges $1.10 per hour or fraction of an hour for airport parking. The maximum charge per day is $7.25.

(a) Write a formula that gives the charge for x hours with $0 \leq x \leq 24$. (*Hint:* See Exercise 52.)

(b) Graph the function in part (a). At what values of x is it continuous?

Standardized Test Questions

You may use a graphing calculator to solve the following problems.

54. **True or False** A continuous function cannot have a point of discontinuity. Justify your answer.

55. **True or False** It is possible to extend the definition of a function f at a jump discontinuity $x = a$ so that f is continuous at $x = a$. Justify your answer.

56. **Multiple Choice** On which of the following intervals is $f(x) = \dfrac{1}{\sqrt{x}}$ not continuous?

(A) $(0, \infty)$ (B) $[0, \infty)$ (C) $(0, 2)$

(D) $(1, 2)$ (E) $[1, \infty)$

57. **Multiple Choice** Which of the following points is not a point of discontinuity of $f(x) = \sqrt{x - 1}$?

(A) $x = -1$ (B) $x = -1/2$ (C) $x = 0$

(D) $x = 1/2$ (E) $x = 1$

58. **Multiple Choice** Which of the following statements about the function

$$f(x) = \begin{cases} 2x, & 0 < x < 1 \\ 1, & x = 1 \\ -x + 3, & 1 < x < 2 \end{cases}$$

is not true?

(A) $f(1)$ does not exist.

(B) $\lim_{x \to 0^+} f(x)$ exists.

(C) $\lim_{x \to 2^-} f(x)$ exists.

(D) $\lim_{x \to 1} f(x)$ exists.

(E) $\lim_{x \to 1} f(x) \neq f(1)$

59. **Multiple Choice** Which of the following points of discontinuity of

$$f(x) = \frac{x(x - 1)(x - 2)^2 (x + 1)^2 (x - 3)^2}{x(x - 1)(x - 2)(x + 1)^2 (x - 3)^3}$$

is not removable?

(A) $x = -1$ (B) $x = 0$ (C) $x = 1$

(D) $x = 2$ (E) $x = 3$

Exploration

60. Let $f(x) = \left(1 + \dfrac{1}{x}\right)^x$.

(a) Find the domain of f.   (b) Draw the graph of f.

(c) **Writing to Learn** Explain why $x = -1$ and $x = 0$ are points of discontinuity of f.

(d) **Writing to Learn** Is either of the discontinuities in part (c) removable? Explain.

(e) Use graphs and tables to estimate $\lim_{x \to \infty} f(x)$.

Extending the Ideas

61. *Continuity at a Point* Show that $f(x)$ is continuous at $x = a$ if and only if

$$\lim_{h \to 0} f(a + h) = f(a).$$

62. *Continuity on Closed Intervals* Let f be continuous and never zero on $[a, b]$. Show that either $f(x) > 0$ for all x in $[a, b]$ or $f(x) < 0$ for all x in $[a, b]$.

63. *Properties of Continuity* Prove that if f is continuous on an interval, then so is $|f|$.

64. *Everywhere Discontinuous* Give a convincing argument that the following function is not continuous at any real number.

$$f(x) = \begin{cases} 1, & \text{if } x \text{ is rational} \\ 0, & \text{if } x \text{ is irrational} \end{cases}$$

2.4 Rates of Change, Tangent Lines, and Sensitivity

You will be able to use limits to determine instantaneous rates of change, slopes of tangent lines, and sensitivity to change.

• Tangent lines
• Slopes of curves
• Instantaneous rate of change
• Sensitivity

Average Rates of Change

We encounter average rates of change in such forms as average speed (in miles per hour), growth rates of populations (in percent per year), and average monthly rainfall (in inches per month). The **average rate of change** of a quantity over a period of time is the amount of change divided by the time it takes. In general, the *average rate of change* of a function over an interval is the amount of change divided by the length of the interval.

EXAMPLE 1 Finding Average Rate of Change

Find the average rate of change of $f(x) = x^3 - x$ over the interval $[1, 3]$.

SOLUTION

Since $f(1) = 0$ and $f(3) = 24$, the average rate of change over the interval $[1, 3]$ is

$$\frac{f(3) - f(1)}{3 - 1} = \frac{24 - 0}{2} = 12. \qquad \textit{Now Try Exercise 1.}$$

Experimental biologists often want to know the rates at which populations grow under controlled laboratory conditions. Figure 2.27 shows how the number of fruit flies *(Drosophila)* grew in a controlled 50-day experiment. The graph was made by counting flies at regular intervals, plotting a point for each count, and drawing a smooth curve through the plotted points.

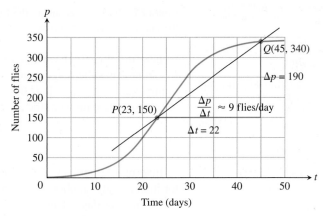

Figure 2.27 Growth of a fruit fly population in a controlled experiment. *Source: Elements of Mathematical Biology.* (Example 2)

Secant to a Curve

A line through two points on a curve is a **secant to the curve.**

Marjorie Lee Browne *(1914–1979)*

When Marjorie Browne graduated from the University of Michigan in 1949, she was one of the first two African American women to be awarded a Ph.D. in Mathematics. Browne went on to become chairperson of the mathematics department at North Carolina Central University, and succeeded in obtaining grants for retraining high school mathematics teachers.

EXAMPLE 2 Growing *Drosophila* in a Laboratory

Use the points $P(23, 150)$ and $Q(45, 340)$ in Figure 2.27 to compute the average rate of change and the slope of the secant line PQ.

SOLUTION

There were 150 flies on day 23 and 340 flies on day 45. This gives an increase of $340 - 150 = 190$ flies in $45 - 23 = 22$ days.

The average rate of change in the population p from day 23 to day 45 was

$$\textit{Average rate of change:} \quad \frac{\Delta p}{\Delta t} = \frac{340 - 150}{45 - 23} = \frac{190}{22} \approx 8.6 \text{ flies/day,}$$

or about 9 flies per day.

continued

This average rate of change is also the slope of the secant line through the two points P and Q on the population curve. We can calculate the slope of the secant PQ from the coordinates of P and Q.

$$\textit{Secant slope:} \quad \frac{\Delta p}{\Delta t} = \frac{340 - 150}{45 - 23} = \frac{190}{22} \approx 8.6 \text{ flies/day}$$

Now Try Exercise 7.

As suggested by Example 2, *we can always think of an average rate of change as the slope of a secant line.*

In addition to knowing the average rate at which the population grew from day 23 to day 45, we may also want to know how fast the population was growing on day 23 itself. To find out, we can watch the slope of the secant PQ change as we back Q along the curve toward P. The results for four positions of Q are shown in Figure 2.28.

Why Find Tangents to Curves?

In mechanics, the tangent determines the direction of a body's motion at every point along its path.

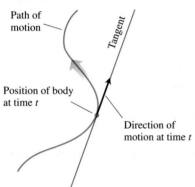

In geometry, the tangents to two curves at a point of intersection determine the angle at which the curves intersect.

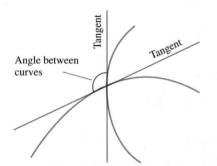

In optics, the tangent determines the angle at which a ray of light enters a curved lens (more about this in Section 4.2). The problem of how to find a tangent to a curve became the dominant mathematical problem of the early 17th century, and it is hard to overestimate how badly the scientists of the day wanted to know the answer. Descartes went so far as to say that the problem was the most useful and most general problem not only that he knew but that he had any desire to know.

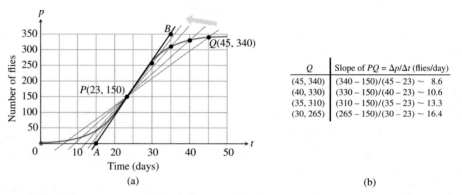

Q	Slope of $PQ = \Delta p/\Delta t$ (flies/day)
(45, 340)	$(340 - 150)/(45 - 23) \sim 8.6$
(40, 330)	$(330 - 150)/(40 - 23) \sim 10.6$
(35, 310)	$(310 - 150)/(35 - 23) \sim 13.3$
(30, 265)	$(265 - 150)/(30 - 23) \sim 16.4$

Figure 2.28 (a) Four secants to the fruit fly graph of Figure 2.27, through the point $P(23, 150)$. (b) The slopes of the four secants.

In terms of geometry, what we see as Q approaches P along the curve is this: The secant PQ approaches the tangent line AB that we drew by eye at P. This means that within the limitations of our drawing, the slopes of the secants approach the slope of the tangent, which we calculate from the coordinates of A and B to be

$$\frac{350 - 0}{35 - 15} = 17.5 \text{ flies/day}.$$

In terms of population, what we see as Q approaches P is this: The average growth rates for increasingly smaller time intervals approach the slope of the tangent to the curve at P (17.5 flies per day). The slope of the tangent line is therefore the number we take as the rate at which the fly population was growing on day $t = 23$.

Tangent to a Curve

The moral of the fruit fly story would seem to be that we should define the rate at which the value of the function $y = f(x)$ is changing with respect to x at any particular value $x = a$ to be the slope of the tangent to the curve $y = f(x)$ at $x = a$. But how are we to define the tangent line at an arbitrary point P on the curve and find its slope from the formula $y = f(x)$? The problem here is that we know only one point. Our usual definition of slope requires two points.

The solution that mathematician Pierre Fermat found in 1629 proved to be one of that century's major contributions to calculus. We still use his method of defining tangents to produce formulas for slopes of curves and rates of change:

1. We start with what we can calculate, namely, the slope of a secant through P and a point Q nearby on the curve.

2. We find the limiting value of the secant slope (if it exists) as Q approaches P along the curve.

3. We define the *slope of the curve* at P to be this number and define the *tangent to the curve* at P to be the line through P with this slope.

EXAMPLE 3 Finding Slope and Tangent Line

Find the slope of the parabola $y = x^2$ at the point $P(2, 4)$. Write an equation for the tangent to the parabola at this point.

SOLUTION

We begin with a secant line through $P(2, 4)$ and a nearby point $Q(2 + h, (2 + h)^2)$ on the curve (Figure 2.29).

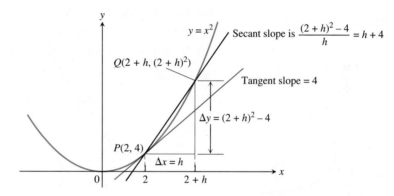

Figure 2.29 The slope of the tangent to the parabola $y = x^2$ at $P(2, 4)$ is 4.

We then write an expression for the slope of the secant line and find the limiting value of this slope as Q approaches P along the curve.

$$\text{Secant slope} = \frac{\Delta y}{\Delta x} = \frac{(2 + h)^2 - 4}{h}$$

$$= \frac{h^2 + 4h + 4 - 4}{h}$$

$$= \frac{h^2 + 4h}{h} = h + 4$$

The limit of the secant slope as Q approaches P along the curve is

$$\lim_{Q \to P} (\text{secant slope}) = \lim_{h \to 0} (h + 4) = 4.$$

Thus, the slope of the parabola at P is 4.

The tangent to the parabola at P is the line through $P(2, 4)$ with slope $m = 4$.

$$y - 4 = 4(x - 2)$$
$$y = 4x - 8 + 4$$
$$y = 4x - 4 \qquad \textbf{Now Try Exercise 11 (a, b).}$$

Slope of a Curve

To find the tangent to a curve $y = f(x)$ at a point $P(a, f(a))$ we use the same dynamic procedure. We calculate the slope of the secant line through P and a point $Q(a + h, f(a + h))$. We then investigate the limit of the slope as $h \to 0$ (Figure 2.30). If the limit exists, it is the slope of the curve at P and we define the tangent at P to be the line through P having this slope.

Pierre de Fermat (1601–1665)

Fermat was a lawyer who worked for the regional parliament in Toulouse, France. He invented his method of tangents in 1629 to solve the problem of finding the cone of greatest volume that can be formed by cutting a sector out of a circle and then folding the circle to join the cut edges (see Exploration 1, Section 5.4, page 225). Fermat shares with René Descartes the honor of having invented what today we know as the Cartesian coordinate system, enabling us to express algebraic equations graphically and so connect algebra and geometry. Fermat made many contributions to the development of calculus, but he did not publish his discoveries. Most of his mathematical writing was confined to professional correspondence and papers written for personal friends.

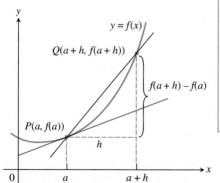

Figure 2.30 The tangent slope is

$$\lim_{h \to 0} \frac{f(a + h) - f(a)}{h}.$$

DEFINITION **Slope of a Curve at a Point**

The **slope of the curve** $y = f(x)$ at the point $P(a, f(a))$ is the number

$$m = \lim_{h \to 0} \frac{f(a + h) - f(a)}{h},$$

provided the limit exists.

The **tangent line to the curve** at P is the line through P with this slope.

EXAMPLE 4 Exploring Slope and Tangent

Let $f(x) = 1/x$.

(a) Find the slope of the curve at $x = a$.

(b) Where does the slope equal $-1/4$?

(c) What happens to the tangent to the curve at the point $(a, 1/a)$ for different values of a?

SOLUTION

(a) The slope at $x = a$ is

$$\lim_{h \to 0} \frac{f(a + h) - f(a)}{h} = \lim_{h \to 0} \frac{\dfrac{1}{a + h} - \dfrac{1}{a}}{h}$$

$$= \lim_{h \to 0} \frac{1}{h} \cdot \frac{a - (a + h)}{a(a + h)}$$

$$= \lim_{h \to 0} \cdot \frac{-h}{ha(a + h)}$$

$$= \lim_{h \to 0} \frac{-1}{a(a + h)} = -\frac{1}{a^2}$$

(b) The slope will be $-1/4$ if

$$-\frac{1}{a^2} = -\frac{1}{4}$$

$$a^2 = 4 \qquad \text{Multiply by } -4a^2.$$

$$a = \pm 2$$

The curve has the slope $-1/4$ at the two points $(2, 1/2)$ and $(-2, -1/2)$ (Figure 2.31).

(c) The slope $-1/a^2$ is always negative. As $a \to 0^+$, the slope approaches $-\infty$ and the tangent becomes increasingly steep. We see this again as $a \to 0^-$. As a moves away from the origin in either direction, the slope approaches 0 and the tangent becomes increasingly horizontal. ***Now Try Exercise 19.***

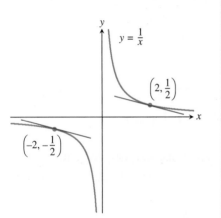

Figure 2.31 The two tangent lines to $y = 1/x$ having slope $-1/4$. (Example 4)

All of These Are the Same:

1. the slope of $y = f(x)$ at $x = a$
2. the slope of the tangent to $y = f(x)$ at $x = a$
3. the (instantaneous) rate of change of $f(x)$ with respect to x at $x = a$
4. $\displaystyle \lim_{h \to 0} \frac{f(a + h) - f(a)}{h}$

An Alternate Form

In Chapter 3, we will introduce the expression

$$\frac{f(x) - f(a)}{x - a}$$

as an important and useful alternate form of the **difference quotient of *f* at *a*.** (See Exercise 57.)

The expression

$$\frac{f(a + h) - f(a)}{h}$$

is the **difference quotient of *f* at *a*.** Suppose the difference quotient has a limit as h approaches zero. If we interpret the difference quotient as a secant slope, the limit is the slope of both the curve and the tangent to the curve at the point $x = a$. If we interpret the difference quotient as an average rate of change, the limit is the function's rate of change with respect to x at the point $x = a$. This limit is one of the two most important mathematical objects considered in calculus. We will begin a thorough study of it in Chapter 3.

About the Word *Normal*

When analytic geometry was developed in the 17th century, European scientists still wrote about their work and ideas in Latin, the one language that all educated Europeans could read and understand. The Latin word *normalis,* which scholars used for *perpendicular,* became *normal* when they discussed geometry in English.

Normal to a Curve

The **normal line** to a curve at a point is the line perpendicular to the tangent at that point.

EXAMPLE 5 Finding a Normal Line

Write an equation for the normal to the curve $f(x) = 4 - x^2$ at $x = 1$.

SOLUTION

The slope of the tangent to the curve at $x = 1$ is

$$\lim_{h \to 0} \frac{f(1 + h) - f(1)}{h} = \lim_{h \to 0} \frac{4 - (1 + h)^2 - 3}{h}$$

$$= \lim_{h \to 0} \frac{4 - 1 - 2h - h^2 - 3}{h}$$

$$= \lim_{h \to 0} \frac{-h(2 + h)}{h} = -2$$

Thus, the slope of the normal is $1/2$, the negative reciprocal of -2. The normal to the curve at $(1, f(1)) = (1, 3)$ is the line through $(1, 3)$ with slope $m = 1/2$.

$$y - 3 = \frac{1}{2}(x - 1)$$

$$y = \frac{1}{2}x - \frac{1}{2} + 3$$

$$y = \frac{1}{2}x + \frac{5}{2}$$

You can support this result by drawing the graphs in a square viewing window.

Now Try Exercise 11 (c, d).

Speed Revisited

The function $y = 16t^2$ that gave the distance fallen by the rock in Example 1, Section 2.1, was the rock's *position function.* A body's average speed along a coordinate axis (here, the *y*-axis) for a given period of time is the average rate of change of its *position* $y = f(t)$. Its *instantaneous speed* at any time t is the *instantaneous rate of change* of position with respect to time at time t, or

$$\lim_{h \to 0} \frac{f(t + h) - f(t)}{h}.$$

We saw in Example 1, Section 2.1, that the rock's instantaneous speed at $t = 2$ sec was 64 ft/sec.

Particle Motion

We have considered only objects moving in one direction in this chapter. In Chapter 3, we will deal with more complicated motion.

EXAMPLE 6 Finding Instantaneous Rate of Change

Find

$$\lim_{h \to 0} \frac{f(t + h) - f(t)}{h}$$

for the function $f(t) = 2t^2 - 1$ at $t = 2$. Interpret the answer if $f(t)$ represents a position function in feet of an object at time t seconds.

continued

SOLUTION

$$\lim_{h \to 0} \frac{f(t+h) - f(t)}{h} = \lim_{h \to 0} \frac{2(2+h)^2 - 1 - (2 \cdot 2^2 - 1)}{h}$$

$$= \lim_{h \to 0} \frac{8 + 8h + 2h^2 - 1 - 7}{h}$$

$$= \lim_{h \to 0} \frac{8h + 2h^2}{h}$$

$$= \lim_{h \to 0} (8 + 2h) = 8$$

The instantaneous rate of change of the object is 8 ft/sec.

Now Try Exercise 23.

EXAMPLE 7   Investigating Free Fall

Find the speed of the falling rock in Example 1, Section 2.1, at $t = 1$ sec.

SOLUTION

The position function of the rock is $f(t) = 16t^2$. The average speed of the rock over the interval between $t = 1$ and $t = 1 + h$ sec was

$$\frac{f(1+h) - f(1)}{h} = \frac{16(1+h)^2 - 16(1)^2}{h} = \frac{16(h^2 + 2h)}{h} = 16(h + 2).$$

The rock's speed at the instant $t = 1$ was

$$\lim_{h \to 0} 16(h + 2) = 32 \text{ ft/sec.}$$ *Now Try Exercise 31.*

Sensitivity

We live in an interconnected world where changes in one quantity cause changes in another. For example, crop yields per acre depend on rainfall. If rainfall has been low, each small increase in the amount of rain creates a small increase in crop yield. For a drug that works to lower a patient's temperature, each small increase in the amount of the drug will lower the temperature a small amount. The mathematical connection between such changes is known as **sensitivity.** Sensitivity describes how one variable responds to small changes in another variable.

How much the patient's temperature drops depends not just on how much more of the drug is given, but also on how large the dose already is. Sensitivity changes as the dosage changes. If we let T denote the patient's temperature and D the dosage, then the sensitivity is given by

$$\text{sensitivity} = \lim_{\Delta D \to 0} \frac{\Delta T}{\Delta D}.$$

If we know the sensitivity and we have a very small change in the dosage, then we can approximate the change in the patient's temperature by

$$\Delta T \approx \text{sensitivity} \times \Delta D.$$

EXAMPLE 8   Measuring Sensitivity to Medicine

A patient enters the hospital with a temperature of 102°F and is given medicine to lower the temperature. As a function of the dosage, D, measured in milligrams, the patient's temperature will be

$$T(D) = 99 + \frac{3}{1 + D}.$$

Find and interpret the sensitivity of the patient's temperature to the medicine dosage when $D = 1$ mg.

continued

SOLUTION

Let h be the increase in the dosage, $\Delta D = h$, so that the sensitivity is

$$\lim_{h \to 0} \frac{\Delta T}{h} = \lim_{h \to 0} \frac{99 + \dfrac{3}{1 + (1 + h)} - \left(99 + \dfrac{3}{1 + 1}\right)}{h}$$

$$= \lim_{h \to 0} \frac{\dfrac{3}{2 + h} - \dfrac{3}{2}}{h} = \lim_{h \to 0} \frac{6 - 6 - 3h}{2(2 + h)h} = \frac{-3}{4} \text{ degrees per mg.}$$

This means that when the dosage is 1 mg, a small additional dosage, ΔD mg, will result in a drop in the patient's temperature of approximately $3/4 \; \Delta D$ degrees.

Now Try Exercise 37.

Quick Review 2.4 *(For help, go to Section 1.1.)*

Exercise numbers with a gray background indicate problems that the authors have designed to be solved *without a calculator.*

In Exercises 1 and 2, find the increments Δx and Δy from point A to point B.

1. $A(-5, 2), \quad B(3, 5)$　　　**2.** $A(1, 3), \quad B(a, b)$

In Exercises 3 and 4, find the slope of the line determined by the points.

3. $(-2, 3), \quad (5, -1)$　　　**4.** $(-3, -1), \quad (3, 3)$

In Exercises 5–9, write an equation for the specified line.

5. through $(-2, 3)$ with slope $= 3/2$

6. through $(1, 6)$ and $(4, -1)$

7. through $(1, 4)$ and parallel to $y = -\dfrac{3}{4}x + 2$

8. through $(1, 4)$ and perpendicular to $y = -\dfrac{3}{4}x + 2$

9. through $(-1, 3)$ and parallel to $2x + 3y = 5$

10. For what value of b will the slope of the line through $(2, 3)$ and $(4, b)$ be $5/3$?

Section 2.4 Exercises

In Exercises 1–6, find the average rate of change of the function over each interval.

1. $f(x) = x^3 + 1$
  (a) $[2, 3]$ **(b)** $[-1, 1]$

2. $f(x) = \sqrt{4x + 1}$
  (a) $[0, 2]$ **(b)** $[10, 12]$

3. $f(x) = e^x$
  (a) $[-2, 0]$ **(b)** $[1, 3]$

4. $f(x) = \ln x$
  (a) $[1, 4]$ **(b)** $[100, 103]$

5. $f(x) = \cot x$
  (a) $[\pi/4, 3\pi/4]$ **(b)** $[\pi/6, \pi/2]$

6. $f(x) = 2 + \cos x$
  (a) $[0, \pi]$ **(b)** $[-\pi, \pi]$

In Exercises 7 and 8, a distance-time graph is shown.

  (a) Estimate the slopes of the secants PQ_1, PQ_2, PQ_3, and PQ_4, arranging them in order in a table. What is the appropriate unit for these slopes?

  (b) Estimate the speed at point P.

7. *Accelerating from a Standstill* The figure shows the distance-time graph for a 1994 Ford® Mustang Cobra™ accelerating from a standstill.

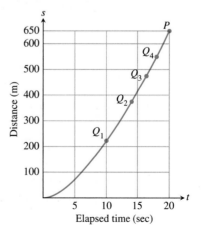

8. *Lunar Data* The accompanying figure shows a distance-time graph for a wrench that fell from the top platform of a communication mast on the moon to the station roof 80 m below.

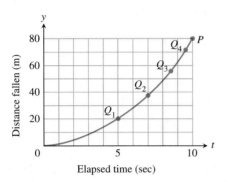

In Exercises 9–12, at the indicated point find

(a) the slope of the curve,

(b) an equation of the tangent, and

(c) an equation of the normal.

(d) Then draw a graph of the curve, tangent line, and normal line in the same square viewing window.

9. $y = x^2$ at $x = -2$ **10.** $y = x^2 - 4x$ at $x = 1$

11. $y = \dfrac{1}{x - 1}$ at $x = 2$ **12.** $y = x^2 - 3x - 1$ at $x = 0$

In Exercises 13 and 14, find the slope of the curve at the indicated point.

13. $f(x) = |x|$ at **(a)** $x = 2$ **(b)** $x = -3$

14. $f(x) = |x - 2|$ at $x = 1$

In Exercises 15–18, determine whether the curve has a tangent at the indicated point. If it does, give its slope. If not, explain why not.

15. $f(x) = \begin{cases} 2 - 2x - x^2, & x < 0 \\ 2x + 2, & x \geq 0 \end{cases}$ at $x = 0$

16. $f(x) = \begin{cases} -x, & x < 0 \\ x^2 - x, & x \geq 0 \end{cases}$ at $x = 0$

17. $f(x) = \begin{cases} 1/x, & x \leq 2 \\ \dfrac{4 - x}{4}, & x > 2 \end{cases}$ at $x = 2$

18. $f(x) = \begin{cases} \sin x, & 0 \leq x < 3\pi/4 \\ \cos x, & 3\pi/4 \leq x \leq 2\pi \end{cases}$ at $x = 3\pi/4$

In Exercises 19–22, **(a)** find the slope of the curve at $x = a$.
(b) Writing to Learn Describe what happens to the tangent at $x = a$ as a changes.

19. $y = x^2 + 2$

20. $y = 2/x$

21. $y = \dfrac{1}{x - 1}$

22. $y = 9 - x^2$

Find the instantaneous rate of change of the position function $y = f(t)$ in feet at the given time t in seconds.

23. $f(t) = 3t - 7, t = 1$

24. $f(t) = 3t^2 + 2t, \quad t = 3$

25. $f(t) = \dfrac{t + 1}{t}, \quad t = 2$

26. $f(t) = t^3 - 1, \quad t = 2$

27. *Free Fall* An object is dropped from the top of a 100-m tower. Its height above ground after t sec is $100 - 4.9t^2$ m. How fast is it falling 2 sec after it is dropped?

28. *Rocket Launch* At t sec after lift-off, the height of a rocket is $3t^2$ ft. How fast is the rocket climbing after 10 sec?

29. *Area of Circle* What is the rate of change of the area of a circle with respect to the radius when the radius is $r = 3$ in.?

30. *Volume of Sphere* What is the rate of change of the volume of a sphere with respect to the radius when the radius is $r = 2$ in.?

31. *Free Fall on Mars* The equation for free fall at the surface of Mars is $s = 1.86t^2$ m with t in seconds. Assume a rock is dropped from the top of a 200-m cliff. Find the speed of the rock at $t = 1$ sec.

32. *Free Fall on Jupiter* The equation for free fall at the surface of Jupiter is $s = 11.44t^2$ m with t in seconds. Assume a rock is dropped from the top of a 500-m cliff. Find the speed of the rock at $t = 2$ sec.

33. *Horizontal Tangent* At what point is the tangent to $f(x) = x^2 + 4x - 1$ horizontal?

34. *Horizontal Tangent* At what point is the tangent to $f(x) = 3 - 4x - x^2$ horizontal?

35. Finding Tangents and Normals

  (a) Find an equation for each tangent to the curve $y = 1/(x - 1)$ that has slope -1. (See Exercise 21.)

  (b) Find an equation for each normal to the curve $y = 1/(x - 1)$ that has slope 1.

36. Finding Tangents Find the equations of all lines tangent to $y = 9 - x^2$ that pass through the point $(1, 12)$.

37. Sensitivity A patient's temperature T as a function of the dosage D of a medicine is given by $T(D) = 99 + 4/(1 + D)$. Find and interpret the sensitivity of the patient's temperature to the dosage when $D = 2$ mg.

38. Sensitivity If a ball is thrown straight up with an initial velocity of v feet per second, it will reach a maximum height of $H = v^2/64$ feet. Find and interpret the sensitivity of the height to the initial velocity when the initial velocity is 40 ft/sec.

39. Table 2.2 gives the total amount of all U.S. exported wheat in millions of bushels for several years.

TABLE 2.2 U.S. Exported Wheat

Year	Exported Wheat (millions of bushels)
2008	1015
2009	879
2010	1291
2011	1051
2012	1007
2013	900

Source: U.S. Department of Agriculture, Economic Research Service, Wheat Data, Table 21.

  (a) Make a scatter plot of the data in the table.

  (b) Let P represent the point corresponding to 2008, Q_1 the point corresponding to 2011, Q_2 the point corresponding to 2012, and Q_3 the point corresponding to 2013. Find the slope of the secant line PQ_i for $i = 1, 2, 3$.

40. Table 2.3 gives the amount of federal spending in billions of dollars for national defense for several years.

TABLE 2.3 National Defense Spending

Year	National Defense Spending ($ billion)
2008	616
2009	661
2010	693
2011	706
2012	678
2013	633

Source: U.S. Office of Management and Budget, *Budget Authority by Function and Subfunction, Outlay by Function and Subfunction,* Table 492.

  (a) Find the average rate of change in spending from 2008 to 2013.

  (b) Find the average rate of change in spending from 2008 to 2011.

  (c) Find the average rate of change in spending from 2011 to 2013.

  (d) **Writing to Learn** Explain why someone might be hesitant to make predictions about the rate of change of national defense spending based on the data given in Table 2.3.

Standardized Test Questions

41. True or False If the graph of a function has a tangent line at $x = a$, then the graph also has a normal line at $x = a$. Justify your answer.

42. True or False The graph of $f(x) = |x|$ has a tangent line at $x = 0$. Justify your answer.

43. Multiple Choice If the line L tangent to the graph of a function f at the point $(2, 5)$ passes through the point $(-1, -3)$, what is the slope of L?

  (A) $-3/8$ **(B)** $3/8$ **(C)** $-8/3$ **(D)** $8/3$ **(E)** undefined

44. Multiple Choice Find the average rate of change of $f(x) = x^2 + x$ over the interval $[1, 3]$.

  (A) -5 **(B)** $1/5$ **(C)** $1/4$ **(D)** 4 **(E)** 5

45. Multiple Choice Which of the following is an equation of the tangent to the graph of $f(x) = 2/x$ at $x = 1$?

  (A) $y = -2x$ **(B)** $y = 2x$ **(C)** $y = -2x + 4$

  (D) $y = -x + 3$ **(E)** $y = x + 3$

46. Multiple Choice Which of the following is an equation of the normal to the graph of $f(x) = 2/x$ at $x = 1$?

  (A) $y = \dfrac{1}{2}x + \dfrac{3}{2}$ **(B)** $y = -\dfrac{1}{2}x$ **(C)** $y = \dfrac{1}{2}x + 2$

  (D) $y = -\dfrac{1}{2}x + 2$ **(E)** $y = 2x + 5$

Explorations

In Exercises 47 and 48, complete the following for the function.

  (a) Compute the difference quotient

$$\frac{f(1 + h) - f(1)}{h}.$$

  (b) Use graphs and tables to estimate the limit of the difference quotient in part (a) as $h \to 0$.

  (c) Compare your estimate in part (b) with the given number.

  (d) **Writing to Learn** Based on your computations, do you think the graph of f has a tangent at $x = 1$? If so, estimate its slope. If not, explain why not.

47. $f(x) = e^x, \quad e$ **48.** $f(x) = 2^x, \quad \ln 4$

Group Activity In Exercises 49–52, the curve $y = f(x)$ has a **vertical tangent** at $x = a$ if

$$\lim_{h \to 0} \frac{f(a + h) - f(a)}{h} = \infty$$

or if

$$\lim_{h \to 0} \frac{f(a + h) - f(a)}{h} = -\infty.$$

In each case, the right- and left-hand limits are required to be the same: both $+\infty$ or both $-\infty$.

Use graphs to investigate whether the curve has a vertical tangent at $x = 0$.

49. $y = x^{2/5}$ **50.** $y = x^{3/5}$

51. $y = x^{1/3}$ **52.** $y = x^{2/3}$

Extending the Ideas

In Exercises 53 and 54, determine whether the graph of the function has a tangent at the origin. Explain your answer.

53. $f(x) = \begin{cases} x^2 \sin \dfrac{1}{x}, & x \neq 0 \\ 0, & x = 0 \end{cases}$

54. $f(x) = \begin{cases} x \sin \dfrac{1}{x}, & x \neq 0 \\ 0, & x = 0 \end{cases}$

55. *Sine Function* Estimate the slope of the curve $y = \sin x$ at $x = 1$. (*Hint:* See Exercises 47 and 48.)

56. Consider the function f given in Example 1. Explain how the average rate of change of f over the interval $[3, 3 + h]$ is the same as the difference quotient of f at $a = 3$.

57. (a) Let $x = a + h$. Show algebraically how the difference quotient of f at a,

$$\frac{f(a + h) - f(a)}{h},$$

is equivalent to an alternate form given by

$$\frac{f(x) - f(a)}{x - a}.$$

(b) Writing to Learn Why do you think we discuss two forms of the difference quotient of f at a?

Quick Quiz for AP* Preparation: Sections 2.3 and 2.4

You may use a calculator with these problems.

1. Multiple Choice Which of the following values is the average rate of $f(x) = \sqrt{x + 1}$ over the interval $(0, 3)$?

(A) -3 **(B)** -1 **(C)** $-1/3$ **(D)** $1/3$ **(E)** 3

2. Multiple Choice Which of the following statements is false for the function

$$f(x) = \begin{cases} \dfrac{3}{4}x, & 0 \leq x < 4 \\ 2, & x = 4 \\ -x + 7, & 4 < x \leq 6 \\ 1, & 6 < x < 8? \end{cases}$$

(A) $\lim_{x \to 4} f(x)$ exists.   **(B)** $f(4)$ exists.

(C) $\lim_{x \to 6} f(x)$ exists.   **(D)** $\lim_{x \to 8^-} f(x)$ exists.

(E) f is continuous at $x = 4$.

3. Multiple Choice Which of the following is an equation for the tangent line to $f(x) = 9 - x^2$ at $x = 2$?

(A) $y = \dfrac{1}{4}x + \dfrac{9}{2}$ **(B)** $y = -4x + 13$

(C) $y = -4x - 3$ **(C)** $y = 4x - 3$

(E) $y = 4x + 13$

4. Free Response Let $f(x) = 2x - x^2$.

(a) Find $f(3)$.   **(b)** Find $f(3 + h)$.

(c) Find $\dfrac{f(3 + h) - f(3)}{h}$.

(d) Find the instantaneous rate of change of f at $x = 3$.

CHAPTER 2   Key Terms

average rate of change (p. 59, 87)	continuous at an interior point (p. 79)	end behavior model (p. 74)
average speed (p. 59)	continuous extension (p. 81)	floor function (p. 64)
composite of continuous functions (p. 82)	continuous function (p. 81)	free fall (p. 59)
connected graph (p. 83)	continuous on an interval (p. 81)	horizontal asymptote (p. 70)
Constant Multiple Rule for Limits (p. 71)	difference quotient (p. 90)	infinite discontinuity (p. 80)
continuity at a point (p. 78)	Difference Rule for Limits (p. 71)	instantaneous rate of change (p. 59)
continuous at an endpoint (p. 79)	discontinuous (p. 79)	instantaneous speed (p. 59)

intermediate value property (p. 83)

Intermediate Value Theorem for Continuous Functions (p. 83)

jump discontinuity (p. 80)

left end behavior model (p. 74)

left-hand limit (p. 63)

limit of a function (p. 60)

normal line to a curve (p. 91)

oscillating discontinuity (p. 80)

point of discontinuity (p. 79)

Power Rule for Limits (p. 71)

Product Rule for Limits (p. 71)

Properties of Continuous Functions (p. 82)

Quotient Rule for Limits (p. 71)

removable discontinuity (p. 80)

right end behavior model (p. 74)

right-hand limit (p. 63)

secant to a curve (p. 87)

sensitivity (p. 92)

slope of a curve (p. 90)

Squeeze Theorem (p. 65)

Sum Rule for Limits (p. 71)

tangent line to a curve (p. 90)

two-sided limit (p. 64)

vertical asymptote (p. 72)

vertical tangent (p. 96)

CHAPTER 2 Review Exercises

Exercise numbers with a gray background indicate problems that the authors have designed to be solved *without a calculator.*

The collection of exercises marked in red could be used as a chapter test.

In Exercises 1–14, find the limits.

1. $\lim\limits_{x \to -2} (x^3 - 2x^2 + 1)$

2. $\lim\limits_{x \to -2} \dfrac{x^2 + 1}{3x^2 - 2x + 5}$

3. $\lim\limits_{x \to 4} \sqrt{1 - 2x}$

4. $\lim\limits_{x \to 5} \sqrt[4]{9 - x^2}$

5. $\lim\limits_{x \to 0} \dfrac{\dfrac{1}{2 + x} - \dfrac{1}{2}}{x}$

6. $\lim\limits_{x \to \pm\infty} \dfrac{2x^2 + 3}{5x^2 + 7}$

7. $\lim\limits_{x \to \pm\infty} \dfrac{x^4 + x^3}{12x^3 + 128}$

8. $\lim\limits_{x \to 0} \dfrac{\sin 2x}{4x}$

9. $\lim\limits_{x \to 0} \dfrac{x \csc x + 1}{x \csc x}$

10. $\lim\limits_{x \to 0} e^x \sin x$

11. $\lim\limits_{x \to 7/2^+} \text{int} (2x - 1)$

12. $\lim\limits_{x \to 7/2^-} \text{int} (2x - 1)$

13. $\lim\limits_{x \to \infty} e^{-x} \cos x$

14. $\lim\limits_{x \to \infty} \dfrac{x + \sin x}{x + \cos x}$

In Exercises 15–20, determine whether the limit exists on the basis of the graph of $y = f(x)$. The domain of f is the set of real numbers.

15. $\lim\limits_{x \to d} f(x)$

16. $\lim\limits_{x \to c^+} f(x)$

17. $\lim\limits_{x \to c^-} f(x)$

18. $\lim\limits_{x \to c} f(x)$

19. $\lim\limits_{x \to b} f(x)$

20. $\lim\limits_{x \to a} f(x)$

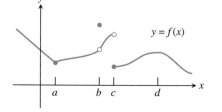

In Exercises 21–24, determine whether the function f used in Exercises 15–20 is continuous at the indicated point.

21. $x = a$

22. $x = b$

23. $x = c$

24. $x = d$

In Exercises 25 and 26, use the graph of the function with domain $-1 \le x \le 3$.

25. Determine

   (a) $\lim\limits_{x \to 3^-} g(x)$.   (b) $g(3)$.

   (c) whether $g(x)$ is continuous at $x = 3$.

   (d) the points of discontinuity of $g(x)$.

   (e) **Writing to Learn** whether any points of discontinuity are removable. If so, describe the new function. If not, explain why not.

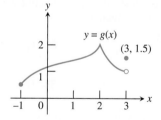

26. Determine

   (a) $\lim\limits_{x \to 1^-} k(x)$.   (b) $\lim\limits_{x \to 1^+} k(x)$.   (c) $k(1)$.

   (d) whether $k(x)$ is continuous at $x = 1$.

   (e) the points of discontinuity of $k(x)$.

   (f) **Writing to Learn** whether any points of discontinuity are removable. If so, describe the new function. If not, explain why not.

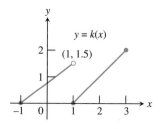

In Exercises 27 and 28, **(a)** find the vertical asymptotes of the graph of $y = f(x)$, and **(b)** describe the behavior of $f(x)$ to the left and right of any vertical asymptote.

27. $f(x) = \dfrac{x + 3}{x + 2}$

28. $f(x) = \dfrac{x - 1}{x^2(x + 2)}$

In Exercises 29 and 30, answer the questions for the piecewise-defined function.

29. $f(x) = \begin{cases} 1, & x \le -1 \\ -x, & -1 < x < 0 \\ 1, & x = 0 \\ -x, & 0 < x < 1 \\ 1, & x \ge 1 \end{cases}$

    (a) Find the right-hand and left-hand limits of f at $x = -1, 0$, and 1.

    (b) Does f have a limit as x approaches -1? 0? 1? If so, what is it? If not, why not?

    (c) Is f continuous at $x = -1$? 0? 1? Explain.

30. $f(x) = \begin{cases} |x^3 - 4x|, & x < 1 \\ x^2 - 2x - 2, & x \ge 1 \end{cases}$

    (a) Find the right-hand and left-hand limits of f at $x = 1$.

    (b) Does f have a limit as $x \to 1$? If so, what is it? If not, why not?

    (c) At what points is f continuous?

    (d) At what points is f discontinuous?

In Exercises 31 and 32, find all points of discontinuity of the function.

31. $f(x) = \dfrac{x + 1}{4 - x^2}$

32. $g(x) = \sqrt[3]{3x + 2}$

In Exercises 33–36, find **(a)** a power function end behavior model and **(b)** any horizontal asymptotes.

33. $f(x) = \dfrac{2x + 1}{x^2 - 2x + 1}$

34. $f(x) = \dfrac{2x^2 + 5x - 1}{x^2 + 2x}$

35. $f(x) = \dfrac{x^3 - 4x^2 + 3x + 3}{x - 3}$

36. $f(x) = \dfrac{x^4 - 3x^2 + x - 1}{x^3 - x + 1}$

In Exercises 37 and 38, find **(a)** a right end behavior model and **(b)** a left end behavior model for the function.

37. $f(x) = x + e^x$

38. $f(x) = \ln|x| + \sin x$

Group Activity In Exercises 39 and 40, what value should be assigned to k to make f a continuous function?

39. $f(x) = \begin{cases} \dfrac{x^2 + 2x - 15}{x - 3}, & x \ne 3 \\ k, & x = 3 \end{cases}$

40. $f(x) = \begin{cases} \dfrac{\sin x}{2x}, & x \ne 0 \\ k, & x = 0 \end{cases}$

Group Activity In Exercises 41 and 42, sketch a graph of a function f that satisfies the given conditions.

41. $\lim\limits_{x \to \infty} f(x) = 3$, $\quad \lim\limits_{x \to -\infty} f(x) = \infty$,

$\quad \lim\limits_{x \to 3^+} f(x) = \infty$, $\quad \lim\limits_{x \to 3^-} f(x) = -\infty$

42. $\lim\limits_{x \to 2} f(x)$ does not exist, $\lim\limits_{x \to 2^+} f(x) = f(2) = 3$

43. *Average Rate of Change* Find the average rate of change of $f(x) = 1 + \sin x$ over the interval $[0, \pi/2]$.

44. *Rate of Change* Find the instantaneous rate of change of the volume $V = (1/3)\pi r^2 H$ of a cone with respect to the radius r at $r = a$ if the height H does not change.

45. *Rate of Change* Find the instantaneous rate of change of the surface area $S = 6x^2$ of a cube with respect to the edge length x at $x = a$.

46. *Slope of a Curve* Find the slope of the curve $y = x^2 - x - 2$ at $x = a$.

47. *Tangent and Normal* Let $f(x) = x^2 - 3x$ and $P = (1, f(1))$. Find **(a)** the slope of the curve $y = f(x)$ at P, **(b)** an equation of the tangent at P, and **(c)** an equation of the normal at P.

48. *Horizontal Tangents* At what points, if any, are the tangents to the graph of $f(x) = x^2 - 3x$ horizontal? (See Exercise 47.)

49. *Sensitivity* A ball is thrown straight up with an initial velocity of v feet per second. The maximum height is $H = v^2/64$ feet. Find and interpret the sensitivity of the height to the initial velocity when the initial velocity is 30 ft/sec.

50. *Sensitivity* An error in the measurement of the radius of a circle results in an error in the computation of its area. Find and interpret the sensitivity of the area, A, of a circle to the measurement of its radius, r, when the radius is 2 meters.

51. *Bear Population* The number of bears in a federal wildlife reserve is given by the population equation

$$p(t) = \dfrac{200}{1 + 7e^{-0.1t}},$$

where t is in years.

    (a) **Writing to Learn** Find $p(0)$. Give a possible interpretation of this number.

    (b) Find $\lim\limits_{t \to \infty} p(t)$.

    (c) **Writing to Learn** Give a possible interpretation of the result in part (b).

52. *Taxi Fares* Bluetop Cab charges $3.20 for the first mile and $1.35 for each additional mile or part of a mile.

    (a) Write a formula that gives the charge for x miles with $0 \le x \le 20$.

    (b) Graph the function in (a). At what values of x is it discontinuous?

53. Table 2.4 gives the population of Florida for several years. All data are for July 1 except in 2010, when it is for April 1.

TABLE 2.4	Population of Florida
Year	Population (in thousands)
2006	18,019
2008	18,328
2009	18,538
2010	18,803
2012	19,321
2013	19,553

Source: U.S. Census Bureau, 2012 Statistical Abstract of the United States.

(a) Make a scatter plot of the data in the table.

(b) Let P represent the point corresponding to 2006, Q_1 the point corresponding to 2009, Q_2 the point corresponding to 2012, and Q_3 the point corresponding to 2013. Find the slope of the secant line PQ_i for $i = 1, 2, 3$.

(c) Using the same information given in part (b), find the average rates of change from P to Q_i.

(d) Estimate the instantaneous rate of change of the population on July 1, 2013.

(e) **Writing to Learn** Assuming the population growth in Table 2.4 *is linear*, estimate the population of Florida in 2020. Explain why linear growth may or may not be a bad assumption over longer periods of time.

54. *Limit Properties* Assume that

$$\lim_{x \to c} [f(x) + g(x)] = 2,$$
$$\lim_{x \to c} [f(x) - g(x)] = 1,$$

and that $\lim_{x \to c} f(x)$ and $\lim_{x \to c} g(x)$ exist. Find $\lim_{x \to c} f(x)$ and $\lim_{x \to c} g(x)$.

AP* Examination Preparation

55. Free Response Let $f(x) = \dfrac{x}{|x^2 - 9|}$.

(a) Find the domain of f.

(b) Write an equation for each vertical asymptote of the graph of f.

(c) Write an equation for each horizontal asymptote of the graph of f.

(d) Is f odd, even, or neither? Justify your answer.

(e) Find all values of x for which f is discontinuous and classify each discontinuity as removable or nonremovable.

56. Free Response Let $f(x) = \begin{cases} x^2 - a^2x & \text{if } x < 2, \\ 4 - 2x^2 & \text{if } x \geq 2. \end{cases}$

(a) Find $\lim_{x \to 2^-} f(x)$.

(b) Find $\lim_{x \to 2^+} f(x)$.

(c) Find all values of a that make f continuous at 2. Justify your answer.

57. Free Response Let $f(x) = \dfrac{x^3 - 2x^2 + 1}{x^2 + 3}$.

(a) Find all zeros of f.

(b) Find a right end behavior model $g(x)$ for f.

(c) Determine $\lim_{x \to \infty} f(x)$ and $\lim_{x \to \infty} \dfrac{f(x)}{g(x)}$.

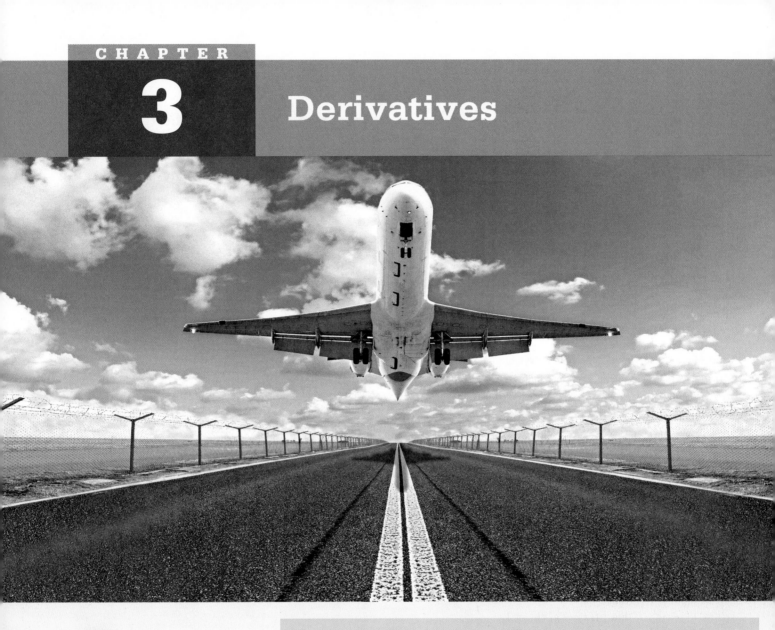

3.1 Derivative of
     a Function

3.2 Differentiability

3.3 Rules for
     Differentiation

3.4 Velocity and Other
     Rates of Change

3.5 Derivatives of
     Trigonometric
     Functions

Shown here is an airplane lifting off after moving down the runway. The airplane speed at lift-off can be determined from the equation $D = (10/9)t^2$, where D is the distance traveled in meters down the runway before lift-off at time t in seconds after the plane's brakes are released. If the airplane becomes airborne when its speed down the runway reaches 200 km/hr, how long will it take it to be airborne and what distance will it have traveled by that time? This problem can be solved with the information covered in Section 3.4.

CHAPTER 3   Overview

In Chapter 2, we learned how to find the slope of a tangent to a curve as the limit of the slopes of secant lines. In Example 4 of Section 2.4, we derived a formula for the slope of the tangent at an arbitrary point $(a, 1/a)$ on the graph of the function $f(x) = 1/x$ and showed that it was $-1/a^2$.

This seemingly unimportant result is more powerful than it might appear at first glance, as it gives us a simple way to calculate the instantaneous rate of change of f at any point. The study of rates of change of functions is called *differential calculus,* and the formula $-1/a^2$ was our first look at a *derivative.* The derivative was the 17th-century breakthrough that enabled mathematicians to unlock the secrets of planetary motion and gravitational attraction—of objects changing position over time. We will learn many uses for derivatives in Chapter 5, but first, in the next two chapters, we will focus on what derivatives are and how they work.

3.1 | Derivative of a Function

You will be able to compute the derivative of a function at $x = a$ using both forms of the limit definition and explain its relationship to slope.

- The meaning of differentiable
- Different ways of denoting the derivative of a function
- Graphing $y = f(x)$ given the graph of $y = f'(x)$
- Graphing $y = f'(x)$ given the graph of $y = f(x)$
- One-sided derivatives
- Graphing the derivative from data

Definition of Derivative

In Section 2.4, we defined the slope of a curve $y = f(x)$ at the point where $x = a$ to be

$$m = \lim_{h \to 0} \frac{f(a + h) - f(a)}{h}.$$

When it exists, this limit is called the **derivative of f at a.** In this section, we investigate the derivative as a *function* derived from f by considering the limit at each point of the domain of f.

DEFINITION   Derivative

The **derivative** of the function f with respect to the variable x is the function f' whose value at x is

$$f'(x) = \lim_{h \to 0} \frac{f(x + h) - f(x)}{h}, \qquad (1)$$

provided the limit exists.

The domain of f', the set of points in the domain of f for which the limit exists, may be smaller than the domain of f. If $f'(x)$ exists, we say that f **has a derivative (is differentiable)** at x. A function that is differentiable at every point of its domain is a **differentiable function.**

EXAMPLE 1 Applying the Definition

Differentiate (that is, find the derivative of) $f(x) = x^3$.

continued

SOLUTION

Applying the definition, we have

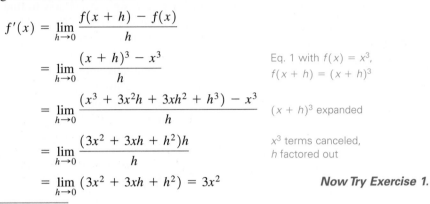

$$f'(x) = \lim_{h \to 0} \frac{f(x+h) - f(x)}{h}$$

$$= \lim_{h \to 0} \frac{(x+h)^3 - x^3}{h} \qquad \text{Eq. 1 with } f(x) = x^3,$$
$$\text{} \qquad f(x+h) = (x+h)^3$$

$$= \lim_{h \to 0} \frac{(x^3 + 3x^2h + 3xh^2 + h^3) - x^3}{h} \qquad (x+h)^3 \text{ expanded}$$

$$= \lim_{h \to 0} \frac{(3x^2 + 3xh + h^2)h}{h} \qquad x^3 \text{ terms canceled,} \\ h \text{ factored out}$$

$$= \lim_{h \to 0} (3x^2 + 3xh + h^2) = 3x^2 \qquad \textbf{\textit{Now Try Exercise 1.}}$$

The derivative of $f(x)$ at a point where $x = a$ is found by taking the limit as $h \to 0$ of slopes of secant lines, as shown in Figure 3.1.

By relabeling the picture as in Figure 3.2, we arrive at a useful alternate formula for calculating the derivative. This time, the limit is taken as x approaches a.

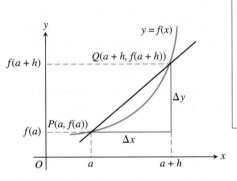

Figure 3.1 The slope of the secant line PQ is

$$\frac{\Delta y}{\Delta x} = \frac{f(a+h) - f(a)}{(a+h) - a}$$

$$= \frac{f(a+h) - f(a)}{h}.$$

DEFINITION (ALTERNATE) **Derivative at a Point**

The **derivative** of the function f **at the point** $x = a$ is the limit

$$f'(a) = \lim_{x \to a} \frac{f(x) - f(a)}{x - a}, \qquad (2)$$

provided the limit exists.

After we find the derivative of f at a point $x = a$ using the alternate form, we can find the derivative of f as a function by applying the resulting formula to an arbitrary x in the domain of f.

EXAMPLE 2 **Applying the Alternate Definition**

Differentiate $f(x) = \sqrt{x}$ using the alternate definition.

SOLUTION

At the point $x = a$,

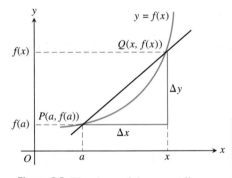

Figure 3.2 The slope of the secant line PQ is

$$\frac{\Delta y}{\Delta x} = \frac{f(x) - f(a)}{x - a}.$$

$$f'(a) = \lim_{x \to a} \frac{f(x) - f(a)}{x - a}$$

$$= \lim_{x \to a} \frac{\sqrt{x} - \sqrt{a}}{x - a} \qquad \text{Eq. 2 with } f(x) = \sqrt{x}$$

$$= \lim_{x \to a} \frac{\sqrt{x} - \sqrt{a}}{x - a} \cdot \frac{\sqrt{x} + \sqrt{a}}{\sqrt{x} + \sqrt{a}} \qquad \text{Rationalize} \dots$$

$$= \lim_{x \to a} \frac{x - a}{(x - a)(\sqrt{x} + \sqrt{a})} \qquad \dots \text{the numerator.}$$

$$= \lim_{x \to a} \frac{1}{\sqrt{x} + \sqrt{a}} \qquad \text{We can now take the limit.}$$

$$= \frac{1}{2\sqrt{a}}$$

Applying this formula to an arbitrary $x > 0$ in the domain of f identifies the derivative as the function $f'(x) = 1/(2\sqrt{x})$ with domain $(0, \infty)$. $\qquad$ **_Now Try Exercise 5._**

Notation

There are many ways to denote the derivative of a function $y = f(x)$. Besides $f'(x)$, the most common notations are these:

y'	"y prime"	Nice and brief, but does not name the independent variable.
$\dfrac{dy}{dx}$	"dy dx" or "the derivative of y with respect to x"	Names both variables and uses d for derivative.
$\dfrac{df}{dx}$	"df dx" or "the derivative of f with respect to x"	Emphasizes the function's name.
$\dfrac{d}{dx}f(x)$	"d dx of f at x" or "the derivative of f at x"	Emphasizes the idea that differentiation is an operation performed on f.

Relationships Between the Graphs of *f* and *f* ′

When we have the explicit formula for $f(x)$, we can derive a formula for $f'(x)$ using methods like those in Examples 1 and 2. We have already seen, however, that functions are encountered in other ways: graphically, for example, or in tables of data.

Because we can think of the derivative at a point in graphical terms as *slope*, we can get a good idea of what the graph of the function f' looks like by *estimating the slopes* at various points along the graph of f.

EXAMPLE 3 Graphing *f* ′ from *f*

Graph the derivative of the function f whose graph is shown in Figure 3.3a. Discuss the behavior of f in terms of the signs and values of f'.

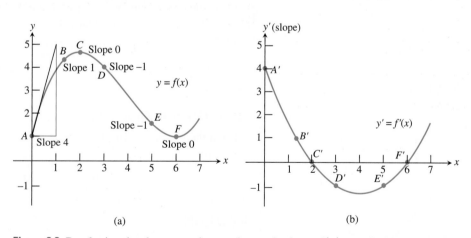

(a) (b)

Figure 3.3 By plotting the slopes at points on the graph of $y = f(x)$, we obtain a graph of $y' = f'(x)$. The slope at point A of the graph of f in part (a) is the y-coordinate of point A' on the graph of f' in part (b), and so on. (Example 3)

SOLUTION

First, we draw a pair of coordinate axes, marking the horizontal axis in x-units and the vertical axis in slope units (Figure 3.3b). Next, we estimate the slope of the graph of f at various points, plotting the corresponding slope values using the new axes. At $A(0, f(0))$, the graph of f has slope 4, so $f'(0) = 4$. At B, the graph of f has slope 1, so $f' = 1$ at B', and so on.

continued

We complete our estimate of the graph of f' by connecting the plotted points with a smooth curve.

Although we do not have a formula for either f or f', the graph of each reveals important information about the behavior of the other. In particular, notice that f is decreasing where f' is negative and increasing where f' is positive. Where f' is zero, the graph of f has a horizontal tangent, changing from increasing to decreasing at point C and from decreasing to increasing at point F. *Now Try Exercise 23.*

EXPLORATION 1 Reading the Graphs

Suppose that the function f in Figure 3.3a represents the depth y (in inches) of water in a ditch alongside a dirt road as a function of time x (in days). How would you answer the following questions?

1. What does the graph in Figure 3.3b represent? What units would you use along the y'-axis?
2. Describe as carefully as you can what happened to the water in the ditch over the course of the 7-day period.
3. Can you describe the weather during the 7 days? When was it the wettest? When was it the driest?
4. How does the graph of the derivative help in finding when the weather was wettest or driest?
5. Interpret the significance of point C in terms of the water in the ditch. How does the significance of point C' reflect that in terms of rate of change?
6. It is tempting to say that it rains right up until the beginning of the second day, but that overlooks a fact about rainwater that is important in flood control. Explain.

Construct your own "real-world" scenario for the function in Example 3, and pose a similar set of questions that could be answered by considering the two graphs in Figure 3.3.

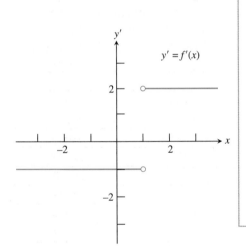

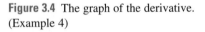

Figure 3.4 The graph of the derivative. (Example 4)

EXAMPLE 4 Graphing *f* from *f'*

Sketch the graph of a function f that has the following properties:

  i. $f(0) = 0$;

  ii. the graph of f', the derivative of f, is as shown in Figure 3.4;

  iii. f is continuous for all x.

SOLUTION

To satisfy property (i), we begin with a point at the origin.

To satisfy property (ii), we consider what the graph of the derivative tells us about slopes. To the left of $x = 1$, the graph of f has a constant slope of -1; therefore we draw a line with slope -1 to the left of $x = 1$, making sure that it goes through the origin.

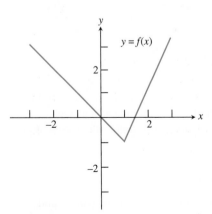

Figure 3.5 The graph of f, constructed from the graph of f' and two other conditions. (Example 4)

To the right of $x = 1$, the graph of f has a constant slope of 2, so it must be a line with slope 2. There are infinitely many such lines but only one—the one that meets the left side of the graph at $(1, -1)$—will satisfy the continuity requirement. The resulting graph is shown in Figure 3.5. *Now Try Exercise 27.*

What's happening at x = 1?

Notice that *f* in Figure 3.5 is defined at *x* = 1, while *f'* is not. It is the continuity of *f* that enables us to conclude that *f*(1) = −1. Looking at the graph of *f*, can you see why *f'* could not possibly be defined at *x* = 1? We will explore the reason for this in Example 6.

Graphing the Derivative from Data

Discrete points plotted from sets of data do not yield a continuous curve, but we have seen that the shape and pattern of the graphed points (called a scatter plot) can be meaningful nonetheless. It is often possible to fit a curve to the points using regression techniques. If the fit is good, we could use the curve to get a graph of the derivative visually, as in Example 3. However, it is also possible to get a scatter plot of the derivative numerically, directly from the data, by computing the slopes between successive points, as in Example 5.

EXAMPLE 5 Estimating the Probability of Shared Birthdays

Suppose 30 people are in a room. What is the probability that two of them share the same birthday? Ignore the year of birth.

SOLUTION

It may surprise you to learn that the probability of a shared birthday among 30 people is at least 0.706, well above two-thirds! In fact, if we assume that no one day is more likely to be a birthday than any other day, the probabilities shown in Table 3.1 are not hard to determine (see Exercise 45).

David H. Blackwell (1919–2010)

By the age of 22, David Blackwell had earned a Ph.D. in Mathematics from the University of Illinois. He taught at Howard University, where his research included statistics, Markov chains, and sequential analysis. He then went on to teach and continue his research at the University of California at Berkeley. Dr. Blackwell served as president of the American Statistical Association and was the first African American mathematician of the National Academy of Sciences.

TABLE 3.1 Probabilities of Shared Birthdays	
People in Room (x)	Probability (y)
0	0
5	0.027
10	0.117
15	0.253
20	0.411
25	0.569
30	0.706
35	0.814
40	0.891
45	0.941
50	0.970
55	0.986
60	0.994
65	0.998
70	0.999

TABLE 3.2 Estimates of Slopes on the Probability Curve	
Midpoint of Interval (x)	Change (Slope $\Delta y/\Delta x$)
2.5	0.0054
7.5	0.0180
12.5	0.0272
17.5	0.0316
22.5	0.0316
27.5	0.0274
32.5	0.0216
37.5	0.0154
42.5	0.0100
47.5	0.0058
52.5	0.0032
57.5	0.0016
62.5	0.0008
67.5	0.0002

A scatter plot of the data in Table 3.1 is shown in Figure 3.6.

Notice that the probabilities grow slowly at first, then faster, then much more slowly past *x* = 45. At which *x* are they growing the fastest? To answer the question, we consider the graph of the derivative.

Using the data in Table 3.1, we compute the slopes between successive points on the probability plot. For example, from *x* = 0 to *x* = 5 the slope is

$$\frac{0.027 - 0}{5 - 0} = 0.0054.$$

We make a new table showing the slopes, beginning with slope 0.0054 on the interval [0, 5] (Table 3.2). A logical *x* value to use to represent the interval is its midpoint, 2.5.

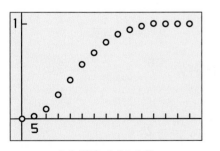

[−5, 75] by [−0.2, 1.1]

Figure 3.6 Scatter plot of the probabilities (*y*) of shared birthdays among *x* people, for *x* = 0, 5, 10, . . . , 70. (Example 5)

continued

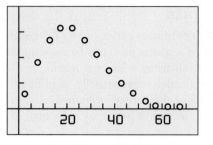

[−5, 75] by [−0.01, 0.04]

Figure 3.7 A scatter plot of the derivative data in Table 3.2. (Example 5)

A scatter plot of the derivative data in Table 3.2 is shown in Figure 3.7.

From the derivative plot, we can see that the rate of change peaks near $x = 20$. You can impress your friends with your "psychic powers" by predicting a shared birthday in a room of just 25 people (since you will be right about 57% of the time), but the derivative warns you to be cautious: A few less people can make quite a difference. On the other hand, going from 40 people to 100 people will not improve your chances much at all.

Now Try Exercise 29.

Generating shared birthday probabilities: If you know a little about probability, you might try generating the probabilities in Table 3.1. Extending the Idea Exercise 45 at the end of this section shows how to generate them on a calculator.

One-Sided Derivatives

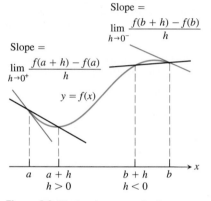

Figure 3.8 Derivatives at endpoints are one-sided limits.

A function $y = f(x)$ is **differentiable on a closed interval $[a, b]$** if it has a derivative at every interior point of the interval, and if the limits

$$\lim_{h \to 0^+} \frac{f(a + h) - f(a)}{h} \quad \text{[the \textbf{right-hand derivative at} } a\text{]}$$

$$\lim_{h \to 0^-} \frac{f(b + h) - f(b)}{h} \quad \text{[the \textbf{left-hand derivative at} } b\text{]}$$

exist at the endpoints. In the right-hand derivative, h is positive and $a + h$ approaches a from the right. In the left-hand derivative, h is negative and $b + h$ approaches b from the left (Figure 3.8).

Right-hand and left-hand derivatives may be defined at any point of a function's domain.

The usual relationship between one-sided and two-sided limits holds for derivatives. Theorem 3, Section 2.1, allows us to conclude that a function has a (two-sided) derivative at a point if and only if the function's right-hand and left-hand derivatives are defined and equal at that point.

EXAMPLE 6 One-Sided Derivatives Can Differ at a Point

Show that the following function has left-hand and right-hand derivatives at $x = 0$, but no derivative there (Figure 3.9).

$$y = \begin{cases} x^2, & x \le 0 \\ 2x, & x > 0 \end{cases}$$

SOLUTION

We verify the existence of the left-hand derivative:

$$\lim_{h \to 0^-} \frac{(0 + h)^2 - 0^2}{h} = \lim_{h \to 0^-} \frac{h^2}{h} = 0$$

We verify the existence of the right-hand derivative:

$$\lim_{h \to 0^+} \frac{2(0 + h) - 0^2}{h} = \lim_{h \to 0^+} \frac{2h}{h} = 2$$

Since the left-hand derivative equals zero and the right-hand derivative equals 2, the derivatives are not equal at $x = 0$. The function does not have a derivative at 0.

Now Try Exercise 31.

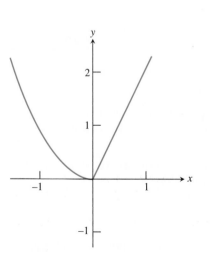

Figure 3.9 A function with different one-sided derivatives at $x = 0$. (Example 6)

Quick Review 3.1 *(For help, go to Sections 2.1 and 2.4.)*

Exercise numbers with a gray background indicate problems that the authors have designed to be solved *without a calculator*.

In Exercises 1–4, evaluate the indicated limit algebraically.

1. $\lim\limits_{h\to 0} \dfrac{(2+h)^2 - 4}{h}$

2. $\lim\limits_{x\to 2^+} \dfrac{x+3}{2}$

3. $\lim\limits_{y\to 0^-} \dfrac{|y|}{y}$

4. $\lim\limits_{x\to 4} \dfrac{2x-8}{\sqrt{x}-2}$

5. Find the slope of the line tangent to the parabola $y = x^2 + 1$ at its vertex.

6. By considering the graph of $f(x) = x^3 - 3x^2 + 2$, find the intervals on which f is increasing.

In Exercises 7–10, let

$$f(x) = \begin{cases} x + 2, & x \le 1 \\ (x-1)^2, & x > 1. \end{cases}$$

7. Find $\lim\limits_{x\to 1^+} f(x)$ and $\lim\limits_{x\to 1^-} f(x)$.

8. Find $\lim\limits_{h\to 0^+} f(1+h)$.

9. Does $\lim\limits_{x\to 1} f(x)$ exist? Explain.

10. Is f continuous? Explain.

Section 3.1 Exercises

In Exercises 1–4, use the definition

$$f'(a) = \lim_{h\to 0} \frac{f(a+h) - f(a)}{h}$$

to find the derivative of the given function at the given value of a.

1. $f(x) = 1/x, a = 2$

2. $f(x) = x^2 + 4, a = 1$

3. $f(x) = 3 - x^2, a = -1$

4. $f(x) = x^3 + x, a = 0$

In Exercises 5–8, use the definition

$$f'(a) = \lim_{x\to a} \frac{f(x) - f(a)}{x - a}$$

to find the derivative of the given function at the given value of a.

5. $f(x) = 1/x, a = 2$

6. $f(x) = x^2 + 4, a = 1$

7. $f(x) = \sqrt{x+1}, a = 3$

8. $f(x) = 2x + 3, a = -1$

9. Find $f'(x)$ if $f(x) = 3x - 12$.

10. Find dy/dx if $y = 7x$.

11. Find $\dfrac{d}{dx}(x^2)$.

12. Find $\dfrac{d}{dx} f(x)$ if $f(x) = 3x^2$.

In Exercises 13–16, match the graph of the function with the graph of the derivative shown here:

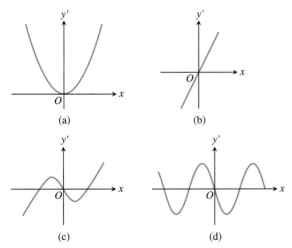

(a) (b)

(c) (d)

13.

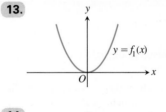

$y = f_1(x)$

14.

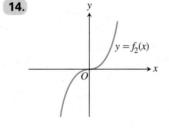

$y = f_2(x)$

15.

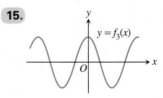

$y = f_3(x)$

16.

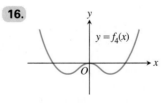

$y = f_4(x)$

17. If $f(2) = 3$ and $f'(2) = 5$, find an equation of **(a)** the *tangent* line, and **(b)** the *normal* line to the graph of $y = f(x)$ at the point where $x = 2$.
[*Hint:* Recall that the normal line is perpendicular to the tangent line.]

18. Find the derivative of the function $y = 2x^2 - 13x + 5$ and use it to find an equation of the line tangent to the curve at $x = 3$.

19. Find the lines that are **(a)** tangent and **(b)** normal to the curve $y = x^3$ at the point $(1, 1)$.

20. Find the lines that are **(a)** tangent and **(b)** normal to the curve $y = \sqrt{x}$ at $x = 4$.

21. *Daylight in Fairbanks* The viewing window below shows the number of hours of daylight in Fairbanks, Alaska, on each day for a typical 365-day period from January 1 to December 31. Answer the following questions by estimating slopes on the graph in hours per day. For the purposes of estimation, assume that each month has 30 days.

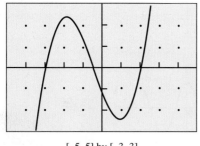

[0, 365] by [0, 24]

(a) On about what date is the amount of daylight increasing at the fastest rate? What is that rate?

(b) Do there appear to be days on which the rate of change in the amount of daylight is zero? If so, which ones?

(c) On what dates is the rate of change in the number of daylight hours positive? negative?

22. *Graphing f′ from f* Given the graph of the function f below, sketch a graph of the *derivative* of f.

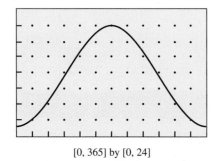

[–5, 5] by [–3, 3]

23. *Lynxes and Hares* In some northern parts of its range, the snowshoe hare is known to have a population that varies dramatically over time. The variation is cyclic and is tied to the population cycle of the Canada lynx, which preys almost exclusively on snowshoe hares. A simplified version of the "predator-prey population model" is shown in Figure 3.10. Figure 3.10a shows populations of hares (blue) and lynxes (red) varying over a 9-year period in the 1800's, while Figure 3.10b shows the graph of the derivative of the hare population, determined by the slopes of the blue curve in Figure 3.10a.

(a) What is the derivative of the hare population in Figure 3.10 when the number of hares is the largest? smallest?

(b) What is the size of the hare population in Figure 3.10 when the population of hares is largest? smallest?

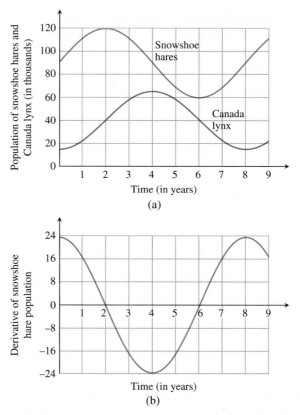

Figure 3.10 Lynxes and hares in a Canadian predator-prey food chain.

(c) Approximately how many years elapse between a peak in the prey population and a peak in the predator population?

24. Shown below is the graph of $f(x) = x \ln x - x$. From what you know about the graphs of functions (i) through (v), pick out the one that is the *derivative* of f for $x > 0$.

  i. $y = e^{x-1}$ **ii.** $y = \ln x$ **iii.** $y = -\ln(x)$

  iv. $y = \ln(x) - 1$ **v.** $y = 3x - 1$

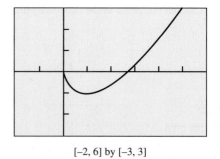

[–2, 6] by [–3, 3]

25. From what you know about the graphs of functions (i) through (v), pick out the one that is *its own derivative*.

  i. $y = \sin x$ **ii.** $y = x$ **iii.** $y = \sqrt{x}$

  iv. $y = e^x$ **v.** $y = x^2$

26. The graph of the function $y = f(x)$ shown here is made of line segments joined end to end.

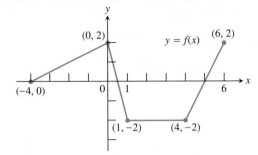

(a) Graph the function's derivative.

(b) At what values of x between $x = -4$ and $x = 6$ is the function not differentiable?

27. *Graphing f from f′* Sketch the graph of a continuous function f with $f(0) = -1$ and

$$f'(x) = \begin{cases} 1, & x < -1 \\ -2, & x > -1. \end{cases}$$

28. *Graphing f from f′* Sketch the graph of a continuous function f with $f(0) = 1$ and

$$f'(x) = \begin{cases} 2, & x < 2 \\ -1, & x > 2. \end{cases}$$

In Exercises 29 and 30, use the data to answer the questions.

29. *A Downhill Skier* Table 3.3 gives the approximate distance traveled by a downhill skier after t seconds for $0 \le t \le 10$. Use the method of Example 5 to sketch a graph of the derivative; then answer the following questions:

(a) What does the derivative represent?

(b) In what units would the derivative be measured?

(c) Can you guess an equation of the derivative by considering its graph?

TABLE 3.3 Skiing Distances

Time t (seconds)	Distance Traveled (feet)
0	0
1	3.3
2	13.3
3	29.9
4	53.2
5	83.2
6	119.8
7	163.0
8	212.9
9	269.5
10	332.7

30. *A Whitewater River* Bear Creek, a Georgia river known to kayaking enthusiasts, drops more than 770 feet over one stretch of 3.24 miles. By reading a contour map, one can estimate the elevations (y) at various distances (x) downriver from the start of the kayaking route (Table 3.4).

TABLE 3.4 Elevations Along Bear Creek

Distance Downriver (miles)	River Elevation (feet)
0.00	1577
0.56	1512
0.92	1448
1.19	1384
1.30	1319
1.39	1255
1.57	1191
1.74	1126
1.98	1062
2.18	998
2.41	933
2.64	869
3.24	805

(a) Sketch a graph of elevation (y) as a function of distance downriver (x).

(b) Use the technique of Example 5 to get an approximate graph of the derivative, dy/dx.

(c) The average change in elevation over a given distance is called a *gradient*. In this problem, what units of measure would be appropriate for a gradient?

(d) In this problem, what units of measure would be appropriate for the derivative?

(e) How would you identify the most dangerous section of the river (ignoring rocks) by analyzing the graph in (a)? Explain.

(f) How would you identify the most dangerous section of the river by analyzing the graph in (b)? Explain.

31. Using one-sided derivatives, show that the function

$$f(x) = \begin{cases} x^2 + x, & x \le 1 \\ 3x - 2, & x > 1 \end{cases}$$

does not have a derivative at $x = 1$.

32. Using one-sided derivatives, show that the function

$$f(x) = \begin{cases} x^3, & x \le 1 \\ 3x, & x > 1 \end{cases}$$

does not have a derivative at $x = 1$.

33. Writing to Learn Graph $y = \sin x$ and $y = \cos x$ in the same viewing window. Which function could be the derivative of the other? Defend your answer in terms of the behavior of the graphs.

34. In Example 2 of this section we showed that the derivative of $y = \sqrt{x}$ is a function with domain $(0, \infty)$. However, the function $y = \sqrt{x}$ itself has domain $[0, \infty)$, so it could have a *right-hand* derivative at $x = 0$. Prove that it does not.

35. Writing to Learn Use the concept of the derivative to define what it might mean for two parabolas to be parallel. Construct equations for two such parallel parabolas and graph them. Are the parabolas "everywhere equidistant," and if so, in what sense?

Standardized Test Questions

36. True or False If $f(x) = x^2 + x$, then $f'(x)$ exists for every real number x. Justify your answer.

37. True or False If the left-hand derivative and the right-hand derivative of f exist at $x = a$, then $f'(a)$ exists. Justify your answer.

38. Multiple Choice Let $f(x) = 4 - 3x$. Which of the following is equal to $f'(-1)$?

(A) -7 (B) 7 (C) -3 (D) 3 (E) does not exist

39. Multiple Choice Let $f(x) = 1 - 3x^2$. Which of the following is equal to $f'(1)$?

(A) -6 (B) -5 (C) 5 (D) 6 (E) does not exist

In Exercises 40 and 41, let

$$f(x) = \begin{cases} x^2 - 1, & x < 0 \\ 2x - 1, & x \geq 0. \end{cases}$$

40. Multiple Choice Which of the following is equal to the left-hand derivative of f at $x = 0$?

(A) -2 (B) 0 (C) 2 (D) ∞ (E) $-\infty$

41. Multiple Choice Which of the following is equal to the right-hand derivative of f at $x = 0$?

(A) -2 (B) 0 (C) 2 (D) ∞ (E) $-\infty$

Explorations

42. Let $f(x) = \begin{cases} x^2, & x \leq 1 \\ 2x, & x > 1. \end{cases}$

(a) Find $f'(x)$ for $x < 1$.   (b) Find $f'(x)$ for $x > 1$.

(c) Find $\lim_{x \to 1^-} f'(x)$.   (d) Find $\lim_{x \to 1^+} f'(x)$.

(e) Does $\lim_{x \to 1} f'(x)$ exist? Explain.

(f) Use the definition to find the left-hand derivative of f at $x = 1$ if it exists.

(g) Use the definition to find the right-hand derivative of f at $x = 1$ if it exists.

(h) Does $f'(1)$ exist? Explain.

43. Group Activity Using graphing calculators, have each person in your group do the following:

(a) pick two numbers a and b between 1 and 10;

(b) graph the function $y = (x - a)(x + b)$;

(c) graph the *derivative* of your function (it will be a line with slope 2);

(d) find the y-intercept of your derivative graph.

(e) Compare your answers and determine a simple way to predict the y-intercept, given the values of a and b. Test your result.

Extending the Ideas

44. Find the unique value of k that makes the function

$$f(x) = \begin{cases} x^3, & x \leq 1 \\ 3x + k, & x > 1 \end{cases}$$

differentiable at $x = 1$.

45. *Generating the Birthday Probabilities* Example 5 of this section concerns the probability that, in a group of n people, at least two people will share a common birthday. You can generate these probabilities on your calculator for values of n from 1 to 365.

Step 1: Set the values of N and P to zero:

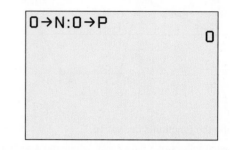

Step 2: Type in this single, multi-step command:

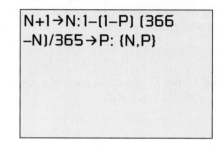

Now each time you press the ENTER key, the command will print a new value of N (the number of people in the room) along-side P (the probability that at least two of them share a common birthday):

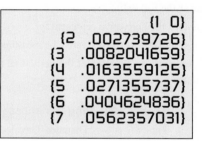

If you have some experience with probability, try to answer the following questions without looking at the table:

(a) If there are three people in the room, what is the probability that they all have *different* birthdays? (Assume that there are 365 possible birthdays, all of them equally likely.)

(b) If there are three people in the room, what is the probability that at least two of them share a common birthday?

(c) Explain how you can use the answer in part (b) to find the probability of a shared birthday when there are *four* people in the room. (This is how the calculator statement in Step 2 generates the probabilities.)

(d) Is it reasonable to assume that all calendar dates are equally likely birthdays? Explain your answer.

46. *Algebraic Challenge* Construct polynomial functions that fit the graphs of f and f' that are shown in Example 3 of this section.

3.2 | Differentiability

You will be able to analyze and discuss the differentiability of functions.

- Why $f'(a)$ might fail to exist at $x = a$
- Differentiability implies local linearity
- Numerical derivatives on a calculator
- Differentiability implies continuity
- Intermediate Value Theorem for derivatives

How $f'(a)$ Might Fail to Exist

A function will not have a derivative at a point $P(a, f(a))$ where the slopes of the secant lines,

$$\frac{f(x) - f(a)}{x - a},$$

fail to approach a limit as x approaches a. Figures 3.11–3.14 illustrate four different instances where this occurs. For example, a function whose graph is otherwise smooth will fail to have a derivative at a point where the graph has

1. a *corner,* where the one-sided derivatives differ; Example: $f(x) = |x|$

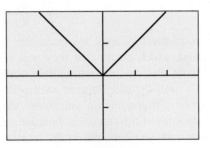

[−3, 3] by [−2, 2]

Figure 3.11 There is a "corner" at $x = 0$.

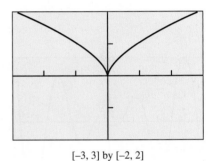

[−3, 3] by [−2, 2]

Figure 3.12 There is a "cusp" at $x = 0$.

2. a *cusp,* where the slopes of the secant lines approach ∞ from one side and $-\infty$ from the other (an extreme case of a corner); Example: $f(x) = x^{2/3}$

3. a *vertical tangent,* where the slopes of the secant lines approach either ∞ or $-\infty$ from both sides (in this example, ∞); Example: $f(x) = \sqrt[3]{x}$

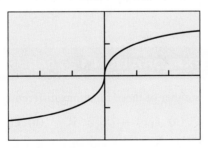

[−3, 3] by [−2, 2]

Figure 3.13 There is a vertical tangent line at $x = 0$.

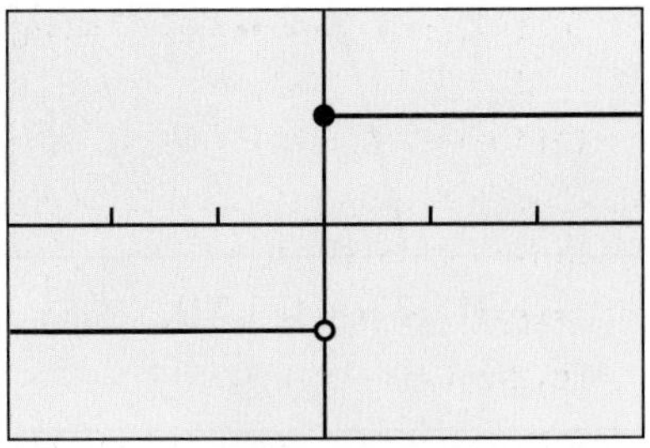

[−3, 3] by [−2, 2]

Figure 3.14 There is a discontinuity at $x = 0$.

4. a *discontinuity* (which will cause one or both of the one-sided derivatives to be nonexistent). Example: The *Unit Step Function*

$$U(x) = \begin{cases} -1, & x < 0 \\ 1, & x \geq 0 \end{cases}$$

In this example, the left-hand derivative fails to exist:

$$\lim_{h \to 0^-} \frac{U(0 + h) - U(0)}{h} = \lim_{h \to 0^-} \frac{(-1) - (1)}{h} = \lim_{h \to 0^-} \frac{-2}{h} = \infty$$

How Rough Can the Graph of a Continuous Function Be?

The graph of the absolute value function fails to be differentiable at a single point. If you graph $y = \sin^{-1}(\sin(x))$ on your calculator, you will see a continuous function with an *infinite* number of points of nondifferentiability. But can a continuous function fail to be differentiable at *every* point?

The answer, surprisingly enough, is yes, as Karl Weierstrass showed in 1872. One of his formulas (there are many like it) was

$$f(x) = \sum_{n=0}^{\infty} \left(\frac{2}{3}\right)^n \cos(9^n \pi x),$$

a formula that expresses f as an infinite (but converging) sum of cosines with increasingly higher frequencies. By adding wiggles to wiggles infinitely many times, so to speak, the formula produces a function whose graph is too bumpy in the limit to have a tangent anywhere!

Later in this section we will prove a theorem that states that a function *must* be continuous at *a* to be differentiable at *a*. This theorem would provide a quick and easy verification that *U* is not differentiable at $x = 0$.

EXAMPLE 1 Finding Where a Function Is Not Differentiable

Find all points in the domain of $f(x) = |x - 2| + 3$ where f is not differentiable.

SOLUTION

Think graphically! The graph of this function is the same as that of $y = |x|$, translated 2 units to the right and 3 units up. This puts the corner at the point $(2, 3)$, so this function is not differentiable at $x = 2$.

At every other point, the graph is (locally) a straight line and f has derivative $+1$ or -1 (again, just like $y = |x|$).   *Now Try Exercise 1.*

Most of the functions we encounter in calculus are differentiable wherever they are defined, which means that they will *not* have corners, cusps, vertical tangent lines, or points of discontinuity within their domains. Their graphs will be unbroken and smooth, with a well-defined slope at each point. Polynomials are differentiable, as are rational functions, trigonometric functions, exponential functions, and logarithmic functions. Composites of differentiable functions are differentiable, and so are sums, products, integer powers, and quotients of differentiable functions, where defined. We will see why all of this is true as Chapters 3 and 4 unfold.

Differentiability Implies Local Linearity

A good way to think of differentiable functions is that they are **locally linear;** that is, a function that is differentiable at *a* closely resembles its own tangent line very close to *a*. In the jargon of graphing calculators, differentiable curves will "straighten out" when we zoom in on them at a point of differentiability. (See Figure 3.15.)

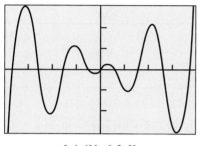

[–4, 4] by [–3, 3]

(a)

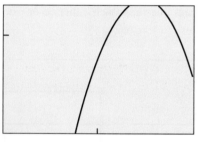

[1.7, 2.3] by [1.7, 2.1]

(b)

[1.93, 2.07] by [1.85, 1.95]

(c)

Figure 3.15 Three different views of the differentiable function $f(x) = x \cos{(3x)}$. We have zoomed in here at the point $(2, 1.9)$.

EXPLORATION 1 Zooming in to "See" Differentiability

Is either of these functions differentiable at $x = 0$?

(a) $f(x) = |x| + 1$ **(b)** $g(x) = \sqrt{x^2 + 0.0001} + 0.99$

1. We already know that f is not differentiable at $x = 0$; its graph has a corner there. Graph f and zoom in at the point $(0, 1)$ several times. Does the corner show signs of straightening out?
2. Now do the same thing with g. Does the graph of g show signs of straightening out? We will learn a quick way to differentiate g in Section 4.1, but for now suffice it to say that it *is* differentiable at $x = 0$, and in fact has a horizontal tangent there.
3. How many zooms does it take before the graph of g looks exactly like a horizontal line?
4. Now graph f and g *together* in a standard square viewing window. They appear to be identical until you start zooming in. The differentiable function eventually straightens out, while the nondifferentiable function remains impressively unchanged.

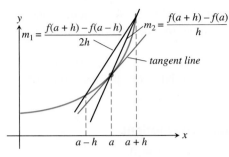

Figure 3.16 The symmetric difference quotient (slope m_1) usually gives a better approximation of the derivative for a given value of h than does the regular difference quotient (slope m_2), which is why the symmetric difference quotient is used in the numerical derivative.

A Word on Notation

Some newer graphing calculators may have two modes of displaying functions when graphing or computing. The new mode is sometimes called **Pretty Print** or **Mathprint,** and the other is the traditional calculator **Classic mode.** These two commands are illustrated below for the derivative of the function $f(x) = x^3$ at $x = 2$ shown in Example 2.

Classic mode: nDeriv(x^3, x, 2):

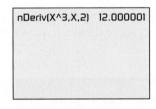

and Pretty Print or Mathprint mode:

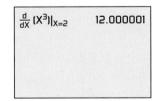

Note that both results are the same and equal to that shown in Example 2. Both Mathprint and Classic modes give the *same numerical approximation* because they are identical computationally on the calculator! Mathprint mode is *not* a Computer Algebra System (CAS) mode giving exact results like $\frac{d}{dx}x^3 = 3x^2$ or 12 when $x = 2$. Also remember that in our textbook we use **NDER ($f(x)$, a)** to represent the numerical derivative of $f(x)$ at $x = a$, as defined on this page.

Numerical Derivatives on a Calculator

For small values of h, the difference quotient

$$\frac{f(a + h) - f(a)}{h}$$

is often a good numerical approximation of $f'(a)$. However, as suggested by Figure 3.16, the same value of h will usually yield a *better* approximation of $f'(a)$ if we use the **symmetric difference quotient**

$$\frac{f(a + h) - f(a - h)}{2h}$$

to compute the slope between two nearby points on opposite sides of a. In fact, this approximation (which calculators can easily compute) is close enough to be used as a substitute for the derivative at a point in most applications.

> ### DEFINITION The Numerical Derivative
>
> The **numerical derivative of f at a,** which we will denote NDER $(f(x), a)$, is the *number*
>
> $$\frac{f(a + 0.001) - f(a - 0.001)}{0.002}.$$
>
> The **numerical derivative of f,** which we will denote NDER $(f(x), x)$, is the *function*
>
> $$\frac{f(x + 0.001) - f(x - 0.001)}{0.002}.$$

Some calculators have a name for the numerical derivative, like nDeriv($f(x), x, a$), which is similar to the one we use in the definition. Others use the Leibniz notation for the actual derivative at a:

$$\left.\frac{d}{dx}(f(x))\right|_{x=a}$$

We do not want to suggest that the numerical derivative and the derivative are the same, so we will continue to use our generic term NDER when referring to the numerical derivative. Thus, in this textbook,

$$\text{NDER}(f(x), a) = \frac{f(a + 0.001) - f(a - 0.001)}{0.002},$$

while

$$\left.\frac{d}{dx}(f(x))\right|_{x=a} = \lim_{h \to 0}\frac{f(a + h) - f(a)}{h}.$$

Be aware, however, that $\left.\frac{d}{dx}(f(x))\right|_{x=a}$ on your calculator might well refer to the numerical derivative.

EXAMPLE 2 Computing a Numerical Derivative

If $f(x) = x^3$, use the numerical derivative to approximate $f'(2)$.

SOLUTION

$$f'(2) = \left.\frac{d}{dx}(x^3)\right|_{x=2} \approx \text{NDER}(x^3, 2) = \frac{(2.001)^3 - (1.999)^3}{0.002} = 12.000001$$

Now Try Exercise 17.

In Example 1 of Section 3.1, we found the derivative of x^3 to be $3x^2$, whose value at $x = 2$ is $3(2)^2 = 12$. The numerical derivative is accurate to 5 decimal places. Not bad for the push of a button.

Example 2 gives dramatic evidence that NDER is very accurate when $h = 0.001$. Such accuracy is usually the case, although it is also possible for NDER to produce some surprisingly inaccurate results, as in Example 3.

EXAMPLE 3 Fooling the Symmetric Difference Quotient

Compute NDER $(|x|, 0)$, the numerical derivative of $|x|$ at $x = 0$.

SOLUTION

We saw at the start of this section that $y = |x|$ is not differentiable at $x = 0$, since its right-hand and left-hand derivatives at $x = 0$ are not the same. Nonetheless,

$$\text{NDER}(|x|, 0) = \frac{|0 + 0.001| - |0 - 0.001|}{2(0.001)}$$

$$= \frac{0.001 - 0.001}{0.002}$$

$$= 0$$

Even in the limit,

$$\lim_{h \to 0} \frac{|0 + h| - |0 - h|}{2h} = \lim_{h \to 0} \frac{0}{2h} = 0.$$

This proves that the derivative *cannot* be defined as the limit of the symmetric difference quotient. The symmetric difference quotient, which works on opposite sides of 0, has no chance of detecting the corner! ***Now Try Exercise 23.***

In light of Example 3, it is worth repeating here that the symmetric difference quotient actually does approach $f'(a)$ *when $f'(a)$ exists,* and in fact approximates it quite well (as in Example 2).

EXPLORATION 2 Looking at the Symmetric Difference Quotient Analytically

Let $f(x) = x^2$ and let $h = 0.01$.

1. Find
$$\frac{f(10 + h) - f(10)}{h}.$$
How close is it to $f'(10)$?

2. Find
$$\frac{f(10 + h) - f(10 - h)}{2h}.$$
How close is it to $f'(10)$?

3. Repeat this comparison for $f(x) = x^3$.

EXAMPLE 4 Graphing a Derivative Using NDER

Let $f(x) = \ln x$. Use NDER to graph $y = f'(x)$. Can you guess what function $f'(x)$ is by analyzing its graph?

continued

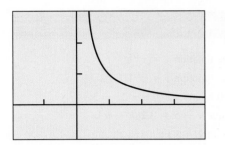

[–2, 4] by [–1, 3]

(a)

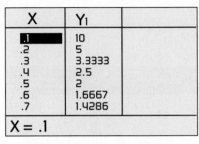

X	Y₁	
.1	10	
.2	5	
.3	3.3333	
.4	2.5	
.5	2	
.6	1.6667	
.7	1.4286	

X = .1

(b)

Figure 3.17 (a) The graph of NDER (ln (x), x) and (b) a table of values. What graph could this be? (Example 4)

Notice that we can obtain the graph and table of values in Figure 3.17 by entering Y1 = nDeriv(ln (x), x, x).

SOLUTION

The graph is shown in Figure 3.17a. The shape of the graph suggests, and the table of values in Figure 3.17b supports, the conjecture that this is the graph of $y = 1/x$. We will prove in Section 4.4 (using analytic methods) that this is indeed the case.

Now Try Exercise 27.

Differentiability Implies Continuity

We began this section with a look at the typical ways that a function could fail to have a derivative at a point. As one example, we indicated graphically that a discontinuity in the graph of f would cause one or both of the one-sided derivatives to be nonexistent. It is actually not difficult to give an analytic proof that continuity is an essential condition for the derivative to exist, so we include that as a theorem here.

THEOREM 1 Differentiability Implies Continuity

If f has a derivative at $x = a$, then f is continuous at $x = a$.

Proof Our task is to show that $\lim_{x \to a} f(x) = f(a)$, or, equivalently, that

$$\lim_{x \to a} [f(x) - f(a)] = 0.$$

Using the Limit Product Rule (and noting that $x - a$ is not zero), we can write

$$\lim_{x \to a} [f(x) - f(a)] = \lim_{x \to a} \left[(x - a) \frac{f(x) - f(a)}{x - a} \right]$$

$$= \lim_{x \to a} (x - a) \cdot \lim_{x \to a} \frac{f(x) - f(a)}{x - a}$$

$$= 0 \cdot f'(a)$$

$$= 0$$ ∎

The converse of Theorem 1 is false, as we have already seen. A continuous function might have a corner, a cusp, or a vertical tangent line, and hence not be differentiable at a given point.

Intermediate Value Theorem for Derivatives

Not every function can be a derivative. A derivative must have the intermediate value property, as stated in the following theorem (the proof of which can be found in advanced texts).

THEOREM 2 Intermediate Value Theorem for Derivatives

If a and b are any two points in an interval on which f is differentiable, then f' takes on every value between $f'(a)$ and $f'(b)$.

Absolutely Not

You might think that the absolute value function would work in Example 5, but it does not work at $x = 0$. Pondering how to overcome that difficulty is futile, but it will give you further insight into Theorem 2.

EXAMPLE 5 Applying Theorem 2

Does any function have the Unit Step Function (see Figure 3.14) as its derivative?

SOLUTION

No. Choose some $a < 0$ and some $b > 0$. Then $U(a) = -1$ and $U(b) = 1$, but U does not take on any value between -1 and 1. *Now Try Exercise 37.*

The question of when a function is a derivative of some function is one of the central questions in all of calculus. The answer, found by Newton and Leibniz, would revolutionize the world of mathematics. We will see what that answer is when we reach Chapter 6.

Quick Review 3.2   *(For help, go to Sections 1.2 and 2.1.)*

Exercise numbers with a gray background indicate problems that the authors have designed to be solved *without a calculator.*

In Exercises 1–5, tell whether the limit could be used to define $f'(a)$ (assuming that f is differentiable at a).

1. $\displaystyle\lim_{h\to 0} \frac{f(a+h) - f(a)}{h}$

2. $\displaystyle\lim_{h\to 0} \frac{f(a+h) - f(h)}{h}$

3. $\displaystyle\lim_{x\to a} \frac{f(x) - f(a)}{x - a}$

4. $\displaystyle\lim_{x\to a} \frac{f(a) - f(x)}{a - x}$

5. $\displaystyle\lim_{h\to 0} \frac{f(a+h) + f(a-h)}{h}$

6. Find the domain of the function $y = x^{4/3}$.

7. Find the domain of the function $y = x^{3/4}$.

8. Find the range of the function $y = |x - 2| + 3$.

9. Find the slope of the line $y - 5 = 3.2(x + \pi)$.

10. If $f(x) = 5x$, find
$$\frac{f(3 + 0.001) - f(3 - 0.001)}{0.002}.$$

Section 3.2 Exercises

In Exercises 1–4, compare the right-hand and left-hand derivatives to show that the function is not differentiable at the point P.

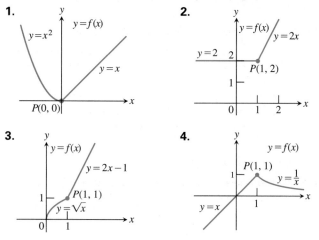

1. $y = f(x)$, $y = x^2$, $y = x$, $P(0,0)$

2. $y = f(x)$, $y = 2x$, $y = 2$, $P(1,2)$

3. $y = f(x)$, $y = 2x - 1$, $y = \sqrt{x}$, $P(1,1)$

4. $y = f(x)$, $P(1,1)$, $y = \frac{1}{x}$, $y = x$

In Exercises 5–10, the graph of a function over a closed interval D is given. At what domain points does the function appear to be

(a) differentiable?   (b) continuous but not differentiable?

(c) neither continuous nor differentiable?

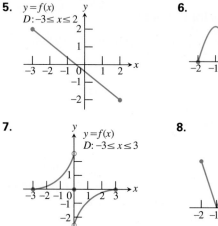

5. $y = f(x)$, $D: -3 \le x \le 2$

6. $y = f(x)$, $D: -2 \le x \le 3$

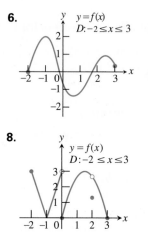

7. $y = f(x)$, $D: -3 \le x \le 3$

8. $y = f(x)$, $D: -2 \le x \le 3$

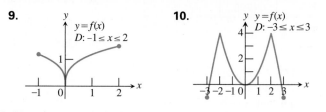

9. $y = f(x)$, $D: -1 \le x \le 2$

10. $y = f(x)$, $D: -3 \le x \le 3$

In Exercises 11–16, the function fails to be differentiable at $x = 0$. Tell whether the problem is a corner, a cusp, a vertical tangent, or a discontinuity.

11. $y = \begin{cases} \tan^{-1}x, & x \ne 0 \\ 1, & x = 0 \end{cases}$

12. $y = x^{4/5}$

13. $y = x + \sqrt{x^2 + 2}$

14. $y = 3 - \sqrt[3]{x}$

15. $y = 3x - 2|x| - 1$

16. $y = \sqrt[3]{|x|}$

In Exercises 17–26, find the numerical derivative of the given function at the indicated point. Use $h = 0.001$. Is the function differentiable at the indicated point?

17. $f(x) = 4x - x^2$, $x = 0$

18. $f(x) = 4x - x^2$, $x = 3$

19. $f(x) = 4x - x^2$, $x = 1$

20. $f(x) = x^3 - 4x$, $x = 0$

21. $f(x) = x^3 - 4x$, $x = -2$

22. $f(x) = x^3 - 4x$, $x = 2$

23. $f(x) = x^{2/3}$, $x = 0$

24. $f(x) = |x - 3|$, $x = 3$

25. $f(x) = x^{2/5}$, $x = 0$

26. $f(x) = x^{4/5}$, $x = 0$

Group Activity In Exercises 27–30, use NDER to graph the derivative of the function. If possible, identify the derivative function by looking at the graph.

27. $y = -\cos x$

28. $y = 0.25x^4$

29. $y = \dfrac{x|x|}{2}$

30. $y = -\ln|\cos x|$

In Exercises 31–36, find all values of x for which the function is differentiable.

31. $f(x) = \dfrac{x^3 - 8}{x^2 - 4x - 5}$

32. $h(x) = \sqrt[3]{3x - 6} + 5$

33. $P(x) = \sin(|x|) - 1$

34. $Q(x) = 3\cos(|x|)$

35. $g(x) = \begin{cases} (x+1)^2, & x \le 0 \\ 2x + 1, & 0 < x < 3 \\ (4 - x)^2, & x \ge 3 \end{cases}$

36. $C(x) = x|x|$

37. Show that the function

$$f(x) = \begin{cases} 0, & -1 \le x < 0 \\ 1, & 0 \le x \le 1 \end{cases}$$

is not the derivative of any function on the interval $-1 \le x \le 1$.

38. Writing to Learn Recall that the numerical derivative (NDER) can give meaningless values at points where a function is not differentiable. In this exercise, we consider the numerical derivatives of the functions $1/x$ and $1/x^2$ at $x = 0$.

(a) Explain why neither function is differentiable at $x = 0$.

(b) Find NDER at $x = 0$ for each function.

(c) By analyzing the definition of the symmetric difference quotient, explain why NDER returns wrong responses that are so different from each other for these two functions.

39. Let f be the function defined as

$$f(x) = \begin{cases} 3 - x, & x < 1 \\ ax^2 + bx, & x \ge 1 \end{cases}$$

where a and b are constants.

(a) If the function is continuous for all x, what is the relationship between a and b?

(b) Find the unique values for a and b that will make f both continuous and differentiable.

Standardized Test Questions

You may use a graphing calculator to solve the following problems.

40. True or False If f has a derivative at $x = a$, then f is continuous at $x = a$. Justify your answer.

41. True or False If f is continuous at $x = a$, then f has a derivative at $x = a$. Justify your answer.

42. Multiple Choice Which of the following is true about the graph of $f(x) = x^{4/5}$ at $x = 0$?

(A) It has a corner.

(B) It has a cusp.

(C) It has a vertical tangent.

(D) It has a discontinuity.

(E) $f(0)$ does not exist.

43. Multiple Choice Let $f(x) = \sqrt[3]{x - 1}$. At which of the following points is $f'(a) \neq \text{NDER}(f(x), a)$?

(A) $a = 1$ (B) $a = -1$ (C) $a = 2$ (D) $a = -2$

(E) $a = 0$

In Exercises 44 and 45, let

$$f(x) = \begin{cases} 2x + 1, & x \le 0 \\ x^2 + 1, & x > 0 \end{cases}$$

44. Multiple Choice Which of the following is equal to the left-hand derivative of f at $x = 0$?

(A) $2x$ (B) 2 (C) 0 (D) $-\infty$ (E) ∞

45. Multiple Choice Which of the following is equal to the right-hand derivative of f at $x = 0$?

(A) $2x$ (B) 2 (C) 0 (D) $-\infty$ (E) ∞

Explorations

46. (a) Enter the expression "$x < 0$" into Y1 of your calculator using "$<$" from the TEST menu. Graph Y1 in DOT MODE in the window $[-4.7, 4.7]$ by $[-3.1, 3.1]$.

(b) Describe the graph in part (a).

(c) Enter the expression "$x \ge 0$" into Y1 of your calculator using "$\ge$" from the TEST menu. Graph Y1 in DOT MODE in the window $[-4.7, 4.7]$ by $[-3.1, 3.1]$.

(d) Describe the graph in part (c).

47. *Graphing Piecewise Functions on a Calculator* Let

$$f(x) = \begin{cases} x^2, & x \le 0 \\ 2x, & x > 0. \end{cases}$$

(a) Enter the expression "$(X^2)(X \le 0) + (2X)(X > 0)$" into Y1 of your calculator and draw its graph in the window $[-4.7, 4.7]$ by $[-3, 5]$.

(b) Explain why the values of Y1 and $f(x)$ are the same.

(c) Enter the numerical derivative of Y1 into Y2 of your calculator and draw its graph in the same window. Turn off the graph of Y1.

(d) Use TRACE to calculate NDER $(Y1, -0.1)$, NDER $(Y1, 0)$, and NDER $(Y1, 0.1)$. Compare with Section 3.1, Example 6. Did the numerical derivative get all three right?

Extending the Ideas

48. *Oscillation* There is another way that a function might fail to be differentiable, and that is by *oscillation*. Let

$$f(x) = \begin{cases} x \sin \dfrac{1}{x}, & x \neq 0 \\ 0, & x = 0. \end{cases}$$

(a) Show that f is continuous at $x = 0$.

(b) Show that

$$\frac{f(0 + h) - f(0)}{h} = \sin \frac{1}{h}.$$

(c) Explain why

$$\lim_{h \to 0} \frac{f(0 + h) - f(0)}{h}$$

does not exist.

(d) Does f have either a left-hand or right-hand derivative at $x = 0$?

(e) Now consider the function

$$g(x) = \begin{cases} x^2 \sin \dfrac{1}{x}, & x \neq 0 \\ 0, & x = 0. \end{cases}$$

Use the definition of the derivative to show that g is differentiable at $x = 0$ and that $g'(0) = 0$.

3.3 | Rules for Differentiation

You will be able to apply the rules for differentiation.

- Power functions
- Sum and difference rules
- Product and quotient rules
- Negative integer powers of *x*
- Second and higher order derivatives

Positive Integer Powers, Multiples, Sums, and Differences

The first rule of differentiation is that the derivative of every constant function is the zero function.

RULE 1 Derivative of a Constant Function

If f is the function with the constant value c, then

$$\frac{df}{dx} = \frac{d}{dx}(c) = 0.$$

Proof of Rule 1 If $f(x) = c$ is a function with a constant value c, then

$$\lim_{h \to 0} \frac{f(x+h) - f(x)}{h} = \lim_{h \to 0} \frac{c - c}{h} = \lim_{h \to 0} 0 = 0. \qquad \blacksquare$$

The next rule is a first step toward a rule for differentiating any polynomial.

More Powerful Rules to Come

The Power Rule actually applies to all real exponents, not just positive integers; we just cannot prove that yet. You will see this same rule several more times in Chapters 3 and 4 as we gradually prove it for more and more kinds of exponents.

RULE 2   Power Rule for Positive Integer Powers of *x*

If n is a positive integer, then

$$\frac{d}{dx}(x^n) = nx^{n-1}.$$

Proof of Rule 2 If $f(x) = x^n$, then

$$\frac{d}{dx}(x^n) = \lim_{h \to 0} \frac{(x+h)^n - x^n}{h}.$$

We can expand $(x + h)^n$ using the Binomial Theorem as follows:

$$(x+h)^n = x^n + n \cdot x^{n-1}h + \frac{n(n-1)}{2} \cdot x^{n-2}h^2 + \cdots + n \cdot xh^{n-1} + h^n$$

$$= x^n + n \cdot x^{n-1}h + h^2 \cdot [\text{stuff}]$$

Notice that after the first two terms of the expansion, every term has a factor of h to a power greater than or equal to 2. This means we can factor h^2 out of all the remaining terms (leaving a polynomial expression we have chosen to call "stuff," since its particulars become irrelevant). Now we can complete the proof.

$$\frac{d}{dx}(x^n) = \lim_{h \to 0} \frac{(x+h)^n - x^n}{h}$$

$$= \lim_{h \to 0} \frac{x^n + n \cdot x^{n-1}h + h^2 \cdot [\text{stuff}] - x^n}{h}$$

$$= \lim_{h \to 0} \frac{n \cdot x^{n-1}h + h^2 \cdot [\text{stuff}]}{h}$$

$$= \lim_{h \to 0} (n \cdot x^{n-1} + h \cdot [\text{stuff}])$$

$$= nx^{n-1} + 0 \cdot [\text{stuff}]$$

$$= nx^{n-1} \qquad \blacksquare$$

The Power Rule says: To differentiate x^n, multiply by n and subtract 1 from the exponent. For example, the derivatives of x^2, x^3, and x^4 are $2x^1$, $3x^2$, and $4x^3$, respectively.

RULE 3   The Constant Multiple Rule

If u is a differentiable function of x and c is a constant, then

$$\frac{d}{dx}(cu) = c\frac{du}{dx}.$$

Proof of Rule 3

$$\frac{d}{dx}(cu) = \lim_{h \to 0} \frac{cu(x + h) - cu(x)}{h}$$

$$= c \lim_{h \to 0} \frac{u(x + h) - u(x)}{h}$$

$$= c\frac{du}{dx} \qquad \blacksquare$$

Rule 3 says that if a differentiable function is multiplied by a constant, then its derivative is multiplied by the same constant. Combined with Rule 2, it enables us to find the derivative of any monomial quickly; for example, the derivative of $7x^4$ is $7(4x^3) = 28x^3$.

To find the derivatives of polynomials, we need to be able to differentiate sums and differences of monomials. We can accomplish this by applying the Sum and Difference Rule.

Denoting Functions by *u* and *v*

The functions we work with when we need a differentiation formula are likely to be denoted by letters like *f* and *g*. When we apply the formula, we do not want to find the formula using these same letters in some other way. To guard against this, we denote the functions in differentiation rules by letters like *u* and *v* that are not likely to be already in use.

RULE 4   The Sum and Difference Rule

If u and v are differentiable functions of x, then their sum and difference are differentiable at every point where u and v are differentiable. At such points,

$$\frac{d}{dx}(u \pm v) = \frac{du}{dx} \pm \frac{dv}{dx}.$$

Proof of Rule 4

We use the difference quotient for $f(x) = u(x) + v(x)$.

$$\frac{d}{dx}[u(x) + v(x)] = \lim_{h \to 0} \frac{[u(x + h) + v(x + h)] - [u(x) + v(x)]}{h}$$

$$= \lim_{h \to 0} \left[\frac{u(x + h) - u(x)}{h} + \frac{v(x + h) - v(x)}{h} \right]$$

$$= \lim_{h \to 0} \frac{u(x + h) - u(x)}{h} + \lim_{h \to 0} \frac{v(x + h) - v(x)}{h}$$

$$= \frac{du}{dx} + \frac{dv}{dx}$$

The proof of the rule for the difference of two functions is similar. $\blacksquare$

EXAMPLE 1 Differentiating a Polynomial

Find $\dfrac{dp}{dt}$ if $p = t^3 + 6t^2 - \dfrac{5}{3}t + 16$.

SOLUTION

By Rule 4 we can differentiate the polynomial term-by-term, applying Rules 1 through 3 as we go.

$$\frac{dp}{dt} = \frac{d}{dt}(t^3) + \frac{d}{dt}(6t^2) - \frac{d}{dt}\left(\frac{5}{3}t\right) + \frac{d}{dt}(16) \qquad \text{Sum and Difference Rule}$$

$$= 3t^2 + 6 \cdot 2t - \frac{5}{3} + 0 \qquad\qquad\qquad \text{Constant and Power Rules}$$

$$= 3t^2 + 12t - \frac{5}{3} \qquad\qquad\qquad\qquad \textbf{\textit{Now Try Exercise 5.}}$$

EXAMPLE 2 Finding Horizontal Tangents

Does the curve $y = x^4 - 2x^2 + 2$ have any horizontal tangents? If so, where?

SOLUTION

The horizontal tangents, if any, occur where the slope dy/dx is zero. To find these points, we

(a) calculate dy/dx:

$$\frac{dy}{dx} = \frac{d}{dx}(x^4 - 2x^2 + 2) = 4x^3 - 4x$$

(b) solve the equation $dy/dx = 0$ for x:

$$4x^3 - 4x = 0$$
$$4x(x^2 - 1) = 0$$
$$x = 0, 1, -1$$

The curve has horizontal tangents at $x = 0$, 1, and -1. The corresponding points on the curve (found from the equation $y = x^4 - 2x^2 + 2$) are $(0, 2)$, $(1, 1)$, and $(-1, 1)$. You might wish to graph the curve to see where the horizontal tangents go.

Now Try Exercise 7.

The derivative in Example 2 was easily factored, making an algebraic solution of the equation $dy/dx = 0$ correspondingly simple. When a simple algebraic solution is not possible, the solutions to $dy/dx = 0$ can still be found to a high degree of accuracy by using the SOLVE capability of your calculator.

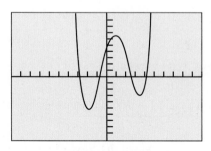

[−10, 10] by [−10, 10]

Figure 3.18 The graph of
$y = 0.2x^4 - 0.7x^3 - 2x^2 + 5x + 4$
has three horizontal tangents. (Example 3)

EXAMPLE 3 Using Calculus and Calculator

As can be seen in the viewing window $[-10, 10]$ by $[-10, 10]$, the graph of $y = 0.2x^4 - 0.7x^3 - 2x^2 + 5x + 4$ has three horizontal tangents (Figure 3.18). At what points do these horizontal tangents occur?

continued

On Rounding Calculator Values

Notice in Example 3 that we rounded the *x* values to four significant digits when we presented the answers. The calculator actually presented many more digits, but there was no practical reason for writing all of them. When we used the calculator to compute the corresponding *y* values, however, we *used the x values stored in the calculator,* not the rounded values. We then rounded the *y* values to four significant digits when we presented the ordered pairs. Significant "round-off errors" can accumulate in a problem if you use rounded intermediate values for doing additional computations, so avoid rounding until the final answer.

SOLUTION

First we find the derivative

$$\frac{dy}{dx} = 0.8x^3 - 2.1x^2 - 4x + 5.$$

Using the calculator solver, we find that $0.8x^3 - 2.1x^2 - 4x + 5 = 0$ when $x \approx -1.862$, 0.9484, and 3.539. We use the calculator again to evaluate the original function at these *x* values and find the corresponding points to be approximately $(-1.862, -5.321)$, $(0.9484, 6.508)$, and $(3.539, -3.008)$. **Now Try Exercise 11.**

Products and Quotients

While the derivative of the sum of two functions is the sum of their derivatives and the derivative of the difference of two functions is the difference of their derivatives, the derivative of the product of two functions is *not* the product of their derivatives.

For instance,

$$\frac{d}{dx}(x \cdot x) = \frac{d}{dx}(x^2) = 2x, \qquad \text{while} \qquad \frac{d}{dx}(x) \cdot \frac{d}{dx}(x) = 1 \cdot 1 = 1.$$

The derivative of a product is actually the sum of *two* products, as we now explain.

Formula Tip

You can remember the Product Rule with the phrase "the first times the derivative of the second plus the second times the derivative of the first."

Gottfried Wilhelm Leibniz (1646–1716)

The method of limits used in this book was not discovered until nearly a century after Newton and Leibniz, the discoverers of calculus, had died.

To Leibniz, the key idea was the *differential,* an infinitely small quantity that was almost like zero, but which—unlike zero—could be used in the denominator of a fraction. Thus, Leibniz thought of the derivative *dy/dx* as the quotient of two differentials, *dy* and *dx*.

The problem was explaining why these differentials sometimes became zero and sometimes did not! See Exercise 59.

Some 17th-century mathematicians were confident that the calculus of Newton and Leibniz would eventually be found to be fatally flawed because of these mysterious quantities. It was only after later generations of mathematicians had found better ways to prove their results that the calculus of Newton and Leibniz was accepted by the entire scientific community.

> **RULE 5   The Product Rule**
>
> The product of two differentiable functions *u* and *v* is differentiable, and
>
> $$\frac{d}{dx}(uv) = u\frac{dv}{dx} + v\frac{du}{dx}.$$

Proof of Rule 5 We begin, as usual, by applying the definition.

$$\frac{d}{dx}(uv) = \lim_{h \to 0} \frac{u(x + h)v(x + h) - u(x)v(x)}{h}$$

To change the fraction into an equivalent one that contains difference quotients for the derivatives of *u* and *v*, we subtract and add $u(x + h)v(x)$ in the numerator. Then,

$$\frac{d}{dx}(uv) = \lim_{h \to 0} \frac{u(x + h)v(x + h) - u(x + h)v(x) + u(x + h)v(x) - u(x)v(x)}{h}$$

$$= \lim_{h \to 0} \left[u(x + h)\frac{v(x + h) - v(x)}{h} + v(x)\frac{u(x + h) - u(x)}{h} \right] \quad \text{Factor and separate.}$$

$$= \lim_{h \to 0} u(x + h) \cdot \lim_{h \to 0} \frac{v(x + h) - v(x)}{h} + v(x) \cdot \lim_{h \to 0} \frac{u(x + h) - u(x)}{h}.$$

As *h* approaches 0, $u(x + h)$ approaches $u(x)$ because *u*, being differentiable at *x*, is continuous at *x*. The two fractions approach the values of *dv/dx* and *du/dx*, respectively, at *x*. Therefore

$$\frac{d}{dx}(uv) = u\frac{dv}{dx} + v\frac{du}{dx}.$$

■

EXAMPLE 4 Differentiating a Product

Find $f'(x)$ if $f(x) = (x^2 + 1)(x^3 + 3)$.

SOLUTION

From the Product Rule with $u = x^2 + 1$ and $v = x^3 + 3$, we find

$$f'(x) = \frac{d}{dx}[(x^2 + 1)(x^3 + 3)] = (x^2 + 1)(3x^2) + (x^3 + 3)(2x)$$

$$= 3x^4 + 3x^2 + 2x^4 + 6x$$

$$= 5x^4 + 3x^2 + 6x \qquad \textit{Now Try Exercise 13.}$$

We could also have done Example 4 by multiplying out the original expression and then differentiating the resulting polynomial. That alternate strategy will not work, however, on a product like $x^2 \sin x$.

Just as the derivative of the product of two differentiable functions is not the product of their derivatives, the derivative of a quotient of two functions is not the quotient of their derivatives. What happens instead is this:

RULE 6   The Quotient Rule

At a point where $v \neq 0$, the quotient $y = u/v$ of two differentiable functions is differentiable, and

$$\frac{d}{dx}\left(\frac{u}{v}\right) = \frac{v\dfrac{du}{dx} - u\dfrac{dv}{dx}}{v^2}.$$

Proof of Rule 6

$$\frac{d}{dx}\left(\frac{u}{v}\right) = \lim_{h \to 0} \frac{\dfrac{u(x + h)}{v(x + h)} - \dfrac{u(x)}{v(x)}}{h}$$

$$= \lim_{h \to 0} \frac{v(x)u(x + h) - u(x)v(x + h)}{hv(x + h)v(x)}$$

To change the last fraction into an equivalent one that contains the difference quotients for the derivatives of u and v, we subtract and add $v(x)u(x)$ in the numerator. This allows us to continue with

$$\frac{d}{dx}\left(\frac{u}{v}\right) = \lim_{h \to 0} \frac{v(x)u(x + h) - v(x)u(x) + v(x)u(x) - u(x)v(x + h)}{hv(x + h)v(x)}$$

$$= \lim_{h \to 0} \frac{v(x)\dfrac{u(x + h) - u(x)}{h} - u(x)\dfrac{v(x + h) - v(x)}{h}}{v(x + h)v(x)}$$

Taking the limits in both the numerator and denominator now gives us the Quotient Rule. ∎

EXAMPLE 5 Supporting Computations Graphically

Differentiate $f(x) = \dfrac{x^2 - 1}{x^2 + 1}$. Support graphically.

continued

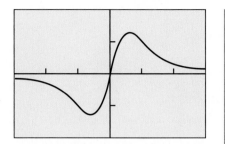

[–3, 3] by [–2, 2]

Figure 3.19 The graph of

$$y = \frac{4x}{(x^2 + 1)^2}$$

and the graph of

$$y = \text{NDER}\left(\frac{x^2 - 1}{x^2 + 1}, x\right)$$

appear to be the same. (Example 5)

SOLUTION

We apply the Quotient Rule with $u = x^2 - 1$ and $v = x^2 + 1$:

$$f'(x) = \frac{(x^2 + 1) \cdot 2x - (x^2 - 1) \cdot 2x}{(x^2 + 1)^2} \qquad \frac{v(du/dx) - u(dv/dx)}{v^2}$$

$$= \frac{2x^3 + 2x - 2x^3 + 2x}{(x^2 + 1)^2}.$$

$$= \frac{4x}{(x^2 + 1)^2}$$

The graphs of $y_1 = f'(x)$ calculated above and of $y_2 = \text{NDER}\,(f(x), x)$ are shown in Figure 3.19. The fact that they appear to be identical provides strong graphical support that our calculations are indeed correct. *Now Try Exercise 19.*

EXAMPLE 6 Working with Numerical Values

Let $y = uv$ be the product of the functions u and v. Find $y'(2)$ if

$$u(2) = 3, \qquad u'(2) = -4, \qquad v(2) = 1, \qquad \text{and} \qquad v'(2) = 2.$$

SOLUTION

From the Product Rule, $y' = (uv)' = uv' + vu'$. In particular,

$$y'(2) = u(2)v'(2) + v(2)u'(2)$$

$$= (3)(2) + (1)(-4)$$

$$= 2 \qquad\qquad \textit{Now Try Exercise 23.}$$

Negative Integer Powers of *x*

The rule for differentiating negative powers of x is the same as Rule 2 for differentiating positive powers of x, although our proof of Rule 2 does not work for negative values of n. We can now extend the Power Rule to negative integer powers by a clever use of the Quotient Rule.

RULE 7   Power Rule for Negative Integer Powers of *x*

If n is a negative integer and $x \neq 0$, then

$$\frac{d}{dx}(x^n) = nx^{n-1}.$$

Proof of Rule 7 If n is a negative integer, then $n = -m$, where m is a positive integer. Hence, $x^n = x^{-m} = 1/x^m$, and

$$\frac{d}{dx}(x^n) = \frac{d}{dx}\left(\frac{1}{x^m}\right) = \frac{x^m \cdot \dfrac{d}{dx}(1) - 1 \cdot \dfrac{d}{dx}(x^m)}{(x^m)^2}$$

$$= \frac{0 - mx^{m-1}}{x^{2m}}$$

$$= -mx^{-m-1}$$

$$= nx^{n-1} \qquad\qquad\qquad \blacksquare$$

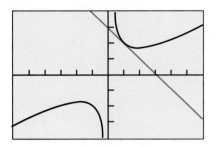

[–6, 6] by [–4, 4]

Figure 3.20 The line $y = -x + 3$ appears to be tangent to the graph of

$$y = \frac{x^2 + 3}{2x}$$

at the point $(1, 2)$. (Example 7)

EXAMPLE 7 Using the Power Rule

Find an equation for the line tangent to the curve

$$y = \frac{x^2 + 3}{2x}$$

at the point $(1, 2)$. Support your answer graphically.

SOLUTION

We could find the derivative by the Quotient Rule, but it is easier to first simplify the function as a sum of two powers of x.

$$\frac{dy}{dx} = \frac{d}{dx}\left(\frac{x^2}{2x} + \frac{3}{2x}\right)$$

$$= \frac{d}{dx}\left(\frac{1}{2}x + \frac{3}{2}x^{-1}\right)$$

$$= \frac{1}{2} - \frac{3}{2}x^{-2}$$

The slope at $x = 1$ is

$$\left.\frac{dy}{dx}\right|_{x=1} = \left[\frac{1}{2} - \frac{3}{2}x^{-2}\right]_{x=1} = \frac{1}{2} - \frac{3}{2} = -1.$$

The line through $(1, 2)$ with slope $m = -1$ is

$$y - 2 = (-1)(x - 1)$$

or, equivalently,

$$y = -x + 3$$

We graph $y = (x^2 + 3)/2x$ and $y = -x + 3$ (Figure 3.20), observing that the line appears to be tangent to the curve at $(1, 2)$. Thus, we have graphical support that our computations are correct. ***Now Try Exercise 27.***

Second and Higher Order Derivatives

The derivative $y' = dy/dx$ is called the *first derivative* of y with respect to x. The first derivative may itself be a differentiable function of x. If so, its derivative,

$$y'' = \frac{dy'}{dx} = \frac{d}{dx}\left(\frac{dy}{dx}\right) = \frac{d^2y}{dx^2},$$

is called the *second derivative* of y with respect to x. If y'' ("y double-prime") is differentiable, its derivative,

$$y''' = \frac{dy''}{dx} = \frac{d^3y}{dx^3},$$

is called the *third derivative* of y with respect to x. The names continue as you might expect they would, except that the multiple-prime notation begins to lose its usefulness after about three primes. We use

$$y^{(n)} = \frac{dy^{(n-1)}}{dx} = \frac{d^ny}{dx^n} \qquad \text{"y super } n\text{"}$$

to denote the **nth derivative** of y with respect to x. (We also use d^ny/dx^n.) Do not confuse $y^{(n)}$ with the nth power of y, which is y^n.

Technology Tip

You can find second derivatives numerically on a calculator by "nesting" the NDER command. For example, the second derivative of x^3 at $x = 2$ is NDER (NDER (x^3, x), 2). In MATHPRINT, that becomes

$$\left.\frac{d}{dx}\left(\left.\frac{d}{dx}(x^3)\right|_{x=x}\right)\right|_{x=2}. \text{ It is not advisable}$$

to use this trick for orders higher than 2, though. Not only does the syntax get even more cumbersome, but error accumulation in the algorithm makes the results unreliable.

EXAMPLE 8 Finding Higher Order Derivatives

Find the first four derivatives of $y = x^3 - 5x^2 + 2$.

SOLUTION

The first four derivatives are

First derivative: $y' = 3x^2 - 10x$;

Second derivative: $y'' = 6x - 10$;

Third derivative: $y''' = 6$;

Fourth derivative: $y^{(4)} = 0$.

This function has derivatives of all orders, the fourth and higher order derivatives all being zero.   ***Now Try Exercise 33.***

EXAMPLE 9 Finding Instantaneous Rate of Change

An orange farmer currently has 200 trees yielding an average of 15 bushels of oranges per tree. She is expanding her farm at the rate of 15 trees per year, while improved husbandry is improving her average annual yield by 1.2 bushels per tree. What is the current (instantaneous) rate of increase of her total annual production of oranges?

SOLUTION

Let the functions t and y be defined as follows.

$t(x) = $ the number of trees x years from now.

$y(x) = $ yield per tree x years from now.

Then $p(x) = t(x)y(x)$ is the total production of oranges in year x. We know the following values.

$$t(0) = 200, \quad y(0) = 15$$
$$t'(0) = 15, \quad y'(0) = 1.2$$

We need to find $p'(0)$, where $p = ty$.

$$p'(0) = t(0)y'(0) + y(0)t'(0)$$
$$= (200)(1.2) + (15)(15)$$
$$= 465$$

The rate we seek is 465 bushels per year.   ***Now Try Exercise 51.***

Quick Review 3.3   *(For help, go to Sections 1.2 and 3.1.)*

Exercise numbers with a gray background indicate problems that the authors have designed to be solved *without a calculator*.

In Exercises 1–6, write the expression as a sum of powers of x.

1. $(x^2 - 2)(x^{-1} + 1)$

2. $\left(\dfrac{x}{x^2 + 1}\right)^{-1}$

3. $3x^2 - \dfrac{2}{x} + \dfrac{5}{x^2}$

4. $\dfrac{3x^4 - 2x^3 + 4}{2x^2}$

5. $(x^{-1} + 2)(x^{-2} + 1)$

6. $\dfrac{x^{-1} + x^{-2}}{x^{-3}}$

7. Find the positive roots of the equation

$$2x^3 - 5x^2 - 2x + 6 = 0$$

and evaluate the function $y = 500x^6$ at each root. Round your answers to the nearest integer, but only in the final step.

8. If $f(x) = 7$ for all real numbers x, find

(a) $f(10)$.

(b) $f(0)$.

(c) $f(x + h)$.

(d) $\displaystyle\lim_{x \to 0} \frac{f(x) - f(a)}{x - a}$.

9. Find the derivatives of these functions with respect to x.

(a) $f(x) = \pi$ (b) $f(x) = \pi^2$ (c) $f(x) = \pi^{15}$

10. Find the derivatives of these functions with respect to x using the definition of the derivative.

(a) $f(x) = \dfrac{x}{\pi}$ (b) $f(x) = \dfrac{\pi}{x}$

Section 3.3 Exercises

In Exercises 1–6, find dy/dx.

1. $y = -x^2 + 3$

2. $y = \dfrac{x^3}{3} - x$

3. $y = 2x + 1$

4. $y = x^2 + x + 1$

5. $y = \dfrac{x^3}{3} + \dfrac{x^2}{2} + x$

6. $y = 1 - x + x^2 - x^3$

In Exercises 7–12, find the values of x for which the curve has horizontal tangents.

7. $y = x^3 - 2x^2 + x + 1$

8. $y = x^3 - 4x^2 + x + 2$

9. $y = x^4 - 4x^2 + 1$

10. $y = 4x^3 - 6x^2 - 1$

11. $y = 5x^3 - 3x^5$

12. $y = x^4 - 7x^3 + 2x^2 + 15$

13. Let $y = (x + 1)(x^2 + 1)$. Find dy/dx **(a)** by applying the Product Rule, and **(b)** by multiplying the factors first and then differentiating.

14. Let $y = (x^2 + 3)/x$. Find dy/dx **(a)** by using the Quotient Rule, and **(b)** by first dividing the terms in the numerator by the denominator and then differentiating.

In Exercises 15–22, find dy/dx. (You can support your answer graphically.)

15. $(x^3 + x + 1)(x^4 + x^2 + 1)$

16. $(x^2 + 1)(x^3 + 1)$

17. $y = \dfrac{2x + 5}{3x - 2}$

18. $y = \dfrac{x^2 + 5x - 1}{x^2}$

19. $y = \dfrac{(x - 1)(x^2 + x + 1)}{x^3}$

20. $y = (1 - x)(1 + x^2)^{-1}$

21. $y = \dfrac{x^2}{1 - x^3}$

22. $y = \dfrac{(x + 1)(x + 2)}{(x - 1)(x - 2)}$

23. Suppose u and v are functions of x that are differentiable at $x = 0$, and that $u(0) = 5$, $u'(0) = -3$, $v(0) = -1$, and $v'(0) = 2$. Find the values of the following derivatives at $x = 0$.

(a) $\dfrac{d}{dx}(uv)$

(b) $\dfrac{d}{dx}\left(\dfrac{u}{v}\right)$

(c) $\dfrac{d}{dx}\left(\dfrac{v}{u}\right)$

(d) $\dfrac{d}{dx}(7v - 2u)$

24. Suppose u and v are functions of x that are differentiable at $x = 2$ and that $u(2) = 3$, $u'(2) = -4$, $v(2) = 1$, and $v'(2) = 2$. Find the values of the following derivatives at $x = 2$.

(a) $\dfrac{d}{dx}(uv)$

(b) $\dfrac{d}{dx}\left(\dfrac{u}{v}\right)$

(c) $\dfrac{d}{dx}\left(\dfrac{v}{u}\right)$

(d) $\dfrac{d}{dx}(3u - 2v + 2uv)$

25. Which of the following numbers is the slope of the line tangent to the curve $y = x^2 + 5x$ at $x = 3$?

i. 24   ii. $-5/2$ iii. 11   iv. 8

26. Which of the following numbers is the slope of the line $3x - 2y + 12 = 0$?

i. 6   ii. 3   iii. $3/2$ iv. $2/3$

In Exercises 27 and 28, find an equation for the line tangent to the curve at the given point.

27. $y = \dfrac{x^3 + 1}{2x}, x = 1$

28. $y = \dfrac{x^4 + 2}{x^2}, x = -1$

In Exercises 29–32, find dy/dx.

29. $y = 4x^{-2} - 8x + 1$

30. $y = \dfrac{x^{-4}}{4} - \dfrac{x^{-3}}{3} + \dfrac{x^{-2}}{2} - x^{-1} + 3$

31. $y = \dfrac{\sqrt{x} - 1}{\sqrt{x} + 1}$

32. $y = 2\sqrt{x} - \dfrac{1}{\sqrt{x}}$

In Exercises 33–36, find the first four derivatives of the function.

33. $y = x^4 + x^3 - 2x^2 + x - 5$

34. $y = x^2 + x + 3$

35. $y = x^{-1} + x^2$

36. $y = \dfrac{x + 1}{x}$

37. Find an equation of the line perpendicular to the tangent to the curve $y = x^3 - 3x + 1$ at the point $(2, 3)$.

38. Find the tangents to the curve $y = x^3 + x$ at the points where the slope is 4. What is the smallest slope of the curve? At what value of x does the curve have this slope?

39. Find the points on the curve $y = 2x^3 - 3x^2 - 12x + 20$ where the tangent is parallel to the x-axis.

40. Find the x- and y-intercepts of the line that is tangent to the curve $y = x^3$ at the point $(-2, -8)$.

41. Find the tangents to *Newton's serpentine,*

$$y = \frac{4x}{x^2 + 1},$$

at the origin and the point $(1, 2)$.

42. Find the tangent to the *witch of Agnesi,*

$$y = \frac{8}{4 + x^2},$$

at the point $(2, 1)$.

43. Use the definition of derivative (given in Section 3.1, Equation 1) to show that

(a) $\dfrac{d}{dx}(x) = 1$.

(b) $\dfrac{d}{dx}(-u) = -\dfrac{du}{dx}$.

44. Use the Product Rule to show that

$$\frac{d}{dx}(c \cdot f(x)) = c \cdot \frac{d}{dx}f(x)$$

for any constant c.

45. Devise a rule for $\dfrac{d}{dx}\left(\dfrac{1}{f(x)}\right)$.

When we work with functions of a single variable in mathematics, we often call the independent variable x and the dependent variable y. Applied fields use many different letters, however. Here are some examples.

46. *Cylinder Pressure* If gas in a cylinder is maintained at a constant temperature T, the pressure P is related to the volume V by a formula of the form

$$P = \frac{nRT}{V - nb} - \frac{an^2}{V^2},$$

in which a, b, n, and R are constants. Find dP/dV.

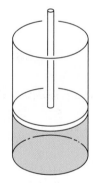

47. *Free Fall* When a rock falls from rest near the surface of the earth, the distance it covers during the first few seconds is given by the equation

$$s = 4.9t^2.$$

In this equation, s is the distance in meters and t is the elapsed time in seconds. Find ds/dt and d^2s/dt^2.

Group Activity In Exercises 48–52, *work in groups of two or three* to solve the problems.

48. *The Body's Reaction to Medicine* The reaction of the body to a dose of medicine can often be represented by an equation of the form

$$R = M^2\left(\frac{C}{2} - \frac{M}{3}\right),$$

where C is a positive constant and M is the amount of medicine absorbed in the blood. If the reaction is a change in blood pressure, R is measured in millimeters of mercury. If the reaction is a change in temperature, R is measured in degrees, and so on.

Find dR/dM. This derivative, as a function of M, is called the sensitivity of the body to medicine. In Chapter 5, we shall see how to find the amount of medicine to which the body is most sensitive. [*Source: Some Mathematical Models in Biology*, Revised Edition, December 1967, PB-202 364, p. 221; distributed by N.T.I.S., U.S. Department of Commerce.]

49. Writing to Learn Recall that the area A of a circle with radius r is πr^2 and that the circumference C is $2\pi r$. Notice that $dA/dr = C$. Explain in terms of geometry why the instantaneous rate of change of the area with respect to the radius should equal the circumference.

50. Writing to Learn Recall that the volume V of a sphere of radius r is $(4/3)\pi r^3$ and that the surface area A is $4\pi r^2$. Notice that $dV/dr = A$. Explain in terms of geometry why the instantaneous rate of change of the volume with respect to the radius should equal the surface area.

51. *Orchard Farming* An apple farmer currently has 156 trees yielding an average of 12 bushels of apples per tree. He is expanding his farm at a rate of 13 trees per year, while improved husbandry is boosting his average annual yield by 1.5 bushels per tree. What is the current (instantaneous) rate of increase of his total annual production of apples? Answer in appropriate units of measure.

52. *Picnic Pavilion Rental* The members of the Blue Boar society always divide the pavilion rental fee for their picnics equally among the members. Currently there are 65 members and the pavilion rents for $250. The pavilion cost is increasing at a rate of $10 per year, while the Blue Boar membership is increasing at a rate of 6 members per year. What is the current (instantaneous) rate of change in each member's share of the pavilion rental fee? Answer in appropriate units of measure.

Standardized Test Questions

53. True or False $\dfrac{d}{dx}(\pi^3) = 3\pi^2$. Justify your answer.

54. True or False The graph of $f(x) = 1/x$ has no horizontal tangents. Justify your answer.

55. Multiple Choice Let $y = uv$ be the product of the functions u and v. Find $y'(1)$ if $u(1) = 2$, $u'(1) = 3$, $v(1) = -1$, and $v'(1) = 1$.

(A) -4 (B) -1 (C) 1 (D) 4 (E) 7

56. Multiple Choice Let $f(x) = x - \dfrac{1}{x}$. Find $f''(x)$.

(A) $1 + \dfrac{1}{x^2}$ (B) $1 - \dfrac{1}{x^2}$ (C) $\dfrac{2}{x^3}$

(D) $-\dfrac{2}{x^3}$ (E) does not exist

57. Multiple Choice Which of the following is $\dfrac{d}{dx}\left(\dfrac{x+1}{x-1}\right)$?

(A) $\dfrac{2}{(x-1)^2}$ (B) 0 (C) $-\dfrac{x^2+1}{x^2}$

(D) $2x - \dfrac{1}{x^2} - 1$ (E) $-\dfrac{2}{(x-1)^2}$

58. Multiple Choice Assume $f(x) = (x^2 - 1)(x^2 + 1)$. Which of the following gives the number of horizontal tangents of f?

(A) 0 (B) 1 (C) 2 (D) 3 (E) 4

Extending the Ideas

59. ***Leibniz's Proof of the Product Rule*** Here's how Leibniz explained the Product Rule in a letter to his colleague John Wallis:

It is useful to consider quantities infinitely small such that when their ratio is sought, they may not be considered zero, but which are rejected as often as they occur with quantities incomparably greater. Thus if we have $x + dx$, dx is rejected. Similarly we cannot have xdx and $dxdx$ standing together, as xdx is incomparably greater than $dxdx$. Hence if we are to differentiate uv, we write

$$d(uv) = (u + du)(v + dv) - uv$$
$$= uv + vdu + udv + dudv - uv$$
$$= vdu + udv.$$

Answer the following questions about Leibniz's proof.

(a) What does Leibniz mean by a quantity being "rejected"?

(b) What happened to $dudv$ in the last step of Leibniz's proof?

(c) Divide both sides of Leibniz's formula
$$d(uv) = vdu + udv$$
by the differential dx. What formula results?

(d) Why would the critics of Leibniz's time have objected to dividing both sides of the equation by dx?

(e) Leibniz had a similar simple (but not-so-clean) proof of the Quotient Rule. Can you reconstruct it?

Quick Quiz for AP* Preparation: Sections 3.1–3.3

1. Multiple Choice Let $f(x) = |x + 1|$. Which of the following statements about f are true?

   I. f is continuous at $x = -1$.

   II. f is differentiable at $x = -1$.

   III. f has a corner at $x = -1$.

(A) I only   (B) II only   (C) III only

(D) I and III only   (E) I and II only

2. Multiple Choice If the line normal to the graph of f at the point $(1, 2)$ passes through the point $(-1, 1)$, then which of the following gives the value of $f'(1) = $?

(A) -2 (B) 2 (C) $-1/2$ (D) $1/2$ (E) 3

3. Multiple Choice Find dy/dx if $y = \dfrac{4x - 3}{2x + 1}$.

(A) $\dfrac{10}{(4x-3)^2}$ (B) $-\dfrac{10}{(4x-3)^2}$ (C) $\dfrac{10}{(2x+1)^2}$

(D) $-\dfrac{10}{(2x+1)^2}$ (E) 2

4. Free Response Let $f(x) = x^4 - 4x^2$.

(a) Find all the points where f has horizontal tangents.

(b) Find an equation of the tangent line at $x = 1$.

(c) Find an equation of the normal line at $x = 1$.

3.4   Velocity and Other Rates of Change

You will be able to interpret the derivative as representing velocity and other rates of change.

- Instantaneous rates of change
- Motion on a line
- Acceleration as the second derivative
- Modeling vertical motion and particle motion
- The derivative as a measure of sensitivity to change
- Marginal cost and marginal revenue

Instantaneous Rates of Change

In this section we examine some applications in which derivatives as functions are used to represent the rates at which things change in the world around us. It is natural to think of change as change with respect to time, but other variables can be treated in the same way. For example, a physician may want to know how change in dosage affects the body's response to a drug. An economist may want to study how the cost of producing steel varies with the number of tons produced.

If we interpret the difference quotient

$$\frac{f(x + h) - f(x)}{h}$$

as the average rate of change of the function f over the interval from x to $x + h$, we can interpret its limit as h approaches 0 to be the rate at which f is changing at the point x.

DEFINITION   Instantaneous Rate of Change

The **(instantaneous) rate of change** of f with respect to x at a is the derivative

$$f'(a) = \lim_{h \to 0} \frac{f(a + h) - f(a)}{h},$$

provided the limit exists.

It is conventional to use the word *instantaneous* even when x does not represent time. The word, however, is frequently omitted in practice. When we say *rate of change*, we mean *instantaneous rate of change*.

EXAMPLE 1   Enlarging Circles

(a) Find the rate of change of the area A of a circle with respect to its radius r.

(b) Evaluate the rate of change of A at $r = 5$ and at $r = 10$.

(c) If r is measured in inches and A is measured in square inches, what units would be appropriate for dA/dr?

SOLUTION

The area of a circle is related to its radius by the equation $A = \pi r^2$.

(a) The (instantaneous) rate of change of A with respect to r is

$$\frac{dA}{dr} = \frac{d}{dr}(\pi r^2) = \pi \cdot 2r = 2\pi r.$$

(b) At $r = 5$, the rate is 10π ($10\pi \approx 31.416$). At $r = 10$, the rate is 20π ($20\pi \approx 62.832$).

Notice that the rate of change gets bigger as r gets bigger. As can be seen in Figure 3.21, the same change in radius brings about a bigger change in area as the circles grow radially away from the center.

(c) The appropriate units for dA/dr are square inches (of area) per inch (of radius).

Now Try Exercise 1.

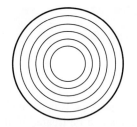

Figure 3.21 The same change in radius brings about a larger change in area as the circles grow radially away from the center. (Example 1, Exploration 1)

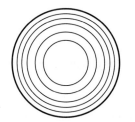

Figure 3.22 Which is the more appropriate model for the growth of rings in a tree—the circles here or those in Figure 3.21? (Exploration 1)

EXPLORATION 1 Growth Rings on a Tree

The phenomenon observed in Example 1, that the rate of change in area of a circle with respect to its radius gets larger as the radius gets larger, is reflected in nature in many ways. When trees grow, they add layers of wood directly under the inner bark during the growing season, then form a darker, protective layer for protection during the winter. This results in concentric rings that can be seen in a cross-sectional slice of the trunk. The age of the tree can be determined by counting the rings.

1. Look at the concentric rings in Figure 3.21 and Figure 3.22. Which is a better model for the pattern of growth rings in a tree? Is it likely that a tree could find the nutrients and light necessary to increase its amount of growth every year?
2. Considering how trees grow, explain why the change in *area* of the rings remains relatively constant from year to year.
3. If the change in area is constant, and if

$$\frac{dA}{dr} = \frac{\text{change in area}}{\text{change in radius}} = 2\pi r,$$

explain why the change in radius must get smaller as r gets bigger.

Motion Along a Line

Suppose that an object is moving along a coordinate line (say an s-axis) so that we know its position s on that line as a function of time t:

$$s = f(t)$$

The **displacement** of the object over the time interval from t to $t + \Delta t$ is

$$\Delta s = f(t + \Delta t) - f(t)$$

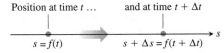

Position at time t ...   and at time $t + \Delta t$

$s = f(t)$ $s + \Delta s = f(t + \Delta t)$

Figure 3.23 The positions of an object moving along a coordinate line at time t and shortly later at time $t + \Delta t$.

(Figure 3.23) and the **average velocity** of the object over that time interval is

$$v_{\text{av}} = \frac{\text{displacement}}{\text{travel time}} = \frac{\Delta s}{\Delta t} = \frac{f(t + \Delta t) - f(t)}{\Delta t}.$$

To find the object's velocity at the exact instant t, we take the limit of the average velocity over the interval from t to $t + \Delta t$ as Δt shrinks to zero. The limit is the derivative of f with respect to t.

DEFINITION **Instantaneous Velocity**

The **(instantaneous) velocity** is the derivative of the position function $s = f(t)$ with respect to time. At time t the velocity is

$$v(t) = \frac{ds}{dt} = \lim_{\Delta t \to 0} \frac{f(t + \Delta t) - f(t)}{\Delta t}.$$

EXAMPLE 2 Finding the Velocity of a Race Car

Figure 3.24 shows the time-to-distance graph of a 1996 Riley & Scott Mk III-Olds WSC race car. The slope of the secant *PQ* is the average velocity for the 3-second interval from $t = 2$ to $t = 5$ sec, in this case, about 100 ft/sec or 68 mph. The slope of the tangent at *P* is the speedometer reading at $t = 2$ sec, about 57 ft/sec or 39 mph. The acceleration for the period shown is a nearly constant 28.5 ft/sec during each second, which is about $0.89g$ where *g* is the acceleration due to gravity. The race car's top speed is an estimated 190 mph. *Source: Road and Track,* March 1997.

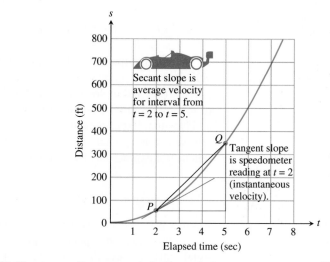

Figure 3.24 The time-to-distance graph for Example 2.

Now Try Exercise 7.

Besides telling how fast an object is moving, velocity tells the direction of motion. When the object is moving forward (when *s* is increasing), the velocity is positive; when the object is moving backward (when *s* is decreasing), the velocity is negative.

If we drive to a friend's house and back at 30 mph, the speedometer will show 30 on the way over but will not show -30 on the way back, even though our distance from home is decreasing. The speedometer always shows *speed,* which is the absolute value of velocity. Speed measures the rate of motion regardless of direction.

DEFINITION Speed

Speed is the absolute value of velocity.

$$\text{Speed} = |v(t)| = \left|\frac{ds}{dt}\right|$$

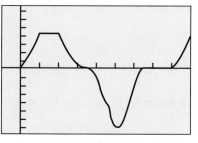

[−4, 36] by [−7.5, 7.5]

Figure 3.25 A student's velocity graph from data recorded by a motion detector. (Example 3)

EXAMPLE 3 Reading a Velocity Graph

A student walks around in front of a motion detector that records her velocity at 1-second intervals for 36 seconds. She stores the data in her graphing calculator and uses it to generate the time-velocity graph shown in Figure 3.25. Describe her motion as a function of time by reading the velocity graph. When is her *speed* a maximum?

SOLUTION

The student moves forward for the first 14 seconds, moves backward for the next 12 seconds, stands still for 6 seconds, and then moves forward again. She achieves her maximum speed at $t \approx 20$, while moving backward.

Now Try Exercise 9.

The rate at which a body's velocity changes is called the body's *acceleration*. The acceleration measures how quickly the body picks up or loses speed.

DEFINITION **Acceleration**

Acceleration is the derivative of velocity with respect to time. If a body's velocity at time t is $v(t) = ds/dt$, then the body's acceleration at time t is

$$a(t) = \frac{dv}{dt} = \frac{d^2s}{dt^2}.$$

The earliest questions that motivated the discovery of calculus were concerned with velocity and acceleration, particularly the motion of freely falling bodies under the force of gravity. (See Examples 1 and 2 in Section 2.1.) The mathematical description of this type of motion captured the imagination of many great scientists, including Aristotle, Galileo, and Newton. Experimental and theoretical investigations revealed that the distance a body released from rest falls freely is proportional to the square of the amount of time it has fallen. We express this by saying that

$$s = \frac{1}{2}gt^2,$$

where s is distance, g is the acceleration due to Earth's gravity, and t is time. The value of g in the equation depends on the units used to measure s and t. With t in seconds (the usual unit), we have the following values:

Free-fall Constants (Earth)

English units: $g = 32\dfrac{\text{ft}}{\text{sec}^2}$, $s = \dfrac{1}{2}(32)t^2 = 16t^2$ (s in feet)

Metric units: $g = 9.8\dfrac{\text{m}}{\text{sec}^2}$, $s = \dfrac{1}{2}(9.8)t^2 = 4.9t^2$ (s in meters)

The abbreviation ft/sec^2 is read "feet per second squared" or "feet per second per second," and m/sec^2 is read "meters per second squared."

EXAMPLE 4 Modeling Vertical Motion

A dynamite blast propels a heavy rock straight up with a launch velocity of 160 ft/sec (about 109 mph) (Figure 3.26a). It reaches a height of $s = 160t - 16t^2$ ft after t seconds.

(a) How high does the rock go?

(b) What is the velocity and speed of the rock when it is 256 ft above the ground on the way up? on the way down?

(c) What is the acceleration of the rock at any time t during its flight (after the blast)?

(d) When does the rock hit the ground?

SOLUTION

In the coordinate system we have chosen, s measures height from the ground up, so velocity is positive on the way up and negative on the way down.

continued

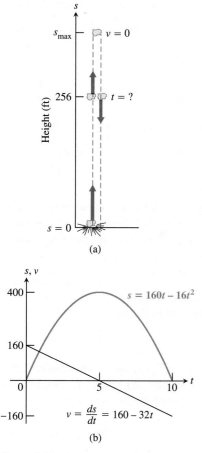

Figure 3.26 (a) The rock in Example 4. (b) The graphs of s and v as functions of time t, showing that s is largest when $v = ds/dt = 0$. (The graph of s is *not* the path of the rock; it is a plot of height as a function of time.) (Example 4)

(a) The instant when the rock is at its highest point is the one instant during the flight when the velocity is 0. At any time t, the velocity is

$$v = \frac{ds}{dt} = \frac{d}{dt}(160t - 16t^2) = 160 - 32t \text{ ft/sec}.$$

The velocity is zero when $160 - 32t = 0$, or at $t = 5$ sec.

The maximum height is the height of the rock at $t = 5$ sec. That is,

$$s_{max} = s(5) = 160(5) - 16(5)^2 = 400 \text{ ft}.$$

See Figure 3.26b.

(b) To find the velocity when the height is 256 ft, we determine the two values of t for which $s(t) = 256$ ft.

$$s(t) = 160t - 16t^2 = 256$$
$$16t^2 - 160t + 256 = 0$$
$$16(t^2 - 10t + 16) = 0$$
$$(t - 2)(t - 8) = 0$$
$$t = 2 \text{ sec} \quad \text{or} \quad t = 8 \text{ sec}$$

The velocity of the rock at each of these times is

$$v(2) = 160 - 32(2) = 96 \text{ ft/sec},$$
$$v(8) = 160 - 32(8) = -96 \text{ ft/sec}$$

At both instants, the speed of the rock is 96 ft/sec.

(c) At any time during its flight after the explosion, the rock's acceleration is

$$a = \frac{dv}{dt} = \frac{d}{dt}(160 - 32t) = -32 \text{ ft/sec}^2.$$

The acceleration is always downward. When the rock is rising, it is slowing down; when it is falling, it is speeding up.

(d) The rock hits the ground at the positive time for which $s = 0$. The equation $160t - 16t^2 = 0$ has two solutions: $t = 0$ and $t = 10$. The blast initiated the flight of the rock from ground level at $t = 0$. The rock returned to the ground 10 seconds later.

Now Try Exercise 13.

EXAMPLE 5 Studying Particle Motion

A particle moves along a line so that its position at any time $t \geq 0$ is given by the function $s(t) = t^2 - 4t + 3$, where s is measured in meters and t is measured in seconds.

(a) Find the displacement of the particle during the first 2 seconds.

(b) Find the average velocity of the particle during the first 4 seconds.

(c) Find the instantaneous velocity of the particle when $t = 4$.

(d) Find the acceleration of the particle when $t = 4$.

(e) Describe the motion of the particle. At what values of t does the particle change directions?

(f) Use parametric graphing to view the motion of the particle on the horizontal line $y = 2$.

continued

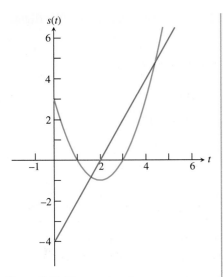

Figure 3.27 The graphs of $s(t) = t^2 - 4t + 3, t \geq 0$ (blue) and its derivative $v(t) = 2t - 4, t \geq 0$ (red). (Example 5)

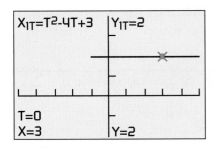

$[-5, 5]$ by $[-2, 4]$

Figure 3.28 The graph of $X_{1T} = T^2 - 4T + 3$, $Y_{1T} = 2$ in parametric mode. (Example 5)

SOLUTION

(a) The displacement is given by $s(2) - s(0) = (-1) - 3 = -4$. This value means that the particle is 4 units left of where it started.

(b) The average velocity we seek is

$$\frac{s(4) - s(0)}{4 - 0} = \frac{3 - 3}{4} = 0 \text{ m/sec.}$$

(c) The velocity $v(t)$ at any time t is $v(t) = ds/dt = 2t - 4$. So $v(4) = 4$ m/sec.

(d) The acceleration $a(t)$ at any time t is $a(t) = dv/dt = 2$ m/sec^2. So $a(4) = 2$.

(e) The graphs of $s(t) = t^2 - 4t + 3$ for $t \geq 0$ and its derivative $v(t) = 2t - 4$ shown in Figure 3.27 will help us analyze the motion.

For $0 \leq t < 2$, $v(t) < 0$, so the particle is moving to the left. Notice that $s(t)$ is decreasing. The particle starts ($t = 0$) at $s = 3$ and moves left, arriving at the origin $t = 1$ when $s = 0$. The particle continues moving to the left until it reaches the point $s = -1$ at $t = 2$.

At $t = 2$, $v = 0$, so the particle is at rest.

For $t > 2$, $v(t) > 0$, so the particle is moving to the right. Notice that $s(t)$ is increasing. In this interval, the particle starts at $s = -1$, moving to the right through the origin and continuing to the right for the rest of time.

The particle changes direction at $t = 2$ when $v = 0$.

(f) Enter $X_{1T} = T^2 - 4T + 3$, $Y_{1T} = 2$ in parametric mode and graph in the window $[-5, 5]$ by $[-2, 4]$ with Tmin = 0, Tmax = 10 (it really should be ∞), and Xscl=Yscl=1 (Figure 3.28). By using TRACE you can follow the path of the particle. You will learn more ways to visualize motion in Explorations 2 and 3.

Now Try Exercise 19.

EXPLORATION 2 Modeling Horizontal Motion

The position (x-coordinate) of a particle moving on the horizontal line $y = 2$ is given by $x(t) = 4t^3 - 16t^2 + 15t$ for $t \geq 0$.

1. Graph the parametric equations $x_1(t) = 4t^3 - 16t^2 + 15t, y_1(t) = 2$ in $[-4, 6]$ by $[-3, 5]$. Use TRACE to support that the particle starts at the point $(0, 2)$, moves to the right, then to the left, and finally to the right. At what times does the particle reverse direction?

2. Graph the parametric equations $x_2(t) = x_1(t), y_2(t) = t$ in the same viewing window. Explain how this graph shows the back and forth motion of the particle. Use this graph to find when the particle reverses direction.

3. Graph the parametric equations $x_3(t) = t, y_3(t) = x_1(t)$ in the same viewing window. Explain how this graph shows the back and forth motion of the particle. Use this graph to find when the particle reverses direction.

4. Use the methods in parts 1, 2, and 3 to represent and describe the *velocity* of the particle.

EXPLORATION 3 Seeing Motion on a Graphing Calculator

The graphs in Figure 3.26b give us plenty of information about the flight of the rock in Example 4, but neither graph shows the path of the rock in flight. We can simulate the moving rock by graphing the parametric equations

$$x_1(t) = 3(t < 5) + 3.1(t \geq 5), \qquad y_1(t) = 160t - 16t^2$$

in dot mode.

This will show the upward flight of the rock along the vertical line $x = 3$, and the downward flight of the rock along the line $x = 3.1$.

1. To see the flight of the rock from beginning to end, what should we use for tMin and tMax in our graphing window?
2. Set xMin $= 0$, xMax $= 6$, and yMin $= -10$. Use the results from Example 4 to determine an appropriate value for yMax. (You will want the entire flight of the rock to fit within the vertical range of the screen.)
3. Set tStep initially at 0.1. (A higher number will make the simulation move faster. A lower number will slow it down.)
4. Can you explain why the grapher actually slows down when the rock would slow down, and speeds up when the rock would speed up?

Sensitivity to Change

We introduced sensitivity in Section 2.4 as a measure of how change in one variable affects the change in another variable. The derivative gives us an easy way to compute this sensitivity.

EXAMPLE 6 Sensitivity to Change

The Austrian monk Gregor Johann Mendel (1822–1884), working with garden peas and other plants, provided the first scientific explanation of hybridization. His careful records showed that if p (a number between 0 and 1) is the relative frequency of the gene for smooth skin in peas (dominant) and $(1 - p)$ is the relative frequency of the gene for wrinkled skin in peas (recessive), then the proportion of smooth-skinned peas in the next generation will be

$$y = 2p(1 - p) + p^2 = 2p - p^2.$$

Compare the graphs of y and dy/dp to determine what values of y are more sensitive to a change in p. The graph of y versus p in Figure 3.29a suggests that the value of y is more sensitive to a change in p when p is small than it is to a change in p when p is large. Indeed, this is borne out by the derivative graph in Figure 3.29b, which shows that dy/dp is close to 2 when p is near 0 and close to 0 when p is near 1.

Now Try Exercise 25.

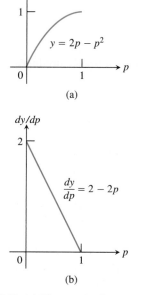

Figure 3.29 (a) The graph of $y = 2p - p^2$ describing the proportion of smooth-skinned peas. (b) The graph of dy/dp. (Example 6)

Derivatives in Economics

Engineers use the terms *velocity* and *acceleration* to refer to the derivatives of functions describing motion. Economists, too, have a specialized vocabulary for rates of change and derivatives. They call them *marginals*.

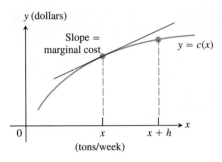

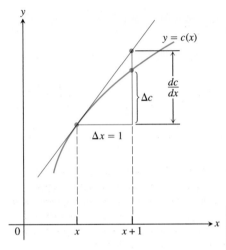

Figure 3.30 Weekly steel production: $c(x)$ is the cost of producing x tons per week. The cost of producing an additional h tons per week is $c(x + h) - c(x)$.

Figure 3.31 Because dc/dx is the slope of the tangent at x, the marginal cost dc/dx approximates the extra cost Δc of producing $\Delta x = 1$ more unit.

In a manufacturing operation, *the cost of production $c(x)$ is a function of x*, the number of units produced. The *marginal cost of production* is the rate of change of cost with respect to the level of production, so it is dc/dx.

Suppose $c(x)$ represents the dollars needed to produce x tons of steel in one week. It costs more to produce $x + h$ tons per week, and the cost difference divided by h is the average cost of producing each additional ton.

$$\frac{c(x + h) - c(x)}{h} = \begin{cases} \text{the average cost of each of the} \\ \text{additional } h \text{ tons produced} \end{cases}$$

The limit of this ratio as $h \to 0$ is the **marginal cost** of producing more steel per week when the current production is x tons (Figure 3.30).

$$\frac{dc}{dx} = \lim_{h \to 0} \frac{c(x + h) - c(x)}{h} = \text{marginal cost of production}$$

Sometimes the marginal cost of production is loosely defined to be the extra cost of producing one more unit,

$$\frac{\Delta c}{\Delta x} = \frac{c(x + 1) - c(x)}{1},$$

which is approximated by the value of dc/dx at x. This approximation is acceptable if the slope of c does not change quickly near x, for then the difference quotient is close to its limit dc/dx even if $\Delta x = 1$ (Figure 3.31). The approximation works best for large values of x.

EXAMPLE 7 Marginal Cost and Marginal Revenue

Suppose it costs

$$c(x) = x^3 - 6x^2 + 15x$$

dollars to produce x radiators when 8 to 10 radiators are produced, and that

$$r(x) = x^3 - 3x^2 + 12x$$

gives the dollar revenue from selling x radiators. Your shop currently produces 10 radiators a day. Find the marginal cost and **marginal revenue.**

SOLUTION

The marginal cost of producing one more radiator a day when 10 are being produced is $c'(10)$.

$$c'(x) = \frac{d}{dx}(x^3 - 6x^2 + 15x) = 3x^2 - 12x + 15$$

$$c'(10) = 3(100) - 12(10) + 15 = 195 \text{ dollars}$$

The marginal revenue is

$$r'(x) = \frac{d}{dx}(x^3 - 3x^2 + 12x) = 3x^2 - 6x + 12,$$

so,

$$r'(10) = 3(100) - 6(10) + 12 = 252 \text{ dollars}.$$

Now Try Exercises 27 and 28.

Quick Review 3.4 *(For help, go to Sections 1.2, 3.1, and 3.3.)*

Exercise numbers with a gray background indicate problems that the authors have designed to be solved *without a calculator*.

In Exercises 1–10, answer the questions about the graph of the quadratic function $y = f(x) = -16x^2 + 160x - 256$ by analyzing the equation algebraically. Then support your answers graphically.

1. Does the graph open upward or downward?

2. What is the *y*-intercept?

3. What are the *x*-intercepts?

4. What is the range of the function?

5. What point is the vertex of the parabola?

6. At what *x* values does $f(x) = 80$?

7. For what *x* value does $dy/dx = 100$?

8. On what interval is $dy/dx > 0$?

9. Find $\lim_{h \to 0} \dfrac{f(3 + h) - f(3)}{h}$.

10. Find d^2y/dx^2 at $x = 7$.

Section 3.4 Exercises

1. (a) Write the volume V of a cube as a function of the side length s.

(b) Find the (instantaneous) rate of change of the volume V with respect to a side s.

(c) Evaluate the rate of change of V at $s = 1$ and $s = 5$.

(d) If s is measured in inches and V is measured in cubic inches, what units would be appropriate for dV/ds?

2. (a) Write the area A of a circle as a function of the circumference C.

(b) Find the (instantaneous) rate of change of the area A with respect to the circumference C.

(c) Evaluate the rate of change of A at $C = \pi$ and $C = 6\pi$.

(d) If C is measured in inches and A is measured in square inches, what units would be appropriate for dA/dC?

3. (a) Write the area A of an equilateral triangle as a function of the side length s.

(b) Find the (instantaneous) rate of change of the area A with respect to a side s.

(c) Evaluate the rate of change of A at $s = 2$ and $s = 10$.

(d) If s is measured in inches and A is measured in square inches, what units would be appropriate for dA/ds?

4. A square of side length s is inscribed in a circle of radius r.

(a) Write the area A of the square as a function of the radius r of the circle.

(b) Find the (instantaneous) rate of change of the area A with respect to the radius r of the circle.

(c) Evaluate the rate of change of A at $r = 1$ and $r = 8$.

(d) If r is measured in inches and A is measured in square inches, what units would be appropriate for dA/dr?

Group Activity In Exercises 5 and 6, the coordinates s of a moving body for various values of t are given. **(a)** Plot s versus t on coordinate paper, and sketch a smooth curve through the given points. **(b)** Assuming that this smooth curve represents the motion of the body, estimate the velocity at $t = 1.0$, $t = 2.5$, and $t = 3.5$.

5.

t (sec)	0	0.5	1.0	1.5	2.0	2.5	3.0	3.5	4.0
s (ft)	12.5	26	36.5	44	48.5	50	48.5	44	36.5

6.

t (sec)	0	0.5	1.0	1.5	2.0	2.5	3.0	3.5	4.0
s (ft)	3.5	−4	−8.5	−10	−8.5	−4	3.5	14	27.5

7. Group Activity Fruit Flies *(Example 2, Section 2.4 continued)* Populations starting out in closed environments grow slowly at first, when there are relatively few members, then more rapidly as the number of reproducing individuals increases and resources are still abundant, then slowly again as the population reaches the carrying capacity of the environment.

(a) Use the graphical technique of Section 3.1, Example 3, to graph the derivative of the fruit fly population introduced in Section 2.4. The graph of the population is reproduced below. What units should be used on the horizontal and vertical axes for the derivative's graph?

(b) During what days does the population seem to be increasing fastest? slowest?

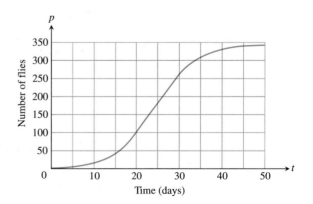

8. *Draining a Tank* The number of gallons of water in a tank t minutes after the tank has started to drain is $Q(t) = 200(30 - t)^2$. How fast is the water running out at the end of 10 min? What is the average rate at which the water flows out during the first 10 min?

9. *Particle Motion* The accompanying figure shows the velocity $v = f(t)$ of a particle moving on a coordinate line.

  (a) When does the particle move forward? move backward? speed up? slow down?

  (b) When is the particle's acceleration positive? negative? zero?

  (c) When does the particle move at its greatest speed?

  (d) When does the particle stand still for more than an instant?

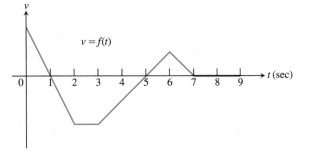

10. *Particle Motion* A particle P moves on the number line shown in part (a) of the accompanying figure. Part (b) shows the position of P as a function of time t.

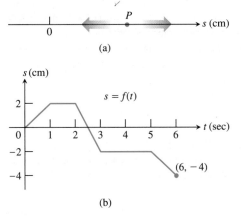

  (a) When is P moving to the left? moving to the right? standing still?

  (b) Graph the particle's velocity and speed (where defined).

11. *Particle Motion* The accompanying figure shows the velocity $v = ds/dt = f(t)$ (m/sec) of a body moving along a coordinate line.

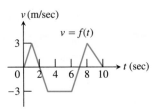

(a) When does the body reverse direction?

(b) When (approximately) is the body moving at a constant speed?

(c) Graph the body's speed for $0 \le t \le 10$.

(d) Graph the acceleration, where defined.

12. *Thoroughbred Racing* A racehorse is running a 10-furlong race. (A furlong is 220 yards, although we will use furlongs and seconds as our units in this exercise.) As the horse passes each furlong marker (F), a steward records the time elapsed (t) since the beginning of the race, as shown in the table below:

F	0	1	2	3	4	5	6	7	8	9	10
t	0	20	33	46	59	73	86	100	112	124	135

(a) How long does it take the horse to finish the race?

(b) What is the average speed of the horse over the first 5 furlongs?

(c) What is the approximate speed of the horse as it passes the 3-furlong marker?

(d) During which portion of the race is the horse running the fastest?

(e) During which portion of the race is the horse accelerating the fastest?

13. *Lunar Projectile Motion* A rock thrown vertically upward from the surface of the moon at a velocity of 24 m/sec (about 86 km/h) reaches a height of $s = 24t - 0.8t^2$ meters in t seconds.

(a) Find the rock's velocity and acceleration as functions of time. (The acceleration in this case is the acceleration of gravity on the moon.)

(b) How long did it take the rock to reach its highest point?

(c) How high did the rock go?

(d) When did the rock reach half its maximum height?

(e) How long was the rock aloft?

14. *Free Fall* The equations for free fall near the surfaces of Mars and Jupiter (s in meters, t in seconds) are: Mars, $s = 1.86t^2$; Jupiter, $s = 11.44t^2$. How long would it take a rock falling from rest to reach a velocity of 16.6 m/sec (about 60 km/h) on each planet?

15. *Projectile Motion* On Earth, in the absence of air, the rock in Exercise 13 would reach a height of $s = 24t - 4.9t^2$ meters in t seconds. How high would the rock go?

16. *Speeding Bullet* A bullet fired straight up from the moon's surface would reach a height of $s = 832t - 2.6t^2$ ft after t sec. On Earth, in the absence of air, its height would be $s = 832t - 16t^2$ ft after t sec. How long would it take the bullet to get back down in each case?

17. *Parametric Graphing* Devise a grapher simulation of the problem situation in Exercise 16. Use it to support the answers obtained analytically.

18. *Launching a Rocket* When a model rocket is launched, the propellant burns for a few seconds, accelerating the rocket upward. After burnout, the rocket coasts upward for a while and then begins to fall. A small explosive charge pops out a parachute shortly after the rocket starts downward. The parachute slows the rocket to keep it from breaking when it lands. This graph shows velocity data from the flight.

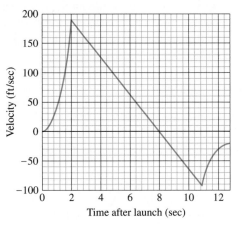

Use the graph to answer the following.

(a) How fast was the rocket climbing when the engine stopped?

(b) For how many seconds did the engine burn?

(c) When did the rocket reach its highest point? What was its velocity then?

(d) When did the parachute pop out? How fast was the rocket falling then?

(e) How long did the rocket fall before the parachute opened?

(f) When was the rocket's acceleration greatest? When was the acceleration constant?

19. *Particle Motion* A particle moves along a line so that its position at any time $t \geq 0$ is given by the function

$$s(t) = t^2 - 3t + 2,$$

where s is measured in meters and t is measured in seconds.

(a) Find the displacement during the first 5 seconds.

(b) Find the average velocity during the first 5 seconds.

(c) Find the instantaneous velocity when $t = 4$.

(d) Find the acceleration of the particle when $t = 4$.

(e) At what values of t does the particle change direction?

(f) Where is the particle when s is a minimum?

20. *Particle Motion* A particle moves along a line so that its position at any time $t \geq 0$ is given by the function $s(t) = -t^3 + 7t^2 - 14t + 8$ where s is measured in meters and t is measured in seconds.

(a) Find the instantaneous velocity at any time t.

(b) Find the acceleration of the particle at any time t.

(c) When is the particle at rest?

(d) Describe the motion of the particle. At what values of t does the particle change directions?

21. *Particle Motion* A particle moves along a line so that its position at any time $t \geq 0$ is given by the function $s(t) = (t - 2)^2(t - 4)$ where s is measured in meters and t is measured in seconds.

(a) Find the instantaneous velocity at any time t.

(b) Find the acceleration of the particle at any time t.

(c) When is the particle at rest?

(d) Describe the motion of the particle. At what values of t does the particle change directions?

22. *Particle Motion* A particle moves along a line so that its position at any time $t \geq 0$ is given by the function $s(t) = t^3 - 6t^2 + 8t + 2$ where s is measured in meters and t is measured in seconds.

(a) Find the instantaneous velocity at any time t.

(b) Find the acceleration of the particle at any time t.

(c) When is the particle at rest?

(d) Describe the motion of the particle. At what values of t does the particle change directions?

23. *Particle Motion* The position of a body at time t sec is $s = t^3 - 6t^2 + 9t$ m. Find the body's acceleration each time the velocity is zero.

24. *Finding Speed* A body's velocity at time t sec is $v = 2t^3 - 9t^2 + 12t - 5$ m/sec. Find the body's speed each time the acceleration is zero.

25. *Draining a Tank* It takes 12 hours to drain a storage tank by opening the valve at the bottom. The depth y of fluid in the tank t hours after the valve is opened is given by the formula

$$y = 6\left(1 - \frac{t}{12}\right)^2 \text{ m}.$$

(a) Find the rate dy/dt (m/h) at which the water level is changing at time t.

(b) When is the fluid level in the tank falling fastest? slowest? What are the values of dy/dt at these times?

(c) Graph y and dy/dt together and discuss the behavior of y in relation to the signs and values of dy/dt.

26. *Moving Truck* The graph here shows the position s of a truck traveling on a highway. The truck starts at $t = 0$ and returns 15 hours later at $t = 15$.

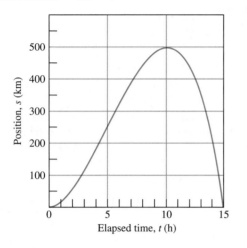

(a) Use the technique described in Section 3.1, Example 3, to graph the truck's velocity $v = ds/dt$ for $0 \le t \le 15$. Then repeat the process, with the velocity curve, to graph the truck's acceleration dv/dt.

(b) Suppose $s = 15t^2 - t^3$. Graph ds/dt and d^2s/dt^2, and compare your graphs with those in part (a).

27. *Marginal Cost* Suppose that the dollar cost of producing x washing machines is $c(x) = 2000 + 100x - 0.1x^2$.

(a) Find the average cost of producing 100 washing machines.

(b) Find the marginal cost when 100 machines are produced.

(c) Show that the marginal cost when 100 washing machines are produced is approximately the cost of producing one more washing machine after the first 100 have been made, by calculating the latter cost directly.

28. *Marginal Revenue* Suppose the weekly revenue in dollars from selling x custom-made office desks is

$$r(x) = 2000\left(1 - \frac{1}{x + 1}\right).$$

(a) Draw the graph of r. What values of x make sense in this problem situation?

(b) Find the marginal revenue when x desks are sold.

(c) Use the function $r'(x)$ to estimate the increase in revenue that will result from increasing sales from 5 desks a week to 6 desks a week.

(d) **Writing to Learn** Find the limit of $r'(x)$ as $x \to \infty$. How would you interpret this number?

29. *Finding Profit* The monthly profit (in thousands of dollars) of a software company is given by

$$P(x) = \frac{10}{1 + 50 \cdot 2^{5-0.1x}},$$

where x is the number of software packages sold.

(a) Graph $P(x)$.

(b) What values of x make sense in the problem situation?

(c) Use NDER to graph $P'(x)$. For what values of x is P relatively sensitive to changes in x?

(d) What is the profit when the marginal profit is greatest?

(e) What is the marginal profit when 50 units are sold? 100 units, 125 units, 150 units, 175 units, and 300 units?

(f) What is $\lim_{x \to \infty} P(x)$? What is the maximum profit possible?

(g) **Writing to Learn** Is there a practical explanation to the maximum profit answer? Explain your reasoning.

30. In Step 1 of Exploration 2, at what time is the particle at the point $(5, 2)$?

31. Group Activity The graphs in Figure 3.32 show as functions of time t the position s, velocity $v = ds/dt$, and acceleration $a = d^2s/dt^2$ of a body moving along a coordinate line. Which graph is which? Give reasons for your answers.

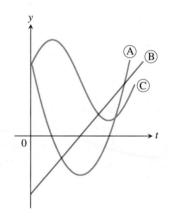

Figure 3.32 The graphs for Exercise 31.

32. Group Activity The graphs in Figure 3.33 show as functions of time t the position s, the velocity $v = ds/dt$, and the acceleration $a = d^2s/dt^2$ of a body moving along a coordinate line. Which graph is which? Give reasons for your answers.

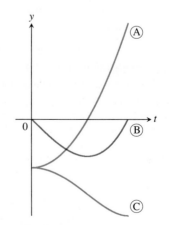

Figure 3.33 The graphs for Exercise 32.

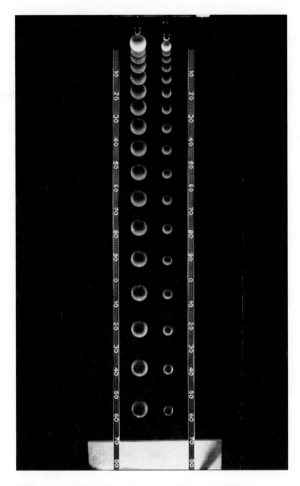

Figure 3.34 Two balls falling from rest. (Exercise 38)

33. *Pisa by Parachute* *(continuation of Exercise 18)* In 1988, Mike McCarthy parachuted 179 ft from the top of the Tower of Pisa. Make a rough sketch to show the shape of the graph of his downward velocity during the jump.

34. *Inflating a Balloon* The volume $V = (4/3)\pi r^3$ of a spherical balloon changes with the radius.

   (a) At what rate does the volume change with respect to the radius when $r = 2$ ft?

   (b) By approximately how much does the volume increase when the radius changes from 2 to 2.2 ft?

35. *Volcanic Lava Fountains* Although the November 1959 Kilauea Iki eruption on the island of Hawaii began with a line of fountains along the wall of the crater, activity was later confined to a single vent in the crater's floor, which at one point shot lava 1900 ft straight into the air (a world record). What was the lava's exit velocity in feet per second? in miles per hour? [*Hint:* If v_0 is the exit velocity of a particle of lava, its height t seconds later will be $s = v_0 t - 16t^2$ feet. Begin by finding the time at which $ds/dt = 0$. Neglect air resistance.]

36. **Writing to Learn** Suppose you are looking at a graph of velocity as a function of time. How can you estimate the acceleration at a given point in time?

37. *Particle Motion* The position (x-coordinate) of a particle moving on the line $y = 2$ is given by $x(t) = 2t^3 - 13t^2 + 22t - 5$ where t is time in seconds.

   (a) Describe the motion of the particle for $t \geq 0$.

   (b) When does the particle speed up? slow down?

   (c) When does the particle change direction?

   (d) When is the particle at rest?

   (e) Describe the velocity and speed of the particle.

   (f) When is the particle at the point $(5, 2)$?

38. *Falling Objects* The multiflash photograph in Figure 3.34 shows two balls falling from rest. The vertical rulers are marked in centimeters. Use the equation $s = 490t^2$ (the free-fall equation for s in centimeters and t in seconds) to answer the following questions.

   (a) How long did it take the balls to fall the first 160 cm? What was their average velocity for the period?

   (b) How fast were the balls falling when they reached the 160-cm mark? What was their acceleration then?

   (c) About how fast was the light flashing (flashes per second)?

39. **Writing to Learn** Explain how the Sum and Difference Rule (Rule 4 in Section 3.3) can be used to derive a formula for *marginal profit* in terms of marginal revenue and marginal cost.

Standardized Test Questions

You may use a graphing calculator to solve the following problems.

40. **True or False** The speed of a particle at $t = a$ is given by the value of the velocity at $t = a$. Justify your answer.

41. **True or False** The acceleration of a particle is the second derivative of the position function. Justify your answer.

42. **Multiple Choice** Find the instantaneous rate of change of $f(x) = x^2 - 2/x + 4$ at $x = -1$.

   (A) -7 **(B)** -4 **(C)** 0 **(D)** 4 **(E)** 7

43. **Multiple Choice** Find the instantaneous rate of change of the volume of a cube with respect to a side length x.

   (A) x **(B)** $3x$ **(C)** $6x$ **(D)** $3x^2$ **(E)** x^3

In Exercises 44 and 45, a particle moves along a line so that its position at any time $t \geq 0$ is given by $s(t) = 2 + 7t - t^2$.

44. **Multiple Choice** At which of the following times is the particle moving to the left?

   (A) $t = 0$ **(B)** $t = 1$ **(C)** $t = 2$ **(D)** $t = 7/2$ **(E)** $t = 4$

45. **Multiple Choice** When is the particle at rest?

   (A) $t = 1$ **(B)** $t = 2$ **(C)** $t = 7/2$ **(D)** $t = 4$ **(E)** $t = 5$

Explorations

46. *Bacterium Population* When a bactericide was added to a nutrient broth in which bacteria were growing, the bacterium population continued to grow for a while but then stopped growing and began to decline. The size of the population at time t (hours) was $b(t) = 10^6 + 10^4 t - 10^3 t^2$. Find the growth rates at $t = 0$, $t = 5$, and $t = 10$ hours.

47. *Finding f from f′* Let $f'(x) = 3x^2$.

(a) Compute the derivatives of $g(x) = x^3$, $h(x) = x^3 - 2$, and $t(x) = x^3 + 3$.

(b) Graph the numerical derivatives of g, h, and t.

(c) Describe a *family* of functions, $f(x)$, that have the property that $f'(x) = 3x^2$.

(d) Is there a function f such that $f'(x) = 3x^2$ and $f(0) = 0$? If so, what is it?

(e) Is there a function f such that $f'(x) = 3x^2$ and $f(0) = 3$? If so, what is it?

48. *Pole Vaulting* In her running approach to begin her vault, a pole vaulter covered a distance of $1.5t^2$ feet in t seconds. When she planted her pole and began her ascent, she had achieved a speed of 22 feet per second. How long was her approach, both in time and in distance?

Extending the Ideas

49. *Even and Odd Functions*

(a) Show that if f is a differentiable even function, then f' is an odd function.

(b) Show that if f is a differentiable odd function, then f' is an even function.

50. *Extended Product Rule* Derive a formula for the derivative of the product fgh of three differentiable functions.

3.5 Derivatives of Trigonometric Functions

You will be able to determine the derivatives of trigonometric functions.

- Derivatives of the sine and cosine functions
- Modeling harmonic motion
- Jerk as the derivative of acceleration
- Derivatives of the tangent, cotangent, secant, and cosecant functions
- Tangent and normal lines

Derivative of the Sine Function

Trigonometric functions are important because so many of the phenomena we want information about are periodic (heart rhythms, earthquakes, tides, weather). It is known that continuous periodic functions can always be expressed in terms of sines and cosines, so the derivatives of sines and cosines play a key role in describing periodic change. This section introduces the derivatives of the six basic trigonometric functions.

EXPLORATION 1 Making a Conjecture by Graphing the Derivative

Graph $y_1 = \sin(x)$ and $y_2 = \dfrac{d}{dx}(\sin x)$ in the window $[-2\pi, 2\pi]$ by $[-4, 4]$

(Figure 3.35). Use the numerical derivative to graph $y_2 = \dfrac{d}{dx}(\sin x)$. See page 113.

1. When the graph of $y_1 = \sin x$ is increasing, what is true about the graph of $y_2 = \dfrac{d}{dx}(\sin x)$?

2. When the graph of $y_1 = \sin x$ is decreasing, what is true about the graph of $y_2 = \dfrac{d}{dx}(\sin x)$?

3. When the graph of $y_1 = \sin x$ stops increasing and starts decreasing, what is true about the graph of $y_2 = \dfrac{d}{dx}(\sin x)$?

4. At the places where $y_2 = \dfrac{d}{dx}(\sin x) = \pm 1$, what appears to be the slope of the graph of $y_1 = \sin x$?

5. Make a conjecture about what function the derivative of sine might be. Test your conjecture by graphing your function and $y_2 = \dfrac{d}{dx}(\sin x)$ in the same viewing window.

6. Now let $y_1 = \cos x$ and $y_2 = \dfrac{d}{dx}(\cos x)$. Answer questions (1) through (5) *without* looking at the graph of $y_2 = \dfrac{d}{dx}(\cos x)$ until you are ready to test your conjecture about what function the derivative of cosine might be.

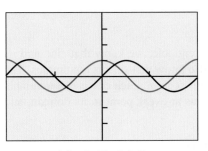

$[-2\pi, 2\pi]$ by $[-4, 4]$

Figure 3.35 Sine and its derivative. What is the derivative? (Exploration 1)

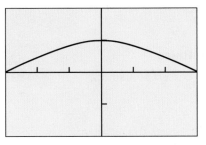

$[-3, 3]$ by $[-2, 2]$

(a)

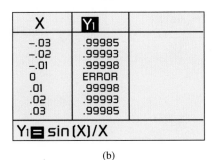

X	Y₁
−.03	.99985
−.02	.99993
−.01	.99998
0	ERROR
.01	.99998
.02	.99993
.03	.99985

Y₁ $\blacksquare$ sin (X)/X

(b)

Figure 3.36 (a) Graphical and (b) numerical support that $\displaystyle\lim_{h \to 0} \frac{\sin(h)}{h} = 1$.

If you conjectured that the derivative of the sine function is the cosine function, then you are right. We will confirm this analytically, but first we appeal to technology one more time to evaluate two limits needed in the proof (see Figure 3.36 in the margin and Figure 3.37 on the next page):

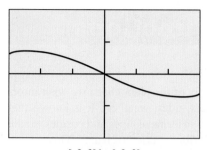

[−3, 3] by [−2, 2]

(a)

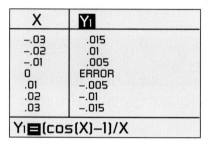

$Y_1 \blacksquare (\cos(X)-1)/X$

(b)

Figure 3.37 (a) Graphical and (b) numerical support that $\lim\limits_{h \to 0} \dfrac{\cos(h) - 1}{h} = 0$.

Numerical Derivatives Revisited

We now know that the exact derivative of $\sin(x)$ at $x = \pi$ is $\cos(\pi) = -1$. You can see below that the numerical derivative (either in MathPrint or Classic mode) gives a slightly different answer, but remember that it is a numerical approximation.

MathPrint Mode

$\dfrac{d}{dx}(\sin(X))|_{X=\pi}$
$-.9999998333$

Classic Mode

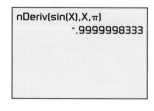

$\text{nDeriv}(\sin(X),X,\pi)$
$-.9999998333$

The proof that the derivative of the sine function is the cosine function follows. Now, let $y = \sin x$. Then

$$\frac{dy}{dx} = \lim_{h \to 0} \frac{\sin(x + h) - \sin x}{h}$$

$$= \lim_{h \to 0} \frac{\sin x \cos h + \cos x \sin h - \sin x}{h} \qquad \text{Angle sum identity}$$

$$= \lim_{h \to 0} \frac{(\sin x)(\cos h - 1) + \cos x \sin h}{h}$$

$$= \lim_{h \to 0} \sin x \cdot \lim_{h \to 0} \frac{(\cos h - 1)}{h} + \lim_{h \to 0} \cos x \cdot \lim_{h \to 0} \frac{\sin h}{h}$$

$$= \sin x \cdot 0 + \cos x \cdot 1$$

$$= \cos x$$

So, the derivative of the sine is the cosine.

$$\frac{d}{dx}\sin x = \cos x$$

Now that we know that the sine function is differentiable, we know that sine and its derivative obey all the rules for differentiation. We also know that $\sin x$ is continuous. The same holds for the other trigonometric functions in this section. Each one is differentiable at every point in its domain, so each one is continuous at every point in its domain, and the differentiation rules apply for each one.

Derivative of the Cosine Function

If you conjectured in Exploration 1 that the derivative of the cosine function is the negative of the sine function, you were correct. You can confirm this analytically in Exercise 24.

$$\frac{d}{dx}\cos x = -\sin x$$

EXAMPLE 1 Revisiting the Differentiation Rules

Find the derivatives of **(a)** $y = x^2 \sin x$ and **(b)** $u = \cos x/(1 - \sin x)$.

SOLUTION

(a) $\dfrac{dy}{dx} = x^2 \cdot \dfrac{d}{dx}(\sin x) + \sin x \cdot \dfrac{d}{dx}(x^2)$ Product Rule

$\qquad = x^2 \cos x + 2x \sin x$

(b) $\dfrac{du}{dx} = \dfrac{(1 - \sin x) \cdot \dfrac{d}{dx}(\cos x) - \cos x \cdot \dfrac{d}{dx}(1 - \sin x)}{(1 - \sin x)^2}$ Quotient Rule

$\qquad = \dfrac{(1 - \sin x)(-\sin x) - \cos x\,(0 - \cos x)}{(1 - \sin x)^2}$

$\qquad = \dfrac{-\sin x + \sin^2 x + \cos^2 x}{(1 - \sin x)^2}$

$\qquad = \dfrac{1 - \sin x}{(1 - \sin x)^2}$ $\sin^2 x + \cos^2 x = 1$

$\qquad = \dfrac{1}{1 - \sin x}$

Now Try Exercises 5 and 9.

Radian Measure in Calculus

In case you have been wondering why calculus uses radian measure instead of degrees, you are now ready to understand the answer. The derivative of sin x is cos x *only* if x is measured in radians! If you look at the analytic confirmation, you will note that the derivative comes down to

$$\cos x \text{ times } \lim_{h \to 0} \frac{\sin h}{h}.$$

We saw that

$$\lim_{h \to 0} \frac{\sin h}{h} = 1$$

in Figure 3.36, but only because the graph in Figure 3.36 is in *radian mode*. If you look at the limit of the same function in *degree* mode you will get a very different limit (and hence a different derivative for sine). See Exercise 50.

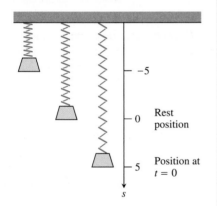

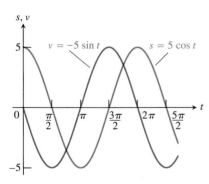

Figure 3.38 The weighted spring in Example 2.

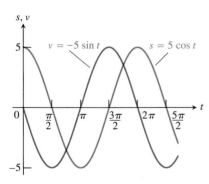

Figure 3.39 Graphs of the position and velocity of the weight in Example 2.

Simple Harmonic Motion

The motion of a weight bobbing up and down on the end of a spring is an example of **simple harmonic motion.** Example 2 describes a case in which there are no opposing forces like friction or buoyancy to slow down the motion.

EXAMPLE 2 The Motion of a Weight on a Spring

A weight hanging from a spring (Figure 3.38) is stretched 5 units beyond its rest position ($s = 0$) and released at time $t = 0$ to bob up and down. Its position at any later time t is

$$s = 5 \cos t.$$

What are its velocity and acceleration at time t? Describe its motion.

SOLUTION We have:

Position: $\quad\quad s = 5 \cos t;$

Velocity: $\quad\quad v = \dfrac{ds}{dt} = \dfrac{d}{dt}(5 \cos t) = -5 \sin t;$

Acceleration: $\quad a = \dfrac{dv}{dt} = \dfrac{d}{dt}(-5 \sin t) = -5 \cos t.$

Notice how much we can learn from these equations:

1. As time passes, the weight moves down and up between $s = -5$ and $s = 5$ on the s-axis. The amplitude of the motion is 5. The period of the motion is 2π.

2. The velocity $v = -5 \sin t$ attains its greatest magnitude, 5, when $\cos t = 0$, as the graphs show in Figure 3.39. Hence the speed of the weight, $|v| = 5 |\sin t|$, is greatest when $\cos t = 0$, that is, when $s = 0$ (the rest position). The speed of the weight is zero when $\sin t = 0$. This occurs when $s = 5 \cos t = \pm 5$, at the endpoints of the interval of motion.

3. The acceleration value is always the exact opposite of the position value. When the weight is above the rest position, gravity is pulling it back down; when the weight is below the rest position, the spring is pulling it back up.

4. The acceleration, $a = -5 \cos t$, is zero only at the rest position where $\cos t = 0$ and the force of gravity and the force from the spring offset each other. When the weight is anywhere else, the two forces are unequal and acceleration is nonzero. The acceleration is greatest in magnitude at the points farthest from the rest position, where $\cos t = \pm 1$.   ***Now Try Exercise 11.***

Jerk

A sudden change in acceleration is called a "jerk." When a ride in a car or a bus is jerky, it is not that the accelerations involved are necessarily large but that the changes in acceleration are abrupt. Jerk is what spills your soft drink. The derivative responsible for jerk is the *third* derivative of position.

DEFINITION Jerk

Jerk is the derivative of acceleration. If a body's position at time t is $s(t)$, the body's jerk at time t is

$$j(t) = \frac{da}{dt} = \frac{d^3s}{dt^3}.$$

Tests have shown that motion sickness comes from accelerations whose changes in magnitude or direction take us by surprise. Keeping an eye on the road helps us to see the changes coming. A driver is less likely to become sick than a passenger who is reading in the back seat.

EXAMPLE 3 A Couple of Jerks

(a) The jerk caused by the constant acceleration of gravity ($g = -32$ ft/sec^2) is zero:

$$j = \frac{d}{dt}(g) = 0$$

This explains why we don't experience motion sickness while just sitting around.

(b) The jerk of the simple harmonic motion in Example 2 is

$$j = \frac{da}{dt} = \frac{d}{dt}(-5 \cos t)$$

$$= 5 \sin t$$

It has its greatest magnitude when $\sin t = \pm 1$. This does not occur at the extremes of the displacement, but at the rest position, where the acceleration changes direction and sign.

Now Try Exercise 19.

Derivatives of the Other Basic Trigonometric Functions

Because $\sin x$ and $\cos x$ are differentiable functions of x, the related functions

$$\tan x = \frac{\sin x}{\cos x}, \qquad \sec x = \frac{1}{\cos x},$$

$$\cot x = \frac{\cos x}{\sin x}, \qquad \csc x = \frac{1}{\sin x}$$

are differentiable at every value of x for which they are defined. Their derivatives (Exercises 25 and 26) are given by the following formulas.

$$\frac{d}{dx}\tan x = \sec^2 x, \qquad \frac{d}{dx}\sec x = \sec x \tan x$$

$$\frac{d}{dx}\cot x = -\csc^2 x, \qquad \frac{d}{dx}\csc x = -\csc x \cot x$$

EXAMPLE 4 Finding Tangent and Normal Lines

Find equations for the lines that are tangent and normal to the graph of

$$f(x) = \frac{\tan x}{x}$$

at $x = 2$.

SOLUTION

First, we use the Quotient Rule to find that $f'(x) = \dfrac{x \cdot \sec^2 x - 1 \cdot \tan x}{x^2} = \dfrac{x \sec^2 x - \tan x}{x^2}$.

The slope of the tangent line, then, is $f'(2) = \dfrac{2 \sec^2 2 - \tan 2}{2^2} = 3.433$, and the slope of the normal line is $-1/(3.433) = -0.291$.

continued

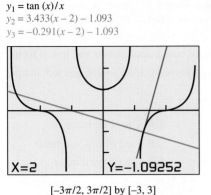

$y_1 = \tan(x)/x$
$y_2 = 3.433(x-2) - 1.093$
$y_3 = -0.291(x-2) - 1.093$

X=2   Y=-1.09252

$[-3\pi/2, 3\pi/2]$ by $[-3, 3]$

Figure 3.40 Graphical support for Example 4.

Calculator Note

Example 4 already makes extensive use of your calculator, but remember that your calculator will also compute the numerical derivative at $x = 2$. In this case, NDER$(\tan(x)/x, 2) = 3.433$.

Both lines go through the point $\left(2, \dfrac{\tan 2}{2}\right) = (2, -1.093)$.

Finally, we write the equations in point-slope form:

Tangent line: $y = 3.433(x - 2) - 1.093$ Normal line: $y = -0.291(x - 2) - 1.093$

If you graph both lines and the original function, you can support your answers with a graphing calculator. Figure 3.40 shows the tangent line in red and the normal line in blue.

Now Try Exercise 23

EXAMPLE 5 A Trigonometric Second Derivative

Find y'' if $y = \sec x$.

SOLUTION

$$y = \sec x$$
$$y' = \sec x \tan x$$
$$y'' = \frac{d}{dx}(\sec x \tan x)$$
$$= \sec x \frac{d}{dx}(\tan x) + \tan x \frac{d}{dx}(\sec x)$$
$$= \sec x (\sec^2 x) + \tan x (\sec x \tan x)$$
$$= \sec^3 x + \sec x \tan^2 x$$

Now Try Exercise 36.

Quick Review 3.5   *(For help, go to Sections 1.6, 3.1, and 3.4.)*

Exercise numbers with a gray background indicate problems that the authors have designed to be solved *without a calculator*.

1. Convert 135 degrees to radians.

2. Convert 1.7 radians to degrees.

3. Find the exact value of $\sin(\pi/3)$ without a calculator.

4. State the domain and the range of the cosine function.

5. State the domain and the range of the tangent function.

6. If $\sin a = -1$, what is $\cos a$?

7. If $\tan a = -1$, what are two possible values of $\sin a$?

8. Verify the identity:
$$\frac{1 - \cos h}{h} = \frac{\sin^2 h}{h(1 + \cos h)}$$

9. Find an equation of the line tangent to the curve $y = 2x^3 - 7x^2 + 10$ at the point $(3, 1)$.

10. A particle moves along a line with velocity $v = 2t^3 - 7t^2 + 10$ for time $t \geq 0$. Find the acceleration of the particle at $t = 3$.

Section 3.5 Exercises

In Exercises 1–10, find dy/dx. Use your grapher to support your analysis if you are unsure of your answer.

1. $y = 1 + x - \cos x$

2. $y = 2 \sin x - \tan x$

3. $y = \dfrac{1}{x} + 5 \sin x$

4. $y = x \sec x$

5. $y = 4 - x^2 \sin x$

6. $y = 3x + x \tan x$

7. $y = \dfrac{4}{\cos x}$

8. $y = \dfrac{x}{1 + \cos x}$

9. $y = \dfrac{\cot x}{1 + \cot x}$

10. $y = \dfrac{\cos x}{1 + \sin x}$

In Exercises 11 and 12, a weight hanging from a spring (see Figure 3.38) bobs up and down with position function $s = f(t)$ (s in meters, t in seconds). What are its velocity and acceleration at time t? Describe its motion.

11. $s = 5 \sin t$

12. $s = 7 \cos t$

In Exercises 13–16, a body is moving in simple harmonic motion with position function $s = f(t)$ (s in meters, t in seconds).

(a) Find the body's velocity, speed, and acceleration at time t.

(b) Find the body's velocity, speed, and acceleration at time $t = \pi/4$.

(c) Describe the motion of the body.

13. $s = 2 + 3 \sin t$　　　　**14.** $s = 1 - 4 \cos t$

15. $s = 2 \sin t + 3 \cos t$　　**16.** $s = \cos t - 3 \sin t$

In Exercises 17–20, a body is moving in simple harmonic motion with position function $s = f(t)$ (s in meters, t in seconds). Find the jerk at time t.

17. $s = 2 \cos t$　　　　**18.** $s = 1 + 2 \cos t$

19. $s = \sin t - \cos t$　　**20.** $s = 2 + 2 \sin t$

21. Find equations for the lines that are tangent and normal to the graph of $y = \sin x + 3$ at $x = \pi$.

22. Find equations for the lines that are tangent and normal to the graph of $y = \sec x$ at $x = \pi/4$.

23. Find equations for the lines that are tangent and normal to the graph of $y = x^2 \sin x$ at $x = 3$.

24. Use the definition of the derivative to prove that $(d/dx)(\cos x) = -\sin x$. (You will need the limits found at the beginning of this section.)

25. Assuming that $(d/dx)(\sin x) = \cos x$ and $(d/dx)(\cos x) = -\sin x$, prove each of the following.

(a) $\dfrac{d}{dx} \tan x = \sec^2 x$　　(b) $\dfrac{d}{dx} \sec x = \sec x \tan x$

26. Assuming that $(d/dx)(\sin x) = \cos x$ and $(d/dx)(\cos x) = -\sin x$, prove each of the following.

(a) $\dfrac{d}{dx} \cot x = -\csc^2 x$　　(b) $\dfrac{d}{dx} \csc x = -\csc x \cot x$

27. Show that the graphs of $y = \sec x$ and $y = \cos x$ have horizontal tangents at $x = 0$.

28. Show that the graphs of $y = \tan x$ and $y = \cot x$ have no horizontal tangents.

29. Find equations for the lines that are tangent and normal to the curve $y = \sqrt{2} \cos x$ at the point $(\pi/4, 1)$.

30. Find the points on the curve $y = \tan x$, $-\pi/2 < x < \pi/2$, where the tangent is parallel to the line $y = 2x$.

In Exercises 31 and 32, find an equation for (a) the tangent to the curve at P and (b) the horizontal tangent to the curve at Q.

31.

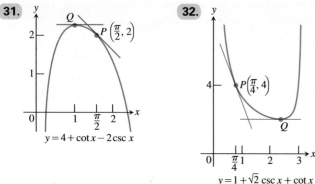

$y = 4 + \cot x - 2 \csc x$

32.

$y = 1 + \sqrt{2} \csc x + \cot x$

Group Activity In Exercises 33 and 34, a body is moving in simple harmonic motion with position $s = f(t)$ (s in meters, t in seconds).

(a) Find the body's velocity, speed, acceleration, and jerk at time t.

(b) Find the body's velocity, speed, acceleration, and jerk at time $t = \pi/4$ sec.

(c) Describe the motion of the body.

33. $s = 2 - 2 \sin t$　　　　**34.** $s = \sin t + \cos t$

35. Find y'' if $y = \csc x$.　　**36.** Find y'' if $y = \theta \tan \theta$.

37. **Writing to Learn** Is there a value of b that will make

$$g(x) = \begin{cases} x + b, & x < 0 \\ \cos x, & x \geq 0 \end{cases}$$

continuous at $x = 0$? differentiable at $x = 0$? Give reasons for your answers.

38. Find $\dfrac{d^{999}}{dx^{999}} (\cos x)$.　　**39.** Find $\dfrac{d^{725}}{dx^{725}} (\sin x)$.

40. *Local Linearity* This is the graph of the function $y = \sin x$ close to the origin. Since $\sin x$ is differentiable, this graph resembles a line. Find an equation for this line.

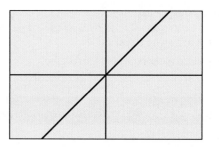

41. *(Continuation of Exercise 40)* For values of x close to 0, the linear equation found in Exercise 40 gives a good approximation of $\sin x$.

(a) Use this fact to estimate $\sin(0.12)$.

(b) Find $\sin(0.12)$ with a calculator. How close is the approximation in part (a)?

42. Use the identity $\sin 2x = 2 \sin x \cos x$ to find the derivative of $\sin 2x$. Then use the identity $\cos 2x = \cos^2 x - \sin^2 x$ to express that derivative in terms of $\cos 2x$.

43. Use the identity $\cos 2x = \cos x \cos x - \sin x \sin x$ to find the derivative of $\cos 2x$. Express the derivative in terms of $\sin 2x$.

Standardized Test Questions

You may use a graphing calculator to solve the following problems.

In Exercises 44 and 45, a weight is bobbing up and down on the end of a spring according to $s(t) = -3 \sin t$.

44. **True or False** The weight is traveling upward at $t = 3\pi/4$. Justify your answer.

45. **True or False** The velocity and speed of the weight are the same at $t = \pi/4$. Justify your answer.

46. Multiple Choice Which of the following is an equation of the tangent line to $y = \sin x + \cos x$ at $x = \pi$?

(A) $y = -x + \pi - 1$ (B) $y = -x + \pi + 1$

(C) $y = -x - \pi + 1$ (D) $y = -x - \pi - 1$

(E) $y = x - \pi + 1$

47. Multiple Choice Which of the following is an equation of the normal line to $y = \sin x + \cos x$ at $x = \pi$?

(A) $y = -x + \pi - 1$ (B) $y = x - \pi - 1$

(C) $y = x - \pi + 1$ (D) $y = x + \pi + 1$

(E) $y = x + \pi - 1$

48. Multiple Choice Find y'' if $y = x \sin x$.

(A) $-x \sin x$ (B) $x \cos x + \sin x$ (C) $-x \sin x + 2 \cos x$

(D) $x \sin x$ (E) $-\sin x + \cos x$

49. Multiple Choice A body is moving in simple harmonic motion with position $s = 3 + \sin t$. At which of the following times is the velocity zero?

(A) $t = 0$ (B) $t = \pi/4$ (C) $t = \pi/2$

(D) $t = \pi$ (E) none of these

Exploration

50. *Radians vs. Degrees* What happens to the derivatives of $\sin x$ and $\cos x$ if x is measured in degrees instead of radians? To find out, take the following steps.

(a) With your grapher in degree mode, graph

$$f(h) = \frac{\sin h}{h}$$

and estimate $\lim_{h \to 0} f(h)$. Compare your estimate with $\pi/180$. Is there any reason to believe the limit should be $\pi/180$?

(b) With your grapher in degree mode, estimate

$$\lim_{h \to 0} \frac{\cos h - 1}{h}.$$

(c) Now go back to the derivation of the formula for the derivative of $\sin x$ in the text and carry out the steps of the derivation using degree-mode limits. What formula do you obtain for the derivative?

(d) Derive the formula for the derivative of $\cos x$ using degree-mode limits.

(e) The disadvantages of the degree-mode formulas become even more apparent as you start taking derivatives of higher order. What are the second and third degree-mode derivatives of $\sin x$ and $\cos x$?

Extending the Ideas

51. Use analytic methods to show that

$$\lim_{h \to 0} \frac{\cos h - 1}{h} = 0.$$

[*Hint:* Multiply numerator and denominator by $(\cos h + 1)$.]

52. Find A and B in $y = A \sin x + B \cos x$ so that $y'' - y = \sin x$.

Quick Quiz for AP* Preparation: Sections 3.4–3.5

1. Multiple Choice If the line tangent to the graph of the function f at the point $(1, 6)$ passes through the point $(-1, -4)$, then $f'(1)$ is

(A) -1 (B) 1 (C) 5 (D) 6 (E) undefined

2. Multiple Choice Which of the following gives y'' for $y = \cos x + \tan x$?

(A) $-\cos x + 2\sec^2 x \tan x$ (B) $\cos x + 2\sec^2 x \tan x$

(C) $-\sin x + \sec^2 x$ (D) $-\cos x + \sec^2 x \tan x$

(E) $\cos x + \sec^2 x \tan x$

3. Multiple Choice If $y = \dfrac{3x + 2}{2x + 3}$, then $\dfrac{dy}{dx} =$

(A) $\dfrac{12x - 13}{(2x + 3)^2}$ (B) $\dfrac{12x - 13}{(2x + 3)^2}$ (C) $\dfrac{-5}{(2x + 3)^2}$

(D) $\dfrac{5}{(2x + 3)^2}$ (E) $\dfrac{2}{3}$

4. Free Response A particle moves along a line so that its position at any time $t \geq 0$ is given by $s(t) = -t^2 + t + 2$, where s is measured in meters and t is measured in seconds.

(a) What is the initial position of the particle?

(b) Find the initial velocity of the particle at any time t.

(c) When is the particle moving to the right?

(d) Find the acceleration of the particle at any time t.

(e) Find the speed of the particle at the moment when $s(t) = 0$.

CHAPTER 3 | Key Terms

acceleration (p. 132)
average velocity (p. 130)
Constant Multiple Rule (p. 119)
Derivative of a Constant Function (p. 118)
derivative of f (p. 101)
derivative of f at a (p. 101, 102)
differentiable function (p. 101)
differentiable on a closed interval
    (p. 106)
displacement (p. 130)
free-fall constants (p. 132)
instantaneous rate of change (p. 129)

instantaneous velocity (p. 130)
Intermediate Value Theorem for
    Derivatives (p. 115)
jerk (p. 145)
left-hand derivative (p. 106)
local linearity (p. 112)
marginal cost (p. 136)
marginal revenue (p. 136)
nth derivative (p. 124)
numerical derivative (NDER) (p. 113)
Power Rule for Negative Integer Powers
    of x (p. 123)

Power Rule for Positive Integer Powers
    of x (p. 118)
Product Rule (p. 121)
Quotient Rule (p. 122)
right-hand derivative (p. 106)
sensitivity to change (p. 135)
simple harmonic motion (p. 145)
speed (p. 131)
Sum and Difference Rule (p. 119)
symmetric difference quotient (p. 113)
velocity (p. 130)

CHAPTER 3 | Review Exercises

Exercise numbers with a gray background indicate problems that the authors have designed to be solved *without a calculator*.

The collection of exercises marked in red could be used as a chapter test.

In Exercises 1–30, find the derivative of the function.

1. $y = x^5 - \dfrac{1}{8}x^2 + \dfrac{1}{4}x$

2. $y = 3 - 7x^3 + 3x^7$

3. $y = 2 \sin x \cos x$

4. $y = \dfrac{2x + 1}{2x - 1}$

5. $s = (t^2 - 1)(t^2 + 1)$

6. $s = \dfrac{t^2 + 1}{1 - t^2}$

7. $y = \sqrt{x} + 1 + \dfrac{1}{\sqrt{x}}$

8. $y = (x^5 + 1)(3x^2 - x)$

9. $r = 5\theta^2 \sec \theta$

10. $r = \dfrac{\tan \theta}{\theta^3 + \theta + 1}$

11. $y = x^2 \sin x + x \cos x$

12. $y = x^2 \sin x - x \cos x$

13. $y = \dfrac{\tan x}{2x^3}$

14. $y = \tan x - \cot x$

15. $y = \dfrac{1}{\sin x + \cos x}$

16. $y = \dfrac{1}{\sin x} + \dfrac{1}{\cos x}$

17. $V = \dfrac{4}{3}\pi r^3 + 8\pi r^2$

18. $A = \dfrac{\sqrt{3}}{4}s^2 + \dfrac{3\pi}{8}s^2$

19. $s = \dfrac{1 + \sin t}{1 + \tan t}$

20. $s = \dfrac{1 + \sin t}{1 + \cos t}$

21. $s = \dfrac{t^{-1} + t^{-2}}{t^{-3}}$

22. $y = x^{-2} \cos x - 4x^{-3}$

23. $y = \dfrac{\sin u}{\csc u} + \dfrac{\cos u}{\sec u}$

24. $y = \dfrac{\cot u}{\tan u} - \dfrac{\csc u}{\sin u}$

25. $y = 2x^{-2}(x^5 - x^3)$

26. $y = 4x^2(x^{-1} + 3x^{-4})$

27. $y = \dfrac{t^2}{\pi^3} - \dfrac{\pi^2}{t^3}$

28. $y = \dfrac{t^3}{\pi^2} - \dfrac{\pi^3}{t^2}$

29. $y = \sec x \tan x \cos x$

30. $y = \dfrac{\sin x \cot x}{\cos x}$

In Exercises 31–34, find all values of x for which the function is differentiable.

31. $y = \dfrac{\sin x}{x}$

32. $y = \sin x - x \cos x$

33. $y = \dfrac{3 \cos x}{x - 2}$

34. $y = (2x - 7)^{-1}(x + 5)$

In Exercises 35–38, find the slope of the curve at $x = \pi$.

35. $y = \sec x$

36. $y = \sin x \cos x$

37. $y = \dfrac{\cos x}{x}$

38. $y = \dfrac{x}{x + \sin x}$

In Exercises 39–42, find $\dfrac{d^2y}{dx^2}$.

39. $y = \dfrac{1}{\cos x}$

40. $y = \csc x$

41. $y = x \sin x$

42. $y = x - x \cos x$

In Exercises 43 and 44, find all derivatives of the function.

43. $y = \dfrac{x^4}{2} - \dfrac{3}{2}x^2 - x$

44. $y = \dfrac{x^5}{120}$

In Exercises 45–48, find an equation for the **(a)** tangent and **(b)** normal to the curve at the indicated point.

45. $y = 8x^{-2}$, $x = 2$

46. $y = 4 + \cot x - 2 \csc x$, $x = \pi/2$

47. $y = \sin x + \cos x$, $x = \dfrac{\pi}{4}$ **48.** $y = 2x^2 + \dfrac{1}{x^4}$, $x = 1$

In Exercises 49–52, find the coordinates of all points on the curve at which the tangent line has slope 6. If no such point exists, write "none."

49. $y = 2x^3$

50. $y = \dfrac{2x^3 - 3x^2}{6}$

51. $y = \dfrac{6x}{x + 1}$

52. $y = 2 \sin x$

53. Writing to Learn

(a) Graph the function

$$f(x) = \begin{cases} x, & 0 \le x \le 1 \\ 2 - x, & 1 < x \le 2. \end{cases}$$

(b) Is f continuous at $x = 1$? Explain.

(c) Is f differentiable at $x = 1$? Explain.

54. Writing to Learn For what values of the constant m is

$$f(x) = \begin{cases} 2 \sin x, & x \le 0 \\ mx, & x > 0 \end{cases}$$

(a) continuous at $x = 0$? Explain.

(b) differentiable at $x = 0$? Explain.

In Exercises 55–58, determine where the function is **(a)** differentiable, **(b)** continuous but not differentiable, and **(c)** neither continuous nor differentiable.

55. $f(x) = x^{4/5}$

56. $y = x^{3/5}$

57. $f(x) = \begin{cases} 2x - 3, & -1 \le x < 0 \\ x - 3, & 0 \le x \le 4 \end{cases}$

58. $g(x) = \begin{cases} \dfrac{x - 1}{x}, & -2 \le x < 0 \\ \dfrac{x + 1}{x}, & 0 \le x \le 2 \end{cases}$

In Exercises 59 and 60, use the graph of f to sketch the graph of f'.

59. Sketching f' from f

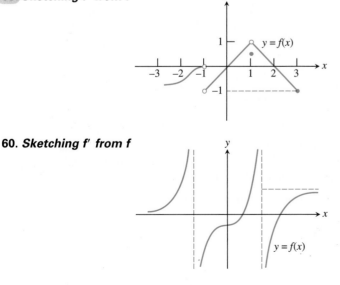

60. Sketching f' from f

61. Recognizing Graphs The following graphs show the distance traveled, velocity, and acceleration for each second of a 2-minute automobile trip. Which graph shows

(a) distance?   (b) velocity?   (c) acceleration?

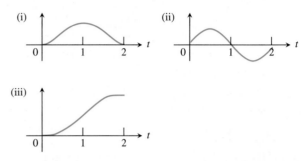

62. Sketching f from f' Sketch the graph of a continuous function f with $f(0) = 5$ and

$$f'(x) = \begin{cases} -2, & x < 2 \\ -0.5, & x > 2. \end{cases}$$

63. Sketching f from f' Sketch the graph of a continuous function f with $f(-1) = 2$ and

$$f'(x) = \begin{cases} -2, & x < 1 \\ 1, & 1 < x < 4 \\ -1, & 4 < x < 6. \end{cases}$$

64. Which of the following statements could be true if $f''(x) = x^{1/3}$?

i. $f(x) = \dfrac{9}{28}x^{7/3} + 9$ **ii.** $f'(x) = \dfrac{9}{28}x^{7/3} - 2$

iii. $f'(x) = \dfrac{3}{4}x^{4/3} + 6$ **iv.** $f(x) = \dfrac{3}{4}x^{4/3} - 4$

A. i only   **B.** iii only

C. ii and iv only   **D.** i and iii only

65. Derivative from Data The following data give the coordinates of a moving body for various values of t.

t (sec)	0	0.5	1	1.5	2	2.5	3	3.5	4
s (ft)	10	38	58	70	74	70	58	38	10

(a) Make a scatter plot of the (t, s) data and sketch a smooth curve through the points.

(b) Compute the average velocity between consecutive points of the table.

(c) Make a scatter plot of the data in part (b) using the midpoints of the t values to represent the data. Then sketch a smooth curve through the points.

(d) **Writing to Learn** Why does the curve in part (c) approximate the graph of ds/dt?

66. Factorial Fact Prove that the nth derivative of x^n is $n!$ for any positive integer n.

67. Working with Numerical Values Suppose that a function f and its first derivative have the following values at $x = 0$ and $x = 1$.

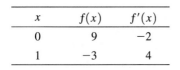

x	$f(x)$	$f'(x)$
0	9	-2
1	-3	4

Find the first derivative of the following functions at the given value of x.

(a) $3f(x)$, $x = 1$

(b) $xf(x)$, $x = 1$

(c) $x^2 f(x)$, $x = 1$

(d) $\dfrac{f(x)}{x}$, $x = 1$

(e) $\dfrac{f(x)}{x^2 + 2}$, $x = 0$

(f) $f(x) \cdot f(x)$, $x = 0$

68. Working with Numerical Values Suppose that functions f and g and their first derivatives have the following values at $x = -1$ and $x = 0$.

x	$f(x)$	$g(x)$	$f'(x)$	$g'(x)$
-1	0	-1	2	1
0	-1	-3	-2	4

Find the first derivative of the following combinations at the given value of x.

(a) $3f(x) - g(x)$, $x = -1$

(b) $f(x)g(x)$, $x = 0$

(c) $f(x)g(x)$, $x = -1$

(d) $\dfrac{f(x)}{g(x)}$, $x = 0$

(e) $\dfrac{f(x)}{g(x)}$, $x = -1$

(f) $\dfrac{f(x)}{g(x) + 2}$, $x = 0$

69. If two functions f and g have positive slopes at $x = 0$, must the function $f + g$ have a positive slope at $x = 0$? Justify your answer.

70. If two functions f and g have positive slopes at $x = 0$, must the function $f \cdot g$ have a positive slope at $x = 0$? Justify your answer.

71. Vertical Motion On Earth, if you shoot a paper clip 64 ft straight up into the air with a rubber band, the paper clip will be $s(t) = 64t - 16t^2$ feet above your hand at t sec after firing.

(a) Find ds/dt and d^2s/dt^2.

(b) How long does it take the paper clip to reach its maximum height?

(c) With what velocity does it leave your hand?

(d) On the moon, the same force will send the paper clip to a height of $s(t) = 64t - 2.6t^2$ ft in t sec. About how long will it take the paper clip to reach its maximum height, and how high will it go?

72. Free Fall Suppose two balls are falling from rest at a certain height in centimeters above the ground. Use the equation $s = 490t^2$ to answer the following questions.

(a) How long does it take the balls to fall the first 160 cm? What is their average velocity for the period?

(b) How fast are the balls falling when they reach the 160-cm mark? What is their acceleration then?

73. Filling a Bowl If a hemispherical bowl of radius 10 in. is filled with water to a depth of x in., the volume of water is given by $V = \pi [10 - (x/3)] x^2$. Find the rate of increase of the volume per inch increase of depth.

74. Marginal Revenue A bus will hold 60 people. The fare charged (p dollars) is related to the number x of people who use the bus by the formula $p = [3 - (x/40)]^2$.

(a) Write a formula for the total revenue per trip received by the bus company.

(b) What number of people per trip will make the marginal revenue equal to zero? What is the corresponding fare?

(c) Writing to Learn Do you think the bus company's fare policy is good for its business?

75. Searchlight The figure shows a boat 1 km offshore sweeping the shore with a searchlight. The light turns at a constant rate, $d\theta/dt = -0.6$ rad/sec.

(a) How fast is the light moving along the shore when it reaches point A?

(b) How many revolutions per minute is 0.6 rad/sec?

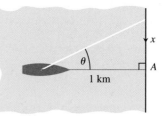

76. Calculator Exploration Use your calculator to graph the functions

$$y_1 = \cos^{-1}(\cos(x)) \quad \text{and} \quad y_2 = \frac{|\sin(x)|}{\sin(x)}.$$

(a) Based on the graphical information, find a relationship between these two functions that involves the derivative.

(b) Can you find a find a function y_2 that relates to the function $y_1 = \sin^{-1}(\sin(x))$ in the same way?

77. Finding a Range The range of the function $y = \dfrac{3x}{x^4 + 6}$ is the interval $[-a, a]$, where a is a certain irrational number. Use a calculator to graph the function, and then find the exact value of a algebraically. [*Hint:* Do you see how solving the equation $\dfrac{dy}{dx} = 0$ might be useful for finding the exact value of a?]

78. *Finding a Range* The range of the function $y = \dfrac{4x}{x^2 + 2}$ is the interval $[-a, a]$, where a is a certain irrational number. Use a calculator to graph the function, and then find the exact value of a algebraically.

79. Graph the function $f(x) = \tan^{-1}(\tan 2x)$ in the window $[-\pi, \pi]$ by $[-4, 4]$. Then answer the following questions.

(a) What is the domain of f?

(b) What is the range of f?

(c) At which points is f not differentiable?

(d) Describe the graph of f'.

80. *Fundamental Frequency of a Vibrating Piano String* We measure the frequencies at which wires vibrate in cycles (trips back and forth) per sec. The unit of measure is a *hertz:* 1 cycle per sec. Middle A on a piano has a frequency 440 hertz. For any given wire, the fundamental frequency y is a function of four variables:

r: the radius of the wire;

l: the length;

d: the density of the wire;

T: the tension (force) holding the wire taut.

With r and l in centimeters, d in grams per cubic centimeter, and T in dynes (it takes about 100,000 dynes to lift an apple), the fundamental frequency of the wire is

$$y = \frac{1}{2rl}\sqrt{\frac{T}{\pi d}}.$$

If we keep all the variables fixed except one, then y can be alternatively thought of as four different functions of one variable, $y(r)$, $y(l)$, $y(d)$, and $y(T)$. How would changing each variable affect the string's fundamental frequency? To find out, calculate $y'(r)$, $y'(l)$, $y'(d)$, and $y'(T)$.

AP* Examination Preparation

You may use a graphing calculator to solve the following problems.

81. A particle moves along the x-axis so that at any time $t \geq 0$ its position is given by $x(t) = t^3 - 12t + 5$.

(a) Find the velocity of the particle at any time t.

(b) Find the acceleration of the particle at any time t.

(c) Find all values of t for which the particle is at rest.

(d) Find the speed of the particle when its acceleration is zero.

(e) Is the particle moving toward the origin or away from the origin when $t = 3$? Justify your answer.

82. The function f is differentiable for all real numbers and satisfies the conditions in the table below. The function g is defined by

$$g(x) = \frac{f(x)}{f(x) - 3}.$$

x	$f(x)$	$f'(x)$
2	-1	3
4	3	5

(a) Write an equation of the line tangent to the graph of f at $x = 4$.

(b) Is f continuous at $x = 3$? Justify your answer.

(c) Is there a zero of f in the interval $[2, 4]$? Justify your answer.

(d) Find $g'(2)$.

(e) Explain why g is not differentiable at $x = 4$.

83. Let $f(x) = \dfrac{\cos(x)}{\cos(x) - 2}$ for $-2\pi \leq x \leq 2\pi$.

(a) Sketch a graph of f in the window $[-2\pi, 2\pi]$ by $[-2, 2]$.

(b) Find $f'(x)$.

(c) Find all values in the domain of f for which $f'(x) = 0$.

(d) Use information obtained from parts (a) and (c) to find the range of f.

4 More Derivatives

the sea. Several silent swans swim serenely as seven

sail southward to the sea. Several silent swans

en swift sailboats sail southward to the sea. Se

wim serenely as seven swift sailboats sail south

eral silent swans swim serenely as seven swi

l to the sea. Several silent swans swim serene

sail southward to the sea. Several si

en swift sailboats sail southward to the sea

wim serenely as seven swift sailboats s

eral silent swans swim serenely as

4.1 Chain Rule

4.2 Implicit Differentiation

4.3 Derivatives of Inverse Trigonometric Functions

4.4 Derivatives of Exponential and Logarithmic Functions

The letter S above is pieced together from curves joined at the red dots. Each piece of the outline is defined by parametric equations $x = f(t)$ and $y = g(t)$, where f and g are cubic polynomials and the parameter t runs from 0 to 1. In a font design program such as Fontlab™ you can drag the control points (blue dots) to change the shape of each piece of the outline. (We show control points for just two pieces of the outline.) As you drag the control points, you are actually changing the coefficients of the polynomials f and g. Using the techniques of Example 6 in Section 4.1 you can show that as long as a joint (or *node*) lies on the line joining its adjacent control points, the two curves that meet at the node will have the same slope there, making a smooth transition. When you send the letter to an output device like a printer, it uses the parametric equations to render the outline at the highest possible resolution.

CHAPTER 4 **Overview**

Now that you have completed a chapter filled with derivative rules and their proofs (most of which we hope you were able to understand rather than simply memorize), you are about to embark on another derivative chapter, this one devoted to a single rule: the Chain Rule. This rule certainly deserves its own chapter, but we also want you to become sufficiently familiar with the rich variety of applications that are accessible once you know how to apply it. You might think of Chapter 3 as the chapter that showed you how to make the bricks; now Chapter 4 will show you how to use those bricks to build houses.

4.1 | Chain Rule

You will be able to differentiate composite functions and parametrically defined functions using the Chain Rule.

- The Chain Rule for differentiating a composite function
- The Chain Rule in prime and Leibniz notations
- Differentiating parametrically defined functions
- The Power Chain Rule
- Using the Chain Rule to show how degree measure affects the calculus of trig functions

Derivative of a Composite Function

We now know how to differentiate $\sin x$ and $x^2 - 4$, but how do we differentiate a composite like $\sin(x^2 - 4)$? The answer is with the Chain Rule, which is probably the most widely used differentiation rule in mathematics. This section describes the rule and how to use it.

EXAMPLE 1 Relating Derivatives

The function $y = 6x - 10 = 2(3x - 5)$ is the composite of the functions $y = 2u$ and $u = 3x - 5$. How are the derivatives of these three functions related?

SOLUTION

We have

$$\frac{dy}{dx} = 6, \quad \frac{dy}{du} = 2, \quad \frac{du}{dx} = 3.$$

Since $6 = 2 \cdot 3$,

$$\frac{dy}{dx} = \frac{dy}{du} \cdot \frac{du}{dx}.$$

Now Try Exercise 1.

Is it an accident that $dy/dx = dy/du \cdot du/dx$?

If we think of the derivative as a rate of change, our intuition allows us to see that this relationship is reasonable. For $y = f(u)$ and $u = g(x)$, if y changes twice as fast as u and u changes three times as fast as x, then we expect y to change six times as fast as x. This is much like the effect of a multiple gear train (Figure 4.1).

Let us try again on another function.

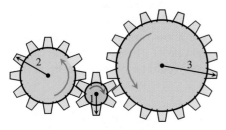

C: *y* turns   B: *u* turns   A: *x* turns

Figure 4.1 When gear A makes x turns, gear B makes u turns, and gear C makes y turns. By comparing circumferences or counting teeth, we see that $y = u/2$ and $u = 3x$, so $y = 3x/2$. Thus $dy/du = 1/2$, $du/dx = 3$, and $dy/dx = 3/2 = (dy/du)(du/dx)$.

EXAMPLE 2 Relating Derivatives

The polynomial $y = 9x^4 + 6x^2 + 1 = (3x^2 + 1)^2$ is the composite of $y = u^2$ and $u = 3x^2 + 1$. Calculating derivatives, we see that

$$\frac{dy}{du} \cdot \frac{du}{dx} = 2u \cdot 6x$$

$$= 2(3x^2 + 1) \cdot 6x$$

$$= 36x^3 + 12x$$

continued

Also,

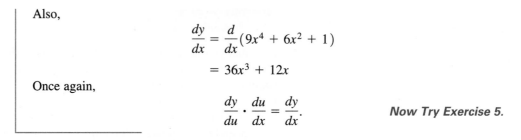

$$\frac{dy}{dx} = \frac{d}{dx}(9x^4 + 6x^2 + 1)$$

$$= 36x^3 + 12x$$

Once again,

$$\frac{dy}{du} \cdot \frac{du}{dx} = \frac{dy}{dx}.$$

Now Try Exercise 5.

The derivative of the composite function $f(g(x))$ at x is the derivative of f at $g(x)$ times the derivative of g at x (Figure 4.2). This is known as the Chain Rule.

Figure 4.2 Rates of change multiply: The derivative of $f \circ g$ at x is the derivative of f at the point $g(x)$ times the derivative of g at x.

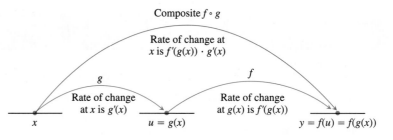

RULE 8 The Chain Rule

If f is differentiable at the point $u = g(x)$, and g is differentiable at x, then the composite function $(f \circ g)(x) = f(g(x))$ is differentiable at x, and

$$(f \circ g)'(x) = f'(g(x)) \cdot g'(x).$$

In Leibniz notation, if $y = f(u)$ and $u = g(x)$, then

$$\frac{dy}{dx} = \frac{dy}{du} \cdot \frac{du}{dx},$$

where dy/du is evaluated at $u = g(x)$.

It would be tempting to try to prove the Chain Rule by writing

$$\frac{\Delta y}{\Delta x} = \frac{\Delta y}{\Delta u} \cdot \frac{\Delta u}{\Delta x}$$

(a true statement about fractions with nonzero denominators) and taking the limit as $\Delta x \to 0$. This is essentially what is happening, and it would work as a proof if we knew that Δu, the change in u, was nonzero; but we do not know this. A small change in x could conceivably produce no change in u. An air-tight proof of the Chain Rule can be constructed to handle all cases, but the limit arguments would be better understood in a future course.

EXAMPLE 3 Applying the Chain Rule

An object moves along the x-axis so that its position at any time $t \geq 0$ is given by $x(t) = \cos(t^2 + 1)$. Find the velocity of the object as a function of t.

SOLUTION

We know that the velocity is dx/dt. In this instance, x is a composite function: $x = \cos(u)$ and $u = t^2 + 1$. We have

$$\frac{dx}{du} = -\sin(u) \qquad x = \cos(u)$$

$$\frac{du}{dt} = 2t \qquad u = t^2 + 1$$

continued

By the Chain Rule,

$$\frac{dx}{dt} = \frac{dx}{du} \cdot \frac{du}{dt}$$

$$= -\sin(u) \cdot 2t$$

$$= -\sin(t^2 + 1) \cdot 2t$$

$$= -2t \sin(t^2 + 1) \qquad \textbf{\textit{Now Try Exercise 9.}}$$

"Outside-Inside" Rule

It sometimes helps to think about the Chain Rule this way: If $y = f(g(x))$, then

$$\frac{dy}{dx} = f'(g(x)) \cdot g'(x).$$

In words, differentiate the "outside" function f and evaluate it at the "inside" function $g(x)$ left alone; then multiply by the derivative of the "inside function."

EXAMPLE 4 Differentiating from the Outside In

Differentiate $\sin(x^2 + x)$ with respect to x.

SOLUTION

$$\frac{d}{dx}\sin\underbrace{(x^2 + x)}_{\text{inside}} = \cos\underbrace{(x^2 + x)}_{\substack{\text{inside} \\ \text{left alone}}} \cdot \underbrace{(2x + 1)}_{\substack{\text{derivative of} \\ \text{the inside}}}$$

\textit{Now Try Exercise 13.}

Repeated Use of the Chain Rule

We sometimes have to use the Chain Rule two or more times to find a derivative. Here is an example:

EXAMPLE 5 A Three-Link "Chain"

Find the derivative of $g(t) = \tan(5 - \sin 2t)$.

SOLUTION

Notice here that tan is a function of $5 - \sin 2t$, while sin is a function of $2t$, which is itself a function of t. Therefore, by the Chain Rule,

$$g'(t) = \frac{d}{dt}(\tan(5 - \sin 2t))$$

$$= \sec^2(5 - \sin 2t) \cdot \frac{d}{dt}(5 - \sin 2t) \qquad \begin{array}{l}\text{Derivative of } \tan u \\ \text{with } u = 5 - \sin 2t\end{array}$$

$$= \sec^2(5 - \sin 2t) \cdot \left(0 - \cos 2t \cdot \frac{d}{dt}(2t)\right) \qquad \begin{array}{l}\text{Derivative of } 5 - \sin u \\ \text{with } u = 2t\end{array}$$

$$= \sec^2(5 - \sin 2t) \cdot (-\cos 2t) \cdot 2$$

$$= -2(\cos 2t)\sec^2(5 - \sin 2t).$$

\textit{Now Try Exercise 23.}

Slopes of Parametrized Curves

A parametrized curve $(x(t), y(t))$ is *differentiable at t* if x and y are differentiable at t. At a point on a differentiable parametrized curve where y is also a differentiable function of x, the derivatives dy/dt, dx/dt, and dy/dx are related by the Chain Rule:

$$\frac{dy}{dt} = \frac{dy}{dx} \cdot \frac{dx}{dt}$$

If $dx/dt \neq 0$, we may divide both sides of this equation by dx/dt to solve for dy/dx.

> **Finding *dy/dx* Parametrically**
>
> If all three derivatives exist and $dx/dt \neq 0$,
>
> $$\frac{dy}{dx} = \frac{dy/dt}{dx/dt}. \tag{1}$$

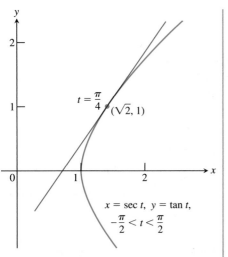

Figure 4.3 The hyperbola branch in Example 6. Equation 1 applies for every point on the graph except $(1, 0)$. Can you state why Equation 1 fails at $(1, 0)$?

EXAMPLE 6   Differentiating with a Parameter

Find the line tangent to the right-hand hyperbola branch defined parametrically by

$$x = \sec t, \quad y = \tan t, \qquad -\frac{\pi}{2} < t < \frac{\pi}{2}$$

at the point $\left(\sqrt{2}, 1\right)$, where $t = \pi/4$ (Figure 4.3).

SOLUTION

All three of the derivatives in Equation 1 exist and $dx/dt = \sec t \tan t$, which is nonzero at the indicated point. Therefore, Equation 1 applies and

$$\frac{dy}{dx} = \frac{dy/dt}{dx/dt}$$

$$= \frac{\sec^2 t}{\sec t \tan t}$$

$$= \frac{\sec t}{\tan t}$$

$$= \csc t$$

Setting $t = \pi/4$ gives

$$\left.\frac{dy}{dx}\right|_{t=\pi/4} = \csc(\pi/4) = \sqrt{2}.$$

The equation of the tangent line is

$$y - 1 = \sqrt{2}\left(x - \sqrt{2}\right). \qquad \textbf{\textit{Now Try Exercise 41.}}$$

Power Chain Rule

If f is a differentiable function of u, and u is a differentiable function of x, then substituting $y = f(u)$ into the Chain Rule formula

$$\frac{dy}{dx} = \frac{dy}{du} \cdot \frac{du}{dx}$$

leads to the formula

$$\frac{d}{dx} f(u) = f'(u) \frac{du}{dx}.$$

Here's an example of how it works: If n is an integer and $f(u) = u^n$, the Power Rules (Rules 2 and 7) tell us that $f'(u) = nu^{n-1}$. If u is a differentiable function of x, then we can use the Chain Rule to extend this to the **Power Chain Rule:**

$$\frac{d}{dx}u^n = nu^{n-1}\frac{du}{dx} \qquad \frac{d}{du}(u^n) = nu^{n-1}$$

EXAMPLE 7 Finding Slope

(a) Find the slope of the line tangent to the curve $y = \sin^5 x$ at the point where $x = \pi/3$.

(b) Show that the slope of every line tangent to the curve $y = 1/(1 - 2x)^3$ is positive.

SOLUTION

(a) $\dfrac{dy}{dx} = 5\sin^4 x \cdot \dfrac{d}{dx}\sin x$ Power Chain Rule with $u = \sin x, n = 5$

$\qquad = 5\sin^4 x \cos x$

The tangent line has slope

$$\left.\frac{dy}{dx}\right|_{x=\pi/3} = 5\left(\frac{\sqrt{3}}{2}\right)^4\left(\frac{1}{2}\right) = \frac{45}{32}.$$

(b) $\dfrac{dy}{dx} = \dfrac{d}{dx}(1 - 2x)^{-3}$

$\qquad = -3(1 - 2x)^{-4} \cdot \dfrac{d}{dx}(1 - 2x)$ Power Chain Rule with $u = (1 - 2x), n = -3$

$\qquad = -3(1 - 2x)^{-4} \cdot (-2)$

$\qquad = \dfrac{6}{(1 - 2x)^4}$

At any point (x, y) on the curve, $x \neq 1/2$ and the slope of the tangent line is

$$\frac{dy}{dx} = \frac{6}{(1 - 2x)^4},$$

the quotient of two positive numbers.   ***Now Try Exercise 53.***

EXAMPLE 8 Radians Versus Degrees

It is important to remember that the formulas for the derivatives of both $\sin x$ and $\cos x$ were obtained under the assumption that x is measured in radians, *not* degrees. The Chain Rule gives us new insight into the difference between the two. Since $180° = \pi$ radians, $x° = \pi x/180$ radians. By the Chain Rule,

$$\frac{d}{dx}\sin(x°) = \frac{d}{dx}\sin\left(\frac{\pi x}{180}\right) = \frac{\pi}{180}\cos\left(\frac{\pi x}{180}\right) = \frac{\pi}{180}\cos(x°).$$

See Figure 4.4.

The factor $\pi/180$, annoying in the first derivative, would compound with repeated differentiation. We see at a glance the compelling reason for the use of radian measure.

continued

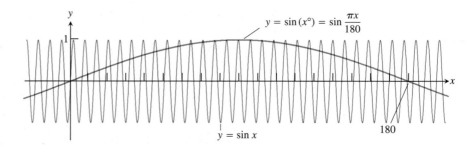

Figure 4.4 $\sin(x°)$ oscillates only $\pi/180$ times as often as $\sin x$ oscillates. Its maximum slope is $\pi/180$. (Example 8)

Quick Review 4.1   *(For help, go to Sections 1.2 and 1.6.)*

Exercise numbers with a gray background indicate problems that the authors have designed to be solved *without a calculator*.

In Exercises 1–5, let $f(x) = \sin x$, $g(x) = x^2 + 1$, and $h(x) = 7x$. Write a simplified expression for the composite function.

1. $f(g(x))$

2. $f(g(h(x)))$

3. $(g \circ h)(x)$

4. $(h \circ g)(x)$

5. $f\left(\dfrac{g(x)}{h(x)}\right)$

In Exercises 6–10, let $f(x) = \cos x$, $g(x) = \sqrt{x + 2}$, and $h(x) = 3x^2$. Write the given function as a composite of two or more of f, g, and h. For example, $\cos 3x^2$ is $f(h(x))$.

6. $\sqrt{\cos x + 2}$

7. $\sqrt{3 \cos^2 x + 2}$

8. $3 \cos x + 6$

9. $\cos 27x^4$

10. $\cos \sqrt{2 + 3x^2}$

Section 4.1 Exercises

In Exercises 1–8, use the given substitution and the Chain Rule to find dy/dx.

1. $y = \sin(3x + 1)$, $u = 3x + 1$
2. $y = \sin(7 - 5x)$, $u = 7 - 5x$

3. $y = \cos(\sqrt{3}x)$, $u = \sqrt{3}x$
4. $y = \tan(2x - x^3)$, $u = 2x - x^3$

5. $y = \left(\dfrac{\sin x}{1 + \cos x}\right)^2$, $u = \dfrac{\sin x}{1 + \cos x}$

6. $y = 5 \cot\left(\dfrac{2}{x}\right)$, $u = \dfrac{2}{x}$
7. $y = \cos(\sin x)$, $u = \sin x$

8. $y = \sec(\tan x)$, $u = \tan x$

In Exercises 9–12, an object moves along the x-axis so that its position at any time $t \geq 0$ is given by $x(t) = s(t)$. Find the velocity of the object as a function of t.

9. $s = \cos\left(\dfrac{\pi}{2} - 3t\right)$
10. $s = t\cos(\pi - 4t)$

11. $s = \dfrac{4}{3\pi}\sin 3t + \dfrac{4}{5\pi}\cos 5t$

12. $s = \sin\left(\dfrac{3\pi}{2}t\right) + \cos\left(\dfrac{7\pi}{4}t\right)$

In Exercises 13–24, find dy/dx.

13. $y = (x + \sqrt{x})^{-2}$
14. $y = (\csc x + \cot x)^{-1}$

15. $y = \sin^{-5} x - \cos^3 x$
16. $y = x^3(2x - 5)^4$

17. $y = \sin^3 x \tan 4x$
18. $y = 4\sqrt{\sec x + \tan x}$

19. $y = \dfrac{3}{\sqrt{2x + 1}}$
20. $y = \dfrac{x}{\sqrt{1 + x^2}}$

21. $y = \sin^2(3x - 2)$
22. $y = (1 + \cos 2x)^2$

23. $y = (1 + \cos^2 7x)^3$
24. $y = \sqrt{\tan 5x}$

In Exercises 25–28, find $dr/d\theta$.

25. $r = \tan(2 - \theta)$
26. $r = \sec 2\theta \tan 2\theta$

27. $r = \sqrt{\theta \sin \theta}$
28. $r = 2\theta\sqrt{\sec \theta}$

In Exercises 29–32, find y''.

29. $y = \tan x$
30. $y = \cot x$

31. $y = \cot(3x - 1)$
32. $y = 9\tan(x/3)$

In Exercises 33–38, find the value of $(f \circ g)'$ at the given value of x.

33. $f(u) = u^5 + 1$, $u = g(x) = \sqrt{x}$, $x = 1$

34. $f(u) = 1 - \dfrac{1}{u}$, $u = g(x) = \dfrac{1}{1 - x}$, $x = -1$

35. $f(u) = \cot\dfrac{\pi u}{10}$, $u = g(x) = 5\sqrt{x}$, $x = 1$

36. $f(u) = u + \dfrac{1}{\cos^2 u}$, $u = g(x) = \pi x$, $x = \dfrac{1}{4}$

37. $f(u) = \dfrac{2u}{u^2 + 1}$, $u = g(x) = 10x^2 + x + 1$, $x = 0$

38. $f(u) = \left(\dfrac{u - 1}{u + 1}\right)^2$, $u = g(x) = \dfrac{1}{x^2} - 1$, $x = -1$

What happens if you can write a function as a composite in different ways? Do you get the same derivative each time? The Chain Rule says you should. Try it with the functions in Exercises 39 and 40.

39. Find dy/dx if $y = \cos(6x + 2)$ by writing y as a composite with

    (a) $y = \cos u$ and $u = 6x + 2$.

    (b) $y = \cos 2u$ and $u = 3x + 1$.

40. Find dy/dx if $y = \sin(x^2 + 1)$ by writing y as a composite with

    (a) $y = \sin(u + 1)$ and $u = x^2$.

    (b) $y = \sin u$ and $u = x^2 + 1$.

In Exercises 41–48, find the equation of the line tangent to the curve at the point defined by the given value of t.

41. $x = 2 \cos t$, $y = 2 \sin t$, $t = \pi/4$

42. $x = \sin 2\pi t$, $y = \cos 2\pi t$, $t = -1/6$

43. $x = \sec^2 t - 1$, $y = \tan t$, $t = -\pi/4$

44. $x = \sec t$, $y = \tan t$, $t = \pi/6$

45. $x = t$, $y = \sqrt{t}$, $t = 1/4$

46. $x = 2t^2 + 3$, $y = t^4$, $t = -1$

47. $x = t - \sin t$, $y = 1 - \cos t$, $t = \pi/3$

48. $x = \cos t$, $y = 1 + \sin t$, $t = \pi/2$

49. Let $x = t^2 + t$, and let $y = \sin t$.

    (a) Find dy/dx as a function of t.

    (b) Find $\dfrac{d}{dt}\left(\dfrac{dy}{dx}\right)$ as a function of t.

    (c) Find $\dfrac{d}{dx}\left(\dfrac{dy}{dx}\right)$ as a function of t.

    Use the Chain Rule and your answer from part (b).

    (d) Which of the expressions in parts (b) and (c) is d^2y/dx^2?

50. A circle of radius 2 and center $(0, 0)$ can be parametrized by the equations $x = 2 \cos t$ and $y = 2 \sin t$. Show that for any value of t, the line tangent to the circle at $(2 \cos t, 2 \sin t)$ is perpendicular to the radius.

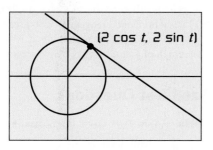
(2 cos t, 2 sin t)

51. Let $s = \cos \theta$. Evaluate ds/dt when $\theta = 3\pi/2$ and $d\theta/dt = 5$.

52. Let $y = x^2 + 7x - 5$. Evaluate dy/dt when $x = 1$ and $dx/dt = 1/3$.

53. What is the largest value possible for the slope of the curve $y = \sin(x/2)$?

54. Write an equation for the tangent to the curve $y = \sin mx$ at the origin.

55. Find the lines that are tangent and normal to the curve $y = 2 \tan(\pi x/4)$ at $x = 1$. Support your answer graphically.

56. *Working with Numerical Values* Suppose that functions f and g and their derivatives have the following values at $x = 2$ and $x = 3$.

x	$f(x)$	$g(x)$	$f'(x)$	$g'(x)$
2	8	2	$1/3$	-3
3	3	-4	2π	5

Evaluate the derivatives with respect to x of the following combinations at the given value of x.

    (a) $2f(x)$ at $x = 2$ **(b)** $f(x) + g(x)$ at $x = 3$

    (c) $f(x) \cdot g(x)$ at $x = 3$ **(d)** $f(x)/g(x)$ at $x = 2$

    (e) $f(g(x))$ at $x = 2$ **(f)** $\sqrt{f(x)}$ at $x = 2$

    (g) $1/g^2(x)$ at $x = 3$ **(h)** $\sqrt{f^2(x) + g^2(x)}$ at $x = 2$

57. *Extension of Example 8* Show that $\dfrac{d}{dx} \cos(x°)$ is $-\dfrac{\pi}{180} \sin(x°)$.

58. *Working with Numerical Values* Suppose that the functions f and g and their derivatives with respect to x have the following values at $x = 0$ and $x = 1$.

x	$f(x)$	$g(x)$	$f'(x)$	$g'(x)$
0	1	1	5	$1/3$
1	3	-4	$-1/3$	$-8/3$

Evaluate the derivatives with respect to x of the following combinations at the given value of x.

    (a) $5f(x) - g(x)$, $x = 1$ **(b)** $f(x)g^3(x)$, $x = 0$

    (c) $\dfrac{f(x)}{g(x) + 1}$, $x = 1$ **(d)** $f(g(x))$, $x = 0$

    (e) $g(f(x))$, $x = 0$ **(f)** $(g(x) + f(x))^{-2}$, $x = 1$

    (g) $f(x + g(x))$, $x = 0$

59. *Orthogonal Curves* Two curves are said to cross at right angles if their tangents are perpendicular at the crossing point. The technical word for "crossing at right angles" is **orthogonal.** Show that the curves $y = \sin 2x$ and $y = -\sin(x/2)$ are orthogonal at the origin. Draw both graphs and both tangents in a square viewing window.

60. *Writing to Learn* Explain why the Chain Rule formula

$$\frac{dy}{dx} = \frac{dy}{du} \cdot \frac{du}{dx}$$

is not simply the well-known rule for multiplying fractions.

61. *Running Machinery Too Fast* Suppose that a piston is moving straight up and down and that its position at time *t* seconds is

$$s = A \cos(2\pi b t),$$

with *A* and *b* positive. The value of *A* is the amplitude of the motion, and *b* is the frequency (number of times the piston moves up and down each second). What effect does doubling the frequency have on the piston's velocity, acceleration, and jerk? (Once you find out, you will know why machinery breaks when you run it too fast.)

Figure 4.5 The internal forces in the engine get so large that they tear the engine apart when the velocity is too great.

62. Group Activity *Tempe Temperatures.* The graph in Figure 4.6 shows the variation in average daily temperature in Tempe, Arizona, during a typical 365-day year. The equation that approximates the Fahrenheit temperature on day *x* is

$$y = 19.3 \sin\left[\frac{2\pi}{365}(x - 101)\right] + 70.$$

(a) On approximately what day of the year does the daily temperature show the greatest increase from the previous day?

(b) About how many degrees per day is the temperature increasing at that time of the year?

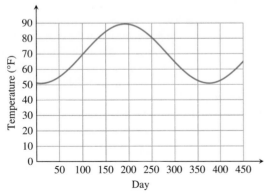

Figure 4.6 Average daily temperatures in Tempe, AZ, for a typical 365-day year are modeled by a sinusoid (Exercise 62).

63. *Particle Motion* The position of a particle moving along a coordinate line is $s = \sqrt{1 + 4t}$, with *s* in meters and *t* in seconds. Find the particle's velocity and acceleration at $t = 6 \sec$.

64. *Constant Acceleration* Suppose the velocity of a falling body is $v = k\sqrt{s}$ m/sec (*k* a constant) at the instant the body has fallen *s* meters from its starting point. Show that the body's acceleration is constant.

65. *Falling Meteorite* The velocity of a heavy meteorite entering the earth's atmosphere is inversely proportional to $\sqrt{s}$ when it is *s* kilometers from the earth's center. Show that the meteorite's acceleration is inversely proportional to s^2.

66. *Particle Acceleration* A particle moves along the *x*-axis with velocity $dx/dt = f(x)$. Show that the particle's acceleration is $f(x)f'(x)$.

67. *Temperature and the Period of a Pendulum* For oscillations of small amplitude (short swings), we may safely model the relationship between the period *T* and the length *L* of a simple pendulum with the equation

$$T = 2\pi\sqrt{\frac{L}{g}},$$

where *g* is the constant acceleration of gravity at the pendulum's location. If we measure *g* in centimeters per second squared, we measure *L* in centimeters and *T* in seconds. If the pendulum is made of metal, its length will vary with temperature, either increasing or decreasing at a rate that is roughly proportional to *L*. In symbols, with *u* being temperature and *k* the proportionality constant,

$$\frac{dL}{du} = kL.$$

Assuming this to be the case, show that the rate at which the period changes with respect to temperature is $kT/2$.

68. Writing to Learn *Chain Rule* Suppose that $f(x) = x^2$ and $g(x) = |x|$. Then the composites

$$(f \circ g)(x) = |x|^2 = x^2 \quad \text{and} \quad (g \circ f)(x) = |x^2| = x^2$$

are both differentiable at $x = 0$ even though *g* itself is not differentiable at $x = 0$. Does this contradict the Chain Rule? Explain.

69. *Tangents* Suppose that $u = g(x)$ is differentiable at $x = 1$ and that $y = f(u)$ is differentiable at $u = g(1)$. If the graph of $y = f(g(x))$ has a horizontal tangent at $x = 1$, can we conclude anything about the tangent to the graph of *g* at $x = 1$ or the tangent to the graph of *f* at $u = g(1)$? Give reasons for your answer.

Standardized Test Questions

70. True or False $\dfrac{d}{dx}(\sin x) = \cos x$, if *x* is measured in degrees or radians. Justify your answer.

71. True or False The slope of the normal line to the curve $x = 3 \cos t$, $y = 3 \sin t$ at $t = \pi/4$ is -1. Justify your answer.

72. Multiple Choice Which of the following is dy/dx if $y = \tan(4x)$?

(A) $4 \sec(4x) \tan(4x)$ **(B)** $\sec(4x) \tan(4x)$ **(C)** $4 \cot(4x)$

(D) $\sec^2(4x)$ **(E)** $4 \sec^2(4x)$

73. Multiple Choice Which of the following is dy/dx if $y = \cos^2(x^3 + x^2)$?

(A) $-2(3x^2 + 2x)$

(B) $-(3x^2 + 2x)\cos(x^3 + x^2)\sin(x^3 + x^2)$

(C) $-2(3x^2 + 2x)\cos(x^3 + x^2)\sin(x^3 + x^2)$

(D) $2(3x^2 + 2x)\cos(x^3 + x^2)\sin(x^3 + x^2)$

(E) $2(3x^2 + 2x)$

In Exercises 74 and 75, use the curve defined by the parametric equations $x = t - \cos t$, $y = -1 + \sin t$.

74. Multiple Choice Which of the following is an equation of the tangent line to the curve at $t = 0$?

(A) $y = x$ **(B)** $y = -x$ **(C)** $y = x + 2$

(D) $y = x - 2$ **(E)** $y = -x - 2$

75. Multiple Choice At which of the following values of t is $dy/dx = 0$?

(A) $t = \pi/4$ **(B)** $t = \pi/2$ **(C)** $t = 3\pi/4$

(D) $t = \pi$ **(E)** $t = 2\pi$

Explorations

76. *The Derivative of sin 2x* Graph the function $y = 2\cos 2x$ for $-2 \le x \le 3.5$. Then, on the same screen, graph

$$y = \frac{\sin 2(x + h) - \sin 2x}{h}$$

for $h = 1.0, 0.5$, and 0.2. Experiment with other values of h, including negative values. What do you see happening as $h \to 0$? Explain this behavior.

77. *The Derivative of cos (x^2)* Graph $y = -2x\sin(x^2)$ for $-2 \le x \le 3$. Then, on the same screen, graph

$$y = \frac{\cos[(x + h)^2] - \cos(x)^2}{h}$$

for $h = 1.0, 0.7$, and 0.3. Experiment with other values of h. What do you see happening as $h \to 0$? Explain this behavior.

Extending the Ideas

78. *Absolute Value Functions* Let u be a differentiable function of x.

(a) Show that $\dfrac{d}{dx}|u| = u'\dfrac{u}{|u|}$.

(b) Use part (a) to find the derivatives of $f(x) = |x^2 - 9|$ and $g(x) = |x| \sin x$.

79. *Geometric and Arithmetic Mean* The geometric mean of u and v is $G = \sqrt{uv}$ and the arithmetic mean is $A = (u + v)/2$. Show that if $u = x$, $v = x + c$, c a real number, then

$$\frac{dG}{dx} = \frac{A}{G}.$$

4.2 | Implicit Differentiation

You will be able to find derivatives of implicitly defined functions and thereby analyze parametrically defined curves.

- Implicitly defined functions
- Using the Chain Rule to find derivatives of functions defined implicitly
- Tangent and normal lines to implicitly defined curves
- Finding higher order derivatives of implicitly defined functions
- Extending the Power Rule from integer powers to rational powers

Implicitly Defined Functions

The graph of the equation $x^3 + y^3 - 9xy = 0$ (Figure 4.7) has a well-defined slope at nearly every point because it is the union of the graphs of the functions $y = f_1(x)$, $y = f_2(x)$, and $y = f_3(x)$, which are differentiable except at O and A. But how do we find the slope when we cannot conveniently solve the equation to find the functions? The answer is to treat y as a differentiable function of x and differentiate both sides of the equation with respect to x, using the differentiation rules for sums, products, and quotients, and the Chain Rule. Then solve for dy/dx in terms of x and y *together* to obtain a formula that calculates the slope at any point (x, y) on the graph from the values of x and y.

The process by which we find dy/dx is called **implicit differentiation.** The phrase derives from the fact that the equation

$$x^3 + y^3 - 9xy = 0$$

defines the functions f_1, f_2, and f_3 implicitly (i.e., hidden inside the equation), without giving us *explicit* formulas to work with.

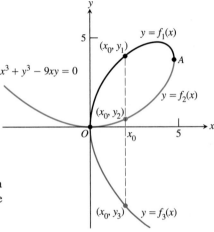

Figure 4.7 The graph of $x^3 + y^3 - 9xy = 0$ (called a *folium*). Although not the graph of a function, it is the union of the graphs of three separate functions. This particular curve dates to Descartes in 1638.

EXAMPLE 1 Differentiating Implicitly

Find dy/dx if $y^2 = x$.

SOLUTION

To find dy/dx, we simply differentiate both sides of the equation $y^2 = x$ with respect to x, treating y as a differentiable function of x and applying the Chain Rule:

$$y^2 = x$$

$$2y\frac{dy}{dx} = 1 \qquad \frac{d}{dx}(y^2) = \frac{d}{dy}(y^2) \cdot \frac{dy}{dx}$$

$$\frac{dy}{dx} = \frac{1}{2y}$$

Now Try Exercise 3.

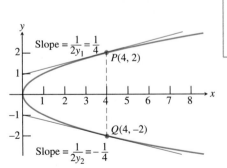

Figure 4.8 The derivative found in Example 1 gives the slope for the tangent lines at both P and Q, because it is a function of y.

In the previous example we differentiated with respect to x, and yet the derivative we obtained appeared as a function of y. Not only is this acceptable, it is actually quite useful. Figure 4.8, for example, shows that the curve has two different tangent lines when $x = 4$: one at the point $(4, 2)$ and the other at the point $(4, -2)$. Since the formula for dy/dx depends on y, our single formula gives the slope in both cases.

Implicit differentiation will frequently yield a derivative that is expressed in terms of both x and y, as in Example 2.

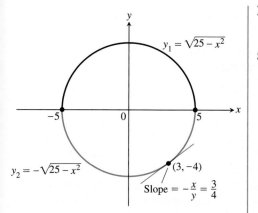

Figure 4.9 The circle combines the graphs of two functions. The graph of y_2 is the lower semicircle and passes through $(3, -4)$. (Example 2)

EXAMPLE 2 Finding Slope on a Circle

Find the slope of the circle $x^2 + y^2 = 25$ at the point $(3, -4)$.

SOLUTION

The circle is not the graph of a single function of x, but it is the union of the graphs of two differentiable functions, $y_1 = \sqrt{25 - x^2}$ and $y_2 = -\sqrt{25 - x^2}$ (Figure 4.9). The point $(3, -4)$ lies on the graph of y_2, so it is possible to find the slope by calculating explicitly:

$$\frac{dy_2}{dx}\bigg|_{x=3} = -\frac{-2x}{2\sqrt{25 - x^2}}\bigg|_{x=3} = -\frac{-6}{2\sqrt{25 - 9}} = \frac{3}{4}$$

But we can also find this slope more easily by differentiating both sides of the equation of the circle implicitly with respect to x:

$$\frac{d}{dx}(x^2 + y^2) = \frac{d}{dx}(25) \qquad \text{Differentiate both sides with respect to } x.$$

$$2x + 2y\frac{dy}{dx} = 0$$

$$\frac{dy}{dx} = -\frac{x}{y}$$

The slope at $(3, -4)$ is

$$-\frac{x}{y}\bigg|_{(3, -4)} = -\frac{3}{-4} = \frac{3}{4}.$$

The implicit solution, besides being computationally easier, yields a formula for dy/dx that applies at any point on the circle (except, of course, $(\pm 5, 0)$, where slope is undefined). The explicit solution derived from the formula for y_2 applies only to the lower half of the circle.

Now Try Exercise 11.

To calculate the derivatives of other implicitly defined functions, we proceed as in Examples 1 and 2. We treat y as a differentiable function of x and apply the usual rules to differentiate both sides of the defining equation.

EXAMPLE 3 Solving for *dy/dx*

Show that the slope dy/dx is defined at every point on the graph of $2y = x^2 + \sin y$.

SOLUTION

First we need to know dy/dx, which we find by implicit differentiation:

$$2y = x^2 + \sin y$$

$$\frac{d}{dx}(2y) = \frac{d}{dx}(x^2 + \sin y) \qquad \text{Differentiate both sides with respect to } x \ldots$$

$$= \frac{d}{dx}(x^2) + \frac{d}{dx}(\sin y)$$

$$2\frac{dy}{dx} = 2x + \cos y\frac{dy}{dx} \qquad \ldots \text{treating } y \text{ as a function of } x \text{ and using the Chain Rule.}$$

$$2\frac{dy}{dx} - (\cos y)\frac{dy}{dx} = 2x \qquad \text{Collect terms with } dy/dx$$

$$(2 - \cos y)\frac{dy}{dx} = 2x \qquad \text{and factor out } dy/dx.$$

$$\frac{dy}{dx} = \frac{2x}{2 - \cos y} \qquad \text{Solve for } dy/dx \text{ by dividing.}$$

The formula for dy/dx is defined at every point (x, y), except for those points at which $\cos y = 2$. Since $\cos y$ cannot be greater than 1, this never happens.

Now Try Exercise 13.

Ellen Ochoa (1958–)

After earning a doctorate degree in electrical engineering from Stanford University, Ellen Ochoa became a research engineer and, within a few years, received three patents in the field of optics. In 1990, Ochoa joined the NASA astronaut program, and, three years later, became the first Hispanic female to travel in space. Ochoa's message to young people is: "If you stay in school you have the potential to achieve what you want in the future."

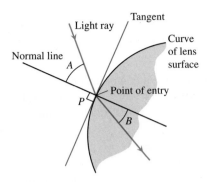

Figure 4.10 The profile of a lens, showing the bending (refraction) of a ray of light as it passes through the lens surface.

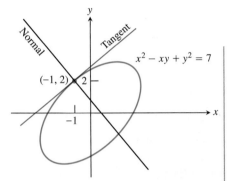

Figure 4.11 Tangent and normal lines to the ellipse $x^2 - xy + y^2 = 7$ at the point $(-1, 2)$. (Example 4)

Implicit Differentiation Process

1. Differentiate both sides of the equation with respect to x.
2. Collect the terms with dy/dx on one side of the equation.
3. Factor out dy/dx.
4. Solve for dy/dx.

Lenses, Tangents, and Normal Lines

In the law that describes how light changes direction as it enters a lens, the important angles are the angles the light makes with the line perpendicular to the surface of the lens at the point of entry (angles A and B in Figure 4.10). This line is called the **normal to the surface** at the point of entry. In a profile view of a lens like the one in Figure 4.10, the normal is a line perpendicular to the tangent to the profile curve at the point of entry.

Profiles of lenses are often described by quadratic curves (see Figure 4.11). When they are, we can use implicit differentiation to find the tangents and normals.

EXAMPLE 4 Tangent and normal to an ellipse

Find the tangent and normal to the ellipse $x^2 - xy + y^2 = 7$ at the point $(-1, 2)$. (See Figure 4.11.)

SOLUTION

We first use implicit differentiation to find dy/dx:

$$x^2 - xy + y^2 = 7$$

$$\frac{d}{dx}(x^2) - \frac{d}{dx}(xy) + \frac{d}{dx}(y^2) = \frac{d}{dx}(7) \qquad \text{Differentiate both sides with respect to } x \ldots$$

$$2x - \left(x\frac{dy}{dx} + y\frac{dx}{dx}\right) + 2y\frac{dy}{dx} = 0 \qquad \ldots \text{treating } xy \text{ as a product and } y \text{ as a function of } x.$$

$$(2y - x)\frac{dy}{dx} = y - 2x \qquad \text{Collect terms.}$$

$$\frac{dy}{dx} = \frac{y - 2x}{2y - x} \qquad \text{Solve for } dy/dx.$$

We then evaluate the derivative at $x = -1, y = 2$ to obtain

$$\left.\frac{dy}{dx}\right|_{(-1, 2)} = \left.\frac{y - 2x}{2y - x}\right|_{(-1, 2)}$$

$$= \frac{2 - 2(-1)}{2(2) - (-1)}$$

$$= \frac{4}{5}$$

The tangent to the curve at $(-1, 2)$ is

$$y - 2 = \frac{4}{5}(x - (-1))$$

$$y - 2 = \frac{4}{5}(x + 1)$$

The normal to the curve at $(-1, 2)$ is

$$y - 2 = -\frac{5}{4}(x + 1) \qquad \qquad \textit{Now Try Exercise 17.}$$

Derivatives of Higher Order

Implicit differentiation can also be used to find derivatives of higher order. Here is an example.

EXAMPLE 5 Finding a Second Derivative Implicitly

Find d^2y/dx^2 if $2x^3 - 3y^2 = 8$.

SOLUTION

To start, we differentiate both sides of the equation with respect to x in order to find $y' = dy/dx$.

$$\frac{d}{dx}(2x^3 - 3y^2) = \frac{d}{dx}(8)$$

$$6x^2 - 6yy' = 0$$

$$x^2 - yy' = 0$$

$$y' = \frac{x^2}{y}, \text{ when } y \neq 0$$

We now apply the Quotient Rule to find y''.

$$y'' = \frac{d}{dx}\left(\frac{x^2}{y}\right) = \frac{2xy - x^2y'}{y^2} = \frac{2x}{y} - \frac{x^2}{y^2} \cdot y'$$

Finally, we substitute $y' = x^2/y$ to express y'' in terms of x and y.

$$y'' = \frac{2x}{y} - \frac{x^2}{y^2}\left(\frac{x^2}{y}\right) = \frac{2x}{y} - \frac{x^4}{y^3}, \text{ when } y \neq 0$$

Now Try Exercise 29.

EXPLORATION 1 An Unexpected Derivative

Consider the set of all points (x, y) satisfying the equation $x^2 - 2xy + y^2 = 4$. What does the graph of the equation look like? You can find out in two ways in this Exploration.

1. Use implicit differentiation to find dy/dx. Are you surprised by this derivative?
2. Knowing the derivative, what do you conjecture about the graph?
3. What are the possible values of y when $x = 0$? Does this information enable you to refine your conjecture about the graph?
4. The original equation can be written as $(x - y)^2 - 4 = 0$. By factoring the expression on the left, write two equations whose graphs combine to give the graph of the original equation. Then sketch the graph.
5. Explain why your graph is consistent with the derivative found in part 1.

Rational Powers of Differentiable Functions

We know that the Power Rule

$$\frac{d}{dx}x^n = nx^{n-1}$$

holds for any integer n (Rules 2 and 7). We can now prove that it holds when n is any rational number.

The Power Rule Again?

This is the third time we have stated this rule, but the first time we are able to prove it for arbitrary rational powers. You will see it one more time (Rule 10) when we have the tools necessary to prove it for all real powers.

RULE 9   Power Rule for Rational Powers of x

If n is any rational number, then

$$\frac{d}{dx}x^n = nx^{n-1}.$$

If $n < 1$, then the derivative does not exist at $x = 0$.

Proof Let p and q be integers with $q > 0$ and suppose that $y = \sqrt[q]{x^p} = x^{p/q}$. Then

$$y^q = x^p.$$

Since p and q are integers (for which we already have the Power Rule), we can differentiate both sides of the equation with respect to x and obtain

$$qy^{q-1}\frac{dy}{dx} = px^{p-1}.$$

If $y \neq 0$, we can divide both sides of the equation by qy^{q-1} to solve for dy/dx, obtaining

$$\frac{dy}{dx} = \frac{px^{p-1}}{qy^{q-1}}$$

$$= \frac{p}{q} \cdot \frac{x^{p-1}}{(x^{p/q})^{q-1}} \qquad y = x^{p/q}$$

$$= \frac{p}{q} \cdot \frac{x^{p-1}}{x^{p-p/q}} \qquad \frac{p}{q}(q-1) = p - \frac{p}{q}$$

$$= \frac{p}{q} \cdot x^{(p-1)-(p-p/q)} \qquad \text{A law of exponents}$$

$$= \frac{p}{q} \cdot x^{(p/q)-1}$$

This proves the rule. ■

By combining this result with the Chain Rule, we get an extension of the Power Chain Rule to rational powers of u:

If n is a rational number and u is a differentiable function of x, then u^n is a differentiable function of x and

$$\frac{d}{dx}u^n = nu^{n-1}\frac{du}{dx},$$

provided that $u \neq 0$ if $n < 1$.

The restriction that $u \neq 0$ when $n < 1$ is necessary because 0 might be in the domain of u^n but not in the domain of u^{n-1}, as we see in the first two parts of Example 6.

EXAMPLE 6 Using the Rational Power Rule

(a) $\dfrac{d}{dx}\left(\sqrt{x}\right) = \dfrac{d}{dx}(x^{1/2}) = \dfrac{1}{2}x^{-1/2} = \dfrac{1}{2\sqrt{x}}$

Notice that $\sqrt{x}$ is defined at $x = 0$, but $1/\left(2\sqrt{x}\right)$ is not.

continued

(b) $\dfrac{d}{dx}(x^{2/3}) = \dfrac{2}{3}(x^{-1/3}) = \dfrac{2}{3x^{1/3}}$

The original function is defined for all real numbers, but the derivative is undefined at $x = 0$. Recall Figure 3.12, which showed that this function's graph has a *cusp* at $x = 0$.

(c) $\dfrac{d}{dx}(\cos x)^{-1/5} = -\dfrac{1}{5}(\cos x)^{-6/5} \cdot \dfrac{d}{dx}(\cos x)$

$= -\dfrac{1}{5}(\cos x)^{-6/5}(-\sin x)$

$= \dfrac{1}{5}\sin x(\cos x)^{-6/5}$ *Now Try Exercise 33.*

EXAMPLE 7 Three Multiple-Choice Challenges

Here are three multiple-choice questions that most calculus students get wrong because they fail to handle the Chain Rule properly. See if you can answer them before looking at the solutions. In any case, be sure to study them carefully so you can avoid making similar mistakes later.

1. If $\dfrac{dy}{dx} = 1 + \sin y$, then $\dfrac{d^2y}{dx^2} =$

   (A) $\cos y$ **(B)** $-\cos y$ **(C)** $\cos^2 y$ **(D)** $(1 + \sin y)^2$ **(E)** $\cos y + \sin y \cos y$

2. If $x = \sin t$ and $y = \cos t$, then $\dfrac{d^2y}{dx^2} =$

   (A) $\sec^2 t$ **(B)** $-\sec^2 t$ **(C)** $\csc^2 t$ **(D)** $-\csc^2 t$ **(E)** $-\sec^3 t$

3. If $y = f(t^2)$ and $f'(x) = \sqrt{2 - \cos x}$, then $\dfrac{dy}{dt} =$

   (A) $\sqrt{2 - \cos(t^2)}$ **(B)** $2t\sqrt{2 - \cos(t^2)}$ **(C)** $2t\sin(t^2)\sqrt{2 - \cos(t^2)}$

   (D) $\dfrac{t}{\sqrt{2 - \cos(t^2)}}$ **(E)** $\dfrac{t\sin(t^2)}{\sqrt{2 - \cos(t^2)}}$

SOLUTION

1. The correct answer is (E), although the popular choice is (A).

Remember that $\dfrac{d^2y}{dx^2} = \dfrac{d}{dx}\left(\dfrac{dy}{dx}\right)$, so you need to differentiate $\dfrac{dy}{dx}$ with respect to x, not y. It is true that $(1 + \sin y)' = \cos y$, but that is the derivative with respect to y. The correct derivative with respect to x is $\dfrac{d}{dx}(1 + \sin y) = \cos y \dfrac{dy}{dx} = \cos y (1 + \sin y) = \cos y + \sin y \cos y$.

2. The correct answer is (E), although the popular choice is (A).

Most students have no problem with the first derivative: $\dfrac{dy}{dx} = \dfrac{dy/dt}{dx/dt} = \dfrac{-\sin t}{\cos t} = -\tan t$. Again, $\dfrac{d^2y}{dx^2} = \dfrac{d}{dx}\left(\dfrac{dy}{dx}\right)$, so you need to differentiate $\dfrac{dy}{dx}$ with respect to x, not t. It is true that $(-\tan t)' = -\sec^2 t$, but that is the derivative with respect to t. The correct derivative with respect to x is $\dfrac{d}{dx}(-\tan t) = \dfrac{d(-\tan t)/dt}{dx/dt} = \dfrac{-\sec^2 t}{\cos t} = -\sec^3 t.$ *continued*

3. The correct answer is (B), although the popular choice is (A).

Distracted by the unusual appearance of prime notation and Leibniz notation in the same sentence, many students forget about the Chain Rule (or else they overcompensate, leading to one of the other distractors).

It is true that $f'(t^2) = \sqrt{2 - \cos(t^2)}$, but that is the derivative of f with respect to t^2. The correct derivative with respect to t is $\dfrac{dy}{dt} = \dfrac{d}{dt}(f(t^2)) = f'(t^2) \cdot 2t = 2t\sqrt{2 - \cos(t^2)}$.

Now Try Exercises 61 and 62.

Quick Review 4.2 *(For help, go to Section 1.2 and Appendix A5.)*

Exercise numbers with a gray background indicate problems that the authors have designed to be solved *without a calculator.*

In Exercises 1–5, sketch the curve defined by the equation and find two functions y_1 and y_2 whose graphs will combine to give the curve.

1. $x - y^2 = 0$

2. $4x^2 + 9y^2 = 36$

3. $x^2 - 4y^2 = 0$

4. $x^2 + y^2 = 9$

5. $x^2 + y^2 = 2x + 3$

In Exercises 6–8, solve for y' in terms of y and x.

6. $x^2 y' - 2xy = 4x - y$

7. $y' \sin x - x \cos x = xy' + y$

8. $x(y^2 - y') = y'(x^2 - y)$

In Exercises 9 and 10, find an expression for the function using rational powers rather than radicals.

9. $\sqrt{x}(x - \sqrt[3]{x})$

10. $\dfrac{x + \sqrt[3]{x^2}}{\sqrt{x^3}}$

Section 4.2 Exercises

In Exercises 1–8, find dy/dx.

1. $x^2 y + xy^2 = 6$

2. $x^3 + y^3 = 18xy$

3. $y^2 = \dfrac{x - 1}{x + 1}$

4. $x^2 = \dfrac{x - y}{x + y}$

5. $x = \tan y$

6. $x = \sin y$

7. $x + \tan(xy) = 0$

8. $x + \sin y = xy$

In Exercises 9–12, find dy/dx and find the slope of the curve at the indicated point.

9. $x^2 + y^2 = 13$, $(-2, 3)$

10. $x^2 + y^2 = 9$, $(0, 3)$

11. $(x - 1)^2 + (y - 1)^2 = 13$, $(3, 4)$

12. $(x + 2)^2 + (y + 3)^2 = 25$, $(1, -7)$

In Exercises 13–16, find where the slope of the curve is defined.

13. $x^2 y - xy^2 = 4$

14. $x = \cos y$

15. $x^3 + y^3 = xy$

16. $x^2 + 4xy + 4y^2 - 3x = 6$

In Exercises 17–26, find the lines that are **(a)** tangent and **(b)** normal to the curve at the given point.

17. $x^2 + xy - y^2 = 1$, $(2, 3)$

18. $x^2 + y^2 = 25$, $(3, -4)$

19. $x^2 y^2 = 9$, $(-1, 3)$

20. $y^2 - 2x - 4y - 1 = 0$, $(-2, 1)$

21. $6x^2 + 3xy + 2y^2 + 17y - 6 = 0$, $(-1, 0)$

22. $x^2 - \sqrt{3}xy + 2y^2 = 5$, $(\sqrt{3}, 2)$

23. $2xy + \pi \sin y = 2\pi$, $(1, \pi/2)$

24. $x \sin 2y = y \cos 2x$, $(\pi/4, \pi/2)$

25. $y = 2 \sin(\pi x - y)$, $(1, 0)$

26. $x^2 \cos^2 y - \sin y = 0$, $(0, \pi)$

In Exercises 27–30, use implicit differentiation to find dy/dx and then d^2y/dx^2.

27. $x^2 + y^2 = 1$

28. $x^{2/3} + y^{2/3} = 1$

29. $y^2 = x^2 + 2x$

30. $y^2 + 2y = 2x + 1$

In Exercises 31–42, find dy/dx.

31. $y = x^{9/4}$

32. $y = x^{-3/5}$

33. $y = \sqrt[3]{x}$

34. $y = \sqrt[4]{x}$

35. $y = (2x + 5)^{-1/2}$

36. $y = (1 - 6x)^{2/3}$

37. $y = x\sqrt{x^2 + 1}$

38. $y = \dfrac{x}{\sqrt{x^2 + 1}}$

39. $y = \sqrt{1 - \sqrt{x}}$

40. $y = 3(2x^{-1/2} + 1)^{-1/3}$

41. $y = 3(\csc x)^{3/2}$

42. $y = [\sin(x + 5)]^{5/4}$

43. Which of the following could be true if $f''(x) = x^{-1/3}$?

(a) $f(x) = \dfrac{3}{2}x^{2/3} - 3$

(b) $f(x) = \dfrac{9}{10}x^{5/3} - 7$

(c) $f'''(x) = -\dfrac{1}{3}x^{-4/3}$

(d) $f'(x) = \dfrac{3}{2}x^{2/3} + 6$

44. Which of the following could be true if $g''(t) = 1/t^{3/4}$?

(a) $g'(t) = 4\sqrt[4]{t} - 4$

(b) $g'''(t) = -4/\sqrt[4]{t}$

(c) $g(t) = t - 7 + (16/5)t^{5/4}$

(d) $g'(t) = (1/4)t^{1/4}$

45. *The Eight Curve* (a) Find the slopes of the figure-eight–shaped curve

$$y^4 = y^2 - x^2$$

at the two points shown on the graph that follows.

(b) Use parametric mode and the two pairs of parametric equations

$$x_1(t) = \sqrt{t^2 - t^4}, \quad y_1(t) = t,$$

$$x_2(t) = -\sqrt{t^2 - t^4}, \quad y_2(t) = t,$$

to graph the curve. Specify a window and a parameter interval.

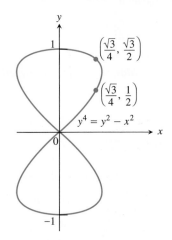

46. *The Cissoid of Diocles (dates from about 200 B.C.E.)*

(a) Find equations for the tangent and normal to the cissoid of Diocles,

$$y^2(2 - x) = x^3,$$

at the point $(1, 1)$ as pictured below.

(b) Explain how to reproduce the graph on a grapher.

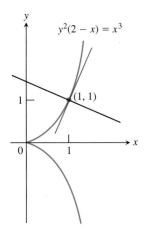

47. (a) Confirm that $(-1, 1)$ is on the curve defined by
$x^3y^2 = \cos(\pi y)$.

(b) Use part (a) to find the slope of the line tangent to the curve at $(-1, 1)$.

48. Group Activity

(a) Show that the relation

$$y^3 - xy = -1$$

cannot be a function of x by showing that there is more than one possible y value when $x = 2$.

(b) On a small enough square with center $(2, 1)$, the part of the graph of the relation within the square will define a function $y = f(x)$. For this function, find $f'(2)$ and $f''(2)$.

49. Find the two points where the curve $x^2 + xy + y^2 = 7$ crosses the x-axis, and show that the tangents to the curve at these points are parallel. What is the common slope of these tangents?

50. Find points on the curve $x^2 + xy + y^2 = 7$ **(a)** where the tangent is parallel to the x-axis and **(b)** where the tangent is parallel to the y-axis. (In the latter case, dy/dx is not defined, but dx/dy is. What value does dx/dy have at these points?)

51. *Orthogonal Curves* Two curves are *orthogonal* at a point of intersection if their tangents at that point cross at right angles. Show that the curves $2x^2 + 3y^2 = 5$ and $y^2 = x^3$ are orthogonal at $(1, 1)$ and $(1, -1)$. Use parametric mode to draw the curves and to show the tangent lines.

52. The position of a body moving along a coordinate line at time t is $s = (4 + 6t)^{3/2}$, with s in meters and t in seconds. Find the body's velocity and acceleration when $t = 2$ sec.

53. The velocity of a falling body is $v = 8\sqrt{s} - t + 1$ feet per second at the instant t (sec) the body has fallen s feet from its starting point. Show that the body's acceleration is 32 ft/sec².

54. *The Devil's Curve (Gabriel Cramer [the Cramer of Cramer's Rule], 1750)* Find the slopes of the devil's curve $y^4 - 4y^2 = x^4 - 9x^2$ at the four indicated points.

$$y^4 - 4y^2 = x^4 - 9x^2$$

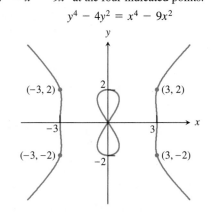

55. *The Folium of Descartes* (See Figure 4.7 on page 164.)

(a) Find the slope of the folium of Descartes, $x^3 + y^3 - 9xy = 0$ at the points $(4, 2)$ and $(2, 4)$.

(b) At what point other than the origin does the folium have a horizontal tangent?

(c) Find the coordinates of point A in Figure 4.7, where the folium has a vertical tangent.

56. The line that is normal to the curve $x^2 + 2xy - 3y^2 = 0$ at $(1, 1)$ intersects the curve at what other point?

57. Find the normals to the curve $xy + 2x - y = 0$ that are parallel to the line $2x + y = 0$.

58. Show that if it is possible to draw these three normals from the point $(a, 0)$ to the parabola $x = y^2$ shown here, then a must be greater than $1/2$. One of the normals is the x-axis. For what value of a are the other two normals perpendicular?

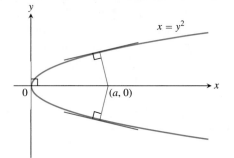

Standardized Test Questions

59. True or False The slope of $xy^2 + x = 1$ at $(1/2, 1)$ is 2. Justify your answer.

60. True or False The derivative of $y = \sqrt[3]{x}$ is $\dfrac{1}{3x^{2/3}}$. Justify your answer.

In Exercises 61 and 62, use the curve $x^2 - xy + y^2 = 1$.

61. Multiple Choice Which of the following is equal to dy/dx?

(A) $\dfrac{y - 2x}{2y - x}$ (B) $\dfrac{y + 2x}{2y - x}$ (C) $\dfrac{2x}{x - 2y}$

(D) $\dfrac{2x + y}{x - 2y}$ (E) $\dfrac{y + 2x}{x}$

62. Multiple Choice Which of the following is equal to $\dfrac{d^2y}{dx^2}$?

(A) $-\dfrac{6}{(2y - x)^3}$ (B) $\dfrac{10y^2 - 10x^2 - 10xy}{(2y - x)^3}$

(C) $\dfrac{8x^2 - 4xy + 8y^2}{(x - 2y)^3}$ (D) $\dfrac{10x^2 + 10y^2}{(x - 2y)^3}$ (E) $\dfrac{2}{x}$

63. Multiple Choice Which of the following is equal to dy/dx if $y = x^{3/4}$?

(A) $\dfrac{3x^{1/3}}{4}$ (B) $\dfrac{4x^{1/4}}{3}$ (C) $\dfrac{3x^{1/4}}{4}$ (D) $\dfrac{4}{3x^{1/4}}$ (E) $\dfrac{3}{4x^{1/4}}$

64. Multiple Choice Which of the following is equal to the slope of the tangent to $y^2 - x^2 = 1$ at $(1, \sqrt{2})$?

(A) $-\dfrac{1}{\sqrt{2}}$ (B) $-\sqrt{2}$ (C) $\dfrac{1}{\sqrt{2}}$ (D) $\sqrt{2}$ (E) 0

Extending the Ideas

65. *Finding Tangents*

(a) Show that the tangent to the ellipse
$$\frac{x^2}{a^2} + \frac{y^2}{b^2} = 1$$
at the point (x_1, y_1) has equation
$$\frac{x_1 x}{a^2} + \frac{y_1 y}{b^2} = 1.$$

(b) Find an equation for the tangent to the hyperbola
$$\frac{x^2}{a^2} - \frac{y^2}{b^2} = 1$$
at the point (x_1, y_1).

66. *End Behavior Model* Consider the hyperbola
$$\frac{x^2}{a^2} - \frac{y^2}{b^2} = 1.$$
Show that

(a) $y = \pm\dfrac{b}{a}\sqrt{x^2 - a^2}$.

(b) $g(x) = (b/a)|x|$ is an end behavior model for
$$f(x) = (b/a)\sqrt{x^2 - a^2}.$$

(c) $g(x) = -(b/a)|x|$ is an end behavior model for
$$f(x) = -(b/a)\sqrt{x^2 - a^2}.$$

Quick Quiz for AP* Preparation: Sections 4.1–4.2

1. Multiple Choice Which of the following gives $\dfrac{dy}{dx}$ for $y = \sin^4(3x)$?

(A) $4\sin^3(3x)\cos(3x)$ (B) $12\sin^3(3x)\cos(3x)$

(C) $12\sin(3x)\cos(3x)$ (D) $12\sin^3(3x)$

(E) $-12\sin^3(3x)\cos(3x)$

2. Multiple Choice What is the slope of the line tangent to the curve $2x^2 - 3y^2 = 2xy - 6$ at the point $(3, 2)$?

(A) 0 (B) $\dfrac{4}{9}$ (C) $\dfrac{7}{9}$ (D) $\dfrac{6}{7}$ (E) $\dfrac{5}{3}$

3. Multiple Choice Which of the following gives $\dfrac{dy}{dx}$ for the parametric curve $x = 3\sin t$, $y = 2\cos t$?

(A) $-\dfrac{3}{2}\cos t$ (B) $\dfrac{3}{2}\cos t$ (C) $-\dfrac{2}{3}\tan t$

(D) $\dfrac{2}{3}\tan t$ (E) $\tan t$

4. Free Response A curve in the xy-plane is defined by $xy^2 - x^3y = 6$.

(a) Find $\dfrac{dy}{dx}$.

(b) Find an equation for the tangent line at each point on the curve with x-coordinate 1.

(c) Find the x-coordinate of each point on the curve where the tangent line is vertical.

4.3 | Derivatives of Inverse Trigonometric Functions

You will be able to use implicit differentiation to find the derivatives of inverses of functions with known derivatives, including inverse trigonometric functions.

- Differentiating inverse functions
- Graphical interpretation of how the derivative of *f* is related to the derivative of f^{-1}
- Derivatives of the inverse trigonometric functions
- Identities for graphing arccot, arcsec, and arccsc functions on a graphing calculator

Derivatives of Inverse Functions

In Section 1.5 we learned that the graph of the inverse of a function f can be obtained by reflecting the graph of f across the line $y = x$. If we combine that with our understanding of what makes a function differentiable, we can gain some quick insights into the differentiability of inverse functions.

As Figure 4.12 suggests, the reflection of a continuous curve with no cusps or corners will be another continuous curve with no cusps or corners. Indeed, if there is a tangent line to the graph of f at the point (a, b), then that line will reflect across $y = x$ to become a tangent line to the graph of f^{-1} at the point (b, a). We can even see geometrically that the *slope* of the reflected tangent line (when it exists and is not zero) will be the *reciprocal* of the slope of the original tangent line, since a change in y becomes a change in x in the reflection, and a change in x becomes a change in y.

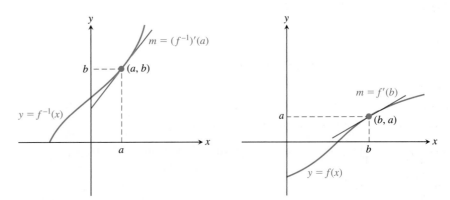

Figure 4.12 The graph of a function and its inverse. Notice that the slopes of the red tangent lines are reciprocals. That is, $(f^{-1})'(a) = \dfrac{1}{f'(b)}$.

All of this serves as an introduction to the following theorem, which we will assume as we proceed to find derivatives of inverse functions. The essence of the proof is contained in the geometry of Figure 4.12, so we will leave the analytic proof for a more advanced course. The important thing to remember is that the slopes have a reciprocal relationship, but the tangent lines are at *different points*.

THEOREM 1   Derivatives of Inverse Functions

If f is differentiable at every point of an interval I and $f'(x)$ is never zero on I, then f has an inverse, and f^{-1} is differentiable at every point of the interval $f(I)$. If $f^{-1}(a) = b$, the **inverse function slope relationship** relates the derivatives by the equation $(f^{-1})'(a) = \dfrac{1}{f'(b)}$. (Figure 4.12)

EXPLORATION 1 Finding a Derivative on an Inverse Graph Geometrically

Let $f(x) = x^5 + 2x - 1$. Since the point $(1, 2)$ is on the graph of f, it follows that the point $(2, 1)$ is on the graph of f^{-1}. Can you find

$$\frac{df^{-1}}{dx}(2),$$

the value of df^{-1}/dx at 2, without knowing a formula for f^{-1}?

1. Graph $f(x) = x^5 + 2x - 1$. A function must be one-to-one to have an inverse function. Is this function one-to-one?
2. Find $f'(x)$. How could this derivative help you to conclude that f has an inverse?
3. Reflect the graph of f across the line $y = x$ to obtain a graph of f^{-1}.
4. Sketch the tangent line to the graph of f^{-1} at the point $(2, 1)$. Call it L.
5. Reflect the line L across the line $y = x$. At what point is the reflection of L tangent to the graph of f?
6. What is the slope of the reflection of L?
7. What is the slope of L?
8. What is $\dfrac{df^{-1}}{dx}(2)$?

Derivative of the Arcsine

We know that the function $x = \sin y$ is differentiable in the open interval $-\pi/2 < y < \pi/2$ and that its derivative, the cosine, is positive there. Theorem 1 therefore assures us that the inverse function $y = \sin^{-1}(x)$ (the *arcsine* of x) is differentiable throughout the interval $-1 < x < 1$. We cannot expect it to be differentiable at $x = -1$ or $x = 1$, however, because the tangents to the graph are vertical at these points (Figure 4.13).

We find the derivative of $y = \sin^{-1}(x)$ as follows:

$$y = \sin^{-1} x$$

$$\sin y = x \qquad \text{Inverse function relationship}$$

$$\frac{d}{dx}(\sin y) = \frac{d}{dx}x \qquad \text{Differentiate both sides.}$$

$$\cos y \frac{dy}{dx} = 1 \qquad \text{Implicit differentiation}$$

$$\frac{dy}{dx} = \frac{1}{\cos y}$$

The division in the last step is safe because $\cos y \neq 0$ for $-\pi/2 < y < \pi/2$. In fact, $\cos y$ is *positive* for $-\pi/2 < y < \pi/2$, so we can replace $\cos y$ with $\sqrt{1 - (\sin y)^2}$, which is $\sqrt{1 - x^2}$. Thus

$$\frac{d}{dx}(\sin^{-1} x) = \frac{1}{\sqrt{1 - x^2}}.$$

If u is a differentiable function of x with $|u| < 1$, we apply the Chain Rule to get

$$\frac{d}{dx}\sin^{-1} u = \frac{1}{\sqrt{1 - u^2}}\frac{du}{dx}, \quad |u| < 1.$$

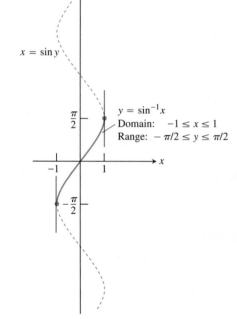

$x = \sin y$

$y = \sin^{-1} x$
Domain: $-1 \leq x \leq 1$
Range: $-\pi/2 \leq y \leq \pi/2$

Figure 4.13 The graph of $y = \sin^{-1} x$ has vertical tangents $x = -1$ and $x = 1$.

EXAMPLE 1 Applying the Formula

$$\frac{d}{dx}(\sin^{-1}x^2) = \frac{1}{\sqrt{1-(x^2)^2}} \cdot \frac{d}{dx}(x^2) = \frac{2x}{\sqrt{1-x^4}}$$

Now Try Exercise 3.

Derivative of the Arctangent

Although the function $y = \sin^{-1}(x)$ has a rather narrow domain of $[-1, 1]$, the function $y = \tan^{-1}x$ is defined for all real numbers, and is differentiable for all real numbers, as we will now see. The differentiation proceeds exactly as with the arcsine function.

$$y = \tan^{-1}x$$

$$\tan y = x \qquad \text{Inverse function relationship}$$

$$\frac{d}{dx}(\tan y) = \frac{d}{dx}x$$

$$\sec^2 y \frac{dy}{dx} = 1 \qquad \text{Implicit differentiation}$$

$$\frac{dy}{dx} = \frac{1}{\sec^2 y}$$

$$= \frac{1}{1 + (\tan y)^2} \qquad \text{Trig identity: } \sec^2 y = 1 + \tan^2 y$$

$$= \frac{1}{1 + x^2}$$

The derivative is defined for all real numbers. If u is a differentiable function of x, we get the Chain Rule form:

$$\frac{d}{dx}\tan^{-1}u = \frac{1}{1+u^2}\frac{du}{dx}$$

EXAMPLE 2 A Moving Particle

A particle moves along the x-axis so that its position at any time $t \geq 0$ is $x(t) = \tan^{-1}\sqrt{t}$. What is the velocity of the particle when $t = 16$?

SOLUTION $v(t) = \dfrac{d}{dt}\tan^{-1}\sqrt{t} = \dfrac{1}{1 + (\sqrt{t})^2} \cdot \dfrac{d}{dt}\sqrt{t} = \dfrac{1}{1+t} \cdot \dfrac{1}{2\sqrt{t}}$

When $t = 16$, the velocity is $\quad v(16) = \dfrac{1}{1+16} \cdot \dfrac{1}{2\sqrt{16}} = \dfrac{1}{136}.$

Now Try Exercise 11.

Derivative of the Arcsecant

We find the derivative of $y = \sec^{-1}x$, $|x| > 1$, beginning as we did with the other inverse trigonometric functions.

$$y = \sec^{-1}x$$

$$\sec y = x \qquad \text{Inverse function relationship}$$

$$\frac{d}{dx}(\sec y) = \frac{d}{dx}x$$

$$\sec y \tan y \frac{dy}{dx} = 1$$

$$\frac{dy}{dx} = \frac{1}{\sec y \tan y} \qquad \begin{array}{l}\text{Since } |x| > 1, \ y \text{ lies in } (0, \pi/2) \cup (\pi/2, \pi) \\ \text{and } \sec y \tan y \neq 0.\end{array}$$

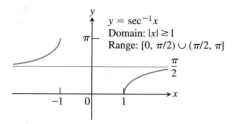

Figure 4.14 The slope of the curve $y = \sec^{-1} x$ is positive for both $x < -1$ and $x > 1$.

To express the result in terms of x, we use the relationships

$$\sec y = x \quad \text{and} \quad \tan y = \pm\sqrt{\sec^2 y - 1} = \pm\sqrt{x^2 - 1}$$

to get

$$\frac{dy}{dx} = \pm\frac{1}{x\sqrt{x^2 - 1}}.$$

Can we do anything about the $\pm$ sign? A glance at Figure 4.14 shows that the slope of the graph $y = \sec^{-1} x$ is always positive. That must mean that

$$\frac{d}{dx}\sec^{-1} x = \begin{cases} +\dfrac{1}{x\sqrt{x^2 - 1}} & \text{if } x > 1 \\[3mm] -\dfrac{1}{x\sqrt{x^2 - 1}} & \text{if } x < -1. \end{cases}$$

With the absolute value symbol we can write a single expression that eliminates the "$\pm$" ambiguity:

$$\frac{d}{dx}\sec^{-1} x = \frac{1}{|x|\sqrt{x^2 - 1}}$$

If u is a differentiable function of x with $|u| > 1$, we have the formula

$$\frac{d}{dx}\sec^{-1} u = \frac{1}{|u|\sqrt{u^2 - 1}}\frac{du}{dx}, \quad |u| > 1.$$

EXAMPLE 3 Using the Formula

$$\frac{d}{dx}\sec^{-1}(5x^4) = \frac{1}{|5x^4|\sqrt{(5x^4)^2 - 1}}\frac{d}{dx}(5x^4)$$

$$= \frac{1}{5x^4\sqrt{25x^8 - 1}}(20x^3)$$

$$= \frac{4}{x\sqrt{25x^8 - 1}}$$

Now Try Exercise 17.

Derivatives of the Other Three

We could use the same technique to find the derivatives of the other three inverse trigonometric functions—arccosine, arccotangent, and arccosecant—but there is a much easier way, thanks to the following identities.

Inverse Function–Inverse Cofunction Identities

$$\cos^{-1} x = \pi/2 - \sin^{-1} x$$
$$\cot^{-1} x = \pi/2 - \tan^{-1} x$$
$$\csc^{-1} x = \pi/2 - \sec^{-1} x$$

It follows easily that the derivatives of the inverse cofunctions are the negatives of the derivatives of the corresponding inverse functions (see Exercises 32–34).

You have probably noticed by now that most calculators do not have buttons for $\cot^{-1}$, $\sec^{-1}$, or $\csc^{-1}$. They are not needed because of the following identities:

Calculator Conversion Identities

$$\sec^{-1} x = \cos^{-1}(1/x)$$
$$\cot^{-1} x = \pi/2 - \tan^{-1} x$$
$$\csc^{-1} x = \sin^{-1}(1/x)$$

Notice that we do not use $\tan^{-1}(1/x)$ as an identity for $\cot^{-1} x$. A glance at the graphs of $y = \tan^{-1}(1/x)$ and $y = \pi/2 - \tan^{-1} x$ reveals the problem (Figure 4.15).

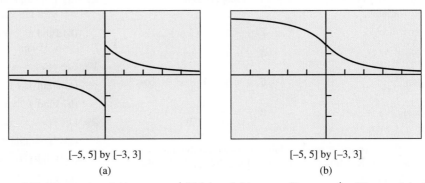

| [–5, 5] by [–3, 3] | [–5, 5] by [–3, 3] |
| (a) | (b) |

Figure 4.15 The graphs of (a) $y = \tan^{-1}(1/x)$ and (b) $y = \pi/2 - \tan^{-1} x$. The graph in (b) is the same as the graph of $y = \cot^{-1} x$.

We cannot replace $\cot^{-1} x$ by the function $y = \tan^{-1}(1/x)$ in the identity for the inverse functions and inverse cofunctions, and so it is not the function we want for $\cot^{-1} x$. The ranges of the inverse trigonometric functions have been chosen in part to make the two sets of identities above hold.

EXAMPLE 4 A Tangent Line to the Arccotangent Curve

Find an equation for the line tangent to the graph of $y = \cot^{-1} x$ at $x = -1$.

SOLUTION

First, we note that

$$\cot^{-1}(-1) = \pi/2 - \tan^{-1}(-1) = \pi/2 - (-\pi/4) = 3\pi/4.$$

The slope of the tangent line is

$$\left.\frac{dy}{dx}\right|_{x=-1} = -\left.\frac{1}{1 + x^2}\right|_{x=-1} = -\frac{1}{1 + (-1)^2} = -\frac{1}{2}.$$

So the tangent line has equation $y - 3\pi/4 = (-1/2)(x + 1)$.

Now Try Exercise 23.

Quick Review 4.3 *(For help, go to Sections 1.2, 1.5, and 1.6.)*

Exercise numbers with a gray background indicate problems that the authors have designed to be solved *without a calculator*.

In Exercises 1–5, give the *domain* and *range* of the function, and evaluate the function at $x = 1$.

1. $y = \sin^{-1} x$

2. $y = \cos^{-1} x$

3. $y = \tan^{-1} x$

4. $y = \sec^{-1} x$

5. $y = \tan(\tan^{-1} x)$

In Exercises 6–10, find the inverse of the given function.

6. $y = 3x - 8$

7. $y = \sqrt[3]{x + 5}$

8. $y = \dfrac{8}{x}$

9. $y = \dfrac{3x - 2}{x}$

10. $y = \arctan(x/3)$

Section 4.3 Exercises

In Exercises 1–8, find the derivative of y with respect to the appropriate variable.

1. $y = \cos^{-1}(x^2)$

2. $y = \cos^{-1}(1/x)$

3. $y = \sin^{-1} \sqrt{2t}$

4. $y = \sin^{-1}(1 - t)$

5. $y = \sin^{-1} \dfrac{3}{t^2}$

6. $y = s\sqrt{1 - s^2} + \cos^{-1} s$

7. $y = x \sin^{-1} x + \sqrt{1 - x^2}$

8. $y = \dfrac{1}{\sin^{-1}(2x)}$

In Exercises 9–12, a particle moves along the x-axis so that its position at any time $t \geq 0$ is given by $x(t)$. Find the velocity at the indicated value of t.

9. $x(t) = \sin^{-1}\left(\dfrac{t}{4}\right)$, $t = 3$

10. $x(t) = \sin^{-1}\left(\dfrac{\sqrt{t}}{4}\right)$, $t = 4$

11. $x(t) = \tan^{-1} t$, $t = 2$

12. $x(t) = \tan^{-1}(t^2)$, $t = 1$

In Exercises 13–22, find the derivative of y with respect to the appropriate variable.

13. $y = \sec^{-1}(2s + 1)$

14. $y = \sec^{-1} 5s$

15. $y = \csc^{-1}(x^2 + 1)$, $x > 0$

16. $y = \csc^{-1} x/2$

17. $y = \sec^{-1} \dfrac{1}{t}$, $0 < t < 1$

18. $y = \cot^{-1} \sqrt{t}$

19. $y = \cot^{-1} \sqrt{t - 1}$

20. $y = \sqrt{s^2 - 1} - \sec^{-1} s$

21. $y = \tan^{-1} \sqrt{x^2 - 1} + \csc^{-1} x$, $x > 1$,

22. $y = \cot^{-1} \dfrac{1}{x} - \tan^{-1} x$

In Exercises 23–26, find an equation for the tangent to the graph of y at the indicated point. Write your answer in the form $y = ax + b$ with a and b correct to the nearest thousandth.

23. $y = \sec^{-1} x$, $x = 2$

24. $y = \tan^{-1} x$, $x = 2$

25. $y = \sin^{-1}\left(\dfrac{x}{4}\right)$, $x = 3$

26. $y = \tan^{-1}(x^2)$, $x = 1$

27. (a) Find an equation for the line tangent to the graph of $y = \tan x$ at the point $(\pi/4, 1)$.

(b) Find an equation for the line tangent to the graph of $y = \tan^{-1} x$ at the point $(1, \pi/4)$.

28. Let $f(x) = x^5 + 2x^3 + x - 1$.

(a) Find $f(1)$ and $f'(1)$.

(b) Find $f^{-1}(3)$ and $(f^{-1})'(3)$.

29. Let $f(x) = \cos x + 3x$.

(a) Show that f has a differentiable inverse.

(b) Find $f(0)$ and $f'(0)$.

(c) Find $f^{-1}(1)$ and $(f^{-1})'(1)$.

30. Group Activity Graph the function $f(x) = \sin^{-1}(\sin x)$ in the viewing window $[-2\pi, 2\pi]$ by $[-4, 4]$. Then answer the following questions:

(a) What is the domain of f?

(b) What is the range of f?

(c) At which points is f not differentiable?

(d) Sketch a graph of $y = f'(x)$ without using NDER or computing the derivative.

(e) Find $f'(x)$ algebraically. Can you reconcile your answer with the graph in part (d)?

31. Group Activity A particle moves along the x-axis so that its position at any time $t \geq 0$ is given by $x = \arctan t$.

(a) Prove that the particle is always moving to the right.

(b) Prove that the particle is always decelerating.

(c) What is the limiting position of the particle as t approaches infinity?

In Exercises 32–34, use the inverse function–inverse cofunction identities to derive the formula for the derivative of the function.

32. arccosine

33. arccotangent

34. arccosecant

Standardized Test Questions

You may use a graphing calculator to solve the following problems.

35. True or False The domain of $y = \sin^{-1} x$ is $-1 \le x \le 1$. Justify your answer.

36. True or False The domain of $y = \tan^{-1} x$ is $-1 \le x \le 1$. Justify your answer.

37. Multiple Choice Which of the following is $\dfrac{d}{dx}\sin^{-1}\left(\dfrac{x}{2}\right)$?

(A) $-\dfrac{2}{\sqrt{4 - x^2}}$ (B) $-\dfrac{1}{\sqrt{4 - x^2}}$ (C) $\dfrac{2}{4 + x^2}$

(D) $\dfrac{2}{\sqrt{4 - x^2}}$ (E) $\dfrac{1}{\sqrt{4 - x^2}}$

38. Multiple Choice Which of the following is $\dfrac{d}{dx}\tan^{-1}(3x)$?

(A) $-\dfrac{3}{1 + 9x^2}$ (B) $-\dfrac{1}{1 + 9x^2}$ (C) $\dfrac{1}{1 + 9x^2}$

(D) $\dfrac{3}{1 + 9x^2}$ (E) $\dfrac{3}{\sqrt{1 - 9x^2}}$

39. Multiple Choice Which of the following is $\dfrac{d}{dx}\sec^{-1}(x^2)$?

(A) $\dfrac{2}{x\sqrt{x^4 - 1}}$ (B) $\dfrac{2}{x\sqrt{x^2 - 1}}$ (C) $\dfrac{2}{x\sqrt{1 - x^4}}$

(D) $\dfrac{2}{x\sqrt{1 - x^2}}$ (E) $\dfrac{2x}{\sqrt{1 - x^4}}$

40. Multiple Choice Which of the following is the slope of the tangent line to $y = \tan^{-1}(2x)$ at $x = 1$?

(A) $-2/5$ (B) $1/5$ (C) $2/5$ (D) $5/2$ (E) 5

Explorations

In Exercises 41–46, find **(a)** the right end behavior model, **(b)** the left end behavior model, and **(c)** any horizontal tangents for the function if they exist.

41. $y = \tan^{-1} x$ **42.** $y = \cot^{-1} x$

43. $y = \sec^{-1} x$ **44.** $y = \csc^{-1} x$

45. $y = \sin^{-1} x$ **46.** $y = \cos^{-1} x$

Extending the Ideas

47. *Identities* Confirm the following identities for $x > 0$.

(a) $\cos^{-1} x + \sin^{-1} x = \pi/2$

(b) $\tan^{-1} x + \cot^{-1} x = \pi/2$

(c) $\sec^{-1} x + \csc^{-1} x = \pi/2$

48. *Proof Without Words* The figure gives a proof without words that $\tan^{-1} 1 + \tan^{-1} 2 + \tan^{-1} 3 = \pi$. Explain what is going on.

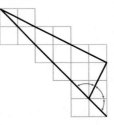

49. *(Continuation of Exercise 48)* Here is a way to construct $\tan^{-1} 1$, $\tan^{-1} 2$, and $\tan^{-1} 3$ by folding a square of paper. Try it and explain what is going on.

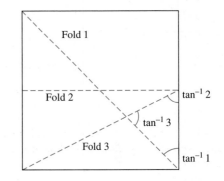

4.4 | Derivatives of Exponential and Logarithmic Functions

You will be able to find derivatives of exponential functions and logarithmic functions with positive base a ($a \neq 1$).

- Derivative of e^x
- Derivative of a^x
- Derivative of $\ln x$
- Derivative of $\log_a x$
- Extending the Power Rule to arbitrary real powers
- Logarithmic differentiation

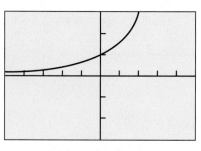

[−4.9, 4.9] by [−2.9, 2.9]

(a)

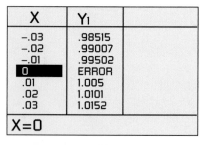

X	Y₁	
−.03	.98515	
−.02	.99007	
−.01	.99502	
0	**ERROR**	
.01	1.005	
.02	1.0101	
.03	1.0152	

X=0

(b)

Figure 4.16 (a) The graph and (b) the table support the conclusion that

$$\lim_{h \to 0} \frac{e^h - 1}{h} = 1.$$

Derivative of e^x

At the end of the brief review of exponential functions in Section 1.3, we mentioned that the function $y = e^x$ was a particularly important function for modeling exponential growth. The number e was defined in that section to be the limit of $(1 + 1/x)^x$ as $x \to \infty$. This intriguing number shows up in other interesting limits as well, but the one with the most interesting implications for the *calculus* of exponential functions is this one:

$$\lim_{h \to 0} \frac{e^h - 1}{h} = 1$$

(The graph and the table in Figure 4.16 provide strong support for this limit being 1. A formal algebraic proof that begins with our limit definition of e would require some rather subtle limit arguments, so we will not include one here.)

The fact that the limit is 1 creates a remarkable relationship between the function e^x and its derivative, as we will now see.

$$\begin{aligned}
\frac{d}{dx}(e^x) &= \lim_{h \to 0} \frac{e^{x+h} - e^x}{h} \\
&= \lim_{h \to 0} \frac{e^x \cdot e^h - e^x}{h} \\
&= \lim_{h \to 0} \left(e^x \cdot \frac{e^h - 1}{h} \right) \\
&= e^x \cdot \lim_{h \to 0} \left(\frac{e^h - 1}{h} \right) \\
&= e^x \cdot 1 \\
&= e^x
\end{aligned}$$

In other words, the derivative of this particular function is itself!

$$\frac{d}{dx}(e^x) = e^x$$

If u is a differentiable function of x, then we have

$$\frac{d}{dx} e^u = e^u \frac{du}{dx}.$$

We will make extensive use of this formula when we study exponential growth and decay in Chapter 7.

EXAMPLE 1 Using the Formula

Find dy/dx if $y = e^{(x + x^2)}$.

SOLUTION

Let $u = x + x^2$ and $y = e^u$. Then

$$\frac{dy}{dx} = e^u \frac{du}{dx}, \quad \text{and} \quad \frac{du}{dx} = 1 + 2x.$$

Thus, $\dfrac{dy}{dx} = e^u \dfrac{du}{dx} = e^{(x+x^2)}(1 + 2x).$

Now Try Exercise 9.

Is Any Other Function Its Own Derivative?

The zero function is also its own derivative, but this hardly seems worth mentioning. (Its value is always 0 and its slope is always 0.) In addition to e^x, however, we can also say that any constant *multiple* of e^x is its own derivative:

$$\frac{d}{dx}(c \cdot e^x) = c \cdot e^x$$

The next obvious question is whether there are still *other* functions that are their own derivatives, and this time the answer is no. The only functions that satisfy the condition $dy/dx = y$ are functions of the form $y = ke^x$ (and notice that the zero function can be included in this category). We will prove this significant fact in Chapter 7.

Derivative of a^x

What about an exponential function with a base other than e? We will assume that the base is positive and different from 1, since negative numbers raised to arbitrary real powers are not always real numbers, and $y = 1^x$ is a constant function.

If $a > 0$ and $a \neq 1$, we can use the properties of logarithms to write a^x in terms of e^x. The formula for doing so is

$$a^x = e^{\ln(a^x)} = e^{x \ln a}.$$

We can then find the derivative of a^x with the Chain Rule.

$$\frac{d}{dx}a^x = \frac{d}{dx}e^{x \ln a} = e^{x \ln a} \cdot \frac{d}{dx}(x \ln a) = e^{x \ln a} \cdot \ln a = a^x \ln a$$

Thus, if u is a differentiable function of x, we get the following rule.

For $a > 0$ and $a \neq 1$,

$$\frac{d}{dx}(a^u) = a^u \ln a \frac{du}{dx}.$$

EXAMPLE 2 Reviewing the Algebra of Logarithms

At what point on the graph of the function $y = 2^t - 3$ does the tangent line have slope 21?

SOLUTION

The slope is the derivative:

$$\frac{d}{dt}(2^t - 3) = 2^t \cdot \ln 2 - 0 = 2^t \ln 2$$

We want the value of t for which $2^t \ln 2 = 21$. We could use the solver on the calculator, but we will use logarithms for the sake of review.

$$2^t \ln 2 = 21$$

$$2^t = \frac{21}{\ln 2}$$

$$\ln 2^t = \ln\left(\frac{21}{\ln 2}\right) \qquad \text{Logarithm of both sides}$$

$$t \cdot \ln 2 = \ln 21 - \ln(\ln 2) \qquad \text{Properties of logarithms}$$

$$t = \frac{\ln 21 - \ln(\ln 2)}{\ln 2}$$

$$t \approx 4.921$$

$$y = 2^t - 3 \approx 27.297 \qquad \text{Using the stored value of } t$$

The point is approximately $(4.9, 27.3)$. *Now Try Exercise 29.*

A glass of cold milk from the refrigerator is left on the counter on a warm summer day. Its temperature y (in degrees Fahrenheit) after sitting on the counter for t minutes is

$$y = 72 - 30(0.98)^t.$$

Answer the following questions by interpreting y and dy/dt.

1. What is the temperature of the refrigerator? How can you tell?
2. What is the temperature of the room? How can you tell?
3. When is the milk warming up the fastest? How can you tell?
4. Determine algebraically when the temperature of the milk reaches 55°F.
5. At what rate is the milk warming when its temperature is 55°F? Answer with an appropriate unit of measure.

Derivative of ln *x*

Now that we know the derivative of e^x, it is relatively easy to find the derivative of its inverse function, ln x.

$$y = \ln x$$
$$e^y = x \qquad \text{Inverse function relationship}$$
$$\frac{d}{dx}(e^y) = \frac{d}{dx}(x) \qquad \text{Differentiate implicitly.}$$
$$e^y \frac{dy}{dx} = 1$$
$$\frac{dy}{dx} = \frac{1}{e^y} = \frac{1}{x}$$

If u is a differentiable function of x and $u > 0$,

$$\frac{d}{dx}\ln u = \frac{1}{u}\frac{du}{dx}.$$

This equation answers what was once a perplexing problem: Is there a function with derivative x^{-1}? All of the other power functions follow the Power Rule,

$$\frac{d}{dx}x^n = nx^{n-1}.$$

However, this formula is not much help if one is looking for a function with x^{-1} as its derivative! Now we know why: The function we should be looking for is not a power function at all; it is the natural logarithm function.

EXAMPLE 3 A Tangent Through the Origin

A line with slope m passes through the origin and is tangent to the graph of $y = \ln x$. What is the value of m?

SOLUTION

This problem is a little harder than it looks, since we do not know the point of tangency. However, we do know two important facts about that point:

1. it has coordinates $(a, \ln a)$ for some positive a, and
2. the tangent line there has slope $m = 1/a$ (Figure 4.17).

Since the tangent line passes through the origin, its slope is

$$m = \frac{\ln a - 0}{a - 0} = \frac{\ln a}{a}.$$

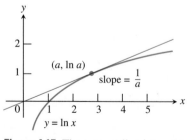

Figure 4.17 The tangent line intersects the curve at some point $(a, \ln a)$, where the slope of the curve is $1/a$. (Example 3)

continued

Setting these two formulas for m equal to each other, we have

$$\frac{\ln a}{a} = \frac{1}{a}$$

$$\ln a = 1$$

$$e^{\ln a} = e^1$$

$$a = e$$

$$m = \frac{1}{e}$$

Now Try Exercise 31.

Derivative of $\log_a x$

To find the derivative of $\log_a x$ for an arbitrary base $(a > 0, a \neq 1)$, we use the change-of-base formula for logarithms to express $\log_a x$ in terms of natural logarithms, as follows:

$$\log_a x = \frac{\ln x}{\ln a}.$$

The rest is easy:

$$\frac{d}{dx}\log_a x = \frac{d}{dx}\left(\frac{\ln x}{\ln a}\right)$$

$$= \frac{1}{\ln a} \cdot \frac{d}{dx}\ln x \quad \text{Since } \ln a \text{ is a constant}$$

$$= \frac{1}{\ln a} \cdot \frac{1}{x}$$

$$= \frac{1}{x \ln a}$$

So, if u is a differentiable function of x and $u > 0$, the formula is as follows.

For $a > 0$ and $a \neq 1$,

$$\frac{d}{dx}\log_a u = \frac{1}{u \ln a}\frac{du}{dx}.$$

EXAMPLE 4 Going the Long Way with the Chain Rule

Find dy/dx if $y = \log_a a^{\sin x}$.

SOLUTION

Carefully working from the outside in, we apply the Chain Rule to get:

$$\frac{d}{dx}(\log_a a^{\sin x}) = \frac{1}{a^{\sin x} \ln a} \cdot \frac{d}{dx}(a^{\sin x}) \qquad \log_a u, \ u = a^{\sin x}$$

$$= \frac{1}{a^{\sin x} \ln a} \cdot a^{\sin x} \ln a \cdot \frac{d}{dx}(\sin x) \qquad a^u, \ u = \sin x$$

$$= \frac{a^{\sin x} \ln a}{a^{\sin x} \ln a} \cdot \cos x$$

$$= \cos x$$

Now Try Exercise 23.

We could have saved ourselves a lot of work in Example 4 if we had noticed at the beginning that $\log_a a^{\sin x}$, being the composite of inverse functions, is equal to $\sin x$. It is always a good idea to simplify functions *before* differentiating, wherever possible. On the other hand, it is comforting to know that all these rules do work if applied correctly.

Power Rule for Arbitrary Real Powers

We are now ready to prove the Power Rule in its final form. As long as $x > 0$, we can write any real power of x as a power of e, specifically

$$x^n = e^{n \ln x}.$$

This enables us to differentiate x^n for any real power n, as follows:

$$\frac{d}{dx}(x^n) = \frac{d}{dx}(e^{n \ln x})$$

$$= e^{n \ln x} \cdot \frac{d}{dx}(n \ln x) \quad e^u, \, u = n \ln x$$

$$= e^{n \ln x} \cdot \frac{n}{x}$$

$$= x^n \cdot \frac{n}{x}$$

$$= nx^{n-1}$$

The Chain Rule extends this result to the Power Rule's final form.

RULE 10   Power Rule for Arbitrary Real Powers

If u is a positive differentiable function of x and n is any real number, then u^n is a differentiable function of x, and

$$\frac{d}{dx} u^n = nu^{n-1} \frac{du}{dx}.$$

EXAMPLE 5 Using the Power Rule in All Its Power

(a) If $y = x^{\sqrt{2}}$, then

$$\frac{dy}{dx} = \sqrt{2} x^{(\sqrt{2}-1)}.$$

(b) If $y = (2 + \sin 3x)^\pi$, then

$$\frac{d}{dx}(2 + \sin 3x)^\pi = \pi(2 + \sin 3x)^{\pi-1}(\cos 3x) \cdot 3$$

$$= 3\pi(2 + \sin 3x)^{\pi-1}(\cos 3x)$$

Now Try Exercise 35.

EXAMPLE 6 Finding a Domain

If $f(x) = \ln(x - 3)$, find $f'(x)$. State the domain of f'.

SOLUTION

The domain of f is $(3, \infty)$ and

$$f'(x) = \frac{1}{x - 3}.$$

continued

The domain of f' appears to be all $x \neq 3$. However, since f is not defined for $x < 3$, neither is f'. Thus,

$$f'(x) = \frac{1}{x - 3}, \quad x > 3.$$

That is, the domain of f' is $(3, \infty)$.

Now Try Exercise 37.

Sometimes the properties of logarithms can be used to simplify the differentiation process, even if we must introduce the logarithms ourselves as a step in the process. Example 7 shows a clever way to differentiate $y = x^x$ for $x > 0$.

EXAMPLE 7 Logarithmic Differentiation

Find dy/dx for $y = x^x$, $x > 0$.

SOLUTION

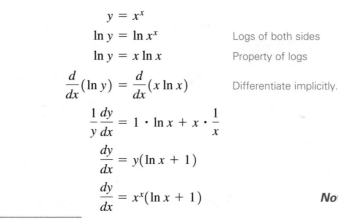

$$y = x^x$$
$$\ln y = \ln x^x \qquad \text{Logs of both sides}$$
$$\ln y = x \ln x \qquad \text{Property of logs}$$
$$\frac{d}{dx}(\ln y) = \frac{d}{dx}(x \ln x) \qquad \text{Differentiate implicitly.}$$
$$\frac{1}{y}\frac{dy}{dx} = 1 \cdot \ln x + x \cdot \frac{1}{x}$$
$$\frac{dy}{dx} = y(\ln x + 1)$$
$$\frac{dy}{dx} = x^x(\ln x + 1) \qquad \qquad \textit{Now Try Exercise 43.}$$

EXAMPLE 8 How Fast Does a Flu Spread?

The spread of a flu in a certain school is modeled by the equation

$$P(t) = \frac{100}{1 + e^{3-t}},$$

where $P(t)$ is the total number of students infected t days after the flu was first noticed. Many of them may already be well again at time t.

(a) Estimate the initial number of students infected with the flu.

(b) How fast is the flu spreading after 3 days?

(c) When will the flu spread at its maximum rate? What is this rate?

SOLUTION

The graph of P as a function of t is shown in Figure 4.18.

(a) $P(0) = 100/(1 + e^3) = 5$ students (to the nearest whole number).

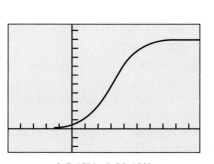

[−5, 10] by [−25, 120]

Figure 4.18 The graph of

$$P(t) = \frac{100}{1 + e^{3-t}},$$

modeling the spread of a flu. (Example 8)

continued

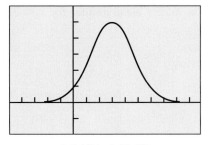

[−5, 10] by [−10, 30]

Figure 4.19 The graph of dP/dt, the rate of spread of the flu in Example 8. The graph of P is shown in Figure 4.18.

(b) To find the rate at which the flu spreads, we find dP/dt. To find dP/dt, we need to invoke the Chain Rule twice:

$$\frac{dP}{dt} = \frac{d}{dt}(100(1 + e^{3-t})^{-1}) = 100 \cdot (-1)(1 + e^{3-t})^{-2} \cdot \frac{d}{dt}(1 + e^{3-t})$$

$$= -100(1 + e^{3-t})^{-2} \cdot \left(0 + e^{3-t} \cdot \frac{d}{dt}(3 - t)\right)$$

$$= -100(1 + e^{3-t})^{-2}(e^{3-t} \cdot (-1))$$

$$= \frac{100e^{3-t}}{(1 + e^{3-t})^2}$$

At $t = 3$, then, $dP/dt = 100/4 = 25$. The flu is spreading to 25 students per day.

(c) We could estimate when the flu is spreading the fastest by seeing where the graph of $y = P(t)$ has the steepest upward slope, but we can answer both the "when" and the "what" parts of this question most easily by finding the maximum point on the graph of the derivative (Figure 4.19).

We see by tracing on the curve that the maximum rate occurs at about 3 days, when (as we have just calculated) the flu is spreading at a rate of 25 students per day.

Now Try Exercise 51.

Quick Review 4.4   *(For help, go to Sections 1.3 and 1.5.)*

Exercise numbers with a gray background indicate problems that the authors have designed to be solved *without a calculator*.

1. Write $\log_5 8$ in terms of natural logarithms.

2. Write 7^x as a power of e.

In Exercises 3–7, simplify the expression using properties of exponents and logarithms.

3. $\ln(e^{\tan x})$

4. $\ln(x^2 - 4) - \ln(x + 2)$

5. $\log_2(8^{x-5})$

6. $(\log_4 x^{15})/(\log_4 x^{12})$

7. $3\ln x - \ln 3x + \ln(12x^2)$

In Exercises 8–10, solve the equation algebraically using logarithms. Give an *exact* answer, such as $(\ln 2)/3$, and also an approximate answer to the nearest hundredth.

8. $3^x = 19$

9. $5^t \ln 5 = 18$

10. $3^{x+1} = 2^x$

Section 4.4 Exercises

In Exercises 1–28, find dy/dx.

1. $y = 2e^x$

2. $y = e^{2x}$

3. $y = e^{-x}$

4. $y = e^{-5x}$

5. $y = e^{2x/3}$

6. $y = e^{-x/4}$

7. $y = xe^2 - e^x$

8. $y = x^2e^x - xe^x$

9. $y = e^{\sqrt{x}}$

10. $y = e^{(x^2)}$

11. $y = 8^x$

12. $y = 9^{-x}$

13. $y = 3^{\csc x}$

14. $y = 3^{\cot x}$

15. $y = \ln(x^2)$

16. $y = (\ln x)^2$

17. $y = \ln(1/x)$

18. $y = \ln(10/x)$

19. $y = \ln(\ln x)$

20. $y = x \ln x - x$

21. $y = \log_4 x^2$

22. $y = \log_5 \sqrt{x}$

23. $y = \log_2(1/x)$

24. $y = 1/\log_2 x$

25. $y = \ln 2 \cdot \log_2 x$

26. $y = \log_3(1 + x \ln 3)$

27. $y = \log_{10} e^x$

28. $y = \ln 10^x$

29. At what point on the graph of $y = 3^x + 1$ is the tangent line parallel to the line $y = 5x - 1$?

30. At what point on the graph of $y = 2e^x - 1$ is the tangent line perpendicular to the line $y = -3x + 2$?

31. A line with slope m passes through the origin and is tangent to $y = \ln(2x)$. What is the value of m?

32. A line with slope m passes through the origin and is tangent to $y = \ln(x/3)$. What is the value of m?

In Exercises 33–36, find dy/dx.

33. $y = x^\pi$

34. $y = x^{1+\sqrt{2}}$

35. $y = x^{-\sqrt{2}}$

36. $y = x^{1-e}$

In Exercises 37–42, find $f'(x)$ and state the domain of f'.

37. $f(x) = \ln(x + 2)$

38. $f(x) = \ln(2x + 2)$

39. $f(x) = \ln(2 - \cos x)$

40. $f(x) = \ln(x^2 + 1)$

41. $f(x) = \log_2(3x + 1)$

42. $f(x) = \log_{10}\sqrt{x + 1}$

Group Activity In Exercises 43–48, use the technique of logarithmic differentiation to find dy/dx.

43. $y = (\sin x)^x, \quad 0 < x < \pi/2$

44. $y = x^{\tan x}, \quad x > 0$

45. $y = \sqrt[5]{\dfrac{(x-3)^4(x^2+1)}{(2x+5)^3}}$

46. $y = \dfrac{x\sqrt{x^2+1}}{(x+1)^{2/3}}$

47. $y = x^{\ln x}$ **48.** $y = x^{(1/\ln x)}$

49. Find an equation for a line that is tangent to the graph of $y = e^x$ and goes through the origin.

50. Find an equation for a line that is normal to the graph of $y = xe^x$ and goes through the origin.

51. *Spread of a Rumor* The spread of a rumor in a certain school is modeled by the equation

$$P(t) = \frac{300}{1 + 2^{4-t}},$$

where $P(t)$ is the total number of students who have heard the rumor t days after the rumor first started to spread.

(a) Estimate the initial number of students who first heard the rumor.

(b) How fast is the rumor spreading after 4 days?

(c) When will the rumor spread at its maximum rate? What is that rate?

52. *Spread of Flu* The spread of flu in a certain school is modeled by the equation

$$P(t) = \frac{200}{1 + e^{5-t}},$$

where $P(t)$ is the total number of students infected t days after the flu first started to spread.

(a) Estimate the initial number of students infected with this flu.

(b) How fast is the flu spreading after 4 days?

(c) When will the flu spread at its maximum rate? What is that rate?

53. *Radioactive Decay* The amount A (in grams) of radioactive plutonium remaining in a 20-gram sample after t days is given by the formula

$$A = 20 \cdot (1/2)^{t/140}.$$

At what rate is the plutonium decaying when $t = 2$ days? Answer in appropriate units.

54. For any positive constant k, the derivative of $\ln(kx)$ is $1/x$. Prove this fact

(a) by using the Chain Rule.

(b) by using a property of logarithms and differentiating.

55. Let $f(x) = 2^x$.

(a) Find $f'(0)$.

(b) Use the definition of the derivative to write $f'(0)$ as a limit.

(c) Deduce the exact value of

$$\lim_{h \to 0} \frac{2^h - 1}{h}.$$

(d) What is the exact value of

$$\lim_{h \to 0} \frac{7^h - 1}{h}?$$

56. **Writing to Learn** The graph of $y = \ln x$ looks as though it might be approaching a horizontal asymptote. Write an argument based on the graph of $y = e^x$ to explain why it does not.

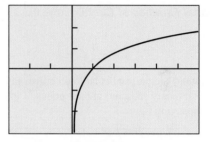

$[-3, 6]$ by $[-3, 3]$

Standardized Test Questions

57. **True or False** The derivative of $y = 2^x$ is 2^x. Justify your answer.

58. **True or False** The derivative of $y = e^{2x}$ is $2(\ln 2)\,e^{2x}$. Justify your answer.

59. **Multiple Choice** If a flu is spreading at the rate of

$$P(t) = \frac{150}{1 + e^{4-t}},$$

which of the following is the initial number of persons infected?

(A) 1   **(B)** 3   **(C)** 7   **(D)** 8   **(E)** 75

60. **Multiple Choice** Which of the following is the domain of $f'(x)$ if $f(x) = \log_2(x + 3)$?

(A) $x < -3$ **(B)** $x \leq 3$ **(C)** $x \neq -3$

(D) $x > -3$ **(E)** $x \geq -3$

61. **Multiple Choice** Which of the following gives dy/dx if $y = \log_{10}(2x - 3)$?

(A) $\dfrac{2}{(2x-3)\ln 10}$ **(B)** $\dfrac{2}{2x-3}$ **(C)** $\dfrac{1}{(2x-3)\ln 10}$

(D) $\dfrac{1}{2x-3}$ **(E)** $\dfrac{1}{2x}$

62. **Multiple Choice** Which of the following gives the slope of the tangent line to the graph of $y = 2^{1-x}$ at $x = 2$?

(A) $-\dfrac{1}{2}$ **(B)** $\dfrac{1}{2}$ **(C)** -2 **(D)** 2 **(E)** $-\dfrac{\ln 2}{2}$

Explorations

63. Let $y_1 = a^x$, $y_2 = \text{NDER}(y_1, x)$, $y_3 = y_2/y_1$, and $y_4 = e^{y_3}$.

(a) Describe the graph of y_4 for $a = 2, 3, 4, 5$. Generalize your description to an arbitrary $a > 1$.

(b) Describe the graph of y_3 for $a = 2, 3, 4, 5$. Compare a table of values for y_3 for $a = 2, 3, 4, 5$ with $\ln a$. Generalize your description to an arbitrary $a > 1$.

(c) Explain how parts (a) and (b) support the statement

$$\frac{d}{dx} a^x = a^x \quad \text{if and only if} \quad a = e.$$

(d) Show algebraically that $y_1 = y_2$ if and only if $a = e$.

Extending the Ideas

64. *Orthogonal Families of Curves* Prove that all curves in the family

$$y = -\frac{1}{2}x^2 + k$$

(k any constant) are perpendicular to all curves in the family $y = \ln x + c$ (c any constant) at their points of intersection. (See accompanying figure.)

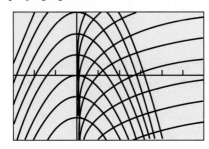

[−3, 6] by [−3, 3]

65. *Which Is Bigger, π^e or e^π?* Calculators have taken some of the mystery out of this once-challenging question. (Go ahead and check; you will see that it is a surprisingly close call.) You can answer the question without a calculator, though, by using the result from Example 3 of this section.

Recall from that example that the line through the origin tangent to the graph of $y = \ln x$ has slope $1/e$.

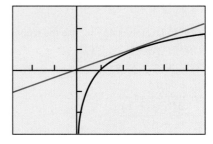

[−3, 6] by [−3, 3]

(a) Find an equation for this tangent line.

(b) Give an argument based on the graphs of $y = \ln x$ and the tangent line to explain why $\ln x < x/e$ for all positive $x \neq e$.

(c) Show that $\ln (x^e) < x$ for all positive $x \neq e$.

(d) Conclude that $x^e < e^x$ for all positive $x \neq e$.

(e) So which is bigger, π^e or e^π?

Quick Quiz for AP* Preparation: Sections 4.3–4.4

1. Multiple Choice If $f(x) = \ln(x + 4 + e^{-3x})$, then $f'(0)$ is

(A) $-\frac{2}{5}$ **(B)** $\frac{1}{5}$ **(C)** $\frac{1}{4}$ **(D)** $\frac{2}{5}$ **(E)** nonexistent

2. Multiple Choice Let f be the function defined by $f(x) = x^3 + x$. If $g(x) = f^{-1}(x)$ and $g(2) = 1$, what is the value of $g'(2)$?

(A) $\frac{1}{13}$ **(B)** $\frac{1}{4}$ **(C)** $\frac{7}{4}$ **(D)** 4 **(E)** 13

3. Multiple Choice Which of the following gives $\dfrac{dy}{dx}$ if $y = \sin^{-1}(2x)$?

(A) $-\dfrac{2}{\sqrt{1 - 4x^2}}$ **(B)** $-\dfrac{1}{\sqrt{1 - 4x^2}}$ **(C)** $\dfrac{2}{\sqrt{1 - 4x^2}}$

(D) $\dfrac{1}{\sqrt{1 - 4x^2}}$ **(E)** $\dfrac{2x}{1 + 4x^2}$

4. Free Response A particle moves along the x-axis with position at time t given by $x(t) = e^t \sin t$ for $0 \le t \le 2\pi$.

(a) Find each time t, $0 \le t \le 2\pi$, for which the particle is at rest.

(b) Find the value of the constant A for which $Ax''(t) + x'(t) = x(t)$ for $0 \le t \le 2\pi$.

CHAPTER 4 Key Terms

Chain Rule (p. 156)
implicit differentiation (p. 164)
inverse function–inverse cofunction
   identities (p. 176)
inverse function slope relationship (p. 173)

logarithmic differentiation (p. 185)
normal to the surface (p. 166)
orthogonal curves (p. 161)
orthogonal families (p. 188)
Power Chain Rule (p. 159)

Power Rule for Arbitrary Real Powers
   (p. 184)
Power Rule for Rational Powers of x
   (p. 168)

CHAPTER 4 Review Exercises

Exercise numbers with a gray background indicate problems that the authors have designed to be solved *without a calculator*.

The collection of exercises marked in red could be used as a chapter test.

In Exercises 1–30, find the derivative of the function.

1. $y = e^{3x-7}$

2. $y = \tan(e^x)$

3. $y = \sin^3 x$

4. $y = \ln(\csc x)$

5. $s = \cos(1 - 2t)$

6. $s = \cot \dfrac{2}{t}$

7. $y = \sqrt{1 + \cos x}$

8. $y = x\sqrt{2x + 1}$

9. $r = \sec(1 + 3\theta)$

10. $r = \tan^2(3 - \theta^2)$

11. $y = x^2 \csc 5x$

12. $y = \ln \sqrt{x}$

13. $y = \ln(1 + e^x)$

14. $y = xe^{-x}$

15. $y = e^{(1 + \ln x)}$

16. $y = \ln(\sin x)$

17. $r = \ln(\cos^{-1} x)$

18. $r = \log_2(\theta^2)$

19. $s = \log_5(t - 7)$

20. $s = 8^{-t}$

21. $y = x^{\ln x}$

22. $y = \dfrac{(2x)2^x}{\sqrt{x^2 + 1}}$

23. $y = e^{\tan^{-1} x}$

24. $y = \sin^{-1}\sqrt{1 - u^2}$

25. $y = t \sec^{-1} t - \dfrac{1}{2}\ln t$

26. $y = (1 + t^2)\cot^{-1} 2t$

27. $y = z\cos^{-1} z - \sqrt{1 - z^2}$

28. $y = 2\sqrt{x - 1}\,\csc^{-1}\sqrt{x}$

29. $y = \csc^{-1}(\sec x),\ 0 \le x < \dfrac{\pi}{2}$

30. $r = \left(\dfrac{1 + \sin\theta}{1 - \cos\theta}\right)^2$

In Exercises 31–34, find all values of x for which the function is differentiable.

31. $y = \ln x^2$

32. $y = \sin(e^{2x})$

33. $y = \sqrt{\dfrac{1 - x}{1 + x^2}}$

34. $y = \dfrac{1}{1 - e^x}$

In Exercises 35–38, find dy/dx.

35. $xy + 2x + 3y = 1$

36. $5x^{4/5} + 10y^{6/5} = 15$

37. $\sqrt{xy} = 1$

38. $y^2 = \dfrac{x}{x + 1}$

In Exercises 39–42, find d^2y/dx^2 by implicit differentiation.

39. $x^3 + y^3 = 1$

40. $y^2 = 1 - \dfrac{2}{x}$

41. $y^3 + y = 2\cos x$

42. $x^{1/3} + y^{1/3} = 4$

In Exercises 43 and 44, find $\dfrac{d^{40}y}{dx^{40}}$.

43. $y = e^{x\sqrt[8]{2}}$

44. $y = \sin(x\sqrt[8]{2})$

In Exercises 45–48, find an equation for the (**a**) tangent and (**b**) normal to the curve at the indicated point.

45. $y = \sqrt{x^2 - 2x},\quad x = 3$

46. $y = \tan 2x,\quad x = \pi/3$

47. $x^2 + 2y^2 = 9,\quad (1, 2)$

48. $x + \sqrt{xy} = 6,\quad (4, 1)$

In Exercises 49–52, find an equation for the line tangent to the curve at the point defined by the given value of t.

49. $x = 2\sin t,\quad y = 2\cos t,\quad t = 3\pi/4$

50. $x = 3\cos t,\quad y = 4\sin t,\quad t = 3\pi/4$

51. $x = 3\sec t,\quad y = 5\tan t,\quad t = \pi/6$

52. $x = \cos t,\quad y = t + \sin t,\quad t = -\pi/4$

53. Writing to Learn

Let $f(x) = \begin{cases} \sin ax + b\cos x, & x < 0 \\ 5x + 3, & x \ge 0 \end{cases}$.

(**a**) If f is continuous at $x = 0$, find the value of b. Justify your answer.

(**b**) If f is differentiable at $x = 0$, find the value of a. Justify your answer.

(**c**) Is f differentiable at $x = 0$ if $a = 5$ and $b = 4$? Justify your answer.

54. Writing to Learn For what values of the constant m is

$$f(x) = \begin{cases} \sin 2x, & x \le 0 \\ mx, & x > 0 \end{cases}$$

(**a**) continuous at $x = 0$? Explain.

(**b**) differentiable at $x = 0$? Explain.

In Exercises 55–58, determine where the function is (**a**) differentiable, (**b**) continuous but not differentiable, and (**c**) neither continuous nor differentiable.

55. $f(x) = \sqrt[3]{(x - 1)^3}$

56. $g(x) = \sin(x^2 + 1)$

57. $f(x) = \begin{cases} \sqrt{x^2 + 3}, & -1 \le x < 1 \\ x + 1, & 1 \le x < 3 \end{cases}$

58. $g(x) = \begin{cases} \sin 2x, & -3 \le x < 0 \\ x^2 + 2x + 1, & 0 \le x \le 3 \end{cases}$

59. Simplify, Simplify Find the derivative of each function easily by simplifying the expression before differentiating.

(a) $y = (\sqrt{3 - \sin x})^2$
(b) $y = \ln (3e^{7x^2 - 13x + 5})$
(c) $s = \tan (\tan^{-1}(t^2 - 3t))$
(d) $s = \sqrt[3]{t^6} - 5(\sin (\sin^{-1} t))^6$

60. Simplify, Simplify Find the derivative of each function relatively easily by simplifying the expression before differentiating.

(a) $y = \ln \left(\dfrac{2x + 7}{3x + 2} \right)$
(b) $y = \dfrac{(x^2 - 1)^2}{(x^2 - 2x + 1)(x + 1)}$

(c) $s = \sin^2 (\cos^{-1} t)$
(d) $s = \left(\dfrac{2\sqrt{t}}{\sqrt[3]{t}} \right)^5$

61. Hitting the Slopes A differentiable function f has the property that $f'(x) > 0$ for all x. The line $y = 3x - 2$ is tangent to the graph of f at the point where $x = 2$.

(a) Find the equation of the line normal to the graph of f at the point where $x = 2$.

(b) Find the equation of the line tangent to the graph of f^{-1} at the point where $y = 2$.

(c) Find the equation of the line tangent to the graph of $y = \dfrac{f(x)}{x}$ at the point where $x = 2$.

62. Hitting the Slopes Again A differentiable function g has the property that $g'(x) < 0$ for all x. The line $y = 5 - 2x$ is tangent to the graph of g at the point where $x = 1$.

(a) Find the equation of the line normal to the graph of g at the point where $x = 1$.

(b) Find the equation of the line tangent to the graph of g^{-1} at the point where $y = 1$.

(c) Find the equation of the line tangent to the graph of $y = g(x^2)$ at the point where $x = 1$.

63. Logarithmic Differentiation Use the technique of logarithmic differentiation to find $\dfrac{dy}{dx}$ when

$y = \dfrac{(x + 2)^5(2x - 3)^4}{(x + 17)^2}$. (See Example 7 of Section 4.4.)

64. Logarithmic Differentiation Use the technique of logarithmic differentiation to find $\dfrac{dy}{dx}$ when $y = (x^2 + 2)^{x+5}$. (See Example 7 of Section 4.4.)

65. Differential Equations Equations that involve derivatives are called *differential equations*. We will have much more to say about them in Chapter 7, but meanwhile try to use what you have learned in Chapters 3 and 4 to find at least one nonzero function that satisfies each of these differential equations.

(a) $f'(x) = x$
(b) $f'(x) = f(x)$
(c) $f'(x) = -f(x)$
(d) $f''(x) = f(x)$
(e) $f''(x) = -f(x)$

66. Working with Numerical Values Suppose that a function f and its first derivative have the following values at $x = 0$ and $x = 1$.

x	$f(x)$	$f'(x)$
0	9	−2
1	−3	1/5

Find the first derivative of the following combinations at the given value of x.

(a) $\sqrt{x}f(x)$, $x = 1$
(b) $\sqrt{f(x)}$, $x = 0$
(c) $f(\sqrt{x})$, $x = 1$
(d) $f(1 - 5\tan x)$, $x = 0$
(e) $\dfrac{f(x)}{2 + \cos x}$, $x = 0$
(f) $10 \sin \left(\dfrac{\pi x}{2} \right) f^2(x)$, $x = 1$

67. Working with Numerical Values Suppose that functions f and g and their first derivatives have the following values at $x = -1$ and $x = 0$.

x	$f(x)$	$g(x)$	$f'(x)$	$g'(x)$
−1	0	−1	2	1
0	−1	−3	−2	4

Find the first derivative of the following combinations at the given value of x.

(a) $\dfrac{f(2x)}{x - 1}$, $x = 0$
(b) $f^2(x)g^3(x)$, $x = 0$
(c) $g(f(x))$, $x = -1$
(d) $f(g(x))$, $x = -1$
(e) $f(g(2x - 1))$, $x = 0$
(f) $g(x + f(x))$, $x = 0$

68. Find the value of dw/ds at $s = 0$ if $w = \sin(\sqrt{r} - 2)$ and $r = 8 \sin (s + \pi/6)$.

69. Find the value of dr/dt at $t = 0$ if $r = (\theta^2 + 7)^{1/3}$ and $\theta^2 t + \theta = 1$.

70. Particle Motion The position at time $t \ge 0$ of a particle moving along the s-axis is

$$s(t) = 10 \cos (t + \pi/4).$$

(a) Give parametric equations that can be used to simulate the motion of the particle.

(b) What is the particle's initial position $(t = 0)$?

(c) What points reached by the particle are farthest to the left and right of the origin?

(d) When does the particle first reach the origin? What are its velocity, speed, and acceleration then?

71. Implicit Hyperbola The hyperbola shown in the graph is defined implicitly by the equation $4x^2 + 8xy + y^2 + 3 = 0$.

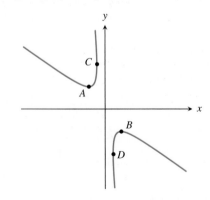

(a) Find the coordinates of points A and B, where the tangent lines are horizontal.

(b) Find the coordinates of points C and D, where the tangent lines are vertical.

72. Implicit Ellipse The ellipse shown in the graph is defined implicitly by the equation $2x^2 - 2xy + y^2 - 4 = 0$.

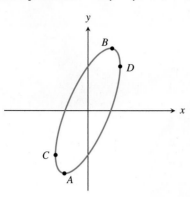

(a) Find the coordinates of points A and B, where the tangent lines are horizontal.

(b) Find the coordinates of points C and D, where the tangent lines are vertical.

73. Implicit Parabola The parabola shown in the graph is defined implicitly by the equation $x^2 - 2xy + y^2 - 4x = 8$.

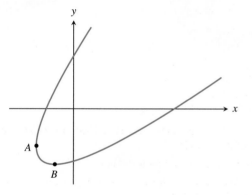

(a) Find the coordinates of point A, where the tangent line is vertical.

(b) Find the coordinates of point B, where the tangent line is horizontal.

74. Problem 73 Revisited Find the slope of the parabola defined implicitly by the equation $x^2 - 2xy + y^2 - 4x = 8$ at each of the points where it crosses the coordinate axes.

75. Slope of a Sinusoid Recall that the general equation of a sinusoid is $y = A \sin(Bx + C) + D$, where only the constants A and B affect the amplitude and period. What is the maximum possible slope for a sinusoid with amplitude 3 and period π?

76. Writing to Learn Write a formula that gives the maximum possible slope for a sinusoid with amplitude A and period p. Justify your answer.

77. Horizontal Tangents The graph of $y = \sin(x - \sin x)$ appears to have horizontal tangents at the x-axis. Does it?

78. *Spread of Measles* The spread of measles in a certain school is given by

$$P(t) = \frac{200}{1 + e^{5-t}},$$

where t is the number of days since the measles first appeared, and $P(t)$ is the total number of students who have caught the measles to date.

(a) Estimate the initial number of students infected with measles.

(b) About how many students in all will get the measles?

(c) When will the rate of spread of measles be greatest? What is this rate?

79. If $x^2 + 2xy + 2y^2 = 5$, find

(a) $\dfrac{dy}{dx}$ at the point $(1, 1)$;

(b) $\dfrac{d^2y}{dx^2}$ at the point $(1, 1)$.

80. If $x^2 - y^2 = 1$, find d^2y/dx^2 at the point $(2, \sqrt{3})$.

AP* Examination Preparation

81. A function f and its first and second derivatives are defined for all real numbers, and it is given that $f(0) = 2$, $f'(0) = 3$, and $f''(0) = -1$.

(a) Define a function g by $g(x) = e^{kx} + f(x)$, where k is a constant. Find $g'(0)$ and $g''(0)$ in terms of k. Show your work.

(b) Define a function h by $h(x) = \cos(bx) f(x)$, where b is a constant. Find $h'(x)$ and write an equation for the line tangent to the graph of h at $x = 0$.

82. Let $y = \dfrac{e^x + e^{-x}}{2}$.

(a) Find $\dfrac{dy}{dx}$.

(b) Find $\dfrac{d^2y}{dx^2}$.

(c) Find an equation of the line tangent to the curve at $x = 1$.

(d) Find an equation of the line normal to the curve at $x = 1$.

(e) Find any points where the tangent line is horizontal.

83. Let $f(x) = \ln(1 - x^2)$.

(a) State the domain of f.

(b) Find $f'(x)$.

(c) State the domain of f'.

(d) Prove that $f''(x) < 0$ for all x in the domain of f.

5.1 Extreme Values
of Functions

5.2 Mean Value Theorem

5.3 Connecting f' and f''
with the Graph of f

5.4 Modeling and
Optimization

5.5 Linearization,
Sensitivity, and
Differentials

5.6 Related Rates

An automobile's gas mileage is a function of many variables, including road surface, tire type, velocity, fuel octane rating, road angle, and the speed and direction of the wind. If we look only at the velocity's effect on gas mileage, then for velocities between 20 and 70 mph the mileage of a certain car can be approximated by

$$m(v) = 0.00027v^3 - 0.051v^2 + 2.9v - 17$$

(where v is velocity).

At what speed should you drive this car to obtain the best gas mileage? The ideas in Section 5.1 will help you find the answer.

CHAPTER 5 Overview

The derivative is supremely useful because there are so many ways to think of it. It is the instantaneous rate of change, enabling us to find velocity when position is given or acceleration when velocity is given. It also describes sensitivity, how change in the input variable is reflected in the change of the output variable. And it has a geometric meaning, as the slope of the tangent to the graph of a function. In this chapter, we will explore how all of these understandings of the derivative lead to applications.

The derivative tells us a great deal about the shape of a curve. Even though we can graph a function quickly, and usually correctly using a grapher, the derivative gives us precise information about how the curve bends and exactly where it turns. We also will see how to deduce rates of change we cannot measure from rates of change we already know, and how to find a function when we know only its first derivative and its value at a single point. The key to recovering functions from derivatives is the Mean Value Theorem, the theorem whose corollaries provide the gateway to *integral calculus*, which we begin in Chapter 6.

This chapter begins where the early developers of calculus began, with the derivative as the slope of the tangent line and the insights this gives us into finding the greatest and least values of a function.

5.1 | Extreme Values of Functions

You will be able to find the maximum or minimum value of a function over a given interval and determine the applicability of the Extreme Value Theorem.

- Absolute (Global) and Local (Relative) Extrema
- The Extreme Value Theorem
- Using the derivative to find extrema

Absolute (Global) Extreme Values

One of the most useful things we can learn from a function's derivative is whether the function assumes any maximum or minimum values on a given interval and where these values are located if it does. Once we know how to find a function's extreme values, we will be able to answer such questions as "What is the most effective size for a dose of medicine?" and "What is the least expensive way to pipe oil from an offshore well to a refinery down the coast?" We will see how to answer questions like these in Section 5.4.

DEFINITION   Absolute Extreme Values

Let f be a function with domain D. Then $f(c)$ is the

(a) absolute maximum value on D if and only if $f(x) \le f(c)$ for all x in D.

(b) absolute minimum value on D if and only if $f(x) \ge f(c)$ for all x in D.

Absolute (or **global**) maximum and minimum values are also called **absolute extrema** (plural of the Latin *extremum*). We often omit the term "absolute" or "global" and just say maximum and minimum.

Example 1 shows that extreme values can occur at interior points or endpoints of intervals.

EXAMPLE 1 Exploring Extreme Values

On $[-\pi/2, \pi/2]$, $f(x) = \cos x$ takes on a maximum value of 1 (once) and a minimum value of 0 (twice). The function $g(x) = \sin x$ takes on a maximum value of 1 and a minimum value of -1 (Figure 5.1). *Now Try Exercise 1.*

Functions with the same defining rule can have different extrema, depending on the domain.

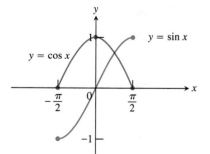

Figure 5.1 (Example 1)

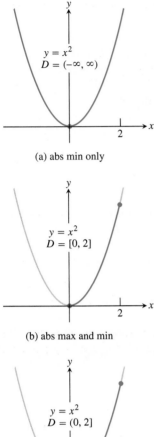

(a) abs min only

(b) abs max and min

(c) abs max only

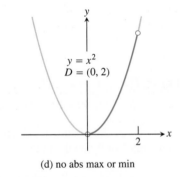

(d) no abs max or min

Figure 5.2 (Example 2)

EXAMPLE 2 Exploring Absolute Extrema

The absolute extrema of the following functions on their domains can be seen in Figure 5.2.

	Function Rule	Domain D	Absolute Extrema on D
(a)	$y = x^2$	$(-\infty, \infty)$	No absolute maximum Absolute minimum of 0 at $x = 0$
(b)	$y = x^2$	$[0, 2]$	Absolute maximum of 4 at $x = 2$ Absolute minimum of 0 at $x = 0$
(c)	$y = x^2$	$(0, 2]$	Absolute maximum of 4 at $x = 2$ No absolute minimum
(d)	$y = x^2$	$(0, 2)$	No absolute extrema

Now Try Exercise 3.

Example 2 shows that a function may fail to have a maximum or minimum value. This cannot happen with a continuous function on a finite closed interval.

THEOREM 1 The Extreme Value Theorem

If f is continuous on a closed interval $[a, b]$, then f has both a maximum value and a minimum value on the interval. (Figure 5.3)

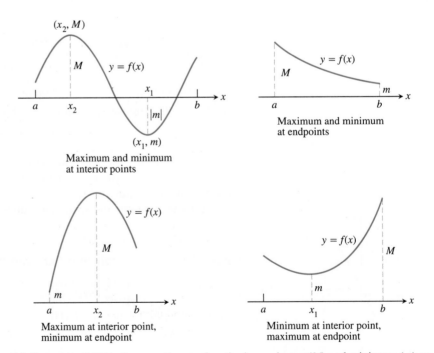

Figure 5.3 Some possibilities for a continuous function's maximum (M) and minimum (m) on a closed interval $[a, b]$.

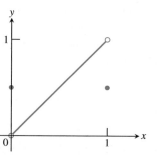

Figure 5.4 A discontinuous function on $[0, 1]$ that has no absolute extrema.

The continuity of f is essential for Theorem 1. Figure 5.4 shows a function on the closed interval $[0, 1]$ that has no absolute extrema.

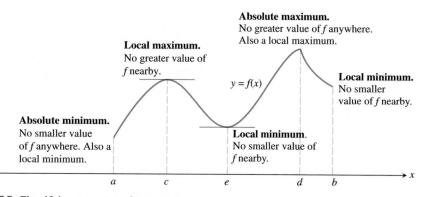

Figure 5.5 Classifying extreme values.

Local (Relative) Extreme Values

Figure 5.5 shows a graph with five points where a function has extreme values on its domain $[a, b]$. The function's absolute minimum occurs at a even though at e the function's value is smaller than at any other point *nearby*. The curve rises to the left and falls to the right around c, making $f(c)$ a maximum locally. The function attains its absolute maximum at d.

DEFINITION Local Extreme Values

Let c be an interior point of the domain of the function f. Then $f(c)$ is a

(a) local maximum value at c if and only if $f(x) \leq f(c)$ for all x in some open interval containing c.

(b) local minimum value at c if and only if $f(x) \geq f(c)$ for all x in some open interval containing c.

A function f has a local maximum or local minimum *at an endpoint* c if the appropriate inequality holds for all x in some half-open domain interval containing c.

Local extrema are also called **relative extrema.**

An **absolute extremum** is also a local extremum, because being an extreme value overall makes it an extreme value in its immediate neighborhood. Hence, *a list of local extrema will automatically include absolute extrema if there are any.*

Finding Extreme Values

The interior domain points where the function in Figure 5.5 has local extreme values are points where either f' is zero or f' does not exist. This is generally the case, as we see from the following theorem, first discovered by Pierre de Fermat (page 89).

THEOREM 2 Local Extreme Values

If a function f has a local maximum value or a local minimum value at an interior point c of its domain, and if f' exists at c, then

$$f'(c) = 0.$$

Because of Theorem 2, we usually need to look at only a few points to find a function's extrema. These consist of the interior domain points where $f' = 0$ or f' does not exist (the domain points covered by the theorem) and the domain endpoints (the domain points not covered by the theorem). At all other domain points, $f' > 0$ or $f' < 0$.

The following definition helps us summarize these findings.

> ### DEFINITION   Critical Point
>
> A point in the interior of the domain of a function f at which $f' = 0$ or f' does not exist is a **critical point** of f.

Thus, in summary, extreme values occur only at critical points and endpoints.

> ### DEFINITION   Stationary Point
>
> A point in the interior of the domain of a function f at which $f' = 0$ is called a **stationary point** of f.

A stationary point can be a minimum, a maximum, or neither. Note that critical points and stationary points of a function f are *not necessarily* the same. See Examples 3 and 5.

EXAMPLE 3   Finding Absolute Extrema

Find the absolute maximum and minimum values of $f(x) = x^{2/3}$ on the interval $[-2, 3]$.

SOLUTION

The graph in Figure 5.6 suggests that f has an absolute maximum value of about 2 at $x = 3$ and an absolute minimum value of 0 at $x = 0$. The critical point $(0, 0)$ is **not** a stationary point.

To find the exact maximum and minimum values, we evaluate the function at the critical points and endpoints and take the largest and smallest of the resulting values.

The first derivative

$$f'(x) = \frac{2}{3}x^{-1/3} = \frac{2}{3\sqrt[3]{x}}$$

has no zeros but is undefined at $x = 0$. The values of f at this one critical point and at the endpoints are

Critical point value: $f(0) = 0$;

Endpoint values: $f(-2) = (-2)^{2/3} = \sqrt[3]{4}$;

$f(3) = (3)^{2/3} = \sqrt[3]{9}$.

We can see from this list that the function's absolute maximum value is $\sqrt[3]{9} \approx 2.08$, and occurs at the right endpoint $x = 3$. The absolute minimum value is 0, and occurs at the interior point $x = 0$.   ***Now Try Exercise 11.***

In Example 4, we investigate the reciprocal of the function whose graph was drawn in Example 3 of Section 1.2 to illustrate "grapher failure."

EXAMPLE 4   Finding Extreme Values

Find the extreme values of $f(x) = \dfrac{1}{\sqrt{4 - x^2}}$.

continued

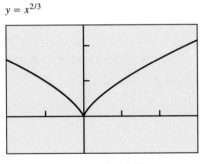

$y = x^{2/3}$

[–2, 3] by [–1, 2.5]

Figure 5.6 (Example 3)

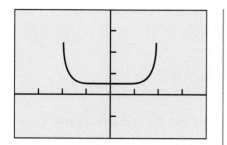

[–4, 4] by [–2, 4]

Figure 5.7 The graph of

$$f(x) = \frac{1}{\sqrt{4 - x^2}}.$$

(Example 4)

SOLUTION

Figure 5.7 suggests that f has an absolute minimum of about 0.5 at $x = 0$. There also appear to be local maxima at $x = -2$ and $x = 2$. However, f is not defined at these points and there do not appear to be maxima anywhere else.

The function f is defined only for $4 - x^2 > 0$, so its domain is the open interval $(-2, 2)$. The domain has no endpoints, so all the extreme values must occur at critical points. We rewrite the formula for f to find f':

$$f(x) = \frac{1}{\sqrt{4 - x^2}} = (4 - x^2)^{-1/2}$$

Thus,

$$f'(x) = -\frac{1}{2}(4 - x^2)^{-3/2}(-2x) = \frac{x}{(4 - x^2)^{3/2}}.$$

The only critical point in the domain $(-2, 2)$ is $x = 0$. The value

$$f(0) = \frac{1}{\sqrt{4 - 0^2}} = \frac{1}{2}$$

is therefore the sole candidate for an extreme value.

To determine whether $1/2$ is an extreme value of f, we examine the formula

$$f(x) = \frac{1}{\sqrt{4 - x^2}}.$$

As x moves away from 0 on either side, the denominator gets smaller, the values of f increase, and the graph rises. We have a minimum value at $x = 0$, and the minimum is absolute.

The function has no maxima, either local or absolute. This does not violate Theorem 1 (The Extreme Value Theorem) because here f is defined on an *open* interval. To invoke Theorem 1's guarantee of extreme points, the interval must be closed.

Now Try Exercise 25.

While a function's extrema can occur only at critical points and endpoints, not every critical point or endpoint signals the presence of an extreme value. Figure 5.8 illustrates this for interior points. Exercise 55 describes a function that fails to assume an extreme value at an endpoint of its domain.

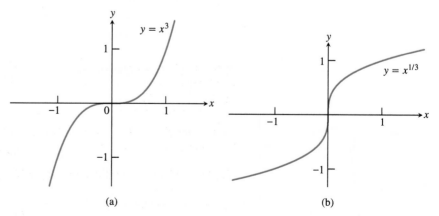

(a)   (b)

Figure 5.8 Critical points without extreme values. (a) $y' = 3x^2$ is 0 at $x = 0$, but $y = x^3$ has no extremum there. (b) $y' = (1/3)x^{-2/3}$ is undefined at $x = 0$, but $y = x^{1/3}$ has no extremum there.

EXAMPLE 5 Finding Extreme Values

Find the extreme values of

$$f(x) = \begin{cases} 5 - 2x^2, & x \leq 1 \\ x + 2, & x > 1. \end{cases}$$

SOLUTION

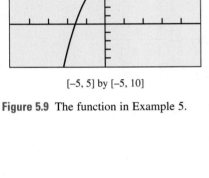

[−5, 5] by [−5, 10]

Figure 5.9 The function in Example 5.

The graph in Figure 5.9 suggests that $f'(0) = 0$ and that $f'(1)$ does not exist. There appears to be a local maximum value of 5 at $x = 0$ and a local minimum value of 3 at $x = 1$. The point $(0, 5)$ is the only stationary point.

To verify the real extrema, we look at the derivative of f. For $x \neq 1$, the derivative is

$$f'(x) = \begin{cases} \dfrac{d}{dx}(5 - 2x^2) = -4x, & x < 1 \\ \dfrac{d}{dx}(x + 2) = 1, & x > 1. \end{cases}$$

The only point where $f' = 0$ is $x = 0$. What happens at $x = 1$?
At $x = 1$, the right- and left-hand derivatives are, respectively,

$$\lim_{h \to 0^+} \frac{f(1 + h) - f(1)}{h} = \lim_{h \to 0^+} \frac{(1 + h) + 2 - 3}{h} = \lim_{h \to 0^+} \frac{h}{h} = 1.$$

$$\lim_{h \to 0^-} \frac{f(1 + h) - f(1)}{h} = \lim_{h \to 0^-} \frac{5 - 2(1 + h)^2 - 3}{h}$$

$$= \lim_{h \to 0^-} \frac{-2h(2 + h)}{h} = -4$$

Since these one-sided derivatives differ, f has no derivative at $x = 1$, and 1 is a second critical point of f.

The domain $(-\infty, \infty)$ has no endpoints, so the only values of f that might be local extrema are those at the critical points:

$$f(0) = 5 \quad \text{and} \quad f(1) = 3$$

From the formula for f, we see that the values of f immediately to either side of $x = 0$ are less than 5, so 5 is a local maximum. Similarly, the values of f immediately to either side of $x = 1$ are greater than 3, so 3 is a local minimum.

Now Try Exercise 41.

Most graphing calculators have built-in methods to find the coordinates of points where extreme values occur. We must, of course, be sure that we use correct graphs to find these values. The calculus that you learn in this chapter should make you feel more confident about working with graphs.

EXAMPLE 6 Using Graphical Methods

Find the extreme values of $f(x) = \ln \left| \dfrac{x}{1 + x^2} \right|$.

SOLUTION

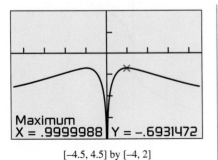

Maximum
X = .9999988   Y = −.6931472

[−4.5, 4.5] by [−4, 2]

Figure 5.10 The function in Example 6.

The domain of f is the set of all nonzero real numbers. Figure 5.10 suggests that f is an even function with a maximum value at two points. The coordinates found in this window suggest an extreme value of about -0.69 at approximately $x = 1$. Because f is even, there is another extreme of the same value at approximately $x = -1$. The figure also suggests a minimum value at $x = 0$, but f is not defined there.

continued

The derivative

$$f'(x) = \frac{1 - x^2}{x(1 + x^2)}$$

is defined at every point of the function's domain. The critical points where $f'(x) = 0$ are $x = 1$ and $x = -1$. The corresponding values of f are both $\ln(1/2) = -\ln 2 \approx -0.69$.

Now Try Exercise 37.

EXPLORATION 1 Finding Extreme Values

Let $f(x) = \left| \dfrac{x}{x^2 + 1} \right|, -2 \le x \le 2$.

1. Determine graphically the extreme values of f and where they occur. Find f' at these values of x.
2. Graph f and f' (or NDER $(f(x), x)$) in the same viewing window. Comment on the relationship between the graphs.
3. Find a formula for $f'(x)$.

Quick Review 5.1 *(For help, go to Sections 1.2, 2.1, 3.5, and 4.1.)*

Exercise numbers with a gray background indicate problems that the authors have designed to be solved *without a calculator.*

In Exercises 1–4, find the first derivative of the function.

1. $f(x) = \sqrt{4 - x}$

2. $f(x) = \dfrac{2}{\sqrt{9 - x^2}}$

3. $g(x) = \cos(\ln x)$

4. $h(x) = e^{2x}$

In Exercises 5–8, match the table with a graph of $f(x)$.

5.

x	$f'(x)$
a	0
b	0
c	5

6.

x	$f'(x)$
a	0
b	0
c	-5

7.

x	$f'(x)$
a	does not exist
b	0
c	-2

8.

x	$f'(x)$
a	does not exist
b	does not exist
c	-1.7

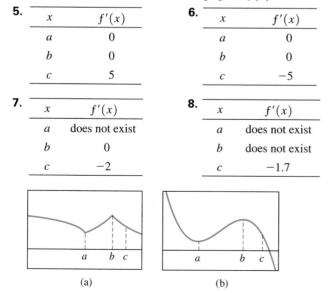

(a)　　　(b)

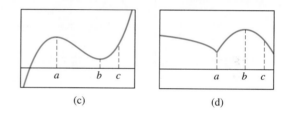

(c)　　　(d)

In Exercises 9 and 10, find the limit for

$$f(x) = \frac{2}{\sqrt{9 - x^2}}.$$

9. $\lim\limits_{x \to 3^-} f(x)$ 　　　**10.** $\lim\limits_{x \to -3^+} f(x)$

In Exercises 11 and 12, let

$$f(x) = \begin{cases} x^3 - 2x, & x \le 2 \\ x + 2, & x > 2. \end{cases}$$

11. Find **(a)** $f'(1)$, **(b)** $f'(3)$, **(c)** $f'(2)$.

12. (a) Find the domain of f'.

　　(b) Write a formula for $f'(x)$.

Section 5.1 Exercises

In Exercises 1–4, find the extreme values and where they occur.

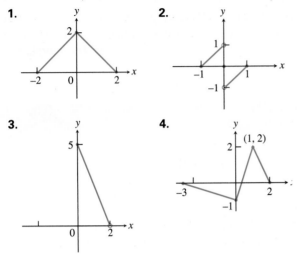

1.

2.

3.

4.

In Exercises 5–10, identify each x value at which any absolute extreme value occurs. Explain how your answer is consistent with the Extreme Value Theorem.

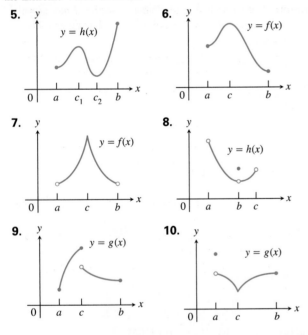

5. $y = h(x)$

6. $y = f(x)$

7. $y = f(x)$

8. $y = h(x)$

9. $y = g(x)$

10. $y = g(x)$

In Exercises 11–18, use analytic methods to find the extreme values of the function on the interval and where they occur. Identify any critical points that are *not* stationary points.

11. $f(x) = \dfrac{1}{x} + \ln x, \quad 0.5 \le x \le 4$

12. $g(x) = e^{-x}, \quad -1 \le x \le 1$

13. $h(x) = \ln(x + 1), \quad 0 \le x \le 3$

14. $k(x) = e^{-x^2}, \quad -\infty < x < \infty$

15. $f(x) = \sin\left(x + \dfrac{\pi}{4}\right), \quad 0 \le x \le \dfrac{7\pi}{4}$

16. $g(x) = \sec x, \quad -\dfrac{\pi}{2} < x < \dfrac{3\pi}{2}$

17. $f(x) = x^{2/5}, \quad -3 \le x < 1$

18. $f(x) = x^{3/5}, \quad -2 < x \le 3$

In Exercises 19–30, find the extreme values of the function and where they occur.

19. $y = 2x^2 - 8x + 9$

20. $y = x^3 - 2x + 4$

21. $y = x^3 + x^2 - 8x + 5$

22. $y = x^3 - 3x^2 + 3x - 2$

23. $y = \sqrt{x^2 - 1}$

24. $y = \dfrac{1}{x^2 - 1}$

25. $y = \dfrac{1}{\sqrt{1 - x^2}}$

26. $y = \dfrac{1}{\sqrt[3]{1 - x^2}}$

27. $y = \sqrt{3 + 2x - x^2}$

28. $y = \dfrac{3}{2}x^4 + 4x^3 - 9x^2 + 10$

29. $y = \dfrac{x}{x^2 + 1}$

30. $y = \dfrac{x + 1}{x^2 + 2x + 2}$

Group Activity In Exercises 31–34, find the extreme values of the function on the interval and where they occur.

31. $f(x) = |x - 2| + |x + 3|, \quad -5 \le x \le 5$

32. $g(x) = |x - 1| - |x - 5|, \quad -2 \le x \le 7$

33. $h(x) = |x + 2| - |x - 3|, \quad -\infty < x < \infty$

34. $k(x) = |x + 1| + |x - 3|, \quad -\infty < x < \infty$

In Exercises 35–42, identify the critical points and determine the local extreme values. Identify which critical points are *not* stationary points.

35. $y = x^{2/3}(x + 2)$

36. $y = x^{2/3}(x^2 - 4)$

37. $y = x\sqrt{4 - x^2}$

38. $y = x^2\sqrt{3 - x}$

39. $y = \begin{cases} 4 - 2x, & x \le 1 \\ x + 1, & x > 1 \end{cases}$

40. $y = \begin{cases} 3 - x, & x < 0 \\ 3 + 2x - x^2, & x \ge 0 \end{cases}$

41. $y = \begin{cases} -x^2 - 2x + 4, & x \le 1 \\ -x^2 + 6x - 4, & x > 1 \end{cases}$

42. $y = \begin{cases} -\dfrac{1}{4}x^2 - \dfrac{1}{2}x + \dfrac{15}{4}, & x \le 1 \\ x^3 - 6x^2 + 8x, & x > 1 \end{cases}$

43. Writing to Learn The function
$$V(x) = x(10 - 2x)(16 - 2x), \quad 0 < x < 5$$
models the volume of a box.

(a) Find the extreme values of V.

(b) Interpret any values found in (a) in terms of volume of the box.

(c) Support your analytic answer to part (a) graphically.

44. Writing to Learn The function
$$P(x) = 2x + \frac{200}{x}, \quad 0 < x < \infty,$$
models the perimeter of a rectangle of dimensions x by $100/x$.

(a) Find any extreme values of P.

(b) Give an interpretation in terms of perimeter of the rectangle for any values found in (a).

Standardized Test Questions

45. True or False If $f(c)$ is a local maximum of a continuous function f on an open interval (a, b), then $f'(c) = 0$. Justify your answer.

46. True or False If m is a local minimum and M is a local maximum of a continuous function f on (a, b), then $m < M$. Justify your answer.

47. Multiple Choice Which of the following values is the absolute maximum of the function $f(x) = 4x - x^2 + 6$ on the interval $[0, 4]$?

(A) 0 (B) 2 (C) 4 (D) 6 (E) 10

48. Multiple Choice If f is a continuous, decreasing function on $[0, 10]$ with a critical point at $(4, 2)$, which of the following statements *must be false*?

(A) $f(10)$ is an absolute minimum of f on $[0, 10]$.

(B) $f(4)$ is neither a relative maximum nor a relative minimum.

(C) $f'(4)$ does not exist.

(D) $f'(4) = 0$

(E) $f'(4) < 0$

49. Multiple Choice Which of the following functions has exactly two local extrema on its domain?

(A) $f(x) = |x - 2|$

(B) $f(x) = x^3 - 6x + 5$

(C) $f(x) = x^3 + 6x - 5$

(D) $f(x) = \tan x$

(E) $f(x) = x + \ln x$

50. Multiple Choice If an even function f with domain all real numbers has a local maximum at $x = a$, then $f(-a)$

(A) is a local minimum.

(B) is a local maximum.

(C) is both a local minimum and a local maximum.

(D) could be either a local minimum or a local maximum.

(E) is neither a local minimum nor a local maximum.

Explorations

In Exercises 51 and 52, give reasons for your answers.

51. Writing to Learn Let $f(x) = (x - 2)^{2/3}$.

(a) Does $f'(2)$ exist?

(b) Show that the only local extreme value of f occurs at $x = 2$.

(c) Does the result in (b) contradict the Extreme Value Theorem?

(d) Repeat parts (a) and (b) for $f(x) = (x - a)^{2/3}$, replacing 2 by a.

52. Writing to Learn Let $f(x) = |x^3 - 9x|$.

(a) Does $f'(0)$ exist?

(b) Does $f'(3)$ exist?

(c) Does $f'(-3)$ exist?

(d) Determine all extrema of f.

Extending the Ideas

53. Cubic Functions Consider the cubic function
$$f(x) = ax^3 + bx^2 + cx + d.$$

(a) Show that f can have 0, 1, or 2 critical points. Give examples and graphs to support your argument.

(b) How many local extreme values can f have?

54. Proving Theorem 2 Assume that the function f has a local maximum value at the interior point c of its domain and that $f'(c)$ exists.

(a) Show that there is an open interval containing c such that $f(x) - f(c) \le 0$ for all x in the open interval.

(b) **Writing to Learn** Now explain why we may say
$$\lim_{x \to c^+} \frac{f(x) - f(c)}{x - c} \le 0.$$

(c) **Writing to Learn** Now explain why we may say
$$\lim_{x \to c^-} \frac{f(x) - f(c)}{x - c} \ge 0.$$

(d) **Writing to Learn** Explain how parts (b) and (c) allow us to conclude $f'(c) = 0$.

(e) **Writing to Learn** Give a similar argument if f has a local minimum value at an interior point.

55. Functions with No Extreme Values at Endpoints

(a) Graph the function
$$f(x) = \begin{cases} \sin\dfrac{1}{x}, & x > 0 \\ 0, & x = 0. \end{cases}$$

Explain why $f(0) = 0$ is not a local extreme value of f.

(b) **Group Activity** Construct a function of your own that fails to have an extreme value at a domain endpoint.

5.2 | Mean Value Theorem

You will be able to apply the Mean Value Theorem to describe the behavior of a function over an interval.

- The Mean Value Theorem
- Increasing and decreasing functions
- Functions whose derivative is zero
- Antidifferentiation

Mean Value Theorem

The Mean Value Theorem connects the average, or mean, rate of change of a function over an interval with the instantaneous rate of change of the function at a point within the interval. It first arose in the 18th century, when it was used by Joseph Louis Lagrange (1736–1813) to determine the distance between a function and its linear approximation (see Exercise 72 in Section 5.5). In the 19th century, it helped to answer many of the questions that faced scientists as they pushed the boundaries of calculus and discovered strange and unexpected effects. For us, it will provide the basis for many applications of the derivative.

The theorem says that somewhere between points A and B on a differentiable curve, there is at least one tangent line parallel to chord AB (Figure 5.11).

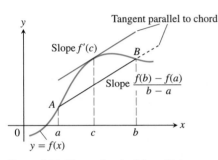

Figure 5.11 Figure for the Mean Value Theorem.

THEOREM 3 Mean Value Theorem for Derivatives

If $y = f(x)$ is continuous at every point of the closed interval $[a, b]$ and differentiable at every point of its interior (a, b), then there is at least one point c in (a, b) at which the instantaneous rate of change equals the mean rate of change,

$$f'(c) = \frac{f(b) - f(a)}{b - a}.$$

The hypotheses of Theorem 3 cannot be relaxed. If they fail at even one point, the graph may fail to have a tangent parallel to the chord. For instance, the function $f(x) = |x|$ is continuous on $[-1, 1]$ and differentiable at every point of the interior $(-1, 1)$ except $x = 0$. The graph has no tangent parallel to chord AB (Figure 5.12a). The function $g(x) = \text{int}(x)$ is differentiable at every point of $(1, 2)$ and continuous at every point of $[1, 2]$ except $x = 2$. Again, the graph has no tangent parallel to chord AB (Figure 5.12b).

The Mean Value Theorem is an *existence theorem*. It tells us the number c exists without telling how to find it. We can sometimes satisfy our curiosity about the value of c but the real importance of the theorem lies in the surprising conclusions we can draw from it.

Rolle's Theorem

Ossian Bonnet (1819–1892) was the first to discover what is now the most common proof of the Mean Value Theorem (Exercise 63). It is based on first proving the simpler case where $f(a) = f(b) = 0$ (Exercise 62). This case is known as Rolle's Theorem, named for Michel Rolle (1652–1719), who proved it only for polynomials.

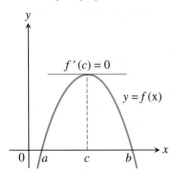

Rolle distrusted calculus and spent most of his life denouncing it. It is ironic that he is known today only for an unintended contribution to a field he tried to suppress.

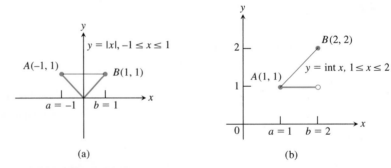

(a)   (b)

Figure 5.12 No tangent parallel to chord AB.

EXAMPLE 1 Exploring the Mean Value Theorem

Show that the function $f(x) = x^2$ satisfies the hypotheses of the Mean Value Theorem on the interval $[0, 2]$. Then find a solution c to the equation

$$f'(c) = \frac{f(b) - f(a)}{b - a}$$

on this interval.

continued

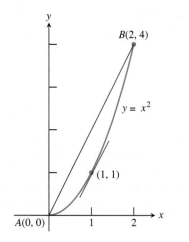

Figure 5.13 (Example 1)

SOLUTION

The function $f(x) = x^2$ is continuous on $[0, 2]$ and differentiable on $(0, 2)$. Since $f(0) = 0$ and $f(2) = 4$, the Mean Value Theorem guarantees a point c in the interval $(0, 2)$ for which

$$f'(c) = \frac{f(b) - f(a)}{b - a}$$

$$2c = \frac{f(2) - f(0)}{2 - 0} = 2 \quad f'(x) = 2x$$

$$c = 1$$

Interpret The tangent line to $f(x) = x^2$ at $x = 1$ has slope 2 and is parallel to the chord joining $A(0, 0)$ and $B(2, 4)$ (Figure 5.13). *Now Try Exercise 1.*

EXAMPLE 2 Exploring the Mean Value Theorem

Explain why each of the following functions fails to satisfy the conditions of the Mean Value Theorem on the interval $[-1, 1]$.

(a) $f(x) = \sqrt{x^2} + 1$ **(b)** $f(x) = \begin{cases} x^3 + 3 & \text{for } x < 1 \\ x^2 + 1 & \text{for } x \geq 1 \end{cases}$

SOLUTION

(a) Note that $\sqrt{x^2} + 1 = |x| + 1$, so this is just a vertical shift of the absolute value function, which has a nondifferentiable "corner" at $x = 0$. (See Section 3.2.) The function f is not differentiable on $(-1, 1)$.

(b) Since $\lim_{x \to 1^-} f(x) = \lim_{x \to 1^-} x^3 + 3 = 4$ and $\lim_{x \to 1^+} f(x) = \lim_{x \to 1^+} x^2 + 1 = 2$, the function has a discontinuity at $x = 1$. The function f is not continuous on $[-1, 1]$.

If the two functions given had satisfied the necessary conditions, the *conclusion* of the Mean Value Theorem would have guaranteed the existence of a number c in $(-1, 1)$ such that $f'(c) = \dfrac{f(1) - f(-1)}{1 - (-1)} = 0$. Such a number c does not exist for the function in part (a), but one happens to exist for the function in part (b) (Figure 5.14).

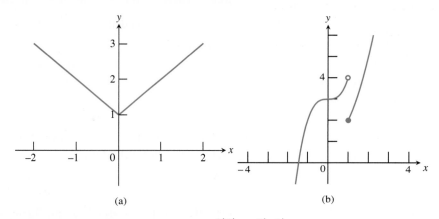

(a)   (b)

Figure 5.14 For both functions in Example 2, $\dfrac{f(1) - f(-1)}{1 - (-1)} = 0$ but neither function satisfies the conditions of the Mean Value Theorem on the interval $[-1, 1]$. For the function in Example 2(a), there is no number c such that $f'(c) = 0$. It happens that $f'(0) = 0$ in Example 2(b).

Now Try Exercise 3.

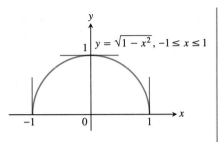

Figure 5.15 (Example 3)

EXAMPLE 3 Applying the Mean Value Theorem

Let $f(x) = \sqrt{1 - x^2}$, $A = (-1, f(-1))$, and $B = (1, f(1))$. Find a tangent to f in the interval $(-1, 1)$ that is parallel to the secant AB.

SOLUTION

The function f (Figure 5.15) is continuous on the interval $[-1, 1]$ and

$$f'(x) = \frac{-x}{\sqrt{1 - x^2}}$$

is defined on the interval $(-1, 1)$. The function is not differentiable at $x = -1$ and $x = 1$, but it does not need to be for the theorem to apply. Since $f(-1) = f(1) = 0$, the tangent we are looking for is horizontal. We find that $f' = 0$ at $x = 0$, where the graph has the horizontal tangent $y = 1$.   *Now Try Exercise 9.*

Physical Interpretation

If we think of the difference quotient $(f(b) - f(a))/(b - a)$ as the average change in f over $[a, b]$ and $f'(c)$ as an instantaneous change, then the Mean Value Theorem says that the instantaneous change at some interior point must equal the average change over the entire interval.

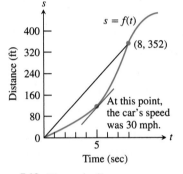

Figure 5.16 (Example 4)

EXAMPLE 4 Interpreting the Mean Value Theorem

If a car accelerating from zero takes 8 sec to go 352 ft, its average velocity for the 8-sec interval is $352/8 = 44$ ft/sec, or 30 mph. At some point during the acceleration, the theorem says, the speedometer must read exactly 30 mph (Figure 5.16).

Now Try Exercise 11.

Increasing and Decreasing Functions

Our first use of the Mean Value Theorem will be its application to increasing and decreasing functions.

Monotonic Functions

A function that is always increasing on an interval or always decreasing on an interval is said to be **monotonic** there.

DEFINITIONS **Increasing Function, Decreasing Function**

Let f be a function defined on an interval I and let x_1 and x_2 be any two points in I.

1. f **increases** on I if $x_1 < x_2$ $\Rightarrow$ $f(x_1) < f(x_2)$.
2. f **decreases** on I if $x_1 < x_2$ $\Rightarrow$ $f(x_1) > f(x_2)$.

The Mean Value Theorem allows us to identify exactly where graphs rise and fall. Functions with positive derivatives are increasing functions; functions with negative derivatives are decreasing functions.

COROLLARY 1 **Increasing and Decreasing Functions**

Let f be continuous on $[a, b]$ and differentiable on (a, b).

1. If $f' > 0$ at each point of (a, b), then f increases on $[a, b]$.
2. If $f' < 0$ at each point of (a, b), then f decreases on $[a, b]$.

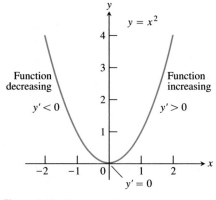

Figure 5.17 (Example 5)

What's Happening at Zero?

Note that 0 appears in both intervals in Example 5, which is consistent both with the definition and with Corollary 1. Does this mean that the function $y = x^2$ is both increasing and decreasing at $x = 0$? No! This is because a function can only be described as increasing or decreasing on an *interval* with more than one point (see the definition). Saying that $y = x^2$ is "increasing at $x = 2$" is not really proper either, but you will often see that statement used as a short way of saying $y = x^2$ is "increasing on an interval containing 2."

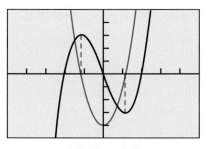

[–5, 5] by [–5, 5]

Figure 5.18 By comparing the graphs of $f(x) = x^3 - 4x$ and $f'(x) = 3x^2 - 4$ we can relate the increasing and decreasing behavior of f to the sign of f'. (Example 6)

Proof Let x_1 and x_2 be any two points in $[a, b]$ with $x_1 < x_2$. The Mean Value Theorem applied to f on $[x_1, x_2]$ gives

$$f(x_2) - f(x_1) = f'(c)(x_2 - x_1)$$

for some c between x_1 and x_2. The sign of the right-hand side of this equation is the same as the sign of $f'(c)$ because $x_2 - x_1$ is positive. Therefore,

(a) $f(x_1) < f(x_2)$ if $f' > 0$ on (a, b) (f is increasing), or

(b) $f(x_1) > f(x_2)$ if $f' < 0$ on (a, b) (f is decreasing). ∎

EXAMPLE 5 Determining Where Graphs Rise or Fall

The function $y = x^2$ (Figure 5.17) is

(a) decreasing on $(-\infty, 0]$ because $y' = 2x < 0$ on $(-\infty, 0)$.

(b) increasing on $[0, \infty)$ because $y' = 2x > 0$ on $(0, \infty)$. *Now Try Exercise 15.*

EXAMPLE 6 Determining Where Graphs Rise or Fall

Where is the function $f(x) = x^3 - 4x$ increasing and where is it decreasing?

SOLUTION

The function is increasing where $f'(x) > 0$.

$$3x^2 - 4 > 0$$

$$x^2 > \frac{4}{3}$$

$$x < -\sqrt{\frac{4}{3}} \quad \text{or} \quad x > \sqrt{\frac{4}{3}}.$$

The function is decreasing where $f'(x) < 0$.

$$3x^2 - 4 < 0$$

$$x^2 < \frac{4}{3}$$

$$-\sqrt{\frac{4}{3}} < x < \sqrt{\frac{4}{3}}.$$

In interval notation, f is increasing on $\left(-\infty, -\sqrt{4/3}\right]$, decreasing on $\left[-\sqrt{4/3}, \sqrt{4/3}\right]$, and increasing on $\left[\sqrt{4/3}, \infty\right)$. See Figure 5.18 for graphical support of the analytic solution. *Now Try Exercise 27.*

Other Consequences

We know that constant functions have the zero function as their derivative. We can now use the Mean Value Theorem to show the converse, that the only functions with the zero function as derivative are constant functions.

COROLLARY 2 Functions with $f' = 0$ Are Constant

If $f'(x) = 0$ at each point of an interval I, then there is a constant C for which $f(x) = C$ for all x in I.

Proof Our plan is to show that $f(x_1) = f(x_2)$ for any two points x_1 and x_2 in I. We can assume the points are numbered so that $x_1 < x_2$. Since f is differentiable at every point of $[x_1, x_2]$ it is continuous at every point as well. Thus, f satisfies the hypotheses of the Mean Value Theorem on $[x_1, x_2]$. Therefore, there is a point c between x_1 and x_2 for which

$$f'(c) = \frac{f(x_2) - f(x_1)}{x_2 - x_1}.$$

Because $f'(c) = 0$, it follows that $f(x_1) = f(x_2)$. ∎

We can use Corollary 2 to show that if two functions have the same derivative, they differ by a constant.

COROLLARY 3   Functions with the Same Derivative Differ by a Constant

If $f'(x) = g'(x)$ at each point of an interval I, then there is a constant C such that $f(x) = g(x) + C$ for all x in I.

Proof Let $h = f - g$. Then for each point x in I,

$$h'(x) = f'(x) - g'(x) = 0.$$

It follows from Corollary 2 that there is a constant C such that $h(x) = C$ for all x in I. Thus, $h(x) = f(x) - g(x) = C$, or $f(x) = g(x) + C$. ∎

We know that the derivative of $f(x) = x^2$ is $2x$ on the interval $(-\infty, \infty)$. So, any other function $g(x)$ with derivative $2x$ on $(-\infty, \infty)$ must have the formula $g(x) = x^2 + C$ for some constant C.

EXAMPLE 7 Applying Corollary 3

Find the function $f(x)$ whose derivative is $\sin x$ and whose graph passes through the point $(0, 2)$.

SOLUTION

Since f has the same derivative as $g(x) = -\cos x$, we know that $f(x) = -\cos x + C$, for some constant C. To identify C, we use the condition that the graph must pass through $(0, 2)$. This is equivalent to saying that

$$f(0) = 2$$
$$-\cos(0) + C = 2 \qquad f(x) = -\cos x + C$$
$$-1 + C = 2$$
$$C = 3.$$

The formula for f is $f(x) = -\cos x + 3$.   ***Now Try Exercise 35.***

In Example 7 we were given a derivative and asked to find a function with that derivative. This type of function is so important that it has a name.

DEFINITION   Antiderivative

A function $F(x)$ is an **antiderivative** of a function $f(x)$ if $F'(x) = f(x)$ for all x in the domain of f. The process of finding an antiderivative is **antidifferentiation.**

We know that if f has one antiderivative F then it has infinitely many antiderivatives, each differing from F by a constant. Corollary 3 says these are all there are. In Example 7, we found the particular antiderivative of $\sin x$ whose graph passed through the point $(0, 2)$.

EXAMPLE 8 Finding Velocity and Position

Find the velocity and position functions of a body falling freely from a height of 0 meters under each of the following sets of conditions:

(a) The acceleration is 9.8 m/sec^2 and the body falls from rest.

(b) The acceleration is 9.8 m/sec^2 and the body is propelled downward with an initial velocity of 1 m/sec.

SOLUTION

(a) *Falling from rest.* We measure distance fallen in meters and time in seconds, and assume that the body is released from rest at time $t = 0$ with downward as the positive direction.

Velocity: We know that the velocity $v(t)$ is an antiderivative of the constant function 9.8. We also know that $g(t) = 9.8t$ is an antiderivative of 9.8. By Corollary 3,

$$v(t) = 9.8t + C$$

for some constant C. Since the body falls from rest, $v(0) = 0$. Thus,

$$9.8(0) + C = 0 \quad \text{and} \quad C = 0.$$

The body's velocity function is $v(t) = 9.8t$.

Position: We know that the position $s(t)$ is an antiderivative of 9.8t. We also know that $h(t) = 4.9t^2$ is an antiderivative of 9.8t. By Corollary 3,

$$s(t) = 4.9t^2 + C$$

for some constant C. Since $s(0) = 0$,

$$4.9(0)^2 + C = 0 \quad \text{and} \quad C = 0.$$

The body's position function is $s(t) = 4.9t^2$.

(b) *Propelled downward.* We measure distance fallen in meters and time in seconds, and assume that the body is propelled downward with a velocity of 1 m/sec at time $t = 0$.

Velocity: The velocity function still has the form $9.8t + C$, but instead of being zero, the initial velocity (velocity at $t = 0$) is now 1 m/sec. Thus,

$$9.8(0) + C = 1 \quad \text{and} \quad C = 1.$$

The body's velocity function is $v(t) = 9.8t + 1$.

Position: We know that the position $s(t)$ is an antiderivative of $9.8t + 1$. We also know that $k(t) = 4.9t^2 + t$ is an antiderivative of $9.8t + 1$. By Corollary 3,

$$s(t) = 4.9t^2 + t + C$$

for some constant C. Since $s(0) = 0$,

$$4.9(0)^2 + 0 + C = 0 \quad \text{and} \quad C = 0.$$

The body's position function is $s(t) = 4.9t^2 + t$.   *Now Try Exercise 43.*

Quick Review 5.2 *(For help, go to Sections 1.2, 2.3, and 3.2.)*

Exercise numbers with a gray background indicate problems that the authors have designed to be solved *without a calculator.*

In Exercises 1 and 2, find exact solutions to the inequality.

1. $2x^2 - 6 < 0$

2. $3x^2 - 6 > 0$

In Exercises 3–5, let $f(x) = \sqrt{8 - 2x^2}$.

3. Find the domain of f.

4. Where is f continuous?

5. Where is f differentiable?

In Exercises 6–8, let $f(x) = \dfrac{x}{x^2 - 1}$.

6. Find the domain of f.

7. Where is f continuous?

8. Where is f differentiable?

In Exercises 9 and 10, find C so that the graph of the function f passes through the specified point.

9. $f(x) = -2x + C$, $(-2, 7)$

10. $g(x) = x^2 + 2x + C$, $(1, -1)$

Section 5.2 Exercises

In Exercises 1–8, **(a)** state whether or not the function satisfies the hypotheses of the Mean Value Theorem on the given interval, and **(b)** if it does, find each value of c in the interval (a, b) that satisfies the equation

$$f'(c) = \frac{f(b) - f(a)}{b - a}.$$

1. $f(x) = x^2 + 2x - 1$ on $[0, 1]$

2. $f(x) = x^{2/3}$ on $[0, 1]$

3. $f(x) = x^{1/3}$ on $[-1, 1]$

4. $f(x) = |x - 1|$ on $[0, 4]$

5. $f(x) = \sin^{-1}x$ on $[-1, 1]$

6. $f(x) = \ln(x - 1)$ on $[2, 4]$

7. $f(x) = \begin{cases} \cos x, & 0 \le x < \pi/2 \\ \sin x, & \pi/2 \le x \le \pi \end{cases}$ on $[0, \pi]$

8. $f(x) = \begin{cases} \sin^{-1}x, & -1 \le x < 1 \\ x/2 + 1, & 1 \le x \le 3 \end{cases}$ on $[-1, 3]$

In Exercises 9 and 10, the interval $a \le x \le b$ is given. Let $A = (a, f(a))$ and $B = (b, f(b))$. Write an equation for

  (a) the secant line AB.

  (b) a tangent line to f in the interval (a, b) that is parallel to AB.

9. $f(x) = x + \dfrac{1}{x}$, $0.5 \le x \le 2$

10. $f(x) = \sqrt{x - 1}$, $1 \le x \le 3$

11. *Speeding* A trucker handed in a ticket at a toll booth showing that in 2 h she had covered 159 mi on a toll road with speed limit 65 mph. The trucker was cited for speeding. Why?

12. *Temperature Change* It took 20 sec for the temperature to rise from 0°F to 212°F when a thermometer was taken from a freezer and placed in boiling water. Explain why at some moment in that interval the mercury was rising at exactly 10.6°F/sec.

13. *Triremes* Classical accounts tell us that a 170-oar trireme (ancient Greek or Roman warship) once covered 184 sea miles in 24 h. Explain why at some point during this feat the trireme's speed exceeded 7.5 knots (sea miles per hour).

14. *Running a Marathon* A marathoner ran the 26.2-mi New York City Marathon in 2.2 h. Show that at least twice, the marathoner was running at exactly 11 mph.

In Exercises 15–22, use analytic methods to find **(a)** the local extrema, **(b)** the intervals on which the function is increasing, and **(c)** the intervals on which the function is decreasing.

15. $f(x) = 5x - x^2$

16. $g(x) = x^2 - x - 12$

17. $h(x) = \dfrac{2}{x}$

18. $k(x) = \dfrac{1}{x^2}$

19. $f(x) = e^{2x}$

20. $f(x) = e^{-0.5x}$

21. $y = 4 - \sqrt{x + 2}$

22. $y = x^4 - 10x^2 + 9$

In Exercises 23–28, find **(a)** the local extrema, **(b)** the intervals on which the function is increasing, and **(c)** the intervals on which the function is decreasing.

23. $f(x) = x\sqrt{4 - x}$ **24.** $g(x) = x^{1/3}(x + 8)$

25. $h(x) = \dfrac{-x}{x^2 + 4}$ **26.** $k(x) = \dfrac{x}{x^2 - 4}$

27. $f(x) = x^3 - 2x - 2\cos x$ **28.** $g(x) = 2x + \cos x$

In Exercises 29–34, find all possible functions f with the given derivative.

29. $f'(x) = x$ **30.** $f'(x) = 2$

31. $f'(x) = 3x^2 - 2x + 1$ **32.** $f'(x) = \sin x$

33. $f'(x) = e^x$ **34.** $f'(x) = \dfrac{1}{x - 1}, \quad x > 1$

In Exercises 35–38, find the function with the given derivative whose graph passes through the point P.

35. $f'(x) = -\dfrac{1}{x^2}, \quad x > 0, \quad P(2, 1)$

36. $f'(x) = \dfrac{1}{4x^{3/4}}, \quad P(1, -2)$

37. $f'(x) = \dfrac{1}{x + 2}, \quad x > -2, \quad P(-1, 3)$

38. $f'(x) = 2x + 1 - \cos x, \quad P(0, 3),$

Group Activity In Exercises 39–42, sketch a graph of a differentiable function $y = f(x)$ that has the given properties.

39. (a) local minimum at $(1, 1)$, local maximum at $(3, 3)$

   (b) local minima at $(1, 1)$ and $(3, 3)$

   (c) local maxima at $(1, 1)$ and $(3, 3)$

40. $f(2) = 3, f'(2) = 0,$ and

   (a) $f'(x) > 0$ for $x < 2$, $f'(x) < 0$ for $x > 2$.

   (b) $f'(x) < 0$ for $x < 2$, $f'(x) > 0$ for $x > 2$.

   (c) $f'(x) < 0$ for $x \neq 2$.

   (d) $f'(x) > 0$ for $x \neq 2$.

41. $f'(-1) = f'(1) = 0,$ $f'(x) > 0$ on $(-1, 1)$,
   $f'(x) < 0$ for $x < -1$, $f'(x) > 0$ for $x > 1$.

42. A local minimum value that is greater than one of its local maximum values.

43. *Free Fall* On the moon, the acceleration due to gravity is 1.6 m/sec².

   (a) If a rock is dropped into a crevasse, how fast will it be going just before it hits bottom 30 sec later?

   (b) How far below the point of release is the bottom of the crevasse?

   (c) If instead of being released from rest, the rock is thrown into the crevasse from the same point with a downward velocity of 4 m/sec, when will it hit the bottom and how fast will it be going when it does?

44. *Diving* (a) With what velocity will you hit the water if you step off from a 10-m diving platform?

   (b) With what velocity will you hit the water if you dive off the platform with an upward velocity of 2 m/sec?

45. Writing to Learn The function

$$f(x) = \begin{cases} x, & 0 \leq x < 1 \\ 0, & x = 1 \end{cases}$$

is zero at $x = 0$ and at $x = 1$. Its derivative is equal to 1 at every point between 0 and 1, so f' is never zero between 0 and 1, and the graph of f has no tangent parallel to the chord from $(0, 0)$ to $(1, 0)$. Explain why this does not contradict the Mean Value Theorem.

46. Writing to Learn Explain why there is a zero of $y = \cos x$ between every two zeros of $y = \sin x$.

47. *Unique Solution* Assume that f is continuous on $[a, b]$ and differentiable on (a, b). Also assume that $f(a)$ and $f(b)$ have opposite signs and $f' \neq 0$ between a and b. Show that $f(x) = 0$ exactly once between a and b.

In Exercises 48 and 49, show that the equation has exactly one solution in the given interval. (*Hint:* See Exercise 47.)

48. $x^4 + 3x + 1 = 0, \qquad -2 \leq x \leq -1$

49. $x + \ln(x + 1) = 0, \qquad 0 \leq x \leq 3$

50. *Parallel Tangents* Assume that f and g are differentiable on $[a, b]$ and that $f(a) = g(a)$ and $f(b) = g(b)$. Show that there is at least one point between a and b where the tangents to the graphs of f and g are parallel or the same line. Illustrate with a sketch.

Standardized Test Questions

You may use a graphing calculator to solve the following problems.

51. True or False If f is differentiable and increasing on (a, b), then $f'(c) > 0$ for every c in (a, b). Justify your answer.

52. True or False If f is differentiable and $f'(c) > 0$ for every c in (a, b), then f is increasing on (a, b). Justify your answer.

53. Multiple Choice If $f(x) = \cos x$, then the Mean Value Theorem guarantees that somewhere between 0 and $\pi/3$, $f'(x) =$

(A) $-\dfrac{3}{2\pi}$ (B) $-\dfrac{\sqrt{3}}{2}$ (C) -1 (D) 0 (E) $\dfrac{1}{2}$

54. Multiple Choice On what interval is the function $g(x) = e^{x^3 - 6x^2 + 8}$ decreasing?

(A) $(-\infty, 2]$ (B) $[0, 4]$ (C) $[2, 4]$

(D) $(4, \infty)$ (E) no interval

55. Multiple Choice Which of the following functions is an anti-derivative of $\dfrac{1}{\sqrt{x}}$?

(A) $-\dfrac{1}{\sqrt{2x^3}}$ (B) $-\dfrac{2}{\sqrt{x}}$ (C) $\dfrac{\sqrt{x}}{2}$

(D) $\sqrt{x} + 5$ (E) $2\sqrt{x} - 10$

56. Multiple Choice All of the following functions satisfy the conditions of the Mean Value Theorem on the interval $[-1, 1]$ *except*

(A) $\sin x$ (B) $\sin^{-1} x$ (C) $x^{5/3}$ (D) $x^{3/5}$ (E) $\dfrac{x}{x - 2}$

Extending the Ideas

57. *Geometric Mean* The **geometric mean** of two positive numbers a and b is $\sqrt{ab}$. Show that for $f(x) = 1/x$ on any interval $[a, b]$ of positive numbers, the value of c in the conclusion of the Mean Value Theorem is $c = \sqrt{ab}$.

58. *Arithmetic Mean* The **arithmetic mean** of two numbers a and b is $(a + b)/2$. Show that for $f(x) = x^2$ on any interval $[a, b]$, the value of c in the conclusion of the Mean Value Theorem is $c = (a + b)/2$.

59. *Upper Bounds* Show that for any numbers a and b $|\sin b - \sin a| \leq |b - a|$.

60. *Sign of f'* Assume that f is differentiable on $a \leq x \leq b$ and that $f(b) < f(a)$. Show that f' is negative at some point between a and b.

61. *Monotonic Functions* Show that monotonic increasing and decreasing functions are one-to-one.

62. Writing to Learn *Proof of Rolle's Theorem* Rolle's Theorem is the special case of the Mean Value Theorem for which $f(a) = f(b) = 0$, and the conclusion is that there is at least one point c for which $f'(c) = 0$. The following steps will lead you through a proof of Rolle's Theorem.

(a) Since f is continuous on $[a, b]$, the Extreme Value Theorem (Theorem 1, p. 194) guarantees that f has both a maximum and a minimum value on this interval. Explain why, if the maximum and minimum occur only at the endpoints, then f is the constant function $f(x) = 0$. It follows that either $f'(x) = 0$ for all x in (a, b) or there is some point c between a and b where f has a local maximum or minimum.

(b) Use Theorem 2 (p. 195) to finish the proof of Rolle's Theorem.

63. Writing to Learn *Proof of the Mean Value Theorem* The following steps will establish the Mean Value Theorem as a corollary of Rolle's Theorem. This is the proof first discovered by Ossian Bonnet in the 1860s. We assume that f is continuous on $[a, b]$ and differentiable on (a, b).

(a) Verify that

$$y = \frac{f(b) - f(a)}{b - a}(x - a) + f(a)$$

is the equation of the secant line through $(a, f(a))$ and $(b, f(b))$.

(b) Define a new function g,

$$g(x) = f(x) - \left(\frac{f(b) - f(a)}{b - a}(x - a) + f(a)\right).$$

Explain why g is continuous on $[a, b]$, differentiable on (a, b), and $g(a) = g(b) = 0$. Rolle's Theorem (Exercise 62) implies that there is at least one point c between a and b for which $g'(c) = 0$.

(c) Use the definition of g to show that

$$g'(c) = f'(c) - \frac{f(b) - f(a)}{b - a}.$$

Now finish the proof of the Mean Value Theorem.

5.3 | Connecting *f'* and *f''* with the Graph of *f*

You will be able to use derivatives to analyze properties of a function.

- Intervals of increase or decrease
- Both First and Second Derivative Tests for local extrema
- Intervals of upward or downward concavity
- Points of inflection
- Identification of key features of functions and their derivatives

First Derivative Test for Local Extrema

As we see once again in Figure 5.19, a function f may have local extrema at some critical points while failing to have local extrema at others. The key is the sign of f' in a critical point's immediate vicinity. As x moves from left to right, the values of f increase where $f' > 0$ and decrease where $f' < 0$.

At the points where f has a minimum value, we see that $f' < 0$ on the interval immediately to the left and $f' > 0$ on the interval immediately to the right. (If the point is an endpoint, there is only the interval on the appropriate side to consider.) This means that the curve is falling (values decreasing) on the left of the minimum value and rising (values increasing) on its right. Similarly, at the points where f has a maximum value, $f' > 0$ on the interval immediately to the left and $f' < 0$ on the interval immediately to the right. This means that the curve is rising (values increasing) on the left of the maximum value and falling (values decreasing) on its right.

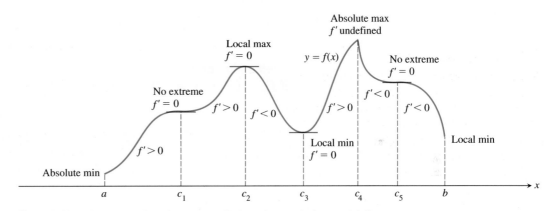

Figure 5.19 A function's first derivative tells how the graph rises and falls.

THEOREM 4   First Derivative Test for Local Extrema

The following test applies to a continuous function $f(x)$.

At a critical point *c*:

1. If f' changes sign from positive to negative at c ($f' > 0$ for $x < c$ and $f' < 0$ for $x > c$), then f has a local maximum value at c.

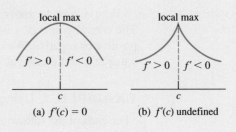

(a) $f'(c) = 0$ (b) $f'(c)$ undefined

continued

2. If f' changes sign from negative to positive at c ($f' < 0$ for $x < c$ and $f' > 0$ for $x > c$) then f has a local minimum value at c.

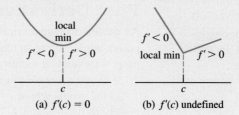

3. If f' does not change sign at c (f' has the same sign on both sides of c), then f has no local extreme value at c.

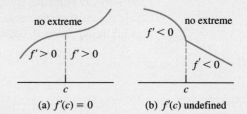

At a left endpoint a:

If $f' < 0$ ($f' > 0$) for $x > a$, then f has a local maximum (minimum) value at a.

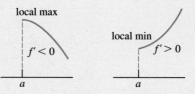

At a right endpoint b:

If $f' < 0$ ($f' > 0$) for $x < b$, then f has a local minimum (maximum) value at b.

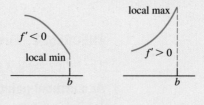

Here is how we apply the First Derivative Test to find the local extrema of a function. The critical points of a function f partition the x-axis into intervals on which f' is either positive or negative. We determine the sign of f' in each interval by evaluating f' for one value of x in the interval. Then we apply Theorem 4 as shown in Examples 1 and 2.

EXAMPLE 1 Using the First Derivative Test

For each of the following functions, use the First Derivative Test to find the local extreme values. Identify any absolute extrema.

(a) $f(x) = x^3 - 12x - 5$ **(b)** $g(x) = (x^2 - 3)e^x$

continued

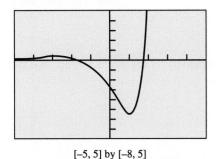

[−5, 5] by [−25, 25]

Figure 5.20 The graph of
$f(x) = x^3 - 12x - 5$.

SOLUTION

(a) Since f is differentiable for all real numbers, the only possible critical points are
the zeros of f'. Solving $f'(x) = 3x^2 - 12 = 0$, we find the zeros to be $x = 2$ and
$x = -2$. The zeros partition the x-axis into three intervals, as shown below:

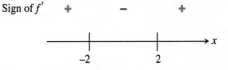

Using the First Derivative Test, we can see from the sign of f' on each interval that
there is a local maximum at $x = -2$ and a local minimum at $x = 2$. The local maximum value is $f(-2) = 11$, and the local minimum value is $f(2) = -21$. There are no
absolute extrema, as the function has range $(-\infty, \infty)$ (Figure 5.20).

(b) Since g is differentiable for all real numbers, the only possible critical points are
the zeros of g'. Since $g'(x) = (x^2 - 3) \cdot e^x + (2x) \cdot e^x = (x^2 + 2x - 3) \cdot e^x$, we
find the zeros of g' to be $x = 1$ and $x = -3$. The zeros partition the x-axis into three
intervals, as shown below:

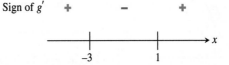

Using the First Derivative Test, we can see from the sign of f' on each interval that there
is a local maximum at $x = -3$ and a local minimum at $x = 1$. The local maximum value
is $g(-3) = 6e^{-3} \approx 0.299$, and the local minimum value is $g(1) = -2e \approx -5.437$.
Although this function has the same increasing–decreasing–increasing pattern as f,
its left end behavior is quite different. We see that $\lim_{x \to -\infty} g(x) = 0$, so the graph
approaches the y-axis asymptotically and is therefore bounded below. This makes
$g(1)$ an *absolute* minimum. Since $\lim_{x \to \infty} g(x) = \infty$, there is no absolute maximum
(Figure 5.21). *Now Try Exercise 3.*

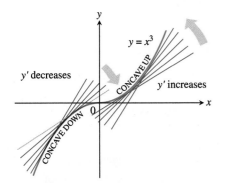

[−5, 5] by [−8, 5]

Figure 5.21 The graph of
$g(x) = (x^2 - 3)e^x$.

Caution: When using a sign chart, as in the
solution to Example 1, be certain to label
it, indicating for which function these are
the signs.

Concavity

As you can see in Figure 5.22, the function $y = x^3$ rises as x increases, but the portions
defined on the intervals $(-\infty, 0)$ and $(0, \infty)$ *turn* in different ways. Looking at tangents
as we scan from left to right, we see that the slope y' of the curve decreases on the interval
$(-\infty, 0)$ and then increases on the interval $(0, \infty)$. The curve $y = x^3$ is *concave down* on
$(-\infty, 0)$ and *concave up* on $(0, \infty)$. The curve lies below the tangents where it is concave
down, and above the tangents where it is concave up.

[figure: graph of $y = x^3$ showing "y' decreases", "CONCAVE DOWN", "CONCAVE UP", "y' increases"]

Figure 5.22 The graph of $y = x^3$ is concave down on $(-\infty, 0)$ and concave up on
$(0, \infty)$.

> **DEFINITION** **Concavity**
>
> The graph of a differentiable function $y = f(x)$ is
>
> **(a) concave up** on an interval I if y' is increasing on I.
> **(b) concave down** on an interval I if y' is decreasing on I.

If a function $y = f(x)$ has a second derivative, then we can conclude that y' increases
if $y'' > 0$ and y' decreases if $y'' < 0$.

Note

Since y' is increasing or decreasing on the interval *I*, we can only speak of concavity on an interval that contains more than one point. There also is a definition of concavity that is independent of the derivative: The graph of $y = f(x)$ is **concave up** on the interval *I* if for any pair of points $x_1 < x_2$ in *I*, the secant line connecting $(x_1, f(x_1))$ and $(x_2, f(x_2))$ lies above the graph of *f*. It is **concave down** if the secant line lies below the graph of *f*.

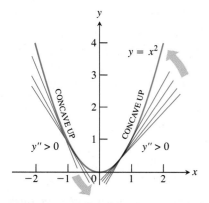

Figure 5.23 The graph of $y = x^2$ is concave up on any interval. (Example 2)

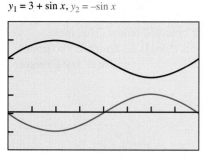

$y_1 = 3 + \sin x, y_2 = -\sin x$

$[0, 2\pi]$ by $[-2, 5]$

Figure 5.24 Using the graph of y'' to determine the concavity of *y*. (Example 2)

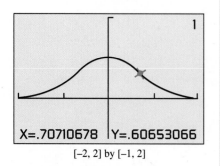

X=.70710678 Y=.60653066

$[-2, 2]$ by $[-1, 2]$

Figure 5.25 Graphical confirmation that the graph of $y = e^{-x^2}$ has a point of inflection at $x = \sqrt{1/2}$ (and hence also at $x = -\sqrt{1/2}$). (Example 3)

Concavity Test

The graph of a twice-differentiable function $y = f(x)$ is

(a) concave up on any interval where $y'' > 0$.

(b) concave down on any interval where $y'' < 0$.

EXAMPLE 2 Determining Concavity

Use the Concavity Test to determine the concavity of the given functions on the given intervals:

(a) $y = x^2$ on $(3, 10)$ **(b)** $y = 3 + \sin x$ on $(0, 2\pi)$

SOLUTION

(a) Since $y'' = 2$ is always positive, the graph of $y = x^2$ is concave up on *any* interval. In particular, it is concave up on $(3, 10)$ (Figure 5.23).

(b) The graph of $y = 3 + \sin x$ is concave down on $(0, \pi)$, where $y'' = -\sin x$ is negative. It is concave up on $(\pi, 2\pi)$, where $y'' = -\sin x$ is positive (Figure 5.24).

Now Try Exercise 7.

Points of Inflection

The curve $y = 3 + \sin x$ in Example 2 changes concavity at the point $(\pi, 3)$. We call $(\pi, 3)$ a *point of inflection* of the curve.

DEFINITION Point of Inflection

A point where the graph of a function has a tangent line and where the concavity changes is a **point of inflection.**

A point on a curve where y'' is positive on one side and negative on the other is a point of inflection. At such a point, y'' is either zero (because derivatives have the Intermediate Value Property) or undefined. If y is a twice differentiable function, $y'' = 0$ at a point of inflection and y' has a local maximum or minimum.

EXAMPLE 3 Finding Points of Inflection

Find all points of inflection of the graph of $y = e^{-x^2}$.

SOLUTION

First we find the second derivative, recalling the Chain and Product Rules:

$$y = e^{-x^2}$$
$$y' = e^{-x^2} \cdot (-2x)$$
$$y'' = e^{-x^2} \cdot (-2x) \cdot (-2x) + e^{-x^2} \cdot (-2)$$
$$= e^{-x^2}(4x^2 - 2)$$

The factor e^{-x^2} is always positive, while the factor $(4x^2 - 2)$ changes sign at $-\sqrt{1/2}$ and at $\sqrt{1/2}$. Since y'' must also change sign at these two numbers, the points of inflection are $\left(-\sqrt{1/2}, 1/\sqrt{e}\right)$ and $\left(\sqrt{1/2}, 1/\sqrt{e}\right)$. We confirm our solution graphically by observing the changes of curvature in Figure 5.25.

Now Try Exercise 13.

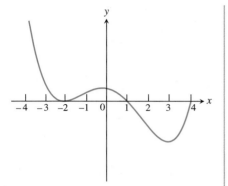

Figure 5.26 The graph of f' the derivative of f, on the interval $[-4, 4]$.

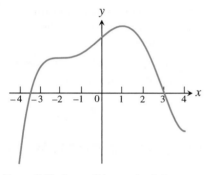

Figure 5.27 A possible graph of f. (Example 4)

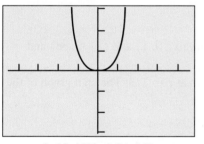

[– 4.7, 4.7] by [–3.1, 3.1]

Figure 5.28 The function $f(x) = x^4$ does not have a point of inflection at the origin, even though $f''(0) = 0$.

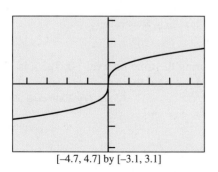

[–4.7, 4.7] by [–3.1, 3.1]

Figure 5.29 The function $f(x) = \sqrt[3]{x}$ has a point of inflection at the origin, even though $f''(0) \neq 0$.

EXAMPLE 4 Reading the Graph of the Derivative

The graph of the *derivative* of a function f on the interval $[-4, 4]$ is shown in Figure 5.26. Answer the following questions about f, justifying each answer with information obtained from the graph of f'.

(a) On what intervals is f increasing?

(b) On what intervals is the graph of f concave up?

(c) At which x-coordinates does f have local extrema?

(d) What are the x-coordinates of all inflection points of the graph of f?

(e) Sketch a possible graph of f on the interval $[-4, 4]$.

SOLUTION

Often, making a chart showing where f' is positive and negative and where f' is increasing and decreasing helps to understand the behavior of the function f (whose derivative is f'). The following chart is based on Figure 5.26.

Intervals	$-4 \leq x < -2$	$-2 < x \leq 0$	$0 < x < 1$	$1 < x \leq 3$	$3 < x \leq 4$
Sign of f'	positive	positive	positive	negative	negative
Graph of f'	decreasing	increasing	decreasing	decreasing	increasing

(a) Since $f' > 0$ on the intervals $[-4, -2)$ and $(-2, 1)$, the function f must be increasing on the entire interval $[-4, 1]$ with a horizontal tangent at $x = -2$ (a "shelf point").

(b) The graph of f is concave up on the intervals where f' is increasing. We see from the graph that f' is increasing on the intervals $(-2, 0)$ and $(3, 4)$.

(c) By the First Derivative Test, there is a local maximum at $x = 1$ because the sign of f' changes from positive to negative there. Note that there is no extremum at $x = -2$, since f' does not change sign. Because the function increases from the left endpoint and decreases to the right endpoint, there are local minima at the endpoints $x = -4$ and $x = 4$.

(d) The inflection points of the graph of f have the same x-coordinates as the turning points of the graph of f', namely, $-2, 0$, and 3.

(e) A possible graph satisfying all the conditions is shown in Figure 5.27.

Now Try Exercise 23.

Caution: It is tempting to oversimplify a point of inflection as a point where the second derivative is zero, but that can be wrong for two reasons:

1. *The second derivative can be zero at a noninflection point.* For example, consider the function $f(x) = x^4$ (Figure 5.28). Since $f''(x) = 12x^2$, we have $f''(0) = 0$; however, $(0, 0)$ is not an inflection point. Note that f'' does not *change sign* at $x = 0$.

2. *The second derivative need not be zero at an inflection point.* For example, consider the function $f(x) = \sqrt[3]{x}$ (Figure 5.29). The concavity changes at $x = 0$, but there is a *vertical* tangent line, so both $f'(0)$ and $f''(0)$ fail to exist.

Therefore, the only safe way to test algebraically for a point of inflection is to confirm a sign change of the second derivative. This *could* occur at a point where the second derivative is zero, but it also could occur at a point where the second derivative fails to exist.

To study the motion of a body moving along a line, we often graph the body's position as a function of time. One reason for doing so is to reveal where the body's acceleration, given by the second derivative, changes sign. On the graph, these are the points of inflection.

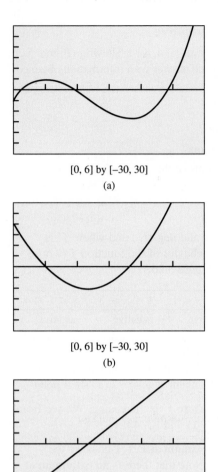

[0, 6] by [–30, 30]
(a)

[0, 6] by [–30, 30]
(b)

[0, 6] by [–30, 30]
(c)

Figure 5.30 The graph of
(a) $x(t) = 2t^3 - 14t^2 + 22t - 5, t \geq 0$,
(b) $x'(t) = 6t^2 - 28t + 22$, and
(c) $x''(t) = 12t - 28$. (Example 5)

EXAMPLE 5 Studying Motion Along a Line

A particle is moving along the *x*-axis with position function

$$x(t) = 2t^3 - 14t^2 + 22t - 5, \quad t \geq 0.$$

Find the velocity and acceleration, and describe the motion of the particle.

SOLUTION

The velocity is

$$v(t) = x'(t) = 6t^2 - 28t + 22 = 2(t - 1)(3t - 11),$$

and the acceleration is

$$a(t) = v'(t) = x''(t) = 12t - 28 = 4(3t - 7).$$

When the function $x(t)$ is increasing, the particle is moving to the right on the *x*-axis; when $x(t)$ is decreasing, the particle is moving to the left. Figure 5.30 shows the graphs of the position, velocity, and acceleration of the particle.

Notice that the first derivative $(v = x')$ is zero when $t = 1$ and $t = 11/3$. These zeros partition the *t*-axis into three intervals, as shown in the sign graph of *v* below:

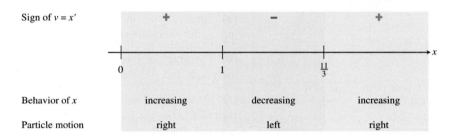

The particle is moving to the right in the time intervals $[0, 1)$ and $(11/3, \infty)$ and moving to the left in $(1, 11/3)$.

The acceleration $a(t) = 12t - 28$ has a single zero at $t = 7/3$. The sign graph of the acceleration is shown below:

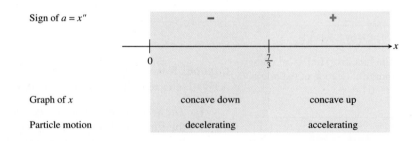

The accelerating force is directed toward the left during the time interval $[0, 7/3)$, is momentarily zero at $t = 7/3$, and is directed toward the right thereafter.

Now Try Exercise 25.

Second Derivative Test for Local Extrema

Instead of looking for sign changes in y' at critical points, we can sometimes use the following test to determine the presence of local extrema.

THEOREM 5   Second Derivative Test for Local Extrema

1. If $f'(c) = 0$ and $f''(c) < 0$, then f has a local maximum at $x = c$.
2. If $f'(c) = 0$ and $f''(c) > 0$, then f has a local minimum at $x = c$.

This test requires us to know f'' *only at c itself* and not in an interval about c. This makes the test easy to apply. That's the good news. The bad news is that the test fails if $f''(c) = 0$ or if $f''(c)$ fails to exist. Sometimes, f'' is just much harder to find than f'. When this happens, go back to the First Derivative Test for local extreme values.

In Example 6, we apply the Second Derivative Test to the function in Example 1.

EXAMPLE 6   Using the Second Derivative Test

Find the local extreme values of $f(x) = x^3 - 12x - 5$.

SOLUTION

We have

$$f'(x) = 3x^2 - 12 = 3(x^2 - 4)$$
$$f''(x) = 6x$$

Testing the critical points $x = \pm 2$ (there are no endpoints), we find

$$f''(-2) = -12 < 0 \Rightarrow f \text{ has a local maximum at } x = -2 \text{ and}$$
$$f''(2) = 12 > 0 \Rightarrow f \text{ has a local minimum at } x = 2.$$

Now Try Exercise 33.

EXAMPLE 7   Using f' and f" to Graph f

Let $f'(x) = 4x^3 - 12x^2$.

(a) Identify where the extrema of f occur.

(b) Find the intervals on which f is increasing and the intervals on which f is decreasing.

(c) Find where the graph of f is concave up and where it is concave down.

(d) Sketch a possible graph for f.

SOLUTION

f is continuous, since f' exists. The domain of f' is $(-\infty, \infty)$, so the domain of f is also $(-\infty, \infty)$. Thus, the critical points of f occur only at the zeros of f'. Since

$$f'(x) = 4x^3 - 12x^2 = 4x^2(x - 3),$$

the first derivative is zero at $x = 0$ and $x = 3$.

Intervals	$x < 0$	$0 < x < 3$	$3 < x$
Sign of f'	−	−	+
Behavior of f	decreasing	decreasing	increasing

(a) Using the First Derivative Test and the table above, we see that there is no extremum at $x = 0$ and a local minimum at $x = 3$.

(b) Using the table above, we see that f is decreasing in $(-\infty, 0]$ and $[0, 3]$, and increasing in $[3, \infty)$. (We also could say that f is decreasing in $(-\infty, 3]$ because 0 is included in both $(-\infty, 0]$ and $[0, 3]$.)

continued

(c) $f''(x) = 12x^2 - 24x = 12x(x - 2)$ is zero at $x = 0$ and $x = 2$.

Intervals	$x < 0$	$0 < x < 2$	$2 < x$
Sign of f''	+	−	+
Behavior of f	concave up	concave down	concave up

We see that f is concave up on the intervals $(-\infty, 0)$ and $(2, \infty)$, and concave down on $(0, 2)$.

(d) Summarizing the information in the two tables above, we obtain

$x < 0$	$0 < x < 2$	$2 < x < 3$	$3 < x$
decreasing	decreasing	decreasing	increasing
concave up	concave down	concave up	concave up

Figure 5.31 shows one possibility for the graph of f.   *Now Try Exercise 37.*

Note

The *Second Derivative Test* does not apply at $x = 0$ because $f''(0) = 0$. We need the First Derivative Test to see that there is no local extremum at $x = 0$.

Figure 5.31 The graph for f has no extremum but has points of inflection where $x = 0$ and $x = 2$, and a local minimum where $x = 3$. (Example 7)

EXPLORATION 1 Finding *f* from *f'*

Let $f'(x) = 4x^3 - 12x^2$.

1. Find three different functions with derivative equal to $f'(x)$. How are the graphs of the three functions related?
2. Compare their behavior with the behavior found in Example 7.

Learning About Functions from Derivatives

We have seen in Example 7 and Exploration 1 that we are able to recover almost everything we need to know about a differentiable function $y = f(x)$ by examining y'. We can find where the graph rises and falls and where any local extrema are assumed. We can differentiate y' to learn how the graph bends as it passes over the intervals of rise and fall. We can determine the shape of the function's graph. The only information we cannot get from the derivative is how to place the graph in the xy-plane. As we discovered in Section 5.2, the only additional information we need to position the graph is the value of f at one point.

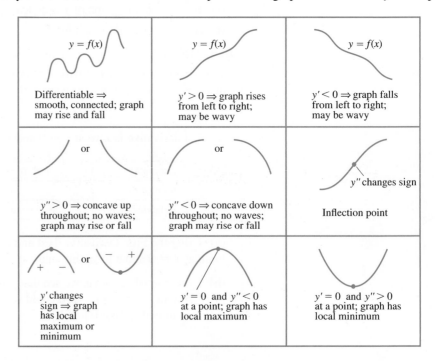

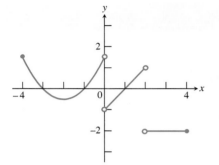

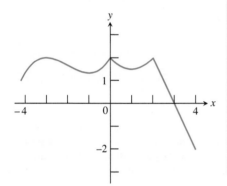

Figure 5.32 The graph of f', a discontinuous derivative.

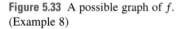

Figure 5.33 A possible graph of f. (Example 8)

Note

Because sign charts are very helpful, you will want to use and analyze them on a regular basis.

Remember also that a function can be continuous and still have points of nondifferentiability (cusps, corners, and points with vertical tangent lines). Thus, a noncontinuous graph of f' could lead to a continuous graph of f, as Example 8 shows.

EXAMPLE 8 Analyzing a Discontinuous Derivative

A function f is continuous on the interval $[-4, 4]$. The discontinuous function f', with domain $[-4, 0) \cup (0, 2) \cup (2, 4]$, is shown in the graph to the left (Figure 5.32).

(a) Find the x-coordinates of all local extrema and points of inflection of f.

(b) Sketch a possible graph of f.

SOLUTION

(a) For extrema, we look for places where f' changes sign. There are local maxima at $x = -3, 0,$ and 2 (where f' goes from positive to negative) and local minima at $x = -1$ and 1 (where f' goes from negative to positive). There are also local minima at the two endpoints $x = -4$ and 4, because f' starts positive at the left endpoint and ends negative at the right endpoint.

For points of inflection, we look for places where f'' changes sign, that is, where the graph of f' changes direction. This occurs only at $x = -2$.

(b) A possible graph of f is shown in Figure 5.33. The derivative information determines the shape of the three components, and the continuity condition determines that the three components must be linked together.   ***Now Try Exercises 47 and 51.***

EXPLORATION 2   Finding f from f' and f''

A function f is continuous on its domain $[-2, 4]$, $f(-2) = 5$, $f(4) = 1$, and f' and f'' have the following properties.

x	$-2 < x < 0$	$x = 0$	$0 < x < 2$	$x = 2$	$2 < x < 4$
f'	+	does not exist	−	0	−
f''	+	does not exist	+	0	−

1. Find where all absolute extrema of f occur.
2. Find where the points of inflection of f occur.
3. Sketch a possible graph of f.

Quick Review 5.3   *(For help, go to Sections 1.3, 2.2, 3.3, and 4.4.)*

Exercise numbers with a gray background indicate problems that the authors have designed to be solved *without a calculator*.

In Exercises 1 and 2, factor the expression and use sign charts to solve the inequality.

1. $x^2 - 9 < 0$ **2.** $x^3 - 4x > 0$

In Exercises 3–6, find the domains of f and f'.

3. $f(x) = xe^x$ **4.** $f(x) = x^{3/5}$

5. $f(x) = \dfrac{x}{x - 2}$ **6.** $f(x) = x^{2/5}$

In Exercises 7–10, find the horizontal asymptotes of the function's graph.

7. $y = (4 - x^2)e^x$ **8.** $y = (x^2 - x)e^{-x}$

9. $y = \dfrac{200}{1 + 10e^{-0.5x}}$ **10.** $y = \dfrac{750}{2 + 5e^{-0.1x}}$

Section 5.3 Exercises

In Exercises 1–6, use the **First Derivative Test** to determine the local extreme values of the function, and identify any absolute extrema. Support your answers graphically.

1. $y = x^2 - x - 1$ **2.** $y = -2x^3 + 6x^2 - 3$

3. $y = 2x^4 - 4x^2 + 1$ **4.** $y = xe^{1/x}$

5. $y = x\sqrt{8 - x^2}$ **6.** $y = \begin{cases} 3 - x^2, & x < 0 \\ x^2 + 1, & x \geq 0 \end{cases}$

In Exercises 7–12, use the Concavity Test to determine the intervals on which the graph of the function is **(a)** concave up and **(b)** concave down.

7. $y = 4x^3 + 21x^2 + 36x - 20$

8. $y = -x^4 + 4x^3 - 4x + 1$

9. $y = 2x^{1/5} + 3$ **10.** $y = 5 - x^{1/3}$

11. $y = \begin{cases} 2x, & x < 1 \\ 2 - x^2, & x \geq 1 \end{cases}$ **12.** $y = e^x, \ \ 0 \leq x \leq 2\pi$

In Exercises 13–20, find all points of inflection of the function.

13. $y = xe^x$ **14.** $y = x\sqrt{9 - x^2}$

15. $y = \tan^{-1} x$ **16.** $y = x^3(4 - x)$

17. $y = x^{1/3}(x - 4)$ **18.** $y = x^{1/2}(x + 3)$

19. $y = \dfrac{x^3 - 2x^2 + x - 1}{x - 2}$ **20.** $y = \dfrac{x}{x^2 + 1}$

In Exercises 21 and 22, use the graph of the function f to estimate where **(a)** f' and **(b)** f'' are 0, positive, and negative.

21.

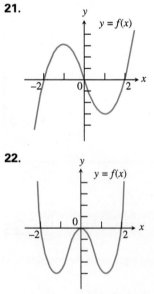

22.

In Exercises 23 and 24, use the graph of the function f' to estimate the intervals on which the function f is **(a)** increasing or **(b)** decreasing. Also, **(c)** estimate the x-coordinates of all local extreme values.

23.

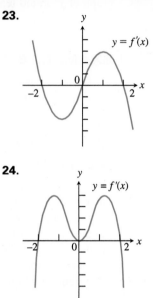

24.

In Exercises 25–28, a particle is moving along the x-axis with position function $x(t)$. Find the **(a)** velocity and **(b)** acceleration, and **(c)** describe the motion of the particle for $t \geq 0$.

25. $x(t) = t^2 - 4t + 3$ **26.** $x(t) = 6 - 2t - t^2$

27. $x(t) = t^3 - 3t + 3$ **28.** $x(t) = 3t^2 - 2t^3$

In Exercises 29 and 30, the graph of the position function $y = s(t)$ of a particle moving along a line is given. At approximately what times is the particle's **(a)** velocity equal to zero? **(b)** acceleration equal to zero?

29.

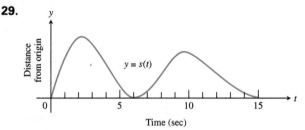

30.

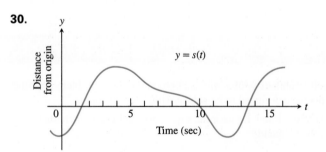

In Exercises 31–36, use the Second Derivative Test to find the local extrema for the function.

31. $y = 3x - x^3 + 5$

32. $y = x^5 - 80x + 100$

33. $y = x^3 + 3x^2 - 2$

34. $y = 3x^5 - 25x^3 + 60x + 20$

35. $y = xe^x$

36. $y = xe^{-x}$

In Exercises 37 and 38, use the derivative of the function $y = f(x)$ to find the points at which f has a

   (a) local maximum,   **(b)** local minimum, or

   (c) point of inflection.

37. $y' = (x - 1)^2(x - 2)$

38. $y' = (x - 1)^2(x - 2)(x - 4)$

Exercises 39 and 40 show the graphs of the first and second derivatives of a function $y = f(x)$. Copy the figure and add a sketch of a possible graph of f that passes through the point P.

39.

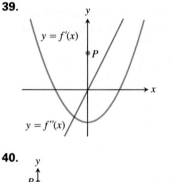

40.

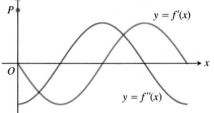

41. Writing to Learn If $f(x)$ is a differentiable function and $f'(c) = 0$ at an interior point c of f's domain, must f have a local maximum or minimum at $x = c$? Explain.

42. Writing to Learn If $f(x)$ is a twice-differentiable function and $f''(c) = 0$ at an interior point c of f's domain, must f have an inflection point at $x = c$? Explain.

43. *Connecting f and f'* Sketch a smooth curve $y = f(x)$ through the origin with the properties that $f'(x) < 0$ for $x < 0$ and $f'(x) > 0$ for $x > 0$.

44. *Connecting f and f"* Sketch a smooth curve $y = f(x)$ through the origin with the properties that $f''(x) < 0$ for $x < 0$ and $f''(x) > 0$ for $x > 0$.

45. *Connecting f, f', and f"* Sketch a continuous curve $y = f(x)$ with the following properties. Label coordinates where possible.

$f(-2) = 8$	$f'(x) > 0$ for $|x| > 2$
$f(0) = 4$	$f'(x) < 0$ for $|x| < 2$
$f(2) = 0$	$f''(x) < 0$ for $x < 0$
$f'(2) = f'(-2) = 0$	$f''(x) > 0$ for $x > 0$

46. *Using Behavior to Sketch* Sketch a continuous curve $y = f(x)$ with the following properties. Label coordinates where possible.

x	y	Curve
$x < 2$		falling, concave up
2	1	horizontal tangent
$2 < x < 4$		rising, concave up
4	4	inflection point
$4 < x < 6$		rising, concave down
6	7	horizontal tangent
$x > 6$		falling, concave down

In Exercises 47 and 48, use the graph of f' to estimate the intervals on which the function f is **(a)** increasing or **(b)** decreasing. Also, **(c)** estimate the x-coordinates of all local extreme values. (Assume that the function f is continuous, even at the points where f' is undefined.)

47. The domain of f' is $[0, 4) \cup (4, 6]$.

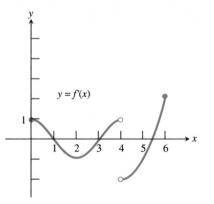

48. The domain of f' is $[0, 1) \cup (1, 2) \cup (2, 3]$.

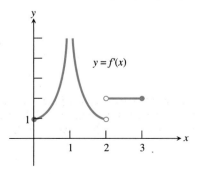

Group Activity In Exercises 49 and 50, do the following.

(a) Find the absolute extrema of f and where they occur.

(b) Find any points of inflection.

(c) Sketch a possible graph of f.

49. f is continuous on $[0, 3]$ and satisfies the following.

x	0	1	2	3
f	0	2	0	-2
f'	3	0	does not exist	-3
f''	0	-1	does not exist	0

x	$0 < x < 1$	$1 < x < 2$	$2 < x < 3$
f	$+$	$+$	$-$
f'	$+$	$-$	$-$
f''	$-$	$-$	$-$

50. f is an even function, continuous on $[-3, 3]$, and satisfies the following.

x	0	1	2
f	2	0	-1
f'	does not exist	0	does not exist
f''	does not exist	0	does not exist

x	$0 < x < 1$	$1 < x < 2$	$2 < x < 3$
f	$+$	$-$	$-$
f'	$-$	$-$	$+$
f''	$+$	$-$	$-$

(d) What can you conclude about $f(3)$ and $f(-3)$?

Group Activity In Exercises 51 and 52, sketch a possible graph of a continuous function f that has the given properties.

51. Domain $[0, 6]$, graph of f' given in Exercise 47, and $f(0) = 2$.

52. Domain $[0, 3]$, graph of f' given in Exercise 48, and $f(0) = -3$.

Standardized Test Questions

53. **True or False** If $f''(c) = 0$, then $(c, f(c))$ is a point of inflection. Justify your answer.

54. **True or False** If $f'(c) = 0$ and $f''(c) < 0$, then $f(c)$ is a local maximum. Justify your answer.

55. **Multiple Choice** If $a < 0$, the graph of $y = ax^3 + 3x^2 + 4x + 5$ is concave up on

(A) $\left(-\infty, -\dfrac{1}{a}\right)$ (B) $\left(-\infty, \dfrac{1}{a}\right)$ (C) $\left(-\dfrac{1}{a}, \infty\right)$

(D) $\left(\dfrac{1}{a}, \infty\right)$ (E) $(-\infty, -1)$

56. **Multiple Choice** If $f(0) = f'(0) = f''(0) = 0$, which of the following *must be true*?

(A) There is a local maximum of f at the origin.

(B) There is a local minimum of f at the origin.

(C) There is no local extremum of f at the origin.

(D) There is a point of inflection of the graph of f at the origin.

(E) There is a horizontal tangent to the graph of f at the origin.

57. **Multiple Choice** The x-coordinates of the points of inflection of the graph of $y = x^5 - 5x^4 + 3x + 7$ are

(A) 0 only   (B) 1 only   (C) 3 only   (D) 0 and 3   (E) 0 and 1

58. **Multiple Choice** Which of the following conditions would enable you to conclude that the graph of f has a point of inflection at $x = c$?

(A) There is a local maximum of f' at $x = c$.

(B) $f''(c) = 0$.

(C) $f''(c)$ does not exist.

(D) The sign of f' changes at $x = c$.

(E) f is a cubic polynomial and $c = 0$.

Exploration

59. ***Graphs of Cubics*** There is almost no leeway in the locations of the inflection point and the extrema of $f(x) = ax^3 + bx^2 + cx + d$, $a \neq 0$, because the one inflection point occurs at $x = -b/(3a)$ and the extrema, if any, must be located symmetrically about this value of x. Check this out by examining (a) the cubic in Exercise 7 and (b) the cubic in Exercise 2. Then (c) prove the general case.

Extending the Ideas

In Exercise 60, feel free to use a CAS (computer algebra system), if you have one, to solve the problem.

60. ***Quartic Polynomial Functions*** Let $f(x) = ax^4 + bx^3 + cx^2 + dx + e$ with $a \neq 0$.

(a) Show that the graph of f has 0 or 2 points of inflection.

(b) Write a condition that must be satisfied by the coefficients if the graph of f has 0 or 2 points of inflection.

Quick Quiz for AP* Preparation: Sections 5.1–5.3

1. **Multiple Choice** How many critical points does the function $f(x) = (x - 2)^5 (x + 3)^4$ have?

(A) One   (B) Two   (C) Three   (D) Five   (E) Nine

2. **Multiple Choice** For what value of x does the function $f(x) = (x - 2)(x - 3)^2$ have a relative maximum?

(A) -3 (B) $-\dfrac{7}{3}$ (C) $-\dfrac{5}{2}$ (D) $\dfrac{7}{3}$ (E) $\dfrac{5}{2}$

3. **Multiple Choice** If g is a differentiable function such that $g(x) < 0$ for all real numbers x, and if $f'(x) = (x^2 - 9)g(x)$, which of the following is true?

(A) f has a relative maximum at $x = -3$ and a relative minimum at $x = 3$.

(B) f has a relative minimum at $x = -3$ and a relative maximum at $x = 3$.

(C) f has relative minima at $x = -3$ and at $x = 3$.

(D) f has relative maxima at $x = -3$ and at $x = 3$.

(E) It cannot be determined if f has any relative extrema.

4. **Free Response** Let f be the function given by $f(x) = 3 \ln (x^2 + 2) - 2x$ with domain $[-2, 4]$.

(a) Find the coordinate of each relative maximum point and each relative minimum point of f. Justify your answer.

(b) Find the x-coordinate of each point of inflection of the graph of f.

(c) Find the absolute maximum value of $f(x)$.

5.4 Modeling and Optimization

You will be able to use derivatives to solve optimization problems.

- Development of a mathematical model
- Analysis of the function used to model the situation
- Identification of critical points and endpoints
- Identification of solution
- Interpretation of solution

A Strategy for Optimization

While optimization problems constantly arise in business and industry, economics, medicine and the life sciences, engineering, physics, chemistry, or anywhere mathematical models are used, it is unlikely that outside of a mathematics class anyone will ever give you a function and ask you to find its maximum or minimum value. Real-world optimization problems almost always involve first finding an appropriate function, then optimizing that function, and finally interpreting the solution. Once you know the function, finding the maximum or minimum is usually the easiest part. In this section, we will practice taking a problem from its original statement to the final interpretation of the solution. Here is a strategy you can use:

Strategy for Solving Max-Min Problems

1. **Understand the Problem** Read the problem carefully. Identify the information you need to solve the problem.
2. **Develop a Mathematical Model of the Problem** Draw pictures and label the parts that are important to the problem. Introduce a variable to represent the quantity that can be controlled. Using that variable, write a function whose extreme value gives the information sought.
3. **Graph the Function** Find the domain of the function. Determine what values of the variable make sense in the problem.
4. **Identify the Critical Points and Endpoints** Find where the derivative is zero or fails to exist.
5. **Solve the Mathematical Model** If unsure of the result, support or confirm your solution with another method.
6. **Interpret the Solution** Translate your mathematical result into the problem setting and decide whether the result makes sense.

Examples from Mathematics

EXAMPLE 1 Using the Strategy

Find two numbers whose sum is 20 and whose product is as large as possible.

SOLUTION

Model If one number is x, the other is $(20 - x)$, and their product is
$$f(x) = x(20 - x).$$

Solve We can see from the graph of f in Figure 5.34 that there is a maximum. From what we know about parabolas, the maximum occurs at $x = 10$. We confirm this solution by observing that $f'(x) = 20 - 2x$ is zero at $x = 10$. Since $f''(x) = -2$ (always negative), a maximum occurs at $x = 10$. The endpoints ($x = 0$ or 20) give us a product of 0, so $x = 10$ is the number we seek. The other number is $20 - x = 10$.

Interpret The two numbers we seek are $x = 10$ and $20 - x = 10$.

Now Try Exercise 1.

Sometimes we find it helpful to use both analytic and graphical methods together, as in Example 2.

EXAMPLE 2 Inscribing Rectangles

A rectangle is to be inscribed under one arch of the sine curve (Figure 5.35). What is the largest area the rectangle can have, and what dimensions give that area?

continued

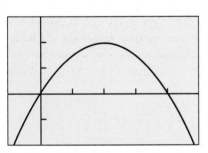

[−5, 25] by [−100, 150]

Figure 5.34 The graph of $f(x) = x(20 - x)$ with domain $(-\infty, \infty)$ has an absolute maximum of 100 at $x = 10$. (Example 1)

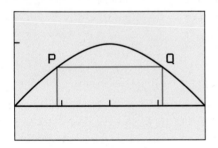

[0, π] by [−0.5, 1.5]

Figure 5.35 A rectangle inscribed under one arch of $y = \sin x$. (Example 2)

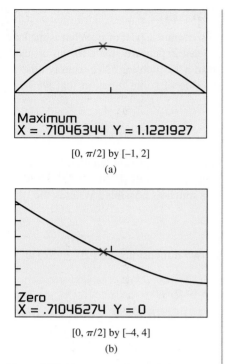

[0, π/2] by [–1, 2]

(a)

Zero
X = .71046274 Y = 0

[0, π/2] by [–4, 4]

(b)

Figure 5.36 The graph of (a) $A(x) = (\pi - 2x) \sin x$ and (b) A' in the interval $0 \le x \le \pi/2$. (Example 2)

Exploration 1, finding the cone of maximum volume that can be constructed from a circular disk of radius R, was a challenge problem that spread among the greatest scientists in Europe in the 1620s. In 1628, Pierre de Fermat invented the derivative in order to solve this problem. His solution made him famous.

SOLUTION

Model Let $(x, \sin x)$ be the coordinates of point P in Figure 5.35. From what we know about the sine function the x-coordinate of point Q is $(\pi - x)$. Thus,

$$\pi - 2x = \text{length of rectangle}$$

and

$$\sin x = \text{height of rectangle.}$$

The area of the rectangle is

$$A(x) = (\pi - 2x) \sin x.$$

Solve We can assume that $0 \le x \le \pi/2$. Notice that $A = 0$ at the endpoints $x = 0$ and $x = \pi/2$. Since A is differentiable, the only critical points occur at the zeros of the first derivative,

$$A'(x) = -2 \sin x + (\pi - 2x) \cos x.$$

It is not possible to solve the equation $A'(x) = 0$ using algebraic methods. We can use the graph of A (Figure 5.36a) to find the maximum value and where it occurs. Or, we can use the graph of A' (Figure 5.36b) to find where the derivative is zero, and then evaluate A at this value of x to find the maximum value. The two x values appear to be the same, as they should.

Interpret The rectangle has a maximum area of about 1.122 square units when $x \approx 0.710$. At this point, the rectangle is $\pi - 2x \approx 1.721$ units long by $\sin x \approx 0.652$ unit high.

Now Try Exercise 5.

EXPLORATION 1 Constructing Cones

A cone of height h and radius r is constructed from a flat, circular disk of radius 4 in. by removing a sector AOC of arc length x in. and then connecting the edges OA and OC. What arc length x will produce the cone of maximum volume, and what is that volume?

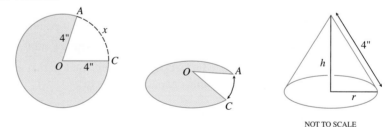

NOT TO SCALE

1. Show that

$$r = \frac{8\pi - x}{2\pi}, \quad h = \sqrt{16 - r^2}, \quad \text{and}$$

$$V(x) = \frac{\pi}{3}\left(\frac{8\pi - x}{2\pi}\right)^2 \sqrt{16 - \left(\frac{8\pi - x}{2\pi}\right)^2}$$

2. Show that the natural domain of V is $0 \le x \le 16\pi$. Graph V over this domain.
3. Explain why the restriction $0 \le x \le 8\pi$ makes sense in the problem situation. Graph V over this domain.
4. Use graphical methods to find where the cone has its maximum volume, and what that volume is.
5. Confirm your findings in part 4 analytically. [*Hint:* Use $V = (1/3)\pi r^2 h$, $h^2 + r^2 = 16$, and the Chain Rule.]

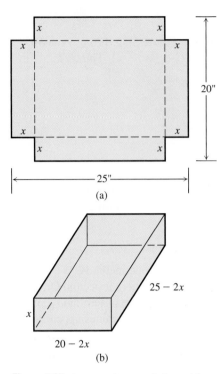

Figure 5.37 An open box made by cutting the corners from a piece of tin. (Example 3)

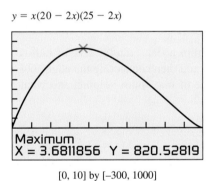

$$y = x(20 - 2x)(25 - 2x)$$

Maximum
X = 3.6811856 Y = 820.52819

[0, 10] by [−300, 1000]

Figure 5.38 We chose the −300 in −300 ≤ y ≤ 1000 so that the coordinates of the local maximum at the bottom of the screen would not interfere with the graph. (Example 3)

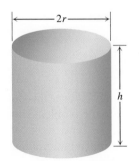

Figure 5.39 This one-liter can uses the least material when $h = 2r$. (Example 4)

Examples from Business and Industry

To *optimize* something means to maximize or minimize some aspect of it. What is the size of the most profitable production run? What is the least expensive shape for an oil can? What is the stiffest rectangular beam we can cut from a 12-inch log? We usually answer such questions by finding the greatest or smallest value of some function that we have used to model the situation.

EXAMPLE 3 Fabricating a Box

An open-top box is to be made by cutting congruent squares of side length x from the corners of a 20- by 25-inch sheet of tin and bending up the sides (Figure 5.37). How large should the squares be to make the box hold as much as possible? What is the resulting maximum volume?

SOLUTION

Model The height of the box is x, and the other two dimensions are $(20 - 2x)$ and $(25 - 2x)$. Thus, the volume of the box is

$$V(x) = x(20 - 2x)(25 - 2x).$$

Solve Because $2x$ cannot exceed 20, we have $0 \le x \le 10$. Figure 5.38 suggests that the maximum value of V is about 820.528 and occurs at $x \approx 3.681$. To verify that this is the solution, we expand $V(x) = 4x^3 - 90x^2 + 500x$. The first derivative of V is

$$V'(x) = 12x^2 - 180x + 500.$$

The two solutions of the quadratic equation $V'(x) = 0$ are

$$c_1 = \frac{180 - \sqrt{180^2 - 48(500)}}{24} \approx 3.681 \quad \text{and}$$

$$c_2 = \frac{180 + \sqrt{180^2 - 48(500)}}{24} \approx 11.317$$

Only c_1 is in the domain $[0, 10]$ of V. The values of V at this one critical point and the two endpoints are

Critical point value: $V(c_1) \approx 820.528$;

Endpoint values: $V(0) = 0, \quad V(10) = 0.$

Interpret Cutout squares that are about 3.681 in. on a side give the maximum volume, about 820.528 in^3. ***Now Try Exercise 7.***

EXAMPLE 4 Designing a Can

You have been asked to design a one-liter oil can shaped like a right circular cylinder (see Figure 5.39). What dimensions will use the least material?

SOLUTION

Volume of can: If r and h are measured in centimeters, then the volume of the can in cubic centimeters is

$$\pi r^2 h = 1000. \quad \text{1 liter = 1000 cm}^3$$

Surface area of can: $A = \underbrace{2\pi r^2}_{\substack{\text{circular} \\ \text{ends}}} + \underbrace{2\pi rh}_{\substack{\text{cylinder} \\ \text{wall}}}$

How can we interpret the phrase "least material"? One possibility is to ignore the thickness of the material and the waste in manufacturing. Then we ask for dimensions r and h that make the total surface area as small as possible while satisfying the constraint $\pi r^2 h = 1000$. (Exercise 17 describes one way to take waste into account.) *continued*

Model To express the surface area as a function of one variable, we solve for one of the variables in $\pi r^2 h = 1000$ and substitute that expression into the surface area formula. Solving for h is easier,

$$h = \frac{1000}{\pi r^2}.$$

Thus,

$$A = 2\pi r^2 + 2\pi rh$$
$$= 2\pi r^2 + 2\pi r\left(\frac{1000}{\pi r^2}\right)$$
$$= 2\pi r^2 + \frac{2000}{r}$$

Solve Our goal is to find a value of $r > 0$ that minimizes the value of A. Figure 5.40 suggests that such a value exists.

Notice from the graph that for small r (a tall thin container, like a piece of pipe), the term $2000/r$ dominates and A is large. For large r (a short wide container, like a pizza pan), the term $2\pi r^2$ dominates and A again is large.

Since A is differentiable on $r > 0$, an interval with no endpoints, it can have a minimum value only where its first derivative is zero.

$$\frac{dA}{dr} = 4\pi r - \frac{2000}{r^2}$$

$$0 = 4\pi r - \frac{2000}{r^2} \qquad \text{Set } dA/dr = 0.$$

$$4\pi r^3 = 2000 \qquad \text{Multiply by } r^2.$$

$$r = \sqrt[3]{\frac{500}{\pi}} \approx 5.419 \qquad \text{Solve for } r.$$

Something happens at $r = \sqrt[3]{500/\pi}$, but what?

If the domain of A were a closed interval, we could find out by evaluating A at this critical point and the endpoints and comparing the results. But the domain is an open interval, so we must learn what is happening at $r = \sqrt[3]{500/\pi}$ by referring to the shape of A's graph. The second derivative

$$\frac{d^2A}{dr^2} = 4\pi + \frac{4000}{r^3}$$

is positive throughout the domain of A. The graph is therefore concave up and the value of A at $r = \sqrt[3]{500/\pi}$ is an absolute minimum.

The corresponding value of h (after a little algebra) is

$$h = \frac{1000}{\pi r^2} = 2\sqrt[3]{\frac{500}{\pi}} = 2r.$$

Interpret The one-liter can that uses the least material has height equal to the diameter, with $r \approx 5.419$ cm and $h \approx 10.839$ cm. *Now Try Exercise 11.*

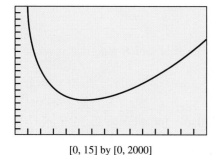

[0, 15] by [0, 2000]

Figure 5.40 The graph of $A = 2\pi r^2 + 2000/r$, $r > 0$, suggests that the minimum occurs when the radius is about 5.419 cm. (Example 4)

Examples from Economics

Here we want to point out two more places where calculus makes a contribution to economic theory. The first has to do with maximizing **profit.** The second has to do with minimizing average cost.

Marginal Analysis

Marginal revenue, cost, and profit are how economists talk about *sensitivity,* the effect of small changes in the input, in this case the number of units, on revenue, costs, or profits. Economists speak of this as *marginal analysis.*

Suppose that

$$r(x) = \text{the revenue from selling } x \text{ items,}$$
$$c(x) = \text{the cost of producing the } x \text{ items,}$$
$$p(x) = r(x) - c(x) = \text{the profit from selling } x \text{ items}$$

The marginal revenue, marginal cost, and marginal profit at this production level (x items) are

$$\frac{dr}{dx} = \text{marginal revenue,} \qquad \frac{dc}{dx} = \text{marginal cost,} \qquad \frac{dp}{dx} = \text{marginal profit.}$$

The first observation is about the relationship of p to these derivatives.

THEOREM 6   Maximum Profit

Maximum profit (if any) occurs at a production level at which marginal revenue equals marginal cost.

Proof We assume that $r(x)$ and $c(x)$ are differentiable for all $x > 0$, so if $p(x) = r(x) - c(x)$ has a maximum value, it occurs at a production level at which $p'(x) = 0$. Since $p'(x) = r'(x) - c'(x)$, $p'(x) = 0$ implies that

$$r'(x) - c'(x) = 0 \quad \text{or} \quad r'(x) = c'(x). \qquad \blacksquare$$

Figure 5.41 gives more information about this situation.

Figure 5.41 The graph of a typical cost function starts concave down and later turns concave up. It crosses the revenue curve at the break-even point *B*. To the left of *B*, the company operates at a loss. To the right, the company operates at a profit, the maximum profit occurring where $r'(x) = c'(x)$. Farther to the right, cost exceeds revenue (perhaps because of a combination of market saturation and rising labor and material costs) and production levels become unprofitable again.

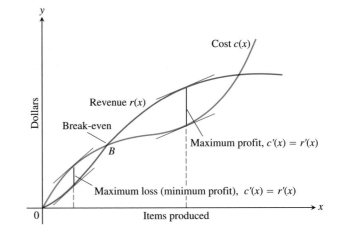

What guidance do we get from this observation? We know that a production level at which $p'(x) = 0$ need not be a level of maximum profit. It might be a level of minimum profit, for example. But if we are making financial projections for our company, we should look for production levels at which marginal cost seems to equal marginal revenue. If there is a most profitable production level, it will be one of these.

EXAMPLE 5   Maximizing Profit

Suppose that $r(x) = 9x$ and $c(x) = x^3 - 6x^2 + 15x$, where x represents thousands of units. Is there a production level that maximizes profit? If so, what is it?

continued

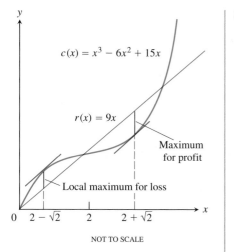

$c(x) = x^3 - 6x^2 + 15x$

$r(x) = 9x$

Maximum for profit

Local maximum for loss

$0 \quad 2-\sqrt{2} \quad 2 \quad 2+\sqrt{2}$

NOT TO SCALE

Figure 5.42 The cost and revenue curves for Example 5.

SOLUTION

Notice that $r'(x) = 9$ and $c'(x) = 3x^2 - 12x + 15$.

$$3x^2 - 12x + 15 = 9 \quad \text{Set } c'(x) = r'(x).$$
$$3x^2 - 12x + 6 = 0$$

The two solutions of the quadratic equation are

$$x_1 = \frac{12 - \sqrt{72}}{6} = 2 - \sqrt{2} \approx 0.586 \quad \text{and}$$

$$x_2 = \frac{12 + \sqrt{72}}{6} = 2 + \sqrt{2} \approx 3.414.$$

The possible production levels for maximum profit are $x \approx 0.586$ thousand units or $x \approx 3.414$ thousand units. The graphs in Figure 5.42 show that maximum profit occurs at about $x = 3.414$ and maximum loss occurs at about $x = 0.586$.

Another way to look for optimal production levels is to look for levels that minimize the average cost of the units produced. Theorem 7 helps us find them.

Now Try Exercise 23.

THEOREM 7 Minimizing Average Cost

The production level (if any) at which average cost is smallest is a level at which the average cost equals the marginal cost.

Proof We assume that $c(x)$ is differentiable.

$$c(x) = \text{cost of producing } x \text{ items, } x > 0.$$

$$\frac{c(x)}{x} = \text{average cost of producing } x \text{ items}$$

If the average cost can be minimized, it will be at a production level at which

$$\frac{d}{dx}\left(\frac{c(x)}{x}\right) = 0$$

$$\frac{xc'(x) - c(x)}{x^2} = 0 \quad \text{Quotient Rule}$$

$$xc'(x) - c(x) = 0 \quad \text{Multiply by } x^2.$$

$$\underbrace{c'(x)}_{\substack{\text{marginal} \\ \text{cost}}} = \underbrace{\frac{c(x)}{x}}_{\substack{\text{average} \\ \text{cost}}}.$$

Again we have to be careful about what Theorem 7 does and does not say. It does not say that there is a production level of minimum average cost—it says where to look to see if there is one. Look for production levels at which average cost and marginal cost are equal. Then check to see if any of them gives a minimum average cost.

EXAMPLE 6 Minimizing Average Cost

Suppose $c(x) = x^3 - 6x^2 + 15x$, where x represents thousands of units. Is there a production level that minimizes average cost? If so, what is it?

continued

SOLUTION

We look for levels at which average cost equals marginal cost.

$$\text{Marginal cost: } c'(x) = 3x^2 - 12x + 15$$

$$\text{Average cost: } \frac{c(x)}{x} = x^2 - 6x + 15$$

$$3x^2 - 12x + 15 = x^2 - 6x + 15 \quad \text{Marginal cost = Average cost}$$

$$2x^2 - 6x = 0$$

$$2x(x - 3) = 0$$

$$x = 0 \quad \text{or} \quad x = 3$$

Since $x > 0$, the only production level that might minimize average cost is $x = 3$ thousand units.

We use the Second Derivative Test.

$$\frac{d}{dx}\left(\frac{c(x)}{x}\right) = 2x - 6$$

$$\frac{d^2}{dx^2}\left(\frac{c(x)}{x}\right) = 2 > 0$$

The second derivative is positive for all $x > 0$, so $x = 3$ gives an absolute minimum.

Now Try Exercise 25.

Modeling Discrete Phenomena with Differentiable Functions

In case you are wondering how we can use differentiable functions $c(x)$ and $r(x)$ to describe the cost and revenue that come from producing a number of items x that can only be an integer, here is the rationale.

When x is large, we can reasonably fit the cost and revenue data with smooth curves $c(x)$ and $r(x)$ that are defined not only at integer values of x but also at the values in between, just as we do when we use regression equations. Once we have these differentiable functions, which are supposed to behave like the real cost and revenue when x is an integer, we can apply calculus to draw conclusions about their values. We then translate these mathematical conclusions into inferences about the real world that we hope will have predictive value. When they do, as is the case with the economic theory here, we say that the functions give a good model of reality.

What do we do when our calculus tells us that the best production level is a value of x that isn't an integer, as it did in Example 5? We use the nearest convenient integer. For $x \approx 3.414$ thousand units in Example 5, we might use 3414, or perhaps 3410 or 3420 if we ship in boxes of 10.

Quick Review 5.4   *(For help, go to Sections 1.6, 5.1, and Appendix A.1.)*

Exercise numbers with a gray background indicate problems that the authors have designed to be solved *without a calculator*.

1. Use the First Derivative Test to identify the local extrema of $y = x^3 - 6x^2 + 12x - 8$.

2. Use the Second Derivative Test to identify the local extrema of $y = 2x^3 + 3x^2 - 12x - 3$.

3. Find the volume of a cone with radius 5 cm and height 8 cm.

4. Find the dimensions of a right circular cylinder with volume 1000 cm^3 and surface area 600 cm^2.

In Exercises 5–8, rewrite the expression as a trigonometric function of the angle α.

5. $\sin(-\alpha)$ **6.** $\cos(-\alpha)$

7. $\sin(\pi - \alpha)$ **8.** $\cos(\pi - \alpha)$

In Exercises 9 and 10, use substitution to find the exact solutions of the system of equations.

9. $\begin{cases} x^2 + y^2 = 4 \\ y = \sqrt{3}x \end{cases}$

10. $\begin{cases} \dfrac{x^2}{4} + \dfrac{y^2}{9} = 1 \\ y = x + 3 \end{cases}$

Section 5.4 Exercises

In Exercises 1–10, solve the problem analytically. Support your answer graphically.

1. *Finding Numbers* The sum of two nonnegative numbers is 20. Find the numbers if

(a) the sum of their squares is as large as possible; as small as possible.

(b) one number plus the square root of the other is as large as possible; as small as possible.

2. *Maximizing Area* What is the largest possible area for a right triangle whose hypotenuse is 5 cm long, and what are its dimensions?

3. *Minimizing Perimeter* What is the smallest perimeter possible for a rectangle whose area is 16 in², and what are its dimensions?

4. *Finding Area* Show that among all rectangles with an 8-m perimeter, the one with largest area is a square.

5. *Inscribing Rectangles* The figure shows a rectangle inscribed in an isosceles right triangle whose hypotenuse is 2 units long.

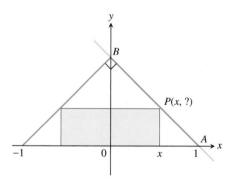

(a) Express the y-coordinate of P in terms of x. (*Hint:* Write an equation for the line AB.)

(b) Express the area of the rectangle in terms of x.

(c) What is the largest area the rectangle can have, and what are its dimensions?

6. *Largest Rectangle* A rectangle has its base on the x-axis and its upper two vertices on the parabola $y = 12 - x^2$. What is the largest area the rectangle can have, and what are its dimensions?

7. *Optimal Dimensions* You are planning to make an open rectangular box from an 8- by 15-in. piece of cardboard by cutting congruent squares from the corners and folding up the sides. What are the dimensions of the box of largest volume you can make this way, and what is its volume?

8. *Closing Off the First Quadrant* You are planning to close off a corner of the first quadrant with a line segment 20 units long running from $(a, 0)$ to $(0, b)$. Show that the area of the triangle enclosed by the segment is largest when $a = b$.

9. *The Best Fencing Plan* A rectangular plot of farmland will be bounded on one side by a river and on the other three sides by a single-strand electric fence. With 800 m of wire at your disposal, what is the largest area you can enclose, and what are its dimensions?

10. *The Shortest Fence* A 216-m² rectangular pea patch is to be enclosed by a fence and divided into two equal parts by another fence parallel to one of the sides. What dimensions for the outer rectangle will require the smallest total length of fence? How much fence will be needed?

11. *Designing a Tank* Your iron works has contracted to design and build a 500-ft³, square-based, open-top, rectangular steel holding tank for a paper company. The tank is to be made by welding thin stainless steel plates together along their edges. As the production engineer, your job is to find dimensions for the base and height that will make the tank weigh as little as possible.

(a) What dimensions do you tell the shop to use?

(b) **Writing to Learn** Briefly describe how you took weight into account.

12. *Catching Rainwater* A 1125-ft³ open-top rectangular tank with a square base x ft on a side and y ft deep is to be built with its top flush with the ground to catch runoff water. The costs associated with the tank involve not only the material from which the tank is made but also an excavation charge proportional to the product xy.

(a) If the total cost is

$$c = 5(x^2 + 4xy) + 10xy,$$

what values of x and y will minimize it?

(b) **Writing to Learn** Give a possible scenario for the cost function in (a).

13. **Designing a Poster** You are designing a rectangular poster to contain 50 in² of printing with a 4-in. margin at the top and bottom and a 2-in. margin at each side. What overall dimensions will minimize the amount of paper used?

14. **Vertical Motion** The height of an object moving vertically is given by

$$s = -16t^2 + 96t + 112,$$

with s in ft and t in sec. Find **(a)** the object's velocity when $t = 0$, **(b)** its maximum height and when it occurs, and **(c)** its velocity when $s = 0$.

15. **Finding an Angle** Two sides of a triangle have lengths a and b, and the angle between them is θ. What value of θ will maximize the triangle's area? [*Hint:* $A = (1/2) \, ab \sin \theta$.]

16. **Designing a Can** What are the dimensions of the lightest open-top right circular cylindrical can that will hold a volume of 1000 cm³? Compare the result here with the result in Example 4.

17. **Designing a Can** You are designing a 1000-cm³ right circular cylindrical can whose manufacture will take waste into account. There is no waste in cutting the aluminum for the side, but the top and bottom of radius r will be cut from squares that measure $2r$ units on a side. The total amount of aluminum used up by the can will therefore be

$$A = 8r^2 + 2\pi rh$$

rather than the $A = 2\pi r^2 + 2\pi rh$ in Example 4. In Example 4 the ratio of h to r for the most economical can was 2 to 1. What is the ratio now?

18. **Designing a Box with Lid** A piece of cardboard measures 10 in. by 15 in. Two equal squares are removed from the corners of a 10-in. side as shown in the figure. Two equal rectangles are removed from the other corners so that the tabs can be folded to form a rectangular box with lid.

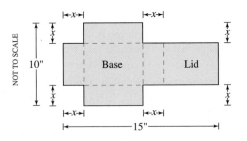

(a) Write a formula $V(x)$ for the volume of the box.

(b) Find the domain of V for the problem situation and graph V over this domain.

(c) Use a graphical method to find the maximum volume and the value of x that gives it.

(d) Confirm your result in part (c) analytically.

19. **Designing a Suitcase** A 24- by 36-in. sheet of cardboard is folded in half to form a 24- by 18-in. rectangle as shown in the figure. Then four congruent squares of side length x are cut from the corners of the folded rectangle. The sheet is unfolded, and the six tabs are folded up to form a box with sides and a lid.

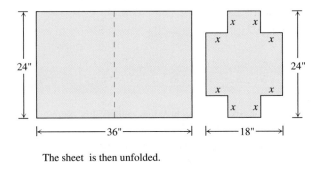

The sheet is then unfolded.

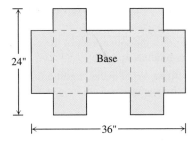

(a) Write a formula $V(x)$ for the volume of the box.

(b) Find the domain of V for the problem situation and graph V over this domain.

(c) Use an analytic method to find the maximum volume and the value of x that gives it.

(d) Support your result in part (c) graphically.

(e) Find a value of x that yields a volume of 1120 in³.

(f) **Writing to Learn** Write a paragraph describing the issues that arise in part (b).

20. **Quickest Route** Jane is 2 mi offshore in a boat and wishes to reach a coastal village 6 mi down a straight shoreline from the point nearest the boat. She can row 2 mph and can walk 5 mph. Where should she land her boat to reach the village in the least amount of time?

21. **Inscribing Rectangles** A rectangle is to be inscribed under the arch of the curve $y = 4 \cos (0.5x)$ from $x = -\pi$ to $x = \pi$. What are the dimensions of the rectangle with largest area, and what is the largest area?

22. **Maximizing Volume** Find the dimensions of a right circular cylinder of maximum volume that can be inscribed in a sphere of radius 10 cm. What is the maximum volume?

23. **Maximizing Profit** Suppose $r(x) = 8\sqrt{x}$ represents revenue and $c(x) = 2x^2$ represents cost, with x measured in thousands of units. Is there a production level that maximizes profit? If so, what is it?

24. *Maximizing Profit* Suppose $r(x) = x^2/(x^2 + 1)$ represents revenue and $c(x) = (x - 1)^3/3 + 1/3$ represents cost, with x measured in thousands of units. Is there a production level that maximizes profit? If so, what is it?

25. *Minimizing Average Cost* Suppose $c(x) = x^3 - 10x^2 - 30x$, where x is measured in thousands of units. Is there a production level that minimizes average cost? If so, what is it?

26. *Minimizing Average Cost* Suppose $c(x) = xe^x - 2x^2$, where x is measured in thousands of units. Is there a production level that minimizes average cost? If so, what is it?

27. *Tour Service* You operate a tour service that offers the following rates:

* $200 per person if 50 people (the minimum number to book the tour) go on the tour.

* For each additional person, up to a maximum of 80 people total, the rate per person is reduced by $2.

It costs $6000 (a fixed cost) plus $32 per person to conduct the tour. How many people does it take to maximize your profit?

28. *Group Activity* The figure shows the graph of $f(x) = xe^{-x}$, $x \geq 0$.

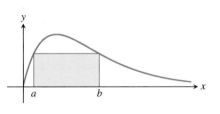

(a) Find where the absolute maximum of f occurs.

(b) Let $a > 0$ and $b > 0$ be given as shown in the figure. Complete the following table where A is the area of the rectangle in the figure.

a	b	A
0.1		
0.2		
0.3		
$\vdots$		
1		

(c) Draw a scatter plot of the data (a, A).

(d) Find the quadratic, cubic, and quartic regression equations for the data in part (b), and superimpose their graphs on a scatter plot of the data.

(e) Use each of the regression equations in part (d) to estimate the maximum possible value of the area of the rectangle.

29. *Cubic Polynomial Functions*
Let $f(x) = ax^3 + bx^2 + cx + d, a \neq 0$.

(a) Show that f has either 0 or 2 local extrema.

(b) Give an example of each possibility in part (a).

30. *Shipping Packages* The U.S. Postal Service will accept a box for domestic shipment only if the sum of its length and girth (distance around), as shown in the figure, does not exceed 108 in. What dimensions will give a box with a square end the largest possible volume?

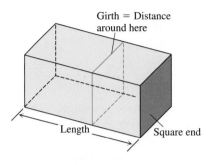

31. *Constructing Cylinders* Compare the answers to the following two construction problems.

(a) A rectangular sheet of perimeter 36 cm and dimensions x cm by y cm is to be rolled into a cylinder as shown in part (a) of the figure. What values of x and y give the largest volume?

(b) The same sheet is to be revolved about one of the sides of length y to sweep out the cylinder as shown in part (b) of the figure. What values of x and y give the largest volume?

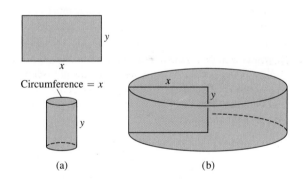

(a)   (b)

32. *Constructing Cones* A right triangle whose hypotenuse is $\sqrt{3}$ m long is revolved about one of its legs to generate a right circular cone. Find the radius, height, and volume of the cone of greatest volume that can be made this way.

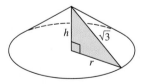

33. *Finding Parameter Values* What value of a makes $f(x) = x^2 + (a/x)$ have **(a)** a local minimum at $x = 2$?
(b) a point of inflection at $x = 1$?

34. *Finding Parameter Values* Show that $f(x) = x^2 + (a/x)$ cannot have a local maximum for any value of a.

35. *Finding Parameter Values* What values of a and b make $f(x) = x^3 + ax^2 + bx$ have **(a)** a local maximum at $x = -1$ and a local minimum at $x = 3$? **(b)** a local minimum at $x = 4$ and a point of inflection at $x = 1$?

36. *Inscribing a Cone* Find the volume of the largest right circular cone that can be inscribed in a sphere of radius 3.

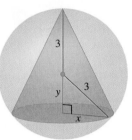

37. *Strength of a Beam* The strength S of a rectangular wooden beam is proportional to its width times the square of its depth.

(a) Find the dimensions of the strongest beam that can be cut from a 12-in.-diameter cylindrical log.

(b) *Writing to Learn* Graph S as a function of the beam's width w, assuming the proportionality constant to be $k = 1$. Reconcile what you see with your answer in part (a).

(c) *Writing to Learn* On the same screen, graph S as a function of the beam's depth d, again taking $k = 1$. Compare the graphs with one another and with your answer in part (a). What would be the effect of changing to some other value of k? Try it.

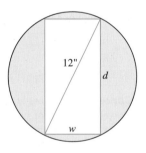

38. *Stiffness of a Beam* The stiffness S of a rectangular beam is proportional to its width times the cube of its depth.

(a) Find the dimensions of the stiffest beam that can be cut from a 12-in.-diameter cylindrical log.

(b) *Writing to Learn* Graph S as a function of the beam's width w, assuming the proportionality constant to be $k = 1$. Reconcile what you see with your answer in part (a).

(c) *Writing to Learn* On the same screen, graph S as a function of the beam's depth d, again taking $k = 1$. Compare the graphs with one another and with your answer in part (a). What would be the effect of changing to some other value of k? Try it.

39. *Frictionless Cart* A small frictionless cart, attached to the wall by a spring, is pulled 10 cm from its rest position and released at time $t = 0$ to roll back and forth for 4 sec. Its position at time t is $s = 10 \cos \pi t$.

(a) What is the cart's maximum speed? When is the cart moving that fast? Where is it then? What is the magnitude of the acceleration then?

(b) Where is the cart when the magnitude of the acceleration is greatest? What is the cart's speed then?

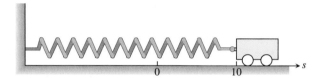

40. *Electrical Current* Suppose that at any time t (sec) the current i (amp) in an alternating current circuit is $i = 2 \cos t + 2 \sin t$. What is the peak (largest magnitude) current for this circuit?

41. *Calculus and Geometry* How close does the curve $y = \sqrt{x}$ come to the point $(3/2, 0)$? (*Hint:* If you minimize the *square* of the distance, you can avoid square roots.)

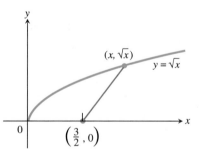

42. *Calculus and Geometry* How close does the semicircle $y = \sqrt{16 - x^2}$ come to the point $(1, \sqrt{3})$?

43. *Writing to Learn* Is the function $f(x) = x^2 - x + 1$ ever negative? Explain.

44. *Writing to Learn* You have been asked to determine whether the function $f(x) = 3 + 4 \cos x + \cos 2x$ is ever negative.

(a) Explain why you need to consider values of x only in the interval $[0, 2\pi]$.

(b) Is f ever negative? Explain.

45. *Vertical Motion* Two masses hanging side by side from springs have positions $s_1 = 2 \sin t$ and $s_2 = \sin 2t$, respectively, with s_1 and s_2 in meters and t in seconds.

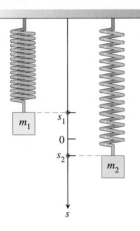

(a) At what times in the interval $t > 0$ do the masses pass each other? (*Hint:* $\sin 2t = 2 \sin t \cos t$.)

(b) When in the interval $0 \le t \le 2\pi$ is the vertical distance between the masses the greatest? What is this distance? (*Hint:* $\cos 2t = 2 \cos^2 t - 1$.)

46. *Motion on a Line* The positions of two particles on the s-axis are $s_1 = \sin t$ and $s_2 = \sin (t + \pi/3)$, with s_1 and s_2 in meters and t in seconds.

(a) At what time(s) in the interval $0 \le t \le 2\pi$ do the particles meet?

(b) What is the farthest apart that the particles ever get?

(c) When in the interval $0 \le t \le 2\pi$ is the distance between the particles changing the fastest?

47. *Finding an Angle* The trough in the figure is to be made to the dimensions shown. Only the angle θ can be varied. What value of θ will maximize the trough's volume?

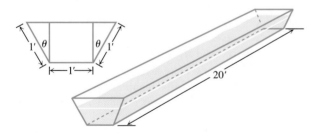

48. Group Activity *Paper Folding* A rectangular sheet of 8 1/2-by 11-in. paper is placed on a flat surface. One of the corners is placed on the opposite longer edge, as shown in the figure, and held there as the paper is smoothed flat. The problem is to make the length of the crease as small as possible. Call the length L. Try it with paper.

(a) Show that $L^2 = 2x^3/(2x - 8.5)$.

(b) What value of x minimizes L^2?

(c) What is the minimum value of L?

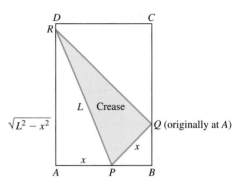

49. *Sensitivity to Medicine* (*continuation of Exercise 48, Section 3.3*) Find the amount of medicine to which the body is most sensitive by finding the value of M that maximizes the derivative dR/dM.

50. *Selling Backpacks* It costs you c dollars each to manufacture and distribute backpacks. If the backpacks sell at x dollars each, the number sold is given by

$$n = \frac{a}{x - c} + b(100 - x),$$

where a and b are certain positive constants. What selling price will bring a maximum profit?

Standardized Test Questions

You may use a graphing calculator to solve the following problems.

51. True or False A continuous function on a closed interval must attain a maximum value on that interval. Justify your answer.

52. True or False If $f'(c) = 0$ and $f(c)$ is not a local maximum, then $f(c)$ is a local minimum. Justify your answer.

53. Multiple Choice Two positive numbers have a sum of 60. What is the maximum product of one number times the square of the second number?

(A) 3481 **(B)** 3600 **(C)** 27,000

(D) 32,000 **(E)** 36,000

54. Multiple Choice A continuous function f has domain $[1, 25]$ and range $[3, 30]$. If $f'(x) < 0$ for all x between 1 and 25, what is $f(25)$?

(A) 1 **(B)** 3 **(C)** 25 **(D)** 30

(E) impossible to determine from the information given

55. Multiple Choice What is the maximum area of a right triangle with hypotenuse 10?

(A) 24 **(B)** 25 **(C)** $25\sqrt{2}$

(D) 48 **(E)** 50

56. Multiple Choice A rectangle is inscribed between the parabolas $y = 4x^2$ and $y = 30 - x^2$ as shown below:

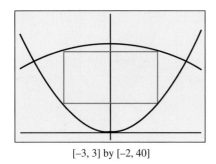

[−3, 3] by [−2, 40]

What is the maximum area of such a rectangle?

(A) $20\sqrt{2}$ (B) 40   (C) $30\sqrt{2}$

(D) 50   (E) $40\sqrt{2}$

Explorations

57. Fermat's Principle in Optics Fermat's principle in optics states that light always travels from one point to another along a path that minimizes the travel time. Light from a source A is reflected by a plane mirror to a receiver at point B, as shown in the figure. Show that for the light to obey Fermat's principle, the angle of incidence must equal the angle of reflection, both measured from the line normal to the reflecting surface. (This result can also be derived without calculus. There is a purely geometric argument, which you may prefer.)

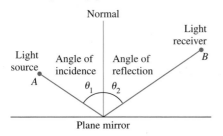

58. Tin Pest When metallic tin is kept below 13.2°C, it slowly becomes brittle and crumbles to a gray powder. Tin objects eventually crumble to this gray powder spontaneously if kept in a cold climate for years. The Europeans who saw tin organ pipes in their churches crumble away years ago called the change *tin pest* because it seemed to be contagious. And indeed it was, for the gray powder is a catalyst for its own formation.

A *catalyst* for a chemical reaction is a substance that controls the rate of reaction without undergoing any permanent change in itself. An *autocatalytic reaction* is one whose product is a catalyst for its own formation. Such a reaction may proceed slowly at first if the amount of catalyst present is small and slowly again at the end, when most of the original substance is used up. But in between, when both the substance and its catalyst product are abundant, the reaction proceeds at a faster pace.

In some cases it is reasonable to assume that the rate $v = dx/dt$ of the reaction is proportional both to the amount of the original substance present and to the amount of product. That is, v may be considered to be a function of x alone, and

$$v = kx(a - x) = kax - kx^2,$$

where

$x =$ the amount of product,

$a =$ the amount of substance at the beginning,

$k =$ a positive constant.

At what value of x does the rate v have a maximum? What is the maximum value of v?

59. How We Cough When we cough, the trachea (windpipe) contracts to increase the velocity of the air going out. This raises the question of how much it should contract to maximize the velocity and whether it really contracts that much when we cough.

Under reasonable assumptions about the elasticity of the tracheal wall and about how the air near the wall is slowed by friction, the average flow velocity v (in cm/sec) can be modeled by the equation

$$v = c(r_0 - r)r^2, \quad \frac{r_0}{2} \le r \le r_0,$$

where r_0 is the rest radius of the trachea in cm and c is a positive constant whose value depends in part on the length of the trachea.

(a) Show that v is greatest when $r = (2/3)r_0$, that is, when the trachea is about 33% contracted. The remarkable fact is that X-ray photographs confirm that the trachea contracts about this much during a cough.

(b) Take r_0 to be 0.5 and c to be 1, and graph v over the interval $0 \le r \le 0.5$. Compare what you see to the claim that v is a maximum when $r = (2/3)r_0$.

60. Wilson Lot Size Formula One of the formulas for inventory management says that the average weekly cost of ordering, paying for, and holding merchandise is

$$A(q) = \frac{km}{q} + cm + \frac{hq}{2},$$

where q is the quantity you order when things run low (shoes, radios, brooms, or whatever the item might be), k is the cost of placing an order (the same, no matter how often you order), c is the cost of one item (a constant), m is the number of items sold each week (a constant), and h is the weekly holding cost per item (a constant that takes into account things such as space, utilities, insurance, and security).

(a) Your job, as the inventory manager for your store, is to find the quantity that will minimize $A(q)$. What is it? (The formula you get for the answer is called the *Wilson lot size formula*.)

(b) Shipping costs sometimes depend on order size. When they do, it is more realistic to replace k by $k + bq$, the sum of k and a constant multiple of q. What is the most economical quantity to order now?

61. Production Level Show that if $r(x) = 6x$ and $c(x) = x^3 - 6x^2 + 15x$ are your revenue and cost functions, then the best you can do is break even (have revenue equal cost).

62. Production Level Suppose $c(x) = x^3 - 20x^2 + 20{,}000x$ is the cost of manufacturing x items. Find a production level that will minimize the average cost of making x items.

Extending the Ideas

63. *Airplane Landing Path* An airplane is flying at altitude H when it begins its descent to an airport runway that is at horizontal ground distance L from the airplane, as shown in the figure. Assume that the landing path of the airplane is the graph of a cubic polynomial function $y = ax^3 + bx^2 + cx + d$ where $y(-L) = H$ and $y(0) = 0$.

(a) What is dy/dx at $x = 0$?

(b) What is dy/dx at $x = -L$?

(c) Use the values for dy/dx at $x = 0$ and $x = -L$ together with $y(0) = 0$ and $y(-L) = H$ to show that

$$y(x) = H\left[2\left(\frac{x}{L}\right)^3 + 3\left(\frac{x}{L}\right)^2\right].$$

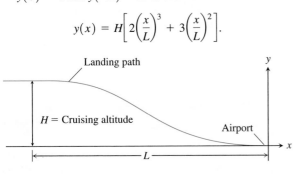

In Exercises 64 and 65, you might find it helpful to use a CAS.

64. *Generalized Cone Problem* A cone of height h and radius r is constructed from a flat, circular disk of radius a in. as described in Exploration 1.

(a) Find a formula for the volume V of the cone in terms of x and a.

(b) Find r and h in the cone of maximum volume for $a = 4$, 5, 6, 8.

(c) Writing to Learn Find a simple relationship between r and h that is independent of a for the cone of maximum volume. Explain how you arrived at your relationship.

65. *Circumscribing an Ellipse* Let $P(x, a)$ and $Q(-x, a)$ be two points on the upper half of the ellipse

$$\frac{x^2}{100} + \frac{(y - 5)^2}{25} = 1$$

centered at $(0, 5)$. A triangle RST is formed by using the tangent lines to the ellipse at Q and P as shown in the figure.

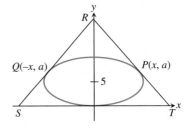

(a) Show that the area of the triangle is

$$A(x) = -f'(x)\left[x - \frac{f(x)}{f'(x)}\right]^2,$$

where $y = f(x)$ is the function representing the upper half of the ellipse.

(b) What is the domain of A? Draw the graph of A. How are the asymptotes of the graph related to the problem situation?

(c) Determine the height of the triangle with minimum area. How is it related to the y-coordinate of the center of the ellipse?

(d) Repeat parts (a)–(c) for the ellipse

$$\frac{x^2}{C^2} + \frac{(y - B)^2}{B^2} = 1$$

centered at $(0, B)$. Show that the triangle has minimum area when its height is $3B$.

5.5 | Linearization, Sensitivity, and Differentials

You will be able to solve problems involving the slope of the tangent line.

- Linear approximation
- Sensitivity analysis
- Differentials
- Newton's method

Linear Approximation

Because the derivative is defined as the limit of the ratio of the change in output to the change in input, $\dfrac{dy}{dx} = \lim\limits_{\Delta x \to 0} \dfrac{\Delta y}{\Delta x}$, we can approximate the derivative by $\Delta y/\Delta x$ when Δx is small. This also works the other way. Very often it is easy to calculate the derivative, which we can use to approximate the change in y when the change in x is known. What is happening is that very close to the point where the derivative is calculated, the graph of the function is very close to a straight line, the tangent line, as we see in Exploration 1. Linear functions are special because the change in output, Δy, is always equal to a constant times the change in input, Δx.

EXPLORATION 1 Appreciating Local Linearity

The function $f(x) = (x^2 + 0.0001)^{1/4} + 0.9$ is differentiable at $x = 0$ and hence "locally linear" there. Let us explore the significance of this fact with the help of a graphing calculator.

1. Graph $y = f(x)$ in the "ZoomDecimal" window. What appears to be the behavior of the function at the point $(0, 1)$?
2. Show algebraically that f is differentiable at $x = 0$. What is the equation of the tangent line at $(0, 1)$?
3. Now zoom in repeatedly, keeping the cursor at $(0, 1)$. What is the long-range outcome of repeated zooming?
4. The graph of $y = f(x)$ eventually looks like the graph of a line. What line is it?

We hope that this exploration gives you a new appreciation for the tangent line. As you zoom in on a differentiable function, its graph at that point actually seems to *become* the graph of the tangent line! This observation—that even the most complicated differentiable curve behaves locally like the simplest graph of all, a straight line—is the basis for most of the applications of differential calculus. It is what allows us, for example, to refer to the derivative as the "slope of the curve" or as "the velocity at time t_0."

Algebraically, the principle of local linearity means that the *equation* of the tangent line defines a function that can be used to *approximate* a differentiable function near the point of tangency. In recognition of this fact, we give the equation of the tangent line a new name: the *linearization of f at a*. Recall that the tangent line at $(a, f(a))$ has point-slope equation $y - f(a) = f'(a)(x - a)$ (Figure 5.43).

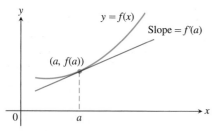

Figure 5.43 The tangent to the curve $y = f(x)$ at $x = a$ is the line $y = f(a) + f'(a)(x - a)$.

DEFINITION Linearization

If f is differentiable at $x = a$, then the equation of the tangent line,

$$L(x) = f(a) + f'(a)(x - a),$$

defines the **linearization of f at a.** The approximation $f(x) \approx L(x)$ is the **standard linear approximation of f at a.** The point $x = a$ is the **center** of the approximation.

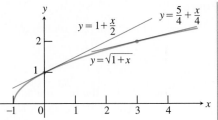

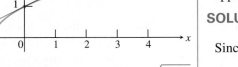

Figure 5.44 The graph of $f(x) = \sqrt{1 + x}$ and its linearization at $x = 0$ and $x = 3$. (Example 1)

Why Not Just Use a Calculator?

We readily admit that linearization will never replace a calculator when it comes to finding square roots. Indeed, historically it was the other way around. Understanding linearization, however, brings you one step closer to understanding how the calculator finds those square roots so easily. You will get many steps closer when you study Taylor polynomials in Chapter 10. (A linearization is just a Taylor polynomial of degree 1.)

EXAMPLE 1 Finding a Linearization

Find the linearization of $f(x) = \sqrt{1 + x}$ at $x = 0$, and use it to approximate $\sqrt{1.02}$ without a calculator. Then use a calculator to determine the accuracy of the approximation.

SOLUTION

Since $f(0) = 1$, the point of tangency is $(0, 1)$. Since $f'(x) = \frac{1}{2}(1 + x)^{-1/2}$, the slope of the tangent line is $f'(0) = \frac{1}{2}$. Thus

$$L(x) = 1 + \frac{1}{2}(x - 0) = 1 + \frac{x}{2}. \qquad \text{(Figure 5.44)}$$

To approximate $\sqrt{1.02}$, we use $x = 0.02$:

$$\sqrt{1.02} = f(0.02) \approx L(0.02) = 1 + \frac{0.02}{2} = 1.01$$

The calculator gives $\sqrt{1.02} = 1.009950494$, so the approximation error is $|1.009950494 - 1.01| \approx 4.95 \times 10^{-5}$. We report that the error is less than 10^{-4}.

Now Try Exercise 1.

Look at how accurate the approximation $\sqrt{1 + x} \approx 1 + \frac{x}{2}$ is for values of x near 0.

Approximation	$\vert$True Value – Approximation$\vert$
$\sqrt{1.002} \approx 1 + \dfrac{0.002}{2} = 1.001$	$<10^{-6}$
$\sqrt{1.02} \approx 1 + \dfrac{0.02}{2} = 1.01$	$<10^{-4}$
$\sqrt{1.2} \approx 1 + \dfrac{0.2}{2} = 1.1$	$<10^{-2}$

As we move away from zero (the center of the approximation), we lose accuracy and the approximation becomes less useful. For example, using $L(2) = 2$ as an approximation for $f(2) = \sqrt{3}$ is not even accurate to one decimal place. We could do slightly better using $L(2)$ to approximate $f(2)$ if we were to use 3 as the center of our approximation (Figure 5.44).

EXAMPLE 2 Finding a Linearization

Find the linearization of $f(x) = \cos x$ at $x = \pi/2$ and use it to approximate $\cos 1.75$ without a calculator. Then use a calculator to determine the accuracy of the approximation.

SOLUTION

Since $f(\pi/2) = \cos(\pi/2) = 0$, the point of tangency is $(\pi/2, 0)$. The slope of the tangent line is $f'(\pi/2) = -\sin(\pi/2) = -1$. Thus

$$L(x) = 0 + (-1)\left(x - \frac{\pi}{2}\right) = -x + \frac{\pi}{2}. \qquad \text{(Figure 5.45)}$$

To approximate $\cos(1.75)$, we use $x = 1.75$:

$$\cos 1.75 = f(1.75) \approx L(1.75) = -1.75 + \frac{\pi}{2}$$

The calculator gives $\cos 1.75 = -0.1782460556$, so the approximation error is $|-0.1782460556 - (-1.75 + \pi/2)| \approx 9.57 \times 10^{-4}$. We report that the error is less than 10^{-3}.

Now Try Exercise 5.

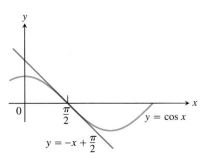

Figure 5.45 The graph of $f(x) = \cos x$ and its linearization at $x = \pi/2$. Near $x = \pi/2$, $\cos x \approx -x + (\pi/2)$. (Example 2)

EXAMPLE 3 Approximating Binomial Powers

Example 1 introduces a special case of a general linearization formula that applies to powers of $1 + x$ for small values of x:

$$(1 + x)^k \approx 1 + kx$$

If k is a positive integer this follows from the Binomial Theorem, but the formula actually holds for *all* real values of k. (We leave the justification to you as Exercise 7.) Use this formula to find polynomials that will approximate the following functions for values of x close to zero:

(a) $\sqrt[3]{1 - x}$ **(b)** $\dfrac{1}{1 - x}$ **(c)** $\sqrt{1 + 5x^4}$ **(d)** $\dfrac{1}{\sqrt{1 - x^2}}$

SOLUTION

We change each expression to the form $(1 + y)^k$, where k is a real number and y is a function of x that is close to 0 when x is close to zero. The approximation is then given by $1 + ky$.

(a) $\sqrt[3]{1 - x} = (1 + (-x))^{1/3} \approx 1 + \dfrac{1}{3}(-x) = 1 - \dfrac{x}{3}$

(b) $\dfrac{1}{1 - x} = (1 + (-x))^{-1} \approx 1 + (-1)(-x) = 1 + x$

(c) $\sqrt{1 + 5x^4} = ((1 + 5x^4))^{1/2} \approx 1 + \dfrac{1}{2}(5x^4) = 1 + \dfrac{5}{2}x^4$

(d) $\dfrac{1}{\sqrt{1 - x^2}} = ((1 + (-x^2)))^{-1/2} \approx 1 + \left(-\dfrac{1}{2}\right)(-x^2) = 1 + \dfrac{1}{2}x^2$

Now Try Exercise 9.

EXAMPLE 4 Approximating Roots

Use linearizations to approximate **(a)** $\sqrt{123}$ and **(b)** $\sqrt[3]{123}$.

SOLUTION

Part of the analysis is to decide where to center the approximations.

(a) Let $f(x) = \sqrt{x}$. The closest perfect square to 123 is 121, so we center the linearization at $x = 121$. The tangent line at $(121, 11)$ has slope

$$f'(121) = \dfrac{1}{2}(121)^{-1/2} = \dfrac{1}{2} \cdot \dfrac{1}{\sqrt{121}} = \dfrac{1}{22}.$$

So

$$\sqrt{123} \approx L(123) = 11 + \dfrac{1}{22}(123 - 121) = 11.\overline{09}.$$

(b) Let $f(x) = \sqrt[3]{x}$. The closest perfect cube to 123 is 125, so we center the linearization at $x = 125$. The tangent line at $(125, 5)$ has slope

$$f'(125) = \dfrac{1}{3}(125)^{-2/3} = \dfrac{1}{3} \cdot \dfrac{1}{(\sqrt[3]{125})^2} = \dfrac{1}{75}.$$

So

$$\sqrt[3]{123} \approx L(123) = 5 + \dfrac{1}{75}(123 - 125) = 4.97\overline{3}.$$

A calculator shows both approximations to be within 10^{-3} of the actual values.

Now Try Exercise 11.

Differentials

Leibniz used the notation dy/dx to represent the derivative of y with respect to x. The notation *looks* like a quotient of real numbers, but it is really a *limit* of quotients in which both numerator and denominator go to zero (without actually equaling zero). That makes it tricky to define dy and dx as separate entities. (See the margin note, "Leibniz and His Notation.") Since we really only need to define dy and dx as formal variables, we define them in terms of each other so that their quotient must be the derivative.

DEFINITION   Differentials

Let $y = f(x)$ be a differentiable function. The **differential dx** is an independent variable. The **differential dy** is

$$dy = f'(x)\, dx.$$

Unlike the independent variable dx, the variable dy is always a dependent variable. It depends on both x and dx.

EXAMPLE 5 Finding the Differential *dy*

Find the differential dy and evaluate dy for the given values of x and dx.

(a) $y = x^5 + 37x$, $x = 1$, $dx = 0.01$ **(b)** $y = \sin 3x$, $x = \pi$, $dx = -0.02$
(c) $x + y = xy$, $x = 2$, $dx = 0.05$

SOLUTION

(a) $dy = (5x^4 + 37)\, dx$. When $x = 1$ and $dx = 0.01$, $dy = (5 + 37)(0.01) = 0.42$.

(b) $dy = (3 \cos 3x)\, dx$. When $x = \pi$ and $dx = -0.02$,
$dy = (3 \cos 3\pi)(-0.02) = 0.06$.

(c) We could solve explicitly for y before differentiating, but it is easier to use implicit differentiation:

$$d(x + y) = d(xy)$$
$$dx + dy = xdy + ydx \quad \text{Sum and Product Rules in differential form}$$
$$dy(1 - x) = (y - 1)dx$$
$$dy = \frac{(y - 1)dx}{1 - x}$$

When $x = 2$ in the original equation, $2 + y = 2y$, so y is also 2. Therefore

$$dy = \frac{(2 - 1)(0.05)}{(1 - 2)} = -0.05. \qquad \textbf{\textit{Now Try Exercise 15.}}$$

If $dx \neq 0$, then the quotient of the differential dy by the differential dx is equal to the derivative $f'(x)$ because

$$\frac{dy}{dx} = \frac{f'(x)dx}{dx} = f'(x).$$

We sometimes write

$$df = f'(x)\, dx$$

in place of $dy = f'(x)\, dx$, calling df the **differential of f**. For instance, if $f(x) = 3x^2 - 6$, then

$$df = d(3x^2 - 6) = 6x\, dx.$$

Every differentiation formula like

$$\frac{d(u + v)}{dx} = \frac{du}{dx} + \frac{dv}{dx} \qquad \text{or} \qquad \frac{d(\sin u)}{dx} = \cos u \frac{du}{dx}$$

has a corresponding differential form like

$$d(u + v) = du + dv \qquad \text{or} \qquad d(\sin u) = \cos u \, du.$$

EXAMPLE 6 Finding Differentials of Functions

(a) $d(\tan 2x) = \sec^2 (2x) \, d(2x) = 2 \sec^2 2x \, dx$

(b) $d\left(\dfrac{x}{x + 1}\right) = \dfrac{(x + 1) \, dx - x \, d(x + 1)}{(x + 1)^2} = \dfrac{x \, dx + dx - x \, dx}{(x + 1)^2} = \dfrac{dx}{(x + 1)^2}$

Now Try Exercise 23.

Differential Estimate of Change

The differential $df = f'(x) \, dx$ has a geometric interpretation. If we think of dx as Δx, the change in x, then the value of df at $x = a$ is ΔL, the change in the linear approximation to f. If f is differentiable at $x = a$, then the approximate change in f when x changes from a to $a + dx$ can be represented by

$$df = f'(a) \, dx.$$

Sensitivity Analysis

We have local linearity because the derivative changes by very little over very small intervals. One of the consequences is that over small intervals the ratio of the change in the output to the change in the input, $\Delta y / \Delta x$, can be treated as constant. This gives us another interpretation of the derivative, as a measure of the sensitivity of the output to small changes in the input.

DEFINITION Sensitivity

Sensitivity is an interpretation of the derivative, describing how small changes in the input variable produce changes in the output variable. For small values of Δx, we can approximate Δy by $\Delta y \approx \frac{dy}{dx} \Delta x$.

Suppose we know the value of a differentiable function $f(x)$ at a point a and we want to predict how much this value will change if we move to a nearby point $a + \Delta x$. If Δx is small, f and its linearization L at a will change by nearly the same amount (Figure 5.46). Since the values of L are simple to calculate, calculating the change in L offers a practical way to estimate the change in f.

In the notation of Figure 5.46, the change in f is

$$\Delta f = f(a + \Delta x) - f(a).$$

The corresponding change in L is

$$\begin{aligned} \Delta L &= L(a + \Delta x) - L(a) \\ &= \underbrace{f(a) + f'(a)[(a + \Delta x) - a]}_{L(a + \Delta x)} - \underbrace{f(a)}_{L(a)} \\ &= f'(a) \, \Delta x \end{aligned}$$

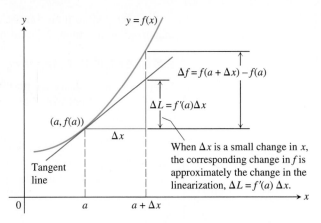

Figure 5.46 Approximating the change in the function f by the change in the linearization of f.

EXAMPLE 7 Estimating Change

The radius r of a circle increases from $a = 10$ m to 10.1 m (Figure 5.47). Use the linearization to estimate the increase in the circle's area A. Compare this estimate with the true change ΔA, and find the approximation error.

SOLUTION

Since $A = \pi r^2$, the estimated increase is

$$A'(a)\, \Delta r = 2\pi a\, \Delta r = 2\pi(10)(0.1) = 2\pi \text{ m}^2.$$

The true change is

$$\Delta A = \pi(10.1)^2 - \pi(10)^2 = (102.01 - 100)\pi = 2.01\pi \text{ m}^2.$$

The approximation error is $\Delta A - A'\Delta r = 2.01\pi - 2\pi = 0.01\pi \text{ m}^2$.

Now Try Exercise 27.

Figure 5.47 When Δr is small compared with a, as it is when $\Delta r = 0.1$ and $a = 10$, $2\pi a\, \Delta r$ gives a good estimate of ΔA. (Example 7)

Caption for left figure: $\Delta r = 0.1$, $a = 10$, $\Delta A = 2\pi a\, \Delta r$

Absolute, Relative, and Percentage Change

As we move from a to a nearby point $a + \Delta x$, we can describe the change in f in three ways:

	True	Estimated
Absolute change	$\Delta f = f(a + \Delta x) - f(a)$	$\Delta f \approx f'(a)\Delta x$
Relative change	$\dfrac{\Delta f}{f(a)}$	$\dfrac{f'(a)}{f(a)}\Delta x$
Percentage change	$\dfrac{\Delta f}{f(a)} \times 100$	$\dfrac{f'(a)}{f(a)}\Delta x \times 100$

Why It's Easy to Estimate Change in Perimeter

Note that the *true* change in Example 8 is $P(13) - P(12) = 26\pi - 24\pi = 2\pi$, so the estimate in this case is perfectly accurate! Why? Since $P = 2\pi r$ is a linear function of r, the linearization of P is the same as P itself. It is useful to keep in mind that local linearity is what makes estimation work.

EXAMPLE 8 Changing Tires

Inflating a bicycle tire changes its radius from 12 inches to 13 inches. Use the linearization to estimate the absolute change, the relative change, and the percentage change in the perimeter of the tire.

SOLUTION

Perimeter $P = 2\pi r$, so $\Delta P \approx 2\pi\Delta r = 2\pi(1) = 2\pi \approx 6.28$.

The absolute change is approximately 6.3 inches.

The relative change (when $P(12) = 24\pi$) is approximately $2\pi/24\pi \approx 0.08$.

The percentage change is approximately 8 percent.

Now Try Exercise 31.

Another way to interpret the change in $f(x)$ resulting from a change in x is the effect that an error in estimating x has on the estimation of $f(x)$. We illustrate this in Example 9.

EXAMPLE 9 Estimating the Earth's Surface Area

Suppose the earth were a perfect sphere and we determined its radius to be 3959 ± 0.1 miles. What effect would the tolerance of ± 0.1 mi have on our estimate of the earth's surface area?

SOLUTION

The surface area of a sphere of radius r is $S = 4\pi r^2$. The uncertainty in the calculation of S that arises from measuring r with a tolerance of Δr miles is

$$\Delta S \approx 8\pi r \, \Delta r.$$

With $r = 3959$ and $\Delta r = 0.1$, our estimate of S could be off by as much as

$$\Delta S \approx 8\pi(3959)(0.1) \approx 9950 \text{ mi}^2,$$

to the nearest square mile, which is about the area of the state of Maryland.

Now Try Exercise 37.

EXAMPLE 10 Determining Tolerance

About how accurately should we measure the radius r of a sphere to calculate the surface area $S = 4\pi r^2$ within 1% of its true value?

SOLUTION

We want any inaccuracy in our measurement to be small enough to make the corresponding increment ΔS in the surface area satisfy the inequality

$$|\Delta S| \leq \frac{1}{100}S = \frac{4\pi r^2}{100}.$$

We replace ΔS in this inequality by its approximation

$$\Delta S \approx \left(\frac{dS}{dr}\right)\Delta r = 8\pi r \, \Delta r.$$

This gives

$$|8\pi r \, \Delta r| \leq \frac{4\pi r^2}{100}, \quad \text{or} \quad |\Delta r| \leq \frac{1}{8\pi r} \cdot \frac{4\pi r^2}{100} = \frac{1}{2} \cdot \frac{r}{100} = 0.005r.$$

We should measure r with an error Δr that is no more than 0.5% of the true value.

Now Try Exercise 45.

Angiography

An opaque dye is injected into a partially blocked artery to make the inside visible under X-rays. This reveals the location and severity of the blockage.

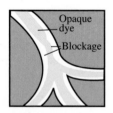

Angioplasty

A balloon-tipped catheter is inflated inside the artery to widen it at the blockage site.

EXAMPLE 11 Unclogging Arteries

In the late 1830s, the French physiologist Jean Poiseuille ("pwa-ZOY") discovered the formula we use today to predict how much the radius of a partially clogged artery has to be expanded to restore normal flow. His formula,

$$V = kr^4,$$

says that the volume V of fluid flowing through a small pipe or tube in a unit of time at a fixed pressure is a constant times the fourth power of the tube's radius r. How will a 10% increase in r affect V?

SOLUTION

The changes in r and V are related by

$$\Delta V \approx \frac{dV}{dr}\Delta r = 4kr^3\Delta r.$$

continued

The relative change in *V* is

$$\frac{\Delta V}{V} \approx \frac{4kr^3 \Delta r}{kr^4} = 4\frac{\Delta r}{r}.$$

The relative change in *V* is 4 times the relative change in *r*, so a 10% increase in *r* will produce a 40% increase in the flow.   ***Now Try Exercise 47.***

Sensitivity to Change

The approximate equality $\Delta f \approx f'(x) \, \Delta x$ tells how *sensitive* the output of *f* is to a change in input at different values of *x*. The larger the value of *f'* at *x*, the greater the effect of a given change Δx.

EXAMPLE 12 Finding Depth of a Well

You want to calculate the depth of a well from the equation $s = 16t^2$ by timing how long it takes a heavy stone you drop to splash into the water below. How sensitive will your calculations be to a 0.1-sec error in measuring the time?

SOLUTION

The size of Δs in the approximation

$$\Delta s \approx 32t \, \Delta t$$

depends on how big *t* is. If $t = 2$ sec, the error caused by $\Delta t = 0.1$ is only

$$\Delta s \approx 32(2)(0.1) = 6.4 \text{ ft.}$$

Three seconds later at $t = 5$ sec, the error caused by the same Δt is

$$\Delta s \approx 32(5)(0.1) = 16 \text{ ft.} \qquad \textbf{\textit{Now Try Exercise 49.}}$$

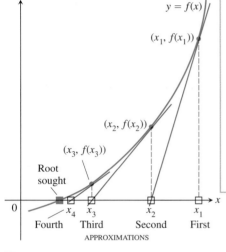

Figure 5.48 Usually the approximations rapidly approach an actual zero of $y = f(x)$.

Newton's Method

Newton's method is a numerical technique for approximating a zero of a function with zeros of its linearizations. Under favorable circumstances, the zeros of the linearizations *converge* rapidly to an accurate approximation. Many calculators use the method because it applies to a wide range of functions and usually gets results in only a few steps. Here is how it works.

To find a solution of an equation $f(x) = 0$, we begin with an initial estimate x_1, found either by looking at a graph or by simply guessing. Then we use the tangent to the curve $y = f(x)$ at $(x_1, f(x_1))$ to approximate the curve (Figure 5.48). The point where the tangent crosses the *x*-axis is the next approximation x_2. The number x_2 is usually a better approximation to the solution than is x_1. The point where the tangent to the curve at $(x_2, f(x_2))$ crosses the *x*-axis is the next approximation x_3. We continue on, using each approximation to generate the next, until we are close enough to the zero to stop.

There is a formula for finding the $(n + 1)$st approximation x_{n+1} from the *n*th approximation x_n, which is shown in the following procedure for Newton's method.

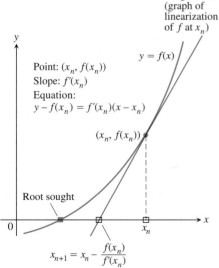

Figure 5.49 From x_n we go up to the curve and follow the tangent line down to find x_{n+1}.

Procedure for Newton's Method

1. Guess a first approximation to a solution of the equation $f(x) = 0$. A graph of $y = f(x)$ may help.
2. Use the first approximation to get a second, the second to get a third, and so on, using the formula

$$x_{n+1} = x_n - \frac{f(x_n)}{f'(x_n)}.$$

See Figure 5.49.

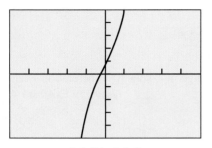

[−5, 5] by [−5, 5]

Figure 5.50 A calculator graph of $y = x^3 + 3x + 1$ suggests that -0.3 is a good first guess at the zero to begin Newton's method. (Example 13)

EXAMPLE 13 Using Newton's Method

Use Newton's method to solve $x^3 + 3x + 1 = 0$.

SOLUTION

Let $f(x) = x^3 + 3x + 1$, then $f'(x) = 3x^2 + 3$ and

$$x_{n+1} = x_n - \frac{f(x_n)}{f'(x_n)} = x_n - \frac{x_n^3 + 3x_n + 1}{3x_n^2 + 3}.$$

The graph of f in Figure 5.50 suggests that $x_1 = -0.3$ is a good first approximation to the zero of f in the interval $-1 \le x \le 0$. Then,

$$x_1 = -0.3,$$
$$x_2 = -0.322324159,$$
$$x_3 = -0.3221853603,$$
$$x_4 = -0.3221853546$$

The x_n for $n \ge 5$ all appear to equal x_4 on the calculator we used for our computations. We conclude that the solution to the equation $x^3 + 3x + 1 = 0$ is about -0.3221853546. *Now Try Exercise 53.*

Newton's Method May Fail

Newton's method does not work if $f'(x_1) = 0$. In that case, choose a new starting point.

Newton's method does not always converge. For instance (see Figure 5.51), successive approximations $r - h$ and $r + h$ can go back and forth between these two values, and no amount of iteration will bring us any closer to the zero r.

If Newton's method does converge, it converges to a zero of f. However, the method may converge to a zero that is different from the expected one if the starting value is not close enough to the zero sought. Figure 5.52 shows how this might happen.

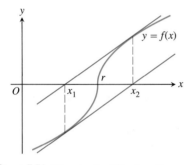

Figure 5.51 The graph of the function

$$f(x) = \begin{cases} -\sqrt{r - x}, & x < r \\ \sqrt{x - r}, & x \ge r. \end{cases}$$

If $x_1 = r - h$, then $x_2 = r + h$. Successive approximations go back and forth between these two values, and Newton's method fails to converge.

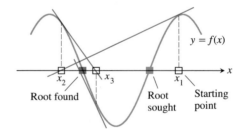

Figure 5.52 Newton's method may miss the zero you want if you start too far away.

Quick Review 5.5 *(For help, go to Sections 3.3, 4.1, and 4.4.)*

Exercise numbers with a gray background indicate problems that the authors have designed to be solved *without a calculator.*

In Exercises 1 and 2, find dy/dx.

1. $y = \sin(x^2 + 1)$ **2.** $y = \dfrac{x + \cos x}{x + 1}$

In Exercises 3 and 4, solve the equation graphically.

3. $xe^{-x} + 1 = 0$ **4.** $x^3 + 3x + 1 = 0$

In Exercises 5 and 6, let $f(x) = xe^{-x} + 1$. Write an equation for the line tangent to f at $x = c$.

5. $c = 0$ **6.** $c = -1$

7. Find where the tangent line in **(a)** Exercise 5 and **(b)** Exercise 6 crosses the x-axis.

8. Let $g(x)$ be the function whose graph is the tangent line to the graph of $f(x) = x^3 - 4x + 1$ at $x = 1$. Complete the table.

x	$f(x)$	$g(x)$
0.7		
0.8		
0.9		
1		
1.1		
1.2		
1.3		

In Exercises 9 and 10, graph $y = f(x)$ and its tangent line at $x = c$.

9. $c = 1.5$, $f(x) = \sin x$

10. $c = 4$, $f(x) = \begin{cases} -\sqrt{3 - x}, & x < 3 \\ \sqrt{x - 3}, & x \geq 3 \end{cases}$

Section 5.5 Exercises

In Exercises 1–6, **(a)** find the linearization $L(x)$ of $f(x)$ at $x = a$. **(b)** How accurate is the approximation $L(a + 0.1) \approx f(a + 0.1)$? See the comparisons following Example 1.

1. $f(x) = x^3 - 2x + 3$, $a = 2$

2. $f(x) = \sqrt{x^2 + 9}$, $a = -4$

3. $f(x) = x + \dfrac{1}{x}$, $a = 1$

4. $f(x) = \ln(x + 1)$, $a = 0$

5. $f(x) = \tan x$, $a = \pi$

6. $f(x) = \cos^{-1} x$, $a = 0$

7. Show that the linearization of $f(x) = (1 + x)^k$ at $x = 0$ is $L(x) = 1 + kx$.

8. Use the linearization $(1 + x)^k \approx 1 + kx$ to approximate the following. State how accurate your approximation is.
  (a) $(1.002)^{100}$ **(b)** $\sqrt[3]{1.009}$

In Exercises 9 and 10, use the linear approximation $(1 + x)^k \approx 1 + kx$ to find an approximation for the function $f(x)$ for values of x near zero.

9. (a) $f(x) = (1 - x)^6$ **(b)** $f(x) = \dfrac{2}{1 - x}$ **(c)** $f(x) = \dfrac{1}{\sqrt{1 + x}}$

10. (a) $f(x) = (4 + 3x)^{1/3}$ **(b)** $f(x) = \sqrt{2 + x^2}$

  (c) $f(x) = \sqrt[3]{\left(1 - \dfrac{1}{2 + x}\right)^2}$

In Exercises 11–14, approximate the root by using a linearization centered at an appropriate nearby number.

11. $\sqrt{101}$ **12.** $\sqrt[3]{26}$

13. $\sqrt[3]{998}$ **14.** $\sqrt{80}$

In Exercises 15–22, **(a)** find dy, and **(b)** evaluate dy for the given value of x and dx.

15. $y = x^3 - 3x$, $x = 2$, $dx = 0.05$

16. $y = \dfrac{2x}{1 + x^2}$, $x = -2$, $dx = 0.1$

17. $y = x^2 \ln x$, $x = 1$, $dx = 0.01$

18. $y = x\sqrt{1 - x^2}$, $x = 0$, $dx = -0.2$

19. $y = e^{\sin x}$, $x = \pi$, $dx = -0.1$

20. $y = 3 \csc\left(1 - \dfrac{x}{3}\right)$, $x = 1$, $dx = 0.1$

21. $y + xy - x = 0$, $x = 0$, $dx = 0.01$

22. $2y = x^2 - xy$, $x = 2$, $dx = -0.05$

In Exercises 23–26, find the differential.

23. $d\left(\sqrt{1 - x^2}\right)$

24. $d(e^{5x} + x^5)$

25. $d(\arctan 4x)$

26. $d(8^x + x^8)$

In Exercises 27–30, the function f changes value when x changes from a to $a + \Delta x$. Find

  (a) the true change $\Delta f = f(a + \Delta x) - f(a)$.

  (b) the estimated change $f'(a)\,\Delta x$.

  (c) the approximation error $|\Delta f - f'(a)\Delta x|$.

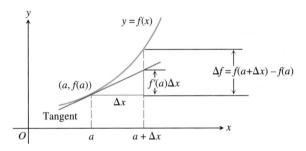

27. $f(x) = x^2 + 2x$, $a = 0$, $\Delta x = 0.1$

28. $f(x) = x^3 - x$, $a = 1$, $\Delta x = 0.1$

29. $f(x) = x^{-1}$, $a = 0.5$, $\Delta x = 0.05$

30. $f(x) = x^4$, $a = 1$, $\Delta x = 0.01$

In Exercises 31–36, write a formula that estimates the given change in volume or surface area. Then use the formula to estimate the change when the independent variable changes from 10 cm to 10.05 cm.

31. *Volume* The change in the volume $V = (4/3)\pi r^3$ of a sphere when the radius changes from a to $a + \Delta r$.

32. *Surface Area* The change in the surface area $S = 4\pi r^2$ of a sphere when the radius changes from a to $a + \Delta r$.

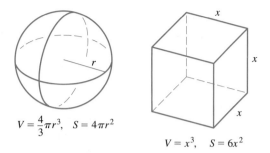

$$V = \frac{4}{3}\pi r^3, \quad S = 4\pi r^2$$

$$V = x^3, \quad S = 6x^2$$

33. Volume The change in the volume $V = x^3$ of a cube when the edge lengths change from a to $a + \Delta x$

34. Surface Area The change in the surface area $S = 6x^2$ of a cube when the edge lengths change from a to $a + \Delta x$

35. Volume The change in the volume $V = \pi r^2 h$ of a right circular cylinder when the radius changes from a to $a + \Delta r$ and the height does not change

36. Surface Area The change in the lateral surface area $S = 2\pi rh$ of a right circular cylinder when the height changes from a to $a + \Delta h$ and the radius does not change

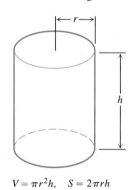

$$V = \pi r^2 h, \quad S = 2\pi rh$$

In Exercises 37–40, use differentials to estimate the maximum error in measurement resulting from the tolerance of error in the independent variable. Express answers to the nearest tenth, since that is the precision used to express the tolerance.

37. The area of a circle with radius 10 ± 0.1 in.

38. The volume of a sphere with radius 8 ± 0.3 in.

39. The volume of a cube with side 15 ± 0.2 cm

40. The area of an equilateral triangle with side 20 ± 0.5 cm

41. Linear Approximation Let f be a function with $f(0) = 1$ and $f'(x) = \cos(x^2)$.

  (a) Find the linearization of f at $x = 0$.

  (b) Estimate the value of f at $x = 0.1$.

  (c) **Writing to Learn** Do you think the actual value of f at $x = 0.1$ is greater than or less than the estimate in part (b)? Explain.

42. Expanding Circle The radius of a circle is increased from 2.00 to 2.02 m.

  (a) Estimate the resulting change in area.

  (b) Estimate as a percentage of the circle's original area.

43. Growing Tree The diameter of a tree was 10 in. During the following year, the circumference increased 2 in. About how much did the tree's diameter increase? the tree's cross-section area?

44. Percentage Error The edge of a cube is measured as 10 cm with an error of 1%. The cube's volume is to be calculated from this measurement. Estimate the percentage error in the volume calculation.

45. Tolerance About how accurately should you measure the side of a square to be sure of calculating the area to within 2% of its true value?

46. Tolerance (a) About how accurately must the interior diameter of a 10-m-high cylindrical storage tank be measured to calculate the tank's volume to within 1% of its true value?

  (b) About how accurately must the tank's exterior diameter be measured to calculate the amount of paint it will take to paint the side of the tank to within 5% of the true amount?

47. Minting Coins A manufacturer contracts to mint coins for the federal government. The coins must weigh within 0.1% of their ideal weight, so the volume must be within 0.1% of the ideal volume. Assuming the thickness of the coins does not change, what is the percentage change in the volume of the coin that would result from a 0.1% increase in the radius?

48. Tolerance The height and radius of a right circular cylinder are equal, so the cylinder's volume is $V = \pi h^3$. The volume is to be calculated with an error of no more than 1% of the true value. Find approximately the greatest error that can be tolerated in the measurement of h, expressed as a percentage of h.

49. Estimating Volume You can estimate the volume of a sphere by measuring its circumference with a tape measure, dividing by 2π to get the radius, then using the radius in the volume formula. Find how sensitive your volume estimate is to a 1/8-in. error in the circumference measurement by filling in the table below for spheres of the given sizes. Use the approximation for ΔV when filling in the last column.

Sphere Type	True Radius	Tape Error	Radius Error	Volume Error
Orange	2 in.	1/8 in.		
Melon	4 in.	1/8 in.		
Beach Ball	7 in.	1/8 in.		

50. Estimating Surface Area Change the heading in the last column of the table in Exercise 49 to "Surface Area Error" and find how sensitive the measure of surface area is to a 1/8-in. error in estimating the circumference of the sphere.

51. The Effect of Flight Maneuvers on the Heart The amount of work done by the heart's main pumping chamber, the left ventricle, is given by the equation

$$W = PV + \frac{V\delta v^2}{2g},$$

where W is the work per unit time, P is the average blood pressure, V is the volume of blood pumped out during the unit of time, δ ("delta") is the density of the blood, v is the average velocity of the exiting blood, and g is the acceleration of gravity.

When P, V, δ, and v remain constant, W becomes a function of g, and the equation takes the simplified form

$$W = a + \frac{b}{g} \quad (a, b \text{ constant}).$$

As a member of NASA's medical team, you want to know how sensitive W is to apparent changes in g caused by flight maneuvers, and this depends on the initial value of g. As part of your investigation, you decide to compare the effect on W of a given change Δg on the moon, where $g = 5.2$ ft/sec^2, with the effect the same change Δg would have on Earth, where $g = 32$ ft/sec^2. Use the simplified equation above to approximate the ratio of ΔW_{moon} to ΔW_{Earth} by finding the ratio of dW_{moon}/dg to dW_{Earth}/dg.

52. ***Measuring Acceleration of Gravity*** When the length L of a clock pendulum is held constant by controlling its temperature, the pendulum's period T depends on the acceleration of gravity g. The period will therefore vary slightly as the clock is moved from place to place on the earth's surface, depending on the change in g. By keeping track of ΔT, we can estimate the variation in g from the equation $T = 2\pi(L/g)^{1/2}$ that relates T, g, and L.

(a) With L held constant and g as the independent variable, estimate ΔT and use it to answer parts (b) and (c).

(b) **Writing to Learn** If g increases, will T increase or decrease? Will a pendulum clock speed up or slow down? Explain.

(c) A clock with a 100-cm pendulum is moved from a location where $g = 980$ cm/sec^2 to a new location. This increases the period by $\Delta T = 0.001$ sec. Approximate Δg and use it to estimate the value of g at the new location.

Using Newton's Method on Your Calculator

Here is a nice way to get your calculator to perform the calculations in Newton's method. Try it with the function $f(x) = x^3 + 3x + 1$ from Example 13.

1. Enter the function in Y1 and its derivative in Y2.

2. On the home screen, store the initial guess into x. For example, using the initial guess in Example 13, you would type $-.3 \rightarrow X$.

3. Type X−Y1/Y2 $\rightarrow$ X and press the ENTER key over and over. Watch as the numbers converge to the zero of f. When

the values stop changing, it means that your calculator has found the zero to the extent of its displayed digits, as shown in the following figure.

```
-.3→X
                          -.3
X−Y₁/Y₂→X
                   -.322324159
                   -.3221853603
                   -.3221853546
                   -.3221853546
```

4. Experiment with different initial guesses and repeat Steps 2 and 3.

5. Experiment with different functions and repeat Steps 1 through 3. Compare each final value you find with the value given by your calculator's built-in zero-finding feature.

In Exercises 53–56, use Newton's method to estimate all real solutions of the equation. Make your answers accurate to 6 decimal places.

53. $x^3 + x - 1 = 0$ 54. $x^4 + x - 3 = 0$

55. $x^2 - 2x + 1 = \sin x$ 56. $x^4 - 2 = 0$

Standardized Test Questions

You may use a graphing calculator to solve the following problems.

57. **True or False** Newton's method will not find the zero of $f(x) = x/(x^2 + 1)$ if the first guess is greater than 1. Justify your answer.

58. **True or False** If u and v are differentiable functions, then $d(uv) = du\, dv$. Justify your answer.

59. **Multiple Choice** What is the linearization of $f(x) = e^x$ at $x = 1$?

(A) $y = e$ (B) $y = ex$ (C) $y = e^x$

(D) $y = x - e$ (E) $y = e(x - 1)$

60. **Multiple Choice** If $y = \tan x$, $x = \pi$, and $dx = 0.5$, what does dy equal?

(A) -0.25 (B) -0.5 (C) 0 (D) 0.5 (E) 0.25

61. **Multiple Choice** If Newton's method is used to find the zero of $f(x) = x - x^3 + 2$, what is the third estimate if the first estimate is 1?

(A) $-\dfrac{3}{4}$ (B) $\dfrac{3}{2}$ (C) $\dfrac{8}{5}$ (D) $\dfrac{18}{11}$ (E) 3

62. **Multiple Choice** If the linearization of $y = \sqrt[3]{x}$ at $x = 64$ is used to approximate $\sqrt[3]{66}$, what is the percentage error?

(A) 0.01% (B) 0.04% (C) 0.4% (D) 1% (E) 4%

Explorations

63. ***Newton's Method*** Suppose your first guess in using Newton's method is lucky in the sense that x_1 is a root of $f(x) = 0$. What happens to x_2 and later approximations?

64. *Oscillation* Show that if $h > 0$, applying Newton's method to

$$f(x) = \begin{cases} \sqrt{x}, & x \geq 0 \\ \sqrt{-x}, & x < 0 \end{cases}$$

leads to $x_2 = -h$ if $x_1 = h$, and to $x_2 = h$ if $x_1 = -h$. Draw a picture that shows what is going on.

65. *Approximations That Get Worse and Worse* Apply Newton's method to $f(x) = x^{1/3}$ with $x_1 = 1$, and calculate x_2, x_3, x_4, and x_5. Find a formula for $|x_n|$. What happens to $|x_n|$ as $n \to \infty$? Draw a picture that shows what is going on.

66. *Quadratic Approximations*

(a) Let $Q(x) = b_0 + b_1(x - a) + b_2(x - a)^2$ be a quadratic approximation to $f(x)$ at $x = a$ with the properties:

    i. $Q(a) = f(a)$,

    ii. $Q'(a) = f'(a)$,

    iii. $Q''(a) = f''(a)$.

Determine the coefficients b_0, b_1, and b_2.

(b) Find the quadratic approximation to $f(x) = 1/(1 - x)$ at $x = 0$.

(c) Graph $f(x) = 1/(1 - x)$ and its quadratic approximation at $x = 0$. Then ZOOM IN on the two graphs at the point $(0, 1)$. Comment on what you see.

(d) Find the quadratic approximation to $g(x) = 1/x$ at $x = 1$. Graph g and its quadratic approximation together. Comment on what you see.

(e) Find the quadratic approximation to $h(x) = \sqrt{1 + x}$ at $x = 0$. Graph h and its quadratic approximation together. Comment on what you see.

(f) What are the linearizations of f, g, and h at the respective points in parts (b), (d), and (e)?

67. *Multiples of Pi* Store any number as X in your calculator. Then enter the command $X - \tan(X) \to X$ and press the ENTER key repeatedly until the displayed value stops changing. The result is always an integral multiple of π. Why is this so? [*Hint:* These are zeros of the sine function.]

Extending the Ideas

68. *Formulas for Differentials* Verify the following formulas.

(a) $d(c) = 0$ (c a constant)

(b) $d(cu) = c\,du$ (c a constant)

(c) $d(u + v) = du + dv$

(d) $d(u \cdot v) = u\,dv + v\,du$

(e) $d\left(\dfrac{u}{v}\right) = \dfrac{v\,du - u\,dv}{v^2}$

(f) $d(u^n) = nu^{n-1}\,du$

69. *The Linearization Is the Best Linear Approximation* Suppose that $y = f(x)$ is differentiable at $x = a$ and that $g(x) = m(x - a) + c$ (m and c constants). If the error $E(x) = f(x) - g(x)$ were small enough near $x = a$, we might think of using g as a linear approximation of f instead of the linearization $L(x) = f(a) + f'(a)(x - a)$. Show that if we impose on g the conditions

    i. $E(a) = 0$,

    ii. $\displaystyle\lim_{x \to a} \frac{E(x)}{x - a} = 0$,

then $g(x) = f(a) + f'(a)(x - a)$. Thus, the linearization gives the only linear approximation whose error is both zero at $x = a$ and negligible in comparison with $(x - a)$.

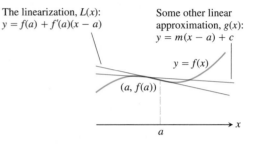

The linearization, $L(x)$:
$y = f(a) + f'(a)(x - a)$

Some other linear approximation, $g(x)$:
$y = m(x - a) + c$

$y = f(x)$

$(a, f(a))$

70. *Writing to Learn* Find the linearization of $f(x) = \sqrt{x + 1} + \sin x$ at $x = 0$. How is it related to the individual linearizations for $\sqrt{x + 1}$ and $\sin x$?

71. *Formula for Newton's Method* Derive the formula for finding the $(n + 1)$st approximation x_{n+1} from the nth approximation x_n. [*Hint:* Write the point-slope equation for the tangent line to the curve at $(x_n, f(x_n))$. See Figure 5.49 on page 245. Then set $y = 0$ and solve for x.]

72. *Bounding the Distance Between Δy and $f'(a)\,\Delta x$* We know that if $y = f(x)$, then Δy is close to $f'(a)\,\Delta x$, where $\Delta x = x - a$ and $\Delta y = f(x) - f(a)$. How close are they? In the late 1700s Joseph Louis Lagrange showed that

$$\left|\Delta y - f'(a)\Delta x\right| = \frac{1}{2}\left|f''(c)\right|(\Delta x)^2$$

for some value of c between x and a. This equality is proven in Exercise 73. While we don't know the exact value of c (if we did, this would no longer be just an approximation), we often can put an upper limit on $f''(c)$.

For the following three examples, find an upper bound on $|f''(c)|$ and use it to bound the difference $|\Delta y - f'(a)\Delta x|$ by a constant times $(\Delta x)^2$.

(a) $y = \sin x$ near $x = \pi/4$,

(b) $y = x^2$ near $x = 1$,

(c) $y = e^x$ within 0.1 unit of $x = 1$.

73. *Writing to Learn* The following steps can be used to prove Lagrange's result that if $y = f(x)$ has a continuous second derivative and we define g to be the difference between $\Delta y = f(x) - f(a)$ and $f'(a)\,\Delta x = f'(a)(x - a)$,

$$g(x) = (f(x) - f(a)) - f'(a)(x - a),$$

then there is some real number c between x and a such that $g(x) = \frac{1}{2}f''(c)(x - a)^2$. This proof assumes that $a < x$, but it is easily modified to handle the case $a > x$.

(a) Show that $g(a) = g'(a) = 0$ and $g''(x) = f''(x)$.

(b) Let A be the minimum value of $\frac{1}{2}g''(t)$ and B the maximum value of $\frac{1}{2}g''(t)$ for t in the interval $[a, x]$. Use the Intermediate Value Theorem to show that for any real number r between A and B, there is some value of c in $[a, x]$ for which $r = \frac{1}{2}g''(c)$.

(c) Explain why $g''(t) - 2A \geq 0$ and $g''(t) - 2B \leq 0$ for all t in the interval $[a, x]$.

(d) Using the fact that $g'(a) - 2A(a - a) = g'(a) - 2B(a - a) = 0$, together with Corollary 1 on page 204, prove that $g'(t) - 2A(t - a) \geq 0$ and $g'(t) - 2B(t - a) \leq 0$ for all t in $[a, x]$.

(e) Using the fact that $g(a) - A(a - a)^2 = g(a) - B(a - a)^2 = 0$, together with Corollary 1 on page 204, prove that $g(t) - A(t - a)^2 \geq 0$ and $g(t) - B(t - a)^2 \leq 0$ for all t in $[a, x]$.

(f) Show that $A \leq \dfrac{g(x)}{(x - a)^2} \leq B$ and therefore, by part (b), there is some value of c in $[a, x]$ for which

$$\frac{g(x)}{(x - a)^2} = \frac{1}{2}g''(c) = \frac{1}{2}f''(c).$$ It follows that

$$(f(x) - f(a)) - f'(a)(x - a) = g(x) = \frac{1}{2}f''(c)(x - a)^2$$

and therefore

$$|\Delta y - f'(a)\Delta x| = \frac{1}{2}|f''(c)|(\Delta x)^2.$$

5.6 | Related Rates

You will be able to solve problems involving rates of change in applied contexts.

- Development of a mathematical model
- Creation of an equation that relates the variable whose rate of change is known to the variable whose rate of change is sought
- Use of Chain Rule to relate the rates of change
- Identification of solution
- Interpretation of solution

Related Rate Equations

Suppose that a particle $P(x, y)$ is moving along a curve C in the plane so that its coordinates x and y are differentiable functions of time t. If D is the distance from the origin to P, then using the Chain Rule we can find an equation that relates dD/dt, dx/dt, and dy/dt.

$$D = \sqrt{x^2 + y^2}$$

$$\frac{dD}{dt} = \frac{1}{2}(x^2 + y^2)^{-1/2}\left(2x\frac{dx}{dt} + 2y\frac{dy}{dt}\right)$$

Any equation involving two or more variables that are differentiable functions of time t can be used to find an equation that relates their corresponding rates.

EXAMPLE 1 Finding Related Rate Equations

(a) Assume that the radius r of a sphere is a differentiable function of t and let V be the volume of the sphere. Find an equation that relates dV/dt and dr/dt.

(b) Assume that the radius r and height h of a cone are differentiable functions of t and let V be the volume of the cone. Find an equation that relates dV/dt, dr/dt, and dh/dt.

SOLUTION

(a) $V = \dfrac{4}{3}\pi r^3$ Volume formula for a sphere

$$\frac{dV}{dt} = 4\pi r^2\frac{dr}{dt}$$

(b) $V = \dfrac{\pi}{3}r^2 h$ Cone volume formula

$$\frac{dV}{dt} = \frac{\pi}{3}\left(r^2 \cdot \frac{dh}{dt} + 2r\frac{dr}{dt} \cdot h\right) = \frac{\pi}{3}\left(r^2\frac{dh}{dt} + 2rh\frac{dr}{dt}\right)$$

Now Try Exercise 3.

Solution Strategy

What has always distinguished calculus from algebra is its ability to deal with variables that change over time. Example 1 illustrates how easy it is to move from a formula relating static variables to a formula that relates their rates of change: Simply differentiate the formula implicitly with respect to t. This introduces an important category of problems called *related rate problems* that constitutes one of the most important applications of calculus.

We introduce a strategy for solving related rate problems, similar to the strategy we introduced for max-min problems earlier in this chapter.

Strategy for Solving Related Rate Problems

1. **Understand the problem.** In particular, identify the variable whose rate of change you *seek* and the variable (or variables) whose rate of change you *know*.
2. **Develop a mathematical model of the problem.** Draw a picture (many of these problems involve geometric figures) and label the parts that are important to the problem. *Be sure to distinguish constant quantities from variables that change over time.* Only constant quantities can be assigned numerical values at the start.

continued

3. **Write an equation relating the variable whose rate of change you seek with the variable(s) whose rate of change you know.** The formula is often geometric, but it could come from a scientific application.
4. **Differentiate both sides of the equation implicitly with respect to time *t*.** Be sure to follow all the differentiation rules. The Chain Rule will be especially critical, as you will be differentiating with respect to the parameter *t*.
5. **Substitute values for any quantities that depend on time.** Notice that it is only safe to do this *after* the differentiation step. Substituting too soon "freezes the picture" and makes changeable variables behave like constants, with zero derivatives.
6. **Interpret the solution.** Translate your mathematical result into the problem setting (with appropriate units) and decide whether the result makes sense.

We illustrate the strategy in Example 2.

EXAMPLE 2 A Rising Balloon

A hot-air balloon rising straight up from a level field is tracked by a range finder 500 feet from the lift-off point. At the moment the range finder's elevation angle is $\pi/4$, the angle is increasing at the rate of 0.14 radians per minute. How fast is the balloon rising at that moment?

SOLUTION

We will carefully identify the six steps of the strategy in this first example.

Step 1: Let *h* be the height of the balloon and let θ be the elevation angle.

We seek: dh/dt.

We know: $d\theta/dt = 0.14$ rad/min.

Step 2: We draw a picture (Figure 5.53). We label the horizontal distance "500 ft" because it does not change over time. We label the height "*h*" and the angle of elevation "θ." Notice that we do not label the angle "$\pi/4$," as that would freeze the picture.

Step 3: We need a formula that relates *h* and θ. Since $\dfrac{h}{500} = \tan \theta$, we get $h = 500 \tan \theta$.

Step 4: Differentiate implicitly:

$$\frac{d}{dt}(h) = \frac{d}{dt}(500 \tan \theta).$$

$$\frac{dh}{dt} = 500 \sec^2 \theta \frac{d\theta}{dt}.$$

Step 5: Let $d\theta/dt = 0.14$ and let $\theta = \pi/4$. (Note that it is now safe to specify our moment in time.)

$$\frac{dh}{dt} = 500 \sec^2\left(\frac{\pi}{4}\right)(0.14) = 500(\sqrt{2})^2(0.14) = 140.$$

Step 6: At the moment in question, the balloon is rising at the rate of 140 ft/min.

Now Try Exercise 11.

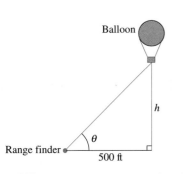

Figure 5.53 The picture shows how *h* and θ are related geometrically. We seek dh/dt when $\theta = \pi/4$ and $d\theta/dt = 0.14$ rad/min. (Example 2)

Unit Analysis in Example 2

A careful analysis of the units in Example 2 gives

$dh/dt = (500 \text{ ft})(\sqrt{2})^2 (0.14 \text{ rad/min})$

$= 140 \text{ ft} \cdot \text{rad/min}.$

Remember that radian measure is actually dimensionless, adaptable to whatever unit is applied to the "unit" circle. The linear units in Example 2 are measured in feet, so "ft • rad" is simply "ft."

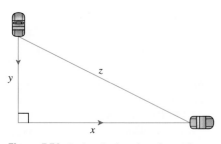

Figure 5.54 A sketch showing the variables in Example 3. We know dy/dt and dz/dt, and we seek dx/dt. The variables x, y, and z are related by the Pythagorean Theorem: $x^2 + y^2 = z^2$.

EXAMPLE 3 A Highway Chase

A police cruiser, approaching a right-angled intersection from the north, is chasing a speeding car that has turned the corner and is now moving straight east. When the cruiser is 0.6 mi north of the intersection and the car is 0.8 mi to the east, the police determine with radar that the distance between them and the car is increasing at 20 mph. If the cruiser is moving at 60 mph at the instant of measurement, what is the speed of the car?

SOLUTION

We carry out the steps of the strategy.

Let x be the distance of the speeding car from the intersection, let y be the distance of the police cruiser from the intersection, and let z be the distance between the car and the cruiser. Distances x and z are increasing, but distance y is decreasing; so dy/dt is negative.

We seek: dx/dt.

We know: $dz/dt = 20$ mph and $dy/dt = -60$ mph.

A sketch (Figure 5.54) shows that x, y, and z form three sides of a right triangle. We need to relate those three variables, so we use the Pythagorean Theorem:

$$x^2 + y^2 = z^2$$

Differentiating implicitly with respect to t, we get

$$2x\frac{dx}{dt} + 2y\frac{dy}{dt} = 2z\frac{dz}{dt}, \text{ which reduces to } x\frac{dx}{dt} + y\frac{dy}{dt} = z\frac{dz}{dt}.$$

We <u>now</u> substitute the numerical values for x, y, dz/dt, dy/dt, and z (which equals $\sqrt{x^2 + y^2}$):

$$(0.8)\frac{dx}{dt} + (0.6)(-60) = \sqrt{(0.8)^2 + (0.6)^2}(20)$$

$$(0.8)\frac{dx}{dt} - 36 = (1)(20)$$

$$\frac{dx}{dt} = 70$$

At the moment in question, the car's speed is 70 mph.   ***Now Try Exercise 13.***

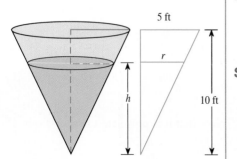

Figure 5.55 In Example 4, the cone of water is increasing in volume inside the reservoir. We know dV/dt and we seek dh/dt. Similar triangles enable us to relate V directly to h.

EXAMPLE 4 Filling a Conical Tank

Water runs into a conical tank at the rate of 9 ft³/min. The tank stands point down and has a height of 10 ft and a base radius of 5 ft. How fast is the water level rising when the water is 6 ft deep?

SOLUTION 1

We carry out the steps of the strategy. Figure 5.55 shows a partially filled conical tank. The tank itself does not change over time; what we are interested in is the changing cone of *water* inside the tank. Let V be the volume, r the radius, and h the height of the cone of water.

We seek: dh/dt.

We know: $dV/dt = 9$ ft³/min.

We need to relate V and h. The volume of the cone of water is $V = \frac{1}{3}\pi r^2 h$, but this formula also involves the variable r, whose rate of change is not given. We need to either

continued

find dr/dt (see Solution 2) or eliminate r from the equation, which we can do by using the similar triangles in Figure 5.55 to relate r and h:

$$\frac{r}{h} = \frac{5}{10}, \text{ or simply } r = \frac{h}{2}$$

Therefore,

$$V = \frac{1}{3}\pi\left(\frac{h}{2}\right)^2 h = \frac{\pi}{12}h^3.$$

Differentiate with respect to t:

$$\frac{dV}{dt} = \frac{\pi}{12} \cdot 3h^2 \frac{dh}{dt} = \frac{\pi}{4}h^2 \frac{dh}{dt}$$

Let $h = 6$ and $dV/dt = 9$; then solve for dh/dt:

$$9 = \frac{\pi}{4}(6)^2 \frac{dh}{dt}$$

$$\frac{dh}{dt} = \frac{1}{\pi} \approx 0.32$$

At the moment in question, the water level is rising at 0.32 ft/min.

SOLUTION 2

The similar triangle relationship

$$r = \frac{h}{2} \text{ also implies that } \frac{dr}{dt} = \frac{1}{2}\frac{dh}{dt}$$

and that $r = 3$ when $h = 6$. So, we could have left all three variables in the formula $V = \frac{1}{3}\pi r^2 h$ and proceeded as follows:

$$\frac{dV}{dt} = \frac{1}{3}\pi\left(2r\frac{dr}{dt}h + r^2\frac{dh}{dt}\right)$$

$$= \frac{1}{3}\pi\left(2r\left(\frac{1}{2}\frac{dh}{dt}\right)h + r^2\frac{dh}{dt}\right)$$

$$9 = \frac{1}{3}\pi\left(2(3)\left(\frac{1}{2}\frac{dh}{dt}\right)(6) + (3)^2\frac{dh}{dt}\right)$$

$$9 = 9\pi\frac{dh}{dt}$$

$$\frac{dh}{dt} = \frac{1}{\pi}$$

This is obviously more complicated than the one-variable approach. In general, it is computationally easier to simplify expressions as much as possible *before* you differentiate.   *Now Try Exercise 17.*

Simulating Related Motion

Parametric mode on a grapher can be used to simulate the motion of moving objects when the motion of each can be expressed as a function of time. In a classic related rate problem, the top end of a ladder slides vertically down a wall as the bottom end is pulled horizontally away from the wall at a steady rate. Exploration 1 shows how you can use your grapher to simulate the related movements of the two ends of the ladder.

EXPLORATION 1 The Sliding Ladder

A 10-foot ladder leans against a vertical wall. The base of the ladder is pulled away from the wall at a constant rate of 2 ft/sec.

1. Explain why the motion of the two ends of the ladder can be represented by the parametric equations given below.

$$X1T = 2T$$
$$Y1T = 0$$
$$X2T = 0$$
$$Y2T = \sqrt{10^2 - (2T)^2}$$

2. What minimum and maximum values of T make sense in this problem?

3. Put your grapher in parametric and simultaneous modes. Enter the parametric equations and change the graphing style to "0" (the little ball) if your grapher has this feature. Set Tmin=0, Tmax=5, Tstep=5/20, Xmin=−1, Xmax=17, Xscl=0, Ymin=−1, Ymax=11, and Yscl=0. You can speed up the action by making the denominator in the Tstep smaller or slow it down by making it larger.

4. Press GRAPH and watch the two ends of the ladder move as time changes. Do both ends seem to move at a constant rate?

5. To see the simulation again, enter "ClrDraw" from the DRAW menu.

6. If y represents the vertical height of the top of the ladder and x the distance of the bottom from the wall, relate y and x and find dy/dt in terms of x and y. (Remember that $dx/dt = 2$.)

7. Find dy/dt when $t = 3$ and interpret its meaning. Why is it negative?

8. In theory, how fast is the top of the ladder moving as it hits the ground?

Figure 5.56 shows you how to write a calculator program that animates the falling ladder as a line segment.

```
PROGRAM:LADDER
: For (A, 0, 5, .25)
: ClrDraw
: Line(2,2+√ (100−
(2A)²), 2+2A, 2)
: If A=0:Pause
: End
```

```
WINDOW
  Xmin=2
  Xmax=20
  Xscl=0
  Ymin=1
  Ymax=13
  Yscl=0
  Xres=1
```

Figure 5.56 This 5-step program (with the viewing window set as shown) will animate the ladder in Exploration 1. Be sure any functions in the "Y=" register are turned off. Run the program and the ladder appears against the wall; push ENTER to start the bottom moving away from the wall.

For an enhanced picture, you can insert the commands ":Pt-On(2,2+$\sqrt{(100 - (2A)^2)}$,2)" and ":Pt-On(2+2A,2,2)" on either side of the middle line of the program.

Quick Review 5.6   *(For help, go to Sections 1.1, 1.4, and 4.2.)*

Exercise numbers with a gray background indicate problems that the authors have designed to be solved *without a calculator*.

In Exercises 1 and 2, find the distance between the points A and B.

1. $A(0, 5)$, $B(7, 0)$ **2.** $A(0, a)$, $B(b, 0)$

In Exercises 3–6, find dy/dx.

3. $2xy + y^2 = x + y$

4. $x \sin y = 1 - xy$

5. $x^2 = \tan y$ **6.** $\ln (x + y) = 2x$

In Exercises 7 and 8, find a parametrization for the line segment with endpoints A and B.

7. $A(-2, 1)$, $B(4, -3)$ **8.** $A(0, -4)$, $B(5, 0)$

In Exercises 9 and 10, let $x = 2 \cos t$, $y = 2 \sin t$. Find a parameter interval that produces the indicated portion of the graph.

9. The portion in the second and third quadrants, including the points on the axes.

10. The portion in the fourth quadrant, including the points on the axes.

Section 5.6 Exercises

In Exercises 1–41, assume all variables are differentiable functions of t.

1. *Area* The radius r and area A of a circle are related by the equation $A = \pi r^2$. Write an equation that relates dA/dt to dr/dt.

2. *Surface Area* The radius r and surface area S of a sphere are related by the equation $S = 4\pi r^2$. Write an equation that relates dS/dt to dr/dt.

3. *Volume* The radius r, height h, and volume V of a right circular cylinder are related by the equation $V = \pi r^2 h$.

(a) How is dV/dt related to dh/dt if r is constant?

(b) How is dV/dt related to dr/dt if h is constant?

(c) How is dV/dt related to dr/dt and dh/dt if neither r nor h is constant?

4. *Electrical Power* The power P (watts) of an electric circuit is related to the circuit's resistance R (ohms) and current I (amperes) by the equation $P = RI^2$.

(a) How is dP/dt related to dR/dt and dI/dt?

(b) How is dR/dt related to dI/dt if P is constant?

5. *Diagonals* If x, y, and z are lengths of the edges of a rectangular box, the common length of the box's diagonals is $s = \sqrt{x^2 + y^2 + z^2}$. How is ds/dt related to dx/dt, dy/dt, and dz/dt?

6. *Area* If a and b are the lengths of two sides of a triangle, and θ the measure of the included angle, the area A of the triangle is $A = (1/2) ab \sin \theta$. How is dA/dt related to da/dt, db/dt, and $d\theta/dt$?

7. *Changing Voltage* The voltage V (volts), current I (amperes), and resistance R (ohms) of an electric circuit like the one shown here are related by the equation $V = IR$. Suppose that V is increasing at the rate of 1 volt/sec while I is decreasing at the rate of $1/3$ amp/sec. Let t denote time in sec.

(a) What is the value of dV/dt?

(b) What is the value of dI/dt?

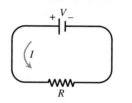

(c) Write an equation that relates dR/dt to dV/dt and dI/dt.

(d) **Writing to Learn** Find the rate at which R is changing when $V = 12$ volts and $I = 2$ amps. Is R increasing or decreasing? Explain.

8. *Heating a Plate* When a circular plate of metal is heated in an oven, its radius increases at the rate of 0.01 cm/sec. At what rate is the plate's area increasing when the radius is 50 cm?

9. *Changing Dimensions in a Rectangle* The length l of a rectangle is decreasing at the rate of 2 cm/sec while the width w is increasing at the rate of 2 cm/sec. When $l = 12$ cm and $w = 5$ cm, find the rates of change of

(a) the area,   (b) the perimeter, and

(c) the length of a diagonal of the rectangle.

(d) **Writing to Learn** Which of these quantities are decreasing, and which are increasing? Explain.

10. *Changing Dimensions in a Rectangular Box* Suppose that the edge lengths x, y, and z of a closed rectangular box are changing at the following rates:

$$\frac{dx}{dt} = 1 \text{ m/sec}, \quad \frac{dy}{dt} = -2 \text{ m/sec}, \quad \frac{dz}{dt} = 1 \text{ m/sec}$$

Find the rates at which the box's **(a)** volume, **(b)** surface area, and **(c)** diagonal length $s = \sqrt{x^2 + y^2 + z^2}$ are changing at the instant when $x = 4$, $y = 3$, and $z = 2$.

11. *Inflating Balloon* A spherical balloon is inflated with helium at the rate of 100π ft³/min.

(a) How fast is the balloon's radius increasing at the instant the radius is 5 ft?

(b) How fast is the surface area increasing at that instant?

12. *Growing Raindrop* Suppose that a droplet of mist is a perfect sphere and that, through condensation, the droplet picks up moisture at a rate proportional to its surface area. Show that under these circumstances the droplet's radius increases at a constant rate.

13. *Air Traffic Control* An airplane is flying at an altitude of 7 mi and passes directly over a radar antenna as shown in the figure. When the plane is 10 mi from the antenna ($s = 10$), the radar detects that the distance s is changing at the rate of 300 mph. What is the speed of the airplane at that moment?

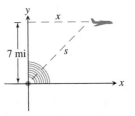

14. *Flying a Kite* Inge flies a kite at a height of 300 ft, the wind carrying the kite horizontally away at a rate of 25 ft/sec. How fast must she let out the string when the kite is 500 ft away from her?

15. *Boring a Cylinder* The mechanics at Lincoln Automotive are reboring a 6-in.-deep cylinder to fit a new piston. The machine they are using increases the cylinder's radius one-thousandth of an inch every 3 min. How rapidly is the cylinder volume increasing when the bore (diameter) is 3.800 in.?

16. *Growing Sand Pile* Sand falls from a conveyor belt at the rate of 10 m³/min onto the top of a conical pile. The height of the pile is always three-eighths of the base diameter. How fast are the **(a)** height and **(b)** radius changing when the pile is 4 m high? Give your answer in cm/min.

17. *Draining Conical Reservoir* Water is flowing at the rate of 50 m³/min from a concrete conical reservoir (vertex down) of base radius 45 m and height 6 m. **(a)** How fast is the water level falling when the water is 5 m deep? **(b)** How fast is the radius of the water's surface changing at that moment? Give your answer in cm/min.

18. *Draining Hemispherical Reservoir* Water is flowing at the rate of 6 m³/min from a reservoir shaped like a hemispherical bowl of radius 13 m, shown here in profile. Answer the following questions given that the volume of water in a hemispherical bowl of radius R is $V = (\pi/3)y^2(3R - y)$ when the water is y units deep.

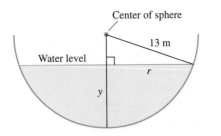

(a) At what rate is the water level changing when the water is 8 m deep?

(b) What is the radius r of the water's surface when the water is y m deep?

(c) At what rate is the radius r changing when the water is 8 m deep?

19. *Sliding Ladder* A 13-ft ladder is leaning against a house (see figure) when its base starts to slide away. By the time the base is 12 ft from the house, the base is moving at the rate of 5 ft/sec.

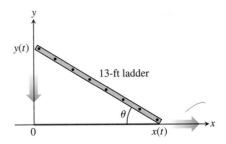

(a) How fast is the top of the ladder sliding down the wall at that moment?

(b) At what rate is the area of the triangle formed by the ladder, wall, and ground changing at that moment?

(c) At what rate is the angle θ between the ladder and the ground changing at that moment?

20. *Filling a Trough* A trough is 15 ft long and 4 ft across the top, as shown in the figure. Its ends are isosceles triangles with height 3 ft. Water runs into the trough at the rate of 2.5 ft³/min. How fast is the water level rising when it is 2 ft deep?

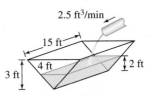

21. *Hauling in a Dinghy* A dinghy is pulled toward a dock by a rope from the bow through a ring on the dock 6 ft above the bow, as shown in the figure. The rope is hauled in at the rate of 2 ft/sec.

(a) How fast is the boat approaching the dock when 10 ft of rope are out?

(b) At what rate is angle θ changing at that moment?

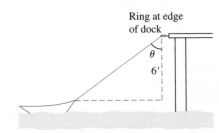

22. *Rising Balloon* A balloon is rising vertically above a level, straight road at a constant rate of 1 ft/sec. Just when the balloon is 65 ft above the ground, a bicycle moving at a constant rate of 17 ft/sec passes under it. How fast is the distance between the bicycle and balloon increasing 3 sec later (see figure)?

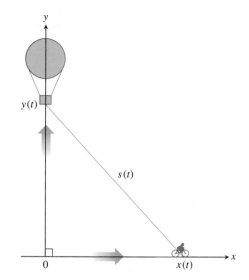

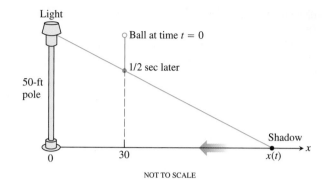

NOT TO SCALE

In Exercises 23 and 24, a particle is moving along the curve $y = f(x)$.

23. Let $y = f(x) = \dfrac{10}{1 + x^2}$.

If $dx/dt = 3$ cm/sec, find dy/dt at the point where

(a) $x = -2$. **(b)** $x = 0$. **(c)** $x = 20$.

24. Let $y = f(x) = x^3 - 4x$.

If $dx/dt = -2$ cm/sec, find dy/dt at the point where

(a) $x = -3$. **(b)** $x = 1$. **(c)** $x = 4$.

25. *Particle Motion* A particle moves along the parabola $y = x^2$ in the first quadrant in such a way that its x-coordinate (in meters) increases at a constant rate of 10 m/sec. How fast is the angle of inclination θ of the line joining the particle to the origin changing when $x = 3$?

26. *Particle Motion* A particle moves from right to left along the parabolic curve $y = \sqrt{-x}$ in such a way that its x-coordinate (in meters) decreases at the rate of 8 m/sec. How fast is the angle of inclination θ of the line joining the particle to the origin changing when $x = -4$?

27. *Melting Ice* A spherical iron ball is coated with a layer of ice of uniform thickness. If the ice melts at the rate of 8 mL/min, how fast is the outer surface area of ice decreasing when the outer diameter (ball plus ice) is 20 cm?

28. *Particle Motion* A particle $P(x, y)$ is moving in the coordinate plane in such a way that $dx/dt = -1$ m/sec and $dy/dt = -5$ m/sec. How fast is the particle's distance from the origin changing as it passes through the point $(5, 12)$?

29. *Moving Shadow* A man 6 ft tall walks at the rate of 5 ft/sec toward a streetlight that is 16 ft above the ground. At what rate is the length of his shadow changing when he is 10 ft from the base of the light?

30. *Moving Shadow* A light shines from the top of a pole 50 ft high. A ball is dropped from the same height from a point 30 ft away from the light, as shown below. How fast is the ball's shadow moving along the ground 1/2 sec later? (Assume the ball falls a distance $s = 16t^2$ in t sec.)

31. *Moving Race Car* You are videotaping a race from a stand 132 ft from the track, following a car that is moving at 180 mph (264 ft/sec), as shown in the figure. About how fast will your camera angle θ be changing when the car is right in front of you? a half second later?

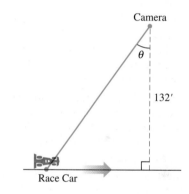

32. *Speed Trap* A highway patrol airplane flies 3 mi above a level, straight road at a constant rate of 120 mph. The pilot sees an oncoming car and with radar determines that at the instant the line-of-sight distance from plane to car is 5 mi the line-of-sight distance is decreasing at the rate of 160 mph. Find the car's speed along the highway.

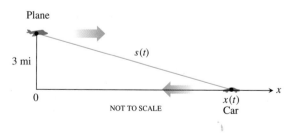

NOT TO SCALE

33. *Building's Shadow* On a morning of a day when the sun will pass directly overhead, the shadow of an 80-ft building on level ground is 60 ft long, as shown in the figure. At the moment in question, the angle θ the sun makes with the ground is increasing at the rate of 0.27°/min. At what rate is the shadow length decreasing? Express your answer in in./min, to the nearest tenth. (Remember to use radians.)

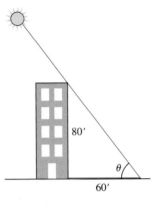

34. *Walkers* A and B are walking on straight streets that meet at right angles. A approaches the intersection at 2 m/sec and B moves away from the intersection at 1 m/sec, as shown in the figure. At what rate is the angle θ changing when A is 10 m from the intersection and B is 20 m from the intersection? Express your answer in degrees per second to the nearest degree.

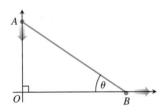

35. *Moving Ships* Two ships are steaming away from a point O along routes that make a 120° angle. Ship A moves at 14 knots (nautical miles per hour; a nautical mile is 2000 yards). Ship B moves at 21 knots. How fast are the ships moving apart when $OA = 5$ and $OB = 3$ nautical miles?

Standardized Test Questions

You may use a graphing calculator to solve the following problems.

36. True or False If the radius of a circle is expanding at a constant rate, then its circumference is increasing at a constant rate. Justify your answer.

37. True or False If the radius of a circle is expanding at a constant rate, then its area is increasing at a constant rate. Justify your answer.

38. Multiple Choice If the volume of a cube is increasing at 24 in³/min and each edge of the cube is increasing at 2 in./min, what is the length of each edge of the cube?

(A) 2 in.   (B) $2\sqrt{2}$ in.   (C) $\sqrt[3]{12}$ in.   (D) 4 in.   (E) 8 in.

39. Multiple Choice If the volume of a cube is increasing at 24 in³/min and the surface area of the cube is increasing at 12 in²/ min, what is the length of each edge of the cube?

(A) 2 in.   (B) $2\sqrt{2}$ in.   (C) $\sqrt[3]{12}$ in.   (D) 4 in.   (E) 8 in.

40. Multiple Choice A particle is moving around the unit circle (the circle of radius 1 centered at the origin). At the point $(0.6, 0.8)$ the particle has horizontal velocity $dx/dt = 3$. What is its vertical velocity dy/dt at that point?

(A) −3.875   (B) −3.75   (C) −2.25   (D) 3.75   (E) 3.875

41. Multiple Choice A cylindrical rubber cord is stretched at a constant rate of 2 cm per second. Assuming the radius is the same along the entire length and its volume does not change, how fast is its radius shrinking when its length is 100 cm and its radius is 1 cm?

(A) 0 cm/sec   (B) 0.01 cm/sec   (C) 0.02 cm/sec

(D) 2 cm/sec   (E) 3.979 cm/sec

Explorations

42. Making Coffee Coffee is draining from a conical filter into a cylindrical coffeepot at the rate of 10 in³/min.

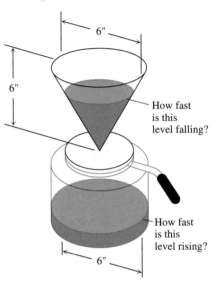

(a) How fast is the level in the pot rising when the coffee in the cone is 5 in. deep?

(b) How fast is the level in the cone falling at that moment?

43. *Cost, Revenue, and Profit* A company can manufacture x items at a cost of $c(x)$ dollars, a sales revenue of $r(x)$ dollars, and a profit of $p(x) = r(x) - c(x)$ dollars (all amounts in thousands). Find dc/dt, dr/dt, and dp/dt for the following values of x and dx/dt.

(a) $r(x) = 9x$, $c(x) = x^3 - 6x^2 + 15x$,
and $dx/dt = 0.1$ when $x = 2$.

(b) $r(x) = 70x$, $c(x) = x^3 - 6x^2 + 45/x$,
and $dx/dt = 0.05$ when $x = 1.5$.

44. Group Activity *Cardiac Output* In the late 1860s, Adolf Fick, a professor of physiology in the Faculty of Medicine in Würtzberg, Germany, developed one of the methods we use today for measuring how much blood your heart pumps in a minute. Your cardiac output as you read this sentence is probably about 7 liters a minute. At rest it is likely to be a bit under 6 L/min. If you are a trained marathon runner running a marathon, your cardiac output can be as high as 30 L/min.

Your cardiac output can be calculated with the formula

$$y = \frac{Q}{D},$$

where Q is the number of milliliters of CO_2 you exhale in a minute and D is the difference between the CO_2 concentration (mL/L) in the blood pumped to the lungs and the CO_2 concentration in the blood returning from the lungs. With $Q = 233$ mL/min and $D = 97 - 56 = 41$ mL/L,

$$y = \frac{233 \text{ mL/min}}{41 \text{ mL/L}} \approx 5.68 \text{ L/min},$$

fairly close to the 6 L/min that most people have at basal (resting) conditions. (Data courtesy of J. Kenneth Herd, M.D., Quillan College of Medicine, East Tennessee State University.)

Suppose that when $Q = 233$ and $D = 41$, we also know that D is decreasing at the rate of 2 units a minute but that Q remains unchanged. What is happening to the cardiac output?

Extending the Ideas

45. *Motion Along a Circle* A wheel of radius 2 ft makes 8 revolutions about its center every second.

(a) Explain how the parametric equations

$$x = 2 \cos \theta, \quad y = 2 \sin \theta$$

can be used to represent the motion of the wheel.

(b) Express θ as a function of time t.

(c) Find the rate of horizontal movement and the rate of vertical movement of a point on the edge of the wheel when it is at the position given by $\theta = \pi/4, \pi/2$, and π.

46. *Ferris Wheel* A Ferris wheel with radius 30 ft makes one revolution every 10 sec.

(a) Assume that the center of the Ferris wheel is located at the point $(0, 40)$, and write parametric equations to model its motion. (*Hint:* See Exercise 45.)

(b) At $t = 0$ the point P on the Ferris wheel is located at $(30, 40)$. Find the rate of horizontal movement, and the rate of vertical movement of the point P when $t = 5$ sec and $t = 8$ sec.

47. *Industrial Production* (a) Economists often use the expression "rate of growth" in relative rather than absolute terms. For example, let $u = f(t)$ be the number of people in the labor force at time t in a given industry. (We treat this function as though it were differentiable even though it is an integer-valued step function.)

Let $v = g(t)$ be the average production per person in the labor force at time t. The total production is then $y = uv$. If the labor force is growing at the rate of 4% per year $(du/dt = 0.04u)$ and the production per worker is growing at the rate of 5% per year $(dv/dt = 0.05v)$, find the rate of growth of the total production, y.

(b) Suppose that the labor force in part (a) is decreasing at the rate of 2% per year while the production per person is increasing at the rate of 3% per year. Is the total production increasing, or is it decreasing, and at what rate?

Quick Quiz for AP* Preparation: Sections 5.4–5.6

You may use a graphing calculator to solve the following problems.

1. Multiple Choice If Newton's method is used to approximate the real root of $x^3 + 2x - 1 = 0$, what would the third approximation, x_3, be if the first approximation is $x_1 = 1$?

(A) 0.453   (B) 0.465   (C) 0.495   (D) 0.600   (E) 1.977

2. Multiple Choice The sides of a right triangle with legs x and y and hypotenuse z increase in such a way that $dz/dt = 1$ and $dx/dt = 3\ dy/dt$. At the instant when $x = 4$ and $y = 3$, what is dx/dt?

(A) $\dfrac{1}{3}$ (B) 1   (C) 2   (D) $\sqrt{5}$ (E) 5

3. Multiple Choice An observer 70 meters south of a railroad crossing watches an eastbound train traveling at 60 meters per second. At how many meters per second is the train moving away from the observer 4 seconds after it passes through the intersection?

(A) 57.60   (B) 57.88   (C) 59.20   (D) 60.00   (E) 67.40

4. Free Response (a) Approximate $\sqrt{26}$ by using the linearization of $y = \sqrt{x}$ at the point $(25, 5)$. Show the computation that leads to your conclusion.

(b) Approximate $\sqrt{26}$ by using a first guess of 5 and one iteration of Newton's method to approximate the zero of $x^2 - 26$. Show the computation that leads to your conclusion.

(c) Approximate $\sqrt[3]{26}$ by using an appropriate linearization. Show the computation that leads to your conclusion.

CHAPTER 5 **Key Terms**

absolute change (p. 243)

absolute extrema (p. 193)

absolute maximum value (p. 193)

absolute minimum value (p. 193)

antiderivative (p. 206)

antidifferentiation (p. 206)

arithmetic mean (p. 210)

average cost (p. 229)

center of linear approximation (p. 238)

concave down (p. 213)

concave up (p. 213)

Concavity Test (p. 214)

critical point (p. 196)

decreasing function (p. 204)

differential (p. 241)

differential estimate of change (p. 242)

differential of a function (p. 241)

extrema (p. 193)

Extreme Value Theorem (p. 194)

First Derivative Test (p. 211)

First Derivative Test for Local Extrema (p. 211)

geometric mean (p. 210)

global maximum value (p. 193)

global minimum value (p. 193)

increasing function (p. 204)

linear approximation (p. 238)

linearization (p. 238)

local linearity (p. 238)

local maximum value (p. 195)

local minimum value (p. 195)

marginal analysis (p. 228)

marginal cost and revenue (p. 228)

Mean Value Theorem (p. 202)

monotonic function (p. 204)

Newton's method (p. 245)

optimization (p. 224)

percentage change (p. 243)

point of inflection (p. 214)

profit (p. 227)

quadratic approximation (p. 250)

related rates (p. 252)

relative change (p. 243)

relative extrema (p. 195)

Rolle's Theorem (p. 202)

Second Derivative Test for Local Extrema (p. 217)

sensitivity (p. 242)

standard linear approximation (p. 238)

stationary point (p. 196)

CHAPTER 5 Review Exercises

Exercise numbers with a gray background indicate problems that the authors have designed to be solved *without a calculator.*

The collection of exercises marked in red could be used as a chapter test.

In Exercises 1 and 2, use analytic methods to find the global extreme values of the function on the interval and state where they occur.

1. $y = x\sqrt{2-x}$, $-2 \le x \le 2$

2. $y = x^3 - 9x^2 - 21x - 11$, $-\infty < x < \infty$

In Exercises 3 and 4, use analytic methods. Find the intervals on which the function is

   (a) increasing,   **(b)** decreasing,

   (c) concave up,   **(d)** concave down.

Then find any

   (e) local extreme values,   **(f)** inflection points.

3. $y = x^2 e^{1/x^2}$ **4.** $y = x\sqrt{4-x^2}$

In Exercises 5–16, use analytic methods to find the intervals on which the function is

   (a) increasing,   **(b)** decreasing,

   (c) concave up,   **(d)** concave down.

Support your answers graphically. Then find any

   (e) local extreme values,   **(f)** inflection points.

5. $y = 1 + x - x^2 - x^4$ **6.** $y = e^{x-1} - x$

7. $y = \dfrac{1}{\sqrt[4]{1-x^2}}$ **8.** $y = \dfrac{x}{x^3 - 1}$

9. $y = \cos^{-1} x$ **10.** $y = \dfrac{x}{x^2 + 2x + 3}$

11. $y = \ln|x|$, $-2 \le x \le 2$, $x \ne 0$

12. $y = \sin 3x + \cos 4x$, $0 \le x \le 2\pi$

13. $y = \begin{cases} e^{-x}, & x \le 0 \\ 4x - x^3, & x > 0 \end{cases}$

14. $y = -x^5 + \dfrac{7}{3}x^3 + 5x^2 + 4x + 2$

15. $y = x^{4/5}(2 - x)$

16. $y = \dfrac{5 - 4x + 4x^2 - x^3}{x - 2}$

In Exercises 17 and 18, use the derivative of the function $y = f(x)$ to find the points at which f has a

   (a) local maximum,   **(b)** local minimum, or

   (c) point of inflection.

17. $y' = 6(x + 1)(x - 2)^2$ **18.** $y' = 6(x + 1)(x - 2)$

In Exercises 19–22, find all possible functions with the given derivative.

19. $f'(x) = x^{-5} + e^{-x}$ **20.** $f'(x) = \sec x \tan x$

21. $f'(x) = \dfrac{2}{x} + x^2 + 1$, $x > 0$ **22.** $f'(x) = \sqrt{x} + \dfrac{1}{\sqrt{x}}$

In Exercises 23 and 24, find the function with the given derivative whose graph passes through the point P.

23. $f'(x) = \sin x + \cos x$, $P(\pi, 3)$

24. $f'(x) = x^{1/3} + x^2 + x + 1$, $P(1, 0)$

In Exercises 25 and 26, the velocity v or acceleration a of a particle is given. Find the particle's position s at time t.

25. $v = 9.8t + 5$, $s = 10$ when $t = 0$

26. $a = 32$, $v = 20$ and $s = 5$ when $t = 0$

In Exercises 27–30, find the linearization $L(x)$ of $f(x)$ at $x = a$.

27. $f(x) = \tan x$, $a = -\pi/4$ **28.** $f(x) = \sec x$, $a = \pi/4$

29. $f(x) = \dfrac{1}{1 + \tan x}$, $a = 0$ **30.** $f(x) = e^x + \sin x$, $a = 0$

In Exercises 31–34, use the graph to answer the questions.

31. Identify any global extreme values of f and the values of x at which they occur.

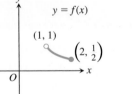

Figure for Exercise 31

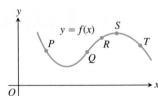

Figure for Exercise 32

32. At which of the five points on the graph of $y = f(x)$ shown here

(a) are y' and y'' both negative?

(b) is y' negative and y'' positive?

33. Estimate the intervals on which the function $y = f(x)$ is (a) increasing; (b) decreasing. (c) Estimate any local extreme values of the function and where they occur.

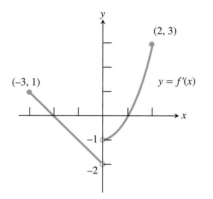

34. Here is the graph of the fruit fly population from Section 2.4, Example 2. On approximately what day did the population's growth rate change from increasing to decreasing?

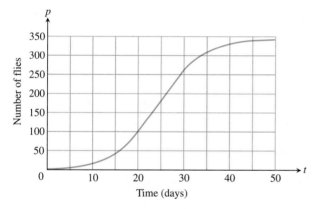

Time (days)

35. *Connecting f and f'* The graph of f' is shown in Exercise 33. Sketch a possible graph of f given that it is continuous with domain $[-3, 2]$ and $f(-3) = 0$.

36. *Connecting f, f', and f''* The function f is continuous on $[0, 3]$ and satisfies the following.

x	0	1	2	3
f	0	-2	0	3
f'	-3	0	does not exist	4
f''	0	1	does not exist	0

x	$0 < x < 1$	$1 < x < 2$	$2 < x < 3$
f	$-$	$-$	$+$
f'	$-$	$+$	$+$
f''	$+$	$+$	$+$

(a) Find the absolute extrema of f and where they occur.

(b) Find any points of inflection.

(c) Sketch a possible graph of f.

37. *Mean Value Theorem* Let $f(x) = x \ln x$.

(a) **Writing to Learn** Show that f satisfies the hypotheses of the Mean Value Theorem on the interval $[a, b] = [0.5, 3]$.

(b) Find the value(s) of c in (a, b) for which

$$f'(c) = \frac{f(b) - f(a)}{b - a}.$$

(c) Write an equation for the secant line AB where $A = (a, f(a))$ and $B = (b, f(b))$.

(d) Write an equation for the tangent line that is parallel to the secant line AB.

38. *Motion Along a Line* A particle is moving along a line with position function $s(t) = 3 + 4t - 3t^2 - t^3$. Find the (a) velocity and (b) acceleration, and (c) describe the motion of the particle for $t \geq 0$.

39. *Approximating Functions* Let f be a function with $f'(x) = \sin x^2$ and $f(0) = -1$.

(a) Find the linearization of f at $x = 0$.

(b) Approximate the value of f at $x = 0.1$.

(c) **Writing to Learn** Is the actual value of f at $x = 0.1$ greater than or less than the approximation in (b)?

40. *Differentials* Let $y = x^2 e^{-x}$. Find (a) dy and (b) evaluate dy for $x = 1$ and $dx = 0.01$.

41. *Newton's Method* Use Newton's method to estimate all real solutions to $2 \cos x - \sqrt{1 + x} = 0$. State your answers accurate to 6 decimal places.

42. *Rocket Launch* A rocket lifts off the surface of Earth with a constant acceleration of 20 m/sec². How fast will the rocket be going 1 min later?

43. *Launching on Mars* The acceleration of gravity near the surface of Mars is 3.72 m/sec². If a rock is blasted straight up from the surface with an initial velocity of 93 m/sec (about 208 mph), how high does it go?

44. *Area of Sector* If the perimeter of the circular sector shown here is fixed at 100 ft, what values of r and s will give the sector the greatest area?

45. *Area of Triangle* An isosceles triangle has its vertex at the origin and its base parallel to the x-axis with the vertices above the axis on the curve $y = 27 - x^2$. Find the largest area the triangle can have.

46. *Storage Bin* Find the dimensions of the largest open-top storage bin with a square base and vertical sides that can be made from 108 ft² of sheet steel. (Neglect the thickness of the steel and assume that there is no waste.)

47. *Designing a Vat* You are to design an open-top rectangular stainless-steel vat. It is to have a square base and a volume of 32 ft³, to be welded from quarter-inch plate, and weigh no more than necessary. What dimensions do you recommend?

48. *Inscribing a Cylinder* Find the height and radius of the largest right circular cylinder that can be put into a sphere of radius $\sqrt{3}$, as described in the figure.

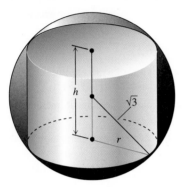

49. *Cone in a Cone* The figure shows two right circular cones, one upside down inside the other. The two bases are parallel, and the vertex of the smaller cone lies at the center of the larger cone's base. What values of r and h will give the smaller cone the largest possible volume?

50. *Box with Lid* Repeat Exercise 18 of Section 5.4 but this time remove the two equal squares from the corners of a 15-in. side.

51. *Inscribing a Rectangle* A rectangle is inscribed under one arch of $y = 8 \cos{(0.3x)}$ with its base on the x-axis and its upper two vertices on the curve symmetric about the y-axis. What is the largest area the rectangle can have?

52. *Oil Refinery* A drilling rig 12 mi offshore is to be connected by a pipe to a refinery onshore, 20 mi down the coast from the rig, as shown in the figure. If underwater pipe costs \$40,000 per mile and land-based pipe costs \$30,000 per mile, what values of x and y give the least expensive connection?

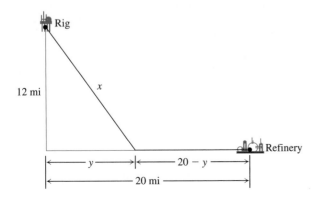

53. *Designing an Athletic Field* An athletic field is to be built in the shape of a rectangle x units long capped by semicircular regions of radius r at the two ends. The field is to be bounded by a 400-m running track. What values of x and r will give the rectangle the largest possible area?

54. *Manufacturing Tires* Your company can manufacture x hundred grade A tires and y hundred grade B tires a day, where $0 \le x \le 4$ and

$$y = \frac{40 - 10x}{5 - x}.$$

Your profit on a grade A tire is twice your profit on a grade B tire. What is the most profitable number of each kind to make?

55. *Particle Motion* The positions of two particles on the s-axis are $s_1 = \cos{t}$ and $s_2 = \cos{(t + \pi/4)}$.

(a) What is the farthest apart the particles ever get? 0.765 unit

(b) When do the particles collide?

56. *Open-top Box* An open-top rectangular box is constructed from a 10- by 16-in. piece of cardboard by cutting squares of equal side length from the corners and folding up the sides. Find analytically the dimensions of the box of largest volume and the maximum volume. Support your answers graphically.

57. *Changing Area* The radius of a circle is changing at the rate of $-2/\pi$ m/sec. At what rate is the circle's area changing when $r = 10$ m?

58. *Particle Motion* The coordinates of a particle moving in the plane are differentiable functions of time t with $dx/dt = -1$ m/sec and $dy/dt = -5$ m/sec. How fast is the particle approaching the origin as it passes through the point $(5, 12)$?

59. *Changing Cube* The volume of a cube is increasing at the rate of 1200 cm³/min at the instant its edges are 20 cm long. At what rate are the edges changing at that instant?

60. *Particle Motion* A point moves smoothly along the curve $y = x^{3/2}$ in the first quadrant in such a way that its distance from the origin increases at the constant rate of 11 units per second. Find dx/dt when $x = 3$.

61. *Draining Water* Water drains from the conical tank shown in the figure at the rate of 5 ft³/min.

(a) What is the relation between the variables h and r?

(b) How fast is the water level dropping when $h = 6$ ft?

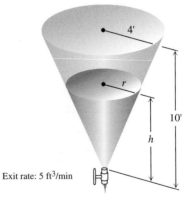

Exit rate: 5 ft³/min

62. *Stringing Telephone Cable* As telephone cable is pulled from a large spool to be strung from the telephone poles along a street, it unwinds from the spool in layers of constant radius, as suggested in the figure. If the truck pulling the cable moves at a constant rate of 6 ft/sec, use the equation $s = r\theta$ to find how fast (in rad/sec) the spool is turning when the layer of radius 1.2 ft is being unwound.

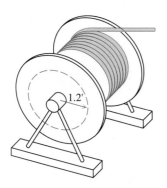

63. *Throwing Dirt* You sling a shovelful of dirt up from the bottom of a 17-ft hole with an initial velocity of 32 ft/sec. Is that enough speed to get the dirt out of the hole, or had you better duck?

64. *Estimating Change* Write a formula that estimates the change that occurs in the volume of a right circular cone (see figure) when the radius changes from a to $a + \Delta r$ and the height does not change.

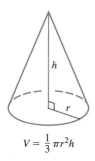

$$V = \frac{1}{3}\pi r^2 h$$

65. *Controlling Error*

(a) How accurately should you measure the edge of a cube to be reasonably sure of calculating the cube's surface area with an error of no more than 2%?

(b) Suppose the edge is measured with the accuracy required in part (a). About how accurately can the cube's volume be calculated from the edge measurement? To find out, estimate the percentage error in the volume calculation that might result from using the edge measurement.

66. *Compounding Error* The circumference of the equator of a sphere is measured as 10 cm with a possible error of 0.4 cm. This measurement is used to calculate the radius. The radius is then used to calculate the surface area and volume of the sphere. Estimate the percentage errors in the calculated values of **(a)** the radius, **(b)** the surface area, and **(c)** the volume.

67. *Finding Height* To find the height of a lamppost (see figure), you stand a 6-ft pole 20 ft from the lamp and measure the length a of its shadow, finding it to be 15 ft, give or take an inch. Calculate the height of the lamppost using the value $a = 15$, and estimate the possible error in the result.

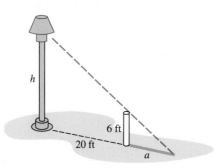

68. *Decreasing Function* Show that the function $y = \sin^2 x - 3x$ decreases on every interval in its domain.

AP* Examination Preparation

69. The accompanying figure shows the graph of the derivative of a function f. The domain of f is the closed interval $[-3, 3]$.

(a) For what values of x in the open interval $(-3, 3)$ does f have a relative maximum? Justify your answer.

(b) For what values of x in the open interval $(-3, 3)$ does f have a relative minimum? Justify your answer.

(c) For what values of x is the graph of f concave up? Justify your answer.

(d) Suppose $f(-3) = 0$. Sketch a possible graph of f on the domain $[-3, 3]$.

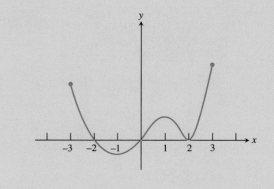

continued

70. The volume V of a cone $\left(V = \frac{1}{3}\pi r^2 h\right)$ is increasing at the rate of 4π cubic inches per second. At the instant when the radius of the cone is 2 inches, its volume is 8π cubic inches and the radius is increasing at $1/3$ inch per second.

(a) At the instant when the radius of the cone is 2 inches, what is the rate of change of the area of its base?

(b) At the instant when the radius of the cone is 2 inches, what is the rate of change of its height h?

(c) At the instant when the radius of the cone is 2 inches, what is the instantaneous rate of change of the area of its base with respect to its height h?

71. A piece of wire 60 inches long is cut into six sections, two of length a and four of length b. Each of the two sections of length a is bent into the form of a circle, and the circles are then joined by the four sections of length b to make a frame for a model of a right circular cylinder, as shown in the accompanying figure.

(a) Find the values of a and b that will make the cylinder of maximum volume.

(b) Use differential calculus to justify your answer in part (a).

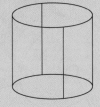

CHAPTER

6

The Definite Integral

6.1 Estimating with Finite Sums

6.2 Definite Integrals

6.3 Definite Integrals and Antiderivatives

6.4 Fundamental Theorem of Calculus

6.5 Trapezoidal Rule

Wind speeds usually follow a Weibull distribution that rises quickly, then trails off (see graph). A typical wind turbine can start producing power with winds of around 7 mph, and achieves peak output with wind speeds between 30 and 55 mph. The average wind speed is defined by

$$A = \frac{k}{\lambda^k} \int_0^{100} x^k e^{-(x/\lambda)^k} dx,$$

(where $k > 0$ is the *shape parameter* and $\lambda > 0$ is the *scale parameter*). How would changes in the values of k and λ affect average wind speed? Section 6.4 can help you answer this question.

This is the graph of $H = \frac{k}{\lambda^k} x^{k-1} e^{-(x/\lambda)^k}$ with $k = 1.667$ and $\lambda = 11.5$, the actual wind distribution for the Mount Batten Weather Station in Plymouth, England.

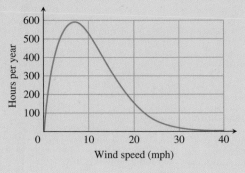

CHAPTER 6 Overview

The need to calculate instantaneous rates of change led the discoverers of calculus to an investigation of the slopes of tangent lines and, ultimately, to the derivative—to what we call differential calculus. But derivatives revealed only half the story. In addition to a calculation method (a "calculus") to describe how functions change at any given instant, they needed a method to describe how those instantaneous changes could accumulate over an interval to produce the function that describes the total change.

Early in the 14th century, a group of scholars at Merton College in Oxford, England, began exploring how to find the accumulated distance from knowledge of the velocity. In 1638, Galileo Galilei used their ideas to explain the motion of falling bodies and justify his claim that the earth circles the sun. Later that century, Isaac Newton studied these accumulation functions and, in 1666, discovered a remarkable insight that connected accumulation functions to what he already knew about derivatives. If there was one moment when calculus was born, this was it.

Today, what we call the *integral* calculus or *integration* has two distinct interpretations. We begin this chapter by looking at integration as accumulation. But it also can be viewed as reversing the process of differentiation, what we call *antidifferentiation*. Newton's insight, that these two are connected, is what is called the Fundamental Theorem of Calculus (also known as the Fundamental Theorem of Integral Calculus).

6.1 Estimating with Finite Sums

You will be able to estimate distance, areas, volumes, and accumulations using finite sums.

- Distance as area under the velocity curve
- Accumulation as area under the curve representing rate of accumulation
- Estimation of area using rectangular approximation
- Estimation of volume using slices
- Use of left, right, and midpoint sums to approximate areas

Accumulation Problems as Area

We know why a scientist pondering motion problems might have been led to consider slopes of curves, but what do those same motion problems have to do with areas under curves? Consider the following problem from a typical elementary school textbook:

A ship moves along an ocean at a steady rate of 7.5 nautical miles per hour (knots) from 7:00 A.M. to 9:00 A.M. What is the total distance traveled by the ship?

Applying the well-known formula *distance = rate × time*, we find that the answer is 15 nautical miles. Simple. Now suppose that you are Nicole Oresme trying to make a connection between this formula and the graph of the velocity function.

You might notice that the distance traveled by the ship (15 miles) is exactly the *area* of the rectangle whose base is the time interval [7, 9] and whose height at each point is the value of the constant velocity function $v = 7.5$ (Figure 6.1). This is no accident, either, since *the distance traveled* and *the area* in this case are both found by multiplying the rate (7.5) by the change in time (2).

This same connection between distance traveled and rectangle area could be made no matter how fast the ship was going or how long or short the time interval was.

Nicole Oresme (c. 1320–1382)

Oresme was a medieval bishop and a philosopher who contributed to mathematics, physics, astronomy, and economics. He was the first to realize that if we represent speed by a graph over a period of time, then the area under this graph is the total distance that is traveled.

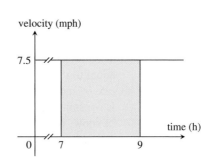

Figure 6.1 The distance traveled in 2 hours by a ship moving at 7.5 nautical miles per hour, which corresponds to the area of the shaded rectangle.

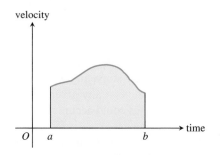

velocity

Figure 6.2 If the velocity varies over the time interval $[a, b]$, does the shaded region give the distance traveled?

But what if the ship had a velocity v that *varied* as a function of time? The graph (Figure 6.2) would no longer be a horizontal line, so the region under the graph would no longer be rectangular.

Would the area of this irregular region still give the total distance traveled over the time interval? Nicole Oresme thought that it obviously would, and the scientists who followed him, from Galileo through Newton and Leibniz, agreed. Because of this, there was tremendous interest throughout the 1600s in finding areas under curves. These scientists imagined the time interval being partitioned into many tiny subintervals, each one so small that the velocity over it would essentially be constant. Geometrically, this was equivalent to slicing the irregular region into narrow strips, each of which would be nearly indistinguishable from a narrow rectangle (Figure 6.3).

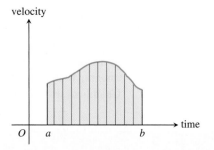

velocity

Figure 6.3 The region is partitioned into vertical strips. If the strips are narrow enough, they are almost indistinguishable from rectangles. The sum of the areas of these "rectangles" will give the total area and can be interpreted as distance traveled.

They argued that, just as the total area could be found by summing the areas of the (essentially rectangular) strips, the total distance traveled could be found by summing the small distances traveled over the tiny time intervals.

Finding the distance traveled when one knows the velocity at each instant of time is a process of accumulating distances; the area of each narrow rectangle is an approximation to the distance traveled over that short interval of time. Other accumulation problems can be viewed as areas.

EXAMPLE 1   Calculating Snowfall

Consider a snowstorm that starts at 3 A.M. Over the first two hours, the rate of snowfall increases from 0 to 1.2 inches per hour. For the next three hours, it continues to fall at 1.2 inches per hour. At 8 A.M., it begins to taper off, decreasing at a steady rate until the snowfall ends at 10:30 A.M. (Figure 6.4). Find the total amount of snow that falls during this storm.

SOLUTION

The amount of snow is the rate at which snow is falling times the time interval. It is equal to the area of the trapezoid in Figure 6.4. Over the first two hours, the average rate of snowfall is 0.6 inch per hour, producing 1.2 inches of snow. The rate of snowfall is constant at 1.2 inches per hour for the next 3 hours, producing a further 3.6 inches of snow. In the last 2.5 hours, the average rate is again 0.6 inch per hour, producing 1.5 inches. Total snowfall is

$$2 \times 0.6 + 3 \times 1.2 + 2.5 \times 0.6 = 6.3 \text{ inches.}$$

Now Try Exercise 3.

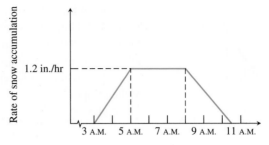

Figure 6.4 The total amount of snow that accumulates from 3 A.M. until 10:30 A.M. is equal to the area under the graph of the rate at which snow is falling.

EXAMPLE 2 Finding Distance Traveled When Velocity Varies

A particle starts at $x = 0$ and moves along the x-axis with velocity $v(t) = t^2$ for time $t \geq 0$. Where is the particle at $t = 3$?

SOLUTION

We graph v and partition the time interval $[0, 3]$ into subintervals of length Δt. (Figure 6.5 shows twelve subintervals of length $3/12$ each.)

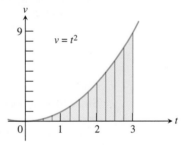

Figure 6.5 The region under the parabola $v = t^2$ from $t = 0$ to $t = 3$ is partitioned into 12 thin strips, each with base $\Delta t = 1/4$. The strips have curved tops. (Example 2)

Notice that the region under the curve is partitioned into thin strips with bases of length $1/4$ and *curved* tops that slope upward from left to right. You might not know how to find the area of such a strip, but you can get a good approximation of it by finding the area of a suitable rectangle. In Figure 6.6, we use the rectangle whose height is the y-coordinate of the function at the midpoint of its base.

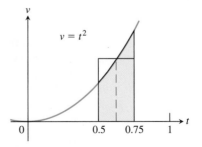

Figure 6.6 The area of the shaded region is approximated by the area of the rectangle whose height is the function value at the midpoint of the interval. (Example 2)

continued

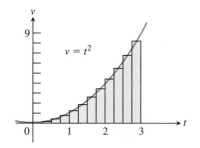

Figure 6.7 These rectangles have approximately the same areas as the strips in Figure 6.5. Each rectangle has height m_i^2, where m_i is the midpoint of its base. (Example 2)

The area of this narrow rectangle approximates the distance traveled over the time subinterval. Adding all the areas (distances) gives an approximation of the total area under the curve (total distance traveled) from $t = 0$ to $t = 3$ (Figure 6.7).

Computing this sum of areas is straightforward. Each rectangle has a base of length $\Delta t = 1/4$, while the height of each rectangle can be found by evaluating the function at the midpoint of the subinterval. Table 6.1 shows the computations for the first four rectangles.

TABLE 6.1				
Subinterval	$\left[0, \dfrac{1}{4}\right]$	$\left[\dfrac{1}{4}, \dfrac{1}{2}\right]$	$\left[\dfrac{1}{2}, \dfrac{3}{4}\right]$	$\left[\dfrac{3}{4}, 1\right]$
Midpoint m_i	$\dfrac{1}{8}$	$\dfrac{3}{8}$	$\dfrac{5}{8}$	$\dfrac{7}{8}$
Height $= (m_i)^2$	$\dfrac{1}{64}$	$\dfrac{9}{64}$	$\dfrac{25}{64}$	$\dfrac{49}{64}$
Area $= (1/4)(m_i)^2$	$\dfrac{1}{256}$	$\dfrac{9}{256}$	$\dfrac{25}{256}$	$\dfrac{49}{256}$

Continuing in this manner, we derive the area $(1/4)(m_i)^2$ for each of the twelve subintervals and add them:

$$\frac{1}{256} + \frac{9}{256} + \frac{25}{256} + \frac{49}{256} + \frac{81}{256} + \frac{121}{256} + \frac{169}{256} + \frac{225}{256}$$
$$+ \frac{289}{256} + \frac{361}{256} + \frac{441}{256} + \frac{529}{256} = \frac{2300}{256} \approx 8.98$$

Since this number approximates the area and hence the total distance traveled by the particle, we conclude that the particle has moved approximately 9 units in 3 seconds. If it starts at $x = 0$, then it is very close to $x = 9$ when $t = 3$. *Now Try Exercise 5.*

Approximation by Rectangles

Approximating irregularly shaped regions by regularly shaped regions for the purpose of computing areas is not new. Archimedes used the idea more than 2200 years ago to find the area of a circle, demonstrating in the process that π was located between 3.140845 and 3.142857. He also used approximations to find the area under a parabolic arch, anticipating the answer to an important 17-century question nearly 2000 years before anyone thought to ask it.

To make it easier to talk about approximations with rectangles, we now introduce some new terminology.

Rectangular Approximation Method (RAM)

In Example 2 we used the *Midpoint Rectangular Approximation Method* (*MRAM*) to approximate the area under the curve. The name suggests the choice we made when determining the heights of the approximating rectangles: We evaluated the function at the midpoint of each subinterval. If instead we had evaluated the function at the left-hand endpoint we would have obtained the *LRAM* approximation, and if we had used the right-hand endpoints we would have obtained the *RRAM* approximation. Figure 6.8 shows what the three approximations look like graphically when we approximate the area under the curve $y = x^2$ from $x = 0$ to $x = 3$ with six subintervals.

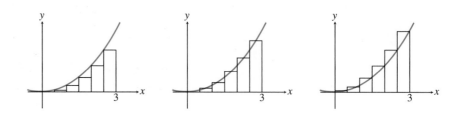

Figure 6.8 LRAM, MRAM, and RRAM approximations to the area under the graph of $y = x^2$ from $x = 0$ to $x = 3$.

No matter which RAM approximation we compute, we are adding products of the form $f(x_i) \cdot \Delta x$, or, in this case, $(x_i)^2 \cdot (3/6)$.

LRAM:

$$\left(0\right)^2\left(\frac{1}{2}\right) + \left(\frac{1}{2}\right)^2\left(\frac{1}{2}\right) + \left(1\right)^2\left(\frac{1}{2}\right) + \left(\frac{3}{2}\right)^2\left(\frac{1}{2}\right) + \left(2\right)^2\left(\frac{1}{2}\right) + \left(\frac{5}{2}\right)^2\left(\frac{1}{2}\right) = 6.875$$

MRAM:

$$\left(\frac{1}{4}\right)^2\left(\frac{1}{2}\right) + \left(\frac{3}{4}\right)^2\left(\frac{1}{2}\right) + \left(\frac{5}{4}\right)^2\left(\frac{1}{2}\right) + \left(\frac{7}{4}\right)^2\left(\frac{1}{2}\right) + \left(\frac{9}{4}\right)^2\left(\frac{1}{2}\right) + \left(\frac{11}{4}\right)^2\left(\frac{1}{2}\right) = 8.9375$$

RRAM:

$$\left(\frac{1}{2}\right)^2\left(\frac{1}{2}\right) + \left(1\right)^2\left(\frac{1}{2}\right) + \left(\frac{3}{2}\right)^2\left(\frac{1}{2}\right) + \left(2\right)^2\left(\frac{1}{2}\right) + \left(\frac{5}{2}\right)^2\left(\frac{1}{2}\right) + \left(3\right)^2\left(\frac{1}{2}\right) = 11.375$$

As we can see from Figure 6.8, LRAM is smaller than the true area and RRAM is larger. MRAM appears to be the closest of the three approximations. However, observe what happens as the number n of subintervals increases:

n	LRAM$_n$	MRAM$_n$	RRAM$_n$
6	6.875	8.9375	11.375
12	7.90625	8.984375	10.15625
24	8.4453125	8.99609375	9.5703125
48	8.720703125	8.999023438	9.283203125
100	8.86545	8.999775	9.13545
1000	8.9865045	8.99999775	9.0135045

We computed the numbers in this table using a graphing calculator and a summing program called RAM. A version of this program for most graphing calculators can be found in the *Technology Resource Manual* that accompanies this textbook. *All three sums* approach the same number (in this case, 9).

EXAMPLE 3   Estimating Area Under the Graph of a Nonnegative Function

Figure 6.9 shows the graph of $f(x) = x^2 \sin x$ on the interval $[0, 3]$. Estimate the area under the curve from $x = 0$ to $x = 3$.

SOLUTION

We apply our RAM program to get the numbers in this table.

n	LRAM$_n$	MRAM$_n$	RRAM$_n$
5	5.15480	5.89668	5.91685
10	5.52574	5.80685	5.90677
25	5.69079	5.78150	5.84320
50	5.73615	5.77788	5.81235
100	5.75701	5.77697	5.79511
1000	5.77476	5.77667	5.77857

It is not necessary to compute all three sums each time just to approximate the area, but we wanted to show again how all three sums approach the same number. With 1000 subintervals, all three agree in the first three digits. (The *exact* area is $-7 \cos 3 + 6 \sin 3 - 2$, which is 5.77666752456 to twelve digits.)   *Now Try Exercise 9.*

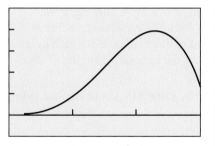

[0, 3] by [−1, 5]

Figure 6.9 The graph of $y = x^2 \sin x$ over the interval $[0, 3]$. (Example 3)

EXPLORATION 1 Which RAM Is the Biggest?

You might think from the previous two RAM tables that LRAM is always a little low and RRAM a little high, with MRAM somewhere in between. That, however, depends on n and on the shape of the curve.

1. Graph $y = 5 - 4\sin(x/2)$ in the window $[0, 3]$ by $[0, 5]$. Copy the graph on paper and sketch the rectangles for the LRAM, MRAM, and RRAM sums with $n = 3$. Order the three approximations from greatest to smallest.
2. Graph $y = 2\sin(5x) + 3$ in the same window. Copy the graph on paper and sketch the rectangles for the LRAM, MRAM, and RRAM sums with $n = 3$. Order the three approximations from greatest to smallest.
3. If a positive, continuous function is increasing on an interval, what can we say about the relative sizes of LRAM, MRAM, and RRAM? Explain.
4. If a positive, continuous function is decreasing on an interval, what can we say about the relative sizes of LRAM, MRAM, and RRAM? Explain.

Volume of a Sphere

Although the visual representation of RAM approximation focuses on area, remember that our original motivation for looking at sums of this type was to find distance traveled by an object moving with a nonconstant velocity. The connection between Examples 1 and 2 is that in each case, we have a function f defined on a closed interval and estimate what we want to know with a sum of function values multiplied by interval lengths. Many other physical quantities can be estimated this way.

EXAMPLE 4 Estimating the Volume of a Sphere

Estimate the volume of a solid sphere of radius 4.

SOLUTION

We picture the sphere as if its surface were generated by revolving the graph of the function $f(x) = \sqrt{16 - x^2}$ about the x-axis (Figure 6.10a). We partition the interval $-4 \le x \le 4$ into n subintervals of equal length $\Delta x = 8/n$. We then slice the sphere with planes perpendicular to the x-axis at the partition points, cutting it like a round loaf of bread into n parallel slices of width Δx. When n is large, each slice can be approximated by a cylinder, a familiar geometric shape of known volume, $\pi r^2 h$. In our case, the cylinders lie on their sides and h is Δx while r varies according to where we are on the x-axis (Figure 6.10b). A logical radius to choose for each cylinder is $f(m_i) = \sqrt{16 - m_i^2}$, where m_i is the midpoint of the interval where the ith slice intersects the x-axis (Figure 6.10c).

We can now approximate the volume of the sphere by using MRAM to sum the cylinder volumes,

$$\pi r^2 h = \pi\left(\sqrt{16 - m_i^2}\right)^2 \Delta x.$$

The function we use in the RAM program is $\pi\left(\sqrt{16 - x^2}\right)^2 = \pi(16 - x^2)$. The interval is $[-4, 4]$.

Number of Slices (n)	MRAM$_n$
10	269.42299
25	268.29704
50	268.13619
100	268.09598
1000	268.08271

continued

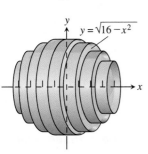

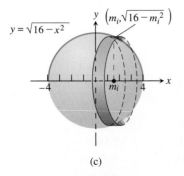

Figure 6.10 (a) The semicircle $y = \sqrt{16 - x^2}$ revolved about the x-axis to generate a sphere. (b) Slices of the solid sphere approximated with cylinders (drawn for $n = 8$). (c) The typical approximating cylinder has radius $f(m_i) = \sqrt{16 - m_i^2}$. (Example 4)

Keeping Track of Units

Notice in Example 4 that we are summing products of the form $\pi(16 - x^2)$ (a cross-section area, measured in square units) times Δx (a length, measured in units). The products are therefore measured in cubic units, which are the correct units for volume.

The value for $n = 1000$ compares *very* favorably with the true volume,

$$V = \frac{4}{3}\pi r^3 = \frac{4}{3}\pi(4)^3 = \frac{256\pi}{3} \approx 268.0825731.$$

Even for $n = 10$ the difference between the MRAM approximation and the true volume is a small percentage of V:

$$\frac{|MRAM_{10} - V|}{V} = \frac{MRAM_{10} - 256\pi/3}{256\pi/3} \leq 0.005$$

That is, the error percentage is about one half of one percent!   *Now Try Exercise 15.*

Cardiac Output

So far we have seen applications of the RAM process to finding distance traveled and volume. These applications hint at the usefulness of this technique. To suggest its versatility we will present an application from human physiology.

The number of liters of blood your heart pumps in a fixed time interval is called your *cardiac output*. For a person at rest, the rate might be 5 or 6 liters per minute. During strenuous exercise the rate might be as high as 30 liters per minute. It might also be altered significantly by disease. How can a physician measure a patient's cardiac output without interrupting the flow of blood?

One technique is to inject a dye into a main vein near the heart. The dye is drawn into the right side of the heart and pumped through the lungs and out the left side of the heart into the aorta, where its concentration can be measured every few seconds as the blood flows past. The data in Table 6.2 and the plot in Figure 6.11 (obtained from the data) show the response of a healthy, resting patient to an injection of 5.6 mg of dye.

TABLE 6.2 Dye Concentration Data	
Seconds After Injection t	Dye Concentration (adjusted for recirculation) c
5	0
7	3.8
9	8.0
11	6.1
13	3.6
15	2.3
17	1.45
19	0.91
21	0.57
23	0.36
25	0.23
27	0.14
29	0.09
31	0

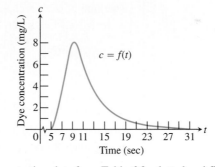

Figure 6.11 The dye concentration data from Table 6.2, plotted and fitted with a smooth curve. Time is measured with $t = 0$ at the time of injection. The dye concentration is zero at the beginning while the dye passes through the lungs. It then rises to a maximum at about $t = 9$ sec and tapers to zero by $t = 31$ sec.

The graph shows dye concentration (measured in milligrams of dye per liter of blood) as a function of time (in seconds). How can we use this graph to obtain the cardiac output (measured in liters of blood per second)? The trick is to divide the *number of mg of dye* by the *area under the dye concentration curve*. You can see why this works if you consider what happens to the units:

$$\frac{\text{mg of dye}}{\text{units of area under curve}} = \frac{\text{mg of dye}}{\dfrac{\text{mg of dye}}{\text{L of blood}} \cdot \text{sec}}$$

$$= \frac{\text{mg of dye}}{\text{sec}} \cdot \frac{\text{L of blood}}{\text{mg of dye}}$$

$$= \frac{\text{L of blood}}{\text{sec}}$$

So you are now ready to compute like a cardiologist.

Charles Richard Drew
(1904–1950)

Millions of people are alive today because of Charles Drew's pioneering work on blood plasma and the preservation of human blood for transfusion. After directing the Red Cross program that collected plasma for the Armed Forces in World War II, Dr. Drew went on to become Head of Surgery at Howard University and Chief of Staff at Freedmen's Hospital in Washington, D.C.

EXAMPLE 5 Computing Cardiac Output from Dye Concentration

Estimate the cardiac output of the patient whose data appear in Table 6.2 and Figure 6.11. Give the estimate in liters per minute.

SOLUTION

We have seen that we can obtain the cardiac output by dividing the amount of dye (5.6 mg for our patient) by the area under the curve in Figure 6.11. Now we need to find the area. Our geometry formulas do not apply to this irregularly shaped region, and the RAM program is useless without a formula for the function. Nonetheless, we can draw the MRAM rectangles ourselves and estimate their heights from the graph. In Figure 6.12 each rectangle has a base 2 units long and a height $f(m_i)$ equal to the height of the curve above the midpoint of the base.

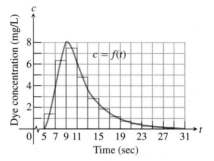

Figure 6.12 The region under the concentration curve of Figure 6.11 is approximated with rectangles. We ignore the portion from $t = 29$ to $t = 31$; its concentration is negligible. (Example 5)

The area of each rectangle, then, is $f(m_i)$ times 2, and the sum of the rectangular areas is the MRAM estimate for the area under the curve:

$$
\begin{aligned}
\text{Area} &\approx f(6) \cdot 2 + f(8) \cdot 2 + f(10) \cdot 2 + \cdots + f(28) \cdot 2 \\
&\approx 2 \cdot (1.4 + 6.3 + 7.5 + 4.8 + 2.8 + 1.9 + 1.1 \\
&\qquad + 0.7 + 0.5 + 0.3 + 0.2 + 0.1) \\
&= 2 \cdot (27.6) = 55.2 \, (\text{mg/L}) \cdot \text{sec}
\end{aligned}
$$

Dividing 5.6 mg by this figure gives an estimate for cardiac output in liters per second. Multiplying by 60 converts the estimate to liters per minute:

$$
\frac{5.6 \text{ mg}}{55.2 \text{ mg} \cdot \text{sec/L}} \cdot \frac{60 \text{ sec}}{1 \text{ min}} \approx 6.09 \text{ L/min} \quad \textbf{\textit{Now Try Exercise 17.}}
$$

Quick Review 6.1

Exercise numbers with a gray background indicate problems that the authors have designed to be solved *without a calculator*.

As you answer the questions in Exercises 1–10, try to associate the answers with area, as in Figure 6.1.

1. A train travels at 80 mph for 5 hours. How far does it travel?

2. A truck travels at an average speed of 48 mph for 3 hours. How far does it travel?

3. Beginning at a standstill, a car maintains a constant acceleration of 10 ft/sec² for 10 seconds. What is its velocity after 10 seconds? Give your answer in ft/sec and then convert it to mi/h.

4. In a vacuum, light travels at a speed of 300,000 kilometers per second. How many kilometers does it travel in a year? (This distance equals one *light-year*.)

5. A long distance runner ran a race in 5 hours, averaging 6 mph for the first 3 hours and 5 mph for the last 2 hours. How far did she run?

6. A pump working at 20 gallons/minute pumps for an hour. How many gallons are pumped?

7. At 8:00 P.M. the temperature began dropping at a rate of 1 degree Celsius per hour. Twelve hours later it began rising at a rate of 1.5 degrees per hour for six hours. What was the net change in temperature over the 18-hour period?

8. Water flows over a spillway at a steady rate of 300 cubic feet per second. How many cubic feet of water pass over the spillway in one day?

9. A town has a population density of 350 people per square mile in an area of 50 square miles. What is the population of the town?

10. A hummingbird in flight beats its wings at a rate of 70 times per second. How many times does it beat its wings in an hour if it is in flight 70% of the time?

Section 6.1 Exercises

1. A particle starts at $x = 0$ and moves along the x-axis with velocity $v(t) = 5$ for time $t \geq 0$. Where is the particle at $t = 4$?

2. A particle starts at $x = 0$ and moves along the x-axis with velocity $v(t) = 2t + 1$ for time $t \geq 0$. Where is the particle at $t = 4$?

3. A beach is eroding at a rate of 3 cubic yards per day. How much of the beach will be lost over a year (365 days)?

4. Water enters a pool at an increasing rate given by $W(t) = 1 + 3t$ gallons per minute from $t = 0$ to $t = 5$ minutes. Find the amount of water that has entered the pool over these five minutes.

5. A particle starts at $x = 0$ and moves along the x-axis with velocity $v(t) = t^2 + 1$ for time $t \geq 0$. Where is the particle at $t = 4$? Approximate the area under the curve using four rectangles of equal width and heights determined by the midpoints of the intervals, as in Example 2.

6. A particle starts at $x = 0$ and moves along the x-axis with velocity $v(t) = t^2 + 1$ for time $t \geq 0$. Where is the particle at $t = 5$? Approximate the area under the curve using five rectangles of equal width and heights determined by the midpoints of the intervals, as in Example 2.

Exercises 7–10 refer to the region R enclosed between the graph of the function $y = 2x - x^2$ and the x-axis for $0 \leq x \leq 2$.

7. (a) Sketch the region R.

(b) Partition $[0, 2]$ into 4 subintervals and show the four rectangles that LRAM uses to approximate the area of R. Compute the LRAM sum without a calculator.

8. Repeat Exercise 7(b) for RRAM and MRAM.

9. Using a calculator program, find the RAM sums that complete the following table.

n	LRAM$_n$	MRAM$_n$	RRAM$_n$
10			
50			
100			
500			

10. Make a conjecture about the area of the region R.

In Exercises 11–14, use RRAM with $n = 100$ to estimate the area of the region enclosed between the graph of f and the x-axis for $a \leq x \leq b$.

11. $f(x) = x^2 - x + 3$, $a = 0$, $b = 3$

12. $f(x) = \dfrac{1}{x}$, $a = 1$, $b = 3$

13. $f(x) = e^{-x^2}$, $a = 0$, $b = 2$

14. $f(x) = \sin x$, $a = 0$, $b = \pi$

15. (*Continuation of Example 4*) Use the slicing technique of Example 4 to find the MRAM sums that approximate the volume of a sphere of radius 5. Use $n = 10, 20, 40, 80,$ and 160.

16. (*Continuation of Exercise 15*) Use a geometry formula to find the volume V of the sphere in Exercise 15 and find **(a)** the error and **(b)** the percentage error in the MRAM approximation for each value of n given.

17. *Cardiac Output* The following table gives dye concentrations for a dye-concentration cardiac-output determination like the one in Example 5. The amount of dye injected in this patient was 5 mg instead of 5.6 mg. Use rectangles to estimate the area under the dye concentration curve and then go on to estimate the patient's cardiac output.

Seconds After Injection t	Dye Concentration (adjusted for recirculation) c
2	0
4	0.6
6	1.4
8	2.7
10	3.7
12	4.1
14	3.8
16	2.9
18	1.7
20	1.0
22	0.5
24	0

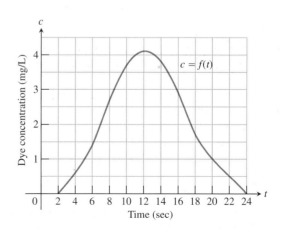

18. Distance Traveled The table below shows the velocity of a model train engine moving along a track for 10 sec. Estimate the distance traveled by the engine, using 10 subintervals of length 1 with **(a)** left-endpoint values (LRAM) and **(b)** right-endpoint values (RRAM).

Time (sec)	Velocity (in./sec)	Time (sec)	Velocity (in./sec)
0	0	6	11
1	12	7	6
2	22	8	2
3	10	9	6
4	5	10	0
5	13		

19. Distance Traveled Upstream You are walking along the bank of a tidal river watching the incoming tide carry a bottle upstream. You record the velocity of the flow every 5 minutes for an hour, with the results shown in the table below. About how far upstream does the bottle travel during that hour? Find the **(a)** LRAM and **(b)** RRAM estimates using 12 subintervals of length 5.

Time (min)	Velocity (m/sec)	Time (min)	Velocity (m/sec)
0	1	35	1.2
5	1.2	40	1.0
10	1.7	45	1.8
15	2.0	50	1.5
20	1.8	55	1.2
25	1.6	60	0
30	1.4		

20. Length of a Road You and a companion are driving along a twisty stretch of dirt road in a car whose speedometer works but whose odometer (mileage counter) is broken. To find out how long this particular stretch of road is, you record the car's velocity at 10-sec intervals, with the results shown in the table below. (The velocity was converted from mi/h to ft/sec using 30 mi/h = 44 ft/sec.) Estimate the length of the road by averaging the LRAM and RRAM sums.

Time (sec)	Velocity (ft/sec)	Time (sec)	Velocity (ft/sec)
0	0	70	15
10	44	80	22
20	15	90	35
30	35	100	44
40	30	110	30
50	44	120	35
60	35		

21. Distance from Velocity Data The table below gives data for the velocity of a vintage sports car accelerating from 0 to 142 mi/h in 36 sec (10 thousandths of an hour).

Time (h)	Velocity (mi/h)	Time (h)	Velocity (mi/h)
0.0	0	0.006	116
0.001	40	0.007	125
0.002	62	0.008	132
0.003	82	0.009	137
0.004	96	0.010	142
0.005	108		

(a) Use rectangles to estimate how far the car traveled during the 36 sec it took to reach 142 mi/h.

(b) Roughly how many seconds did it take the car to reach the halfway point? About how fast was the car going then?

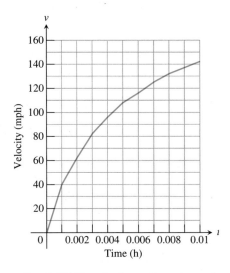

22. Volume of a Solid Hemisphere To estimate the volume of a solid hemisphere of radius 4, imagine its axis of symmetry to be the interval $[0, 4]$ on the *x*-axis. Partition $[0, 4]$ into eight subintervals of equal length and approximate the solid with cylinders based on the circular cross sections of the hemisphere perpendicular to the *x*-axis at the subintervals' left endpoints. (See the accompanying profile view.)

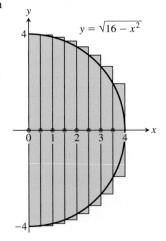

(a) **Writing to Learn** Find the sum S_8 of the volumes of the cylinders. Do you expect S_8 to overestimate *V*? Give reasons for your answer.

(b) Express $|V - S_8|$ as a percentage of *V* to the nearest percent.

23. Repeat Exercise 22 using cylinders based on cross sections at the right endpoints of the subintervals.

24. Volume of Water in a Reservoir A reservoir shaped like a hemispherical bowl of radius 8 m is filled with water to a depth of 4 m.

  (a) Find an estimate S of the water's volume by approximating the water with eight circumscribed solid cylinders.

  (b) It can be shown that the water's volume is $V = (320\pi)/3$ m³. Find the error $|V - S|$ as a percentage of V to the nearest percent.

25. Volume of Water in a Swimming Pool A rectangular swimming pool is 30 ft wide and 50 ft long. The table below shows the depth $h(x)$ of the water at 5-ft intervals from one end of the pool to the other. Estimate the volume of water in the pool using **(a)** left-endpoint values and **(b)** right-endpoint values.

Position (ft) x	Depth (ft) $h(x)$	Position (ft) x	Depth (ft) $h(x)$
0	6.0	30	11.5
5	8.2	35	11.9
10	9.1	40	12.3
15	9.9	45	12.7
20	10.5	50	13.0
25	11.0		

26. Volume of a Nose Cone The nose "cone" of a rocket is a *paraboloid* obtained by revolving the curve $y = \sqrt{x}$, $0 \le x \le 5$ about the x-axis, where x is measured in feet. Estimate the volume V of the nose cone by partitioning $[0, 5]$ into five subintervals of equal length, slicing the cone with planes perpendicular to the x-axis at the subintervals' left end-points, constructing cylinders of height 1 based on cross sections at these points, and finding the volumes of these cylinders. (See the accompanying figure.)

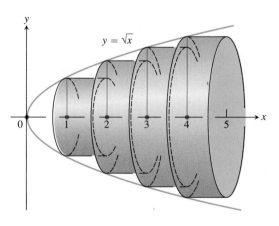

27. Volume of a Nose Cone Repeat Exercise 26 using cylinders based on cross sections at the *midpoints* of the subintervals.

28. Free Fall with Air Resistance An object is dropped straight down from a helicopter. The object falls faster and faster but its acceleration (rate of change of its velocity) decreases over time because of air resistance. The acceleration is measured in ft/sec² and recorded every second after the drop for 5 sec, as shown in the table below.

t	0	1	2	3	4	5
a	32.00	19.41	11.77	7.14	4.33	2.63

  (a) Use LRAM_5 to find an upper estimate for the speed when $t = 5$.

  (b) Use RRAM_5 to find a lower estimate for the speed when $t = 5$.

  (c) Use upper estimates for the speed during the first second, second second, and third second to find an upper estimate for the distance fallen when $t = 3$.

29. Distance Traveled by a Projectile An object is shot straight upward from sea level with an initial velocity of 400 ft/sec.

  (a) Assuming gravity is the only force acting on the object, give an upper estimate for its velocity after 5 sec have elapsed. Use $g = 32$ ft/sec² for the gravitational constant.

  (b) Use RRAM_5 to find a lower estimate for the height attained after 5 sec.

30. Water Pollution Oil is leaking out of a tanker damaged at sea. The damage to the tanker is worsening, as evidenced by the increased leakage each hour, recorded in the table below.

Time (h)	0	1	2	3	4
Leakage (gal/h)	50	70	97	136	190

Time (h)	5	6	7	8
Leakage (gal/h)	265	369	516	720

  (a) Give an upper and lower estimate of the total quantity of oil that has escaped after 5 hours.

  (b) Repeat part (a) for the quantity of oil that has escaped after 8 hours.

  (c) The tanker continues to leak 720 gal/h after the first 8 hours. If the tanker originally contained 25,000 gal of oil, approximately how many more hours will elapse in the worst case before all of the oil has leaked? in the best case?

31. Air Pollution A power plant generates electricity by burning oil. Pollutants produced by the burning process are removed by scrubbers in the smokestacks. Over time the scrubbers become less efficient and eventually must be replaced when the amount of pollutants released exceeds government standards. Measurements taken at the end of each month determine the rate at which pollutants are released into the atmosphere, as recorded in the table below.

Month	Jan	Feb	Mar	Apr	May	Jun
Pollutant Release Rate (tons/day)	0.20	0.25	0.27	0.34	0.45	0.52

Month	Jul	Aug	Sep	Oct	Nov	Dec
Pollutant Release Rate (tons/day)	0.63	0.70	0.81	0.85	0.89	0.95

(a) Assuming a 30-day month and that new scrubbers allow only 0.05 ton/day released, give an upper estimate of the total tonnage of pollutants released by the end of June. What is a lower estimate?

(b) In the best case, approximately when will a total of 125 tons of pollutants have been released into the atmosphere?

32. Writing to Learn The graph shows the sales record for a company over a 10-year period. If sales are measured in millions of units per year, explain what information can be obtained from the area of the region, and why.

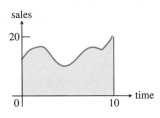

Standardized Test Questions

33. True or False If f is a positive, continuous, increasing function on $[a, b]$, then LRAM gives an area estimate that is less than the true area under the curve. Justify your answer.

34. True or False For a given number of rectangles, MRAM always gives a more accurate approximation to the true area under the curve than RRAM or LRAM. Justify your answer.

35. Multiple Choice If an MRAM sum with four rectangles of equal width is used to approximate the area enclosed between the x-axis and the graph of $y = 4x - x^2$, the approximation is

(A) 10   (B) 10.5   (C) $10.\overline{6}$ (D) 10.75   (E) 11

36. Multiple Choice If f is a positive, continuous function on an interval $[a, b]$, which of the following rectangular approximation methods has a limit equal to the actual area under the curve from a to b as the number of rectangles approaches infinity?

I. LRAM

II. RRAM

III. MRAM

(A) I and II only

(B) III only

(C) I and III only

(D) I, II, and III

(E) None of these

37. Multiple Choice An LRAM sum with 4 equal subdivisions is used to approximate the area under the sine curve from $x = 0$ to $x = \pi$. What is the approximation?

(A) $\dfrac{\pi}{4}\left(0 + \dfrac{\pi}{4} + \dfrac{\pi}{2} + \dfrac{3\pi}{4}\right)$ (B) $\dfrac{\pi}{4}\left(0 + \dfrac{1}{2} + \dfrac{\sqrt{3}}{2} + 1\right)$

(C) $\dfrac{\pi}{4}\left(0 + \dfrac{\sqrt{2}}{2} + 1 + \dfrac{\sqrt{2}}{2}\right)$ (D) $\dfrac{\pi}{4}\left(0 + \dfrac{1}{2} + \dfrac{\sqrt{2}}{2} + \dfrac{\sqrt{3}}{2}\right)$

(E) $\dfrac{\pi}{4}\left(\dfrac{1}{2} + \dfrac{\sqrt{2}}{2} + \dfrac{\sqrt{3}}{2} + 1\right)$

38. Multiple Choice A truck moves with positive velocity $v(t)$ from time $t = 3$ to time $t = 15$. The area under the graph of $y = v(t)$ between 3 and 15 gives

(A) the velocity of the truck at $t = 15$.

(B) the acceleration of the truck at $t = 15$.

(C) the position of the truck at $t = 15$.

(D) the distance traveled by the truck from $t = 3$ to $t = 15$.

(E) the average position of the truck in the interval from $t = 3$ to $t = 15$.

Exploration

39. Group Activity *Area of a Circle* Inscribe a regular n-sided polygon inside a circle of radius 1 and compute the area of the polygon for the following values of n.

(a) 4 (square)   (b) 8 (octagon)   (c) 16

(d) Compare the areas in parts (a), (b), and (c) with the area of the circle.

Extending the Ideas

40. *Rectangular Approximation Methods* Prove or disprove the following statement: MRAM_n is always the average of LRAM_n and RRAM_n.

41. *Rectangular Approximation Methods* Show that if f is a nonnegative function on the interval $[a, b]$ and the line $x = (a + b)/2$ is a line of symmetry of the graph of $y = f(x)$, then $\text{LRAM}_n f = \text{RRAM}_n f$ for every positive integer n.

42. *(Continuation of Exercise 39)*

(a) Inscribe a regular n-sided polygon inside a circle of radius 1 and compute the area of one of the n congruent triangles formed by drawing radii to the vertices of the polygon.

(b) Compute the limit of the area of the inscribed polygon as $n \to \infty$.

(c) Repeat the computations in parts (a) and (b) for a circle of radius r.

6.2 | Definite Integrals

You will be able to interpret the definite integral as the limit of a Riemann sum and express the limit of a Riemann sum in integral notation as well as calculate definite integrals using areas.

- Existence of definite integrals for continuous functions
- Terminology and notation of definite integration
- Definite integral as area
- Definite integral as accumulator
- Definite integrals with discontinuities

Riemann Sums

In the preceding section, we estimated distances, accumulations, areas, and volumes with finite sums. The terms in the sums were obtained by multiplying selected function values by the lengths of intervals. In this section we move beyond finite sums to see what happens in the limit, as the terms become infinitely small and their number infinitely large.

Sigma notation enables us to express a large sum in compact form:

$$\sum_{k=1}^{n} a_k = a_1 + a_2 + a_3 + \cdots + a_{n-1} + a_n$$

The Greek capital letter Σ (sigma) stands for "sum." The index k tells us where to begin the sum (at the number below the Σ) and where to end (at the number above). If the symbol ∞ appears above the Σ, it indicates that the terms go on indefinitely.

The sums in which we will be interested are called *Riemann* ("*ree*-mahn") *sums,* after Georg Friedrich Bernhard Riemann (1826–1866). LRAM, MRAM, and RRAM in the previous section are all examples of Riemann sums—not because they estimated area, but because they were constructed in a particular way. We now describe that construction formally, in a more general context that does not confine us to nonnegative functions.

We begin with an arbitrary continuous function $f(x)$ defined on a closed interval $[a, b]$. Like the function graphed in Figure 6.13, it may have negative values as well as positive values.

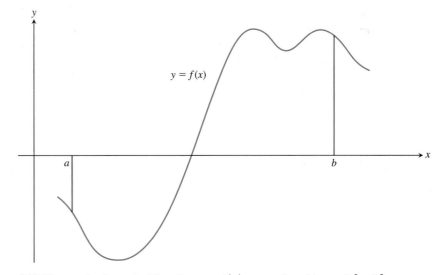

Figure 6.13 The graph of a typical function $y = f(x)$ over a closed interval $[a, b]$.

We then partition the interval $[a, b]$ into n subintervals by choosing $n - 1$ points, say $x_1, x_2, \cdots, x_{n-1}$, between a and b subject only to the condition that

$$a < x_1 < x_2 < \cdots < x_{n-1} < b.$$

To make the notation consistent, we denote a by x_0 and b by x_n. The set

$$P = \{x_0, x_1, x_2, \cdots, x_n\}$$

is called a **partition** of $[a, b]$.

The partition P determines n closed **subintervals,** as shown in Figure 6.14. The kth subinterval is $[x_{k-1}, x_k]$, which has length $\Delta x_k = x_k - x_{k-1}$.

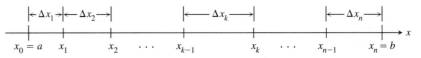

Figure 6.14 The partition $P = \{a = x_0, x_1, x_2, \cdots, x_n = b\}$ divides $[a, b]$ into n subintervals of lengths $\Delta x_1, \Delta x_2, \cdots, \Delta x_n$. The kth subinterval has length Δx_k.

In each subinterval we select some number. Denote the number chosen from the kth subinterval by c_k.

Then, on each subinterval we stand a vertical rectangle that reaches from the x-axis to touch the curve at $(c_k, f(c_k))$. These rectangles could lie either above or below the x-axis (Figure 6.15).

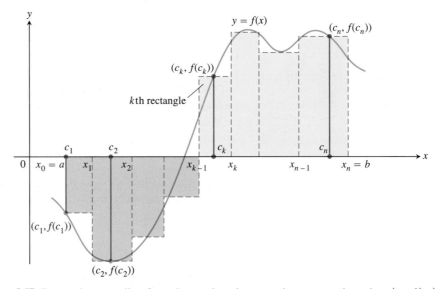

Figure 6.15 Rectangles extending from the x-axis to intersect the curve at the points $(c_k, f(c_k))$. The rectangles approximate the region between the x-axis and the graph of the function.

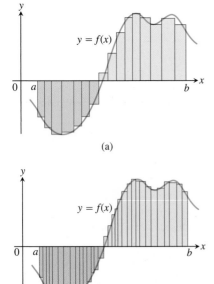

Figure 6.16 The curve of Figure 6.13 with rectangles from finer partitions of $[a, b]$. Finer partitions create more rectangles, with shorter bases.

On each subinterval, we form the product $f(c_k) \cdot \Delta x_k$. This product can be positive, negative, or zero, depending on $f(c_k)$.

Finally, we take the sum of these products:

$$S_n = \sum_{k=1}^{n} f(c_k) \cdot \Delta x_k$$

This sum, which depends on the partition P and the choice of the numbers c_k, is a **Riemann sum for f on the interval $[a, b]$.**

As the partitions of $[a, b]$ become finer and finer, we would expect the rectangles defined by the partitions to approximate the region between the x-axis and the graph of f with increasing accuracy (Figure 6.16).

Just as LRAM, MRAM, and RRAM in our earlier examples converged to a common value in the limit, *all* Riemann sums for a given function on $[a, b]$ converge to a common value, as long as the lengths of the subintervals all tend to zero. This latter condition is assured by requiring the longest subinterval length (called the **norm** of the partition and denoted by $\|P\|$) to tend to zero.

DEFINITION   **The Definite Integral as a Limit of Riemann Sums**

Let f be a function defined on a closed interval $[a, b]$. For any partition P of $[a, b]$, let the numbers c_k be chosen arbitrarily in the subintervals $[x_{k-1}, x_k]$.

If there exists a number I such that

$$\lim_{\|P\| \to 0} \sum_{k=1}^{n} f(c_k) \Delta x_k = I$$

no matter how P and the c_k's are chosen, then f is **integrable** on $[a, b]$ and I is the **definite integral** of f over $[a, b]$.

Despite the potential for variety in the sums $\sum f(c_k) \Delta x_k$ as the partitions change and as the c_k's are chosen arbitrarily in the intervals of each partition, the sums always have the same limit as $\|P\| \to 0$ as long as f is *continuous* on $[a, b]$. This important property of continuous functions was first proved by Augustin-Louis Cauchy in 1821.

Georg Riemann (1826–1866)

Two of the greatest mathematicians of the 19th century, Carl Friedrich Gauss and Gustav Lejeune-Dirichlet, were teachers of the young Riemann, who went on to build on their knowledge and create our modern understandings of both calculus and geometry. Einstein's discoveries in physics rely on Riemann's geometry. While the idea of the Riemann sum as an approximation to the definite integral can be found in the work of Newton and Leibniz, Riemann showed how to use these sums to investigate the question of when a *discontinuous* function can be integrated.

THEOREM 1   **The Existence of Definite Integrals**

All continuous functions are integrable. That is, if a function f is continuous on an interval $[a, b]$, then its definite integral over $[a, b]$ exists.

Because of Theorem 1, we can get by with a simpler construction for definite integrals of continuous functions. Since we know for these functions that the Riemann sums tend to the same limit for *all* partitions in which $\|P\| \to 0$, we need only to consider the limit of the so-called **regular partitions,** in which all the subintervals have the same length.

The Definite Integral of a Continuous Function on $[a, b]$

Let f be continuous on $[a, b]$, and let $[a, b]$ be partitioned into n subintervals of equal length $\Delta x = (b - a)/n$. Then the definite integral of f over $[a, b]$ is given by

$$\lim_{n \to \infty} \sum_{k=1}^{n} f(c_k) \Delta x,$$

where each c_k is chosen arbitrarily in the kth subinterval.

Terminology and Notation of Integration

Leibniz's clever choice of notation for the derivative, dy/dx, had the advantage of retaining an identity as a "fraction" even though both numerator and denominator had tended to zero. Although not really fractions, derivatives can *behave* like fractions, so the notation makes profound results like the Chain Rule

$$\frac{dy}{dx} = \frac{dy}{du} \cdot \frac{du}{dx}$$

seem almost simple.

The notation that Leibniz introduced for the integral was equally inspired. In his derivative notation, the Greek letters ("Δ" for "difference") switch to Roman letters ("d" for "differential") in the limit,

$$\lim_{\Delta x \to 0} \frac{\Delta y}{\Delta x} = \frac{dy}{dx}.$$

In his definite integral notation, the Greek letters again become Roman letters in the limit,

$$\lim_{n \to \infty} \sum_{k=1}^{n} f(c_k) \Delta x = \int_a^b f(x)\, dx.$$

Notice that the difference Δx has again tended to zero, becoming a differential dx. The Greek "Σ" has become an elongated Roman "S," so that the integral can retain its identity as a "sum." The c_k's have become so crowded together in the limit that we no longer think of a choppy selection of x values between a and b, but rather of a continuous, unbroken sampling of x values from a to b. It is as if we were summing *all* products of the form $f(x)\, dx$ as x goes from a to b, so we can abandon the k and the n used in the finite sum expression.

The symbol

$$\int_a^b f(x)\, dx$$

is read as "the integral from a to b of f of x dee x," or sometimes as "the integral from a to b of f of x with respect to x." The component parts also have names:

Joseph Fourier (1768–1830)

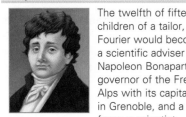

The twelfth of fifteen children of a tailor, Fourier would become a scientific adviser to Napoleon Bonaparte, governor of the French Alps with its capital in Grenoble, and a famous scientist.

He studied how heat is transferred and created one of the most important tools of modern science, Fourier Series. It was his idea to put the lower and upper limits of a definite integral next to the integral sign, $\int_a^b$.

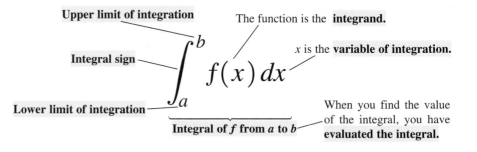

The value of the definite integral of a function over any particular interval depends on the function and not on the letter we choose to represent its independent variable. If we decide to use t or u instead of x, we simply write the integral as

$$\int_a^b f(t)\, dt \quad \text{or} \quad \int_a^b f(u)\, du \quad \text{instead of} \quad \int_a^b f(x)\, dx.$$

No matter how we represent the integral, it is the same *number,* defined as a limit of Riemann sums. Since it does not matter what letter we use to run from a to b, the variable of integration is called a **dummy variable.**

EXAMPLE 1 Using the Notation

The interval $[-1, 3]$ is partitioned into n subintervals of equal length $\Delta x = 4/n$. Let m_k denote the midpoint of the kth subinterval. Express the limit

$$\lim_{n \to \infty} \sum_{k=1}^{n} \left(3(m_k)^2 - 2m_k + 5\right) \Delta x$$

as an integral.

continued

SOLUTION

Since the midpoints m_k have been chosen from the subintervals of the partition, this expression is indeed a limit of Riemann sums. (The points chosen did not have to be midpoints; they could have been chosen from the subintervals in any arbitrary fashion.) The function being integrated is $f(x) = 3x^2 - 2x + 5$ over the interval $[-1, 3]$. Therefore,

$$\lim_{n \to \infty} \sum_{k=1}^{n} (3(m_k)^2 - 2m_k + 5)\, \Delta x = \int_{-1}^{3} (3x^2 - 2x + 5)\, dx.$$

Now Try Exercise 5.

Definite Integral and Area

If an integrable function $y = f(x)$ is nonnegative throughout an interval $[a, b]$, each nonzero term $f(c_k)\Delta x_k$ is the area of a rectangle reaching from the x-axis up to the curve $y = f(x)$. (See Figure 6.17.)

The Riemann sum

$$\sum f(c_k)\, \Delta x_k,$$

which is the sum of the areas of these rectangles, gives an estimate of the area of the region between the curve and the x-axis from a to b. Since the rectangles give an increasingly good approximation of the region as we use partitions with smaller and smaller norms, we call the limiting value the area under the curve.

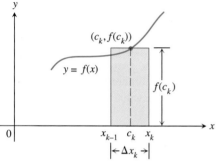

Figure 6.17 A term of a Riemann sum $\sum f(c_k)\Delta x_k$ for a nonnegative function f is either zero or the area of a rectangle such as the one shown.

> **DEFINITION   Area Under a Curve (as a Definite Integral)**
>
> If $y = f(x)$ is nonnegative and integrable over a closed interval $[a, b]$, then the **area under the curve $y = f(x)$ from a to b** is the integral of f from a to b,
>
> $$A = \int_{a}^{b} f(x)\, dx.$$

This definition works both ways: We can use integrals to calculate areas *and* we can use areas to calculate integrals.

EXAMPLE 2 Revisiting Area Under a Curve

Evaluate the integral $\int_{-2}^{2} \sqrt{4 - x^2}\, dx$.

SOLUTION

We recognize $f(x) = \sqrt{4 - x^2}$ as a function whose graph is a semicircle of radius 2 centered at the origin (Figure 6.18).

The area between the semicircle and the x-axis from -2 to 2 can be computed using the geometry formula

$$\text{Area} = \frac{1}{2} \cdot \pi r^2 = \frac{1}{2} \cdot \pi(2)^2 = 2\pi.$$

Because the area is also the value of the integral of f from -2 to 2,

$$\int_{-2}^{2} \sqrt{4 - x^2}\, dx = 2\pi.$$

Now Try Exercise 15.

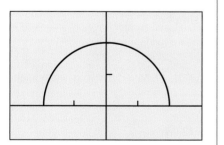

[−3, 3] by [−1, 3]

Figure 6.18 A square viewing window on $y = \sqrt{4 - x^2}$. The graph is a semi-circle because $y = \sqrt{4 - x^2}$ is the same as $y^2 = 4 - x^2$, or $x^2 + y^2 = 4$, with $y \geq 0$. (Example 2)

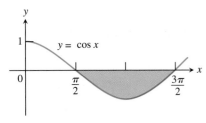

Figure 6.19 Because $f(x) = \cos x$ is nonpositive on $[\pi/2, 3\pi/2]$, the integral of f is a negative number. The area of the shaded region is the opposite of this integral,

$$\text{Area} = -\int_{\pi/2}^{3\pi/2} \cos x \, dx.$$

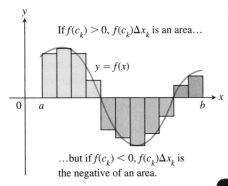

...but if $f(c_k) < 0$, $f(c_k)\Delta x_k$ is the negative of an area.

Figure 6.20 An integrable function f with negative as well as positive values.

Net Area

Sometimes $\int_a^b f(x)\,dx$ is called the *net area* of the region determined by the curve $y = f(x)$ and the x-axis between $x = a$ and $x = b$.

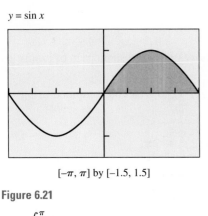

$[-\pi, \pi]$ by $[-1.5, 1.5]$

Figure 6.21

$$\int_0^\pi \sin x \, dx = 2. \text{ (Exploration 1)}$$

If an integrable function $y = f(x)$ is nonpositive, the nonzero terms $f(c_k)\Delta x_k$ in the Riemann sums for f over an interval $[a, b]$ are negatives of rectangle areas. The limit of the sums, the integral of f from a to b, is therefore the *negative* of the area of the region between the graph of f and the x-axis (Figure 6.19).

$$\int_a^b f(x) \, dx = -(\text{the area}) \quad \text{if} \quad f(x) \le 0.$$

Or, turning this around,

$$\text{Area} = -\int_a^b f(x) \, dx \quad \text{when} \quad f(x) \le 0.$$

If an integrable function $y = f(x)$ has both positive and negative values on an interval $[a, b]$, then the Riemann sums for f on $[a, b]$ add areas of rectangles that lie above the x-axis to the negatives of areas of rectangles that lie below the x-axis, as in Figure 6.20. The resulting cancellations mean that the limiting value is a number whose magnitude is less than the total area between the curve and the x-axis. The value of the integral is the area above the x-axis minus the area below.

For any integrable function,

$$\int_a^b f(x) \, dx = (\text{area above the } x\text{-axis}) - (\text{area below the } x\text{-axis}).$$

EXPLORATION 1 Finding Integrals by Signed Areas

It is a fact (which we will revisit) that $\int_0^\pi \sin x \, dx = 2$ (Figure 6.21). With that information, what you know about integrals and areas, what you know about graphing curves, and sometimes a bit of intuition, determine the values of the following integrals. Give as convincing an argument as you can for each value, based on the graph of the function.

1. $\displaystyle\int_\pi^{2\pi} \sin x \, dx$ **2.** $\displaystyle\int_0^{2\pi} \sin x \, dx$

3. $\displaystyle\int_0^{\pi/2} \sin x \, dx$ **4.** $\displaystyle\int_0^\pi (2 + \sin x) \, dx$

5. $\displaystyle\int_0^\pi 2 \sin x \, dx$ **6.** $\displaystyle\int_2^{\pi+2} \sin(x-2) \, dx$

7. $\displaystyle\int_{-\pi}^\pi \sin u \, du$ **8.** $\displaystyle\int_0^{2\pi} \sin(x/2) \, dx$

9. $\displaystyle\int_0^\pi \cos x \, dx$

10. Suppose k is *any* positive number. Make a conjecture about $\int_{-k}^k \sin x \, dx$ and support your conjecture.

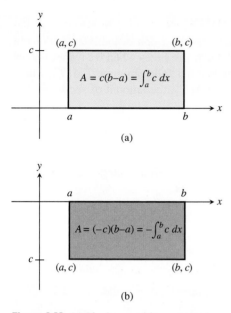

Figure 6.22 (a) If c is a positive constant, then $\int_a^b c\,dx$ is the area of the rectangle shown. (b) If c is negative, then $\int_a^b c\,dx$ is the opposite of the area of the rectangle.

Constant Functions

Integrals of constant functions are easy to evaluate. Over a closed interval, they are simply the constant times the length of the interval (Figure 6.22).

THEOREM 2   The Integral of a Constant

If $f(x) = c$, where c is a constant, on the interval $[a, b]$, then

$$\int_a^b f(x)\,dx = \int_a^b c\,dx = c(b - a).$$

Proof A constant function is continuous, so the integral exists, and we can evaluate it as a limit of Riemann sums with subintervals of equal length $(b - a)/n$. Any such sum looks like

$$\sum_{k=1}^n f(c_k) \cdot \Delta x, \quad \text{which is} \quad \sum_{k=1}^n c \cdot \frac{b - a}{n}.$$

Then

$$\sum_{k=1}^n c \cdot \frac{b - a}{n} = c \cdot (b - a) \sum_{k=1}^n \frac{1}{n}$$

$$= c(b - a) \cdot n\left(\frac{1}{n}\right)$$

$$= c(b - a)$$

Since the sum is *always* $c(b - a)$ for any value of n, it follows that the limit of the sums, the integral to which they converge, is also $c(b - a)$. ∎

EXAMPLE 3 Revisiting the Ship Problem

A ship sails at a steady 7.5 nautical miles per hour (knots) from 7:00 A.M. to 9:00 A.M. Express its total distance traveled as an integral. Evaluate the integral using Theorem 2.

SOLUTION

(See Figure 6.23.)

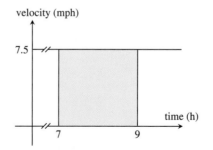

Figure 6.23 The area of the rectangle is a special case of Theorem 2. (Example 3)

$$\text{Distance traveled} = \int_7^9 7.5\,dt = 7.5 \cdot (9 - 7) = 15$$

Since the 7.5 is measured in nautical miles/hour and the $(9 - 7)$ is measured in hours, the 15 is measured in nautical miles. The ship traveled 15 nautical miles.

Now Try Exercise 29.

Definite Integral as an Accumulator Function

In Example 1 on page 270, we saw how the area under the graph of the rate of snowfall describes the total amount of snow that has fallen. There are times when we want to know not just the total snowfall, but the amount of snow that has fallen by time T, $S(T)$, where $3 \leq T \leq 10.5$ hours after midnight. We can express $S(T)$, the amount of snow that has fallen by time T, as a definite integral,

$$S(T) = \int_3^T r(t)\, dt,$$

where $r(t)$ is the rate at which snow is falling at time t. The definite integral makes it possible to build new functions called **accumulator functions.**

DEFINITION   Accumulator Function

If the function f is integrable over the closed interval $[a, b]$, then the definite integral of f from a to x defines a new function for $a \leq x \leq b$, the accumulator function,

$$A(x) = \int_a^x f(t)\, dt.$$

EXAMPLE 4 An Accumulator Function

Let $f(t) = 1 + 2t$ for $1 \leq t \leq 6$. Write the accumulator function $A(x)$ as a polynomial in x where

$$A(x) = \int_1^x (1 + 2t)\, dt, \quad 1 \leq x \leq 6.$$

SOLUTION

The accumulation from 1 to x is the area under the graph of $y = 1 + 2t$ over the interval $[1, x]$ (Figure 6.24). The area of this trapezoid is the length of the base times the average of the heights of the left and right sides,

$$A(x) = (x - 1)\frac{(1 + 2(1)) + (1 + 2(x))}{2} = (x - 1)(2 + x) = x^2 + x - 2.$$

Now Try Exercise 33.

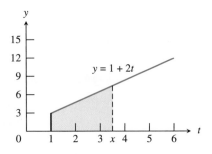

Figure 6.24 The accumulator function $A(x)$ is the area under the graph of $y = 1 + 2t$ for $1 \leq t \leq x$.

Integrals on a Calculator

You do not have to know much about your calculator to realize that finding the limit of a Riemann sum is exactly the kind of thing that it does best. We have seen how effectively it can approximate areas using MRAM, but most modern calculators have sophisticated built-in programs that converge to integrals with much greater speed and precision than that. We will assume that your calculator has such a numerical integration capability, which we will denote as **NINT.** In particular, we will use NINT $(f(x), x, a, b)$ to denote a calculator (or computer) approximation of $\int_a^b f(x)\, dx$. When we write

$$\int_a^b f(x)\, dx = \text{NINT}\,(f(x), x, a, b),$$

we do so with the understanding that the right-hand side of the equation is an approximation of the left-hand side.

EXAMPLE 5 Using NINT

Evaluate the following integrals numerically.

(a) $\displaystyle\int_{-1}^{2} x \sin x \, dx$ **(b)** $\displaystyle\int_{0}^{1} \frac{4}{1 + x^2}\, dx$ **(c)** $\displaystyle\int_{0}^{5} e^{-x^2}\, dx$

SOLUTION

(a) NINT $(x \sin x, x, -1, 2) \approx 2.04$

(b) NINT $(4/(1 + x^2), x, 0, 1) \approx 3.14$

(c) NINT $(e^{-x^2}, x, 0, 5) \approx 0.89$ ***Now Try Exercise 37.***

We will eventually be able to confirm that the exact value for the integral in Example 4a is $-2 \cos 2 + \sin 2 - \cos 1 + \sin 1$. You might want to conjecture for yourself what the exact answer to Example 4b might be. As for Example 4c, no explicit *exact* value has ever been found for this integral! The best we can do in this case (and in many like it) is to approximate the integral numerically. Here, technology is not only useful, it is essential.

We also can use NINT to graph an accumulator function. Consider the function f defined by

$$f(x) = \int_0^x (1 + t \cos t)\, dt.$$

Graphing both $y = 1 + x \cos x$ and $y = \text{NINT}\,(1 + t \cos t, t, 0, x)$ produces the graphs in Figure 6.25. (See if you can decide which is which.)

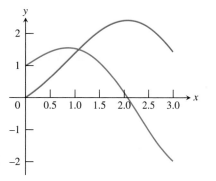

Figure 6.25 The graphs of $y = 1 + x \cos x$ and $y = \text{NINT}\,(1 + t \cos t, t, 0, x)$.

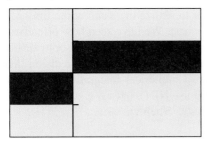

$y = |x|/x$

[−1, 2] by [−2, 2]

Figure 6.26 A discontinuous integrable function:

$$\int_{-1}^{2} \frac{|x|}{x}\, dx = -(\text{area below } x\text{-axis}) + (\text{area above } x\text{-axis}).$$

(Example 6)

Bounded Functions

We say a function is *bounded* on a given domain if its range is confined between some minimum value m and some maximum value M. That is, given any x in the domain, $m \le f(x) \le M$. Equivalently, the graph of $y = f(x)$ lies between the horizontal lines $y = m$ and $y = M$.

A Nonintegrable Function

How "bad" does a function have to be before it is *not* integrable? One way to defeat integrability is to be unbounded (like $y = 1/x$ near $x = 0$), which can prevent the Riemann sums from tending to a finite limit. Another, more subtle, way is to be bounded but badly discontinuous, like the *characteristic function of the rationals*:

$$f(x) = \begin{cases} 1 & \text{if } x \text{ is rational} \\ 0 & \text{if } x \text{ is irrational} \end{cases}$$

No matter what partition we take of the closed interval $[0, 1]$, every subinterval contains both rational and irrational numbers. That means that we can always form a Riemann sum with all rational c_k's (a Riemann sum of 1) or all irrational c_k's (a Riemann sum of 0). The sums can therefore never tend toward a unique limit.

This method is *very* slow. The problem is that for each point on the graph of the accumulator function, the calculator or computer has to go all the way back to the beginning and calculate the whole Riemann sum from 0 up to that value of x. Surely life would be easier if it used the last calculated value and just figured out how much the function changed as we moved from the last to the current value of x. This simple observation will be the key to one of the most important results in all of calculus, the Fundamental Theorem of Calculus.

Discontinuous Integrable Functions

Theorem 1 guarantees that all continuous functions are integrable. But some functions with discontinuities are also integrable. For example, a bounded function (see margin note) that has a finite number of points of discontinuity on an interval $[a, b]$ will still be integrable on the interval if it is continuous everywhere else. The function can even be undefined at a single point of discontinuity (as in Example 6). We just avoid that one value in the Riemann sum approximation.

EXAMPLE 6 Integrating a Discontinuous Function

Find $\displaystyle\int_{-1}^{2} \frac{|x|}{x}\, dx$.

SOLUTION

This function has a discontinuity at $x = 0$, where the graph jumps from $y = -1$ to $y = 1$. The graph, however, determines two rectangles, one below the x-axis and one above (Figure 6.26).

Using the idea of net area, we have

$$\int_{-1}^{2} \frac{|x|}{x}\, dx = -1 + 2 = 1. \qquad \textbf{\textit{Now Try Exercise 41.}}$$

EXPLORATION 2 More Discontinuous Integrands

1. Explain why the function

$$f(x) = \frac{x^2 - 4}{x - 2}$$

   is not continuous on $[0, 3]$. What kind of discontinuity occurs?

2. Use areas to show that

$$\int_{0}^{3} \frac{x^2 - 4}{x - 2}\, dx = 10.5.$$

3. Use areas to show that

$$\int_{0}^{5} \text{int}\,(x)\, dx = 10.$$

Quick Review 6.2

Exercise numbers with a gray background indicate problems that the authors have designed to be solved *without a calculator.*

In Exercises 1–3, evaluate the sum.

1. $\displaystyle\sum_{n=1}^{5} n^2$

2. $\displaystyle\sum_{k=0}^{4} (3k - 2)$

3. $\displaystyle\sum_{j=0}^{4} 100\,(j + 1)^2$

In Exercises 4–6, write the sum in sigma notation.

4. $1 + 2 + 3 + \cdots + 98 + 99$

5. $0 + 2 + 4 + \cdots + 48 + 50$

6. $3(1)^2 + 3(2)^2 + \cdots + 3(500)^2$

In Exercises 7 and 8, write the expression as a single sum in sigma notation.

7. $2\sum_{x=1}^{50} x^2 + 3\sum_{x=1}^{50} x$

8. $\sum_{k=0}^{8} x^k + \sum_{k=9}^{20} x^k$

9. Find $\sum_{k=0}^{n} (-1)^k$ if n is odd.

10. Find $\sum_{k=0}^{n} (-1)^k$ if n is even.

Section 6.2 Exercises

In Exercises 1–6, each c_k is chosen from the kth subinterval of a regular partition of the indicated interval into n subintervals of length Δx. Express the limit as a definite integral.

1. $\lim_{n \to \infty} \sum_{k=1}^{n} c_k^2 \Delta x, \quad [0, 2]$

2. $\lim_{n \to \infty} \sum_{k=1}^{n} (c_k^2 - 3c_k) \Delta x, \quad [-7, 5]$

3. $\lim_{n \to \infty} \sum_{k=1}^{n} \frac{1}{c_k} \Delta x, \quad [1, 4]$

4. $\lim_{n \to \infty} \sum_{k=1}^{n} \frac{1}{1 - c_k} \Delta x, \quad [2, 3]$

5. $\lim_{n \to \infty} \sum_{k=1}^{n} \sqrt{4 - c_k^2}\, \Delta x, \quad [0, 1]$

6. $\lim_{n \to \infty} \sum_{k=1}^{n} (\sin^3 c_k)\, \Delta x, \quad [-\pi, \pi]$

In Exercises 7–12, evaluate the integral.

7. $\int_{-2}^{1} 5\, dx$

8. $\int_{3}^{7} (-20)\, dx$

9. $\int_{0}^{3} (-160)\, dt$

10. $\int_{-4}^{-1} \frac{\pi}{2}\, d\theta$

11. $\int_{-2.1}^{3.4} 0.5\, ds$

12. $\int_{\sqrt{2}}^{\sqrt{18}} \sqrt{2}\, dr$

In Exercises 13–22, use the graph of the integrand and areas to evaluate the integral.

13. $\int_{-2}^{4} \left(\frac{x}{2} + 3 \right) dx$

14. $\int_{1/2}^{3/2} (-2x + 4)\, dx$

15. $\int_{-3}^{3} \sqrt{9 - x^2}\, dx$

16. $\int_{-4}^{0} \sqrt{16 - x^2}\, dx$

17. $\int_{-2}^{1} |x|\, dx$

18. $\int_{-1}^{1} (1 - |x|)\, dx$

19. $\int_{-1}^{1} (2 - |x|)\, dx$

20. $\int_{-1}^{1} (1 + \sqrt{1 - x^2})\, dx$

21. $\int_{\pi}^{2\pi} \theta\, d\theta$

22. $\int_{\sqrt{2}}^{5\sqrt{2}} r\, dr$

In Exercises 23–28, use areas to evaluate the integral.

23. $\int_{0}^{b} x\, dx, \quad b > 0$

24. $\int_{0}^{b} 4x\, dx, \quad b > 0$

25. $\int_{a}^{b} 2s\, ds, \quad 0 < a < b$

26. $\int_{a}^{b} 3t\, dt, \quad 0 < a < b$

27. $\int_{a}^{2a} x\, dx, \quad a > 0,$

28. $\int_{a}^{\sqrt{3}a} x\, dx, \quad a > 0$

In Exercises 29–32, express the desired quantity as a definite integral and evaluate the integral using Theorem 2.

29. Find the distance traveled by a train moving at 87 mph from 8:00 A.M. to 11:00 A.M.

30. Find the output from a pump producing 25 gallons per minute during the first hour of its operation.

31. Find the calories burned by a walker burning 300 calories per hour between 6:00 P.M. and 7:30 P.M.

32. Find the amount of water lost from a bucket leaking 0.4 liter per hour between 8:30 A.M. and 11:00 A.M.

In Exercises 33–36, write the accumulator function $A(x)$ as a polynomial in x.

33. $A(x) = \int_{2}^{x} 3\, dt, \ 2 \le x \le 5$

34. $A(x) = \int_{0}^{x} 3t\, dt, \ 0 \le x \le 3$

35. $A(x) = \int_{0}^{x} (4 - 2t)\, dt, \ 0 \le x \le 2$

36. $A(x) = \int_{1}^{x} (5 - 2t)\, dt, \ 1 \le x \le 2$

In Exercises 37–40, use NINT to evaluate the expression.

37. $\int_{0}^{5} \frac{x}{x^2 + 4}\, dx$

38. $3 + 2\int_{0}^{\pi/3} \tan x\, dx$

39. Find the area enclosed between the x-axis and the graph of $y = 4 - x^2$ from $x = -2$ to $x = 2$.

40. Find the area enclosed between the x-axis and the graph of $y = x^2 e^{-x}$ from $x = -1$ to $x = 3$.

In Exercises 41–44, **(a)** find the points of discontinuity of the integrand on the interval of integration, and **(b)** use area to evaluate the integral.

41. $\int_{-2}^{3} \frac{x}{|x|}\, dx$

42. $\int_{-6}^{5} 2\operatorname{int}(x - 3)\, dx$

43. $\int_{-3}^{4} \frac{x^2 - 1}{x + 1}\, dx$

44. $\int_{-5}^{6} \frac{9 - x^2}{x - 3}\, dx$

Standardized Test Questions

45. True or False If $\int_a^b f(x)\, dx > 0$, then $f(x)$ is positive for all x in $[a, b]$. Justify your answer.

46. True or False If $f(x)$ is positive for all x in $[a, b]$, then $\int_a^b f(x)\, dx > 0$. Justify your answer.

47. Multiple Choice If $\int_2^5 f(x)\, dx = 18$, then $\int_2^5 (f(x) + 4)\, dx =$

(A) 20   (B) 22   (C) 23   (D) 25   (E) 30

48. Multiple Choice $\int_{-4}^4 (4 - |x|)\, dx =$

(A) 0   (B) 4   (C) 8   (D) 16   (E) 32

49. Multiple Choice If the interval $[0, \pi]$ is divided into n subintervals of length π/n and c_k is chosen from the kth subinterval, which of the following is a Riemann sum?

(A) $\sum_{k=1}^{n} \sin(c_k)$ (B) $\sum_{k=1}^{\infty} \sin(c_k)$ (C) $\sum_{k=1}^{n} \sin(c_k)\left(\dfrac{\pi}{n}\right)$

(D) $\sum_{k=1}^{n} \sin\left(\dfrac{\pi}{n}\right)(c_k)$ (E) $\sum_{k=1}^{n} \sin(c_k)\left(\dfrac{\pi}{k}\right)$

50. Multiple Choice Which of the following quantities would *not* be represented by the definite integral $\int_0^8 70\, dt$?

(A) The distance traveled by a train moving at 70 mph for 8 minutes

(B) The volume of ice cream produced by a machine making 70 gallons per hour for 8 hours

(C) The length of a track left by a snail traveling at 70 cm per hour for 8 hours

(D) The total sales of a company selling $70 of merchandise per hour for 8 hours

(E) The amount the tide has risen 8 minutes after low tide if it rises at a rate of 70 mm per minute during that period

Explorations

In Exercises 51–60, use graphs, your knowledge of area, and the fact that

$$\int_0^1 x^3\, dx = \frac{1}{4}$$

to evaluate the integral.

51. $\int_{-1}^1 x^3\, dx$

52. $\int_0^1 (x^3 + 3)\, dx$

53. $\int_2^3 (x - 2)^3\, dx$

54. $\int_{-1}^1 |x|^3\, dx$

55. $\int_0^1 (1 - x^3)\, dx$

56. $\int_{-1}^2 (|x| - 1)^3\, dx$

57. $\int_0^2 \left(\dfrac{x}{2}\right)^3 dx$

58. $\int_{-8}^8 x^3\, dx$

59. $\int_0^1 (x^3 - 1)\, dx$

60. $\int_0^1 \sqrt[3]{x}\, dx$

Extending the Ideas

61. Writing to Learn The function

$$f(x) = \begin{cases} \dfrac{1}{x^2}, & 0 < x \le 1 \\ 0, & x = 0 \end{cases}$$

is defined on $[0, 1]$ and has a single point of discontinuity at $x = 0$.

(a) What happens to the graph of f as x approaches 0 from the right?

(b) The function f is not integrable on $[0, 1]$. Give a convincing argument based on Riemann sums to explain why it is not.

62. It can be shown by mathematical induction (see Appendix 2) that

$$\sum_{k=1}^n k^2 = \frac{n(n + 1)(2n + 1)}{6}.$$

Use this fact to give a formal proof that

$$\int_0^1 x^2\, dx = \frac{1}{3}$$

by following the steps given below.

(a) Partition $[0, 1]$ into n subintervals of length $1/n$. Show that the RRAM Riemann sum for the integral is

$$\sum_{k=1}^n \left(\left(\frac{k}{n}\right)^2 \cdot \frac{1}{n}\right).$$

(b) Show that this sum can be written as

$$\frac{1}{n^3} \cdot \sum_{k=1}^n k^2.$$

(c) Show that the sum can therefore be written as

$$\frac{(n + 1)(2n + 1)}{6n^2}.$$

(d) Show that

$$\lim_{n \to \infty} \sum_{k=1}^n \left(\left(\frac{k}{n}\right)^2 \cdot \frac{1}{n}\right) = \frac{1}{3}.$$

(e) Explain why the equation in part (d) proves that

$$\int_0^1 x^2\, dx = \frac{1}{3}.$$

6.3 | Definite Integrals and Antiderivatives

You will be able to calculate a definite integral using areas and properties of definite integrals and apply definite integrals to problems involving the average value of a function.

- Properties of definite integrals
- Average value of a function
- Mean Value Theorem for Definite Integrals

Properties of Definite Integrals

Because $\int_a^b f(x)\, dx$ is accumulating the area from a to b under the graph of f, we define $\int_a^a f(x)\, dx = 0$. Since we have not moved off the starting point, nothing has accumulated. We also want the accumulation from a to b plus the accumulation from b to c to equal the accumulation from a to c,

$$\int_a^b f(x)\, dx + \int_b^c f(x)\, dx = \int_a^c f(x)\, dx.$$

What happens if we reverse the usual order so that the right-hand end of the interval is on the bottom and the left-hand end on top? If we want to stick with our last decision for all values of a, b, and c, then when we accumulate from a to b and then b back to a, we are just accumulating from a to a,

$$\int_a^b f(x)\, dx + \int_b^a f(x)\, dx = \int_a^a f(x)\, dx = 0,$$

and therefore

$$\int_b^a f(x)\, dx = -\int_a^b f(x)\, dx.$$

Other rules for definite integrals (Table 6.3) follow from similar rules that hold for Riemann sums. However, the limit step required to *prove* that these rules hold in the limit (as the norms of the partitions tend to zero) places their mathematical verification beyond the scope of this course. They should make good sense nonetheless.

TABLE 6.3 Rules for Definite Integrals

1. *Zero:*
$$\int_a^a f(x)\, dx = 0$$

2. *Additivity:*
$$\int_a^b f(x)\, dx + \int_b^c f(x)\, dx = \int_a^c f(x)\, dx$$

3. *Order of Integration:*
$$\int_b^a f(x)\, dx = -\int_a^b f(x)\, dx$$

4. *Constant Multiple:*
$$\int_a^b k f(x)\, dx = k \int_a^b f(x)\, dx \qquad \text{Any number } k$$
$$\int_a^b -f(x)\, dx = -\int_a^b f(x)\, dx \qquad k = -1$$

5. *Sum and Difference:*
$$\int_a^b (f(x) \pm g(x))\, dx = \int_a^b f(x)\, dx \pm \int_a^b g(x)\, dx$$

6. *Max-Min Inequality:* If max f and min f are the maximum and minimum values of f on $[a, b]$, then
$$\min f \cdot (b - a) \le \int_a^b f(x)\, dx \le \max f \cdot (b - a).$$

7. *Domination:* $f(x) \ge g(x)$ on $[a, b] \Rightarrow \int_a^b f(x)\, dx \ge \int_a^b g(x)\, dx$
$$f(x) \ge 0 \text{ on } [a, b] \Rightarrow \int_a^b f(x)\, dx \ge 0 \qquad g = 0$$

EXAMPLE 1 Using the Rules for Definite Integrals

Suppose

$$\int_{-1}^{1} f(x)\, dx = 5, \quad \int_{1}^{4} f(x)\, dx = -2, \quad \text{and} \quad \int_{-1}^{1} h(x)\, dx = 7.$$

Find each of the following integrals, if possible.

(a) $\displaystyle\int_{4}^{1} f(x)\, dx$ **(b)** $\displaystyle\int_{-1}^{4} f(x)\, dx$ **(c)** $\displaystyle\int_{-1}^{1} [\,2f(x) + 3h(x)\,]\, dx$

(d) $\displaystyle\int_{0}^{1} f(x)\, dx$ **(e)** $\displaystyle\int_{-2}^{2} h(x)\, dx$ **(f)** $\displaystyle\int_{-1}^{4} [\,f(x) + h(x)\,]\, dx$

SOLUTION

(a) $\displaystyle\int_{4}^{1} f(x)\, dx = -\int_{1}^{4} f(x)\, dx = -(-2) = 2$

(b) $\displaystyle\int_{-1}^{4} f(x)\, dx = \int_{-1}^{1} f(x)\, dx + \int_{1}^{4} f(x)\, dx = 5 + (-2) = 3$

(c) $\displaystyle\int_{-1}^{1} [\,2f(x) + 3h(x)\,]\, dx = 2\int_{-1}^{1} f(x)\, dx + 3\int_{-1}^{1} h(x)\, dx = 2(5) + 3(7) = 31$

(d) Not enough information given. (We cannot assume, for example, that integrating over half the interval would give half the integral!)

(e) Not enough information given. (We have no information about the function h outside the interval $[-1, 1]$.)

(f) Not enough information given (same reason as in part (e)). ***Now Try Exercise 1.***

EXAMPLE 2 Finding Bounds for an Integral

Show that the value of $\int_{0}^{1} \sqrt{1 + \cos x}\, dx$ is less than $3/2$.

SOLUTION

The Max-Min Inequality for definite integrals (Rule 6) says that min $f \cdot (b - a)$ is a *lower bound* for the value of $\int_{a}^{b} f(x)\, dx$ and that max $f \cdot (b - a)$ is an *upper bound*.

The maximum value of $\sqrt{1 + \cos x}$ on $[0, 1]$ is $\sqrt{2}$, so

$$\int_{0}^{1} \sqrt{1 + \cos x}\, dx \le \sqrt{2} \cdot (1 - 0) = \sqrt{2}.$$

Since $\int_{0}^{1} \sqrt{1 + \cos x}\, dx$ is bounded above by $\sqrt{2}$ (which is $1.414\ldots$), it is less than $3/2$. ***Now Try Exercise 7.***

Average Value of a Function

The *average* of n numbers is the sum of the numbers divided by n. How would we define the average value of an arbitrary function f over a closed interval $[a, b]$? As there are infinitely many values to consider, adding them and then dividing by infinity is not an option.

Consider, then, what happens if we take a large *sample* of n numbers from regular subintervals of the interval $[a, b]$. One way would be to take some number c_k from each of the n subintervals of length

$$\Delta x = \frac{b - a}{n}.$$

The average of the n sampled values is

$$\frac{f(c_1) + f(c_2) + \cdots + f(c_n)}{n} = \frac{1}{n} \cdot \sum_{k=1}^{n} f(c_k)$$

$$= \frac{\Delta x}{b - a} \sum_{k=1}^{n} f(c_k) \qquad \frac{1}{n} = \frac{\Delta x}{b - a}$$

$$= \frac{1}{b - a} \cdot \sum_{k=1}^{n} f(c_k) \Delta x$$

Does this last sum look familiar? It is $1/(b - a)$ times a Riemann sum for f on $[a, b]$. That means that when we consider this averaging process as $n \to \infty$, we find it *has a limit,* namely $1/(b - a)$ times the integral of f over $[a, b]$. We are led by this remarkable fact to the following definition.

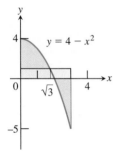

Figure 6.27 The rectangle with base $[0, 3]$ and with height equal to 1 (the average value of the function $f(x) = (4 - x^2)$) has area equal to the net area between f and the x-axis from 0 to 3. (Example 3)

DEFINITION   Average (Mean) Value

If f is integrable on $[a, b]$, its **average (mean) value** on $[a, b]$ is

$$av(f) = \frac{1}{b - a} \int_a^b f(x)\, dx.$$

EXAMPLE 3 Applying the Definition

Find the average value of $f(x) = 4 - x^2$ on $[0, 3]$. Does f actually take on this value at some point in the given interval?

SOLUTION

$$av(f) = \frac{1}{b - a} \int_a^b f(x)\, dx$$

$$= \frac{1}{3 - 0} \int_0^3 (4 - x^2)\, dx$$

$$= \frac{1}{3 - 0} \cdot 3 \qquad \text{Using NINT}$$

$$= 1$$

The average value of $f(x) = 4 - x^2$ over the interval $[0, 3]$ is 1. The function assumes this value when $4 - x^2 = 1$ or $x = \pm\sqrt{3}$. Since $x = \sqrt{3}$ lies in the interval $[0, 3]$, the function does assume its average value in the given interval (Figure 6.27).

Now Try Exercise 11.

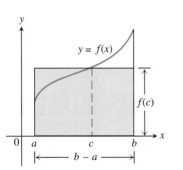

Figure 6.28 The value $f(c)$ in the Mean Value Theorem is, in a sense, the average (or *mean*) height of f on $[a, b]$. When $f \geq 0$, the area of the shaded rectangle

$$f(c)(b - a) = \int_a^b f(x)\, dx,$$

is the area under the graph of f from a to b.

Mean Value Theorem for Definite Integrals

It was no mere coincidence that the function in Example 3 took on its average value at some point in the interval. Look at the graph in Figure 6.28 and imagine rectangles with base $(b - a)$ and heights ranging from the minimum of f (a rectangle too small to give the integral) to the maximum of f (a rectangle too large). Somewhere in between there is a "just right" rectangle, and its topside will intersect the graph of f if f is continuous. The statement that a continuous function on a closed interval *always* assumes its average value at least once in the interval is known as the Mean Value Theorem for Definite Integrals.

THEOREM 3   The Mean Value Theorem for Definite Integrals

If f is continuous on $[a, b]$, then at some point c in $[a, b]$,

$$f(c) = \frac{1}{b - a} \int_a^b f(x)\, dx.$$

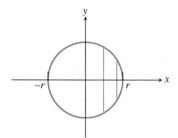

Figure 6.29 Chords perpendicular to the diameter $[-r, r]$ in a circle of radius r centered at the origin. (Exploration 1)

EXPLORATION 1   How Long Is the Average Chord of a Circle?

Suppose we have a circle of radius r centered at the origin. We want to know the average length of the chords perpendicular to the diameter $[-r, r]$ on the x-axis.

1. Show that the length of the chord at x is $2\sqrt{r^2 - x^2}$ (Figure 6.29).
2. Set up an integral expression for the average value of $2\sqrt{r^2 - x^2}$ over the interval $[-r, r]$.
3. Evaluate the integral by identifying its value as an area.
4. So, what is the average length of a chord of a circle of radius r?
5. Explain how we can use the Mean Value Theorem for Definite Integrals (Theorem 3) to show that the function assumes the value in Step 4.

Connecting Differential and Integral Calculus

Before we move on to the next section, let us pause for a moment of historical perspective that can help you to appreciate the power of the theorem that you are about to encounter. In Example 3 we used NINT to find the integral, and in Section 6.2, Example 2, we were fortunate that we could use our knowledge of the area of a circle. The area of a circle has been around for a long time, but NINT has not; so how did people evaluate definite integrals when they could not apply some known area formula? For example, in Exploration 1 of the previous section we used the fact that

$$\int_0^\pi \sin x\, dx = 2.$$

Would Newton and Leibniz have known this fact? How?

They did know that *quotients of infinitely small quantities,* as they put it, could be used to get velocity functions from position functions, and that *sums of infinitely thin "rectangle areas"* could be used to get position functions from velocity functions. In some way, then, there had to be a connection between these two seemingly different processes. Newton and Leibniz were able to picture that connection, and it led them to the Fundamental Theorem of Calculus. Can you picture it? Try Exploration 2.

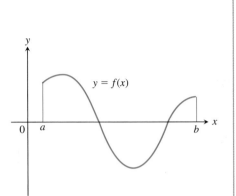

Figure 6.30 The graph of the function in Exploration 2.

EXPLORATION 2 Finding the Derivative of an Integral

Group Activity Suppose we are given the graph of a continuous function f, as in Figure 6.30.

1. Copy the graph of f onto your own paper. Choose any x greater than a in the interval $[a, b]$ and mark it on the x-axis.
2. Using only *vertical line segments,* shade in the region between the graph of f and the x-axis from a to x. (Some shading might be below the x-axis.)
3. Your shaded region represents the accumulator function, which we will call F, $F(x) = \int_a^x f(t)\, dt$.
4. Recall that $F'(x)$ is the limit of $\Delta F/\Delta x$ as Δx gets smaller and smaller. Represent ΔF in your picture by drawing *one more vertical shading segment* to the right of the last one you drew in step 2. ΔF is the (signed) *area* of your vertical segment.
5. Represent Δx in your picture by moving x to beneath your newly drawn segment. That small change in Δx is the *thickness* of your vertical segment.
6. What is now the *height* of your vertical segment?
7. Can you see why Newton and Leibniz concluded that $F'(x) = f(x)$?

If all went well in Exploration 2, you concluded that the derivative with respect to x of the integral of f from a to x is simply f. Specifically,

$$\frac{d}{dx}\int_a^x f(t)\, dt = f(x).$$

This means that the integral is an *antiderivative* of f, a fact we can exploit in the following way.

If F is any antiderivative of f, then

$$\int_a^x f(t)\, dt = F(x) + C$$

for some constant C. Setting x in this equation equal to a gives

$$\int_a^a f(t)\, dt = F(a) + C$$
$$0 = F(a) + C$$
$$C = -F(a).$$

Putting it all together,

$$\int_a^x f(t)\, dt = F(x) - F(a).$$

The implications of the previous last equation were enormous for the discoverers of calculus. It meant that they could evaluate the definite integral of f from a to any number x simply by computing $F(x) - F(a)$, where F is any antiderivative of f.

EXAMPLE 4 Finding an Integral Using Antiderivatives

Find $\int_0^{\pi} \sin x \, dx$ using the formula $\int_a^x f(t) \, dt = F(x) - F(a)$.

SOLUTION

Since $\sin x$ is the rate of change of the quantity $F(x) = -\cos x$, that is $F'(x) = \sin x$,

$$\int_0^{\pi} \sin x \, dx = -\cos(\pi) - (-\cos(0))$$

$$= -(-1) - (-1)$$

$$= 2$$

This explains how we obtained the value for Exploration 1 of the previous section.

Now Try Exercise 21.

Quick Review 6.3 *(For help, go to Sections 4.1, 4.3, and 4.4.)*

Exercise numbers with a gray background indicate problems that the authors have designed to be solved *without a calculator*.

In Exercises 1–10, find dy/dx.

1. $y = -\cos x$

2. $y = \sin x$

3. $y = \ln(\sec x)$

4. $y = \ln(\sin x)$

5. $y = \ln(\sec x + \tan x)$

6. $y = x \ln x - x$

7. $y = \dfrac{x^{n+1}}{n+1}$ $(n \neq -1)$

8. $y = \dfrac{1}{2^x + 1}$

9. $y = xe^x$

10. $y = \tan^{-1} x$

Section 6.3 Exercises

The exercises in this section are designed to reinforce your understanding of the definite integral from the algebraic and geometric points of view. For this reason, you should not use the numerical integration capability of your calculator (NINT) except perhaps to support an answer.

1. Suppose that f and g are continuous functions and that

$$\int_1^2 f(x) \, dx = -4, \quad \int_1^5 f(x) \, dx = 6, \quad \int_1^5 g(x) \, dx = 8.$$

Use the rules in Table 6.3 to find each integral.

(a) $\displaystyle \int_2^2 g(x) \, dx$

(b) $\displaystyle \int_5^1 g(x) \, dx$

(c) $\displaystyle \int_1^2 3f(x) \, dx$

(d) $\displaystyle \int_2^5 f(x) \, dx$

(e) $\displaystyle \int_1^5 [f(x) - g(x)] \, dx$

(f) $\displaystyle \int_1^5 [4f(x) - g(x)] \, dx$

2. Suppose that f and h are continuous functions and that

$$\int_1^9 f(x) \, dx = -1, \quad \int_7^9 f(x) \, dx = 5, \quad \int_7^9 h(x) \, dx = 4.$$

Use the rules in Table 6.3 to find each integral.

(a) $\displaystyle \int_1^9 -2f(x) \, dx$

(b) $\displaystyle \int_7^9 [f(x) + h(x)] \, dx$

(c) $\displaystyle \int_7^9 [2f(x) - 3h(x)] \, dx$

(d) $\displaystyle \int_9^1 f(x) \, dx$

(e) $\displaystyle \int_1^7 f(x) \, dx$

(f) $\displaystyle \int_9^7 [h(x) - f(x)] \, dx$

3. Suppose that $\int_1^2 f(x) \, dx = 5$. Find each integral.

(a) $\displaystyle \int_1^2 f(u) \, du$

(b) $\displaystyle \int_1^2 \sqrt{3} \, f(z) \, dz$

(c) $\displaystyle \int_2^1 f(t) \, dt$

(d) $\displaystyle \int_1^2 [-f(x)] \, dx$

4. Suppose that $\int_{-3}^0 g(t) \, dt = \sqrt{2}$. Find each integral.

(a) $\displaystyle \int_0^{-3} g(t) \, dt$

(b) $\displaystyle \int_{-3}^0 g(u) \, du$

(c) $\displaystyle \int_{-3}^0 [-g(x)] \, dx$

(d) $\displaystyle \int_{-3}^0 \frac{g(r)}{\sqrt{2}} \, dr$

5. Suppose that f is continuous and that

$$\int_0^3 f(z)\, dz = 3 \quad \text{and} \quad \int_0^4 f(z)\, dz = 7.$$

Find each integral.

(a) $\int_3^4 f(z)\, dz$ (b) $\int_4^3 f(t)\, dt$

6. Suppose that h is continuous and that

$$\int_{-1}^1 h(r)\, dr = 0 \quad \text{and} \quad \int_{-1}^3 h(r)\, dr = 6.$$

Find each integral.

(a) $\int_1^3 h(r)\, dr$ (b) $-\int_3^1 h(u)\, du$

7. Show that the value of $\int_0^1 \sin(x^2)\, dx$ cannot possibly be 2.

8. Show that the value of $\int_0^1 \sqrt{x+8}\, dx$ lies between $2\sqrt{2} \approx 2.8$ and 3.

9. *Integrals of Nonnegative Functions* Use the Max-Min Inequality to show that if f is integrable then

$$f(x) \geq 0 \text{ on } [a, b] \implies \int_a^b f(x)\, dx \geq 0.$$

10. *Integrals of Nonpositive Functions* Show that if f is integrable then

$$f(x) \leq 0 \text{ on } [a, b] \implies \int_a^b f(x)\, dx \leq 0.$$

In Exercises 11–14, use NINT to find the average value of the function on the interval. At what point(s) in the interval does the function assume its average value?

11. $y = x^2 - 1$, $[0, \sqrt{3}]$ **12.** $y = -\dfrac{x^2}{2}$, $[0, 3]$

13. $y = -3x^2 - 1$, $[0, 1]$ **14.** $y = (x-1)^2$, $[0, 3]$

In Exercises 15–18, find the average value of the function on the interval without integrating, by appealing to the geometry of the region between the graph and the x-axis.

15. $f(x) = \begin{cases} x + 4, & -4 \leq x \leq -1, \\ -x + 2, & -1 < x \leq 2, \end{cases}$ on $[-4, 2]$

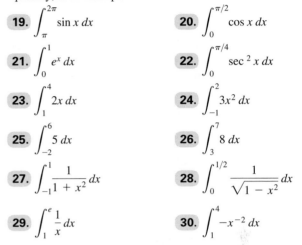

16. $f(t) = 1 - \sqrt{1 - t^2}$, $[-1, 1]$

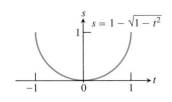

17. $f(t) = \sin t$, $[0, 2\pi]$

18. $f(\theta) = \tan \theta$, $\left[-\dfrac{\pi}{4}, \dfrac{\pi}{4}\right]$

In Exercises 19–30, interpret the integrand as the rate of change of a quantity and evaluate the integral using the antiderivative of the quantity, as in Example 4.

19. $\int_\pi^{2\pi} \sin x\, dx$ **20.** $\int_0^{\pi/2} \cos x\, dx$

21. $\int_0^1 e^x\, dx$ **22.** $\int_0^{\pi/4} \sec^2 x\, dx$

23. $\int_{-1}^4 2x\, dx$ **24.** $\int_{-1}^2 3x^2\, dx$

25. $\int_{-2}^6 5\, dx$ **26.** $\int_3^7 8\, dx$

27. $\int_{-1}^1 \dfrac{1}{1 + x^2}\, dx$ **28.** $\int_0^{1/2} \dfrac{1}{\sqrt{1 - x^2}}\, dx$

29. $\int_1^e \dfrac{1}{x}\, dx$ **30.** $\int_1^4 -x^{-2}\, dx$

In Exercises 31–36, find the average value of the function on the interval, using antiderivatives to compute the integral.

31. $y = \sin x$, $[0, \pi]$ **32.** $y = \dfrac{1}{x}$, $[e, 2e]$

33. $y = \sec^2 x$, $\left[0, \dfrac{\pi}{4}\right]$ **34.** $y = \dfrac{1}{1 + x^2}$, $[0, 1]$

35. $y = 3x^2 + 2x$, $[-1, 2]$ **36.** $y = \sec x \tan x$, $\left[0, \dfrac{\pi}{3}\right]$

37. Group Activity Use the Max-Min Inequality to find upper and lower bounds for the value of

$$\int_0^1 \dfrac{1}{1 + x^4}\, dx.$$

38. Group Activity *(Continuation of Exercise 37)* Use the Max-Min Inequality to find upper and lower bounds for the values of

$$\int_0^{0.5} \dfrac{1}{1 + x^4}\, dx \quad \text{and} \quad \int_{0.5}^1 \dfrac{1}{1 + x^4}\, dx.$$

Add these to arrive at an improved estimate for

$$\int_0^1 \dfrac{1}{1 + x^4}\, dx.$$

39. Writing to Learn If $av(f)$ really is a typical value of the integrable function $f(x)$ on $[a, b]$, then the number $av(f)$ should have the same integral over $[a, b]$ that f does. Does it? That is, does

$$\int_a^b av(f)\, dx = \int_a^b f(x)\, dx?$$

Give reasons for your answer.

40. Writing to Learn A driver averaged 30 mph on a 150-mile trip and then returned over the same 150 miles at the rate of 50 mph. He figured that his average speed was 40 mph for the entire trip.

(a) What was his total distance traveled?

(b) What was his total time spent for the trip?

(c) What was his average speed for the trip?

(d) Explain the error in the driver's reasoning.

41. Writing to Learn A dam released 1000 m³ of water at 10 m³/min and then released another 1000 m³ at 20 m³/min. What was the average rate at which the water was released? Give reasons for your answer.

42. Use the inequality $\sin x \leq x$, which holds for $x \geq 0$, to find an upper bound for the value of $\int_0^1 \sin x \, dx$.

43. The inequality $\sec x \geq 1 + (x^2/2)$ holds on $(-\pi/2, \pi/2)$. Use it to find a lower bound for the value of $\int_0^1 \sec x \, dx$.

44. Show that the average value of a linear function $L(x)$ on $[a, b]$ is

$$\frac{L(a) + L(b)}{2}.$$

(*Caution:* This simple formula for average value does *not* work for functions in general!)

Standardized Test Questions

You may use a graphing calculator to solve the following problems.

45. True or False The average value of a function f on $[a, b]$ always lies between $f(a)$ and $f(b)$. Justify your answer.

46. True or False If $\int_a^b f(x) \, dx = 0$, then $f(a) = f(b)$. Justify your answer.

47. Multiple Choice If $\int_3^7 f(x) \, dx = 5$ and $\int_3^7 g(x) \, dx = 3$, then all of the following must be true *except*

(A) $\int_3^7 f(x)g(x) \, dx = 15$

(B) $\int_3^7 [f(x) + g(x)] \, dx = 8$

(C) $\int_3^7 2 f(x) \, dx = 10$

(D) $\int_3^7 [f(x) - g(x)] \, dx = 2$

(E) $\int_7^3 [g(x) - f(x)] \, dx = 2$

48. Multiple Choice If $\int_2^5 f(x) \, dx = 12$ and $\int_5^8 f(x) \, dx = 4$, then all of the following must be true *except*

(A) $\int_2^8 f(x) \, dx = 16$

(B) $\int_2^5 f(x) \, dx - \int_5^8 3 f(x) \, dx = 0$

(C) $\int_5^2 f(x) \, dx = -12$

(D) $\int_{-5}^{-8} f(x) \, dx = -4$

(E) $\int_2^6 f(x) \, dx + \int_6^8 f(x) \, dx = 16$

49. Multiple Choice What is the average value of the cosine function on the interval $[1, 5]$?

(A) -0.990 (B) -0.450 (C) -0.128

(D) 0.412 (E) 0.998

50. Multiple Choice If the average value of the function f on the interval $[a, b]$ is 10, then $\int_a^b f(x) \, dx =$

(A) $\dfrac{10}{b - a}$ (B) $\dfrac{f(a) + f(b)}{10}$ (C) $10b - 10a$

(D) $\dfrac{b - a}{10}$ (E) $\dfrac{f(b) + f(a)}{20}$

Exploration

51. *Comparing Area Formulas* Consider the region in the first quadrant under the curve $y = (h/b)x$ from $x = 0$ to $x = b$ (see figure).

(a) Use a geometry formula to calculate the area of the region.

(b) Find all antiderivatives of y.

(c) Use an antiderivative of y to evaluate $\int_0^b y(x) \, dx$.

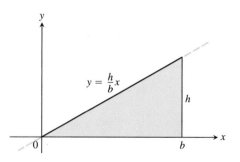

Extending the Ideas

52. *Graphing Calculator Challenge* If $k > 1$, and if the average value of x^k on $[0, k]$ is k, what is k? Check your result with a CAS if you have one available.

53. Show that if $F'(x) = G'(x)$ on $[a, b]$, then

$$F(b) - F(a) = G(b) - G(a).$$

Quick Quiz for AP* Preparation: Sections 6.1–6.3

1. Multiple Choice If $\int_a^b f(x)\, dx = a + 2b$, then $\int_a^b (f(x) + 3)\, dx =$

(A) $a + 2b + 3$ (B) $3b - 3a$

(C) $4a - b$ (D) $5b - 2a$

(E) $5b - 3a$

2. Multiple Choice The expression

$$\frac{1}{20}\left(\sqrt{\frac{1}{20}} + \sqrt{\frac{2}{20}} + \sqrt{\frac{3}{20}} + \cdots + \sqrt{\frac{20}{20}} \right)$$

is a Riemann sum approximation for

(A) $\displaystyle\int_0^1 \sqrt{\frac{x}{20}}\, dx$ (B) $\displaystyle\int_0^1 \sqrt{x}\, dx$

(C) $\displaystyle\frac{1}{20}\int_0^1 \sqrt{\frac{x}{20}}\, dx$ (D) $\displaystyle\frac{1}{20}\int_0^1 \sqrt{x}\, dx$

(E) $\displaystyle\frac{1}{20}\int_0^{20} \sqrt{x}\, dx$

3. Multiple Choice What are all values of k for which $\int_2^k x^2\, dx = 0$?

(A) -2 (B) 0 (C) 2

(D) -2 and 2 (E) -2, 0, and 2

4. Free Response Let f be a function such that $f''(x) = 6x + 12$.

(a) Find $f(x)$ if the graph of f is tangent to the line $4x - y = 5$ at the point $(0, -5)$.

(b) Find the average value of $f(x)$ on the closed interval $[-1, 1]$.

6.4 | Fundamental Theorem of Calculus

You will be able to analyze functions defined by an integral and evaluate definite integrals.

- The Antiderivative Part of the Fundamental Theorem of Calculus
- Use of definite integrals to define new functions (accumulator functions)
- The Evaluation Part of the Fundamental Theorem of Calculus
- Evaluation of definite integrals using antiderivatives

Fundamental Theorem, Antiderivative Part

In the last section, we saw how to compute areas and accumulations by reversing differentiation, what we call *antidifferentiation*. This was first discovered by Newton in 1666. A few years later and totally independently, Gottfried Leibniz rediscovered the same connection. But while Newton kept his discovery to himself, Leibniz proclaimed it to the world, drawing other scientists into the work of exploring its consequences.

This relationship between areas or accumulations and antidifferentiation is often referred to as the Fundamental Theorem of Calculus. That is a contraction of its original name: the Fundamental Theorem of Integral Calculus. While we will use "Fundamental Theorem of Calculus" to refer to this result, it is important to remember that this is really a theorem about integration. It says that the definite integral can be understood as accumulation (a limit of Riemann sums) or as antidifferentiation (the change in the value of an antiderivative). As long as we are working with continuous functions, these two ways of thinking about the definite integral are equally valid.

This connection provides powerful insight in both directions. It says that if we have an accumulation problem, there is an easy way to evaluate it if we can find an antiderivative (the Evaluation Part). It also says that if we need an antiderivative, we can always build one using the accumulation given by the limit of a Riemann sum (the Antiderivative Part).

THEOREM 4   The Fundamental Theorem of Calculus, Antiderivative Part

If f is continuous on $[a, b]$, then the function

$$F(x) = \int_a^x f(t)\, dt$$

has a derivative at every point x in $[a, b]$, and

$$\frac{dF}{dx} = \frac{d}{dx} \int_a^x f(t)\, dt = f(x).$$

Proof The geometric exploration at the end of the previous section contained the idea of the proof, but it glossed over the necessary limit arguments. Here we will be more precise.

Apply the definition of the derivative directly to the function F. That is,

$$\frac{dF}{dx} = \lim_{h \to 0} \frac{F(x+h) - F(x)}{h}$$

$$= \lim_{h \to 0} \frac{\displaystyle\int_a^{x+h} f(t)\, dt - \int_a^x f(t)\, dt}{h}$$

$$= \lim_{h \to 0} \frac{\displaystyle\int_x^{x+h} f(t)\, dt}{h} \qquad \text{Rules for integrals, Section 6.3}$$

$$= \lim_{h \to 0} \left[\frac{1}{h} \int_x^{x+h} f(t)\, dt \right]$$

The expression in brackets in the last line is the average value of f from x to $x + h$. We know from the Mean Value Theorem for Definite Integrals (Theorem 3, Section 6.3) that f, being continuous, takes on its average value at least once in the interval; that is,

$$\frac{1}{h} \int_x^{x+h} f(t)\, dt = f(c) \quad \text{for some } c \text{ between } x \text{ and } x + h.$$

We can therefore continue our proof, letting $(1/h)\int_x^{x+h} f(t)\, dt = f(c)$,

$$\frac{dF}{dx} = \lim_{h \to 0} \frac{1}{h} \int_x^{x+h} f(t)\, dt$$

$$= \lim_{h \to 0} f(c), \quad \text{where } c \text{ lies between } x \text{ and } x + h.$$

Augustin-Louis Cauchy (1789–1857)

In a series of textbooks written for his students at the École Polytechnique in Paris, Cauchy demonstrated the importance of continuity and created our modern definitions of limit, derivative, and definite integral. He also gave the first complete proofs of both the Antiderivative and Evaluation Parts of the Fundamental Theorem of Calculus for any continuous function. Cauchy was largely responsible for the creation of complex analysis, played an important role in the early development of linear algebra, and made significant contributions to understanding light propagation, mechanics, and elasticity.

What happens to c as h goes to zero? As $x + h$ gets closer to x, it carries c along with it like a bead on a wire, forcing c to approach x. Since f is continuous, this means that $f(c)$ approaches $f(x)$:

$$\lim_{h \to 0} f(c) = f(x).$$

Putting it all together,

$$\frac{dF}{dx} = \lim_{h \to 0} \frac{F(x + h) - F(x)}{h} \qquad \text{Definition of derivatives}$$

$$= \lim_{h \to 0} \frac{\int_x^{x+h} f(t)\, dt}{h} \qquad \text{Rules for integrals}$$

$$= \lim_{h \to 0} f(c) \quad \text{for some } c \text{ between } x \text{ and } x + h.$$

$$= f(x) \qquad \text{Because } f \text{ is continuous}$$

This concludes the proof. ∎

It is difficult to overestimate the power of the equation

$$\frac{d}{dx} \int_a^x f(t)\, dt = f(x). \tag{1}$$

It says that every continuous function f is the derivative of some other function, namely, $\int_a^x f(t)\, dt$. It says that every continuous function has an antiderivative. And it says that the processes of integration and differentiation are inverses of one another. If any equation deserves to be called the Fundamental Theorem of Calculus, this equation is surely the one.

EXAMPLE 1 Applying the Fundamental Theorem

Find

$$\frac{d}{dx} \int_{-\pi}^x \cos t\, dt \quad \text{and} \quad \frac{d}{dx} \int_0^x \frac{1}{1 + t^2}\, dt$$

by using the Fundamental Theorem.

SOLUTION

$$\frac{d}{dx} \int_{-\pi}^x \cos t\, dt = \cos x \qquad \text{Eq. 1 with } f(t) = \cos t$$

$$\frac{d}{dx} \int_0^x \frac{1}{1 + t^2}\, dt = \frac{1}{1 + x^2} \qquad \text{Eq. 1 with } f(t) = \frac{1}{1 + t^2}$$

Now Try Exercise 3.

EXAMPLE 2 The Fundamental Theorem with the Chain Rule

Find dy/dx if $y = \int_1^{x^2} \cos t \, dt$.

SOLUTION

The upper limit of integration is not x but x^2. This makes y a composite of

$$y = \int_1^u \cos t \, dt \quad \text{and} \quad u = x^2.$$

We must therefore apply the Chain Rule when finding dy/dx.

$$\frac{dy}{dx} = \frac{dy}{du} \cdot \frac{du}{dx}$$

$$= \left(\frac{d}{du} \int_1^u \cos t \, dt \right) \cdot \frac{du}{dx}$$

$$= \cos u \cdot \frac{du}{dx}$$

$$= \cos (x^2) \cdot 2x$$

$$= 2x \cos x^2 \qquad \qquad \textbf{\textit{Now Try Exercise 9.}}$$

EXAMPLE 3 Variable Lower Limits of Integration

Find dy/dx.

(a) $y = \int_x^5 3t \sin t \, dt$ **(b)** $y = \int_{2x}^{x^2} \frac{1}{2 + e^t} \, dt$

SOLUTION

The rules for integrals set these up for the Fundamental Theorem.

(a) $\dfrac{d}{dx}\displaystyle\int_x^5 3t \sin t \, dt = \dfrac{d}{dx}\left(-\int_5^x 3t \sin t \, dt \right)$

$$= -\frac{d}{dx}\int_5^x 3t \sin t \, dt$$

$$= -3x \sin x$$

(b) $\dfrac{d}{dx}\displaystyle\int_{2x}^{x^2} \frac{1}{2 + e^t} \, dt = \dfrac{d}{dx}\left(\int_0^{x^2} \frac{1}{2 + e^t} \, dt - \int_0^{2x} \frac{1}{2 + e^t} \, dt \right)$

$$= \frac{1}{2 + e^{x^2}}\frac{d}{dx}(x^2) - \frac{1}{2 + e^{2x}}\frac{d}{dx}(2x) \qquad \text{Chain Rule}$$

$$= \frac{1}{2 + e^{x^2}} \cdot 2x - \frac{1}{2 + e^{2x}} \cdot 2$$

$$= \frac{2x}{2 + e^{x^2}} - \frac{2}{2 + e^{2x}} \qquad \qquad \textbf{\textit{Now Try Exercise 19.}}$$

EXAMPLE 4 Constructing a Function with a Given Derivative and Value

Find a function $y = f(x)$ with derivative

$$\frac{dy}{dx} = \tan x$$

that satisfies the condition $f(3) = 5$.

SOLUTION

The Fundamental Theorem makes it easy to construct a function with derivative $\tan x$:

$$y = \int_3^x \tan t \, dt$$

Since $y(3) = 0$, we have only to add 5 to this function to construct one with derivative $\tan x$ whose value at $x = 3$ is 5:

$$f(x) = \int_3^x \tan t \, dt + 5 \qquad \textbf{\textit{Now Try Exercise 25.}}$$

Although the solution to the problem in Example 4 satisfies the two required conditions, you might question whether it is in a useful form. Not many years ago, this form might have posed a computation problem. Indeed, for such problems much effort has been expended over the centuries trying to find solutions that do not involve integrals. We will see some in Chapter 7, where we will learn (for example) how to write the solution in Example 4 as

$$y = \ln \left| \frac{\cos 3}{\cos x} \right| + 5.$$

However, now that computers and calculators are capable of evaluating integrals, the form given in Example 4 is not only useful, but in some ways preferable. It is certainly easier to find and is always available.

Graphing the Function $\int_a^x f(t) \, dt$

Consider for a moment the two forms of the function we have just been discussing,

$$F(x) = \int_3^x \tan t \, dt + 5 \quad \text{and} \quad F(x) = \ln \left| \frac{\cos 3}{\cos x} \right| + 5.$$

With which expression is it easier to evaluate, say, $F(4)$? From the time of Newton almost to the present, there has been no contest: the expression on the right. At least it provides something to compute, and there have always been tables or slide rules or calculators to facilitate that computation. The expression on the left involved at best a tedious summing process and almost certainly an increased opportunity for error.

Today we can find $F(4)$ from either expression on the same machine. The choice is between NINT $(\tan x, x, 3, 4) + 5$ and $\ln (\text{abs}(\cos (3)/\cos (4))) + 5$. Both calculations give 5.415135083 in approximately the same amount of time.

We can even use NINT to graph the function. This modest technology feat would have absolutely dazzled the mathematicians of the 18th and 19th centuries, who knew how the solutions of differential equations, such as $dy/dx = \tan x$, could be written as integrals, but for whom integrals were of no practical use computationally unless they could be written in exact form. Since so few integrals could, in fact, be written in exact form, NINT would have spared generations of scientists much frustration.

Nevertheless, one must not proceed blindly into the world of calculator computation. Exploration 1 will demonstrate the need for caution.

Graphing NINT *f*

Some graphers can graph the numerical integral $y = \text{NINT}\,(f(x), x, a, x)$ directly as a function of x. Others will require a toolbox program such as the one called NINTGRAF provided in the *Technology Resource Manual*.

EXPLORATION 1 Graphing NINT *f*

Let us use NINT to attempt to graph the function we just discussed,

$$F(x) = \int_3^x \tan t\, dt + 5.$$

1. Graph the function $y = F(x)$ in the window $[-10, 10]$ by $[-10, 10]$. You will probably wait a long time and see no graph. Break out of the graphing program if necessary.
2. Recall that the graph of the function $y = \tan x$ has vertical asymptotes. Where do they occur on the interval $[-10, 10]$?
3. When attempting to graph the function $F(x) = \int_3^x \tan t\, dt + 5$ on the interval $[-10, 10]$, your grapher begins by trying to find $F(-10)$. Explain why this might cause a problem for your calculator.
4. Set your viewing window so that your calculator graphs only over the domain of the continuous branch of the tangent function that contains the point $(3, \tan 3)$.
5. What is the domain in step 4? Is it an open interval or a closed interval?
6. What is the domain of $F(x)$? Is it an open interval or a closed interval?
7. Your calculator graphs over the closed interval $[x_{\min}, x_{\max}]$. Find a viewing window that will give you a good look at the graph of F and produce the graph on your calculator.
8. Describe the graph of F.

You have probably noticed that your grapher moves slowly when graphing NINT. This is because it must compute each value as a limit of sums—comparatively slow work even for a microprocessor. Here are some ways to speed up the process:

1. Change the *tolerance* on your grapher. The smaller the tolerance, the more accurate the calculator will try to be when finding the limiting value of each sum (and the longer it will take to do so). The default value is usually quite small (like 0.00001), but a value as large as 1 can be used for graphing in a typical viewing window.

2. Change the *x-resolution.* The default resolution is 1, which means that the grapher will compute a function value for every vertical column of pixels. At resolution 2 it computes only every second value, and so on. With higher resolutions, some graph smoothness is sacrificed for speed.

3. Switch to parametric mode. To graph $y = \text{NINT}\,(f(x), x, a, x)$ in parametric mode, let $x(t) = t$ and let $y(t) = \text{NINT}\,(f(t), t, a, t)$. You can then control the speed of the grapher by changing the t-step. (Choosing a bigger t-step has the same effect as choosing a larger x-resolution.)

EXPLORATION 2 The Effect of Changing a in $\int_a^x f(t)\,dt$

The first part of the Fundamental Theorem of Calculus asserts that the derivative of $\int_a^x f(t)\,dt$ is $f(x)$, regardless of the value of a.

1. Graph NDER (NINT $(t^2, t, 0, x), x$).
2. Graph NDER (NINT $(t^2, t, 5, x), x$).
3. Without graphing, tell what the x-intercept of (NINT $(t^2, t, 0, x), x$) is. Explain.
4. Without graphing, tell what the x-intercept of NDER (NINT $(t^2, t, 5, x), x$) is. Explain.
5. How does changing a affect the graph of $y = (d/dx) \int_a^x f(t)\,dt$?
6. How does changing a affect the graph of $y = \int_a^x f(t)\,dt$?

Fundamental Theorem, Evaluation Part

The second part of the Fundamental Theorem of Calculus shows how to evaluate definite integrals directly from antiderivatives.

THEOREM 4 (continued) **The Fundamental Theorem of Calculus, Evaluation Part**

If f is continuous at every point of $[a, b]$, and if F is any antiderivative of f on $[a, b]$, then

$$\int_a^b f(x)\,dx = F(b) - F(a).$$

This part of the Fundamental Theorem is also called the **Integral Evaluation Theorem.**

Proof The Antiderivative Part of the Fundamental Theorem tells us that an antiderivative of f exists, namely,

$$G(x) = \int_a^x f(t)\,dt.$$

Thus, if F is *any* antiderivative of f, then $F(x) = G(x) + C$ for some constant C (by Corollary 3 of the Mean Value Theorem for Derivatives, Section 5.2).

Evaluating $F(b) - F(a)$, we have

$$F(b) - F(a) = [G(b) + C] - [G(a) + C]$$

$$= G(b) - G(a)$$

$$= \int_a^b f(t)\,dt - \int_a^a f(t)\,dt$$

$$= \int_a^b f(t)\,dt - 0$$

$$= \int_a^b f(t)\,dt \qquad \blacksquare$$

At the risk of repeating ourselves: It is difficult to overestimate the power of the simple equation

$$\int_a^b f(x)\, dx = F(b) - F(a).$$

It says that any definite integral of any continuous function f can be calculated without taking limits, without calculating Riemann sums, and often without effort—so long as an antiderivative of f can be found. If you can imagine what it was like before this theorem (and before computing machines), when approximations by tedious sums were the only alternative for solving many real-world problems, then you can imagine what a miracle calculus was thought to be. If any equation deserves to be called the Fundamental Theorem of Calculus, this equation is surely the (second) one.

EXAMPLE 5 Evaluating an Integral

Evaluate $\int_{-1}^{3}(x^3 + 1)\, dx$ using an antiderivative.

SOLUTION

A simple antiderivative of $x^3 + 1$ is $(x^4/4) + x$. Therefore,

$$\int_{-1}^{3}(x^3 + 1)\, dx = \left[\frac{x^4}{4} + x\right]_{-1}^{3}$$

$$= \left(\frac{81}{4} + 3\right) - \left(\frac{1}{4} - 1\right)$$

$$= 24 \qquad\qquad \textit{Now Try Exercise 29.}$$

Integral Evaluation Notation

The usual notation for $F(b) - F(a)$ is

$$F(x)\Big]_a^b \quad \text{or} \quad \left[F(x)\right]_a^b,$$

depending on whether F has one or more terms. This notation provides a compact "recipe" for the evaluation, allowing us to show the antiderivative in an intermediate step.

Area Connection

In Section 6.2 we saw that the definite integral could be interpreted as the net area between the graph of a function and the x-axis. We can therefore compute areas using antiderivatives, but we must again be careful to distinguish net area (in which area below the x-axis is counted as negative) from total area. The unmodified word "area" will be taken to mean *total area*.

EXAMPLE 6 Finding Area Using Antiderivatives

Find the area of the region between the curve $y = 4 - x^2$, $0 \le x \le 3$, and the x-axis.

SOLUTION

The curve crosses the x-axis at $x = 2$, partitioning the interval $[0, 3]$ into two subintervals, on each of which $f(x) = 4 - x^2$ will not change sign.

We can see from the graph (Figure 6.31) that $f(x) > 0$ on $[0, 2)$ and $f(x) < 0$ on $(2, 3]$.

Over $[0, 2]$: $\displaystyle\int_0^2 (4 - x^2)\, dx = \left[4x - \frac{x^3}{3}\right]_0^2 = \frac{16}{3}.$

Over $[2, 3]$: $\displaystyle\int_2^3 (4 - x^2)\, dx = \left[4x - \frac{x^3}{3}\right]_2^3 = -\frac{7}{3}.$

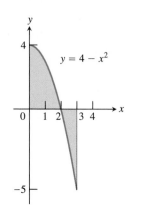

Figure 6.31 The function $f(x) = 4 - x^2$ changes sign only at $x = 2$ on the interval $[0, 3]$. (Example 6)

The area of the region is $\left|\dfrac{16}{3}\right| + \left|-\dfrac{7}{3}\right| = \dfrac{23}{3}.$ \qquad\qquad *Now Try Exercise 41.*

How to Find Total Area Analytically

To find the area between the graph of $y = f(x)$ and the x-axis over the interval $[a, b]$ analytically,

1. partition $[a, b]$ with the zeros of f,
2. integrate f over each subinterval,
3. add the absolute values of the integrals.

We can find area numerically by using NINT to integrate the *absolute value* of the function over the given interval. There is no need to partition. By taking absolute values, we automatically reflect the negative portions of the graph across the x-axis to count all area as positive (Figure 6.32).

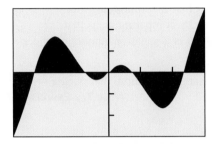

[−3, 3] by [−3, 3]

(a)

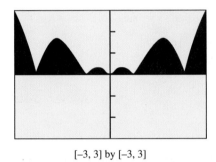

[−3, 3] by [−3, 3]

(b)

Figure 6.32 The graphs of (a) $y = x \cos 2x$ and (b) $y = |x \cos 2x|$ over $[−3, 3]$. The shaded regions have the same area.

EXAMPLE 7 Finding Area Using NINT

Find the area of the region between the curve $y = x \cos 2x$ and the x-axis over the interval $-3 \leq x \leq 3$ (Figure 6.32).

SOLUTION

Rounded to two decimal places, we have

$$\text{NINT}\,(|x \cos 2x|, x, -3, 3) = 5.43. \qquad \textbf{\textit{Now Try Exercise 51.}}$$

How to Find Total Area Numerically

To find the area between the graph of $y = f(x)$ and the x-axis over the interval $[a, b]$ numerically, evaluate

$$\text{NINT}\,(|f(x)|, x, a, b).$$

Analyzing Antiderivatives Graphically

A good way to put several calculus concepts together at this point is to start with the graph of a function f and consider a new function h defined as a definite integral of f. If $h(x) = \int_a^x f(t)\, dt$, for example, the Fundamental Theorem guarantees that $h'(x) = f(x)$, so the graph of f is also the graph of h'. We can therefore make conclusions about the behavior of h by considering the graphical behavior of its derivative f, just as we did in Section 5.3.

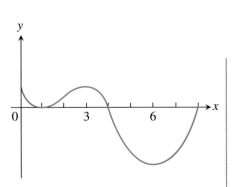

Figure 6.33 The graph of f in Example 8, in which questions are asked about the function $h(x) = \int_1^x f(t)\, dt$.

EXAMPLE 8 Using the Graph of *f* to Analyze $h(x) = \int_a^x f(t)\, dt$

The graph of a continuous function f with domain $[0, 8]$ is shown in Figure 6.33. Let h be the function defined by $h(x) = \int_1^x f(t)\, dt$.

(a) Find $h(1)$.

(b) Is $h(0)$ positive or negative? Justify your answer.

(c) Find the value of x for which $h(x)$ is a maximum.

(d) Find the value of x for which $h(x)$ is a minimum.

(e) Find the x-coordinates of all points of inflection of the graph of $y = h(x)$.

continued

SOLUTION

First, we note that $h'(x) = f(x)$, so the graph of f is also the graph of the derivative of h. Also, h is continuous because it is differentiable.

(a) $h(1) = \int_1^1 f(t)\,dt = 0$.

(b) $h(0) = \int_1^0 f(t)\,dt < 0$, because we are integrating from right to left under a positive function.

(c) The derivative of h is positive on $(0, 1)$, positive on $(1, 4)$, and negative on $(4, 8)$, so the continuous function h is increasing on $[0, 4]$ and decreasing on $[4, 8]$. Thus $h(4)$ is a maximum.

(d) The sign analysis of the derivative above shows that the minimum value occurs at an endpoint of the interval $[0, 8]$. We see by comparing areas that $h(0) = \int_1^0 f(t)\,dt \approx -0.5$, while $h(8) = \int_1^8 f(t)\,dt$ is a negative number considerably less than -1. Thus $h(8)$ is a minimum.

(e) The points of inflection occur where $h' = f$ changes direction, that is, at $x = 1$, $x = 3$, and $x = 6$.

Now Try Exercise 57.

Quick Review 6.4   (For help, go to Sections 4.1, 4.2, and 4.4.)

Exercise numbers with a gray background indicate problems that the authors have designed to be solved *without a calculator*.

In Exercises 1–10, find dy/dx.

1. $y = \sin(x^2)$

2. $y = (\sin x)^2$

3. $y = \sec^2 x - \tan^2 x$

4. $y = \ln(3x) - \ln(7x)$

5. $y = 2^x$

6. $y = \sqrt{x}$

7. $y = \dfrac{\cos x}{x}$

8. $y = \sin t$ and $x = \cos t$

9. $xy + x = y^2$

10. $dx/dy = 3x$

Section 6.4 Exercises

In Exercises 1–20, find dy/dx.

1. $y = \displaystyle\int_0^x (\sin^2 t)\,dt$

2. $y = \displaystyle\int_2^x (3t + \cos t^2)\,dt$

3. $y = \displaystyle\int_0^x (t^3 - t)^5\,dt$

4. $y = \displaystyle\int_{-2}^x \sqrt{1 + e^{5t}}\,dt$

5. $y = \displaystyle\int_2^x (\tan^3 u)\,du$

6. $y = \displaystyle\int_4^x e^u \sec u\,du$

7. $y = \displaystyle\int_7^x \frac{1 + t}{1 + t^2}\,dt$

8. $y = \displaystyle\int_{-\pi}^x \frac{2 - \sin t}{3 + \cos t}\,dt$

9. $y = \displaystyle\int_0^{x^2} e^{t^2}\,dt$

10. $y = \displaystyle\int_6^{x^2} \cot 3t\,dt$

11. $y = \displaystyle\int_2^{5x} \frac{\sqrt{1 + u^2}}{u}\,du$

12. $y = \displaystyle\int_\pi^{\pi - x} \frac{1 + \sin^2 u}{1 + \cos^2 u}\,du$

13. $y = \displaystyle\int_x^6 \ln(1 + t^2)\,dt$

14. $y = \displaystyle\int_x^7 \sqrt{2t^4 + t + 1}\,dt$

15. $y = \displaystyle\int_{x^3}^5 \frac{\cos t}{t^2 + 2}\,dt$

16. $y = \displaystyle\int_{5x^2}^{25} \frac{t^2 - 2t + 9}{t^3 + 6}\,dt$

17. $y = \displaystyle\int_{\sqrt{x}}^x \sin(r^2)\,dr$

18. $y = \displaystyle\int_{3x^2}^{5x} \ln(2 + p^2)\,dp$

19. $\displaystyle\int_{x^2}^{x^3} \cos(2t)\,dt$

20. $y = \displaystyle\int_{\sin x}^{\cos x} t^2\,dt$

In Exercises 21–26, construct a function of the form $y = \int_a^x f(t)\,dt + C$ that satisfies the given conditions.

21. $\dfrac{dy}{dx} = \sin^3 x$, and $y = 0$ when $x = 5$.

22. $\dfrac{dy}{dx} = e^x \tan x$, and $y = 0$ when $x = 8$.

23. $\dfrac{dy}{dx} = \ln(\sin x + 5)$, and $y = 3$ when $x = 2$.

24. $\dfrac{dy}{dx} = \sqrt{3 - \cos x}$, and $y = 4$ when $x = -3$.

25. $\dfrac{dy}{dx} = \cos^2 5x$, and $y = -2$ when $x = 7$.

26. $\dfrac{dy}{dx} = e^{\sqrt{x}}$, and $y = 1$ when $x = 0$.

In Exercises 27–40, evaluate each integral using the Evaluation Part of the Fundamental Theorem.

27. $\displaystyle\int_{1/2}^{3}\left(2 - \dfrac{1}{x}\right) dx$

28. $\displaystyle\int_{2}^{-1} 3^x\, dx$

29. $\displaystyle\int_{0}^{1} (x^2 + \sqrt{x})\, dx$

30. $\displaystyle\int_{0}^{5} x^{3/2}\, dx$

31. $\displaystyle\int_{1}^{32} x^{-6/5}\, dx$

32. $\displaystyle\int_{-2}^{-1} \dfrac{2}{x^2}\, dx$

33. $\displaystyle\int_{0}^{\pi} \sin x\, dx$

34. $\displaystyle\int_{0}^{\pi} (1 + \cos x)\, dx$

35. $\displaystyle\int_{0}^{\pi/3} 2 \sec^2 \theta\, d\theta$

36. $\displaystyle\int_{\pi/6}^{5\pi/6} \csc^2 \theta\, d\theta$

37. $\displaystyle\int_{\pi/4}^{3\pi/4} \csc x \cot x\, dx$

38. $\displaystyle\int_{0}^{\pi/3} 4 \sec x \tan x\, dx$

39. $\displaystyle\int_{-1}^{1} (r + 1)^2\, dr$

40. $\displaystyle\int_{1}^{4} \dfrac{1 - \sqrt{u}}{\sqrt{u}}\, du$

In Exercises 41–44, find the total area of the region between the curve and the *x*-axis.

41. $y = 2 - x, \quad 0 \le x \le 3$

42. $y = 3x^2 - 3, \quad -2 \le x \le 2$

43. $y = x^3 - 3x^2 + 2x, \quad 0 \le x \le 2$

44. $y = x^3 - 4x, \quad -2 \le x \le 2$

In Exercises 45–48, find the area of the shaded region.

45.

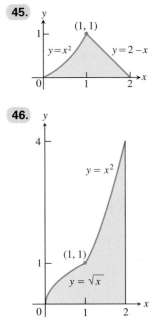

46.

47.

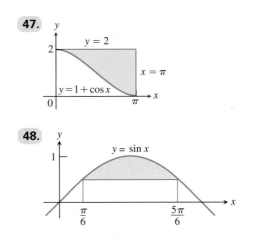

48.

In Exercises 49–54, use NINT to solve the problem.

49. Evaluate $\displaystyle\int_{0}^{10} \dfrac{1}{3 + 2\sin x}\, dx$.

50. Evaluate $\displaystyle\int_{-0.8}^{0.8} \dfrac{2x^4 - 1}{x^4 - 1}\, dx$.

51. Find the area of the semielliptical region between the *x*-axis and the graph of $y = \sqrt{8 - 2x^2}$.

52. Find the average value of $\sqrt{\cos x}$ on the interval $[-1, 1]$.

53. For what value of *x* does $\int_{0}^{x} e^{-t^2}\, dt = 0.6$?

54. Find the area of the region in the first quadrant enclosed by the coordinate axes and the graph of $x^3 + y^3 = 1$.

In Exercises 55 and 56, find *K* so that

$$\int_{a}^{x} f(t)\, dt + K = \int_{b}^{x} f(t)\, dt.$$

55. $f(x) = x^2 - 3x + 1; \quad a = -1; \quad b = 2$

56. $f(x) = \sin^2 x; \quad a = 0; \quad b = 2$

57. Let

$$H(x) = \int_{0}^{x} f(t)\, dt,$$

where *f* is the continuous function with domain $[0, 12]$ graphed here.

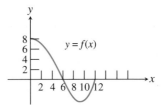

(a) Find $H(0)$.

(b) On what interval is *H* increasing? Explain.

(c) On what interval is the graph of *H* concave up? Explain.

(d) Is $H(12)$ positive or negative? Explain.

(e) Where does *H* achieve its maximum value? Explain.

(f) Where does *H* achieve its minimum value? Explain.

In Exercises 58 and 59, f is the differentiable function whose graph is shown in the given figure. The position at time t (sec) of a particle moving along a coordinate axis is

$$s = \int_0^t f(x)\, dx$$

meters. Use the graph to answer the questions. Give reasons for your answers.

58.

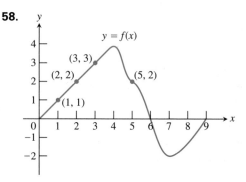

(a) What is the particle's velocity at time $t = 5$?

(b) Is the acceleration of the particle at time $t = 5$ positive or negative?

(c) What is the particle's position at time $t = 3$?

(d) At what time during the first 9 sec does s have its largest value?

(e) Approximately when is the acceleration zero?

(f) When is the particle moving toward the origin? away from the origin?

(g) On which side of the origin does the particle lie at time $t = 9$?

59.

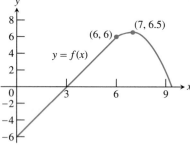

(a) What is the particle's velocity at time $t = 3$?

(b) Is the acceleration of the particle at time $t = 3$ positive or negative?

(c) What is the particle's position at time $t = 3$?

(d) When does the particle pass through the origin?

(e) Approximately when is the acceleration zero?

(f) When is the particle moving toward the origin? away from the origin?

(g) On which side of the origin does the particle lie at time $t = 9$?

60. Suppose $\int_1^x f(t)\, dt = x^2 - 2x + 1$. Find $f(x)$.

61. *Linearization* Find the linearization of

$$f(x) = 2 + \int_0^x \frac{10}{1 + t}\, dt \quad \text{at} \quad x = 0.$$

62. Find $f(4)$ if $\int_0^x f(t)\, dt = x \cos \pi x$.

63. *Finding Area* Show that if k is a positive constant, then the area between the x-axis and one arch of the curve $y = \sin kx$ is always $2/k$.

64. *Archimedes' Area Formula for Parabolas* Archimedes (287–212 B.C.), inventor, military engineer, physicist, and the greatest mathematician of classical times, discovered that the area under a parabolic arch like the one shown here is always two-thirds the base times the height.

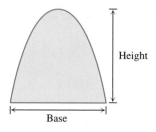

(a) Find the area under the parabolic arch

$$y = 6 - x - x^2, \quad -3 \le x \le 2.$$

(b) Find the height of the arch.

(c) Show that the area is two-thirds the base times the height.

Standardized Test Questions

You may use a graphing calculator to solve the following problems.

65. True or False If f is continuous on an open interval I containing a, then F defined by $F(x) = \int_a^x f(t)\, dt$ is continuous on I. Justify your answer.

66. True or False If $b > a$, then $\dfrac{d}{dx} \int_a^b e^{x^2}\, dx$ is positive. Justify your answer.

67. Multiple Choice Let $f(x) = \int_a^x \ln(2 + \sin t)\, dt$. If $f(3) = 4$, then $f(5) =$

(A) 0.040　(B) 0.272　(C) 0.961　(D) 4.555　(E) 6.667

68. Multiple Choice What is $\displaystyle\lim_{h \to 0} \frac{1}{h} \int_x^{x+h} f(t)\, dt$?

(A) 0　(B) 1　(C) $f'(x)$　(D) $f(x)$　(E) nonexistent

69. Multiple Choice At $x = \pi$, the linearization of $f(x) = \int_\pi^x \cos^3 t\, dt$ is

(A) $y = -1$　　(B) $y = -x$　　(C) $y = \pi$

(D) $y = x - \pi$　　(E) $y = \pi - x$

70. Multiple Choice The area of the region enclosed between the graph of $y = \sqrt{1 - x^4}$ and the x-axis is

(A) 0.886　　(B) 1.253　　(C) 1.414

(D) 1.571　　(E) 1.748

Explorations

71. *The Sine Integral Function* The sine integral function

$$\text{Si}(x) = \int_0^x \frac{\sin t}{t}\, dt$$

is one of the many useful functions in engineering that are defined as integrals. Although the notation does not show it, the function being integrated is

$$f(t) = \begin{cases} \dfrac{\sin t}{t}, & t \neq 0 \\ 1, & t = 0, \end{cases}$$

the continuous extension of $(\sin t)/t$ to the origin.

(a) Show that $\text{Si}(x)$ is an odd function of x.

(b) What is the value of $\text{Si}(0)$?

(c) Find the values of x at which $\text{Si}(x)$ has a local extreme value.

(d) Use NINT to graph $\text{Si}(x)$.

72. *Cost from Marginal Cost* The marginal cost of printing a poster when x posters have been printed is

$$\frac{dc}{dx} = \frac{1}{2\sqrt{x}}$$

dollars. Find

(a) $c(100) - c(1)$, the cost of printing posters 2 to 100.

(b) $c(400) - c(100)$, the cost of printing posters 101 to 400.

73. *Revenue from Marginal Revenue* Suppose that a company's marginal revenue from the manufacture and sale of eggbeaters is

$$\frac{dr}{dx} = 2 - \frac{2}{(x+1)^2},$$

where r is measured in thousands of dollars and x in thousands of units. How much money should the company expect from a production run of $x = 3$ thousand eggbeaters? To find out, integrate the marginal revenue from $x = 0$ to $x = 3$.

74. *Average Daily Holding Cost* Solon Container receives 450 drums of plastic pellets every 30 days. The inventory function (drums on hand as a function of days) is $I(x) = 450 - x^2/2$.

(a) Find the average daily inventory (that is, the average value of $I(x)$ for the 30-day period).

(b) If the holding cost for one drum is $0.02 per day, find the average daily holding cost (that is, the per-drum holding cost times the average daily inventory).

75. Suppose that f has a negative derivative for all values of x and that $f(1) = 0$. Which of the following statements must be true of the function

$$h(x) = \int_0^x f(t)\, dt?$$

Give reasons for your answers.

(a) h is a twice-differentiable function of x.

(b) h and dh/dx are both continuous.

(c) The graph of h has a horizontal tangent at $x = 1$.

(d) h has a local maximum at $x = 1$.

(e) h has a local minimum at $x = 1$.

(f) The graph of h has an inflection point at $x = 1$.

(g) The graph of dh/dx crosses the x-axis at $x = 1$.

Extending the Ideas

76. Writing to Learn If f is an odd continuous function, give a graphical argument to explain why $\int_0^x f(t)\, dt$ is even.

77. Writing to Learn If f is an even continuous function, give a graphical argument to explain why $\int_0^x f(t)\, dt$ is odd.

78. Writing to Learn Explain why we can conclude from Exercises 76 and 77 that every even continuous function is the derivative of an odd continuous function and vice versa.

79. Give a convincing argument that the equation

$$\int_0^x \frac{\sin t}{t}\, dt = 1$$

has exactly one solution. Give its approximate value.

6.5 | Trapezoidal Rule

You will be able to approximate definite integrals using the Trapezoidal Rule.

• Trapezoidal approximations
• Comparison to other numerical approximations
• Bounding the error in the Trapezoidal Rule

Trapezoidal Approximations

You probably noticed in Section 6.1 that MRAM was generally more efficient in approximating integrals than either LRAM or RRAM, even though all three RAM approximations approached the same limit. All three RAM approximations, however, depend on the areas of rectangles. Are there other geometric shapes with known areas that can do the job more efficiently? The answer is yes, and the most obvious one is the trapezoid.

As shown in Figure 6.34, if $[a, b]$ is partitioned into n subintervals of equal length $h = (b - a)/n$, the graph of f on $[a, b]$ can be approximated by a straight line segment over each subinterval.

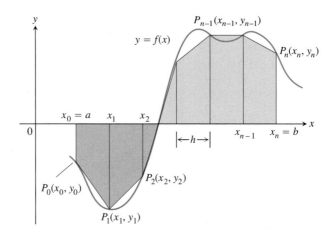

Figure 6.34 The trapezoidal rule approximates short stretches of the curve $y = f(x)$ with line segments. To approximate the integral of f from a to b, we add the "signed" areas of the trapezoids made by joining the ends of the segments to the x-axis.

The region between the curve and the x-axis is then approximated by the trapezoids, the area of each trapezoid being the length of its horizontal "altitude" times the average of its two vertical "bases." That is,

$$\int_a^b f(x)\,dx \approx h \cdot \frac{y_0 + y_1}{2} + h \cdot \frac{y_1 + y_2}{2} + \cdots + h \cdot \frac{y_{n-1} + y_n}{2}$$

$$= h\left(\frac{y_0}{2} + y_1 + y_2 + \cdots + y_{n-1} + \frac{y_n}{2}\right)$$

$$= \frac{h}{2}(y_0 + 2y_1 + 2y_2 + \cdots + 2y_{n-1} + y_n),$$

where

$$y_0 = f(a), \quad y_1 = f(x_1), \quad \cdots, \quad y_{n-1} = f(x_{n-1}), \quad y_n = f(b)$$

This is algebraically equivalent to finding the numerical average of LRAM and RRAM; indeed, that is how some texts define the Trapezoidal Rule.

The Trapezoidal Rule

To approximate $\int_a^b f(x)\, dx$, use

$$T = \frac{h}{2}(y_0 + 2y_1 + 2y_2 + \cdots + 2y_{n-1} + y_n),$$

where $[a, b]$ is partitioned into n subintervals of equal length $h = (b - a)/n$. Equivalently,

$$T = \frac{\text{LRAM}_n + \text{RRAM}_n}{2},$$

where LRAM_n and RRAM_n are the Riemann sums using the left and right endpoints, respectively, for f for the partition.

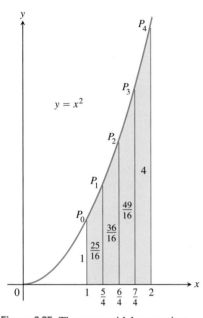

Figure 6.35 The trapezoidal approximation of the area under the graph of $y = x^2$ from $x = 1$ to $x = 2$ is a slight overestimate. (Example 1)

EXAMPLE 1 Applying the Trapezoidal Rule

Use the Trapezoidal Rule with $n = 4$ to estimate $\int_1^2 x^2\, dx$. Compare the estimate with the value of NINT $(x^2, x, 1, 2)$ and with the exact value.

SOLUTION

Partition $[1, 2]$ into four subintervals of equal length (Figure 6.35). Then evaluate $y = x^2$ at each partition point (Table 6.4).

Using these y values, $n = 4$, and $h = (2 - 1)/4 = 1/4$ in the Trapezoidal Rule, we have

$$T = \frac{h}{2}(y_0 + 2y_1 + 2y_2 + 2y_3 + y_4)$$

$$= \frac{1}{8}\left(1 + 2\left(\frac{25}{16}\right) + 2\left(\frac{36}{16}\right) + 2\left(\frac{49}{16}\right) + 4\right)$$

$$= \frac{75}{32} = 2.34375$$

The value of NINT $(x^2, x, 1, 2)$ is 2.333333333.

The exact value of the integral is

$$\int_1^2 x^2\, dx = \frac{x^3}{3}\bigg]_1^2 = \frac{8}{3} - \frac{1}{3} = \frac{7}{3}.$$

The T approximation overestimates the integral by about half a percent of its true value of $7/3$. The percentage error is $(2.34375 - 7/3)/(7/3) \approx 0.446\%$.

Now Try Exercise 3.

TABLE 6.4

x	$y = x^2$
1	1
$\frac{5}{4}$	$\frac{25}{16}$
$\frac{6}{4}$	$\frac{36}{16}$
$\frac{7}{4}$	$\frac{49}{16}$
2	4

We could have predicted that the Trapezoidal Rule would overestimate the integral in Example 1 by considering the geometry of the graph in Figure 6.35. Since the parabola is concave *up*, the approximating segments lie above the curve, giving each trapezoid slightly more area than the corresponding strip under the curve. In Figure 6.34 we see that the straight segments lie *under* the curve on those intervals where the curve is concave *down*, causing the Trapezoidal Rule to *underestimate* the integral on those intervals. The interpretation of "area" changes where the curve lies below the *x*-axis but it is still the case that the higher *y* values give the greater signed area. So we can always say that *T* overestimates the integral where the graph is concave up and underestimates the integral where the graph is concave down.

EXAMPLE 2 Averaging Temperatures

An observer measures the outside temperature every hour from noon until midnight, recording the temperatures in the following table.

Time	N	1	2	3	4	5	6	7	8	9	10	11	M
Temp	63	65	66	68	70	69	68	68	65	64	62	58	55

What was the average temperature for the 12-hour period?

SOLUTION

We are looking for the average value of a continuous function (temperature) for which we know values at discrete times that are one unit apart. We need to find

$$av(f) = \frac{1}{b-a} \int_a^b f(x)\, dx,$$

without having a formula for $f(x)$. The integral, however, can be approximated by the Trapezoidal Rule, using the temperatures in the table as function values at the points of a 12-subinterval partition of the 12-hour interval (making $h = 1$).

$$T = \frac{h}{2}(y_0 + 2y_1 + 2y_2 + \cdots + 2y_{11} + y_{12})$$

$$= \frac{1}{2}(63 + 2 \cdot 65 + 2 \cdot 66 + \cdots + 2 \cdot 58 + 55)$$

$$= 782$$

Using *T* to approximate $\int_a^b f(x)\, dx$, we have

$$av(f) \approx \frac{1}{b-a} \cdot T = \frac{1}{12} \cdot 782 \approx 65.17.$$

Rounding to be consistent with the data given, we estimate the average temperature as 65 degrees.   *Now Try Exercise 7.*

Other Algorithms

LRAM, MRAM, RRAM, and the Trapezoidal Rule all give reasonable approximations to the integral of a continuous function over a closed interval. The Trapezoidal Rule is more efficient, giving a better approximation for small values of *n*, which makes it a faster algorithm for numerical integration.

Indeed, the only shortcoming of the Trapezoidal Rule seems to be that it depends on approximating curved arcs with straight segments. You might think that an algorithm that approximates the curve with *curved* pieces would be even more efficient (and hence faster for machines), and you would be right. All we need to do is find a geometric figure with a straight base, straight sides, and a curved top that has a known area. You might not know one, but the ancient Greeks did; it is one of the things they knew about parabolas.

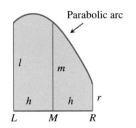

Figure 6.36 The area under the parabolic arc can be computed from the length of the base *LR* and the lengths of the altitudes constructed at *L*, *R*, and midpoint *M*. (Exploration 1)

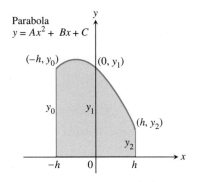

Figure 6.37 A convenient coordinatization of Figure 6.36. The parabola has equation $y = Ax^2 + Bx + C$, and the midpoint of the base is at the origin. (Exploration 1)

EXPLORATION 1 Area Under a Parabolic Arc

The area A_P of a figure having a horizontal base, vertical sides, and a parabolic top (Figure 6.36) can be computed by the formula

$$A_P = \frac{h}{3}(l + 4m + r),$$

where h is half the length of the base, l and r are the lengths of the left and right sides, and m is the altitude at the midpoint of the base. This formula, once a profound discovery of ancient geometers, is readily verified today with calculus.

1. Coordinatize Figure 6.36 by centering the base at the origin, as shown in Figure 6.37. Let $y = Ax^2 + Bx + C$ be the equation of the parabola. Using this equation, show that $y_0 = Ah^2 - Bh + C$, $y_1 = C$, and $y_2 = Ah^2 + Bh + C$.
2. Show that $y_0 + 4y_1 + y_2 = 2Ah^2 + 6C$.
3. Integrate to show that the area A_P is

$$\frac{h}{3}(2Ah^2 + 6C).$$

4. Combine these results to derive the formula

$$A_P = \frac{h}{3}(y_0 + 4y_1 + y_2).$$

This last formula leads to an efficient rule for approximating integrals numerically. Partition the interval of integration into an even number of subintervals, apply the formula for A_P to successive interval pairs, and add the results. This algorithm is known as Simpson's Rule.

What's in a Name?

The formula that underlies Simpson's Rule (see Exploration 1) was discovered long before Thomas Simpson (1720–1761) was born. Just as Pythagoras did not discover the Pythagorean Theorem, Simpson did not discover Simpson's Rule. It is another of history's beautiful quirks that one of the ablest mathematicians of 18th-century England is remembered not for his successful textbooks and his contributions to mathematical analysis, but for a rule that was never his, that he never laid claim to, and that bears his name only because he happened to mention it in one of his books.

Simpson's Rule

To approximate $\int_a^b f(x)\, dx$, use

$$S = \frac{h}{3}(y_0 + 4y_1 + 2y_2 + 4y_3 + \cdots + 2y_{n-2} + 4y_{n-1} + y_n),$$

where $[a, b]$ is partitioned into an *even* number n of subintervals of equal length $h = (b - a)/n$.

EXAMPLE 3 Applying Simpson's Rule

Use Simpson's Rule with $n = 4$ to approximate $\int_0^2 5x^4\, dx$.

SOLUTION

Partition $[0, 2]$ into four subintervals and evaluate $y = 5x^4$ at the partition points. (See Table 6.5 on the next page.)

continued

TABLE 6.5	
x	y = 5x⁴
0	0
$\frac{1}{2}$	$\frac{5}{16}$
1	5
$\frac{3}{2}$	$\frac{405}{16}$
2	80

Then apply Simpson's Rule with $n = 4$ and $h = 1/2$:

$$S = \frac{h}{3}(y_0 + 4y_1 + 2y_2 + 4y_3 + y_4)$$

$$= \frac{1}{6}\left(0 + 4\left(\frac{5}{16}\right) + 2(5) + 4\left(\frac{405}{16}\right) + 80\right)$$

$$= \frac{385}{12}$$

This estimate differs from the exact value (32) by only $1/12$, a percentage error of less than three-tenths of one percent—and this was with just 4 subintervals.

Now Try Exercise 17.

There are still other algorithms for approximating definite integrals, most of them involving fancy numerical analysis designed to make the calculations more efficient for high-speed computers. Some are kept secret by the companies that design the machines. In any case, we will not deal with them here.

Error Analysis

After finding that the trapezoidal approximation in Example 1 overestimated the integral, we pointed out that this could have been predicted from the concavity of the curve we were approximating.

Knowing something about the error in an approximation is more than just an interesting sidelight. Despite what your years of classroom experience might have suggested, exact answers are not always easy to find in mathematics. It is fortunate that for all *practical* purposes exact answers are also rarely necessary. (For example, a carpenter who computes the need for a board of length $\sqrt{34}$ feet will happily settle for an approximation when cutting the board.)

Suppose that an exact answer really *cannot* be found, but that we know that an approximation within 0.001 unit is good enough. How can we tell that our approximation is within 0.001 if we do not know the exact answer? This is where knowing something about the error is critical.

In Exercise 72 on page 250, we saw that if we approximate a function by the tangent line at $(a, f(a))$, then the difference between the true value of f at x and the value given by the linear approximation is equal to $\frac{1}{2}f''(c)(\Delta x)^2$, where Δx is the distance from x to a and c is some value between a and x. While we do not know the value of c, we can put a bound on this difference if we know that for c between a and x, $|f''(c)|$ is always less than or equal to some maximum value, $M_{f''}$. We get a similar bound for E_T, the error in the trapezoidal approximation,

$$|E_T| \leq \frac{b-a}{12}h^2 M_{f''},$$

where $[a, b]$ is the interval of integration, h is the length of each subinterval, and $M_{f''}$ is the maximum value of $|f''(c)|$ for c in $[a, b]$.

It can also be shown that the error E_S in Simpson's Rule depends on h and the *fourth* derivative. It satisfies the inequality

$$|E_S| \leq \frac{b-a}{180}h^4 M_{f^{(4)}},$$

where $[a, b]$ is the interval of integration, h is the length of each subinterval, and $M_{f^{(4)}}$ is the maximum value of $|f^{(4)}|$ on $[a, b]$, provided that $f^{(4)}$ is continuous.

For comparison's sake, if all the assumptions hold, we have the following *error bounds*.

Error Bounds

If T and S represent the approximations to $\int_a^b f(x)\, dx$ given by the Trapezoidal Rule and Simpson's Rule, respectively, then the errors E_T and E_S satisfy

$$|E_T| \le \frac{b-a}{12} h^2 M_{f''} \quad \text{and} \quad |E_S| \le \frac{b-a}{180} h^4 M_{f^{(4)}}.$$

If we disregard possible differences in magnitude between $M_{f''}$ and $M_{f^{(4)}}$, we notice immediately that $(b-a)/180$ is one-fifteenth the size of $(b-a)/12$, giving S an obvious advantage over T as an approximation. That, however, is almost insignificant when compared to the fact that the trapezoid error varies as the *square* of h, while Simpson's error varies as the *fourth power* of h. (Remember that h is already a small number in most partitions.)

Table 6.6 shows T and S values for approximations of $\int_1^2 (1/x)\, dx$ using various values of n. Notice how Simpson's Rule dramatically improves over the Trapezoidal Rule. In particular, notice that when we double the value of n (thereby halving the value of h), the T error is divided by 2 *squared*, while the S error is divided by 2 *to the fourth*.

TABLE 6.6 Trapezoidal Rule Approximations (T_n) and Simpson's Rule Approximations (S_n) of ln 2 $= \int_1^2 (1/x)\, dx$

n	T_n	$|$Error$|$ less than ...	S_n	$|$Error$|$ less than ...
10	0.6937714032	0.0006242227	0.6931502307	0.0000030502
20	0.6933033818	0.0001562013	0.6931473747	0.0000001942
30	0.6932166154	0.0000694349	0.6931472190	0.0000000385
40	0.6931862400	0.0000390595	0.6931471927	0.0000000122
50	0.6931721793	0.0000249988	0.6931471856	0.0000000050
100	0.6931534305	0.0000062500	0.6931471809	0.0000000004

This has a dramatic effect as h gets very small. The Simpson approximation for $n = 50$ rounds accurately to seven places, and for $n = 100$ agrees to nine decimal places (billionths)!

We close by showing you the values (Table 6.7) we found for $\int_1^5 (\sin x)/x\, dx$ by six different calculator methods. The exact value of this integral to six decimal places is 0.603848, so both Simpson's method with 50 subintervals and NINT give results accurate to at least six places (millionths).

TABLE 6.7
Approximations of $\int_1^5 (\sin x)/x\, dx$

Method	Subintervals	Value
LRAM	50	0.6453898
RRAM	50	0.5627293
MRAM	50	0.6037425
TRAP	50	0.6040595
SIMP	50	0.6038481
NINT	Tol $= 0.00001$	0.6038482

Quick Review 6.5   *(For help, go to Sections 4.4 and 5.3.)*

Exercise numbers with a gray background indicate problems that the authors have designed to be solved *without a calculator*.

In Exercises 1–10, tell whether the curve is concave up or concave down on the given interval.

1. $y = \cos x$ on $[-1, 1]$

2. $y = x^4 - 12x - 5$ on $[8, 17]$

3. $y = 4x^3 - 3x^2 + 6$ on $[-8, 0]$

4. $y = \sin(x/2)$ on $[48\pi, 50\pi]$

5. $y = e^{2x}$ on $[-5, 5]$

6. $y = \ln x$ on $[100, 200]$

7. $y = \dfrac{1}{x}$ on $[3, 6]$

8. $y = \csc x$ on $[0, \pi]$

9. $y = 10^{10} - 10x^{10}$ on $[10, 10^{10}]$

10. $y = \sin x - \cos x$ on $[1, 2]$

Section 6.5 Exercises

In Exercises 1–6, **(a)** use the Trapezoidal Rule with $n = 4$ to approximate the value of the integral. **(b)** Use the concavity of the function to predict whether the approximation is an overestimate or an underestimate. Finally, **(c)** find the integral's exact value to check your answer.

1. $\displaystyle\int_0^2 x\,dx$

2. $\displaystyle\int_0^2 x^2\,dx$

3. $\displaystyle\int_0^2 x^3\,dx$

4. $\displaystyle\int_1^2 \frac{1}{x}\,dx$

5. $\displaystyle\int_0^4 \sqrt{x}\,dx$

6. $\displaystyle\int_0^\pi \sin x\,dx$

7. Use the function values in the following table and the Trapezoidal Rule with $n = 6$ to approximate $\int_0^6 f(x)\,dx$.

x	0	1	2	3	4	5	6
$f(x)$	12	10	9	11	13	16	18

8. Use the function values in the following table and the Trapezoidal Rule with $n = 6$ to approximate $\int_2^8 f(x)\,dx$.

x	2	3	4	5	6	7	8
$f(x)$	16	19	17	14	13	16	20

9. *Volume of Water in a Swimming Pool* A rectangular swimming pool is 30 ft wide and 50 ft long. The table below shows the depth $h(x)$ of the water at 5-ft intervals from one end of the pool to the other. Estimate the volume of water in the pool using the Trapezoidal Rule with $n = 10$, applied to the integral

$$V = \int_0^{50} 30 \cdot h(x)\,dx.$$

Position (ft) x	Depth (ft) $h(x)$	Position (ft) x	Depth (ft) $h(x)$
0	6.0	30	11.5
5	8.2	35	11.9
10	9.1	40	12.3
15	9.9	45	12.7
20	10.5	50	13.0
25	11.0		

10. *Stocking a Fish Pond* As the fish and game warden of your township, you are responsible for stocking the town pond with fish before the fishing season. The average depth of the pond is 20 feet. Using a scaled map, you measure distances across the pond at 200-foot intervals, as shown in the diagram.

(a) Use the Trapezoidal Rule to estimate the volume of the pond.

(b) You plan to start the season with one fish per 1000 cubic feet. You intend to have at least 25% of the opening day's fish population left at the end of the season. What is the maximum number of licenses the town can sell if the average seasonal catch is 20 fish per license?

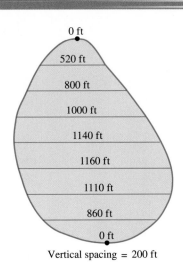

0 ft

520 ft

800 ft

1000 ft

1140 ft

1160 ft

1110 ft

860 ft

0 ft

Vertical spacing = 200 ft

11. *Scarpellone Panther I* The accompanying table shows time-to-speed data for a 2011 Scarpellone Panther I accelerating from rest to 130 mph. How far had the Panther I traveled by the time it reached this speed? (Use trapezoids to estimate the area under the velocity curve, but be careful: the time intervals vary in length.)

Speed Change: Zero to	Time (sec)
30 mph	1.8
40 mph	3.1
50 mph	4.2
60 mph	5.5
70 mph	7.4
80 mph	9.2
90 mph	11.5
100 mph	14.6
120 mph	20.9
130 mph	25.7

12. The table below records the velocity of a bobsled at 1-second intervals for the first eight seconds of its run. Use the Trapezoidal Rule to approximate the distance the bobsled travels during that 8-second interval. (Give your final answer in feet.)

Time (seconds)	Speed (miles/hr)
0	0
1	3
2	7
3	12
4	17
5	25
6	33
7	41
8	48

In Exercises 13–18, **(a)** use Simpson's Rule with $n = 4$ to approximate the value of the integral and **(b)** find the exact value of the integral to check your answer. (Note that these are the same integrals as Exercises 1–6, so you can also compare it with the Trapezoidal Rule approximation.)

13. $\int_0^2 x \, dx$

14. $\int_0^2 x^2 \, dx$

15. $\int_0^2 x^3 \, dx$

16. $\int_1^2 \frac{1}{x} \, dx$

17. $\int_0^4 \sqrt{x} \, dx$

18. $\int_0^\pi \sin x \, dx$

19. Consider the integral $\int_{-1}^3 (x^3 - 2x) \, dx$.

(a) Use Simpson's Rule with $n = 4$ to approximate its value.

(b) Find the exact value of the integral. What is the error, $|E_S|$?

(c) Explain how you could have predicted what you found in (b) from knowing the error-bound formula.

(d) **Writing to Learn** Is it possible to make a general statement about using Simpson's Rule to approximate integrals of cubic polynomials? Explain.

20. Writing to Learn In Example 2 (before rounding) we found the average temperature to be 65.17 degrees when we used the integral approximation, yet the average of the 13 discrete temperatures is only 64.69 degrees. Considering the shape of the temperature curve, explain why you would expect the average of the 13 discrete temperatures to be less than the average value of the temperature function on the entire interval.

21. *(Continuation of Exercise 20)*

(a) In the Trapezoidal Rule, every function value in the sum is doubled except for the two endpoint values. Show that if you double the endpoint values, you get 70.08 for the average temperature.

(b) Explain why it makes more sense to not double the endpoint values if we are interested in the average temperature over the entire 12-hour period.

22. Group Activity For most functions, Simpson's Rule gives a better approximation to an integral than the Trapezoidal Rule for a given value of n. Sketch the graph of a function on a closed interval for which the Trapezoidal Rule obviously gives a better approximation than Simpson's Rule for $n = 4$.

In Exercises 23–26, use a calculator program to find the Simpson's Rule approximations with $n = 50$ and $n = 100$.

23. $\int_{-1}^1 2\sqrt{1 - x^2} \, dx$

24. $\int_0^1 \sqrt{1 + x^4} \, dx$

25. $\int_0^{\pi/2} \frac{\sin x}{x} \, dx$

26. $\int_0^{\pi/2} \sin(x^2) \, dx$

27. Consider the integral $\int_0^\pi \sin x \, dx$.

(a) Use a calculator program to find the Trapezoidal Rule approximations for $n = 10$, 100, and 1000.

(b) Record the errors with as many decimal places of accuracy as you can.

(c) What pattern do you see?

(d) **Writing to Learn** Explain how the error bound for E_T accounts for the pattern.

28. *(Continuation of Exercise 27)* Repeat Exercise 27 with Simpson's Rule and E_S.

29. *Aerodynamic Drag* A vehicle's aerodynamic drag is determined in part by its cross-section area, so, all other things being equal, engineers try to make this area as small as possible. Use Simpson's Rule to estimate the cross-section area of the body of James Worden's solar-powered Solectria® automobile at M.I.T. from the diagram below.

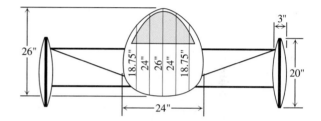

30. *Wing Design* The design of a new airplane requires a gasoline tank of constant cross-section area in each wing. A scale drawing of a cross section is shown here. The tank must hold 5000 lb of gasoline, which has a density of 42 lb/ft³. Estimate the length of the tank.

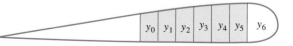

$y_0 = 1.5$ ft, $y_1 = 1.6$ ft, $y_2 = 1.8$ ft, $y_3 = 1.9$ ft,
$y_4 = 2.0$ ft, $y_5 = y_6 = 2.1$ ft   Horizontal spacing = 1 ft

Standardized Test Questions

31. True or False The Trapezoidal Rule will underestimate $\int_a^b f(x)\,dx$ if the graph of f is concave up on $[a, b]$. Justify your answer.

32. True or False For a given value of n, the Trapezoidal Rule with n subdivisions will always give a more accurate estimate of $\int_a^b f(x)\,dx$ than a right Riemann sum with n subdivisions. Justify your answer.

33. Multiple Choice Using 8 equal subdivisions of the interval $[2, 12]$, the LRAM approximation of $\int_2^{12} f(x)\,dx$ is 16.6 and the trapezoidal approximation is 16.4. What is the RRAM approximation?

(A) 16.2   (B) 16.5

(C) 16.6   (D) 16.8

(E) It cannot be determined from the given information.

34. Multiple Choice If three equal subdivisions of $[-2, 4]$ are used, what is the trapezoidal approximation of $\int_{-2}^{4} \dfrac{e^x}{2}\,dx$?

(A) $e^4 + e^2 + e^0 + e^{-2}$

(B) $e^4 + 2e^2 + 2e^0 + e^{-2}$

(C) $\dfrac{1}{2}(e^4 + e^2 + e^0 + e^{-2})$

(D) $\dfrac{1}{2}(e^4 + 2e^2 + 2e^0 + e^{-2})$

(E) $\dfrac{1}{4}(e^4 + 2e^2 + 2e^0 + e^{-2})$

35. Multiple Choice The trapezoidal approximation of $\int_0^{\pi} \sin x\,dx$ using 4 equal subdivisions of the interval of integration is

(A) $\dfrac{\pi}{2}$

(B) π

(C) $\dfrac{\pi}{4}\left(1 + \sqrt{2}\right)$

(D) $\dfrac{\pi}{2}\left(1 + \sqrt{2}\right)$

(E) $\dfrac{\pi}{4}\left(2 + \sqrt{2}\right)$

36. Multiple Choice Suppose f, f', and f'' are all positive on the interval $[a, b]$, and suppose we compute LRAM, RRAM, and trapezoidal approximations of $I = \int_a^b f(x)\,dx$ using the same number of equal subdivisions of $[a, b]$. If we denote the three

approximations of I as L, R, and T respectively, which of the following is true?

(A) $R < T < I < L$ (B) $R < I < T < L$

(C) $L < I < T < R$ (D) $L < T < I < R$

(E) $L < I < R < T$

Explorations

37. Consider the integral $\int_{-1}^{1} \sin\left(x^2\right)\,dx$.

(a) Find f'' for $f(x) = \sin\left(x^2\right)$.

(b) Graph $y = f''(x)$ in the viewing window $[-1, 1]$ by $[-3, 3]$.

(c) Explain why the graph in part (b) suggests that $|f''(x)| \le 3$ for $-1 \le x \le 1$.

(d) Show that the error estimate for the Trapezoidal Rule in this case becomes

$$|E_T| \le \frac{h^2}{2}.$$

(e) Show that the Trapezoidal Rule error will be less than or equal to 0.01 if $h \le 0.1$.

(f) How large must n be for $h \le 0.1$?

38. Consider the integral $\int_{-1}^{1} \sin\left(x^2\right)\,dx$.

(a) Find $f^{(4)}$ for $f(x) = \sin\left(x^2\right)$. (You may want to check your work with a CAS if you have one available.)

(b) Graph $y = f^{(4)}(x)$ in the viewing window $[-1, 1]$ by $[-30, 10]$.

(c) Explain why the graph in part (b) suggests that $|f^{(4)}(x)| \le 30$ for $-1 \le x \le 1$.

(d) Show that the error estimate for Simpson's Rule in this case becomes

$$|E_S| \le \frac{h^4}{3}.$$

(e) Show that the Simpson's Rule error will be less than or equal to 0.01 if $h \le 0.4$.

(f) How large must n be for $h \le 0.4$?

Extending the Ideas

39. Using the definitions, prove that, in general,

$$T_n = \frac{\text{LRAM}_n + \text{RRAM}_n}{2}.$$

40. Using the definitions, prove that, in general,

$$S_{2n} = \frac{\text{MRAM}_n + 2T_{2n}}{3}.$$

Quick Quiz for AP* Preparation: Sections 6.4 and 6.5

You may use a graphing calculator to solve the following problems.

1. Multiple Choice The function f is continuous on the closed interval $[1, 7]$ and has values that are given in the table below.

x	1	4	6	7
$f(x)$	10	30	40	20

Using the subintervals $[1, 4]$, $[4, 6]$, and $[6, 7]$, what is the trapezoidal approximation of $\int_1^7 f(x)\, dx$?

(A) 110   (B) 130   (C) 160   (D) 190   (E) 210

2. Multiple Choice Let $F(x)$ be an antiderivative of $\sin^3 x$. If $F(1) = 0$, then $F(8) =$

(A) 0.00   (B) 0.021   (C) 0.373   (D) 0.632   (E) 0.968

3. Multiple Choice Let $f(x) = \int_{-2}^{x^2 - 3x} e^{t^2}\, dt$. At what value of x is $f(x)$ a minimum?

(A) For no value of x (B) $\dfrac{1}{2}$ (C) $\dfrac{3}{2}$ (D) 2   (E) 3

4. Free Response Let $F(x) = \int_0^x \sin(t^2)\, dt$ for $0 \le x \le 3$.

(a) Use the Trapezoidal Rule with four equal subdivisions of the closed interval $[0, 2]$ to approximate $F(2)$.

(b) On what interval or intervals is F increasing? Justify your answer.

(c) If the average rate of change of F on the closed interval $[0, 3]$ is k, find $\int_0^3 \sin(t^2)\, dt$ in terms of k.

CHAPTER 6   Key Terms

accumulator function (p. 288)
area under a curve (p. 285)
average value (p. 295)
bounded function (p. 289)
cardiac output (p. 275)
characteristic function of the rationals
    (p. 290)
definite integral (p. 283)
differential calculus (p. 269)
dummy variable (p. 284)
error bounds (p. 319)
Fundamental Theorem of Calculus,
    Antiderivative Part (p. 302)
Fundamental Theorem of Calculus,
    Evaluation Part (p. 307)
integrable function (p. 283)

integral calculus (p. 269)
Integral Evaluation Theorem (p. 307)
integral of f from a to b (p. 284)
integral sign (p. 284)
integrand (p. 284)
lower bound (p. 294)
lower limit of integration (p. 284)
LRAM (p. 272)
mean value (p. 295)
Mean Value Theorem for Definite Integrals
    (p. 296)
MRAM (p. 272)
net area (p. 286)
NINT (p. 289)
norm of a partition (p. 282)
partition (p. 281)

Rectangular Approximation Method
    (RAM) (p. 272)
regular partition (p. 283)
Riemann sum (p. 281)
Riemann sum for f on the interval $[a, b]$
    (p. 282)
RRAM (p. 272)
sigma notation (p. 281)
Simpson's Rule (p. 317)
subinterval (p. 282)
total area (p. 308)
Trapezoidal Rule (p. 315)
upper bound (p. 294)
upper limit of integration (p. 284)
variable of integration (p. 284)

CHAPTER 6   Review Exercises

Exercise numbers with a gray background indicate problems that the authors have designed to be solved *without a calculator*.

The collection of exercises marked in red could be used as a chapter test.

Exercises 1–6 refer to the region R in the first quadrant enclosed by the x-axis and the graph of the function $y = 4x - x^3$.

1. Sketch R and partition it into four subregions, each with a base of length $\Delta x = 1/2$.

2. Sketch the rectangles and compute (by hand) the area for the LRAM_4 approximation.

3. Sketch the rectangles and compute (by hand) the area for the MRAM_4 approximation.

4. Sketch the rectangles and compute (by hand) the area for the RRAM_4 approximation.

5. Sketch the trapezoids and compute (by hand) the area for the T_4 approximation.

6. Find the exact area of R by using the Fundamental Theorem of Calculus.

7. Use a calculator program to compute the RAM approximations in the following table for the area under the graph of $y = 1/x$ from $x = 1$ to $x = 5$.

n	LRAM_n	MRAM_n	RRAM_n
10			
20			
30			
50			
100			
1000			

8. *(Continuation of Exercise 7)* Use the Fundamental Theorem of Calculus to determine the value to which the sums in the table are converging.

9. Suppose

$$\int_{-2}^{2} f(x)\,dx = 4, \quad \int_{2}^{5} f(x)\,dx = 3, \quad \int_{-2}^{5} g(x)\,dx = 2.$$

Which of the following statements are true, and which, if any, are false?

(a) $\int_{5}^{2} f(x)\,dx = -3$

(b) $\int_{-2}^{5} [f(x) + g(x)]\,dx = 9$

(c) $f(x) \le g(x)$ on the interval $-2 \le x \le 5$

10. The region under one arch of the curve $y = \sin x$ is revolved around the x-axis to form a solid. **(a)** Use the method of Example 4, Section 6.1, to set up a Riemann sum that approximates the volume of the solid. **(b)** Write the limit of the Riemann sum as a definite integral and then find the volume using NINT.

11. The accompanying graph shows the velocity (m/sec) of a body moving along the s-axis during the time interval from $t = 0$ to $t = 10$ sec. **(a)** About how far did the body travel during those 10 seconds?

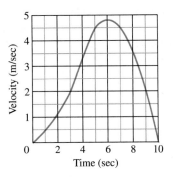

(b) Sketch a graph of position (s) as a function of time (t) for $0 \le t \le 10$, assuming $s(0) = 0$.

12. The interval $[0, 10]$ is partitioned into n subintervals of length $\Delta x = 10/n$. We form the following Riemann sums, choosing each c_k in the kth subinterval. Write the limit as $n \to \infty$ of each Riemann sum as a definite integral.

(a) $\sum_{k=1}^{n} (c_k)^3 \Delta x$

(b) $\sum_{k=1}^{n} c_k(\sin c_k) \Delta x$

(c) $\sum_{k=1}^{n} c_k(3c_k - 2)^2 \Delta x$

(d) $\sum_{k=1}^{n} (1 + c_k^2)^{-1} \Delta x$

(e) $\sum_{k=1}^{n} \pi(9 - \sin^2(\pi c_k/10)) \Delta x$

In Exercises 13 and 14, find the total area between the curve and the x-axis.

13. $y = 4 - x, \quad 0 \le x \le 6$

14. $y = \cos x, \quad 0 \le x \le \pi$

In Exercises 15–24, evaluate the integral analytically by using the Integral Evaluation Theorem (Evaluation Part of the Fundamental Theorem, Theorem 4).

15. $\int_{-2}^{2} 5\,dx$

16. $\int_{2}^{5} 4x\,dx$

17. $\int_{0}^{\pi/4} \cos x\,dx$

18. $\int_{-1}^{1} (3x^2 - 4x + 7)\,dx$

19. $\int_{0}^{1} (8s^3 - 12s^2 + 5)\,ds$

20. $\int_{1}^{2} \frac{4}{x^2}\,dx$

21. $\int_{1}^{27} y^{-4/3}\,dy$

22. $\int_{1}^{4} \frac{dt}{t\sqrt{t}}$

23. $\int_{0}^{\pi/3} \sec^2 \theta\,d\theta$

24. $\int_{1}^{e} (1/x)\,dx$

In Exercises 25–29, evaluate the integral.

25. $\int_{0}^{1} \frac{36}{(2x + 1)^3}\,dx$

26. $\int_{1}^{2} \left(x + \frac{1}{x^2}\right)\,dx$

27. $\int_{-\pi/3}^{0} \sec x \tan x\,dx$

28. $\int_{-1}^{1} 2x \sin(1 - x^2)\,dx$

29. $\int_{0}^{2} \frac{2}{y + 1}\,dy$

In Exercises 30–32, evaluate the integral by interpreting it as area and using formulas from geometry.

30. $\int_{0}^{2} \sqrt{4 - x^2}\,dx$

31. $\int_{-4}^{8} |x|\,dx$

32. $\int_{-8}^{8} 2\sqrt{64 - x^2}\,dx$

33. *Oil Consumption on Pathfinder Island* A diesel generator runs continuously, consuming oil at a gradually increasing rate until it must be temporarily shut down to have the filters replaced.

Day	Oil Consumption Rate (liters/hour)
Sun	0.019
Mon	0.020
Tue	0.021
Wed	0.023
Thu	0.025
Fri	0.028
Sat	0.031
Sun	0.035

(a) Give an upper estimate and a lower estimate for the amount of oil consumed by the generator during that week.

(b) Use the Trapezoidal Rule to estimate the amount of oil consumed by the generator during that week.

34. *Rubber-Band–Powered Sled* A sled powered by a wound rubber band moves along a track until friction and the unwinding of the rubber band gradually slow it to a stop. A speedometer in the sled monitors its speed, which is recorded at 3-second intervals during the 27-second run.

Time (sec)	Speed (ft/sec)
0	5.30
3	5.25
6	5.04
9	4.71
12	4.25
15	3.66
18	2.94
21	2.09
24	1.11
27	0

(a) Give an upper estimate and a lower estimate for the distance traveled by the sled.

(b) Use the Trapezoidal Rule to estimate the distance traveled by the sled.

35. *Writing to Learn* Your friend knows how to compute integrals but never could understand what difference the "*dx*" makes, claiming that it is irrelevant. How would you explain to your friend why it is necessary?

36. The function

$$f(x) = \begin{cases} x^2, & x \ge 0 \\ x - 2, & x < 0 \end{cases}$$

is discontinuous at 0, but integrable on $[-4, 4]$. Find $\int_{-4}^{4} f(x)\,dx$.

37. Show that $0 \le \int_{0}^{1} \sqrt{1 + \sin^2 x}\,dx \le \sqrt{2}$.

38. Find the average value of

(a) $y = \sqrt{x}$ over the interval $[0, 4]$.

(b) $y = a\sqrt{x}$ over the interval $[0, a]$.

In Exercises 39–42, find dy/dx.

39. $y = \int_{2}^{x} \sqrt{2 + \cos^3 t}\,dt$ **40.** $y = \int_{2}^{7x^2} \sqrt{2 + \cos^3 t}\,dt$

41. $y = \int_{x}^{1} \dfrac{6}{3 + t^4}\,dt$ **42.** $y = \int_{x}^{2x} \dfrac{1}{t^2 + 1}\,dt$

43. *Printing Costs* Including start-up costs, it costs a printer $50 to print 25 copies of a newsletter, after which the marginal cost at *x* copies is

$$\frac{dc}{dx} = \frac{2}{\sqrt{x}} \text{ dollars per copy.}$$

Find the total cost of printing 2500 newsletters.

44. *Average Daily Inventory* Rich Wholesale Foods, a manufacturer of cookies, stores its cases of cookies in an air-conditioned warehouse for shipment every 14 days. Rich tries to keep 600 cases on reserve to meet occasional peaks in demand, so a typical 14-day inventory function is $I(t) = 600 + 600t$, $0 \le t \le 14$. The holding cost for each case is 4¢ per day. Find Rich's average daily inventory and average daily holding cost (that is, the average of $I(x)$ for the 14-day period, and this average multiplied by the holding cost).

45. Solve for *x*: $\int_{0}^{x}(t^3 - 2t + 3)\,dt = 4$.

46. Suppose $f(x)$ has a positive derivative for all values of *x* and that $f(1) = 0$. Which of the following statements must be true of

$$g(x) = \int_{0}^{x} f(t)\,dt?$$

(a) *g* is a differentiable function of *x*.

(b) *g* is a continuous function of *x*.

(c) The graph of *g* has a horizontal tangent line at $x = 1$.

(d) *g* has a local maximum at $x = 1$.

(e) *g* has a local minimum at $x = 1$.

(f) The graph of *g* has an inflection point at $x = 1$.

(g) The graph of dg/dx crosses the *x*-axis at $x = 1$.

47. Suppose $F(x)$ is an antiderivative of $f(x) = \sqrt{1 + x^4}$. Express $\int_{0}^{1}\sqrt{1 + x^4}\,dx$ in terms of *F*.

48. Express the function $y(x)$ with

$$\frac{dy}{dx} = \frac{\sin x}{x} \quad \text{and} \quad y(5) = 3$$

as a definite integral.

49. Show that $y = x^2 + \int_{1}^{x}(1/t)\,dt + 1$ satisfies both of the following conditions:

i. $y'' = 2 - \dfrac{1}{x^2}$

ii. $y = 2$ and $y' = 3$ when $x = 1$.

50. *Writing to Learn* Which of the following is the graph of the function whose derivative is $dy/dx = 2x$ and whose value at $x = 1$ is 4? Explain your answer.

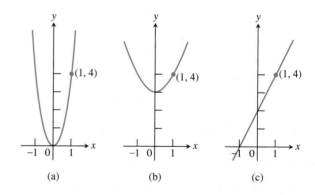

(a)   (b)   (c)

51. *Fuel Efficiency* An automobile computer gives a digital readout of fuel consumption in gallons per hour. During a trip, a passenger recorded the fuel consumption every 5 minutes for a full hour of travel.

time	gal/h	time	gal/h
0	2.5	35	2.5
5	2.4	40	2.4
10	2.3	45	2.3
15	2.4	50	2.4
20	2.4	55	2.4
25	2.5	60	2.3
30	2.6		

(a) Use the Trapezoidal Rule to approximate the total fuel consumption during the hour.

(b) If the automobile covered 60 miles in the hour, what was its fuel efficiency (in miles per gallon) for that portion of the trip?

52. *Skydiving* Skydivers A and B are in a helicopter hovering at 6400 feet. Skydiver A jumps and descends for 4 sec before opening her parachute. The helicopter then climbs to 7000 feet and hovers there. Forty-five seconds after A leaves the aircraft, B jumps and descends for 13 sec before opening her parachute. Both skydivers descend at 16 ft/sec with parachutes open. Assume that the skydivers fall freely (with acceleration -32 ft/sec^2) before their parachutes open.

(a) At what altitude does A's parachute open?

(b) At what altitude does B's parachute open?

(c) Which skydiver lands first?

53. *Relating Simpson's Rule, MRAM, and T* The figure below shows an interval of length $2h$ with a trapezoid, a midpoint rectangle, and a parabolic region on it.

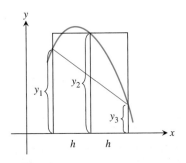

(a) Show that the area of the trapezoid plus twice the area of the rectangle equals

$$h(y_1 + 4y_2 + y_3).$$

(b) Use the result in part (a) to prove that

$$S_{2_n} = \frac{2 \cdot \text{MRAM}_n + T_n}{3}.$$

54. The graph of a function f consists of a semicircle and two line segments as shown below.

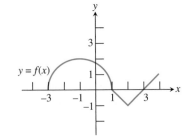

Let $g(x) = \int_1^x f(t)\, dt$.

(a) Find $g(1)$.

(b) Find $g(3)$.

(c) Find $g(-1)$.

(d) Find all values of x on the open interval $(-3, 4)$ at which g has a relative maximum.

(e) Write an equation for the line tangent to the graph of g at $x = -1$.

(f) Find the x-coordinate of each point of inflection of the graph of g on the open interval $(-3, 4)$.

(g) Find the range of g.

55. What is the total area under the curve $y = e^{-x^2/2}$?

The graph approaches the x-axis as an asymptote both to the left and the right, but quickly enough so that the total area is a finite number. In fact,

$$\text{NINT}\left(e^{-x^2/2}, x, -10, 10\right)$$

computes all but a negligible amount of the area.

(a) Find this number on your calculator. Verify that NINT $\left(e^{-x^2/2}, x, -20, 20\right)$ does not increase the number enough for the calculator to distinguish the difference.

(b) This area has an interesting relationship to π. Perform various (simple) algebraic operations on the number to discover what it is.

56. *Filling a Swamp* A town wants to drain and fill the small polluted swamp shown below. The swamp averages 5 ft deep. About how many cubic yards of dirt will it take to fill the area after the swamp is drained?

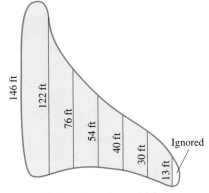

Horizontal spacing = 20 ft

57. *Household Electricity* We model the voltage V in our homes with the sine function

$$V = V_{\text{max}} \sin\left(120\, \pi t\right),$$

which expresses V in volts as a function of time t in seconds. The function runs through 60 cycles each second. The number V_{max} is the *peak voltage*.

To measure the voltage effectively, we use an instrument that measures the square root of the average value of the square of the voltage over a 1-second interval:

$$V_{\text{rms}} = \sqrt{(V^2)_{\text{av}}}$$

The subscript "rms" stands for "root mean square." It turns out that

$$V_{\text{rms}} = \frac{V_{\text{max}}}{\sqrt{2}}. \tag{1}$$

The familiar phrase "115 volts ac" means that the rms voltage is 115. The peak voltage, obtained from Equation 1 as $V_{\text{max}} = 115\sqrt{2}$, is about 163 volts.

(a) Find the average value of V^2 over a 1-sec interval. Then find V_{rms}, and verify Equation 1.

(b) The circuit that runs your electric stove is rated 240 volts rms. What is the peak value of the allowable voltage?

AP* Examination Preparation

You may use a graphing calculator to solve the following problems.

58. The rate at which water flows out of a pipe is given by a differentiable function R of time t. The table below records the rate at 4-hour intervals for a 24-hour period.

t (hours)	$R(t)$ (gallons per hour)
0	9.6
4	10.3
8	10.9
12	11.1
16	10.9
20	10.5
24	9.6

(a) Use the Trapezoidal Rule with 6 subdivisions of equal length to approximate $\int_0^{24} R(t)\, dt$. Explain the meaning of your answer in terms of water flow, using correct units.

(b) Is there some time t between 0 and 24 such that $R'(t) = 0$? Justify your answer.

(c) Suppose the rate of water flow is approximated by $Q(t) = 0.01(950 + 25x - x^2)$. Use $Q(t)$ to approximate the average rate of water flow during the 24-hour period. Indicate units of measure.

59. Let f be a differentiable function with the following properties.

    i. $f'(x) = ax^2 + bx$ **ii.** $f'(1) = -6$ and $f''(x) = 6$

    iii. $\int_1^2 f(x)\, dx = 14$

Find $f(x)$. Show your work.

60. The graph of the function f, consisting of three line segments, is shown below.

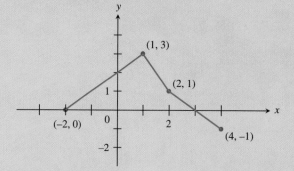

Let $g(x) = \int_1^x f(t)\, dt$.

(a) Compute $g(4)$ and $g(-2)$.

(b) Find the instantaneous rate of change of g, with respect to x, at $x = 2$.

(c) Find the absolute minimum value of g on the closed interval $[-2, 4]$. Justify your answer.

(d) The second derivative of g is not defined at $x = 1$ and $x = 2$. Which of these values are x-coordinates of points of inflection of the graph of g? Justify your answer.

7.1 Slope Fields and Euler's Method

7.2 Antidifferentiation by Substitution

7.3 Antidifferentiation by Parts

7.4 Exponential Growth and Decay

7.5 Logistic Growth

The lovely image above is actually a two-dimensional projection of a three-dimensional graph that is determined by three differential equations:

$$\frac{dx}{dt} = 10(y - x)$$

$$\frac{dy}{dt} = x(28 - z) - y$$

$$\frac{dz}{dt} = xy - \frac{8}{3}z$$

These equations were first used by Edward Lorenz (1917–2008), an MIT professor who had served as a meteorologist during World War II. He had hoped to use three-dimensional computer simulations of atmospheric convection to predict future weather conditions. What he discovered was somewhat discouraging for weather predictors but very exciting for mathematicians: the first insights into what is widely known today as Chaos Theory. You may have read of the "butterfly effect," the whimsical name for the chaotic impact that small perturbations can have on the solutions to such systems. (The fact that this classic solution, known as the Lorenz attractor, resembles a butterfly is just a happy coincidence.) You will learn more about differential equations and their graphs in this chapter.

CHAPTER 7 Overview

One of the early accomplishments of calculus was predicting the future position of a planet from its present position and velocity. Today this is just one of many situations in which we deduce everything we need to know about a function from one of its known values and its rate of change. From this kind of information, we can tell how long a sample of radioactive polonium will last; whether, given current trends, a population will grow or become extinct; and how large major league baseball salaries are likely to be in the year 2020. In this chapter, we examine the analytic, graphical, and numerical techniques on which such predictions are based.

7.1 | Slope Fields and Euler's Method

You will be able to use slope fields to analyze solution curves to differential equations, and you will be able to use Euler's method to construct solutions numerically.

- Differential equations
- General and particular solutions of differential equations
- Solving exact differential equations
- Slope fields
- Euler's Method

Differential Equations

We have already seen how the discovery of calculus enabled mathematicians to solve problems that had befuddled them for centuries because the problems involved moving objects. Leibniz and Newton were able to model these problems of motion by using equations involving derivatives—what we call *differential equations* today, after the notation of Leibniz. Much energy and creativity has been spent over the years on techniques for solving such equations, which continue to arise in all areas of applied mathematics.

> **DEFINITION   Differential Equation**
>
> An equation involving a derivative is called a **differential equation.** The **order of a differential equation** is the order of the highest derivative involved in the equation.

EXAMPLE 1   Solving a Differential Equation

Find all functions y that satisfy $dy/dx = \sec^2 x + 2x + 5$.

SOLUTION

We first encountered this sort of differential equation (called **exact** because it gives the derivative exactly) in Chapter 5. The solution can be any antiderivative of $\sec^2 x + 2x + 5$, which can be any function of the form $y = \tan x + x^2 + 5x + C$. That family of functions is the **general solution** to the differential equation.

Now Try Exercise 1.

Notice that we cannot find a unique solution to a differential equation unless we are given further information. If the general solution to a first-order differential equation is continuous, the only additional information needed is the value of the function at a single point, called an **initial condition.** A differential equation with an initial condition is called an **initial value problem.** It has a unique solution, called the **particular solution** to the differential equation.

EXAMPLE 2   Solving an Initial Value Problem

Find the particular solution to the equation $dy/dx = e^x - 6x^2$ whose graph passes through the point $(1, 0)$.

SOLUTION

The general solution is $y = e^x - 2x^3 + C$. Applying the initial condition that $y = 0$ when $x = 1$, we have $0 = e - 2 + C$, from which we conclude that $C = 2 - e$. Therefore, the particular solution is $y = e^x - 2x^3 + 2 - e$.   *Now Try Exercise 13.*

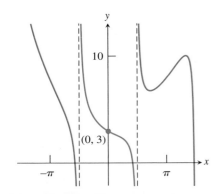

Figure 7.1 A graph of the discontinuous function $y = x^2/2 - \tan x + 3$, which satisfies the conditions of the initial value problem in Example 3. Note that the initial condition $y = 3$ when $x = 0$ "pins down" only the blue section of the curve. The red sections could move up and down, and the function would still solve the initial value problem. (Example 3)

An initial condition determines a particular solution by requiring that a solution curve pass through a given point. If the curve is continuous, this pins down the solution on the entire domain. If the curve is discontinuous, the initial condition pins down only the continuous *piece of the curve* that passes through the given point. In this case, the domain of the solution must be specified.

EXAMPLE 3 Handling Discontinuity in an Initial Value Problem

Find the particular solution to the differential equation $dy/dx = x - \sec^2 x$ with the initial condition that $y = 3$ when $x = 0$.

SOLUTION

The general solution is $y = x^2/2 - \tan x + C$. Applying the initial condition, we have $3 = 0 - 0 + C$. Therefore, the particular solution is $y = x^2/2 - \tan x + 3$. Since the function is discontinuous, the initial condition guarantees a unique solution only over the interval $(-\pi/2, \pi/2)$. (See Figure 7.1.) We must therefore add the domain stipulation that the particular solution is valid for $-\pi/2 < x < \pi/2$.

Now Try Exercise 15.

Sometimes we are unable to find an antiderivative to solve an initial value problem, but we can still find a solution using the Fundamental Theorem of Calculus.

EXAMPLE 4 Using the Fundamental Theorem to Solve an Initial Value Problem

Find the solution to the differential equation $f'(x) = e^{-x^2}$ for which $f(7) = 3$.

SOLUTION

This almost seems too simple, but $f(x) = \int_7^x e^{-t^2} \, dt + 3$ has both of the necessary properties! Clearly, $f(7) = \int_7^7 e^{-t^2} \, dt + 3 = 0 + 3 = 3$, and $f'(x) = e^{-x^2}$ by the Fundamental Theorem. The integral form of the solution in Example 4 might seem less desirable than the explicit form of the solutions in Examples 2 and 3, but (thanks to modern technology) it does enable us to find $f(x)$ for any x. For example,

$$f(-2) = \int_7^{-2} e^{-t^2} \, dt + 3 = \text{NINT} \left(e^{\wedge}(-t^2), t, 7, -2\right) + 3 \approx 1.2317.$$

Now Try Exercise 21.

EXAMPLE 5 Graphing a General Solution

Graph the family of functions that solve the differential equation $dy/dx = \cos x$.

SOLUTION

Any function of the form $y = \sin x + C$ solves the differential equation. We cannot graph them all, but we can graph enough of them to see what a family of solutions would look like. The command $\{-3, -2, -1, 0, 1, 2, 3,\} \rightarrow L_1$ stores seven values of C in the list L_1. Figure 7.2 shows the result of graphing the function $Y_1 = \sin(x) + L_1$.

Now Try Exercises 25–28.

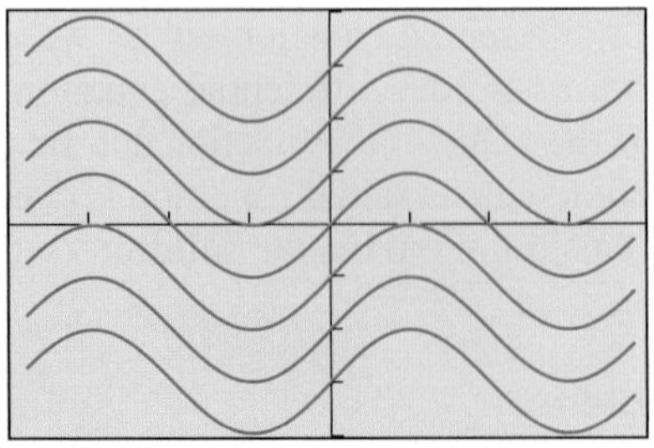

[$-2\pi, 2\pi$] by [$-4, 4$]

Figure 7.2 A graph of the family of functions $Y_1 = \sin(x) + L_1$, where $L_1 = \{-3, -2, -1, 0, 1, 2, 3\}$. This graph shows some of the functions that satisfy the differential equation $dy/dx = \cos x$. (Example 5)

Notice that the graph in Figure 7.2 consists of a family of parallel curves. This should come as no surprise, since functions of the form $\sin(x) + C$ are all vertical translations of the basic sine curve. It might be less obvious that we could have predicted the appearance of this family of curves from *the differential equation itself.* Exploration 1 gives you a new way to look at the solution graph.

Exploration 1 suggests the interesting possibility that we could have produced the family of curves in Figure 7.2 without even solving the differential equation, simply by looking carefully at slopes. That is exactly the idea behind *slope fields.*

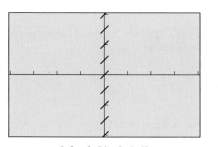

[−2π, 2π] by [−4, 4]

(a)

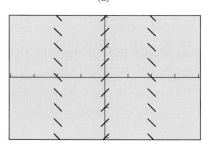

[−2π, 2π] by [−4, 4]

(b)

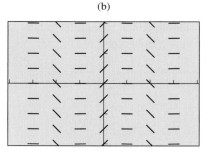

[−2π, 2π] by [−4, 4]

(c)

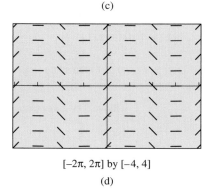

[−2π, 2π] by [−4, 4]

(d)

Figure 7.3 The steps in constructing a slope field for the differential equation $dy/dx = \cos x$. (Example 6)

EXPLORATION 1 Seeing the Slopes

Figure 7.2 shows the general solution to the exact differential equation $dy/dx = \cos x$.

1. Since $\cos x = 0$ at odd multiples of $\pi/2$, we should "see" that $dy/dx = 0$ at the odd multiples of $\pi/2$ in Figure 7.2. Is that true? How can you tell?
2. Algebraically, the y-coordinate does not affect the value of $dy/dx = \cos x$. Why not?
3. Does the graph show that the y-coordinate does not affect the value of dy/dx? How can you tell?
4. According to the differential equation $dy/dx = \cos x$, what should be the slope of the solution curves when $x = 0$? Can you see this in the graph?
5. According to the differential equation $dy/dx = \cos x$, what should be the slope of the solution curves when $x = \pi$? Can you see this in the graph?
6. Since $\cos x$ is an even function, the slope at any point should be the same as the slope at its reflection across the y-axis. Is this true? How can you tell?

Slope Fields

Suppose we want to produce Figure 7.2 without actually solving the differential equation $dy/dx = \cos x$. Since the differential equation gives the *slope* at any point (x, y), we can use that information to draw a small piece of the linearization at that point, which (thanks to local linearity) approximates the solution curve that passes through that point. Repeating that process at many points yields an approximation of Figure 7.2 called a **slope field.** Example 6 shows how this is done.

EXAMPLE 6 Constructing a Slope Field

Construct a slope field for the differential equation $dy/dx = \cos x$.

SOLUTION

We know that the slope at any point $(0, y)$ will be $\cos 0 = 1$, so we can start by drawing tiny segments with slope 1 at several points along the y-axis (Figure 7.3a). Then, since the slope at any point (π, y) or $(-\pi, y)$ will be -1, we can draw tiny segments with slope -1 at several points along the vertical lines $x = \pi$ and $x = -\pi$ (Figure 7.3b). The slope at all odd multiples of $\pi/2$ will be zero, so we draw tiny horizontal segments along the lines $x = \pm\pi/2$ and $x = \pm 3\pi/2$ (Figure 7.3c). Finally, we add tiny segments of slope 1 along the lines $x = \pm 2\pi$ (Figure 7.3d).

Now Try Exercise 29.

To illustrate how a family of solution curves conforms to a slope field, we superimpose the solutions in Figure 7.2 on the slope field in Figure 7.3d. The result is shown in Figure 7.4 on the next page.

We could get a smoother-looking slope field by drawing shorter line segments at more points, but that can get tedious. Happily, the algorithm is simple enough to be programmed into a graphing calculator. One such program, using a lattice of 150 sample points, produced in a matter of seconds the graph in Figure 7.5 on the next page.

It is also possible to produce slope fields for differential equations that are not of the form $dy/dx = f(x)$. We will study analytic techniques for solving certain types of these nonexact differential equations later in this chapter, but you should keep in mind that you can graph the general solution with a slope field even if you cannot find it analytically.

Differential Equation Mode

If your calculator has a *differential equation mode* for graphing, it is intended for graphing slope fields. The usual "Y=" turns into a "*dy/dx* = " screen, and you can enter a function of *x* and/or *y*. The grapher draws a slope field for the differential equation when you press the GRAPH button.

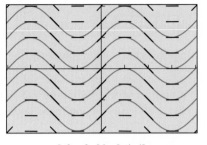

$[-2\pi, 2\pi]$ by $[-4, 4]$

Figure 7.4 The graph of the general solution in Figure 7.2 conforms nicely to the slope field of the differential equation. (Example 6)

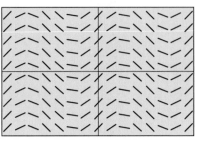

$[-2\pi, 2\pi]$ by $[-4, 4]$

Figure 7.5 A slope field produced by a graphing calculator program.

Can We Solve the Differential Equation in Example 7?

Although it looks harmless enough, the differential equation $dy/dx = x + y$ is not easy to solve until you have seen how it is done. It is an example of a *first-order linear differential equation,* and its general solution is

$$y = Ce^x - x - 1$$

(which you can easily check by verifying that $dy/dx = x + y$). We will defer the analytic solution of such equations to a later course.

EXAMPLE 7 Constructing a Slope Field for a Nonexact Differential Equation

Use a calculator to construct a slope field for the differential equation $dy/dx = x + y$ and sketch a graph of the particular solution that passes through the point $(2, 0)$.

SOLUTION

The calculator produces a graph like the one in Figure 7.6a. Notice the following properties of the graph, all of them easily predictable from the differential equation:

1. The slopes are zero along the line $x + y = 0$ (The horizontal segments do not exactly appear in this calculator window, but you can see where they would be.)

2. The slopes are -1 along the line $x + y = -1$.

3. The slopes get steeper as x increases.

4. The slopes get steeper as y increases.

The particular solution can be found by drawing a smooth curve through the point $(2, 0)$ that follows the slopes in the slope field, as shown in Figure 7.6b.

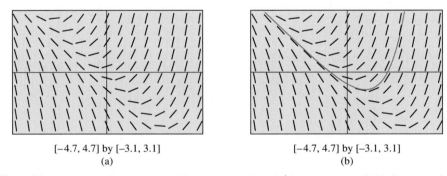

$[-4.7, 4.7]$ by $[-3.1, 3.1]$
(a)

$[-4.7, 4.7]$ by $[-3.1, 3.1]$
(b)

Figure 7.6 (a) A slope field for the differential equation $dy/dx = x + y$, and (b) the same slope field with the graph of the particular solution through $(2, 0)$ superimposed. (Example 7)

Now Try Exercise 35.

EXAMPLE 8 Matching Slope Fields with Differential Equations

Use slope analysis to match each of the following differential equations with one of the slope fields (a) through (d). (Do not use your graphing calculator.)

continued

1. $\dfrac{dy}{dx} = x - y$ **2.** $\dfrac{dy}{dx} = xy$ **3.** $\dfrac{dy}{dx} = \dfrac{x}{y}$ **4.** $\dfrac{dy}{dx} = \dfrac{y}{x}$

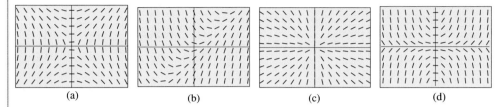

(a)   (b)   (c)   (d)

SOLUTION

To match Equation 1, we look for a graph that has zero slope along the line $x - y = 0$. That is graph (b).

To match Equation 2, we look for a graph that has zero slope along both axes. That is graph (d).

To match Equation 3, we look for a graph that has horizontal segments when $x = 0$ and vertical segments when $y = 0$. That is graph (a).

To match Equation 4, we look for a graph that has vertical segments when $x = 0$ and horizontal segments when $y = 0$. That is graph (c).

Now Try Exercise 39.

Euler's Method

In Example 7 we graphed the particular solution to an initial value problem by first producing a slope field and then finding a smooth curve through the slope field that passed through the given point. In fact, we could have graphed the particular solution directly, by starting at the given point and piecing together little line segments to build a continuous approximation of the curve. This clever application of local linearity to graph a solution without knowing its equation is called **Euler's Method.**

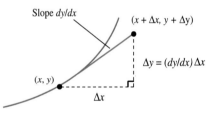

Figure 7.7 How Euler's Method moves along the linearization at the point (x, y) to define a new point $(x + \Delta x, y + \Delta y)$. The process is then repeated, starting with the new point.

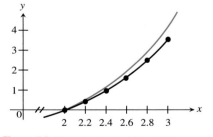

Figure 7.8 Euler's Method is used to construct an approximate solution to an initial value problem between $x = 2$ and $x = 3$. (Example 9)

Euler's Method for Graphing a Solution to an Initial Value Problem

1. Begin at the point (x, y) specified by the initial condition. This point will be on the graph, as required.
2. Use the differential equation to find the slope dy/dx at the point.
3. Increase x by a small amount, Δx. Increase y by a small amount, Δy, where $\Delta y = (dy/dx)\Delta x$. This defines a new point $(x + \Delta x, y + \Delta y)$ that lies along the linearization (Figure 7.7).
4. Using this new point, return to step 2. Repeating the process constructs the graph to the right of the initial point.
5. To construct the graph moving to the left from the initial point, repeat the process using negative values for Δx.

We illustrate the method in Example 9.

EXAMPLE 9 Applying Euler's Method

Let f be the function that satisfies the initial value problem in Example 7 (that is, $dy/dx = x + y$ and $f(2) = 0$). Use Euler's Method and increments of $\Delta x = 0.2$ to approximate $f(3)$.

SOLUTION

We use Euler's Method to construct an approximation of the curve from $x = 2$ to $x = 3$, pasting together five small linearization segments (Figure 7.8). Each segment

continued

will extend from a point (x, y) to a point $(x + \Delta x, y + \Delta y)$, where $\Delta x = 0.2$ and $\Delta y = (dy/dx)\Delta x$. The following table shows how we construct each new point from the previous one.

(x, y)	$dy/dx = x + y$	Δx	$\Delta y = (dy/dx)\Delta x$	$(x + \Delta x, y + \Delta y)$
$(2, 0)$	2	0.2	0.4	$(2.2, 0.4)$
$(2.2, 0.4)$	2.6	0.2	0.52	$(2.4, 0.92)$
$(2.4, 0.92)$	3.32	0.2	0.664	$(2.6, 1.584)$
$(2.6, 1.584)$	4.184	0.2	0.8368	$(2.8, 2.4208)$
$(2.8, 2.4208)$	5.2208	0.2	1.04416	$(3, 3.46496)$

Euler's Method leads us to an approximation $f(3) \approx 3.46496$, which we would more reasonably report as $f(3) \approx 3.465$.   ***Now Try Exercise 51.***

You can see from Figure 7.8 that Euler's Method leads to an underestimate when the curve is concave up, just as it will lead to an overestimate when the curve is concave down. You can also see that the error increases as the distance from the original point increases. In fact, the true value of $f(3)$ is about 4.155, so the approximation error is about 16.6%. We could increase the accuracy by taking smaller increments—a reasonable option if we have a calculator program to do the work. For example, 100 increments of 0.01 give an estimate of 4.1144, cutting the error to about 1%.

EXAMPLE 10 Moving Backward with Euler's Method

If $dy/dx = 2x - y$ and if $y = 3$ when $x = 2$, use Euler's Method with five equal steps to approximate y when $x = 1.5$.

SOLUTION

Starting at $x = 2$, we need five equal steps of $\Delta x = -0.1$.

(x, y)	$dy/dx = 2x - y$	Δx	$\Delta y = (dy/dx)\Delta x$	$(x + \Delta x, y + \Delta y)$
$(2, 3)$	1	−0.1	−0.1	$(1.9, 2.9)$
$(1.9, 2.9)$	0.9	−0.1	−0.09	$(1.8, 2.81)$
$(1.8, 2.81)$	0.79	−0.1	−0.079	$(1.7, 2.731)$
$(1.7, 2.731)$	0.669	−0.1	−0.0669	$(1.6, 2.6641)$
$(1.6, 2.6641)$	0.5359	−0.1	−0.05359	$(1.5, 2.61051)$

The value at $x = 1.5$ is approximately 2.61. (The actual value is about 2.649, so the percentage error in this case is about 1.4%.)   ***Now Try Exercise 55.***

If we program a grapher to do the work of finding the points, Euler's Method can be used to graph (approximately) the solution to an initial value problem without actually solving it. For example, a graphing calculator program starting with the initial value problem in Example 10 produced the graph in Figure 7.9, using increments of ± 0.1. The graph of the actual solution is shown in red. Notice that Euler's Method does a better job of approximating the curve when the curve is nearly straight, as should be expected.

Euler's Method is one example of a **numerical method** for solving differential equations. The table of values is the **numerical solution.** The analysis of error in a numerical solution and the investigation of methods to reduce it are important, but appropriate for a more advanced course (which would also describe more accurate numerical methods than the one shown here).

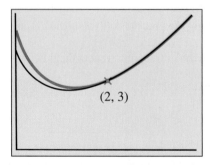

[0, 4] by [0, 6]

Figure 7.9 A grapher program using Euler's Method and increments of ± 0.1 produced this approximation to the solution curve for the initial value problem in Example 10. The actual solution curve is shown in red.

Quick Review 7.1

Exercise numbers with a gray background indicate problems that the authors have designed to be solved *without a calculator*.

In Exercises 1–8, determine whether or not the function y satisfies the differential equation.

1. $\dfrac{dy}{dx} = y \qquad y = e^x$

2. $\dfrac{dy}{dx} = 4y \qquad y = e^{4x}$

3. $\dfrac{dy}{dx} = 2xy \qquad y = x^2 e^x$

4. $\dfrac{dy}{dx} = 2xy \qquad y = e^{x^2}$

5. $\dfrac{dy}{dx} = 2xy \qquad y = e^{x^2} + 5$

6. $\dfrac{dy}{dx} = \dfrac{1}{y} \qquad y = \sqrt{2x}$

7. $\dfrac{dy}{dx} = y \tan x \qquad y = \sec x$

8. $\dfrac{dy}{dx} = y^2 \qquad y = x^{-1}$

In Exercises 9–12, find the constant C.

9. $y = 3x^2 + 4x + C$ and $y = 2$ when $x = 1$

10. $y = 2 \sin x - 3 \cos x + C$ and $y = 4$ when $x = 0$

11. $y = e^{2x} + \sec x + C$ and $y = 5$ when $x = 0$

12. $y = \tan^{-1} x + \ln(2x - 1) + C$ and $y = \pi$ when $x = 1$

Section 7.1 Exercises

In Exercises 1–10, find the general solution to the exact differential equation.

1. $\dfrac{dy}{dx} = 5x^4 - \sec^2 x$

2. $\dfrac{dy}{dx} = \sec x \tan x - e^x$

3. $\dfrac{dy}{dx} = \sin x - e^{-x} + 8x^3$

4. $\dfrac{dy}{dx} = \dfrac{1}{x} - \dfrac{1}{x^2} \ (x > 0)$

5. $\dfrac{dy}{dx} = 5^x \ln 5 + \dfrac{1}{x^2 + 1}$

6. $\dfrac{dy}{dx} = \dfrac{1}{\sqrt{1 - x^2}} - \dfrac{1}{\sqrt{x}}$

7. $\dfrac{dy}{dt} = 3t^2 \cos(t^3)$

8. $\dfrac{dy}{dt} = (\cos t) \, e^{\sin t}$

9. $\dfrac{du}{dx} = (\sec^2 x^5)(5x^4)$

10. $\dfrac{dy}{du} = 4 (\sin u)^3 (\cos u)$

In Exercises 11–20, solve the initial value problem explicitly.

11. $\dfrac{dy}{dx} = 3 \sin x$ and $y = 2$ when $x = 0$

12. $\dfrac{dy}{dx} = 2e^x - \cos x$ and $y = 3$ when $x = 0$

13. $\dfrac{du}{dx} = 7x^6 - 3x^2 + 5$ and $u = 1$ when $x = 1$

14. $\dfrac{dA}{dx} = 10x^9 + 5x^4 - 2x + 4$ and $A = 6$ when $x = 1$

15. $\dfrac{dy}{dx} = -\dfrac{1}{x^2} - \dfrac{3}{x^4} + 12$ and $y = 3$ when $x = 1$

16. $\dfrac{dy}{dx} = 5 \sec^2 x - \dfrac{3}{2}\sqrt{x}$ and $y = 7$ when $x = 0$

17. $\dfrac{dy}{dt} = \dfrac{1}{1 + t^2} + 2^t \ln 2$ and $y = 3$ when $t = 0$

18. $\dfrac{dx}{dt} = \dfrac{1}{t} - \dfrac{1}{t^2} + 6$ and $x = 0$ when $t = 1$

19. $\dfrac{dv}{dt} = 4 \sec t \tan t + e^t + 6t$ and $v = 5$ when $t = 0$

20. $\dfrac{ds}{dt} = t(3t - 2)$ and $s = 0$ when $t = 1$

In Exercises 21–24, solve the initial value problem using the Fundamental Theorem. (Your answer will contain a definite integral.)

21. $\dfrac{dy}{dx} = \sin (x^2)$ and $y = 5$ when $x = 1$

22. $\dfrac{du}{dx} = \sqrt{2 + \cos x}$ and $u = -3$ when $x = 0$

23. $F'(x) = e^{\cos x}$ and $F(2) = 9$

24. $G'(s) = \sqrt[3]{\tan s}$ and $G(0) = 4$

In Exercises 25–28, match the differential equation with the graph of a family of functions (a)–(d) at the top of the next page that solve it. Use slope analysis, not your graphing calculator.

25. $\dfrac{dy}{dx} = (\sin x)^2$

26. $\dfrac{dy}{dx} = (\sin x)^3$

27. $\dfrac{dy}{dx} = (\cos x)^2$

28. $\dfrac{dy}{dx} = (\cos x)^3$

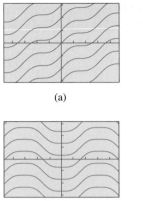

(a)

(b)

(c)

(d)

In Exercises 29–34, construct a slope field for the differential equation. In each case, copy the graph at the right and draw tiny segments through the twelve lattice points shown in the graph. Use slope analysis, not your graphing calculator.

29. $\dfrac{dy}{dx} = x$ **30.** $\dfrac{dy}{dx} = y$ **31.** $\dfrac{dy}{dx} = 2x + y$

32. $\dfrac{dy}{dx} = 2x - y$ **33.** $\dfrac{dy}{dx} = x + 2y$ **34.** $\dfrac{dy}{dx} = x - 2y$

In Exercises 35–40, match the differential equation with the appropriate slope field. Then use the slope field to sketch the graph of the particular solution through the highlighted point $(3, 2)$. (All slope fields are shown in the window $[-6, 6]$ by $[-4, 4]$.)

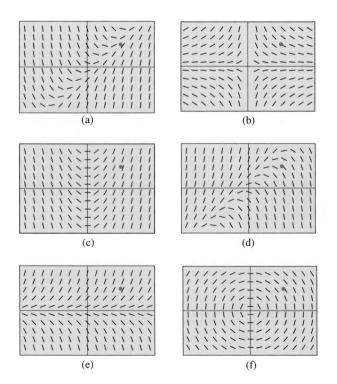

(a)

(b)

(c)

(d)

(e)

(f)

35. $\dfrac{dy}{dx} = x$ **36.** $\dfrac{dy}{dx} = y$

37. $\dfrac{dy}{dx} = x - y$ **38.** $\dfrac{dy}{dx} = y - x$

39. $\dfrac{dy}{dx} = -\dfrac{y}{x}$ **40.** $\dfrac{dy}{dx} = -\dfrac{x}{y}$

In Exercises 41–46, match the differential equation with the appropriate slope field. Then use the slope field to sketch the graph of the particular solution through the highlighted point $(0, 2)$. (All slope fields are shown in the window $[-6, 6]$ by $[-4, 4]$.)

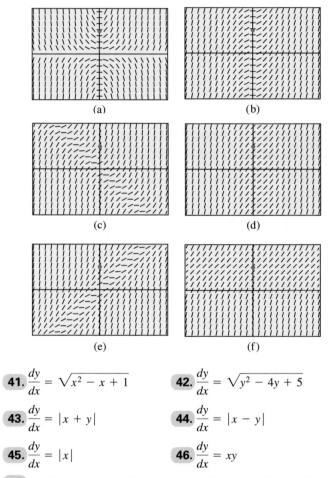

(a)

(b)

(c)

(d)

(e)

(f)

41. $\dfrac{dy}{dx} = \sqrt{x^2 - x + 1}$ **42.** $\dfrac{dy}{dx} = \sqrt{y^2 - 4y + 5}$

43. $\dfrac{dy}{dx} = |x + y|$ **44.** $\dfrac{dy}{dx} = |x - y|$

45. $\dfrac{dy}{dx} = |x|$ **46.** $\dfrac{dy}{dx} = xy$

47. (a) Sketch a graph of the solution to the initial value problem

$$\frac{dy}{dx} = \sec^2 x \text{ and } y = 1 \text{ when } x = \pi.$$

(b) Writing to Learn A student solved part (a) and used a graphing calculator to produce the following graph:

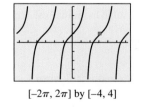

$[-2\pi, 2\pi]$ by $[-4, 4]$

How would you explain to this student why this graph is *not* the correct answer to part (a)?

48. (a) Sketch a graph of the solution to the initial value problem

$$\frac{dy}{dx} = -x^{-2} \text{ and } y = 1 \text{ when } x = 1.$$

(b) Writing to Learn A student solved part (a) and used a graphing calculator to produce the following graph:

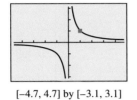

[−4.7, 4.7] by [−3.1, 3.1]

How would you explain to this student why this graph is *not* the correct answer to part (a)?

49. *Left Field Line* A single line from the slope field for $\dfrac{dy}{dx} = 2y + x$ is shown in the second quadrant of one of the following three graphs. Choose the only possible graph and draw a line for the same slope field through the reflected point in the first quadrant. All graphs are shown in the window $[-4.7, 4.7]$ by $[-3.1, 3.1]$.

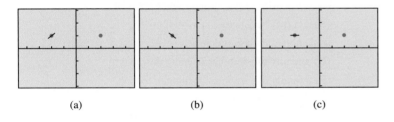

(a)   (b)   (c)

50. *Right Field Line* A single line from the slope field for $\dfrac{dy}{dx} = y^2 - x$ is shown in the first quadrant of one of the following three graphs. Choose the only possible graph and draw a line for the same slope field through the reflected point in the second quadrant. All graphs are shown in the window $[-4.7, 4.7]$ by $[-3.1, 3.1]$.

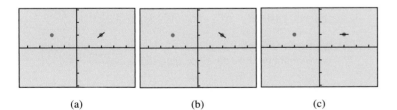

(a)   (b)   (c)

In Exercises 51–54, use Euler's Method with increments of $\Delta x = 0.1$ to approximate the value of y when $x = 1.3$.

51. $\dfrac{dy}{dx} = x - 1$ and $y = 2$ when $x = 1$

52. $\dfrac{dy}{dx} = y - 1$ and $y = 3$ when $x = 1$

53. $\dfrac{dy}{dx} = y - x$ and $y = 2$ when $x = 1$

54. $\dfrac{dy}{dx} = 2x - y$ and $y = 0$ when $x = 1$

In Exercises 55–58, use Euler's Method with increments of $\Delta x = -0.1$ to approximate the value of y when $x = 1.7$.

55. $\dfrac{dy}{dx} = 2 - x$ and $y = 1$ when $x = 2$

56. $\dfrac{dy}{dx} = 1 + y$ and $y = 0$ when $x = 2$

57. $\dfrac{dy}{dx} = x - y$ and $y = 2$ when $x = 2$

58. $\dfrac{dy}{dx} = x - 2y$ and $y = 1$ when $x = 2$

In Exercises 59 and 60, **(a)** determine which graph shows the solution of the initial value problem without actually solving the problem.

(b) Writing to Learn Explain how you eliminated two of the possibilities.

59. $\dfrac{dy}{dx} = \dfrac{1}{1 + x^2}, \quad y(0) = \dfrac{\pi}{2}$

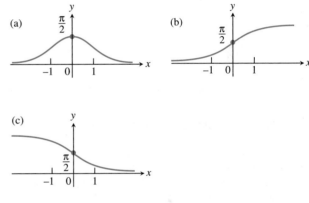

60. $\dfrac{dy}{dx} = -x, \quad y(-1) = 1$

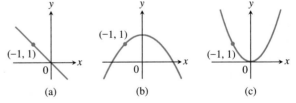

(a)   (b)   (c)

61. Writing to Learn Explain why $y = x^2$ could not be a solution to the differential equation with slope field shown below.

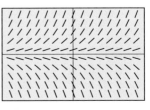

[−4.7, 4.7] by [−3.1, 3.1]

62. Writing to Learn Explain why $y = \sin x$ could not be a solution to the differential equation with slope field shown below.

[-4.7, 4.7] by [-3.1, 3.1]

63. Percentage Error Let $y = f(x)$ be the solution to the initial value problem $dy/dx = 2x + 1$ such that $f(1) = 3$. Find the percentage error if Euler's Method with $\Delta x = 0.1$ is used to approximate $f(1.4)$.

64. Percentage Error Let $y = f(x)$ be the solution to the initial value problem $dy/dx = 2x - 1$ such that $f(2) = 3$. Find the percentage error if Euler's Method with $\Delta x = -0.1$ is used to approximate $f(1.6)$.

65. Perpendicular Slope Fields The figure below shows the slope fields for the differential equations $dy/dx = e^{(x-y)/2}$ and $dy/dx = -e^{(y-x)/2}$ superimposed on the same grid. It appears that the slope lines are perpendicular wherever they intersect. Prove algebraically that this must be so.

66. Perpendicular Slope Fields If the slope fields for the differential equations $dy/dx = \sec x$ and $dy/dx = g(x)$ are perpendicular (as in Exercise 65), find $g(x)$.

67. Plowing Through a Slope Field The slope field for the differential equation $dy/dx = \csc x$ is shown below. Find a function that will be *perpendicular* to every line it crosses in the slope field. [*Hint:* First find a differential equation that will produce a perpendicular slope field.]

[-4.7, 4.7] by [-3.1, 3.1]

68. Plowing Through a Slope Field The slope field for the differential equation $dy/dx = 1/x$ is shown below. Find a function that will be *perpendicular* to every line it crosses in the slope field. [*Hint:* First find a differential equation that will produce a perpendicular slope field.]

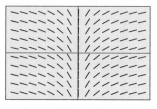

[-4.7, 4.7] by [-3.1, 3.1]

Standardized Test Questions

69. True or False Any two solutions to the differential equation $dy/dx = 5$ are parallel lines. Justify your answer.

70. True or False If $f(x)$ is a solution to $dy/dx = 2x$, then $f^{-1}(x)$ is a solution to $dy/dx = 2y$. Justify your answer.

71. Multiple Choice A slope field for the differential equation $dy/dx = 42 - y$ will show

(A) a line with slope -1 and y-intercept 42.

(B) a vertical asymptote at $x = 42$.

(C) a horizontal asymptote at $y = 42$.

(D) a family of parabolas opening downward.

(E) a family of parabolas opening to the left.

72. Multiple Choice For which of the following differential equations will a slope field show nothing but negative slopes in the fourth quadrant?

(A) $\dfrac{dy}{dx} = -\dfrac{x}{y}$ (B) $\dfrac{dy}{dx} = xy + 5$ (C) $\dfrac{dy}{dx} = xy^2 - 2$

(D) $\dfrac{dy}{dx} = \dfrac{x^3}{x^2}$ (E) $\dfrac{dy}{dx} = \dfrac{y}{x^2} - 3$

73. Multiple Choice If $dy/dx = 2xy$ and $y = 1$ when $x = 0$, then $y =$

(A) y^{2x} (B) e^{x^2} (C) x^2y (D) $x^2y + 1$ (E) $\dfrac{x^2y^2}{2} + 1$

74. Multiple Choice Which of the following differential equations would produce the slope field shown below?

(A) $\dfrac{dy}{dx} = y - |x|$ (B) $\dfrac{dy}{dx} = |y| - x$

(C) $\dfrac{dy}{dx} = |y - x|$ (D) $\dfrac{dy}{dx} = |y + x|$

(E) $\dfrac{dy}{dx} = |y| - |x|$

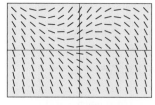

[-3, 3] by [-1.98, 1.98]

Explorations

75. Solving Differential Equations Let $\dfrac{dy}{dx} = x - \dfrac{1}{x^2}$.

(a) Find a solution to the differential equation in the interval $(0, \infty)$ that satisfies $y(1) = 2$.

(b) Find a solution to the differential equation in the interval $(-\infty, 0)$ that satisfies $y(-1) = 1$.

(c) Show that the following piecewise function is a solution to the differential equation for any values of C_1 and C_2.

$$y = \begin{cases} \dfrac{1}{x} + \dfrac{x^2}{2} + C_1 & x < 0 \\[2mm] \dfrac{1}{x} + \dfrac{x^2}{2} + C_2 & x > 0 \end{cases}$$

(d) Choose values for C_1 and C_2 so that the solution in part (c) agrees with the solutions in parts (a) and (b).

(e) Choose values for C_1 and C_2 so that the solution in part (c) satisfies $y(2) = -1$ and $y(-2) = 2$.

76. Solving Differential Equations Let $\dfrac{dy}{dx} = \dfrac{1}{x}$.

(a) Show that $y = \ln x + C$ is a solution to the differential equation in the interval $(0, \infty)$.

(b) Show that $y = \ln(-x) + C$ is a solution to the differential equation in the interval $(-\infty, 0)$.

(c) **Writing to Learn** Explain why $y = \ln |x| + C$ is a solution to the differential equation in the domain $(-\infty, 0) \cup (0, \infty)$.

(d) Show that the function

$$y = \begin{cases} \ln(-x) + C_1, & x < 0 \\ \ln x + C_2, & x > 0 \end{cases}$$

is a solution to the differential equation for any values of C_1 and C_2.

Extending the Ideas

77. Second-Order Differential Equations Find the general solution to each of the following second-order differential equations by first finding dy/dx and then finding y. The general solution will have two unknown constants.

(a) $\dfrac{d^2y}{dx^2} = 12x + 4$ (b) $\dfrac{d^2y}{dx^2} = e^x + \sin x$

(c) $\dfrac{d^2y}{dx^2} = x^3 + x^{-3}$

78. Second-Order Differential Equations Find the specific solution to each of the following second-order initial value problems by first finding dy/dx and then finding y.

(a) $\dfrac{d^2y}{dx^2} = 24x^2 - 10$. When $x = 1$, $\dfrac{dy}{dx} = 3$ and $y = 5$.

(b) $\dfrac{d^2y}{dx^2} = \cos x - \sin x$. When $x = 0$, $\dfrac{dy}{dx} = 2$ and $y = 0$.

(c) $\dfrac{d^2y}{dx^2} = e^x - x$. When $x = 0$, $\dfrac{dy}{dx} = 0$ and $y = 1$.

79. Differential Equation Potpourri For each of the following differential equations, find at least one particular solution. You will need to call on past experience with functions you have differentiated. For a greater challenge, find the general solution.

(a) $y' = x$ (b) $y' = -x$ (c) $y' = y$
(d) $y' = -y$ (e) $y' = xy$

80. Second-Order Potpourri For each of the following second-order differential equations, find at least one particular solution. You will need to call on past experience with functions you have differentiated. For a significantly greater challenge, find the general solution (which will involve two unknown constants).

(a) $y'' = x$ (b) $y'' = -x$ (c) $y'' = -\sin x$
(d) $y'' = y$ (e) $y'' = -y$

7.2 | Antidifferentiation by Substitution

You will be able to find antiderivatives of functions using the technique of substitution to reverse the effect of the chain rule in differentiation.

- Indefinite integrals
- Properties of indefinite integrals
- Antiderivative formulas arising from known derivatives
- Leibniz notation (differentials) in integrals
- Using substitution to evaluate indefinite integrals
- Using substitution to evaluate definite integrals

Indefinite Integrals

If $y = f(x)$ we can denote the derivative of f by either dy/dx or $f'(x)$. What can we use to denote the *antiderivative* of f? We have seen that the general solution to the differential equation $dy/dx = f(x)$ actually consists of an infinite family of functions of the form $F(x) + C$, where $F'(x) = f(x)$. Both the name for this family of functions and the symbol we use to denote it are closely related to the definite integral because of the Fundamental Theorem of Calculus.

DEFINITION Indefinite Integral

The family of all antiderivatives of a function $f(x)$ is the **indefinite integral of f with respect to x** and is denoted by $\int f(x)dx$.

If F is any function such that $F'(x) = f(x)$, then $\int f(x)dx = F(x) + C$, where C is an arbitrary constant, called the **constant of integration.**

As in Chapter 6, the symbol $\int$ is an **integral sign,** the function f is the **integrand** of the integral, and x is the **variable of integration.**

Notice that an indefinite integral is not at all like a definite integral, despite the similarities in notation and name. A definite integral is a *number*, the limit of a sequence of Riemann sums. An indefinite integral is a *family of functions* having a common derivative. If the Fundamental Theorem of Calculus had not provided such a dramatic link between antiderivatives and integration, we would surely be using a different name and symbol for the general antiderivative today.

EXAMPLE 1 Evaluating an Indefinite Integral

Evaluate $\int (x^2 - \sin x)\, dx$.

SOLUTION

Evaluating this indefinite integral is just like solving the differential equation $dy/dx = x^2 - \sin x$. Our past experience with derivatives leads us to conclude that

$$\int (x^2 - \sin x)\, dx = \frac{x^3}{3} + \cos x + C$$

(as you can check by differentiating). *Now Try Exercise 3.*

You have actually been finding antiderivatives since Section 6.3, so Example 1 should hardly have seemed new. Indeed, each derivative formula in Chapters 3 and 4 could be turned around to yield a corresponding indefinite integral formula. We list some of the most useful such indefinite integral formulas on the next page. Be sure to familiarize yourself with these before moving on to the next section, in which function composition becomes an issue. (Incidentally, it is in anticipation of the next section that we give some of these formulas in terms of the variable u rather than x.)

Properties of Indefinite Integrals

$$\int k\,f(x)\,dx = k\int f(x)\,dx \quad \text{for any constant } k$$

$$\int (f(x) \pm g(x))\,dx = \int f(x)\,dx \pm \int g(x)\,dx$$

Power Formulas

$$\int u^n\,du = \frac{u^{n+1}}{n+1} + C \text{ when } n \neq -1 \qquad \int u^{-1}\,du = \int \frac{1}{u}\,du = \ln|u| + C$$

(see Example 2)

Trigonometric Formulas

$$\int \cos u\,du = \sin u + C \qquad\qquad \int \sin u\,du = -\cos u + C$$

$$\int \sec^2 u\,du = \tan u + C \qquad\qquad \int \csc^2 u\,du = -\cot u + C$$

$$\int \sec u \tan u\,du = \sec u + C \qquad\qquad \int \csc u \cot u\,du = -\csc u + C$$

Exponential and Logarithmic Formulas

$$\int e^u\,du = e^u + C \qquad\qquad \int a^u\,du = \frac{a^u}{\ln a} + C$$

$$\int \ln u\,du = u \ln u - u + C \quad \text{(See Example 2)}$$

$$\int \log_a u\,du = \int \frac{\ln u}{\ln a}\,du = \frac{u \ln u - u}{\ln a} + C$$

A Note on Absolute Value

Since the indefinite integral does not specify a domain, you should always use the absolute value when finding $\int 1/u\,du$. The function $\ln u + C$ is defined only on positive u-intervals, while the function $\ln|u| + C$ is defined on both the positive *and* negative intervals in the domain of $1/u$ (see Example 2).

EXAMPLE 2 Verifying Antiderivative Formulas

Verify the antiderivative formulas:

(a) $\displaystyle\int u^{-1}\,du = \int \frac{1}{u}\,du = \ln|u| + C$ **(b)** $\displaystyle\int \ln u\,du = u \ln u - u + C$

SOLUTION

We can verify antiderivative formulas by differentiating.

(a) For $u > 0$, we have $\dfrac{d}{du}(\ln|u| + C) = \dfrac{d}{du}(\ln u + C) = \dfrac{1}{u} + 0 = \dfrac{1}{u}$.

For $u < 0$, we have $\dfrac{d}{du}(\ln|u| + C) = \dfrac{d}{du}(\ln(-u) + C) = \dfrac{1}{-u}(-1) + 0 = \dfrac{1}{u}$.

Since $\dfrac{d}{du}(\ln|u| + C) = \dfrac{1}{u}$ in either case, $\ln|u| + C$ is the general antiderivative of the function $\dfrac{1}{u}$ on its entire domain.

(b) $\dfrac{d}{du}(u \ln u - u + C) = 1 \cdot \ln u + u\left(\dfrac{1}{u}\right) - 1 + 0 = \ln u + 1 - 1 = \ln u$.

Now Try Exercise 11.

Leibniz Notation and Antiderivatives

The appearance of the differential "*dx*" in the definite integral $\int_a^b f(x)\,dx$ is easily explained by the fact that it is the limit of a Riemann sum of the form $\sum_{k=1}^{n} f(x_k) \cdot \Delta x$ (see Section 6.2). The same "*dx*" almost seems unnecessary when we use the indefinite integral $\int f(x)\,dx$ to represent the general antiderivative of f, but in fact it is quite useful for *dealing with the effects of the Chain Rule* when function composition is involved. Exploration 1 will show you why this is an important consideration.

EXPLORATION 1 Are $\int f(u)\,du$ and $\int f(u)\,dx$ the Same Thing?

Let $u = x^2$ and let $f(u) = u^3$.

1. Find $\int f(u)\,du$ as a function of u.
2. Use your answer to question 1 to write $\int f(u)\,du$ as a function of x.
3. Show that $f(u) = x^6$ and find $\int f(u)\,dx$ as a function of x.
4. Are the answers to questions 2 and 3 the same?

Exploration 1 shows that the notation $\int f(u)$ is not sufficient to describe an antiderivative when u is a function of another variable. Just as du/du is different from du/dx when differentiating, $\int f(u)\,du$ is different from $\int f(u)\,dx$ when antidifferentiating. We will use this fact to our advantage in the next section, where the importance of "*dx*" or "*du*" in the integral expression will become even more apparent.

EXAMPLE 3 Paying Attention to the Differential

Let $f(x) = x^3 + 1$ and let $u = x^2$. Find each of the following antiderivatives in terms of x:

(a) $\displaystyle\int f(x)\,dx$ (b) $\displaystyle\int f(u)\,du$ (c) $\displaystyle\int f(u)\,dx$

SOLUTION

(a) $\displaystyle\int f(x)\,dx = \int (x^3 + 1)\,dx = \frac{x^4}{4} + x + C$

(b) $\displaystyle\int f(u)\,du = \int (u^3 + 1)\,du = \frac{u^4}{4} + u + C = \frac{(x^2)^4}{4} + x^2 + C = \frac{x^8}{4} + x^2 + C$

(c) $\displaystyle\int f(u)\,dx = \int (u^3 + 1)\,dx = \int ((x^2)^3 + 1)\,dx = \int (x^6 + 1)\,dx = \frac{x^7}{7} + x + C$

Now Try Exercise 15.

Substitution in Indefinite Integrals

A change of variables can often turn an unfamiliar integral into one that we can evaluate. The important point to remember is that it is *not sufficient* to change an integral of the form $\int f(x)\,dx$ into an integral of the form $\int g(u)\,dx$. The differential matters. A complete substitution changes the integral $\int f(x)\,dx$ into an integral of the form $\int g(u)\,du$.

EXAMPLE 4 Using Substitution

Evaluate $\int \sin x\, e^{\cos x}\,dx$.

continued

SOLUTION

Let $u = \cos x$. Then $du/dx = -\sin x$, from which we conclude that $du = -\sin x\, dx$. We rewrite the integral and proceed as follows:

$$\int \sin x\, e^{\cos x}\, dx = -\int (-\sin x) e^{\cos x}\, dx$$

$$= -\int e^{\cos x} \cdot (-\sin x)\, dx$$

$$= -\int e^u\, du \qquad \text{Substitute } u \text{ for } \cos x \text{ and } du \text{ for } -\sin x\, dx.$$

$$= -e^u + C$$

$$= -e^{\cos x} + C \qquad \text{Resubstitute } \cos x \text{ for } u \text{ after antidifferentiating.}$$

Now Try Exercise 19.

If you differentiate $-e^{\cos x} + C$, you will find that a factor of $-\sin x$ appears when you apply the Chain Rule. The technique of *antidifferentiation by substitution* reverses that effect by absorbing the $-\sin x$ into the differential du when you change $\int \sin x\, e^{\cos x}\, dx$ into $-\int e^u\, du$. That is why a "*u*-substitution" always involves a "*du*-substitution" to convert the integral into a form ready for antidifferentiation.

EXAMPLE 5 Using Substitution

Evaluate $\int x^2 \sqrt{5 + 2x^3}\, dx$.

SOLUTION

This integral invites the substitution $u = 5 + 2x^3$, $du = 6x^2\, dx$.

$$\int x^2 \sqrt{5 + 2x^3}\, dx = \int (5 + 2x^3)^{1/2} \cdot x^2\, dx$$

$$= \frac{1}{6} \int (5 + 2x^3)^{1/2} \cdot 6x^2\, dx \quad \text{Set up the substitution with a factor of 6.}$$

$$= \frac{1}{6} \int u^{1/2}\, du \qquad \text{Substitute } u \text{ for } 5 + 2x^3 \text{ and } du \text{ for } 6x^2\, dx.$$

$$= \frac{1}{6}\left(\frac{2}{3}\right) u^{3/2} + C$$

$$= \frac{1}{9}(5 + 2x^3)^{3/2} + C \qquad \text{Resubstitute after antidifferentiating.}$$

Now Try Exercise 27.

EXAMPLE 6 Using Substitution

Evaluate $\int \cot 7x\, dx$.

SOLUTION

We do not recall a function whose derivative is $\cot 7x$, but a basic trigonometric identity changes the integrand into a form that invites the substitution $u = \sin 7x$, $du = 7 \cos 7x\, dx$. We rewrite the integrand as shown below.

$$\int \cot 7x\, dx = \int \frac{\cos 7x}{\sin 7x}\, dx \qquad \text{Trigonometric identity}$$

$$= \frac{1}{7} \int \frac{7 \cos 7x\, dx}{\sin 7x} \qquad \text{Note that } du = 7 \cos 7x\, dx \text{ when } u = \sin 7x.$$
$$\text{We multiply by } \frac{1}{7} \cdot 7, \text{ or 1.}$$

continued

$$= \frac{1}{7} \int \frac{du}{u} \qquad \text{Substitute } u \text{ for sin } 7x \text{ and } du \text{ for 7 cos } 7x \, dx.$$

$$= \frac{1}{7} \ln |u| + C \qquad \text{Notice the absolute value!}$$

$$= \frac{1}{7} \ln |\sin 7x| + C \qquad \text{Resubstitute sin } 7x \text{ for } u \text{ after antidifferentiating.}$$

Now Try Exercise 29.

EXAMPLE 7 Setting Up a Substitution with a Trigonometric Identity

Find the indefinite integrals. In each case you can use a trigonometric identity to set up a substitution.

(a) $\displaystyle\int \frac{dx}{\cos^2 2x}$ **(b)** $\displaystyle\int \cot^2 3x \, dx$ **(c)** $\displaystyle\int \cos^3 x \, dx$

SOLUTION

(a) $\displaystyle\int \frac{dx}{\cos^2 2x} = \int \sec^2 2x \, dx = \frac{1}{2} \int \sec^2 2x \cdot 2 \, dx$

$$= \frac{1}{2} \int \sec^2 u \, du \qquad \text{Let } u = 2x \text{ and } du = 2dx.$$

$$= \frac{1}{2} \tan u + C$$

$$= \frac{1}{2} \tan 2x + C \qquad \text{Resubstitute after antidifferentiating.}$$

(b) $\displaystyle\int \cot^2 3x \, dx = \int (\csc^2 3x - 1) \, dx$

$$= \frac{1}{3} \int (\csc^2 3x - 1) \cdot 3 \, dx$$

$$= \frac{1}{3} \int (\csc^2 u - 1) \cdot du \qquad \text{Let } u = 3x \text{ and } du = 3dx.$$

$$= \frac{1}{3} (-\cot u - u) + C$$

$$= \frac{1}{3} (-\cot 3x - 3x) + C \qquad \text{Resubstitute after antidifferentiation.}$$

$$= -\frac{1}{3} \cot 3x - x + C$$

(c) $\displaystyle\int \cos^3 x \, dx = \int (\cos^2 x) \cos x \, dx$

$$= \int (1 - \sin^2 x) \cos x \, dx$$

$$= \int (1 - u^2) \, du \qquad \text{Let } u = \sin x \text{ and } du = \cos x \, dx.$$

$$= u - \frac{u^3}{3} + C$$

$$= \sin x - \frac{\sin^3 x}{3} + C \qquad \text{Resubstitute after antidifferentiating.}$$

Now Try Exercise 47.

Substitution in Definite Integrals

Antiderivatives play an important role when we evaluate a definite integral by the Fundamental Theorem of Calculus, and so, consequently, does substitution. In fact, if we make full use of our substitution of variables and change the interval of integration to match the *u*-substitution in the integrand, we can avoid the "resubstitution" step in the previous four examples.

EXAMPLE 8 Evaluating a Definite Integral by Substitution

Evaluate $\displaystyle\int_0^{\pi/3} \tan x \sec^2 x \, dx$.

SOLUTION

Let $u = \tan x$ and $du = \sec^2 x \, dx$.

Note also that $u(0) = \tan 0 = 0$ and $u(\pi/3) = \tan(\pi/3) = \sqrt{3}$.

So

$$\int_0^{\pi/3} \tan x \sec^2 x \, dx = \int_0^{\sqrt{3}} u \, du \quad \text{Substitute } u\text{-interval for } x\text{-interval.}$$

$$= \frac{u^2}{2}\Big|_0^{\sqrt{3}} = \frac{3}{2} - 0 = \frac{3}{2}$$

Now Try Exercise 55.

EXAMPLE 9 That Absolute Value Again

Evaluate $\displaystyle\int_0^1 \frac{x}{x^2 - 4} \, dx$.

SOLUTION

Let $u = x^2 - 4$ and $du = 2x \, dx$. Then $u(0) = 0^2 - 4 = -4$ and $u(1) = 1^2 - 4 = -3$.

So

$$\int_0^1 \frac{x}{x^2 - 4} \, dx = \frac{1}{2} \int_0^1 \frac{2x \, dx}{x^2 - 4}$$

$$= \frac{1}{2} \int_{-4}^{-3} \frac{du}{u} \quad \text{Substitute } u\text{-interval for } x\text{-interval.}$$

$$= \frac{1}{2} \ln |u| \,\Big|_{-4}^{-3}$$

$$= \frac{1}{2}(\ln 3 - \ln 4) = \frac{1}{2} \ln \left(\frac{3}{4}\right)$$

Notice that $\ln u$ would not have existed over the interval of integration $[-4, -3]$. The absolute value in the antiderivative is important.   *Now Try Exercise 63.*

Finally, consider this historical note. The technique of *u*-substitution derived its importance from the fact that it was a powerful tool for antidifferentiation. Antidifferentiation derived its importance from the Fundamental Theorem, which established it as the way to evaluate definite integrals. Definite integrals derived their importance from real-world applications. While the applications are no less important today, the fact that the definite integrals can be easily evaluated by technology has made the world less reliant on antidifferentiation, and hence less reliant on *u*-substitution. Consequently, you have seen in this book only a sampling of the substitution tricks calculus students would have routinely studied in the past. You may see more of them in a differential equations course.

Quick Review 7.2   *(For help, go to Sections 4.1 and 4.4.)*

Exercise numbers with a gray background indicate problems that the authors have designed to be solved *without a calculator*.

In Exercises 1 and 2, evaluate the definite integral.

1. $\displaystyle\int_0^2 x^4 \, dx$ **2.** $\displaystyle\int_1^5 \sqrt{x-1} \, dx$

In Exercises 3–10, find dy/dx.

3. $y = \displaystyle\int_2^x 3^t \, dt$ **4.** $y = \displaystyle\int_0^x 3^t \, dt$

5. $y = (x^3 - 2x^2 + 3)^4$

6. $y = \sin^2 (4x - 5)$

7. $y = \ln \cos x$

8. $y = \ln \sin x$

9. $y = \ln (\sec x + \tan x)$

10. $y = \ln (\csc x + \cot x)$

Section 7.2 Exercises

In Exercises 1–6, find the indefinite integral.

1. $\displaystyle\int (\cos x - 3x^2) \, dx$ **2.** $\displaystyle\int x^{-2} \, dx$

3. $\displaystyle\int \left(t^2 - \frac{1}{t^2}\right) dt$ **4.** $\displaystyle\int \frac{dt}{t^2 + 1}$

5. $\displaystyle\int (3x^4 - 2x^{-3} + \sec^2 x) \, dx$

6. $\displaystyle\int \left(2e^x + \sec x \tan x - \sqrt{x}\right) dx$

In Exercises 7–12, use differentiation to verify the antiderivative formula.

7. $\displaystyle\int \csc^2 u \, du = -\cot u + C$ **8.** $\displaystyle\int \csc u \cot u = -\csc u + C$

9. $\displaystyle\int e^{2x} \, dx = \frac{1}{2} e^{2x} + C$ **10.** $\displaystyle\int 5^x \, dx = \frac{1}{\ln 5} 5^x + C$

11. $\displaystyle\int \frac{1}{1 + u^2} \, du = \tan^{-1} u + C$ **12.** $\displaystyle\int \frac{1}{\sqrt{1 - u^2}} \, du = \sin^{-1} u + C$

In Exercises 13–16, verify that $\int f(u) \, du \neq \int f(u) \, dx$.

13. $f(u) = \sqrt{u}$ and $u = x^2 \, (x > 0)$

14. $f(u) = u^2$ and $u = x^5$

15. $f(u) = e^u$ and $u = 7x$ **16.** $f(u) = \sin u$ and $u = 4x$

In Exercises 17–24, use the indicated substitution to evaluate the integral. Confirm your answer by differentiation.

17. $\displaystyle\int \sin 3x \, dx, \quad u = 3x$

18. $\displaystyle\int x \cos (2x^2) \, dx, \quad u = 2x^2$

19. $\displaystyle\int \sec 2x \tan 2x \, dx, \quad u = 2x$

20. $\displaystyle\int 28(7x - 2)^3 \, dx, \quad u = 7x - 2$

21. $\displaystyle\int \frac{dx}{x^2 + 9}, \quad u = \frac{x}{3}$ **22.** $\displaystyle\int \frac{9r^2 \, dr}{\sqrt{1 - r^3}}, \quad u = 1 - r^3$

23. $\displaystyle\int \left(1 - \cos \frac{t}{2}\right)^2 \sin \frac{t}{2} \, dt, \quad u = 1 - \cos \frac{t}{2}$

24. $\displaystyle\int 8(y^4 + 4y^2 + 1)^2(y^3 + 2y) \, dy, \quad u = y^4 + 4y^2 + 1$

In Exercises 25–46, use substitution to evaluate the integral.

25. $\displaystyle\int \frac{dx}{(1 - x)^2}$ **26.** $\displaystyle\int \sec^2 (x + 2) \, dx$

27. $\displaystyle\int \sqrt{\tan x} \sec^2 x \, dx$

28. $\displaystyle\int \sec \left(\theta + \frac{\pi}{2}\right) \tan \left(\theta + \frac{\pi}{2}\right) d\theta$

29. $\displaystyle\int \tan(4x + 2) \, dx$ **30.** $\displaystyle\int 3(\sin x)^{-2} \, dx$

31. $\displaystyle\int \cos (3z + 4) \, dz$ **32.** $\displaystyle\int \sqrt{\cot x} \csc^2 x \, dx$

33. $\displaystyle\int \frac{\ln^6 x}{x} \, dx$ **34.** $\displaystyle\int \tan^7 \left(\frac{x}{2}\right) \sec^2 \left(\frac{x}{2}\right) dx$

35. $\displaystyle\int s^{1/3} \cos (s^{4/3} - 8) \, ds$ **36.** $\displaystyle\int \frac{dx}{\sin^2 3x}$

37. $\displaystyle\int \frac{\sin (2t + 1)}{\cos^2 (2t + 1)} \, dt$ **38.** $\displaystyle\int \frac{6 \cos t}{(2 + \sin t)^2} \, dt$

39. $\displaystyle\int \frac{dx}{x \ln x}$ **40.** $\displaystyle\int \tan^2 x \sec^2 x \, dx$

41. $\int \dfrac{x\,dx}{x^2+1}$

42. $\int \dfrac{40\,dx}{x^2+25}$

43. $\int \dfrac{dx}{\cot 3x}$

44. $\int \dfrac{dx}{\sqrt{5x+8}}$

45. $\int \sec x\,dx$ (*Hint:* Multiply the integrand by

$$\frac{\sec x+\tan x}{\sec x+\tan x}$$

and then use a substitution to integrate the result.)

46. $\int \csc x\,dx$ (*Hint:* Multiply the integrand by

$$\frac{\csc x+\cot x}{\csc x+\cot x}$$

and then use a substitution to integrate the result.)

In Exercises 47–52, use the given trigonometric identity to set up a *u*-substitution and then evaluate the indefinite integral.

47. $\int \sin^3 2x\,dx, \quad \sin^2 2x = 1 - \cos^2 2x$

48. $\int \sec^4 x\,dx, \quad \sec^2 x = 1 + \tan^2 x$

49. $\int 2\sin^2 x\,dx, \quad \cos 2x = 1 - 2\sin^2 x$

50. $\int 4\cos^2 x\,dx, \quad \cos 2x = 2\cos^2 x - 1$

51. $\int \tan^4 x\,dx, \quad \tan^2 x = \sec^2 x - 1$

52. $\int (\cos^4 x - \sin^4 x)\,dx, \quad \cos 2x = \cos^2 x - \sin^2 x$

In Exercises 53–66, make a *u*-substitution and integrate from $u(a)$ to $u(b)$.

53. $\displaystyle\int_0^3 \sqrt{y+1}\,dy$

54. $\displaystyle\int_0^1 r\sqrt{1-r^2}\,dr$

55. $\displaystyle\int_{-\pi/4}^0 \tan x\sec^2 x\,dx$

56. $\displaystyle\int_{-1}^1 \dfrac{5r}{(4+r^2)^2}\,dr$

57. $\displaystyle\int_0^1 \dfrac{10\sqrt{\theta}}{(1+\theta^{3/2})^2}\,d\theta$

58. $\displaystyle\int_{-\pi}^{\pi} \dfrac{\cos x}{\sqrt{4+3\sin x}}\,dx$

59. $\displaystyle\int_0^1 \sqrt{t^5+2t}\,(5t^4+2)\,dt$

60. $\displaystyle\int_0^{\pi/6} \cos^{-3} 2\theta \sin 2\theta\,d\theta$

61. $\displaystyle\int_0^7 \dfrac{dx}{x+2}$

62. $\displaystyle\int_2^5 \dfrac{dx}{2x-3}$

63. $\displaystyle\int_1^2 \dfrac{dt}{t-3}$

64. $\displaystyle\int_{\pi/4}^{3\pi/4} \cot x\,dx$

65. $\displaystyle\int_{-1}^3 \dfrac{x\,dx}{x^2+1}$

66. $\displaystyle\int_0^2 \dfrac{e^x\,dx}{3+e^x}$

Two Routes to the Integral In Exercises 67 and 68, make a substitution $u = \cdots$ (an expression in x), $du = \cdots$. Then

  (a) integrate with respect to u from $u(a)$ to $u(b)$.

  (b) find an antiderivative with respect to u, replace u by the expression in x, then evaluate from a to b.

67. $\displaystyle\int_0^1 \dfrac{x^3}{\sqrt{x^4+9}}\,dx$

68. $\displaystyle\int_{\pi/6}^{\pi/3} (1-\cos 3x)\sin 3x\,dx$

69. Show that

$$y = \ln\left|\frac{\cos 3}{\cos x}\right| + 5$$

is the solution to the initial value problem

$$\frac{dy}{dx} = \tan x, \quad f(3) = 5.$$

(See the discussion following Example 4, Section 6.4.)

70. Show that

$$y = \ln\left|\frac{\sin x}{\sin 2}\right| + 6$$

is the solution to the initial value problem

$$\frac{dy}{dx} = \cot x, \quad f(2) = 6.$$

Standardized Test Questions

71. **True or False** By *u*-substitution, $\int_0^{\pi/4}\tan^3 x\sec^2 x\,dx = \int_0^{\pi/4} u^3\,du$. Justify your answer.

72. **True or False** If f is positive and differentiable on $[a,b]$, then

$$\int_a^b \frac{f'(x)\,dx}{f(x)} = \ln\left(\frac{f(b)}{f(a)}\right).$$ Justify your answer.

73. **Multiple Choice** $\int \tan x\,dx =$

  (A) $\dfrac{\tan^2 x}{2} + C$ **(B)** $\ln|\cot x| + C$ **(C)** $\ln|\cos x| + C$

  (D) $-\ln|\cos x| + C$ **(E)** $-\ln|\cot x| + C$

74. **Multiple Choice** $\int_0^2 e^{2x}\,dx =$

  (A) $\dfrac{e^4}{2}$ **(B)** $e^4 - 1$ **(C)** $e^4 - 2$ **(D)** $2e^4 - 2$ **(E)** $\dfrac{e^4-1}{2}$

75. **Multiple Choice** If $\int_3^5 f(x-a)\,dx = 7$ where a is a constant, then $\int_{3-a}^{5-a} f(x)\,dx =$

  (A) $7+a$ **(B)** 7 **(C)** $7-a$ **(D)** $a-7$ **(E)** -7

76. **Multiple Choice** If the differential equation $dy/dx = f(x)$ leads to the slope field shown below, which of the following could be $\int f(x)\,dx$?

  (A) $\sin x + C$ **(B)** $\cos x + C$ **(C)** $-\sin x + C$

  (D) $-\cos x + C$ **(E)** $\dfrac{\sin^2 x}{2} + C$

Explorations

77. Constant of Integration Consider the integral

$$\int \sqrt{x + 1}\, dx.$$

(a) Show that $\int \sqrt{x + 1}\, dx = \frac{2}{3}(x + 1)^{3/2} + C.$

(b) Writing to Learn Explain why

$$y_1 = \int_0^x \sqrt{t + 1}\, dt \quad \text{and} \quad y_2 = \int_3^x \sqrt{t + 1}\, dt$$

are antiderivatives of $\sqrt{x + 1}$.

(c) Use a table of values for $y_1 - y_2$ to find the value of C for which $y_1 = y_2 + C$.

(d) Writing to Learn Give a convincing argument that

$$C = \int_0^3 \sqrt{x + 1}\, dx.$$

78. Group Activity Making Connections Suppose that

$$\int f(x)\, dx = F(x) + C.$$

(a) Explain how you can use the derivative of $F(x) + C$ to confirm the integration is correct.

(b) Explain how you can use a slope field for $dy/dx = f(x)$ and the graph of $y = F(x)$ to support your evaluation of the integral.

(c) Explain how you can use the graphs of $y_1 = F(x)$ and $y_2 = \int_0^x f(t)\, dt$ to support your evaluation of the integral.

(d) Explain how you can use a table of values for $y_1 - y_2$, y_1 and y_2 defined as in part (c), to support your evaluation of the integral.

(e) Explain how you can use graphs of f and NDER of $F(x)$ to support your evaluation of the integral.

(f) Illustrate parts (a)–(e) for $f(x) = \dfrac{x}{\sqrt{x^2 + 1}}.$

79. Different Solutions? Consider the integral $\int 2 \sin x \cos x\, dx.$

(a) Evaluate the integral using the substitution $u = \sin x$.

(b) Evaluate the integral using the substitution $u = \cos x$.

(c) Writing to Learn Explain why the different-looking answers in parts (a) and (b) are actually equivalent.

80. Different Solutions? Consider the integral $\int 2 \sec^2 x \tan x\, dx.$

(a) Evaluate the integral using the substitution $u = \tan x$.

(b) Evaluate the integral using the substitution $u = \sec x$.

(c) Writing to Learn Explain why the different-looking answers in parts (a) and (b) are actually equivalent.

Extending the Ideas

81. Trigonometric Substitution Suppose $u = \sin^{-1} x$. Then $\cos u > 0$.

(a) Use the substitution $x = \sin u, dx = \cos u\, du$ to show that

$$\int \frac{dx}{\sqrt{1 - x^2}} = \int 1\, du.$$

(b) Evaluate $\int 1\, du$ to show that $\int \dfrac{dx}{\sqrt{1 - x^2}} = \sin^{-1} x + C.$

82. Trigonometric Substitution Suppose $u = \tan^{-1} x$.

(a) Use the substitution $x = \tan u, dx = \sec^2 u\, du$ to show that

$$\int \frac{dx}{1 + x^2} = \int 1\, du.$$

(b) Evaluate $\int 1\, du$ to show that $\int \dfrac{dx}{1 + x^2} = \tan^{-1} x + C.$

83. Trigonometric Substitution Suppose $\sqrt{x} = \sin y$.

(a) Use the substitution $x = \sin^2 y, dx = 2 \sin y \cos y\, dy$ to show that

$$\int_0^{1/2} \frac{\sqrt{x}\, dx}{\sqrt{1 - x}} = \int_0^{\pi/4} 2 \sin^2 y\, dy.$$

(b) Use the identity given in Exercise 49 to evaluate the definite integral without a calculator.

84. Trigonometric Substitution Suppose $u = \tan^{-1} x$.

(a) Use the substitution $x = \tan u, dx = \sec^2 u\, du$ to show that

$$\int_0^{\sqrt{3}} \frac{dx}{\sqrt{1 + x^2}} = \int_0^{\pi/3} \sec u\, du.$$

(b) Use the hint in Exercise 45 to evaluate the definite integral without a calculator.

7.3 Antidifferentiation by Parts

Product Rule in Integral Form

When u and v are differentiable functions of x, the Product Rule for differentiation tells us that

$$\frac{d}{dx}(uv) = u\frac{dv}{dx} + v\frac{du}{dx}.$$

Integrating both sides with respect to x and rearranging leads to the integral equation

$$\int \left(u\frac{dv}{dx}\right)dx = \int \left(\frac{d}{dx}(uv)\right)dx - \int \left(v\frac{du}{dx}\right)dx$$

$$= uv - \int \left(v\frac{du}{dx}\right)dx$$

When this equation is written in the simpler differential notation we obtain the following formula.

Integration by Parts Formula

$$\int u\,dv = uv - \int v\,du$$

LIPET

Some teachers recommend the acronym LIPET for choosing u when integrating by parts. Look first for a natural logarithm (L). If there is none, look for an inverse trigonometric function (I). If there is not one of those either, look for a polynomial (P). If none of those pan out, look for an exponential (E) or trigonometric (T) function. In general, you want u to be something that simplifies when differentiated, while you want dv to be something that remains manageable when antidifferentiated.

This formula expresses one integral, $\int u\,dv$, in terms of a second integral, $\int v\,du$. With a proper choice of u and v, the second integral may be easier to evaluate than the first. This is the reason for the importance of the formula. When faced with an integral that we cannot handle analytically, we can replace it by one with which we might have more success.

EXAMPLE 1 Using Integration by Parts

Evaluate $\int x\cos x\,dx$.

SOLUTION

We use the formula $\int u\,dv = uv - \int v\,du$ with

$$u = x, \quad dv = \cos x\,dx.$$

To complete the formula, we take the differential of u and find the simplest antiderivative of $\cos x$.

$$du = dx \quad v = \sin x$$

Then,

$$\int \overset{u}{x}\,\overset{dv}{\cos x\,dx} = \overset{u}{x}\overset{v}{\sin x} - \int \overset{v}{\sin x}\,\overset{du}{dx} = x\sin x + \cos x + C.$$

Now Try Exercise 1.

The goal of integration by parts is to go from an integral $\int u\,dv$ that we don't see how to evaluate to an integral $\int v\,du$ that we can evaluate. Keep in mind that integration by parts does not always work.

Let's examine the choices available for u and dv in Example 1.

EXPLORATION 1 Choosing the Right *u* and *dv*

Not every choice of *u* and *dv* leads to success in antidifferentiation by parts. There is always a trade-off when we replace $\int u\, dv$ with $\int v\, du$, and we gain nothing if $\int v\, du$ is no easier to find than the integral we started with. Let us look at the other choices we might have made in Example 1 to find $\int x \cos x\, dx$.

1. Apply the parts formula to $\int x \cos x\, dx$, letting $u = 1$ and $dv = x \cos x\, dx$. Analyze the result to explain why the choice of $u = 1$ is never a good one.
2. Apply the parts formula to $\int x \cos x\, dx$, letting $u = x \cos x$ and $dv = dx$. Analyze the result to explain why this is not a good choice for this integral.
3. Apply the parts formula to $\int x \cos x\, dx$, letting $u = \cos x$ and $dv = x\, dx$. Analyze the result to explain why this is not a good choice for this integral.
4. What makes *x* a good choice for *u* and $\cos x\, dx$ a good choice for *dv*?

Sometimes we have to use integration by parts more than once to evaluate an integral.

EXAMPLE 2 Repeated Use of Integration by Parts

Evaluate $\int x^2 e^x\, dx$.

SOLUTION

With $u = x^2$, $dv = e^x\, dx$, $du = 2x\, dx$, and $v = e^x$, we have

$$\int \overset{u}{\overbrace{x^2}}\ \overset{dv}{\overbrace{e^x\, dx}} = \overset{u}{x^2}\ \overset{v}{e^x} - \int \overset{v}{e^x}\ \overset{du}{\overbrace{2x\, dx}}$$

$$= x^2 e^x - 2 \int x e^x\, dx$$

The new integral is less complicated than the original because the exponent of *x* is reduced by one. To evaluate the integral on the right, we integrate by parts again, with $u = x$, $dv = e^x\, dx$. Then $du = dx$, $v = e^x$, and

$$\int \overset{u}{x}\ \overset{dv}{\overbrace{e^x\, dx}} = \overset{u}{x}\ \overset{v}{e^x} - \int \overset{v\ du}{e^x\, dx} = x e^x - e^x + C.$$

Hence,

$$\int x^2 e^x\, dx = x^2 e^x - 2 \int x e^x\, dx$$

$$= x^2 e^x - 2x e^x + 2e^x + C$$

The technique of Example 2 can be applied repeatedly for any integral of the form $\int x^n e^x\, dx$ in which *n* is a positive integer, because differentiating x^n will eventually reduce the exponent to zero and lead to a final integral involving only e^x. Repeated integration by parts can be done most easily by the method of *tabular integration,* covered later in this section.

Now Try Exercise 5.

EXAMPLE 3 Solving an Initial Value Problem

Solve the differential equation $dy/dx = x \ln (x)$ subject to the initial condition $y = -1$ when $x = 1$. Confirm the solution graphically by showing that it conforms to the slope field.

continued

SOLUTION

We find the antiderivative of $x \ln (x)$ by using parts. It is usually a better idea to differentiate $\ln (x)$ than to antidifferentiate it. (Do you see why?) So we let $u = \ln (x)$ and $dv = x \, dx$.

$$y = \int x \ln (x) \, dx = \int \overset{u}{\ln (x)} \overset{dv}{x \, dx}$$

$$= \overset{u}{\ln (x)} \overset{v}{\left(\frac{x^2}{2}\right)} - \int \overset{v}{\left(\frac{x^2}{2}\right)} \overset{du}{\left(\frac{1}{x}\right)} \, dx$$

$$= \left(\frac{x^2}{2}\right) \ln (x) - \int \left(\frac{x}{2}\right) \, dx$$

$$= \left(\frac{x^2}{2}\right) \ln (x) - \frac{x^2}{4} + C$$

Using the initial condition,

$$-1 = \left(\frac{1}{2}\right) \ln (1) - \frac{1}{4} + C$$

$$-\frac{3}{4} = 0 + C$$

$$C = -\frac{3}{4}$$

Thus

$$y = \left(\frac{x^2}{2}\right) \ln (x) - \frac{x^2}{4} - \frac{3}{4}.$$

Figure 7.10 shows a graph of this function superimposed on a slope field for $dy/dx = x \ln(x)$, to which it conforms nicely.

Now Try Exercise 11.

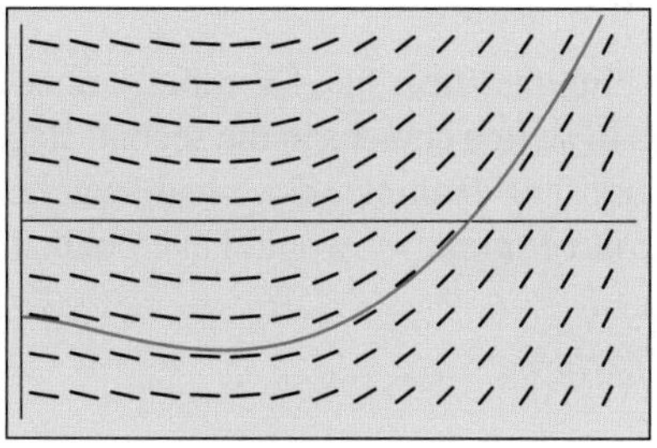

[0, 3] by [−1.5, 1.5]

Figure 7.10 The solution to the initial value problem in Example 3 conforms nicely to a slope field of the differential equation. (Example 3)

Solving for the Unknown Integral

Integrals like the one in the next example occur in electrical engineering. Their evaluation requires two integrations by parts, followed by solving for the unknown integral.

EXAMPLE 4 **Solving for the Unknown Integral**

Evaluate $\int e^x \cos x \, dx$.

SOLUTION

Let $u = e^x$, $dv = \cos x \, dx$. Then $du = e^x \, dx$, $v = \sin x$, and

$$\int \overset{u}{e^x} \overset{dv}{\cos x \, dx} = \overset{u}{e^x} \overset{v}{\sin x} - \int \overset{v}{\sin x} \overset{du}{e^x \, dx}$$

$$= e^x \sin x - \int e^x \sin x \, dx$$

The second integral is like the first, except it has $\sin x$ in place of $\cos x$. To evaluate it, we use integration by parts again, with

$$u = e^x, \quad dv = \sin x \, dx, \quad v = -\cos x, \quad du = e^x \, dx.$$

continued

Then

$$\int e^x \cos x \, dx = e^x \sin x - \int \overset{u}{e^x} \overset{dv}{\overline{\sin x \, dx}}$$

$$= e^x \sin x - \left(\overset{u}{e^x} \overset{v}{(-\cos x)} - \int \overset{v}{(-\cos x)} \overset{du}{\overline{e^x \, dx}} \right)$$

$$= e^x \sin x + e^x \cos x - \int e^x \cos x \, dx$$

The unknown integral now appears on both sides of the equation. Adding the integral to both sides gives

$$2 \int e^x \cos x \, dx = e^x \sin x + e^x \cos x + C.$$

Dividing by 2 and renaming the constant of integration gives

$$\int e^x \cos x \, dx = \frac{e^x \sin x + e^x \cos x}{2} + C.$$

Now Try Exercise 17.

When making repeated use of integration by parts in circumstances like Example 4, once a choice for *u* and *dv* is made, it is usually not a good idea to switch choices in the second stage of the problem. Doing so will result in undoing the work. For example, if we had switched to the substitution $u = \sin x$, $dv = e^x \, dx$ in the second integration, we would have obtained

$$\int e^x \cos x \, dx = e^x \sin x - \int \overset{u}{\sin x} \overset{dv}{\overline{e^x \, dx}}$$

$$= e^x \sin x - \left(\overset{u}{\sin x} \overset{v}{e^x} - \int \overset{v}{e^x} \overset{du}{\overline{\cos x \, dx}} \right)$$

$$= \int e^x \cos x \, dx,$$

undoing the first integration by parts.

Tic-Tac-Toe Method

A scene in the 1988 movie *Stand and Deliver* showed calculus teacher Jaime Escalante (played by Edward James Olmos) referring to this tabular method as the "Tic-Tac-Toe" method. Although the connection to the classic X-and-O grid game is not readily apparent, the name has endured in many classrooms ever since.

Tabular Integration

We have seen that integrals of the form $\int f(x)g(x)dx$, in which f can be differentiated repeatedly to become zero and g can be integrated repeatedly without difficulty, are natural candidates for integration by parts. However, if many repetitions are required, the calculations can be cumbersome. In situations like this, there is a way to organize the calculations that saves a great deal of work. It is **tabular integration,** as shown in Examples 5 and 6.

EXAMPLE 5 Using Tabular Integration

Evaluate $\int x^2 e^x \, dx$.

SOLUTION

With $f(x) = x^2$ and $g(x) = e^x$, we list:

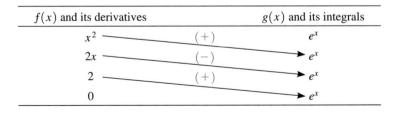

$f(x)$ and its derivatives		$g(x)$ and its integrals
x^2	$(+)$	e^x
$2x$	$(-)$	e^x
2	$(+)$	e^x
0		e^x

continued

We combine the products of the functions connected by the arrows according to the operation signs above the arrows to obtain

$$\int x^2 e^x \, dx = x^2 e^x - 2x e^x + 2 e^x + C.$$

Compare this with the result in Example 2.   *Now Try Exercise 21.*

EXAMPLE 6 Using Tabular Integration

Evaluate $\int x^3 \sin x \, dx$.

SOLUTION

With $f(x) = x^3$ and $g(x) = \sin x$, we list:

$f(x)$ and its derivatives		$g(x)$ and its integrals
x^3	$(+)$	$\sin x$
$3x^2$	$(-)$	$-\cos x$
$6x$	$(+)$	$-\sin x$
6	$(-)$	$\cos x$
0		$\sin x$

Again we combine the products of the functions connected by the arrows according to the operation signs above the arrows to obtain

$$\int x^3 \sin x \, dx = -x^3 \cos x + 3x^2 \sin x + 6x \cos x - 6 \sin x + C.$$

Now Try Exercise 23.

Inverse Trigonometric and Logarithmic Functions

The method of parts is useful only when the integrand can be written as a product of two functions (u and dv). In fact, *any* integrand $f(x) \, dx$ satisfies that requirement, since we can let $u = f(x)$ and $dv = dx$. There are not many antiderivatives of the form $\int f(x) \, dx$ that you would want to find by parts, but there are some, most notably the antiderivatives of logarithmic and inverse trigonometric functions.

EXAMPLE 7 Antidifferentiating ln x

Find $\int \ln x \, dx$.

SOLUTION

If we want to use parts, we have little choice but to let $u = \ln x$ and $dv = dx$.

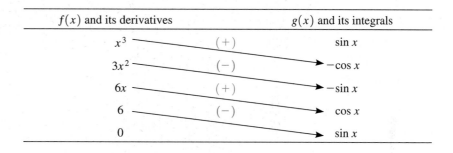

$$\int \overset{u}{\ln x} \overset{dv}{dx} = \overset{u}{(\ln x)} \overset{v}{(x)} - \int (x) \left(\frac{1}{x} \right) dx$$

$$= x \ln x - \int 1 \, dx$$

$$= x \ln x - x + C$$

Now Try Exercise 9.

EXAMPLE 8 Antidifferentiating $\sin^{-1} x$

Find the solution to the differential equation $dy/dx = \sin^{-1} x$ if the graph of the solution passes through the point $(0, 0)$.

SOLUTION

We find $\displaystyle\int \sin^{-1} x\, dx$, letting $u = \sin^{-1} x$, $dv = dx$.

$$\int \overset{u}{\sin^{-1} x}\, \overset{dv}{dx} = (\overset{u}{\sin^{-1} x})(\overset{v}{x}) - \int \overset{v}{x} \left(\overset{du}{\frac{1}{\sqrt{1 - x^2}}} \right) dx$$

$$= x \sin^{-1} x - \int \frac{x\, dx}{\sqrt{1 - x^2}}$$

$$= x \sin^{-1} x + \frac{1}{2} \int \frac{-2x\, dx}{\sqrt{1 - x^2}} \qquad \text{Set up substitution.}$$

$$= x \sin^{-1} x + \frac{1}{2} \int u^{-1/2}\, du \qquad \text{Let } u = 1 - x^2,\ du = -2x\, dx.$$

$$= x \sin^{-1} x + u^{1/2} + C$$

$$= x \sin^{-1} x + \sqrt{1 - x^2} + C \qquad \text{Resubstitute.}$$

Applying the initial condition $y = 0$ when $x = 0$, we conclude that the particular solution is $y = x \sin^{-1} x + \sqrt{1 - x^2} - 1$.

A graph of $y = x \sin^{-1} x + \sqrt{1 - x^2} - 1$ conforms nicely to the slope field for $dy/dx = \sin^{-1} x$, as shown in Figure 7.11.   ***Now Try Exercise 10.***

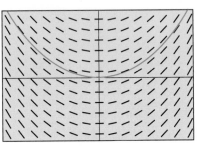

[−1, 1] by [−0.5, 0.5]

Figure 7.11 The solution to the initial value problem in Example 8 conforms nicely to the slope field of the differential equation. (Example 8)

Quick Review 7.3 *(For help, go to Sections 4.3 and 4.4.)*

Exercise numbers with a gray background indicate problems that the authors have designed to be solved *without a calculator*.

In Exercises 1–4, find dy/dx.

1. $y = x^3 \sin 2x$

2. $y = e^{2x} \ln (3x + 1)$

3. $y = \tan^{-1} 2x$

4. $y = \sin^{-1} (x + 3)$

In Exercises 5 and 6, solve for x in terms of y.

5. $y = \tan^{-1} 3x$

6. $y = \cos^{-1} (x + 1)$

7. Find the area under the arch of the curve $y = \sin \pi x$ from $x = 0$ to $x = 1$.

8. Solve the differential equation $dy/dx = e^{2x}$.

9. Solve the initial value problem $dy/dx = x + \sin x$, $y(0) = 2$.

10. Use differentiation to confirm the integration formula

$$\int e^x \sin x\, dx = \frac{1}{2} e^x (\sin x - \cos x).$$

Section 7.3 Exercises

In Exercises 1–10, find the indefinite integral.

1. $\displaystyle\int x \sin x\, dx$

2. $\displaystyle\int x\, e^x\, dx$

3. $\displaystyle\int 3t\, e^{2t}\, dt$

4. $\displaystyle\int 2t \cos (3t)\, dt$

5. $\displaystyle\int x^2 \cos x\, dx$

6. $\displaystyle\int x^2 e^{-x}\, dx$

7. $\displaystyle\int y \ln y\, dy$

8. $\displaystyle\int t^2 \ln t\, dt$

9. $\displaystyle\int \log_2 x\, dx$

10. $\displaystyle\int \tan^{-1} x\, dx$

In Exercises 11–16, solve the initial value problem. (Then you can confirm your answer by checking that it conforms to the slope field of the differential equation.)

11. $\dfrac{dy}{dx} = (x + 2) \sin x$ and $y = 2$ when $x = 0$

12. $\dfrac{dy}{dx} = 2xe^{-x}$ and $y = 3$ when $x = 0$

13. $\dfrac{du}{dx} = x \sec^2 x$ and $u = 1$ when $x = 0$

14. $\dfrac{dz}{dx} = x^3 \ln x$ and $z = 5$ when $x = 1$

15. $\dfrac{dy}{dx} = x\sqrt{x-1}$ and $y = 2$ when $x = 1$

16. $\dfrac{dy}{dx} = 2x\sqrt{x+2}$ and $y = 0$ when $x = -1$

In Exercises 17–20, use parts and solve for the unknown integral.

17. $\displaystyle\int e^x \sin x \, dx$

18. $\displaystyle\int e^{-x} \cos x \, dx$

19. $\displaystyle\int e^x \cos 2x \, dx$

20. $\displaystyle\int e^{-x} \sin 2x \, dx$

In Exercises 21–24, use tabular integration to find the antiderivative.

21. $\displaystyle\int x^4 e^{-x} \, dx$

22. $\displaystyle\int (x^2 - 5x)e^x \, dx$

23. $\displaystyle\int x^3 e^{-2x} \, dx$

24. $\displaystyle\int x^3 \cos 2x \, dx$

In Exercises 25–28, evaluate the integral analytically. Support your answer using NINT.

25. $\displaystyle\int_0^{\pi/2} x^2 \sin 2x \, dx$

26. $\displaystyle\int_0^{\pi/2} x^3 \cos 2x \, dx$

27. $\displaystyle\int_{-2}^{3} e^{2x} \cos 3x \, dx$

28. $\displaystyle\int_{-3}^{2} e^{-2x} \sin 2x \, dx$

In Exercises 29–32, solve the differential equation.

29. $\dfrac{dy}{dx} = x^2 e^{4x}$

30. $\dfrac{dy}{dx} = x^2 \ln x$

31. $\dfrac{dy}{d\theta} = \theta \sec^{-1} \theta, \quad \theta > 1$

32. $\dfrac{dy}{d\theta} = \theta \sec \theta \tan \theta$

33. *Finding Area* Find the area of the region enclosed by the x-axis and the curve $y = x \sin x$ for

(a) $0 \le x \le \pi$,   (b) $\pi \le x \le 2\pi$,   (c) $0 \le x \le 2\pi$.

34. *Finding Area* Find the area of the region enclosed by the y-axis and the curves $y = x^2$ and $y = (x^2 + x + 1)e^{-x}$.

35. *Average Value* A retarding force, symbolized by the dashpot in the figure, slows the motion of the weighted spring so that the mass's position at time t is

$$y = 2e^{-t} \cos t, \quad t \ge 0.$$

Find the average value of y over the interval $0 \le t \le 2\pi$.

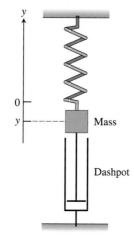

Standardized Test Questions

36. True or False If $f'(x) = g(x)$, then $\int x \, g(x) \, dx = x \, f(x) - \int f(x) \, dx$. Justify your answer.

37. True or False If $f'(x) = g(x)$, then $\int x^2 \, g(x) \, dx = x^2 \, f(x) - 2\int x \, f(x) \, dx$. Justify your answer.

38. Multiple Choice If $\int x^2 \cos x \, dx = h(x) - \int 2x \sin x \, dx$, then $h(x) =$

(A) $2 \sin x + 2x \cos x + C$

(B) $x^2 \sin x + C$

(C) $2x \cos x - x^2 \sin x + C$

(D) $4 \cos x - 2x \sin x + C$

(E) $(2 - x^2) \cos x - 4 \sin x + C$

39. Multiple Choice $\int x \sin (5x) \, dx =$

(A) $-x \cos (5x) + \sin (5x) + C$

(B) $-\dfrac{x}{5} \cos (5x) + \dfrac{1}{25} \sin (5x) + C$

(C) $-\dfrac{x}{5} \cos (5x) + \dfrac{1}{5} \sin (5x) + C$

(D) $\dfrac{x}{5} \cos (5x) + \dfrac{1}{25} \sin (5x) + C$

(E) $5x \cos (5x) - \sin (5x) + C$

40. Multiple Choice $\int x \csc^2 x \, dx =$

(A) $\dfrac{x^2 \csc^3 x}{6} + C$

(B) $x \cot x - \ln |\sin x| + C$

(C) $-x \cot x + \ln |\sin x| + C$

(D) $-x \cot x - \ln |\sin x| + C$

(E) $-x \sec^2 x - \tan x + C$

41. Multiple Choice The graph of $y = f(x)$ conforms to the slope field for the differential equation $dy/dx = 4x \ln x$, as shown in the graph below. Which of the following could be $f(x)$?

(A) $2x^2 (\ln x)^2 + 3$

(B) $x^3 \ln x + 3$

(C) $2x^2 \ln x - x^2 + 3$

(D) $(2x^2 + 3) \ln x - 1$

(E) $2x(\ln x)^2 - \dfrac{4}{3}(\ln x)^3 + 3$

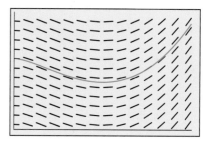

[0, 2] by [0, 5]

Explorations

42. Consider the integral $\int x^n e^x \, dx$. Use integration by parts to evaluate the integral if

(a) $n = 1$.

(b) $n = 2$.

(c) $n = 3$.

(d) Conjecture the value of the integral for any positive integer n.

(e) **Writing to Learn** Give a convincing argument that your conjecture in part (d) is true.

In Exercises 43–46, evaluate the integral by using a substitution prior to integration by parts.

43. $\displaystyle\int \sin \sqrt{x} \, dx$

44. $\displaystyle\int e^{\sqrt{3x+9}} \, dx$

45. $\displaystyle\int x^7 e^{x^2} \, dx$

46. $\displaystyle\int \sin(\ln r) \, dr$

In Exercises 47–50, use integration by parts to establish the *reduction formula*.

47. $\displaystyle\int x^n \cos x \, dx = x^n \sin x - n \int x^{n-1} \sin x \, dx$

48. $\displaystyle\int x^n \sin x \, dx = -x^n \cos x + n \int x^{n-1} \cos x \, dx$

49. $\displaystyle\int x^n e^{ax} \, dx = \frac{x^n e^{ax}}{a} - \frac{n}{a} \int x^{n-1} e^{ax} \, dx, \, a \neq 0$

50. $\displaystyle\int (\ln x)^n \, dx = x(\ln x)^n - n \int (\ln x)^{n-1} \, dx$

Extending the Ideas

51. *Integrating Inverse Functions* Assume that the function f has an inverse.

(a) Show that $\int f^{-1}(x) \, dx = \int y f'(y) \, dy$. [*Hint:* Use the substitution $y = f^{-1}(x)$.]

(b) Use integration by parts on the second integral in part (a) to show that

$$\int f^{-1}(x) \, dx = \int y f'(y) \, dy = x f^{-1}(x) - \int f(y) \, dy.$$

52. *Integrating Inverse Functions* Assume that the function f has an inverse. Use integration by parts directly to show that

$$\int f^{-1}(x) \, dx = x f^{-1}(x) - \int x \left(\frac{d}{dx} f^{-1}(x) \right) dx.$$

In Exercises 53–56, evaluate the integral using

(a) the technique of Exercise 51.

(b) the technique of Exercise 52.

(c) Show that the expressions (with $C = 0$) obtained in parts (a) and (b) are the same.

53. $\displaystyle\int \sin^{-1} x \, dx$

54. $\displaystyle\int \tan^{-1} x \, dx$

55. $\displaystyle\int \cos^{-1} x \, dx$

56. $\displaystyle\int \log_2 x \, dx$

57. *A Challenging Antiderivative* Use integration by parts to find $\int \sec^3 x \, dx$. (*Hint:* Start with $\int \sec^3 x \, dx = \int \sec x \cdot \sec^2 x \, dx$. Eventually you might want to look at Exercise 45 in the previous section.)

58. *An Equally Challenging Antiderivative* Use integration by parts to find $\int \csc^3 x \, dx$. (*Hint:* Start with $\int \csc^3 x \, dx = \int \csc x \cdot \csc^2 x \, dx$. Eventually you might want to look at Exercise 46 in the previous section.)

Quick Quiz for AP* Preparation: Sections 7.1–7.3

1. Multiple Choice Which of the following differential equations would produce the slope field shown below?

(A) $\dfrac{dy}{dx} = y - 3x$ (B) $\dfrac{dy}{dx} = y - \dfrac{x}{3}$

(C) $\dfrac{dy}{dx} = y + \dfrac{x}{3}$ (D) $\dfrac{dy}{dx} = x + \dfrac{y}{3}$

(E) $\dfrac{dy}{dx} = x - \dfrac{y}{3}$

2. Multiple Choice If the substitution $\sqrt{x} = \sin y$ is made in the integrand of $\displaystyle\int_0^{1/2} \dfrac{\sqrt{x}}{\sqrt{1-x}}\, dx$, the resulting integral is

(A) $\displaystyle\int_0^{1/2} \sin^2 y\, dy$ (B) $\displaystyle 2\int_0^{1/2} \dfrac{\sin^2 y}{\cos y}\, dy$

(C) $\displaystyle 2\int_0^{\pi/4} \sin^2 y\, dy$ (D) $\displaystyle\int_0^{\pi/4} \sin^2 y\, dy$

(E) $\displaystyle 2\int_0^{\pi/6} \sin^2 y\, dy$

3. Multiple Choice $\displaystyle\int x\, e^{2x}\, dx =$

(A) $\dfrac{x\, e^{2x}}{2} - \dfrac{e^{2x}}{4} + C$ (B) $\dfrac{x\, e^{2x}}{2} - \dfrac{e^{2x}}{2} + C$

(C) $\dfrac{x\, e^{2x}}{2} + \dfrac{e^{2x}}{4} + C$ (D) $\dfrac{x\, e^{2x}}{2} + \dfrac{e^{2x}}{2} + C$

(E) $\dfrac{x^2\, e^{2x}}{4} + C$

4. Free Response Consider the differential equation $dy/dx = 2y - 4x$.

(a) The slope field for the differential equation is shown below. Sketch the solution curve that passes through the point $(0, 1)$ and sketch the solution curve that goes through the point $(0, -1)$.

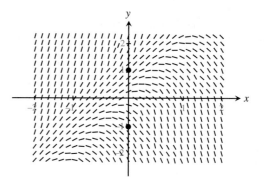

(b) There is a value of b for which $y = 2x + b$ is a solution to the differential equation. Find this value of b. Justify your answer.

(c) Let g be the function that satisfies the given differential equation with the initial condition $g(0) = 0$. It appears from the slope field that g has a local maximum at the point $(0, 0)$. Using the differential equation, prove analytically that this is so.

7.4 Exponential Growth and Decay

You will be able to solve separable differential equations, including those arising in problems of exponential growth, exponential decay, and logistic growth.

- The differential equation $dy/dt = ky$ and the law of exponential change
- Continuously compounded interest
- Radioactive decay
- Modeling growth in convenient bases
- Newton's Law of Cooling

Separable Differential Equations

Before we revisit the topic of exponential growth (last seen as a precalculus topic in Chapter 1), we need to introduce the concept of separable differential equations.

DEFINITION **Separable Differential Equation**

A differential equation of the form $dy/dx = f(y)g(x)$ is called **separable.** We **separate the variables** by writing it in the form

$$\frac{1}{f(y)} \, dy = g(x) \, dx.$$

The solution is found by antidifferentiating each side with respect to its thusly isolated variable.

EXAMPLE 1 Solving by Separation of Variables

Solve for y if $dy/dx = (xy)^2$ and $y = 1$ when $x = 1$.

SOLUTION

The equation is separable because it can be written in the form $dy/dx = y^2x^2$, where $f(y) = y^2$ and $g(x) = x^2$. We separate the variables and antidifferentiate as follows.

$$y^{-2} \, dy = x^2 \, dx \qquad \text{Separate the variables.}$$

$$\int y^{-2} \, dy = \int x^2 \, dx \qquad \text{Prepare to antidifferentiate.}$$

$$-y^{-1} = \frac{x^3}{3} + C \qquad \text{Note that only one constant is needed.}$$

We then apply the initial condition to find C.

$$-1 = \frac{1}{3} + C \Rightarrow C = -\frac{4}{3}$$

$$-y^{-1} = \frac{x^3}{3} - \frac{4}{3}$$

$$y^{-1} = \frac{4 - x^3}{3}$$

$$y = \frac{3}{4 - x^3}$$

This solution is valid for the continuous section of the function that goes through the point $(1, 1)$, that is, on the domain $\left(-\infty, \sqrt[3]{4}\right)$.

It is apparent that $y = 1$ when $x = 1$, but it is worth checking that $dy/dx = (xy)^2$.

$$y = \frac{3}{4 - x^3}$$

$$\frac{dy}{dx} = -3(4 - x^3)^{-2} (-3x^2)$$

$$\frac{dy}{dx} = \frac{9x^2}{(4 - x^3)^2} = x^2\left(\frac{3}{4 - x^3}\right)^2 = x^2y^2 = (xy)^2$$

Now Try Exercise 1.

Law of Exponential Change

You have probably solved enough exponential growth problems by now to recognize that they involve growth in which the rate of change is proportional to the amount present. The more bacteria in the dish, the faster they multiply. The more radioactive material present, the faster it decays. The greater your bank account (assuming it earns compounded interest), the faster it grows.

The differential equation that describes this growth is $dy/dt = ky$, where k is the *exponential growth constant* (if positive) or the *exponential decay constant* (if negative). We can solve this equation by separating the variables.

$$\frac{dy}{dt} = ky$$

$$\frac{1}{y}dy = k\,dt \qquad \text{Separate the variables.}$$

$$\ln|y| = kt + C \qquad \text{Antidifferentiate both sides.}$$

$$|y| = e^{kt+C} \qquad \text{Exponentiate both sides.}$$

$$|y| = e^C e^{kt} \qquad \text{Property of exponents.}$$

$$y = \pm e^C e^{kt} \qquad \text{Definition of absolute value.}$$

$$y = Ae^{kt} \qquad \text{Let } A = \pm e^C.$$

What if $A = 0$?

If $A = 0$, then the solution to $dy/dt = ky$ is the constant function $y = 0$. This function is technically of the form $y = Ae^{kt}$, but we do not consider it to be an exponential function. The initial condition in this case leads to a "trivial" solution.

This solution shows that the *only* growth function that results in a growth rate proportional to the amount present is, in fact, exponential. Note that the constant A is the amount present when $t = 0$, so it is usually denoted y_0.

The Law of Exponential Change

If y changes at a rate proportional to the amount present (that is, if $dy/dt = ky$), and if $y = y_0$ when $t = 0$, then

$$y = y_0\,e^{kt}.$$

The constant k is the *exponential growth constant* if $k > 0$ or the *exponential decay constant* if $k < 0$.

Now Try Exercise 11.

Continuously Compounded Interest

Suppose that P dollars are invested at a fixed annual interest rate r (expressed as a decimal). If interest is added to the account n times a year, the amount of money present after t years is

$$A(t) = P\left(1 + \frac{r}{n}\right)^{nt}.$$

The interest might be added ("compounded," bankers say) monthly ($n = 12$), weekly ($n = 52$), daily ($n = 365$), or even more frequently, by the hour or by the minute.

If, instead of being added at discrete intervals, the interest is added continuously at a rate proportional to the amount in the account, we can model the growth of the account with the following initial value problem.

Differential equation: $\dfrac{dA}{dt} = rA$

Initial condition: $A(0) = P$

It can be shown that

$$\lim_{n \to \infty} P\left(1 + \frac{r}{n}\right)^{nt} = Pe^{rt}.$$

We will see how this limit is evaluated in Section 9.2, Exercise 57.

The amount of money in the account after t years is then

$$A(t) = Pe^{rt}.$$

Interest paid according to this formula is said to be **compounded continuously.** The number r is the **continuous interest rate.**

EXAMPLE 2 Compounding Interest Continuously

Suppose you deposit $800 in an account that pays 6.3% annual interest. How much will you have 8 years later if the interest is **(a)** compounded continuously? **(b)** compounded quarterly?

SOLUTION

Here $P = 800$ and $r = 0.063$. The amount in the account to the nearest cent after 8 years is

(a) $A(8) = 800e^{(0.063)(8)} = 1324.26.$

(b) $A(8) = 800\left(1 + \dfrac{0.063}{4}\right)^{(4)(8)} = 1319.07.$

You might have expected to generate more than an additional $5.19 with interest compounded continuously.

Now Try Exercise 19.

For radium-226, which used to be painted on watch dials to make them glow at night (a dangerous practice for the painters, who licked their brush-tips), t is measured in years and $k = 4.3 \times 10^{-4}$. For radon-222 gas, t is measured in days and $k = 0.18$. The decay of radium in the earth's crust is the source of the radon we sometimes find in our basements.

Radioactivity

When an atom emits some of its mass as radiation, the remainder of the atom re-forms to make an atom of some new element. This process of radiation and change is **radioactive decay,** and an element whose atoms go spontaneously through this process is **radioactive.** Radioactive carbon-14 decays into nitrogen. Radium, through a number of intervening radioactive steps, decays into lead.

Experiments have shown that at any given time the rate at which a radioactive element decays (as measured by the number of nuclei that change per unit of time) is approximately proportional to the number of radioactive nuclei present. Thus, the decay of a radioactive element is described by the equation $dy/dt = -ky, k > 0$. If y_0 is the number of radioactive nuclei present at time zero, the number still present at any later time t will be

$$y = y_0 e^{-kt}, \quad k > 0.$$

Convention

It is conventional to use $-k\,(k > 0)$ here instead of $k\,(k < 0)$ to emphasize that y is decreasing.

The **half-life** of a radioactive element is the time required for half of the radioactive nuclei present in a sample to decay. Example 3 shows the surprising fact that the half-life is a constant that depends only on the radioactive substance and not on the number of radioactive nuclei present in the sample.

EXAMPLE 3 Finding Half-Life

Find the half-life of a radioactive substance with decay equation $y = y_0 e^{-kt}$ and show that the half-life depends only on k.

SOLUTION

Model The half-life is the solution to the equation

$$y_0 e^{-kt} = \frac{1}{2}y_0.$$

continued

Solve Algebraically

$$e^{-kt} = \frac{1}{2}$$ Divide by y_0.

$$-kt = \ln \frac{1}{2}$$ Take ln of both sides.

$$t = -\frac{1}{k} \ln \frac{1}{2} = \frac{\ln 2}{k}$$ $\ln \frac{1}{a} = -\ln a$

Interpret This value of t is the half-life of the element. It depends only on the value of k. Note that the number y_0 does not appear. ***Now Try Exercise 21.***

DEFINITION   Half-life

The **half-life** of a radioactive substance with rate constant k ($k > 0$) is

$$\text{half-life} = \frac{\ln 2}{k}.$$

Modeling Growth with Other Bases

As we have seen, the differential equation $dy/dt = ky$ leads to the exponential solution

$$y = y_0 \, e^{kt},$$

where y_0 is the value of y at $t = 0$. We can also write this solution in the form

$$y = y_0 \, b^{ht},$$

where b is any positive number not equal to 1, and h is another rate constant, related to k by the equation $k = h \ln b$. This means that exponential growth can be modeled in *any* positive base not equal to 1, enabling us to choose a convenient base to fit a given growth pattern, as the following exploration shows.

EXPLORATION 1 Choosing a Convenient Base

A certain population y is growing at a continuous rate so that the population doubles every 5 years.

1. Let $y = y_0 \, 2^{ht}$. Since $y = 2 \, y_0$ when $t = 5$, what is h? What is the relationship of h to the doubling period?

2. How long does it take for the population to triple?

A certain population y is growing at a continuous rate so that the population triples every 10 years.

3. Let $y = y_0 \, 3^{ht}$. Since $y = 3 \, y_0$ when $t = 10$, what is h? What is the relationship of h to the tripling period?

4. How long does it take for the population to double?

A certain isotope of sodium (Na-24) has a half-life of 15 hours. That is, half the atoms of Na-24 disintegrate into another nuclear form in fifteen hours.

5. Let $A = A_0 (1/2)^{ht}$. Since $y = (1/2) \, y_0$ when $t = 15$, what is h? What is the relationship of h to the half-life?

6. How long does it take for the amount of radioactive material to decay to 10% of the original amount?

Hornets Aplenty

The hornet population in Example 4 can grow exponentially for a while, but the ecosystem cannot sustain such growth all summer. The model will eventually become logistic, as we will see in the next section. Nevertheless, given the right conditions, a bald-faced hornet nest can grow to be bigger than a basketball and house more than 600 workers.

Carbon-14 Dating

The decay of radioactive elements can sometimes be used to date events from Earth's past. The ages of rocks more than 2 billion years old have been measured by the extent of the radioactive decay of uranium (half-life 4.5 billion years!). In a living organism, the ratio of radioactive carbon, carbon-14, to ordinary carbon stays fairly constant during the lifetime of the organism, being approximately equal to the ratio in the organism's surroundings at the time. After the organism's death, however, no new carbon is ingested, and the proportion of carbon-14 decreases as the carbon-14 decays. It is possible to estimate the ages of fairly old organic remains by comparing the proportion of carbon-14 they contain with the proportion assumed to have been in the organism's environment at the time it lived. Archeologists have dated shells (which contain $CaCO_3$), seeds, and wooden artifacts this way. The estimate of 15,500 years for the age of the cave paintings at Lascaux, France, is based on carbon-14 dating. After generations of controversy, the Shroud of Turin, long believed by many to be the burial cloth of Christ, was shown by carbon-14 dating in 1988 to have been made after 1200 C.E.

It is important to note that while the exponential growth model $y = y_0 b^{ht}$ satisfies the differential equation $dy/dt = ky$ for any positive base b, it is only when $b = e$ that the growth constant k appears in the exponent as the coefficient of t. In general, the coefficient of t is the reciprocal of the time period required for the population to grow (or decay) by a factor of b.

EXAMPLE 4 Choosing a Base

At the beginning of the summer, the population of a hive of bald-faced hornets (which are actually wasps) is growing at a rate proportional to the population. From a population of 10 on May 1, the number of hornets grows to 50 in thirty days. If the growth continues to follow the same model, how many days after May 1 will the population reach 100?

SOLUTION

Since $dy/dt = ky$, the growth is exponential. Noting that the population grows by a factor of 5 in 30 days, we model the growth in base 5: $y = 10 \times 5^{(1/30)t}$. Now we need only solve the equation $100 = 10 \times 5^{(1/30)t}$ for t:

$$100 = 10 \times 5^{(1/30)t}$$
$$10 = 5^{(1/30)t}$$
$$\ln 10 = (1/30)t \ln 5$$
$$t = 30\left(\frac{\ln 10}{\ln 5}\right) = 42.920$$

Approximately 43 days will pass after May 1 before the population reaches 100.

Now Try Exercise 23.

EXAMPLE 5 Using Carbon-14 Dating

Scientists who use carbon-14 dating use 5700 years for its half-life. Find the age of a sample in which 10% of the radioactive nuclei originally present have decayed.

SOLUTION

We model the exponential decay in base $1/2$: $A = A_0(1/2)^{t/5700}$. We seek the value of t for which $0.9A_0 = A_0(1/2)^{t/5700}$, or $(1/2)^{t/5700} = 0.9$.

Solving algebraically with logarithms,

$$(1/2)^{t/5700} = 0.9$$
$$(t/5700)\ln(1/2) = \ln(0.9)$$
$$t = 5700\left(\frac{\ln(0.9)}{\ln(0.5)}\right)$$
$$t \approx 866$$

Interpreting the answer, we conclude that the sample is about 866 years old.

Now Try Exercise 25.

Newton's Law of Cooling

Soup left in a cup cools to the temperature of the surrounding air. A hot silver ingot immersed in water cools to the temperature of the surrounding water. In situations like these, the rate at which an object's temperature is changing at any given time is roughly proportional to

J. Ernest Wilkins, Jr. (1923–2011)

By the age of nineteen, J. Ernest Wilkins had earned a Ph.D. degree in Mathematics from the University of Chicago. He then taught, served on the Manhattan project (the goal of which was to build the first atomic bomb), and worked as a mathematician and physicist for several corporations. In 1970, Dr. Wilkins joined the faculty at Howard University and served as head of the electrical engineering, physics, chemistry, and mathematics departments before retiring. He was also Distinguished Professor of Applied Mathematics and Mathematical Physics at Clark Atlanta University.

the difference between its temperature and the temperature of the surrounding medium. This observation is *Newton's Law of Cooling,* although it applies to warming as well, and there is an equation for it.

If T is the temperature of the object at time t, and T_s is the surrounding temperature, then

$$\frac{dT}{dt} = -k(T - T_s). \tag{1}$$

Since $dT = d(T - T_s)$, equation (1) can be written as

$$\frac{d}{dt}(T - T_s) = -k(T - T_s).$$

Its solution, by the law of exponential change, is

$$T - T_s = (T_0 - T_s)e^{-kt},$$

where T_0 is the temperature at time $t = 0$. This equation also bears the name **Newton's Law of Cooling.**

EXAMPLE 6 Using Newton's Law of Cooling

A hard-boiled egg at 98°C is put in a pan under running 18°C water to cool. After 5 minutes, the egg's temperature is found to be 38°C. How much longer will it take the egg to reach 20°C?

SOLUTION

Model Using Newton's Law of Cooling with $T_s = 18$ and $T_0 = 98$, we have

$$T - 18 = (98 - 18)e^{-kt} \quad \text{or} \quad T = 18 + 80e^{-kt}.$$

To find k we use the information that $T = 38$ when $t = 5$.

$$38 = 18 + 80e^{-5k}$$

$$e^{-5k} = \frac{1}{4}$$

$$-5k = \ln\frac{1}{4} = -\ln 4$$

$$k = \frac{1}{5}\ln 4$$

The egg's temperature at time t is $T = 18 + 80e^{-(0.2\ln 4)t}$.

Solve Graphically We can now use a grapher to find the time when the egg's temperature is 20°C. Figure 7.12 shows that the graphs of

$$y = 20 \quad \text{and} \quad y = T = 18 + 80e^{-(0.2\ln 4)t}$$

intersect at about $t = 13.3$.

Interpret The egg's temperature will reach 20°C in about 13.3 min after it is put in the pan under running water to cool. Because it took 5 min to reach 38°C, it will take slightly more than 8 additional minutes to reach 20°C.

Now Try Exercise 31.

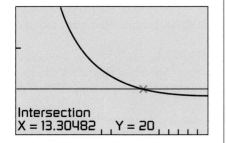

Intersection
X = 13.30482   Y = 20

[0, 20] by [10, 40]

Figure 7.12 The egg will reach 20°C about 13.3 min after being placed in the pan to cool. (Example 6)

Quick Review 7.4

Exercise numbers with a gray background indicate problems that the authors have designed to be solved *without a calculator.*

In Exercises 1 and 2, rewrite the equation in exponential form or logarithmic form.

1. $\ln a = b$

2. $e^c = d$

In Exercises 3–8, solve the equation.

3. $\ln (x + 3) = 2$

4. $100e^{2x} = 600$

5. $0.85^x = 2.5$

6. $2^{k+1} = 3^k$

7. $1.1^t = 10$

8. $e^{-2t} = \dfrac{1}{4}$

In Exercises 9 and 10, solve for y.

9. $\ln (y + 1) = 2x - 3$

10. $\ln |y + 2| = 3t - 1$

Section 7.4 Exercises

In Exercises 1–10, use separation of variables to solve the initial value problem. Indicate the domain over which the solution is valid.

1. $\dfrac{dy}{dx} = \dfrac{x}{y}$ and $y = 2$ when $x = 1$

2. $\dfrac{dy}{dx} = -\dfrac{x}{y}$ and $y = 3$ when $x = 4$

3. $\dfrac{dy}{dx} = \dfrac{y}{x}$ and $y = 2$ when $x = 2$

4. $\dfrac{dy}{dx} = 2xy$ and $y = 3$ when $x = 0$

5. $\dfrac{dy}{dx} = (y + 5)(x + 2)$ and $y = 1$ when $x = 0$

6. $\dfrac{dy}{dx} = \cos^2 y$ and $y = 0$ when $x = 0$

7. $\dfrac{dy}{dx} = (\cos x)e^{y+\sin x}$ and $y = 0$ when $x = 0$

8. $\dfrac{dy}{dx} = e^{x-y}$ and $y = 2$ when $x = 0$

9. $\dfrac{dy}{dx} = -2xy^2$ and $y = 0.25$ when $x = 1$

10. $\dfrac{dy}{dx} = \dfrac{4\sqrt{y} \ln x}{x}$ and $y = 1$ when $x = e$

In Exercises 11–14, find the solution of the differential equation $dy/dt = ky$, k a constant, that satisfies the given conditions.

11. $k = 1.5$, $y(0) = 100$

12. $k = -0.5$, $y(0) = 200$

13. $y(0) = 50$, $y(5) = 100$

14. $y(0) = 60$, $y(10) = 30$

In Exercises 15–18, complete the table for an investment if interest is compounded continuously.

	Initial Deposit ($)	Annual Rate (%)	Doubling Time (yr)	Amount in 30 yr ($)
15.	1000	8.6		
16.	2000		15	
17.		5.25		2898.44
18.	1200			10,405.37

In Exercises 19 and 20, find the amount of time required for a $2000 investment to double if the annual interest rate r is compounded **(a)** annually, **(b)** monthly, **(c)** quarterly, and **(d)** continuously.

19. $r = 4.75\%$ **20.** $r = 8.25\%$

21. *Half-Life* The radioactive decay of Sm-151 (an isotope of samarium) can be modeled by the differential equation $dy/dt = -0.0077y$, where t is measured in years. Find the half-life of Sm-151.

22. *Half-Life* An isotope of neptunium (Np-240) has a half-life of 65 minutes. If the decay of Np-240 is modeled by the differential equation $dy/dt = -ky$, where t is measured in minutes, what is the decay constant k?

23. *Growth of Cholera Bacteria* Suppose that the cholera bacteria in a colony grow unchecked according to the Law of Exponential Change. The colony starts with 1 bacterium and doubles in number every half hour.

(a) How many bacteria will the colony contain at the end of 24 h?

(b) *Writing to Learn* Use part (a) to explain why a person who feels well in the morning may be dangerously ill by evening even though, in an infected person, many bacteria are destroyed.

24. *Bacterial Growth* A colony of bacteria is grown under ideal conditions in a laboratory so that the population increases exponentially with time. At the end of 3 h there are 10,000 bacteria. At the end of 5 h there are 40,000 bacteria. How many bacteria were present initially?

25. *Radon-222* The decay equation for radon-222 gas is known to be $y = y_0 e^{-0.18t}$, with t in days. About how long will it take the amount of radon in a sealed sample of air to decay to 90% of its original value?

26. *Polonium-210* The number of radioactive atoms remaining after t days in a sample of polonium-210 that starts with y_0 radioactive atoms is $y = y_0 e^{-0.005t}$.

(a) Find the element's half-life.

(b) Your sample will not be useful to you after 95% of the radioactive nuclei present on the day the sample arrives have disintegrated. For about how many days after the sample arrives will you be able to use the polonium?

In Exercises 27 and 28, find the exponential function $y = y_0 e^{kt}$ whose graph passes through the two points.

27.

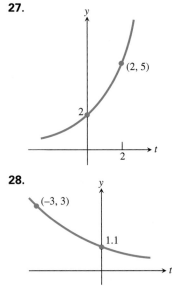

28.

29. Mean Life of Radioactive Nuclei Physicists using the radioactive decay equation $y = y_0 e^{-kt}$ call the number $1/k$ the *mean life* of a radioactive nucleus. The mean life of a radon-222 nucleus is about $1/0.18 \approx 5.6$ days. The mean life of a carbon-14 nucleus is more than 8000 years. Show that 95% of the radioactive nuclei originally present in any sample will disintegrate within three mean lifetimes, that is, by time $t = 3/k$. Thus, the mean life of a nucleus gives a quick way to estimate how long the radioactivity of a sample will last.

30. Finding the Original Temperature of a Beam An aluminum beam was brought from the outside cold into a machine shop where the temperature was held at 65°F. After 10 min, the beam warmed to 35°F and after another 10 min its temperature was 50°F. Use Newton's Law of Cooling to estimate the beam's initial temperature.

31. Cooling Soup Suppose that a cup of soup cooled from 90°C to 60°C in 10 min in a room whose temperature was 20°C. Use Newton's Law of Cooling to answer the following questions.

(a) How much longer would it take the soup to cool to 35°C?

(b) Instead of being left to stand in the room, the cup of 90°C soup is put into a freezer whose temperature is −15°C. How long will it take the soup to cool from 90°C to 35°C?

32. Cooling Silver The temperature of an ingot of silver is 60°C above room temperature right now. Twenty minutes ago, it was 70°C above room temperature. How far above room temperature will the silver be

(a) 15 minutes from now?

(b) 2 hours from now?

(c) When will the silver be 10°C above room temperature?

33. Avian Development The rate at which a baby bird gains weight is proportional to the difference between its adult weight and its current weight. At time $t = 0$, when the bird is first

weighed, its weight is 20 grams. If $B(t)$ is the weight of the bird, in grams, t days after it is first weighed, then $dB/dt = 0.2(100 - B)$.

(a) Is the bird gaining weight faster when it weighs 40 grams or when it weighs 70 grams? Explain your reasoning.

(b) Find $\dfrac{d^2B}{dt^2}$ in terms of t. Use $\dfrac{d^2B}{dt^2}$ to explain why the graph of B cannot resemble the following graph:

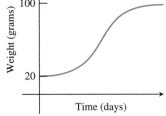

(c) Use separation of variables to find $y = B(t)$, the particular solution to the differential equation with initial condition $B(0) = 20$.

34. Solid Waste Accumulation A landfill at time $t = 0$ years contains 1200 tons of solid waste. The increasing function W models the total amount of solid waste stored at the landfill. Planners estimate that W will satisfy the differential equation $dW/dt = 0.04(W - 300)$ for the years $0 \le t \le 20$, where W is measured in tons.

(a) Use the line tangent to the graph of W at $t = 0$ to approximate the amount of solid waste in the landfill 3 months later.

(b) Find $\dfrac{d^2W}{dt^2}$ in terms of W. Use $\dfrac{d^2W}{dt^2}$ to determine whether your answer in part (a) is an underestimate or an overestimate of the amount of solid waste that the landfill contains at time $t = 1/4$.

(c) Find the particular solution $W = W(t)$ to the differential equation $dW/dt = 0.04(W - 300)$ with initial condition $W(0) = 1200$.

35. Dating Crater Lake The charcoal from a tree killed in the volcanic eruption that formed Crater Lake in Oregon contained 44.5% of the carbon-14 found in living matter. About how old is Crater Lake?

36. Carbon-14 Dating Measurement Sensitivity To see the effect of a relatively small error in the estimate of the amount of carbon-14 in a sample being dated, answer the following questions about this hypothetical situation.

(a) A fossilized bone found in central Illinois in the year 2000 C.E. contains 17% of its original carbon-14 content. Estimate the year the animal died.

(b) Repeat part (a) assuming 18% instead of 17%.

(c) Repeat part (a) assuming 16% instead of 17%.

37. What is the half-life of a substance that decays to $1/3$ of its original radioactive amount in 5 years?

38. A savings account earning compound interest triples in value in 10 years. How long will it take for the original investment to quadruple?

39. ***The Inversion of Sugar*** The processing of raw sugar has an "inversion" step that changes the sugar's molecular structure. Once the process has begun, the rate of change of the amount of raw sugar is proportional to the amount of raw sugar remaining. If 1000 kg of raw sugar reduces to 800 kg of raw sugar during the first 10 h, how much raw sugar will remain after another 14 h?

40. ***Oil Depletion*** Suppose the amount of oil pumped from one of the canyon wells in Whittier, California, decreases at the continuous rate of 10% per year. When will the well's output fall to one-fifth of its present level?

41. ***Atmospheric Pressure*** Earth's atmospheric pressure p is often modeled by assuming that the rate dp/dh at which p changes with the altitude h above sea level is proportional to p. Suppose that the pressure at sea level is 1013 millibars (about 14.7 lb/in^2) and that the pressure at an altitude of 20 km is 90 millibars.

(a) Solve the initial value problem

Differential equation: $\dfrac{dp}{dh} = kp,$

Initial condition: $p = p_0$ when $h = 0,$

to express p in terms of h. Determine the values of p_0 and k from the given altitude-pressure data.

(b) What is the atmospheric pressure at $h = 50$ km?

(c) At what altitude does the pressure equal 900 millibars?

42. ***First-Order Chemical Reactions*** In some chemical reactions the rate at which the amount of a substance changes with time is proportional to the amount present. For the change of δ-glucono lactone into gluconic acid, for example,

$$\frac{dy}{dt} = -0.6y$$

when y is measured in grams and t is measured in hours. If there are 100 grams of a δ-glucono lactone present when $t = 0$, how many grams will be left after the first hour?

43. ***Discharging Capacitor Voltage*** Suppose that electricity is draining from a capacitor at a rate proportional to the voltage V across its terminals and that, if t is measured in seconds,

$$\frac{dV}{dt} = -\frac{1}{40}V.$$

(a) Solve this differential equation for V, using V_0 to denote the value of V when $t = 0$.

(b) How long will it take the voltage to drop to 10% of its original value?

44. ***John Napier's Answer*** John Napier (1550–1617), the Scottish laird who invented logarithms, was the first person to answer the question, "What happens if you invest an amount of money at 100% yearly interest, compounded continuously?"

(a) **Writing to Learn** What does happen? Explain.

(b) How long does it take to triple your money?

(c) **Writing to Learn** How much can you earn in a year?

45. ***Benjamin Franklin's Will*** The Franklin Technical Institute of Boston owes its existence to a provision in a codicil to Benjamin Franklin's will. In part the codicil reads:

I wish to be useful even after my Death, if possible, in forming and advancing other young men that may be serviceable to their Country in both Boston and Philadelphia. To this end I devote Two thousand Pounds Sterling, which I give, one thousand thereof to the Inhabitants of the Town of Boston in Massachusetts, and the other thousand to the inhabitants of the City of Philadelphia, in Trust and for the Uses, Interests and Purposes hereinafter mentioned and declared.

Franklin's plan was to lend money to young apprentices at 5% interest with the provision that each borrower should pay each year along

... with the yearly Interest, one tenth part of the Principal, which sums of Principal and Interest shall be again let to fresh Borrowers. ... If this plan is executed and succeeds as projected without interruption for one hundred Years, the Sum will then be one hundred and thirty-one thousand Pounds of which I would have the Managers of the Donation to the Inhabitants of the Town of Boston, then lay out at their discretion one hundred thousand Pounds in Public Works. ... The remaining thirty-one thousand Pounds, I would have continued to be let out on Interest in the manner above directed for another hundred Years. ... At the end of this second term if no unfortunate accident has prevented the operation the sum will be Four Millions and Sixty-one Thousand Pounds.

It was not always possible to find as many borrowers as Franklin had planned, but the managers of the trust did the best they could. At the end of 100 years from the receipt of the Franklin gift, in January 1894, the fund had grown from 1000 pounds to almost 90,000 pounds. In 100 years the original capital had multiplied about 90 times instead of the 131 times Franklin had imagined.

(a) What annual rate of interest, compounded continuously for 100 years, would have multiplied Benjamin Franklin's original capital by 90?

(b) In Benjamin Franklin's estimate that the original 1000 pounds would grow to 131,000 in 100 years, he was using an annual rate of 5% and compounding once each year. What rate of interest per year when compounded continuously for 100 years would multiply the original amount by 131?

46. ***Rules of 70 and 72*** The rules state that it takes about $70/i$ or $72/i$ years for money to double at i percent, compounded continuously, using whichever of 70 or 72 is easier to divide by i.

(a) Show that it takes $t = (\ln 2)/r$ years for money to double if it is invested at annual interest rate r (in decimal form) compounded continuously.

(b) Graph the functions

$$y_1 = \frac{\ln 2}{r}, \quad y_2 = \frac{70}{100\,r}, \quad \text{and} \quad y_3 = \frac{72}{100r}$$

in the $[0, 0.1]$ by $[0, 100]$ viewing window.

(c) **Writing to Learn** Explain why these two rules of thumb for mental computation are reasonable.

(d) Use the rules to estimate how long it takes to double money at 5% compounded continuously.

(e) Invent a rule for estimating the number of years needed to triple your money.

Standardized Test Questions

You may use a graphing calculator to solve the following problems.

47. True or False If $dy/dx = ky$, then $y = e^{kx} + C$. Justify your answer.

48. True or False The general solution to $dy/dt = 2y$ can be written in the form $y = C(3^{kt})$ for some constants C and k. Justify your answer.

49. Multiple Choice A bank account earning continuously compounded interest doubles in value in 7.0 years. At the same interest rate, how long would it take the value of the account to triple?

(A) 4.4 years   **(B)** 9.8 years   **(C)** 10.5 years

(D) 11.1 years   **(E)** 21.0 years

50. Multiple Choice A sample of Ce-143 (an isotope of cerium) loses 99% of its radioactive matter in 199 hours. What is the half-life of Ce-143?

(A) 4 hours   **(B)** 6 hours   **(C)** 30 hours

(D) 100.5 hours   **(E)** 143 hours

51. Multiple Choice In which of the following models is dy/dt directly proportional to y?

$$\text{I. } y = e^{kt} + C$$

$$\text{II. } y = Ce^{kt}$$

$$\text{III. } y = 28^{kt}$$

(A) I only   **(B)** II only   **(C)** I and II only

(D) II and III only   **(E)** I, II, and III

52. Multiple Choice An apple pie comes out of the oven at 425°F and is placed on a counter in a 68°F room to cool. In 30 minutes it has cooled to 195°F. According to Newton's Law of Cooling, how many additional minutes must pass before it cools to 100°F?

(A) 12.4   **(B)** 15.4   **(C)** 25.0   **(D)** 35.0   **(E)** 40.0

Explorations

53. Resistance Proportional to Velocity It is reasonable to assume that the air resistance encountered by a moving object, such as a car coasting to a stop, is proportional to the object's velocity. The resisting force on an object of mass m moving with velocity v is thus $-kv$ for some positive constant k.

(a) Use the law *Force = Mass × Acceleration* to show that the velocity of an object slowed by air resistance (and no other forces) satisfies the differential equation

$$m\frac{dv}{dt} = -kv$$

(b) Solve the differential equation to show that $v = v_0\, e^{-(k/m)t}$, where v_0 is the velocity of the object at time $t = 0$.

(c) If k is the same for two objects of different masses, which one will slow to half its starting velocity in the shortest time? Justify your answer.

54. Coasting to a Stop Assume that the resistance encountered by a moving object is proportional to the object's velocity so that its velocity is $v = v_0 e^{-(k/m)t}$.

(a) Integrate the velocity function with respect to t to obtain the distance function s. Assume that $s(0) = 0$ and show that

$$s(t) = \frac{v_0 m}{k}\left(1 - e^{-(k/m)t}\right).$$

(b) Show that the total coasting distance traveled by the object as it coasts to a complete stop is $v_0 m/k$.

55. Coasting to a Stop Table 7.1 shows the distance s (meters) coasted in t seconds by Kelly Schmitzer on her in-line skates. Her initial velocity was $v_0 = 1$ m/sec, her mass was $m = 49.90$ kg (110 lb), and her total coasting distance was 1.32 m. Find a model for her position function using the form in Exercise 54(a), and superimpose the graph of the function on a scatter plot of the data. (*Note:* You should use your calculator to find the value of k in the formula, but do not use your calculator to fit a regression curve to the data.)

TABLE 7.1   Kelly Schmitzer Skating Data

t (sec)	0	0.1	0.3	0.5	0.7	0.9	1.1	1.3	1.5	1.7
s (m)	0	0.07	0.22	0.36	0.49	0.60	0.71	0.81	0.89	0.97

t (sec)	1.9	2.1	2.3	2.5	2.7	2.9	3.1	3.3	3.5	3.7
s (m)	1.05	1.11	1.17	1.22	1.25	1.28	1.30	1.31	1.32	1.32

Source: Valerie Sharritts, St. Francis de Sales H.S., Columbus, OH.

Extending the Ideas

56. Continuously Compounded Interest

(a) Use tables to give a numerical argument that

$$\lim_{x \to \infty}\left(1 + \frac{1}{x}\right)^x = e.$$

Support your argument graphically.

(b) For several different values of r, give numerical and graphical evidence that

$$\lim_{x \to \infty}\left(1 + \frac{r}{x}\right)^x = e^r.$$

(c) Writing to Learn Explain why compounding interest over smaller and smaller periods of time leads to the concept of interest compounded continuously.

57. **_Skydiving_** If a body of mass m falling from rest under the action of gravity encounters an air resistance proportional to the square of the velocity, then the body's velocity $v(t)$ is modeled by the initial value problem

Differential equation: $m\dfrac{dv}{dt} = mg - kv^2,$

Initial condition: $v(0) = 0,$

where t represents time in seconds, g is the acceleration due to gravity, and k is a constant that depends on the body's aerodynamic properties and the density of the air. (We assume that the fall is short enough so that variation in the air's density will not affect the outcome.)

(a) Show that the function

$$v(t) = \sqrt{\frac{mg}{k}}\,\frac{e^{at} - e^{-at}}{e^{at} + e^{-at}},$$

where $a = \sqrt{gk/m}$, is a solution of the initial value problem.

(b) Find the body's limiting velocity, $\lim\limits_{t \to \infty} v(t)$.

(c) For a 160-lb skydiver ($mg = 160$), and with time in seconds and distance in feet, a typical value for k is 0.005. What is the diver's limiting velocity in feet per second? in miles per hour?

Skydivers can vary their limiting velocities by changing the amount of body area opposing the fall. Their velocities can vary from 94 to 321 miles per hour.

7.5 | Logistic Growth

You will be able to solve the logistic differential equation using the technique of partial fractions and then by the general formula.

- Logistic growth as a reasonable model for population growth
- The technique of partial fractions
- Solving a logistic differential equation by partial fractions
- Real-world applications of logistic growth
- The general logistic formula

How Populations Grow

In Section 7.4 we showed that when the rate of change of a population is directly proportional to the size of the population, the population grows exponentially. This seems like a reasonable model for population growth in the short term, but populations in nature cannot sustain exponential growth for very long. Available food, habitat, and living space are just a few of the constraints that will eventually impose limits on the growth of any real-world population.

EXPLORATION 1 Exponential Growth Revisited

Almost any algebra book will include a problem like this: A culture of bacteria in a Petri dish is doubling every hour. If there are 100 bacteria at time $t = 0$, how many bacteria will there be in 12 hours?

1. Answer the algebra question.
2. Suppose a textbook editor, seeking to add a little unit conversion to the problem to satisfy a reviewer, changes "12 hours" to "12 days" in the second edition of the textbook. What is the answer to the revised question?
3. Is the new answer reasonable? (*Hint:* It has been estimated that there are about 10^{79} atoms in the entire universe.)
4. Suppose the maximal sustainable population of bacteria in this Petri dish is 500,000 bacteria. How many hours will it take the bacteria to reach this population if the exponential model continues to hold?
5. The graph below shows what the graph of the population would look like if it were to remain exponential until hitting 500,000. Draw a more reasonable graph that shows how the population might approach 500,000 after growing exponentially up to the marked point.

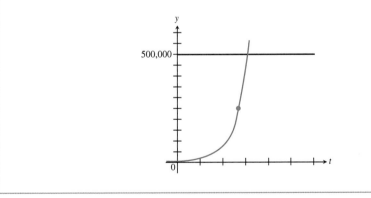

Logistic growth, which starts off exponentially and then changes concavity to approach a maximal sustainable population, is a better model for real-world populations, for all the reasons mentioned above.

Partial Fractions

Before we introduce the differential equation that describes logistic growth, we need to review a bit of algebra that is needed to solve it.

Partial Fraction Decomposition with Distinct Linear Denominators

If $f(x) = \dfrac{P(x)}{Q(x)}$, where P and Q are polynomials with the degree of P less than the degree of Q, and if $Q(x)$ can be written as a product of distinct linear factors, then $f(x)$ can be written as a sum of rational functions with distinct linear denominators.

We will illustrate this principle with examples.

EXAMPLE 1 Finding a Partial Fraction Decomposition

Write the function $f(x) = \dfrac{x - 13}{2x^2 - 7x + 3}$ as a sum of rational functions with linear denominators.

SOLUTION

Since $f(x) = \dfrac{x - 13}{(2x - 1)(x - 3)}$, we will find numbers A and B so that

$$f(x) = \frac{A}{2x - 1} + \frac{B}{x - 3}.$$

Note that $\dfrac{A}{2x - 1} + \dfrac{B}{x - 3} = \dfrac{A(x - 3) + B(2x - 1)}{(2x - 1)(x - 3)}$, so it follows that

$$A(x - 3) + B(2x - 1) = x - 13. \tag{1}$$

Setting $x = 3$ in equation (1), we get

$$A(0) + B(5) = -10, \text{ so } B = -2.$$

Setting $x = \dfrac{1}{2}$ in equation (1), we get

$$A\left(-\frac{5}{2}\right) + B(0) = -\frac{25}{2}, \text{ so } A = 5.$$

Therefore $f(x) = \dfrac{x - 13}{(2x - 1)(x - 3)} = \dfrac{5}{2x - 1} - \dfrac{2}{x - 3}.$

Now Try Exercise 3.

You might already have guessed that partial fraction decomposition can be of great value when antidifferentiating rational functions.

EXAMPLE 2 Antidifferentiating with Partial Fractions

Find $\displaystyle \int \frac{3x^4 + 1}{x^2 - 1} \, dx.$

SOLUTION

First we note that the degree of the numerator is not less than the degree of the denominator. We use the division algorithm to find the quotient and remainder:

$$
\begin{array}{r}
3x^2 + 3 \\
x^2 - 1 \overline{)\,3x^4 \qquad\quad + 1} \\
\underline{3x^4 - 3x^2} \qquad\quad \\
3x^2 + 1 \\
\underline{3x^2 - 3} \\
4
\end{array}
$$

continued

Thus

$$\int \frac{3x^4 + 1}{x^2 - 1} dx = \int \left(3x^2 + 3 + \frac{4}{x^2 - 1}\right) dx$$

$$= x^3 + 3x + \int \frac{4}{(x-1)(x+1)} dx$$

$$= x^3 + 3x + \int \left(\frac{A}{x-1} + \frac{B}{x+1}\right) dx$$

We know that $A(x + 1) + B(x - 1) = 4$.

Setting $x = 1$,

$$A(2) + B(0) = 4, \text{ so } A = 2.$$

Setting $x = -1$,

$$A(0) + B(-2) = 4, \text{ so } B = -2.$$

Thus

$$\int \frac{3x^4 + 1}{x^2 - 1} dx = x^3 + 3x + \int \left(\frac{2}{x-1} + \frac{-2}{x+1}\right) dx$$

$$= x^3 + 3x + 2 \ln |x - 1| - 2 \ln |x + 1| + C$$

$$= x^3 + 3x + 2 \ln \left|\frac{x-1}{x+1}\right| + C$$

Now Try Exercise 7.

EXAMPLE 3 Finding Three Partial Fractions

This example will be our most laborious problem.

Find the general solution to $\dfrac{dy}{dx} = \dfrac{6x^2 - 8x - 4}{(x^2 - 4)(x - 1)}$.

SOLUTION

$$y = \int \frac{6x^2 - 8x - 4}{(x-2)(x+2)(x-1)} dx = \int \left(\frac{A}{x-2} + \frac{B}{x+2} + \frac{C}{x-1}\right) dx.$$

We know that $A(x + 2)(x - 1) + B(x - 2)(x - 1) + C(x - 2)(x + 2) = 6x^2 - 8x - 4$.

Setting $x = 2$:

$$A(4)(1) + B(0) + C(0) = 4, \text{ so } A = 1.$$

Setting $x = -2$:

$$A(0) + B(-4)(-3) + C(0) = 36, \text{ so } B = 3.$$

Setting $x = 1$,

$$A(0) + B(0) + C(-1)(3) = -6, \text{ so } C = 2.$$

Thus

$$\int \frac{6x^2 - 8x - 4}{(x-2)(x+2)(x-1)} dx = \int \left(\frac{1}{x-2} + \frac{3}{x+2} + \frac{2}{x-1}\right) dx$$

$$= \ln |x - 2| + 3 \ln |x + 2| + 2 \ln |x - 1| + C$$

$$= \ln \left(|x - 2||x + 2|^3 |x - 1|^2\right) + C.$$

Now Try Exercise 17.

The technique of partial fractions can actually be extended to apply to all rational functions, but the method has to be adapted slightly if there are repeated linear factors or irreducible quadratic factors in the denominator. Both of these cases lead to partial fractions with quadratic denominators, and we will not deal with them in this book.

The Logistic Differential Equation

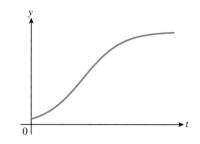

Figure 7.13 A logistic curve.

Now consider the case of a population P with a growth curve as a function of time that begins increasing and concave up (as in exponential growth), then turns increasing and concave down as it approaches the carrying capacity of its habitat. A **logistic curve,** like the one shown in Figure 7.13, has the shape to model this growth.

We have seen that the exponential growth at the beginning can be modeled by the differential equation

$$\frac{dP}{dt} = kP \text{ for some } k > 0.$$

If we want the growth rate to approach zero as P approaches a maximal **carrying capacity** M, we can introduce a limiting factor of $M - P$:

$$\frac{dP}{dt} = kP(M - P)$$

This is the **logistic differential equation.** Before we find its general solution, let us see how much we can learn about logistic growth just by studying the differential equation itself.

EXPLORATION 2 Learning from the Differential Equation

Consider a (positive) population P that satisfies $dP/dt = kP(M - P)$, where k and M are positive constants.

1. For what values of P will the growth rate dP/dt be close to zero?
2. As a function of P, $y = kP(M - P)$ has a graph that is an upside-down parabola. What is the value of P at the vertex of that parabola?
3. Use the answer to part (2) to explain why the growth rate is maximized when the population reaches half the carrying capacity.
4. If the initial population is less than M, is the initial growth rate positive or negative?
5. If the initial population is greater than M, is the initial growth rate positive or negative?
6. If the initial population equals M, what is the initial growth rate?
7. What is $\lim\limits_{t \to \infty} P(t)$? Does it depend on the initial population?

You can use the results of Exploration 2 in the following example.

EXAMPLE 4

The growth rate of a population P of bears in a newly established wildlife preserve is modeled by the differential equation $dP/dt = 0.008P(100 - P)$, where t is measured in years.

(a) What is the carrying capacity for bears in this wildlife preserve?

(b) What is the bear population when the population is growing the fastest?

(c) What is the rate of change of the population when it is growing the fastest?

continued

SOLUTION

(a) The carrying capacity is 100 bears.

(b) The bear population is growing the fastest when it is half the carrying capacity, 50 bears.

(c) When $P = 50$, $dP/dt = 0.008(50)(100 - 50) = 20$ bears per year. Although the derivative represents the instantaneous growth rate, it is reasonable to say that the population grows by about 20 bears that year.

Now Try Exercise 25.

In this next example we will find the solution to a logistic differential equation with an initial condition.

EXAMPLE 5 Tracking a Moose Population

In 1985 and 1987, the Michigan Department of Natural Resources airlifted 61 moose from Algonquin Park, Ontario, to Marquette County in the Upper Peninsula. It was originally hoped that the population P would reach carrying capacity in about 25 years with a growth rate of

$$\frac{dP}{dt} = 0.0003P(1000 - P).$$

(a) According to the model, what is the carrying capacity?

(b) With a calculator, generate a slope field for the differential equation.

(c) Solve the differential equation with the initial condition $P(0) = 61$ and show that it conforms to the slope field.

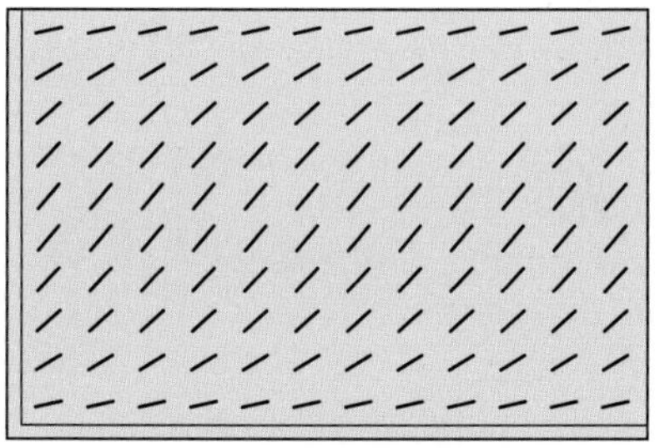

SOLUTION

(a) The carrying capacity is 1000 moose.

(b) The slope field is shown in Figure 7.14. Since the population approaches a horizontal asymptote at 1000 in about 25 years, we use the window $[0, 25]$ by $[0, 1000]$.

(c) After separating the variables, we encounter an antiderivative to be found using partial fractions.

$$\frac{dP}{P(1000 - P)} = 0.0003 \, dt$$

$$\int \frac{1}{P(1000 - P)} \, dP = \int 0.0003 \, dt$$

$$\int \left(\frac{A}{P} + \frac{B}{1000 - P}\right) dP = \int 0.0003 \, dt$$

We know that $A(1000 - P) + B(P) = 1$.

Setting $P = 0$: $A(1000) + B(0) = 1$, so $A = 0.001$.

Setting $P = 1000$: $A(0) + B(1000) = 1$, so $B = 0.001$.

continued

[0, 25] by [0, 1000]

Figure 7.14 The slope field for the moose differential equation in Example 5.

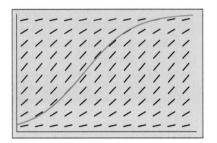

[0, 25] by [0, 1000]

Figure 7.15 The particular solution

$$P = \frac{1000}{1 + 15.393e^{-0.3t}}$$

conforms nicely to the slope field for
$dP/dt = 0.0003P(1000 - P)$.
(Example 5)

$$\int \left(\frac{0.001}{P} + \frac{0.001}{1000 - P} \right) dP = \int 0.0003 \, dt$$

$$\int \left(\frac{1}{P} + \frac{1}{1000 - P} \right) dP = \int 0.3 \, dt \qquad \text{Multiplied both integrals by 1000}$$

$$\ln P - \ln(1000 - P) = 0.3t + C$$

$$\ln(1000 - P) - \ln P = -0.3t - C$$

$$\ln \left(\frac{1000 - P}{P} \right) = -0.3t - C$$

$$\frac{1000}{P} - 1 = e^{-0.3t - C}$$

$$\frac{1000}{P} = 1 + e^{-0.3t} e^{-C}$$

Setting $P = 61$ and $t = 0$, we find that $e^{-C} \approx 15.393$. Thus

$$\frac{1000}{P} = 1 + 15.393e^{-0.3t}$$

$$P = \frac{1000}{1 + 15.393e^{-0.3t}}$$

The graph conforms nicely to the slope field, as shown in Figure 7.15.

Now Try Exercise 29.

Logistic Growth Models

We could solve many more logistic differential equations and the algebra would look the same every time. In fact, it is almost as simple to solve the equation using letters for all the constants, thereby arriving at a general formula. In Exercise 35 we will ask you to verify the result in the box below.

The General Logistic Formula

The solution of the general logistic differential equation

$$\frac{dP}{dt} = kP(M - P)$$

is

$$P = \frac{M}{1 + Ae^{-(Mk)t}}$$

where A is a constant determined by an appropriate initial condition. The **carrying capacity** M and the **logistic growth constant** k are positive constants.

EXAMPLE 6 Finding a Logistic Model Formulaically

The growth of the population of Aurora, CO, for the years between 1950 and 2003 was roughly logistic, satisfying the differential equation $\dfrac{dP}{dt} = P(0.1 - 3.125 \times 10^{-7}P)$.
Model the growth with a logistic function, using the initial condition $P(0) = 12{,}800$.

continued

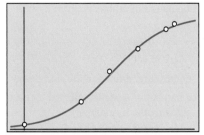

Figure 7.16 The logistic curve fits the data for population growth in Aurora, CO, from 1950 to 2003. (Example 6)

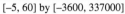

[−5, 60] by [−3600, 337000]

Figure 7.17 The slope field for the differential equation fits the data and the logistic curve nicely. (Example 6)

SOLUTION

First write the differential equation in the form $\dfrac{dP}{dt} = kP(M - P)$ by factoring

out 3.125×10^{-7}. Thus, $\dfrac{dP}{dt} = (3.125 \times 10^{-7})P(320{,}000 - P)$, and we see that

$k = 3.125 \times 10^{-7}$ and $M = 320{,}000$. By knowing the general solution to the differential equation, we can directly write

$$P = \frac{320{,}000}{1 + Ae^{-0.1t}}.$$

Finally, we use the initial condition to find A:

$$12{,}800 = \frac{320{,}000}{1 + Ae^{0}} \Rightarrow 1 + A = \frac{320{,}000}{12{,}800} \Rightarrow A = 24$$

The model that satisfies the initial value problem is $P(t) = \dfrac{320{,}000}{1 + 24e^{-0.1t}}.$

Figure 7.16 shows that this model fits a scatter plot of actual population data for Aurora in those years quite nicely. Figure 7.17 shows that the curve fits a slope field of the differential equation, as expected.

Now Try Exercise 33.

We caution readers once again not to assume that logistic models work perfectly in real-world problems involving population growth. For example, the curve in Example 6 that fits the Aurora data so well from 1950 to 2003 predicts a maximal population of 320,000, whereas the actual population of Aurora surpassed that number by 2010—and is still growing.

Quick Review 7.5 *(For help, go to Sections 2.2 and 2.3.)*

Exercise numbers with a gray background indicate problems that the authors have designed to be solved *without a calculator*.

In Exercises 1–4, use the polynomial division algorithm (as in Example 2 of this section) to write the rational function in the form $Q(x) + \dfrac{R(x)}{D(x)}$, where the degree of R is less than the degree of D.

1. $\dfrac{x^2}{x - 1}$

2. $\dfrac{x^2}{x^2 - 4}$

3. $\dfrac{x^2 + x + 1}{x^2 + x - 2}$

4. $\dfrac{x^3 - 5}{x^2 - 1}$

In Exercises 5–10, let $f(x) = \dfrac{60}{1 + 5e^{-0.1x}}$.

5. Find where f is continuous.

6. Find $\displaystyle\lim_{x \to \infty} f(x)$.

7. Find $\displaystyle\lim_{x \to -\infty} f(x)$.

8. Find the y-intercept of the graph of f.

9. Find all horizontal asymptotes of the graph of f.

10. Draw the graph of $y = f(x)$.

Section 7.5 Exercises

In Exercises 1–4, find the values of A and B that complete the partial fraction decomposition.

1. $\dfrac{x - 12}{x^2 - 4x} = \dfrac{A}{x} + \dfrac{B}{x - 4}$

2. $\dfrac{2x + 16}{x^2 + x - 6} = \dfrac{A}{x + 3} + \dfrac{B}{x - 2}$

3. $\dfrac{16 - x}{x^2 + 3x - 10} = \dfrac{A}{x - 2} + \dfrac{B}{x + 5}$

4. $\dfrac{3}{x^2 - 9} = \dfrac{A}{x - 3} + \dfrac{B}{x + 3}$

In Exercises 5–14, evaluate the integral.

5. $\int \dfrac{x - 12}{x^2 - 4x}\, dx$

6. $\int \dfrac{2x + 16}{x^2 + x - 6}\, dx$

7. $\int \dfrac{2x^3}{x^2 - 4}\, dx$

8. $\int \dfrac{x^2 - 6}{x^2 - 9}\, dx$

9. $\int \dfrac{2\, dx}{x^2 + 1}$

10. $\int \dfrac{3\, dx}{x^2 + 9}$

11. $\int \dfrac{7\, dx}{2x^2 - 5x - 3}$

12. $\int \dfrac{1 - 3x}{3x^2 - 5x + 2}\, dx$

13. $\int \dfrac{8x - 7}{2x^2 - x - 3}\, dx$

14. $\int \dfrac{5x + 14}{x^2 + 7x}\, dx$

In Exercises 15–18, solve the differential equation.

15. $\dfrac{dy}{dx} = \dfrac{2x - 6}{x^2 - 2x}$

16. $\dfrac{du}{dx} = \dfrac{2}{x^2 - 1}$

17. $F'(x) = \dfrac{2}{x^3 - x}$

18. $G'(t) = \dfrac{2t^3}{t^3 - t}$

In Exercises 19–22, find the integral *without* using the technique of partial fractions.

19. $\int \dfrac{2x}{x^2 - 4}\, dx$

20. $\int \dfrac{4x - 3}{2x^2 - 3x + 1}\, dx$

21. $\int \dfrac{x^2 + x - 1}{x^2 - x}\, dx$

22. $\int \dfrac{2x^3}{x^2 - 1}\, dx$

In Exercises 23–26, the logistic equation describes the growth of a population P, where t is measured in years. In each case, find **(a)** the carrying capacity of the population, **(b)** the size of the population when it is growing the fastest, and **(c)** the rate at which the population is growing when it is growing the fastest.

23. $\dfrac{dP}{dt} = 0.006P(200 - P)$

24. $\dfrac{dP}{dt} = 0.0008P(700 - P)$

25. $\dfrac{dP}{dt} = 0.0002P(1200 - P)$

26. $\dfrac{dP}{dt} = 10^{-5}P(5000 - P)$

In Exercises 27–30, solve the initial value problem using partial fractions. Use a graphing utility to generate a slope field for the differential equation and verify that the solution conforms to the slope field.

27. $\dfrac{dP}{dt} = 0.006P(200 - P)$ and $P = 8$ when $t = 0$.

28. $\dfrac{dP}{dt} = 0.0008P(700 - P)$ and $P = 10$ when $t = 0$.

29. $\dfrac{dP}{dt} = 0.0002P(1200 - P)$ and $P = 20$ when $t = 0$.

30. $\dfrac{dP}{dt} = 10^{-5}P(5000 - P)$ and $P = 50$ when $t = 0$.

In Exercises 31 and 32, a population function is given.

   (a) Show that the function is a solution of a logistic differential equation. Identify k and the carrying capacity.

   (b) Writing to Learn Estimate $P(0)$. Explain its meaning in the context of the problem.

31. *Rabbit Population* A population of rabbits is given by the formula

$$P(t) = \frac{1000}{1 + e^{4.8 - 0.7t}},$$

where t is the number of months after a few rabbits are released.

32. *Spread of Measles* The number of students infected by measles in a certain school is given by the formula

$$P(t) = \frac{200}{1 + e^{5.3 - t}},$$

where t is the number of days after students are first exposed to an infected student.

33. *Guppy Population* A 2000-gallon tank can support no more than 150 guppies. Six guppies are introduced into the tank. Assume that the rate of growth of the population is

$$\frac{dP}{dt} = 0.0015P(150 - P),$$

where time t is in weeks.

   (a) Find a formula for the guppy population in terms of t.

   (b) How long will it take for the guppy population to be 100? 125?

34. *Gorilla Population* A certain wild animal preserve can support no more than 250 lowland gorillas. Twenty-eight gorillas were known to be in the preserve in 1970. Assume that the rate of growth of the population is

$$\frac{dP}{dt} = 0.0004P(250 - P),$$

where time t is in years.

   (a) Find a formula for the gorilla population in terms of t.

   (b) How long will it take for the gorilla population to reach the carrying capacity of the preserve?

35. *Logistic Differential Equation* Show that the solution of the differential equation

$$\frac{dP}{dt} = kP(M - P) \quad \text{is} \quad P = \frac{M}{1 + Ae^{-Mkt}},$$

where A is a constant determined by an appropriate initial condition.

36. *Limited Growth Equation* Another differential equation that models limited growth of a population P in an environment with carrying capacity M is $dP/dt = k(M - P)$ (where $k > 0$ and $M > 0$).

   (a) Show that $P = M - Ae^{-kt}$, where A is a constant determined by an appropriate initial condition.

   (b) What is $\lim\limits_{t \to \infty} P(t)$?

   (c) For what time $t \geq 0$ is the population growing the fastest?

   (d) Writing to Learn How does the growth curve in this model differ from the growth curve in the logistic model?

37. *Growing Boys* Between the ages of 2 and 20, the weight W of an American boy is a logistic function of his age. For boys at the 50th percentile, the differential equation for W can be approximated by $dW/dt = 0.0008W(216 - W)$, where W is measured in pounds and t is measured in years beyond the age of 2. Express W as a function of t subject to the initial condition $W(0) = 24$.

38. *Growing Girls* Between the ages of 2 and 20, the weight W of an American girl is a logistic function of her age. For girls at the 50th percentile, the differential equation for W can be approximated by $dW/dt = 0.0015W(147 - W)$, where W is measured in pounds and t is measured in years beyond the age of 2. Express W as a function of t subject to the initial condition $W(0) = 24.5$.

Standardized Test Questions

39. True or False For small values of t, the solution to the logistic differential equation $dP/dt = kP(100 - P)$ that passes through the point $(0, 10)$ resembles the solution to the differential equation $dP/dt = kP$ that passes through the point $(0, 10)$. Justify your answer.

40. True or False If $0 < P(0) < M$, then the graph of the solution to the differential equation $dP/dt = kP(100 - P)$ has asymptotes $y = 0$ and $y = 100$. Justify your answer.

41. Multiple Choice The spread of a disease through a community can be modeled with the logistic equation

$$y = \frac{600}{1 + 59e^{-0.1t}},$$

where y is the number of people infected after t days. How many people are infected when the disease is spreading the fastest?

(A) 10   (B) 59   (C) 60   (D) 300   (E) 600

42. Multiple Choice The spread of a disease through a community can be modeled with the logistic equation

$$y = \frac{0.9}{1 + 45e^{-0.15t}},$$

where y is the proportion of people infected after t days. According to the model, what percentage of the people in the community will not become infected?

(A) 2%   (B) 10%   (C) 15%   (D) 45%   (E) 90%

43. Multiple Choice $\displaystyle\int_2^3 \frac{3}{(x - 1)(x + 2)} \, dx =$

(A) $-\dfrac{33}{20}$ (B) $-\dfrac{9}{20}$ (C) $\ln\left(\dfrac{5}{2}\right)$ (D) $\ln\left(\dfrac{8}{5}\right)$ (E) $\ln\left(\dfrac{2}{5}\right)$

44. Multiple Choice Which of the following differential equations would produce the slope field shown below?

(A) $\dfrac{dy}{dx} = 0.01x(120 - x)$ (B) $\dfrac{dy}{dx} = 0.01y(120 - y)$

(C) $\dfrac{dy}{dx} = 0.01y(100 - x)$ (D) $\dfrac{dy}{dx} = \dfrac{120}{1 + 60e^{-1.2x}}$

(E) $\dfrac{dy}{dx} = \dfrac{120}{1 + 60e^{-1.2y}}$

[−3, 8] by [−50, 150]

Explorations

45. *Extinct Populations* One theory states that if the size of a population falls below a minimum m, the population will become extinct. This condition leads to the *extended* logistic differential equation

$$\frac{dP}{dt} = kP\left(1 - \frac{P}{M}\right)\left(1 - \frac{m}{P}\right)$$

$$= \frac{k}{M}(M - P)(P - m),$$

with $k > 0$ the proportionality constant and M the population maximum.

(a) Show that dP/dt is positive for $m < P < M$ and negative if $P < m$ or $P > M$.

(b) Let $m = 100, M = 1200$, and assume that $m < P < M$. Show that the differential equation can be rewritten in the form

$$\left[\frac{1}{1200 - P} + \frac{1}{P - 100}\right]\frac{dP}{dt} = \frac{11}{12}k.$$

Use a procedure similar to that used in Example 5 in Section 7.5 to solve this differential equation.

(c) Find the solution to part (b) that satisfies $P(0) = 300$.

(d) Superimpose the graph of the solution in part (c) with $k = 0.1$ on a slope field of the differential equation.

(e) Solve the general extended differential equation with the restriction $m < P < M$.

46. *Integral Tables* Antiderivatives of various generic functions can be found as formulas in *integral tables*. See if you can derive the formulas that would appear in an integral table for the following functions. (Here, a is an arbitrary constant.)

(a) $\displaystyle\int \frac{dx}{a^2 + x^2}$ (b) $\displaystyle\int \frac{dx}{a^2 - x^2}$ (c) $\displaystyle\int \frac{dx}{(a + x)^2}$

Extending the Ideas

47. *Partial Fractions with Repeated Linear Factors*

If

$$f(x) = \frac{P(x)}{(x - r)^m}$$

is a rational function with the degree of P less than m, then the partial fraction decomposition of f is

$$f(x) = \frac{A_1}{x - r} + \frac{A_2}{(x - r)^2} + \cdots + \frac{A_m}{(x - r)^m}.$$

For example,

$$\frac{4x}{(x - 2)^2} = \frac{4}{x - 2} + \frac{8}{(x - 2)^2}.$$

Use partial fractions to find the following integrals:

(a) $\displaystyle\int \frac{5x}{(x + 3)^2} \, dx$

(b) $\displaystyle\int \frac{5x}{(x + 3)^3} \, dx$ [*Hint:* Use part (a).]

48. *More on Repeated Linear Factors* The Heaviside Method is not very effective at finding the unknown numerators for partial fraction decompositions with repeated linear factors, but here is another way to find them.

(a) If $\dfrac{x^2 + 3x + 5}{(x-1)^3} = \dfrac{A}{x-1} + \dfrac{B}{(x-1)^2} + \dfrac{C}{(x-1)^3}$, show

that $A(x-1)^2 + B(x-1) + C = x^2 + 3x + 5$.

(b) Expand and equate coefficients of like terms to show that $A = 1, -2A + B = 3$, and $A - B + C = 5$. Then find A, B, and C.

(c) Use partial fractions to evaluate $\displaystyle\int \dfrac{x^2 + 3x + 5}{(x-1)^3}\,dx$.

Quick Quiz: Sections 7.4 and 7.5

You may use a graphing calculator to solve the following problems.

1. Multiple Choice The rate at which acreage is being consumed by a plot of kudzu is proportional to the number of acres already consumed at time t. If there are 2 acres consumed when $t = 1$ and 3 acres consumed when $t = 5$, how many acres will be consumed when $t = 8$?

(A) 3.750   **(B)** 4.000   **(C)** 4.066   **(D)** 4.132   **(E)** 4.600

2. Multiple Choice Let $F(x)$ be an antiderivative of $\cos{(x^2)}$. If $F(1) = 0$, then $F(5) =$

(A) −0.099   **(B)** −0.153   **(C)** −0.293   **(D)** −0.992   **(E)** −1.833

3. Multiple Choice $\displaystyle\int \dfrac{dx}{(x-1)(x+3)} =$

(A) $\dfrac{1}{4}\ln\left|\dfrac{x-1}{x+3}\right| + C$ **(B)** $\dfrac{1}{4}\ln\left|\dfrac{x+3}{x-1}\right| + C$

(C) $\dfrac{1}{2}\ln|(x-1)(x+3)| + C$ **(D)** $\dfrac{1}{2}\ln\left|\dfrac{2x+2}{(x-1)(x+3)}\right| + C$

(E) $\ln|(x-1)(x+3)| + C$

4. Free Response A population is modeled by a function P that satisfies the logistic differential equation

$$\frac{dP}{dt} = \frac{P}{5}\left(1 - \frac{P}{10}\right).$$

(a) If $P(0) = 3$, what is $\displaystyle\lim_{t\to\infty} P(t)$?

(b) If $P(0) = 20$, what is $\displaystyle\lim_{t\to\infty} P(t)$?

(c) A different population is modeled by a function Y that satisfies the separable differential equation

$$\frac{dY}{dt} = \frac{Y}{5}\left(1 - \frac{t}{10}\right).$$

Find $Y(t)$ if $Y(0) = 3$.

(d) For the function Y found in part (c), what is $\displaystyle\lim_{t\to\infty} Y(t)$?

CHAPTER 7 **Key Terms**

antidifferentiation by parts (p. 349)
antidifferentiation by substitution (p. 343)
carbon-14 dating (p. 362)
carrying capacity (p. 374)
compounded continuously (p. 360)
constant of integration (p. 340)
continuous interest rate (p. 360)
differential equation (p. 329)
Euler's Method (p. 333)
evaluate an integral (p. 340)
exact differential equation (p. 329)
exponential decay constant (p. 359)
exponential growth constant (p. 359)
first-order differential equation (p. 329)
first-order linear differential
  equation (p. 332)
general solution to a differential
  equation (p. 329)

graphical solution of a differential
  equation (p. 330)
half-life (p. 360)
Heaviside Method (p. 370)
indefinite integral (p. 340)
initial condition (p. 329)
initial value problem (p. 329)
integral sign (p. 340)
integrand (p. 340)
integration by parts (p. 349)
Law of Exponential Change (p. 359)
Leibniz notation for integrals (p. 342)
logistic curve (p. 372)
logistic differential equation (p. 372)
logistic growth constant (p. 374)
logistic growth model (p. 374)
Newton's Law of Cooling (p. 363)
numerical method (p. 334)

numerical solution of a differential
  equation (p. 334)
order of a differential equation (p. 329)
partial fraction decomposition (p. 370)
particular solution (p. 329)
proper rational function (p. 370)
properties of indefinite integrals (p. 341)
radioactive (p. 360)
radioactive decay (p. 360)
resistance proportional to velocity (p. 367)
second-order differential equation (p. 339)
separable differential equations (p. 358)
separation of variables (p. 358)
slope field (p. 331)
solution of a differential equation (p. 329)
substitution in definite integrals (p. 345)
tabular integration (p. 352)
variable of integration (p. 340)

CHAPTER 7 Review Exercises

Exercise numbers with a gray background indicate problems that the authors have designed to be solved *without a calculator*.

The collection of exercises marked in red could be used as a chapter test.

In Exercises 1–10, evaluate the integral analytically. You may use NINT to support your result.

1. $\int_0^{\pi/3} \sec^2 \theta \, d\theta$

2. $\int_1^2 \left(x + \frac{1}{x^2} \right) dx$

3. $\int_0^1 \frac{36 \, dx}{(2x + 1)^3}$

4. $\int_{-1}^1 2x \sin (1 - x^2) \, dx$

5. $\int_0^{\pi/2} 5 \sin^{3/2} x \cos x \, dx$

6. $\int_{1/2}^4 \frac{x^2 + 3x}{x} \, dx$

7. $\int_0^{\pi/4} e^{\tan x} \sec^2 x \, dx$

8. $\int_1^e \frac{\sqrt{\ln r}}{r} \, dr$

9. $\int_0^1 \frac{x}{x^2 + 5x + 6} \, dx$

10. $\int_1^2 \frac{2x + 6}{x^2 - 3x} \, dx$

In Exercises 11–24, evaluate the integral.

11. $\int \frac{\cos x}{2 - \sin x} \, dx$

12. $\int \frac{dx}{\sqrt[3]{3x + 4}}$

13. $\int \frac{t \, dt}{t^2 + 5}$

14. $\int \frac{1}{\theta^2} \sec \frac{1}{\theta} \tan \frac{1}{\theta} \, d\theta$

15. $\int \frac{\tan (\ln y)}{y} \, dy$

16. $\int e^x \sec (e^x) \, dx$

17. $\int \frac{dx}{x \ln x}$

18. $\int \frac{dt}{t \sqrt{t}}$

19. $\int x^3 \cos x \, dx$

20. $\int x^4 \ln x \, dx$

21. $\int e^{3x} \sin x \, dx$

22. $\int x^2 e^{-3x} \, dx$

23. $\int \frac{25}{x^2 - 25} \, dx$

24. $\int \frac{5x + 2}{2x^2 + x - 1} \, dx$

In Exercises 25–34, solve the initial value problem analytically. Support your solution by overlaying its graph on a slope field of the differential equation.

25. $\frac{dy}{dx} = 1 + x + \frac{x^2}{2}, \quad y(0) = 1$

26. $\frac{dy}{dx} = \left(x + \frac{1}{x} \right)^2, \quad y(1) = 1$

27. $\frac{dy}{dt} = \frac{1}{t + 4}, \quad y(-3) = 2$

28. $\frac{dy}{d\theta} = \csc 2\theta \cot 2\theta, \quad y(\pi/4) = 1$

29. $\frac{d^2y}{dx^2} = 2x - \frac{1}{x^2}, \quad x > 0, \quad y'(1) = 1, \quad y(1) = 0$

30. $\frac{d^3r}{dt^3} = -\cos t, \quad r''(0) = r'(0) = r(0) = -1$

31. $\frac{dy}{dx} = y + 2, \quad y(0) = 2$

32. $\frac{dy}{dx} = (2x + 1)(y + 1), \quad y(-1) = 1$

33. $\frac{dy}{dt} = y(1 - y), \quad y(0) = 0.1$

34. $\frac{dy}{dx} = 0.001y(100 - y), \quad y(0) = 5$

35. Find an integral equation $y = \int_a^x f(t) \, dt + b$ such that $dy/dx = \sin^3 x$ and $y = 5$ when $x = 4$.

36. Find an integral equation $y = \int_a^x f(t) \, dt + b$ such that $dy/dx = \sqrt{1 + x^4}$ and $y = 2$ when $x = 1$.

In Exercises 37 and 38, construct a slope field for the differential equation. In each case, copy the graph shown and draw tiny segments through the twelve lattice points shown in the graph. Use slope analysis, not your graphing calculator.

37. $\frac{dy}{dx} = -x$

38. $\frac{dy}{dx} = 1 - y$

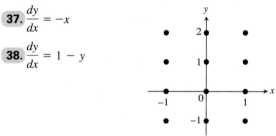

In Exercises 39–42, match the differential equation with the appropriate slope field. (All slope fields are shown in the window $[-6, 6]$ by $[-4, 4]$.)

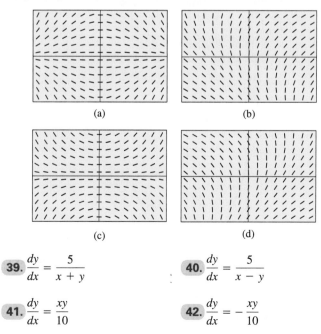

(a)

(b)

(c)

(d)

39. $\frac{dy}{dx} = \frac{5}{x + y}$

40. $\frac{dy}{dx} = \frac{5}{x - y}$

41. $\frac{dy}{dx} = \frac{xy}{10}$

42. $\frac{dy}{dx} = -\frac{xy}{10}$

43. Suppose $dy/dx = x + y - 1$ and $y = 1$ when $x = 1$. Use Euler's Method with increments of $\Delta x = 0.1$ to approximate the value of y when $x = 1.3$.

44. Suppose $dy/dx = x - y$ and $y = 2$ when $x = 1$. Use Euler's Method with increments of $\Delta x = -0.1$ to approximate the value of y when $x = 0.7$.

In Exercises 45 and 46, match the indefinite integral with the graph of one of the antiderivatives of the integrand.

45. $\displaystyle\int \frac{\sin x}{x}\, dx$ **46.** $\displaystyle\int e^{-x^2}\, dx$

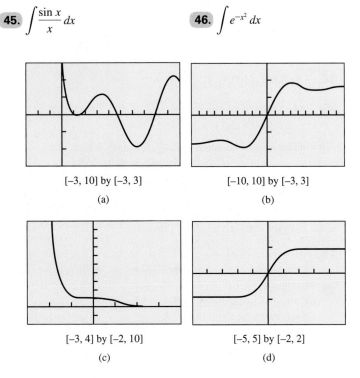

[–3, 10] by [–3, 3]
(a)

[–10, 10] by [–3, 3]
(b)

[–3, 4] by [–2, 10]
(c)

[–5, 5] by [–2, 2]
(d)

47. Writing to Learn The figure shows the graph of the function $y = f(x)$ that is the solution of one of the following initial value problems. Which one? How do you know?

    i. $dy/dx = 2x, \quad y(1) = 0$

    ii. $dy/dx = x^2, \quad y(1) = 1$

    iii. $dy/dx = 2x + 2, \quad y(1) = 1$

    iv. $dy/dx = 2x, \quad y(1) = 1$

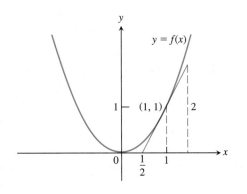

48. Writing to Learn Does the following initial value problem have a solution? Explain.

$$\frac{d^2y}{dx^2} = 0, \quad y'(0) = 1, \quad y(0) = 0$$

49. Moving Particle The acceleration of a particle moving along a coordinate line is

$$\frac{d^2s}{dt^2} = 2 + 6t \text{ m/sec}^2.$$

At $t = 0$ the velocity is 4 m/sec.

(a) Find the velocity as a function of time t.

(b) How far does the particle move during the first second of its trip, from $t = 0$ to $t = 1$?

50. Sketching Solutions Draw a possible graph for the function $y = f(x)$ with slope field given in the figure that satisfies the initial condition $y(0) = 0$.

[–10, 10] by [–10, 10]

51. Californium-252 What costs $27 million per gram and can be used to treat brain cancer, analyze coal for its sulfur content, and detect explosives in luggage? The answer is californium-252, a radioactive isotope so rare that only about 8 g of it have been made in the Western world since its discovery by Glenn Seaborg in 1950. The half-life of the isotope is 2.645 years—long enough for a useful service life and short enough to have a high radioactivity per unit mass. One microgram of the isotope releases 170 million neutrons per second.

(a) What is the value of k in the decay equation for this isotope?

(b) What is the isotope's mean life? (See Exercise 29, Section 7.4.)

52. Cooling a Pie A deep-dish apple pie, whose internal temperature was 220°F when removed from the oven, was set out on a 40°F breezy porch to cool. Fifteen minutes later, the pie's internal temperature was 180°F. How long did it take the pie to cool from there to 70°F?

53. Finding Temperature A pan of warm water (46°C) was put into a refrigerator. Ten minutes later, the water's temperature was 39°C; 10 minutes after that, it was 33°C. Use Newton's Law of Cooling to estimate how cold the refrigerator was.

54. Art Forgery A painting attributed to Vermeer (1632–1675), which should contain no more than 96.2% of its original carbon-14, contains 99.5% instead. About how old is the forgery?

55. *Carbon-14* What is the age of a sample of charcoal in which 90% of the carbon-14 that was originally present has decayed?

56. *Appreciation* A violin made in 1785 by John Betts, one of England's finest violin makers, cost $250 in 1924 and sold for $7500 in 1988. Assuming a constant relative rate of appreciation, what was that rate?

57. *Working Underwater* The intensity $L(x)$ of light x feet beneath the surface of the ocean satisfies the differential equation

$$\frac{dL}{dx} = -kL,$$

where k is a constant. As a diver you know from experience that diving to 18 ft in the Caribbean Sea cuts the intensity in half. You cannot work without artificial light when the intensity falls below a tenth of the surface value. About how deep can you expect to work without artificial light?

58. *Transport Through a Cell Membrane* Under certain conditions, the result of the movement of a dissolved substance across a cell's membrane is described by the equation

$$\frac{dy}{dt} = k\frac{A}{V}(c - y),$$

where y is the concentration of the substance inside the cell, and dy/dt is the rate with which y changes over time. The letters k, A, V, and c stand for constants, k being the *permeability coefficient* (a property of the membrane), A the surface area of the membrane, V the cell's volume, and c the concentration of the substance outside the cell. The equation says that the rate at which the concentration changes within the cell is proportional to the difference between it and the outside concentration.

(a) Solve the equation for $y(t)$, using $y_0 = y(0)$.

(b) Find the steady-state concentration, $\lim_{t\to\infty} y(t)$.

59. *Logistic Equation* The spread of flu in a certain school is given by the formula

$$P(t) = \frac{150}{1 + e^{4.3-t}},$$

where t is the number of days after students are first exposed to infected students.

(a) Show that the function is a solution of a logistic differential equation. Identify k and the carrying capacity.

(b) *Writing to Learn* Estimate $P(0)$. Explain its meaning in the context of the problem.

(c) Estimate the number of days it will take for a total of 125 students to become infected.

60. *Confirming a Solution* Show that

$$y = \int_0^x \sin\left(t^2\right) dt + x^3 + x + 2$$

is the solution of the initial value problem.

Differential equation: $y'' = 2x\cos\left(x^2\right) + 6x$

Initial conditions: $y'(0) = 1, \quad y(0) = 2$

61. *Finding an Exact Solution* Use analytic methods to find the exact solution to

$$\frac{dP}{dt} = 0.002P\left(1 - \frac{P}{800}\right), \quad P(0) = 50.$$

62. *Supporting a Solution* Give two ways to provide graphical support for the integral formula

$$\int x^2 \ln x \, dx = \frac{x^3}{3}\ln x - \frac{x^3}{9} + C.$$

63. *Doubling Time* Find the amount of time required for $10,000 to double if the 6.3% annual interest is compounded **(a)** annually, **(b)** continuously.

64. *Constant of Integration* Let

$$f(x) = \int_0^x u(t)\, dt \quad \text{and} \quad g(x) = \int_3^x u(t)\, dt.$$

(a) Show that f and g are antiderivatives of $u(x)$.

(b) Find a constant C so that $f(x) = g(x) + C$.

65. *Putting a Solution Through a Slope Field* Consider the differential equation $dy/dx = (3 - y)\cos x$. Let $y = f(x)$ be the particular solution to the differential equation with initial condition $f(0) = 1$. The function f is defined for all real numbers.

(a) A portion of the slope field of the differential equation is shown below. Use the slope field to sketch the solution curve through the point $(0, 1)$.

(b) Write an equation for the line tangent to the solution given in part (a) at the point $(0, 1)$. Use the equation to approximate $f(0.2)$.

(c) Find the particular solution to the differential equation with initial condition $f(0) = 1$.

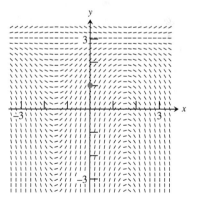

66. *One Last Differential Equation* Consider the differential equation $dy/dx = e^y(3x^2 - 6x)$. Let $y = f(x)$ be the particular solution to the differential equation that passes through $(1, 0)$.

(a) Write an equation for the line tangent to the graph of f at the point $(1, 0)$. Use the tangent line to approximate $f(1.2)$.

(b) Find the particular solution to the differential equation that passes through $(1, 0)$.

AP* Examination Preparation

You may use a graphing calculator to solve the following problems.

67. The spread of a rumor through a small town is modeled by $dy/dt = 1.2y(1 - y)$, where y is the proportion of the townspeople who have heard the rumor at time t in days. At time $t = 0$, ten percent of the townspeople have heard the rumor.

   (a) What proportion of the townspeople have heard the rumor when it is spreading the fastest?

   (b) Find y explicitly as a function of t.

   (c) At what time t is the rumor spreading the fastest?

68. A population P of wolves at time t years $(t \geq 0)$ is increasing at a rate directly proportional to $600 - P$, where the constant of proportionality is k.

   (a) If $P(0) = 200$, find $P(t)$ in terms of t and k.

   (b) If $P(2) = 500$, find k.

   (c) Find $\lim_{t \to \infty} P(t)$.

69. Let $v(t)$ be the velocity, in feet per second, of a skydiver at time t seconds, $t \geq 0$. After her parachute opens, her velocity satisfies the differential equation $dv/dt = -2(v + 17)$, with initial condition $v(0) = -47$.

   (a) Use separation of variables to find an expression for v in terms of t, where t is measured in seconds.

   (b) Terminal velocity is defined as $\lim_{t \to \infty} v(t)$. Find the terminal velocity of the skydiver to the nearest foot per second.

   (c) It is safe to land when her speed is 20 feet per second. At what time t does she reach this speed?

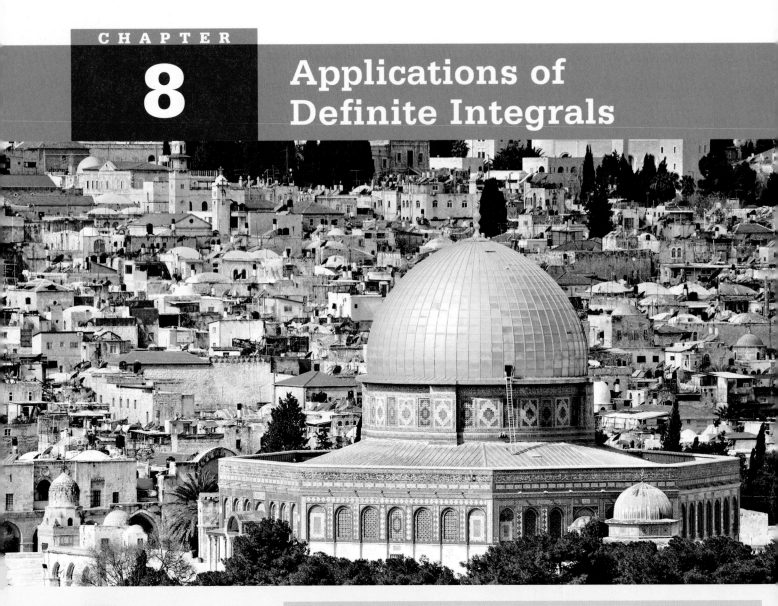

CHAPTER
8 Applications of Definite Integrals

8.1 Accumulation and Net Change

8.2 Areas in the Plane

8.3 Volumes

8.4 Lengths of Curves

8.5 Applications from Science and Statistics

Ever since antiquity, scientists, architects, and engineers have searched for a simple way to calculate the volume of solids that have rotational symmetry, such as the cylinder and cone. Around 250 B.C.E., Archimedes discovered the formula for the volume of a sphere and considered it his proudest accomplishment. One of the greatest advances in our ability to find these volumes occurred over a thousand years ago when Abu Ali al-Hasan ibn al-Haytham (c. 965–1040) discovered how to compute the volume of the shape obtained by rotating the curve $y = b\sqrt{x/a}$, $0 \le x \le a$, around the line $x = a$, a shape that can be found today in the dome of many Islamic mosques. In Section 8.3, we will see how to calculate the volume of this and other solids.

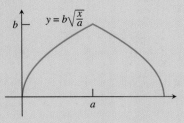

CHAPTER 8 **Overview**

By this point it should be apparent that finding the limits of Riemann sums is not just an intellectual exercise; it is a natural way to calculate mathematical or physical quantities that appear to be irregular when viewed as a whole, but which can be fragmented into regular pieces. We calculate values for the regular pieces using known formulas, then sum them to find a value for the irregular whole. This approach to problem solving was around for thousands of years before calculus came along, but it was tedious work and the more accurate you wanted to be the more tedious it became.

With calculus it became possible to get *exact* answers for these problems with almost no effort, because in the limit these sums became definite integrals and definite integrals could be evaluated with antiderivatives. With calculus, the challenge became one of fitting an integrable function to the situation at hand (the "modeling" step) and then finding an antiderivative for it.

Today we can finesse the antidifferentiation step (occasionally an insurmountable hurdle for our predecessors) with programs like NINT, but the modeling step is no less crucial. Ironically, it is the modeling step that is thousands of years old. Before either calculus or technology can be of assistance, we must still break down the irregular whole into regular parts and set up a function to be integrated. We have already seen how the process works with area, volume, and average value, for example. Now we will focus more closely on the underlying modeling step: how to set up the function to be integrated.

8.1 Accumulation and Net Change

You will be able to apply the definite integral to problems involving motion and use the definite integral to solve problems involving accumulation.

- Displacement as integral of velocity
- Total distance as integral of absolute value of velocity
- Modeling accumulation using Riemann sum approximations
- Interpretation of limits of Riemann sums as definite integrals
- Finding net change given graphical and/or tabular representations of rate of change

Linear Motion Revisited

In many applications, the integral is viewed as net change over time. The classic example of this kind is distance traveled, a problem we discussed in Chapter 6.

EXAMPLE 1 Interpreting a Velocity Function

Figure 8.1 shows the velocity

$$\frac{ds}{dt} = v(t) = t^2 - \frac{8}{(t+1)^2} \quad \frac{\text{cm}}{\text{sec}}$$

of a particle moving along a horizontal *s*-axis for $0 \le t \le 5$. Describe the motion.

SOLUTION

The graph of *v* (Figure 8.1) starts with $v(0) = -8$, which we interpret as saying that the particle has an initial velocity of 8 cm/sec to the left. It slows to a halt at about $t = 1.25$ sec, after which it moves to the right ($v > 0$) with increasing speed, reaching a velocity of $v(5) \approx 24.8$ cm/sec at the end. ***Now Try Exercise 1(a).***

At a constant velocity, displacement—the distance an object has moved from its starting position—is simply velocity times time. If the velocity is not constant and we want to find $s(a) - s(0)$, the displacement over the time interval $t = 0$ to $t = a$, we can partition the time interval into small increments, Δt, evaluate the velocity at some point on each interval, $v(t_k)$, and approximate the displacement over each time interval by $v(t_k)\Delta t$. Adding these up, we get a Riemann sum approximation to the displacement

$$s(a) - s(0) \approx \sum v(t_k)\Delta t,$$

which becomes the definite integral representing the exact value of the displacement

$$s(a) - s(0) = \int_0^a v(t)\, dt$$

in the limit as Δt approaches 0.

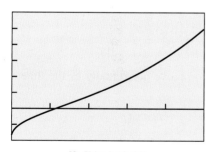

[0, 5] by [−10, 30]

Figure 8.1 The velocity function in Example 1.

Reminder from Section 3.4

A change in position is a **displacement.** If $s(t)$ is a body's position at time t, the displacement over the time interval from t to $t + \Delta t$ is $s(t + \Delta t) - s(t)$. The displacement may be positive, negative, or zero, depending on the motion.

EXAMPLE 2 **Finding Position from Displacement**

Suppose the initial position of the particle in Example 1 is $s(0) = 9$. What is the particle's position at (a) $t = 1$ sec? (b) $t = 5$ sec?

SOLUTION

(a) Displacement from time $t = 0$ to $t = 1$ is the definite integral of velocity,

$$\text{Displacement} = \int_0^1 v(t)\, dt$$

$$= \int_0^1 \left(t^2 - \frac{8}{(t+1)^2} \right) dt$$

$$= \left[\frac{t^3}{3} + \frac{8}{t+1} \right]_0^1$$

$$= \frac{1}{3} + \frac{8}{2} - 8 = -\frac{11}{3}$$

During the first second of motion, the particle moves $11/3$ cm to the left. It starts at $s(0) = 9$, so its position at $t = 1$ is

$$\text{New position} = \text{initial position} + \text{displacement} = 9 - \frac{11}{3} = \frac{16}{3}.$$

(b) If we model the displacement from $t = 0$ to $t = 5$ in the same way, we arrive at

$$\text{Displacement} = \int_0^5 v(t)\, dt = \left[\frac{t^3}{3} + \frac{8}{t+1} \right]_0^5 = 35.$$

The motion has the net effect of displacing the particle 35 cm to the right of its starting point. The particle's final position is

$$\text{Final position} = \text{initial position} + \text{displacement}$$
$$= s(0) + 35 = 9 + 35 = 44.$$

Now Try Exercise 1(b).

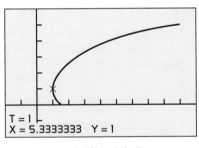

[–10, 50] by [–2, 6]

(a)

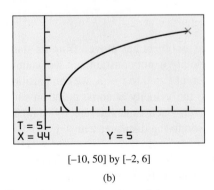

[–10, 50] by [–2, 6]

(b)

Figure 8.2 Using TRACE and the parametrization in Exploration 1 you can "see" the left and right motion of the particle.

EXPLORATION 1 Revisiting Example 2

The position of the particle in Example 1 at time t is its initial position plus its displacement,

$$s(t) = 9 + \int_0^t \left(u^2 - \frac{8}{(u+1)^2} \right) du$$

$$= 9 + \left[\frac{u^3}{3} + \frac{8}{u+1} \right]_0^t$$

$$= 9 + \left(\frac{t^3}{3} + \frac{8}{t+1} \right) - 8 = 1 + \frac{t^3}{3} + \frac{8}{t+1}$$

Using a parametric plot, we can watch the position move horizontally as the time variable moves vertically by setting

$$x(t) = 1 + t^3/3 + 8/(t+1), \quad y(t) = t$$

(See Figure 8.2).

Use both the function $s(t)$ and the TRACE feature to determine the position of the particle at times $t = 1$ and $t = 5$. Compare your answers with the answers to Example 2.

We know now that the particle in Example 1 was at $s(0) = 9$ at the beginning of the motion and at $s(5) = 44$ at the end. But it did not travel from 9 to 44 directly—it began its trip by moving to the left (Figure 8.2). How much distance did the particle actually travel? We find out in Example 3.

EXAMPLE 3   Calculating Total Distance Traveled

Find the *total distance traveled* by the particle in Example 1.

SOLUTION

We approximate the total distance with a Riemann sum in which each position shift is *positive,* so we use the absolute value of the velocity. The Riemann sum is

$$\sum |v(t_k)| \Delta t,$$

and we are led to the integral

$$\text{Total distance traveled} = \int_0^5 |v(t)| \, dt = \int_0^5 \left| t^2 - \frac{8}{(t+1)^2} \right| \, dt.$$

We can evaluate this numerically,

$$\text{NINT}\left(\left| t^2 - \frac{8}{(t+1)^2} \right|, t, 0, 5 \right) \approx 42.59.$$

We also can evaluate this by integrating $-v(t)$, where v is negative, and $v(t)$, where v is positive:

$$\text{Total distance traveled} = -\int_0^{1.25} v(t)dt + \int_{1.25}^5 v(t)dt$$

$$= -(s(1.25) - s(0)) + (s(5) - s(1.25)) \approx 42.59$$

Now Try Exercise 1(c).

What we learn from Examples 2 and 3 is this: Integrating velocity gives displacement (net area between the velocity curve and the time axis). Integrating the *absolute value* of velocity gives total distance traveled (total area between the velocity curve and the time axis).

General Strategy

The idea of fragmenting net effects into finite sums of easily estimated small changes is not new. We used it in Section 6.1 to estimate snowfall, distance, volume, and cardiac output. What *is* new is that we can now identify many of these sums as Riemann sums and express their limits as integrals. The advantages of doing so are twofold. First, we can evaluate one of these integrals to get an accurate result in less time than it takes to crank out even the crudest estimate from a finite sum. Second, the integral itself becomes a formula that enables us to solve similar problems without having to repeat the modeling step.

The strategy that we began in Section 6.1 and have continued here is the following:

Strategy for Modeling with Integrals

1. *Approximate what you want to find as a Riemann sum* of values of a continuous function multiplied by interval lengths. If $f(x)$ is the function and $[a, b]$ the interval, and you partition the interval into subintervals of length Δx, the approximating sums will have the form $\sum f(c_k)\Delta x$ with c_k a point in the kth subinterval.

2. *Write a definite integral,* here $\int_a^b f(x) \, dx$, to express the limit of these sums as the norms of the partitions go to zero.

3. *Evaluate the integral* numerically or with an antiderivative.

EXAMPLE 4 Modeling the Effects of Acceleration

A car moving with initial velocity of 5 mph accelerates at the rate of $a(t) = 2.4t$ mph per second for 8 seconds.

(a) How fast is the car going when the 8 seconds are up?

(b) How far did the car travel during those 8 seconds?

SOLUTION

(a) We first model the effect of the acceleration on the car's velocity.

Step 1:

Approximate the net change in velocity as a Riemann sum. When acceleration is constant,

$$\text{velocity change} = \text{acceleration} \times \text{time applied.} \quad \text{Rate of change} \times \text{time}$$

To apply this formula, we partition $[0, 8]$ into short subintervals of length Δt. On each subinterval the acceleration is nearly constant, so if t_k is any point in the kth subinterval, the change in velocity imparted by the acceleration in the subinterval is approximately

$$a(t_k)\,\Delta t \text{ mph.} \quad \frac{\text{mph}}{\text{sec}} \times \text{sec}$$

The net change in velocity for $0 \le t \le 8$ is approximately

$$\sum a(t_k)\,\Delta t \text{ mph.}$$

Step 2:

Write a definite integral. The limit of these sums as the norms of the partitions go to zero is

$$\int_0^8 a(t)\,dt.$$

Step 3:

Evaluate the integral. Using an antiderivative, we have

$$\text{Net velocity change} = \int_0^8 2.4t\,dt = 1.2t^2 \Big]_0^8 = 76.8 \text{ mph.}$$

So, how fast is the car going when the 8 seconds are up? Its initial velocity is 5 mph and the acceleration adds another 76.8 mph for a total of 81.8 mph.

(b) There is nothing special about the upper limit 8 in the preceding calculation. Applying the acceleration for any length of time t adds

$$\int_0^t 2.4u\,du \text{ mph} \quad u \text{ is just a dummy variable here.}$$

to the car's velocity, giving

$$v(t) = 5 + \int_0^t 2.4\,u\,du = 5 + 1.2t^2 \text{ mph.}$$

The distance traveled from $t = 0$ to $t = 8$ sec is

$$\int_0^8 |v(t)|\,dt = \int_0^8 (5 + 1.2t^2)\,dt \quad \text{Extension of Example 3}$$

$$= \Big[5t + 0.4t^3\Big]_0^8$$

$$= 244.8 \text{ mph} \times \text{seconds} \qquad \qquad \textit{continued}$$

Miles-per-hour second is not a distance unit that we normally work with! To convert to miles we multiply by hours/second = $1/3600$, obtaining

$$244.8 \times \frac{1}{3600} = 0.068 \text{ mile.} \qquad \frac{\text{mi}}{\text{h}} \times \text{sec} \times \frac{\text{h}}{\text{sec}} = \text{mi}$$

The car traveled $0.068 \text{ mi} \approx 359$ ft during the 8 seconds of acceleration.

Now Try Exercise 9.

Consumption over Time

The integral is a natural tool to calculate net change and total **accumulation** of more quantities than just distance and velocity. Integrals can be used to calculate growth, decay, and, as in the next example, consumption. Whenever you want to find the cumulative effect of a varying rate of change, integrate it.

EXAMPLE 5 Potato Consumption

From 1970 to 1980, the rate of potato consumption in a particular country was $C(t) = 2.2 + 1.1^t$ millions of bushels per year, with t being years since the beginning of 1970. How many bushels were consumed from the beginning of 1972 to the end of 1973?

SOLUTION

We seek the cumulative effect of the consumption rate for $2 \le t \le 4$.

Step 1:
Riemann sum. We partition $[2, 4]$ into subintervals of length Δt and let t_k be a time in the kth subinterval. The amount consumed during this interval is approximately

$$C(t_k)\Delta t \quad \text{million bushels.}$$

The consumption for $2 \le t \le 4$ is approximately

$$\sum C(t_k)\Delta t \quad \text{million bushels.}$$

Step 2:
Definite integral. The amount consumed from $t = 2$ to $t = 4$ is the limit of these sums as the norms of the partitions go to zero.

$$\int_2^4 C(t)\, dt = \int_2^4 (2.2 + 1.1^t)\, dt \quad \text{million bushels}$$

Step 3:
Evaluate. Evaluating numerically, we obtain

$$\text{NINT}\,(2.2 + 1.1^t, t, 2, 4) \approx 7.066 \quad \text{million bushels.} \qquad \textit{Now Try Exercise 21.}$$

Coming and Going

Many problems involve simultaneous flows in and out. To find the net change, we need to consider both how much is added and how much is removed. The following example also shows how to work with rates that are given graphically.

EXAMPLE 6 At the Amusement Park

From noon until 6 P.M., the rate at which people enter an amusement park at time t is given by $E(t)$, for which the graph is shown in Figure 8.3, where $t = 0$ corresponds to noon and $t = 6$ is 6 P.M. People are also leaving at the rate $L(t) = 50(2 + t^2\, e^{-t/5})$. If 3000 people are in the park at noon, how many people are in the park at 6 P.M., rounded to the nearest multiple of 100?

continued

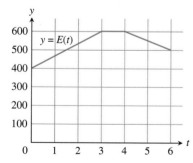

Figure 8.3 The graph of $y = E(t)$, with t measuring hours after noon and y measuring the rate at which people are entering the park in people per hour.

SOLUTION

The number of people who enter the park between noon and 6 P.M. is the integral of $E(t)$ from $t = 0$ to $t = 6$, which is the area under the graph of $y = E(t)$,

$$\text{Number of people who enter the park} = \int_0^6 E(t)\, dt.$$

From noon to 3 P.M., the area of the trapezoid is 1500, from 3 to 4 P.M. the area is 600, and from 4 to 6 P.M. the area is 1100, totaling 3200. The units are people/hours × hours = people. A total of 3200 people enter the park from noon until 6 P.M.

To the nearest person, the number of people who leave the park is

$$\int_0^6 50(2 + t^2 e^{-t/5})\, dt = 2106 \text{ people.}$$

The number of people in the park at 6 P.M. is the number we started with plus the number who entered minus the number who left,

$$3000 + 3200 - 2106 = 4094 \text{ people.}$$

To the nearest multiple of 100, there are 4100 people in the park at 6 P.M.

Now Try Exercise 23.

Net Change from Data

Many real applications begin with data, not a fully modeled function. In the next example, we are given data on the rate at which a pump operates in consecutive 5-minute intervals and asked to find the total amount pumped.

TABLE 8.1 Pumping Rates	
Time (min)	Rate (gal/min)
0	58
5	60
10	65
15	64
20	58
25	57
30	55
35	55
40	59
45	60
50	60
55	63
60	63

EXAMPLE 7 Finding Gallons Pumped from Rate Data

A pump connected to a generator operates at a varying rate, depending on how much power is being drawn from the generator to operate other machinery. The rate (gallons per minute) at which the pump operates is recorded at 5-minute intervals for one hour as shown in Table 8.1. How many gallons were pumped during that hour?

SOLUTION

Let $R(t)$, $0 \le t \le 60$, be the pumping rate as a continuous function of time for the hour. We can partition the hour into short subintervals of length Δt on which the rate is nearly constant and form the sum $\sum R(t_k)\, \Delta t$ as an approximation to the amount pumped during the hour. This reveals the integral formula for the number of gallons pumped to be

$$\text{Gallons pumped} = \int_0^{60} R(t)\, dt.$$

We have no formula for R in this instance, but the 13 equally spaced values in Table 8.1 enable us to estimate the integral with the Trapezoidal Rule:

$$\int_0^{60} R(t)\, dt \approx \frac{60}{2 \cdot 12}\left[58 + 2(60) + 2(65) + \cdots + 2(63) + 63 \right]$$

$$= 3582.5$$

The total amount pumped during the hour is about 3580 gal. *Now Try Exercise 27.*

Density

EXAMPLE 8 A Gopher Problem

A ten-mile stretch of rural Minnesota road is bounded on the north by colonies of pocket gophers. Along the road, the density of the gopher population is 500 per square mile. The density increases linearly until it reaches 2000 per square mile three miles from the road. Find the total population of gophers in this stretch of land that is ten miles long and three miles wide.

SOLUTION

Step 1:

Riemann Sum. Let y be the distance from the road. We divide the land into narrow strips, each 10 miles long and Δy miles wide (Figure 8.4). Let y_k be the distance from the road in the kth strip. Let $P(y)$ be the population density at distance y from the road. Because population density is a linear function of y that is 500 when $y = 0$ and 2000 when $y = 3$, we know that

$$P(y) = 500 + 500\,y.$$

Now we can construct our Riemann sum. The total number of gophers in the kth strip is the population density times the area of the strip,

$$(500 + 500y_k) \times 10\,\Delta y,$$

and the Riemann sum is

$$\sum (5000 + 5000y_k)\Delta y.$$

Steps 2 and 3:

Integrate. The limit of these sums as Δy approaches 0 is

$$\int_0^3 (5000 + 5000y)\,dy = \left[5000y + 2500y^2 \right]_0^3 = 37{,}500 \text{ gophers.}$$

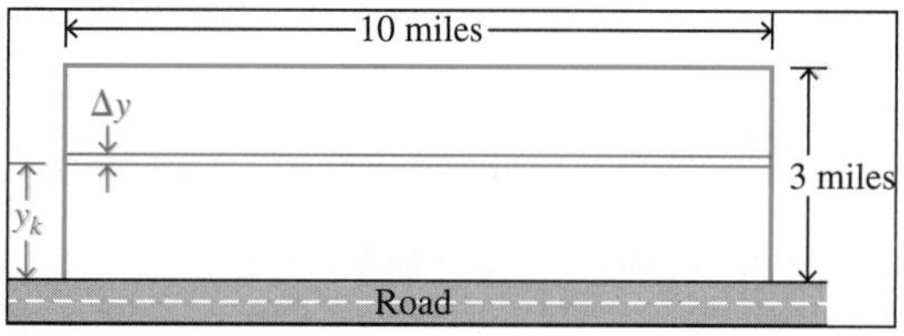

Figure 8.4 The ten-mile stretch of land with pocket gophers, showing the long, narrow strip in which the gopher population density is close to $P(y_k)$. ***Now Try Exercise 31.***

Now Try Exercise 31.

Joules

The **joule**, abbreviated J and pronounced "jewel," is named after the English physicist James Prescott Joule (1818–1889). The defining equation is

1 joule = (1 newton)(1 meter).

In symbols, 1 J = 1 N · m.

It takes a force of about 1 N to lift an apple from a table. If you lift it 1 m you have done about 1 J of work on the apple. If you eat the apple, you will have consumed about 80 food calories, the heat equivalent of nearly 335,000 joules. If this energy were directly useful for mechanical work (it's not), it would enable you to lift 335,000 more apples up 1 m.

Work

In everyday life, *work* means an activity that requires muscular or mental effort. In science, the term refers specifically to a force acting on a body and the body's subsequent displacement. When a body moves a distance d along a straight line as a result of the action of a force of constant magnitude F in the direction of motion, the **work** done by the force is

$$W = Fd.$$

The equation $W = Fd$ is the **constant-force formula** for work.

The units of work are force $\times$ distance. In the metric system, the unit is the newton-meter, which, for historical reasons, is called a joule (see margin note). In the U.S. customary system, the most common unit of work is the **foot-pound.**

Hooke's Law for springs says that the force it takes to stretch or compress a spring x units from its natural (unstressed) length is a constant times x. In symbols,

$$F = kx,$$

where k, measured in force units per unit length, is a characteristic of the spring called the **force constant.**

EXAMPLE 9 A Bit of Work

It takes a force of 10 N to stretch a spring 2 m beyond its natural length. How much work is done in stretching the spring 4 m from its natural length?

SOLUTION

We let $F(x)$ represent the force in newtons required to stretch the spring x meters from its natural length. By Hooke's Law, $F(x) = kx$ for some constant k. We are told that

$$F(2) = 10 = k \cdot 2, \qquad \text{The force required to stretch the spring 2 m is 10 newtons.}$$

so $k = 5$ N/m and $F(x) = 5x$ for this particular spring.

We construct an integral for the work done in applying F over the interval from $x = 0$ to $x = 4$.

Step 1:

Riemann sum. We partition the interval into subintervals on each of which F is so nearly constant that we can apply the constant-force formula for work. If x_k is any point in the kth subinterval, the value of F throughout the interval is approximately $F(x_k) = 5x_k$. The work done by F across the interval is approximately $5x_k \Delta x$, where Δx is the length of the interval. The sum

$$\sum F(x_k) \Delta x = \sum 5x_k \Delta x$$

approximates the work done by F from $x = 0$ to $x = 4$.

Steps 2 and 3:

Integrate. The limit of these sums as the norms of the partitions go to zero is

$$\int_0^4 F(x)\, dx = \int_0^4 5x\, dx = 5\frac{x^2}{2}\Big]_0^4 = 40 \text{ N} \cdot \text{m}. \qquad \textit{Now Try Exercise 35.}$$

Numerically, work is the area under the force graph.

We will revisit work in Section 8.5.

Quick Review 8.1 *(For help, go to Section 1.2.)*

Exercise numbers with a gray background indicate problems that the authors have designed to be solved *without a calculator.*

In Exercises 1–10, find all values of x (if any) at which the function changes sign on the given interval. Sketch a number line graph of the interval, and indicate the sign of the function on each subinterval.

Example: $f(x) = x^2 - 1$ on $[-2, 3]$

Changes sign at $x = \pm 1$.

1. $\sin 2x$ on $[-3, 2]$

2. $x^2 - 3x + 2$ on $[-2, 4]$

3. $x^2 - 2x + 3$ on $[-4, 2]$

4. $2x^3 - 3x^2 + 1$ on $[-2, 2]$

5. $x \cos 2x$ on $[0, 4]$

6. xe^{-x} on $[0, \infty)$

7. $\dfrac{x}{x^2 + 1}$ on $[-5, 30]$

8. $\dfrac{x^2 - 2}{x^2 - 4}$ on $[-3, 3]$

9. $\sec(1 + \sqrt{1 - \sin^2 x})$ on $(-\infty, \infty)$

10. $\sin(1/x)$ on $[0.1, 0.2]$

Section 8.1 Exercises

In Exercises 1–8, the function $v(t)$ is the velocity in m/sec of a particle moving along the x-axis. Use analytic methods to do each of the following:

(a) Determine when the particle is moving to the right, to the left, and stopped.

(b) Find the particle's displacement for the given time interval. If $s(0) = 3$, what is the particle's final position?

(c) Find the total distance traveled by the particle.

1. $v(t) = 5 \cos t, \quad 0 \le t \le 2\pi$

2. $v(t) = 6 \sin 3t, \quad 0 \le t \le \pi/2$

3. $v(t) = 49 - 9.8t, \quad 0 \leq t \leq 10$

4. $v(t) = 6t^2 - 18t + 12, \quad 0 \leq t \leq 2$

5. $v(t) = 5 \sin^2 t \cos t, \quad 0 \leq t \leq 2\pi$

6. $v(t) = \sqrt{4 - t}, \quad 0 \leq t \leq 4$

7. $v(t) = e^{\sin t} \cos t, \quad 0 \leq t \leq 2\pi$

8. $v(t) = \dfrac{t}{1 + t^2}, \quad 0 \leq t \leq 3$

9. An automobile accelerates from rest at $1 + 3\sqrt{t}$ mph/sec for 9 seconds.

    (a) What is its velocity after 9 seconds?

    (b) How far does it travel in those 9 seconds?

10. A particle travels with velocity

$$v(t) = (t - 2) \sin t \text{ m/sec}$$

for $0 \leq t \leq 4$ sec.

    (a) What is the particle's displacement?

    (b) What is the total distance traveled?

11. *Projectile* Recall that the acceleration due to Earth's gravity is 32 ft/sec². From ground level, a projectile is fired straight upward with velocity 90 feet per second.

    (a) What is its velocity after 3 seconds?

    (b) When does it hit the ground?

    (c) When it hits the ground, what is the net distance it has traveled?

    (d) When it hits the ground, what is the total distance it has traveled?

In Exercises 12–16, a particle moves along the *x*-axis (units in cm). Its initial position at $t = 0$ sec is $x(0) = 15$. The figure shows the graph of the particle's velocity $v(t)$. The numbers are the *areas* of the enclosed regions.

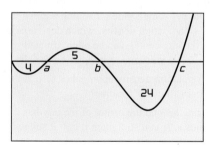

12. What is the particle's displacement between $t = 0$ and $t = c$?

13. What is the total distance traveled by the particle in the same time period?

14. Give the positions of the particle at times a, b, and c.

15. Approximately where does the particle achieve its greatest positive acceleration on the interval $[0, b]$?

16. Approximately where does the particle achieve its greatest positive acceleration on the interval $[0, c]$?

In Exercises 17–20, the graph of the velocity of a particle moving on the *x*-axis is given. The particle starts at $x = 2$ when $t = 0$.

    (a) Find where the particle is at the end of the trip.

    (b) Find the total distance traveled by the particle.

17.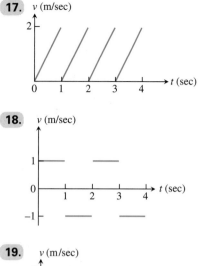

18.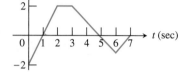

19.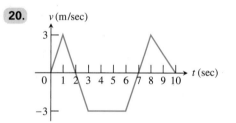

20.

21. *U.S. Oil Consumption* The rate of consumption of oil in the United States during the 1980s (in billions of barrels per year) is modeled by the function $C = 27.08 \cdot e^{t/25}$, where t is the number of years after January 1, 1980. Find the total consumption of oil in the United States from January 1, 1980, to January 1, 1990.

22. *Home Electricity Use* The rate at which your home consumes electricity is measured in kilowatts. If your home consumes electricity at the rate of 1 kilowatt for 1 hour, you will be charged for 1 "kilowatt-hour" of electricity. Suppose that the average consumption rate for a certain home is modeled by the function $C(t) = 3.9 - 2.4 \sin(\pi t/12)$, where $C(t)$ is measured in kilowatts and t is the number of hours past midnight. Find the average daily consumption for this home, measured in kilowatt-hours.

23. *Light Bulbs* A thousand compact fluorescent light bulbs from a certain company burn out at a rate of $\frac{7}{4}e^{-0.00175t}$ bulbs per day if they are left burning continually, where t is measured in days from when they are first turned on. To the nearest whole light bulb, how many will have burned out after 100 days of continuous use?

24. *Traffic Flow* Midday traffic through an intersection can be modeled by the function $74 + 6\cos(t/3)$ cars per minute, where t is measured in minutes after noon. Find the number of cars that pass through this intersection between noon and 12:30 P.M.

25. *Getting onto the Ride* People join the line for a particular amusement park ride at a rate R, measured in people per hour, given by the graph shown below.

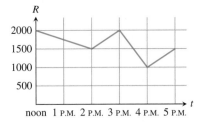

There are 500 people waiting in line at noon. If the ride can take 1500 people per hour, how many are waiting in line at 5 P.M.?

26. *Water In, Water Out* At 6 A.M., a tank holds 2500 gallons of water. Over the next 18 hours, it is being filled at a constant rate of 100 gallons per hour while water is taken out at a rate given by $W(t) = 120 + 60 \sin\left(4\sqrt{t}\right)$ gallons per hour, where t is measured in hours after 6 A.M. How much water is in the tank at midnight, when $t = 18$?

27. *Filling Milk Cartons* A machine fills milk cartons with milk at an approximately constant rate, but backups along the assembly line cause some variation. The rates (in cases per hour) are recorded at hourly intervals during a 10-hour period, from 8:00 A.M. to 6:00 P.M.

Time	Rate (cases/h)
8	120
9	110
10	115
11	115
12	119
1	120
2	120
3	115
4	112
5	110
6	121

Use the Trapezoidal Rule with $n = 10$ to determine approximately how many cases of milk were filled by the machine over the 10-hour period.

28. *Fuel Consumption* The table shows the rate of fuel consumption in a small plane at different times during a 90-minute flight, where t is measured in minutes since the start of the flight. Use a trapezoidal approximation to estimate the total fuel consumption during the flight. (Watch your units.)

Time (minutes)	Fuel Consumption (gallons per hour)
0	4
10	16
30	12
45	6
60	7
80	5
90	4

29. *Hot Dogs* A popular hot dog stand opens at noon. At different times between noon and 3 P.M., the manager stops by to measure how fast the hot dogs are selling, with the results given in the table. Use a trapezoidal approximation to estimate the total number of hot dogs sold during the first three hours.

Time (minutes after noon)	Rate of Hot Dog Sales (hot dogs per minute)
0	3
10	6
30	18
45	16
60	12
90	8
120	10
180	6

30. *Writing to Learn* As a school project, Anna accompanies her mother on a trip to the grocery store and keeps a log of the car's speed at 10-second intervals. Explain how she can use the data to estimate the distance from her home to the store. What is the connection between this process and the definite integral?

31. *Finding Mass* A two-meter-long rod of uniform diameter 6 cm has density $3/(5 + x)$ grams per cubic centimeter at distance x, measured in meters, from the left-hand endpoint. Find the total mass of the rod.

32. *Weight of Air* Within the troposphere (up to about 17 km above sea level), the density of air at h meters above sea level is given by

$$\text{density of air} = 4.17 \times 10^{-11}(288.15 - 0.0065h)^{4.256} \text{ kg/m}^3.$$

Find the mass of a cylindrical column of air one meter in diameter from sea level up to 10 km.

33. *Population Density* Population density measures the number of people per square mile inhabiting a given living area. Washerton's population density, which decreases as you move away from the city center, can be approximated by the function $10{,}000(2 - r)$ at a distance r miles from the city center.

(a) If the population density approaches zero at the edge of the city, what is the city's radius?

(b) A thin ring around the center of the city has thickness Δr and radius r. If you straighten it out, it suggests a rectangular strip. Approximately what is its area?

(c) *Writing to Learn* Explain why the population of the ring in part (b) is approximately

$$10{,}000(2 - r)(2\pi r)\Delta r.$$

(d) Estimate the total population of Washerton by setting up and evaluating a definite integral.

34. *Oil Flow* Oil flows through a cylindrical pipe of radius 3 inches, but friction from the pipe slows the flow toward the outer edge. The speed at which the oil flows at a distance r inches from the center is $8(10 - r^2)$ inches per second.

(a) In a plane cross section of the pipe, a thin ring with thickness Δr at a distance r inches from the center approximates a rectangular strip when you straighten it out. What is the area of the strip (and hence the approximate area of the ring)?

(b) Explain why we know that oil passes through this ring at approximately $8(10 - r^2)(2\pi r)\Delta r$ cubic inches per second.

(c) Set up and evaluate a definite integral that will give the rate (in cubic inches per second) at which oil is flowing through the pipe.

35. Hooke's Law A certain spring requires a force of 6 N to stretch it 3 cm beyond its natural length.

(a) What force would be required to stretch the spring 9 cm beyond its natural length?

(b) What would be the work done in stretching the spring 9 cm beyond its natural length?

36. Hooke's Law Hooke's Law also applies to *compressing* springs; that is, it requires a force of kx to compress a spring a distance x from its natural length. Suppose a 10,000-lb force compressed a spring from its natural length of 12 inches to a length of 11 inches. How much work was done in compressing the spring

(a) the first half-inch? **(b)** the second half-inch?

Standardized Test Questions

You may use a graphing calculator to solve the following problems.

37. True or False The figure below shows the velocity for a particle moving along the *x*-axis. The displacement for this particle is negative. Justify your answer.

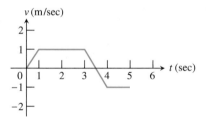

38. True or False If the velocity of a particle moving along the *x*-axis is always positive, then the displacement is equal to the total distance traveled. Justify your answer.

39. Multiple Choice The graph below shows the rate at which water is pumped from a storage tank. Approximate the total gallons of water pumped from the tank in 24 hours.

(A) 600 **(B)** 2400 **(C)** 3600 **(D)** 4200 **(E)** 4800

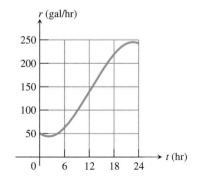

40. Multiple Choice The data for the acceleration $a(t)$ of a car from 0 to 15 seconds are given in the table below. If the velocity at $t = 0$ is 5 ft/sec, which of the following gives the approximate velocity at $t = 15$ using the Trapezoidal Rule?

(A) 47 ft/sec **(B)** 52 ft/sec **(C)** 120 ft/sec

(D) 125 ft/sec **(E)** 141 ft/sec

t (sec)	0	3	6	9	12	15
$a(t)$ (ft/sec^2)	4	8	6	9	10	10

41. Multiple Choice The rate at which customers arrive at a counter to be served is modeled by the function F defined by

$$F(t) = 12 + 6 \cos\left(\frac{t}{\pi}\right)$$ for $0 \le t \le 60$, where $F(t)$ is measured in customers per minute and t is measured in minutes. To the nearest whole number, how many customers arrive at the counter over the 60-minute period?

(A) 720 **(B)** 725 **(C)** 732

(D) 744 **(E)** 756

42. Multiple Choice Pollution is being removed from a lake at a rate modeled by the function $y = 20e^{-0.5t}$ tons/yr, where t is the number of years since 2005. Estimate the amount of pollution removed from the lake between 2005 and 2015. Round your answer to the nearest ton.

(A) 40 **(B)** 47 **(C)** 56

(D) 61 **(E)** 71

Extending the Ideas

43. Inflation Although the economy is continuously changing, we analyze it with discrete measurements. The following table records the *annual* inflation rate as measured each month for 13 consecutive months. Use the Trapezoidal Rule with $n = 12$ to find the overall inflation rate for the year.

Month	Annual Rate
January	0.04
February	0.04
March	0.05
April	0.06
May	0.05
June	0.04
July	0.04
August	0.05
September	0.04
October	0.06
November	0.06
December	0.05
January	0.05

44. Inflation Rate The table below shows the *monthly* inflation rate (in *thousandths*) for energy prices for thirteen consecutive months. Use the Trapezoidal Rule with $n = 12$ to approximate the *annual* inflation rate for the 12-month period running from the middle of the first month to the middle of the last month.

Month	Monthly Rate (in thousandths)
January	3.6
February	4.0
March	3.1
April	2.8
May	2.8
June	3.2
July	3.3
August	3.1
September	3.2
October	3.4
November	3.4
December	3.9
January	4.0

45. In Exercise 25, the rate at which people join the line from noon $(t = 0)$ until 5 P.M. $(t = 5)$ can be described by the piecewise defined function

$$R(t) = \begin{cases} 2000 - 250t, & 0 \le t < 2 \\ 500 + 500t, & 2 \le t < 3 \\ 5000 - 1000t, & 3 \le t < 4 \\ -1000 + 500t, & 4 \le t \le 5. \end{cases}$$

Given that 500 people are waiting in line at noon, find the piecewise defined function $L(T)$ that describes the total number of people waiting in line at time $T, 0 \le T \le 5$.

46. Continuing Exercises 25 and 45:

(a) Since the ride can accommodate 1500 people per hour, find the piecewise defined function that describes the wait time in minutes for a person who arrives at time T.

(b) Find the average wait time between noon and 5 P.M.

47. Center of Mass Suppose we have a finite collection of masses in the coordinate plane, the mass m_k located at the point (x_k, y_k) as shown in the figure.

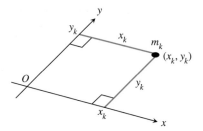

Each mass m_k has **moment $m_k y_k$ with respect to the x-axis** and **moment $m_k x_k$ about the y-axis.** The moments of the entire system with respect to the two axes are

$$\text{Moment about } x\text{-axis: } M_x = \sum m_k y_k,$$

$$\text{Moment about } y\text{-axis: } M_y = \sum m_k x_k.$$

The **center of mass** is $(\bar{x}, \bar{y})$ where

$$\bar{x} = \frac{M_y}{M} = \frac{\sum m_k x_k}{\sum m_k} \quad \text{and} \quad \bar{y} = \frac{M_x}{M} = \frac{\sum m_k y_k}{\sum m_k}.$$

Suppose we have a thin, flat plate occupying a region in the plane.

(a) Imagine the region cut into thin strips parallel to the y-axis. Show that

$$\bar{x} = \frac{\int x \, dm}{\int dm},$$

where $dm = \delta \, dA$, $\delta =$ density (mass per unit area), and $A =$ area of the region.

(b) Imagine the region cut into thin strips parallel to the x-axis. Show that

$$\bar{y} = \frac{\int y \, dm}{\int dm},$$

where $dm = \delta \, dA$, $\delta =$ density, and $A =$ area of the region.

In Exercises 48 and 49, use Exercise 47 to find the center of mass of the region with given density.

48. the region bounded by the parabola $y = x^2$ and the line $y = 4$ with constant density δ

49. the region bounded by the lines $y = x, y = -x, x = 2$ with constant density δ

8.2 | Areas in the Plane

You will be able to apply the definite integral to solve problems involving areas.

- Areas as limits of Riemann sums
- Areas between curves
- Areas for which integration is with respect to *y*

Area Between Curves

We know how to find the area of a region between a curve and the *x*-axis but many times we want to know the area of a region that is bounded above by one curve, $y = f(x)$, and below by another, $y = g(x)$ (Figure 8.5).

We find the area as an integral by applying the first two steps of the modeling strategy developed in Section 8.1.

1. We partition the region into vertical strips of equal width Δx and approximate each strip with a rectangle with base parallel to $[a, b]$ (Figure 8.6). Each rectangle has area

$$[f(c_k) - g(c_k)]\Delta x$$

for some c_k in its respective subinterval (Figure 8.7). This expression will be non-negative even if the region lies below the *x*-axis. We approximate the area of the region with the Riemann sum

$$\sum [f(c_k) - g(c_k)]\Delta x.$$

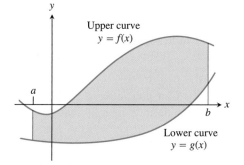

Figure 8.5 The region between $y = f(x)$ and $y = g(x)$ and the lines $x = a$ and $x = b$.

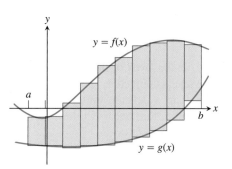

Figure 8.6 We approximate the region with rectangles perpendicular to the *x*-axis.

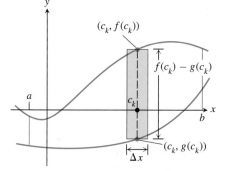

Figure 8.7 The area of a typical rectangle is $[f(c_k) - g(c_k)]\Delta x$.

2. The limit of these sums as $\Delta x \rightarrow 0$ is

$$\int_a^b [f(x) - g(x)]\, dx.$$

This approach to finding area captures the properties of area, so it can serve as a definition.

DEFINITION Area Between Curves

If f and g are continuous with $f(x) \geq g(x)$ throughout $[a, b]$, then the **area between the curves** $y = f(x)$ and $y = g(x)$ **from** a **to** b is the integral of $[f - g]$ from a to b,

$$A = \int_a^b [f(x) - g(x)]\, dx.$$

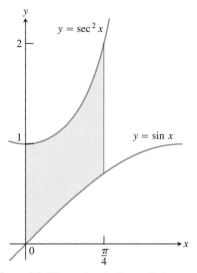

Figure 8.8 The region in Example 1.

EXAMPLE 1 Applying the Definition

Find the area of the region between $y = \sec^2 x$ and $y = \sin x$ from $x = 0$ to $x = \pi/4$.

SOLUTION

We graph the curves (Figure 8.8) to find their relative positions in the plane, and see that $y = \sec^2 x$ lies *above* $y = \sin x$ on $[0, \pi/4]$. The area is therefore

$$A = \int_0^{\pi/4} [\sec^2 x - \sin x]\, dx$$

$$= \left[\tan x + \cos x \right]_0^{\pi/4}$$

$$= \frac{\sqrt{2}}{2} \text{ units squared} \qquad \textit{Now Try Exercise 1.}$$

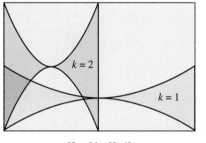

Figure 8.9 Two members of the family of butterfly-shaped regions described in Exploration 1.

EXPLORATION 1 A Family of Butterflies

For each positive integer k, let A_k denote the area of the butterfly-shaped region enclosed between the graphs of $y = k \sin kx$ and $y = 2k - k \sin kx$ on the interval $[0, \pi/k]$. The regions for $k = 1$ and $k = 2$ are shown in Figure 8.9.

1. Find the areas of the two regions in Figure 8.9.
2. Make a conjecture about the areas A_k for $k \geq 3$.
3. Set up a definite integral that gives the area A_k. Can you make a simple *u*-substitution that will transform this integral into the definite integral that gives the area A_1?
4. What is $\lim_{k \to \infty} A_k$?
5. If P_k denotes the perimeter of the kth butterfly-shaped region, what is $\lim_{k \to \infty} P_k$? (You can answer this question without an explicit formula for P_k.)

Area Enclosed by Intersecting Curves

When a region is enclosed by intersecting curves, the intersection points give the limits of integration.

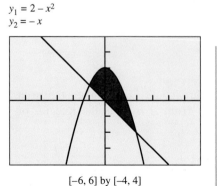

Figure 8.10 The region in Example 2.

EXAMPLE 2 Area of an Enclosed Region

Find the area of the region enclosed by the parabola $y = 2 - x^2$ and the line $y = -x$.

SOLUTION

We graph the curves to view the region (Figure 8.10).

The limits of integration are found by solving the equation

$$2 - x^2 = -x$$

either algebraically or by calculator. The solutions are $x = -1$ and $x = 2$.

continued

Since the parabola lies above the line on $[-1, 2]$, the area integrand is $2 - x^2 - (-x)$.

$$A = \int_{-1}^{2} [2 - x^2 - (-x)] \, dx$$

$$= \left[2x - \frac{x^3}{3} + \frac{x^2}{2} \right]_{-1}^{2}$$

$$= \frac{9}{2} \text{ units squared}$$

Now Try Exercise 5.

EXAMPLE 3 Using a Calculator

Find the area of the region enclosed by the graphs of $y = 2 \cos x$ and $y = x^2 - 1$.

SOLUTION

The region is shown in Figure 8.11.

Using a calculator, we solve the equation

$$2 \cos x = x^2 - 1$$

to find the x-coordinates of the points where the curves intersect. These are the limits of integration. The solutions are $x = \pm 1.265423706$. We store the negative value as A and the positive value as B. The area is

$$\text{NINT} (2 \cos x - (x^2 - 1), x, A, B) \approx 4.994907788.$$

This is the final calculation, so we are now free to round. The area is about 4.99.

Now Try Exercise 7.

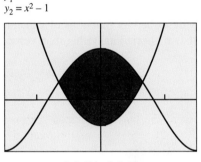

$y_1 = 2 \cos x$
$y_2 = x^2 - 1$

[−3, 3] by [−2, 3]

Figure 8.11 The region in Example 3.

Finding Intersections by Calculator

The coordinates of the points of intersection of two curves are sometimes needed for other calculations. To take advantage of the accuracy provided by calculators, use them to solve for the values and *store* the ones you want.

Boundaries with Changing Functions

If a boundary of a region is defined by more than one function, we can partition the region into subregions that correspond to the function changes and proceed as usual.

EXAMPLE 4 Finding Area Using Subregions

Find the area of the region R in the first quadrant that is bounded above by $y = \sqrt{x}$ and below by the x-axis and the line $y = x - 2$.

SOLUTION

The region is shown in Figure 8.12.

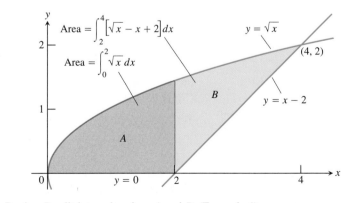

$$\text{Area} = \int_{2}^{4} \left[\sqrt{x} - x + 2 \right] dx$$

$$\text{Area} = \int_{0}^{2} \sqrt{x} \, dx$$

$y = \sqrt{x}$

(4, 2)

B

$y = x - 2$

A

$y = 0$

Figure 8.12 Region R split into subregions A and B. (Example 4)

continued

While it appears that no single integral can give the area of R (the bottom boundary is defined by two different curves), we can split the region at $x = 2$ into two regions A and B. The area of R can be found as the sum of the areas of A and B.

$$\text{Area of } R = \underbrace{\int_0^2 \sqrt{x}\, dx}_{\text{area of } A} + \underbrace{\int_2^4 \left[\sqrt{x} - (x - 2) \right] dx}_{\text{area of } B}$$

$$= \left[\frac{2}{3} x^{3/2} \right]_0^2 + \left[\frac{2}{3} x^{3/2} - \frac{x^2}{2} + 2x \right]_2^4$$

$$= \frac{10}{3} \text{ units squared}$$

Now Try Exercise 9.

Integrating with Respect to *y*

Sometimes the boundaries of a region are more easily described by functions of y than by functions of x. We can use approximating rectangles that are horizontal rather than vertical and the resulting basic formula has y in place of x.

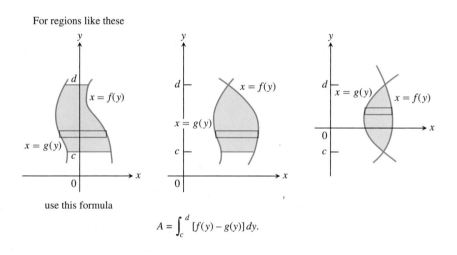

For regions like these

use this formula

$$A = \int_c^d [f(y) - g(y)]\, dy.$$

EXAMPLE 5 Integrating with Respect to *y*

Find the area of the region in Example 4 by integrating with respect to y.

SOLUTION

We remarked in solving Example 4 that "it appears that no single integral can give the area of R," but notice how appearances change when we think of our rectangles being summed over y. The interval of integration is $[0, 2]$, and the rectangles run between the same two curves on the entire interval. There is no need to split the region (Figure 8.13).

We need to solve for x in terms of y in both equations:

$$y = x - 2 \quad \text{becomes} \quad x = y + 2,$$

$$y = \sqrt{x} \quad \text{becomes} \quad x = y^2, \quad y \geq 0$$

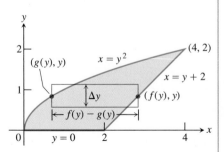

Figure 8.13 It takes two integrations to find the area of this region if we integrate with respect to x. It takes only one if we integrate with respect to y. (Example 5)

continued

$y_1 = x^3, y_2 = \sqrt{x + 2}, y_3 = -\sqrt{x + 2}$

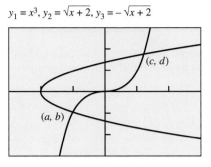

[−3, 3] by [−3, 3]

Figure 8.14 The region in Example 6.

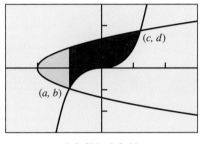

[−3, 3] by [−3, 3]

Figure 8.15 If we integrate with respect to *x* in Example 6, we must split the region at *x* = *a*.

We must still be careful to subtract the lower number from the higher number when forming the integrand. In this case, the higher numbers are the higher *x* values, which are on the line $x = y + 2$ because the line lies to the *right* of the parabola. So,

$$\text{Area of } R = \int_0^2 (y + 2 - y^2)\, dy = \left[\frac{y^2}{2} + 2y - \frac{y^3}{3} \right]_0^2 = \frac{10}{3} \text{ units squared.}$$

Now Try Exercise 11.

EXAMPLE 6 Making the Choice

Find the area of the region enclosed by the graphs of $y = x^3$ and $x = y^2 - 2$.

SOLUTION

We can produce a graph of the region on a calculator by graphing the three curves $y = x^3$, $y = \sqrt{x + 2}$, and $y = -\sqrt{x + 2}$ (Figure 8.14).

This conveniently gives us all of our bounding curves as functions of *x*. If we integrate in terms of *x*, however, we need to split the region at $x = a$ (Figure 8.15).

On the other hand, we can integrate from $y = b$ to $y = d$ and handle the entire region at once. We solve the cubic for *x* in terms of *y*:

$$y = x^3 \quad \text{becomes} \quad x = y^{1/3}$$

To find the limits of integration, we solve $y^{1/3} = y^2 - 2$. It is easy to see that the lower limit is $b = -1$, but a calculator is needed to find that the upper limit $d = 1.793003715$. We store this value as D.

The cubic lies to the right of the parabola, so

$$\text{Area} = \text{NINT} \left(y^{1/3} - (y^2 - 2), y, -1, D \right) = 4.214939673.$$

The area is about 4.21.

Now Try Exercise 27.

Saving Time with Geometry Formulas

Here is yet another way to handle Example 4.

EXAMPLE 7 Using Geometry

Find the area of the region in Example 4 by subtracting the area of the triangular region from the area under the square root curve.

SOLUTION

Figure 8.16 illustrates the strategy, which enables us to integrate with respect to *x* without splitting the region.

$$\text{Area} = \int_0^4 \sqrt{x}\, dx - \frac{1}{2}(2)(2) = \frac{2}{3} x^{3/2} \Big]_0^4 - 2 = \frac{10}{3} \text{ units squared}$$

Now Try Exercise 35.

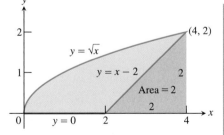

Figure 8.16 The area of the blue region is the area under the parabola $y = \sqrt{x}$ minus the area of the triangle. (Example 7)

The moral behind Examples 4, 5, and 7 is that you often have options for finding the area of a region, some of which may be easier than others. You can integrate with respect to *x* or with respect to *y*, you can partition the region into subregions, and sometimes you can even use traditional geometry formulas. Sketch the region first and take a moment to determine the best way to proceed.

Quick Review 8.2 *(For help, go to Sections 1.2 and 6.1.)*

Exercise numbers with a gray background indicate problems that the authors have designed to be solved *without a calculator*.

In Exercises 1–5, find the area between the *x*-axis and the graph of the given function over the given interval.

1. $y = \sin x$ over $[0, \pi]$

2. $y = e^{2x}$ over $[0, 1]$

3. $y = \sec^2 x$ over $[-\pi/4, \pi/4]$

4. $y = 4x - x^3$ over $[0, 2]$

5. $y = \sqrt{9 - x^2}$ over $[-3, 3]$

In Exercises 6–10, find the *x*- and *y*-coordinates of all points where the graphs of the given functions intersect. If the curves never intersect, write "NI."

6. $y = x^2 - 4x$ and $y = x + 6$

7. $y = e^x$ and $y = x + 1$

8. $y = x^2 - \pi x$ and $y = \sin x$

9. $y = \dfrac{2x}{x^2 + 1}$ and $y = x^3$

10. $y = \sin x$ and $y = x^3$

Section 8.2 Exercises

In Exercises 1–6, find the area of the shaded region analytically.

1.

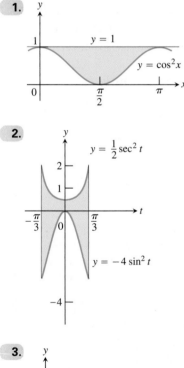

$y = 1$

$y = \cos^2 x$

2.

$y = \frac{1}{2}\sec^2 t$

$y = -4\sin^2 t$

3.

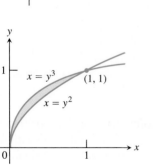

$x = y^3$

$(1, 1)$

$x = y^2$

4.

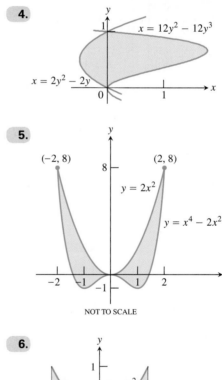

$x = 12y^2 - 12y^3$

$x = 2y^2 - 2y$

5.

$(-2, 8)$ $(2, 8)$

$y = 2x^2$

$y = x^4 - 2x^2$

NOT TO SCALE

6.

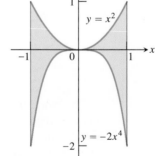

$y = x^2$

$y = -2x^4$

In Exercises 7 and 8, use a calculator to find the area of the region enclosed by the graphs of the two functions.

7. $y = \sin x, y = 1 - x^2$ **8.** $y = \cos(2x), y = x^2 - 2$

In Exercises 9 and 10, find the area of the shaded region analytically.

9.

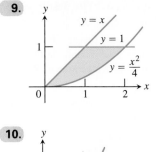

10.

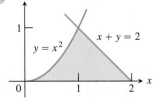

In Exercises 11 and 12, find the area enclosed by the graphs of the two curves by integrating with respect to y.

11. $y^2 = x + 1, y^2 = 3 - x$ **12.** $y^2 = x + 3, y = 2x$

In Exercises 13 and 14, find the total shaded area.

13.

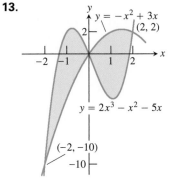

14.

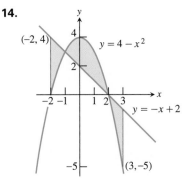

In Exercises 15–34, find the area of the regions enclosed by the lines and curves.

15. $y = x^2 - 2$ and $y = 2$

16. $y = 2x - x^2$ and $y = -3$

17. $y = 7 - 2x^2$ and $y = x^2 + 4$

18. $y = x^4 - 4x^2 + 4$ and $y = x^2$

19. $y = x\sqrt{a^2 - x^2}$, $a > 0$,   and $y = 0$

20. $y = \sqrt{|x|}$ and $5y = x + 6$
(How many intersection points are there?)

21. $y = |x^2 - 4|$ and $y = (x^2/2) + 4$

22. $x = y^2$ and $x = y + 2$

23. $y^2 - 4x = 4$ and $4x - y = 16$

24. $x - y^2 = 0$ and $x + 2y^2 = 3$

25. $x + y^2 = 0$ and $x + 3y^2 = 2$

26. $4x^2 + y = 4$ and $x^4 - y = 1$

27. $x + y^2 = 3$ and $4x + y^2 = 0$

28. $y = 2\sin x$ and $y = \sin 2x$, $0 \le x \le \pi$

29. $y = 8\cos x$ and $y = \sec^2 x, -\pi/3 \le x \le \pi/3$

30. $y = \cos(\pi x/2)$ and $y = 1 - x^2$

31. $y = \sin(\pi x/2)$ and $y = x$

32. $y = \sec^2 x$, $y = \tan^2 x$, $x = -\pi/4$, $x = \pi/4$

33. $x = \tan^2 y$ and $x = -\tan^2 y$, $-\pi/4 \le y \le \pi/4$

34. $x = 3\sin y \sqrt{\cos y}$ and $x = 0$, $0 \le y \le \pi/2$

In Exercises 35 and 36, find the area of the region by subtracting the area of a triangular region from the area of a larger region.

35. The region on or above the x-axis bounded by the curves $y^2 = x + 3$ and $y = 2x$

36. The region on or above the x-axis bounded by the curves $y = 4 - x^2$ and $y = 3x$

37. Find the area of the propeller-shaped region enclosed by the curve $x - y^3 = 0$ and the line $x - y = 0$.

38. Find the area of the region in the first quadrant bounded by the line $y = x$, the line $x = 2$, the curve $y = 1/x^2$, and the x-axis.

39. Find the area of the "triangular" region in the first quadrant bounded on the left by the y-axis and on the right by the curves $y = \sin x$ and $y = \cos x$.

40. Find the area of the region between the curve $y = 3 - x^2$ and the line $y = -1$ by integrating with respect to **(a)** x, **(b)** y.

41. The region bounded below by the parabola $y = x^2$ and above by the line $y = 4$ is to be partitioned into two subsections of equal area by cutting across it with the horizontal line $y = c$.

  (a) Sketch the region and draw a line $y = c$ across it that looks about right. In terms of c, what are the coordinates of the points where the line and parabola intersect? Add them to your figure.

  (b) Find c by integrating with respect to y. (This puts c in the limits of integration.)

  (c) Find c by integrating with respect to x. (This puts c into the integrand as well.)

42. Find the area of the region in the first quadrant bounded on the left by the y-axis, below by the line $y = x/4$, above left by the curve $y = 1 + \sqrt{x}$, and above right by the curve $y = 2/\sqrt{x}$.

43. The figure here shows triangle *AOC* inscribed in the region cut from the parabola $y = x^2$ by the line $y = a^2$. Find the limit of the ratio of the area of the triangle to the area of the parabolic region as a approaches zero.

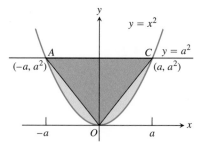

44. Suppose the area of the region between the graph of a positive continuous function f and the *x*-axis from $x = a$ to $x = b$ is 4 square units. Find the area between the curves $y = f(x)$ and $y = 2f(x)$ from $x = a$ to $x = b$.

45. Writing to Learn Which of the following integrals, if either, calculates the area of the shaded region shown here? Give reasons for your answer.

i. $\int_{-1}^{1} (x - (-x))\, dx = \int_{-1}^{1} 2x\, dx$

ii. $\int_{-1}^{1} (-x - (x))\, dx = \int_{-1}^{1} -2x\, dx$

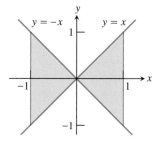

46. Writing to Learn Is the following statement true, sometimes true, or never true? The area of the region between the graphs of the continuous functions $y = f(x)$ and $y = g(x)$ and the vertical lines $x = a$ and $x = b$ $(a < b)$ is

$$\int_{a}^{b} [f(x) - g(x)]\, dx.$$

Give reasons for your answer.

47. Find the area of the propeller-shaped region enclosed between the graphs of

$$y = \frac{2x}{x^2 + 1} \quad \text{and} \quad y = x^3.$$

48. Find the area of the propeller-shaped region enclosed between the graphs of $y = \sin x$ and $y = x^3$.

49. Find the positive value of k such that the area of the region enclosed between the graph of $y = k \cos x$ and the graph of $y = kx^2$ is 2.

Standardized Test Questions

50. True or False The area of the region enclosed by the graph of $y = x^2 + 1$ and the line $y = 10$ is 36. Justify your answer.

51. True or False The area of the region in the first quadrant enclosed by the graphs of $y = \cos x$, $y = x$, and the *y*-axis is given by the definite integral $\int_{0}^{0.739} (x - \cos x)\, dx$. Justify your answer.

52. Multiple Choice Let R be the region in the first quadrant bounded by the *x*-axis, the graph of $x = y^2 + 2$, and the line $x = 4$. Which of the following integrals gives the area of R?

(A) $\int_{0}^{\sqrt{2}} [4 - (y^2 + 2)]\, dy$ **(B)** $\int_{0}^{\sqrt{2}} [(y^2 + 2) - 4]\, dy$

(C) $\int_{-\sqrt{2}}^{\sqrt{2}} [4 - (y^2 + 2)]\, dy$ **(D)** $\int_{-\sqrt{2}}^{\sqrt{2}} [(y^2 + 2) - 4]\, dy$

(E) $\int_{2}^{4} [4 - (y^2 + 2)]\, dy$

53. Multiple Choice Which of the following gives the area of the region between the graphs of $y = x^2$ and $y = -x$ from $x = 0$ to $x = 3$?

(A) 2 **(B)** 9/2 **(C)** 13/2 **(D)** 13 **(E)** 27/2

54. Multiple Choice Let R be the shaded region enclosed by the graphs of $y = e^{-x^2}$, $y = -\sin(3x)$, and the *y*-axis as shown in the figure below. Which of the following gives the approximate area of the region R?

(A) 1.139 **(B)** 1.445 **(C)** 1.869 **(D)** 2.114 **(E)** 2.340

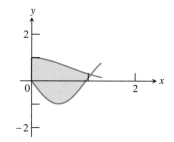

55. Multiple Choice Let f and g be the functions given by $f(x) = e^x$ and $g(x) = 1/x$. Which of the following gives the area of the region enclosed by the graphs of f and g between $x = 1$ and $x = 2$?

(A) $e^2 - e - \ln 2$

(B) $\ln 2 - e^2 + e$

(C) $e^2 - \dfrac{1}{2}$

(D) $e^2 - e - \dfrac{1}{2}$

(E) $\dfrac{1}{e} - \ln 2$

Exploration

56. Group Activity *Area of Ellipse*

An ellipse with major axis of length $2a$ and minor axis of length $2b$ can be coordinatized with its center at the origin and its major axis horizontal, in which case it is defined by the equation

$$\frac{x^2}{a^2} + \frac{y^2}{b^2} = 1.$$

(a) Find the equations that define the upper and lower semi-ellipses as functions of x.

(b) Write an integral expression that gives the area of the ellipse.

(c) With your group, use NINT to find the areas of ellipses for various lengths of a and b.

(d) There is a simple formula for the area of an ellipse with major axis of length $2a$ and minor axis of length $2b$. Can you tell what it is from the areas you and your group have found?

(e) Work with your group to write a *proof* of this area formula by showing that it is the exact value of the integral expression in part (b).

Extending the Ideas

57. *Cavalieri's Theorem* Bonaventura Cavalieri (1598–1647) discovered that if two plane regions can be arranged to lie over the same interval of the x-axis in such a way that they have identical vertical cross sections at every point (see figure), then the regions have the same area. Show that this theorem is true.

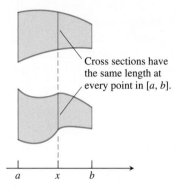

Cross sections have the same length at every point in $[a, b]$.

58. Find the area of the region enclosed by the curves

$$y = \frac{x}{x^2 + 1} \quad \text{and} \quad y = mx, \quad 0 < m < 1.$$

8.3 | Volumes

You will be able to apply the definite integral to solve problems involving volumes.

- Volumes as limits of Riemann sums
- Volumes with circular, square, or other cross sections
- Volumes of solids of revolution using washers or cylindrical shells

Volume as an Integral

In Section 6.1, Example 4, we estimated the volume of a sphere by partitioning it into thin slices that were nearly cylindrical and summing the cylinders' volumes using MRAM. MRAM sums are Riemann sums, and had we known how at the time, we could have continued on to express the volume of the sphere as a definite integral.

Starting the same way, we can now find the volumes of a great many solids by integration. Suppose we want to find the volume of a solid like the one in Figure 8.17. The cross section of the solid at each point x in the interval $[a, b]$ is a region $S(x)$ of area $A(x)$. If A is a continuous function of x, we can use it to define and calculate the volume of the solid as an integral in the following way.

We partition $[a, b]$ into subintervals of length Δx and slice the solid, as we would a loaf of bread, by planes perpendicular to the x-axis at the partition points. If the surface of our solid is continuous, we can expect that the cross sections between the plane at x_{k-1} and the plane at x_k are almost identical. If we replace the solid between these planes by the cylinder whose base is $S(x_k)$ and whose height is $\Delta x = x_k - x_{k-1}$ (Figure 8.18), we will get a good approximation to the volume of this slice of the solid.

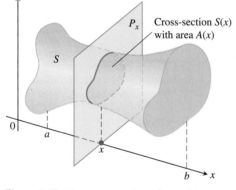

Figure 8.17 The cross section of an arbitrary solid at point x.

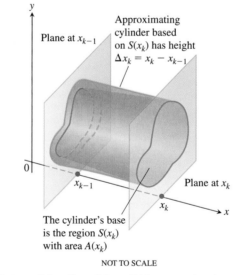

NOT TO SCALE

Figure 8.18 Enlarged view of the slice of the solid between the planes at x_{k-1} and x_k.

The volume of the cylinder is

$$V_k = \text{base area} \times \text{height} = A(x_k) \times \Delta x.$$

The sum

$$\sum V_k = \sum A(x_k) \times \Delta x$$

approximates the volume of the solid.

This is a Riemann sum for $A(x)$ on $[a, b]$. We expect the approximations to improve as the norms of the partitions go to zero, so we define their limiting integral to be the *volume of the solid.*

> **DEFINITION   Volume of a Solid**
>
> The **volume of a solid** of known integrable cross-section area $A(x)$ from $x = a$ to $x = b$ is the integral of A from a to b,
>
> $$V = \int_a^b A(x)\, dx.$$

To apply the formula in the previous definition, we proceed as follows.

> **How to Find Volume by the Method of Slicing**
>
> 1. Sketch the solid and a typical cross section.
> 2. Find a formula for $A(x)$.
> 3. Find the limits of integration.
> 4. Integrate $A(x)$ to find the volume.

Square Cross Sections

Let us apply the volume formula to a solid with square cross sections.

EXAMPLE 1 A Square-Based Pyramid

A pyramid 3 m high has congruent triangular sides and a square base that is 3 m on each side. Each cross section of the pyramid parallel to the base is a square. Find the volume of the pyramid.

SOLUTION

We follow the steps for the method of slicing.

1. *Sketch.* We draw the pyramid with its vertex at the origin and its altitude along the interval $0 \le x \le 3$. We sketch a typical cross section at a point x between 0 and 3 (Figure 8.19).

2. *Find a formula for $A(x)$.* The cross section at x is a square x meters on a side, so

$$A(x) = x^2.$$

3. *Find the limits of integration.* The squares go from $x = 0$ to $x = 3$.

4. *Integrate to find the volume.*

$$V = \int_0^3 A(x)\, dx = \int_0^3 x^2\, dx = \left.\frac{x^3}{3}\right]_0^3 = 9 \text{ m}^3 \qquad \textbf{\textit{Now Try Exercise 3.}}$$

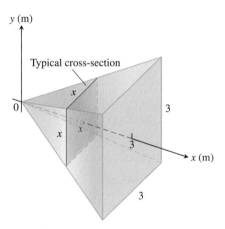

y (m)

Typical cross-section

Figure 8.19 A cross section of the pyramid in Example 1.

Circular Cross Sections

The only thing that changes when the cross sections of a solid are circular is the formula for $A(x)$. Many such solids are **solids of revolution,** as in the next example.

EXAMPLE 2 A Solid of Revolution

The region between the graph of $f(x) = 2 + x \cos x$ and the *x*-axis over the interval $[-2, 2]$ is revolved about the *x*-axis to generate a solid. Find the volume of the solid.

continued

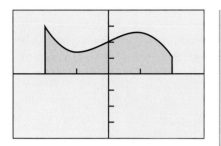

[−3, 3] by [−4, 4]

Figure 8.20 The region in Example 2.

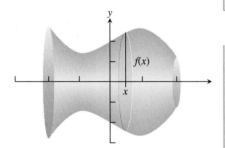

Figure 8.21 The region in Figure 8.20 is revolved about the *x*-axis to generate a solid. A typical cross section is circular, with radius $f(x) = 2 + x \cos x$. (Example 2)

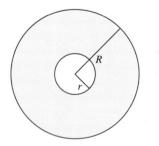

Figure 8.24 The area of a washer is $\pi R^2 - \pi r^2$. (Example 3)

Caution!

The area of a washer is $\pi R^2 - \pi r^2$, which you can simplify to $\pi(R^2 - r^2)$, but *not* to $\pi(R - r)^2$. No matter how tempting it is to make the latter simplification, it's wrong. Don't do it.

SOLUTION

Revolving the region (Figure 8.20) about the *x*-axis generates the vase-shaped solid in Figure 8.21. The cross section at a typical point *x* is circular, with radius equal to $f(x)$. Its area is

$$A(x) = \pi(f(x))^2.$$

The volume of the solid is

$$V = \int_{-2}^{2} A(x)\, dx$$

$$\approx \text{NINT}\left(\pi(2 + x \cos x)^2, x, -2, 2\right) \approx 52.43 \text{ units cubed}$$

Now Try Exercise 7.

EXAMPLE 3 Washer Cross Sections

The region in the first quadrant enclosed by the *y*-axis and the graphs of $y = \cos x$ and $y = \sin x$ is revolved about the *x*-axis to form a solid. Find its volume.

SOLUTION

The region is shown in Figure 8.22.

We revolve it about the *x*-axis to generate a solid with a cone-shaped cavity in its center (Figure 8.23).

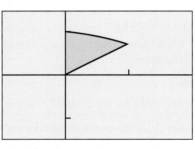

[−π/4, π/2] by [−1.5, 1.5]

Figure 8.22 The region in Example 3.

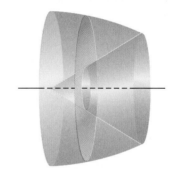

Figure 8.23 The solid generated by revolving the region in Figure 8.22 about the *x*-axis. A typical cross section is a washer: a circular region with a circular region cut out of its center. (Example 3)

This time each cross section perpendicular to the *axis of revolution* is a *washer*, a circular region with a circular region cut from its center. The area of a washer can be found by subtracting the inner area from the outer area (Figure 8.24).

In our region the cosine curve defines the outer radius, and the curves intersect at $x = \pi/4$. The volume is

$$V = \int_{0}^{\pi/4} \pi(\cos^2 x - \sin^2 x)\, dx$$

$$= \pi \int_{0}^{\pi/4} \cos 2x\, dx \quad \text{identity: } \cos^2 x - \sin^2 x = \cos 2x$$

$$= \pi \left[\frac{\sin 2x}{2}\right]_{0}^{\pi/4} = \frac{\pi}{2} \text{ units cubed} \qquad \textit{Now Try Exercise 17.}$$

We could have done the integration in Example 3 with NINT, but we wanted to demonstrate how a trigonometric identity can be useful under unexpected circumstances in calculus. The double-angle identity turned a difficult integrand into an easy one and enabled us to get an exact answer by antidifferentiation.

The solid of revolution found by al-Haytham around the year 1000 (see page 384) requires revolving a region around the vertical line $x = a$, but the idea is exactly the same. We approximate our volume using thin discs. Because *we* can use the Fundamental Theorem of Calculus, once we have found the cross-section area we can write the volume as an integral, and the rest is easy. For al-Haytham, finding what today we call the Riemann sum was just the start. To determine its limit was the hard part.

EXAMPLE 4 Rotation Around Another Axis

The region bounded by the graph of $y = 3\sqrt{\dfrac{x}{4}}$, the x-axis, and the line $x = 4$

(Figure 8.25) is revolved about the line $x = 4$ to generate a solid (Figure 8.26). Find the volume of the solid.

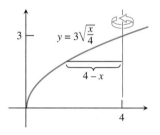

Figure 8.25 The region in Example 4 showing the distance from the axis of rotation to the graph.

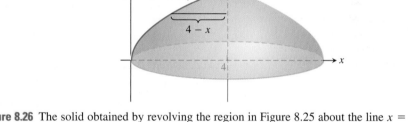

Figure 8.26 The solid obtained by revolving the region in Figure 8.25 about the line $x = 4$. (Example 4)

SOLUTION

We take horizontal slices of our solid. The cross section at height y is circular with radius $4 - x$, where x is the x-coordinate of the point on the graph of $y = 3\sqrt{\dfrac{x}{4}}$

(Figure 8.25). Solving for x as a function of y, we get $x = \dfrac{4y^2}{9}$. The radius of the cross

section at height y is $4 - \dfrac{4y^2}{9}$, and the area of this cross section is

$$A(y) = \pi\left(4 - \frac{4y^2}{9}\right)^2 = \frac{16\pi}{81}(9 - y^2)^2.$$

The volume of the solid is

$$V = \int_0^3 \frac{16\pi}{81}(9 - y^2)^2 \, dy = \frac{16\pi}{81}\int_0^3 (81 - 18y^2 + y^4) \, dy$$

$$= \frac{16\pi}{81}\left[81y - 6y^3 + \frac{y^5}{5}\right]_0^3 = \frac{128\pi}{5} \text{ units cubed} \qquad \textit{Now Try Exercise 21.}$$

Abu Ali al-Hasan ibn al-Haytham (c. 965–1040)

Ibn al-Haytham, also known as al-Basri because he was from Basra in what is now Iraq, was hired by the Egyptian caliph to engineer control of the Nile. Although that project was beyond the capabilities of the time, al-Haytham remained in Cairo, where he made major advances in astronomy, physics, and mathematics. He is best known for his study of curved mirrors that concentrate light rays and is considered one of the fathers of solar technology.

Cylindrical Shells

There is another way to find volumes of solids of rotation that can be useful when the axis of revolution is perpendicular to the axis containing the natural interval of integration. Instead of summing volumes of thin slices, we sum volumes of thin cylindrical shells that grow outward from the axis of revolution like tree rings.

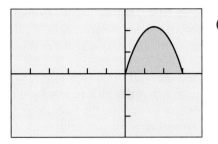

[–6, 4] by [–3, 3]

Figure 8.27 The graph of the region in Exploration 1, before revolution.

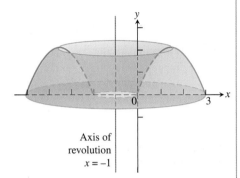

Axis of revolution
x = –1

Figure 8.28 The region in Figure 8.27 is revolved about the line $x = -1$ to form a solid cake. The natural interval of integration is along the x-axis, perpendicular to the axis of revolution. (Exploration 1)

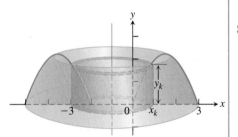

Figure 8.29 Cutting the cake into thin cylindrical slices, working from the inside out. Each slice occurs at some x_k between 0 and 3 and has thickness Δx. (Exploration 1)

EXPLORATION 1   Volume by Cylindrical Shells

The region enclosed by the x-axis and the parabola $y = f(x) = 3x - x^2$ is revolved about the line $x = -1$ to generate the shape of a cake (Figures 8.27, 8.28). (Such a cake is often called a bundt cake.) What is the volume of the cake?

Integrating with respect to y would be awkward here, as it is not easy to get the original parabola in terms of y. (Try finding the volume by washers and you will soon see what we mean.) To integrate with respect to x, you can do the problem by *cylindrical shells,* which requires that you cut the cake in a rather unusual way.

1. Instead of cutting the usual wedge shape, cut a *cylindrical* slice by cutting straight down all the way around close to the inside hole. Then cut another cylindrical slice around the enlarged hole, then another, and so on. The radii of the cylinders gradually increase, and the heights of the cylinders follow the contour of the parabola: smaller to larger, then back to smaller (Figure 8.29). Each slice is sitting over a subinterval of the x-axis of length Δx. Its radius is approximately $(1 + x_k)$. What is its height?

2. If you unroll the cylinder at x_k and flatten it out, it becomes (essentially) a rectangular slab with thickness Δx. Show that the volume of the slab is approximately $2\pi(x_k + 1)(3x_k - x_k^2)\Delta x$.

3. $\sum 2\pi(x_k + 1)(3x_k - x_k^2)\Delta x$ is a Riemann sum. What is the limit of these Riemann sums as $\Delta x \rightarrow 0$?

4. Evaluate the integral you found in step 3 to find the volume of the cake!

EXAMPLE 5   Finding Volumes Using Cylindrical Shells

The region bounded by the curve $y = \sqrt{x}$, the x-axis, and the line $x = 4$ is revolved about the x-axis to generate a solid. Find the volume of the solid.

SOLUTION

1. Sketch the region and draw a line segment across it parallel to the axis of revolution (Figure 8.30). Label the segment's length (shell height) and distance from the axis of revolution (shell radius). The width of the segment is the shell thickness dy. (We drew the shell in Figure 8.31, but you need not do that.)

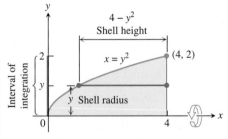

Figure 8.30 The region, shell dimensions, and interval of integration in Example 5.

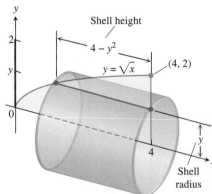

Figure 8.31 The shell swept out by the line segment in Figure 8.30.

2. Identify the limits of integration: y runs from 0 to 2.

3. Integrate to find the volume.   *continued*

$$V = \int_0^2 2\pi \binom{\text{shell}}{\text{radius}}\binom{\text{shell}}{\text{height}} dy$$

$$= \int_0^2 2\pi(y)(4 - y^2)\, dy$$

$$= 2\pi \int (4y - y^3)\, dy$$

$$= 2\pi \left[2y^2 - \frac{y^4}{4} \right]_0^2 = 8\pi \qquad \text{\textit{Now Try Exercise 35(a).}}$$

EXAMPLE 6 Finding Volumes Using Cylindrical Shells

The region bounded by the curves $y = 4 - x^2$, $y = x$, and $x = 0$ is revolved about the y-axis to form a solid. Use cylindrical shells to find the volume of the solid.

SOLUTION

1. Sketch the region and draw a line segment across it parallel to the y-axis (Figure 8.32). The segment's length (shell height) is $4 - x^2 - x$. The distance of the segment from the axis of revolution (shell radius) is x.

2. Identify the limits of integration: The x-coordinate of the point of intersection of the curves $y = 4 - x^2$ and $y = x$ in the first quadrant is about 1.562. So x runs from 0 to 1.562.

3. Integrate to find the volume.

$$V = \int_0^{1.562} 2\pi \binom{\text{shell}}{\text{radius}}\binom{\text{shell}}{\text{height}} dx$$

$$= \int_0^{1.562} 2\pi(x)(4 - x^2 - x)\, dx$$

$$= 2\pi \int_0^{1.562} (4x - x^3 - x^2)\, dx$$

$$= 2\pi \left[2x^2 - \frac{x^4}{4} - \frac{x^3}{3} \right]_0^{1.562}$$

$$\approx 13.327 \qquad \text{\textit{Now Try Exercise 37.}}$$

Figure 8.32 The region and the height of a typical shell in Example 6.

EXAMPLE 7 Comparing Different Methods for Finding a Volume

We found the volume of the solid in Example 5 by using cylindrical shells. Use circular cross sections (or disks) to find the volume of the same solid.

SOLUTION

The following sketch shows drawing a line segment across the region bounded by $y = \sqrt{x}$, the x-axis, and the line $x = 4$ perpendicular to the axis of revolution.

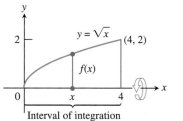

radius of
cross section $= f(x)$
$$A(x) = \pi(f(x))^2$$
$$= \pi(\sqrt{x})^2 = \pi x \qquad \text{\textit{continued}}$$

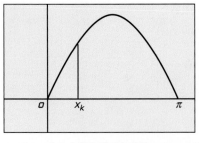

[–1, 3.5] by [–0.8, 2.2]

Figure 8.33 The base of the paperweight in Example 8. The segment perpendicular to the x-axis at x_k is the diameter of a semicircle that is perpendicular to the base.

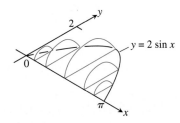

Figure 8.34 Cross sections perpendicular to the region in Figure 8.33 are semicircular. (Example 8)

Bonaventura Cavalieri
(1598–1647)

Cavalieri, a student of Galileo, discovered that if two plane regions can be arranged to lie over the same interval of the x-axis in such a way that they have identical vertical cross sections at every point, then the regions have the same area. This theorem and a letter of recommendation from Galileo were enough to win Cavalieri a chair at the University of Bologna in 1629. The solid geometry version in Example 9, which Cavalieri never proved, was named after him by later geometers.

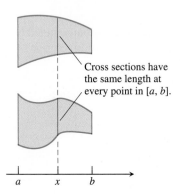

Cross sections have the same length at every point in [a, b].

The volume of the solid is

$$V = \int_0^4 A(x)\, dx = \int_0^4 \pi x\, dx = \pi \left[\frac{x^2}{2} \right]_0^4 = 8\pi.$$

Either method gives the same volume, 8π.   *Now Try Exercise 39.*

Other Cross Sections

The method of cross-section slicing can be used to find volumes of a wide variety of unusually shaped solids, so long as the cross sections have areas that we can describe with some formula. Admittedly, it does take a special artistic talent to *draw* some of these solids, but a crude picture is usually enough to suggest how to set up the integral.

EXAMPLE 8 A Mathematician's Paperweight

A mathematician has a paperweight made so that its base is the shape of the region between the x-axis and one arch of the curve $y = 2 \sin x$ (linear units in inches). Each cross section cut perpendicular to the x-axis (and hence to the xy-plane) is a semicircle whose diameter runs from the x-axis to the curve. (Think of the cross section as a semicircular fin sticking up out of the plane.) Find the volume of the paperweight.

SOLUTION

The paperweight is not easily drawn, but we know what it looks like. Its base is the region in Figure 8.33, and the cross sections perpendicular to the base are semicircular fins like those in Figure 8.34.

The semicircle at each point x has

$$\text{radius} = \frac{2 \sin x}{2} = \sin x \quad \text{and area} \quad A(x) = \frac{1}{2}\pi (\sin x)^2.$$

The volume of the paperweight is

$$V = \int_0^\pi A(x)\, dx$$

$$= \frac{\pi}{2} \int_0^\pi (\sin x)^2\, dx$$

$$\approx \frac{\pi}{2}\, \text{NINT}\, ((\sin x)^2, x, 0, \pi)$$

$$\approx \frac{\pi}{2}(1.570796327)$$

The number in parentheses looks like half of π, an observation that can be confirmed analytically, and which we support numerically by dividing by π to get 0.5. The volume of the paperweight is

$$\frac{\pi}{2} \cdot \frac{\pi}{2} = \frac{\pi^2}{4} \approx 2.47 \text{ in}^3. \qquad \textbf{\textit{Now Try Exercise 41(a).}}$$

EXAMPLE 9 Cavalieri's Volume Theorem

Cavalieri's volume theorem says that solids with equal altitudes and identical cross-section areas at each height have the same volume (Figure 8.35). This follows immediately from the definition of volume, because the cross-section area function $A(x)$ and the interval $[a, b]$ are the same for both solids.

continued

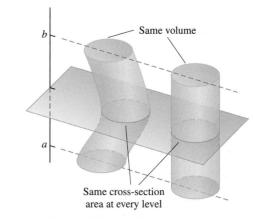

Figure 8.35 *Cavalieri's volume theorem:* These solids have the same volume. You can illustrate this yourself with stacks of coins. (Example 9)

Now Try Exercise 45.

EXPLORATION 2 Surface Area

We know how to find the volume of a solid of revolution, but how would we find the *surface area*? As before, we partition the solid into thin slices, but now we wish to form a Riemann sum of approximations to *surface areas of slices* (rather than of volumes of slices).

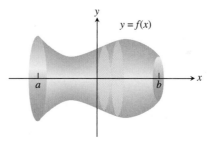

A typical slice has a surface area that can be approximated by $2\pi \cdot f(x) \cdot \Delta s$, where Δs is the tiny *slant height* of the slice. We will see in Section 8.4, when we study arc length, that $\Delta s = \sqrt{\Delta x^2 + \Delta y^2}$, and that this can be written as $\Delta s = \sqrt{1 + (f'(x_k))^2}\, \Delta x$.

Thus, the surface area is approximated by the Riemann sum

$$\sum_{k=1}^{n} 2\pi f(x_k) \sqrt{1 + (f'(x_k))^2}\, \Delta x.$$

1. Write the limit of the Riemann sums as a definite integral from a to b. When will the limit exist?
2. Use the formula from part 1 to find the surface area of the solid generated by revolving a single arch of the curve $y = \sin x$ about the x-axis.
3. The region enclosed by the graphs of $y^2 = x$ and $x = 4$ is revolved about the x-axis to form a solid. Find the surface area of the solid.

Quick Review 8.3 *(For help, go to Section 1.2.)*

Exercise numbers with a gray background indicate problems that the authors have designed to be solved *without a calculator*.

In Exercises 1–10, give a formula for the area of the plane region in terms of the single variable x.

1. a square with sides of length x

2. a square with diagonals of length x

3. a semicircle of radius x

4. a semicircle of diameter x

5. an equilateral triangle with sides of length x

6. an isosceles right triangle with legs of length x

7. an isosceles right triangle with hypotenuse x

8. an isosceles triangle with two sides of length $2x$ and one side of length x

9. a triangle with sides $3x$, $4x$, and $5x$

10. a regular hexagon with sides of length x

Section 8.3 Exercises

In Exercises 1 and 2, find a formula for the area $A(x)$ of the cross sections of the solid that are perpendicular to the x-axis.

1. The solid lies between planes perpendicular to the x-axis at $x = -1$ and $x = 1$. The cross sections perpendicular to the x-axis between these planes run from the semicircle $y = -\sqrt{1 - x^2}$ to the semicircle $y = \sqrt{1 - x^2}$.

(a) The cross sections are circular disks with diameters in the xy-plane.

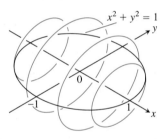

(b) The cross sections are squares with bases in the xy-plane.

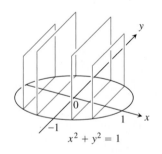

(c) The cross sections are squares with diagonals in the xy-plane. (The length of a square's diagonal is $\sqrt{2}$ times the length of its sides.)

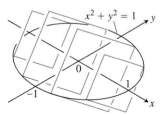

(d) The cross sections are equilateral triangles with bases in the xy-plane.

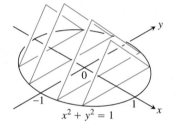

2. The solid lies between planes perpendicular to the x-axis at $x = 0$ and $x = 4$. The cross sections perpendicular to the x-axis between these planes run from $y = -\sqrt{x}$ to $y = \sqrt{x}$.

(a) The cross sections are circular disks with diameters in the xy-plane.

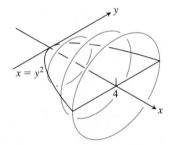

(b) The cross sections are squares with bases in the xy-plane.

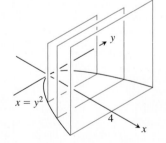

(c) The cross sections are squares with diagonals in the xy-plane.

(d) The cross sections are equilateral triangles with bases in the xy-plane.

In Exercises 3–6, find the volume of the solid analytically.

3. The solid lies between planes perpendicular to the *x*-axis at $x = 0$ and $x = 4$. The cross sections perpendicular to the axis on the interval $0 \le x \le 4$ are squares whose diagonals run from $y = -\sqrt{x}$ to $y = \sqrt{x}$.

4. The solid lies between planes perpendicular to the *x*-axis at $x = -1$ and $x = 1$. The cross sections perpendicular to the *x*-axis are circular disks whose diameters run from the parabola $y = x^2$ to the parabola $y = 2 - x^2$.

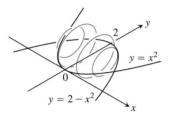

5. The solid lies between planes perpendicular to the *x*-axis at $x = -1$ and $x = 1$. The cross sections perpendicular to the *x*-axis between these planes are squares whose bases run from the semicircle $y = -\sqrt{1 - x^2}$ to the semicircle $y = \sqrt{1 - x^2}$.

6. The solid lies between planes perpendicular to the *x*-axis at $x = -1$ and $x = 1$. The cross sections perpendicular to the *x*-axis between these planes are squares whose diagonals run from the semicircle $y = -\sqrt{1 - x^2}$ to the semicircle $y = \sqrt{1 - x^2}$.

In Exercises 7–10, find the volume of the solid generated by revolving the shaded region about the given axis.

7. about the *x*-axis   **8.** about the *y*-axis

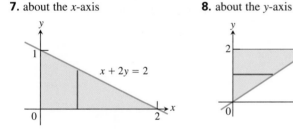

9. about the *y*-axis   **10.** about the *x*-axis

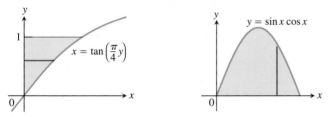

In Exercises 11–20, find the volume of the solid generated by revolving the region bounded by the lines and curves about the *x*-axis.

11. $y = x^2$, $y = 0$, $x = 2$ **12.** $y = x^3$, $y = 0$, $x = 2$

13. $y = \sqrt{9 - x^2}$, $y = 0$ **14.** $y = x - x^2$, $y = 0$

15. $y = x$, $y = 1$, $x = 0$ **16.** $y = 2x$, $y = x$, $x = 1$

17. $y = x^2 + 1, y = x + 3$ **18.** $y = 4 - x^2$, $y = 2 - x$

19. $y = \sec x$, $y = \sqrt{2}$, $-\pi/4 \le x \le \pi/4$

20. $y = -\sqrt{x}$, $y = -2$, $x = 0$

In Exercises 21–24, find the volume of the solid generated by revolving the region about the given line.

21. the region bounded by $y = x^2, y = 0$, and $x = 2$ about the line $x = 2$

22. the region bounded by $y = \sin x, y = 0$, and $x = \pi/2$ about the line $x = \pi/2$

23. the region in the first quadrant bounded above by the line $y = \sqrt{2}$, below by the curve $y = \sec x \tan x$, and on the left by the *y*-axis, about the line $y = \sqrt{2}$

24. the region in the first quadrant bounded above by the line $y = 2$, below by the curve $y = 2 \sin x, 0 \le x \le \pi/2$, and on the left by the *y*-axis, about the line $y = 2$

In Exercises 25–30, find the volume of the solid generated by revolving the region about the *y*-axis.

25. the region enclosed by $x = \sqrt{5}y^2$, $x = 0$, $y = -1$, $y = 1$

26. the region enclosed by $x = y^{3/2}$, $x = 0$, $y = 2$

27. the region enclosed by the triangle with vertices $(1, 0), (2, 1)$, and $(1, 1)$

28. the region enclosed by the triangle with vertices $(0, 1), (1, 0)$, and $(1, 1)$

29. the region in the first quadrant bounded above by the parabola $y = x^2$, below by the *x*-axis, and on the right by the line $x = 2$

30. the region bounded above by the curve $y = \sqrt{x}$ and below by the line $y = x$

Group Activity In Exercises 31–34, find the volume of the solid described.

31. Find the volume of the solid generated by revolving the region bounded by $y = \sqrt{x}$ and the lines $y = 2$ and $x = 0$ about

(a) the *x*-axis.   (b) the *y*-axis.

(c) the line $y = 2$.   (d) the line $x = 4$.

32. Find the volume of the solid generated by revolving the triangular region bounded by the lines $y = 2x, y = 0$, and $x = 1$ about

(a) the line $x = 1$.   (b) the line $x = 2$.

33. Find the volume of the solid generated by revolving the region bounded by the parabola $y = x^2$ and the line $y = 1$ about

(a) the line $y = 1$.   (b) the line $y = 2$.

(c) the line $y = -1$.

34. By integration, find the volume of the solid generated by revolving the triangular region with vertices $(0, 0), (b, 0), (0, h)$ about

(a) the *x*-axis.   (b) the *y*-axis.

In Exercises 35 and 36, use the cylindrical shell method to find the volume of the solid generated by revolving the shaded region about the indicated axis.

35. (a) the *x*-axis　　　　(b) the line $y = 1$

(c) the line $y = 8/5$　　(d) the line $y = -2/5$

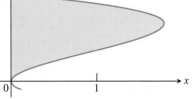

36. (a) the *x*-axis　　　　(b) the line $y = 2$

(c) the line $y = 5$　　　(d) the line $y = -5/8$

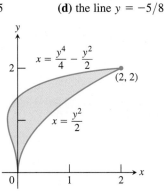

In Exercises 37–40, use the cylindrical shell method to find the volume of the solid generated by revolving the region bounded by the curves about the *y*-axis.

37. $y = x$,　$y = -x/2$,　$x = 2$

38. $y = x^2$,　$y = 2 - x$,　$x = 0$,　for　$x \geq 0$

39. $y = \sqrt{x}$,　$y = 0$,　$x = 4$

40. $y = 2x - 1$,　$y = \sqrt{x}$,　$x = 0$

In Exercises 41–44, find the volume of the solid analytically.

41. The base of a solid is the region between the curve $y = 2\sqrt{\sin x}$ and the interval $[0, \pi]$ on the *x*-axis. The cross sections perpendicular to the *x*-axis are

(a) equilateral triangles with bases running from the *x*-axis to the curve as shown in the figure.

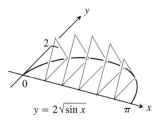

(b) squares with bases running from the *x*-axis to the curve.

42. The solid lies between planes perpendicular to the *x*-axis at $x = -\pi/3$ and $x = \pi/3$. The cross sections perpendicular to the *x*-axis are

(a) circular disks with diameters running from the curve $y = \tan x$ to the curve $y = \sec x$.

(b) squares whose bases run from the curve $y = \tan x$ to the curve $y = \sec x$.

43. The solid lies between planes perpendicular to the *y*-axis at $y = 0$ and $y = 2$. The cross sections perpendicular to the *y*-axis are circular disks with diameters running from the *y*-axis to the parabola $x = \sqrt{5}y^2$.

44. The base of the solid is the disk $x^2 + y^2 \leq 1$. The cross sections by planes perpendicular to the *y*-axis between $y = -1$ and $y = 1$ are isosceles right triangles with one leg in the disk.

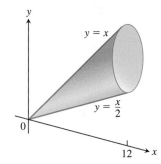

45. Writing to Learn A solid lies between planes perpendicular to the *x*-axis at $x = 0$ and $x = 12$. The cross sections by planes perpendicular to the *x*-axis are circular disks whose diameters run from the line $y = x/2$ to the line $y = x$ as shown in the figure. Explain why the solid has the same volume as a right circular cone with base radius 3 and height 12.

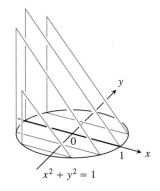

46. A Twisted Solid A square of side length *s* lies in a plane perpendicular to a line *L*. One vertex of the square lies on *L*. As this square moves a distance *h* along *L*, the square turns one revolution about *L* to generate a corkscrew-like column with square cross sections.

(a) Find the volume of the column.

(b) **Writing to Learn** What will the volume be if the square turns twice instead of once? Give reasons for your answer.

47. Find the volume of the solid generated by revolving the region in the first quadrant bounded by $y = x^3$ and $y = 4x$ about

(a) the *x*-axis,

(b) the line $y = 8$.

48. Find the volume of the solid generated by revolving the region bounded by $y = 2x - x^2$ and $y = x$ about

(a) the y-axis,

(b) the line $x = 1$.

49. The region in the first quadrant that is bounded above by the curve $y = 1/\sqrt{x}$, on the left by the line $x = 1/4$, and below by the line $y = 1$ is revolved about the y-axis to generate a solid. Find the volume of the solid by **(a)** the washer method and **(b)** the cylindrical shell method.

50. Let $f(x) = \begin{cases} (\sin x)/x, & 0 < x \leq \pi \\ 1, & x = 0. \end{cases}$

(a) Show that $x f(x) = \sin x$, $0 \leq x \leq \pi$.

(b) Find the volume of the solid generated by revolving the shaded region about the y-axis.

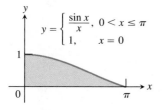

51. *Designing a Plumb Bob* Having been asked to design a brass plumb bob that will weigh in the neighborhood of 190 g, you decide to shape it like the solid of revolution shown here.

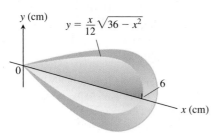

(a) Find the plumb bob's volume.

(b) If you specify a brass that weighs 8.5 g/cm³, how much will the plumb bob weigh to the nearest gram?

52. *Volume of a Bowl* A bowl has a shape that can be generated by revolving the graph of $y = x^2/2$ between $y = 0$ and $y = 5$ about the y-axis.

(a) Find the volume of the bowl.

(b) If we fill the bowl with water at a constant rate of 3 cubic units per second, how fast will the water level in the bowl be rising when the water is 4 units deep?

53. *The Classical Bead Problem* A round hole is drilled through the center of a spherical solid of radius r. The resulting cylindrical hole has height 4 cm.

(a) What is the volume of the solid that remains?

(b) What is unusual about the answer?

54. **Writing to Learn** Explain how you could estimate the volume of a solid of revolution by measuring the shadow cast on a table parallel to its axis of revolution by a light shining directly above it.

55. *Same Volume About Each Axis* The region in the first quadrant enclosed between the graph of $y = ax - x^2$ and the x-axis generates the same volume whether it is revolved about the x-axis or the y-axis. Find the value of a.

56. *(Continuation of Exploration 2)* Let $x = g(y) > 0$ have a continuous first derivative on $[c, d]$. Show that the area of the surface generated by revolving the curve $x = g(y)$ about the y-axis is

$$S = \int_c^d 2\pi g(y) \sqrt{1 + (g'(y))^2}\, dy.$$

In Exercises 57–64, find the area of the surface generated by revolving the curve about the indicated axis.

57. $x = \sqrt{y}$, $0 \leq y \leq 2$; y-axis

58. $x = y^3/3$, $0 \leq y \leq 1$; y-axis

59. $x = y^{1/2} - (1/3)^{3/2}$, $1 \leq y \leq 3$; y-axis

60. $x = \sqrt{2y - 1}$, $(5/8) \leq y \leq 1$; y-axis

61. $y = x^2$, $0 \leq x \leq 2$; x-axis

62. $y = 3x - x^2$, $0 \leq x \leq 3$; x-axis

63. $y = \sqrt{2x - x^2}$, $0.5 \leq x \leq 1.5$; x-axis

64. $y = \sqrt{x + 1}$, $1 \leq x \leq 5$; x-axis

Standardized Test Questions

You may use a graphing calculator to solve the following problems.

65. True or False The volume of a solid of a known integrable cross section area $A(x)$ from $x = a$ to $x = b$ is $\int_a^b A(x)\, dx$. Justify your answer.

66. True or False If the region enclosed by the y-axis, the line $y = 2$, and the curve $y = \sqrt{x}$ is revolved about the y-axis, the volume of the solid is given by the definite integral $\int_0^2 \pi y^2\, dy$. Justify your answer.

67. Multiple Choice The base of a solid S is the region enclosed by the graph of $y = \ln x$, the line $x = e$, and the x-axis. If the cross sections of S perpendicular to the x-axis are squares, which of the following gives the best approximation of the volume of S?

(A) 0.718   (B) 1.718   (C) 2.718

(D) 3.171   (E) 7.388

68. Multiple Choice Let R be the region in the first quadrant bounded by the graph of $y = 8 - x^{3/2}$, the x-axis, and the y-axis. Which of the following gives the best approximation of the volume of the solid generated when R is revolved about the x-axis?

(A) 60.3   (B) 115.2   (C) 225.4

(D) 319.7   (E) 361.9

69. Multiple Choice Let R be the region enclosed by the graph of $y = x^2$, the line $x = 4$, and the x-axis. Which of the following gives the best approximation of the volume of the solid generated when R is revolved about the y-axis?

(A) 64π (B) 128π (C) 256π

(D) 360   (E) 512

70. Multiple Choice Let R be the region enclosed by the graphs of $y = e^{-x}$, $y = e^x$, and $x = 1$. Which of the following gives the volume of the solid generated when R is revolved about the x-axis?

(A) $\displaystyle\int_0^1 (e^x - e^{-x})\, dx$ **(B)** $\displaystyle\int_0^1 (e^{2x} - e^{-2x})\, dx$

(C) $\displaystyle\int_0^1 (e^x - e^{-x})^2\, dx$ **(D)** $\pi\displaystyle\int_0^1 (e^{2x} - e^{-2x})\, dx$

(E) $\pi\displaystyle\int_0^1 (e^x - e^{-x})^2\, dx$

Explorations

71. Max-Min The arch $y = \sin x$, $0 \le x \le \pi$, is revolved about the line $y = c$, $0 \le c \le 1$, to generate the solid in the figure.

(a) Find the value of c that minimizes the volume of the solid. What is the minimum volume?

(b) What value of c in $[0, 1]$ maximizes the volume of the solid?

(c) **Writing to Learn** Graph the solid's volume as a function of c, first for $0 \le c \le 1$ and then on a larger domain. What happens to the volume of the solid as c moves away from $[0, 1]$? Does this make sense physically? Give reasons for your answers.

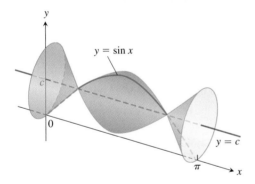

72. A Vase We wish to estimate the volume of a flower vase using only a calculator, a string, and a ruler. We measure the height of the vase to be 6 inches. We then use the string and the ruler to find circumferences of the vase (in inches) at half-inch intervals. (We list them from the top down to correspond with the picture of the vase.)

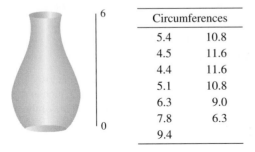

Circumferences	
5.4	10.8
4.5	11.6
4.4	11.6
5.1	10.8
6.3	9.0
7.8	6.3
9.4	

(a) Find the areas of the cross sections that correspond to the given circumferences.

(b) Express the volume of the vase as an integral with respect to y over the interval $[0, 6]$.

(c) Approximate the integral using the Trapezoidal Rule with $n = 12$.

Extending the Ideas

73. Volume of a Hemisphere Derive the formula $V = (2/3)\pi R^3$ for the volume of a hemisphere of radius R by comparing its cross sections with the cross sections of a solid right circular cylinder of radius R and height R from which a solid right circular cone of base radius R and height R has been removed, as suggested by the figure.

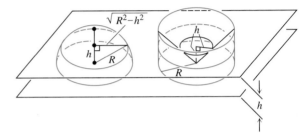

74. Volume of a Torus The disk $x^2 + y^2 \le a^2$ is revolved about the line $x = b$ $(b > a)$ to generate a solid shaped like a doughnut, called a *torus*. Find its volume. (*Hint:* $\int_{-a}^{a} \sqrt{a^2 - y^2}\, dy = \pi a^2/2$, since it is the area of a semicircle of radius a.)

75. Filling a Bowl

(a) **Volume** A hemispherical bowl of radius a contains water to a depth h. Find the volume of water in the bowl.

(b) **Related Rates** Water runs into a sunken concrete hemispherical bowl of radius 5 m at a rate of 0.2 m^3/sec. How fast is the water level in the bowl rising when the water is 4 m deep?

76. Consistency of Volume Definitions The volume formulas in calculus are consistent with the standard formulas from geometry in the sense that they agree on objects to which both apply.

(a) As a case in point, show that if you revolve the region enclosed by the semicircle $y = \sqrt{a^2 - x^2}$ and the x-axis about the x-axis to generate a solid sphere, the calculus formula for volume at the beginning of the section will give $(4/3)\pi a^3$ for the volume, just as it should.

(b) Use calculus to find the volume of a right circular cone of height h and base radius r.

Quick Quiz for AP* Preparation: Sections 8.1–8.3

You may use a graphing calculator to solve the following problems.

1. **Multiple Choice** The base of a solid is the region in the first quadrant bounded by the x-axis, the graph of $y = \sin^{-1} x$, and the vertical line $x = 1$. For this solid, each cross section perpendicular to the x-axis is a square. What is the volume?

   (A) 0.117   **(B)** 0.285   **(C)** 0.467   **(D)** 0.571   **(E)** 1.571

2. **Multiple Choice** Let R be the region in the first quadrant bounded by the graph of $y = 3x - x^2$ and the x-axis. A solid is generated when R is revolved about the horizontal line $y = -1$. Set up, but do not evaluate, the definite integral that gives the volume of this solid.

   (A) $\pi \displaystyle\int_0^3 (3x - x^2 - 1)^2\, dx$

   (B) $\pi \displaystyle\int_0^3 (3x - x^2 + 1)^2\, dx$

   (C) $\pi \displaystyle\int_0^3 ((3x - x^2)^2 - 1)\, dx$

   (D) $\pi \displaystyle\int_0^3 ((3x - x^2 - 1)^2 - 1)\, dx$

   (E) $\pi \displaystyle\int_0^3 ((3x - x^2 + 1)^2 - 1)\, dx$

3. **Multiple Choice** A developing country consumes oil at a rate given by $r(t) = 20e^{0.2t}$ million barrels per year, where t is time measured in years, for $0 \le t \le 10$. Which of the following expressions gives the amount of oil consumed by the country during the time interval $0 \le t \le 10$?

   (A) $r(10)$

   (B) $r(10) - r(0)$

   (C) $\displaystyle\int_0^{10} r'(t)\, dt$

   (D) $\displaystyle\int_0^{10} r(t)\, dt$

   (E) $10 \cdot r(10)$

4. **Free Response** Let R be the region bounded by the graphs of $y = \sqrt{x}$, $y = e^{-x}$, and the y-axis.

   (a) Find the area of R.

   (b) Find the volume of the solid generated when R is revolved about the horizontal line $y = -1$.

   (c) The region R is the base of a solid. For this solid, each cross section perpendicular to the x-axis is a semicircle whose diameter runs from the graph of $y = \sqrt{x}$ to the graph of $y = e^{-x}$. Find the volume of this solid.

8.4 Lengths of Curves

You will be able to apply the definite integral to solve problems involving lengths of curves.

- Lengths of smooth curves
- Lengths of curves with vertical tangents, corners, or cusps

A Sine Wave

How long is a sine wave (Figure 8.36)?

The usual meaning of *wavelength* refers to the fundamental period, which for $y = \sin x$ is 2π. But how long is the curve itself? If you straightened it out like a piece of string along the positive *x*-axis with one end at 0, where would the other end be?

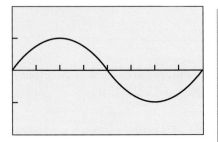

[0, 2π] by [−2, 2]

Figure 8.36 One wave of a sine curve has to be longer than 2π.

EXAMPLE 1 The Length of a Sine Wave

What is the length of the curve $y = \sin x$ from $x = 0$ to $x = 2\pi$?

SOLUTION

We answer this question with integration, following our usual plan of breaking the whole into measurable parts. We partition $[0, 2\pi]$ into intervals so short that the pieces of curve (call them "arcs") lying directly above the intervals are nearly straight. That way, each arc is nearly the same as the line segment joining its two ends and we can take the length of the segment as an approximation to the length of the arc.

Figure 8.37 shows the segment approximating the arc above the subinterval $[x_{k-1}, x_k]$. The length of the segment is $\sqrt{\Delta x_k{}^2 + \Delta y_k{}^2}$. The sum

$$\sum \sqrt{\Delta x_k{}^2 + \Delta y_k{}^2}$$

over the entire partition approximates the length of the curve. All we need now is to find the limit of this sum as the norms of the partitions go to zero. That's the usual plan, but this time there is a problem. Do you see it?

The problem is that the sums as written are not Riemann sums. They do not have the form $\sum f(c_k)\Delta x$. We can rewrite them as Riemann sums if we multiply and divide each square root by Δx_k.

$$\sum \sqrt{\Delta x_k{}^2 + \Delta y_k{}^2} = \sum \frac{\sqrt{(\Delta x_k)^2 + (\Delta y_k)^2}}{\Delta x_k} \Delta x_k$$

$$= \sum \sqrt{1 + \left(\frac{\Delta y_k}{\Delta x_k}\right)^2} \Delta x_k$$

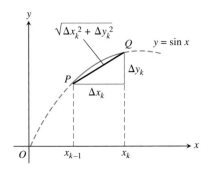

Figure 8.37 The line segment approximating the arc *PQ* of the sine curve above the subinterval $[x_{k-1}, x_k]$. (Example 1)

This is better, but we still need to write the last square root as a function evaluated at some c_k in the *k*th subinterval. For this, we call on the Mean Value Theorem for differentiable functions (Section 5.2), which says that since $\sin x$ is continuous on $[x_{k-1}, x_k]$ and is differentiable on (x_{k-1}, x_k) there is a point c_k in (x_{k-1}, x_k) at which $\Delta y_k/\Delta x_k = \sin' c_k$ (Figure 8.38). That gives us

$$\sum \sqrt{1 + (\sin' c_k)^2}\, \Delta x_k,$$

which *is* a Riemann sum.

Now we take the limit as the norms of the subdivisions go to zero and find that the length of one wave of the sine function is

$$\int_0^{2\pi} \sqrt{1 + (\sin' x)^2}\, dx = \int_0^{2\pi} \sqrt{1 + \cos^2 x}\, dx \approx 7.64. \quad \text{Using NINT}$$

How close was your estimate?

Now Try Exercise 9.

Group Exploration

Later in this section we will use an integral to find the length of the sine wave with great precision. But there are ways to get good approximations without integrating. Take five minutes to come up with a written estimate of the curve's length. No fair looking ahead.

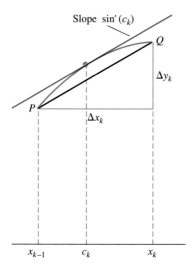

Figure 8.38 The portion of the sine curve above $[x_{k-1}, x_k]$. At some c_k in the interval, $\sin'(c_k) = \Delta y_k / \Delta x_k$, the slope of segment PQ. (Example 1)

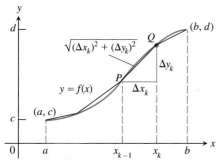

Figure 8.39 The graph of f, approximated by line segments.

Length of a Smooth Curve

We are almost ready to define the length of a curve as a definite integral, using the procedure of Example 1. We first call attention to two properties of the sine function that came into play along the way.

We obviously used *differentiability* when we invoked the Mean Value Theorem to replace $\Delta y_k / \Delta x_k$ by $\sin'(c_k)$ for some c_k in the interval (x_{k-1}, x_k). Less obviously, we used the continuity of the derivative of sine in passing from $\sum \sqrt{1 + (\sin'(c_k))^2}\,\Delta x_k$ to the Riemann integral. The requirement for finding the length of a curve by this method, then, is that the function have a continuous first derivative. We call this property *smoothness*. A function with a continuous first derivative is **smooth** and its graph is a **smooth curve.**

Let us review the process, this time with a general smooth function $f(x)$. Suppose the graph of f begins at the point (a, c) and ends at (b, d), as shown in Figure 8.39. We partition the interval $a \le x \le b$ into subintervals so short that the arcs of the curve above them are nearly straight. The length of the segment approximating the arc above the subinterval $[x_{k-1}, x_k]$ is $\sqrt{\Delta x_k^2 + \Delta y_k^2}$. The sum $\sum \sqrt{\Delta x_k^2 + \Delta y_k^2}$ approximates the length of the curve. We apply the Mean Value Theorem to f on each subinterval to rewrite the sum as a Riemann sum,

$$\sum \sqrt{\Delta x_k^2 + \Delta y_k^2} = \sum \sqrt{1 + \left(\frac{\Delta y_k}{\Delta x_k}\right)^2}\,\Delta x_k$$

$$= \sum \sqrt{1 + (f'(c_k))^2}\,\Delta x_k \quad \text{For some point } c_k \text{ in } (x_{k-1}, x_k)$$

Passing to the limit as the norms of the subdivisions go to zero gives the length of the curve as

$$L = \int_a^b \sqrt{1 + (f'(x))^2}\,dx = \int_a^b \sqrt{1 + \left(\frac{dy}{dx}\right)^2}\,dx.$$

We could as easily have transformed $\sum \sqrt{\Delta x_k^2 + \Delta y_k^2}$ into a Riemann sum by dividing and multiplying by Δy_k, giving a formula that involves x as a function of y (say, $x = g(y)$) on the interval $[c, d]$:

$$L \approx \sum \frac{\sqrt{(\Delta x_k)^2 + (\Delta y_k)^2}}{\Delta y_k}\,\Delta y_k = \sum \sqrt{1 + \left(\frac{\Delta x_k}{\Delta y_k}\right)^2}\,\Delta y_k$$

$$= \sum \sqrt{1 + (g'(c_k))^2}\,\Delta y_k \quad \text{For some } c_k \text{ in } (y_{k-1}, y_k)$$

The limit of these sums, as the norms of the subdivisions go to zero, gives another reasonable way to calculate the curve's length,

$$L = \int_c^d \sqrt{1 + (g'(y))^2}\,dy = \int_c^d \sqrt{1 + \left(\frac{dx}{dy}\right)^2}\,dy.$$

Putting these two formulas together, we have the following definition for the length of a smooth curve.

DEFINITION   Arc Length: Length of a Smooth Curve

If a smooth curve begins at (a, c) and ends at (b, d), $a < b, c < d$, then the **length (arc length) of the curve** is

$$L = \int_a^b \sqrt{1 + \left(\frac{dy}{dx}\right)^2}\,dx \qquad \text{if } y \text{ is a smooth function of } x \text{ on } [a, b];$$

$$L = \int_c^d \sqrt{1 + \left(\frac{dx}{dy}\right)^2}\,dy \qquad \text{if } x \text{ is a smooth function of } y \text{ on } [c, d].$$

EXAMPLE 2 **Applying the Definition**

Find the *exact* length of the curve

$$y = \frac{4\sqrt{2}}{3} x^{3/2} - 1 \quad \text{for} \quad 0 \le x \le 1.$$

SOLUTION

$$\frac{dy}{dx} = \frac{4\sqrt{2}}{3} \cdot \frac{3}{2} x^{1/2} = 2\sqrt{2}\, x^{1/2},$$

which is continuous on $[0, 1]$. Therefore,

$$L = \int_0^1 \sqrt{1 + \left(\frac{dy}{dx}\right)^2}\, dx$$

$$= \int_0^1 \sqrt{1 + (2\sqrt{2}x^{1/2})^2}\, dx$$

$$= \int_0^1 \sqrt{1 + 8x}\, dx$$

$$= \frac{2}{3} \cdot \frac{1}{8} (1 + 8x)^{3/2} \Big]_0^1$$

$$= \frac{13}{6}$$ *Now Try Exercise 11.*

We asked for an exact length in Example 2 to take advantage of the rare opportunity it afforded of taking the antiderivative of an arc length integrand. When you add 1 to the square of the derivative of an arbitrary smooth function and then take the square root of that sum, the result is rarely antidifferentiable by reasonable methods. We know a few more functions that give "nice" integrands, but we are saving those for the exercises.

Vertical Tangents, Corners, and Cusps

Sometimes a curve has a vertical tangent, corner, or cusp where the derivative we need to work with is undefined. We can sometimes get around such a difficulty in ways illustrated by the following examples.

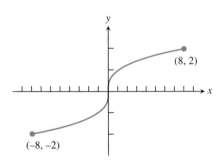

Figure 8.40 The graph of $y = x^{1/3}$ has a vertical tangent line at the origin where dy/dx does not exist. (Example 3)

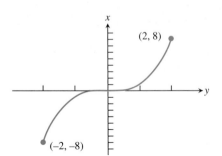

Figure 8.41 The curve in Figure 8.40 plotted with x as a function of y. The tangent at the origin is now horizontal. (Example 3)

EXAMPLE 3 **A Vertical Tangent**

Find the length of the curve $y = x^{1/3}$ between $(-8, -2)$ and $(8, 2)$.

SOLUTION

The derivative

$$\frac{dy}{dx} = \frac{1}{3} x^{-2/3} = \frac{1}{3x^{2/3}}$$

is not defined at $x = 0$. Graphically, there is a vertical tangent at $x = 0$ where the derivative becomes infinite (Figure 8.40). If we change to x as a function of y, the tangent at the origin will be horizontal (Figure 8.41) and the derivative will be zero instead of undefined. Solving $y = x^{1/3}$ for x gives $x = y^3$, and we have

$$L = \int_{-2}^2 \sqrt{1 + \left(\frac{dx}{dy}\right)^2}\, dy = \int_{-2}^2 \sqrt{1 + (3y^2)^2}\, dy \approx 17.26. \quad \text{Using NINT}$$

Now Try Exercise 25.

What happens if you fail to notice that dy/dx is undefined at $x = 0$ and ask your calculator to compute

$$\text{NINT}\left(\sqrt{1 + ((1/3)\,x^{-2/3})^2}, x, -8, 8\right)?$$

This actually depends on your calculator. If, in the process of its calculations, it tries to evaluate the function at $x = 0$, then some sort of domain error will result. If it tries to find convergent Riemann sums near $x = 0$, it might get into a long, futile loop of computations that you will have to interrupt. Or it might actually produce an answer—in which case you hope it would be sufficiently bizarre for you to realize that it should not be trusted.

EXAMPLE 4 Getting Around a Corner

Find the length of the curve $y = x^2 - 4|x| - x$ from $x = -4$ to $x = 4$.

SOLUTION

We should always be alert for abrupt slope changes when absolute value is involved. We graph the function to check (Figure 8.42).

There is clearly a corner at $x = 0$ where neither dy/dx nor dx/dy can exist. To find the length, we split the curve at $x = 0$ to write the function *without* absolute values:

$$x^2 - 4|x| - x = \begin{cases} x^2 + 3x & \text{if } x < 0, \\ x^2 - 5x & \text{if } x \geq 0 \end{cases}$$

Then,

$$L = \int_{-4}^{0} \sqrt{1 + (2x + 3)^2}\, dx + \int_{0}^{4} \sqrt{1 + (2x - 5)^2}\, dx$$

$$\approx 19.56 \quad \text{By NINT}$$

Now Try Exercise 27.

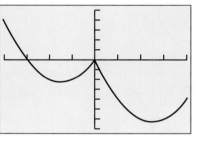

[-4, 4] by [-7, 5]

Figure 8.42 The graph of

$$y = x^2 - 4|x| - x, -4 \leq x \leq 4,$$

has a corner at $x = 0$ where neither dy/dx nor dx/dy exists. We find the lengths of the two smooth pieces and add them together. (Example 4)

Finally, cusps are handled the same way corners are: split the curve into smooth pieces and add the lengths of those pieces.

Quick Review 8.4 *(For help, go to Sections 1.3 and 3.2.)*

Exercise numbers with a gray background indicate problems that the authors have designed to be solved *without a calculator*.

In Exercises 1–5, simplify the function.

1. $\sqrt{1 + 2x + x^2}$ on $[1, 5]$

2. $\sqrt{1 - x + \dfrac{x^2}{4}}$ on $[-3, -1]$

3. $\sqrt{1 + (\tan x)^2}$ on $[0, \pi/3]$

4. $\sqrt{1 + (x/4 - 1/x)^2}$ on $[4, 12]$

5. $\sqrt{1 + \cos 2x}$ on $[0, \pi/2]$

In Exercises 6–10, identify all values of x for which the function fails to be differentiable.

6. $f(x) = |x - 4|$

7. $f(x) = 5x^{2/3}$

8. $f(x) = \sqrt[5]{x + 3}$

9. $f(x) = \sqrt{x^2 - 4x + 4}$

10. $f(x) = 1 + \sqrt[3]{\sin x}$

Section 8.4 Exercises

In Exercises 1–10,

   (a) set up an integral for the length of the curve;

   (b) graph the curve to see what it looks like;

   (c) use NINT to find the length of the curve.

1. $y = x^2, \quad -1 \le x \le 2$

2. $y = \tan x, \quad -\pi/3 \le x \le 0$

3. $x = \sin y, \quad 0 \le y \le \pi$

4. $x = \sqrt{1 - y^2}, \quad -1/2 \le y \le 1/2$

5. $y^2 + 2y = 2x + 1, \quad$ from $(-1, -1)$ to $(7, 3)$

6. $y = \sin x - x \cos x, \quad 0 \le x \le \pi$

7. $y = \int_0^x \tan t \, dt, \quad 0 \le x \le \pi/6$

8. $x = \int_0^y \sqrt{\sec^2 t - 1} \, dt, \quad -\pi/3 \le y \le \pi/4$

9. $y = \sec x, \quad -\pi/3 \le x \le \pi/3$

10. $y = (e^x + e^{-x})/2, \quad -3 \le x \le 3$

In Exercises 11–18, find the exact length of the curve analytically by antidifferentiation. You will need to simplify the integrand algebraically before finding an antiderivative.

11. $y = (1/3)(x^2 + 2)^{3/2} \quad$ from $\quad x = 0$ to $x = 3$

12. $y = x^{3/2} \quad$ from $\quad x = 0$ to $x = 4$

13. $x = (y^3/3) + 1/(4y) \quad$ from $\quad y = 1$ to $y = 3$

   [*Hint:* $1 + (dx/dy)^2$ is a perfect square.]

14. $x = (y^4/4) + 1/(8y^2) \quad$ from $\quad y = 1$ to $y = 2$

   [*Hint:* $1 + (dx/dy)^2$ is a perfect square.]

15. $x = (y^3/6) + 1/(2y) \quad$ from $\quad y = 1$ to $y = 2$

   [*Hint:* $1 + (dx/dy)^2$ is a perfect square.]

16. $y = (x^3/3) + x^2 + x + 1/(4x + 4), \quad 0 \le x \le 2$

17. $x = \int_0^y \sqrt{\sec^4 t - 1} \, dt, \quad -\pi/4 \le y \le \pi/4$

18. $y = \int_{-2}^x \sqrt{3t^4 - 1} \, dt, \quad -2 \le x \le -1$

19. (a) Group Activity Find a curve through the point $(1, 1)$ whose length integral is

$$L = \int_1^4 \sqrt{1 + \frac{1}{4x}} \, dx.$$

   (b) Writing to Learn How many such curves are there? Give reasons for your answer.

20. (a) Group Activity Find a curve through the point $(0, 1)$ whose length integral is

$$L = \int_1^2 \sqrt{1 + \frac{1}{y^4}} \, dy.$$

   (b) Writing to Learn How many such curves are there? Give reasons for your answer.

21. Find the length of the curve

$$y = \int_0^x \sqrt{\cos 2t} \, dt$$

from $x = 0$ to $x = \pi/4$.

22. *The Length of an Astroid* The graph of the equation $x^{2/3} + y^{2/3} = 1$ is one of the family of curves called *astroids* (not "asteroids") because of their starlike appearance (see figure). Find the length of this particular astroid by finding the length of half the first quadrant portion, $y = (1 - x^{2/3})^{3/2}, \sqrt{2}/4 \le x \le 1$, and multiplying by 8.

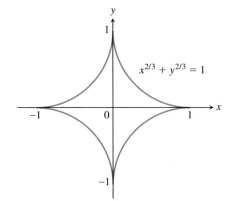

23. *Fabricating Metal Sheets* Your metal fabrication company is bidding for a contract to make sheets of corrugated steel roofing like the one shown here. The cross sections of the corrugated sheets are to conform to the curve

$$y = \sin\left(\frac{3\pi}{20} x\right), 0 \le x \le 20 \text{ in.}$$

If the roofing is to be stamped from flat sheets by a process that does not stretch the material, how wide should the original material be? Give your answer to two decimal places.

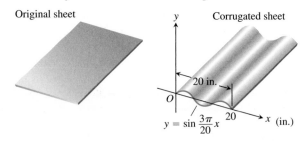

24. *Tunnel Construction* Your engineering firm is bidding for the contract to construct the tunnel shown on the next page. The tunnel is 300 ft long and 50 ft wide at the base. The cross section is shaped like one arch of the curve $y = 25 \cos(\pi x/50)$. Upon completion, the tunnel's inside surface (excluding the roadway) will be treated with a waterproof sealer that costs

$1.75 per square foot to apply. How much will it cost to apply the sealer?

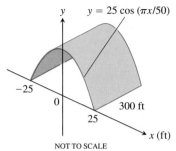

y = 25 cos (πx/50)

NOT TO SCALE

In Exercises 25 and 26, find the length of the curve.

25. $f(x) = x^{1/3} + x^{2/3}, \quad 0 \le x \le 2$

26. $f(x) = \dfrac{x-1}{4x^2+1}, \quad -\dfrac{1}{2} \le x \le 1$

In Exercises 27–29, find the length of the nonsmooth curve.

27. $y = x^3 + 5|x|$ from $x = -2$ to $x = 1$

28. $\sqrt{x} + \sqrt{y} = 1$

29. $y = \sqrt[4]{x}$ from $x = 0$ to $x = 16$

30. Writing to Learn Explain geometrically why it does not work to use short *horizontal* line segments to approximate the lengths of small arcs when we search for a Riemann sum that leads to the formula for arc length.

31. Writing to Learn A curve is totally contained inside the square with vertices $(0,0)$, $(1,0)$, $(1,1)$, and $(0,1)$. Is there any limit to the possible length of the curve? Explain.

Standardized Test Questions

32. True or False If a function $y = f(x)$ is continuous on an interval $[a, b]$, then the length of its curve is given by

$$\int_a^b \sqrt{1 + \left(\frac{dy}{dx}\right)^2}\, dx.$$ Justify your answer.

33. True or False If a function $y = f(x)$ is differentiable on an interval $[a, b]$, then the length of its curve is given by

$$\int_a^b \sqrt{1 + \left(\frac{dy}{dx}\right)^2}\, dx.$$ Justify your answer.

34. Multiple Choice Which of the following gives the best approximation of the length of the arc of $y = \cos(2x)$ from $x = 0$ to $x = \pi/4$?

(A) 0.785 **(B)** 0.955 **(C)** 1.0 **(D)** 1.318 **(E)** 1.977

35. Multiple Choice Which of the following expressions gives the length of the graph of $x = y^3$ from $y = -2$ to $y = 2$?

(A) $\displaystyle\int_{-2}^{2} (1 + y^6)\, dy$ **(B)** $\displaystyle\int_{-2}^{2} \sqrt{1 + y^6}\, dy$

(C) $\displaystyle\int_{-2}^{2} \sqrt{1 + 9y^4}\, dy$ **(D)** $\displaystyle\int_{-2}^{2} \sqrt{1 + x^2}\, dx$

(E) $\displaystyle\int_{-2}^{2} \sqrt{1 + x^4}\, dx$

36. Multiple Choice Find the length of the curve described by $y = \dfrac{2}{3}x^{3/2}$ from $x = 0$ to $x = 8$.

(A) $\dfrac{26}{3}$ **(B)** $\dfrac{52}{3}$ **(C)** $\dfrac{512\sqrt{2}}{15}$

(D) $\dfrac{512\sqrt{2}}{15} + 8$ **(E)** 96

37. Multiple Choice Which of the following expressions should be used to find the length of the curve $y = x^{2/3}$ from $x = -1$ to $x = 1$?

(A) $2\displaystyle\int_{0}^{1} \sqrt{1 + \frac{9}{4}y}\, dy$

(B) $\displaystyle\int_{-1}^{1} \sqrt{1 + \frac{9}{4}y}\, dy$

(C) $\displaystyle\int_{0}^{1} \sqrt{1 + y^3}\, dy$

(D) $\displaystyle\int_{0}^{1} \sqrt{1 + y^6}\, dy$

(E) $\displaystyle\int_{0}^{1} \sqrt{1 + y^{9/4}}\, dy$

Exploration

38. *Modeling Running Tracks* Two lanes of a running track are modeled by the semiellipses as shown. The equation for lane 1 is $y = \sqrt{100 - 0.2x^2}$, and the equation for lane 2 is $y = \sqrt{150 - 0.2x^2}$. The starting point for lane 1 is at the negative x-intercept $(-\sqrt{500}, 0)$. The finish points for both lanes are the positive x-intercepts. Where should the starting point be placed on lane 2 so that the two lane lengths will be equal (running clockwise)?

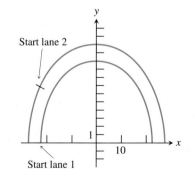

Start lane 2

Start lane 1

Extending the Ideas

39. *Using Tangent Fins to Find Arc Length* Assume f is smooth on $[a, b]$ and partition the interval $[a, b]$ in the usual way. In each subinterval $[x_{k-1}, x_k]$ construct the *tangent fin* at the point $(x_{k-1}, f(x_{k-1}))$ as shown in the figure.

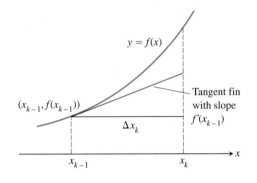

(a) Show that the length of the kth tangent fin over the interval $[x_{k-1}, x_k]$ equals

$$\sqrt{(\Delta x_k)^2 + (f'(x_{k-1})\Delta x_k)^2}.$$

(b) Show that

$$\lim_{n \to \infty} \sum_{k=1}^{n} (\text{length of } k\text{th tangent fin}) = \int_a^b \sqrt{1 + (f'(x))^2}\, dx,$$

which is the length L of the curve $y = f(x)$ from $x = a$ to $x = b$.

40. Is there a smooth curve $y = f(x)$ whose length over the interval $0 \le x \le a$ is always $a\sqrt{2}$? Give reasons for your answer.

8.5 | Applications from Science and Statistics

You will be able to apply the definite integral to solve problems involving work, fluid pressure, and probabilities.

- Work done by variable force
- Total fluid pressure
- Normal probability distribution

4.4 newtons ≈ 1 lb

$(1 \text{ newton})(1 \text{ meter}) = 1 \text{ N} \cdot \text{m} = 1 \text{ Joule}$

Our goal in this section is to hint at the diversity of ways in which the definite integral can be used. The contexts may be new to you, but we will explain what you need to know as we go along.

Work Revisited

Recall from Section 8.1 that *work* is defined as force (in the direction of motion) times displacement. A familiar example is to move against the force of gravity to lift an object. The object has to move, incidentally, before "work" is done, no matter how tired you get *trying*.

If the force $F(x)$ is not constant, then the work done in moving an object from $x = a$ to $x = b$ is the definite integral $W = \int_a^b F(x)\, dx$.

EXAMPLE 1 Finding the Work Done by a Force

Find the work done by the force $F(x) = \cos(\pi x)$ newtons along the *x*-axis from $x = 0$ meters to $x = 1/2$ meter.

SOLUTION

$$W = \int_0^{1/2} \cos(\pi x)\, dx$$

$$= \frac{1}{\pi} \sin(\pi x)\Big|_0^{1/2}$$

$$= \frac{1}{\pi}\left(\sin\left(\frac{\pi}{2}\right) - \sin(0)\right)$$

$$= \frac{1}{\pi} \approx 0.318$$

Now Try Exercise 1.

EXAMPLE 2 Work Done Lifting

A leaky bucket weighs 22 newtons (N) empty. It is lifted from the ground at a constant rate to a point 20 m above the ground by a rope weighing 0.4 N/m. The bucket starts with 70 N (approximately 7.1 liters) of water, but it leaks at a constant rate and just finishes draining as the bucket reaches the top. Find the amount of work done

(a) lifting the bucket alone;

(b) lifting the water alone;

(c) lifting the rope alone;

(d) lifting the bucket, water, and rope together.

SOLUTION

(a) *The bucket alone.* This is easy because the bucket's weight is constant. To lift it, you must exert a force of 22 N through the entire 20-meter interval.

$$\text{Work} = (22\,\text{N}) \times (20\,\text{m}) = 440\,\text{N} \cdot \text{m} = 440\,\text{J}$$

Figure 8.43 shows the graph of force vs. distance applied. The work corresponds to the area under the force graph.

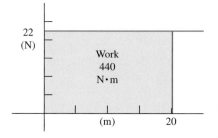

Figure 8.43 The work done by a constant 22-N force lifting a bucket 20 m is 440 N · m. (Example 2)

continued

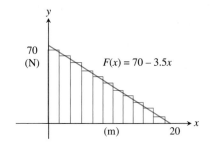

Figure 8.44 The force required to lift the water varies with distance but the work still corresponds to the area under the force graph. (Example 2)

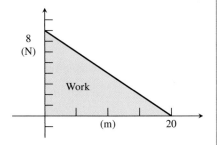

Figure 8.45 The work done lifting the rope to the top corresponds to the area of another triangle. (Example 2)

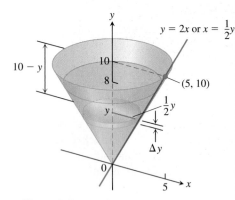

Figure 8.46 The conical tank in Example 3.

(b) *The water alone.* The force needed to lift the water is equal to the water's weight, which decreases steadily from 70 N to 0 N over the 20-m lift. When the bucket is x m off the ground, the water weighs

$$F(x) = 70\left(\frac{20 - x}{20}\right) = 70\left(1 - \frac{x}{20}\right) = 70 - 3.5x \text{ N}.$$

original weight of water   proportion left at elevation x

The work done is (Figure 8.44)

$$W = \int_a^b F(x)\, dx$$

$$= \int_0^{20} (70 - 3.5x)\, dx = \left[70x - 1.75x^2\right]_0^{20} = 1400 - 700 = 700 \text{ J}$$

(c) *The rope alone.* The force needed to lift the rope is also variable, starting at $(0.4)(20) = 8$ N when the bucket is on the ground and ending at 0 N when the bucket and rope are all at the top. As with the leaky bucket, the rate of decrease is constant. At elevation x meters, the $(20 - x)$ meters of rope still there to lift weigh $F(x) = (0.4)(20 - x)$ N. Figure 8.45 shows the graph of F. The work done lifting the rope is

$$\int_0^{20} F(x)\, dx = \int_0^{20} (0.4)(20 - x)\, dx$$

$$= \left[8x - 0.2x^2\right]_0^{20} = 160 - 80 = 80 \text{ N} \cdot \text{m} = 80 \text{ J}$$

(d) *The bucket, water, and rope together.* The total work is

$$440 + 700 + 80 = 1220 \text{ J}. \qquad \textbf{\textit{Now Try Exercise 5.}}$$

EXAMPLE 3 Work Done Pumping

The conical tank in Figure 8.46 is filled to within 2 ft of the top with olive oil weighing 57 lb/ft³. How much work does it take to pump the oil to the rim of the tank?

SOLUTION

We imagine the oil partitioned into thin slabs by planes perpendicular to the y-axis at the points of a partition of the interval $[0, 8]$. (The 8 represents the top of the oil, not the top of the tank.)

The typical slab between the planes at y and $y + \Delta y$ has a volume of about

$$\Delta V = \pi(\text{radius})^2(\text{thickness}) = \pi\left(\frac{1}{2}y\right)^2 \Delta y = \frac{\pi}{4}y^2 \Delta y \text{ ft}^3.$$

The force $F(y)$ required to lift this slab is equal to its weight,

$$F(y) = 57\,\Delta V = \frac{57\pi}{4}y^2 \Delta y \text{ lb}. \quad \text{Weight} = \left(\begin{array}{c}\text{weight per}\\\text{unit volume}\end{array}\right) \times \text{volume}$$

The distance through which $F(y)$ must act to lift this slab to the level of the rim of the cone is about $(10 - y)$ ft, so the work done lifting the slab is about

$$\Delta W = \frac{57\pi}{4}(10 - y)y^2 \Delta y \text{ ft} \cdot \text{lb}.$$

The work done lifting all the slabs from $y = 0$ to $y = 8$ to the rim is approximately

$$W \approx \sum \frac{57\pi}{4}(10 - y)y^2 \Delta y \text{ ft} \cdot \text{lb}. \qquad \textit{continued}$$

This is a Riemann sum for the function $(57\pi/4)(10 - y)y^2$ on the interval from $y = 0$ to $y = 8$. The work of pumping the oil to the rim is the limit of these sums as the norms of the partitions go to zero.

$$W = \int_0^8 \frac{57\pi}{4}(10 - y)y^2 \, dy = \frac{57\pi}{4}\int_0^8 (10y^2 - y^3)\, dy$$

$$= \frac{57\pi}{4}\left[\frac{10y^3}{3} - \frac{y^4}{4}\right]_0^8 \approx 30{,}561 \text{ ft} \cdot \text{lb} \qquad \textit{Now Try Exercise 17.}$$

Fluid Force and Fluid Pressure

We make dams thicker at the bottom than at the top (Figure 8.47) because the pressure against them increases with depth. It is a remarkable fact that the pressure at any point on a dam depends only on how far below the surface the point lies and not on how much water the dam is holding back. In any liquid, the **fluid pressure** p (force per unit area) at depth h is

$$p = wh, \quad \text{Dimensions check: } \frac{\text{lb}}{\text{ft}^2} = \frac{\text{lb}}{\text{ft}^3} \times \text{ft, for example}$$

where w is the *weight-density* (weight per unit volume) of the liquid.

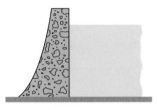

Figure 8.47 To withstand the increasing pressure, dams are built thicker toward the bottom.

Typical Weight-Densities (lb/ft³)

Gasoline	42
Mercury	849
Milk	64.5
Molasses	100
Seawater	64
Water	62.4

EXAMPLE 4 The Great Molasses Flood of 1919

At 1:00 P.M. on January 15, 1919 (an unseasonably warm day), a 90-ft-high, 90-foot-diameter cylindrical metal tank in which the Puritan Distilling Company stored molasses at the corner of Foster and Commercial streets in Boston's North End exploded. Molasses flooded the streets 30 feet deep, trapping pedestrians and horses, knocking down buildings, and oozing into homes. It was eventually tracked all over town and even made its way into the suburbs via trolley cars and people's shoes. It took weeks to clean up.

(a) Given that the tank was full of molasses weighing 100 lb/ft³, what was the total force exerted by the molasses on the bottom of the tank at the time it ruptured?

(b) What was the total force against the bottom foot-wide band of the tank wall (Figure 8.48)?

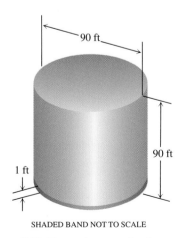

90 ft

90 ft

1 ft

SHADED BAND NOT TO SCALE

Figure 8.48 The molasses tank of Example 4.

continued

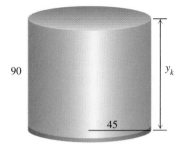

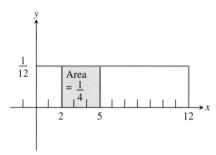

SOLUTION

(a) At the bottom of the tank, the molasses exerted a constant pressure of

$$p = wh = \left(100 \frac{\text{lb}}{\text{ft}^3}\right)(90 \text{ ft}) = 9000 \frac{\text{lb}}{\text{ft}^2}.$$

Since the area of the base was $\pi(45)^2$, the total force on the base was

$$\left(9000 \frac{\text{lb}}{\text{ft}^2}\right)(2025 \pi \text{ ft}^2) \approx 57{,}255{,}526 \text{ lb}.$$

Figure 8.49 The 1-ft band at the bottom of the tank wall can be partitioned into thin strips on which the pressure is approximately constant. (Example 4)

(b) We partition the band from depth 89 ft to depth 90 ft into narrower bands of width Δy and choose a depth y_k in each one. The pressure at this depth y_k is $p = wh = 100 \, y_k$ lb/ft² (Figure 8.49). The force against each narrow band is approximately

$$\text{pressure} \times \text{area} = (100 y_k)(90\pi \, \Delta y) = 9000\pi \, y_k \, \Delta y \text{ lb}.$$

Adding the forces against all the bands in the partition and passing to the limit as the norms go to zero, we arrive at

$$F = \int_{89}^{90} 9000\pi y \, dy = 9000\pi \int_{89}^{90} y \, dy \approx 2{,}530{,}553 \text{ lb}$$

for the force against the bottom foot of tank wall. *Now Try Exercise 25.*

Normal Probabilities

Suppose you find an old clock in the attic. What is the probability that it has stopped somewhere between 2:00 and 5:00?

If you imagine time being measured continuously over a 12-hour interval, it is easy to conclude that the answer is $1/4$ (since the interval from 2:00 to 5:00 contains one-fourth of the time), and that is correct. Mathematically, however, the situation is not quite that clear because both the 12-hour interval and the 3-hour interval contain an *infinite* number of times. In what sense does the ratio of one infinity to another infinity equal $1/4$?

The easiest way to resolve that question is to look at area. We represent the total probability of the 12-hour interval as a rectangle of area 1 sitting above the interval (Figure 8.50).

Not only does it make perfect sense to say that the rectangle over the time interval $[2, 5]$ has an area that is one-fourth the area of the total rectangle, the area actually *equals* $1/4$, since the total rectangle has area 1. That is why mathematicians represent probabilities as areas, and that is where definite integrals enter the picture.

Figure 8.50 The probability that the clock has stopped between 2:00 and 5:00 can be represented as an area of $1/4$. The rectangle over the entire interval has area 1.

DEFINITION   Probability Density Function (pdf)

A **probability density function** is a function $f(x)$ with domain all reals such that

$$f(x) \geq 0 \text{ for all } x \quad \text{and} \quad \int_{-\infty}^{\infty} f(x) \, dx = 1.$$

Then the probability associated with an interval $[a, b]$ is

$$\int_a^b f(x) \, dx.$$

Improper Integrals

More information about improper integrals like $\int_{-\infty}^{\infty} f(x) \, dx$ can be found in Section 9.3. (You will not need that information here.)

Probabilities of events, such as the clock stopping between 2:00 and 5:00, are integrals of an appropriate pdf.

EXAMPLE 5 Probability of the Clock Stopping

Find the probability that the clock stopped between 2:00 and 5:00.

SOLUTION

The pdf of the clock is

$$f(t) = \begin{cases} 1/12, & 0 \le t \le 12 \\ 0, & \text{otherwise.} \end{cases}$$

The probability that the clock stopped at some time t with $2 \le t \le 5$ is

$$\int_2^5 f(t)\, dt = \frac{1}{4}. \qquad \textit{Now Try Exercise 27.}$$

By far the most useful kind of pdf is the *normal* kind. ("Normal" here is a technical term, referring to a curve with the shape in Figure 8.51.) The **normal curve,** often called the "bell curve," is one of the most significant curves in applied mathematics because it enables us to describe entire populations based on the statistical measurements taken from a reasonably sized sample. The measurements needed are the *mean* (μ) and the *standard deviation* (σ), which your calculators will approximate for you from the data. The symbols on the calculator will probably be $\bar{x}$ and s (see your *Owner's Manual*), but go ahead and use them as μ and σ, respectively. Once you have the numbers, you can find the curve by using the following remarkable formula discovered by Karl Friedrich Gauss.

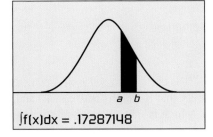

∫f(x)dx = .17287148

Figure 8.51 A normal probability density function. The probability associated with the interval $[a, b]$ is the area under the curve, as shown.

DEFINITION Normal Probability Density Function (pdf)

The **normal probability density function (Gaussian curve)** for a population with mean μ and standard deviation σ is

$$f(x) = \frac{1}{\sigma\sqrt{2\pi}}\, e^{-(x-\mu)^2/(2\sigma^2)}.$$

The **mean** μ represents the average value of the variable x. The **standard deviation** σ measures the "scatter" around the mean. For a normal curve, the mean and standard deviation tell you where most of the probability lies. The rule of thumb, illustrated in Figure 8.52, is this:

The 68-95-99.7 Rule for Normal Distributions

Given a normal curve,

- 68% of the area will lie within σ of the mean μ,
- 95% of the area will lie within 2σ of the mean μ,
- 99.7% of the area will lie within 3σ of the mean μ.

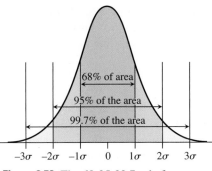

Figure 8.52 The 68-95-99.7 rule for normal distributions.

Even with the 68-95-99.7 rule, the area under the curve can spread quite a bit, depending on the size of σ. Figure 8.53 shows three normal pdfs with mean $\mu = 2$ and standard deviations equal to 0.5, 1, and 2.

EXAMPLE 6 A Telephone Help Line

Suppose a telephone help line takes a mean of 2 minutes to answer calls. If the standard deviation is $\sigma = 0.5$, then 68% of the calls are answered in the range of 1.5 to 2.5 minutes and 99.7% of the calls are answered in the range of 0.5 to 3.5 minutes. Assume that the time to answer calls is normally distributed. *Now Try Exercise 29.*

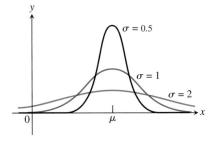

Figure 8.53 Normal pdf curves with mean $\mu = 2$ and $\sigma = 0.5$, 1, and 2.

EXAMPLE 7 Weights of Spinach Boxes

Suppose that frozen spinach boxes marked as "10 ounces" of spinach have a mean weight of 10.3 ounces and a standard deviation of 0.2 ounce. Assume that the weights of the spinach boxes are normally distributed.

(a) What percentage of *all* such spinach boxes can be expected to weigh between 10 and 11 ounces?

(b) What percentage would we expect to weigh less than 10 ounces?

(c) What is the probability that a box weighs *exactly* 10 ounces?

SOLUTION

Assuming that some person or machine is *trying* to pack 10 ounces of spinach into these boxes, we expect that most of the weights will be around 10, with probabilities tailing off for boxes being heavier or lighter. We expect, in other words, that a normal pdf will model these probabilities. First, we define $f(x)$ using the formula

$$f(x) = \frac{1}{0.2\sqrt{2\pi}} e^{-(x-10.3)^2/(0.08)}.$$

The graph (Figure 8.54) has the look we are expecting.

(a) For an arbitrary box of this spinach, the probability that it weighs between 10 and 11 ounces is the area under the curve from 10 to 11, which is

$$\text{NINT}\,(f(x), x, 10, 11) \approx 0.933.$$

So without doing any more measuring, we can predict that about 93.3% of all such spinach boxes will weigh between 10 and 11 ounces.

(b) For the probability that a box weighs less than 10 ounces, we use the entire area under the curve to the left of $x = 10$. The curve actually approaches the x-axis as an asymptote, but you can see from the graph (Figure 8.54) that $f(x)$ approaches zero quite quickly. Indeed, $f(9)$ is only slightly larger than a billionth. So getting the area from 9 to 10 should do it:

$$\text{NINT}\,(f(x), x, 9, 10) \approx 0.067$$

We would expect only about 6.7% of the boxes to weigh less than 10 ounces.

(c) This would be the integral from 10 to 10, which is zero. This zero probability might seem strange at first, but remember that we are assuming a continuous, unbroken interval of possible spinach weights, and 10 is but one of an infinite number of them.

Now Try Exercise 31.

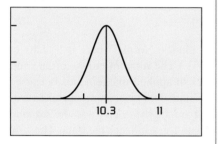

[9, 11.5] by [−1, 2.5]

Figure 8.54 The normal pdf for the spinach weights in Example 7. The mean is at the center.

Quick Review 8.5 *(For help, go to Section 6.2.)*

Exercise numbers with a gray background indicate problems that the authors have designed to be solved *without a calculator.*

In Exercises 1–5, find the definite integral by **(a)** antiderivatives and **(b)** using NINT.

1. $\displaystyle\int_0^1 e^{-x}\,dx$

2. $\displaystyle\int_0^1 e^x\,dx$

3. $\displaystyle\int_{\pi/4}^{\pi/2} \sin x\,dx$

4. $\displaystyle\int_0^3 (x^2 + 2)\,dx$

5. $\displaystyle\int_1^2 \frac{x^2}{x^3 + 1}\,dx$

In Exercises 6–10 find, but do not evaluate, the definite integral that is the limit as the norms of the partitions go to zero of the Riemann sums on the closed interval $[0, 7]$.

6. $\sum 2\pi(x_k + 2)(\sin x_k)\, \Delta x$

7. $\sum (1 - x_k{}^2)(2\pi x_k)\, \Delta x$

8. $\sum \pi(\cos x_k)^2\, \Delta x$

9. $\sum \pi\left(\dfrac{y_k}{2}\right)^2(10 - y_k)\, \Delta y$

10. $\sum \dfrac{\sqrt{3}}{4}(\sin^2 x_k)\, \Delta x$

Section 8.5 Exercises

In Exercises 1–4, find the work done by the force of $F(x)$ newtons along the *x*-axis from $x = a$ meters to $x = b$ meters.

1. $F(x) = xe^{-x/3}, \quad a = 0, \quad b = 5$

2. $F(x) = x \sin(\pi x/4), \quad a = 0, \quad b = 3$

3. $F(x) = x\sqrt{9 - x^2}, \quad a = 0, \quad b = 3$

4. $F(x) = e^{\sin x}\cos x + 2, \quad a = 0, \quad b = 10$

5. *Leaky Bucket* The workers in Example 2 changed to a larger bucket that held 50 L (490 N) of water, but the new bucket had an even larger leak so that it too was empty by the time it reached the top. Assuming the water leaked out at a steady rate, how much work was done lifting the water to a point 20 meters above the ground? (Do not include the rope and bucket.)

6. *Leaky Bucket* The bucket in Exercise 5 is hauled up more quickly so that there is still 10 L (98 N) of water left when the bucket reaches the top. How much work is done lifting the water this time? (Do not include the rope and bucket.)

7. *Leaky Sand Bag* A bag of sand originally weighing 144 lb was lifted at a constant rate. As it rose, sand leaked out at a constant rate. The sand was half gone by the time the bag had been lifted 18 ft. How much work was done lifting the sand this far? (Neglect the weights of the bag and lifting equipment.)

8. *Stretching a Spring* A spring has a natural length of 10 in. An 800-lb force stretches the spring to 14 in.

(a) Find the force constant.

(b) How much work is done in stretching the spring from 10 in. to 12 in.?

(c) How far beyond its natural length will a 1600-lb force stretch the spring?

9. *Subway Car Springs* It takes a force of 21,714 lb to compress a coil spring assembly on a New York City Transit Authority subway car from its free height of 8 in. to its fully compressed height of 5 in.

(a) What is the assembly's force constant?

(b) How much work does it take to compress the assembly the first half-inch? the second half-inch? Answer to the nearest inch-pound.

(*Source:* Data courtesy of Bombardier, Inc., Mass Transit Division, for spring assemblies in subway cars delivered to the New York City Transit Authority from 1985 to 1987.)

10. *Bathroom Scale* A bathroom scale is compressed 1/16 in. when a 150-lb person stands on it. Assuming the scale behaves like a spring that obeys Hooke's Law,

(a) how much does someone who compresses the scale 1/8 in. weigh?

(b) how much work is done in compressing the scale 1/8 in.?

11. *Hauling a Rope* A mountain climber is about to haul up a 50-m length of hanging rope. How much work will it take if the rope weighs 0.624 N/m?

12. *Compressing Gas* Suppose that gas in a circular cylinder of cross-section area A is being compressed by a piston (see figure).

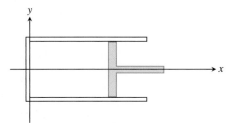

(a) If p is the pressure of the gas in pounds per square inch and V is the volume in cubic inches, show that the work done in compressing the gas from state (p_1, V_1) to state (p_2, V_2) is given by the equation

$$\text{Work} = \int_{(p_1, V_1)}^{(p_2, V_2)} (-p\, dV) \text{ in.} \cdot \text{lb,}$$

where the force against the piston is $-pA$.

(b) Find the work done in compressing the gas from $V_1 = 243$ in.^{3} to $V_2 = 32$ in.^{3} if $p_1 = 50$ lb/in.^{3} and p and V obey the gas law $pV^{1.4} = $ constant (for adiabatic processes).

Group Activity In Exercises 13–16, the vertical end of a tank containing water (blue shading) weighing 62.4 lb/ft³ has the given shape.

(a) **Writing to Learn** Explain how to approximate the force against the end of the tank by a Riemann sum.

(b) Find the force as an integral and evaluate it.

13. semicircle

14. semiellipse

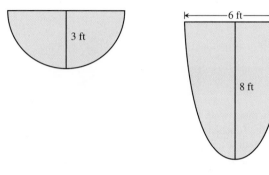

15. triangle

16. parabola

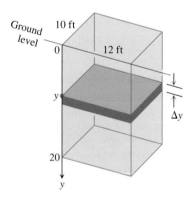

17. *Pumping Water* The rectangular tank shown here, with its top at ground level, is used to catch runoff water. Assume that the water weighs 62.4 lb/ft³.

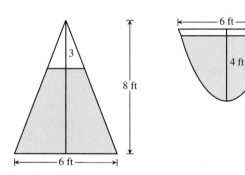

(a) How much work does it take to empty the tank by pumping the water back to ground level once the tank is full?

(b) If the water is pumped to ground level with a (5/11)-horsepower motor (work output 250 ft · lb/sec), how long will it take to empty the full tank (to the nearest minute)?

(c) Show that the pump in part (b) will lower the water level 10 ft (halfway) during the first 25 min of pumping.

(d) ***The Weight of Water*** Because of differences in the strength of Earth's gravitational field, the weight of a cubic foot of water at sea level can vary from as little as 62.26 lb at the equator to as much as 62.59 lb near the poles, a variation of about 0.5%. A cubic foot of water that weighs 62.4 lb in Melbourne or New York City will weigh 62.5 lb in Juneau or Stockholm. What are the answers to parts (a) and (b) in a location where water weighs 62.26 lb/ft³? 62.5 lb/ft³?

18. *Emptying a Tank* A vertical right cylindrical tank measures 30 ft high and 20 ft in diameter. It is full of kerosene weighing 51.2 lb/ft³. How much work does it take to pump the kerosene to the level of the top of the tank?

19. Writing to Learn The cylindrical tank shown here is to be filled by pumping water from a lake 15 ft below the bottom of the tank. There are two ways to go about this. One is to pump the water through a hose attached to a valve in the bottom of the tank. The other is to attach the hose to the rim of the tank and let the water pour in. Which way will require less work? Give reasons for your answer.

20. *Drinking a Milkshake* The truncated conical container shown here is full of strawberry milkshake that weighs $(4/9)$ oz/in³. As you can see, the container is 7 in. deep, 2.5 in. across at the base, and 3.5 in. across at the top (a standard size at Brigham's in Boston). The straw sticks up an inch above the top. About how much work does it take to drink the milkshake through the straw (neglecting friction)? Answer in inch-ounces.

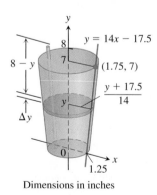

Dimensions in inches

21. *Revisiting Example 3* How much work will it take to pump the oil in Example 3 to a level 3 ft above the cone's rim?

22. Pumping Milk Suppose the conical tank in Example 3 contains milk weighing 64.5 lb/ft^3 instead of olive oil. How much work will it take to pump the contents to the rim?

23. Writing to Learn You are in charge of the evacuation and repair of the storage tank shown here. The tank is a hemisphere of radius 10 ft and is full of benzene weighing 56 lb/ft^3.

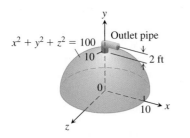

A firm you contacted says it can empty the tank for $1/2$ cent per foot-pound of work. Find the work required to empty the tank by pumping the benzene to an outlet 2 ft above the tank. If you have budgeted \$5000 for the job, can you afford to hire the firm?

24. Water Tower Your town has decided to drill a well to increase its water supply. As the town engineer, you have determined that a water tower will be necessary to provide the pressure needed for distribution, and you have designed the system shown here. The water is to be pumped from a 300-ft well through a vertical 4-in. pipe into the base of a cylindrical tank 20 ft in diameter and 25 ft high. The base of the tank will be 60 ft above ground. The pump is a 3-hp pump, rated at 1650 ft · lb/sec. To the nearest hour, how long will it take to fill the tank the first time? (Include the time it takes to fill the pipe.) Assume water weighs 62.4 lb/ft^3.

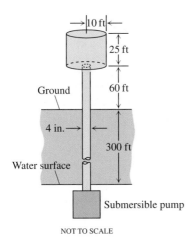

NOT TO SCALE

25. Fish Tank A rectangular freshwater fish tank with base 2 × 4 ft and height 2 ft (interior dimensions) is filled to within 2 in. of the top.

(a) Find the fluid force against each end of the tank.

(b) Suppose the tank is sealed and stood on end (without spilling) so that one of the square ends is the base. What does that do to the fluid forces on the rectangular sides?

26. Milk Carton A rectangular milk carton measures 3.75 in. by 3.75 in. at the base and is 7.75 in. tall. Find the force of the milk (weighing 64.5 lb/ft^3) on one side when the carton is full.

27. Find the probability that a clock stopped between 1:00 and 5:00.

28. Find the probability that a clock stopped between 3:00 and 6:00.

For problems 29, 30, and 31, assume a normal distribution.

29. Suppose a telephone help line takes a mean of 5 minutes to answer calls. If the standard deviation is $\sigma = 2$, what percentage of the calls are answered in the range of 3 to 7 minutes?

30. Test Scores The mean score on a national aptitude test is 498 with a standard deviation of 100 points.

(a) What percentage of the population has scores between 400 and 500?

(b) If we sample 300 test-takers at random, about how many should have scores above 700?

31. Heights of Females The mean height of an adult female in New York City is estimated to be 63.4 inches with a standard deviation of 3.2 inches. What proportion of the adult females in New York City are

(a) less than 63.4 inches tall?

(b) between 63 and 65 inches tall?

(c) taller than 6 feet?

(d) exactly 5 feet tall?

32. Writing to Learn Exercises 30 and 31 are subtly different, in that the heights in Exercise 31 are measured *continuously* and the scores in Exercise 30 are measured *discretely*. The discrete probabilities determine rectangles above the individual test scores, so that there actually is a nonzero probability of scoring, say, 560. The rectangles would look like the figure below, and would have total area 1.

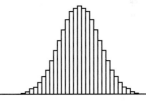

Explain why integration gives a good estimate for the probability, even in the discrete case.

33. Writing to Learn Suppose that $f(t)$ is the probability density function for the lifetime of a certain type of light bulb where t is in hours. What is the meaning of the integral

$$\int_{100}^{800} f(t)\, dt?$$

Standardized Test Questions

You may use a graphing calculator to solve the following problems.

34. True or False A force is applied to compress a spring several inches. Assume the spring obeys Hooke's Law. Twice as much work is required to compress the spring the second inch than is required to compress the spring the first inch. Justify your answer.

35. True or False An aquarium contains water weighing 62.4 lb/ft^3. The aquarium is in the shape of a cube where the length of each edge is 3 ft. Each side of the aquarium is engineered to withstand 1000 pounds of force. This should be sufficient to withstand the force from water pressure. Justify your answer.

36. Multiple Choice A force of $F(x) = 350x$ newtons moves a particle along a line from $x = 0$ m to $x = 5$ m. Which of the following gives the best approximation of the work done by the force?

(A) 1750 J

(B) 2187.5 J

(C) 2916.67 J

(D) 3281.25 J

(E) 4375 J

37. Multiple Choice A leaky bag of sand weighs 50 N. It is lifted from the ground at a constant rate, to a height of 20 m above the ground. The sand leaks at a constant rate and just finishes draining as the bag reaches the top. Which of the following gives the work done to lift the sand to the top? (Neglect the bag.)

(A) 50 J

(B) 100 J

(C) 250 J

(D) 500 J

(E) 1000 J

38. Multiple Choice A spring has a natural length of 0.10 m. A 200-N force stretches the spring to a length of 0.15 m. Which of the following gives the work done in stretching the spring from 0.10 m to 0.15 m?

(A) 0.05 J

(B) 5 J

(C) 10 J

(D) 200 J

(E) 4000 J

39. Multiple Choice A vertical right cylindrical tank measures 12 ft high and 16 ft in diameter. It is full of water weighing 62.4 lb/ft^3. How much work does it take to pump the water to the level of the top of the tank? Round your answer to the nearest ft-lb.

(A) 149,490 ft-lb

(B) 285,696 ft-lb

(C) 360,240 ft-lb

(D) 448,776 ft-lb

(E) 903,331 ft-lb

Extending the Ideas

40. *Putting a Satellite into Orbit* The strength of Earth's gravitational field varies with the distance r from Earth's center, and the magnitude of the gravitational force experienced by a satellite of mass m during and after launch is

$$F(r) = \frac{mMG}{r^2}.$$

Here, $M = 5.975 \times 10^{24}$ kg is Earth's mass, $G = 6.6726 \times 10^{-11}$ N · m^2 kg^{-2} is the *universal gravitational constant*, and r is measured in meters. The work it takes to lift a 1000-kg satellite from Earth's surface to a circular orbit 35,780 km above Earth's center is therefore given by the integral

$$\text{Work} = \int_{6,370,000}^{35,780,000} \frac{1000 \, MG}{r^2} \, dr \text{ joules.}$$

The lower limit of integration is Earth's radius in meters at the launch site. Evaluate the integral. (This calculation does not take into account energy spent lifting the launch vehicle or energy spent bringing the satellite to orbit velocity.)

41. *Forcing Electrons Together* Two electrons r meters apart repel each other with a force of

$$F = \frac{23 \times 10^{-29}}{r^2} \text{ newton.}$$

(a) Suppose one electron is held fixed at the point $(1, 0)$ on the x-axis (units in meters). How much work does it take to move a second electron along the x-axis from the point $(-1, 0)$ to the origin?

(b) Suppose an electron is held fixed at each of the points $(-1, 0)$ and $(1, 0)$. How much work does it take to move a third electron along the x-axis from $(5, 0)$ to $(3, 0)$?

42. *Kinetic Energy* If a variable force of magnitude $F(x)$ moves a body of mass m along the x-axis from x_1 to x_2, the body's velocity v can be written as dx/dt (where t represents time). Use Newton's second law of motion, $F = m(dv/dt)$, and the Chain Rule

$$\frac{dv}{dt} = \frac{dv}{dx}\frac{dx}{dt} = v\frac{dv}{dx}$$

to show that the net work done by the force in moving the body from x_1 to x_2 is

$$W = \int_{x_1}^{x_2} F(x) \, dx = \frac{1}{2}mv_2^2 - \frac{1}{2}mv_1^2, \qquad (1)$$

where v_1 and v_2 are the body's velocities at x_1 and x_2. In physics the expression $(1/2)mv^2$ is the *kinetic energy* of the body moving with velocity v. Therefore, *the work done by the force equals the change in the body's kinetic energy,* and we can find the work by calculating this change.

In Exercises 43–48, use Equation 1 from Exercise 42.

43. *Tennis* A 58-gram tennis ball was served at 50 m/sec. How much work was done to make it go this fast?

44. *Baseball* How many joules of work does it take to throw a baseball 40 m/sec (about 90 mph)? A baseball has a mass of 143 g.

45. *Golf* A 45-gram golf ball is driven off the tee at a speed of 85 m/sec. How many joules of work are done getting the ball into the air?

46. *Football* A quarterback threw a 0.42-kg football 144 km/hour. How many joules of work were done on the ball to get it to that speed?

47. Softball How much work has to be performed on a 0.19-kg softball to pitch it at 40 m/sec?

48. A Ball Bearing A 60-g steel ball bearing is placed on a vertical spring whose force constant is $k = 2.5$ newtons/cm. The spring is compressed 8 cm and released. About how high does

the ball bearing go? [*Hint*: The kinetic (compression) energy is $mgh = \frac{1}{2}ks^2$, where s is the distance the spring is compressed, m is the mass, g is the acceleration due to gravity, and h is the height.]

Quick Quiz for AP* Preparation: Sections 8.4 and 8.5

1. Multiple Choice The length of a curve from $x = 0$ to $x = 1$ is given by $\int_0^1 \sqrt{1 + 16x^6} \, dx$. If the curve contains the point $(1, 4)$, which of the following could be an equation for this curve?

(A) $y = x^4 + 3$

(B) $y = x^4 + 1$

(C) $y = 1 + 16x^6$

(D) $y = \sqrt{1 + 16x^6}$

(E) $y = x + \dfrac{x^7}{7}$

2. Multiple Choice Which of the following gives the length of the curve $y = 2x^{5/4}$ over the interval $0 \le x \le 2$?

(A) $\displaystyle\int_0^2 \sqrt{1 + 4x^{5/2}} \, dx$

(B) $\displaystyle\int_0^2 \sqrt{1 + \frac{5}{2}x^{5/2}} \, dx$

(C) $\dfrac{1}{2}\displaystyle\int_0^2 \sqrt{1 + 25x^{1/2}} \, dx$

(D) $\dfrac{1}{2}\displaystyle\int_0^2 \sqrt{4 + 25x^{1/2}} \, dx$

(E) $\dfrac{1}{2}\displaystyle\int_0^2 \sqrt{4 + 25x^{5/2}} \, dx$

3. Multiple Choice The base of a solid is a circle of radius 2 inches. Each cross section perpendicular to a certain diameter is a square with one side lying in the circle. The volume of the solid in cubic inches is

(A) 16

(B) 16π

(C) $\dfrac{128}{3}$

(D) $\dfrac{128\pi}{3}$

(E) 32π

4. Free Response The front of a fish tank is rectangular and measures 2 ft wide by 1.5 ft tall. The water in the tank exerts pressure on the front of the tank. The pressure at any point on the front of the tank depends only on how far below the surface the point lies and is given by the equation $p = 62.4h$, where h is depth below the surface measured in feet and p is pressure measured in pounds/ft^2.

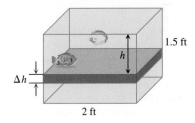

The front of the tank can be partitioned into narrow horizontal bands of height Δh. The force exerted by the water on a band at depth h_i is approximately

$$\text{pressure} \cdot \text{area} = 62.4h_i \cdot 2\Delta h.$$

(a) Write the Riemann sum that approximates the force exerted on the entire front of the tank.

(b) Use the Riemann sum from part (a) to write and evaluate a definite integral that gives the force exerted on the front of the tank. Include correct units.

(c) Find the total force exerted on the front of the tank if the front (and back) are semicircles with diameter 2 ft. Include correct units.

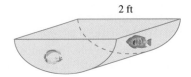

CHAPTER 8 Key Terms

accumulation (p. 389)

arc length (p. 421)

area between curves (p. 397)

Cavalieri's theorems (p. 412)

center of mass (p. 396)

constant-force formula (p. 391)

cylindrical shells (p. 410)

displacement (p. 386)

fluid force (p. 429)

fluid pressure (p. 429)

foot-pound (p. 391)

force constant (p. 391)

Gaussian curve (p. 431)

Hooke's Law (p. 391)

inflation rate (p. 396)

joule (p. 391)

length of a curve (p. 421)

mean (p. 431)

moment (p. 396)

net change (p. 385)

newton (p. 391)

normal curve (p. 431)

normal pdf (p. 431)

probability density function (pdf) (p. 430)

68-95-99.7 rule (p. 431)

smooth curve (p. 421)

smooth function (p. 421)

solid of revolution (p. 407)

standard deviation (p. 431)

surface area (p. 413)

total distance traveled (p. 387)

universal gravitational constant (p. 436)

volume by cylindrical shells (p. 410)

volume by slicing (p. 407)

volume of a solid (p. 407)

weight-density (p. 429)

work (p. 391)

CHAPTER 8 Review Exercises

Exercise numbers with a gray background indicate problems that the authors have designed to be solved *without a calculator.*

The collection of exercises marked in red could be used as a chapter test.

In Exercises 1–5, the application involves the accumulation of small changes over an interval to give the net change over that entire interval. Set up an integral to model the accumulation and evaluate it to answer the question.

1. A toy car slides down a ramp and coasts to a stop after 5 sec. Its velocity from $t = 0$ to $t = 5$ is modeled by $v(t) = t^2 - 0.2t^3$ ft/sec. How far does it travel?

2. The fuel consumption of a diesel motor between weekly maintenance periods is modeled by the function $c(t) = 4 + 0.001t^4$ gal/day, $0 \le t \le 7$. How many gallons does it consume in a week?

3. The number of billboards per mile along a 100-mile stretch of an interstate highway approaching a certain city is modeled by the function $B(x) = 21 - e^{0.03x}$, where x is the distance from the city in miles. About how many billboards are along that stretch of highway?

4. A 2-meter rod has a variable density modeled by the function $\rho(x) = 11 - 4x$ g/m, where x is the distance in meters from the base of the rod. What is the total mass of the rod?

5. The electrical power consumption (measured in kilowatts) at a factory t hours after midnight during a typical day is modeled by $E(t) = 300(2 - \cos(\pi t/12))$. How many kilowatt-hours of electrical energy does the company consume in a typical day?

In Exercises 6–19, find the area of the region enclosed by the lines and curves. You may use a graphing calculator to graph the functions.

6. $y = x, \quad y = 0, \quad y = 1/x^2, \quad x = 2$

7. $y = x + 1, \quad y = 3 - x^2$

8. $\sqrt{x} + \sqrt{y} = 1, \quad x = 0, \quad y = 0$

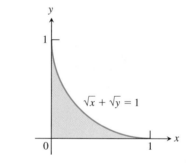

9. $x = 2y^2, \quad x = 0, \quad y = 3$

10. $4x = y^2 - 4, \quad 4x = y + 16$

11. $y = \sin x, \quad y = x, \quad x = \pi/4$

12. $y = 2 \sin x, \quad y = \sin 2x, \quad 0 \le x \le \pi$

13. $y = \cos x, \quad y = 4 - x^2$

14. $y = \sec^2 x, \quad y = 3 - |x|$

15. *The Necklace* one of the smaller bead-shaped regions enclosed by the graphs of $y = 1 + \cos x$ and $y = 2 - \cos x$

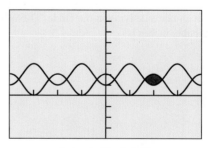

$[-4\pi, 4\pi]$ by $[-4, 8]$

16. one of the larger bead-shaped regions enclosed by the curves in Exercise 15

17. *The Bow Tie* the region enclosed by the graphs of

$$y = x^3 - x \quad \text{and} \quad y = \frac{x}{x^2 + 1}$$

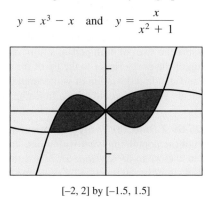

[−2, 2] by [−1.5, 1.5]

18. *The Bell* the region enclosed by the graphs of

$$y = 3^{1-x^2} \quad \text{and} \quad y = \frac{x^2 - 3}{10}$$

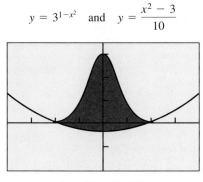

[−4, 4] by [−2, 3.5]

19. *The Kissing Fish* the region enclosed between the graphs of $y = x \sin x$ and $y = -x \sin x$ over the interval $[-\pi, \pi]$

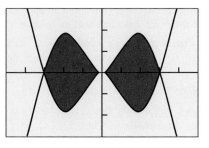

[−5, 5] by [−3, 3]

20. Find the volume of the solid generated by revolving the region bounded by the *x*-axis, the curve $y = 3x^4$, and the lines $x = -1$ and $x = 1$ about the *x*-axis.

21. Find the volume of the solid generated by revolving the region enclosed by the parabola $y^2 = 4x$ and the line $y = x$ about

  (a) the *x*-axis.   **(b)** the *y*-axis.

  (c) the line $x = 4$.   **(d)** the line $y = 4$.

22. The section of the parabola $y = x^2/2$ from $y = 0$ to $y = 2$ is revolved about the *y*-axis to form a bowl.

  (a) Find the volume of the bowl.

  (b) Find how much the bowl is holding when it is filled to a depth of *k* units $(0 < k < 2)$.

  (c) If the bowl is filled at a rate of 2 cubic units per second, how fast is the depth *k* increasing when $k = 1$?

23. The profile of a football resembles the ellipse shown here (all dimensions in inches). Find the volume of the football to the nearest cubic inch.

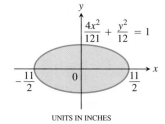

UNITS IN INCHES

24. The base of a solid is the region enclosed between the graphs of $y = \sin x$ and $y = -\sin x$ from $x = 0$ to $x = \pi$. Each cross section perpendicular to the *x*-axis is a semicircle with diameter connecting the two graphs. Find the volume of the solid.

25. The region enclosed by the graphs of $y = e^{x/2}$, $y = 1$, and $x = \ln 3$ is revolved about the *x*-axis. Find the volume of the solid generated.

26. A round hole of radius $\sqrt{3}$ feet is bored through the center of a sphere of radius 2 feet. Find the volume of the piece cut out.

27. Find the length of the arch of the parabola $y = 9 - x^2$ that lies above the *x*-axis.

28. Find the *perimeter* of the bow-tie-shaped region enclosed between the graphs of $y = x^3 - x$ and $y = x - x^3$.

29. A particle travels at 2 units per second along the curve $y = x^3 - 3x^2 + 2$. How long does it take to travel from the local maximum to the local minimum?

30. Group Activity One of the following statements is true for all positive integers *k* and one is false. Which is which? Explain.

  (a) The graphs of $y = k \sin x$ and $y = \sin kx$ have the same length on the interval $[0, 2\pi]$.

  (b) The graph of $y = k \sin x$ is *k* times as long as the graph of $y = \sin x$ on the interval $[0, 2\pi]$.

31. Let $F(x) = \int_1^x \sqrt{t^4 - 1}\, dt$. Find the *exact* length of the graph of *F* from $x = 2$ to $x = 5$ without using a calculator.

32. *Rock Climbing* A rock climber is about to haul up 100 N (about 22.5 lb) of equipment that has been hanging beneath her on 40 m of rope weighing 0.8 N/m. How much work will it take to lift

  (a) the equipment?   **(b)** the rope?

  (c) the rope and equipment together?

33. *Hauling Water* You drove an 800-gallon tank truck from the base of Mt. Washington to the summit and discovered on arrival that the tank was only half full. You had started out with a full tank of water, had climbed at a steady rate, and had taken 50 minutes to accomplish the 4750-ft elevation change. Assuming that the water leaked out at a steady rate, how much work was spent in carrying the water to the summit? Water weighs 8 lb/gal. (Do not count the work done getting you and the truck to the top.)

34. *Stretching a Spring* If a force of 80 N is required to hold a spring 0.3 m beyond its unstressed length, how much work does it take to stretch the spring this far? How much work does it take to stretch the spring an additional meter?

35. Writing to Learn It takes a lot more effort to roll a stone up a hill than to roll the stone down the hill, but the weight of the stone and the distance it covers are the same. Does this mean that the same amount of work is done? Explain.

36. *Emptying a Bowl* A hemispherical bowl with radius 8 inches is filled with punch (weighing 0.04 pound per cubic inch) to within 2 inches of the top. How much work is done emptying the bowl if the contents are pumped just high enough to get over the rim?

37. *Fluid Force* The vertical triangular plate shown below is the end plate of a feeding trough full of hog slop, weighing 80 pounds per cubic foot. What is the force against the plate?

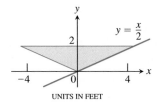

UNITS IN FEET

38. *Fluid Force* A standard olive oil can measures 5.75 in. by 3.5 in. by 10 in. Find the fluid force against the base and each side of the can when it is full. (Olive oil has a weight-density of 57 pounds per cubic foot.)

39. *Volume* A solid lies between planes perpendicular to the *x*-axis at $x = 0$ and at $x = 6$. The cross sections between the planes are squares whose bases run from the *x*-axis up to the curve $\sqrt{x} + \sqrt{y} = \sqrt{6}$. Find the volume of the solid.

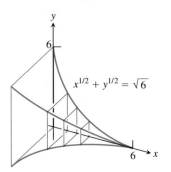

40. *Yellow Perch* A researcher measures the lengths of 3-year-old yellow perch in a fish hatchery and finds that they have a mean length of 17.2 cm with a standard deviation of 3.4 cm. What proportion of 3-year-old yellow perch raised under similar conditions can be expected to reach a length of 20 cm or more?

41. Group Activity Using as large a sample of classmates as possible, measure the span of each person's fully stretched hand, from the tip of the pinky finger to the tip of the thumb. Based on the mean and standard deviation of your sample, what percentage of students your age would have a finger span of more than 10 inches?

42. *The 68-95-99.7 Rule* (a) Verify that for every normal pdf, the proportion of the population lying within one standard deviation of the mean is close to 68%. (*Hint:* Since it is the same for every pdf, you can simplify the function by assuming that $\mu = 0$ and $\sigma = 1$. Then integrate from -1 to 1.)

(b) Verify the two remaining parts of the rule.

43. Writing to Learn Explain why the area under the graph of a probability density function has to equal 1.

In Exercises 44–48, use the cylindrical shell method to find the volume of the solid generated by revolving the region bounded by the curves about the *y*-axis.

44. $y = 2x$, $y = x/2$, $x = 1$

45. $y = 1/x$, $y = 0$, $x = 1/2$, $x = 2$

46. $y = \sin x$, $y = 0$, $0 \le x \le \pi$

47. $y = x - 3$, $y = x^2 - 3x$

48. the bell-shaped region in Exercise 18

49. *Bundt Cake* A bundt cake (see Exploration 1, Section 8.3) has a hole of radius 2 inches and an outer radius of 6 inches at the base. It is 5 inches high, and each cross-sectional slice is parabolic.

(a) Model a typical slice by finding the equation of the parabola with *y*-intercept 5 and *x*-intercepts ± 2.

(b) Revolve the parabolic region about an appropriate line to generate the bundt cake and find its volume.

50. *Finding a Function* Find a function *f* that has a continuous derivative on $(0, \infty)$ and that has both of the following properties.

   i. The graph of *f* goes through the point $(1, 1)$.

   ii. The length *L* of the curve from $(1, 1)$ to any point $(x, f(x))$ is given by the formula $L = \ln x + f(x) - 1$.

In Exercises 51 and 52, find the area of the surface generated by revolving the curve about the indicated axis.

51. $y = \tan x$, $0 \le x \le \pi/4$;   *x*-axis

52. $xy = 1$, $1 \le y \le 2$;   *y*-axis

AP* Examination Preparation

You may use a graphing calculator to solve the following problems.

53. Let R be the region in the first quadrant enclosed by the y-axis and the graphs of $y = 2 + \sin x$ and $y = \sec x$.

   (a) Find the area of R.

   (b) Find the volume of the solid generated when R is revolved about the x-axis.

   (c) Find the volume of the solid whose base is R and whose cross sections cut by planes perpendicular to the x-axis are squares.

54. The temperature outside a house during a 24-hour period is given by

$$F(t) = 80 - 10 \cos\left(\frac{\pi t}{12}\right), 0 \le t \le 24,$$

where $F(t)$ is measured in degrees Fahrenheit and t is measured in hours.

   (a) Find the average temperature, to the nearest degree Fahrenheit, between $t = 6$ and $t = 14$.

   (b) An air conditioner cooled the house whenever the outside temperature was at or above 78 degrees Fahrenheit. For what values of t was the air conditioner cooling the house?

   (c) The cost of cooling the house accumulates at the rate of $0.05 per hour for each degree the outside temperature exceeds 78 degrees Fahrenheit. What was the total cost, to the nearest cent, to cool the house for this 24-hour period?

55. The rate at which people enter an amusement park on a given day is modeled by the function E defined by

$$E(t) = \frac{15600}{t^2 - 24t + 160}.$$

The rate at which people leave the same amusement park on the same day is modeled by the function L defined by

$$L(t) = \frac{9890}{t^2 - 38t + 370}.$$

Both $E(t)$ and $L(t)$ are measured in people per hour, and time t is measured in hours after midnight. These functions are valid for $9 \le t \le 23$, which are the hours that the park is open. At time $t = 9$, there are no people in the park.

   (a) How many people have entered the park by 5:00 P.M. ($t = 17$)? Round your answer to the nearest whole number.

   (b) The price of admission to the park is $15 until 5:00 P.M. ($t = 17$). After 5:00 P.M., the price of admission to the park is $11. How many dollars are collected from admissions to the park on the given day? Round your answer to the nearest whole number.

   (c) Let $H(t) = \int_9^t (E(x) - L(x))\, dx$ for $9 \le t \le 23$. The value of $H(17)$ to the nearest whole number is 3725. Find the value of $H'(17)$ and explain the meaning of $H(17)$ and $H'(17)$ in the context of the park.

   (d) At what time t, for $9 \le t \le 23$, does the model predict that the number of people in the park is a maximum?

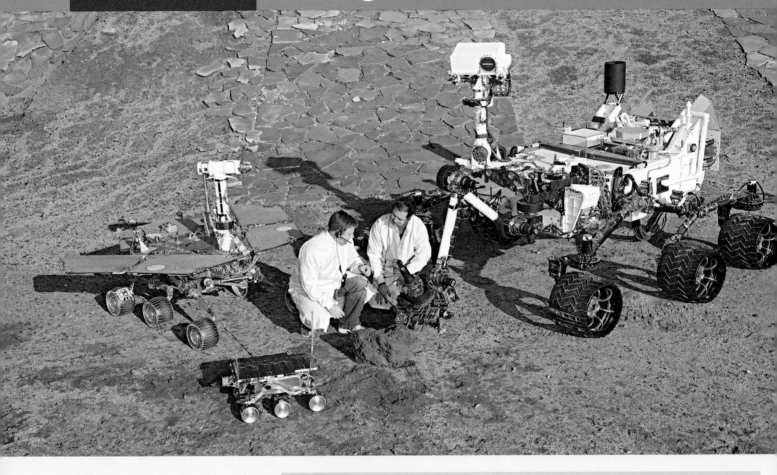

9.1 Sequences

9.2 L'Hospital's Rule

9.3 Relative Rates of Growth

9.4 Improper Integrals

NASA's Mars Pathfinder rover *Sojourner* was launched into space using a Delta II launch rocket vehicle. The *Sojourner* rover landed successfully on the Martian surface and began transmitting data back to Earth.

To launch a heavy payload on its way to Mars, scientists must calculate the "escape velocity" necessary to overcome Earth's gravitational pull. This requires computing an integral over the entire distance affected by Earth's gravity, which extends infinitely into space. Such an integral is called *improper* because it is defined on an interval of the form $[a, \infty)$ rather than an interval $[a, b]$. You will learn how to handle improper integrals in Section 9.4.

CHAPTER 9 | **Overview**

In the late 17th century, John Bernoulli discovered a rule for calculating limits of fractions whose numerators and denominators both approach zero. The rule is known today as l'Hospital's Rule, after Guillaume François Antoine de l'Hospital (1661–1704), Marquis de St. Mesme, a French nobleman who wrote the first differential calculus text, where the rule first appeared in print. We will also use l'Hospital's Rule to compare the rates at which functions of x grow as $|x|$ becomes large.

In Chapter 6 we saw how to evaluate definite integrals of continuous functions and bounded functions with a finite number of discontinuities on finite closed intervals. These ideas are extended to integrals where one or both limits of integration are infinite, and to integrals whose integrands become unbounded on the interval of integration. Sequences are introduced in preparation for the study of infinite series in Chapter 10.

9.1 | Sequences

You will be able to construct and manipulate sequences of various kinds and analyze them for convergence or divergence.

- Explicit and recursive definitions
- Arithmetic and geometric sequences
- Graphs of sequences
- Limits of sequences; convergent and divergent sequences
- The Squeeze Theorem

Defining a Sequence

We have seen sequences before, such as sequences $x_0, x_1, \ldots, x_n, \ldots$ of numerical approximations generated by Newton's method in Chapter 5. A **sequence** $\{a_n\}$ is a list of numbers written in an explicit order. For example, in the sequence

$$\{a_n\} = \{a_1, a_2, a_3, \ldots, a_n, \ldots\},$$

a_1 is the *first term*, a_2 is the *second term*, a_3 is the *third term*, and so forth. The numbers $a_1, a_2, a_3, \ldots, a_n, \ldots$ are the **terms** of the sequence and a_n is the **nth term** of the sequence. We may also think of the sequence $\{a_1, a_2, a_3, \ldots, a_n, \ldots\}$ as a function with domain the set of positive integers and range $\{a_1, a_2, a_3, \ldots, a_n, \ldots\}$.

Any real-valued function with domain a subset of the set of positive integers is considered a sequence. If the domain is finite, then the sequence is a **finite sequence.** Generally we will concentrate on **infinite sequences,** that is, sequences with domains that are infinite subsets of the positive integers.

EXAMPLE 1 Defining a Sequence Explicitly

Find the first six terms and the 100th term of the sequence $\{a_n\}$ where

$$a_n = \frac{(-1)^n}{n^2 + 1}.$$

SOLUTION

Set n equal to 1, 2, 3, 4, 5, 6, and we obtain

$$a_1 = \frac{(-1)^1}{1^2 + 1} = -\frac{1}{2}, a_2 = \frac{(-1)^2}{2^2 + 1} = \frac{1}{5}, a_3 = -\frac{1}{10}, a_4 = \frac{1}{17}, a_5 = -\frac{1}{26}, a_6 = \frac{1}{37}.$$

For $n = 100$ we find

$$a_{100} = \frac{(-1)^{100}}{100^2 + 1} = \frac{1}{10001}.$$

Now Try Exercise 1.

Bernard A. Harris Jr. (1956–)

Bernard Harris, M.D., became an astronaut in 1991. In 1995, as the Payload Commander on the STS-63 mission, he became the first African American to walk in space. During this mission, which included a rendezvous with the Russian Space Station, *Mir*, Harris traveled over 2.9 million miles. Dr. Harris left NASA in 1996 to become Vice President of Microgravity and Life Sciences for SPACEHAB Incorporated.

The sequence of Example 1 is defined **explicitly** because the formula for a_n is defined in terms of n. Another way to define a sequence is **recursively** by giving a formula for a_n relating it to previous terms, as shown in Example 2.

EXAMPLE 2 **Defining a Sequence Recursively**

Find the first four terms and the eighth term for the sequence defined recursively by the following conditions:

$$b_1 = 4$$
$$b_n = b_{n-1} + 2 \quad \text{for all} \quad n \geq 2$$

SOLUTION

We proceed one term at a time, starting with $b_1 = 4$ and obtaining each succeeding term by adding 2 to the term just before it:

$$b_1 = 4$$
$$b_2 = b_1 + 2 = 6$$
$$b_3 = b_2 + 2 = 8$$
$$b_4 = b_3 + 2 = 10$$

and so forth

Continuing in this way we arrive at $b_8 = 18$.   *Now Try Exercise 5.*

Explicit and Recursive Formulas for Arithmetic Sequences

From the sequence $\{a, a + d, a + 2d, \ldots, a + (n - 1)d, \ldots\}$ we have $a_1 = a$ and $a_n = a + (n - 1)d$ for any positive integer n. So, for any arithmetic sequence, we have an explicit formula and a recursive formula for a_n.

Arithmetic and Geometric Sequences

There are a variety of rules by which we can construct sequences, but two particular types of sequence are dominant in mathematical applications: those in which pairs of successive terms all have a *common difference* (*arithmetic sequences*), and those in which pairs of successive terms all have a *common quotient,* or *common ratio* (*geometric sequences*).

DEFINITION **Arithmetic Sequence**

A sequence $\{a_n\}$ is an **arithmetic sequence** if it can be written in the form

$$\{a, a + d, a + 2d, \ldots, a + (n - 1)d, \ldots\}$$

for some constant d. The number d is the **common difference.**

Each term in an arithmetic sequence can be obtained recursively from its preceding term by adding d:

$$a_n = a_{n-1} + d \quad \text{for all} \quad n \geq 2$$

EXAMPLE 3 **Defining Arithmetic Sequences**

For each of the following arithmetic sequences, find **(a)** the common difference, **(b)** the ninth term, **(c)** a recursive rule for the nth term, and **(d)** an explicit rule for the nth term.

Sequence 1: $-5, -2, 1, 4, 7, \ldots$ **Sequence 2:** $\ln 2, \ln 6, \ln 18, \ln 54, \ldots$

SOLUTION

Sequence 1

(a) The difference between successive terms is 3.

(b) $a_9 = -5 + (9 - 1)(3) = 19$

(c) The sequence is defined recursively by $a_1 = -5$ and $a_n = a_{n-1} + 3$ for all $n \geq 2$.

(d) The sequence is defined explicitly by $a_n = -5 + (n - 1)(3) = 3n - 8$.

Sequence 2

(a) The difference between the first two terms is $\ln 6 - \ln 2 = \ln (6/2) = \ln 3$. You can check that $\ln 18 - \ln 6 = \ln 54 - \ln 18$ are also equal to $\ln 3$.

continued

(b) $a_9 = \ln 2 + (9 - 1)(\ln 3) = \ln 2 + 8 \ln 3 = \ln (2 \cdot 3^8) = \ln 13,122$

(c) The sequence is defined recursively by $a_1 = \ln 2$ and $a_n = a_{n-1} + \ln 3$ for all $n \geq 2$.

(d) The sequence is defined explicitly by $a_n = \ln 2 + (n - 1)(\ln 3) = \ln (2 \cdot 3^{n-1})$.

Now Try Exercise 13.

DEFINITION   **Geometric Sequence**

A sequence $\{a_n\}$ is a **geometric sequence** if it can be written in the form

$$\{a, a \cdot r, a \cdot r^2, \dots, a \cdot r^{n-1}, \dots\}$$

for some nonzero constant r. The number r is the **common ratio.**

Each term in a geometric sequence can be obtained recursively from its preceding term by multiplying by r:

$$a_n = a_{n-1} \cdot r \quad \text{for all} \quad n \geq 2$$

EXAMPLE 4 Defining Geometric Sequences

For each of the following geometric sequences, find **(a)** the common ratio, **(b)** the tenth term, **(c)** a recursive rule for the nth term, and **(d)** an explicit rule for the nth term.

Sequence 1: $1, -2, 4, -8, 16, \dots$ **Sequence 2:** $10^{-2}, 10^{-1}, 1, 10, 10^2, \dots$

SOLUTION

Sequence 1

(a) The ratio between successive terms is -2.

(b) $a_{10} = (1) \cdot (-2)^9 = -512$

(c) The sequence is defined recursively by $a_1 = 1$ and $a_n = (-2)a_{n-1}$ for $n \geq 2$.

(d) The sequence is defined explicitly by $a_n = (1) \cdot (-2)^{n-1} = (-2)^{n-1}$.

Sequence 2

(a) The ratio between successive terms is 10.

(b) $a_{10} = (10^{-2}) \cdot (10^9) = 10^7$

(c) The sequence is defined recursively by $a_1 = 10^{-2}$ and $a_n = (10)a_{n-1}$ for $n \geq 2$.

(d) The sequence is defined explicitly by $a_n = (10^{-2}) \cdot (10^{n-1}) = 10^{n-3}$.

Now Try Exercise 17.

EXAMPLE 5 Constructing a Sequence

The second and fifth terms of a geometric sequence are 6 and -48, respectively. Find the first term, the common ratio, and an explicit rule for the nth term.

SOLUTION

Because the sequence is geometric the second term is $a_1 \cdot r$ and the fifth term is $a_1 \cdot r^4$, where a_1 is the first term and r is the common ratio. Dividing, we have

$$\frac{a_1 \cdot r^4}{a_1 \cdot r} = -\frac{48}{6}$$

$$r^3 = -8$$

$$r = -2$$

continued

Then $a_1 \cdot r = 6$ implies that $a_1 = -3$. The sequence is defined explicitly by

$$a_n = (-3)(-2)^{n-1} = (-1)^n (3)(2^{n-1}).$$

Now Try Exercise 21.

Graphing a Sequence

As with other kinds of functions, it helps to represent a sequence geometrically with its graph. One way to produce a graph of a sequence on a graphing calculator is to use parametric mode, as shown in Example 6.

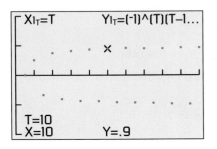

Figure 9.1 The graph of the sequence of Example 6. The TRACE feature shows the coordinates of the 10th point of the sequence graphed in parametric mode.

EXAMPLE 6 Graphing a Sequence Using Parametric Mode

Draw a graph of the sequence $\{a_n\}$ with $a_n = (-1)^n \dfrac{n-1}{n}, n = 1, 2, \ldots$.

SOLUTION

Let $X_{1T} = T$, $Y_{1T} = (-1)^T \dfrac{T-1}{T}$, and graph in dot mode. Set Tmin $= 1$, Tmax $= 20$, and Tstep $= 1$. Even though the domain of the sequence is all positive integers, we are required to choose a value for Tmax to use parametric graphing mode. Finally, we choose Xmin $= 0$, Xmax $= 20$, Xscl $= 2$, Ymin $= -2$, Ymax $= 2$, Yscl $= 1$, and draw the graph (Figure 9.1). We have also activated the TRACE feature in Figure 9.1.

Now Try Exercise 23.

Some graphing calculators have a built-in sequence graphing mode that makes it easy to graph sequences defined recursively. The function names used in this mode are u, v, and w. We will use this procedure to graph the sequence of Example 7.

EXAMPLE 7 Graphing a Sequence Using Sequence Graphing Mode

Graph the sequence defined recursively by

$$b_1 = 4$$
$$b_n = b_{n-1} + 2 \quad \text{for all} \quad n \geq 2.$$

SOLUTION

We set the calculator in Sequence graphing mode and dot mode (Figure 9.2a). Replace b_n by $u(n)$. Then select nMin $= 1$, $u(n) = u(n-1) + 2$, and $u(n\text{Min}) = \{4\}$ (Figure 9.2b).

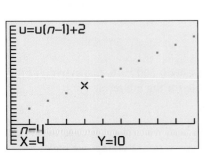

[0, 10] by [−5, 25]

Figure 9.3 The graph of the sequence of Example 7. The TRACE feature shows the coordinates of the fourth point $(4, 10)$ of the sequence

$$b_1 = 4, b_n = b_{n-1} + 2, n \geq 2.$$

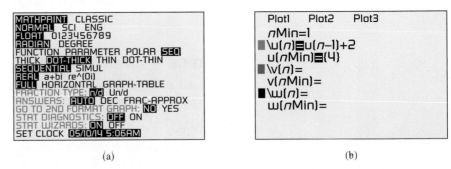

Figure 9.2 (a) Setting sequence mode and dot mode on the calculator, and (b) entering the sequence of Example 7 in the calculator.

Then set nMin $= 1$, nMax $= 10$, PlotStart $= 1$, PlotStep $= 1$, and graph in the $[0, 10]$ by $[-5, 25]$ viewing window (Figure 9.3). We have also activated TRACE in Figure 9.3.

Now Try Exercise 27.

Limit of a Sequence

The sequence $\{1, 2, 3, \dots, n, \dots\}$ of positive integers has no limit. As with functions, we can use a grapher to suggest what a limiting value may be, and then we can confirm the limit analytically with theorems based on a formal definition, as we did in Chapter 2.

DEFINITION   Limit of a Sequence

Let L be a real number. The sequence $\{a_n\}$ has **limit L as n approaches ∞** if we can force a_n to be as close to L as we wish for all sufficiently large n. More formally, given any positive number ϵ, there is a positive number M such that for all $n > M$ we have

$$|a_n - L| < \epsilon.$$

We write $\lim\limits_{n\to\infty} a_n = L$ and say that the sequence **converges to L.** Sequences that do not have limits **diverge.**

Just as in Chapter 2, there are important properties of limits that help us compute limits of sequences.

THEOREM 1   Properties of Limits

If L and M are real numbers and $\lim\limits_{n\to\infty} a_n = L$ and $\lim\limits_{n\to\infty} b_n = M$, then

1. *Sum Rule:*
$$\lim_{n\to\infty} (a_n + b_n) = L + M$$

2. *Difference Rule:*
$$\lim_{n\to\infty} (a_n - b_n) = L - M$$

3. *Product Rule:*
$$\lim_{n\to\infty} (a_n b_n) = L \cdot M$$

4. *Constant Multiple Rule:*
$$\lim_{n\to\infty} (c \cdot a_n) = c \cdot L$$

5. *Quotient Rule:*
$$\lim_{n\to\infty} \frac{a_n}{b_n} = \frac{L}{M}, \quad M \neq 0$$

EXAMPLE 8 Finding the Limit of a Sequence

Determine whether the sequence converges or diverges. If it converges, find its limit.

$$a_n = \frac{2n - 1}{n}$$

SOLUTION

The graph of the sequence in Figure 9.4 suggests that the sequence converges and the limit exists. The TRACE feature shows that the number 2 is a reasonable conjecture for the limit. We can prove it is 2 by using the properties of limits; we have

$$\lim_{n\to\infty} \frac{2n - 1}{n} = \lim_{n\to\infty} \left(2 - \frac{1}{n}\right)$$

$$= \lim_{n\to\infty} (2) - \lim_{n\to\infty} \left(\frac{1}{n}\right)$$

$$= 2 - 0 = 2.$$

So the sequence converges and its limit is 2.   ***Now Try Exercise 31.***

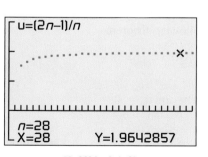

u=(2n–1)/n

n=28
X=28   Y=1.9642857

[0, 30] by [–1, 3]

Figure 9.4 The graph of the sequence in Example 8 with TRACE activated, showing for $n = 28$, $a_{28} = 1.9642857$.

Leonardo Pisano (c. 1170–c. 1250)

Leonardo was from Italy and is known today as **Fibonacci**. In his *Liber Abaci* (book of calculations), published in 1202, he introduced the so-called *modus Indorum* (method of the Indians) which introduced the western world to Arabic numerals. The book advocated numeration with the digits 0–9 and place value. His book showed the practical importance of the new Arabic numeral system by applying it to commercial bookkeeping. The book was very well received throughout educated Europe and had great impact on European thought.

Recursive Sequences in Nature and Design—the Golden Ratio

The successive quotients of the numbers in the Fibonacci sequence—1, 1, 2, 3, 5, 8, 13, 21, ... (see Exercise 56 in this section)—form another interesting sequence, 1/1, 2/1, 3/2, 5/3, 8/5, 13/8, 21/13, ..., which converges to the number $\dfrac{1 + \sqrt{5}}{2}$.

This number, denoted ϕ, is sometimes called the *golden ratio* because it seems to appear so commonly in nature and human design. For example, the stars on the American flag contain segments of four different lengths, all of which can be paired in golden ratios.

EXAMPLE 9 Determining Convergence or Divergence

Determine whether the sequence with given nth term converges or diverges. If it converges, find its limit.

(a) $a_n = (-1)^n \dfrac{n - 1}{n}, n = 1, 2, \dots$ **(b)** $b_1 = 4, b_n = b_{n-1} + 2$ for all $n \geq 2$

SOLUTION

(a) This is the sequence of Example 6 with graph shown in Figure 9.1. This sequence diverges. In fact, we can see that the terms with n even approach 1 while the terms with n odd approach -1.

(b) This is the sequence of Example 7 with graph shown in Figure 9.3. This sequence also diverges. In fact, we can say that $\lim_{n \to \infty} b_n = \infty$.   *Now Try Exercise 35.*

An important theorem that can be rewritten for sequences is the Squeeze Theorem from Chapter 2.

THEOREM 2   The Squeeze Theorem for Sequences

If $\lim_{n \to \infty} a_n = \lim_{n \to \infty} c_n = L$ and if there is an integer N for which $a_n \leq b_n \leq c_n$ for all $n > N$, then $\lim_{n \to \infty} b_n = L$.

EXAMPLE 10 Using the Squeeze Theorem

Show that the sequence $\left\{ \dfrac{\cos n}{n} \right\}$ converges, and find its limit.

SOLUTION

Because $|\cos x| \leq 1$ for all x, it follows that

$$\left| \frac{\cos n}{n} \right| \leq \frac{|\cos n|}{|n|} \leq \frac{1}{n}$$

for all integers $n \geq 1$. Thus,

$$-\frac{1}{n} \leq \frac{\cos n}{n} \leq \frac{1}{n}.$$

Then, $\lim_{n \to \infty} \dfrac{\cos n}{n} = 0$ because $\lim_{n \to \infty} \left(-\dfrac{1}{n} \right) = \lim_{n \to \infty} \left(\dfrac{1}{n} \right) = 0$. The sequence $\left\{ \dfrac{\cos n}{n} \right\}$ converges.   *Now Try Exercise 41.*

We can use the Squeeze Theorem to prove the following theorem.

THEOREM 3   Absolute Value Theorem

Consider the sequence $\{ a_n \}$. If $\lim_{n \to \infty} |a_n| = 0$, then $\lim_{n \to \infty} a_n = 0$.

Proof We know that $-|a_n| \leq a_n \leq |a_n|$. Thus, $\lim_{n \to \infty} |a_n| = 0$ and $\lim_{n \to \infty} -|a_n| = 0$ implies that $\lim_{n \to \infty} a_n = 0$ because of the Squeeze Theorem. ∎

Another way to state the Absolute Value Theorem is that if the absolute value sequence converges to 0, then the original sequence also converges to 0.

Quick Review 9.1 *(For help, go to Sections 1.2, 2.1, and 2.2.)*

Exercise numbers with a gray background indicate problems that the authors have designed to be solved *without a calculator*.

In Exercises 1 and 2, let $f(x) = \dfrac{x}{x + 3}$. Find the values of f.

1. $f(5)$ **2.** $f(-2)$

In Exercises 3 and 4, evaluate the expression $a + (n - 1)d$ for the given values of a, n, and d.

3. $a = -2, n = 3, d = 1.5$

4. $a = -7, n = 5, d = 3$

In Exercises 5 and 6, evaluate the expression ar^{n-1} for the given values of a, r, and n.

5. $a = 1.5, r = 2, n = 4$ **6.** $a = -2, r = 1.5, n = 3$

In Exercises 7–10, find the value of the limit.

7. $\displaystyle\lim_{x\to\infty} \frac{5x^3 + 2x^2}{3x^4 + 16x^2}$ **8.** $\displaystyle\lim_{x\to 0} \frac{\sin(3x)}{x}$

9. $\displaystyle\lim_{x\to\infty}\left(x \sin\left(\frac{1}{x}\right)\right)$ **10.** $\displaystyle\lim_{x\to\infty} \frac{2x^3 + x^2}{x + 1}$

Section 9.1 Exercises

In Exercises 1–4, find the first six terms and the 50th term of the sequence with specified nth term.

1. $a_n = \dfrac{n}{n + 1}$ **2.** $b_n = 3 - \dfrac{1}{n}$

3. $c_n = \left(1 + \dfrac{1}{n}\right)^n$ **4.** $d_n = n^2 - 3n$

In Exercises 5–10, find the first four terms and the eighth term of the recursively defined sequence.

5. $a_1 = 3, a_n = a_{n-1} - 2$ for all $n \geq 2$

6. $b_1 = -2, b_n = b_{n-1} + 1$ for all $n \geq 2$

7. $c_1 = 2, c_n = 2c_{n-1}$ for all $n \geq 2$

8. $d_1 = 10, d_n = 1.1d_{n-1}$ for all $n \geq 2$

9. $u_1 = 1, u_2 = 1, u_n = u_{n-1} + u_{n-2}$ for all $n \geq 3$

10. $v_1 = -3, v_2 = 2, v_n = v_{n-1} + v_{n-2}$ for all $n \geq 3$

In Exercises 11–14, the sequences are arithmetic. Find

(a) the common difference,

(b) the eighth term,

(c) a recursive rule for the nth term, and

(d) an explicit rule for the nth term.

11. $-2, 1, 4, 7, \ldots$ **12.** $15, 13, 11, 9, \ldots$

13. $1, 3/2, 2, 5/2, \ldots$ **14.** $3, 3.1, 3.2, 3.3, \ldots$

In Exercises 15–18, the sequences are geometric. Find

(a) the common ratio,

(b) the ninth term,

(c) a recursive rule for the nth term, and

(d) an explicit rule for the nth term.

15. $8, 4, 2, 1, \ldots$ **16.** $1, 1.5, 2.25, 3.375, \ldots$

17. $-3, 9, -27, 81, \ldots$ **18.** $5, -5, 5, -5, \ldots$

19. The second and fifth terms of an arithmetic sequence are -2 and 7, respectively. Find the first term and a recursive rule for the nth term.

20. The fifth and ninth terms of an arithmetic sequence are 5 and -3, respectively. Find the first term and an explicit rule for the nth term.

21. The fourth and seventh terms of a geometric sequence are 3010 and 3,010,000, respectively. Find the first term, common ratio, and an explicit rule for the nth term.

22. The second and seventh terms of a geometric sequence are $-1/2$ and 16, respectively. Find the first term, common ratio, and an explicit rule for the nth term.

In Exercises 23–30, draw a graph of the sequence $\{a_n\}$.

23. $a_n = \dfrac{n}{n^2 + 1}$, $n = 1, 2, 3, \ldots$

24. $a_n = \dfrac{n - 2}{n + 2}$, $n = 1, 2, 3, \ldots$

25. $a_n = (-1)^n \dfrac{2n + 1}{n}$, $n = 1, 2, 3, \ldots$

26. $a_n = \left(1 + \dfrac{2}{n}\right)^n$, $n = 1, 2, 3, \ldots$

27. $u_1 = 2$, $u_n = 3u_{n-1}$ for all $n \geq 2$

28. $u_1 = 2$, $u_n = u_{n-1} + 3$ for all $n \geq 2$

29. $u_1 = 3$, $u_n = 5 - \dfrac{1}{2} u_{n-1}$ for all $n \geq 2$

30. $u_1 = 5$, $u_n = u_{n-1} - 2$ for all $n \geq 2$

In Exercises 31–40, determine the convergence or divergence of the sequence with given nth term. If the sequence converges, find its limit.

31. $a_n = \dfrac{3n + 1}{n}$ **32.** $a_n = \dfrac{2n}{n + 3}$

33. $a_n = \dfrac{2n^2 - n - 1}{5n^2 + n + 2}$ **34.** $a_n = \dfrac{n}{n^2 + 1}$

35. $a_n = (-1)^n \dfrac{n - 1}{n + 3}$ **36.** $a_n = (-1)^n \dfrac{n + 1}{n^2 + 2}$

37. $a_n = (1.1)^n$ **38.** $a_n = (0.9)^n$

39. $a_n = n \sin\left(\dfrac{1}{n}\right)$ **40.** $a_n = \cos\left(n\dfrac{\pi}{2}\right)$

In Exercises 41–44, use the Squeeze Theorem to show that the sequence with given nth term converges and find its limit.

41. $a_n = \dfrac{\sin n}{n}$ **42.** $a_n = \dfrac{1}{2^n}$

43. $a_n = \dfrac{1}{n!}$ **44.** $a_n = \dfrac{\sin^2 n}{2^n}$

In Exercises 45–48, match the graph or table with the sequence with given nth term.

45. $a_n = \dfrac{2n - 1}{n}$

46. $b_n = (-1)^n \dfrac{3n + 1}{n + 3}$

47. $c_n = \dfrac{n + 1}{n}$

48. $d_n = \dfrac{4}{n + 2}$

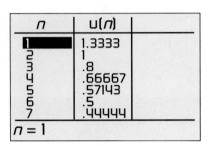

n	$u(n)$
1	1.3333
2	1
3	.8
4	.66667
5	.57143
6	.5
7	.44444

$n = 1$

(a)

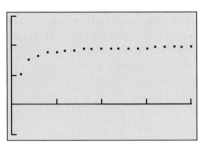

[0, 20] by [–1, 3]

(b)

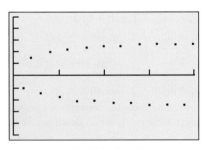

[0, 20] by [–5, 5]

(c)

n	$u(n)$
1	2
2	1.5
3	1.3333
4	1.25
5	1.2
6	1.1667
7	1.1429

$n = 1$

(d)

Standardized Test Questions

49. True or False If the first two terms of an arithmetic sequence are negative, then all its terms are negative. Justify your answer.

50. True or False If the first two terms of a geometric sequence are positive, then all its terms are positive. Justify your answer.

51. Multiple Choice The first and third terms of an arithmetic sequence are -1 and 5, respectively. Which of the following is the sixth term?

(A) -25 (B) 11 (C) 14 (D) 29 (E) 3125

52. Multiple Choice The second and third terms of a geometric sequence are 2.5 and 1.25, respectively. Which of the following is the first term?

(A) -5 (B) -2.5 (C) 0.625 (D) 3.75 (E) 5

53. Multiple Choice Which of the following is the limit of the sequence with nth term $a_n = n \sin\left(\dfrac{3\pi}{n}\right)$?

(A) 1 (B) π (C) 2π (D) 3π (E) 4π

54. Multiple Choice Which of the following is the limit of the sequence with nth term $a_n = (-1)^n \dfrac{3n - 1}{n + 2}$?

(A) -3 (B) 0 (C) 2 (D) 3 (E) diverges

Explorations

55. *Connecting Geometry and Sequences* In the sequence of diagrams that follow, regular polygons are inscribed in unit circles with at least one side of each polygon perpendicular to the x-axis.

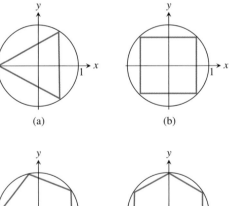

(a)   (b)

(c)   (d)

(a) Prove that the perimeter of each polygon in the sequence is given by $a_n = 2n \sin(\pi/n)$, where n is the number of sides in the polygon.

(b) Determine $\lim\limits_{n \to \infty} a_n$.

56. *Fibonacci Sequence* The **Fibonacci sequence** can be defined recursively by $a_1 = 1$, $a_2 = 1$, and $a_n = a_{n-2} + a_{n-1}$ for all integers $n \geq 3$.

(a) Write out the first 10 terms of the sequence.

(b) Draw a graph of the sequence using the Sequence Graphing mode on your grapher. Enter $u(n) = u(n - 1) + u(n - 2)$ and $u(n\text{Min}) = \{1, 1\}$.

(c) Write out the first 10 terms of the sequence a_n/a_{n-1} $(a_1 = 1 = a_2)$ and $n > 2$ that determine the golden ratio from page 448 (margin) and compute the ratio a_n/a_{n-1} for $n = 10$.

(d) The sequence in (c) converges to $\dfrac{1 + \sqrt{5}}{2} = 1.618$ (to three decimal places). What is the first term of the sequence that approximates $\dfrac{1 + \sqrt{5}}{2}$ with an error of less than 0.001?

Extending the Ideas

57. **Writing to Learn** If $\{a_n\}$ is a geometric sequence with all positive terms, explain why $\{\log a_n\}$ must be arithmetic.

58. **Writing to Learn** If $\{a_n\}$ is an arithmetic sequence, explain why $\{10^{a_n}\}$ must be geometric.

59. *Proving Limits* Use the formal definition of limit to prove that
$$\lim_{n \to \infty} \frac{1}{n} = 0.$$

9.2 | L'Hospital's Rule

You will be able to use l'Hospital's Rule to determine limits of indeterminate forms.

- L'Hospital's Rule and its stronger form for repeated iterations
- Indeterminate forms $0/0$ and ∞/∞
- Indeterminate forms $\infty \cdot 0$ and $\infty - \infty$
- Indeterminate forms 1^{∞}, 0^{0}, and ∞^{0}

Indeterminate Form 0/0

If functions $f(x)$ and $g(x)$ are both zero at $x = a$, then

$$\lim_{x \to a} \frac{f(x)}{g(x)}$$

cannot be found by substituting $x = a$. The substitution produces $0/0$, a meaningless expression known as an **indeterminate form.** Our experience so far has been that limits that lead to indeterminate forms may or may not be hard to find algebraically. It took a lot of analysis in Exercise 75 of Section 2.1 to find $\lim_{x \to 0} (\sin x)/x$. But we have had remarkable success with the limit used to calculate derivatives:

$$f'(a) = \lim_{x \to a} \frac{f(x) - f(a)}{x - a},$$

which always produces the equivalent of $0/0$. L'Hospital's Rule enables us to draw on our success with derivatives to evaluate limits that otherwise lead to indeterminate forms.

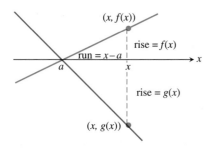

Figure 9.5 A zoom-in view of the graphs of the differentiable functions f and g at $x = a$. (Theorem 4)

THEOREM 4 L'Hospital's Rule (First Form)

Suppose that $f(a) = g(a) = 0$, that $f'(a)$ and $g'(a)$ exist, and that $g'(a) \neq 0$. Then

$$\lim_{x \to a} \frac{f(x)}{g(x)} = \frac{f'(a)}{g'(a)}.$$

Proof Before proving the theorem, we can gain insight by looking at a geometric argument. Refer to Figure 9.5. If we zoom in on the graphs of f and g at $(a, f(a)) = (a, g(a)) = (a, 0)$, the graphs (Figure 9.5) appear to be straight lines because differentiable functions are locally linear. Let m_1 and m_2 be the slopes of the lines for f and g, respectively. Then for x near a,

$$\frac{f(x)}{g(x)} = \frac{\dfrac{f(x)}{x - a}}{\dfrac{g(x)}{x - a}} = \frac{m_1}{m_2}.$$

As $x \to a$, m_1 and m_2 approach $f'(a)$ and $g'(a)$, respectively. Therefore,

$$\lim_{x \to a} \frac{f(x)}{g(x)} = \lim_{x \to a} \frac{m_1}{m_2} = \frac{f'(a)}{g'(a)}.$$

To prove the theorem, we work backward, recognizing that $f'(a)$ and $g'(a)$ are themselves limits. So,

$$\frac{f'(a)}{g'(a)} = \frac{\displaystyle \lim_{x \to a} \frac{f(x) - f(a)}{x - a}}{\displaystyle \lim_{x \to a} \frac{g(x) - g(a)}{x - a}} = \lim_{x \to a} \frac{\dfrac{f(x) - f(a)}{x - a}}{\dfrac{g(x) - g(a)}{x - a}}$$

$$= \lim_{x \to a} \frac{f(x) - f(a)}{g(x) - g(a)} = \lim_{x \to a} \frac{f(x) - 0}{g(x) - 0} = \lim_{x \to a} \frac{f(x)}{g(x)}. \quad \blacksquare$$

Guillaume de l'Hospital (1661–1704)

Although the rule did not originate with l'Hospital, it appeared in print for the first time in his treatise on the infinitesimal calculus. His book was the first systematic exposition of differential calculus. Several editions and translations to other languages were published, and it became a model for subsequent treatments of calculus.

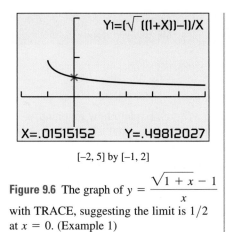

Y1=(√ ((1+X))−1)/X

X=.01515152   Y=.49812027

[−2, 5] by [−1, 2]

Figure 9.6 The graph of $y = \dfrac{\sqrt{1+x}-1}{x}$ with TRACE, suggesting the limit is 1/2 at $x = 0$. (Example 1)

EXAMPLE 1 Indeterminate Form 0/0

Estimate the limit graphically and then use l'Hospital's Rule to find the limit.

$$\lim_{x\to 0}\frac{\sqrt{1+x}-1}{x}$$

SOLUTION

From the graph in Figure 9.6 we can estimate the limit to be about 1/2. If we set $f(x) = \sqrt{1+x}-1$ and $g(x) = x$ we have $f(0) = g(0) = 0$. Thus, l'Hospital's Rule applies in this case. Because $f'(x) = (1/2)(1+x)^{-1/2}$ and $g'(x) = 1$ it follows that

$$\lim_{x\to 0}\frac{\sqrt{1+x}-1}{x} = \frac{(1/2)(1+0)^{-1/2}}{1} = \frac{1}{2}.$$

Now Try Exercise 3.

Sometimes after differentiation the new numerator and denominator both equal zero at $x = a$, as we will see in Example 2. In these cases we apply a stronger form of l'Hospital's Rule.

Augustin-Louis Cauchy
(1789–1857)

An engineer with a genius for mathematics and mathematical modeling, Cauchy created an early modeling of surface wave propagation that is now a classic in hydrodynamics. Cauchy (pronounced "CO-she") invented our notion of continuity and proved the Intermediate Value Theorem for continuous functions. He invented modern limit notation and was the first to prove the convergence of $(1 + 1/n)^n$. His Mean Value Theorem, the subject of Exercise 71, is the key to proving the stronger form of l'Hospital's Rule. His work advanced not only calculus and mathematical analysis, but also the fields of complex function theory, error theory, differential equations, and celestial mechanics.

THEOREM 5   L'Hospital's Rule (Stronger Form)

Suppose that $f(a) = g(a) = 0$, that f and g are differentiable on an open interval I containing a, and that $g'(x) \neq 0$ on I if $x \neq a$. Then

$$\lim_{x\to a}\frac{f(x)}{g(x)} = \lim_{x\to a}\frac{f'(x)}{g'(x)},$$

if the latter limit exists.

When you apply l'Hospital's Rule, look for a change from 0/0 into something else. This is where the limit is revealed.

EXAMPLE 2 Applying a Stronger Form of l'Hospital's Rule

Evaluate $\displaystyle\lim_{x\to 0}\frac{\sqrt{1+x}-1-x/2}{x^2}$.

SOLUTION

Substituting $x = 0$ leads to the indeterminate form 0/0 because the numerator and denominator of the fraction are 0 when 0 is substituted for x. So we apply l'Hospital's Rule.

$$\lim_{x\to 0}\frac{\sqrt{1+x}-1-x/2}{x^2} = \lim_{x\to 0}\frac{(1/2)(1+x)^{-1/2}-1/2}{2x}$$ Differentiate numerator and denominator

Substituting 0 for x leads to 0 in both the numerator and denominator of the second fraction, so we differentiate again.

$$\lim_{x\to 0}\frac{\sqrt{1+x}-1-x/2}{x^2} = \lim_{x\to 0}\frac{(1/2)(1+x)^{-1/2}-1/2}{2x} = \lim_{x\to 0}\frac{-(1/4)(1+x)^{-3/2}}{2}$$

The third limit in the above line is $-1/8$. Thus,

$$\lim_{x\to 0}\frac{\sqrt{1+x}-1-x/2}{x^2} = -\frac{1}{8}.$$

Now Try Exercise 5.

EXPLORATION 1 Exploring L'Hospital's Rule Graphically

Consider the function $f(x) = \dfrac{\sin x}{x}$.

1. Use l'Hospital's Rule to find $\lim_{x \to 0} f(x)$.
2. Let $y_1 = \sin x$, $y_2 = x$, $y_3 = y_1/y_2$, $y_4 = y_1'/y_2'$. Explain how graphing y_3 and y_4 in the same viewing window provides support for l'Hospital's Rule in part 1.
3. Let $y_5 = y_3'$. Graph y_3, y_4, and y_5 in the same viewing window. Based on what you see in the viewing window, make a statement about what l'Hospital's Rule does *not* say.

L'Hospital's Rule applies to one-sided limits as well.

EXAMPLE 3 Using L'Hospital's Rule with One-Sided Limits

Evaluate the following limits using l'Hospital's Rule:

(a) $\displaystyle\lim_{x \to 0^+} \frac{\sin x}{x^2}$

(b) $\displaystyle\lim_{x \to 0^-} \frac{\sin x}{x^2}$

Support your answer graphically.

SOLUTION

(a) Substituting $x = 0$ leads to the indeterminate form $0/0$. Apply l'Hospital's Rule by differentiating numerator and denominator.

$$\lim_{x \to 0^+} \frac{\sin x}{x^2} = \lim_{x \to 0^+} \frac{\cos x}{2x} \quad \frac{1}{0}$$
$$= \infty$$

(b) $\displaystyle\lim_{x \to 0^-} \frac{\sin x}{x^2} = \lim_{x \to 0^-} \frac{\cos x}{2x} \quad \frac{1}{-0}$
$$= -\infty$$

Figure 9.7 supports the results. **Now Try Exercise 11.**

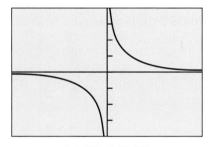

[−1, 1] by [−20, 20]

Figure 9.7 The graph of $f(x) = (\sin x)/x^2$. (Example 3)

When we reach a point where one of the derivatives approaches 0, as in Example 3, and the other does not, then the limit in question is 0 (if only the numerator approaches 0) or $\pm$ infinity (if only the denominator approaches 0).

Indeterminate Forms ∞/∞, $\infty \cdot 0$, $\infty - \infty$

A version of l'Hospital's Rule also applies to quotients that lead to the indeterminate form ∞/∞. If $f(x)$ and $g(x)$ both approach infinity as $x \to a$, then

$$\lim_{x \to a} \frac{f(x)}{g(x)} = \lim_{x \to a} \frac{f'(x)}{g'(x)},$$

provided the latter limit exists. The a here (and in the indeterminate form $0/0$) may itself be finite or infinite, and may be an endpoint of the interval I of Theorem 5.

EXAMPLE 4 Working with Indeterminate Form ∞/∞

Identify the indeterminate form and evaluate the limit using l'Hospital's Rule. Support your answer graphically.

$$\lim_{x \to \pi/2} \frac{\sec x}{1 + \tan x}$$

continued

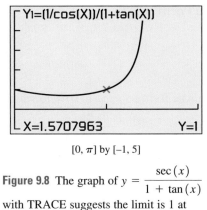

[0, π] by [−1, 5]

Figure 9.8 The graph of $y = \dfrac{\sec(x)}{1 + \tan(x)}$ with TRACE suggests the limit is 1 at $x = \pi/2$. (Example 4)

SOLUTION

The numerator and denominator are discontinuous at $x = \pi/2$, so we investigate the one-sided limits there. To apply l'Hospital's Rule we can choose I to be any open interval containing $x = \pi/2$.

$$\lim_{x \to (\pi/2)^-} \frac{\sec x}{1 + \tan x} \qquad \frac{\infty}{\infty} \text{ from the left}$$

Next differentiate the numerator and denominator.

$$\lim_{x \to (\pi/2)^-} \frac{\sec x}{1 + \tan x} = \lim_{x \to (\pi/2)^-} \frac{\sec x \tan x}{\sec^2 x} = \lim_{x \to (\pi/2)^-} \sin x = 1$$

The right-hand limit is 1 also, with $(-\infty)/(-\infty)$ as the indeterminate form. Therefore, the two-sided limit is equal to 1. The graph of $(\sec x)/(1 + \tan x)$ in Figure 9.8 appears to pass right through the point $(\pi/2, 1)$ and supports the work above.

Now Try Exercise 13.

EXAMPLE 5 Working with Indeterminate Form ∞/∞

Identify the indeterminate form and evaluate the limit using l'Hospital's Rule. Support your answer graphically.

$$\lim_{x \to \infty} \frac{\ln x}{2\sqrt{x}}$$

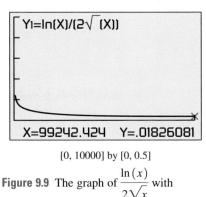

[0, 10000] by [0, 0.5]

Figure 9.9 The graph of $\dfrac{\ln(x)}{2\sqrt{x}}$ with TRACE suggests the limit is 0 as $x \to \infty$. (Example 5)

SOLUTION

$$\frac{\infty}{\infty}$$

$$\lim_{x \to \infty} \frac{\ln x}{2\sqrt{x}} = \lim_{x \to \infty} \frac{1/x}{1/\sqrt{x}} = \lim_{x \to \infty} \frac{1}{\sqrt{x}} = 0$$

The graph in Figure 9.9 supports the result.   *Now Try Exercise 15.*

We can sometimes handle the indeterminate forms $\infty \cdot 0$ and $\infty - \infty$ by using algebra to get $0/0$ or ∞/∞ instead. Here again we do not mean to suggest that there is a number $\infty \cdot 0$ or $\infty - \infty$ any more than we mean to suggest that there is a number $0/0$ or ∞/∞. These forms are not numbers but descriptions of function behavior.

EXAMPLE 6 Working with Indeterminate Form $\infty \cdot 0$

Find   **(a)** $\displaystyle\lim_{x \to \infty} \left(x \sin \frac{1}{x} \right)$ **(b)** $\displaystyle\lim_{x \to -\infty} \left(x \sin \frac{1}{x} \right)$.

SOLUTION

Figure 9.10 suggests that the limits exist.

(a)
$$\lim_{x \to \infty} \left(x \sin \frac{1}{x} \right) \qquad \infty \cdot 0$$

$$= \lim_{h \to 0^+} \left(\frac{1}{h} \sin h \right) \qquad \text{Let } h = 1/x.$$

$$= 1$$

(b) Similarly,

$$\lim_{x \to -\infty} \left(x \sin \frac{1}{x} \right) = 1.$$

Now Try Exercise 17.

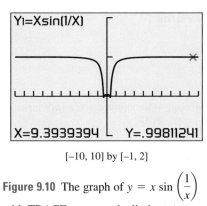

[−10, 10] by [−1, 2]

Figure 9.10 The graph of $y = x \sin\left(\dfrac{1}{x}\right)$ with TRACE suggests the limit at $+\infty$ and $-\infty$ is 1. (Example 6)

EXAMPLE 7 Working with Indeterminate Form $\infty - \infty$

Find $\displaystyle \lim_{x \to 1} \left(\frac{1}{\ln x} - \frac{1}{x-1} \right)$.

SOLUTION

Combining the two fractions converts the indeterminate form $\infty - \infty$ to $0/0$, to which we can apply l'Hospital's Rule.

$$\lim_{x \to 1} \left(\frac{1}{\ln x} - \frac{1}{x-1} \right) \qquad \infty - \infty$$

$$= \lim_{x \to 1} \frac{x - 1 - \ln x}{(x-1)\ln x} \qquad \text{Now } \frac{0}{0}$$

$$= \lim_{x \to 1} \frac{1 - 1/x}{\dfrac{x-1}{x} + \ln x}$$

$$= \lim_{x \to 1} \frac{x-1}{x \ln x + x - 1} \qquad \text{Still } \frac{0}{0}$$

$$= \lim_{x \to 1} \frac{1}{2 + \ln x}$$

$$= \frac{1}{2}$$

Now Try Exercise 19.

Indeterminate Forms 1^{∞}, 0^0, ∞^0

Limits that lead to the indeterminate forms 1^{∞}, 0^0, and ∞^0 can sometimes be handled by taking logarithms first. We use l'Hospital's Rule to find the limit of the logarithm and then exponentiate to reveal the original function's behavior.

Since $b = e^{\ln b}$ for every positive number b, we can write $f(x)$ as

$$f(x) = e^{\ln f(x)}$$

for any positive function $f(x)$.

$$\lim_{x \to a} \ln f(x) = L \implies \lim_{x \to a} f(x) = \lim_{x \to a} e^{\ln f(x)} = e^L$$

Here a can be finite or infinite.

In Section 1.3 we used graphs and tables to investigate the values of $f(x) = (1 + 1/x)^x$ as $x \to \infty$. Now we find this limit with l'Hospital's Rule.

EXAMPLE 8 Working with Indeterminate Form 1^{∞}

Find $\displaystyle \lim_{x \to \infty} \left(1 + \frac{1}{x} \right)^x$.

SOLUTION

Let $f(x) = (1 + 1/x)^x$. Then taking logarithms of both sides converts the indeterminate form 1^{∞} to $0/0$, to which we can apply l'Hospital's Rule.

$$\ln f(x) = \ln \left(1 + \frac{1}{x} \right)^x = x \ln \left(1 + \frac{1}{x} \right) = \frac{\ln \left(1 + \dfrac{1}{x} \right)}{\dfrac{1}{x}}$$

continued

We apply l'Hospital's Rule to the previous expression.

$$\lim_{x \to \infty} \ln f(x) = \lim_{x \to \infty} \frac{\ln\left(1 + \dfrac{1}{x}\right)}{\dfrac{1}{x}} \qquad \frac{0}{0}$$

$$= \lim_{x \to \infty} \frac{\dfrac{1}{1 + \dfrac{1}{x}}\left(-\dfrac{1}{x^2}\right)}{-\dfrac{1}{x^2}} \qquad \begin{array}{l}\text{Differentiate numerator}\\ \text{and denominator}\end{array}$$

$$= \lim_{x \to \infty} \frac{1}{1 + \dfrac{1}{x}} = 1$$

Therefore,

$$\lim_{x \to \infty} \left(1 + \frac{1}{x}\right)^x = \lim_{x \to \infty} f(x) = \lim_{x \to \infty} e^{\ln f(x)} = e^1 = e.$$

Now Try Exercise 21.

EXAMPLE 9 Working with Indeterminate Form 0^0

Determine whether $\lim_{x \to 0^+} x^x$ exists and find its value if it does.

SOLUTION

Figure 9.11 suggests that the limit from the right exists and has a value of 1.

The limit leads to the indeterminate form 0^0. To convert the problem to one involving $0/0$, we let $f(x) = x^x$ and take the logarithm of both sides.

$$\ln f(x) = x \ln x = \frac{\ln x}{1/x}$$

Applying l'Hospital's Rule to $(\ln x)/(1/x)$ we obtain

$$\lim_{x \to 0^+} \ln f(x) = \lim_{x \to 0^+} \frac{\ln x}{1/x} \qquad \frac{-\infty}{\infty}$$

$$= \lim_{x \to 0^+} \frac{1/x}{-1/x^2} \qquad \text{Differentiate.}$$

$$= \lim_{x \to 0^+} (-x) = 0$$

Therefore,

$$\lim_{x \to 0^+} x^x = \lim_{x \to 0^+} f(x) = \lim_{x \to 0^+} e^{\ln f(x)} = e^0 = 1.$$

Now Try Exercise 23.

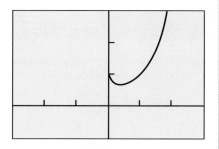

[−3, 3] by [−1, 3]

Figure 9.11 The graph of $y = x^x$. (Example 9)

EXAMPLE 10 Working with Indeterminate Form ∞^0

Find $\lim_{x \to \infty} x^{1/x}$.

SOLUTION

Let $f(x) = x^{1/x}$. Then

$$\ln f(x) = \frac{\ln x}{x}.$$

continued

Applying l'Hospital's Rule to $\ln f(x)$ we obtain

$$\lim_{x\to\infty} \ln f(x) = \lim_{x\to\infty} \frac{\ln x}{x} \qquad \frac{\infty}{\infty}$$

$$= \lim_{x\to\infty} \frac{1/x}{1} \qquad \text{Differentiate.}$$

$$= \lim_{x\to\infty} \frac{1}{x} = 0.$$

Therefore,

$$\lim_{x\to\infty} x^{1/x} = \lim_{x\to\infty} f(x) = \lim_{x\to\infty} e^{\ln f(x)} = e^0 = 1.$$

Now Try Exercise 25.

Quick Review 9.2 *(For help, go to Sections 2.1 and 2.2.)*

Exercise numbers with a gray background indicate problems that the authors have designed to be solved *without a calculator*.

In Exercises 1 and 2, use tables to estimate the value of the limit.

1. $\lim_{x\to\infty} \left(1 + \frac{0.1}{x}\right)^x$

2. $\lim_{x\to 0^+} x^{1/(\ln x)}$

In Exercises 3–8, use graphs or tables to estimate the value of the limit.

3. $\lim_{x\to 0^-} \left(1 - \frac{1}{x}\right)^x$

4. $\lim_{x\to -1^-} \left(1 + \frac{1}{x}\right)^x$

5. $\lim_{t\to 1} \frac{t-1}{\sqrt{t}-1}$

6. $\lim_{x\to\infty} \frac{\sqrt{4x^2+1}}{x+1}$

7. $\lim_{x\to 0} \frac{\sin 3x}{x}$

8. $\lim_{\theta\to\pi/2} \frac{\tan\theta}{2+\tan\theta}$

In Exercises 9 and 10, substitute $x = 1/h$ to express y as a function of h.

9. $y = x \sin\frac{1}{x}$

10. $y = \left(1 + \frac{1}{x}\right)^x$

Section 9.2 Exercises

In Exercises 1–4, estimate the limit graphically and then use l'Hospital's Rule to find the limit.

1. $\lim_{x\to 2} \frac{x-2}{x^2-4}$

2. $\lim_{x\to 0} \frac{\sin(5x)}{x}$

3. $\lim_{x\to 2} \frac{\sqrt{2+x}-2}{x-2}$

4. $\lim_{x\to 1} \frac{\sqrt[3]{x}-1}{x-1}$

In Exercises 5–8, apply the stronger form of l'Hospital's Rule to find the limit.

5. $\lim_{x\to 0} \frac{1-\cos x}{x^2}$

6. $\lim_{\theta\to\pi/2} \frac{1-\sin\theta}{1+\cos(2\theta)}$

7. $\lim_{t\to 0} \frac{\cos t - 1}{e^t - t - 1}$

8. $\lim_{x\to 2} \frac{x^2-4x+4}{x^3-12x+16}$

In Exercises 9–12, use l'Hospital's Rule to evaluate the one-sided limits. Support your answer graphically.

9. (a) $\lim_{x\to 0^-} \frac{\sin 4x}{\sin 2x}$

(b) $\lim_{x\to 0^+} \frac{\sin 4x}{\sin 2x}$

10. (a) $\lim_{x\to 0^-} \frac{\tan x}{x}$

(b) $\lim_{x\to 0^+} \frac{\tan x}{x}$

11. (a) $\lim_{x\to 0^-} \frac{\sin x}{x^3}$

(b) $\lim_{x\to 0^+} \frac{\sin x}{x^3}$

12. (a) $\lim_{x\to 0^-} \frac{\tan x}{x^2}$

(b) $\lim_{x\to 0^+} \frac{\tan x}{x^2}$

In Exercises 13–16, identify the indeterminate form and evaluate the limit using l'Hospital's Rule. Support your answer graphically.

13. $\lim_{x\to\pi} \frac{\csc x}{1+\cot x}$

14. $\lim_{x\to\pi/2} \frac{1+\sec x}{\tan x}$

15. $\lim_{x\to\infty} \frac{\ln(x+1)}{\log_2 x}$

16. $\lim_{x\to\infty} \frac{5x^2-3x}{7x^2+1}$

In Exercises 17–26, identify the indeterminate form and evaluate the limit using l'Hospital's Rule.

17. $\lim_{x\to 0^+} (x \ln x)$

18. $\lim_{x\to\infty} \left(x \tan\frac{1}{x}\right)$

19. $\lim_{x\to 0^+} (\csc x - \cot x + \cos x)$

20. $\lim_{x\to\infty} (\ln(2x) - \ln(x+1))$

21. $\lim_{x\to 0} (e^x + x)^{1/x}$

22. $\lim_{x\to 1} x^{1/(x-1)}$

23. $\lim_{x\to 1} (x^2 - 2x + 1)^{x-1}$

24. $\lim_{x\to 0^+} (\sin x)^x$

25. $\lim_{x\to 0^+} \left(1 + \frac{1}{x}\right)^x$

26. $\lim_{x\to\infty} (\ln x)^{1/x}$

In Exercises 27 and 28, **(a)** complete the table and estimate the limit. **(b)** Use l'Hospital's Rule to confirm your estimate.

27. $\lim_{x\to\infty} f(x), f(x) = \frac{\ln x^5}{x}$

x	10	10^2	10^3	10^4	10^5
$f(x)$					

28. $\lim\limits_{x\to 0^+} f(x),\ f(x) = \dfrac{x - \sin x}{x^3}$

x	10^0	10^{-1}	10^{-2}	10^{-3}	10^{-4}
$f(x)$					

In Exercises 29–32, use tables to estimate the limit. Confirm your estimate using l'Hospital's Rule.

29. $\lim\limits_{\theta\to 0} \dfrac{\sin 3\theta}{\sin 4\theta}$

30. $\lim\limits_{t\to 0} \left(\dfrac{1}{\sin t} - \dfrac{1}{t} \right)$

31. $\lim\limits_{x\to\infty} (1 + x)^{1/x}$

32. $\lim\limits_{x\to\infty} \dfrac{x - 2x^2}{3x^2 + 5x}$

In Exercises 33–52, use l'Hospital's Rule to evaluate the limit.

33. $\lim\limits_{\theta\to 0} \dfrac{\sin\theta^2}{\theta}$

34. $\lim\limits_{t\to 1} \dfrac{t - 1}{\ln t - \sin \pi t}$

35. $\lim\limits_{x\to\infty} \dfrac{\log_2 x}{\log_3 (x + 3)}$

36. $\lim\limits_{y\to 0^+} \dfrac{\ln (y^2 + 2y)}{\ln y}$

37. $\lim\limits_{y\to\pi/2} \left(\dfrac{\pi}{2} - y \right) \tan y$

38. $\lim\limits_{x\to 0^+} (\ln x - \ln \sin x)$

39. $\lim\limits_{x\to 0^+} \left(\dfrac{1}{x} - \dfrac{1}{\sqrt{x}} \right)$

40. $\lim\limits_{x\to 0} \left(\dfrac{1}{x^2} \right)^x$

41. $\lim\limits_{x\to\pm\infty} \dfrac{3x - 5}{2x^2 - x + 2}$

42. $\lim\limits_{x\to 0} \dfrac{\sin 7x}{\tan 11x}$

43. $\lim\limits_{x\to\infty} (1 + 2x)^{1/(2 \ln x)}$

44. $\lim\limits_{x\to(\pi/2)^-} (\cos x)^{\cos x}$

45. $\lim\limits_{x\to 0^+} (1 + x)^{1/x}$

46. $\lim\limits_{x\to 0^+} (\sin x)^{\tan x}$

47. $\lim\limits_{x\to 1^+} x^{1/(1-x)}$

48. $\lim\limits_{x\to\infty} \displaystyle\int_x^{2x} \dfrac{dt}{t}$

49. $\lim\limits_{x\to 1} \dfrac{x^3 - 1}{4x^3 - x - 3}$

50. $\lim\limits_{x\to\infty} \dfrac{2x^2 + 3x}{x^3 + x + 1}$

51. $\lim\limits_{x\to 1} \dfrac{\int_1^x \cos t\, dt}{x^2 - 1}$

52. $\lim\limits_{x\to 1} \dfrac{\int_1^x \dfrac{dt}{t}}{x^3 - 1}$

Group Activity In Exercises 53 and 54, do the following.

(a) **Writing to Learn** Explain why l'Hospital's Rule does not help you to find the limit.

(b) Use a graph to estimate the limit.

(c) Evaluate the limit analytically, using the techniques of Chapter 2.

53. $\lim\limits_{x\to\infty} \dfrac{\sqrt{9x + 1}}{\sqrt{x + 1}}$

54. $\lim\limits_{x\to\pi/2} \dfrac{\sec x}{\tan x}$

55. *Continuous Extension* Find a value of c that makes the function

$$f(x) = \begin{cases} \dfrac{9x - 3\sin 3x}{5x^3}, & x \neq 0 \\ c, & x = 0 \end{cases}$$

continuous at $x = 0$. Explain why your value of c works.

56. *Continuous Extension* Let $f(x) = |x|^x, x \neq 0$. Show that f has a removable discontinuity at $x = 0$ and extend the definition of f to $x = 0$ so that the extended function is continuous there.

57. *Interest Compounded Continuously*

(a) Show that $\lim\limits_{k\to\infty} A_0 \left(1 + \dfrac{r}{k} \right)^{kt} = A_0 e^{rt}$.

(b) **Writing to Learn** Explain how the limit in part (a) connects interest compounded k times per year with interest compounded continuously.

58. *L'Hospital's Rule* Let

$$f(x) = \begin{cases} x + 2, & x \neq 0 \\ 0, & x = 0 \end{cases} \quad \text{and} \quad g(x) = \begin{cases} x + 1, & x \neq 0 \\ 0, & x = 0. \end{cases}$$

(a) Show that

$$\lim\limits_{x\to 0} \dfrac{f'(x)}{g'(x)} = 1 \quad \text{but} \quad \lim\limits_{x\to 0} \dfrac{f(x)}{g(x)} = 2.$$

(b) **Writing to Learn** Explain why this does not contradict l'Hospital's Rule.

59. *Solid of Revolution* Let $A(t)$ be the area of the region in the first quadrant enclosed by the coordinate axes, the curve $y = e^{-x}$, and the line $x = t > 0$ as shown in the figure. Let $V(t)$ be the volume of the solid generated by revolving the region about the x-axis. Find the following limits.

(a) $\lim\limits_{t\to\infty} A(t)$ (b) $\lim\limits_{t\to\infty} \dfrac{V(t)}{A(t)}$ (c) $\lim\limits_{t\to 0^+} \dfrac{V(t)}{A(t)}$

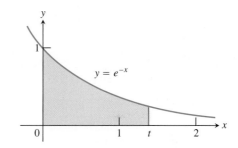

60. *L'Hospital's Trap* Let $f(x) = \dfrac{1 - \cos x}{x + x^2}$.

(a) Use graphs or tables to estimate $\lim\limits_{x\to 0} f(x)$.

(b) Find the error in the following incorrect application of l'Hospital's Rule.

$$\lim\limits_{x\to 0} \dfrac{1 - \cos x}{x + x^2} = \lim\limits_{x\to 0} \dfrac{\sin x}{1 + 2x}$$
$$= \lim\limits_{x\to 0} \dfrac{\cos x}{2}$$
$$= \dfrac{1}{2}$$

61. *Exponential Functions* (a) Use the equation

$$a^x = e^{x \ln a}$$

to find the domain of

$$f(x) = \left(1 + \dfrac{1}{x} \right)^x.$$

(a) Find $\lim\limits_{x\to -1^-} f(x)$.

(b) Find $\lim\limits_{x\to -\infty} f(x)$.

Standardized Test Questions

62. True or False If $f(a) = g(a) = 0$ and $f'(a)$ and $g'(a)$

exist, then

$$\lim_{x \to a} \frac{f(x)}{g(x)} = \frac{f'(a)}{g'(a)}.$$ Justify your answer.

63. True or False $\lim_{x \to 0^+} x^x$ does not exist. Justify your answer.

64. Multiple Choice Which of the following gives the value of

$$\lim_{x \to 0} \frac{x}{\tan x}?$$

(A) −1 **(B)** 0 **(C)** 1 **(D)** π **(E)** Does not exist

65. Multiple Choice Which of the following gives the value of

$$\lim_{x \to 1} \frac{1 - \dfrac{1}{x}}{1 - \dfrac{1}{x^2}}?$$

(A) Does not exist **(B)** 2 **(C)** 1 **(D)** 1/2 **(E)** 0

66. Multiple Choice Which of the following gives the value of

$$\lim_{x \to \infty} \frac{\log_2 x}{\log_3 x}?$$

(A) 1 **(B)** $\dfrac{\ln 3}{\ln 2}$ **(C)** $\dfrac{\ln 2}{\ln 3}$ **(D)** $\ln\left(\dfrac{3}{2}\right)$ **(E)** $\ln\left(\dfrac{2}{3}\right)$

67. Multiple Choice Which of the following gives the value of

$$\lim_{x \to \infty} \left(1 + \frac{1}{x}\right)^{3x}?$$

(A) 0 **(B)** 1 **(C)** e **(D)** e^2 **(E)** e^3

Explorations

68. Give an example of two differentiable functions f and g with $\lim_{x \to 3} f(x) = \lim_{x \to 3} g(x) = 0$ that satisfy the following.

(a) $\lim_{x \to 3} \dfrac{f(x)}{g(x)} = 7$ **(b)** $\lim_{x \to 3} \dfrac{f(x)}{g(x)} = 0$

(c) $\lim_{x \to 3} \dfrac{f(x)}{g(x)} = \infty$

69. Give an example of two differentiable functions f and g with $\lim_{x \to \infty} f(x) = \lim_{x \to \infty} g(x) = \infty$ that satisfy the following.

(a) $\lim_{x \to \infty} \dfrac{f(x)}{g(x)} = 3$ **(b)** $\lim_{x \to \infty} \dfrac{f(x)}{g(x)} = 0$

(c) $\lim_{x \to \infty} \dfrac{f(x)}{g(x)} = \infty$

Extending the Ideas

70. Grapher Precision Let $f(x) = \dfrac{1 - \cos x^6}{x^{12}}$.

(a) Explain why some graphs of f may give false information about $\lim_{x \to 0} f(x)$. Try the window $[-0.3, 0.3]$ by $[-0.5, 1]$. Illustrate your answer with a graph.

(b) Explain why tables may give false information about $\lim_{x \to 0} f(x)$. (*Hint:* Try tables with increments of 0.01.)

(c) Use l'Hospital's Rule to find $\lim_{x \to 0} f(x)$.

(d) Writing to Learn This is an example of a function for which graphers do not have enough precision to give reliable information. Explain this statement in your own words.

71. Cauchy's Mean Value Theorem Suppose that functions f and g are continuous on $[a, b]$ and differentiable throughout (a, b) and suppose also that $g' \neq 0$ throughout (a, b). Then there exists a number c in (a, b) at which

$$\frac{f'(c)}{g'(c)} = \frac{f(b) - f(a)}{g(b) - g(a)}.$$

Find all values of c in (a, b) that satisfy this property for the following given functions and intervals.

(a) $f(x) = x^3 + 1$, $g(x) = x^2 - x$, $[a, b] = [-1, 1]$

(b) $f(x) = \cos x$, $g(x) = \sin x$, $[a, b] = [0, \pi/2]$

72. Why 0^∞ and $0^{-\infty}$ Are Not Indeterminate Forms Assume that $f(x)$ is nonnegative in an open interval containing c and $\lim_{x \to 0} f(x) = 0$.

(a) If $\lim_{x \to c} g(x) = \infty$, show that $\lim_{x \to c} f(x)^{g(x)} = 0$.

(b) If $\lim_{x \to c} g(x) = -\infty$, show that $\lim_{x \to c} f(x)^{g(x)} = \infty$.

Quick Quiz for AP* Preparation: Sections 9.1 and 9.2

1. Multiple Choice Which of the following gives the value of

$$\lim_{x \to 0} \frac{(x + 1)^{4/3} - (4/3)x - 1}{x^2}?$$

(A) −1/3 **(B)** 0 **(C)** 2/9
(D) 4/9 **(E)** Does not exist

2. Multiple Choice Which of the following gives the value of $\lim_{x \to 0^+} (3x^{2x})$?

(A) 0 **(B)** 1 **(C)** 2
(D) 3 **(E)** Does not exist

3. Multiple Choice Which of the following gives the value of

$$\lim_{x \to 2} \frac{\int_2^x \sin t \, dt}{x^2 - 4}?$$

(A) $-\dfrac{\sin 2}{4}$ **(B)** $\dfrac{\sin 2}{4}$ **(C)** $-\dfrac{\sin 2}{2}$

(D) $\dfrac{\sin 2}{2}$ **(E)** Does not exist

4. Free Response The second and fifth terms of a geometric sequence are −4 and 1/2, respectively. Find

(a) the first term, **(b)** the common ratio,

(c) an explicit rule for the nth term, and

(d) a recursive rule for the nth term.

9.3 Relative Rates of Growth

You will be able to compare growth rates of various function types as the independent variable increases without bound.

- Comparing growth rates
- Comparing growth rates using l'Hospital's Rule
- Relative efficiency of sequential and binary search algorithms

Comparing Rates of Growth

We restrict our attention to functions whose values eventually become and remain positive as $x \to \infty$.

The exponential function e^x grows so rapidly and the logarithm function $\ln x$ grows so slowly that they set standards by which we can judge the growth of other functions. The graphs (Figure 9.12) of e^x, $\ln x$, and x suggest how rapidly and slowly e^x and $\ln x$, respectively, grow in comparison to x.

In fact, all the functions a^x, $a > 1$, grow faster (eventually) than any power of x, even $x^{1,000,000}$ (Exercise 39), and hence faster (eventually) than any polynomial function.

To get a feeling for how rapidly the values of e^x grow with increasing x, think of graphing the function on a large blackboard, with the axes scaled in centimeters. At $x = 1$ cm, the graph is $e^1 \approx 3$ cm above the x-axis. At $x = 6$ cm, the graph is $e^6 \approx 403$ cm ≈ 4 m high. (It is about to go through the ceiling if it hasn't done so already.) At $x = 10$ cm, the graph is $e^{10} \approx 22{,}026$ cm ≈ 220 m high, higher than most buildings. At $x = 24$ cm, the graph is more than halfway to the moon, and at $x = 43$ cm from the origin, the graph is high enough to reach well past the sun's closest stellar neighbor, the red dwarf star Proxima Centauri:

$$
\begin{aligned}
e^{43} &\approx 4.7 \times 10^{18} \text{ cm} \\
&= 4.7 \times 10^{13} \text{ km} \\
&\approx 1.57 \times 10^8 \text{ light-seconds} \\
&\approx 5.0 \text{ light-years}
\end{aligned}
$$

Light travels about 300,000 km/sec in a vacuum.

The distance to Proxima Centauri is 4.2 light-years. Yet with $x = 43$ cm from the origin, the graph is still less than 2 feet to the right of the y-axis.

In contrast, the logarithm function $\ln x$ grows more slowly as $x \to \infty$ than any positive power of x, even $x^{1/1,000,000}$ (Exercise 41). Because $\ln x$ and e^x are inverse functions, the calculations above show that with axes scaled in centimeters, you have to go nearly 5 light-years out on the x-axis to find where the graph of $\ln x$ is even 43 cm high.

In fact, all the functions $\log_a x$, $a > 1$, grow slower (eventually) than any positive power of x.

These comparisons of exponential, polynomial, and logarithmic functions can be made precise by defining what it means for a function $f(x)$ to *grow faster* than another function $g(x)$ as $x \to \infty$.

$y = e^x$
$y = \ln x$
$y = x$

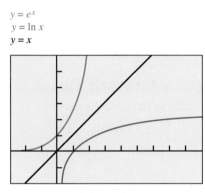

[–3, 9] by [–2, 6]

Figure 9.12 The graphs of $y = e^x$, $y = \ln x$, and $y = x$.

Grace Murray Hopper (1906–1992)

Computer scientists use function comparisons like the ones in this section to measure the relative efficiencies of computer programs. The pioneering work of Rear Admiral Grace Murray Hopper in the field of computer technology led the navy, and the country, into the computer age. Hopper graduated from Yale in 1934 with a Ph.D. in Mathematics. During World War II she joined the navy and became director of a project that resulted in the development of COBOL, a computer language that enabled computers to "talk to one another." On September 6, 1997, the navy commissioned a multi-mission ship, the USS *Hopper*.

DEFINITIONS   Faster, Slower, Same-Rate Growth as $x \to \infty$

Let $f(x)$ and $g(x)$ be positive for x sufficiently large.

1. *f* **grows faster** than *g* (and *g* **grows slower** than *f*) as $x \to \infty$ if

$$
\lim_{x \to \infty} \frac{f(x)}{g(x)} = \infty, \quad \text{or, equivalently, if} \quad \lim_{x \to \infty} \frac{g(x)}{f(x)} = 0.
$$

2. *f* and *g* **grow at the same rate** as $x \to \infty$ if

$$
\lim_{x \to \infty} \frac{f(x)}{g(x)} = L \neq 0. \quad \text{\small *L* finite and not zero}
$$

According to these definitions, $y = 2x$ does not grow faster than $y = x$ as $x \to \infty$. The two functions grow at the same rate because

$$
\lim_{x \to \infty} \frac{2x}{x} = \lim_{x \to \infty} 2 = 2,
$$

which is a finite nonzero limit. The reason for this apparent disregard of common sense is that we want "f grows faster than g" to mean that for large x values, g is negligible in comparison to f.

If $L = 1$ in part 2 of the definition, then f and g are right end behavior models for each other (Section 2.2). If f grows faster than g, then

$$\lim_{x \to \infty} \frac{f(x) + g(x)}{f(x)} = \lim_{x \to \infty}\left(1 + \frac{g(x)}{f(x)}\right) = 1 + 0 = 1,$$

so f is a right end behavior model for $f + g$. Thus, for large x values, g can be ignored in the sum $f + g$. This explains why, for large x values, we can ignore the terms

$$g(x) = a_{n-1}x^{n-1} + \cdots + a_0$$

in

$$f(x) = a_n x^n + a_{n-1}x^{n-1} + \cdots + a_0;$$

that is, why $a_n x^n$ is an end behavior model for

$$a_n x^n + a_{n-1}x^{n-1} + \cdots + a_0.$$

Using L'Hospital's Rule to Compare Growth Rates

L'Hospital's Rule can help us to compare rates of growth, as shown in Example 1.

EXAMPLE 1 Comparing e^x and x^2 as $x \to \infty$

Show that the function e^x grows faster than x^2 as $x \to \infty$.

SOLUTION

We need to show that $\lim_{x \to \infty} (e^x/x^2) = \infty$. Notice this limit is of indeterminate type ∞/∞, so we can apply l'Hospital's Rule and take the derivative of the numerator and the derivative of the denominator. In fact, we have to apply l'Hospital's Rule twice.

$$\lim_{x \to \infty} \frac{e^x}{x^2} = \lim_{x \to \infty} \frac{e^x}{2x} = \lim_{x \to \infty} \frac{e^x}{1} = \infty$$

Now Try Exercise 1.

> **EXPLORATION 1** Comparing Rates of Growth as $x \to \infty$
>
> 1. Show that a^x, $a > 1$, grows faster than x^2 as $x \to \infty$.
> 2. Show that 3^x grows faster than 2^x as $x \to \infty$.
> 3. If $a > b > 1$, show that a^x grows faster than b^x as $x \to \infty$.

EXAMPLE 2 Comparing ln x with x and x^2 as $x \to \infty$

Show that ln x grows slower than (a) x and (b) x^2 as $x \to \infty$.

SOLUTION

(a) $\lim_{x \to \infty} \dfrac{\ln x}{x} = \lim_{x \to \infty} \dfrac{1/x}{1}$ l'Hospital's Rule

$\qquad = \lim_{x \to \infty} \dfrac{1}{x} = 0$

continued

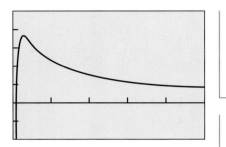

[0, 50] by [−0.2, 0.5]

Figure 9.13 The *x*-axis is a horizontal asymptote of the function $f(x) = (\ln x)/x$. (Example 2)

Figure 9.13 suggests that the graph of the function $f(x) = (\ln x)/x$ drops dramatically toward the *x*-axis as *x* outstrips $\ln x$.

(b) $\displaystyle \lim_{x \to \infty} \frac{\ln x}{x^2} = \lim_{x \to \infty} \left(\frac{\ln x}{x} \cdot \frac{1}{x} \right) = 0 \cdot 0 = 0$

Now Try Exercise 5.

EXAMPLE 3 Comparing *x* with *x* + sin *x* as *x* → ∞

Show that *x* grows at the same rate as $x + \sin x$ as $x \to \infty$.

SOLUTION

We need to show that $\displaystyle \lim_{x \to \infty} ((x + \sin x)/x)$ is finite and not 0. The limit can be computed directly.

$$\lim_{x \to \infty} \frac{x + \sin x}{x} = \lim_{x \to \infty} \left(1 + \frac{\sin x}{x} \right) = 1$$

Graphical support for the limit is shown in Figure 9.14. *Now Try Exercise 9.*

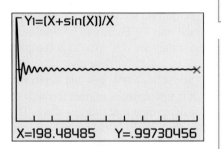

Y1=(X+sin(X))/X

X=198.48485   Y=.99730456

[0, 200] by [0, 2]

Figure 9.14 TRACE on the graph suggests that the limit in Example 3 is 1.

EXAMPLE 4 Comparing Logarithmic Functions as *x* → ∞

Let *a* and *b* be numbers greater than 1. Show that $\log_a x$ and $\log_b x$ grow at the same rate as $x \to \infty$.

SOLUTION

$$\lim_{x \to \infty} \frac{\log_a x}{\log_b x} = \lim_{x \to \infty} \frac{\ln x/\ln a}{\ln x/\ln b} = \frac{\ln b}{\ln a}$$

The limiting value is finite and nonzero. *Now Try Exercise 13.*

Growing at the same rate is a *transitive relation*.

Transitivity of Growing Rates

If *f* grows at the same rate as *g* as $x \to \infty$ and *g* grows at the same rate as *h* as $x \to \infty$, then *f* grows at the same rate as *h* as $x \to \infty$.

The reason is that

$$\lim_{x \to \infty} \frac{f}{g} = L \quad \text{and} \quad \lim_{x \to \infty} \frac{g}{h} = M$$

together imply that

$$\lim_{x \to \infty} \frac{f}{h} = \lim_{x \to \infty} \left(\frac{f}{g} \cdot \frac{g}{h} \right) = LM.$$

If *L* and *M* are finite and nonzero, then so is *LM*.

EXAMPLE 5 Growing at the Same Rate as *x* → ∞

Show that $f(x) = \sqrt{x^2 + 5}$ and $g(x) = \left(2\sqrt{x} - 1 \right)^2$ grow at the same rate as $x \to \infty$.

SOLUTION

We show that *f* and *g* grow at the same rate by showing that they both grow at the same rate as $h(x) = x$.

$$\lim_{x \to \infty} \frac{f(x)}{h(x)} = \lim_{x \to \infty} \frac{\sqrt{x^2 + 5}}{x} = \lim_{x \to \infty} \sqrt{1 + \frac{5}{x^2}} = 1$$

continued

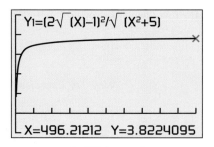

[0, 500] by [−1, 5]

Figure 9.15 The graph of g/f appears to have the line $y = 4$ as a horizontal asymptote. (Example 5)

and

$$\lim_{x \to \infty} \frac{g(x)}{h(x)} = \lim_{x \to \infty} \frac{(2\sqrt{x} - 1)^2}{x} = \lim_{x \to \infty} \left(\frac{2\sqrt{x} - 1}{\sqrt{x}}\right)^2 = \lim_{x \to \infty} \left(2 - \frac{1}{\sqrt{x}}\right)^2 = 4$$

Thus,

$$\lim_{x \to \infty} \frac{f}{g} = \lim_{x \to \infty} \left(\frac{f}{h} \cdot \frac{h}{g}\right) = 1 \cdot \frac{1}{4} = \frac{1}{4},$$

and f and g grow at the same rate as $x \to \infty$.

The graph of $y = g/f$ in Figure 9.15 suggests that the quotient g/f is an increasing function with horizontal asymptote $y = 4$. This supports that f and g grow at the same rate.

Now Try Exercise 31.

Sequential Versus Binary Search

Computer scientists sometimes measure the efficiency of an algorithm by counting the number of steps a computer must take to make the algorithm do something. (Your graphing calculator works according to algorithms programmed into it.) There can be significant differences in how efficiently algorithms perform, even if they are designed to accomplish the same task. Here is an example.

Webster's *Third New International Dictionary* lists about 26,000 words that begin with the letter *a*. One way to look up a word, or to learn if it is not there, is to read through the list one word at a time until you either find the word or determine that it is not there. This **sequential search** method makes no particular use of the words' alphabetical arrangement. You are sure to get an answer, but it might take about 26,000 steps.

Another way to find the word or to learn that it is not there is to go straight to the middle of the list (give or take a few words). If you do not find the word, then go to the middle of the half that would contain it and forget about the half that would not. (You know which half would contain it because you know the list is ordered alphabetically.) This **binary search** method eliminates roughly 13,000 words in this first step. If you do not find the word on the second try, then jump to the middle of the half that would contain it. Continue this way until you have found the word or divided the list in half so many times that there are no words left. How many times do you have to divide the list to find the word or learn that it is not there? At most 15, because

$$\frac{26,000}{2^{15}} < 1.$$

This certainly beats a possible 26,000 steps.

For a list of length n, a sequential search algorithm takes on the order of n steps to find a word or determine that it is not in the list.

EXAMPLE 6 Finding the Order of a Binary Search

For a list of length n, how many steps are required for a binary search?

SOLUTION

A binary search takes on the order of $\log_2 n$ steps. The reason is if $2^{m-1} < n \le 2^m$, then $m - 1 < \log_2 n \le m$, and the number of bisections required to narrow the list to one word will be at most m, the smallest integer greater than or equal to $\log_2 n$.

Now Try Exercise 43.

On a list of length n, there is a big difference between a sequential search (order n) and a binary search (order $\log_2 n$) because n grows faster than $\log_2 n$ as $n \to \infty$. In fact,

$$\lim_{n \to \infty} \frac{n}{\log_2 n} = \lim_{n \to \infty} \frac{1}{1/(n \ln 2)} = \infty.$$

Note

You would not use a sequential search method to find a word, but you might program a computer to search for a word using this technique.

Computer scientists look for the most efficient algorithms when they program searches.

Quick Review 9.3 *(For help, go to Sections 2.2 and 5.1.)*

Exercise numbers with a gray background indicate problems that the authors have designed to be solved *without a calculator*.

In Exercises 1–4, evaluate the limit.

1. $\lim\limits_{x \to \infty} \dfrac{\ln x}{e^x}$

2. $\lim\limits_{x \to \infty} \dfrac{e^x}{x^3}$

3. $\lim\limits_{x \to -\infty} \dfrac{x^2}{e^{2x}}$

4. $\lim\limits_{x \to \infty} \dfrac{x^2}{e^{2x}}$

In Exercises 5 and 6, find an end behavior model (Section 2.2) for the function.

5. $f(x) = -3x^4 + 5x^3 - x + 1$

6. $f(x) = \dfrac{2x^3 - 3x + 1}{x + 2}$

In Exercises 7 and 8, show that g is a right end behavior model for f.

7. $g(x) = x, \quad f(x) = x + \ln x$

8. $g(x) = 2x, \quad f(x) = \sqrt{4x^2 + 5x}$

9. Let $f(x) = \dfrac{e^x + x^2}{e^x}$. Find the

  (a) local extreme values of f and where they occur.

  (b) intervals on which f is increasing.

  (c) intervals on which f is decreasing.

10. Let $f(x) = \dfrac{x + \sin x}{x}$.

  Find the absolute maximum value of f and where it occurs.

Section 9.3 Exercises

In Exercises 1–4, show that e^x grows faster than the given function.

1. $x^3 - 3x + 1$

2. x^{20}

3. $e^{\cos x}$

4. $(5/2)^x$

In Exercises 5–8, show that $\ln x$ grows slower than the given function.

5. $x - \ln x$

6. $\sqrt{x}$

7. $\sqrt[3]{x}$

8. x^3

In Exercises 9–12, show that x^2 grows at the same rate as the given function.

9. $x^2 + 4x$

10. $\sqrt{x^4 + 5x}$

11. $\sqrt[3]{x^6 + x^2}$

12. $x^2 + \sin x$

In Exercises 13 and 14, show that the two functions grow at the same rate.

13. $\ln x, \log \sqrt{x}$

14. e^{x+1}, e^x

In Exercises 15–20, determine whether the function grows faster than e^x, at the same rate as e^x, or slower than e^x as $x \to \infty$.

15. $\sqrt{1 + x^4}$

16. 4^x

17. $x \ln x - x$

18. xe^x

19. x^{1000}

20. $(e^x + e^{-x})/2$

In Exercises 21–24, determine whether the function grows faster than x^2, at the same rate as x^2, or slower than x^2 as $x \to \infty$.

21. $x^3 + 3$

22. $15x + 3$

23. $\ln x$

24. 2^x

In Exercises 25–28, determine whether the function grows faster than $\ln x$, at the same rate as $\ln x$, or slower than $\ln x$ as $x \to \infty$.

25. $\log_2 x^2$

26. $\sqrt{x}$

27. $\log x$

28. $5 \ln x$

In Exercises 29 and 30, order the functions from slowest-growing to fastest-growing as $x \to \infty$.

29. $e^x, \quad x^x, \quad (\ln x)^x, \quad e^{x/2}$

30. $2^x, \quad x^2, \quad (\ln 2)^x, \quad e^x$

In Exercises 31–34, show that the three functions grow at the same rate as $x \to \infty$.

31. $f_1(x) = \sqrt{x}, \quad f_2(x) = \sqrt{10x + 1}, \quad f_3(x) = \sqrt{x + 1}$

32. $f_1(x) = x^2, \quad f_2(x) = \sqrt{x^4 + x}, \quad f_3(x) = \sqrt{x^4 - x^3}$

33. $f_1(x) = 3^x, \quad f_2(x) = \sqrt{9^x + 2^x}, \quad f_3(x) = \sqrt{9^x - 4^x}$

34. $f_1(x) = x^3, \quad f_2(x) = \dfrac{x^4 + 2x^2 - 1}{x + 1}, \quad f_3(x) = \dfrac{2x^5 - 1}{x^2 + 1}$

In Exercises 35–38, only one of the following is true.

  i. f grows faster than g.

  ii. g grows faster than f.

  iii. f and g grow at the same rate.

Use the given graph of f/g to determine which one is true.

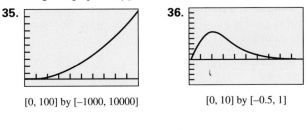

35.

[0, 100] by [−1000, 10000]

36.

[0, 10] by [−0.5, 1]

37.

[0, 100] by [−1, 1.5]

38.

[0, 20] by [−1, 3]

Group Activity In Exercises 39–41, do the following comparisons.

39. *Comparing Exponential and Power Functions*

  (a) Writing to Learn Explain why e^x grows faster than x^n as $x \to \infty$ for any positive integer n, even $n = 1{,}000{,}000$. (*Hint:* What is the nth derivative of x^n?)

(b) Writing to Learn Explain why a^x, $a > 1$, grows faster than x^n as $x \to \infty$ for any positive integer n.

40. Comparing Exponential and Polynomial Functions

(a) Writing to Learn Show that e^x grows faster than any polynomial

$$a_n x^n + a_{n-1} x^{n-1} + \cdots + a_1 x + a_0, a_n > 0,$$

as $x \to \infty$. Explain.

(b) Writing to Learn Show that a^x, $a > 1$, grows faster than any polynomial

$$a_n x^n + a_{n-1} x^{n-1} + \cdots + a_1 x + a_0, a_n > 0,$$

as $x \to \infty$. Explain.

41. Comparing Logarithm and Power Functions

(a) Writing to Learn Show that $\ln x$ grows slower than $x^{1/n}$ as $x \to \infty$ for any positive integer n, even $n = 1{,}000{,}000$. Explain.

(b) Writing to Learn Show that for any number $a > 0$, $\ln x$ grows slower than x^a as $x \to \infty$. Explain.

42. Comparing Logarithm and Polynomial Functions Show that $\ln x$ grows slower than any nonconstant polynomial

$$a_n x^n + a_{n-1} x^{n-1} + \cdots + a_1 x + a_0, a_n > 0,$$

as $x \to \infty$.

43. Search Algorithms Suppose you have three different algorithms for solving the same problem and each algorithm provides for a number of steps that is of order of one of the functions listed here.

$$n \log_2 n, \quad n^{3/2}, \quad n(\log_2 n)^2$$

Which of the algorithms is likely the most efficient in the long run? Give reasons for your answer.

44. Sequential and Binary Search Suppose you are looking for an item in an ordered list one million items long. How many steps might it take to find the item with **(a)** a sequential search? **(b)** a binary search?

45. Growing at the Same Rate Suppose that polynomials $p(x)$ and $q(x)$ grow at the same rate as $x \to \infty$. What can you conclude about

(a) $\displaystyle\lim_{x \to \infty} \frac{p(x)}{q(x)}$?   **(b)** $\displaystyle\lim_{x \to -\infty} \frac{p(x)}{q(x)}$?

Standardized Test Questions

You may use a graphing calculator to solve the following problems.

46. True or False A search of order $n \log_2 n$ is more efficient than a search of order $n^{3/2}$. Justify your answer.

47. True or False The function $f(x) = 100x^2 + 50x + 1$ grows faster than the function $x^2 + 1$ as $x \to \infty$. Justify your answer.

48. Multiple Choice Which of the following functions grows faster than $x^5 + x^2 + 1$ as $x \to \infty$?

(A) $x^2 + 1$ **(B)** $x^3 + 2$ **(C)** $x^4 - x^2$ **(D)** x^5 **(E)** $x^6 + 1$

49. Multiple Choice Which of the following functions grows faster than $\log_{13} x$ as $x \to \infty$?

(A) e^{-x} **(B)** $\log_2 x$ **(C)** $\ln x$ **(D)** $\log x$ **(E)** $x \ln x$

50. Multiple Choice Which of the following functions grows at the same rate as e^x as $x \to \infty$?

(A) e^{2x} **(B)** e^{3x} **(C)** e^{x+2} **(D)** e^{-x} **(E)** e^{-x+1}

51. Multiple Choice Which of the following functions grows at the same rate as $\sqrt{x^8 + x^4}$ as $x \to \infty$?

(A) x **(B)** x^2 **(C)** x^3 **(D)** x^4 **(E)** x^5

Explorations

52. Let

$$f(x) = a_n x^n + a_{n-1} x^{n-1} + \cdots + a_1 x + a_0$$

and

$$g(x) = b_m x^m + b_{m-1} x^{m-1} + \cdots + b_1 x + b_0$$

be any two polynomial functions with $a_n > 0$, $b_m > 0$.

(a) Compare the rates of growth of x^5 and x^2 as $x \to \infty$.

(b) Compare the rates of growth of $5x^3$ and $2x^3$ as $x \to \infty$.

(c) If x^m grows faster than x^n as $x \to \infty$, what can you conclude about m and n?

(d) If x^m grows at the same rate as x^n as $x \to \infty$, what can you conclude about m and n?

(e) If $g(x)$ grows faster than $f(x)$ as $x \to \infty$, what can you conclude about their degrees?

(f) If $g(x)$ grows at the same rate as $f(x)$ as $x \to \infty$, what can you conclude about their degrees?

Extending the Ideas

53. Suppose that the values of the functions $f(x)$ and $g(x)$ eventually become and remain negative as $x \to \infty$. We say that

i. f **decreases faster** than g as $x \to \infty$ if

$$\lim_{x \to \infty} \frac{f(x)}{g(x)} = \infty.$$

ii. f and g **decrease at the same rate** as $x \to \infty$ if

$$\lim_{x \to \infty} \frac{f(x)}{g(x)} = L \neq 0.$$

(a) Show that if f decreases faster than g as $x \to \infty$, then $|f|$ grows faster than $|g|$ as $x \to \infty$.

(b) Show that if f and g decrease at the same rate as $x \to \infty$, then $|f|$ and $|g|$ grow at the same rate as $x \to \infty$.

54. Suppose that the values of the functions $f(x)$ and $g(x)$ eventually become and remain positive as $x \to -\infty$. We say that

i. f **grows faster** than g as $x \to -\infty$ if

$$\lim_{x \to -\infty} \frac{f(x)}{g(x)} = \infty.$$

ii. f and g **grow at the same rate** as $x \to -\infty$ if

$$\lim_{x \to -\infty} \frac{f(x)}{g(x)} = L \neq 0.$$

(a) Show that if f grows faster than g as $x \to -\infty$, then $f(-x)$ grows faster than $g(-x)$ as $x \to \infty$.

(b) Show that if f and g grow at the same rate as $x \to -\infty$, then $f(-x)$ and $g(-x)$ grow at the same rate as $x \to \infty$.

9.4 | Improper Integrals

You will be able to evaluate improper integrals of various kinds as limits of definite integrals.

- Improper integrals
- Horizontally improper integrals (infinite limits of integration)
- Vertically improper integrals (intervals with points of infinite discontinuity)
- Comparison tests for convergence and divergence of improper integrals

Infinite Limits of Integration

Consider the infinite region that lies under the curve $y = e^{-x/2}$ in the first quadrant (Figure 9.16a). You might think this region has infinite area, but we will see that it is finite. Here is how we assign a value to the area. First we find the area $A(b)$ of the portion of the region that is bounded on the right by $x = b$ (Figure 9.16b).

$$A(b) = \int_0^b e^{-x/2} \, dx = -2e^{-x/2} \Big]_0^b = -2e^{-b/2} + 2$$

Then we find the limit of $A(b)$ as $b \to \infty$.

$$\lim_{b \to \infty} A(b) = \lim_{b \to \infty} (-2e^{-b/2} + 2) = 2$$

The area under the curve from 0 to ∞ is

$$\int_0^\infty e^{-x/2} \, dx = \lim_{b \to \infty} \int_0^b e^{-x/2} \, dx = 2.$$

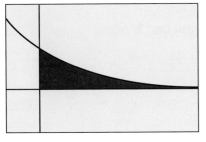

(a)

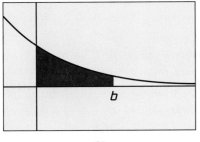

(b)

Figure 9.16 (a) The area in the first quadrant under the curve $y = e^{-x/2}$ is (b)

$$\lim_{b \to \infty} \int_0^b e^{-x/2} \, dx.$$

DEFINITION   Improper Integrals with Infinite Integration Limits

Integrals with infinite limits of integration are **improper integrals**.

1. If $f(x)$ is continuous on $[a, \infty)$, then

$$\int_a^\infty f(x) \, dx = \lim_{b \to \infty} \int_a^b f(x) \, dx.$$

2. If $f(x)$ is continuous on $(-\infty, b]$, then

$$\int_{-\infty}^b f(x) \, dx = \lim_{a \to -\infty} \int_a^b f(x) \, dx.$$

3. If $f(x)$ is continuous on $(-\infty, \infty)$, then

$$\int_{-\infty}^\infty f(x) \, dx = \int_{-\infty}^c f(x) \, dx + \int_c^\infty f(x) \, dx,$$

where c is any real number.

In parts 1 and 2, if the limit is finite the improper integral **converges** and the limit is the **value** of the improper integral. If the limit fails to exist, the improper integral **diverges.** In part 3, the integral on the left-hand side of the equation **converges** if both improper integrals on the right-hand side converge; otherwise it **diverges** and has no value. It can be shown that the choice of c in part 3 is unimportant. We can evaluate or determine the convergence or divergence of $\int_{-\infty}^\infty f(x) \, dx$ with any convenient choice.

EXAMPLE 1 Writing Improper Integrals as Limits

Express the improper integral $\int_{-\infty}^\infty e^x \, dx$ in terms of limits of definite integrals and then evaluate the integral.

continued

SOLUTION

Choosing $c = 0$ in part 3 of the definition, then applying parts 1 and 2, we can write the integral as

$$\int_{-\infty}^{\infty} e^x \, dx = \lim_{a \to -\infty} \int_a^0 e^x \, dx + \lim_{b \to \infty} \int_0^b e^x \, dx.$$

Next we evaluate the definite integrals and compute the corresponding limits.

$$\int_{-\infty}^{\infty} e^x \, dx = \lim_{a \to -\infty} \int_a^0 e^x \, dx + \lim_{b \to \infty} \int_0^b e^x \, dx$$
$$= \lim_{a \to -\infty} (1 - e^a) + \lim_{b \to \infty} (e^b - 1)$$
$$= 1 + \infty$$

The integral diverges because the second part diverges. *Now Try Exercise 3.*

EXAMPLE 2 **Evaluating an Improper Integral on** $[1, \infty)$

Does the improper integral $\int_1^{\infty} \dfrac{dx}{x}$ converge or diverge?

SOLUTION

$$\int_1^{\infty} \frac{dx}{x} = \lim_{b \to \infty} \int_1^b \frac{dx}{x} \qquad \text{Definition}$$
$$= \lim_{b \to \infty} \ln x \Big]_1^b$$
$$= \lim_{b \to \infty} (\ln b - \ln 1) = \infty$$

Thus, the integral diverges. *Now Try Exercise 5.*

EXAMPLE 3 **Using Partial Fractions with Improper Integrals**

Evaluate $\int_0^{\infty} \dfrac{2 \, dx}{x^2 + 4x + 3}$ or state that it diverges.

SOLUTION

By definition, $\int_0^{\infty} \dfrac{2 \, dx}{x^2 + 4x + 3} = \lim_{b \to \infty} \int_0^b \dfrac{2 \, dx}{x^2 + 4x + 3}$. We use partial fractions to integrate the definite integral. Set

$$\frac{2}{x^2 + 4x + 3} = \frac{A}{x + 1} + \frac{B}{x + 3}$$

and solve for A and B.

$$\frac{2}{x^2 + 4x + 3} = \frac{A(x + 3)}{(x + 1)(x + 3)} + \frac{B(x + 1)}{(x + 3)(x + 1)}$$
$$= \frac{(A + B)x + (3A + B)}{(x + 1)(x + 3)}$$

continued

Thus, $A + B = 0$ and $3A + B = 2$. Solving, we find $A = 1$ and $B = -1$. Therefore,

$$\frac{2}{x^2 + 4x + 3} = \frac{1}{x + 1} - \frac{1}{x + 3}$$

and

$$\int_0^b \frac{2\,dx}{x^2 + 4x + 3} = \int_0^b \frac{dx}{x + 1} - \int_0^b \frac{dx}{x + 3}$$

$$= \ln(x + 1) \Big]_0^b - \ln(x + 3) \Big]_0^b$$

$$= \ln(b + 1) - \ln(b + 3) + \ln 3$$

$$= \ln \frac{b + 1}{b + 3} + \ln 3$$

So,

$$\lim_{b \to \infty} \left[\ln\left(\frac{b + 1}{b + 3}\right) + \ln 3 \right] = \lim_{b \to \infty} \left[\ln\left(\frac{1 + 1/b}{1 + 3/b}\right) + \ln 3 \right] = \ln 3.$$

Thus, $\displaystyle\int_0^\infty \frac{2\,dx}{x^2 + 4x + 3} = \ln 3.$ ***Now Try Exercise 13.***

In Example 4 we use l'Hospital's Rule to help evaluate the improper integral.

EXAMPLE 4   Using L'Hospital's Rule with Improper Integrals

Evaluate $\int_1^\infty xe^{-x}\,dx$ or state that it diverges.

SOLUTION

By definition $\int_1^\infty xe^{-x}\,dx = \lim_{b \to \infty} \int_1^b xe^{-x}\,dx$. We use integration by parts to evaluate the definite integral. Let

$$u = x \qquad dv = e^{-x}\,dx$$
$$du = dx \qquad v = -e^{-x}$$

Then

$$\int_1^b xe^{-x}\,dx = \left[-xe^{-x} \right]_1^b + \int_1^b e^{-x}\,dx$$

$$= \left[-xe^{-x} - e^{-x} \right]_1^b$$

$$= \left[-(x + 1)e^{-x} \right]_1^b$$

$$= -(b + 1)e^{-b} + 2e^{-1}$$

So,

$$\lim_{b \to \infty} \left[-(b + 1)e^{-b} + 2e^{-1} \right] = \lim_{b \to \infty} \frac{-(b + 1)}{e^b} + \frac{2}{e}$$

$$= \lim_{b \to \infty} \frac{-1}{e^b} + \frac{2}{e} \qquad \text{L'Hospital's Rule}$$

$$= \frac{2}{e}$$

Thus $\int_1^\infty xe^{-x}\,dx = 2/e$.   ***Now Try Exercise 17.***

EXAMPLE 5 Evaluating an Integral on $(-\infty, \infty)$

Evaluate $\displaystyle\int_{-\infty}^{\infty} \frac{dx}{1 + x^2}$.

SOLUTION

According to the definition (part 3) we can write

$$\int_{-\infty}^{\infty} \frac{dx}{1 + x^2} = \int_{-\infty}^{0} \frac{dx}{1 + x^2} + \int_{0}^{\infty} \frac{dx}{1 + x^2}.$$

Next, we evaluate each improper integral on the right-hand side of the equation above.

$$\int_{-\infty}^{0} \frac{dx}{1 + x^2} = \lim_{a \to -\infty} \int_{a}^{0} \frac{dx}{1 + x^2}$$

$$= \lim_{a \to -\infty} \tan^{-1} x \Big]_{a}^{0}$$

$$= \lim_{a \to -\infty} (\tan^{-1} 0 - \tan^{-1} a) = 0 - \left(-\frac{\pi}{2}\right) = \frac{\pi}{2}$$

$$\int_{0}^{\infty} \frac{dx}{1 + x^2} = \lim_{b \to \infty} \int_{0}^{b} \frac{dx}{1 + x^2}$$

$$= \lim_{b \to \infty} \tan^{-1} x \Big]_{0}^{b}$$

$$= \lim_{b \to \infty} (\tan^{-1} b - \tan^{-1} 0) = \frac{\pi}{2} - 0 = \frac{\pi}{2}$$

Thus,
$$\int_{-\infty}^{\infty} \frac{dx}{1 + x^2} = \frac{\pi}{2} + \frac{\pi}{2} = \pi. \qquad \textbf{\textit{Now Try Exercise 21.}}$$

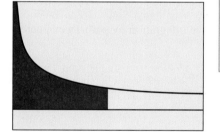

[0, 2] by [−1, 5]

(a)

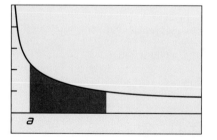

[0, 2] by [−1, 5]

(b)

Figure 9.17 (a) The area under the curve $y = 1/\sqrt{x}$ from $x = 0$ to $x = 1$ is (b)

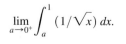

$\displaystyle\lim_{a \to 0^+} \int_{a}^{1} (1/\sqrt{x})\, dx.$

Integrands with Infinite Discontinuities

Another type of improper integral arises when the integrand has a vertical asymptote—an infinite discontinuity—at a limit of integration or at some point between the limits of integration.

Consider the infinite region in the first quadrant that lies under the curve $y = 1/\sqrt{x}$ from $x = 0$ to $x = 1$ (Figure 9.17a). First we find the area of the portion from a to 1 (Figure 9.17b).

$$\int_{a}^{1} \frac{dx}{\sqrt{x}} = 2\sqrt{x} \Big]_{a}^{1} = 2 - 2\sqrt{a}$$

Then, we find the limit of this area as $a \to 0^+$.

$$\lim_{a \to 0^+} \int_{a}^{1} \frac{dx}{\sqrt{x}} = \lim_{a \to 0^+} (2 - 2\sqrt{a}) = 2$$

The area under the curve from 0 to 1 is

$$\int_{0}^{1} \frac{dx}{\sqrt{x}} = \lim_{a \to 0^+} \int_{a}^{1} \frac{dx}{\sqrt{x}} = 2.$$

DEFINITION   Improper Integrals with Infinite Discontinuities

Integrals of functions that become infinite at a point within the interval of integration
are **improper integrals.**

1. If $f(x)$ is continuous on $(a, b]$, then

$$\int_a^b f(x)\, dx = \lim_{c \to a^+} \int_c^b f(x)\, dx.$$

2. If $f(x)$ is continuous on $[a, b)$, then

$$\int_a^b f(x)\, dx = \lim_{c \to b^-} \int_a^c f(x)\, dx.$$

3. If $f(x)$ is continuous on $[a, c) \cup (c, b]$, then

$$\int_a^b f(x)\, dx = \int_a^c f(x)\, dx + \int_c^b f(x)\, dx.$$

In parts 1 and 2, if the limit is finite the improper integral **converges** and the limit is the
value of the improper integral. If the limit fails to exist, the improper integral **diverges.** In
part 3, the integral on the left-hand side of the equation **converges** if both integrals on the
right-hand side have values; otherwise it **diverges.**

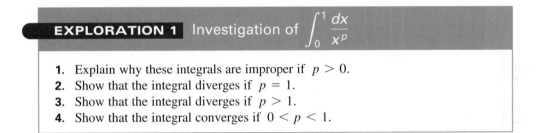

EXPLORATION 1 Investigation of $\displaystyle\int_0^1 \frac{dx}{x^p}$

1. Explain why these integrals are improper if $p > 0$.
2. Show that the integral diverges if $p = 1$.
3. Show that the integral diverges if $p > 1$.
4. Show that the integral converges if $0 < p < 1$.

EXAMPLE 6 Infinite Discontinuity at an Interior Point

Evaluate $\displaystyle\int_0^3 \frac{dx}{(x - 1)^{2/3}}$.

SOLUTION

The integrand has a vertical asymptote at $x = 1$ and is continuous on $[0, 1)$ and $(1, 3]$.
Thus, by part 3 of the definition above

$$\int_0^3 \frac{dx}{(x - 1)^{2/3}} = \int_0^1 \frac{dx}{(x - 1)^{2/3}} + \int_1^3 \frac{dx}{(x - 1)^{2/3}}.$$

Next, we evaluate each improper integral on the right-hand side of this equation.

$$\int_0^1 \frac{dx}{(x - 1)^{2/3}} = \lim_{c \to 1^-} \int_0^c \frac{dx}{(x - 1)^{2/3}}$$

$$= \lim_{c \to 1^-} 3(x - 1)^{1/3} \Big]_0^c$$

$$= \lim_{c \to 1^-} \left[3(c - 1)^{1/3} + 3 \right] = 3$$

continued

$$\int_1^3 \frac{dx}{(x-1)^{2/3}} = \lim_{c \to 1^+} \int_c^3 \frac{dx}{(x-1)^{2/3}}$$

$$= \lim_{c \to 1^+} 3(x-1)^{1/3} \Big]_c^3$$

$$= \lim_{c \to 1^+} [3(3-1)^{1/3} - 3(c-1)^{1/3}] = 3\sqrt[3]{2}$$

We conclude that

$$\int_0^3 \frac{dx}{(x-1)^{2/3}} = 3 + 3\sqrt[3]{2}.$$

Now Try Exercise 25.

EXAMPLE 7 Infinite Discontinuity at an Endpoint

Evaluate $\displaystyle\int_1^2 \frac{dx}{(x-2)}$.

SOLUTION

The integrand has an infinite discontinuity at $x = 2$ and is continuous on $[1, 2)$. Thus,

$$\int_1^2 \frac{dx}{x-2} = \lim_{c \to 2^-} \int_1^c \frac{dx}{x-2}$$

$$= \lim_{c \to 2^-} \ln|x-2| \Big]_1^c$$

$$= \lim_{c \to 2^-} (\ln|c-2| - \ln|-1|) = -\infty$$

The original integral diverges and has no value.   *Now Try Exercise 29.*

Test for Convergence and Divergence

When we cannot evaluate an improper integral directly (often the case in practice) we first try to determine whether it converges or diverges. If the integral diverges, that's the end of the story. If it converges, we can then use numerical methods to approximate its value. In such cases the following theorem is useful.

THEOREM 6   Comparison Test

Let f and g be continuous on $[a, \infty)$ with $0 \le f(x) \le g(x)$ for all $x \ge a$. Then

1. $\displaystyle\int_a^\infty f(x)\, dx$ converges if $\displaystyle\int_a^\infty g(x)\, dx$ converges.

2. $\displaystyle\int_a^\infty g(x)\, dx$ diverges if $\displaystyle\int_a^\infty f(x)\, dx$ diverges.

EXAMPLE 8 Investigating Convergence

(a) Does the integral $\int_1^\infty e^{-x^2}\, dx$ converge?

(b) If it converges, use a calculator to estimate its value.

SOLUTION

(a) By definition, $\displaystyle\int_1^\infty e^{-x^2}\, dx = \lim_{b \to \infty} \int_1^b e^{-x^2}\, dx.$

continued

We cannot evaluate the latter integral directly because there is no simple formula for the antiderivative of e^{-x^2}. We must therefore determine its convergence or divergence some other way. Because $e^{-x^2} > 0$ for all x, $\int_1^b e^{-x^2} dx$ is an increasing function of b. Therefore, as $b \to \infty$, the integral either becomes infinite as $b \to \infty$ or it is bounded from above and is forced to converge (have a finite limit).

The two curves $y = e^{-x^2}$ and $y = e^{-x}$ intersect at $(1, e^{-1})$, and $0 < e^{-x^2} \le e^{-x}$ for $x \ge 1$ (Figure 9.18). Thus, for any $b > 1$,

$$0 < \int_1^b e^{-x^2} dx \le \int_1^b e^{-x} dx = -e^{-b} + e^{-1} < e^{-1} \approx 0.368. \quad \text{Rounded up to be safe}$$

As an increasing function of b bounded above by 0.368, the integral $\int_1^\infty e^{-x^2} dx$ must converge. This does not tell us much about the value of the improper integral, however, except that it is positive and less than 0.368.

(b) The graph of NINT $(e^{-x^2}, x, 1, x)$ is shown in Figure 9.19. The value of the integral rises rapidly as x first moves away from 1 but changes little past $x = 3$. Values sampled along the curve suggest a limit of about 0.13940 as $x \to \infty$. (Exercise 57 shows how to confirm the accuracy of this estimate.) *Now Try Exercise 31.*

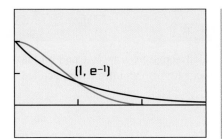

[0, 3] by [−0.5, 1.5]

Figure 9.18 The graph of $y = e^{-x^2}$ lies below the graph of $y = e^{-x}$ for $x > 1$. (Example 8)

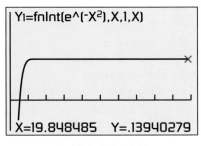

[0, 20] by [−0.1, 0.3]

Figure 9.19 TRACE is used to suggest that the limiting value for NINT $(e^{-x^2}, x, 1, x)$ is approximately 0.1394 in Example 8b.

Applications

EXAMPLE 9 Finding Circumference

Use the arc length formula (Section 8.4) to show that the circumference of the circle $x^2 + y^2 = 4$ is 4π.

SOLUTION

One fourth of this circle is given by $y = \sqrt{4 - x^2}, 0 \le x \le 2$. Its arc length is

$$L = \int_0^2 \sqrt{1 + (y')^2} \, dx, \quad \text{where} \quad y' = -\frac{x}{\sqrt{4 - x^2}}.$$

The integral is improper because y' is not defined at $x = 2$. We evaluate it as a limit.

$$L = \int_0^2 \sqrt{1 + (y')^2} \, dx = \int_0^2 \sqrt{1 + \frac{x^2}{4 - x^2}} \, dx$$

$$= \int_0^2 \sqrt{\frac{4}{4 - x^2}} \, dx$$

$$= \lim_{b \to 2^-} \int_0^b \sqrt{\frac{4}{4 - x^2}} \, dx$$

$$= \lim_{b \to 2^-} \int_0^b \sqrt{\frac{1}{1 - (x/2)^2}} \, dx$$

$$= \lim_{b \to 2^-} 2 \sin^{-1} \frac{x}{2} \Big]_0^b$$

$$= \lim_{b \to 2^-} 2 \left[\sin^{-1} \frac{b}{2} - 0 \right] = \pi$$

The circumference of the quarter circle is π; the circumference of the circle is 4π.

Now Try Exercise 47.

EXPLORATION 2 Gabriel's Horn

Consider the region R in the first quadrant bounded above by $y = 1/x$ and on the left by $x = 1$. The region is revolved about the x-axis to form an infinite solid called Gabriel's Horn, which is shown in the figure.

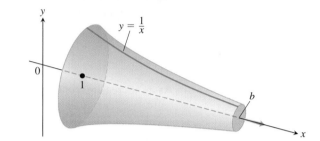

1. Explain how Example 2 shows that the region R has infinite area.
2. Find the volume of the solid.
3. Find the area of the shadow that would be cast by Gabriel's Horn.
4. Why is Gabriel's Horn sometimes described as a solid that has finite volume but casts an infinite shadow?

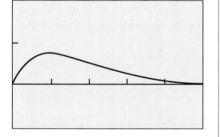

[0, 5] by [–0.5, 1]

Figure 9.20 The graph of $y = xe^{-x}$. (Example 10)

EXAMPLE 10 Finding the Volume of an Infinite Solid

Find the volume of the solid obtained by revolving the curve $y = xe^{-x}, 0 \le x < \infty$ about the x-axis.

SOLUTION

Figure 9.20 shows a portion of the region to be revolved about the x-axis. The area of a typical cross section of the solid is

$$\pi(\text{radius})^2 = \pi y^2 = \pi x^2 e^{-2x}.$$

The volume of the solid is

$$V = \pi \int_0^\infty x^2 e^{-2x}\, dx = \pi \lim_{b \to \infty} \int_0^b x^2 e^{-2x}\, dx.$$

Integrating by parts twice we obtain the following.

$$\int x^2 e^{-2x}\, dx = -\frac{x^2}{2} e^{-2x} + \int x e^{-2x}\, dx \qquad \begin{aligned} u &= x^2,\ dv = e^{-2x}\, dx \\ du &= 2x\, dx,\ v = -\tfrac{1}{2} e^{-2x} \end{aligned}$$

$$= -\frac{x^2}{2} e^{-2x} - \frac{x}{2} e^{-2x} + \frac{1}{2} \int e^{-2x}\, dx \qquad \begin{aligned} u &= x,\ dv = e^{-2x}\, dx \\ du &= dx,\ v = -\tfrac{1}{2} e^{-2x} \end{aligned}$$

$$= -\frac{x^2}{2} e^{-2x} - \frac{x}{2} e^{-2x} - \frac{1}{4} e^{-2x} + C$$

$$= -\frac{2x^2 + 2x + 1}{4e^{2x}} + C$$

Thus,

$$V = \pi \lim_{b \to \infty} \left[-\frac{2x^2 + 2x + 1}{4e^{2x}} \right]_0^b$$

$$= \pi \lim_{b \to \infty} \left[-\frac{2b^2 + 2b + 1}{4e^{2b}} + \frac{1}{4} \right] = \frac{\pi}{4},$$

and the volume of the solid is $\pi/4$. ***Now Try Exercise 55.***

Quick Review 9.4 *(For help, go to Sections 1.2, 6.3, and 9.2.)*

Exercise numbers with a gray background indicate problems that the authors have designed to be solved *without a calculator*.

In Exercises 1–4, evaluate the integral.

1. $\displaystyle\int_0^3 \frac{dx}{x+3}$

2. $\displaystyle\int_{-1}^1 \frac{x\,dx}{x^2+1}$

3. $\displaystyle\int \frac{dx}{x^2+4}$

4. $\displaystyle\int \frac{dx}{x^4}$

In Exercises 5 and 6, find the domain of the function.

5. $g(x) = \dfrac{1}{\sqrt{9-x^2}}$

6. $h(x) = \dfrac{1}{\sqrt{x-1}}$

In Exercises 7 and 8, confirm the inequality.

7. $\left|\dfrac{\cos x}{x^2}\right| \le \dfrac{1}{x^2}, \quad -\infty < x < \infty$

8. $\dfrac{1}{\sqrt{x^2-1}} \ge \dfrac{1}{x}, \quad x > 1$

In Exercises 9 and 10, show that the functions f and g grow at the same rate as $x \to \infty$.

9. $f(x) = 4e^x - 5, \quad g(x) = 3e^x + 7$

10. $f(x) = \sqrt{2x-1}, \quad g(x) = \sqrt{x+3}$

Section 9.4 Exercises

In Exercises 1–4, **(a)** express the improper integral as a limit of definite integrals, and **(b)** evaluate the integral.

1. $\displaystyle\int_0^\infty \frac{2x}{x^2+1}\,dx$

2. $\displaystyle\int_1^\infty \frac{dx}{x^{1/3}}$

3. $\displaystyle\int_{-\infty}^\infty \frac{2x}{(x^2+1)^2}\,dx$

4. $\displaystyle\int_1^\infty \frac{dx}{\sqrt{x}}$

In Exercises 5–24, evaluate the improper integral or state that it diverges.

5. $\displaystyle\int_1^\infty \frac{dx}{x^4}$

6. $\displaystyle\int_1^\infty \frac{2\,dx}{x^3}$

7. $\displaystyle\int_1^\infty \frac{dx}{\sqrt[3]{x}}$

8. $\displaystyle\int_1^\infty \frac{dx}{\sqrt[4]{x}}$

9. $\displaystyle\int_{-\infty}^{-1} \frac{dx}{x^2}$

10. $\displaystyle\int_{-\infty}^0 \frac{dx}{(x-2)^3}$

11. $\displaystyle\int_{-\infty}^{-2} \frac{2\,dx}{x^2-1}$

12. $\displaystyle\int_2^\infty \frac{3\,dx}{x^2-x}$

13. $\displaystyle\int_{-1}^\infty \frac{dx}{x^2+5x+6}$

14. $\displaystyle\int_{-\infty}^0 \frac{2\,dx}{x^2-4x+3}$

15. $\displaystyle\int_1^\infty \frac{5x+6}{x^2+2x}\,dx$

16. $\displaystyle\int_{-2}^{-\infty} \frac{2\,dx}{x^2-2x}$

17. $\displaystyle\int_1^\infty xe^{-2x}\,dx$

18. $\displaystyle\int_{-\infty}^0 x^2 e^x\,dx$

19. $\displaystyle\int_1^\infty x\ln(x)\,dx$

20. $\displaystyle\int_0^\infty (x+1)e^{-x}\,dx$

21. $\displaystyle\int_{-\infty}^\infty e^{-|x|}\,dx$

22. $\displaystyle\int_{-\infty}^\infty 2xe^{-x^2}\,dx$

23. $\displaystyle\int_{-\infty}^\infty \frac{dx}{e^x+e^{-x}}$

24. $\displaystyle\int_{-\infty}^\infty e^{2x}\,dx$

In Exercises 25–30, **(a)** state why the integral is improper. Then **(b)** evaluate the integral or state that it diverges.

25. $\displaystyle\int_0^2 \frac{dx}{1-x^2}$

26. $\displaystyle\int_0^1 \frac{dx}{\sqrt{1-x^2}}$

27. $\displaystyle\int_0^1 \frac{x+1}{\sqrt{x^2+2x}}\,dx$

28. $\displaystyle\int_0^4 \frac{e^{-\sqrt{x}}}{\sqrt{x}}\,dx$

29. $\displaystyle\int_0^1 x\ln(x)\,dx$

30. $\displaystyle\int_{-1}^4 \frac{dx}{\sqrt{|x|}}$

In Exercises 31–34, use the Comparison Test to determine whether the integral converges or diverges.

31. $\displaystyle\int_1^\infty \frac{dx}{1+e^x}$

32. $\displaystyle\int_1^\infty \frac{dx}{x^3+1}$

33. $\displaystyle\int_\pi^\infty \frac{2+\cos x}{x}\,dx$

34. $\displaystyle\int_{-\infty}^\infty \frac{dx}{\sqrt{x^4+1}}$

In Exercises 35–42, evaluate the integral or state that it diverges.

35. $\displaystyle\int_0^{\ln 2} y^{-2}e^{1/y}\,dy$

36. $\displaystyle\int_0^4 \frac{dr}{\sqrt{4-r}}$

37. $\displaystyle\int_0^\infty \frac{ds}{(1+s)\sqrt{s}}$

38. $\displaystyle\int_1^2 \frac{du}{u\sqrt{u^2-1}}$

39. $\displaystyle\int_0^\infty \frac{16\tan^{-1}v}{1+v^2}\,dv$

40. $\displaystyle\int_{-\infty}^0 \theta e^\theta\,d\theta$

41. $\displaystyle\int_0^2 \frac{dt}{1-t}$

42. $\displaystyle\int_{-1}^1 \ln(|w|)\,dw$

In Exercises 43 and 44, find the area of the region in the first quadrant that lies under the given curve.

43. $y = \dfrac{\ln x}{x^2}$

44. $y = \dfrac{\ln x}{x}$

45. Group Activity

(a) Show that if f is an even function and the necessary integrals exist, then

$$\int_{-\infty}^\infty f(x)\,dx = 2\int_0^\infty f(x)\,dx.$$

(b) Show that if f is odd and the necessary integrals exist, then

$$\int_{-\infty}^\infty f(x)\,dx = 0.$$

46. Writing to Learn

(a) Show that the integral $\displaystyle\int_0^\infty \frac{2x\,dx}{x^2+1}$ diverges.

(b) Explain why we can conclude from part (a) that

$$\int_{-\infty}^\infty \frac{2x\,dx}{x^2+1} \text{ diverges.}$$

(c) Show that $\displaystyle\lim_{b\to\infty}\int_{-b}^b \frac{2x\,dx}{x^2+1} = 0.$

(d) Explain why the result in part (c) does not contradict part (b).

47. Finding Perimeter Find the perimeter of the 4-sided figure $x^{2/3} + y^{2/3} = 1$.

Standardized Test Questions

You may use a graphing calculator to solve the following problems.

In Exercises 48 and 49, let f and g be continuous on $[a, \infty)$ with $0 \le f(x) \le g(x)$ for all $x \ge a$.

48. True or False If $\int_a^\infty f(x)\,dx$ converges then $\int_a^\infty g(x)\,dx$ converges. Justify your answer.

49. True or False If $\int_a^\infty g(x)\,dx$ converges then $\int_a^\infty f(x)\,dx$ converges. Justify your answer.

50. Multiple Choice Which of the following gives the value of the integral $\displaystyle\int_1^\infty \frac{dx}{x^{1.01}}$?

(A) 1   (B) 10   (C) 100   (D) 1000   (E) diverges

51. Multiple Choice Which of the following gives the value of the integral $\displaystyle\int_0^1 \frac{dx}{x^{0.5}}$?

(A) 1   (B) 2   (C) 3   (D) 4   (E) diverges

52. Multiple Choice Which of the following gives the value of the integral $\displaystyle\int_0^1 \frac{dx}{x-1}$?

(A) −1   (B) −1/2   (C) 0   (D) 1   (E) diverges

53. Multiple Choice Which of the following gives the value of the area under the curve $y = 1/(x^2+1)$ in the first quadrant?

(A) $\pi/4$ (B) 1   (C) $\pi/2$ (D) π (E) diverges

Explorations

54. The Integral $\displaystyle\int_1^\infty \frac{dx}{x^p}$.

(a) Evaluate the integral for $p = 0.5$.

(b) Evaluate the integral for $p = 1$.

(c) Evaluate the integral for $p = 1.5$.

(d) Show that $\displaystyle\int_1^\infty \frac{dx}{x^p} = \lim_{b\to\infty}\left[\frac{1}{1-p}\left(\frac{1}{b^{p-1}}-1\right)\right].$

(e) Use part (d) to show that $\displaystyle\int_1^\infty \frac{dx}{x^p} = \begin{cases} \dfrac{1}{p-1}, & p>1 \\ \infty, & p<1. \end{cases}$

(f) For what values of p does the integral converge? diverge?

55. Each cross section of the solid infinite horn shown in the figure cut by a plane perpendicular to the x-axis for $-\infty < x \le \ln 2$ is a circular disc with one diameter reaching from the x-axis to the curve $y = e^x$.

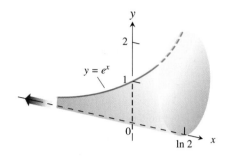

(a) Find the area of a typical cross section.

(b) Express the volume of the horn as an improper integral.

(c) Find the volume of the horn.

56. Normal Probability Distribution Function In Section 8.5, we encountered the bell-shaped normal distribution curve that is the graph of

$$f(x) = \frac{1}{\sigma\sqrt{2\pi}} e^{-\frac{1}{2}\left(\frac{x-\mu}{\sigma}\right)^2},$$

the normal probability density function with mean μ and standard deviation σ. The number μ tells where the distribution is centered, and σ measures the "scatter" around the mean.

From the theory of probability, it is known that

$$\int_{-\infty}^\infty f(x)\,dx = 1.$$

In what follows, let $\mu = 0$ and $\sigma = 1$.

(a) Draw the graph of f. Find the intervals on which f is increasing, the intervals on which f is decreasing, and any local extreme values and where they occur.

(b) Evaluate $\displaystyle\int_{-n}^n f(x)\,dx$ for $n = 1, 2, 3$.

(c) Give a convincing argument that $\displaystyle\int_{-\infty}^\infty f(x)\,dx = 1$.

[*Hint:* Show that $0 < f(x) < e^{-x/2}$ for $x > 1$, and for $b > 1$,

$$\int_b^\infty e^{-x/2}\,dx \to 0 \quad\text{as}\quad b \to \infty.]$$

57. Approximating the Value of $\int_1^\infty e^{-x^2}\,dx$

(a) Show that $\displaystyle\int_6^\infty e^{-x^2}\,dx \le \int_6^\infty e^{-6x}\,dx < 4\times 10^{-17}$.

(b) **Writing to Learn** Explain why

$$\int_1^\infty e^{-x^2}\,dx \approx \int_1^6 e^{-x^2}\,dx$$

with error of at most 4×10^{-17}.

(c) Use the approximation in part (b) to estimate the value of $\int_1^\infty e^{-x^2}\,dx$. Compare this estimate with the value displayed in Figure 9.19.

(d) Writing to Learn Explain why

$$\int_0^\infty e^{-x^2}\,dx \approx \int_0^3 e^{-x^2}\,dx$$

with error of at most 0.000042.

Extending the Ideas

58. Use properties of integrals to give a convincing argument that Theorem 6 is true.

59. Consider the integral

$$f(n + 1) = \int_0^\infty x^n e^{-x}\,dx$$

where $n \geq 0$.

(a) Show that $\int_0^\infty x^n e^{-x}\,dx$ converges for $n = 0, 1, 2$.

(b) Use integration by parts to show that $f(n + 1) = nf(n)$.

(c) Give a convincing argument that $\int_0^\infty x^n e^{-x}\,dx$ converges for all integers $n \geq 0$.

60. Let $f(x) = \displaystyle\int_0^x \frac{\sin t}{t}\,dt$.

(a) Use graphs and tables to investigate the values of $f(x)$ as $x \to \infty$.

(b) Does the integral $\int_0^\infty (\sin x)/x\,dx$ converge? Give a convincing argument.

61. (a) Show that we get the same value for the improper integral in Example 5 if we express

$$\int_{-\infty}^\infty \frac{dx}{1 + x^2} = \int_{-\infty}^1 \frac{dx}{1 + x^2} + \int_1^\infty \frac{dx}{1 + x^2},$$

and then evaluate these two integrals.

(b) Show that it doesn't matter what we choose for c in (Improper Integrals with Infinite Integration Limits, part 3)

$$\int_{-\infty}^\infty f(x)\,dx = \int_{-\infty}^c f(x)\,dx + \int_c^\infty f(x)\,dx.$$

Quick Quiz for AP* Preparation: Sections 9.3 and 9.4

You may use a graphing calculator to solve the following problems.

1. Multiple Choice Which of the following functions grows faster than x^2 as $x \to \infty$?

(A) e^{-x} (B) $\ln(x)$ (C) $7x + 10$ (D) $2x^2 - 3x$ (E) $0.1x^3$

2. Multiple Choice Find all the values of p for which the integral converges $\displaystyle\int_1^\infty \frac{dx}{x^{p+1}}$.

(A) $p < -1$ (B) $p < 0$ (C) $p > 0$
(D) $p > 1$ (E) diverges for all p

3. Multiple Choice Find all the values of p for which the integral converges $\displaystyle\int_0^1 \frac{dx}{x^{p+1}}$.

(A) $p < -1$ (B) $p < 0$ (C) $p > 0$
(D) $p > 1$ (E) diverges for all p

4. Free Response Consider the region R in the first quadrant under the curve $y = \dfrac{2\ln(x)}{x^2}$.

(a) Write the area of R as an improper integral.

(b) Express the integral in part (a) as a limit of a definite integral.

(c) Find the area of R.

CHAPTER 9 Key Terms

Absolute Value Theorem for Sequences (p. 448)

arithmetic sequence (p. 444)

binary search (p. 464)

common difference (p. 444)

common ratio (p. 445)

Comparison Test (p. 472)

Constant Multiple Rule for limits (p. 447)

convergence of improper integral (pp. 467, 471)

convergent sequence (p. 447)

Difference Rule for limits (p. 447)

divergence of improper integral (pp. 467, 471)

divergent sequence (p. 447)

explicitly defined sequence (p. 443)

finite sequence (p. 443)

geometric sequence (p. 445)

grows at the same rate (p. 461)

grows faster (p. 461)

grows slower (p. 461)

improper integral (pp. 467, 471)

indeterminate form (p. 452)

infinite sequence (p. 443)

l'Hospital's Rule, first form (p. 452)

l'Hospital's Rule, stronger form (p. 453)

limit of a sequence (p. 447)

nth term of a sequence (p. 443)

Product Rule for limits (p. 447)

Quotient Rule for limits (p. 447)

recursively defined sequence (p. 443)

sequence (p. 443)

sequential search (p. 464)

Squeeze Theorem for Sequences (p. 448)

Sum Rule for limits (p. 447)

terms of sequence (p. 443)

transitivity of growing rates (p. 463)

value of improper integral (p. 467, 471)

CHAPTER 9 Review Exercises

Exercise numbers with a gray background indicate problems that the authors have designed to be solved *without a calculator*.

The collection of exercises marked in red could be used as a Chapter Test.

In Exercises 1 and 2, find the first four terms and the fortieth term of the given sequence.

1. $a_n = (-1)^n \dfrac{n+1}{n+3}$ for all $n \geq 1$

2. $a_1 = -3$, $a_n = 2a_{n-1}$ for all $n \geq 2$

3. The sequence $-1, 1/2, 2, 7/2, \ldots$ is arithmetic. Find **(a)** the common difference, **(b)** the tenth term, and **(c)** an explicit rule for the nth term.

4. The sequence $1/2, -2, 8, -32, \ldots$ is geometric. Find **(a)** the common ratio, **(b)** the seventh term, and **(c)** an explicit rule for the nth term.

In Exercises 5 and 6, draw a graph of the sequence with given nth term.

5. $a_n = \dfrac{2^{n+1} + (-1)^n}{2^n}$, $n = 1, 2, 3, \ldots$

6. $a_n = (-1)^{n-1} \dfrac{n-1}{n}$

In Exercises 7 and 8, determine the convergence or divergence of the sequence with given nth term. If the sequence converges, find its limit.

7. $a_n = \dfrac{3n^2 - 1}{2n^2 + 1}$

8. $a_n = (-1)^n \dfrac{3n - 1}{n + 2}$

In Exercises 9–22, find the limit.

9. $\displaystyle \lim_{t \to 0} \dfrac{t - \ln(1 + 2t)}{t^2}$

10. $\displaystyle \lim_{t \to 0} \dfrac{\tan 3t}{\tan 5t}$

11. $\displaystyle \lim_{x \to 0} \dfrac{x \sin x}{1 - \cos x}$

12. $\displaystyle \lim_{x \to 1} x^{1/(1-x)}$

13. $\displaystyle \lim_{x \to \infty} x^{1/x}$

14. $\displaystyle \lim_{x \to \infty} \left(1 + \dfrac{3}{x}\right)^x$

15. $\displaystyle \lim_{r \to \infty} \dfrac{\cos r}{\ln r}$

16. $\displaystyle \lim_{\theta \to \pi/2} \left(\theta - \dfrac{\pi}{2}\right) \sec \theta$

17. $\displaystyle \lim_{x \to 1} \left(\dfrac{1}{x - 1} - \dfrac{1}{\ln x}\right)$

18. $\displaystyle \lim_{x \to 0^+} \left(1 + \dfrac{1}{x}\right)^x$

19. $\displaystyle \lim_{\theta \to 0^+} (\tan \theta)^\theta$

20. $\displaystyle \lim_{\theta \to \infty} \theta^2 \sin\left(\dfrac{1}{\theta}\right)$

21. $\displaystyle \lim_{x \to \infty} \dfrac{x^3 - 3x^2 + 1}{2x^2 + x - 3}$

22. $\displaystyle \lim_{x \to \infty} \dfrac{3x^2 - x + 1}{x^4 - x^3 + 2}$

In Exercises 23–30, determine whether f grows faster than, slower than, or at the same rate as g as $x \to \infty$. Give reasons for your answer.

23. $f(x) = x$, $g(x) = 5x$

24. $f(x) = \log_2 x$, $g(x) = \log_3 x$

25. $f(x) = x$, $g(x) = x + \dfrac{1}{x}$

26. $f(x) = \dfrac{x}{100}$, $g(x) = xe^{-x}$

27. $f(x) = x$, $g(x) = \tan^{-1} x$

28. $f(x) = e^{\ln x}$, $g(x) = x \log_2 x$

29. $f(x) = \ln 2x$, $g(x) = \ln x^2$

30. $f(x) = 10x^3 + 2x^2$, $g(x) = e^x$

In Exercises 31–36,

    (a) show that f has a removable discontinuity at $x = 0$.

    (b) define f at $x = 0$ so that it is continuous there.

31. $f(x) = \dfrac{1 - \cos^2 x}{3x^2}$

32. $f(x) = \dfrac{e^x - 1}{\tan x}$

33. $f(x) = x \sec\left(x + \dfrac{\pi}{2}\right)$

34. $f(x) = x^2(1 + \cot^2 x)$

35. $f(x) = \dfrac{2^{\sin x} - 1}{e^x - 1}$

36. $f(x) = x \ln x$

In Exercises 37–48, evaluate the improper integral or state that it diverges.

37. $\displaystyle \int_1^\infty \dfrac{dx}{x^{3/2}}$

38. $\displaystyle \int_1^\infty \dfrac{dx}{(x^2 + 7x + 12)}$

39. $\displaystyle \int_{-\infty}^{-1} \dfrac{3\,dx}{3x - x^2}$

40. $\displaystyle \int_0^3 \dfrac{dx}{\sqrt{9 - x^2}}$

41. $\displaystyle \int_0^1 \ln(x)\,dx$

42. $\displaystyle \int_{-1}^1 \dfrac{dy}{y^{2/3}}$

43. $\displaystyle \int_{-2}^0 \dfrac{d\theta}{(\theta + 1)^{3/5}}$

44. $\displaystyle \int_3^\infty \dfrac{2\,dx}{x^2 - 2x}$

45. $\displaystyle \int_0^\infty x^2 e^{-x}\,dx$

46. $\displaystyle \int_{-\infty}^0 xe^{3x}\,dx$

47. $\displaystyle \int_{-\infty}^\infty \dfrac{dx}{e^x + e^{-x}}$

48. $\displaystyle \int_{-\infty}^\infty \dfrac{4\,dx}{x^2 + 16}$

In Exercises 49 and 50, use the Comparison Test to determine whether the improper integral converges or diverges.

49. $\displaystyle \int_1^\infty \dfrac{\ln z}{z}\,dz$

50. $\displaystyle \int_1^\infty \dfrac{e^{-t}}{\sqrt{t}}\,dt$

51. The second and fifth terms of a geometric sequence are -3 and $-3/8$, respectively. Find **(a)** the first term, **(b)** the common ratio, and **(c)** an explicit formula for the nth term.

52. The second and sixth terms of an arithmetic sequence are 11.5 and 5.5, respectively. Find **(a)** the first term, **(b)** the common difference, and **(c)** an explicit formula for the nth term.

53. Consider the improper integral $\int_{-\infty}^\infty e^{-2|x|}\,dx$.

    (a) Express the improper integral as a limit of definite integrals.

    (b) Evaluate the integral.

54. *Infinite Solid* The infinite region bounded by the coordinate axes and the curve $y = -\ln x$ in the first quadrant (see figure) is revolved about the x-axis to generate a solid. Find the volume of the solid.

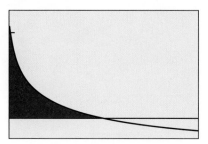

[0, 2] by [−1, 5]

55. *Infinite Region* Find the area of the region in the first quadrant under the curve $y = xe^{-x}$ (see figure).

[0, 5] by [−0.5, 1]

AP* Examination Preparation

56. Consider the infinite region R in the first quadrant under the curve $y = xe^{-x/2}$.

 (a) Write the area of R as an improper integral.

 (b) Express the integral in part (a) as a limit of a definite integral.

 (c) Find the area of R.

57. The infinite region in the first quadrant bounded by the coordinate axes and the curve $y = \dfrac{1}{x} - 1$ is revolved about the y-axis to generate a solid.

 (a) Write the volume of the solid as an improper integral.

 (b) Express the integral in part (a) as a limit of a definite integral.

 (c) Find the volume of the solid.

58. Determine whether or not $\int_0^\infty xe^{-x}\,dx$ converges. If it converges, give its value. Show your reasoning.

CHAPTER

10 Infinite Series

10.1 Power Series

10.2 Taylor Series

10.3 Taylor's Theorem

10.4 Radius of Convergence

10.5 Testing Convergence at Endpoints

$$\frac{1}{1^2} + \frac{1}{2^2} + \frac{1}{3^2} + \frac{1}{4^2} + \cdots + \frac{1}{n^2} + \cdots = ?$$

This is a modern photograph of the beautiful city of Basel, Switzerland, located on the Rhine River. Basel's university was an important center of European mathematics in the 17th century, largely due to a talented faculty that included the eminent Jakob Bernoulli. Bernoulli had become intrigued by a challenging problem first posed by Pietro Mengoli in 1644: What is the exact sum of the reciprocals of the squares of all the natural numbers? It was well known to be a finite number and had been approximated with some accuracy, but nobody recognized what it was, including Jakob Bernoulli. He challenged the greatest minds in Europe to find the exact sum and to give a proof that it was correct, a challenge that came to be known simply as the Basel Problem. In 1735, another talented Basel mathematician, the 28-year-old Leonhard Euler, announced to the world that the sum was $\pi^2/6$. The stunning insights into infinite sums that led him to that conclusion are some of the most elegant in the history of mathematical discovery. You will encounter this series (and Euler again, for yet another great formula) in this chapter.

CHAPTER 10 Overview

One consequence of the early and dramatic successes that scientists enjoyed when using calculus to explain natural phenomena was that there suddenly seemed to be no limits, so to speak, on how infinite processes might be exploited. There was still considerable mystery about "infinite sums" and "division by infinitely small quantities" in the years after Newton and Leibniz, but even mathematicians normally insistent on rigorous proof were inclined to throw caution to the wind while things were working. The result was a century of unprecedented progress in understanding the physical universe. (Moreover, we can note happily in retrospect, the proofs eventually followed.)

One infinite process that had puzzled mathematicians for centuries was the summing of infinite series. Sometimes an infinite series of terms added up to a number, as in

$$\frac{1}{2} + \frac{1}{4} + \frac{1}{8} + \frac{1}{16} + \cdots = 1.$$

(You can see this by adding the areas in the "infinitely halved" unit square at the right.) But sometimes the infinite sum was infinite, as in

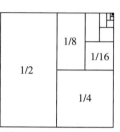

$$\frac{1}{1} + \frac{1}{2} + \frac{1}{3} + \frac{1}{4} + \frac{1}{5} + \cdots = \infty$$

(although this is far from obvious), and sometimes the infinite sum was difficult to pin down, as in

$$1 - 1 + 1 - 1 + 1 - 1 + \cdots$$

(Is it 0? Is it 1? Is it neither?).

Nonetheless, mathematicians like Gauss and Euler successfully used infinite series to derive previously inaccessible results. Laplace used infinite series to prove the stability of the solar system (although that does not stop some people from worrying about it today when they feel that "too many" planets have swung to the same side of the sun). It was years later that careful analysts like Cauchy developed the theoretical foundation for series computations, sending many mathematicians (including Laplace) back to their desks to verify their results.

Our approach in this chapter will be to discover the calculus of infinite series as the pioneers of calculus did: proceeding intuitively, accepting what works and rejecting what does not. Toward the end of the chapter we will return to the crucial question of convergence and take a careful look at it.

10.1 Power Series

You will be able to appreciate the difference between finite sums and infinite series and between polynomials and power series. Building on a knowledge of geometric series, you will explore some power series that are equivalent to familiar functions.

- Geometric series
- Convergence and divergence of series; the sequence of partial sums
- Power series
- Representing functions by power series
- Differentiating and integrating power series term by term
- Power series for $\frac{1}{1-x}$, $\frac{1}{1+x}$, $\ln(1+x)$, $\frac{1}{1+x^2}$, $\tan^{-1}x$, and e^x

Geometric Series

The first thing to get straight about an infinite series is that it is not simply an example of addition. Addition of real numbers is a *binary* operation, meaning that we really add numbers two at a time. The only reason that $1 + 2 + 3$ makes sense as "addition" is that we can *group* the numbers and then add them two at a time. The associative property of addition guarantees that we get the same sum no matter how we group them:

$$1 + (2 + 3) = 1 + 5 = 6$$

and

$$(1 + 2) + 3 = 3 + 3 = 6$$

In short, a *finite sum* of real numbers always produces a real number (the result of a finite number of binary additions), but an *infinite sum* of real numbers is something else entirely. That is why we need the following definition.

> **DEFINITION** **Infinite Series**
>
> An **infinite series** is an expression of the form
>
> $$a_1 + a_2 + a_3 + \cdots + a_n + \cdots, \qquad \text{or} \qquad \sum_{k=1}^{\infty} a_k.$$
>
> The numbers $a_1, a_2, \ldots$ are the **terms** of the series; a_n is the **nth term.**

The **partial sums** of the series form a sequence

$$s_1 = a_1$$
$$s_2 = a_1 + a_2$$
$$s_3 = a_1 + a_2 + a_3$$
$$\vdots$$
$$s_n = \sum_{k=1}^{n} a_k$$
$$\vdots$$

of real numbers, each defined as a finite sum. If the sequence of partial sums has a limit S as $n \to \infty$, we say the series **converges** to the sum S, and we write

$$a_1 + a_2 + a_3 + \cdots + a_n + \cdots = \sum_{k=1}^{\infty} a_k = S.$$

Otherwise, we say the series **diverges.**

EXAMPLE 1 Identifying a Divergent Series

Does the series $1 - 1 + 1 - 1 + 1 - 1 + \cdots$ converge?

SOLUTION

You might be tempted to pair the terms as

$$(1 - 1) + (1 - 1) + (1 - 1) + \cdots.$$

That strategy, however, requires an *infinite* number of pairings, so it cannot be justified by the associative property of addition. This is an infinite series, not a finite sum, so if it has a sum it *has to be* the limit of its sequence of partial sums,

$$1, 0, 1, 0, 1, 0, 1, \ldots.$$

Since this sequence has no limit, the series has no sum. It diverges. *Now Try Exercise 7.*

EXAMPLE 2 Identifying a Convergent Series

Does the series

$$\frac{3}{10} + \frac{3}{100} + \frac{3}{1000} + \cdots + \frac{3}{10^n} + \cdots$$

converge?

SOLUTION

Here is the sequence of partial sums, written in decimal form.

$$0.3, 0.33, 0.333, 0.3333, \ldots$$

This sequence has a limit $0.\overline{3}$, which we recognize as the fraction $1/3$. The series converges to the sum $1/3$. *Now Try Exercise 9.*

There is an easy way to identify some divergent series. In Exercise 62 you are asked to show that whenever an infinite series $\sum_{k=1}^{\infty} a_k$ converges, the limit of the *n*th term as $n \to \infty$ must be zero.

> If the **infinite series**
>
> $$\sum_{k=1}^{\infty} a_k = a_1 + a_2 + \cdots + a_k + \cdots$$
>
> converges, then $\lim_{k \to \infty} a_k = 0$.
> This means that if $\lim_{k \to \infty} a_k \neq 0$ the series must diverge.

The series in Example 2 is a **geometric series** because each term is obtained from its preceding term by multiplying by the same number *r*—in this case, $r = 1/10$. (The series of areas for the infinitely halved square at the beginning of this chapter is also geometric.) The convergence of geometric series is one of the few infinite processes with which mathematicians were reasonably comfortable prior to calculus. You may have already seen the following result in a previous course.

> The **geometric series**
>
> $$a + ar + ar^2 + ar^3 + \cdots + ar^{n-1} + \cdots = \sum_{n=1}^{\infty} ar^{n-1}$$
>
> converges to the sum $a/(1-r)$ if $|r| < 1$, and diverges if $|r| \geq 1$.

This completely settles the issue for geometric series. We know which ones converge and which ones diverge, and for the convergent ones we know what the sums must be. The interval $-1 < r < 1$ is the **interval of convergence.**

EXAMPLE 3 Analyzing Geometric Series

Tell whether each series converges or diverges. If it converges, give its sum.

(a) $\displaystyle\sum_{n=1}^{\infty} 3\left(\frac{1}{2}\right)^{n-1}$

(b) $1 - \dfrac{1}{2} + \dfrac{1}{4} - \dfrac{1}{8} + \cdots + \left(-\dfrac{1}{2}\right)^{n-1} + \cdots$

(c) $\displaystyle\sum_{k=0}^{\infty} \left(\frac{3}{5}\right)^k$

(d) $\dfrac{\pi}{2} + \dfrac{\pi^2}{4} + \dfrac{\pi^3}{8} + \cdots$

SOLUTION

(a) First term is $a = 3$ and $r = 1/2$. The series converges to

$$\frac{3}{1 - (1/2)} = 6.$$

(b) First term is $a = 1$ and $r = -1/2$. The series converges to

$$\frac{1}{1 - (-1/2)} = \frac{2}{3}.$$

continued

Partial Sums

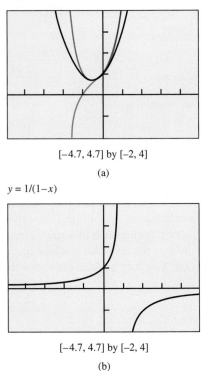

[−4.7, 4.7] by [−2, 4]

(a)

$y = 1/(1-x)$

[−4.7, 4.7] by [−2, 4]

(b)

Figure 10.1 (a) Partial sums converging to $1/(1 - x)$ on the interval $(-1; 1)$. The partial sums graphed here are $1 + x + x^2$, $1 + x + x^2 + x^3$, and $1 + x + x^2 + x^3 + x^4$. (b) Notice how the graphs in (a) resemble the graph of $1/(1 - x)$ on the interval $(-1, 1)$ but are not even close when $|x| \geq 1$.

When we set $x = 0$ in the expression

$$\sum_{n=0}^{\infty} c_n x^n = c_0 + c_1 x + c_2 x^2 + \cdots + c_n x^n + \cdots,$$

we get c_0 on the right but $c_0 \cdot 0^0$ on the left. Since 0^0 is not a number, this is a slight flaw in the notation, which we agree to overlook. The same situation arises when we set $x = a$ in

$$\sum_{n=0}^{\infty} c_n (x - a)^n.$$

In either case, we agree that the expression will equal c_0. (It really *should* equal c_0, so we are not compromising the mathematics; we are clarifying the notation we use to convey the mathematics.)

(c) First term is $a = (3/5)^0 = 1$ and $r = 3/5$. The series converges to

$$\frac{1}{1 - (3/5)} = \frac{5}{2}.$$

(d) In this series, $r = \pi/2 > 1$. The series diverges.   *Now Try Exercises 11 and 19.*

We have hardly begun our study of infinite series, but knowing everything there is to know about the convergence and divergence of an *entire class* of series (geometric) is an impressive start. Like the Renaissance mathematicians, we are ready to explore where this might lead. We are ready to bring in x.

Representing Functions by Series

If $|x| < 1$, then the geometric series formula assures us that

$$1 + x + x^2 + x^3 + \cdots + x^n + \cdots = \frac{1}{1 - x}.$$

Consider this statement for a moment. The expression on the right defines a function whose domain is the set of all numbers $x \neq 1$. The expression on the left defines a function whose domain is the interval of convergence, $|x| < 1$. The equality is understood to hold only on this latter domain, where both sides of the equation are defined. On this domain, the series *represents* the function $1/(1 - x)$.

The partial sums of the infinite series on the left are all polynomials, so we can graph them (Figure 10.1). As expected, we see that the convergence is strong in the interval $(-1, 1)$ but breaks down when $|x| \geq 1$.

The expression $\sum_{n=0}^{\infty} x^n$ is like a polynomial in that it is a sum of coefficients times powers of x, but polynomials have *finite* degrees and do not suffer from divergence for the wrong values of x. Just as an infinite series of numbers is not a mere sum, this series of powers of x is not a mere polynomial.

DEFINITION   Power Series

An expression of the form

$$\sum_{n=0}^{\infty} c_n x^n = c_0 + c_1 x + c_2 x^2 + \cdots + c_n x^n + \cdots$$

is a **power series centered at $x = 0$.** An expression of the form

$$\sum_{n=0}^{\infty} c_n (x - a)^n = c_0 + c_1(x - a) + c_2(x - a)^2 + \cdots + c_n(x - a)^n + \cdots$$

is a **power series centered at $x = a$.** The term $c_n(x - a)^n$ is the **nth term**; the number a is the **center.**

The geometric series

$$\sum_{n=0}^{\infty} x^n = 1 + x + x^2 + \cdots + x^n + \cdots$$

is a power series centered at $x = 0$. It converges on the interval $-1 < x < 1$, also centered at $x = 0$. This is typical behavior, as we will see in Section 10.4. A power series either converges for all x, converges on a finite interval with the same center as the series, or converges only at the center itself.

We have seen that the power series $\sum_{n=0}^{\infty} x^n$ represents the function $1/(1 - x)$ on the domain $(-1, 1)$. Can we find power series to represent other functions?

EXPLORATION 1 Finding Power Series for Other Functions

1. Given that $1/(1 - x)$ is represented by the power series

$$1 + x + x^2 + \cdots + x^n + \cdots$$

on the interval $(-1, 1)$,
   (a) find a power series that represents $1/(1 + x)$ on $(-1, 1)$.
   (b) find a power series that represents $x/(1 + x)$ on $(-1, 1)$.
   (c) find a power series that represents $1/(1 - 2x)$ on $(-1/2, 1/2)$.
   (d) find a power series that represents

$$\frac{1}{x} = \frac{1}{1 + (x - 1)}$$

on $(0, 2)$.

Could you have found the intervals of convergence yourself?

2. Find a power series that represents

$$\frac{1}{3x} = \frac{1}{3} \cdot \left(\frac{1}{1 + (x - 1)} \right)$$

and give its interval of convergence.

Differentiation and Integration

So far we have only represented functions by power series that happen to be geometric. The partial sums that converge to those power series, however, are *polynomials,* and we can apply calculus to polynomials. It would seem logical that the calculus of polynomials (the first rules we encountered in Chapter 3) would also apply to power series.

EXAMPLE 4 Finding a Power Series by Differentiation

Given that $1/(1 - x)$ is represented by the power series

$$1 + x + x^2 + \cdots + x^n + \cdots$$

on the interval $(-1, 1)$, find a power series to represent $1/(1 - x)^2$.

SOLUTION

Notice that $1/(1 - x)^2$ is the derivative of $1/(1 - x)$. To find the power series, we differentiate both sides of the equation

$$\frac{1}{1 - x} = 1 + x + x^2 + x^3 + \cdots + x^n + \cdots.$$

$$\frac{d}{dx}\left(\frac{1}{1 - x}\right) = \frac{d}{dx}(1 + x + x^2 + x^3 + \cdots + x^n + \cdots)$$

$$\frac{1}{(1 - x)^2} = 1 + 2x + 3x^2 + 4x^3 + \cdots + nx^{n-1} + \cdots$$

continued

Partial Sums

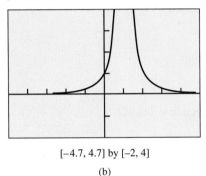

[−4.7, 4.7] by [−2, 4]

(a)

$y = 1/(1-x)^2$

[−4.7, 4.7] by [−2, 4]

(b)

Figure 10.2 (a) The polynomial partial sums of the power series we derived for (b) $1/(1 - x)^2$ seem to converge on the open interval $(−1, 1)$. (Example 4)

Antiderivative or Definite Integral?

Notice in Example 5 that we used a *definite* integral from 0 to *x* in the antidifferentation step. This is just a simple way of imposing the initial condition $F(0) = 0$, eliminating the step of solving for *C*. For the same reason, if we had been integrating a series in powers of $x − a$, we would have used a definite integral from *a* to *x* to impose the initial condition $F(a) = 0$. (See Theorem 2.)

What about the interval of convergence? Since the original series converges for $−1 < x < 1$, it would seem that the differentiated series ought to converge on the same open interval. Graphs (Figure 10.2) of the partial sums $1 + 2x + 3x^2$, $1 + 2x + 3x^2 + 4x^3$, and $1 + 2x + 3x^2 + 4x^3 + 5x^4$ suggest that this is the case (although such empirical evidence does not constitute a proof).   ***Now Try Exercise 27.***

The basic theorem about differentiating power series is the following.

> ### THEOREM 1   Term-by-Term Differentiation
>
> If $f(x) = \sum_{n=0}^{\infty} c_n(x − a)^n = c_0 + c_1(x − a) + c_2(x − a)^2 +$
>
> $$\cdots + c_n(x − a)^n + \cdots$$
>
> converges for $|x − a| < R$, then the series
>
> $$\sum_{n=1}^{\infty} nc_n(x − a)^{n-1} = c_1 + 2c_2(x − a) + 3c_3(x − a)^2 +$$
>
> $$\cdots + nc_n(x − a)^{n-1} + \cdots,$$
>
> obtained by differentiating the series for *f* term by term, converges for $|x − a| < R$ and represents $f'(x)$ on that interval. If the series for *f* converges for all *x*, then so does the series for f'.

Theorem 1 says that if a power series is differentiated term by term, the new series will converge on the same interval to the derivative of the function represented by the original series. This gives a way to generate new connections between functions and series.

Another way to reveal new connections between functions and series is by integration.

EXAMPLE 5   Finding a Power Series by Integration

Given that

$$\frac{1}{1 + x} = 1 − x + x^2 − x^3 + \cdots + (−x)^n + \cdots, \quad −1 < x < 1$$

(Exploration 1, Part 1), find a power series to represent $\ln(1 + x)$.

SOLUTION

Recall that $1/(1 + x)$ is the derivative of $\ln(1 + x)$. We can therefore integrate the series for $1/(1 + x)$ to obtain a series for $\ln(1 + x)$ (no absolute value bars are necessary because $(1 + x)$ is positive for $−1 < x < 1$).

$$\frac{1}{1 + x} = 1 − x + x^2 − x^3 + \cdots + (−x)^n + \cdots$$

$$= 1 − x + x^2 − x^3 + \cdots + (−1)^n x^n + \cdots$$

$$\int_0^x \frac{1}{1 + t} \, dt = \int_0^x \left(1 − t + t^2 − t^3 + \cdots + (−1)^n t^n + \cdots\right) dt \quad \text{\footnotesize t is a dummy variable.}$$

$$\ln(1 + t) \Big]_0^x = \left[t − \frac{t^2}{2} + \frac{t^3}{3} − \frac{t^4}{4} + \cdots + (−1)^n \frac{t^{n+1}}{n + 1} + \cdots\right]_0^x \quad \text{\footnotesize $(−1)^n$ is just a constant.}$$

$$\ln(1 + x) = x − \frac{x^2}{2} + \frac{x^3}{3} − \frac{x^4}{4} + \cdots + (−1)^n \frac{x^{n+1}}{n + 1} + \cdots$$

continued

It would seem logical for the new series to converge where the original series converges, on the open interval $(-1, 1)$. The graphs of the partial sums in Figure 10.3 support this idea.

Now Try Exercise 33.

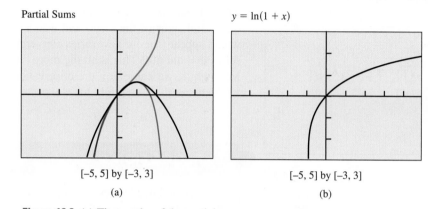

Partial Sums $\qquad\qquad\qquad\qquad\qquad y = \ln(1 + x)$

[−5, 5] by [−3, 3] $\qquad\qquad\qquad\qquad$ [−5, 5] by [−3, 3]

(a) $\qquad\qquad\qquad\qquad\qquad\qquad$ (b)

Figure 10.3 (a) The graphs of the partial sums

$$x - \frac{x^2}{2}, \qquad x - \frac{x^2}{2} + \frac{x^3}{3}, \qquad \text{and} \qquad x - \frac{x^2}{2} + \frac{x^3}{3} - \frac{x^4}{4}$$

closing in on (b) the graph of $\ln(1 + x)$ over the interval $(-1, 1)$. (Example 5)

The idea that the integrated series in Example 5 converges to $\ln(1 + x)$ for all x between -1 and 1 is confirmed by the following theorem.

Remember the Constants in Life

Do not be intimidated when differentiating or antidifferentiating the nth term of a power series. Keep in mind that the *variable* is x, while n is (for any given term) a constant. If you can antidifferentiate $7(x - a)^5$ to get $7 \cdot \frac{(x - a)^6}{6}$, you should be able to antidifferentiate $(-1)^n \frac{3^n}{n!}(x - a)^n$ to get $(-1)^n \frac{3^n}{n!} \cdot \frac{(x - a)^{n+1}}{n + 1}$.

THEOREM 2 Term-by-Term Integration

If $f(x) = \displaystyle\sum_{n=0}^{\infty} c_n(x - a)^n = c_0 + c_1(x - a) + c_2(x - a)^2 +$

$$\cdots + c_n(x - a)^n + \cdots$$

converges for $|x - a| < R$, then the series

$$\sum_{n=0}^{\infty} c_n \frac{(x - a)^{n+1}}{n + 1} = c_0(x - a) + c_1 \frac{(x - a)^2}{2} + c_2 \frac{(x - a)^3}{3} +$$

$$\cdots + c_n \frac{(x - a)^{n+1}}{n + 1} + \cdots,$$

obtained by integrating the series for f term by term, converges for $|x - a| < R$ and represents $\int_a^x f(t)\, dt$ on that interval. If the series for f converges for all x, then so does the series for the integral.

Theorem 2 says that if a power series is integrated term by term, the new series will converge on the same interval to the integral of the function represented by the original series.

There is still more to be learned from Example 5. The original equation

$$\frac{1}{1 + x} = 1 - x + x^2 - x^3 + \cdots + (-x)^n + \cdots$$

clearly diverges at $x = 1$ (see Example 1). The behavior is not so apparent, however, for the equation we obtained by integrating:

$$\ln(1 + x) = x - \frac{x^2}{2} + \frac{x^3}{3} - \frac{x^4}{4} + \cdots + (-1)^n \frac{x^{n+1}}{n + 1} + \cdots$$

Some calculators have a *sequence mode* that enables you to generate a sequence of partial sums, but you can also do it with simple commands on the home screen. Try entering the two multiple-step commands shown on the first screen below.

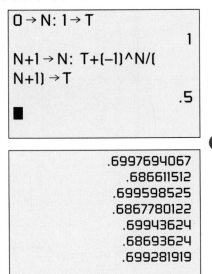

If you are successful, then every time you hit ENTER, the calculator will display the next partial sum of the series

$$1 - \frac{1}{2} + \frac{1}{3} - \frac{1}{4} + \cdots + \frac{(-1)^n}{n+1} + \cdots.$$

The second screen shows the result of about 80 ENTERs. The sequence certainly seems to be converging to $\ln 2 = 0.6931471806 \ldots$.

If we let $x = 1$ on both sides of this equation, we get

$$\ln 2 = 1 - \frac{1}{2} + \frac{1}{3} - \frac{1}{4} + \cdots + \frac{(-1)^n}{n+1} + \cdots,$$

which looks like a reasonable statement. It looks even more reasonable if you look at the partial sums of the series and watch them converge toward $\ln 2$ (see margin note). It would appear that our new series converges at 1 despite the fact that we obtained it from a series that did not! This is all the more reason to take a careful look at convergence later. Meanwhile, we can enjoy the observation that we have created a series that apparently works better than we might have expected and better than Theorem 2 could guarantee.

EXPLORATION 2 Finding a Power Series for $\tan^{-1} x$

1. Find a power series that represents $1/(1 + x^2)$ on $(-1, 1)$.
2. Use the technique of Example 5 to find a power series that represents $\tan^{-1} x$ on $(-1, 1)$.
3. Graph the first four partial sums. Do the graphs suggest convergence on the open interval $(-1, 1)$?
4. Do you think that the series for $\tan^{-1} x$ converges at $x = 1$? Can you support your answer with evidence?

Identifying a Series

So far we have been finding power series to represent functions. Let us now try to find the function that a given power series represents.

EXPLORATION 3 A Series with a Curious Property

Define a function f by a power series as follows:

$$f(x) = 1 + x + \frac{x^2}{2!} + \frac{x^3}{3!} + \frac{x^4}{4!} + \cdots + \frac{x^n}{n!} + \cdots$$

1. Find $f'(x)$.
2. Find $f(0)$.
3. What well-known function do you suppose f is?
4. Use your responses to parts 1 and 2 to set up an initial value problem that the function f must solve. You will need a differential equation and an initial condition.
5. Solve the initial value problem to prove your conjecture in part 3.
6. Graph the first three partial sums. What appears to be the interval of convergence?
7. Graph the next three partial sums. Did you underestimate the interval of convergence?

The correct answer to part 7 in Exploration 3 above is "yes," unless you had the keen insight (or reckless bravado) to answer "all real numbers" in part 6. You will be able to prove the remarkable fact that this series converges *for all x* in Section 10.3.

Quick Review 10.1 *(For help, go to Section 9.1.)*

In Exercises 1 and 2, find the first four terms and the 30th term of the sequence

$$\{u_n\}_{n=1}^{\infty} = \{u_1, u_2, \ldots, u_n, \ldots\}.$$

1. $u_n = \dfrac{4}{n+2}$ **2.** $u_n = \dfrac{(-1)^n}{n}$

In Exercises 3 and 4, the sequences are geometric ($a_{n+1}/a_n = r$, a constant). Find

  (a) the common ratio r.   **(b)** the tenth term.

  (c) a rule for the nth term.

3. $\{2, 6, 18, 54, \ldots\}$ **4.** $\{8, -4, 2, -1, \ldots\}$

In Exercises 5–10,

  (a) graph the sequence $\{a_n\}$.

  (b) determine $\lim\limits_{n \to \infty} a_n$.

5. $a_n = \dfrac{1-n}{n^2}$ **6.** $a_n = \left(1 + \dfrac{1}{n}\right)^n$

7. $a_n = (-1)^n$ **8.** $a_n = \dfrac{1-2n}{1+2n}$

9. $a_n = 2 - \dfrac{1}{n}$ **10.** $a_n = \dfrac{\ln(n+1)}{n}$

Section 10.1 Exercises

Exercise numbers with a gray background indicate problems that the authors have designed to be solved *without a calculator*.

1. Replace the * with an expression that will generate the series

$$1 - \frac{1}{4} + \frac{1}{9} - \frac{1}{16} + \cdots.$$

  (a) $\displaystyle\sum_{n=1}^{\infty} (-1)^{n-1}\left(\frac{1}{*}\right)$ **(b)** $\displaystyle\sum_{n=0}^{\infty} (-1)^n\left(\frac{1}{*}\right)$

  (c) $\displaystyle\sum_{n=*}^{\infty} (-1)^n\left(\frac{-1}{(n-2)^2}\right)$

2. Write an expression for the nth term, a_n.

  (a) $\displaystyle\sum_{n=0}^{\infty} a_n = 1 + \frac{1}{3} + \frac{1}{9} + \frac{1}{27} + \frac{1}{81} + \cdots$

  (b) $\displaystyle\sum_{n=1}^{\infty} a_n = 1 - \frac{1}{2} + \frac{1}{3} - \frac{1}{4} + \frac{1}{5} - \cdots$

  (c) $\displaystyle\sum_{n=0}^{\infty} a_n = 5 + 0.5 + 0.05 + 0.005 + 0.0005 + \cdots$

In Exercises 3–6, tell whether the series is the same as

$$\sum_{n=1}^{\infty} \left(-\frac{1}{2}\right)^{n-1}.$$

3. $\displaystyle\sum_{n=1}^{\infty} -\left(\frac{1}{2}\right)^{n-1}$ **4.** $\displaystyle\sum_{n=0}^{\infty} \left(-\frac{1}{2}\right)^{n}$

5. $\displaystyle\sum_{n=0}^{\infty} (-1)^n\left(\frac{1}{2}\right)^{n}$ **6.** $\displaystyle\sum_{n=1}^{\infty} \frac{(-1)^n}{2^{n-1}}$

In Exercises 7–10, compute the limit of the partial sums to determine whether the series converges or diverges.

7. $1 + 1.1 + 1.11 + 1.111 + 1.1111 + \cdots$

8. $2 - 1 + 1 - 1 + 1 - 1 + \cdots$

9. $\dfrac{1}{2} + \dfrac{1}{4} + \dfrac{1}{8} + \cdots + \dfrac{1}{2^k} + \cdots$

10. $3 + 0.5 + 0.05 + 0.005 + 0.0005 + \cdots$

In Exercises 11–20, tell whether the series converges or diverges. If it converges, give its sum.

11. $1 + \dfrac{2}{3} + \left(\dfrac{2}{3}\right)^2 + \left(\dfrac{2}{3}\right)^3 + \cdots + \left(\dfrac{2}{3}\right)^n + \cdots$

12. $1 - 2 + 3 - 4 + 5 - \cdots + (-1)^n(n+1) + \cdots$

13. $\displaystyle\sum_{n=0}^{\infty} \left(\frac{5}{4}\right)\left(\frac{2}{3}\right)^n$ **14.** $\displaystyle\sum_{n=0}^{\infty} \left(\frac{2}{3}\right)\left(\frac{5}{4}\right)^n$

15. $\displaystyle\sum_{n=0}^{\infty} \cos(n\pi)$

16. $3 - 0.3 + 0.03 - 0.003 + 0.0003 - \cdots + 3(-0.1)^n + \cdots$

17. $\displaystyle\sum_{n=0}^{\infty} \sin^n\left(\frac{\pi}{4} + n\pi\right)$

18. $\dfrac{1}{2} + \dfrac{2}{3} + \dfrac{3}{4} + \dfrac{4}{5} + \cdots + \dfrac{n}{n+1} + \cdots$

19. $\displaystyle\sum_{n=1}^{\infty} \left(\frac{e}{\pi}\right)^n$ **20.** $\displaystyle\sum_{n=0}^{\infty} \frac{5^n}{6^{n+1}}$

In Exercises 21–24, find the interval of convergence and the function of x represented by the **geometric** series.

21. $\displaystyle\sum_{n=0}^{\infty} 2^n x^n$ **22.** $\displaystyle\sum_{n=0}^{\infty} (-1)^n(x+1)^n$

23. $\displaystyle\sum_{n=0}^{\infty} \left(-\frac{1}{2}\right)^n (x-3)^n$ **24.** $\displaystyle\sum_{n=0}^{\infty} 3\left(\frac{x-1}{2}\right)^n$

In Exercises 25 and 26, find the values of x for which the geometric series converges and find the function of x it represents.

25. $\displaystyle\sum_{n=0}^{\infty} \sin^n x$ **26.** $\displaystyle\sum_{n=0}^{\infty} \tan^n x$

In Exercises 27–30, use the series and the function $f(x)$ that it represents from the indicated exercise to find a power series for $f'(x)$.

27. Exercise 21   **28.** Exercise 22

29. Exercise 23   **30.** Exercise 24

In Exercises 31–34, use the series centered at a and the function it represents to find a power series for $\int_a^x f(t)\,dt$.

31. Exercise 21   **32.** Exercise 22

33. Exercise 23   **34.** Exercise 24

35. Writing to Learn Each of the following series diverges in a slightly different way. Explain what is happening to the sequence of partial sums in each case.

  (a) $\sum_{n=1}^{\infty} 2n$ **(b)** $\sum_{n=0}^{\infty} (-1)^n$ **(c)** $\sum_{n=1}^{\infty} (-1)^n (2n)$

36. Prove that $\sum_{n=0}^{\infty} \dfrac{e^n \pi}{\pi^n e}$ diverges.

37. Solve for x: $\sum_{n=0}^{\infty} x^n = 20$.

38. Writing to Learn Explain how it is possible, given any real number at all, to construct an infinite series of nonzero terms that converges to it.

39. Make up a geometric series $\sum ar^{n-1}$ that converges to the number 5 if

  (a) $a = 2$ **(b)** $a = 13/2$

In Exercises 40 and 41, express the repeating decimal as a geometric series and find its sum.

40. $0.\overline{21}$ **41.** $0.\overline{234}$

In Exercises 42–47, express the number as the ratio of two integers.

42. $0.\overline{7} = 0.7777\ldots$

43. $0.\overline{d} = 0.dddd\ldots$,   where d is a digit

44. $0.0\overline{6} = 0.06666\ldots$ **45.** $1.\overline{414} = 1.414\,414\,414\ldots$

46. $1.24\overline{123} = 1.24\,123\,123\,123\ldots$

47. $3.\overline{142857} = 3.142857\,142857\ldots$

48. Bouncing Ball A ball is dropped from a height of 4 m. Each time it strikes the pavement after falling from a height of h m, it rebounds to a height of $0.6h$ m. Find the total distance the ball travels up and down.

49. (Continuation of Exercise 48) Find the total number of seconds that the ball in Exercise 48 travels. [*Hint:* A freely falling ball travels $4.9t^2$ meters in t seconds, so it will fall h meters in $\sqrt{h/4.9}$ seconds. Bouncing from ground to apex takes the same time as falling from apex to ground.]

50. Summing Areas The figure below shows the first five of an infinite sequence of squares. The outermost square has an area of 4 m^2. Each of the other squares is obtained by joining the midpoints of the sides of the preceding square. Find the sum of the areas of all the squares.

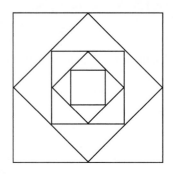

51. Summing Areas The accompanying figure shows the first three rows and part of the fourth row of a sequence of rows of semicircles. There are 2^n semicircles in the nth row, each of radius $1/(2^n)$. Find the sum of the areas of all the semicircles.

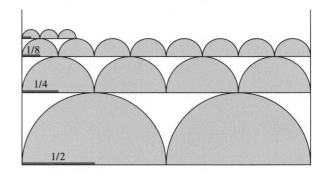

52. Sum of a Finite Geometric Progression Let a and r be real numbers with $r \neq 1$, and let

$$S = a + ar + ar^2 + ar^3 + \cdots + ar^{n-1}.$$

  (a) Find $S - rS$.

  (b) Use the result in part (a) to show that $S = \dfrac{a - ar^n}{1 - r}$.

53. Sum of a Convergent Geometric Series Exercise 52 gives a formula for the nth partial sum of an infinite geometric series. Use this formula to show that $\sum_{n=1}^{\infty} ar^{n-1}$ diverges when $|r| \geq 1$ and converges to $a/(1-r)$ when $|r| < 1$.

In Exercises 54–59, find a *geometric* power series to represent the given function and identify its interval of convergence. When writing the power series, include a formula for the nth term.

54. $\dfrac{1}{1 + 3x}$ **55.** $\dfrac{x}{1 - 2x}$

56. $\dfrac{3}{1 - x^3}$ **57.** $\dfrac{1}{1 + (x - 4)}$

58. $\dfrac{1}{4x} = \dfrac{1}{4}\left(\dfrac{1}{1 + (x - 1)}\right)$ **59.** $\dfrac{1}{2 - x}$ [*Hint:* Rewrite $2 - x$.]

60. Find the value of b for which $1 + e^b + e^{2b} + e^{3b} + \cdots = 9$.

61. Let S be the series $\sum_{n=0}^{\infty} \left(\dfrac{t}{1+t}\right)^n$, $t \neq 0$.

(a) Find the value to which S converges when $t = 1$.

(b) Determine all values of t for which S converges.

(c) Find all values of t that make the sum of S greater than 10.

62. nth Term Test Assume that the series $\sum_{k=1}^{\infty} a_k$ converges to S.

(a) **Writing to Learn** Explain why $\lim_{n \to \infty} \sum_{k=1}^{k=n} a_k = S$.

(b) Show that $S_n = S_{n-1} + a_n$, where S_n denotes the nth partial sum of the series.

(c) Show that $\lim_{n \to \infty} a_n = 0$.

63. A Series for ln x Starting with the power series found for $1/x$ in Exploration 1, Part 1(d), find a power series for $\ln x$ centered at $x = 1$.

64. Differentiation Use differentiation to find a series for $f(x) = 2/(1 - x)^3$. What is the interval of convergence of your series?

65. Group Activity Intervals of Convergence How much can the interval of convergence of a power series be changed by integration or differentiation? To be specific, suppose that the power series

$$f(x) = c_0 + c_1 x + c_2 x^2 + \cdots + c_n x^n + \cdots$$

converges for $-1 < x < 1$ and diverges for all other values of x.

(a) **Writing to Learn** Could the series obtained by integrating the series for f term by term possibly converge for $-2 < x < 2$? Explain. [*Hint:* Apply Theorem 1, not Theorem 2.]

(b) **Writing to Learn** Could the series obtained by differentiating the series for f term by term possibly converge for $-2 < x < 2$? Explain.

Standardized Test Questions

66. True or False The series

$$\frac{1}{2} + \frac{1.01}{2} + \frac{(1.01)^2}{2} + \cdots + \frac{(1.01)^n}{2} + \cdots$$

converges. Justify your answer.

67. True or False The series $1 + \dfrac{1}{2} + \dfrac{1}{4} + \dfrac{1}{8} + \dfrac{1}{16} + \cdots$ diverges. Justify your answer.

68. Multiple Choice To which of the following numbers does the series $1 + \dfrac{1}{3} + \dfrac{1}{9} + \dfrac{1}{27} + \cdots$ converge?

(A) 2/3   (B) 9/8   (C) 3/2   (D) 2   (E) It diverges

In Exercises 69–71, use the geometric series $\sum_{n=0}^{\infty}(x - 1)^n$, which represents the function $f(x)$.

69. Multiple Choice Find the values of x for which the series converges.

(A) $0 < x < 2$ (B) $0 < x < 1$ (C) $-1 < x < 0$

(D) $-1 < x < 1$ (E) $-2 < x < 0$

70. Multiple Choice Which of the following is the function that the power series represents?

(A) $\dfrac{1}{x - 1}$ (B) $\dfrac{1}{1 - 2x}$ (C) $-\dfrac{1}{x}$ (D) $\dfrac{1}{x - 2}$ (E) $\dfrac{1}{2 - x}$.

71. Multiple Choice Which of the following is a function that $\int_0^x f(t)\,dt$ represents?

(A) $-\ln\left(\dfrac{x - 2}{2}\right)$ (B) $\ln\left(\dfrac{x - 2}{2}\right)$ (C) $\dfrac{1}{(x - 2)^2}$

(D) $-\ln\left(\dfrac{|x - 2|}{2}\right)$ (E) $\ln\left(\dfrac{|x - 2|}{2}\right)$

Exploration

72. Let $f(t) = \dfrac{4}{1 + t^2}$ and $G(x) = \displaystyle\int_0^x f(t)\,dt$.

(a) Find the first four nonzero terms and the general term for a power series for $f(t)$ centered at $t = 0$.

(b) Find the first four nonzero terms and the general term for a power series for $G(x)$ centered at $x = 0$.

(c) Find the interval of convergence of the power series in part (a).

(d) The interval of convergence of the power series in part (b) is almost the same as the interval in part (c), but includes two more numbers. What are the numbers?

Extending the Ideas

The sequence $\{a_n\}$ **converges** to the number L if to every positive number ε there corresponds an integer N such that for all n,

$$n > N \implies |a_n - L| < \varepsilon.$$

L is the **limit** of the sequence and we write $\lim_{n \to \infty} a_n = L$. If no such number L exists, we say that $\{a_n\}$ **diverges.**

73. Tail of a Sequence Prove that if $\{a_n\}$ is a convergent sequence, then to every positive number ε there corresponds an integer N such that for all m and n,

$$m > N \quad \text{and} \quad n > N \implies |a_m - a_n| < \varepsilon.$$

[*Hint:* Let $\lim_{n \to \infty} a_n = L$. As the terms approach L, how far apart can they be?]

74. Uniqueness of Limits Prove that limits of sequences are unique. That is, show that if L_1 and L_2 are numbers such that $\lim_{n \to \infty} a_n = L_1$ and $\lim_{n \to \infty} a_n = L_2$, then $L_1 = L_2$.

75. Limits and Subsequences Prove that if two subsequences of a sequence $\{a_n\}$ have different limits $L_1 \neq L_2$, then $\{a_n\}$ diverges.

76. Limits and Asymptotes

(a) Show that the sequence with nth term $a_n = (3n + 1)/(n + 1)$ converges.

(b) If $\lim_{n \to \infty} a_n = L$, explain why $y = L$ is a horizontal asymptote of the graph of the function

$$f(x) = \frac{3x + 1}{x + 1}$$

obtained by replacing n by x in the nth term.

10.2 Taylor Series

You will learn how to build a power series to represent a function by choosing the coefficients judiciously, using the function and its derivatives at a point. You will construct power series for some familiar functions and explore the convergence of such series graphically.

- Constructing a Maclaurin polynomial using derivatives at 0
- Maclaurin series for sin x and cos x
- Taylor series and Taylor polynomials
- Observing the convergence of Maclaurin polynomials graphically
- Combining and manipulating Taylor series to form new series
- A table of Maclaurin series and their intervals of convergence

Constructing a Series

A comprehensive understanding of geometric series served us well in Section 10.1, enabling us to find power series to represent certain functions and functions that are equivalent to certain power series (all of these equivalencies being subject to the condition of convergence). In this section we learn a more general technique for constructing power series, one that makes good use of the tools of calculus.

Let us start by constructing a polynomial.

EXPLORATION 1 Designing a Polynomial to Specifications

Construct a polynomial $P(x) = a_0 + a_1x + a_2x^2 + a_3x^3 + a_4x^4$ with the following behavior at $x = 0$:

$$P(0) = 5,$$
$$P'(0) = 7,$$
$$P''(0) = 11,$$
$$P'''(0) = 13, \text{ and}$$
$$P^{(4)}(0) = 17$$

This task might look difficult at first, but when you try it you will find that the predictability of differentiation when applied to polynomials makes it straightforward. (Be sure to check this out before you move on.)

There is nothing special about the number of derivatives in Exploration 1. We could have prescribed the value of the polynomial and its first n derivatives at $x = 0$ for any n and found a polynomial of degree at most n to match. Our plan now is to use the technique of Exploration 1 to construct polynomials that approximate functions by emulating their behavior at 0.

EXAMPLE 1 Approximating ln $(1 + x)$ by a Polynomial

Construct a polynomial $P(x) = a_0 + a_1x + a_2x^2 + a_3x^3 + a_4x^4$ that matches the behavior of ln $(1 + x)$ at $x = 0$ through its first four derivatives. That is,

$$P(0) = \ln (1 + x) \qquad \text{at } x = 0,$$
$$P'(0) = (\ln (1 + x))' \qquad \text{at } x = 0,$$
$$P''(0) = (\ln (1 + x))'' \qquad \text{at } x = 0,$$
$$P'''(0) = (\ln (1 + x))''' \qquad \text{at } x = 0, \text{ and}$$
$$P^{(4)}(0) = (\ln (1 + x))^{(4)} \qquad \text{at } x = 0$$

SOLUTION

This is just like Exploration 1, except that first we need to find out what the numbers are.

$$P(0) = \ln (1 + x) \Big|_{x=0} = 0$$

$$P'(0) = \frac{1}{1 + x} \Big|_{x=0} = 1$$

continued

$$P''(0) = -\frac{1}{(1+x)^2}\Big|_{x=0} = -1$$

$$P'''(0) = \frac{2}{(1+x)^3}\Big|_{x=0} = 2$$

$$P^{(4)}(0) = -\frac{6}{(1+x)^4}\Big|_{x=0} = -6$$

In working through Exploration 1, you probably noticed that the coefficient of the term x^n in the polynomial we seek is $P^{(n)}(0)$ divided by $n!$. The polynomial is

$$P(x) = 0 + x - \frac{x^2}{2} + \frac{x^3}{3} - \frac{x^4}{4}. \qquad \textbf{\textit{Now Try Exercise 1.}}$$

We have just constructed the fourth-order **Taylor polynomial** for the function $\ln(1+x)$ at $x = 0$. You might recognize it as the beginning of the power series we discovered for $\ln(1+x)$ in Example 5 of Section 10.1, when we came upon it by integrating a geometric series. If we keep going, of course, we will gradually reconstruct that entire series one term at a time, improving the approximation near $x = 0$ with every term we add. The series is called the **Taylor series** generated by the function $\ln(1+x)$ at $x = 0$.

You might also recall Figure 10.3, which shows how the polynomial approximations converge nicely to $\ln(1+x)$ near $x = 0$, but then gradually peel away from the curve as x gets farther away from 0 in either direction. Given that the coefficients are totally determined by specifying behavior at $x = 0$, that is exactly what we ought to expect.

Series for sin *x* and cos *x*

We can use the technique of Example 1 to construct Taylor series about $x = 0$ for any function, as long as we can keep taking derivatives there. Two functions that are particularly well suited for this treatment are the sine and cosine.

EXAMPLE 2 Constructing a Power Series for sin *x*

Construct the seventh-order Taylor polynomial and the Taylor series for sin x at $x = 0$.

SOLUTION

We need to evaluate sin x and its first seven derivatives at $x = 0$. Fortunately, this is not hard to do.

$$\sin(0) = 0$$
$$\sin'(0) = \cos(0) = 1$$
$$\sin''(0) = -\sin(0) = 0$$
$$\sin'''(0) = -\cos(0) = -1$$
$$\sin^{(4)}(0) = \sin(0) = 0$$
$$\sin^{(5)}(0) = \cos(0) = 1$$
$$\vdots$$

The pattern $0, 1, 0, -1$ will keep repeating forever. *continued*

The unique seventh-order Taylor polynomial that matches all these derivatives at $x = 0$ is

$$P_7(x) = 0 + 1x - 0x^2 - \frac{1}{3!}x^3 + 0x^4 + \frac{1}{5!}x^5 - 0x^6 - \frac{1}{7!}x^7$$

$$= x - \frac{x^3}{3!} + \frac{x^5}{5!} - \frac{x^7}{7!}$$

P_7 is the seventh-order Taylor polynomial for $\sin x$ at $x = 0$. (It also happens to be of seventh degree, but that does not always happen. For example, you can see that P_8 for $\sin x$ will be the same polynomial as P_7.)

To form the Taylor series, we just keep on going:

$$x - \frac{x^3}{3!} + \frac{x^5}{5!} - \frac{x^7}{7!} + \frac{x^9}{9!} - \cdots = \sum_{n=0}^{\infty} (-1)^n \frac{x^{2n+1}}{(2n + 1)!}$$

Now Try Exercise 3.

EXPLORATION 2 A Power Series for the Cosine

Group Activity

1. Construct the sixth-order Taylor polynomial and the Taylor series at $x = 0$ for $\cos x$.
2. Compare your method for attacking part 1 with the methods of other groups. Did anyone find a shortcut?

Beauty Bare

Edna St. Vincent Millay, an American poet of the early 20th century, in referring to the experience of simultaneously seeing and understanding the geometric underpinnings of nature, wrote, "Euclid alone has looked on Beauty bare." In case you have never experienced that sort of reverie when gazing upon something geometric, we intend to give you that opportunity now.

In Example 2 we constructed a power series for $\sin x$ by matching the behavior of $\sin x$ at $x = 0$. Let us graph the first nine partial sums together with $y = \sin x$ to see how well we did (Figure 10.4).

Behold what is occurring here! These polynomials were constructed to mimic the behavior of $\sin x$ near $x = 0$. The *only* information we used to construct the coefficients of these polynomials was information about the sine function and its derivatives at 0. Yet, somehow, the information at $x = 0$ is producing a series whose graph not only looks like sine near the origin, but appears to be a clone of the *entire* sine curve. This is no deception, either; we will show in Section 10.3, Example 3, that the Taylor series for $\sin x$ does, in fact, converge to $\sin x$ over the entire real line. We have managed to construct an entire function by knowing its behavior at a single point! (The same is true about the series for $\cos x$ found in Exploration 2.)

We still must remember that convergence is an infinite process. Even the one-billionth–order Taylor polynomial begins to peel away from $\sin x$ as we move away from 0, although imperceptibly at first, and eventually becomes unbounded, as any polynomial must. Nonetheless, we can approximate the sine of *any* number to whatever accuracy we want if we just have the patience to work out enough terms of this series!

This kind of dramatic convergence does not occur for all Taylor series. The Taylor polynomials for $\ln (1 + x)$ do not converge outside the interval from -1 to 1, no matter how many terms we add.

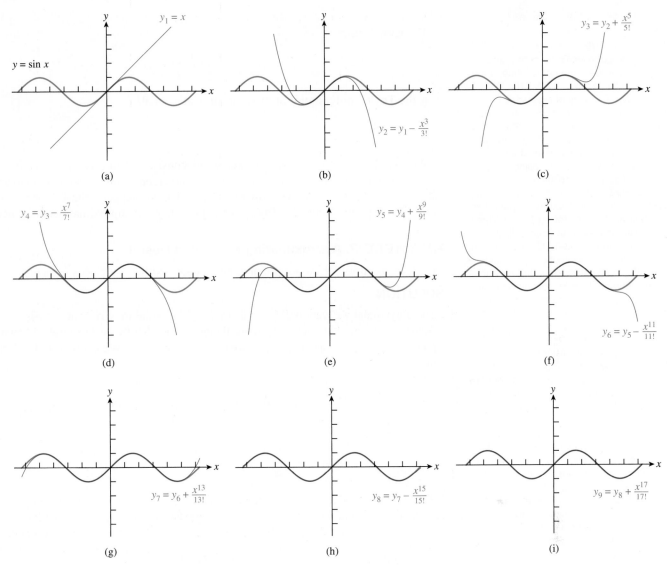

Figure 10.4 $y = \sin x$ and its nine Taylor polynomials $P_1, P_3, \ldots, P_{17}$ for $-2\pi \le x \le 2\pi$. Try graphing these functions in the window $[-2\pi, 2\pi]$ by $[-5, 5]$.

Maclaurin and Taylor Series

If we generalize the steps we followed in constructing the coefficients of the power series in this section so far, we arrive at the following definition.

DEFINITION **Taylor Series Generated by *f* at *x* = 0 (Maclaurin Series)**

Let f be a function with derivatives of all orders throughout some open interval containing 0. Then the **Taylor series generated by f at $x = 0$** is

$$f(0) + f'(0)x + \frac{f''(0)}{2!}x^2 + \cdots + \frac{f^{(n)}(0)}{n!}x^n + \cdots = \sum_{k=0}^{\infty} \frac{f^{(k)}(0)}{k!}x^k.$$

This series is also called the **Maclaurin series generated by f.**

continued

The partial sum

$$P_n(x) = \sum_{k=0}^{n} \frac{f^{(k)}(0)}{k!} x^k$$

is the **Taylor polynomial of order n for f at $x = 0$.**

We use $f^{(0)}$ to mean f. *Every* power series constructed in this way converges to the function f at $x = 0$, but we have seen that the convergence might well extend to an interval containing 0, or even to the entire real line. When this happens, the Taylor polynomials that form the partial sums of a Taylor series provide good approximations for f near 0.

EXAMPLE 3 Approximating a Function Near 0

Find the fourth-order Taylor polynomial that approximates $y = \cos 2x$ near $x = 0$.

SOLUTION

The polynomial we want is $P_4(x)$, the Taylor polynomial for $\cos 2x$ at $x = 0$. Before we go cranking out derivatives, though, remember that we can use a known power series to generate another, as we did in Section 10.1. We know from Exploration 2 that

$$\cos x = 1 - \frac{x^2}{2!} + \frac{x^4}{4!} - \cdots + (-1)^n \frac{x^{2n}}{(2n)!} + \cdots.$$

Therefore,

$$\cos 2x = 1 - \frac{(2x)^2}{2!} + \frac{(2x)^4}{4!} - \cdots + (-1)^n \frac{(2x)^{2n}}{(2n)!} + \cdots.$$

So,

$$P_4(x) = 1 - \frac{(2x)^2}{2!} + \frac{(2x)^4}{4!}$$
$$= 1 - 2x^2 + (2/3)x^4$$

The graph in Figure 10.5 shows how well the polynomial approximates the cosine near $x = 0$.

Now Try Exercise 5.

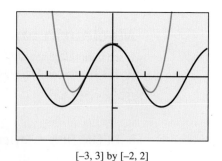

[−3, 3] by [−2, 2]

Figure 10.5 The graphs of $y = 1 - 2x^2 + (2/3)x^4$ and $y = \cos 2x$ near $x = 0$. (Example 3)

These polynomial approximations can be useful in a variety of ways. For one thing, it is easy to do calculus with polynomials. For another thing, polynomials are built using only the two basic operations of addition and multiplication, so computers can handle them easily.

EXPLORATION 3 Approximating sin 13

How many terms of the series

$$\sum_{n=0}^{\infty} (-1)^n \frac{x^{2n+1}}{(2n+1)!}$$

are required to approximate sin 13 accurate to the third decimal place?

1. Find sin 13 on your calculator (radians, of course).
2. Enter these two multiple-step commands on your home screen. They will give you the first-order and second-order Taylor polynomial approximations for sin 13. Notice that the second-order approximation, in particular, is not very good.

```
0 → N: 13 → T
                          13
N+1 → N: T+(−1)^N*1
3^(2N+1)/(2N+1)!
→ T
                −353.1666667
```

3. Continue to hit ENTER. Each time you will add one more term to the Taylor polynomial approximation. Be patient; things will get worse before they get better.
4. How many terms are required before the polynomial approximations stabilize in the thousandths place for $x = 13$?

This strategy for approximation would be of limited practical value if we were restricted to power series at $x = 0$—but we are not. We can match a power series with f in the same way at *any* value $x = a$, provided we can take the derivatives. In fact, we can get a formula for doing that by simply "shifting horizontally" the formula we already have.

DEFINITION **Taylor Series Generated by *f* at *x* = *a***

Let f be a function with derivatives of all orders throughout some open interval containing a. Then the **Taylor series generated by f at $x = a$** is

$$f(a) + f'(a)(x - a) + \frac{f''(a)}{2!}(x - a)^2 + \cdots + \frac{f^{(n)}(a)}{n!}(x - a)^n + \cdots$$

$$= \sum_{k=0}^{\infty} \frac{f^{(k)}(a)}{k!}(x - a)^k$$

The partial sum

$$P_n(x) = \sum_{k=0}^{n} \frac{f^{(k)}(a)}{k!}(x - a)^k$$

is the **Taylor polynomial of order n for f at $x = a$.**

Order and Degree

As noted in the solution to Example 2, the Taylor polynomial of order n might not have degree n, since the coefficient of the term with degree n might be zero.

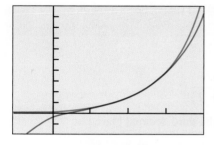

[-1, 4] by [-10, 50]

Figure 10.6 The graphs of $y = e^x$ and $y = P_3(x)$ (the third-order Taylor polynomial for e^x at $x = 2$). (Example 4)

EXAMPLE 4 A Taylor Series at *x* = 2

Find the Taylor series generated by $f(x) = e^x$ at $x = 2$.

SOLUTION

We first observe that $f(2) = f'(2) = f''(2) = \cdots = f^{(n)}(2) = e^2$. The series, therefore, is

$$e^x = e^2 + e^2(x - 2) + \frac{e^2}{2!}(x - 2)^2 + \cdots + \frac{e^2}{n!}(x - 2)^n + \cdots$$

$$= \sum_{k=0}^{\infty}\left(\frac{e^2}{k!}\right)(x - 2)^k$$

We illustrate the convergence near $x = 2$ by sketching the graphs of $y = e^x$ and $y = P_3(x)$ in Figure 10.6.   ***Now Try Exercise 13.***

EXAMPLE 5 Taylor Polynomials for a Polynomial

Find the third-order Taylor polynomial for $f(x) = 2x^3 - 3x^2 + 4x - 5$

(a) at $x = 0$.   **(b)** at $x = 1$.

SOLUTION

(a) This is easy. This polynomial is already written in powers of x and is of degree three, so it is its own third-order (and fourth-order, etc.) Taylor polynomial at $x = 0$.

(b) This would also be easy if we could quickly rewrite the formula for f as a polynomial in powers of $x - 1$, but that would require some messy tinkering. Instead, we apply the Taylor series formula.

$$f(1) = 2x^3 - 3x^2 + 4x - 5\Big|_{x=1} = -2$$

$$f'(1) = 6x^2 - 6x + 4\Big|_{x=1} = 4$$

$$f''(1) = 12x - 6\Big|_{x=1} = 6$$

$$f'''(1) = 12$$

So,

$$P_3(x) = -2 + 4(x - 1) + \frac{6}{2!}(x - 1)^2 + \frac{12}{3!}(x - 1)^3$$

$$= 2(x - 1)^3 + 3(x - 1)^2 + 4(x - 1) - 2$$

This polynomial function agrees with f at every value of x (as you can verify by multiplying it out) but it is written in powers of $(x - 1)$ instead of x.   ***Now Try Exercise 15.***

Combining Taylor Series

On the intersection of their intervals of convergence, Taylor series can be added, subtracted, and multiplied by constants and powers of x, and the results are once again Taylor series. The Taylor series for $f(x) + g(x)$ is the sum of the Taylor series for $f(x)$ and the Taylor series for $g(x)$ because the nth derivative of $f + g$ is $f^{(n)} + g^{(n)}$, and so on. We can obtain the Maclaurin series for $(1 + \cos 2x)/2$ by substituting $2x$ in the Maclaurin series for cos x, adding 1, and dividing the result by 2. The Maclaurin series for sin x + cos x is the term-by-term sum of the series for sin x and cos x. We obtain the Maclaurin series for x sin x by multiplying all the terms of the Maclaurin series for sin x by x.

EXAMPLE 6 Building Series from Known Series

Find a Maclaurin series to represent the function $f(x) = \dfrac{e^{2x} - 1}{3}$. What is its interval of convergence?

First, recall that $e^x = 1 + x + \dfrac{x^2}{2!} + \dfrac{x^3}{3!} + \cdots + \dfrac{x^n}{n!} + \cdots$.

Therefore, $e^{2x} = 1 + 2x + \dfrac{(2x)^2}{2!} + \dfrac{(2x)^3}{3!} + \cdots + \dfrac{(2x)^n}{n!} + \cdots$.

Therefore, $e^{2x} - 1 = 2x + \dfrac{(2x)^2}{2!} + \dfrac{(2x)^3}{3!} + \cdots + \dfrac{(2x)^n}{n!} + \cdots$.

Finally, $\dfrac{e^{2x} - 1}{3} = \dfrac{1}{3}\left(2x + \dfrac{(2x)^2}{2!} + \dfrac{(2x)^3}{3!} + \cdots + \dfrac{(2x)^n}{n!} + \cdots\right)$

$= \dfrac{2}{3}x + \dfrac{2^2}{3 \cdot 2!}x^2 + \dfrac{2^3}{3 \cdot 3!}x^3 + \dfrac{2^4}{3 \cdot 4!}x^4 + \cdots + \dfrac{2^n}{3 \cdot n!}x^n + \cdots$

Since the Maclaurin series for e^x converges for all real numbers, the series we have constructed from it also converges for all real numbers. ***Now Try Exercise 25.***

Table of Maclaurin Series

We conclude the section by listing some of the most useful Maclaurin series, all of which have been derived in one way or another in the first two sections of this chapter. The exercises will ask you to use these series as basic building blocks for constructing other series (e.g., $\tan^{-1} x^2$ or $7xe^x$). We also list the intervals of convergence, although rigorous proofs of convergence are deferred until we develop convergence tests in Sections 10.4 and 10.5.

Maclaurin Series (Taylor Series at $x = 0$)

$$\frac{1}{1-x} = 1 + x + x^2 + \cdots + x^n + \cdots = \sum_{n=0}^{\infty} x^n \quad (|x| < 1)$$

$$\frac{1}{1+x} = 1 - x + x^2 - \cdots + (-x)^n + \cdots = \sum_{n=0}^{\infty} (-1)^n x^n \quad (|x| < 1)$$

$$e^x = 1 + x + \frac{x^2}{2!} + \cdots + \frac{x^n}{n!} + \cdots = \sum_{n=0}^{\infty} \frac{x^n}{n!} \quad (\text{all real } x)$$

$$\sin x = x - \frac{x^3}{3!} + \frac{x^5}{5!} - \cdots + (-1)^n \frac{x^{2n+1}}{(2n+1)!} + \cdots$$

$$= \sum_{n=0}^{\infty} (-1)^n \frac{x^{2n+1}}{(2n+1)!} \quad (\text{all real } x)$$

$$\cos x = 1 - \frac{x^2}{2!} + \frac{x^4}{4!} - \cdots + (-1)^n \frac{x^{2n}}{(2n)!} + \cdots$$

$$= \sum_{n=0}^{\infty} (-1)^n \frac{x^{2n}}{(2n)!} \quad (\text{all real } x)$$

continued

$$\ln(1 + x) = x - \frac{x^2}{2} + \frac{x^3}{3} - \cdots + (-1)^{n-1}\frac{x^n}{n} + \cdots$$

$$= \sum_{n=1}^{\infty} (-1)^{n-1}\frac{x^n}{n} \quad (-1 < x \le 1)$$

$$\tan^{-1}x = x - \frac{x^3}{3} + \frac{x^5}{5} - \cdots + (-1)^n\frac{x^{2n+1}}{2n+1} + \cdots$$

$$= \sum_{n=0}^{\infty} (-1)^n\frac{x^{2n+1}}{2n+1} \quad (|x| \le 1)$$

Quick Review 10.2   *(For help, go to Sections 3.3 and 4.1.)*

Exercise numbers with a gray background indicate problems that the authors have designed to be solved *without a calculator*.

In Exercises 1–5, find a formula for the *n*th derivative of the function.

1. e^{2x}

2. $\dfrac{1}{x-1}$

3. 3^x

4. $\ln x$

5. x^n

In Exercises 6–10, find dy/dx. (Assume that letters other than x represent constants.)

6. $y = \dfrac{x^n}{n!}$

7. $y = \dfrac{2^n(x-a)^n}{n!}$

8. $y = (-1)^n\dfrac{x^{2n+1}}{(2n+1)!}$

9. $y = \dfrac{(x+a)^{2n}}{(2n)!}$

10. $y = \dfrac{(1-x)^n}{n!}$

Section 10.2 Exercises

In Exercises 1 and 2, use the formula in the definition to construct the fourth-order Taylor polynomial at $x = 0$ for the function.

1. $f(x) = \sqrt{1+x^2}$ **2.** $f(x) = e^{2x}$

In Exercises 3 and 4, use the formula in the definition to construct the fifth-order Taylor polynomial and the Taylor series for the function at $x = 0$.

3. $f(x) = \dfrac{1}{x+2}$ **4.** $f(x) = e^{1-x}$

In Exercises 5–12, *use the table of Maclaurin series at the end of this section.* Construct the first three nonzero terms and the general term of the Maclaurin series generated by the function and give the interval of convergence.

5. $\sin 2x$ **6.** $\ln(1-x)$

7. $\tan^{-1}x^2$ **8.** $7x\,e^x$

9. $\cos\left(\dfrac{x}{2}\right)$ **10.** $x^2\cos x$

11. $\dfrac{x}{1-x^3}$ **12.** e^{-2x}

In Exercises 13 and 14, find the Taylor series generated by the function at the given point.

13. $f(x) = \dfrac{1}{x+1}$, $x = 2$ **14.** $f(x) = e^{x/2}$, $x = 1$

In Exercises 15–17, use the methods of Example 5 to find the Taylor polynomial of order 3 generated by f

    (a) at $x = 0$;   **(b)** at $x = 1$.

15. $f(x) = x^3 - 2x + 4$ **16.** $f(x) = 2x^3 + x^2 + 3x - 8$

17. $f(x) = x^4$

In Exercises 18–21, find the Taylor polynomials of orders 0, 1, 2, and 3 generated by f at $x = a$.

18. $f(x) = \dfrac{1}{x}$, $a = 2$ **19.** $f(x) = \sin x$, $a = \pi/4$

20. $f(x) = \cos x$, $a = \pi/4$ **21.** $f(x) = \sqrt{x}$, $a = 4$

22. Let f be a function that has derivatives of all orders for all real numbers. Assume $f(0) = 4, f'(0) = 5, f''(0) = -8$, and $f'''(0) = 6$.

    (a) Write the third-order Taylor polynomial for f at $x = 0$ and use it to approximate $f(0.2)$.

    (b) Write the second-order Taylor polynomial for f', the derivative of f, at $x = 0$ and use it to approximate $f'(0.2)$.

23. Let f be a function that has derivatives of all orders for all real numbers. Assume $f(1) = 4$, $f'(1) = -1$, $f''(1) = 3$, and $f'''(1) = 2$.

    (a) Write the third-order Taylor polynomial for f at $x = 1$ and use it to approximate $f(1.2)$.

    (b) Write the second-order Taylor polynomial for f', the derivative of f, at $x = 1$ and use it to approximate $f'(1.2)$.

24. The Maclaurin series for $f(x)$ is

$$f(x) = 1 + \frac{x}{2!} + \frac{x^2}{3!} + \frac{x^3}{4!} + \cdots + \frac{x^n}{(n+1)!} + \cdots.$$

(a) Find $f'(0)$ and $f^{(10)}(0)$.

(b) Let $g(x) = xf(x)$. Write the Maclaurin series for $g(x)$, showing the first three nonzero terms and the general term.

(c) Write $g(x)$ in terms of a familiar function without using series.

25. (a) Write the first three nonzero terms and the general term of the Taylor series generated by $e^{x/2}$ at $x = 0$.

(b) Write the first three nonzero terms and the general term of a power series to represent

$$g(x) = \frac{e^x - 1}{x}.$$

(c) For the function g in part (b), find $g'(1)$ and use it to show that

$$\sum_{n=1}^{\infty} = \frac{n}{(n+1)!} = 1.$$

26. Let

$$f(t) = \frac{2}{1 - t^2} \quad \text{and} \quad G(x) = \int_0^x f(t)\, dt.$$

(a) Find the first four terms and the general term for the Maclaurin series generated by f.

(b) Find the first four nonzero terms and the Maclaurin series for G.

27. (a) Find the first four nonzero terms in the Taylor series generated by $f(x) = \sqrt{1 + x}$ at $x = 0$.

(b) Use the results found in part (a) to find the first four nonzero terms in the Taylor series for $g(x) = \sqrt{1 + x^2}$ at $x = 0$.

(c) Find the first four nonzero terms in the Taylor series at $x = 0$ for the function h such that $h'(x) = \sqrt{1 + x^2}$ and $h(0) = 5$.

28. Consider the power series

$$\sum_{n=0}^{\infty} a_n x^n, \quad \text{where } a_0 = 1 \text{ and } a_n = \left(\frac{3}{n}\right) a_{n-1} \text{ for } n \geq 1.$$

(This defines the coefficients *recursively*.)

(a) Find the first four terms and the general term of the series.

(b) What function f is represented by this power series?

(c) Find the exact value of $f'(1)$.

29. Use the technique of Exploration 3 to determine the number of terms of the Maclaurin series for $\cos x$ that are needed to approximate the value of $\cos 18$ accurate to within 0.001 of the true value.

30. Writing to Learn Based on what you know about polynomial functions, explain why no Taylor polynomial of any order could actually equal $\sin x$.

31. Writing to Learn Your friend has memorized the Maclaurin series for both $\sin x$ and $\cos x$ but is having a hard time remembering which is which. Assuming that your friend knows the trigonometric functions well, what are some tips you could give that would help match $\sin x$ and $\cos x$ with their correct series?

32. What is the coefficient of x^5 in the Maclaurin series generated by $\sin 3x$?

33. What is the coefficient of $(x - 2)^3$ in the Taylor series generated by $\ln x$ at $x = 2$?

34. Writing to Learn Review the definition of the *linearization* of a differentiable function f at a in Chapter 5. What is the connection between the linearization of f and Taylor polynomials?

35. *Linearizations at Inflection Points*

(a) As the figure below suggests, linearizations fit particularly well at inflection points. As another example, graph *Newton's serpentine* $f(x) = 4x/(x^2 + 1)$ together with its linearizations at $x = 0$ and $x = \sqrt{3}$.

(b) Show that if the graph of a twice-differentiable function $f(x)$ has an inflection point at $x = a$, then the linearization of f at $x = a$ is also the second-order Taylor polynomial of f at $x = a$. This explains why tangent lines fit so well at inflection points.

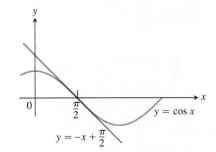

The graph of $f(x) = \cos x$ and its linearization at $\pi/2$. (Exercise 35)

36. According to the table of Maclaurin series, the power series

$$x - \frac{x^3}{3} + \frac{x^5}{5} - \cdots + (-1)^n \frac{x^{2n+1}}{2n + 1} + \cdots$$

converges at $x = \pm 1$. To what number does it converge when $x = 1$? To what number does it converge when $x = -1$?

Standardized Test Questions

In Exercises 37 and 38, the Taylor series generated by $f(x)$ at $x = 0$ is

$$x - \frac{x^3}{3} + \frac{x^5}{5} - \cdots + (-1)^n \frac{x^{2n+1}}{2n + 1} + \cdots.$$

37. True or False $f(0) = 0$. Justify your answer.

38. True or False $f'''(0) = -1/3$. Justify your answer.

39. Multiple Choice If $f(0) = 0, f'(0) = 1, f''(0) = 0$, and $f'''(0) = 2$, then which of the following is the third-order Taylor polynomial generated by $f(x)$ at $x = 0$?

(A) $2x^3 + x$ (B) $\frac{1}{3}x^3 + \frac{1}{2}x$ (C) $\frac{2}{3}x^3 + x$

(D) $2x^3 - x$ (E) $\frac{1}{3}x^3 + x$

40. Multiple Choice Which of the following is the coefficient of x^4 in the Maclaurin series generated by $\cos(3x)$?

(A) $27/8$ (B) 9   (C) $1/24$ (D) 0   (E) $-27/8$

41. **Multiple Choice** Which of the following is the fourth-order Taylor polynomial for $\sin(x)$ at $x = \pi/2$?

(A) $(x - \pi/2) - \dfrac{(x - \pi/2)^2}{2!} + \dfrac{(x - \pi/2)^4}{4!}$

(B) $1 + \dfrac{(x - \pi/2)^2}{2!} + \dfrac{(x - \pi/2)^4}{4!}$

(C) $1 - \dfrac{(x - \pi/2)^2}{2!} + \dfrac{(x - \pi/2)^4}{4!}$

(D) $1 - (x - \pi/2)^2 + (x - \pi/2)^4$

(E) $1 + (x - \pi/2)^2 + (x - \pi/2)^4$

42. **Multiple Choice** Which of the following is the Taylor series for $\sin(x)$ at $x = \pi/2$?

(A) $\displaystyle\sum_{n=0}^{\infty} (-1)^n \dfrac{(x - \pi/2)^{2n}}{(2n)!}$

(B) $\displaystyle\sum_{n=0}^{\infty} (-1)^n \dfrac{(x - \pi/2)^{2n+1}}{(2n)!}$

(C) $\displaystyle\sum_{n=0}^{\infty} \dfrac{(x - \pi/2)^{2n}}{(2n)!}$

(D) $\displaystyle\sum_{n=0}^{\infty} (-1)^n (x - \pi/2)^{2n}$

(E) $\displaystyle\sum_{n=0}^{\infty} (x - \pi/2)^{2n}$

Explorations

43. **(a)** Using the table of Maclaurin series, find a power series to represent $f(x) = (\sin x)/x$.

(b) The power series you found in part (a) is not quite a Maclaurin series for f, because f is technically not eligible to have a Maclaurin series. Why not?

(c) If we redefine f as follows, then the power series in part (a) *will* be a Maclaurin series for f. What is the value of k?

$$f(x) = \begin{cases} \dfrac{\sin x}{x}, & x \neq 0, \\ k, & x = 0 \end{cases}$$

44. **Group Activity** Find a function f whose Maclaurin series is

$$1x^1 + 2x^2 + 3x^3 + \cdots + nx^n + \cdots.$$

Extending the Ideas

45. **The Binomial Series** Let $f(x) = (1 + x)^m$ for some nonzero constant m.

(a) Show that $f'''(x) = m(m - 1)(m - 2)(1 + x)^{m-3}$.

(b) Extend the result of part (a) to show that

$$f^{(k)}(0) = m(m - 1)(m - 2) \cdots (m - k + 1).$$

(c) Find the coefficient of x^k in the Maclaurin series generated by f.

(d) We define the symbol $\dbinom{m}{k}$ as follows:

$$\binom{m}{k} = \frac{m(m - 1)(m - 2) \cdots (m - k + 1)}{k!},$$

with the understanding that

$$\binom{m}{0} = 1 \quad \text{and} \quad \binom{m}{1} = m.$$

With this notation, show that the Maclaurin series generated by $f(x) = (1 + x)^m$ is

$$\sum_{k=0}^{\infty} \binom{m}{k} x^k.$$

This is called the **binomial series.**

46. **(Continuation of Exercise 45)** If m is a positive integer, explain why the Maclaurin series generated by f is a polynomial of degree m. (This means that

$$(1 + x)^m = \sum_{k=0}^{m} \binom{m}{k} x^k.$$

You may recognize this result as the **Binomial Theorem** from algebra.)

10.3 Taylor's Theorem

You will be able to analyze truncation error for Taylor polynomials using the alternating series error bound and the Lagrange error bound found in Taylor's Theorem.

- Taylor polynomials and truncation error
- Truncation error for a geometric series
- Truncation error bound for certain alternating series
- Taylor's Theorem with Remainder
- The Lagrange error bound
- The Remainder Bounding Theorem
- Deriving Euler's Formula from Maclaurin series

Taylor Polynomials

While there is a certain unspoiled beauty in the exactness of a convergent Taylor series, it is the inexact Taylor polynomials that essentially do all the work. It is satisfying to know, for example, that sin x can be found *exactly* by summing an infinite Taylor series, but if we want to use that information to find sin 3, we will have to evaluate Taylor polynomials until we arrive at an *approximation* with which we are satisfied. Even a computer must deal with finite sums.

EXAMPLE 1 Approximating a Function to Specifications

Find a Taylor polynomial that will serve as an adequate substitute for sin x on the interval $[-\pi, \pi]$.

SOLUTION

You do not have to be a professional mathematician to appreciate the imprecision of this problem as written. We are simply unable to proceed until someone decides what an "adequate" substitute is! We will revisit this issue shortly, but for now let us accept the following clarification of "adequate."

By "adequate," we mean that the polynomial should differ from sin x by less than 0.0001 anywhere on the interval.

Now we have a clear mission: Choose $P_n(x)$ so that $|P_n(x) - \sin x| < 0.0001$ for every x in the interval $[-\pi, \pi]$. How do we do this?

Recall the nine graphs of the partial sums of the Maclaurin series for sin x in Section 10.2. They show that the approximations get worse as x moves away from 0, suggesting that if we can make $|P_n(\pi) - \sin \pi| < 0.0001$, then P_n will be adequate throughout the interval. Since sin $\pi = 0$, this means that we need to make $|P_n(\pi)| < 0.0001$.

We evaluate the partial sums at $x = \pi$, adding a term at a time, eventually arriving at the following:

$$\pi - \pi^3/3! + \pi{}^{\wedge}5/5! - \pi$$
$${}^{\wedge}7/7! + \pi{}^{\wedge}9/9! - \pi{}^{\wedge}1$$
$$1/11! + \pi{}^{\wedge}13/13!$$
$$2.114256749\text{E}^-5$$

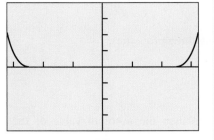

$[-\pi, \pi]$ by $[-0.00004, 0.00004]$

Figure 10.7 The graph shows that $|P_{13}(x) - \sin x| < 0.00010$ throughout the interval $[-\pi, \pi]$. (Example 1)

As graphical support that the polynomial $P_{13}(x)$ is adequate throughout the interval, we graph the *absolute error* of the approximation, namely $|P_{13}(x) - \sin x|$, in the window $[-\pi, \pi]$ by $[-0.00004, 0.00004]$ (Figure 10.7). ***Now Try Exercise 11.***

   In practical terms, then, we would like to be able to use Taylor polynomials to approximate functions over the intervals of convergence of the Taylor series, and we would like to keep the error of the approximation within specified bounds. Since the error results from *truncating* the series down to a polynomial (that is, cutting it off after some number of terms), we call it the **truncation error.**

$y = x^8/(1 - x^2)$

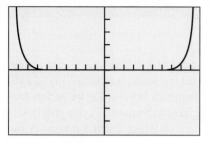

[–1, 1] by [–5, 5]

Figure 10.8 A graph of the truncation error on $(-1, 1)$ if $P_6(x)$ is used to approximate $1/(1 - x^2)$. (Example 2)

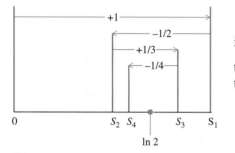

Figure 10.9 The partial sums of this alternating series oscillate back and forth on either side of their eventual sum, ln 2. This guarantees that the truncation error is always less than the first omitted term of the series in magnitude.

EXAMPLE 2 Truncation Error for a Geometric Series

Find a formula for the truncation error if we use $1 + x^2 + x^4 + x^6$ to approximate $1/(1 - x^2)$ over the interval $(-1, 1)$.

SOLUTION

We recognize this polynomial as the fourth partial sum of the geometric series for $1/(1 - x^2)$. Since this series converges to $1/(1 - x^2)$ on $(-1, 1)$, the truncation error is the absolute value of the part that we threw away, namely,

$$\left| x^8 + x^{10} + \cdots + x^{2n} + \cdots \right|.$$

This is the absolute value of a geometric series with first term x^8 and $r = x^2$. Therefore,

$$\left| x^8 + x^{10} + \cdots + x^{2n} + \cdots \right| = \left| \frac{x^8}{1 - x^2} \right| = \frac{x^8}{1 - x^2}.$$

Figure 10.8 shows that the error is small near 0, but increases as x gets closer to 1 or -1.

Now Try Exercise 13.

You may recall in Section 10.1 that we had you look at calculator evidence that the infinite series $1 - \dfrac{1}{2} + \dfrac{1}{3} - \dfrac{1}{4} + \cdots$ converges to ln 2. In fact, this particular series has three properties that also enable us to say something simple about the truncation error. The three properties are:

1. the terms alternate in sign;
2. the terms decrease in absolute value;
3. the terms approach 0 as a limit.

Because of these three properties, the partial sums oscillate back and forth on either side of their eventual sum as they converge to ln 2 in the limit (Figure 10.9).

Since the nth partial sum and the $(n + 1)$st partial sum are on opposite sides of ln 2, this means that the $(n + 1)$st term of the series is bigger than the truncation error! We will revisit this important fact when we study Leibniz's Theorem in Section 10.5, but for now let us accept it as another special case for analyzing truncation error.

Alternating Series Error Bound

Suppose the terms of a series have the following three properties:

1. the terms alternate in sign;
2. the terms decrease in absolute value;
3. the terms approach 0 as a limit.

Then the truncation error after n terms is less than the absolute value of the $(n + 1)$st term.

So we have a way of *computing* the truncation error for geometric series and a way of *bounding* the truncation error for particular kinds of alternating series, but what can we say about the truncation error for series that do not fit into either of these categories? That practical question sets the stage for Taylor's Theorem.

The Remainder

Every truncation splits a Taylor series into two equally significant pieces: the Taylor polynomial $P_n(x)$ that gives us the approximation, and the *remainder* $R_n(x)$ that tells us whether the approximation is any good. Taylor's Theorem is about both pieces.

THEOREM 3 Taylor's Theorem with Remainder

If f has derivatives of all orders in an open interval I containing a, then for each positive integer n and for each x in I,

$$f(x) = f(a) + f'(a)(x - a) + \frac{f''(a)}{2!}(x - a)^2 + \cdots$$

$$+ \frac{f^{(n)}(a)}{n!}(x - a)^n + R_n(x),$$

where

$$R_n(x) = \frac{f^{(n+1)}(c)}{(n + 1)!}(x - a)^{n+1}$$

for some c between a and x.

Pause for a moment to consider how remarkable this theorem is. If we wish to approximate f by a polynomial of degree n over an interval I, the theorem gives us both a formula for the *polynomial* and a formula for the *error* involved in using that approximation over the interval I.

The first equation in Taylor's Theorem is **Taylor's formula.** The function $R_n(x)$ is the **remainder of order n** or the **error term** for the approximation of f by $P_n(x)$ over I. It is also called the **Lagrange form of the remainder,** and bounds on $R_n(x)$ found using this form are **Lagrange error bounds.**

The introduction of $R_n(x)$ finally gives us a mathematically precise way to define what we mean when we say that a Taylor series converges to a function on an interval. If $R_n(x) \to 0$ as $n \to \infty$ for all x in I, we say that the Taylor series generated by f at $x = a$ **converges to f** on I, and we write

$$f(x) = \sum_{k=0}^{\infty} \frac{f^{(k)}(a)}{k!}(x - a)^k.$$

EXAMPLE 3 Proving Convergence of a Maclaurin Series

Prove that the series

$$\sum_{k=0}^{\infty} (-1)^k \frac{x^{2k+1}}{(2k + 1)!}$$

converges to $\sin x$ for all real x.

SOLUTION

We need to consider what happens to $R_n(x)$ as $n \to \infty$.

By Taylor's Theorem,

$$R_n(x) = \frac{f^{(n+1)}(c)}{(n + 1)!}(x - 0)^{n+1},$$

where $f^{(n+1)}(c)$ is the $(n + 1)$st derivative of $\sin x$ evaluated at some c between x and 0. This does not seem at first glance to give us much information, but *for this*
continued

particular function we can say something very significant about $f^{(n+1)}(c)$: It lies between -1 and 1 inclusive. Therefore, no matter what x is, we have

$$|R_n(x)| = \left| \frac{f^{(n+1)}(c)}{(n+1)!}(x-0)^{n+1} \right|$$

$$= \frac{|f^{(n+1)}(c)|}{(n+1)!}|x^{n+1}|$$

$$\leq \frac{1}{(n+1)!}|x^{n+1}| = \frac{|x|^{n+1}}{(n+1)!}$$

What happens to $|x|^{n+1}/(n+1)!$ as $n \to \infty$? The numerator is a product of $n+1$ factors, all of them $|x|$. The denominator is a product of $n+1$ factors, the largest of which eventually exceed $|x|$ and keep on growing as $n \to \infty$. The factorial growth in the denominator, therefore, eventually outstrips the exponential growth in the numerator, and we have $|x|^{n+1}/(n+1)! \to 0$ for all x. This means that $R_n(x) \to 0$ for all x, which completes the proof. ***Now Try Exercise 15.***

EXPLORATION 1 Your Turn

Modify the steps of the proof in Example 3 to prove that

$$\sum_{k=0}^{\infty} (-1)^k \frac{x^{2k}}{(2k)!}$$

converges to $\cos x$ for all real x.

Bounding the Remainder

Notice in Example 3 and Exploration 1 that we were able to use the remainder formula in Taylor's Theorem to verify the convergence of two Taylor series to their generating functions ($\sin x$ and $\cos x$) for all real numbers, and yet in neither case did we have to find an actual value for $f^{(n+1)}(c)$. Let us take a closer look at the error term to see how we might generalize this approach.

Behavior as $n \to \infty$ depends on f and c.

Gets bigger exponentially if $|x-a| > 1$, but gets smaller exponentially if $|x-a| < 1$.

$$R_n(x) = f^{(n+1)}(c)\frac{(x-a)^{n+1}}{(n+1)!}$$

Gets bigger no matter what, and factorial growth outstrips exponential growth.

The Lagrange formula for the error suggests that $\lim_{n\to\infty} R_n(x)$ will be zero *unless* the $f^{(n+1)}(c)$ factor grows without bound. In fact, it will still be zero if the $f^{(n+1)}(c)$ factor only contributes more exponential growth to the numerator. That is the idea conveyed in the following Remainder Bounding Theorem.

THEOREM 4 Remainder Bounding Theorem

If there are positive constants M and r such that $\left|f^{(n+1)}(t)\right| \le Mr^{n+1}$ for all t between a and x, then the remainder $R_n(x)$ in Taylor's Theorem satisfies the inequality

$$\left|R_n(x)\right| \le M\frac{r^{n+1}\left|x-a\right|^{n+1}}{(n+1)!}.$$

If these conditions hold for every n and all the other conditions of Taylor's Theorem are satisfied by f, then the series converges to $f(x)$.

It does not matter if M and r are huge; the important thing is that they do not get any *more huge* as $n \to \infty$. This allows the factorial growth to outstrip the exponential growth and thereby sweep $R_n(x)$ to zero.

EXAMPLE 4 Proving Convergence with the Remainder Bounding Theorem

The Maclaurin series for e^{7x} is $\displaystyle\sum_{n=0}^{\infty} \frac{(7x)^n}{n!}$. Prove that it converges to e^{7x} for all x.

SOLUTION

First, note that if $f(t) = e^{7t}$, then $f^{(n+1)}(t) = 7^{n+1}e^{7t}$. On any interval $[0, x]$, the increasing function e^{7t} is bounded by $M = e^{7x}$, so $\left|f^{(n+1)}(t)\right| \le M \cdot 7^{n+1}$ for all t between 0 and x. On any interval $[x, 0]$, the increasing function e^{7t} is bounded by $M = 1$, so again $\left|f^{(n+1)}(t)\right| \le M \cdot 7^{n+1}$ for all t between 0 and x. By the Remainder Bounding Theorem, the series converges to e^{7x} in either case. Since x is arbitrary, the series therefore converges for all x.   ***Now Try Exercise 17.***

Analyzing Truncation Error

You now have three different ways to analyze the error when approximating a function at a point by a truncated series. Let us review them briefly.

Geometric Series Error: If you happen to be truncating a convergent geometric series $\displaystyle\sum_{n=0}^{\infty} ar^n$ after n terms, then the remaining terms form a geometric series. The error can be found exactly by using the usual formula with first term a_{n+1} and ratio r. Thus, $error = \left|\dfrac{a_{n+1}}{1-r}\right|$. In practice, of course, there is no real need to approximate the sum of a convergent geometric series, since you can find the sum exactly.

Alternating Series Error Bound: If you happen to be truncating a series $\displaystyle\sum_{n=1}^{\infty} a_n$ that *is alternating in sign*, with terms that *decrease in absolute value* with a *limit of zero*, then there is a convenient upper bound on the error: the absolute value of the first discarded term. Thus, if the series is truncated after n terms, $error < \left|a_{n+1}\right|$. Notice that this is *not* a formula for the error itself, which might be considerably smaller than the bound.

Lagrange Error Formula: If you truncate *any* Taylor series $\displaystyle\sum_{n=0}^{\infty} f^{(n)}(a)\frac{(x-a)^n}{n!}$ after n terms, then the exact error is given by $error = \left|f^{(n+1)}(c)\frac{(x-a)^{n+1}}{(n+1)!}\right|$ for some c

between x and a. When using an nth-degree Taylor polynomial about a to approximate some $f(x)$, you will know n, a, and x, but not c. However, you can still *bound* the error if you can find an upper bound on $f^{(n+1)}(c)$ for all c between a and x.

EXAMPLE 5 Bounding the Remainder (Two Ways)

Suppose we use the first two terms of the Maclaurin series for $f(x) = \ln(1 + x)$ to approximate $f(0.1)$. Find a bound on the error by using (a) the alternating series error bound, and (b) the Lagrange error formula.

SOLUTION

The truncated polynomial is $P_2(x) = x - \dfrac{x^2}{2}$, so $f(0.1) \approx 0.1 - 0.1^2/2 = 0.095$.

(a) Since the Maclaurin series for $f(x) = \ln(1 + x)$ satisfies the three criteria for using the alternating series error bound, we can say that the error is less than the magnitude of the third term of the series: $error < |0.1^3/3| = 3.33 \times 10^{-4}$.

(b) We first compute that $f^{(3)}(c) = 2(1 + c)^{-3}$. Then, using the Lagrange error formula,

we find $error = \left| f^{(n+1)}(c)\dfrac{(x - a)^{n+1}}{(n + 1)!} \right| = 2(1 + c)^{-3}\dfrac{(0.1 - 0)^3}{3!} = \dfrac{(0.1)^3}{3(1 + c)^3}$.

Since $0 < c < 0.1$, the denominator is greater than 3, and so $error < |0.1^3/3| = 3.33 \times 10^{-4}$.

The actual error can be computed with a calculator: $error = |\ln(1 + 0.1) - 0.095| = 3.102 \times 10^{-4}$. We see that the error is less than the bound, as predicted.

Now Try Exercise 19.

It is also possible to find an upper bound for the error when a Taylor polynomial is used to approximate a function on an *entire interval*. In this case, it is necessary to find an upper bound for $f^{(n+1)}(c)$ on the interval (as before), and it is also necessary to find an upper bound on the magnitude of $|(x - a)^{n+1}|$. This amounts to finding the value of x in the interval that is the greatest distance from a.

EXAMPLE 6 Bounding the Error on an Interval

Suppose the second-order Taylor polynomial for $f(x)$ about $x = 2$ is used as an approximation for $f(x)$, and suppose that $|f^{(3)}(x)| < 2.3$ for all x in the interval $[2, 2.5]$. Show that $|f(x) - P_2(x)| < 0.05$ for all x in the interval $[2, 2.5]$.

SOLUTION

First, observe that the value of x in the interval $[2, 2.5]$ that maximizes $(x - 2)^3$ is $x = 2.5$.

$$|f(x) - P_2(x)| = error = \left| f^{(3)}(c) \cdot \dfrac{(x - 2)^3}{3!} \right| < 2.3 \cdot \dfrac{(2.5 - 2)^3}{3!}$$

$$= \dfrac{2.3}{48} < \dfrac{2.4}{48} = 0.05$$

Now Try Exercise 21.

Euler's Formula

We have seen that $\sin x$, $\cos x$, and e^x equal their respective Maclaurin series for all real numbers x. It can also be shown that this is true for all *complex* numbers, although we would need to extend our concept of limit to know what convergence would mean in that context. Accept for the moment that we can substitute complex numbers into these power series, and let us see where that might lead.

Srinivasa Ramanujan
(1887–1920)

Ramanujan, from southern India, wrote with amazing originality and depth on a wide range of topics in mathematics, including infinite series, prime and composite numbers, integers as the sum of squares, function theory, and combinatorics. His theorems have influenced medical research and statistical mechanics. One of his identities has been used by computer programmers to calculate the decimal expansion of π to millions of digits. There are still areas of his work that have not been explored. Ramanujan was largely self taught and, although he worked with the British mathematician G. H. Hardy of Cambridge, he never graduated from college because he neglected his other studies for mathematics.

We mentioned at the beginning of the chapter that Leonhard Euler had derived some powerful results using infinite series. One of the most impressive was the surprisingly simple relationship he discovered that connects the exponential function e^x to the trigonometric functions sin x and cos x. You do not need a deep understanding of complex numbers to understand what Euler did, but you do need to recall the powers of $i = \sqrt{-1}$.

$$i^1 = i \qquad i^5 = i$$
$$i^2 = -1 \qquad i^6 = -1$$
$$i^3 = -i \qquad i^7 = -i$$
$$i^4 = 1 \qquad i^8 = 1 \quad \text{etc.}$$

Now try this exploration!

EXPLORATION 2   *Euler's Formula*

Assume that e^x, cos x, and sin x equal their Maclaurin series (as in the table in Section 10.2) for complex numbers as well as for real numbers.

1. Find the Maclaurin series for e^{ix}.
2. Use the result of part 1 and the Maclaurin series for cos x and sin x to prove that $e^{ix} = \cos x + i \sin x$. This equation is known as **Euler's formula.**
3. Use Euler's formula to prove that $e^{i\pi} + 1 = 0$. This beautiful equation, which brings together the five most celebrated numbers in mathematics in such a stunningly unexpected way, is also widely known as Euler's formula. (There are still others. The prolific Euler had more than his share.)

Quick Review 10.3   *(For help, go to Sections 3.3 and 4.1.)*

Exercise numbers with a gray background indicate problems that the authors have designed to be solved *without a calculator.*

In Exercises 1–5, find the smallest number M that bounds $|f|$ from above on the interval I (that is, find the smallest M such that $|f(x)| \le M$ for all x in I).

1. $f(x) = 2 \cos (3x)$, $I = [-2\pi, 2\pi]$

2. $f(x) = x^2 + 3$, $I = [1, 2]$

3. $f(x) = 2^x$, $I = [-3, 0]$

4. $f(x) = \dfrac{x}{x^2 + 1}$, $I = [-2, 2]$

5. $f(x) = \begin{cases} 2 - x^2, & x \le 1, \\ 2x - 1, & x > 1, \end{cases}$ $I = [-3, 3]$

In Exercises 6–10, tell whether the function has derivatives of all orders at the given value of a.

6. $\dfrac{x}{x + 1}$, $a = 0$

7. $|x^2 - 4|$, $a = 2$

8. $\sin x + \cos x$, $a = \pi$

9. e^{-x}, $a = 0$

10. $x^{3/2}$, $a = 0$

Section 10.3 Exercises

In Exercises 1–10, give the first four nonzero terms and the general term of the Maclaurin series for the function. You may use the Table of Maclaurin Series found at the end of Section 10.2.

1. e^{-2x}

2. $\cos (\pi x/2)$

3. $5 \sin (-x)$

4. $\ln (1 + x^2)$

5. $(1 - x)^{-2}$

6. $\sin x - x + x^3/3!$

7. xe^x

8. $\cos^2 x$ [*Hint:* $\cos^2 x = (1/2)(1 + \cos 2x)$.]

9. $\sin^2 x$ [*Hint:* Adapt the hint for #8.]

10. $\dfrac{x^2}{1 - 2x}$

11. Use graphs to find the minimal degree of a Taylor polynomial $P_n(x)$ for $\ln(1+x)$ so that $|P_n(x) - \ln(1+x)| < 0.001$ for every x in $[-0.5, 0.5]$.

12. Use graphs to find the minimal degree of a Taylor polynomial $P_n(x)$ for $\cos x$ so that $|P_n(x) - \cos x| < 0.001$ for every x in $[-\pi, \pi]$.

13. Find a formula for the truncation error if we use $P_6(x)$ to approximate $\dfrac{1}{1-2x}$ on $(-1/2, 1/2)$.

14. Find a formula for the truncation error if we use $P_9(x)$ to approximate $\dfrac{1}{1-x}$ on $(-1, 1)$.

In Exercises 15–18, use the Remainder Bounding Theorem to prove that the Maclaurin series for the given function converges to that function for all real x.

15. $\cos x$

16. $\sin 5x$

17. $\cos 8x$

18. e^{5x}

19. Suppose you use $P_3(x) = x - (x^3/6)$ to approximate $\sin(0.5)$. Give a bound on the error of the approximation based on **(a)** the alternating series error bound and **(b)** the Lagrange error formula.

20. Suppose you use $P_2(x) = 1 - (x^2/2)$ to approximate $\cos(0.5)$. Give a bound on the error of the approximation based on **(a)** the alternating series error bound and **(b)** the Lagrange error formula.

21. If $P_2(x) = 1 - (x^2/2)$ is used to approximate $\cos x$ for $|x| < 0.5$, find a bound for the maximum error based on **(a)** the alternating series error bound and **(b)** the Lagrange error formula. Will the approximation be too large or too small?

22. Find a bound based on **(a)** the alternating series error bound and **(b)** the Lagrange error formula for the closeness of the approximation $\sin x \approx x$ when $|x| < 0.1$. **(c)** For which of these values is $x < \sin x$?

23. The approximation $\sqrt{1+x} \approx 1 + (x/2)$ can be used when x is small. If $|x| < 0.01$, estimate the maximum error graphically.

24. Hyperbolic sine and cosine The hyperbolic sine and hyperbolic cosine functions, denoted sinh and cosh respectively, are defined as

$$\sinh x = \frac{e^x - e^{-x}}{2} \quad \text{and} \quad \cosh x = \frac{e^x + e^{-x}}{2}.$$

(Appendix A6 gives more information about hyperbolic functions.)

Find the Maclaurin series generated by $\sinh x$ and $\cosh x$.

25. Use the Remainder Bounding Theorem to prove that $\cosh x$ equals its Maclaurin series for all real numbers x.

26. Writing to Learn Review the statement of the Mean Value Theorem (Section 5.2) and explain its relationship to Taylor's Theorem.

Quadratic Approximations Just as we call the Taylor polynomial of order 1 generated by f at $x = a$ the *linearization* of f at a, we call the Taylor polynomial of order 2 generated by f at $x = a$ the *quadratic approximation* of f at a. The graph of the linearization matches the value and slope of f at a, while the graph of the quadratic approximation matches the value, slope, and curvature.

In Exercises 27–31, find **(a)** the linearization and **(b)** the quadratic approximation of the given function at $x = 0$. Then use your grapher to verify the expected graphical behavior.

27. $f(x) = \ln(\cos x)$

28. $f(x) = e^{\sin x}$

29. $f(x) = 1/\sqrt{1-x^2}$

30. $f(x) = \sec x$

31. $f(x) = \tan x$

32. Let f be the function given by $f(x) = \sin\left(5x + \dfrac{\pi}{4}\right)$, and let $P_3(x)$ be the third-degree Taylor polynomial for f about $x = 0$.

(a) Find $P(x)$ by computing the coefficients.

(b) Find the coefficient of x^{22} in the Taylor series for f about $x = 0$.

(c) Use the Lagrange error bound to show that

$$\left| f\left(\frac{1}{10}\right) - P_3\left(\frac{1}{10}\right) \right| < \frac{1}{100}.$$

(d) Let G be the function given by $G(x) = \displaystyle\int_0^x f(t)\, dt$. Write the third-degree Taylor polynomial for G about $x = 0$.

33. Let f be the function given by $f(x) = \dfrac{2x}{1+x^2}$.

(a) Write the first four nonzero terms and the general term of the Taylor series for f about $x = 0$.

(b) Does the series found in part (a), when evaluated at $x = 1$, converge to $f(1)$? Explain why or why not.

(c) The derivative of $\ln(1+x^2)$ is $\dfrac{2x}{1+x^2}$. Write the first four nonzero terms of the Taylor series for $\ln(1+x^2)$ about $x = 0$.

(d) Use the series found in part (c) to find a rational number A such that $\left| A - \ln\left(\dfrac{5}{4}\right) \right| < \dfrac{1}{100}$. Justify your answer.

34. Let $f(x) = \sin(x^2) + \cos x$.

The graph of $y = |f^{(5)}(x)|$ is shown below.

(a) Write the first four nonzero terms of the Taylor series for f about $x = 0$.

(b) Find the value of $f^{(6)}(0)$.

(c) Let $P_4(x)$ be the fourth-degree Taylor polynomial for f about $x = 0$. Using information from the graph of $y = |f^{(5)}(x)|$, show that $\left| P_4\left(\dfrac{1}{4}\right) - f\left(\dfrac{1}{4}\right) \right| < \dfrac{1}{3000}$.

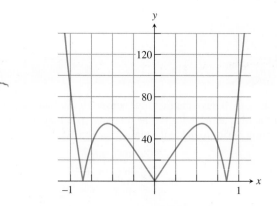

35. Consider the initial value problem,

$$\frac{dy}{dx} = e^{-x^2} \quad \text{and} \quad y = 2 \quad \text{when } x = 0.$$

(a) Can you find a formula for the function y that does not involve any integrals?

(b) Can you represent y by a power series?

(c) For what values of x does this power series actually equal the function y? Give a reason for your answer.

36. (a) Construct the Maclaurin series for $\ln(1 - x)$.

(b) Use this series and the series for $\ln(1 + x)$ to construct a Maclaurin series for

$$\ln\left(\frac{1 + x}{1 - x}\right).$$

37. *Identifying Graphs* Which well-known functions are approximated on the interval $(-\pi/2, \pi/2)$ by the following Taylor polynomials?

(a) $x + \dfrac{x^3}{3} + \dfrac{2x^5}{15} + \dfrac{17x^7}{315} + \dfrac{62x^9}{2835}$

(b) $1 + \dfrac{x^2}{2} + \dfrac{5x^4}{24} + \dfrac{61x^6}{720} + \dfrac{277x^8}{8064}$

Standardized Test Questions

You may use a graphing calculator to solve the following problems.

38. True or False The degree of the linearization of a function f at $x = a$ must be 1. Justify your answer.

39. True or False If $\displaystyle\sum_{n=0}^{\infty} \frac{x^{n+1}}{n!} = x + x^2 + \frac{x^3}{2!} + \cdots$ is the Maclaurin series for the function $f(x)$, then $f'(0) = 1$. Justify your answer.

40. Multiple Choice Which of the following gives the Taylor polynomial of order 5 approximation to $\sin(1.5)$?

(A) 0.965   **(B)** 0.985   **(C)** 0.997   **(D)** 1.001   **(E)** 1.005

41. Multiple Choice Let $\displaystyle\sum_{n=0}^{\infty} \frac{x^{n+1}}{n!} = x + x^2 + \frac{x^3}{2!} + \cdots$ be the Maclaurin series for $f(x)$. Which of the following is $f^{(12)}(0)$, the 12th derivative of f at $x = 0$?

(A) $1/11!$ **(B)** $1/12!$ **(C)** 0   **(D)** 1   **(E)** 12

42. Multiple Choice Let $\displaystyle\sum_{n=0}^{\infty} (-1)^n \frac{x^{2n}}{(2n)!} = 1 - \frac{x^2}{2!} + \frac{x^4}{4!} - \cdots$ be the Maclaurin series for $\cos x$. Which of the following gives the smallest value of n for which $|P_n(x) - \cos x| < 0.01$ for all x in the interval $[-\pi, \pi]$?

(A) 12   **(B)** 10   **(C)** 8   **(D)** 6   **(E)** 4

43. Multiple Choice Which of the following is the quadratic approximation for $f(x) = e^{-x}$ at $x = 0$?

(A) $1 - x + \dfrac{1}{2}x^2$ **(B)** $1 - x - \dfrac{1}{2}x^2$

(C) $1 + x + \dfrac{1}{2}x^2$ **(D)** $1 + x$

(E) $1 - x$

Explorations

44. *Group Activity* Try to reinforce each other's ideas and verify your computations at each step.

(a) Use the identity

$$\sin^2 x = \frac{1}{2}(1 - \cos 2x)$$

to obtain the Maclaurin series for $\sin^2 x$.

(b) Differentiate this series to obtain the Maclaurin series for $2 \sin x \cos x$.

(c) Verify that this is the series for $\sin 2x$.

45. *Improving Approximations to π*

(a) Let P be an approximation of π accurate to n decimal places. Check with a calculator to see that $P + \sin P$ gives an approximation correct to at least $3n$ decimal places!

(b) Use the alternating series error bound and the Maclaurin series for $\sin x$ to explain what is happening in part (a). [*Hint:* Let $P = \pi + x$, where x is the error of the estimate. Why should $(P + \sin P) - \pi$ be less than x^3?]

46. *Euler's Identities* Use Euler's formula to show that

(a) $\cos\theta = \dfrac{e^{i\theta} + e^{-i\theta}}{2}$, and   **(b)** $\sin\theta = \dfrac{e^{i\theta} - e^{-i\theta}}{2i}$.

47. *A Divergent Remainder* Recall that the Maclaurin series for

$$f(x) = \frac{1}{1 - x}$$

converges only if $|x| < 1$. By analyzing partial sums of the series, find a formula for the remainder $R_n(x)$ when $x = -1$ and show that $\displaystyle\lim_{n\to\infty} R_n(x) \neq 0$.

48. *Follow-up to Exercise 47* Show that the value of c in the Lagrange error formula that will yield the error $R_n(-1)$ found in Exercise 47 is $c = 1 - 2^{\left(\frac{1}{n+2}\right)}$.

Extending the Ideas

49. When a and b are real numbers, we define $e^{(a+ib)x}$ with the equation

$$e^{(a+ib)x} = e^{ax} \cdot e^{ibx} = e^{ax}(\cos bx + i \sin bx).$$

Differentiate the right-hand side of this equation to show that

$$\frac{d}{dx} e^{(a+ib)x} = (a + ib) e^{(a+ib)x}.$$

Thus, the familiar rule

$$\frac{d}{dx} e^{kx} = k e^{kx}$$

holds for complex values of k as well as for real values.

50. *(Continuation of Exercise 49)*

(a) Confirm the antiderivative formula

$$\int e^{(a+ib)x} dx = \frac{a - ib}{a^2 + b^2} e^{(a+ib)x} + C$$

by differentiating both sides. (In this case, $C = C_1 + iC_2$ is a complex constant of integration.)

(b) Two complex numbers $a + ib$ and $c + id$ are equal if and only if $a = c$ and $b = d$. Use this fact and the formula in part (a) to evaluate $\int e^{ax} \cos bx\, dx$ and $\int e^{ax} \sin bx\, dx$.

Quick Quiz for AP* Preparation: Sections 10.1–10.3

1. Multiple Choice Which of the following is the sum of the series $\sum_{n=0}^{\infty} \dfrac{\pi^n}{e^{2n}}$?

(A) $\dfrac{e}{e - \pi}$ (B) $\dfrac{\pi}{\pi - e}$ (C) $\dfrac{\pi}{\pi - e^2}$

(D) $\dfrac{e^2}{e^2 - \pi}$ (E) The series diverges.

2. Multiple Choice Assume that f has derivatives of all orders for all real numbers x, $f(0) = 2$, $f'(0) = -1$, $f''(0) = 6$, and $f'''(0) = 12$. Which of the following is the third-order Taylor polynomial for f at $x = 0$?

(A) $2 - x + 3x^2 + 2x^3$ (B) $2 - x + 6x^2 + 12x^3$

(C) $2 - \dfrac{1}{2}x + 3x^2 + 2x^3$ (D) $-2 + x - 3x^2 - 2x^3$

(E) $2 - x + 6x^2$

3. Multiple Choice Which of the following is the Taylor series generated by $f(x) = 1/x$ at $x = 1$?

(A) $\sum_{n=0}^{\infty} (x - 1)^n$ (B) $\sum_{n=0}^{\infty} (-1)^n x^n$

(C) $\sum_{n=0}^{\infty} (-1)^n(x + 1)^n$ (D) $\sum_{n=0}^{\infty} (-1)^n \dfrac{(x - 1)^n}{n!}$

(e) $\sum_{n=0}^{\infty} (-1)^n(x - 1)^n$

4. Free Response Let f be the function defined by

$$f(x) = \sum_{n=0}^{\infty} 2\left(\frac{x + 2}{3}\right)^n$$

for all values of x for which the series converges.

(a) Find the interval of convergence for the series.

(b) Find the function that the series represents.

10.4 Radius of Convergence

You will understand the importance of convergence and will be able to use the Ratio Test to find the radius of convergence for power series.

- The importance of convergence
- The *n*th-Term Test
- The Direct Comparison Test
- Absolute and conditional convergence
- The Ratio Test
- The radius of convergence of a power series
- Possible behavior at the endpoints of an interval of convergence
- Telescoping series

Convergence

Throughout our explorations of infinite series we stressed the importance of convergence. In terms of numbers, the difference between a convergent series and a divergent series could hardly be more stark: A convergent series is a number and may be treated as such; a divergent series is not a number and must not be treated as one.

Recall that the symbol "=" means many different things in mathematics.

1. $1 + 1 = 2$ signifies *equality of real numbers.* It is a true sentence.

2. $2(x - 3) = 2x - 6$ signifies *equivalent expressions.* It is a true sentence.

3. $x^2 + 3 = 7$ is an *equation.* It is an *open sentence,* because it can be true or false, depending on whether x is a solution to the equation.

4. $(x^2 - 1)/(x + 1) = x - 1$ is an *identity.* It is a true sentence (very much like the equation in (2)), but with the important qualification that x *must be in the domain of both expressions.* If either side of the equality is undefined, the sentence is meaningless. Substituting -1 into both sides of the equation in (3) gives a sentence that is mathematically false (i.e., $4 = 7$); substituting -1 into both sides of this identity gives a sentence that is meaningless.

EXAMPLE 1 The Importance of Convergence

Consider the sentence

$$\frac{1}{1 + x^2} = 1 - x^2 + x^4 - x^6 + \cdots + (-1)^n x^{2n} + \cdots.$$

For what values of x is this an identity?

SOLUTION

The function on the left has domain all real numbers. The function on the right can be viewed as a limit of Taylor polynomials. Each Taylor polynomial has domain all real numbers, but the polynomial values *converge* only when $|x| < 1$, so the *series* has the domain $(-1, 1)$. If we graph the Taylor polynomials (Figure 10.10), we can see the dramatic convergence to $1/(1 + x^2)$ over the interval $(-1, 1)$. The divergence is just as dramatic for $|x| \geq 1$.

For values of x outside the interval, the statement in this example is meaningless. The Taylor series on the right diverges, so it is not a number. The sentence is an identity for x in $(-1, 1)$.   ***Now Try Exercise 1.***

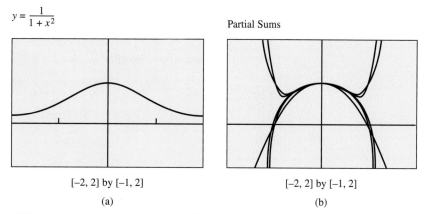

$y = \dfrac{1}{1 + x^2}$

Partial Sums

[-2, 2] by [-1, 2]

(a)

[-2, 2] by [-1, 2]

(b)

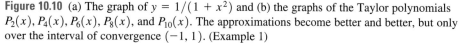

Figure 10.10 (a) The graph of $y = 1/(1 + x^2)$ and (b) the graphs of the Taylor polynomials $P_2(x)$, $P_4(x)$, $P_6(x)$, $P_8(x)$, and $P_{10}(x)$. The approximations become better and better, but only over the interval of convergence $(-1, 1)$. (Example 1)

Seki Kowa   *(1642–1708)*

Child prodigy, brilliant mathematician, and inspirational teacher, Seki Kowa was born into a samurai warrior family in Fujioka, Kozuke, Japan, and adopted by the family of an accountant.
Among his contributions were an improved method of solving higher-degree equations, the use of determinants in solving simultaneous equations, and a form of calculus known in Japan as *yenri*. It is difficult to know the full extent of his work because the samurai code demanded great modesty. Seki Kowa is credited with awakening in Japan a scientific spirit that continues to this day.

As convincing as these graphs are, they do not *prove* convergence or divergence as $n \to \infty$. The series in Example 1 happens to be geometric, so we do have an analytic proof that it converges for $|x| < 1$ and diverges for $|x| \geq 1$, but for nongeometric series we do not have such undeniable assurance about convergence (yet).

In this section we develop a strategy for finding the interval of convergence of an arbitrary power series and backing it up with proof. We begin by noting that any power series of the form $\sum_{n=0}^{\infty} c_n(x - a)^n$ always converges at $x = a$, thus assuring us of at least one coordinate on the real number line where the series must converge. We have encountered power series that converge for all real numbers (the Maclaurin series for $\sin x$, $\cos x$, and e^x), and we have encountered power series like the series in Example 1 that converge only on a finite interval centered at a. A useful fact about power series is that those are the only possibilities, as the following theorem attests.

THEOREM 5   The Convergence Theorem for Power Series

There are three possibilities for $\sum_{n=0}^{\infty} c_n(x - a)^n$ with respect to convergence:

1. There is a positive number R such that the series diverges for $|x - a| > R$ but converges for $|x - a| < R$. The series may or may not converge at either of the endpoints $x = a - R$ and $x = a + R$.
2. The series converges for every x $(R = \infty)$.
3. The series converges at $x = a$ and diverges elsewhere $(R = 0)$.

The number R is the **radius of convergence,** and the set of all values of x for which the series converges is the **interval of convergence.** The radius of convergence completely determines the interval of convergence if R is either zero or infinite. For $0 < R < \infty$, however, there remains the question of what happens at the endpoints of the interval. The table of Maclaurin series at the end of Section 10.2 includes intervals of convergence that are open, half-open, and closed.

We will learn how to find the radius of convergence first, and then we will settle the endpoint question in Section 10.5.

nth-Term Test

The most obvious requirement for convergence of a series is that the *n*th term must go to zero as $n \to \infty$. If the partial sums are approaching a limit S, then they also must be getting close to one another, so that for a convergent series $\sum a_n$,

$$\lim_{n \to \infty} a_n = \lim_{n \to \infty} (S_n - S_{n-1}) = S - S = 0.$$

This gives a handy test for divergence:

THEOREM 6   The *n*th-Term Test for Divergence

$\sum_{n=1}^{\infty} a_n$ diverges if $\lim_{n \to \infty} a_n$ fails to exist or is different from zero.

Comparing Nonnegative Series

An effective way to show that a series $\sum a_n$ of nonnegative numbers *converges* is to compare it term by term with a known convergent series $\sum c_n$.

THEOREM 7 **The Direct Comparison Test**

Let $\sum a_n$ be a series with no negative terms.

(a) $\sum a_n$ converges if there is a convergent series $\sum c_n$ with $a_n \leq c_n$ for all $n > N$, for some integer N.

(b) $\sum a_n$ diverges if there is a divergent series $\sum d_n$ of nonnegative terms with $a_n \geq d_n$ for all $n > N$, for some integer N.

If we can show that $\sum a_n$, $a_n \geq 0$ is eventually dominated by a convergent series, that will establish the convergence of $\sum a_n$. If we can show that $\sum a_n$ eventually dominates a divergent series of nonnegative terms, that will establish the divergence of $\sum a_n$.

We leave the proof to Exercises 61 and 62.

EXAMPLE 2 Proving Convergence by Comparison

Prove that $\displaystyle\sum_{n=0}^{\infty} \frac{x^{2n}}{(n!)^2}$ converges for all real x.

SOLUTION

Let x be any real number. The series

$$\sum_{n=0}^{\infty} \frac{x^{2n}}{(n!)^2}$$

has no negative terms.

For any n, we have

$$\frac{x^{2n}}{(n!)^2} \leq \frac{x^{2n}}{n!} = \frac{(x^2)^n}{n!}.$$

We recognize

$$\sum_{n=0}^{\infty} \frac{(x^2)^n}{n!}$$

as the Taylor series for e^{x^2}, which we know converges to e^{x^2} for all real numbers. Since the e^{x^2} series dominates

$$\sum_{n=0}^{\infty} \frac{x^{2n}}{(n!)^2}$$

term by term, the latter series must also converge for all real numbers by the Direct Comparison Test. *Now Try Exercise 3.*

For the Direct Comparison Test to apply, the terms of the unknown series must be *nonnegative*. The fact that $\sum a_n$ is dominated by a convergent positive series means nothing if $\sum a_n$ diverges to $-\infty$. You might think that the requirement of nonnegativity would limit the usefulness of the Direct Comparison Test, but in practice this does not turn out to be the case. We can apply our test to $\sum |a_n|$ (which certainly has no negative terms); if $\sum |a_n|$ converges, then $\sum a_n$ converges.

DEFINITION **Absolute Convergence**

If the series $\sum |a_n|$ of absolute values converges, then $\sum a_n$ **converges absolutely.**

THEOREM 8 **Absolute Convergence Implies Convergence**

If $\sum |a_n|$ converges, then $\sum a_n$ converges.

Proof For each n,

$$-|a_n| \le a_n \le |a_n|, \quad \text{so} \quad 0 \le a_n + |a_n| \le 2|a_n|.$$

If $\sum |a_n|$ converges, then $\sum 2|a_n|$ converges, and by the Direct Comparison Test, the nonnegative series $\sum (a_n + |a_n|)$ converges. The equality $a_n = (a_n + |a_n|) - |a_n|$ now allows us to express $\sum a_n$ as the difference of two convergent series:

$$\sum a_n = \sum (a_n + |a_n| - |a_n|) = \sum (a_n + |a_n|) - \sum |a_n|$$

Therefore, $\sum a_n$ converges. ∎

EXAMPLE 3 **Using Absolute Convergence**

Show that

$$\sum_{n=0}^{\infty} \frac{(\sin x)^n}{n!}$$

converges for all x.

SOLUTION

Let x be any real number. The series

$$\sum_{n=0}^{\infty} \frac{|\sin x|^n}{n!}$$

has no negative terms, and it is term-by-term less than or equal to the series $\sum_{n=0}^{\infty} (1/n!)$, which we know converges to e. Therefore,

$$\sum_{n=0}^{\infty} \frac{|\sin x|^n}{n!}$$

converges by direct comparison. Since

$$\sum_{n=0}^{\infty} \frac{(\sin x)^n}{n!}$$

converges absolutely, it converges. *Now Try Exercise 5.*

Ratio Test

Our strategy for finding the radius of convergence for an arbitrary power series will be to check for absolute convergence using a powerful test called the *Ratio Test*.

L'Hospital's rule is occasionally helpful in determining the limits that arise here.

THEOREM 9   The Ratio Test

Let $\Sigma\, a_n$ be a series with positive terms, and with

$$\lim_{n\to\infty} \frac{a_{n+1}}{a_n} = L.$$

Then,

(a) the series *converges* if $L < 1$,
(b) the series *diverges* if $L > 1$,
(c) the test is *inconclusive* if $L = 1$.

Proof

(a) $L < 1$:

Choose some number r such that $L < r < 1$. Since

$$\lim_{n\to\infty} \frac{a_{n+1}}{a_n} = L,$$

we know that there is some N large enough so that a_{n+1}/a_n is arbitrarily close to L for all $n \geq N$. In particular, we can guarantee that for some N large enough, $(a_{n+1}/a_n) < r$ for all $n \geq N$. (See Figure 10.11.)
Thus,

$$\frac{a_{N+1}}{a_N} < r \qquad \text{so} \qquad a_{N+1} < ra_N$$

$$\frac{a_{N+2}}{a_{N+1}} < r \qquad \text{so} \qquad a_{N+2} < ra_{N+1} < r^2 a_N$$

$$\frac{a_{N+3}}{a_{N+2}} < r \qquad \text{so} \qquad a_{N+3} < ra_{N+2} < r^3 a_N$$

$$\vdots$$

This shows that for $n \geq N$ we can dominate $\Sigma\, a_n$ by $a_N\,(1 + r + r^2 + \cdots)$. Since $0 < r < 1$, this latter series is a convergent geometric series, and so $\Sigma\, a_n$ converges by the Direct Comparison Test.

(b) $L > 1$:

From some index M,

$$\frac{a_{n+1}}{a_n} > 1$$

for all $n \geq M$. In particular,

$$a_M < a_{M+1} < a_{M+2} < \cdots.$$

The terms of the series do not approach 0, so $\Sigma\, a_n$ diverges by the nth-Term Test.

(c) $L = 1$:

In Exploration 1 you will finish the proof by showing that the Ratio Test is inconclusive when $L = 1$. ∎

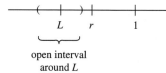

Figure 10.11 Since

$$\lim_{n\to\infty} \frac{a_{n+1}}{a_n} = L,$$

there is some N large enough so that a_{n+1}/a_n lies inside this open interval around L for all $n \geq N$. This guarantees that $a_{n+1}/a_n < r < 1$ for all $n \geq N$.

A Note on Absolute Convergence: The proof of the Ratio Test shows that the convergence of a power series inside its radius of convergence is *absolute* convergence, a stronger result than we first stated in Theorem 5. We will learn more about the distinction between convergence and absolute convergence in Section 10.5.

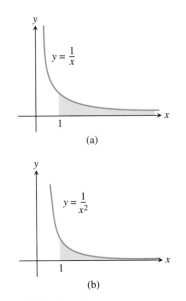

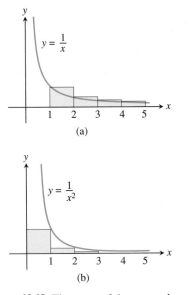

Figure 10.12 Find these areas. (Exploration 1)

Figure 10.13 The areas of the rectangles form a series in each case. (Exploration 1)

EXPLORATION 1   Finishing the Proof of the Ratio Test

Consider

$$\sum_{n=1}^{\infty} \frac{1}{n} \quad \text{and} \quad \sum_{n=1}^{\infty} \frac{1}{n^2}.$$

(We will refer to them hereafter in this exploration as $\sum 1/n$ and $\sum 1/n^2$.)

1. Show that the Ratio Test yields $L = 1$ for both series.
2. Use improper integrals to find the areas shaded in Figures 10.12a and 10.12b for $1 \leq x < \infty$.
3. Explain how Figure 10.13a shows that $\sum 1/n$ diverges, while Figure 10.13b shows that $\sum 1/n^2$ converges.
4. Explain how this proves the last part of the Ratio Test.

EXAMPLE 4 Finding the Radius of Convergence

Find the radius of convergence of

$$\sum_{n=0}^{\infty} \frac{nx^n}{10^n}.$$

SOLUTION

We check for absolute convergence using the Ratio Test.

$$\lim_{n \to \infty} \frac{|a_{n+1}|}{|a_n|} = \lim_{n \to \infty} \frac{(n+1)\,|x^{n+1}|}{10^{n+1}} \cdot \frac{10^n}{n\,|x^n|}$$

$$= \lim_{n \to \infty} \left(\frac{n+1}{n}\right)\frac{|x|}{10} = \frac{|x|}{10}$$

Setting $|x|/10 < 1$, we see that the series converges absolutely (and hence converges) for $-10 < x < 10$. The series diverges for $|x| > 10$, which means (by Theorem 5, the Convergence Theorem for Power Series) that it diverges for $x > 10$ and for $x < -10$. The radius of convergence is 10.   ***Now Try Exercise 9.***

EXAMPLE 5 A Series with Radius of Convergence 0

Find the radius of convergence of the series $\displaystyle\sum_{n=0}^{\infty} n!x^n$.

SOLUTION

We check for absolute convergence using the Ratio Test.

$$\lim_{n \to \infty} \frac{|a_{n+1}|}{|a_n|} = \lim_{n \to \infty} \frac{(n+1)!|x|^{n+1}}{n!|x|^n}$$

$$= \lim_{n \to \infty} (n+1)|x|$$

$$= \infty, \qquad x \neq 0$$

The series converges only for $x = 0$. The radius of convergence is $R = 0$.   ***Now Try Exercise 17.***

Endpoint Convergence

The Ratio Test, which is really a test for absolute convergence, establishes the radius of convergence for $\sum |c_n(x - a)^n|$. Theorem 5 guarantees that this is the same as the radius of convergence of $\sum c_n(x - a)^n$. Therefore, all that remains to be resolved about the convergence of an arbitrary power series is the question of convergence at the endpoints of the convergence interval when the radius of convergence is a finite, nonzero number.

EXPLORATION 2 Revisiting a Maclaurin Series

For what values of x does the series

$$x - \frac{x^2}{2} + \frac{x^3}{3} - \cdots + (-1)^{n-1}\frac{x^n}{n} + \cdots$$

converge?

1. Apply the Ratio Test to determine the radius of convergence.
2. Substitute the left-hand endpoint of the interval into the power series. Use Figure 10.13a of Exploration 1 to help you decide whether the resulting series converges or diverges.
3. Substitute the right-hand endpoint of the interval into the power series. You should get

$$1 - \frac{1}{2} + \frac{1}{3} - \frac{1}{4} + \cdots + \frac{(-1)^{n-1}}{n} + \cdots.$$

   Chart the progress of the partial sums of this series geometrically on a number line as follows: Start at 0. Go forward 1. Go back $1/2$. Go forward $1/3$. Go back $1/4$. Go forward $1/5$, and so on.
4. Does the series converge at the right-hand endpoint? Give a convincing argument based on your geometric journey in part 3.
5. Does the series converge *absolutely* at the right-hand endpoint?

EXAMPLE 6 Determining Convergence of a Series

Determine the convergence or divergence of the series $\sum\limits_{n=0}^{\infty} \dfrac{3^n}{5^n + 1}$.

SOLUTION

We use the Ratio Test.

$$\lim_{n\to\infty} \frac{a_{n+1}}{a_n} = \lim_{n\to\infty} \frac{\dfrac{3^{n+1}}{5^{n+1} + 1}}{\dfrac{3^n}{5^n + 1}} = \lim_{n\to\infty} \left(\frac{3^{n+1}}{5^{n+1} + 1}\right)\left(\frac{5^n + 1}{3^n}\right)$$

$$= \lim_{n\to\infty} 3\left(\frac{5^n + 1}{5^{n+1} + 1}\right)$$

$$= \lim_{n\to\infty} 3\,\frac{1 + \dfrac{1}{5^n}}{5 + \dfrac{1}{5^n}} \qquad \text{Divide numerator and denominator by } 5^n.$$

$$= \frac{3}{5}$$

The series converges because the ratio $3/5 < 1$. 　　　　　　　　　 *Now Try Exercise 31.*

The question of convergence of a power series at an endpoint is really a question about the convergence of a series of numbers. If the series is geometric with first term a and common ratio r, then the series converges to $a/(1 - r)$ if $|r| < 1$ and diverges if $|r| \geq 1$. Another type of series whose sums are easily found are **telescoping series,** as illustrated in Example 7.

EXAMPLE 7 Summing a Telescoping Series

Find the sum of $\displaystyle\sum_{n=1}^{\infty} \frac{1}{n(n + 1)}$.

SOLUTION

Use partial fractions to rewrite the nth term.

$$\frac{1}{n(n + 1)} = \frac{1}{n} - \frac{1}{n + 1}$$

We compute a few partial sums to find a general formula.

$$s_1 = 1 - \frac{1}{2}$$

$$s_2 = \left(1 - \frac{1}{2}\right) + \left(\frac{1}{2} - \frac{1}{3}\right) = 1 - \frac{1}{3}$$

$$s_3 = \left(1 - \frac{1}{2}\right) + \left(\frac{1}{2} - \frac{1}{3}\right) + \left(\frac{1}{3} - \frac{1}{4}\right) = 1 - \frac{1}{4}$$

We can see that, in general,

$$s_n = 1 - \frac{1}{n + 1},$$

because all the terms between the first and last cancel when the parentheses are removed. Therefore, the sum of the series is

$$S = \lim_{n \to \infty} s_n = 1. \qquad \textit{Now Try Exercise 48.}$$

Telescoping Series

We call the series in Example 7 a *telescoping series* because its partial sums collapse like an old handheld telescope.

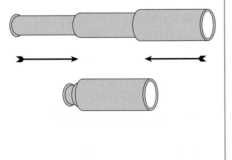

The final section of this chapter will formalize some of the strategies used in Exploration 2 and Example 7 and will develop additional tests that can be used to determine series behavior at endpoints.

Quick Review 10.4 *(For help, go to Sections 2.2 and 10.1.)*

Exercise numbers with a gray background indicate problems that the authors have designed to be solved *without a calculator*.

In Exercises 1–5, find the limit of the expression as $n \to \infty$. Assume x remains fixed as n changes.

1. $\dfrac{n|x|}{n + 1}$

2. $\dfrac{n^2|x - 3|}{n(n - 1)}$

3. $\dfrac{|x|^n}{n!}$

4. $\dfrac{(n + 1)^4 x^2}{(2n)^4}$

5. $\dfrac{|2x + 1|^{n+1} 2^n}{2^{n+1}|2x + 1|^n}$

In Exercises 6–10, the terms of one of the series (call it $\Sigma\, a_n$) will eventually be greater than the terms of the other series (call it $\Sigma\, b_n$). Identify which series is which, and find the smallest positive integer N for which $a_n > b_n$ for all $n \geq N$.

6. $\Sigma\, 5n, \quad \Sigma\, n^2$

7. $\Sigma\, n^5, \quad \Sigma\, 5^n$

8. $\Sigma\, \ln n, \quad \Sigma\, \sqrt{n},$

9. $\Sigma\, \dfrac{1}{10^n}, \quad \Sigma\, \dfrac{1}{n!}$

10. $\Sigma\, \dfrac{1}{n^2}, \quad \Sigma\, n^{-3}$

Section 10.4 Exercises

In Exercises 1 and 2, find the values of x for which the equation is an identity. Support your answer graphically.

1. $\dfrac{-1}{x+4} = 1 + (x+5) + (x+5)^2 + (x+5)^3 + \cdots$

2. $\dfrac{1}{1-x} = 1 + x + x^2 + x^3 + \cdots$

In Exercises 3 and 4, use a comparison test to show that the series converges for all x.

3. $\displaystyle\sum_{n=0}^{\infty} \dfrac{x^{4n}}{2n!+1}$

4. $\displaystyle\sum_{n=0}^{\infty} \dfrac{x^{2n}}{n!+2}$

In Exercises 5 and 6, show that the series converges absolutely.

5. $\displaystyle\sum_{n=0}^{\infty} \dfrac{(\cos x)^n}{n!+1}$

6. $\displaystyle\sum_{n=0}^{\infty} \dfrac{2(\sin x)^n}{n!+3}$

In Exercises 7–22, find the *radius* of convergence of the power series.

7. $\displaystyle\sum_{n=0}^{\infty} x^n$

8. $\displaystyle\sum_{n=0}^{\infty} (x+5)^n$

9. $\displaystyle\sum_{n=0}^{\infty} (-1)^n (4x+1)^n$

10. $\displaystyle\sum_{n=1}^{\infty} \dfrac{(3x-2)^n}{n}$

11. $\displaystyle\sum_{n=0}^{\infty} \dfrac{(x-2)^n}{10^n}$

12. $\displaystyle\sum_{n=0}^{\infty} \dfrac{nx^n}{n+2}$

13. $\displaystyle\sum_{n=1}^{\infty} \dfrac{x^n}{n\sqrt{n}\,3^n}$

14. $\displaystyle\sum_{n=0}^{\infty} \dfrac{x^{2n+1}}{n!}$

15. $\displaystyle\sum_{n=0}^{\infty} \dfrac{n(x+3)^n}{5^n}$

16. $\displaystyle\sum_{n=0}^{\infty} \dfrac{nx^n}{4^n(n^2+1)}$

17. $\displaystyle\sum_{n=0}^{\infty} n!(x-4)^n$

18. $\displaystyle\sum_{n=0}^{\infty} \dfrac{\sqrt{n}\,x^n}{3^n}$

19. $\displaystyle\sum_{n=0}^{\infty} (-2)^n(n+1)(x-1)^n$

20. $\displaystyle\sum_{n=1}^{\infty} \dfrac{(4x-5)^{2n+1}}{n^{3/2}}$

21. $\displaystyle\sum_{n=1}^{\infty} \dfrac{(x+\pi)^n}{\sqrt{n}}$

22. $\displaystyle\sum_{n=0}^{\infty} \dfrac{(x-\sqrt{2})^{2n+1}}{2^n}$

In Exercises 23–28, find the *interval* of convergence of the series and, within this interval, the sum of the series as a function of x.

23. $\displaystyle\sum_{n=0}^{\infty} \dfrac{(x-1)^{2n}}{4^n}$

24. $\displaystyle\sum_{n=0}^{\infty} \dfrac{(x+1)^{2n}}{9^n}$

25. $\displaystyle\sum_{n=0}^{\infty} \left(\dfrac{\sqrt{x}}{2} - 1\right)^n$

26. $\displaystyle\sum_{n=0}^{\infty} (\ln x)^n$

27. $\displaystyle\sum_{n=0}^{\infty} \left(\dfrac{x^2-1}{3}\right)^n$

28. $\displaystyle\sum_{n=0}^{\infty} \left(\dfrac{\sin x}{2}\right)^n$

In Exercises 29–44, determine the convergence or divergence of the series. Identify the test (or tests) you use. There may be more than one correct way to determine convergence or divergence of a given series.

29. $\displaystyle\sum_{n=1}^{\infty} \dfrac{n}{n+1}$

30. $\displaystyle\sum_{n=1}^{\infty} \dfrac{2^n}{n+1}$

31. $\displaystyle\sum_{n=1}^{\infty} \dfrac{n^2-1}{2^n}$

32. $\displaystyle\sum_{n=1}^{\infty} -\dfrac{1}{8^n}$

33. $\displaystyle\sum_{n=1}^{\infty} \dfrac{2^n}{3^n+1}$

34. $\displaystyle\sum_{n=1}^{\infty} n \sin\left(\dfrac{1}{n}\right)$

35. $\displaystyle\sum_{n=0}^{\infty} n^2 e^{-n}$

36. $\displaystyle\sum_{n=0}^{\infty} \dfrac{n^{10}}{10^n}$

37. $\displaystyle\sum_{n=1}^{\infty} \dfrac{(n+3)!}{3!\,n!\,3^n}$

38. $\displaystyle\sum_{n=1}^{\infty} \left(1 + \dfrac{1}{n}\right)^n$

39. $\displaystyle\sum_{n=0}^{\infty} \dfrac{(-2)^n}{3^n}$

40. $\displaystyle\sum_{n=1}^{\infty} n!\,e^{-n}$

41. $\displaystyle\sum_{n=1}^{\infty} \dfrac{3^n}{n^3 2^n}$

42. $\displaystyle\sum_{n=1}^{\infty} \dfrac{n \ln n}{2^n}$

43. $\displaystyle\sum_{n=1}^{\infty} \dfrac{n!}{(2n+1)!}$

44. $\displaystyle\sum_{n=1}^{\infty} \dfrac{n!}{n^n}$ [*Hint:* If you do not recognize L, try recognizing the reciprocal of L.]

45. Give an example to show that the converse of the nth-Term Test is false. That is, $\sum a_n$ might diverge even though $\lim_{n\to\infty} a_n = 0$.

46. Find two convergent series $\sum a_n$ and $\sum b_n$ such that $\sum (a_n/b_n)$ diverges.

47. Writing to Learn We reviewed in Section 10.1 how to find the interval of convergence for the geometric series $\sum_{n=0}^{\infty} x^n$. Can we find the interval of convergence of a geometric series by using the Ratio Test? Explain.

In Exercises 48–54, find the sum of the telescoping series.

48. $\displaystyle\sum_{n=1}^{\infty} \dfrac{4}{(4n-3)(4n+1)}$

49. $\displaystyle\sum_{n=1}^{\infty} \dfrac{6}{(2n-1)(2n+1)}$

50. $\displaystyle\sum_{n=1}^{\infty} \dfrac{40n}{(2n-1)^2(2n+1)^2}$

51. $\displaystyle\sum_{n=1}^{\infty} \dfrac{2n+1}{n^2(n+1)^2}$

52. $\displaystyle\sum_{n=1}^{\infty} \left(\dfrac{1}{\sqrt{n}} - \dfrac{1}{\sqrt{n+1}}\right)$

53. $\displaystyle\sum_{n=1}^{\infty} \left(\dfrac{1}{\ln(n+2)} - \dfrac{1}{\ln(n+1)}\right)$

54. $\displaystyle\sum_{n=1}^{\infty} \left(\tan^{-1}(n) - \tan^{-1}(n+1)\right)$

Standardized Test Questions

You may use a graphing calculator to solve the following problems.

55. True or False If a series converges absolutely, then it converges. Justify your answer.

56. True or False If the radius of convergence of a power series is 0, then the series diverges for all real numbers. Justify your answer.

57. Multiple Choice Which of the following gives $\lim\limits_{n\to\infty}\dfrac{a_{n+1}}{a_n}$ for the series $\sum\limits_{n=0}^{\infty}\dfrac{2^n}{(-3)^n}$?

(A) 3/2   (B) 2/3   (C) 1   (D) 0   (E) ∞

58. Multiple Choice Which of the following gives the radius of convergence of the series $\sum\limits_{n=1}^{\infty}\dfrac{(2x-3)^n}{n}$?

(A) 2   (B) 1   (C) 1/2   (D) 0   (E) ∞

59. Multiple Choice Which of the following describes the behavior of the series $\sum\limits_{n=1}^{\infty}\dfrac{(\sin x)^n}{2^n\,n^2}$?

      I. diverges

      II. converges

      III. converges absolutely

(A) I only   (B) II only   (C) III only

(D) I & II only   (E) II & III only

60. Multiple Choice Which of the following gives the sum of the telescoping series $\sum\limits_{n=1}^{\infty}\dfrac{3}{(3n-1)(3n+2)}$?

(A) 3/10 (B) 3/8 (C) 9/22 (D) 1/2 (E) The series diverges.

Explorations

Group Activity *Nondecreasing Sequences* As you already know, a nondecreasing (or increasing) function $f(x)$ that is bounded from above on an interval $[a,\infty)$ has a limit as $x\to\infty$ that is less than or equal to the bound. The same is true of sequences of numbers. If $s_1\le s_2\le s_3\le\ldots\le s_n\ldots$ and there is a number M such that $|s_n|\le M$ for all n, then the sequence converges to a limit $S\le M$. You will need this fact as you work through Exercises 61 and 62.

61. *Proof of the Direct Comparison Test, Part a* Let $\sum a_n$ be a series with no negative terms, and let $\sum c_n$ be a convergent series such that $a_n\le c_n$ for all $n\ge N$, for some integer N.

(a) Show that the partial sums of $\sum a_n$ are bounded above by

$$a_1+\cdots+a_N+\sum_{n=N+1}^{\infty}c_n.$$

(b) Explain why this shows that $\sum a_n$ must converge.

62. *Proof of the Direct Comparison Test, Part b* Let $\sum a_n$ be a series with no negative terms, and let $\sum d_n$ be a divergent series of nonnegative terms such that $a_n\ge d_n$ for all $n\ge N$, for some integer N.

(a) Show that the partial sums of $\sum d_n$ are bounded above by

$$d_1+\cdots+d_N+\sum_{n=N+1}^{\infty}a_n.$$

(b) Explain why this leads to a contradiction if we assume that $\sum a_n$ converges.

63. Group Activity Within your group, have each student make up a power series with radius of convergence equal to one of the numbers $1, 2, \ldots, n$. Then exchange series with another group and match the other group's series with the correct radii of convergence.

Extending the Ideas

64. We can show that the series

$$\sum_{n=0}^{\infty}\frac{n^2}{2^n}$$

converges by the Ratio Test, but what is its sum?

To find out, express $1/(1-x)$ as a geometric series. Differentiate both sides of the resulting equation with respect to x, multiply both sides of the result by x, differentiate again, multiply by x again, and set x equal to $1/2$. What do you get? (*Source:* David E. Dobbs's letter to the editor, *Illinois Mathematics Teacher*, Vol. 33, Issue 4, 1982, p. 27.)

10.5 Testing Convergence at Endpoints

You will learn additional tests for convergence of series of constants, and you will be able to test for conditional and absolute convergence at the endpoints of intervals of convergence.

• The Integral Test
• Harmonic series and *p*-series
• The Limit Comparison Test
• The Alternating Series Test and Leibniz's Theorem
• The strange implication of conditional convergence
• Finding intervals of convergence
• Why convergence of a series **for** *f* does not imply convergence **to** *f*

Integral Test

In Exploration 1 of Section 10.4, you showed that $\sum 1/n$ *diverges* by modeling it as a sum of rectangle areas that contain the area under the curve $y = 1/x$ from 1 to ∞. You also showed that $\sum 1/n^2$ *converges* by modeling it as a sum of rectangle areas contained by the area under the curve $y = 1/x^2$ from 1 to ∞. This area-based convergence test in its general form is known as the *Integral Test*.

> **THEOREM 10   The Integral Test**
>
> Let $\{a_n\}$ be a sequence of positive terms. Suppose that $a_n = f(n)$, where f is a continuous, positive, decreasing function of x for all $x \geq N$ (N a positive integer). Then the series $\sum_{n=N}^{\infty} a_n$ and the integral $\int_N^{\infty} f(x)\,dx$ either both converge or both diverge.

Proof We will illustrate the proof for $N = 1$ to keep the notation simple, but the illustration can be shifted horizontally to any value of N without affecting the logic of the proof. The proof is entirely contained in these two pictures (Figure 10.14):

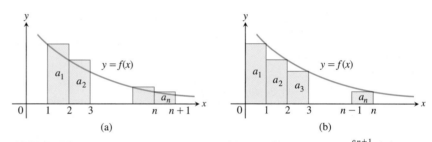

Figure 10.14 (a) The sum $a_1 + a_2 + \cdots + a_n$ provides an upper bound for $\int_1^{n+1} f(x)\,dx$. (b) The sum $a_2 + a_3 + \cdots + a_n$ provides a lower bound for $\int_1^{n} f(x)\,dx$. (Theorem 10)

We leave it to you (in Exercise 52) to supply the words.   ■

EXAMPLE 1   Applying the Integral Test

Does $\displaystyle\sum_{n=1}^{\infty} \frac{1}{n\sqrt{n}}$ converge?

SOLUTION

The Integral Test applies because

$$f(x) = \frac{1}{x\sqrt{x}}$$

is a continuous, positive, decreasing function of x for $x > 1$.
We have

$$\int_1^{\infty} \frac{1}{x\sqrt{x}}\,dx = \lim_{k\to\infty} \int_1^{k} x^{-3/2}\,dx = \lim_{k\to\infty} \left[-2x^{-1/2} \right]_1^{k}$$

$$= \lim_{k\to\infty} \left(-\frac{2}{\sqrt{k}} + 2 \right) = 2$$

Since the integral converges, so must the series.   *Now Try Exercise 1.*

Caution

The series and the integral in the Integral Test need not have the same value in the convergent case. Although the integral converges to 2 in Example 1, the series might have a quite different sum. If you use your calculator to compute or graph partial sums for the series, you can see that the 11th partial sum is already greater than 2.

Harmonic Series and *p*-series

The Integral Test can be used to settle the question of convergence for any series of the form $\sum_{n=1}^{\infty} = (1/n^p)$, *p* a real constant. (The series in Example 1 had this form, with $p = 3/2$.) Such a series is called a *p*-series.

EXPLORATION 1 The *p*-Series Test

1. Use the Integral Test to prove that $\sum_{n=1}^{\infty} (1/n^p)$ converges if $p > 1$.
2. Use the Integral Test to prove that $\sum_{n=1}^{\infty} (1/n^p)$ diverges if $p < 1$.
3. Use the Integral Test to prove that $\sum_{n=1}^{\infty} (1/n^p)$ diverges if $p = 1$.

What Is Harmonic About the Harmonic Series?

The terms in the harmonic series correspond to the nodes on a vibrating string that produce multiples of the fundamental frequency. For example, 1/2 produces the harmonic that is twice the fundamental frequency, 1/3 produces a frequency that is three times the fundamental frequency, and so on. The fundamental frequency is the lowest note or pitch we hear when a string is plucked. (Figure 10.16)

The *p*-series with $p = 1$ is the **harmonic series,** and it is probably the most famous divergent series in mathematics. The *p*-Series Test shows that the harmonic series is just *barely* divergent; if we increase *p* to 1.000000001, for instance, the series converges!

The slowness with which the harmonic series approaches infinity is most impressive. Consider the following example.

EXAMPLE 2 The Slow Divergence of the Harmonic Series

Approximately how many terms of the harmonic series are required to form a partial sum larger than 20?

SOLUTION

Before you set your graphing calculator to the task of finding this number, you might want to estimate how long the calculation might take. The graphs tell the story (Figure 10.15).

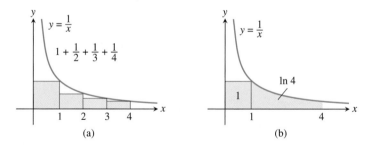

Figure 10.15 Finding an upper bound for one of the partial sums of the harmonic series. (Example 2)

Let H_n denote the *n*th partial sum of the harmonic series. Comparing the two graphs, we see that $H_4 < (1 + \ln 4)$ and (in general) that $H_n \leq (1 + \ln n)$. If we wish H_n to be greater than 20, then

$$1 + \ln n > H_n > 20$$
$$1 + \ln n > 20$$
$$\ln n > 19$$
$$n > e^{19}$$

The exact value of e^{19} rounds up to 178,482,301. It will take *at least* that many terms of the harmonic series to move the partial sums beyond 20. It would take your calculator several weeks to compute a partial sum of this many terms. Nonetheless, the harmonic series really does diverge!

Now Try Exercise 3.

Figure 10.16 On a guitar, the second harmonic note is produced when the finger is positioned halfway between the bridge and nut of the string while the string is plucked with the other hand.

Comparison Tests

The *p*-Series Test tells everything there is to know about the convergence or divergence of series of the form $\sum (1/n^p)$. This is admittedly a rather narrow class of series, but we can test many other kinds (including those in which the *n*th term is any rational function of *n*) by *comparing* them to *p*-series.

The Direct Comparison Test (Theorem 7, Section 10.4) is one method of comparison, but the *Limit Comparison Test* is another.

THEOREM 11   The Limit Comparison Test (LCT)

Suppose that $a_n > 0$ and $b_n > 0$ for all $n \geq N$ (*N* a positive integer).

1. If $\displaystyle\lim_{n \to \infty} \frac{a_n}{b_n} = c, 0 < c < \infty$, then $\sum a_n$ and $\sum b_n$ both converge or both diverge.

2. If $\displaystyle\lim_{n \to \infty} \frac{a_n}{b_n} = 0$ and $\sum b_n$ converges, then $\sum a_n$ converges.

3. If $\displaystyle\lim_{n \to \infty} \frac{a_n}{b_n} = \infty$ and $\sum b_n$ diverges, then $\sum a_n$ diverges.

We omit the proof.

EXAMPLE 3 Using the Limit Comparison Test

Determine whether the series converge or diverge.

(a) $\dfrac{3}{4} + \dfrac{5}{9} + \dfrac{7}{16} + \dfrac{9}{25} + \cdots = \displaystyle\sum_{n=1}^{\infty} \frac{2n + 1}{(n + 1)^2}$

(b) $\dfrac{1}{1} + \dfrac{1}{3} + \dfrac{1}{7} + \dfrac{1}{15} + \cdots = \displaystyle\sum_{n=1}^{\infty} \frac{1}{2^n - 1}$

(c) $\dfrac{8}{4} + \dfrac{11}{21} + \dfrac{14}{56} + \dfrac{17}{115} + \cdots = \displaystyle\sum_{n=2}^{\infty} \frac{3n + 2}{n^3 - 2n}$

(d) $\sin 1 + \sin\dfrac{1}{2} + \sin\dfrac{1}{3} + \cdots = \displaystyle\sum_{n=1}^{\infty} \sin\left(\frac{1}{n}\right)$

SOLUTION

(a) For *n* large, $\dfrac{2n + 1}{(n + 1)^2}$ behaves like $\dfrac{2n}{n^2} = \dfrac{2}{n}$,

so we compare terms of the given series to terms of $\sum (1/n)$ and try the LCT.

$$\lim_{n \to \infty} \frac{a_n}{b_n} = \lim_{n \to \infty} \frac{(2n + 1)/(n + 1)^2}{1/n}$$

$$= \lim_{n \to \infty} \frac{2n + 1}{(n + 1)^2} \cdot \frac{n}{1}$$

Applying l'Hospital's rule, $\displaystyle\lim_{n \to \infty} \frac{2n^2 + n}{(n + 1)^2} = \lim_{n \to \infty} \frac{4n + 1}{2(n + 1)} = 2.$

Since the limit is a nonzero number and $\sum (1/n)$ diverges,

$$\sum_{n=1}^{\infty} \frac{2n + 1}{(n + 1)^2}$$

also diverges.

continued

(b) For n large, $1/(2^n - 1)$ behaves like $1/2^n$, so we compare the given series to $\sum (1/2^n)$.

$$\lim_{n \to \infty} \frac{a_n}{b_n} = \lim_{n \to \infty} \frac{1}{2^n - 1} \cdot \frac{2^n}{1}$$

$$= \lim_{n \to \infty} \frac{2^n}{2^n - 1}$$

$$= \lim_{n \to \infty} \frac{1}{1 - (1/2^n)} = 1$$

Since $\sum (1/2^n)$ converges (geometric, $r = 1/2$), the LCT guarantees that

$$\sum_{n=1}^{\infty} \frac{1}{2^n - 1}$$

also converges.

(c) For n large,

$$\frac{3n + 2}{n^3 - 2n}$$

behaves like $3/n^2$, so we compare the given series to $\sum (1/n^2)$.

$$\lim_{n \to \infty} \frac{a_n}{b_n} = \lim_{n \to \infty} \frac{3n + 2}{n^3 - 2n} \cdot \frac{n^2}{1}$$

$$= \lim_{n \to \infty} \frac{3n^3 + 2n^2}{n^3 - 2n} = 3$$

Since $\sum (1/n^2)$ converges by the p-Series Test,

$$\sum_{n=2}^{\infty} \frac{3n + 2}{n^3 - 2n}$$

also converges (by the LCT).

(d) Recall that

$$\lim_{x \to 0} \frac{\sin x}{x} = 1,$$

so we try the LCT by comparing the given series to $\sum (1/n)$.

$$\lim_{n \to \infty} \frac{a_n}{b_n} = \lim_{n \to \infty} \frac{\sin (1/n)}{(1/n)} = 1$$

Since $\sum (1/n)$ diverges, $\sum_{n=1}^{\infty} \sin (1/n)$ also diverges. ***Now Try Exercise 5.***

As Example 3 suggests, applying the Limit Comparison Test has strong connections to analyzing end behavior in functions. In part (c) of Example 3, we could have reached the same conclusion if a_n had been *any* linear polynomial in n divided by *any* cubic polynomial in n, since any such rational function "in the end" will grow like $1/n^2$.

Alternating Series

A series in which the terms are alternately positive and negative is an **alternating series.**
Here are three examples.

$$1 - \frac{1}{2} + \frac{1}{3} - \frac{1}{4} + \frac{1}{5} - \cdots + \frac{(-1)^{n+1}}{n} + \cdots \tag{1}$$

$$-2 + 1 - \frac{1}{2} + \frac{1}{4} - \frac{1}{8} + \cdots + \frac{(-1)^n 4}{2^n} + \cdots \tag{2}$$

$$1 - 2 + 3 - 4 + 5 - 6 + \cdots + (-1)^{n+1} n + \cdots \tag{3}$$

Series 1, called the **alternating harmonic series,** converges to $\ln 2$, as we have
previously noted. Series 2, a geometric series with $a = -2, r = -1/2$, converges to
$-2/[1 + (1/2)] = -4/3$. Series 3 diverges by the nth-Term Test.

We can prove the convergence of the alternating harmonic series by applying the following test.

THEOREM 12   The Alternating Series Test (Leibniz's Theorem)

The series

$$\sum_{n=1}^{\infty} (-1)^{n+1} u_n = u_1 - u_2 + u_3 - u_4 + \cdots$$

converges if all three of the following conditions are satisfied:

1. each u_n is positive;
2. $u_n \geq u_{n+1}$ for all $n \geq N$, for some integer N;
3. $\lim_{n \to \infty} u_n = 0$.

Figure 10.17 illustrates the convergence of the partial sums to their limit L.

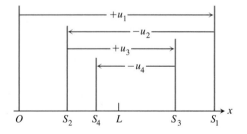

Figure 10.17 Closing in on the sum of a convergent alternating series. (Theorem 12)

As we noted in Section 10.3, the figure that proves the Alternating Series Test actually
proves more than the *fact* of convergence; it also shows the *way* that an alternating series
converges when it satisfies the conditions of the test. The partial sums keep "overshooting"
the limit as they go back and forth on the number line, gradually closing in as the terms
tend to zero. If we stop at the nth partial sum, we know that the next term ($\pm u_{n+1}$)
will again cause us to overshoot the limit in the positive direction or negative direction,
depending on the sign carried by u_{n+1}. This gives us a convenient bound for the truncation
error, which we now restate as another theorem.

THEOREM 13   The Alternating Series Bound Theorem

If the alternating series $\sum_{n=1}^{\infty} (-1)^{n+1} u_n$ satisfies the conditions of Theorem 12, then the truncation error for the *n*th partial sum is less than u_{n+1} and has the same sign as the first unused term.

EXAMPLE 4 The Alternating Harmonic Series

Prove that the alternating harmonic series is convergent, but not absolutely convergent. Find a bound for the truncation error after 99 terms.

SOLUTION

The terms are strictly alternating in sign and decrease in absolute value from the start:

$$1 > \frac{1}{2} > \frac{1}{3} > \cdots. \quad \text{Also,} \quad \frac{1}{n} \to 0$$

By the Alternating Series Test,

$$\sum_{n=1}^{\infty} \frac{(-1)^{n+1}}{n}$$

converges.

On the other hand, the series $\sum_{n=1}^{\infty} (1/n)$ of absolute values is the harmonic series, which diverges, so the alternating harmonic series is not absolutely convergent.

The Alternating Series Bound Theorem guarantees that the truncation error after 99 terms is less than $u_{99+1} = 1/(99 + 1) = 1/100$.   *Now Try Exercise 23.*

A Note on the Error Bound

Theorem 13 does not give a *formula* for the truncation error, but a *bound* for the truncation error. The bound might be fairly conservative. For example, the first 99 terms of the alternating harmonic series add to about 0.6981721793, while the series itself has a sum of ln 2 ≈ 0.6931471806. That makes the actual truncation error very close to 0.005, about half the size of the bound of 0.01 given by Theorem 13.

Absolute and Conditional Convergence

Because the alternating harmonic series is convergent but not absolutely convergent, we say it is **conditionally convergent** (or **converges conditionally**).

We take it for granted that we can rearrange the terms of a *finite* sum without affecting the sum. We can also rearrange a *finite number* of terms of an infinite series without affecting the sum. But if we rearrange an infinite number of terms of an infinite series, we can be sure of leaving the sum unaltered *only if it converges absolutely.*

Rearrangements of Absolutely Convergent Series

If $\sum a_n$ converges absolutely, and if $b_1, b_2, b_3, \ldots, b_n, \ldots$ is any rearrangement of the sequence $\{a_n\}$, then $\sum b_n$ converges absolutely and $\sum_{n=1}^{\infty} b_n = \sum_{n=1}^{\infty} a_n$.

On the other hand, consider this:

Rearrangements of Conditionally Convergent Series

If $\sum a_n$ converges conditionally, then the terms can be rearranged to form a divergent series. The terms can also be rearranged to form a series that converges to *any* preassigned sum.

This seems incredible, but it is a logical consequence of the definition of the sum as the *limit of the sequence of partial sums*. A conditionally convergent series consists of positive terms that sum to ∞ and negative terms that sum to $-\infty$, so we can manipulate the partial sums to do virtually anything we wish. We illustrate the technique with the alternating harmonic series.

EXAMPLE 5 **Rearranging the Alternating Harmonic Series**

Show how to rearrange the terms of

$$\sum_{n=1}^{\infty} \frac{(-1)^{n+1}}{n}$$

to form

(a) a divergent series;   **(b)** a series that converges to π.

SOLUTION

The series of positive terms,

$$1 + \frac{1}{3} + \frac{1}{5} + \cdots + \frac{1}{2n+1} + \cdots,$$

diverges to ∞, while the series of negative terms,

$$-\frac{1}{2} - \frac{1}{4} - \frac{1}{6} - \cdots - \frac{1}{2n} - \cdots,$$

diverges to $-\infty$. No matter what finite number of terms we use, the remaining positive terms or negative terms still diverge. So, we build our series as follows:

(a) Start by adding positive terms until the partial sum is greater than 1. Then add negative terms until the partial sum is less than -2. Then add positive terms until the sum is greater than 3. Then add negative terms until the sum is less than -4. Continue in this manner indefinitely, so that the sequence of partial sums swings arbitrarily far in both directions and hence diverges.

(b) Start by adding positive terms until the partial sum is greater than π. Then add negative terms until the partial sum is less than π. Then add positive terms until the sum is greater than π. Continue in this manner indefinitely, always closing in on π. Since the positive and negative terms of the original series both approach zero, the amount by which the partial sums exceed or fall short of π approaches zero.

Now Try Exercise 33.

Intervals of Convergence

Our purpose in this section has been to develop tests for convergence that can be used at the endpoints of the intervals of absolute convergence of power series. There are three possibilities at each endpoint: The series could diverge, it could converge absolutely, or it could converge conditionally.

How to Test a Power Series $\sum_{n=0}^{\infty} c_n(x - a)^n$ for Convergence

1. Use the Ratio Test to find the values of x for which the series converges absolutely. Ordinarily, this is an open interval

$$a - R < x < a + R.$$

In some instances, the series converges for all values of x. In rare cases, the series converges only at $x = a$.

continued

2. If the interval of absolute convergence is finite, test for convergence or divergence at each endpoint. The Ratio Test fails at these points. Use a comparison test, the Integral Test, or the Alternating Series Test.
3. If the interval of absolute convergence is $a - R < x < a + R$, conclude that the series diverges (it does not even converge conditionally) for $|x - a| > R$, because for those values of x the nth term does not approach zero.

EXAMPLE 6 The Convergence of Your Knowledge About Convergence

For each of the following series, find (a) the radius of convergence and (b) the interval of convergence. Then identify the values of x for which the series converges (c) absolutely and (d) conditionally.

(A) $\displaystyle\sum_{n=1}^{\infty} (-1)^{n+1} \frac{x^{2n}}{2n} = \frac{x^2}{2} - \frac{x^4}{4} + \frac{x^6}{6} - \cdots$

(B) $\displaystyle\sum_{n=0}^{\infty} \frac{(10x)^n}{n!} = 1 + 10x + \frac{100x^2}{2!} + \frac{1000x^3}{3!} + \cdots$

(C) $\displaystyle\sum_{n=0}^{\infty} n!(x + 1)^n = 1 + (x + 1) + 2!(x + 1)^2 + 3!(x + 1)^3 + \cdots$

(D) $\displaystyle\sum_{n=1}^{\infty} \frac{(x - 3)^n}{2n} = \frac{(x - 3)}{2} + \frac{(x - 3)^2}{4} + \frac{(x - 3)^3}{6} + \cdots$

SOLUTION

The strategy is to apply the Ratio Test to determine the interval of absolute convergence, then check the endpoints for conditional convergence (but not with the Ratio Test!).

Series (A):
First, apply the Ratio Test for absolute convergence:

$$\lim_{n \to \infty} \left| \frac{u_{n+1}}{u_n} \right| = \lim_{n \to \infty} \frac{x^{2n+2}}{2n + 2} \cdot \frac{2n}{x^{2n}}$$

$$= \lim_{n \to \infty} \left(\frac{2n}{2n + 2} \right) x^2$$

$$= \lim_{n \to \infty} \left(\frac{2}{2} \right) x^2 \qquad \text{L'Hospital's Rule}$$

$$= x^2$$

The series converges absolutely for $x^2 < 1$, i.e., on the interval $(-1, 1)$. Now check the endpoints:

At $x = \pm 1$, the series is $\displaystyle\sum_{n=1}^{\infty} \frac{(-1)^{n+1}}{2n}$, which converges conditionally by the Alternating Series Test. (In fact, it is half the alternating harmonic series.) Thus, for series (A) we have **(a)** $r = 1$; **(b)** $[-1, 1]$; **(c)** $(-1, 1)$; and **(d)** $x = \pm 1$.

continued

Series (B):

First, apply the Ratio Test for absolute convergence:

$$\lim_{n\to\infty}\left|\frac{u_{n+1}}{u_n}\right| = \lim_{n\to\infty}\frac{|10x|^{n+1}}{(n+1)!}\cdot\frac{n!}{|10x|^n}$$

$$= \lim_{n\to\infty}\frac{|10x|}{n+1}$$

$$= 0$$

The series converges absolutely for all x. There are no endpoints to check. Thus, for series (B) we have **(a)** $r = \infty$; **(b)** $(-\infty, \infty)$; **(c)** $(-\infty, \infty)$; and **(d)** no values of x.

Series (C):

First, apply the Ratio Test for absolute convergence:

$$\lim_{n\to\infty}\left|\frac{u_{n+1}}{u_n}\right| = \lim_{n\to\infty}\frac{(n+1)!(x+1)^{n+1}}{n!(x+1)^n}$$

$$= \lim_{n\to\infty}(n+1)|x+1|$$

$$= \begin{cases} \infty & \text{if } x \neq -1 \\ 0 & \text{if } x = -1 \end{cases}$$

The series converges absolutely at $x = -1$ and diverges for all other x. There are no endpoints to check. Thus, for series (C) we have **(a)** $r = 0$; **(b)** $\{-1\}$; **(c)** $\{-1\}$; and **(d)** no values of x.

Series (D):

First, apply the Ratio Test for absolute convergence:

$$\lim_{n\to\infty}\left|\frac{u_{n+1}}{u_n}\right| = \lim_{n\to\infty}\frac{|x-3|^{n+1}}{2n+2}\cdot\frac{2n}{|x-3|^n}$$

$$= \lim_{n\to\infty}\left(\frac{2n}{2n+2}\right)|x-3|$$

$$= \lim_{n\to\infty}\left(\frac{2}{2}\right)|x-3| \qquad \text{L'Hospital's Rule}$$

$$= |x-3|$$

The series converges absolutely for $|x-3| < 1$, i.e., on the interval $(2, 4)$.
Now check the endpoints:

At $x = 2$, the series is $\displaystyle\sum_{n=1}^{\infty}\frac{(-1)^n}{2n}$, which converges conditionally by the Alternating Series Test.

At $x = 4$, the series is $\displaystyle\sum_{n=1}^{\infty}\frac{1}{2n}$, which diverges by limit comparison with the harmonic series. Thus, for series (D) we have **(a)** $r = 1$; **(b)** $[2, 4)$; **(c)** $(2, 4)$; and **(d)** $x = 2$.

Now Try Exercise 41.

To facilitate testing convergence at endpoints we can use the following flowchart.

Procedure for Determining Convergence

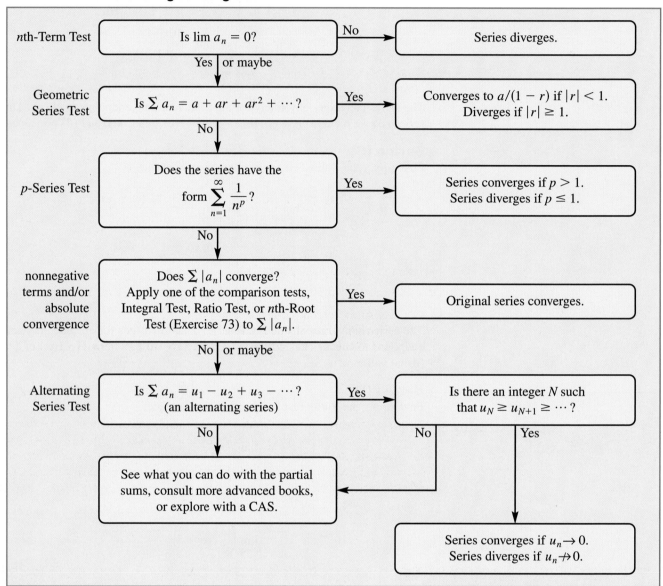

A Word of Caution

Although we can use the tests we have developed to find where a given power series converges, they do not tell us what function that power series is converging *to*. Even if the series is known to be a Maclaurin series generated by a function f, we cannot automatically conclude that the series converges *to the function* f on its interval of convergence. That is why it is so important to estimate the error.

For example, we can use the Ratio Test to show that the Maclaurin series for $\sin x$, $\cos x$, and e^x all converge absolutely for all real numbers. However, the reason we know that they converge to $\sin x$, $\cos x$, and e^x, respectively, is that we used the Remainder Bounding Theorem to show that the respective truncation errors went to zero.

The following exploration shows what can happen with a strange function.

EXPLORATION 2 The Maclaurin Series of a Strange Function

Let $f(x) = \begin{cases} 0, & x = 0 \\ e^{-1/x^2}, & x \neq 0. \end{cases}$

It can be shown (although not easily) that f (Figure 10.18) has derivatives of all orders at $x = 0$ and that $f^{(n)}(0) = 0$ for all n. Use this fact as you proceed with the exploration.

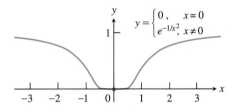

Figure 10.18 The graph of the continuous extension of $y = e^{-1/x^2}$ is so flat at the origin that all of its derivatives there are zero.

1. Construct the Maclaurin series for f.
2. For what values of x does this series converge?
3. Find all values of x for which the series actually converges to $f(x)$.

If you are surprised by the behavior of the series in Exploration 2, remember that we identified it up front as a strange function. It was fortunate for the early history of calculus that the functions that modeled physical behavior in the Newtonian world were much more predictable, enabling the early theories to enjoy encouraging successes before they could be lost in detail. When the subtleties of convergence emerged later, the theory was prepared to confront them.

Quick Review 10.5 *(For help, go to Sections 1.2 and 9.3.)*

Exercise numbers with a gray background indicate problems that the authors have designed to be solved *without a calculator.*

In Exercises 1–5, determine whether the improper integral converges or diverges. Give reasons for your answer. (You do not need to evaluate the integral.)

1. $\int_{1}^{\infty} \frac{1}{x^{4/3}}\,dx$

2. $\int_{1}^{\infty} \frac{x^2}{x^3 + 1}\,dx$

3. $\int_{1}^{\infty} \frac{\ln x}{x}\,dx$

4. $\int_{1}^{\infty} \frac{1 + \cos x}{x^2}\,dx$

5. $\int_{1}^{\infty} \frac{\sqrt{x}}{x + 1}\,dx$

In Exercises 6–10, determine whether the function is both positive and decreasing on some interval (N, ∞). (You do not need to identify N.)

6. $f(x) = \frac{3}{x}$

7. $f(x) = \frac{7x}{x^2 - 8}$

8. $f(x) = \frac{3 + x^2}{3 - x^2}$

9. $f(x) = \frac{\sin x}{x^5}$

10. $f(x) = \ln(1/x)$

Section 10.5 Exercises

In Exercises 1 and 2, use the Integral Test to determine convergence or divergence of the series.

1. $\displaystyle\sum_{n=1}^{\infty} \frac{1}{\sqrt[3]{n}}$
2. $\displaystyle\sum_{n=1}^{\infty} n^{-3/2}$

3. Find the first six partial sums of $\displaystyle\sum_{n=1}^{\infty} \frac{1}{n}$.

4. If S_k is the kth partial sum of $\displaystyle\sum_{n=1}^{\infty} \frac{1}{n}$, find the first value of k for which $S_k > 4$.

In Exercises 5 and 6, use the Limit Comparison Test to determine convergence or divergence of the series.

5. $\displaystyle\sum_{n=1}^{\infty} \frac{3n - 1}{n^2 + 1}$
6. $\displaystyle\sum_{n=0}^{\infty} \frac{2^n}{3^n + 1}$

In Exercises 7–22, determine whether the series converges or diverges. There may be more than one correct way to determine convergence or divergence of a given series.

7. $\displaystyle\sum_{n=1}^{\infty} \frac{5}{n + 1}$
8. $\displaystyle\sum_{n=1}^{\infty} \frac{3}{\sqrt{n}}$

9. $\displaystyle\sum_{n=1}^{\infty} \frac{\ln n}{n}$
10. $\displaystyle\sum_{n=1}^{\infty} \frac{1}{2n - 1}$

11. $\displaystyle\sum_{n=1}^{\infty} \frac{1}{(\ln 2)^n}$
12. $\displaystyle\sum_{n=1}^{\infty} \frac{1}{(\ln 3)^n}$

13. $\displaystyle\sum_{n=1}^{\infty} n \sin\left(\frac{1}{n}\right)$
14. $\displaystyle\sum_{n=0}^{\infty} \frac{e^n}{1 + e^{2n}}$

15. $\displaystyle\sum_{n=1}^{\infty} \frac{\sqrt{n}}{n^2 + 1}$
16. $\displaystyle\sum_{n=1}^{\infty} \frac{5n^3 - 3n}{n^2(n + 2)(n^2 + 5)}$

17. $\displaystyle\sum_{n=1}^{\infty} \frac{3^{n-1} + 1}{3^n}$
18. $\displaystyle\sum_{n=2}^{\infty} (-1)^{n+1} \frac{1}{\ln n}$

19. $\displaystyle\sum_{n=1}^{\infty} (-1)^{n+1} \frac{10^n}{n^{10}}$
20. $\displaystyle\sum_{n=1}^{\infty} (-1)^{n+1} \frac{\sqrt{n} + 1}{n + 1}$

21. $\displaystyle\sum_{n=2}^{\infty} (-1)^{n+1} \frac{\ln n}{\ln n^2}$
22. $\displaystyle\sum_{n=1}^{\infty} \left(\frac{1}{n} - \frac{1}{n^2}\right)$

In Exercises 23–26, determine whether the series converges absolutely, converges conditionally, or diverges. Give reasons for your answer. Find a bound for the truncation error after 99 terms.

23. $\displaystyle\sum_{n=1}^{\infty} (-1)^{n+1} \frac{1 + n}{n^2}$
24. $\displaystyle\sum_{n=1}^{\infty} (-1)^{n+1}(0.1)^n$

25. $\displaystyle\sum_{n=2}^{\infty} (-1)^{n+1} \frac{1}{n \ln n}$
26. $\displaystyle\sum_{n=1}^{\infty} (-1)^n n^2 \left(\frac{2}{3}\right)^n$

In Exercises 27–32, determine whether the series converges absolutely, converges conditionally, or diverges. Give reasons for your answers.

27. $\displaystyle\sum_{n=1}^{\infty} (-1)^{n+1} \frac{n!}{2^n}$
28. $\displaystyle\sum_{n=1}^{\infty} (-1)^{n+1} \frac{\sin n}{n^2}$

29. $\displaystyle\sum_{n=1}^{\infty} \frac{(-1)^n}{1 + \sqrt{n}}$
30. $\displaystyle\sum_{n=1}^{\infty} \frac{\cos n\pi}{n\sqrt{n}}$

31. $\displaystyle\sum_{n=1}^{\infty} \frac{\cos n\pi}{n}$
32. $\displaystyle\sum_{n=1}^{\infty} \frac{(-1)^n}{\sqrt{n} + \sqrt{n + 1}}$

In Exercises 33 and 34, explain how to rearrange the terms of the series from the specified exercise to form **(a)** a divergent series, and **(b)** a series that converges to 4.

33. Exercise 23
34. Exercise 25

In Exercises 35–50, find **(a)** the *interval* of convergence of the series. For what values of x does the series converge **(b)** absolutely, **(c)** conditionally?

35. $\displaystyle\sum_{n=0}^{\infty} x^n$
36. $\displaystyle\sum_{n=0}^{\infty} (x + 5)^n$

37. $\displaystyle\sum_{n=0}^{\infty} (-1)^n(4x + 1)^n$
38. $\displaystyle\sum_{n=1}^{\infty} \frac{(3x - 2)^n}{n}$

39. $\displaystyle\sum_{n=0}^{\infty} \frac{(x - 2)^n}{10^n}$
40. $\displaystyle\sum_{n=0}^{\infty} \frac{nx^n}{n + 2}$

41. $\displaystyle\sum_{n=1}^{\infty} \frac{x^n}{n\sqrt{n}\,3^n}$
42. $\displaystyle\sum_{n=0}^{\infty} \frac{x^{2n+1}}{n!}$

43. $\displaystyle\sum_{n=0}^{\infty} \frac{n(x + 3)^n}{5^n}$
44. $\displaystyle\sum_{n=0}^{\infty} \frac{nx^n}{4^n(n^2 + 1)}$

45. $\displaystyle\sum_{n=0}^{\infty} \frac{\sqrt{n}x^n}{3^n}$
46. $\displaystyle\sum_{n=0}^{\infty} n!(x - 4)^n$

47. $\displaystyle\sum_{n=0}^{\infty} (-2)^n(n + 1)(x - 1)^n$
48. $\displaystyle\sum_{n=1}^{\infty} \frac{(4x - 5)^{2n+1}}{n^{3/2}}$

49. $\displaystyle\sum_{n=1}^{\infty} \frac{(x + \pi)^n}{\sqrt{n}}$
50. $\displaystyle\sum_{n=0}^{\infty} (\ln x)^n$

51. Not only do the figures in Example 2 show that the nth partial sum of the harmonic series is less than $1 + \ln n$; they also show that it is *greater* than $\ln (n + 1)$. Suppose you had started summing the harmonic series with $S_1 = 1$ at the time the universe was formed, 13 billion years ago. If you had been able to add a term every *second* since then, about how large would your partial sum be today? (Assume a 365-day year.)

52. Writing to Learn Write out a proof of the Integral Test (Theorem 10) for $N = 1$, explaining what you see in Figure 10.14.

53. (Continuation of Exercise 52) Relabel the pictures for an arbitrary N and explain why the same conclusions about convergence can be drawn.

54. In each of the following cases, decide whether the infinite series converges. Justify your answer.

(a) $\displaystyle\sum_{k=1}^{\infty} \frac{1}{\sqrt{2k+7}}$

(b) $\displaystyle\sum_{k=1}^{\infty} \left(1 + \frac{1}{k}\right)^k$

(c) $\displaystyle\sum_{k=1}^{\infty} \frac{\cos k}{k^2 + \sqrt{k}}$

(d) $\displaystyle\sum_{k=3}^{\infty} \frac{18}{k(\ln k)}$

In Exercises 55 and 56, find the *radius* of convergence of the series.

55. $\displaystyle\sum_{n=1}^{\infty} \frac{n^n(x+2)^n}{3^n n!}$

56. $\displaystyle\sum_{n=1}^{\infty} \frac{n!x^n}{n^n 5^n}$

57. Construct a series that diverges more slowly than the harmonic series. Justify your answer.

58. Let $a_k = (-1)^{k+1} \int_0^{1/k} 6(kx)^2 \, dx$.

(a) Evaluate a_k.

(b) Show that $\sum_{k=1}^{\infty} a_k$ converges.

(c) Show that

$$1 \le \sum_{k=1}^{\infty} a_k \le \frac{3}{2}.$$

59. (a) Determine whether the series

$$A = \sum_{n=1}^{\infty} \frac{n}{3n^2 + 1}$$

converges or diverges. Justify your answer.

(b) If S is the series formed by multiplying the nth term in A by the nth term in $\sum_{n=1}^{\infty}(3/n)$, write an expression using summation notation for S and determine whether S converges or diverges.

60. (a) Find the Taylor series generated by $f(x) = \ln(1+x)$ at $x = 0$. Include an expression for the general term.

(b) For what values of x does the series in part (a) converge?

(c) Use Theorem 13 to find a bound for the error in evaluating $\ln(3/2)$ by using only the first five nonzero terms of the series in part (a).

(d) Use the result found in part (a) to determine the logarithmic function whose Taylor series is

$$\sum_{n=1}^{\infty} \frac{(-1)^{n+1}x^{2n}}{2n}.$$

61. Determine all values of x for which the series

$$\sum_{k=0}^{\infty} \frac{2^k x^k}{\ln(k+2)}$$

converges. Justify your answer.

62. Consider the series $\displaystyle\sum_{n=2}^{\infty} \frac{1}{n^p \ln n}$, where $p \ge 0$.

(a) Show that the series converges for $p > 1$.

(b) **Writing to Learn** Determine whether the series converges or diverges for $p = 1$. Show your analysis.

(c) Show that the series diverges for $0 \le p < 1$.

63. The Maclaurin series for $1/(1+x)$ converges for $-1 < x < 1$, but when we integrate it term by term, the resulting series for $\ln|1+x|$ converges for $-1 < x \le 1$. Verify the convergence at $x = 1$.

64. The Maclaurin series for $1/(1+x^2)$ converges for $-1 < x < 1$, but when we integrate it term by term, the resulting series for $\arctan x$ converges for $-1 \le x \le 1$. Verify the convergence at $x = 1$ and $x = -1$.

65. (a) The series

$$\frac{1}{3} - \frac{1}{2} + \frac{1}{9} - \frac{1}{4} + \frac{1}{27} - \frac{1}{8} + \cdots + \frac{1}{3^n} - \frac{1}{2^n} + \cdots$$

fails to satisfy one of the conditions of the Alternating Series Test. Which one?

(b) Find the sum of the series in part (a).

Standardized Test Questions

You may use a graphing calculator to solve the following problems.

66. True or False The series

$$\sum_{n=1}^{\infty} (-1)^{n+1} \frac{x^{2n}}{2n}$$

converges at the endpoints of its interval of convergence. Justify your answer.

67. True or False If S_{100} is used to estimate the sum of the series

$$\sum_{n=1}^{\infty} \frac{(-1)^n}{n^2},$$

the estimate is an overestimate. Justify your answer.

In Exercises 68 and 69, use the series $\displaystyle\sum_{n=0}^{\infty} \frac{n(2x-5)^n}{n+2}$.

68. Multiple Choice Which of the following is the radius of convergence of the series?

(A) 1   (B) 1/2   (C) 3/2   (D) 2   (E) 5/2

69. Multiple Choice Which of the following is the interval of convergence of the series?

(A) $2 < x < 3$ (B) $4 < x < 6$ (C) $-\frac{1}{2} < x < \frac{1}{2}$

(D) $-3 < x < -2$ (E) $-6 < x < -4$

70. Multiple Choice Which of the following series converge?

I. $\displaystyle\sum_{n=1}^{\infty} \frac{4}{\sqrt{n}}$ II. $\displaystyle\sum_{n=1}^{\infty} \frac{1}{(\ln 4)^n}$ III. $\displaystyle\sum_{n=1}^{\infty} \frac{(-1)^n}{n^2}$

(A) I only   (B) II only   (C) III only

(D) I & II only   (E) II & III only

71. Multiple Choice Which of the following gives the truncation error if S_{100} is used to approximate the sum of the series

$$\sum_{n=1}^{\infty} \frac{(-1)^n}{2^n}?$$

(A) $\dfrac{1}{3 \cdot 2^{101}}$ (B) $\dfrac{1}{3 \cdot 2^{100}}$ (C) $\dfrac{1}{2^{101}}$

(D) $\dfrac{3}{2^{101}}$ (E) $\dfrac{3}{2^{100}}$

Exploration

72. Group Activity Within your group, have each student construct a series that converges to one of the numbers $1, \ldots, n$. Then exchange your series with another group and try to figure out which number is matched with which series.

Extending the Ideas

Here is a test called the *nth-Root Test*.

---

nth-Root Test Let $\sum a_n$ be a series with $a_n \geq 0$ for $n \geq N$, and suppose that $\lim_{n \to \infty} \sqrt[n]{a_n} = L$.
Then,

    (a) the series *converges* if $L < 1$,

    (b) the series *diverges* if $L > 1$ or L is infinite,

    (c) the test is *inconclusive* if $L = 1$.

---

73. Use the *nth-Root Test* and the fact that $\lim_{n \to \infty} \sqrt[n]{n} = 1$ to test the following series for convergence or divergence.

    (a) $\displaystyle\sum_{n=1}^{\infty} \frac{n^2}{2^n}$

    (b) $\displaystyle\sum_{n=1}^{\infty} \left(\frac{n}{2n-1} \right)^n$

    (c) $\displaystyle\sum_{n=1}^{\infty} a_n$, where $a_n = \begin{cases} n/2^n, & n \text{ is odd} \\ 1/2^n, & n \text{ is even} \end{cases}$

74. Use the *nth-Root Test* and whatever else you need to find the intervals of convergence of the following series.

    (a) $\displaystyle\sum_{n=0}^{\infty} \frac{(x-1)^n}{4^n}$

    (b) $\displaystyle\sum_{n=1}^{\infty} \frac{(x-2)^n}{n \cdot 3^n}$

    (c) $\displaystyle\sum_{n=1}^{\infty} 2^n x^n$

    (d) $\displaystyle\sum_{n=0}^{\infty} (\ln x)^n$

Quick Quiz for AP* Preparation: Sections 10.4 and 10.5

You may use a graphing calculator to solve the following problems.

1. Multiple Choice Which of the following series converge?

    I. $\displaystyle\sum_{n=0}^{\infty} \frac{2}{n^2+1}$ II. $\displaystyle\sum_{n=1}^{\infty} \frac{2^n-1}{3^n+1}$ III. $\displaystyle\sum_{n=1}^{\infty} \frac{\sqrt[4]{n}}{n}$

    (A) I only   (B) II only   (C) III only

    (D) II & III only   (E) I & II only

2. Multiple Choice Which of the following is the sum of the telescoping series

$$\sum_{n=1}^{\infty} \frac{2}{(n+1)(n+2)}?$$

    (A) 1/3   (B) 1/2   (C) 3/5   (D) 2/3   (E) 1

3. Multiple Choice Which of the following describes the behavior of the series

$$\sum_{n=1}^{\infty} (-1)^n \frac{\ln n}{n}?$$

    I. converges   II. diverges   III. converges conditionally

    (A) I only   (B) II only   (C) III only

    (D) I & III only   (E) II & III only

4. Free Response Consider the power series

$$\sum_{n=0}^{\infty} \frac{n(2x+3)^n}{n+2}.$$

    (a) Find all values of x for which the series converges absolutely. Justify your answer.

    (b) Find all values of x for which the series converges conditionally. Justify your answer.

absolute convergence (p. 516)

alternating harmonic series (p. 527)

alternating series (p. 527)

Alternating Series Bound
Theorem (p. 528)

Alternating Series Test (p. 527)

binomial series (p. 502)

Binomial Theorem (p. 502)

center of power series (p. 484)

conditional convergence (p. 528)

Convergence Theorem for Power
Series (p. 514)

convergent sequence (p. 491)

convergent series (p. 482)

converges absolutely (p. 516)

differentiation of series (p. 485)

Direct Comparison Test (p. 515)

divergent sequence (p. 491)

divergent series (p. 482)

error term (p. 505)

Euler's formula (p. 509)

Euler's identities (p. 511)

finite sum (p. 481)

geometric series (p. 483)

harmonic series (p. 524)

hyperbolic sine and cosine (p. 510)

identity (p. 513)

infinite series (p. 482)

Integral Test (p. 523)

integration of series (p. 486)

interval of convergence (p. 483)

Lagrange error bound (p. 505)

Lagrange form of the remainder (p. 505)

Leibniz's Theorem (p. 527)

Limit Comparison Test (p. 525)

limit of a sequence (p. 491)

Maclaurin series (pp. 495, 499)

nth-Root Test (p. 536)

nth term of a series (p. 482)

nth-Term Test for divergence (p. 514)

partial sum (p. 482)

power series centered at $x = a$ (p. 484)

p-series (p. 524)

p-Series Test (p. 524)

quadratic approximation (p. 510)

radius of convergence (p. 514)

Ratio Test (p. 517)

rearrangement of series (p. 528)

Remainder Bounding Theorem (p. 507)

remainder of order n (p. 505)

representing functions by series (p. 484)

sum of a series (p. 481)

Taylor polynomial (p. 493)

Taylor polynomial of order n at
$x = a$ (p. 497)

Taylor series (p. 493)

Taylor series at $x = a$ (p. 497)

Taylor's formula (p. 505)

Taylor's Theorem with Remainder (p. 505)

telescoping series (p. 520)

Term-by-Term Differentiation
Theorem (p. 486)

Term-by-Term Integration
Theorem (p. 487)

terms of a series (p. 482)

truncation error (p. 503)

Exercise numbers with a gray background indicate problems that the authors have designed to be solved *without a calculator*.

The collection of exercises marked in red could be used as a chapter test.

In Exercises 1–16, find **(a)** the radius of convergence for the series and **(b)** its interval of convergence. Then identify the values of x for which the series converges **(c)** absolutely and **(d)** conditionally.

1. $\displaystyle\sum_{n=0}^{\infty} \frac{(-x)^n}{n!}$

2. $\displaystyle\sum_{n=1}^{\infty} \frac{(x + 4)^n}{n3^n}$

3. $\displaystyle\sum_{n=0}^{\infty} \left(\frac{2}{3}\right)^n (x - 1)^n$

4. $\displaystyle\sum_{n=1}^{\infty} \frac{(x - 1)^{2n-2}}{(2n - 1)!}$

5. $\displaystyle\sum_{n=1}^{\infty} \frac{(-1)^{n-1}(3x - 1)^n}{n^2}$

6. $\displaystyle\sum_{n=0}^{\infty} (n + 1)x^{3n}$

7. $\displaystyle\sum_{n=0}^{\infty} \frac{(n + 1)(2x + 1)^n}{(2n + 1)2^n}$

8. $\displaystyle\sum_{n=1}^{\infty} \frac{x^n}{n^n}$

9. $\displaystyle\sum_{n=1}^{\infty} \frac{x^n}{\sqrt{n}}$

10. $\displaystyle\sum_{n=1}^{\infty} \frac{e^n}{n^e} x^n$

11. $\displaystyle\sum_{n=0}^{\infty} \frac{(n + 1)x^{2n-1}}{3^n}$

12. $\displaystyle\sum_{n=0}^{\infty} \frac{(-1)^n(x - 1)^{2n+1}}{2n + 1}$

13. $\displaystyle\sum_{n=1}^{\infty} \frac{n!}{2^n} x^{2n}$

14. $\displaystyle\sum_{n=2}^{\infty} \frac{(10x)^n}{\ln n}$

15. $\displaystyle\sum_{n=1}^{\infty} (n + 1)! \, x^n$

16. $\displaystyle\sum_{n=1}^{\infty} \left(\frac{x^2 - 1}{2}\right)^n$

In Exercises 17–22, the series is the value of the Maclaurin series of a function $f(x)$ at a particular point. What function and what point? What is the sum of the series?

17. $1 - \dfrac{1}{4} + \dfrac{1}{16} - \cdots + (-1)^n \dfrac{1}{4^n} + \cdots$

18. $\dfrac{2}{3} - \dfrac{4}{18} + \dfrac{8}{81} - \cdots + (-1)^{n-1} \dfrac{2^n}{n3^n} + \cdots$

19. $\pi - \dfrac{\pi^3}{3!} + \dfrac{\pi^5}{5!} - \cdots + (-1)^n \dfrac{\pi^{2n+1}}{(2n + 1)!} + \cdots$

20. $1 - \dfrac{\pi^2}{9 \cdot 2!} + \dfrac{\pi^4}{81 \cdot 4!} - \cdots + (-1)^n \dfrac{\pi^{2n}}{3^{2n}(2n)!} + \cdots$

21. $1 + \ln 2 + \dfrac{(\ln 2)^2}{2!} + \cdots + \dfrac{(\ln 2)^n}{n!} + \cdots$

22. $\dfrac{1}{\sqrt{3}} - \dfrac{1}{9\sqrt{3}} + \dfrac{1}{45\sqrt{3}} - \cdots$

$+ (-1)^{n-1} \dfrac{1}{(2n - 1)(\sqrt{3})^{2n-1}} + \cdots$

In Exercises 23–36, find a Maclaurin series for the function.

23. $\dfrac{1}{1 - 6x}$

24. $\dfrac{1}{1 + x^3}$

25. $x^9 - 2x^2 + 1$

26. $\dfrac{4x}{1 - x}$

27. $\sin \pi x$

28. $-\sin \dfrac{2x}{3}$

29. $-x + \sin x$

30. $\dfrac{e^x + e^{-x}}{2}$

31. $\cos \sqrt{5x}$

32. $e^{(\pi x/2)}$

33. xe^{-x^2}

34. $\tan^{-1} 3x$

35. $\ln(1 - 2x)$

36. $x \ln(1 - x)$

In Exercises 37–40, find the first four nonzero terms and the general term of the Taylor series generated by f at $x = a$.

37. $f(x) = \dfrac{1}{3 - x}, \quad a = 2$

38. $f(x) = x^3 - 2x^2 + 5, \quad a = -1$

39. $f(x) = \dfrac{1}{x}, \quad a = 3$

40. $f(x) = \sin x, \quad a = \pi$

In Exercises 41–52, determine if the series converges absolutely, converges conditionally, or diverges. Give reasons for your answer.

41. $\displaystyle\sum_{n=1}^{\infty} \dfrac{-5}{n}$

42. $\displaystyle\sum_{n=1}^{\infty} \dfrac{(-1)^n}{\sqrt{n}}$

43. $\displaystyle\sum_{n=1}^{\infty} \dfrac{\ln n}{n^3}$

44. $\displaystyle\sum_{n=1}^{\infty} \dfrac{n + 1}{n!}$

45. $\displaystyle\sum_{n=1}^{\infty} \dfrac{(-1)^n}{\ln(n + 1)}$

46. $\displaystyle\sum_{n=2}^{\infty} \dfrac{1}{n(\ln n)^2}$

47. $\displaystyle\sum_{n=1}^{\infty} \dfrac{(-3)^n}{n!}$

48. $\displaystyle\sum_{n=1}^{\infty} \dfrac{2^n 3^n}{n^n}$

49. $\displaystyle\sum_{n=1}^{\infty} \dfrac{(-1)^n(n^2 + 1)}{2n^2 + n - 1}$

50. $\displaystyle\sum_{n=1}^{\infty} \dfrac{1}{\sqrt{n(n + 1)(n + 2)}}$

51. $\displaystyle\sum_{n=2}^{\infty} \dfrac{1}{n\sqrt{n^2 - 1}}$

52. $\displaystyle\sum_{n=1}^{\infty} \left(\dfrac{n}{n + 1}\right)^n$

In Exercises 53 and 54, find the sum of the series.

53. $\displaystyle\sum_{n=3}^{\infty} \dfrac{1}{(2n - 3)(2n - 1)}$

54. $\displaystyle\sum_{n=2}^{\infty} \dfrac{-2}{n(n + 1)}$

55. Let f be a function that has derivatives of all orders for all real numbers. Assume that $f(3) = 1, f'(3) = 4, f''(3) = 6$, and $f'''(3) = 12$.

  (a) Write the third-order Taylor polynomial for f at $x = 3$ and use it to approximate $f(3.2)$.

  (b) Write the second-order Taylor polynomial for f' at $x = 3$ and use it to approximate $f'(2.7)$.

  (c) Does the linearization of f underestimate or overestimate the values of $f(x)$ near $x = 3$? Justify your answer.

56. Let

$$P_4(x) = 7 - 3(x - 4) + 5(x - 4)^2 - 2(x - 4)^3 + 6(x - 4)^4$$

be the Taylor polynomial of order 4 for the function f at $x = 4$. Assume f has derivatives of all orders for all real numbers.

  (a) Find $f(4)$ and $f'''(4)$.

  (b) Write the second-order Taylor polynomial for f' at $x = 4$ and use it to approximate $f'(4.3)$.

  (c) Write the fourth-order Taylor polynomial for $g(x) = \int_4^x f(t)\, dt$ at $x = 4$.

  (d) Can the exact value of $f(3)$ be determined from the information given? Justify your answer.

57. **(a)** Write the first three nonzero terms and the general term of the Taylor series generated by $f(x) = 5 \sin(x/2)$ at $x = 0$.

  (b) What is the interval of convergence for the series found in (a)? Show your method.

  (c) **Writing to Learn** What is the minimum number of terms of the series in (a) needed to approximate $f(x)$ on the interval $(-2, 2)$ with an error not exceeding 0.1 in magnitude? Show your method.

58. Let $f(x) = 1/(1 - 2x)$.

  (a) Write the first four terms and the general term of the Taylor series generated by $f(x)$ at $x = 0$.

  (b) What is the interval of convergence for the series found in part (a)? Show your method.

  (c) Find $f(-1/4)$. How many terms of the series are adequate for approximating $f(-1/4)$ with an error not exceeding one percent in magnitude? Justify your answer.

59. Let $f(x) = \displaystyle\sum_{n=1}^{\infty} \dfrac{x^n n^n}{n!}$

for all x for which the series converges.

  (a) Find the radius of convergence of this series.

  (b) Use the first three terms of this series to approximate $f(-1/3)$.

  (c) Estimate the error involved in the approximation in part (b). Justify your answer.

60. Let $f(x) = 1/(x - 2)$.

  (a) Write the first four terms and the general term of the Taylor series generated by $f(x)$ at $x = 3$.

  (b) Use the result from part (a) to find the first four terms and the general term of the series generated by $\ln|x - 2|$ at $x = 3$.

  (c) Use the series in part (b) to compute a number that differs from $\ln(3/2)$ by less than 0.05. Justify your answer.

61. Let $f(x) = e^{-2x^2}$.

(a) Find the first four nonzero terms and the general term for the power series generated by $f(x)$ at $x = 0$.

(b) Find the interval of convergence of the series generated by $f(x)$ at $x = 0$. Show the analysis that leads to your conclusion.

(c) **Writing to Learn** Let g be the function defined by the sum of the first four nonzero terms of the series generated by $f(x)$. Show that $|f(x) - g(x)| < 0.02$ for $-0.6 \leq x \leq 0.6$.

62. (a) Find the Maclaurin series generated by $f(x) = x^2/(1 + x)$.

(b) Does the series converge at $x = 1$? Explain.

63. *Evaluating Nonelementary Integrals* Maclaurin series can be used to express nonelementary integrals in terms of series.

(a) Express $\int_0^x \sin t^2 \, dt$ as a power series.

(b) According to the Alternating Series Bound Theorem, how many terms of the series in part (a) should you use to estimate $\int_0^1 \sin x^2 \, dx$ with an error of less than 0.001?

(c) Use NINT to approximate $\int_0^1 \sin x^2 \, dx$.

(d) How close to the answer in part (c) do you get if you use four terms of the series in part (a)?

64. *Estimating an Integral* Suppose you want a quick noncalculator estimate for the value of $\int_0^1 x^2 e^x \, dx$. There are several ways to get one.

(a) Use the Trapezoidal Rule with $n = 2$ to estimate $\int_0^1 x^2 e^x \, dx$.

(b) Write the first three nonzero terms of the Maclaurin series for $x^2 e^x$ to obtain the fourth-order Maclaurin polynomial $P_4(x)$ for $x^2 e^x$. Use $\int_0^1 P_4(x) \, dx$ to obtain another estimate of $\int_0^1 x^2 e^x \, dx$.

(c) **Writing to Learn** The second derivative of $f(x) = x^2 e^x$ is positive for all $x > 0$. Explain why this enables you to conclude that the Trapezoidal Rule estimate obtained in part (a) is too large.

(d) **Writing to Learn** All the derivatives of $f(x) = x^2 e^x$ are positive for $x > 0$. Explain why this enables you to conclude that all Maclaurin series approximations to $f(x)$ for x in $[0, 1]$ will be too small. [*Hint:* $f(x) = P_n(x) + R_n(x)$.]

(e) Use integration by parts to evaluate $\int_0^1 x^2 e^x \, dx$.

65. *Perpetuities* Suppose you want to give a favorite school or charity $1000 a year forever. This kind of gift is called a *perpetuity*. Assume you can earn 8% annually on your money, i.e., that a payment of a_n today will be worth $a_n(1.08)^n$ in n years.

(a) Show that the amount you must invest today to cover the nth $1000 payment in n years is $1000(1.08)^{-n}$.

(b) Construct an infinite series that gives the amount you must invest today to cover *all* the payments in the perpetuity.

(c) Show that the series in part (b) converges and find its sum. This sum is called the *present value* of the perpetuity. What does it represent?

66. *(Continuation of Exercise 65)* Find the present value of a $1000-per-year perpetuity at 6% annual interest.

67. *Expected Payoff* How much would you expect to win playing the following game?

Toss a *fair* coin (heads and tails equally likely). Every time it comes up heads you win a dollar, but the game is over as soon as it comes up tails.

(a) The *expected payoff* of the game is computed by summing all possible payoffs times their respective probabilities. If the probability of tossing the first tail on the nth toss is $(1/2)^n$, express the expected payoff of this game as an infinite series.

(b) Differentiate both sides of

$$\frac{1}{1 - x} = 1 + x + x^2 + \cdots + x^n + \cdots$$

to get a series for $1/(1 - x)^2$.

(c) Use the series in part (b) to get a series for $x^2/(1 - x)^2$.

(d) Use the series in part (c) to evaluate the expected payoff of the game.

68. *Punching Out Triangles* This exercise refers to the "right side up" equilateral triangle with sides of length $2b$ in the accompanying figure.

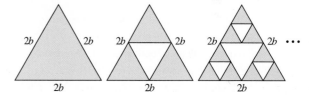

"Upside down" equilateral triangles are removed from the original triangle as the sequence of pictures suggests. The sum of the areas removed from the original triangle forms an infinite series.

(a) Find this infinite series.

(b) Find the sum of this infinite series and hence find the total area removed from the original triangle.

(c) Is every point on the original triangle removed? Explain why or why not.

69. *Nicole Oresme's (pronounced "O-rem's") Theorem* Prove Nicole Oresme's Theorem that

$$1 + \frac{1}{2} \cdot 2 + \frac{1}{4} \cdot 3 + \cdots + \frac{n}{2^{n-1}} + \cdots = 4.$$

[*Hint:* Differentiate both sides of the equation $1/(1 - x) = 1 + \sum_{n=1}^{\infty} x^n$.]

70. (a) Show that

$$\sum_{n=1}^{\infty} \frac{n(n + 1)}{x^n} = \frac{2x^2}{(x - 1)^3}$$

for $|x| > 1$ by differentiating the identity

$$\sum_{n=1}^{\infty} x^{n+1} = \frac{x^2}{1 - x}$$

twice, multiplying the result by x, and then replacing x by $1/x$.

(b) Use part (a) to find the real solution greater than 1 of the equation

$$x = \sum_{n=1}^{\infty} \frac{n(n+1)}{x^n}.$$

AP* Examination Preparation

You may use a graphing calculator to solve the following problems.

71. Let $f(x) = \dfrac{1}{x+1}$.

(a) Find the first three terms and the general term for the Taylor series for f at $x = 1$.

(b) Find the interval of convergence for the series in part (a). Justify your answer.

(c) Find the third-order Taylor polynomial for f at $x = 1$, and use it to approximate $f(0.5)$.

72. Let $f(x) = \sum_{n=0}^{\infty} \dfrac{nx^n}{2^n}$.

(a) Find the interval of convergence of the series. Justify your answer.

(b) Show that the first nine terms of the series are sufficient to approximate $f(-1)$ with an error less than 0.01.

73. Let f be a function that has derivatives of all orders for all real numbers. Assume that $f(0) = -1, f'(0) = 2, f''(0) = -3$, and $f'''(0) = 4$.

(a) Write the linearization for f at $x = 0$.

(b) Write the quadratic approximation for f at $x = 0$.

(c) Write the third-degree Taylor approximation $P_3(x)$ for f at $x = 0$.

(d) Use $P_3(x)$ to approximate $f(0.7)$.

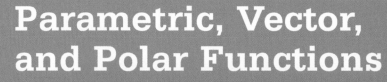

CHAPTER

11 Parametric, Vector, and Polar Functions

11.1 Parametric Functions

11.2 Vectors in the Plane

11.3 Polar Functions

When and how do you make the burn for a translunar injection, taking a spaceship out of earth orbit and onto a trajectory that will lead to a lunar orbit? To solve this problem, we must first understand how gravitational attraction shapes the path of a satellite in the earth or lunar orbit. In his *Mathematical Principles of Natural Philosophy* of 1687, Isaac Newton showed that these paths would always be conic sections: circles, ellipses, parabolas, or hyperbolas. Today, his solution is written in the language of parametric equations, vectors, and—especially—polar coordinates. We will explore this connection in Section 11.3.

CHAPTER 11   Overview

The material in this book is generally described as the calculus of a single variable, since it deals with functions of one independent variable (usually x or t). In this chapter you will apply your understanding of single-variable calculus in three kinds of two-variable contexts, enabling you to analyze some new kinds of curves (parametrically defined and polar) and to analyze motion in the plane that does not proceed along a straight line. Interestingly enough, this will not require the tools of multivariable calculus, which you will probably learn in your next calculus course. We will simply use single-variable calculus in some new and interesting ways.

11.1 | Parametric Functions

You will be able to extend the calculation of derivatives to parametric functions.

- The slope and concavity of a curve given by parametric functions
- The length of a curve (arc length) given by parametric functions

Parametric Curves in the Plane

We reviewed parametrically defined functions in Section 1.4. Instead of defining the points (x, y) on a planar curve by relating y directly to x, we can define both coordinates as functions of a parameter t. The resulting set of points may or may not define y as a function of x (that is, the parametric curve might fail the vertical line test).

EXAMPLE 1   Reviewing Some Parametric Curves

Sketch the parametric curves and identify those which define y as a function of x. In each case, eliminate the parameter to find an equation that relates x and y directly.

(a) $x = \cos t$ and $y = \sin t$ for t in the interval $[0, 2\pi)$

(b) $x = 3 \cos t$ and $y = 2 \sin t$ for t in the interval $[0, 4\pi]$

(c) $x = \sqrt{t}$ and $y = t - 2$ for t in the interval $[0, 4]$

SOLUTION

(a) This is probably the best-known parametrization of all. The curve is the unit circle (Figure 11.1a), and it does not define y as a function of x. To eliminate the parameter, we use the identity $(\cos t)^2 + (\sin t)^2 = 1$ to write $x^2 + y^2 = 1$.

(b) This parametrization stretches the unit circle by a factor of 3 horizontally and by a factor of 2 vertically. The result is an ellipse (Figure 11.1b), which is traced twice as t covers the interval $[0, 4\pi]$. (In fact, the point $(3, 0)$ is visited three times.) It does not define y as a function of x. We use the same identity as in part (a) to write $\left(\dfrac{x}{3}\right)^2 + \left(\dfrac{y}{2}\right)^2 = 1$.

(c) This parametrization produces a segment of a parabola (Figure 11.1c). It does define y as a function of x. Since $t = x^2$, we write $y = x^2 - 2$.   ***Now Try Exercise 1.***

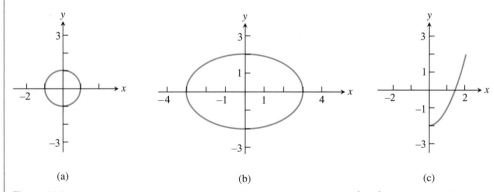

(a)   (b)   (c)

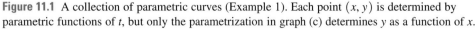

Figure 11.1 A collection of parametric curves (Example 1). Each point (x, y) is determined by parametric functions of t, but only the parametrization in graph (c) determines y as a function of x.

Slope and Concavity

We can analyze the slope and concavity of parametric curves just as we can with explicitly defined curves. The slope of the curve is still dy/dx, and the concavity still depends on d^2y/dx^2, so all that is needed is a way of differentiating with respect to x when everything is given in terms of t. The required parametric differentiation formulas are straightforward applications of the Chain Rule.

Parametric Differentiation Formulas

If x and y are both differentiable functions of t and if $dx/dt \neq 0$, then

$$\frac{dy}{dx} = \frac{dy/dt}{dx/dt}.$$

If $y' = dy/dx$ is also a differentiable function of t, then

$$\frac{d^2y}{dx^2} = \frac{d}{dx}(y') = \frac{dy'/dt}{dx/dt}.$$

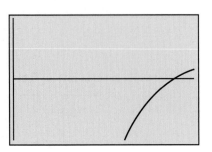

Figure 11.2 The parametric curve defined in Example 2.

EXAMPLE 2 Analyzing a Parametric Curve

Consider the curve defined parametrically by $x = t^2 - 5$ and $y = 2 \sin t$ for $0 \leq t \leq \pi$.

(a) Sketch a graph of the curve in the viewing window $[-7, 7]$ by $[-4, 4]$. Indicate the direction in which it is traced.

(b) Find the highest point on the curve. Justify your answer.

(c) Find all points of inflection on the curve. Justify your answer.

SOLUTION

(a) The curve is shown in Figure 11.2.

(b) We seek to maximize y as a function of t, so we compute $dy/dt = 2 \cos t$. Since dy/dt is positive for $0 \leq t < \pi/2$ and negative for $\pi/2 < t \leq \pi$, the maximum occurs when $t = \pi/2$. Substituting this t-value into the parametrization, we find the highest point to be approximately $(-2.533, 2)$.

(c) First we compute d^2y/dx^2.

$$\frac{dy}{dx} = \frac{dy/dt}{dx/dt} = \frac{2 \cos t}{2t} = \frac{\cos t}{t}$$

$$\frac{d^2y}{dx^2} = \frac{dy'/dt}{dx/dt} = \frac{\dfrac{(-\sin t)(t) - (1)(\cos t)}{t^2}}{2t} = -\frac{t \sin t + \cos t}{2t^3}$$

A graph of

$$z = -\frac{t \sin t + \cos t}{2t^3} \quad \text{on the interval } [0, \pi] \text{ (Figure 11.3)}$$

shows a sign change at $t = 2.798386\ldots$. Substituting this t value into the parametrization, we find the point of inflection to be approximately $(2.831, 0.673)$.

Now Try Exercise 19.

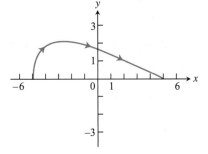

$[0, \pi]$ by $[-0.1, 0.1]$

Figure 11.3 The graph of d^2y/dx^2 for the parametric curve in Example 2 shows a sign change at $t = 2.798386\ldots$, indicating a point of inflection on the curve. (Example 2)

Arc Length

In Section 8.4 we derived two different formulas for arc length, each of them based on an approximation of the curve by tiny straight line segments with length $\sqrt{\Delta x_k{}^2 + \Delta y_k{}^2}$. (See Figure 11.4.)

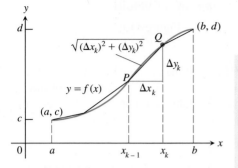

Figure 11.4 The graph of f, approximated by line segments.

Here is a third formula based on the same approximation.

Arc Length of a Parametrized Curve

Let L be the length of a parametric curve that is traversed exactly once as t increases from t_1 to t_2.

If dx/dt and dy/dt are continuous functions of t, then

$$L = \int_{t_1}^{t_2} \sqrt{\left(\frac{dx}{dt}\right)^2 + \left(\frac{dy}{dt}\right)^2}\, dt.$$

$x = \cos^3 t, \, y = \sin^3 t, \, 0 \le t \le 2\pi$

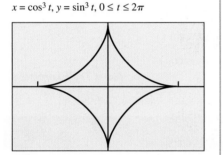

Figure 11.5 The astroid in Example 3.

EXAMPLE 3 Measuring a Parametric Curve

Find the length of the astroid (Figure 11.5)

$$x = \cos^3 t, \quad y = \sin^3 t, \quad 0 \le t \le 2\pi.$$

SOLUTION

The curve is traced once as t goes from 0 to 2π. Because of the curve's symmetry with respect to the coordinate axes, its length is four times the length of the first quadrant portion. We have

$$\left(\frac{dx}{dt}\right)^2 = \left((3\cos^2 t)(-\sin t)\right)^2 = 9\cos^4 t \sin^2 t$$

$$\left(\frac{dy}{dt}\right)^2 = \left((3\sin^2 t)(\cos t)\right)^2 = 9\sin^4 t \cos^2 t$$

$$\sqrt{\left(\frac{dx}{dt}\right)^2 + \left(\frac{dy}{dt}\right)^2} = \sqrt{9\cos^2 t \sin^2 t \underbrace{(\cos^2 t + \sin^2 t)}_{1}}$$

$$= \sqrt{9\cos^2 t \sin^2 t}$$

$$= 3|\cos t \sin t|$$

Thus, the length of the first quadrant portion of the curve is

$$\int_0^{\pi/2} 3|\cos t \sin t|\, dt = 3\int_0^{\pi/2} \cos t \sin t\, dt \quad \text{\small $\cos t \sin t \ge 0, 0 \le t \le \pi/2$}$$

$$= \frac{3}{2}\sin^2 t\,\Big]_0^{\pi/2} \quad \text{\small $u = \sin t, \, du = \cos t\, dt$}$$

$$= \frac{3}{2}$$

The length of the astroid is $4(3/2) = 6$.

Now Try Exercise 29.

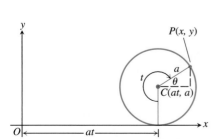

Figure 11.6 The position of $P(x, y)$ on the edge of the wheel when the wheel has turned t radians. (Example 4)

Cycloids

Suppose that a wheel of radius a rolls along a horizontal line without slipping (see Figure 11.6). The path traced by a point P on the wheel's edge is a **cycloid,** where P is originally at the origin.

Huygens's Clock

The problem with a pendulum clock whose bob swings in a circular arc is that the frequency of the swing depends on the amplitude of the swing. The wider the swing, the longer it takes the bob to return to center.

This does not happen if the bob can be made to swing in a cycloid. In 1673, Christiaan Huygens (1629–1695), the Dutch mathematician, physicist, and astronomer who discovered the rings of Saturn, designed a pendulum clock whose bob would swing in a cycloid. Driven by a need to make accurate determinations of longitude at sea, he hung the bob from a fine wire constrained by guards that caused it to draw up as it swung away from center. How were the guards shaped? They were cycloids, too.

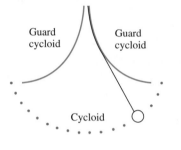

EXAMPLE 4 Finding Parametric Equations for a Cycloid

Find parametric equations for the path of the point P in Figure 11.6.

SOLUTION

We suppose that the wheel rolls to the right, P being at the origin when the turn angle t equals 0. Figure 11.6 shows the wheel after it has turned t radians. The base of the wheel is at distance at from the origin. The wheel's center is at (at, a), and the coordinates of P are

$$x = at + a \cos \theta, \quad y = a + a \sin \theta.$$

To express θ in terms of t, we observe that $t + \theta = 3\pi/2 + 2k\pi$ for some integer k, so

$$\theta = \frac{3\pi}{2} - t + 2k\pi.$$

Thus,

$$\cos \theta = \cos \left(\frac{3\pi}{2} - t + 2k\pi \right) = -\sin t,$$

$$\sin \theta = \sin \left(\frac{3\pi}{2} - t + 2k\pi \right) = -\cos t$$

Therefore,

$$x = at - a \sin t = a(t - \sin t),$$

$$y = a - a \cos t = a(1 - \cos t)$$

Now Try Exercise 41.

EXPLORATION 1 Investigating Cycloids

Consider the cycloids with parametric equations

$$x = a(t - \sin t), \quad y = a(1 - \cos t), \quad a > 0.$$

1. Graph the equations for $a = 1, 2,$ and 3.
2. Find the x-intercepts.
3. Show that $y \geq 0$ for all t.
4. Explain why the arches of a cycloid are congruent.
5. What is the maximum value of y? Where is it attained?
6. Describe the graph of a cycloid.

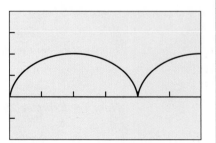

[0, 3π] by [−2, 4]

Figure 11.7 The graph of the cycloid $x = t - \sin t, y = 1 - \cos t, t \geq 0$. (Example 5)

EXAMPLE 5 Finding Length

Find the length of one arch of the cycloid

$$x = a(t - \sin t), \quad y = a(1 - \cos t), \quad a > 0.$$

SOLUTION

Figure 11.7 shows the first arch of the cycloid and part of the next for $a = 1$. In Exploration 1 you found that the x-intercepts occur at t equal to multiples of 2π and that the arches are congruent.

The length of the first arch is

$$\int_0^{2\pi} \sqrt{\left(\frac{dx}{dt} \right)^2 + \left(\frac{dy}{dt} \right)^2} \, dt.$$

continued

We have

$$\left(\frac{dx}{dt}\right)^2 = [a(1 - \cos t)]^2 = a^2(1 - 2\cos t + \cos^2 t)$$

$$\left(\frac{dy}{dt}\right)^2 = [a\sin t]^2 = a^2\sin^2 t$$

$$\sqrt{\left(\frac{dx}{dt}\right)^2 + \left(\frac{dy}{dt}\right)^2} = a\sqrt{2 - 2\cos t} \quad a > 0,\ \sin^2 t + \cos^2 t = 1$$

Therefore,

$$\int_0^{2\pi}\sqrt{\left(\frac{dx}{dt}\right)^2 + \left(\frac{dy}{dt}\right)^2}\,dt = a\int_0^{2\pi}\sqrt{2 - 2\cos t}\,dt = 8a. \quad \text{Using NINT}$$

The length of one arch of the cycloid is $8a$.   ***Now Try Exercise 43.***

Quick Review 11.1   *(For help, go to Appendix A.1.)*

Exercise numbers with a gray background indicate problems that the authors have designed to be solved *without a calculator.*

Use algebra or a trig identity to write an equation relating x and y.

1. $x = t + 1$ and $y = 2t + 3$

2. $x = 3t$ and $y = 54t^3 - 3$

3. $x = \sin t$ and $y = \cos t$

4. $x = \sin t \cos t$ and $y = \sin(2t)$

5. $x = \tan\theta$ and $y = \sec\theta$

6. $x = \csc\theta$ and $y = \cot\theta$

7. $x = \cos\theta$ and $y = \cos(2\theta)$

8. $x = \sin\theta$ and $y = \cos(2\theta)$

9. $x = \cos\theta$ and $y = \sin\theta\ (0 \le \theta \le \pi)$

10. $x = \cos\theta$ and $y = \sin\theta\ (\pi \le \theta \le 2\pi)$

Section 11.1 Exercises

In Exercises 1–6, sketch the parametric curves and identify those which define y as a function of x. In each case, eliminate the parameter to find an equation that relates x and y directly.

1. $x = 2t + 3$ and $y = 4t - 3$ for t in the interval $[0, 3]$

2. $x = \sqrt{t - 2}$ and $y = \dfrac{t + 5}{4}$ for t in the interval $[3, 11]$

3. $x = \tan t$ and $y = \sec t$ for t in the interval $[0, \pi/4]$

4. $x = \sin t$ and $y = 2\cos t$ for t in the interval $[0, \pi]$

5. $x = \sin t$ and $y = \cos(2t)$ for t in the interval $[0, 2\pi]$

6. $x = \sin 6t$ and $y = 2t$ for t in the interval $[0, \pi/2]$

In Exercises 7–16, find (a) dy/dx and (b) d^2y/dx^2 in terms of t.

7. $x = 4\sin t,\quad y = 2\cos t$

8. $x = \cos t,\quad y = \sqrt{3}\cos t$

9. $x = -\sqrt{t + 1},\quad y = \sqrt{3}\,t$

10. $x = 1/t,\quad y = -2 + \ln t$

11. $x = t^2 - 3t,\quad y = t^3$

12. $x = t^2 + t,\quad y = t^2 - t$

13. $x = \tan t,\quad y = \sec t$

14. $x = 2\cos t,\quad y = \cos(2t)$

15. $x = \ln(2t),\quad y = \ln(3t)^4$

16. $x = \ln(5t),\quad y = e^{5t}$

In Exercises 17–22,

(a) sketch the curve over the given t-interval, indicating the direction in which it is traced,

(b) identify the requested point, and

(c) justify that you have found the requested point by analyzing an appropriate derivative. You may use a grapher, as was done in Example 2, part (c).

17. $x = t + 1,\quad y = t^2 + t,\quad -2 \le t \le 2$ Lowest point

18. $x = t^2 + 2t,\quad y = t^2 - 2t + 3,\quad -2 \le t \le 3$ Leftmost point

19. $x = 2\sin t,\quad y = \cos t,\quad 0 \le t \le \pi$ Rightmost point

20. $x = \tan t,\quad y = 2\sec t,\quad -1 \le t \le 1$ Lowest point

21. $x = 2\sin t,\quad y = \cos(2t),\quad 1.5 \le t \le 4.5$ Highest point

22. $x = \ln(5t),\quad y = \ln(4t^2),\quad 0 < t \le 10$ Rightmost point

In Exercises 23–26, find the points at which the tangent line to the curve is (a) horizontal or (b) vertical.

23. $x = 2 + \cos t,\quad y = -1 + \sin t$

24. $x = \sec t,\quad y = \tan t$

25. $x = 2 - t,\quad y = t^3 - 4t$

26. $x = -2 + 3\cos t,\quad y = 1 + 3\sin t$

In Exercises 27–34, find the length of the curve. (For an algebraic challenge, evaluate the integrals in Exercises 29–34 without a calculator.)

27. $x = \cos t, \quad y = \sin t, \quad 0 \le t \le 2\pi$

28. $x = 3 \sin t, \quad y = 3 \cos t, \quad 0 \le t \le \pi$

29. $x = 8 \cos t + 8t \sin t, \quad y = 8 \sin t - 8t \cos t, \quad 0 \le t \le \pi/2$

30. $x = 2 \cos^3 t, \quad y = 2 \sin^3 t, \quad 0 \le t \le 2\pi$

31. $x = \dfrac{(2t + 3)^{3/2}}{3}, \quad y = t + \dfrac{t^2}{2}, \quad 0 \le t \le 3$

32. $x = \dfrac{(8t + 8)^{3/2}}{12}, \quad y = t^2 + t, \quad 0 \le t \le 2$

33. $x = \dfrac{1}{3} t^3, \quad y = \dfrac{1}{2} t^2, \quad 0 \le t \le 1$

34. $x = \ln(\sec t + \tan t) - \sin t, \quad y = \cos t, \quad 0 \le t \le \pi/3$

35. *Length Is Independent of Parametrization* To illustrate the fact that the numbers we get for length do not usually depend on the way we parametrize our curves, calculate the length of the semicircle $y = \sqrt{1 - x^2}$ with these two different parametrizations.

(a) $x = \cos 2t, \quad y = \sin 2t, \quad 0 \le t \le \pi/2$

(b) $x = \sin \pi t, \quad y = \cos \pi t, \quad -1/2 \le t \le 1/2$

36. *Perimeter of an Ellipse* Find the length of the ellipse $x = 3 \cos t, \quad y = 4 \sin t, \quad 0 \le t \le 2\pi$.

37. *Cartesian Length Formula* The graph of a function $y = f(x)$ over an interval $[a, b]$ automatically has the parametrization

$$x = x, \quad y = f(x), \quad a \le x \le b.$$

The parameter in this case is x itself. Show that for this parametrization, the length formula

$$L = \int_a^b \sqrt{\left(\frac{dx}{dt}\right)^2 + \left(\frac{dy}{dt}\right)^2}\, dt$$

reduces to the Cartesian formula

$$L = \int_a^b \sqrt{1 + \left(\frac{dy}{dx}\right)^2}\, dx$$

derived in Section 8.4.

38. *(Continuation of Exercise 37)* Show that the Cartesian formula

$$L = \int_c^d \sqrt{1 + \left(\frac{dx}{dy}\right)^2}\, dy$$

for the length of the curve $x = g(y), c \le y \le d$, from Section 8.4 is a special case of the parametric length formula

$$L = \int_a^b \sqrt{\left(\frac{dx}{dt}\right)^2 + \left(\frac{dy}{dt}\right)^2}\, dt.$$

Exercises 39 and 40 refer to the region bounded by the x-axis and one arch of the cycloid

$$x = a(t - \sin t), \quad y = a(1 - \cos t)$$

that is shaded in the figure shown at the top of the next column.

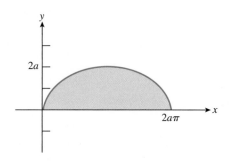

39. Find the area of the shaded region. [*Hint:* $dx = (dx/dt)\, dt$]

40. Find the volume swept out by revolving the region about the x-axis. [*Hint:* $dV = \pi y^2\, dx = \pi y^2 (dx/dt)\, dt$]

41. *Curtate Cycloid* Modify Example 4 slightly to find the parametric equations for the motion of a point in the *interior* of a wheel of radius a as the wheel rolls along the horizontal line without slipping. Assume that the point is at distance b from the center of the wheel, where $0 < b < a$. This curve, known as a *curtate cycloid,* has been used by artisans in designing the arches of violins (*Source:* mathworld.wolfram.com).

42. *Prolate Cycloid* Modify Example 4 slightly to find the parametric equations for the motion of a point on the *exterior* of a wheel of radius a as the wheel rolls along the horizontal line without slipping. Assume that the point is at distance b from the center of the wheel, where $a < b < 2a$. This curve, known as a *prolate cycloid,* is traced out by a point on the outer edge of a train's flanged wheel as the train moves along a track. (If you graph a prolate cycloid, you can see why they say that there is always part of a forward-moving train that is moving backward!)

43. *Arc Length* Find the length of one arch (that is, the curve over one period) of the curtate cycloid defined parametrically by $x = 3t - 2 \sin t$ and $y = 3 - 2 \cos t$.

44. *Arc Length* Find the length of one arch (that is, the curve over one period) of the prolate cycloid defined parametrically by $x = 2t - 3 \sin t$ and $y = 2 - 3 \cos t$.

Standardized Test Questions

45. True or False In a parametrization, if x is a continuous function of t and y is a continuous function of t, then y is a continuous function of x. Justify your answer.

46. True or False If f is a function with domain all real numbers, then the graph of f can be defined parametrically by $x = t$ and $y = f(t)$ for $-\infty < t < \infty$. Justify your answer.

47. Multiple Choice For which of the following parametrizations of the unit circle will the circle be traversed clockwise?

(A) $x = \cos t, \quad y = \sin t, \quad 0 \le t \le 2\pi$

(B) $x = \sin t, \quad y = \cos t, \quad 0 \le t \le 2\pi$

(C) $x = -\cos t, \quad y = -\sin t, \quad 0 \le t \le 2\pi$

(D) $x = -\sin t, \quad y = \cos t, \quad 0 \le t \le 2\pi$

(E) $x = \sin t, \quad y = -\cos t, \quad 0 \le t \le 2\pi$

48. Multiple Choice A parametric curve is defined by $x = \sin t$ and $y = \csc t$ for $0 < t < \pi/2$. This curve is

(A) increasing and concave up.

(B) increasing and concave down.

(C) decreasing and concave up.

(D) decreasing and concave down.

(E) decreasing with a point of inflection.

49. Multiple Choice The parametric curve defined by $x = \ln(t)$, $y = t$ for $t > 0$ is identical to the graph of the function

(A) $y = \ln x$ for all real x.

(B) $y = \ln^x$ for $x > 0$.

(C) $y = e^x$ for all real x.

(D) $y = e^x$ for $x > 0$.

(E) $y = \ln(e^x)$ for $x > 0$.

50. Multiple Choice The curve parametrized by

$$x = 6 \sin t - 3 \sin(7t) \text{ and } y = 6 \cos t - 3 \cos(7t),$$

as shown in the diagram below, is traversed exactly once as t increases from 0 to 2π. The total length of the curve is given by

(A) $\int_0^{2\pi} \sqrt{(6 \sin t - 3 \sin(7t))^2 + (6 \cos t - 3 \cos(7t))^2} \, dt$

(B) $\int_0^{2\pi} \sqrt{(6 \cos t - 3 \cos(7t))^2 + (6 \sin t - 3 \sin(7t))^2} \, dt$

(C) $\int_0^{2\pi} \sqrt{(6 \cos t - 21 \cos(7t))^2 - (6 \sin t - 21 \sin(7t))^2} \, dt$

(D) $\int_0^{2\pi} \sqrt{(6 \cos t - 21 \cos(7t))^2 - (-6 \sin t + 21 \sin(7t))^2} \, dt$

(E) $\int_0^{2\pi} \sqrt{(6 \cos t - 3 \cos(7t))^2 + (6 \sin t + 3 \sin(3t))^2} \, dt$

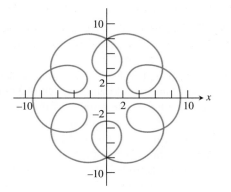

Explorations

51. Group Activity *Involute of a Circle* If a string wound around a fixed circle is unwound while being held taut in the plane of the circle, its end P traces an *involute* of the circle as suggested by the following diagram. In the diagram, the circle is the unit circle in the xy-plane, and the initial position of the tracing point is the point $(1, 0)$ on the x-axis. The unwound portion of the string is tangent to the circle at Q, and t is the radian measure of the angle from the positive x-axis to the segment OQ.

(a) Derive parametric equations for the involute by expressing the coordinates x and y of P in terms of t for $t \geq 0$.

(b) Find the length of the involute for $0 \leq t \leq 2\pi$.

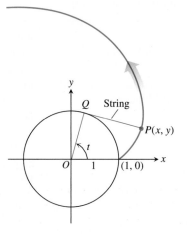

52. (Continuation of Exercise 51) Repeat Exercise 51 using the circle of radius a centered at the origin, $x^2 + y^2 = a^2$.

In Exercises 53–56, a projectile is launched over horizontal ground at an angle θ with the horizontal and with initial velocity v_0 ft/sec. Its path is given by the parametric equations

$$x = (v_0 \cos \theta)t, \quad y = (v_0 \sin \theta)t - 16t^2.$$

(a) Find the length of the path traveled by the projectile.

(b) Estimate the maximum height of the projectile.

53. $\theta = 20°$, $v_0 = 150$ **54.** $\theta = 30°$, $v_0 = 150$

55. $\theta = 60°$, $v_0 = 150$ **56.** $\theta = 90°$, $v_0 = 150$

Extending the Ideas

If dx/dt and dy/dt are continuous, the parametric curve defined by $(x(t), y(t))$ for $a \leq t \leq b$ is called *smooth*. If the curve is traversed exactly once as t increases from a to b, and if y is a positive function of x, then the curve can be revolved about the x-axis to form a surface of revolution (see Section 8.3). The area of such a surface is given by

$$S = \int_a^b 2\pi y \sqrt{\left(\frac{dx}{dt}\right)^2 + \left(\frac{dy}{dt}\right)^2} \, dt.$$

Apply this formula in Exercises 57–60 to find the surface area when the parametric curve is revolved about the x-axis.

57. $x = \cos t$, $y = 2 + \sin t$, $0 \leq t \leq 2\pi$

58. $x = 2\sqrt{t}$, $y = (2/3)t^{3/2}$, $0 \leq t \leq 2$

59. $x = t^2 + 2$, $y = t + 1$, $0 \leq t \leq 3$

60. $x = \ln(\sec t + \tan t) - \sin t$, $y = \cos t$, $0 \leq t \leq \pi/3$

11.2 Vectors in the Plane

You will be able to extend the calculation of derivatives and integrals to vector-valued functions.

- Vector operations
- Velocity and acceleration for vector-valued functions
- Displacement and distance traveled for vector-valued functions

Two-Dimensional Vectors

When an object moves *along a straight line,* its velocity can be determined by a single number that represents both magnitude and direction (forward if the number is positive, backward if it is negative). The speed of an object moving on a path *in a plane* can still be represented by a number, but how can we represent its direction when there are an infinite number of directions possible? Fortunately, we can represent both magnitude and direction with just two numbers, just as we can represent any point in the plane with just two coordinates (which is possible essentially for the same reason). This representation is what two-dimensional vectors were designed to do.

While the pair (a, b) determines a point in the plane, it also determines a **directed line segment** (or **arrow**) with its tail at the origin and its head at (a, b) (Figure 11.8). The length of this arrow represents magnitude, while the direction in which it points represents direction. In this way, the ordered pair (a, b) represents a mathematical object with both magnitude and direction, called the **position vector of (a, b).**

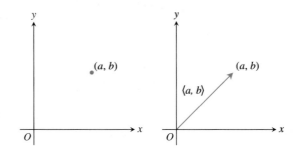

Figure 11.8 The point represents the ordered pair (a, b). The arrow (directed line segment), represents the vector $\langle a, b \rangle$.

Vector Notation

The American physicist J. Willard Gibbs (1839–1903) championed the use of vector notation in the study of electrodynamics and fluid mechanics. In 1893, Oliver Heaviside (1850–1925) became the first person to use **boldface** letters such as **v** to denote vectors.

DEFINITION Two-Dimensional Vector

A **two-dimensional vector v** is an ordered pair of real numbers, denoted in **component form** as $\langle a, b \rangle$. The numbers a and b are the **components** of the vector **v**. The **standard representation** of the vector $\langle a, b \rangle$ is the arrow from the origin to the point (a, b). The **magnitude** (or **absolute value**) of **v**, denoted $|\mathbf{v}|$, is the length of the arrow, and the **direction of v** is the direction in which the arrow is pointing. The vector $\mathbf{0} = \langle 0, 0 \rangle$, called the **zero vector,** has zero length and no direction.

The distance formula in the plane gives a simple computational formula for magnitude.

Magnitude of a Vector

The **magnitude** or **absolute value** of the vector $\langle a, b \rangle$ is the nonnegative real number $|\langle a, b \rangle| = \sqrt{a^2 + b^2}$.

Direction can be quantified in several ways; for example, navigators use bearings from compass points. The simplest choice for us is to measure direction as we do with the trigonometric functions, using the usual position angle formed with the positive x-axis as the initial ray and the vector as the terminal ray. In this way, every nonzero vector determines a unique **direction angle** θ satisfying (in degrees) $0 \leq \theta < 360$ or (in radians) $0 \leq \theta < 2\pi$. (See Figure 11.10 for an example.)

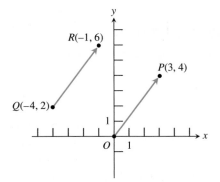

Figure 11.9 The arrows $\overrightarrow{QR}$ and $\overrightarrow{OP}$ both represent the vector $\langle 3, 4 \rangle$, as would any arrow with the same length pointing in the same direction. Such arrows are called *equivalent.*

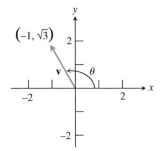

Figure 11.10 The vector **v** in Example 1 is represented by an arrow from the origin to the point $\left(-1, \sqrt{3} \right)$.

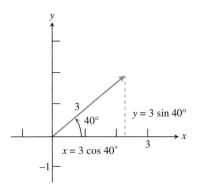

Figure 11.11 The vector in Example 2 is represented by an arrow from the origin to the point $(3 \cos 40°, 3 \sin 40°)$.

Why Not Use Slope for Direction?

Notice that *slope* is inadequate for determining the direction of a vector, since two vectors with the same slope could be pointing in opposite directions. Moreover, vectors are still useful in dimensions higher than 2, while slope is not.

Direction Angle of a Vector

The **direction angle** of a nonzero vector **v** is the smallest nonnegative angle θ formed with the positive *x*-axis as the initial ray and the standard representation of **v** as the terminal ray.

This textbook uses boldface variables to represent vectors (for example, **u** and **v**) to distinguish them from numbers. In handwritten form it is customary to distinguish vector variables by arrows (for example, $\vec{u}$ and $\vec{v}$). We also use angled brackets to distinguish a vector $\langle x, y \rangle$ from a point (x, y) in the plane, although it is not uncommon to see (x, y) used for both, especially in handwritten form.

It is often convenient in applications to represent vectors with arrows that begin at points other than the origin. The important thing to remember is that *any two arrows with the same length and pointing in the same direction represent the same vector.* In Figure 11.9, for example, the vector $\langle 3, 4 \rangle$ is shown represented by $\overrightarrow{QR}$, an arrow with **initial point** Q and **terminal point** R, as well as by its standard representation $\overrightarrow{OP}$. Two arrows that represent the same vector are said to be **equivalent.**

The quick way to associate arrows with the vectors they represent is to use the following rule.

Head Minus Tail (HMT) Rule

If an arrow has initial point (x_1, y_1) and terminal point (x_2, y_2), it represents the vector $\langle x_2 - x_1, y_2 - y_1 \rangle$.

EXAMPLE 1 Finding Magnitude and Direction

Find the magnitude and the direction angle θ of the vector $\mathbf{v} = \left\langle -1, \sqrt{3} \right\rangle$ (Figure 11.10).

SOLUTION

The magnitude of **v** is $|\mathbf{v}| = \sqrt{(-1 - 0)^2 + \left(\sqrt{3} - 0 \right)^2} = 2$. Using triangle ratios, we see that the direction angle θ satisfies $\cos \theta = -1/2$ and $\sin \theta = \sqrt{3}/2$, so $\theta = 120°$ or $2\pi/3$ radians.

Now Try Exercise 5.

EXAMPLE 2 Finding Component Form

Find the component form of a vector with magnitude 3 and direction angle 40°.

SOLUTION

The components of the vector, found trigonometrically, are $x = 3 \cos 40°$ and $y = 3 \sin 40°$ (Figure 11.11).

The vector is $\langle 3 \cos 40°, 3 \sin 40° \rangle \approx \langle 2.298, 1.928 \rangle$. *Now Try Exercise 13.*

Vector Operations

The algebra of vectors sometimes involves working with vectors and numbers at the same time. In this context, we refer to the numbers as **scalars.** The two most basic algebraic operations involving vectors are **vector addition** (adding a vector to a vector) and **scalar multiplication** (multiplying a vector by a number). Both operations are easily represented geometrically.

DEFINITION **Vector Addition and Scalar Multiplication**

Let $\mathbf{u} = \langle u_1, u_2 \rangle$ and $\mathbf{v} = \langle v_1, v_2 \rangle$ be vectors and let k be a real number (scalar).

The **sum** (or **resultant**) **of the vectors u and v** is the vector

$$\mathbf{u} + \mathbf{v} = \langle u_1 + v_1, u_2 + v_2 \rangle.$$

The **product of the scalar k and the vector u** is

$$k\mathbf{u} = k\langle u_1, u_2 \rangle = \langle ku_1, ku_2 \rangle.$$

The **opposite of a vector v** is $-\mathbf{v} = (-1)\mathbf{v}$. We define vector subtraction by

$$\mathbf{u} - \mathbf{v} = \mathbf{u} + (-\mathbf{v}).$$

The vector $\dfrac{\mathbf{v}}{|\mathbf{v}|}$ is a vector of magnitude 1, called a **unit vector.** Its component form is $\langle \cos\theta, \sin\theta \rangle$, where θ is the direction angle of **v.** For this reason, $\dfrac{\mathbf{v}}{|\mathbf{v}|}$ is sometimes called the **direction vector** of **v.**

The sum of two vectors **u** and **v** can be represented geometrically by arrows in two ways. In the **tail-to-head representation,** the arrow from the origin to (u_1, u_2) is the standard representation of **u,** the arrow from (u_1, u_2) to $(u_1 + v_1, u_2 + v_2)$, represents **v** (as you can verify by the HMT Rule), and the arrow from the origin to $(u_1 + v_1, u_2 + v_2)$ then is the standard representation of $u + v$ (Figure 11.12a).

In the **parallelogram representation,** the standard representations of **u** and **v** determine a parallelogram whose diagonal is the standard representation of $\mathbf{u} + \mathbf{v}$ (Figure 11.12b).

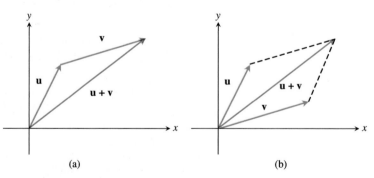

Figure 11.12 Two ways to represent vector addition geometrically: (a) tail-to-head and (b) parallelogram.

The product $k\mathbf{u}$ of the scalar k and the vector **u** can be represented by a stretch (or shrink) of **u** by a factor of k. If $k > 0$, then $k\mathbf{u}$ points in the same direction as **u;** if $k < 0$, then $k\mathbf{u}$ points in the opposite direction (Figure 11.13).

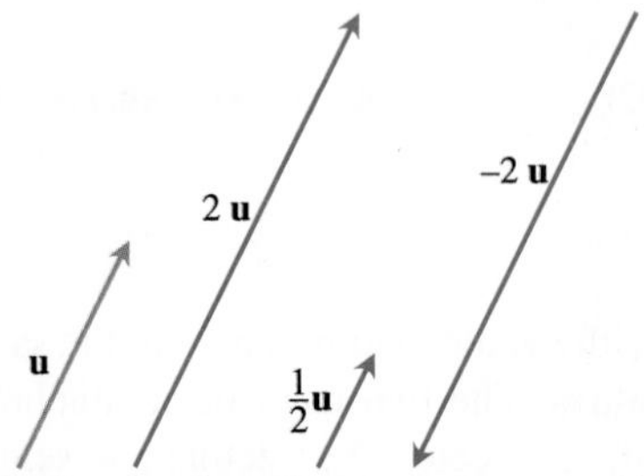

Figure 11.13 Representations of **u** and several scalar multiples of **u.**

EXAMPLE 3 Performing Operations on Vectors

Let $\mathbf{u} = \langle -1, 3 \rangle$ and $\mathbf{v} = \langle 4, 7 \rangle$. Find the following.

(a) $2\mathbf{u} + 3\mathbf{v}$ **(b)** $\mathbf{u} - \mathbf{v}$ **(c)** $\left|\dfrac{1}{2}\mathbf{u}\right|$

SOLUTION

(a) $2\mathbf{u} + 3\mathbf{v} = 2\langle -1, 3 \rangle + 3\langle 4, 7 \rangle$

$= \langle 2(-1) + 3(4), 2(3) + 3(7) \rangle = \langle 10, 27 \rangle$ *continued*

(b) $\mathbf{u} - \mathbf{v} = \langle -1, 3 \rangle - \langle 4, 7 \rangle$

$$= \langle -1 - 4, 3 - 7 \rangle = \langle -5, -4 \rangle$$

(c) $\left| \frac{1}{2} \mathbf{u} \right| = \left| \left\langle -\frac{1}{2}, \frac{3}{2} \right\rangle \right| = \sqrt{\left(-\frac{1}{2} \right)^2 + \left(\frac{3}{2} \right)^2} = \frac{1}{2} \sqrt{10}$

Now Try Exercise 21.

Vector operations have many of the properties of their real-number counterparts.

Properties of Vector Operations

Let $\mathbf{u}$, $\mathbf{v}$, $\mathbf{w}$ be vectors and a, b be scalars.

1. $\mathbf{u} + \mathbf{v} = \mathbf{v} + \mathbf{u}$
2. $(\mathbf{u} + \mathbf{v}) + \mathbf{w} = \mathbf{u} + (\mathbf{v} + \mathbf{w})$
3. $\mathbf{u} + \mathbf{0} = \mathbf{u}$
4. $\mathbf{u} + (-\mathbf{u}) = \mathbf{0}$
5. $0\mathbf{u} = \mathbf{0}$
6. $1\mathbf{u} = \mathbf{u}$
7. $a(b\mathbf{u}) = (ab)\mathbf{u}$
8. $a(\mathbf{u} + \mathbf{v}) = a\mathbf{u} + a\mathbf{v}$
9. $(a + b)\mathbf{u} = a\mathbf{u} + b\mathbf{u}$

Modeling Planar Motion

Although vectors are used in many other physical applications, our primary reason for introducing them into this course is to model the motion of objects moving in a coordinate plane. You may have seen vector problems of the following type in a physics or mechanics course.

EXAMPLE 4 Finding Ground Speed and Direction

A Boeing® 727® airplane, flying due east at 500 mph in still air, encounters a 70-mph tail wind acting in the direction 60° north of east. The airplane holds its compass heading due east but, because of the wind, acquires a new ground speed and direction. What are they?

SOLUTION

If $\mathbf{u} =$ the velocity of the airplane alone and $\mathbf{v} =$ the velocity of the tail wind, then $|\mathbf{u}| = 500$ and $|\mathbf{v}| = 70$ (Figure 11.14).

We need to find the magnitude and direction of the *resultant vector* $\mathbf{u} + \mathbf{v}$. If we let the positive x-axis represent east and the positive y-axis represent north, then the component forms of $\mathbf{u}$ and $\mathbf{v}$ are

$$\mathbf{u} = \langle 500, 0 \rangle \quad \text{and} \quad \mathbf{v} = \langle 70 \cos 60°, 70 \sin 60° \rangle = \langle 35, 35\sqrt{3} \rangle.$$

Therefore,

$$\mathbf{u} + \mathbf{v} = \langle 535, 35\sqrt{3} \rangle,$$

$$|\mathbf{u} + \mathbf{v}| = \sqrt{535^2 + (35\sqrt{3})^2} \approx 538.4,$$

and

$$\theta = \tan^{-1} \frac{35\sqrt{3}}{535} \approx 6.5°.$$

Interpret The new ground speed of the airplane is about 538.4 mph, and its new direction is about 6.5° north of east.

Now Try Exercise 25.

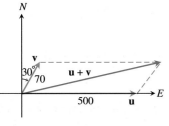

NOT TO SCALE

Figure 11.14 Vectors representing the velocities of the airplane and tail wind in Example 4.

Recall that if the position x of an object moving along a line is given as a function of time t, then the velocity of the object is dx/dt and the acceleration of the object is d^2x/dt^2. It is almost as simple to relate position, velocity, and acceleration for an object moving in the plane, because we can model those functions with vectors and treat *the components of the vectors as separate linear models*. Example 5 shows how simple this modeling actually is.

EXAMPLE 5 Doing Calculus Componentwise

A particle moves in the plane so that its position at any time $t \geq 0$ is given by $(\sin t, t^2/2)$.

(a) Find the position vector of the particle at time t.

(b) Find the velocity vector of the particle at time t.

(c) Find the acceleration of the particle at time t.

(d) Describe the position and motion of the particle at time $t = 6$.

SOLUTION

(a) The position vector, which has the same components as the position point, is $\langle \sin t, t^2/2 \rangle$. In fact, it could also be represented as $(\sin t, t^2/2)$, since the context would identify it as a vector.

(b) Differentiate each component of the position vector to get $\langle \cos t, t \rangle$.

(c) Differentiate each component of the velocity vector to get $\langle -\sin t, 1 \rangle$.

(d) The particle is at the point $(\sin 6, 18)$, with velocity $\langle \cos 6, 6 \rangle$ and acceleration $\langle -\sin 6, 1 \rangle$.

You can graph the path of this particle parametrically, letting $x = \sin(t)$ and $y = t^2/2$. In Figure 11.15 we show the path of the particle from $t = 0$ to $t = 6$. The red arrow at the point $(\sin 6, 18)$ represents the velocity vector $(\cos 6, 6)$. It shows both the magnitude and direction of the velocity at that moment in time.

Now Try Exercise 31.

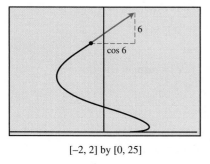

[–2, 2] by [0, 25]

$0 \leq t \leq 6$

Figure 11.15 The path of the particle in Example 5 from $t = 0$ to $t = 6$. The red arrow shows the velocity vector at $t = 6$.

Velocity, Acceleration, and Speed

We are now ready to give some definitions.

DEFINITIONS Velocity, Speed, Acceleration, and Direction of Motion

Suppose a particle moves along a smooth curve in the plane so that its position at any time t is $(x(t), y(t))$, where x and y are differentiable functions of t.

1. The particle's **position vector** is $\mathbf{r}(t) = \langle x(t), y(t) \rangle$.

2. The particle's **velocity vector** is $\mathbf{v}(t) = \left\langle \dfrac{dx}{dt}, \dfrac{dy}{dt} \right\rangle$.

3. The particle's **speed** is the magnitude of $\mathbf{v}$, denoted $|\mathbf{v}|$. Speed is a *scalar*, not a vector.

4. The particle's **acceleration vector** is $\mathbf{a}(t) = \left\langle \dfrac{d^2x}{dt^2}, \dfrac{d^2y}{dt^2} \right\rangle$.

5. The particle's **direction of motion** is the **direction vector** $\dfrac{\mathbf{v}}{|\mathbf{v}|}$.

A Word About Differentiability

Our definitions can be expanded to a **calculus of vectors**, in which (for example) $d\mathbf{v}/dt = \mathbf{a}(t)$, but it is not our intention to get into that here. We have therefore finessed the fine point of vector differentiability by requiring the path of our particle to be "smooth." The path can have vertical tangents, fail the vertical line test, and loop back on itself, but corners and cusps are still problematic.

EXAMPLE 6 Catching a Fly Ball

A baseball leaves a batter's bat at an angle of 60° from the horizontal, traveling at 110 feet per second. A fielder, who is standing in the direct line of the hit with his glove at a vertical reach of 8 feet, catches the ball for the out. His feet do not leave the ground.

continued

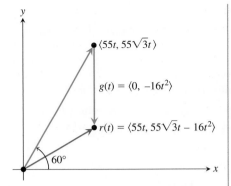

Figure 11.16 A vector diagram showing $\mathbf{r}(t)$, the position vector of a baseball hit by a bat, and the effect of gravity. (Example 6)

(a) Find the position vector of the baseball at time t (in seconds).

(b) Find the velocity vector of the baseball at time t (in seconds).

(c) At what time t does the fielder catch the ball, and how far is he from home plate?

(d) How fast is the ball traveling when he catches the ball?

SOLUTION

(a) From elementary physics we know that the position vector of the ball at any time t is $\mathbf{r}(t) = \langle x(t), y(t) \rangle$, where $x(t) = 110t \cos 60° = 55t$ and $y(t) = 110t \sin 60° - 16t^2 = 55\sqrt{3}t - 16t^2$. See Figure 11.16.

Note that we ignore the height of the batter (the ball is hit a few feet off the ground), air resistance, and wind effects. We consider only gravity in this model of the motion of a baseball hit by a bat.

(b) The velocity vector is $\mathbf{v}(t) = \left\langle \dfrac{dx}{dt}, \dfrac{dy}{dt} \right\rangle$. Evaluating the derivatives, we get

$$\mathbf{v}(t) = \langle 55, 55\sqrt{3} - 32t \rangle.$$

(c) Note that the *vertical component* of the desired position vector must be 8 (feet). So, $y(t) = 55\sqrt{3}t - 16t^2 = 8$. Next, solving for $t(t > 0)$, we have

$$16t^2 - 55\sqrt{3}t + 8 = 0, \text{ which gives } t = \frac{55\sqrt{3} + \sqrt{(55\sqrt{3})^2 - 4 \cdot 16 \cdot 8}}{32}, \text{ or }$$

$t \approx 5.869$ seconds. Thus, the fielder catches the ball in the air 5.869 seconds after the ball was hit. The *horizontal component* of the position vector is $x(t) = 55t$, which gives $x(t) = 55(5.869) \approx 322.780$ feet. So, the fielder is standing about 323 feet from home plate when he catches the ball.

(d) The speed of the ball at any time t is $|\mathbf{v}(t)|$. So, we evaluate $|\mathbf{v}(t)|$ at $t = 5.869$, found in part (c):

$$|\mathbf{v}(t)| = \sqrt{55^2 + (55\sqrt{3} - 32t)^2}$$

$$|\mathbf{v}(5.869)| = \sqrt{55^2 + (55\sqrt{3} - 32 \cdot 5.869)^2} \approx 107.655 \text{ ft/sec, or } 73.402 \text{ mph}$$

So, the ball is traveling at about 73 mph when the fielder catches the ball.

Now Try Exercise 33.

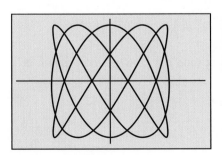

[–1.6, 1.6] by [–1.1, 1.1]

$0 \le t \le 6.3$

Figure 11.17 The path of the busy particle in Example 7.

EXAMPLE 7 Studying Planar Motion

A particle moves in the plane with position vector $\mathbf{r}(t) = \langle \sin(3t), \cos(5t) \rangle$. Find the velocity and acceleration vectors and determine the path of the particle.

SOLUTION

Velocity $\mathbf{v}(t) = \left\langle \dfrac{d}{dt}(\sin(3t)), \dfrac{d}{dt}(\cos(5t)) \right\rangle = \langle 3\cos(3t), -5\sin(5t) \rangle.$

Acceleration $\mathbf{a}(t) = \left\langle \dfrac{d}{dt}(3\cos(3t)), \dfrac{d}{dt}(-5\sin(5t)) \right\rangle = \langle -9\sin(3t), -25\cos(5t) \rangle.$

The path of the particle is found by graphing (in parametric mode) the curve defined by $x = \sin(3t)$ and $y = \cos(5t)$ (Figure 11.17).

Now Try Exercise 35.

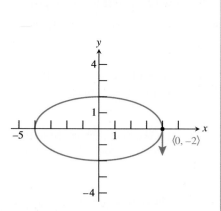

Figure 11.18 The ellipse on which the particle travels in Example 8. The velocity vector at the point $(4, 0)$ is $\langle 0, -2 \rangle$, represented by an arrow tangent to the ellipse at $(4, 0)$ and pointing down. The direction of the velocity at that point indicates that the particle travels clockwise around the origin.

EXAMPLE 8 Studying Planar Motion

A particle moves in an elliptical path so that its position at any time $t \geq 0$ is given by $(4 \sin t, 2 \cos t)$.

(a) Find the velocity and acceleration vectors.

(b) Find the velocity, acceleration, speed, and direction of motion at $t = \pi/4$.

(c) Sketch the path of the particle and show the velocity vector at the point $(4, 0)$.

(d) Does the particle travel clockwise or counterclockwise around the origin?

SOLUTION

(a) Velocity $\mathbf{v}(t) = \left\langle \dfrac{d}{dt}(4 \sin t), \dfrac{d}{dt}(2 \cos t) \right\rangle = \langle 4 \cos t, -2 \sin t \rangle$

Acceleration $\mathbf{a}(t) = \left\langle \dfrac{d}{dt}(4 \cos t), \dfrac{d}{dt}(-2 \sin t) \right\rangle = \langle -4 \sin t, -2 \cos t \rangle$

(b) Velocity $\mathbf{v}(\pi/4) = \langle 4 \cos (\pi/4), -2 \sin (\pi/4) \rangle = \langle 2\sqrt{2}, -\sqrt{2} \rangle$

Acceleration $\mathbf{a}(\pi/4) = \langle -4 \sin (\pi/4), -2 \cos (\pi/4) \rangle = \langle -2\sqrt{2}, -\sqrt{2} \rangle$

Speed $= |\mathbf{v}(\pi/4)| = |\langle 2\sqrt{2}, -\sqrt{2} \rangle| = \sqrt{(2\sqrt{2})^2 + (-\sqrt{2})^2} = \sqrt{10}$

(c) The ellipse defined parametrically by $x = 4 \sin t$ and $y = 2 \cos t$ is shown in Figure 11.18. At the point $(4, 0)$, $\sin t = 1$ and $\cos t = 0$, so $\mathbf{v}(t) = \langle 4 \cos t, -2 \sin t \rangle = \langle 0, -2 \rangle$. The vector $\langle 0, -2 \rangle$ is drawn tangent to the curve at $(4, 0)$.

(d) As the vector in Figure 11.18 shows, the particle travels clockwise around the origin.

Now Try Exercise 37.

Displacement and Distance Traveled

Recall that when a particle moves along a line with velocity $v(t)$, the displacement (or net distance traveled) from time $t = a$ to time $t = b$ is given by $\int_a^b v(t)\, dt$, while the (total) distance traveled in that time interval is given by $\int_a^b |v(t)|\, dt$. When a particle moves in the plane with velocity vector $\mathbf{v}(t)$, displacement and distance traveled can be found by applying the same integrals to the vector $\mathbf{v}$, although in slightly different ways.

DEFINITIONS   Displacement and Distance Traveled

Suppose a particle moves along a path in the plane so that its velocity at any time t is $\mathbf{v}(t) = (v_1(t), v_2(t))$, where v_1 and v_2 are integrable functions of t.

The **displacement** from $t = a$ to $t = b$ is given by the vector

$$\left\langle \int_a^b v_1(t)\, dt, \int_a^b v_2(t)\, dt \right\rangle.$$

The preceding vector is added to the position at time $t = a$ to get the position at time $t = b$.

The **distance traveled** from $t = a$ to $t = b$ is

$$\int_a^b |\mathbf{v}(t)|\, dt = \int_a^b \sqrt{(v_1(t))^2 + (v_2(t))^2}\, dt.$$

There are two things worth noting about the formula for distance traveled. First of all, it is a nice example of the integral as an accumulator, since we are summing up bits of speed multiplied by bits of time, which equals bits of positive distance. Second, it is actually a new look at an old formula. Substitute dx/dt for $v_1(t)$ and dy/dt for $v_2(t)$ and you get the arc length formula for a curve defined parametrically (Section 11.1). This formula makes sense, since the distance the particle travels is precisely the length of the path along which it moves.

EXAMPLE 9 Finding Displacement and Distance Traveled

A particle moves in the plane with velocity vector $\mathbf{v}(t) = (t - 3\pi \cos \pi t, 2t - \pi \sin \pi t)$. At $t = 0$, the particle is at the point $(1, 5)$.

(a) Find the position of the particle at $t = 4$.

(b) What is the total distance traveled by the particle from $t = 0$ to $t = 4$?

SOLUTION

(a) Displacement $= \left\langle \int_0^4 (t - 3\pi \cos \pi t)dt, \int_0^4 (2t - \pi \sin \pi t)dt \right\rangle = \langle 8, 16 \rangle$.

The particle is at the point $(1 + 8, 5 + 16) = (9, 21)$.

(b) Distance traveled $= \int_0^4 \sqrt{(t - 3\pi \cos \pi t)^2 + (2t - \pi \sin \pi t)^2} \, dt \approx 33.533$.

Now Try Exercise 39.

EXAMPLE 10 Finding the Path of the Particle

Determine the path that the particle in Example 9 travels going from $(1, 5)$ to $(9, 21)$.

SOLUTION

The velocity vector and the position at $t = 0$ combine to give us the vector equivalent of an initial value problem. We simply find the components of the position vector separately.

$$\frac{dx}{dt} = t - 3\pi \cos \pi t$$

$$x = \frac{t^2}{2} - 3 \sin \pi t + C \quad \text{Antidifferentiate.}$$

$$x = \frac{t^2}{2} - 3 \sin \pi t + 1 \quad x = 1 \text{ when } t = 0.$$

$$\frac{dy}{dt} = 2t - \pi \sin \pi t$$

$$y = t^2 + \cos \pi t + C \quad \text{Antidifferentiate.}$$

$$y = t^2 + \cos \pi t + 4 \quad y = 5 \text{ when } t = 0.$$

We then graph the position $\langle t^2/2 - 3 \sin \pi t + 1, t^2 + \cos \pi t + 4 \rangle$ parametrically from $t = 0$ to $t = 4$. The path is shown in Figure 11.19.

Now Try Exercise 43.

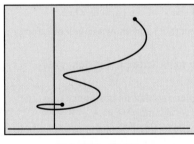

[−5, 15] by [0, 23]

$0 \le t \le 4$

Figure 11.19 The path traveled by the particle in Example 9 as it goes from $(1, 5)$ to $(9, 21)$ in four seconds. (Example 9)

Quick Review 11.2   *(For help, go to Sections 1.1, 5.3, and 11.1.)*

Exercise numbers with a gray background indicate problems that the authors have designed to be solved *without a calculator.*

In Exercises 1–4, let $P = (1, 2)$ and $Q = (5, 3)$.

1. Find the distance between the points P and Q.

2. Find the slope of the line segment PQ.

3. If $R = (3, b)$, determine b so that segments PQ and RQ are collinear.

4. If $R = (3, b)$, determine b so that segments PQ and RQ are perpendicular.

In Exercises 5 and 6, determine the missing coordinate so that the four points form a parallelogram $ABCD$.

5. $A = (0, 0)$, $B = (1, 3)$, $C = (5, 3)$, $D = (a, 0)$

6. $A = (1, 1)$, $B = (3, 5)$, $C = (8, b)$, $D = (6, 2)$

7. Find the velocity and acceleration of a particle moving along a line if its position at time t is given by $x(t) = t \sin t$.

8. A particle moves along the x-axis with velocity $v(t) = 3t^2 - 12t$ for $t \ge 0$. If its position is $x = 40$ when $t = 0$, where is the particle when $t = 4$?

9. A particle moves along the x-axis with velocity $v(t) = 3t^2 - 12t$ for $t \ge 0$. What is the total distance traveled by the particle from $t = 0$ to $t = 4$?

10. Find the length of the curve defined parametrically by $x = \sin(2t)$ and $y = \cos(3t)$ for $0 \le t \le 2\pi$.

Section 11.2 Exercises

In Exercises 1–4, find the component form of the vector.

1. the vector from the origin to the point $A = (2, 3)$

2. the vector from the point $A = (2, 3)$ to the origin

3. the vector $\overrightarrow{PQ}$, where $P = (1, 3)$ and $Q = (2, -1)$

4. the vector $\overrightarrow{OP}$, where O is the origin and P is the midpoint of the segment RS connecting $R = (2, -1)$ and $S = (-4, 3)$.

In Exercises 5–10, find the magnitude of the vector and the direction angle θ it forms with the positive x-axis ($0 \le \theta < 360°$).

5. $\langle 2, 2 \rangle$

6. $\langle -\sqrt{2}, \sqrt{2} \rangle$

7. $\langle \sqrt{3}, 1 \rangle$

8. $\langle -2, -2\sqrt{3} \rangle$

9. $\langle -5, 0 \rangle$

10. $\langle 0, 4 \rangle$

In Exercises 11–16, find the component form of the vector with the given magnitude that forms the given directional angle with the positive x-axis.

11. 4, 180°

12. 6, 270°

13. 5, 100°

14. 13, 200°

15. $3\sqrt{2}$, $\pi/4$ radians

16. $2\sqrt{3}$, $\pi/6$ radians

In Exercises 17–24, let $\mathbf{u} = \langle 3, -2 \rangle$ and $\mathbf{v} = \langle -2, 5 \rangle$. Find the (a) component form and (b) magnitude of the vector.

17. $3\mathbf{u}$

18. $-2\mathbf{v}$

19. $\mathbf{u} + \mathbf{v}$

20. $\mathbf{u} - \mathbf{v}$

21. $2\mathbf{u} - 3\mathbf{v}$

22. $-2\mathbf{u} + 5\mathbf{v}$

23. $\dfrac{3}{5}\mathbf{u} + \dfrac{4}{5}\mathbf{v}$

24. $-\dfrac{5}{13}\mathbf{u} + \dfrac{12}{13}\mathbf{v}$

25. *Navigation* An airplane, flying in the direction 20° east of north at 325 mph in still air, encounters a 40-mph tail wind acting in the direction 40° west of north. The airplane maintains its compass heading but, because of the wind, acquires a new ground speed and direction. What are they?

26. A river is flowing due east at 2 mph. A canoeist paddles across the river at 4 mph with his bow aimed directly northwest (a direction angle of 135°). What is the true direction angle of the canoeist's path, and how fast is the canoe going?

In Exercises 27–32, a particle travels in the plane with position vector $\mathbf{r}(t)$. Find (a) the velocity vector $\mathbf{v}(t)$ and (b) the acceleration vector $a(t)$.

27. $\mathbf{r}(t) = \langle 3t^2, 2t^3 \rangle$

28. $\mathbf{r}(t) = \langle \sin 2t, 2 \cos t \rangle$

29. $\mathbf{r}(t) = \langle te^{-t}, e^{-t} \rangle$

30. $\mathbf{r}(t) = \langle 2 \cos 3t, 2 \sin 4t \rangle$

31. $\mathbf{r}(t) = \langle t^2 + \sin 2t, t^2 - \cos 2t \rangle$

32. $\mathbf{r}(t) = \langle t \sin t, t \cos t \rangle$

33. A baseball leaves the bat at an angle of 55° from the horizontal traveling at 90 feet per second. A 20-foot boundary fence is 230 feet from the batter in a direct line of where the baseball is hit.

(a) Find the position vector of the baseball at time t (in seconds).

(b) Find the velocity vector of the baseball at time t (in seconds).

(c) Is the hit a home run?

(d) At what time t does the ball hit the fence or clear it for a home run? Illustrate with a graph and explain why the graph supports your solution.

(e) How fast is the ball traveling when it either hits the fence or passes over it?

34. *Football* A player punts the ball from his own 30-yard line at an angle of 57 degrees from horizontal, traveling at 81 feet per second. A 6-foot player from the opposing team is standing on his own 10-yard line to receive the punt.

(a) Find the position vector of the football at time t in seconds. Assume a 100-yard playing field.

(b) Find the velocity vector of the football at time t in seconds.

(c) About what time t is the football "over" the player on the 10-yard line?

(d) Can the 6-ft player call for a "fair catch" and likely catch the ball while standing on the 10-yard line downfield? Explain your reasoning and your assumptions.

35. A particle moves in the plane with position vector $\langle \cos 3t, \sin 2t \rangle$. Find the velocity and acceleration vectors and determine the path of the particle.

36. A particle moves in the plane with position vector $\langle \sin 4t, \cos 3t \rangle$. Find the velocity and acceleration vectors and determine the path of the particle.

37. A particle moves in the plane so that its position at any time $t \ge 0$ is given by $x = \sin 4t \cos t$ and $y = \sin 2t$.

(a) Find the velocity and speed of the particle when $t = 5\pi/4$.

(b) Draw the path of the particle and show the velocity vector at $t = 5\pi/4$.

(c) Is the particle moving to the left or to the right when $t = 5\pi/4$?

38. A particle moves in the plane so that its position at any time $t \ge 0$ is given by $x = e^t + e^{-t}$ and $y = e^t - e^{-t}$.

(a) Find the velocity vector.

(b) Find $\displaystyle\lim_{t \to \infty} \dfrac{dy/dt}{dx/dt}$.

(c) Show algebraically that the particle moves on the hyperbola $x^2 - y^2 = 4$.

(d) Sketch the path of the particle, showing the velocity vector at $t = 0$.

In Exercises 39–42, the velocity $\mathbf{v}(t)$ of a particle moving in the plane is given, along with the position of the particle at time $t = 0$. Find (a) the position of the particle at time $t = 3$, and (b) the distance the particle travels from $t = 0$ to $t = 3$.

39. $\mathbf{v}(t) = \langle 3t^2 - 2t, 1 + \cos \pi t \rangle$; $(2, 6)$

40. $\mathbf{v}(t) = \langle 2\pi \cos 4\pi t, 4\pi \sin 2\pi t \rangle$; $(7, 2)$

41. $\mathbf{v}(t) = \langle (t + 1)^{-1}, (t + 2)^{-2} \rangle$; $(3, -2)$

42. $v(t) = \langle e^t - t, e^t + t \rangle$; $(1, 1)$

43. Sketch the path that the particle travels in Exercise 39.

44. Sketch the path that the particle travels in Exercise 40.

45. A point moves in the plane so that $x = 5 \cos (\pi t/6)$ and $y = 3 \sin (\pi t/6)$.

(a) Find the speed of the point at $t = 2$.

(b) Find the acceleration vector at $t = 2$.

(c) Eliminate the parameter and find an equation in x and y that defines the curve on which the point moves.

46. A particle moves with position vector $\langle \sec \pi t, \tan \pi t \rangle$ for $0 \le t < 1/2$.

    (a) Find the velocity and speed of the particle at $t = 1/4$.

    (b) The particle moves along a hyperbola. Eliminate the parameter to find an equation of the hyperbola in terms of x and y.

    (c) Sketch the path of the particle over the time interval $0 \le t < 1/2$.

47. A particle moves on the circle $x^2 + y^2 = 1$ so that its position vector at any time $t \ge 0$ is $\left\langle \dfrac{1 - t^2}{1 + t^2}, \dfrac{2t}{1 + t^2} \right\rangle$.

    (a) Find the velocity vector.

    (b) Is the particle ever at rest? Justify your answer.

    (c) Give the coordinates of the point that the particle approaches as t increases without bound.

48. A particle moves in the plane so that its position at any time $t, 0 \le t \le 2\pi$, is given parametrically by $x = \sin t$ and $y = \cos(2t)$.

    (a) Find the velocity vector for the particle.

    (b) For what values of t is the particle at rest?

    (c) Write an equation for the path of the particle in terms of x and y that does not involve trigonometric functions.

    (d) Sketch the path of the particle.

49. A particle moves in the plane so that its position at any time $t, 0 \le t \le 2\pi$, is given parametrically by $x = e^t \sin t$ and $y = e^t \cos t$.

    (a) Find the slope of the path of the particle at time $t = \pi/2$.

    (b) Find the speed of the particle when $t = 1$.

    (c) Find the distance traveled by the particle along the path from $t = 0$ to $t = 1$.

50. The position of a particle at any time $t \ge 0$ is given by $x(t) = t^2 - 3$ and $y(t) = \dfrac{2}{3} t^3$.

    (a) Find the magnitude of the velocity vector at $t = 4$.

    (b) Find the total distance traveled by the particle from $t = 0$ to $t = 4$.

    (c) Find dy/dx as a function of x.

51. An object moving along a curve in the xy-plane has position $(x(t), y(t))$ at time $t \ge 0$ with $dx/dt = 2 + \sin(t^2)$. The derivative dy/dt is not explicitly given. At time $t = 2$, the object is at position $(3, 5)$.

    (a) Find the x-coordinate of the position of the object at time $t = 4$.

    (b) At time $t = 2$, the value of dy/dt is -6. Write an equation for the line tangent to the curve at the point $(x(2), y(2))$.

    (c) Find the speed of the object at time $t = 2$.

    (d) For $t \ge 3$, the line tangent to the curve at $(x(t), y(t))$ has a slope of $2t - 1$. Find the acceleration vector of the object at time $t = 4$.

52. For $0 \le t \le 3$, an object moving along a curve in the xy-plane has position $(x(t), y(t))$ with $dx/dt = \sin(t^3)$ and $dy/dt = 3 \cos(t^2)$. At time $t = 2$, the object is at position $(4, 5)$.

    (a) Write an equation for the line tangent to the curve at $(4, 5)$.

    (b) Find the speed of the object at time $t = 2$.

    (c) Find the total distance traveled by the object over the time interval $0 \le t \le 1$.

    (d) Find the position of the object at time $t = 3$.

Standardized Test Questions

You may use a graphing calculator to solve the following problems.

53. True or False A scalar multiple of a vector $\mathbf{v}$ has the same direction as $\mathbf{v}$. Justify your answer.

54. True or False If a vector with direction angle $0°$ is added to a vector with direction angle $90°$, the result is a vector with direction angle $45°$. Justify your answer.

55. Multiple Choice The position of a particle in the xy-plane is given by $x = t^2 + 1$ and $y = \ln(2t + 3)$ for all $t \ge 0$. The acceleration vector of the particle is

    (A) $\left(2t, \dfrac{2}{2t + 3} \right)$.   **(B)** $\left(2t, -\dfrac{4}{(2t + 3)^2} \right)$.   **(C)** $\left(2, \dfrac{4}{(2t + 3)^2} \right)$.

    (D) $\left(2, \dfrac{2}{(2t + 3)^2} \right)$.   **(E)** $\left(2, -\dfrac{4}{(2t + 3)^2} \right)$.

56. Multiple Choice An object moving along a curve in the xy-plane has position $(x(t), y(t))$ with $dx/dt = \cos(t^2)$ and $dy/dt = \sin(t^3)$. At time $t = 0$, the object is at position $(4, 7)$. Where is the particle when $t = 2$?

    (A) $\langle -0.654, 0.989 \rangle$ **(B)** $\langle 0.461, 0.452 \rangle$ **(C)** $\langle 3.346, 7.989 \rangle$

    (D) $\langle 4.461, 7.452 \rangle$ **(E)** $\langle 5.962, 8.962 \rangle$

57. Multiple Choice A vector with magnitude 7 and direction angle $40°$ is added to a vector with magnitude 4 and direction angle $140°$. The result is a vector with magnitude

    (A) 4.684.   **(B)** 7.435.   **(C)** 8.062.   **(D)** 9.369.   **(E)** 11.

58. Multiple Choice The path of a particle moving in the plane is defined parametrically as a function of time t by $x = \sin 2t$ and $y = \cos 5t$. What is the speed of the particle when $t = 2$?

    (A) 1.130   **(B)** 3.018   **(C)** $\langle -1.307, 2.720 \rangle$

    (D) $\langle 0.757, 0.839 \rangle$ **(E)** $\langle 1.307, 2.720 \rangle$

Explorations

Two nonzero vectors are said to be *orthogonal* if they are perpendicular to each other. The zero vector is considered to be orthogonal to every vector.

59. *Orthogonal Vectors* A particle with coordinates (x, y) moves along a curve in the first quadrant in such a way that $dx/dt = -x$ and $dy/dt = \sqrt{1 - x^2}$ for every $t \ge 0$. Find the acceleration vector in terms of x and show that it is orthogonal to the corresponding velocity vector.

60. *Orthogonal Vectors* A particle moves around the unit circle with position vector $\langle \cos t, \sin t \rangle$. Use vectors to show that the particle's velocity is always orthogonal to both its position and its acceleration.

61. *Colliding Particles* The paths of two particles for $t \geq 0$ are given by the position vectors

$$\mathbf{r}_1(t) = \langle t - 3, (t - 3)^2 \rangle$$

$$\mathbf{r}_2(t) = \left\langle \frac{3t}{2} - 4, \frac{3t}{2} - 2 \right\rangle$$

(a) Determine the exact time(s) at which the particles collide.

(b) Find the direction of motion of each particle at the time(s) of collision.

62. *A Satellite in Circular Orbit* A satellite of mass m is moving at a constant speed v around a planet of mass M in a circular orbit of radius r_0, as measured from the planet's center of mass. Determine the satellite's orbital period T (the time to complete one full orbit), as follows:

(a) Coordinatize the orbital plane by placing the origin at the planet's center of mass, with the satellite on the x-axis at $t = 0$ and moving counterclockwise, as in the accompanying figure.

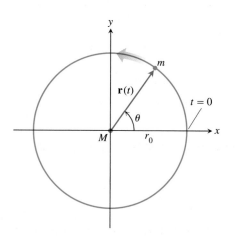

Let $\mathbf{r}(t)$ be the satellite's position vector at time t. Show that $\theta = vt/r_0$ and hence that

$$\mathbf{r}(t) = \left\langle r_0 \cos \frac{vt}{r_0}, r_0 \sin \frac{vt}{r_0} \right\rangle.$$

(b) Find the acceleration of the satellite.

(c) According to Newton's law of gravitation, the gravitational force exerted on the satellite by the planet is directed toward the origin and is given by

$$\mathbf{F} = \left(-\frac{GmM}{r_0^2} \right) \frac{\mathbf{r}}{r_0},$$

where G is the universal constant of gravitation. Using Newton's second law, $\mathbf{F} = m\mathbf{a}$, show that $v^2 = GM/r_0$.

(d) Show that the orbital period T satisfies $vT = 2\pi r_0$.

(e) From parts (c) and (d), deduce that

$$T^2 = \frac{4\pi^2}{GM} r_0^3;$$

that is, the square of the period of a satellite in circular orbit is proportional to the cube of the radius from the orbital center.

63. Use the parametric graphing mode on your calculator to simulate the baseball problem in Example 6. Set $X_{1T} = 110T \cos(60°)$ and $Y_{1T} = 110T \sin(60°)$. Use TRACE to support the analytic results found in the example. [*Hint:* Use a $[0, 350]$ by $[-50, 200]$ window with Tstep $= 0.001$. Note that it will take a few minutes to fully graph with such a small Tstep increment.] Then use TRACE repeatedly (input 5 for 5 seconds, 5.5, 5.65, and so forth). Look at the y-coordinate after each TRACE input.

Extending the Ideas

Let $\mathbf{u} = \langle u_1, u_2 \rangle$ and $\mathbf{v} = \langle v_1, v_2 \rangle$ be vectors in the plane. The **dot product** or **inner product** $\mathbf{u} \cdot \mathbf{v}$ is a scalar defined by

$$\mathbf{u} \cdot \mathbf{v} = \langle u_1, u_2 \rangle \cdot \langle v_1, v_2 \rangle = u_1 v_1 + u_2 v_2.$$

64. *Using the Dot Product* Show that the dot product of two perpendicular vectors is zero.

65. *An Alternate Formula for Dot Product* Let $\mathbf{u} = \langle u_1, u_2 \rangle$ and $\mathbf{v} = \langle v_1, v_2 \rangle$ be vectors in the plane, and let $\mathbf{w} = \mathbf{u} - \mathbf{v}$.

(a) Explain why $\mathbf{w}$ can be represented by the arrow in the accompanying diagram.

(b) Explain why $|\mathbf{w}|^2 = |\mathbf{u}|^2 + |\mathbf{v}|^2 - 2|\mathbf{u}||\mathbf{v}| \cos \theta$, where θ is the angle between vectors $\mathbf{u}$ and $\mathbf{v}$.

(c) Find the component form of $\mathbf{w}$ and use it to prove that

$$|\mathbf{u}|^2 + |\mathbf{v}|^2 - |\mathbf{w}|^2 = 2(u_1 v_1 + u_2 v_2).$$

(d) Finally, prove that $\mathbf{u} \cdot \mathbf{v} = |\mathbf{u}||\mathbf{v}| \cos \theta$, where θ is the angle between vectors $\mathbf{u}$ and $\mathbf{v}$.

11.3 Polar Functions

You will be able to extend the calculation of derivatives and integrals to polar functions.

- The slope of a curve given by a polar function
- Areas bounded by polar curves

Polar Coordinates

When we track the path of a satellite circling the earth, we mark its position by the angle, θ, through which it has traveled and its distance from the center of the earth, r (Figure 11.20). When we look at the plane in which the satellite moves, these two numbers tell us exactly where the satellite is located, and they are much more useful than trying to mark the location by trying to impose a rectangular grid. Each time the satellite circles the earth, it follows the same path. What we want to know is the distance r as a function of the angle θ, $r = f(\theta)$. This function of θ is called a **polar function.**

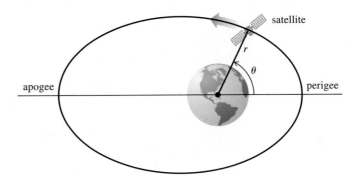

Figure 11.20 The elliptical orbit of a satellite for which the center of the earth lies at one focus of the ellipse.

It was Isaac Newton in 1687 who showed that the **polar equation** of a satellite's path is given by

$$r = \frac{c}{1 + e \cos \theta},$$

where c and e are constants. The constant c depends on the mass of the earth and the velocity of the satellite. The constant e is called the *eccentricity,* and it tells us the shape of the orbit. If $e = 0$, then $r = c$ is constant, and the orbit is a perfect circle. As e increases toward 1, the circle turns into an ellipse that gets longer and longer. For $0 < e < 1$, r has its smallest value when $\theta = 0$, in which case $r = c/(1 + e)$, the point we called the **perigee.** The largest value of r is at $\theta = \pi$, where $r = c/(1 - e)$, the point called the **apogee.** In Figure 11.21a, where $c = 1$ and $e = 0.5$, the distance to the perigee is $1/1.5 = 2/3$ and the distance to the apogee is $1/0.5 = 2$.

As e approaches 1, the distance to the perigee approaches $c/2$, while the distance to the apogee approaches infinity. At $e = 1$, the orbit is no longer periodic because

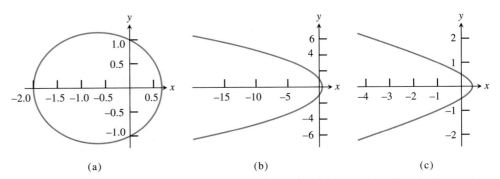

Figure 11.21 Conic sections in polar coordinates with $c = 1$ and (a) $e = 0.5$ (ellipse), (b) $e = 1$ (parabola), (c) $e = 1.2$ (branch of hyperbola with $-\cos^{-1}(-1/1.2) < \theta < \cos^{-1}(-1/1.2)$).

we can never reach the angle $\theta = \pi$. The orbit has opened up into a parabola (Figure 11.21b). If e is greater than 1, then the parabola opens up into a branch of a hyperbola with the distance approaching infinity as $1 + e \cos \theta$ approaches 0, which means that θ approaches $\cos^{-1}(-1/e)$. In Figure 11.21c, where $e = 1.2$, the asymptotes are at $\theta = \pm \cos^{-1}(-1/1.2) \approx \pm 2.556 \approx \pm 146.4°$.

We have entered the world of **polar coordinates,** where we identify points in the plane by (r, θ) where r is the distance to the origin, O, called the **pole,** and θ is the angle from the **initial ray** that we can think of as the positive x-axis. In Figure 11.22 we see that the point P with rectangular (Cartesian) coordinates $(2, 2)$ has polar coordinates $\left(2\sqrt{2}, \pi/4\right)$.

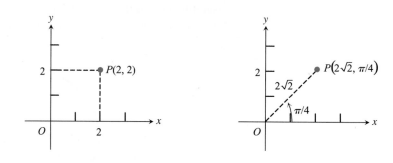

Rectangular coordinates   Polar coordinates

Figure 11.22 Point P has rectangular coordinates $(2, 2)$ and polar coordinates $\left(2\sqrt{2}, \pi/4\right)$.

As you would expect, we can also coordinatize point P with the polar coordinates $\left(2\sqrt{2}, 9\pi/4\right)$ or $\left(2\sqrt{2}, -7\pi/4\right)$, since those angles determine the same ray $\overrightarrow{OP}$. Less obviously, we can also coordinatize P with polar coordinates $\left(-2\sqrt{2}, -3\pi/4\right)$, since the **directed distance** $-2\sqrt{2}$ in the $-3\pi/4$ direction is the same as the directed distance $2\sqrt{2}$ in the $\pi/4$ direction (Figure 11.23). So, although each pair (r, θ) determines a unique point in the plane, each point in the plane can be coordinatized by an infinite number of polar ordered pairs.

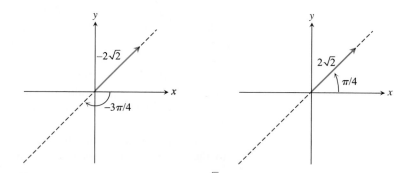

Figure 11.23 The directed *negative* distance $-2\sqrt{2}$ in the $-3\pi/4$ direction is the same as the directed *positive* distance $2\sqrt{2}$ in the $\pi/4$ direction. Thus the polar coordinates $\left(-2\sqrt{2}, -3\pi/4\right)$ and $\left(2\sqrt{2}, \pi/4\right)$ determine the same point.

EXAMPLE 1 Rectangular and Polar Coordinates

(a) Find rectangular coordinates for the points with given polar coordinates.

   (i) $(4, \pi/2)$ **(ii)** $(-3, \pi)$ **(iii)** $(16, 5\pi/6)$ **(iv)** $\left(-\sqrt{2}, -\pi/4\right)$

(b) Find two different sets of polar coordinates for the points with given rectangular coordinates.

   (i) $(1, 0)$ **(ii)** $(-3, 3)$ **(iii)** $(0, -4)$ **(iv)** $\left(1, \sqrt{3}\right)$

continued

SOLUTION

(a) (i) $(0, 4)$ **(ii)** $(3, 0)$ **(iii)** $\left(-8\sqrt{3}, 8\right)$ **(iv)** $(-1, 1)$

(b) A point has infinitely many sets of polar coordinates, so here we list just two typical examples for each given point.

(i) $(1, 0), (1, 2\pi)$ **(ii)** $\left(3\sqrt{2}, 3\pi/4\right), \left(-3\sqrt{2}, -\pi/4\right)$

(iii) $(4, -\pi/2), (4, 3\pi/2)$ **(iv)** $(2, \pi/3), (-2, 4\pi/3)$

Now Try Exercises 1 and 3.

EXAMPLE 2 Graphing with Polar Coordinates

Graph all points in the plane that satisfy the given polar equation.

(a) $r = 2$ **(b)** $r = -2$ **(c)** $\theta = \pi/6$

SOLUTION

First, note that we do *not* label our axes r and θ. We are graphing *polar* equations in the usual *xy*-plane, not renaming our rectangular variables!

(a) The set of all points with directed distance 2 units from the pole is a circle of radius 2 centered at the origin (Figure 11.24a).

(b) The set of all points with directed distance -2 units from the pole is also a circle of radius 2 centered at the origin (Figure 11.24b).

(c) The set of all points of positive or negative directed distance from the pole in the $\pi/6$ direction is a line through the origin with slope $\tan(\pi/6)$ (Figure 11.24c).

Now Try Exercise 7.

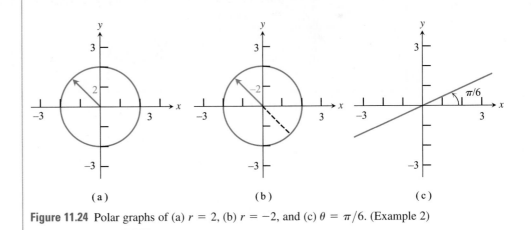

         (a)   (b)   (c)

Figure 11.24 Polar graphs of (a) $r = 2$, (b) $r = -2$, and (c) $\theta = \pi/6$. (Example 2)

Polar Curves

The curves in Example 2 are a start, but we would not introduce a new coordinate system just to graph circles and lines; there are far more interesting polar curves to study. In the past it was hard work to produce reasonable polar graphs by hand, but today, thanks to graphing technology, it is just a matter of finding the right window and pushing the right buttons. Our intent in this section is to use the technology to produce the graphs and then concentrate on how calculus can be used to give us further information.

EXAMPLE 3 Polar Graphing with Technology

Find an appropriate graphing window and produce a graph of the polar curve.

(a) $r = \sin 6\theta$ **(b)** $r = 1 - 2 \cos \theta$ **(c)** $r = 4 \sin \theta$

SOLUTION

For all these graphs, set your calculator to POLAR mode.

(a) First we find the window. Notice that $|r| = |\sin 6\theta| \leq 1$ for all θ, so points on the graph are all within 1 unit from the pole. We want a window at least as large as $[-1, 1]$ by $[-1, 1]$, but we choose the window $[-1.5, 1.5]$ by $[-1, 1]$ in order to keep the *aspect ratio* close to the screen dimensions, which have a ratio of 3:2. We choose a θ-range of $0 \leq \theta \leq 2\pi$ to get a full rotation around the graph, after which we know that $\sin 6\theta$ will repeat the same graph periodically. Choose θ step $= 0.05$. The result is shown in Figure 11.25a.

(b) In this graph we notice that $|r| = |1 - 2 \cos \theta| \leq 3$, so we choose $[-3, 3]$ for our *y*-range and, to get the right aspect ratio, $[-4.5, 4.5]$ for our *x*-range. Due to the cosine's period, $0 \leq \theta \leq 2\pi$ again suffices for our θ-range. The graph is shown in Figure 11.25b.

(c) Since $|r| = |4 \sin \theta| \leq 4$, we choose $[-4, 4]$ for our *y*-range and $[-6, 6]$ for our *x*-range. Due to the sine's period, $0 \leq \theta \leq 2\pi$ again suffices for our θ-range. The graph is shown in Figure 11.25c.

Now Try Exercise 13.

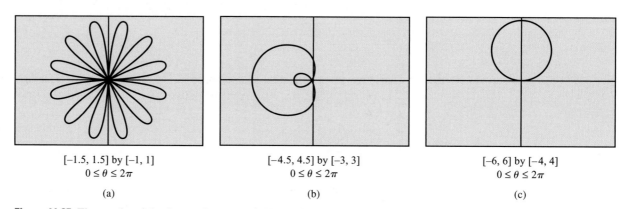

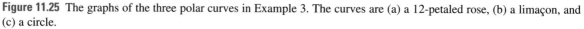

$[-1.5, 1.5]$ by $[-1, 1]$	$[-4.5, 4.5]$ by $[-3, 3]$	$[-6, 6]$ by $[-4, 4]$
$0 \leq \theta \leq 2\pi$	$0 \leq \theta \leq 2\pi$	$0 \leq \theta \leq 2\pi$
(a)	(b)	(c)

Figure 11.25 The graphs of the three polar curves in Example 3. The curves are (a) a 12-petaled rose, (b) a limaçon, and (c) a circle.

A Rose Is a Rose

The graph in Figure 11.25a is called a 12-petaled rose, because it looks like a flower and some flowers are roses. The graph in Figure 11.25b is called a limaçon (LEE-ma-sohn) from an old French word for *snail*. We will have more names for you at the end of the section.

With a little experimentation, it is possible to improve on the "safe" windows we chose in Example 3 (at least in parts (b) and (c)), but it is always a good idea to keep a 3:2 ratio of the *x*-range to the *y*-range so that shapes do not become distorted. Also, an astute observer may have noticed that the graph in part (c) was traversed *twice* as θ went from 0 to 2π, so a range of $0 \leq \theta \leq \pi$ would have sufficed to produce the entire graph. From 0 to π, the circle is swept out by positive *r*-values; then from π to 2π, the same circle is swept out by negative *r*-values.

Although the graph in Figure 11.25c certainly looks like a circle, how can we tell for sure that it really is? One way is to convert the polar equation to a Cartesian equation and verify that it is the equation of a circle. Trigonometry gives us a simple way to convert polar equations to rectangular equations and vice versa.

Polar–Rectangular Conversion Formulas

$$x = r \cos \theta \qquad r^2 = x^2 + y^2$$
$$y = r \sin \theta \qquad \tan \theta = \frac{y}{x}$$

EXAMPLE 4 Converting Polar to Rectangular

Use the polar–rectangular conversion formulas to show that the polar graph of $r = 4 \sin \theta$ is a circle.

SOLUTION

To facilitate the substitutions, multiply both sides of the original equation by r. (This could introduce extraneous solutions with $r = 0$, but the pole is the only such point, and we notice that it is already on the graph.)

$$\begin{aligned} r &= 4 \sin \theta \\ r^2 &= 4r \sin \theta \qquad &\text{Multiply by } r. \\ x^2 + y^2 &= 4y \qquad &\text{Polar–rectangular conversion} \\ x^2 + y^2 - 4y &= 0 \\ x^2 + y^2 - 4y + 4 &= 4 \qquad &\text{Completing the square} \\ x^2 + (y - 2)^2 &= 2^2 \qquad &\text{Circle in standard form} \end{aligned}$$

Sure enough, the graph is a circle centered at $(0, 2)$ with radius 2. See Figure 11.25c for graphing calculator support of the analytic solution.

Now Try Exercise 25.

The polar–rectangular conversion formulas also reveal the calculator's secret to polar graphing: It is really just parametric graphing with θ as the parameter.

Parametric Equations of Polar Curves

The polar graph of $r = f(\theta)$ is the curve defined parametrically by:

$$x = r \cos \theta = f(\theta) \cos \theta$$
$$y = r \sin \theta = f(\theta) \sin \theta$$

EXPLORATION 1 Graphing Polar Curves Parametrically

Switch your grapher to parametric mode and enter the equations

$$x = \sin (6t) \cos t$$
$$y = \sin (6t) \sin t$$

1. Set an appropriate window and see if you can reproduce the polar graph in Figure 11.25a.
2. Then produce the graphs in Figures 11.25b and 11.25c in the same way.

Slopes of Polar Curves

Since polar curves are drawn in the *xy*-plane, the *slope* of a polar curve is still the slope of the tangent line, which is dy/dx. The polar–rectangular conversion formulas enable us to write x and y as functions of θ, so we can find dy/dx as we did with parametrically defined functions:

$$\frac{dy}{dx} = \frac{dy/d\theta}{dx/d\theta}.$$

EXAMPLE 5 Finding Slope of a Polar Curve

Find the slope of the rose curve $r = 2 \sin 3\theta$ at the point where $\theta = \pi/6$ and use it to find the equation of the tangent line (Figure 11.26).

SOLUTION

By substitution using the parametric representation of the polar equation $r = 2 \sin 3\theta$, we have

$$x = r \cos \theta = 2 \sin 3\theta \cos \theta$$
$$y = r \sin \theta = 2 \sin 3\theta \sin \theta$$

So, the slope is

$$\left. \frac{dy}{dx} \right|_{\theta=\frac{\pi}{6}} = \left. \frac{dy/d\theta}{dx/d\theta} \right|_{\theta=\frac{\pi}{6}} = \left. \frac{\dfrac{d}{d\theta}(2 \sin 3\theta \sin \theta)}{\dfrac{d}{d\theta}(2 \sin 3\theta \cos \theta)} \right|_{\theta=\frac{\pi}{6}}$$

Using the derivative product rule on both the numerator and denominator, you can compute analytically that the slope is $-\sqrt{3}$.

When $\theta = \pi/6$,

$$x = 2 \sin(\pi/2) \cos(\pi/6) = \sqrt{3} \quad \text{and} \quad y = 2 \sin(\pi/2) \sin(\pi/6) = 1.$$

So the tangent line has equation $y - 1 = -\sqrt{3}(x - \sqrt{3})$.

Now Try Exercise 39.

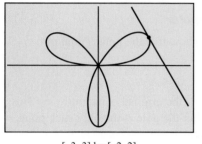

[−3, 3] by [−2, 2]

Figure 11.26 The 3-petaled rose curve $r = 2 \sin 3\theta$. Example 5 shows how to find the tangent line to the curve at $\theta = \pi/6$.

Areas Enclosed by Polar Curves

We would like to be able to use numerical integration to find areas enclosed by polar curves just as we did with curves defined by their rectangular coordinates. Converting the equations to rectangular coordinates is not a reasonable option for most polar curves, so we would like to have a formula involving small changes in θ rather than small changes in x. While a small change Δx produces a thin *rectangular* strip of area, a small change $\Delta \theta$ produces a thin *circular sector* of area (Figure 11.27).

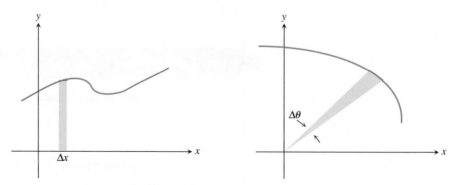

Figure 11.27 A small change in x produces a rectangular strip of area, while a small change in θ produces a thin *sector* of area.

Recall from geometry that the area of a sector of a circle is $\frac{1}{2}r^2\theta$, where r is the radius and θ is the central angle measured in radians. If we replace θ by the differential $d\theta$, we get the **area differential** $dA = \frac{1}{2}r^2 d\theta$ (Figure 11.28), which is exactly the quantity that we need to integrate to get an area in polar coordinates.

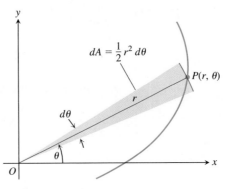

Figure 11.28 The area differential dA.

Area in Polar Coordinates

The area of the region between the origin and the curve $r = f(\theta)$ for $\alpha \le \theta \le \beta$ is

$$A = \int_\alpha^\beta \frac{1}{2}r^2 d\theta = \int_\alpha^\beta \frac{1}{2}(f(\theta))^2 \, d\theta.$$

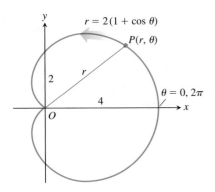

Figure 11.29 The cardioid in Example 6.

EXAMPLE 6   Finding Area

Find the area of the region in the plane enclosed by the cardioid $r = 2(1 + \cos\theta)$.

SOLUTION

We graph the cardioid (Figure 11.29) and determine that the *radius OP* sweeps out the region exactly once as θ runs from 0 to 2π.

The area is therefore

$$\int_{\theta=0}^{\theta=2\pi} \frac{1}{2}r^2 \, d\theta = \int_0^{2\pi} \frac{1}{2} \cdot 4(1 + \cos\theta)^2 \, d\theta$$

$$= \int_0^{2\pi} 2(1 + 2\cos\theta + \cos^2\theta) \, d\theta$$

$$= \int_0^{2\pi} \left(2 + 4\cos\theta + 2\,\frac{1 + \cos 2\theta}{2} \right) d\theta$$

$$= \int_0^{2\pi} (3 + 4\cos\theta + \cos 2\theta) \, d\theta$$

$$= \left[3\theta + 4\sin\theta + \frac{\sin 2\theta}{2} \right]_0^{2\pi} = 6\pi - 0 = 6\pi$$

Now Try Exercise 43.

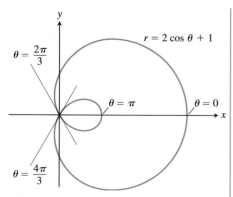

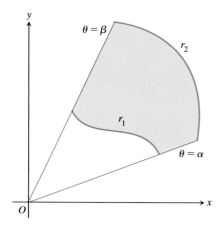

Figure 11.30 The limaçon in Example 7.

Figure 11.31 The area of the shaded region is calculated by subtracting the area of the region between r_1 and the origin from the area of the region between r_2 and the origin.

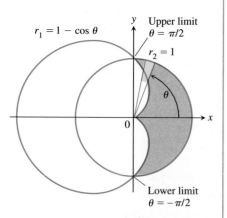

Figure 11.32 The region and limits of integration in Example 8.

EXAMPLE 7 Finding Area

Find the area inside the smaller loop of the limaçon $r = 2 \cos \theta + 1$.

SOLUTION

After watching the grapher generate the curve over the interval $0 \le \theta \le 2\pi$ (Figure 11.30), we see that the smaller loop is traced by the point (r, θ) as θ increases from $\theta = 2\pi/3$ to $\theta = 4\pi/3$ (the values for which $r = 2 \cos \theta + 1 = 0$). The area we seek is

$$A = \int_{2\pi/3}^{4\pi/3} \frac{1}{2} r^2 \, d\theta = \frac{1}{2} \int_{2\pi/3}^{4\pi/3} (2 \cos \theta + 1)^2 \, d\theta.$$

We can evaluate this integral numerically:

$$\frac{1}{2} \text{NINT}((2 \cos \theta + 1)^2, \theta, 2\pi/3, 4\pi/3) \approx 0.544$$

Now Try Exercise 47.

To find the area of a region like the one in Figure 11.31, which lies between two polar curves $r_1 = r_1(\theta)$ and $r_2 = r_2(\theta)$ from $\theta = \alpha$ to $\theta = \beta$, we subtract the integral of $(1/2)r_1^2$ from the integral of $(1/2)r_2^2$. This leads to the following formula.

Area Between Polar Curves

The area of the region between $r_1(\theta)$ and $r_2(\theta)$ for $\alpha \le \theta \le \beta$ is

$$A = \int_\alpha^\beta \frac{1}{2} r_2^2 \, d\theta - \int_\alpha^\beta \frac{1}{2} r_1^2 \, d\theta = \int_\alpha^\beta \frac{1}{2} (r_2^2 - r_1^2) \, d\theta.$$

EXAMPLE 8 Finding Area Between Curves

Find the area of the region that lies inside the circle $r = 1$ and outside the cardioid $r = 1 - \cos \theta$.

SOLUTION

The region is shown in Figure 11.32. The outer curve is $r_2 = 1$, the inner curve is $r_1 = 1 - \cos \theta$, and θ runs from $-\pi/2$ to $\pi/2$. Using the formula for the area between polar curves, the area is

$$A = \int_{-\pi/2}^{\pi/2} \frac{1}{2} (r_2^2 - r_1^2) \, d\theta$$

$$= 2 \int_0^{\pi/2} \frac{1}{2} (r_2^2 - r_1^2) \, d\theta \qquad \text{Symmetry}$$

$$= \int_0^{\pi/2} (1 - (1 - 2 \cos \theta + \cos^2 \theta)) \, d\theta$$

$$= \int_0^{\pi/2} \left(2 \cos \theta - \left(\frac{1 + \cos 2\theta}{2} \right) \right) d\theta$$

$$= 2 \sin \theta - \left(\frac{\theta}{2} + \frac{\sin 2\theta}{4} \right) \Big|_0^{\pi/2} = 2 - \frac{\pi}{4} \approx 1.215$$

Now Try Exercise 53.

A SMALL POLAR GALLERY

Here are a few of the more common polar graphs and the θ-intervals that can be used to produce them.

CIRCLES

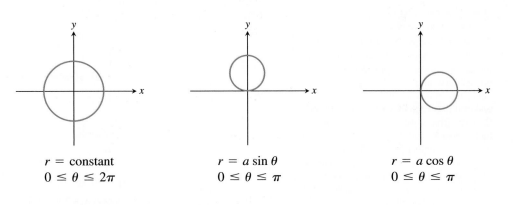

$r = \text{constant}$
$0 \leq \theta \leq 2\pi$

$r = a \sin \theta$
$0 \leq \theta \leq \pi$

$r = a \cos \theta$
$0 \leq \theta \leq \pi$

ROSE CURVES

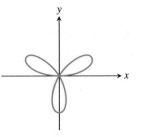

$r = a \sin n\theta, \ n \ \text{odd}$
$0 \leq \theta \leq \pi$
n petals
y-axis symmetry

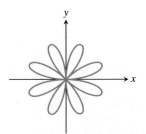

$r = a \sin n\theta, \ n \ \text{even}$
$0 \leq \theta \leq 2\pi$
$2n$ petals
y-axis symmetry and
x-axis symmetry

$r = a \cos n\theta, \ n \ \text{odd}$
$0 \leq \theta \leq \pi$
n petals
x-axis symmetry

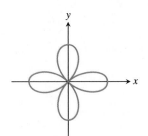

$r = a \cos n\theta, \ n \ \text{even}$
$0 \leq \theta \leq 2\pi$
$2n$ petals
y-axis symmetry and
x-axis symmetry

LIMAÇON CURVES

$r = a \pm b \sin \theta$ or $r = a \pm b \cos \theta$ with $a > 0$ and $b > 0$

($r = a \pm b \sin \theta$ has y-axis symmetry; $r = a \pm b \cos \theta$ has x-axis symmetry.)

Discovery of the Limaçon

The artist Albrecht Dürer (1471–1528) was the first to explain how to draw the curve we call a limaçon. It appeared in his book on compass and straightedge constructions, which was published in 1525 and was the first mathematics book printed in German. The limaçon was rediscovered by Étienne Pascal (1588–1651), father of the famous philosopher and mathematician Blaise Pascal (1623–1662). This curve was given its name, the *limaçon de Pascal*, by a friend of the family, Gilles-Personne Roberval (1602–1675), who used it in 1650 to illustrate how to find slopes of tangent lines.

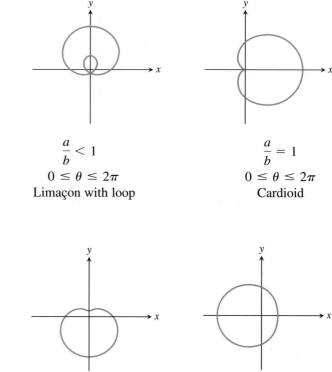

$$\frac{a}{b} < 1$$
$$0 \le \theta \le 2\pi$$
Limaçon with loop

$$\frac{a}{b} = 1$$
$$0 \le \theta \le 2\pi$$
Cardioid

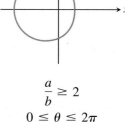

$$1 < \frac{a}{b} < 2$$
$$0 \le \theta \le \pi$$
Dimpled limaçon

$$\frac{a}{b} \ge 2$$
$$0 \le \theta \le 2\pi$$
Convex limaçon

Discovery of the Lemniscate

The lemniscate was discovered by Jacob Bernoulli (1654–1705) in 1694. Its name derives from the Latin *lemniscus*, an ornamental ribbon. It is the special case $b = a$ of a *Cassini oval* given by the polar equation $r^4 = 2a^2r^2 \cos (2\theta) + b^4 - a^4$ and first described by Giovanni Domenico Cassini (1625–1712) in 1680.

LEMNISCATE CURVES

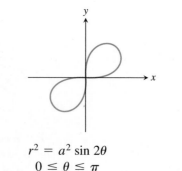

$$r^2 = a^2 \sin 2\theta$$
$$0 \le \theta \le \pi$$

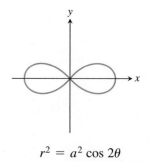

$$r^2 = a^2 \cos 2\theta$$
$$0 \le \theta \le \pi$$

Spiral of Archimedes

Archimedes' *On Spirals*

Archimedes of Syracuse (287–212 B.C.E.) wrote an entire book, *On Spirals*, about this curve. He explained how to find its arc lengths, tangents, and areas.

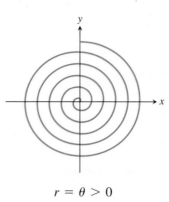

$r = \theta > 0$

Quick Review 11.3 *(For help, go to Sections 11.1 and 11.2.)*

Exercise numbers with a gray background indicate problems that the authors have designed to be solved *without a calculator.*

1. Find the component form of a vector with magnitude 4 and direction angle 30°.

2. Find the area of a 30° sector of a circle of radius 6.

3. Find the area of a sector of a circle of radius 8 that has a central angle of $\pi/8$ radians.

4. Find the rectangular equation of a circle of radius 5 centered at the origin.

5. Explain how to use your calculator in function mode to graph the curve $x^2 + 3y^2 = 4$.

Exercises 6–10 refer to the parametrized curve

$$x = 3 \cos t, \ y = 5 \sin t, \ 0 \le t \le 2\pi.$$

6. Find dy/dx.

7. Find the slope of the curve at $t = 2$.

8. Find the points on the curve where the slope is zero.

9. Find the points on the curve where the slope is undefined.

10. Find the length of the curve from $t = 0$ to $t = \pi$.

Section 11.3 Exercises

In Exercises 1 and 2, plot each point with the given polar coordinates and find the corresponding rectangular coordinates.

1. (a) $\left(\sqrt{2}, \pi/4\right)$ **(b)** $(1, 0)$
   (c) $(0, \pi/2)$ **(d)** $\left(-\sqrt{2}, \pi/4\right)$

2. (a) $(-3, 5\pi/6)$ **(b)** $\left(5, \tan^{-1}(4/3)\right)$
   (c) $(-1, 7\pi)$ **(d)** $\left(2\sqrt{3}, 2\pi/3\right)$

In Exercises 3 and 4, plot each point with the given rectangular coordinates and find two sets of corresponding polar coordinates.

3. (a) $(-1, 1)$ **(b)** $\left(1, -\sqrt{3}\right)$
   (c) $(0, 3)$ **(d)** $(-1, 0)$

4. (a) $\left(-\sqrt{3}, -1\right)$ **(b)** $(3, 4)$
   (c) $(0, -2)$ **(d)** $(2, 0)$

In Exercises 5–10, graph the set of points whose polar coordinates satisfy the given equation.

5. $r = 3$ **6.** $r = -3$

7. $r^2 = 4$ **8.** $\theta = -\pi/4$

9. $|\theta| = \pi/6$ **10.** $r^2 + 8 = 6r$

In Exercises 11–20, find an appropriate window and use a graphing calculator to produce the polar curve. Then sketch the complete curve and identify the type of curve by name.

11. $r = 1 + \cos \theta$ **12.** $r = 2 - 2 \cos \theta$

13. $r = 2 \cos 3\theta$ **14.** $r = -3 \sin 2\theta$

15. $r = 1 - 2 \sin \theta$ **16.** $r = 3/2 + \cos \theta$

17. $r^2 = 4 \cos 2\theta$ **18.** $r^2 = \sin 2\theta$

19. $r = 4 \sin \theta$ **20.** $r = 3 \cos \theta$

In Exercises 21–30, use analytic methods to replace the polar equation by an equivalent Cartesian (rectangular) equation. Then identify or describe the graph without using a grapher.

21. $r = 4 \csc \theta$ **22.** $r = -3 \sec \theta$

23. $r \cos \theta + r \sin \theta = 1$ **24.** $r^2 = 1$

25. $r = \dfrac{5}{\sin \theta - 2 \cos \theta}$ **26.** $r^2 \sin 2\theta = 2$

27. $\cos^2 \theta = \sin^2 \theta$ **28.** $r^2 = -4r \cos \theta$

29. $r = 8 \sin \theta$ **30.** $r = 2 \cos \theta + 2 \sin \theta$

In Exercises 31–38, find an appropriate window and use a graphing calculator to produce the polar curve. Then sketch the complete curve and identify the type of curve by name. (*Note:* You won't find these in the Polar Gallery.)

31. $r = \sec \theta \tan \theta$ **32.** $r = -\csc \theta \cot \theta$

33. $r = \dfrac{1}{1 + \cos \theta}$ **34.** $r = \dfrac{2}{1 - \sin \theta}$

35. $r = \dfrac{14}{5 + 9 \cos \theta}$ **36.** $r = \dfrac{12}{8 + 6 \cos \theta}$

37. $r = \dfrac{1}{1 - 0.8 \cos \theta}$ **38.** $r = \dfrac{1}{1 - 1.3 \cos \theta}$

In Exercises 39–42, find the slope of the curve at each indicated point.

39. $r = -1 + \sin \theta,\ \theta = 0, \pi$

40. $r = \cos 2\theta,\ \theta = 0, \pm \pi/2, \pi$

41. $r = 2 - 3 \sin \theta$

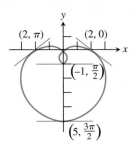

42. $r = 3(1 - \cos \theta)$

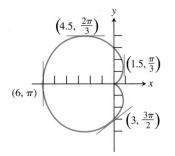

In Exercises 43–56, find the area of the region described.

43. inside the convex limaçon $r = 4 + 2 \cos \theta$

44. inside the cardioid $r = 2 + 2 \sin \theta$

45. inside one petal of the four-petaled rose $r = \cos 2\theta$

46. inside the eight-petaled rose $r = 2 \sin 4\theta$

47. inside one loop of the lemniscate $r^2 = 4 \cos 2\theta$

48. inside the six-petaled rose $r^2 = 2 \sin 3\theta$

49. inside the dimpled limaçon $r = 3 - 2 \cos \theta$

50. inside the inner loop of the limaçon $r = 2 \sin \theta - 1$

51. shared by the circles $r = 2 \cos \theta$ and $r = 2 \sin \theta$

52. shared by the circles $r = 1$ and $r = 2 \sin \theta$

53. shared by the circle $r = 2$ and the cardioid $r = 2(1 - \cos \theta)$

54. shared by the cardioids $r = 2(1 + \cos \theta)$ and $r = 2(1 - \cos \theta)$

55. inside the circle $r = 2$ and outside the cardioid $r = 2(1 - \sin \theta)$

56. inside the four-petaled rose $r = 4 \cos 2\theta$ and outside the circle $r = 2$

57. Sketch the polar curves $r = 3 \cos \theta$ and $r = 1 + \cos \theta$ and find the area that lies inside the circle and outside the cardioid.

58. Sketch the polar curves $r = 2$ and $r = 2(1 - \sin \theta)$ and find the area that lies inside the circle and outside the cardioid.

59. Sketch the polar curve $r = 2 \sin 3\theta$. Find the area enclosed by the curve and find the slope of the curve at the point where $\theta = \pi/4$.

60. The accompanying figure shows the parts of the graphs of the line $x = \frac{5}{3}y$ and the curve $x = \sqrt{1 + y^2}$ that lie in the first quadrant. Region R is enclosed by the line, the curve, and the x-axis.

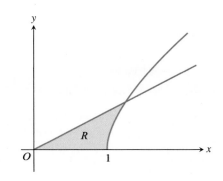

(a) Set up and evaluate an integral expression with respect to y that gives the area of R.

(b) Show that the curve $x = \sqrt{1 + y^2}$ can be described in polar coordinates by $r^2 = \dfrac{1}{\cos^2 \theta - \sin^2 \theta}$.

(c) Use the polar equation in part (b) to set up an integral expression with respect to θ that gives the area of R.

Standardized Test Questions

You may use a graphing calculator to solve the following problems.

61. True or False There is exactly one point in the plane with polar coordinates $(2, 2)$. Justify your answer.

62. True or False The total area enclosed by the 3-petaled rose $r = \sin 3\theta$ is $\int_0^{2\pi} \frac{1}{2} \sin^2 3\theta\, d\theta$. Justify your answer.

63. Multiple Choice The area of the region enclosed by the polar graph of $r = \sqrt{3 + \cos \theta}$ is given by which integral?

(A) $\int_0^{2\pi} \sqrt{3 + \cos \theta}\, d\theta$ **(B)** $\int_0^{\pi} \sqrt{3 + \cos \theta}\, d\theta$

(C) $2\int_0^{\pi/2} (3 + \cos \theta)\, d\theta$ **(D)** $\int_0^{\pi} (3 + \cos \theta)\, d\theta$

(E) $\int_0^{\pi/2} \sqrt{3 + \cos \theta}\, d\theta$

64. Multiple Choice The area enclosed by one petal of the 3-petaled rose $r = 4 \cos(3\theta)$ is given by which integral?

(A) $16 \int_{-\pi/3}^{\pi/3} \cos(3\theta)\, d\theta$ **(B)** $8 \int_{-\pi/6}^{\pi/6} \cos(3\theta)\, d\theta$

(C) $8 \int_{-\pi/3}^{\pi/3} \cos^2(3\theta)\, d\theta$ **(D)** $16 \int_{-\pi/6}^{\pi/6} \cos^2(3\theta)\, d\theta$

(E) $8 \int_{-\pi/6}^{\pi/6} \cos^2(3\theta)\, d\theta$

65. Multiple Choice If $a \neq 0$ and $\theta \neq 0$, all of the following must necessarily represent the same point in polar coordinates *except* which ordered pair?

(A) (a, θ) (B) $(-a, -\theta)$ (C) $(-a, \theta - \pi)$

(D) $(-a, \theta + \pi)$ (E) $(a, \theta - 2\pi)$

66. Multiple Choice Which of the following gives the slope of the polar curve $r = f(\theta)$ graphed in the xy-plane?

(A) $\dfrac{dr}{d\theta}$ (B) $\dfrac{dy}{d\theta}$ (C) $\dfrac{dx}{d\theta}$

(D) $\dfrac{dy/d\theta}{dx/d\theta}$ (E) $\dfrac{dy}{dx}\dfrac{dr}{d\theta}$

Explorations

67. *Rotating Curves* Let $r_1(\theta) = 3(1 - \cos \theta)$ and $r_2(\theta) = r_1(\theta - \alpha)$.

(a) Graph r_2 for $\alpha = \pi/6, \pi/4, \pi/3$, and $\pi/2$ and compare with the graph of r_1.

(b) Graph r_2 for $\alpha = -\pi/6, -\pi/4, -\pi/3$, and $-\pi/2$ and compare with the graph of r_1.

(c) Based on your observations in parts (a) and (b), describe the relationship between the graphs of $r_1 = f(\theta)$ and $r_2 = f(\theta - \alpha)$.

68. Let $r = \dfrac{2}{1 + e \cos \theta}$.

(a) Graph r in a square viewing window for $e = 0.1, 0.3, 0.5, 0.7$, and 0.9. Describe the graphs.

(b) Based on your observations in part (a), conjecture what happens to the graphs for $0 < e < 1$ and $e \to 0^+$.

69. Let $r = \dfrac{2}{1 + e \cos \theta}$.

(a) Graph r in a square viewing window for $e = -0.1, -0.3, -0.5, -0.7$, and -0.9. Describe the graphs.

(b) Based on your observations in part (a), what is the relationship between the graph of a conic section with eccentricity e and the graph with eccentricity $-e$?

70. Let $r = \dfrac{2}{1 + e \cos \theta}$.

(a) Graph r in a square viewing window for $e = 1.1, 1.3, 1.5, 1.7$, and 1.9. Describe the graphs.

(b) Based on your observations in part (a), conjecture what happens to the graphs for $e > 1$ and $e \to 1^+$.

71. Let $r = \dfrac{c}{1 + \cos \theta}$.

(a) Graph r in a square viewing window for $c = 1, 3, 5, 7$, and 9. Describe the graphs.

(b) Based on your observations in part (a), conjecture what happens to the graphs for $c > 0$ and $c \to 0^+$.

Extending the Ideas

72. *Distance Formula* Show that the distance between two points (r_1, θ_1) and (r_2, θ_2) in polar coordinates is
$$d = \sqrt{r_1^2 + r_2^2 - 2r_1 r_2 \cos (\theta_1 - \theta_2)}.$$

73. *Average Value* If f is continuous, the average value of the polar coordinate r over the curve $r = f(\theta), \alpha \leq \theta \leq \beta$, with respect to θ is
$$r_{av} = \frac{1}{\beta - \alpha} \int_\alpha^\beta f(\theta)\, d\theta.$$

Use this formula to find the average value of r with respect to θ over the following curves $(a > 0)$.

(a) the cardioid $r = a(1 - \cos \theta)$

(b) the circle $r = a$

(c) the circle $r = a \cos \theta, -\pi/2 \leq \theta \leq \pi/2$

74. *Length of a Polar Curve* The parametric form of the arc length formula (Section 11.1) gives the length of a polar curve as
$$L = \int_\alpha^\beta \sqrt{\left(\frac{dx}{d\theta}\right)^2 + \left(\frac{dy}{d\theta}\right)^2}\, d\theta.$$

Assuming that the necessary derivatives are continuous, show that the substitutions $x = r \cos \theta$ and $y = r \sin \theta$ transform this expression into
$$L = \int_\alpha^\beta \sqrt{r^2 + \left(\frac{dr}{d\theta}\right)^2}\, d\theta.$$

75. *Length of a Cardioid* Use the formula in Exercise 74 to find the length of the cardioid $r = 1 + \cos \theta$.

76. *Writing to Learn* Let $r = \dfrac{1}{1 + 1.2 \cos \theta}$.

(a) Graph r in a square viewing window. Describe what you see.

(b) Explain why you get both branches of the hyperbola.

(c) Explain why the graphing calculator also appears to show the asymptotes.

77. *Writing to Learn* Show that if $|e| < 1$, then the polar equation of an ellipse $r = \dfrac{c}{1 + e \cos \theta}$ corresponds to the equation in rectangular coordinates $\dfrac{(x + ae)}{a^2} + \dfrac{y^2}{b^2} = 1$, where $a = \dfrac{c}{1 - e^2}$ and $b = \dfrac{c}{\sqrt{1 - e^2}}$. [*Hint:* Rewrite the polar equation as $r = c - e(r \cos \theta) = c - ex$.]

78. For an ellipse with its center at the origin, semimajor axis a, and semiminor axis b, given by the equation $\dfrac{x^2}{a^2} + \dfrac{y^2}{b^2} = 1$, the *foci* (plural of focus) are located at $\left(\pm \sqrt{a^2 - b^2}, 0\right)$. Using the result of Exercise 77, show that for an ellipse given by the polar equation $r = \dfrac{c}{1 + e \cos \theta}$, one of the foci is located at the origin.

79. *Orbital Mechanics* A satellite in orbit sweeps out equal area in equal time, which means that $\dfrac{dA}{dt}$ is constant, say, $\dfrac{dA}{dt} = K$.

Use the integral formula for the area of a polar curve to show that for any integrable polar curve $r = f(\theta)$, the rate at which area is swept out is given by
$$\frac{dA}{dt} = \frac{1}{2} r^2 \frac{d\theta}{dt}.$$

Show that this implies that for a satellite in orbit, $\dfrac{d\theta}{dt} = \dfrac{2K}{r^2}$. In other words, the angular velocity is inversely proportional to the square of the distance.

80. The parametric equations for a conic section are given by

$$x = \frac{c \cos t}{1 + e \cos t},$$

$$y = \frac{c \sin t}{1 + e \cos t}.$$

Using the result of Exercise 79, show that for a satellite following a curve that is a conic section and sweeping out equal area in equal time, the acceleration vector is given by

$$\left\langle \frac{d^2x}{dt^2}, \frac{d^2y}{dt^2} \right\rangle = \frac{-4K^2}{cr^2} \langle \cos t, \sin t \rangle.$$

Explain why this implies that the acceleration is directed toward the origin and has magnitude inversely proportional to the square of the distance. [*Hint:* Use the fact that

$$2K = r^2 \frac{d\theta}{dt} = \frac{c^2}{(1 + e \cos \theta)^2} \frac{d\theta}{dt}.]$$

Quick Quiz for AP* Preparation: Sections 11.1–11.3

You may use a graphing calculator to solve the following problems.

1. Multiple Choice Which of the following is equal to the area of the region inside the polar curve $r = 2 \cos \theta$ and outside the polar curve $r = \cos \theta$?

(A) $3 \int_0^{\pi/2} \cos^2 \theta \, d\theta$ **(B)** $3 \int_0^{\pi} \cos^2 \theta \, d\theta$

(C) $\frac{3}{2} \int_0^{\pi/2} \cos^2 \theta \, d\theta$ **(D)** $3 \int_0^{\pi/2} \cos \theta \, d\theta$

(E) $3 \int_0^{\pi} \cos \theta \, d\theta$

2. Multiple Choice For what values of t does the curve given by the parametric equations $x = t^3 - t^2 - 1$ and $y = t^4 + 2t^2 - 8t$ have a vertical tangent?

(A) 0 only   **(B)** 1 only

(C) 0 and 2/3 only   **(D)** 0, 2/3, and 1

(E) No value

3. Multiple Choice The length of the path described by the parametric equations $x = t^2$ and $y = t$ from $t = 0$ to $t = 4$ is given by which integral?

(A) $\int_0^4 \sqrt{4t + 1} \, dt$ **(B)** $2 \int_0^4 \sqrt{t^2 + 1} \, dt$ **(C)** $\int_0^4 \sqrt{2t^2 + 1} \, dt$

(D) $\int_0^4 \sqrt{4t^2 + 1} \, dt$ **(E)** $2\pi \int_0^4 \sqrt{4t^2 + 1} \, dt$

4. Free Response A polar curve is defined by the equation $r = \theta + \sin 2\theta$ for $0 \le \theta \le \pi$.

(a) Find the area bounded by the curve and the x-axis.

(b) Find the angle θ that corresponds to the point on the curve where $x = -2$.

(c) For $\dfrac{\pi}{3} < \theta < \dfrac{2\pi}{3}$, $\dfrac{dr}{d\theta}$ is negative. How can this be seen from the graph?

(d) At what angle θ in the interval $0 \le \theta \le \pi/2$ is the curve farthest away from the origin? Justify your answer.

CHAPTER 11   Key Terms

Absolute value of a vector (p. 550)

Acceleration vector (p. 554)

Apogee (p. 561)

Arc length of a parametrized curve (p. 545)

Arc length of a polar curve (p. 573)

Area between polar curves (p. 568)

Area differential (p. 567)

Area in polar coordinates (p. 567)

Arrow (p. 550)

Cardioid (p. 570)

Cartesian equation of a curve (p. 564)

Component form of a vector (p. 550)

Components of a vector (p. 550)

Convex limaçon (p. 570)

Cycloid (p. 545)

Dimpled limaçon (p. 570)

Directed distance (p. 562)

Directed line segment (p. 550)

Direction angle of a vector (p. 551)

Direction of motion (p. 554)

Direction vector (p. 550)

Displacement (p. 556)

Distance traveled (p. 556)

Dot product of vectors (p. 560)

Equivalent arrows (p. 551)

Head Minus Tail Rule (p. 551)

Huygens's clock (p. 546)

Initial point of an arrow (p. 551)

Initial ray of angle of direction (p. 562)

Lemniscate (p. 570)

Limaçon (p. 570)

Limaçon with inner loop (p. 570)

Magnitude of a vector (p. 550)

Opposite of a vector (p. 552)

Orthogonal vectors (p. 559)

Parallelogram representation of vector addition (p. 552)

Parametric equations of a polar curve (p. 565)

Parametric formula for dy/dx (p. 544)

Parametric formula for d^2y/dx^2 (p. 544)

Path of a particle (p. 554)

Perigee (p. 561)

Polar coordinates (p. 562)

Polar equation of a curve (p. 561)

Polar function (p. 561)

Polar graphing (p. 563)

Polar–rectangular conversion formulas (p. 565)

Pole (p. 562)

Position of a particle (p. 554)

Position vector (p. 550)

Properties of vectors (p. 553)

Resultant vector (p. 552)

Rose curve (p. 569)

Scalar (p. 551)

Scalar multiple of a vector (p. 552)

Speed (p. 554)

Spiral of Archimedes (p. 571)

Standard representation of a
vector (p. 550)

Sum of vectors (p. 552)

Tail-to-head representation of vector
addition (p. 552)

Terminal point of an arrow (p. 551)

Unit vector (p. 552)

Vector (p. 550)

Vector addition (p. 551)

Velocity vector (p. 554)

Zero vector (p. 550)

CHAPTER 11   Review Exercises

In Exercises 1–4, let $\mathbf{u} = \langle -3, 4 \rangle$ and $\mathbf{v} = \langle 2, -5 \rangle$. Find (**a**) the component form of the vector and (**b**) its magnitude.

1. $3\mathbf{u} - 4\mathbf{v}$ **2.** $\mathbf{u} + \mathbf{v}$ **3.** $-2\mathbf{u}$ **4.** $5\mathbf{v}$

In Exercises 5–8, find the component form of the vector.

5. the vector obtained by rotating $\langle 0, 1 \rangle$ through an angle of $2\pi/3$ radians

6. the unit vector that makes an angle of $\pi/6$ radian with the positive x-axis

7. the vector 2 units long in the direction $4\mathbf{i} - \mathbf{j}$

8. the vector 5 units long in the direction opposite to the direction of $\langle 3/5, 4/5 \rangle$

In Exercises 9 and 10, (**a**) find an equation for the tangent to the curve at the point corresponding to the given value of t, and (**b**) find the value of d^2y/dx^2 at this point.

9. $x = (1/2) \tan t$, $y = (1/2) \sec t$; $t = \pi/3$

10. $x = 1 + 1/t^2$, $y = 1 - 3/t$; $t = 2$

In Exercises 11–14, find the points at which the tangent to the curve is (**a**) horizontal; (**b**) vertical.

11. $x = (1/2) \tan t$, $y = (1/2) \sec t$

12. $x = -2 \cos t$, $y = 2 \sin t$

13. $x = -\cos t$, $y = \cos^2 t$

14. $x = 4 \cos t$, $y = 9 \sin t$

In Exercises 15–20, find an appropriate window and graph the polar curve on a graphing calculator. Then sketch the curve on paper and identify the type of curve.

15. $r = 1 - \sin \theta$ **16.** $r = 2 + \cos \theta$

17. $r = \cos 2\theta$ **18.** $r \cos \theta = 1$

19. $r^2 = \sin 2\theta$ **20.** $r = -\sin \theta$

In Exercises 21 and 22, find the slope of the tangent lines at the point where $\theta = \pi/3$.

21. $r = \cos 2\theta$ **22.** $r = 2 + \cos 2\theta$

In Exercises 23 and 24, find equations for the horizontal and vertical tangent lines to the curves.

23. $r = 1 - \cos(\theta/2)$, $\quad 0 \le \theta \le 4\pi$

24. $r = 2(1 - \sin \theta)$, $\quad 0 \le \theta \le 2\pi$

25. Find equations for the lines that are tangent to the tips of the petals of the four-petaled rose $r = \sin 2\theta$.

26. Find equations for the lines that are tangent to the cardioid $r = 1 + \sin \theta$ at the points where it crosses the x-axis.

In Exercises 27–30, replace the polar equation by an equivalent Cartesian equation. Then identify or describe the graph.

27. $r \cos \theta = r \sin \theta$ **28.** $r = 3 \cos \theta$

29. $r = 4 \tan \theta \sec \theta$ **30.** $r \cos(\theta + \pi/3) = 2\sqrt{3}$

In Exercises 31–34, replace the Cartesian equation by an equivalent polar equation.

31. $x^2 + y^2 + 5y = 0$ **32.** $x^2 + y^2 - 2y = 0$

33. $x^2 + 4y^2 = 16$ **34.** $(x + 2)^2 + (y - 5)^2 = 16$

In Exercises 35–38, find the area of the region described.

35. enclosed by the limaçon $r = 2 - \cos \theta$

36. enclosed by one petal of the three-petaled rose $r = \sin 3\theta$

37. inside the "figure eight" $r = 1 + \cos 2\theta$ and outside the circle $r = 1$

38. inside the cardioid $r = 2(1 + \sin \theta)$ and outside the circle $r = 2 \sin \theta$

In Exercises 39 and 40, $r(t)$ is the position vector of a particle moving in the plane at time t. Find (**a**) the velocity and acceleration vectors, and (**b**) the speed at the given value of t.

39. $\mathbf{r}(t) = \langle 4 \cos t, \sqrt{2} \sin t \rangle$, $t = \pi/4$

40. $\mathbf{r}(t) = \langle \sqrt{3} \sec t, \sqrt{3} \tan t \rangle$, $t = 0$

41. The position of a particle in the plane at time t is
$$\mathbf{r} = \left\langle \frac{1}{\sqrt{1 + t^2}}, \frac{t}{\sqrt{1 + t^2}} \right\rangle.$$ Find the particle's maximum speed.

42. Writing to Learn Suppose that $\mathbf{r}(t) = \langle e^t \cos t, e^t \sin t \rangle$. Show that the angle between $\mathbf{r}$ and the acceleration vector $\mathbf{a}$ never changes. What is the angle?

In Exercises 43–46, find the position vector.

43. $\mathbf{v}(t) = \langle -\sin t, \cos t \rangle$ and $\mathbf{r}(0) = \langle 0, 1 \rangle$

44. $\mathbf{v}(t) = \left\langle \frac{1}{t^2 + 1}, \frac{t}{\sqrt{t^2 + 1}} \right\rangle$ and $\mathbf{r}(0) = \langle 1, 1 \rangle$

45. $\mathbf{a}(t) = \langle 0, 2 \rangle$ and $\mathbf{v}(0) = \langle 0, 0 \rangle$ and $\mathbf{r}(0) = \langle 1, 0 \rangle$

46. $\mathbf{a}(t) = \langle -2, -2 \rangle$ and $\mathbf{v}(1) = \langle 4, 0 \rangle$ and $\mathbf{r}(1) = \langle 3, 3 \rangle$

47. *Particle Motion* A particle moves in the plane in such a manner that its coordinates at time t are

$$x = 3 \cos \frac{\pi}{4} t, \quad y = 5 \sin \frac{\pi}{4} t.$$

(a) Find the length of the velocity vector at $t = 3$.

(b) Find the x- and y-components of the acceleration of the particle at $t = 3$.

(c) Find a single equation in x and y for the path of the particle.

48. *Particle Motion* At time t, $0 \leq t \leq 4$, the position of a particle moving along a path in the plane is given by the parametric equations

$$x = e^t \cos t, \quad y = e^t \sin t.$$

(a) Find the slope of the path of the particle at time $t = \pi$.

(b) Find the speed of the particle when $t = 3$.

(c) Find the distance traveled by the particle along the path from $t = 0$ to $t = 3$.

49. *Particle Motion* The position of a particle at any time $t \geq 0$ is given by

$$x(t) = t^2 - 2, \quad y(t) = \frac{2}{5} t^3.$$

(a) Find the magnitude of the velocity vector at $t = 4$.

(b) Find the total distance traveled by the particle from $t = 0$ to $t = 4$.

(c) Find dy/dx as a function of x.

50. *Navigation* An airplane, flying in the direction 80° east of north at 540 mph in still air, encounters a 55-mph tail wind acting in the direction 100° east of north. The airplane holds its compass heading but, because of the wind, acquires a different ground speed and direction. What are they?

AP* Examination Preparation

You may use a graphing calculator to solve the following problems.

51. A particle moves along the graph of $y = \cos x$ so that its x-component of acceleration is always 2. At time $t = 0$, the particle is at the point $(\pi, -1)$ and the velocity of the particle is $\langle 0, 0 \rangle$.

(a) Find the position vector of the particle.

(b) Find the speed of the particle when it is at the point $(4, \cos 4)$.

52. Two particles move in the xy-plane. For time $t \geq 0$, the position of particle A is given by $x = t - 2$ and $y = (t - 2)^2$, and the position of particle B is given by $x = \frac{3}{2}t - 4$ and $y = \frac{3}{2}t - 2$.

(a) Find the velocity vector for each particle at time $t = 3$.

(b) Find the distance traveled by particle A from $t = 0$ to $t = 3$.

(c) Determine the exact time when the particles collide.

53. A region R in the xy-plane is bounded below by the x-axis and above by the polar curve defined by $r = \dfrac{4}{1 + \sin \theta}$ for $0 \leq \theta \leq \pi$.

(a) Find the area of R by evaluating an integral in polar coordinates.

(b) The curve resembles an arch of the parabola $8y = 16 - x^2$. Convert the polar equation to rectangular coordinates and prove that the curves are the same.

(c) Set up an integral in rectangular coordinates that gives the area of R.

Appendices

A1 | Formulas from Precalculus Mathematics

Algebra

1. Laws of Exponents

$$a^m a^n = a^{m+n}, \quad (ab)^m = a^m b^m, \quad (a^m)^n = a^{mn}, \quad a^{m/n} = \sqrt[n]{a^m}$$

If $a \neq 0$, $\quad \dfrac{a^m}{a^n} = a^{m-n}, \quad a^0 = 1, \quad a^{-m} = \dfrac{1}{a^m}$

2. Zero Division by zero is not defined.

If $a \neq 0$: $\quad \dfrac{0}{a} = 0, \quad a^0 = 1, \quad 0^a = 0$

For any number a: $\quad a \cdot 0 = 0 \cdot a = 0$

3. Fractions

$$\frac{a}{b} + \frac{c}{d} = \frac{ad + bc}{bd}, \quad \frac{a}{b} \cdot \frac{c}{d} = \frac{ac}{bd}, \quad \frac{a/b}{c/d} = \frac{a}{b} \cdot \frac{d}{c}, \quad \frac{-a}{b} = -\frac{a}{b} = \frac{a}{-b},$$

$$\frac{(a/b) + (c/d)}{(e/f) + (g/h)} = \frac{(a/b) + (c/d)}{(e/f) + (g/h)} \cdot \frac{bdfh}{bdfh} = \frac{(ad + bc)fh}{(eh + fg)bd}$$

4. The Binomial Theorem

For any positive integer n,

$$(a + b)^n = a^n + na^{n-1}b + \frac{n(n - 1)}{1 \cdot 2} a^{n-2}b^2$$

$$+ \frac{n(n - 1)(n - 2)}{1 \cdot 2 \cdot 3} a^{n-3}b^3 + \cdots + nab^{n-1} + b^n.$$

For instance, $\quad (a + b)^1 = a + b,$

$(a + b)^2 = a^2 + 2ab + b^2,$

$(a + b)^3 = a^3 + 3a^2b + 3ab^2 + b^3,$

$(a + b)^4 = a^4 + 4a^3b + 6a^2b^2 + 4ab^3 + b^4$

5. Differences of Like Integer Powers, $n > 1$

$$a^n - b^n = (a - b)(a^{n-1} + a^{n-2}b + a^{n-3}b^2 + \cdots + ab^{n-2} + b^{n-1})$$

For instance, $\quad a^2 - b^2 = (a - b)(a + b),$

$a^3 - b^3 = (a - b)(a^2 + ab + b^2),$

$a^4 - b^4 = (a - b)(a^3 + a^2b + ab^2 + b^3)$

6. Completing the Square

If $a \neq 0$, we can rewrite the quadratic $ax^2 + bx + c$ in the form $au^2 + C$ by a process called completing the square:

$$ax^2 + bx + c = a\left(x^2 + \frac{b}{a}x\right) + c$$

Factor a from the first two terms.

$$= a\left(x^2 + \frac{b}{a}x + \frac{b^2}{4a^2} - \frac{b^2}{4a^2}\right) + c$$

Add and subtract the square of half the coefficient of x.

$$= a\left(x^2 + \frac{b}{a}x + \frac{b^2}{4a^2}\right) + a\left(-\frac{b^2}{4a^2}\right) + c$$

Bring out the $-\frac{b^2}{4a^2}$.

$$= a\underbrace{\left(x^2 + \frac{b}{a}x + \frac{b^2}{4a^2}\right)}_{\text{This is } \left(x + \frac{b}{2a}\right)^2.} + \underbrace{c - \frac{b^2}{4a}}_{\substack{\text{Call this} \\ \text{part } C.}}$$

$$= au^2 + C \qquad\qquad u = x + \frac{b}{2a}$$

7. The Quadratic Formula

By completing the square on the first two terms of the equation

$$ax^2 + bx + c = 0$$

and solving the resulting equation for x (details omitted), we obtain

$$x = \frac{-b \pm \sqrt{b^2 - 4ac}}{2a}.$$

This equation is the **quadratic formula.**

For instance, the solutions of the equation $2x^2 + 3x - 1 = 0$ are

$$x = \frac{-3 \pm \sqrt{(3)^2 - 4(2)(-1)}}{2(2)} = \frac{-3 \pm \sqrt{9 + 8}}{4}$$

or

$$x = \frac{-3 + \sqrt{17}}{4} \quad \text{and} \quad x = \frac{-3 - \sqrt{17}}{4}.$$

Geometry

(A = area, B = area of base, C = circumference, h = height, S = lateral area or surface area, V = volume)

1. Triangle   **2. Similar Triangles**   **3. Pythagorean Theorem**

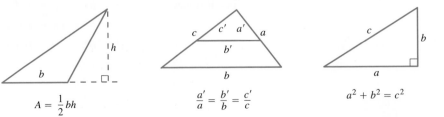

$$A = \frac{1}{2}bh \qquad\qquad \frac{a'}{a} = \frac{b'}{b} = \frac{c'}{c} \qquad\qquad a^2 + b^2 = c^2$$

4. Parallelogram

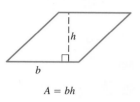

$$A = bh$$

5. Trapezoid

$$A = \frac{1}{2}(a + b)h$$

6. Circle

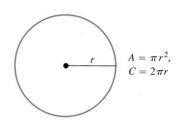

$$A = \pi r^2, \quad C = 2\pi r$$

7. Any Cylinder or Prism with Parallel Bases

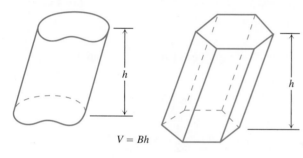

$$V = Bh$$

8. Right Circular Cylinder

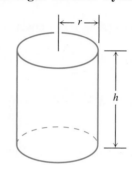

$$V = \pi r^2 h, \quad S = 2\pi rh$$

9. Any Cone or Pyramid

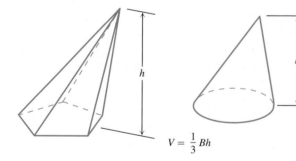

$$V = \frac{1}{3} Bh$$

10. Right Circular Cone

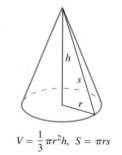

$$V = \frac{1}{3}\pi r^2 h, \quad S = \pi rs$$

11. Sphere

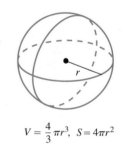

$$V = \frac{4}{3}\pi r^3, \quad S = 4\pi r^2$$

Trigonometry

1. Definitions of Fundamental Identities

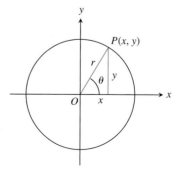

Sine: $\quad \sin\theta = \dfrac{y}{r} = \dfrac{1}{\csc\theta}$

Cosine: $\quad \cos\theta = \dfrac{x}{r} = \dfrac{1}{\sec\theta}$

Tangent: $\quad \tan\theta = \dfrac{y}{x} = \dfrac{1}{\cot\theta}$

2. Identities

$$\sin(-\theta) = -\sin\theta, \qquad \cos(-\theta) = \cos\theta,$$

$$\sin^2\theta + \cos^2\theta = 1, \quad \sec^2\theta = 1 + \tan^2\theta, \quad \csc^2\theta = 1 + \cot^2\theta$$

$$\sin 2\theta = 2\sin\theta\cos\theta, \qquad \cos 2\theta = \cos^2\theta - \sin^2\theta$$

$$\cos^2\theta = \frac{1 + \cos 2\theta}{2}, \qquad \sin^2\theta = \frac{1 - \cos 2\theta}{2}$$

$$\sin(A + B) = \sin A \cos B + \cos A \sin B \qquad \tan(A + B) = \frac{\tan A + \tan B}{1 - \tan A \tan B}$$

$$\sin(A - B) = \sin A \cos B - \cos A \sin B$$

$$\cos(A + B) = \cos A \cos B - \sin A \sin B \qquad \tan(A - B) = \frac{\tan A - \tan B}{1 + \tan A \tan B}$$

$$\cos(A - B) = \cos A \cos B + \sin A \sin B$$

$$\sin\left(A - \frac{\pi}{2}\right) = -\cos A, \qquad\qquad \cos\left(A - \frac{\pi}{2}\right) = \sin A$$

$$\sin\left(A + \frac{\pi}{2}\right) = \cos A, \qquad\qquad \cos\left(A + \frac{\pi}{2}\right) = -\sin A$$

$$\sin A \sin B = \frac{1}{2}\cos(A - B) - \frac{1}{2}\cos(A + B)$$

$$\cos A \cos B = \frac{1}{2}\cos(A - B) + \frac{1}{2}\cos(A + B)$$

$$\sin A \cos B = \frac{1}{2}\sin(A - B) + \frac{1}{2}\sin(A + B)$$

$$\sin A + \sin B = 2\sin\frac{1}{2}(A + B)\cos\frac{1}{2}(A - B)$$

$$\sin A - \sin B = 2\cos\frac{1}{2}(A + B)\sin\frac{1}{2}(A - B)$$

$$\cos A + \cos B = 2\cos\frac{1}{2}(A + B)\cos\frac{1}{2}(A - B)$$

$$\cos A - \cos B = -2\sin\frac{1}{2}(A + B)\sin\frac{1}{2}(A - B)$$

3. Common Reference Triangles

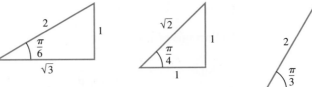

4. Angles and Sides of a Triangle

Law of cosines: $c^2 = a^2 + b^2 - 2ab\cos C$

Law of sines: $\dfrac{\sin A}{a} = \dfrac{\sin B}{b} = \dfrac{\sin C}{c}$

Area $= \dfrac{1}{2}bc\sin A = \dfrac{1}{2}ac\sin B = \dfrac{1}{2}ab\sin C$

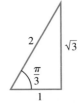
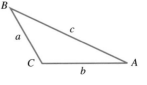

Conic Sections

1. Circle

$$(x - h)^2 + (y - k)^2 = r^2$$

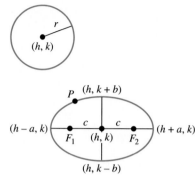

2. Ellipse (horizontal)

$$\frac{(x - h)^2}{a^2} + \frac{(y - k)^2}{b^2} = 1$$

$$a^2 = b^2 + c^2$$

$$eccentricity = \frac{c}{a}$$

$$PF_1 + PF_2 = 2a$$

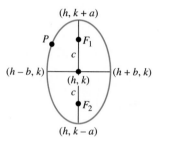

2. Ellipse (vertical)

$$\frac{(y - k)^2}{a^2} + \frac{(x - h)^2}{b^2} = 1$$

$$a^2 = b^2 + c^2$$

$$eccentricity = \frac{c}{a}$$

$$PF_1 + PF_2 = 2a$$

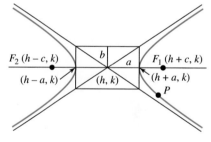

3. Hyperbola (horizontal)

$$\frac{(x - h)^2}{a^2} - \frac{(y - k)^2}{b^2} = 1$$

$$c^2 = a^2 + b^2$$

$$eccentricity = \frac{c}{a}$$

$$\left| PF_1 - PF_2 \right| = 2a$$

$$Asymptotes: \ y - k = \pm \frac{b}{a}(x - h)$$

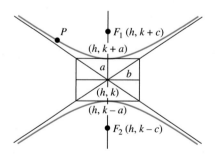

3. Hyperbola (vertical)

$$\frac{(y - k)^2}{a^2} - \frac{(x - h)^2}{b^2} = 1$$

$$c^2 = a^2 + b^2$$

$$eccentricity = \frac{c}{a}$$

$$\left| PF_1 - PF_2 \right| = 2a$$

$$Asymptotes: \ y - k = \pm \frac{a}{b}(x - h)$$

4. Parabola (vertical)

$$(x - h)^2 = 4p(y - k)$$

$$PF = Pd$$

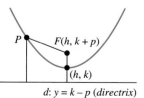

4. **Parabola (horizontal)**

$$(y - k)^2 = 4p(x - h)$$

$$PF = Pd$$

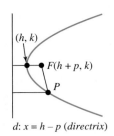

$d: x = h - p$ (*directrix*)

5. **General Conics**

In general, the graph of $Ax^2 + Bxy + Cy^2 + Dx + Ey + F = 0$ is a(n):

circle if $B = 0$ and $A = C$

ellipse if $B^2 - 4AC < 0$ (possibly a circle)

hyperbola if $B^2 - 4AC > 0$

parabola if $B^2 - 4AC = 0$

unless the graph is degenerate:

empty (degenerate ellipse/circle)

a point (degenerate ellipse/circle)

a line (degenerate parabola)

two lines (degenerate hyperbola)

6. **Reflection Properties**

Parabola: A ray parallel to the axis of symmetry will reflect off the parabola toward the focus. A ray emanating from the focus will reflect off the parabola to be parallel to the axis of symmetry.

Ellipse: A ray emanating from one focus will reflect off the ellipse toward the other focus.

Hyperbola: A ray emanating from outside a branch of the hyperbola and directed toward its interior focus will reflect off the hyperbola toward the other focus.

A2 | A Formal Definition of Limit

The Formal Definition

The strange algebra of calculus is constantly invoking the concept of "limit" to make sense of the infinitely large and the infinitely small. When we say that the derivative is

$$\lim_{h \to 0} \frac{f(x + h) - f(x)}{h},$$

what exactly is h? It can't really be 0, because then the fraction would be $0/0$, which is meaningless. It can't be your favorite small number, because *whatever* your favorite small number is, h must be *closer* to 0 than that. Surprisingly, that simple way of looking at what it means to be "arbitrarily close to 0" (closer than any number you can name) led to the formal definition of limit that we use today.

We begin by setting the stage for the definition of limit. Recall that the limit of f of x as x approaches c equals L ($\lim_{x \to c} f(x) = L$) means that the values $f(x)$ of the function f approach or equal L as the values of x approach (but do not equal) c. Suppose we are watching the values of a function $f(x)$ as x approaches c (without taking on the value of c itself). Certainly we want to be able to say that $f(x)$ stays within one-tenth of a unit of L as soon as x stays within some distance δ of c (Figure A2.1). But that in itself is not enough, because as x continues on its course toward c, what is to prevent $f(x)$ from jittering about within the interval from $L - 1/10$ to $L + 1/10$ without tending toward L?

We can insist that $f(x)$ stay within $1/100$ or $1/1000$ or $1/100{,}000$ of L. Each time, we find a new δ-interval about c so that keeping x within that interval keeps $f(x)$ within $\epsilon = 1/100$ or $1/1000$ or $1/100{,}000$ of L. And each time the possibility exists that c jitters away from L at the last minute.

Figure A2.2 illustrates the problem. You can think of this as a quarrel between a skeptic and a scholar. The skeptic presents ϵ-challenges to prove that the limit does not exist or, more precisely, that there is room for doubt, and the scholar answers every challenge with a δ-interval around c.

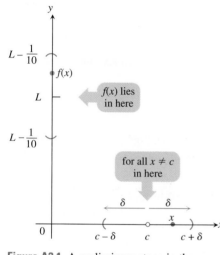

Figure A2.1 A preliminary stage in the development of the definition of limit.

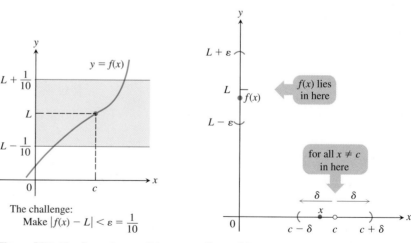

Figure A2.2 The first of a possibly endless sequence of challenges.

Figure A2.3 The relation of the δ and ϵ in the definition of limit.

How do we stop this seemingly endless sequence of challenges and responses? By proving that for every ϵ-distance that the challenger can produce, we can find, calculate, or conjure a matching δ-distance that keeps x "close enough" to c to keep $f(x)$ within that distance of L (Figure A2.3).

The following definition provides a mathematical way to say that the closer x gets to c, the closer $f(x)$ must get to L.

DEFINITION Limit

Let c and L be real numbers. The function f **has limit L as x approaches c** if, given any positive number ϵ, there is a positive number δ such that for all x

$$|f(x) - L| < \epsilon \quad \text{whenever} \quad |x - c| < \delta \text{ and } x \neq c.$$

We write

$$\lim_{x \to c} f(x) = L.$$

Finding Deltas for Given Epsilons

From our work in Chapter 2 we know that $\lim_{x \to 1}(5x - 3) = 2$. In Example 1, we confirm this result using the definition of limit.

EXAMPLE 1 Using the Definition of Limit

Show that $\lim_{x \to 1}(5x - 3) = 2$.

SOLUTION

Set $c = 1$, $f(x) = 5x - 3$, and $L = 2$ in the definition of limit. For any given $\epsilon > 0$ we have to find a suitable $\delta > 0$ so that if $x \neq 1$ and x is within distance δ of $c = 1$, that is, if

$$0 < |x - 1| < \delta,$$

then $f(x)$ is within distance ϵ of $L = 2$, that is,

$$|f(x) - 2| < \epsilon.$$

We find δ by working backward from the ϵ-inequality:

$$|(5x - 3) - 2| = |5x - 5| < \epsilon$$
$$5|x - 1| < \epsilon$$
$$|x - 1| < \epsilon/5$$

Thus we can take $\delta = \epsilon/5$ (Figure A2.4). If $0 < |x - 1| < \delta = \epsilon/5$, then

$$|(5x - 3) - 2| = |5x - 5|$$
$$= 5|x - 1| < 5(\epsilon/5) = \epsilon$$

This proves that $\lim_{x \to 1}(5x - 3) = 2$. *Now Try Exercise 5.*

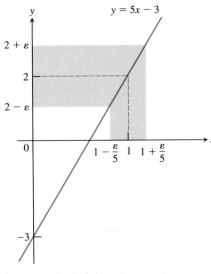

Figure A2.4 If $f(x) = 5x - 3$, then $0 < |x - 1| < \epsilon/5$ guarantees that $|f(x) - 2| < \epsilon$. (Example 1)

The value of $\delta = \epsilon/5$ is not the only value that will make $0 < |x - 1| < \delta$ imply $|f(x) - 2| = |5x - 5| < \epsilon$ in Example 1. Any smaller positive δ will do as well. The definition does not ask for a "best" positive δ, just one that will work.

We can use graphs to find a δ for a specific ϵ as in Example 2.

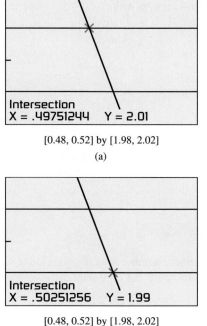

Intersection
X = .49751244   Y = 2.01

[0.48, 0.52] by [1.98, 2.02]
(a)

Intersection
X = .50251256   Y = 1.99

[0.48, 0.52] by [1.98, 2.02]
(b)

Figure A2.5 We can see from the two graphs that if $0.498 < x < 0.502$, then $1.99 < f(x) < 2.01$. (Example 2)

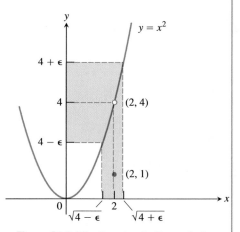

Figure A2.6 The function in Example 3.

EXAMPLE 2   Finding a δ Graphically

For the limit $\lim_{x \to 0.5}(1/x) = 2$, find a δ that works for $\epsilon = 0.01$. That is, find a $\delta > 0$ such that for all x

$$0 < |x - 0.5| < \delta \quad \Rightarrow \quad |f(x) - 2| < 0.01.$$

SOLUTION

Here $f(x) = 1/x$, $c = 0.5$, and $L = 2$. Figure A2.5 shows the graphs of f and the two horizontal lines

$$y = L - \epsilon = 2 - 0.01 = 1.99 \quad \text{and} \quad y = L + \epsilon = 2 + 0.01 = 2.01.$$

Figure A2.5a shows that the graph of f intersects the horizontal line $y = 2.01$ at about $(0.49751244, 2.01)$, and Figure A2.5b shows that the graph of f intersects the horizontal line $y = 1.99$ at about $(0.50251256, 1.99)$. It follows that

$$0 < |x - 0.5| < 0.002 \quad \Rightarrow \quad |f(x) - 2| < 0.01.$$

Thus, $\delta = 0.002$ works. *Now Try Exercise 3.*

EXAMPLE 3   Finding δ Algebraically

Prove that $\lim_{x \to 2} f(x) = 4$ if

$$f(x) = \begin{cases} x^2, & x \neq 2 \\ 1, & x = 2. \end{cases}$$

SOLUTION

Our task is to show that given $\epsilon > 0$ there exists a $\delta > 0$ such that for all $x \neq 2$

$$0 < |x - 2| < \delta \quad \Rightarrow \quad |f(x) - 4| < \epsilon.$$

Step 1: Solve the inequality $|f(x) - 4| < \epsilon$ to find an open interval about $x = 2$ on which the inequality holds for all $x \neq 2$.

For $x \neq 2$, we have $f(x) = x^2$, and the inequality to solve is $|x^2 - 4| < \epsilon$:

$$|x^2 - 4| < \epsilon$$
$$-\epsilon < x^2 - 4 < \epsilon$$
$$4 - \epsilon < x^2 < 4 + \epsilon$$
$$\sqrt{4 - \epsilon} < |x| < \sqrt{4 + \epsilon} \qquad \text{Assume } \epsilon < 4.$$
$$\sqrt{4 - \epsilon} < x < \sqrt{4 + \epsilon} \qquad \begin{array}{l}\text{An open interval about 2} \\ \text{that solves the inequality}\end{array}$$

The inequality $|f(x) - 4| < \epsilon$ holds for all $x \neq 2$ in the open interval $\left(\sqrt{4 - \epsilon}, \sqrt{4 + \epsilon}\right)$ (Figure A2.6).

Step 2: Find a value of $\delta > 0$ that places the *centered* interval $(2 - \delta, 2 + \delta)$ inside the open interval $\left(\sqrt{4 - \epsilon}, \sqrt{4 + \epsilon}\right)$.

Take δ to be the distance from $c = 2$ to the nearer endpoint of $\left(\sqrt{4 - \epsilon}, \sqrt{4 + \epsilon}\right)$. In other words, take

$$\delta = \min\left\{2 - \sqrt{4 - \epsilon}, \sqrt{4 + \epsilon} - 2\right\},$$

the *minimum* (the smaller) of the two numbers $2 - \sqrt{4 - \epsilon}$ and $\sqrt{4 - \epsilon} - 2$. If δ has this or any smaller positive value, the inequality

$$0 < |x - 2| < \delta$$

continued

will automatically place x between $\sqrt{4 - \epsilon}$ and $\sqrt{4 + \epsilon}$ to make

$$|f(x) - 4| < \epsilon.$$

For all x,

$$0 < |x - 2| < \delta \implies |f(x) - 4| < \epsilon.$$

This completes the proof.   *Now Try Exercise 13.*

Why was it all right to assume $\epsilon < 4$ in Example 3? Because, in finding a δ such that, for all x, $0 < |x - 2| < \delta$ implied $|f(x) - 4| < \epsilon < 4$, we found a δ that would work for any larger ϵ as well.

Finally, notice the freedom we gained in letting

$$\delta = \min\left\{2 - \sqrt{4 - \epsilon}, \sqrt{4 + \epsilon} - 2\right\}.$$

We did not have to spend time deciding which, if either, number was the smaller of the two. We just let δ represent the smaller and went on to finish the argument.

Proving Limit Theorems

We use the limit definition to prove parts 1, 3, and 5 of Theorem 1 (Properties of Limits) from Section 2.1.

THEOREM 1   Properties of Limits

If L, M, c, and k are real numbers and

$$\lim_{x \to c} f(x) = L \quad \text{and} \quad \lim_{x \to c} g(x) = M, \quad \text{then}$$

1. *Sum Rule:* $\displaystyle\lim_{x \to c} (f(x) + g(x)) = L + M$

2. *Difference Rule:* $\displaystyle\lim_{x \to c} (f(x) - g(x)) = L - M$

3. *Product Rule:* $\displaystyle\lim_{x \to c} (f(x) \cdot g(x)) = L \cdot M$

4. *Constant Multiple Rule:* $\displaystyle\lim_{x \to c} k \cdot f(x) = k \cdot L$

5. *Quotient Rule:* $\displaystyle\lim_{x \to c} \frac{f(x)}{g(x)} = \frac{L}{M}, \quad M \neq 0$

6. *Power Rule:*   If r and s are integers, $s \neq 0$, then

$$\lim_{x \to c} (f(x))^{r/s} = L^{r/s}$$

provided $L^{r/s}$ is a real number.

Proof of the Limit Sum Rule We need to show that for any $\epsilon > 0$, there is a $\delta > 0$ such that for all x in the common domain D of f and g,

$$0 < |x - c| < \delta \implies |f(x) + g(x) - (L + M)| < \epsilon.$$

Regrouping terms, we get

$$|f(x) + g(x) - (L + M)| = |(f(x) - L) + (g(x) - M)|$$
$$\leq |f(x) - L| + |g(x) - M| \quad \scriptstyle |a + b| \leq |a| + |b|$$

continued

Here we have applied the triangle inequality, which states that for all real numbers a and b, $|a + b| \leq |a| + |b|$. Since $\lim_{x \to c} f(x) = L$, there exists a number $\delta_1 > 0$ such that for all x in D

$$0 < |x - c| < \delta_1 \implies |f(x) - L| < \epsilon/2.$$

Similarly, since $\lim_{x \to c} g(x) = M$, there exists a number $\delta_2 > 0$ such that for all x in D

$$0 < |x - c| < \delta_2 \implies |g(x) - M| < \epsilon/2.$$

Let $\delta = \min\{\delta_1, \delta_2\}$, the smaller of δ_1 and δ_2. If $0 < |x - c| < \delta$ then

$$0 < |x - c| < \delta_1, \quad \text{so} \quad |f(x) - L| < \epsilon/2,$$

and

$$0 < |x - c| < \delta_2, \quad \text{so} \quad |g(x) - M| < \epsilon/2.$$

Therefore, $\left|f(x) + g(x) - (L + M)\right| < \dfrac{\epsilon}{2} + \dfrac{\epsilon}{2} = \epsilon.$

This shows that $\lim_{x \to c} (f(x) + g(x)) = L + M$. ∎

Proof of the Limit Product Rule We show that for any $\epsilon > 0$, there is a $\delta > 0$ such that for all x in the common domain D of f and g,

$$0 < |x - c| < \delta \implies |f(x)g(x) - LM| < \epsilon.$$

Write $f(x)$ and $g(x)$ as $f(x) = L + (f(x) - L), g(x) = M + (g(x) - M)$.

Multiply these expressions together and subtract LM:

$$
\begin{aligned}
f(x) \cdot g(x) - LM &= (L + (f(x) - L))(M + (g(x) - M)) - LM \\
&= LM + L(g(x) - M) + M(f(x) - L) + (f(x) - L)(g(x) - M) - LM \quad (1) \\
&= L(g(x) - M) + M(f(x) - L) + (f(x) - L)(g(x) - M)
\end{aligned}
$$

Since f and g have limits L and M as $x \to c$, there exist positive numbers $\delta_1, \delta_2, \delta_3$, and δ_4 such that for all x in D

$$
\begin{aligned}
0 < |x - c| < \delta_1 &\implies |f(x) - L| < \sqrt{\epsilon/3} \\
0 < |x - c| < \delta_2 &\implies |g(x) - M| < \sqrt{\epsilon/3} \\
0 < |x - c| < \delta_3 &\implies |f(x) - L| < \frac{\epsilon}{3(1 + |M|)} \qquad (2) \\
0 < |x - c| < \delta_4 &\implies |g(x) - M| < \frac{\epsilon}{3(1 + |L|)}
\end{aligned}
$$

If we take δ to be the smallest of the numbers δ_1 through δ_4, the inequalities on the right-hand side of (2) will hold simultaneously for $0 < |x - c| < \delta$. Then, applying the triangle inequality to Equation 1, we have for all x in D, $0 < |x - c| < \delta$ implies

$$
\begin{aligned}
|f(x) \cdot g(x) - LM| \\
\leq |L||g(x) - M| + |M||f(x) - L| + |f(x) - L||g(x) - M| \\
\leq (1 + |L|)|g(x) - M| + (1 + |M|)|f(x) - L| + |f(x) - L||g(x) - M| \\
\leq \frac{\epsilon}{3} + \frac{\epsilon}{3} + \sqrt{\frac{\epsilon}{3}}\sqrt{\frac{\epsilon}{3}} = \epsilon \quad \text{Values from (2)}
\end{aligned}
$$

This completes the proof of the Limit Product Rule. ∎

Proof of the Limit Quotient Rule We show that $\lim_{x \to c} (1/g(x)) = 1/M$. We can then conclude that

$$\lim_{x \to c} \frac{f(x)}{g(x)} = \lim_{x \to c} \left(f(x) \cdot \frac{1}{g(x)} \right) = \lim_{x \to c} f(x) \cdot \lim_{x \to c} \frac{1}{g(x)} = L \cdot \frac{1}{M} = \frac{L}{M}$$

by the Limit Product Rule.

Let $\epsilon > 0$ be given. To show that $\lim_{x \to c} (1/g(x)) = 1/M$, we need to show that there exists a $\delta > 0$ such that for all x

$$0 < |x - c| < \delta \quad \Rightarrow \quad \left| \frac{1}{g(x)} - \frac{1}{M} \right| < \epsilon.$$

Since $|M| > 0$, there exists a positive number δ_1 such that for all x

$$0 < |x - c| < \delta_1 \quad \Rightarrow \quad |g(x) - M| < \frac{|M|}{2}. \tag{3}$$

For any numbers A and B it can be shown that

$$|A| - |B| \le |A - B| \quad \text{and} \quad |B| - |A| \le |A - B|,$$

from which it follows that $||A| - |B|| \le |A - B|$. With $A = g(x)$ and $B = M$, this becomes

$$||g(x)| - |M|| \le |g(x) - M|,$$

which can be combined with the inequality on the right in (3) to get, in turn,

$$||g(x)| - |M|| < \frac{|M|}{2}$$

$$-\frac{|M|}{2} < |g(x)| - |M| < \frac{|M|}{2}$$

$$\frac{|M|}{2} < |g(x)| < \frac{3|M|}{2}$$

$$\frac{1}{|g(x)|} < \frac{2}{|M|} < \frac{3}{|g(x)|} \qquad \text{Multiply by } 2/(|M||g(x)|). \tag{4}$$

Therefore, $0 < |x - c| < \delta$ implies that

$$\left| \frac{1}{g(x)} - \frac{1}{M} \right| = \left| \frac{M - g(x)}{Mg(x)} \right| \le \frac{1}{|M|} \cdot \frac{1}{|g(x)|} \cdot |M - g(x)|$$

$$< \frac{1}{|M|} \cdot \frac{2}{|M|} \cdot |M - g(x)| \qquad \text{Inequality (4)} \tag{5}$$

Since $(1/2)|M|^2 \epsilon > 0$, there exists a number $\delta_2 > 0$ such that for all x in D

$$0 < |x - c| < \delta_2 \quad \Rightarrow \quad |M - g(x)| < \frac{\epsilon}{2} |M|^2. \tag{6}$$

If we take δ to be the smaller of δ_1 and δ_2, the conclusions in (5) and (6) both hold for all x such that $0 < |x - c| < \delta$. Combining these conclusions gives

$$0 < |x - c| < \delta_2 \quad \Rightarrow \quad \left| \frac{1}{g(x)} - \frac{1}{M} \right| < \epsilon.$$

This completes the proof of the Limit Quotient Rule. ■

The last proof we give is of the Squeeze Theorem (Theorem 4) of Section 2.1.

THEOREM 4 The Squeeze Theorem

If $g(x) \le f(x) \le h(x)$ for all $x \ne c$ in some interval about c, and

$$\lim_{x \to c} g(x) = \lim_{x \to c} h(x) = L,$$

then

$$\lim_{x \to c} f(x) = L.$$

Proof for Right-Hand Limits Suppose that $\lim_{x \to c^+} g(x) = \lim_{x \to c^+} h(x) = L$. Then for any $\epsilon > 0$ there exists a $\delta > 0$ such that for all x the inequality $c < x < c + \delta$ implies

$$L - \epsilon < g(x) < L + \epsilon \quad \text{and} \quad L - \epsilon < h(x) < L + \epsilon.$$

These inequalities combine with the inequality $g(x) \le f(x) \le h(x)$ to give

$$L - \epsilon < g(x) \le f(x) \le h(x) < L + \epsilon,$$

$$L - \epsilon < f(x) < L + \epsilon,$$

$$-\epsilon < f(x) - L < \epsilon$$

Thus, for all x, the inequality $c < x < c + \delta$ implies $\left| f(x) - L \right| < \epsilon$. Therefore, $\lim_{x \to c^+} f(x) = L$.

Proof for Left-Hand Limits Suppose that $\lim_{x \to c^-} g(x) = \lim_{x \to c^-} h(x) = L$. Then for any $\epsilon > 0$ there exists a $\delta > 0$ such that for all x the inequality $c - \delta < x < c$ implies

$$L - \epsilon < g(x) < L + \epsilon \quad \text{and} \quad L - \epsilon < h(x) < L + \epsilon.$$

We conclude as before that for all x, $c - \delta < x < c$ implies $\left| f(x) - L \right| < \epsilon$. Therefore, $\lim_{x \to c^-} f(x) = L$.

Proof for Two-Sided Limits If $\lim_{x \to c} g(x) = \lim_{x \to c} h(x) = L$, then $g(x)$ and $h(x)$ both approach L as $x \to c^+$ and $x \to c^-$; so $\lim_{x \to c^+} f(x) = L$ and $\lim_{x \to c^-} f(x) = L$. Hence $\lim_{x \to c} f(x)$ exists and equals L. ∎

Section A2 Exercises

In Exercises 1 and 2, sketch the interval (a, b) on the x-axis with the point c inside. Then find a value of $\delta > 0$ such that for all x,

$$0 < \left| x - c \right| < \delta \quad \Rightarrow \quad a < x < b.$$

1. $a = 4/9, \quad b = 4/7, \quad c = 1/2$

2. $a = 2.7591, \quad b = 3.2391, \quad c = 3$

In Exercises 3 and 4, use the graph to find a $\delta > 0$ such that for all $x, 0 < \left| x - c \right| < \delta \quad \Rightarrow \quad \left| f(x) - L \right| < \epsilon.$

3.

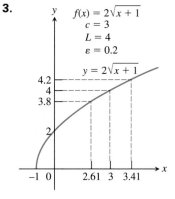

$f(x) = 2\sqrt{x + 1}$
$c = 3$
$L = 4$
$\epsilon = 0.2$

$y = 2\sqrt{x + 1}$

NOT TO SCALE

4.

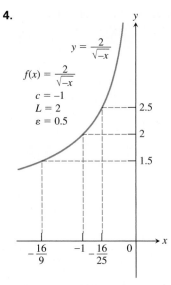

$$y = \frac{2}{\sqrt{-x}}$$

$f(x) = \frac{2}{\sqrt{-x}}$

$c = -1$

$L = 2$

$\varepsilon = 0.5$

Exercises 5–8 give a function $f(x)$ and numbers L, c, and ϵ. Find an open interval about c on which the inequality $|f(x) - L| < \epsilon$ holds. Then give a value for $\delta > 0$ such that for all x satisfying $0 < |x - c| < \delta$ the inequality $|f(x) - L| < \epsilon$ holds. Use algebra to find your answers.

5. $f(x) = 2x - 2$, $L = -6$, $c = -2$, $\epsilon = 0.02$

6. $f(x) = \sqrt{x + 1}$, $L = 1$, $c = 0$, $\epsilon = 0.1$

7. $f(x) = \sqrt{19 - x}$, $L = 3$, $c = 10$, $\epsilon = 1$

8. $f(x) = x^2$, $L = 4$, $c = -2$, $\epsilon = 0.5$

Exercises 9–12 give a function $f(x)$, a point c, and a positive number ϵ. **(a)** Find $L = \lim_{x \to c} f(x)$. Then **(b)** find a number $\delta > 0$ such that for all x

$$0 < |x - c| < \delta \quad \Rightarrow \quad |f(x) - L| < \epsilon.$$

9. $f(x) = \dfrac{x^2 + 6x + 5}{x + 5}$, $c = -5$, $\epsilon = 0.05$

10. $f(x) = \begin{cases} 4 - 2x, & x < 1, \\ 6x - 4, & x \geq 1, \end{cases}$ $c = 1$, $\epsilon = 0.5$

11. $f(x) = \sin x$, $c = 1$, $\epsilon = 0.01$

12. $f(x) = \dfrac{x}{x^2 - 4}$, $c = -1$, $\epsilon = 0.1$

In Exercises 13 and 14, use the definition of limit to prove the limit statement.

13. $\lim_{x \to 1} f(x) = 1$ if $f(x) = \begin{cases} x^2, & x \neq 1 \\ 2, & x = 1 \end{cases}$

14. $\lim_{x \to \sqrt{3}} \dfrac{1}{x^2} = \dfrac{1}{3}$

15. *Relating to Limits* Given $\epsilon > 0$, **(a)** find an interval $I = (5, 5 + \delta)$, $\delta > 0$, such that if x lies in I, then $\sqrt{x - 5} < \epsilon$. **(b)** What limit is being verified?

16. *Relating to Limits* Given $\epsilon > 0$, **(a)** find an interval $I = (4 - \delta, 4)$, $\delta > 0$, such that if x lies in I, then $\sqrt{4 - x} < \epsilon$. **(b)** What limit is being verified?

17. Prove the Constant Multiple Rule for limits.

18. Prove the Difference Rule for limits.

A3 A Proof of the Chain Rule

Error in the Approximation $\Delta f \approx df$

Let $f(x)$ be differentiable at $x = a$ and suppose that Δx is an increment of x. We know that the differential $df = f'(a)\Delta x$ is an approximation for the change $\Delta f = (f(a + \Delta x) - f(a))$ in f as x changes from a to $(a + \Delta x)$. How well does df approximate Δf?

We measure the approximation error by subtracting df from Δf:

$$\text{Approximation error} = \Delta f - df = \Delta f - f'(a)\Delta x$$

$$= \underbrace{f(a + \Delta x) - f(a)}_{\Delta f} - f'(a)\Delta x \qquad \Delta f = f(a + \Delta x) - f(a)$$

$$= \underbrace{\left(\frac{f(a + \Delta x) - f(a)}{\Delta x} - f'(a)\right)}_{\text{Call this part } \epsilon.} \cdot \Delta x = \epsilon \cdot \Delta x$$

As $\Delta x \to 0$, the difference quotient $(f(a + \Delta x) - f(a))/\Delta x$ approaches $f'(a)$ (remember the definition of $f'(a)$), so the quantity in parentheses becomes a very small number (which is why we called it ϵ). In fact, $\epsilon \to 0$ as $\Delta x \to 0$. When Δx is small, the **approximation error** $\epsilon \Delta x$ is smaller still.

$$\underbrace{\Delta f}_{\substack{\text{true} \\ \text{change}}} = \underbrace{f'(a)\Delta x}_{\substack{\text{estimated} \\ \text{change}}} + \underbrace{\epsilon \Delta x}_{\text{error}} \qquad (1)$$

The Proof

We want to show if $f(u)$ is a differentiable function of u and $u = g(x)$ is a differentiable function of x, then $y = f(g(x))$ is a differentiable function of x. More precisely, if g is differentiable at a and f is differentiable at $g(a)$, then the composite is differentiable at a and

$$\left.\frac{dy}{dx}\right|_{x=a} = f'(g(a)) \cdot g'(a).$$

Let Δx be an increment in x and let Δu and Δy be the corresponding increments in u and y. As you can see in Figure A3.1,

$$\left.\frac{dy}{dx}\right|_{x=a} = \lim_{\Delta x \to 0} \frac{\Delta y}{\Delta x},$$

so our goal is to show that the limit is $f'(g(a)) \cdot g'(a)$.

By Equation 1,

$$\Delta u = g'(a)\Delta x + \epsilon_1 \Delta x = (g'(a) + \epsilon_1)\Delta x,$$

where $\epsilon_1 \to 0$ as $\Delta x \to 0$. Similarly, since f is differentiable at $g(a)$,

$$\Delta y = f'(g(a))\Delta u + \epsilon_2 \Delta u = (f'(g(a)) + \epsilon_2)\Delta u,$$

where $\epsilon_2 \to 0$ as $\Delta u \to 0$. Notice also that $\Delta u \to 0$ as $\Delta x \to 0$. Combining the equations for Δu and Δy gives $\Delta y = (f'(g(a)) + \epsilon_2)(g'(a) + \epsilon_1)\Delta x$, so

$$\frac{\Delta y}{\Delta x} = f'(g(a))g'(a) + \epsilon_2 g'(a) + f'(g(a))\epsilon_1 + \epsilon_2 \epsilon_1.$$

Since ϵ_1 and ϵ_2 go to zero as Δx goes to zero, three of the four terms on the right vanish in the limit, leaving

$$\lim_{\Delta x \to 0} \frac{\Delta y}{\Delta x} = f'(g(a))g'(a).$$

This concludes the proof. ∎

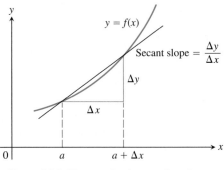

Figure A3.1 The graph of y as a function of x. The derivative of y with respect to x at $x = a$ is $\lim_{\Delta x \to 0}(\Delta y/\Delta x)$.

A4 | Hyperbolic Functions

Background

Suspension cables like those of the Golden Gate Bridge, which support a constant load per horizontal foot, hang in parabolas. Cables like power line cables, which hang freely, hang in curves called hyperbolic cosine curves.

Besides describing the shapes of hanging cables, hyperbolic functions describe the motions of waves in elastic solids, the temperature distributions in metal cooling fins, and the motions of falling bodies that encounter air resistance proportional to the square of the velocity. If a hanging cable were turned upside down (without changing shape) to form an arch, the internal forces, then reversed, would once again be in equilibrium, making the inverted hyperbolic cosine curve the ideal shape for a self-standing arch. The center line of the Gateway Arch to the West in St. Louis follows a hyperbolic cosine curve.

Definitions

The hyperbolic cosine and sine functions are defined by the first two equations in Table A4.1. The table also defines the hyperbolic tangent, cotangent, secant, and cosecant. As we will see, the hyperbolic functions bear a number of similarities to the trigonometric functions after which they are named.

Pronouncing "cosh" and "sinh"

"Cosh" is often pronounced "kosh," rhyming with "gosh" or "gauche." "Sinh" is pronounced as if spelled "cinch" or "shine."

TABLE A4.1 The six basic hyperbolic functions

Hyperbolic cosine of x:	$\cosh x = \dfrac{e^x + e^{-x}}{2}$
Hyperbolic sine of x:	$\sinh x = \dfrac{e^x - e^{-x}}{2}$
Hyperbolic tangent:	$\tanh x = \dfrac{\sinh x}{\cosh x} = \dfrac{e^x - e^{-x}}{e^x + e^{-x}}$
Hyperbolic cotangent:	$\coth x = \dfrac{\cosh x}{\sinh x} = \dfrac{e^x + e^{-x}}{e^x - e^{-x}}$
Hyperbolic secant:	$\operatorname{sech} x = \dfrac{1}{\cosh x} = \dfrac{2}{e^x + e^{-x}}$
Hyperbolic cosecant:	$\operatorname{csch} x = \dfrac{1}{\sinh x} = \dfrac{2}{e^x - e^{-x}}$

See Figure A4.1 for graphs.

**TABLE A4.2
Identities for hyperbolic functions**

$$\sinh 2x = 2 \sinh x \cosh x$$

$$\cosh 2x = \cosh^2 x + \sinh^2 x$$

$$\cosh^2 x = \frac{\cosh 2x + 1}{2}$$

$$\sinh^2 x = \frac{\cosh 2x - 1}{2}$$

$$\cosh^2 x - \sinh^2 x = 1$$

$$\tanh^2 x = 1 - \operatorname{sech}^2 x$$

$$\coth^2 x = 1 + \operatorname{csch}^2 x$$

Identities

Hyperbolic functions satisfy the identities in Table A4.2. Except for differences in sign, these are identities we already know for trigonometric functions.

Derivatives and Integrals

The six hyperbolic functions, being rational combinations of the differentiable functions e^x and e^{-x}, have derivatives at every point at which they are defined (Table A4.3 on the following page). Again, there are similarities with trigonometric functions. The derivative formulas in Table A4.3 lead to the integral formulas seen there.

TABLE A4.3 Derivatives and companion integrals

$\dfrac{d}{dx}(\sinh u) = \cosh u \dfrac{du}{dx}$ $\qquad\qquad \displaystyle\int \sinh u \, du = \cosh u + C$

$\dfrac{d}{dx}(\cosh u) = \sinh u \dfrac{du}{dx}$ $\qquad\qquad \displaystyle\int \cosh u \, du = \sinh u + C$

$\dfrac{d}{dx}(\tanh u) = \operatorname{sech}^2 u \dfrac{du}{dx}$ $\qquad\qquad \displaystyle\int \operatorname{sech}^2 u \, du = \tanh u + C$

$\dfrac{d}{dx}(\coth u) = -\operatorname{csch}^2 u \dfrac{du}{dx}$ $\qquad\qquad \displaystyle\int \operatorname{csch}^2 u \, du = -\coth u + C$

$\dfrac{d}{dx}(\operatorname{sech} u) = -\operatorname{sech} u \tanh u \dfrac{du}{dx}$ $\qquad\qquad \displaystyle\int \operatorname{sech} u \tanh u \, du = -\operatorname{sech} u + C$

$\dfrac{d}{dx}(\operatorname{csch} u) = -\operatorname{csch} u \coth u \dfrac{du}{dx}$ $\qquad\qquad \displaystyle\int \operatorname{csch} u \coth u \, du = -\operatorname{csch} u + C$

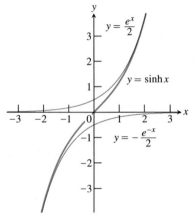

(a) The hyperbolic sine and its component exponentials.

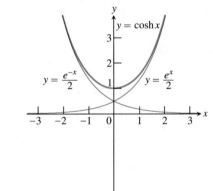

(b) The hyperbolic cosine and its component exponentials.

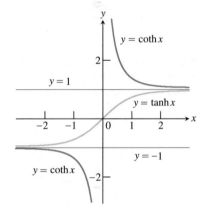

(c) The graphs of $y = \tanh x$ and $y = \coth x = 1/\tanh x$.

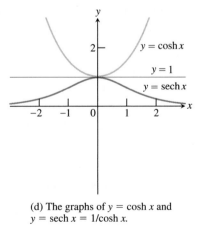

(d) The graphs of $y = \cosh x$ and $y = \operatorname{sech} x = 1/\cosh x$.

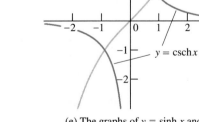

(e) The graphs of $y = \sinh x$ and $y = \operatorname{csch} x = 1/\sinh x$.

Figure A4.1 The graphs of the six hyperbolic functions.

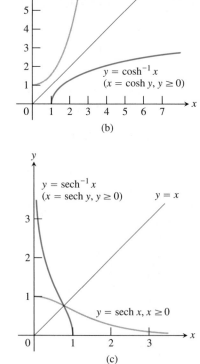

(a)

(b)

(c)

Figure A4.2 The graphs of the inverse hyperbolic sine, cosine, and secant of x. Notice the symmetries about the line $y = x$.

EXAMPLE 1 Finding a Derivative

$$\frac{d}{dt}\left(\tanh\sqrt{1+t^2}\right) = \text{sech}^2\sqrt{1+t^2} \cdot \frac{d}{dt}\left(\sqrt{1+t^2}\right)$$

$$= \frac{t}{\sqrt{1+t^2}}\,\text{sech}^2\sqrt{1+t^2}$$

Now Try Exercise 13.

EXAMPLE 2 Integrating a Hyperbolic Cotangent

$$\int \coth 5x\,dx = \int \frac{\cosh 5x}{\sinh 5x}\,dx = \frac{1}{5}\int \frac{du}{u} \qquad \begin{array}{l} u = \sinh 5x, \\ du = 5\cosh 5x\,dx \end{array}$$

$$= \frac{1}{5}\ln|u| + C = \frac{1}{5}\ln|\sinh 5x| + C$$

Now Try Exercise 41.

EXAMPLE 3 Using an Identity to Integrate

Evaluate $\displaystyle\int_0^1 \sinh^2 x\,dx$.

SOLUTION

$$\int_0^1 \sinh^2 x\,dx = \int_0^1 \frac{\cosh 2x - 1}{2}\,dx \qquad \text{Table A4.2}$$

$$= \frac{1}{2}\int_0^1 (\cosh 2x - 1)\,dx = \frac{1}{2}\left[\frac{\sinh 2x}{2} - x\right]_0^1 = \frac{\sinh 2}{4} - \frac{1}{2} \approx 0.40672$$

Now Try Exercise 47.

Inverse Hyperbolic Functions

We use the inverses of the six basic hyperbolic functions in integration. Since $d(\sinh x)/dx = \cosh x > 0$, the hyperbolic sine is an increasing function of x. We denote its inverse by

$$y = \sinh^{-1} x.$$

For every value of x in the interval $-\infty < x < \infty$, the value of $y = \sinh^{-1} x$ is the number whose hyperbolic sine is x (Figure A4.2a).

The function $y = \cosh x$ is not one-to-one, as we can see from the graph in Figure A4.1. But the restricted function $y = \cosh x$, $x \geq 0$, is one-to-one and therefore has an inverse, denoted by

$$y = \cosh^{-1} x.$$

For every value of $x \geq 1$, $y = \cosh^{-1} x$ is the number in the interval $0 \leq y < \infty$ whose hyperbolic cosine is x (Figure A4.2b).

Like $y = \cosh x$, the function $y = \text{sech } x = 1/\cosh x$ fails to be one-to-one, but its restriction to nonnegative values of x does have an inverse, denoted by

$$y = \text{sech}^{-1} x.$$

For every value of x in the interval $(0, 1]$, $y = \text{sech}^{-1} x$ is the nonnegative number whose hyperbolic secant is x (Figure A4.2c).

The hyperbolic tangent, cotangent, and cosecant are one-to-one on their domains and therefore have inverses, denoted (respectively) by

$$y = \tanh^{-1} x, \quad y = \coth^{-1} x, \quad y = \operatorname{csch}^{-1} x$$

(Figure A4.3).

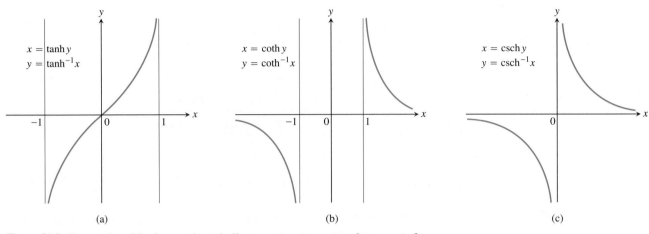

Figure A4.3 The graphs of the inverse hyperbolic tangent, cotangent, and cosecant of x.

EXPLORATION 1 Viewing Inverses

Let $x_1(t) = t, \qquad y_1(t) = t,$
$\quad x_2(t) = t, \qquad y_2(t) = 1/\cosh t,$
$\quad x_3(t) = y_2(t), \quad y_3(t) = x_2(t).$

1. Graph the parametric equations simultaneously in a square viewing window that contains $0 \le x \le 6, 0 \le y \le 4$. Set $t\text{Min} = 0, t\text{Max} = 6$, and t-step $= 0.05$. Explain what you see. Explain the domain of each function.
2. Let $x_4(t) = t, y_4(t) = \cosh^{-1}(1/t)$. Graph and compare (x_3, y_3) and (y_4, x_4). Predict what you should see, and explain what you do see.

Identities for $\operatorname{sech}^{-1} x$, $\operatorname{csch}^{-1} x$, $\coth^{-1} x$

We use the identities in Table A4.4 to calculate the values of $\operatorname{sech}^{-1} x$, $\operatorname{csch}^{-1} x$, and $\coth^{-1} x$ on calculators that give only $\cosh^{-1} x$, $\sinh^{-1} x$, and $\tanh^{-1} x$.

Derivatives of Inverse Hyperbolic Functions; Associated Integrals

The chief use of inverse hyperbolic functions lies in integrations that reverse the derivative formulas in Table A4.5.

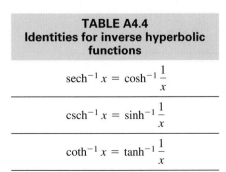

TABLE A4.4
Identities for inverse hyperbolic functions

$$\operatorname{sech}^{-1} x = \cosh^{-1} \frac{1}{x}$$

$$\operatorname{csch}^{-1} x = \sinh^{-1} \frac{1}{x}$$

$$\coth^{-1} x = \tanh^{-1} \frac{1}{x}$$

TABLE A4.5 Derivatives of inverse hyperbolic functions

$$\frac{d(\sinh^{-1} u)}{dx} = \frac{1}{\sqrt{1 + u^2}} \frac{du}{dx}$$

$$\frac{d(\cosh^{-1} u)}{dx} = \frac{1}{\sqrt{u^2 - 1}} \frac{du}{dx}, \quad u > 1$$

$$\frac{d(\tanh^{-1} u)}{dx} = \frac{1}{1 - u^2} \frac{du}{dx}, \quad |u| < 1$$

$$\frac{d(\coth^{-1} u)}{dx} = \frac{1}{1 - u^2} \frac{du}{dx}, \quad |u| > 1$$

$$\frac{d(\operatorname{sech}^{-1} u)}{dx} = \frac{-du/dx}{u\sqrt{1 - u^2}}, \quad 0 < u < 1$$

$$\frac{d(\operatorname{csch}^{-1} u)}{dx} = \frac{-du/dx}{|u|\sqrt{1 - u^2}}, \quad u \neq 0$$

The restrictions $|u| < 1$ and $|u| > 1$ on the derivative formulas for $\tanh^{-1} u$ and $\coth^{-1} u$ come from the natural restrictions on the values of these functions. (See Figures A4.3a and b.) The distinction between $|u| < 1$ and $|u| > 1$ becomes important when we convert the derivative formulas into integral formulas. If $|u| < 1$, the integral of $1/(1 - u^2)$ is $\tanh^{-1} u + C$. If $|u| > 1$, the integral is $\coth^{-1} u + C$.

With appropriate substitutions, the derivative formulas in Table A4.5 lead to the integral formulas in Table A4.6.

TABLE A4.6 Integrals leading to inverse hyperbolic functions

1. $\displaystyle\int \frac{du}{\sqrt{a^2 + u^2}} = \sinh^{-1}\left(\frac{u}{a}\right) + C, \quad a > 0$

2. $\displaystyle\int \frac{du}{\sqrt{u^2 - a^2}} = \cosh^{-1}\left(\frac{u}{a}\right) + C, \quad u > a > 0$

3. $\displaystyle\int \frac{du}{\sqrt{a^2 - u^2}} = \begin{cases} \dfrac{1}{a}\tanh^{-1}\left(\dfrac{u}{a}\right) + C & \text{if } u^2 < a^2 \\[2mm] \dfrac{1}{a}\coth^{-1}\left(\dfrac{u}{a}\right) + C & \text{if } u^2 > a^2 \end{cases}$

4. $\displaystyle\int \frac{du}{u\sqrt{a^2 - u^2}} = -\frac{1}{a}\operatorname{sech}^{-1}\left(\frac{u}{a}\right) + C, \quad 0 < u < a$

5. $\displaystyle\int \frac{du}{u\sqrt{a^2 + u^2}} = -\frac{1}{a}\operatorname{csch}^{-1}\left|\frac{u}{a}\right| + C, \quad u \neq 0$

EXAMPLE 4 Using Table A4.6

Evaluate $\displaystyle\int_0^1 \frac{2\,dx}{\sqrt{3+4x^2}}$.

SOLUTION

The indefinite integral is

$$\int \frac{2\,dx}{\sqrt{3+4x^2}} = \int \frac{du}{\sqrt{a^2+u^2}} \qquad u = 2x,\ du = 2\,dx,\ a = \sqrt{3}$$

$$= \sinh^{-1}\left(\frac{u}{a}\right) + C \qquad \text{Formula from Table A4.6}$$

$$= \sinh^{-1}\left(\frac{2x}{\sqrt{3}}\right) + C.$$

Therefore,

$$\int_0^1 \frac{2\,dx}{\sqrt{3+4x^2}} = \sinh^{-1}\left(\frac{2x}{\sqrt{3}}\right)\Big]_0^1 = \sinh^{-1}\left(\frac{2}{\sqrt{3}}\right) - \sinh^{-1}(0)$$

$$= \sinh^{-1}\left(\frac{2}{\sqrt{3}}\right) - 0 \approx 0.98665.$$

Now Try Exercise 37.

Section A4 Exercises

In Exercises 1–4, find the values of the remaining five hyperbolic functions.

1. $\sinh x = -\dfrac{3}{4}$

2. $\sinh x = \dfrac{4}{3}$

3. $\cosh x = \dfrac{17}{15}, \quad x > 0$

4. $\cosh x = \dfrac{13}{5}, \quad x > 0$

In Exercises 5–10, rewrite the expression in terms of exponentials and simplify the results as much as you can. Support your answers graphically.

5. $2\cosh(\ln x)$

6. $\sinh(2\ln x)$

7. $\cosh 5x + \sinh 5x$

8. $\cosh 3x - \sinh 3x$

9. $(\sinh x + \cosh x)^4$

10. $\ln(\cosh x + \sinh x) + \ln(\cosh x - \sinh x)$

11. Use the identities

$$\sinh(x + y) = \sinh x \cosh y + \cosh x \sinh y$$
$$\cosh(x + y) = \cosh x \cosh y + \sinh x \sinh y$$

to show that

(a) $\sinh 2x = 2\sinh x \cosh x$;

(b) $\cosh 2x = \cosh^2 x + \sinh^2 x$.

12. Use the definitions of $\cosh x$ and $\sinh x$ to show that
$$\cosh^2 x - \sinh^2 x = 1.$$

In Exercises 13–24, find the derivative of y with respect to the appropriate variable.

13. $y = 6\sinh\dfrac{x}{3}$

14. $y = \dfrac{1}{2}\sinh(2x + 1)$

15. $y = 2\sqrt{t}\tanh\sqrt{t}$

16. $y = t^2\tanh\dfrac{1}{t}$

17. $y = \ln(\sinh z)$

18. $y = \ln(\cosh z)$

19. $y = \operatorname{sech}\theta(1 - \ln\operatorname{sech}\theta)$

20. $y = \operatorname{csch}\theta(1 - \ln\operatorname{csch}\theta)$

21. $y = \ln\cosh x - \dfrac{1}{2}\tanh^2 x$

22. $y = \ln\sinh x - \dfrac{1}{2}\coth^2 x$

23. $y = (x^2 + 1)\operatorname{sech}(\ln x)$ [*Hint:* Before differentiating, express in terms of exponentials and simplify.]

24. $y = (4x^2 - 1)\operatorname{csch}(\ln 2x)$

In Exercises 25–36, find the derivative of y with respect to the appropriate variable.

25. $y = \sinh^{-1}\sqrt{x}$

26. $y = \cosh^{-1}(2\sqrt{x + 1})$

27. $y = (1 - \theta)\tanh^{-1}\theta$

28. $y = (\theta^2 + 2\theta) \tanh^{-1}(\theta + 1)$

29. $y = (1 - t) \coth^{-1} \sqrt{t}$

30. $y = (1 - t^2) \coth^{-1} t$

31. $y = \cos^{-1} x - x \sec h^{-1} x$

32. $y = \ln x + \sqrt{1 - x^2} \sec h^{-1} x$

33. $y = \csc h^{-1} \left(\dfrac{1}{2}\right)^{\theta}$

34. $y = \csc h^{-1} 2^{\theta}$

35. $y = \sinh^{-1}(\tan x)$

36. $y = \cosh^{-1}(\sec x), \quad 0 < x < \pi/2$

Verify the integration formulas in Exercises 37–40.

37. (a) $\displaystyle\int \sec h\, x\, dx = \tan^{-1}(\sinh x) + C$

(b) $\displaystyle\int \sec h\, x\, dx = \sin^{-1}(\tanh x) + C$

38. $\displaystyle\int x \sec h^{-1} x\, dx = \dfrac{x^2}{2} \sec h^{-1} x - \dfrac{1}{2}\sqrt{1 - x^2} + C$

39. $\displaystyle\int x \coth^{-1} x\, dx = \dfrac{x^2 - 1}{2} \coth^{-1} x + \dfrac{x}{2} + C$

40. $\displaystyle\int \tanh^{-1} x\, dx = x \tanh^{-1} x + \dfrac{1}{2}\ln(1 - x^2) + C$

Evaluate the integrals in Exercises 41–50.

41. $\displaystyle\int \sinh 2x\, dx$

42. $\displaystyle\int \sinh \dfrac{x}{5}\, dx$

43. $\displaystyle\int 6 \cosh \left(\dfrac{x}{2} - \ln 3\right) dx$

44. $\displaystyle\int 4 \cosh (3x - \ln 2)\, dx$

45. $\displaystyle\int \tanh \dfrac{x}{7}\, dx$

46. $\displaystyle\int \coth \dfrac{\theta}{\sqrt{3}}\, d\theta$

47. $\displaystyle\int \sec h^2 \left(x - \dfrac{1}{2}\right) dx$

48. $\displaystyle\int \csc h^2 (5 - x)\, dx$

49. $\displaystyle\int \dfrac{\sec h\, \sqrt{t} \tanh \sqrt{t}\, dt}{\sqrt{t}}$

50. $\displaystyle\int \dfrac{\csc h\, (\ln t) \coth (\ln t)\, dt}{t}$

Evaluate the integrals in Exercises 51–60 analytically and support with NINT.

51. $\displaystyle\int_{\ln 2}^{\ln 4} \coth x\, dx$

52. $\displaystyle\int_{0}^{\ln 2} \tanh 2x\, dx$

53. $\displaystyle\int_{-\ln 4}^{-\ln 2} 2e^{\theta} \cosh \theta\, d\theta$

54. $\displaystyle\int_{0}^{\ln 2} 4e^{-\theta} \sinh \theta\, d\theta$

55. $\displaystyle\int_{-\pi/4}^{\pi/4} \cosh (\tan \theta) \sec^2 \theta\, d\theta$

56. $\displaystyle\int_{0}^{\pi/2} 2 \sinh (\sin \theta) \cos \theta\, d\theta$

57. $\displaystyle\int_{1}^{2} \dfrac{\cosh (\ln t)}{t}\, dt$ **58.** $\displaystyle\int_{1}^{4} \dfrac{8 \cosh \sqrt{x}}{\sqrt{x}}\, dx$

59. $\displaystyle\int_{-\ln 2}^{0} \cosh^2 \left(\dfrac{x}{2}\right) dx$ **60.** $\displaystyle\int_{0}^{\ln 10} 4 \sinh^2 \left(\dfrac{x}{2}\right) dx$

In Exercises 61 and 62, find the volume of the solid generated by revolving the shaded region about the *x*-axis.

61.

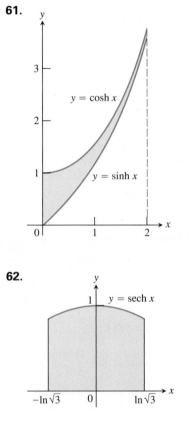

$y = \cosh x$

$y = \sinh x$

62.

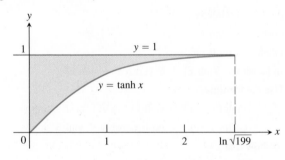

$y = \sec h\, x$

63. Find the volume of the solid generated by revolving the shaded region about the line $y = 1$.

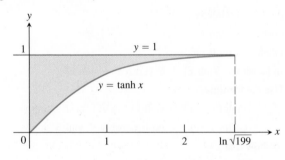

$y = 1$

$y = \tanh x$

64. (a) Find the length of the curve $y = (1/2) \cosh 2x$,
$0 \le x \le \ln \sqrt{5}$.

(b) Find the length of the curve $y = (1/a) \cosh ax, 0 \le x \le b$.

Extending the Ideas

65. *Even-Odd Decompositions*

(a) Show that if a function f is defined on an interval symmetric about the origin (so that f is defined at $-x$ whenever it is defined at x), then

$$f(x) = \frac{f(x) + f(-x)}{2} + \frac{f(x) - f(-x)}{2}. \qquad (1)$$

Then show that

$$\frac{f(x) + f(-x)}{2} \quad \text{is even}$$

and

$$\frac{f(x) - f(-x)}{2} \quad \text{is odd}.$$

(b) In Equation 1, set $f(x) = e^x$. Identify the even and odd parts of f.

66. Writing to Learn *(Continuation of Exercise 65)* Equation 1 in Exercise 65 simplifies considerably if f itself is **(a)** even or **(b)** odd. What are the new equations? Explain.

67. *Skydiving* If a body of mass m falling from rest under the action of gravity encounters an air resistance proportional to the square of the velocity, then the body's velocity t seconds into the fall satisfies the differential equation

$$m\frac{dv}{dt} = mg - kv^2,$$

where k is a constant that depends on the body's aerodynamic properties and the density of the air. (We assume that the fall is short enough so that variation in the air's density will not affect the outcome.)

Show that

$$v = \sqrt{\frac{mg}{k}} \tanh\left(\sqrt{\frac{gk}{m}}\, t\right)$$

satisfies the differential equation and the initial condition that $v = 0$ when $t = 0$.

68. *Accelerations Whose Magnitudes Are Proportional to Displacement* Suppose that the position of a body moving along a coordinate line at time t is

(a) $s = a \cos kt + b \sin kt$,

(b) $s = a \cosh kt + b \sinh kt$.

Show in both cases that the acceleration d^2s/dt^2 is proportional to s but that in the first case it is directed toward the origin while in the second case it is directed away from the origin.

69. *Tractor Trailers and the Tractrix* When a tractor trailer turns into a cross street or driveway, its rear wheels follow a curve like the one shown here. (This is why the rear wheels sometimes ride up over the curb.)

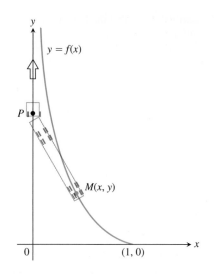

We can find an equation for the curve if we picture the rear wheels as a mass M at the point $(1, 0)$ on the x-axis attached by a rod of unit length to a point P representing the cab at the origin. As P moves up the y-axis, it drags M along behind it. The curve traced by M, called a *tractrix* from the Latin word *tractum* for "drag," can be shown to be the graph of the function $y = f(x)$ that solves the initial value problem

Differential equation: $\quad \dfrac{dy}{dx} = -\dfrac{1}{x\sqrt{1 - x^2}} + \dfrac{x}{\sqrt{1 - x^2}},$

Initial condition: $\qquad y = 0 \quad \text{when} \quad x = 1$

Solve the initial value problem to find an equation for the curve. (You need an inverse hyperbolic function.)

70. *A Minimal Surface* Find the area of the surface swept out by revolving the curve $y = 4 \cosh(x/4), -\ln 16 \le x \le \ln 81$, about the x-axis. See the figure below.

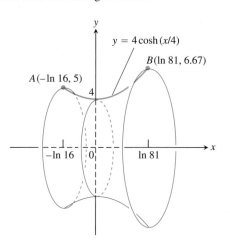

It can be shown that, of all continuously differentiable curves joining points A and B in the figure, the curve $y = 4 \cosh(x/4)$ generates the surface of least area. If you made a rigid wire frame of the end-circles through A and B and dipped them in a soap-film solution, the surface spanning the circles would be the one generated by the curve.

71. *Hanging Cables* Show that the function $y = a \cosh (x/a)$ solves the initial value problem

$$y'' = (1/a)\sqrt{1 + (y')^2}, \quad y'(0) = 0, \quad y(0) = a.$$

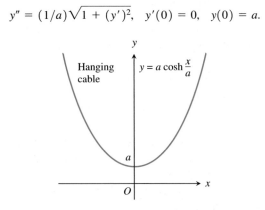

By analyzing the forces on hanging cables, we can show that the curves they hang in always satisfy the differential equation and initial conditions given here. That is how we know that hanging cables hang in hyperbolic cosines.

72. *The Hyperbolic in Hyperbolic Functions* In case you are wondering where the name *hyperbolic* comes from, here is the answer: Just as $x = \cos u$ and $y = \sin u$ are identified with points (x, y) on the unit circle, the functions $x = \cosh u$ and $y = \sinh u$ are identified with points (x, y) on the right-hand branch of the unit hyperbola $x^2 - y^2 = 1$ (Figure A4.4).

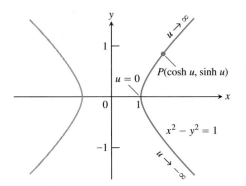

Figure A4.4 Since $\cosh^2 u - \sinh^2 u = 1$, the point $(\cosh u, \sinh u)$ lies on the right-hand branch of the hyperbola $x^2 - y^2 = 1$ for every value of u (Exercise 72).

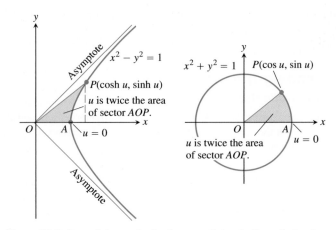

Figure A4.5 One of the analogies between hyperbolic and circular functions is revealed by these two diagrams (Exercise 72).

Another analogy between hyperbolic and circular functions is that the variable u in the coordinates $(\cosh u, \sinh u)$ for the points of the right-hand branch of the hyperbola $x^2 - y^2 = 1$ is twice the area of the sector AOP pictured in Figure A4.5. To see why, carry out the following steps.

(a) Let $A(u)$ be the area of sector AOP. Show that

$$A(u) = \frac{1}{2} \cosh u \sinh u - \int_1^{\cosh u} \sqrt{x^2 - 1} \, dx.$$

(b) Differentiate both sides of the equation in (a) with respect to u to show that

$$A'(u) = \frac{1}{2}.$$

(c) Solve the equation in (b) for $A(u)$. What is the value of $A(0)$? What is the value of the constant of integration C in your solution? With C determined, what does your solution say about the relationship of u to $A(u)$?

A5 A Very Brief Table of Integrals

Back in the old days, when everyone's primary reference sources were books, most calculus textbooks would include a table of integrals as a service to students. Many of the integrals in the table were well beyond the scope of the course, but that was exactly why the students would have needed the table. Now that modern technology has given us calculators to find definite integrals and computer algebra software to find antiderivatives (not to mention the Internet as a more efficient reference source), integral tables are inexorably going the way of trig table and log tables. Rather than completely eliminate our table, we decided to trim it from 141 formulas to a more manageable number of formulas that *students could be expected to prove using the techniques studied in this course.* We also kept a few others that we thought students might find interesting, like the *n*th powers of the basic trig functions. Note that all variables are assumed to take on only those values for which the expressions in the formula are real numbers.

1. $\int u \, dv = uv - \int v \, du$

2. $\int a^u \, du = \frac{a^u}{\ln a} + C, \quad a \neq 1, \quad a > 0$

3. $\int \cos u \, du = \sin u + C$

4. $\int \sin u \, du = -\cos u + C$

5. $\int (ax + b)^n \, dx = \frac{(ax + b)^{n+1}}{a(n + 1)} + C, \quad n \neq -1$

6. $\int (ax + b)^{-1} \, dx = \frac{1}{a} \ln |ax + b| + C$

7. $\int \frac{dx}{x(ax + b)} = \frac{1}{b} \ln \left| \frac{x}{ax + b} \right| + C$

8. $\int (\sqrt{ax + b})^n \, dx = \frac{2}{a} \frac{(\sqrt{ax + b})^{n+2}}{n + 2} + C, \quad n \neq -2$

9. $\int \frac{dx}{a^2 - x^2} = \frac{1}{a} \tan^{-1} \frac{x}{a} + C$

10. $\int \frac{dx}{a^2 - x^2} = \frac{1}{2a} \ln \left| \frac{x + a}{x - a} \right| + C$

11. $\int \frac{dx}{\sqrt{a^2 + x^2}} = \sinh^{-1} \frac{x}{a} + C = \ln \left(x + \sqrt{a^2 + x^2} \right) + C$

12. $\int \frac{dx}{\sqrt{a^2 - x^2}} = \sin^{-1} \frac{x}{a} + C$

13. $\int \frac{dx}{\sqrt{x^2 - a^2}} = \cosh^{-1} \frac{x}{a} + C = \ln \left| x + \sqrt{x^2 - a^2} \right| + C$

14. $\int x \left(\sqrt{x^2 - a^2} \right)^n \, dx = \frac{\left(\sqrt{x^2 - a^2} \right)^{n+2}}{n + 2} + C, \quad n \neq -2$

15. $\int \frac{dx}{x\sqrt{x^2 - a^2}} = \frac{1}{a} \sec^{-1} \left| \frac{x}{a} \right| + C = \frac{1}{a} \cos^{-1} \left| \frac{a}{x} \right| + C$

16. $\int \frac{dx}{\sqrt{2ax - x^2}} = \sin^{-1} \left(\frac{x - a}{a} \right) + C$

17. $\int \sin ax \, dx = -\frac{1}{a} \cos ax + C$

18. $\int \cos ax \, dx = \frac{1}{a} \sin ax + C$

19. $\int \sin^2 ax \, dx = \frac{x}{2} - \frac{\sin 2ax}{4a} + C$

20. $\int \cos^2 ax \, dx = \frac{x}{2} + \frac{\sin 2ax}{4a} + C$

21. $\int \sin^n ax \, dx = -\frac{\sin^{n-1} ax \cos ax}{na} + \frac{n - 1}{n} \int \sin^{n-2} ax \, dx$

22. $\int \cos^n ax \, dx = \frac{\cos^{n-1} ax \sin ax}{na} + \frac{n - 1}{n} \int \cos^{n-2} ax \, dx$

23. $\int \sin ax \cos ax \, dx = -\frac{\cos 2ax}{4a} + C$

24. $\int \sin^n ax \cos ax \, dx = \frac{\sin^{n+1} ax}{(n + 1)a} + C, \quad n \neq -1$

25. $\int \frac{\cos ax}{\sin ax} \, dx = \frac{1}{a} \ln |\sin ax| + C$

26. $\displaystyle\int \cos^n ax \sin ax \, dx = -\frac{\cos^{n+1} ax}{(n+1)a} + C, \quad n \neq -1$

27. $\displaystyle\int \frac{\sin ax}{\cos ax} \, dx = -\frac{1}{a} \ln |\cos ax| + C$

28. $\displaystyle\int x \sin ax \, dx = \frac{1}{a^2} \sin ax - \frac{x}{a} \cos ax + C$

29. $\displaystyle\int x \cos ax \, dx = \frac{1}{a^2} \cos ax + \frac{x}{a} \sin ax + C$

30. $\displaystyle\int x^n \sin ax \, dx = -\frac{x^n}{a} \cos ax + \frac{n}{a} \int x^{n-1} \cos ax \, dx$

31. $\displaystyle\int x^n \cos ax \, dx = \frac{x^n}{a} \sin ax - \frac{n}{a} \int x^{n-1} \sin ax \, dx$

32. $\displaystyle\int \tan ax \, dx = \frac{1}{a} \ln |\sec ax| + C$

33. $\displaystyle\int \cot ax \, dx = \frac{1}{a} \ln |\sin ax| + C$

34. $\displaystyle\int \tan^2 ax \, dx = \frac{1}{a} \tan ax - x + C$

35. $\displaystyle\int \cot^2 ax \, dx = -\frac{1}{a} \cot ax - x + C$

36. $\displaystyle\int \tan^n ax \, dx = \frac{\tan^{n-1} ax}{a(n-1)} - \int \tan^{n-2} ax \, dx, \quad n \neq 1$

37. $\displaystyle\int \cot^n ax \, dx = -\frac{\cot^{n-1} ax}{a(n-1)} - \int \cot^{n-2} ax \, dx, \quad n \neq 1$

38. $\displaystyle\int \sec ax \, dx = \frac{1}{a} \ln |\sec ax + \tan ax| + C$

39. $\displaystyle\int \csc ax \, dx = -\frac{1}{a} \ln |\csc ax - \cot ax| + C$

40. $\displaystyle\int \sec^2 ax \, dx = \frac{1}{a} \tan ax + C$

41. $\displaystyle\int \csc^2 ax \, dx = -\frac{1}{a} \cot ax + C$

42. $\displaystyle\int \sec^n ax \, dx = \frac{\sec^{n-2} ax \tan ax}{a(n-1)} + \frac{n-2}{n-1} \int \sec^{n-2} ax \, dx, \quad n \neq 1$

43. $\displaystyle\int \csc^n ax \, dx = -\frac{\csc^{n-2} ax \cot ax}{a(n-1)} + \frac{n-2}{n-1} \int \csc^{n-2} ax \, dx, \quad n \neq 1$

44. $\displaystyle\int \sec^n ax \tan ax \, dx = \frac{\sec^n ax}{na} + C, \quad n \neq 0$

45. $\displaystyle\int \csc^n ax \cot ax \, dx = -\frac{\csc^n ax}{na} + C, \quad n \neq 0$

46. $\displaystyle\int \sin^{-1} ax \, dx = x \sin^{-1} ax + \frac{1}{a} \sqrt{1 - a^2 x^2} + C$

47. $\displaystyle\int \cos^{-1} ax \, dx = x \cos^{-1} ax - \frac{1}{a} \sqrt{1 - a^2 x^2} + C$

48. $\displaystyle\int \tan^{-1} ax \, dx = x \tan^{-1} ax - \frac{1}{2a} \ln (1 + a^2 x^2) + C$

49. $\displaystyle\int e^{ax} \, dx = \frac{1}{a} e^{ax} + C$

50. $\displaystyle\int b^{ax} \, dx = \frac{1}{a} \frac{b^{ax}}{\ln b} + C, \quad b > 0, \quad b \neq 1$

51. $\displaystyle\int x e^{ax} \, dx = \frac{e^{ax}}{a^2} (ax - 1) + C$

52. $\displaystyle\int x^n e^{ax} \, dx = \frac{1}{a} x^n e^{ax} - \frac{n}{a} \int x^{n-1} e^{ax} \, dx$

53. $\displaystyle\int x^n b^{ax} \, dx = \frac{x^n b^{ax}}{a \ln b} - \frac{n}{a \ln b} \int x^{n-1} b^{ax} \, dx, \quad b > 0, \quad b \neq 1$

54. $\displaystyle\int e^{ax} \sin bx \, dx = \frac{e^{ax}}{a^2 + b^2} (a \sin bx - b \cos bx) + C$

55. $\displaystyle\int e^{ax} \cos bx \, dx = \frac{e^{ax}}{a^2 + b^2} (a \cos bx + b \sin bx) + C$

56. $\displaystyle\int \ln ax \, dx = x \ln ax - x + C$

57. $\displaystyle\int \frac{dx}{x \ln ax} = \ln |\ln ax| + C$

58. $\displaystyle\int \sinh ax \, dx = \frac{1}{a} \cosh ax + C$

59. $\displaystyle\int \cosh ax \, dx = \frac{1}{a} \sinh ax + C$

60. $\displaystyle\int \sinh^2 ax \, dx = \frac{\sinh 2ax}{4a} - \frac{x}{2} + C$

61. $\displaystyle\int \cosh^2 ax\, dx = \frac{\sinh 2ax}{4a} + \frac{x}{2} + C$

62. $\displaystyle\int x \sinh ax\, dx = \frac{x}{a} \cosh ax - \frac{1}{a^2} \sinh ax + C$

63. $\displaystyle\int x \cosh ax\, dx = \frac{x}{a} \sinh ax - \frac{1}{a^2} \cosh ax + C$

64. $\displaystyle\int x^n \sinh ax\, dx = \frac{x^n}{a} \cosh ax - \frac{n}{a} \int x^{n-1} \cosh ax\, dx$

65. $\displaystyle\int x^n \cosh ax\, dx = \frac{x^n}{a} \sinh ax - \frac{n}{a} \int x^{n-1} \sinh ax\, dx$

66. $\displaystyle\int \tanh ax\, dx = \frac{1}{a} \ln\,(\cosh ax) + C$

67. $\displaystyle\int \coth ax\, dx = \frac{1}{a} \ln |\sinh ax| + C$

68. $\displaystyle\int \tanh^2 ax\, dx = x - \frac{1}{a} \tanh ax + C$

69. $\displaystyle\int \coth^2 ax\, dx = x - \frac{1}{a} \coth ax + C$

70. $\displaystyle\int \text{sech}^2 ax\, dx = \frac{1}{a} \tanh ax + C$

71. $\displaystyle\int \text{csch}^2 ax\, dx = -\frac{1}{a} \coth ax + C$

72. $\displaystyle\int \text{sech}^n ax \tanh ax\, dx = -\frac{\text{sech}^n ax}{na} + C, \quad n \neq 0$

73. $\displaystyle\int \text{csch}^n ax \coth ax\, dx = -\frac{\text{csch}^n ax}{na} + C, \quad n \neq 0$

74. $\displaystyle\int e^{ax} \sinh bx\, dx = \frac{e^{ax}}{2}\left[\frac{e^{bx}}{a+b} - \frac{e^{-bx}}{a-b}\right] + C, \quad a^2 \neq b^2$

75. $\displaystyle\int e^{ax} \cosh bx\, dx = \frac{e^{ax}}{2}\left[\frac{e^{bx}}{a+b} + \frac{e^{-bx}}{a-b}\right] + C, \quad a^2 \neq b^2$

Glossary

Absolute convergence: If the series $\Sigma |a_n|$ of absolute values converges, then $\Sigma\, a_n$ is said to converge absolutely.   p. 528

Absolute error: $|(\text{true value}) - (\text{approximate value})|$ p. 239

Absolute maximum: The function f has an absolute maximum value $f(c)$ at a point c in its domain D if and only if $f(x) \le f(c)$ for all x in D.   p. 193

Absolute minimum: The function f has an absolute minimum value $f(c)$ at a point c in its domain D if and only if $f(x) \ge f(c)$ for all x in D.   p. 193

Absolute, relative, and percentage change: As we move from $x = a$ to a nearby point $a + \Delta x$, we can describe the corresponding change in the value of a function $f(x)$ three ways:

Absolute change: $\Delta f = f(a + \Delta x) - f(a)$

Relative change: $\Delta f / f(a)$

Percentage change: $(\Delta f / f(a)) \times 100$.

p. 243

Absolute value function: The function $f(x) = |x|$. See also *Absolute value of a number.*   p. 18

Absolute value of a number: The absolute value of x is

$$|x| = \begin{cases} -x, & x < 0 \\ x, & x \ge 0. \end{cases}$$

Acceleration: The derivative of a velocity function with respect to time.   p. 132

Acceleration vector: If $\langle x(t), y(t) \rangle$ is the position vector of a particle moving along a smooth curve in the plane, then $\langle x''(t), y''(t) \rangle$ is the particle's acceleration vector.   p. 554

Accumulator function: If the function f is integrable on $[a, b]$, then A, the accumulator function of f, is defined by $A(x) = \int_a^x f(t)\, dt$ for x in $[a, b]$.   p. 288

Algebraic function: A function $y = f(x)$ that satisfies an equation of the form $P_n y^n + \cdots + P_1 y + P_0 = 0$ in which the P's are polynomials in x with rational coefficients. The function $y = 1/\sqrt{x + 1}$ is algebraic, for example, because it satisfies the equation $(x + 1)y^2 - 1 = 0$. Here, $P_2 = x + 1$, $P_1 = 0$, and $P_0 = -1$. All polynomials and rational functions are algebraic.

Alternating harmonic series: The series

$$\sum_{n=1}^{\infty} \frac{(-1)^{n-1}}{n}.$$

p. 527

Alternating series: A series in which the terms are alternately positive and negative.   p. 527

Alternating series error bound: If a series $\sum_{k=1}^{\infty} a_k$ has terms that alternate in sign and decrease in absolute value to a limit of 0, then the truncation error for $\sum_{k=1}^{n} a_k$ is less than $|a_{n+1}|$.   p. 504

Amplitude: For a periodic function $f(x)$ continuous for all real x, the number

$$\frac{(\text{absolute max of } f) - (\text{absolute min of } f)}{2},$$

is called the amplitude.

The amplitude of the sine function

$$f(x) = A \sin [B(x - C)] + D,$$

is $|A|$.   p. 47

Angle between curves: At a point of intersection of two differentiable curves, the angle between their tangent lines at the point of intersection.

Angle between vectors u and v: The angle

$$\theta = \cos^{-1}\left(\frac{\mathbf{u} \cdot \mathbf{v}}{|\mathbf{u}||\mathbf{v}|}\right).$$

Antiderivative: A function $F(x)$ is an antiderivative of a function $f(x)$ if $F'(x) = f(x)$ for all x in the domain of f.   p. 206

Antidifferentiation: The process of finding an antiderivative. p. 206

Antidifferentiation by partial fractions: A method for integrating a rational function by writing it as a sum of proper fractions, callled partial fractions, with linear or quadratic denominators.   p. 370

Antidifferentiation by parts: A method of integration in which $\int u\, dv$ is written as $uv - \int v\, du$.   p. 349

Antidifferentiation by substitution: A method of integration in which $\int f(g(x)) \cdot g'(x)\, dx$ is rewritten as $\int f(u)\, du$ by substituting $u = g(x)$ and $du = g'(x)\, dx$.   p. 340

Apogee: The point in a satellite's orbit around the earth at which it is farthest from the earth.   p. 561

Arc length: If the derivatives in the formulas exist and are continuous, the length of a smooth curve from the point (a, b), where $t = t_1$, to the point (c, d), where $t = t_2$, can be found by integrating

with respect to x: $\displaystyle\int_a^c \sqrt{1 + \left(\frac{dy}{dx}\right)^2}\, dx$

with respect to y: $\displaystyle\int_b^d \sqrt{1 + \left(\frac{dx}{dy}\right)^2}\, dy$

with respect to the parameter t: $\displaystyle\int_{t_1}^{t_2} \sqrt{\left(\frac{dx}{dt}\right)^2 + \left(\frac{dy}{dt}\right)^2}\, dt.$

pp. 421, 545

Arccosine or inverse cosine function: The inverse of the cosine function with restricted domain $[0, \pi]$.   p. 49

Arcsine or inverse sine function: The inverse of the sine function with restricted domain $[-\pi/2, \pi/2]$.   p. 48

Arctangent or inverse tangent function: The inverse of the tangent function with restricted domain $(-\pi/2, \pi/2)$.   p. 49

Arithmetic sequence: A sequence that can be written in the form $\{a, a + d, a + 2d, \ldots, a + (n - 1)d, \ldots\}$ for some common difference d.   p. 444

Asymptote: The line $y = b$ is a horizontal asymptote of the graph of a function $y = f(x)$ if either

$$\lim_{x \to \infty} f(x) = b \quad \text{or} \quad \lim_{x \to -\infty} f(x) = b. \quad \text{p. 70}$$

The line $x = a$ is a vertical asymptote of the graph of a function $y = f(x)$ if either

$$\lim_{x \to a^+} f(x) = \pm\infty \quad \text{or} \quad \lim_{x \to a^-} f(x) = \pm\infty. \quad \text{p. 72}$$

Average rate of change of a quantity over a period of time: The amount of change divided by the time it takes. p. 59

Average value of a continuous function f on $[a, b]$:

$$\frac{1}{b - a} \int_a^b f(x)\, dx.$$

p. 295

Average velocity: Displacement (change in position) divided by time traveled.   p. 130

Axis of revolution: The line about which a solid of revolution is generated. See *Solid of revolution.*

Base (exponential and logarithm): See *Exponential function with base a; Logarithm function with base a.*

Basic trigonometric functions: When an angle of measure θ is placed in standard position in the coordinate plane and (x, y) is the point at which its terminal ray intersects a circle with center $(0, 0)$ and radius r, the values of the six basic trigonometric functions of θ are

$$\text{Sine: } \sin\theta = \frac{y}{r} \qquad \text{Cosecant: } \csc\theta = \frac{r}{y}$$

$$\text{Cosine: } \cos\theta = \frac{x}{r} \qquad \text{Secant: } \sec\theta = \frac{r}{x}$$

$$\text{Tangent: } \tan\theta = \frac{y}{x} \qquad \text{Cotangent: } \cot\theta = \frac{x}{y}.$$

p. 45

Binomial series: The Maclaurin series for $f(x) = (1 + x)^m$. p. 502

Bounded: A function f is bounded on a given domain if there are numbers m and M such that $m \leq f(x) \leq M$ for any x in the domain of f. The number m is a lower bound and the number M is an upper bound for f.   p. 290

Bounded above: A function f is bounded above on a given domain if there is a number M such that $f(x) \leq M$ for all x in the domain.   p. 294

Bounded below: A function f is bounded below on a given domain if there is a number m such that $m \leq f(x)$ for all x in the domain.   p. 294

Center of a power series: See *Power series.*

Chain Rule: If $y = f(u)$ is differentiable at the point $u = g(x)$, and g is differentiable at x, then the composite function $(f \circ g)(x) = f(g(x))$ is differentiable at x, and

$$(f \circ g)'(x) = f'(g(x)) \cdot g'(x), \quad \text{or} \quad \frac{dy}{dx} = \frac{dy}{du} \cdot \frac{du}{dx},$$

where dy/du is evaluated at $u = g(x)$.   p. 156

Circular functions: The functions $\cos x$ and $\sin x$ with reference to their function values corresponding to points $(\cos x, \sin x)$, x in radians, on the unit circle. More generally, the six basic trigonometric functions.   p. 45

Closed interval $[a, b]$: The set of all real numbers x with $a \leq x \leq b$.   p. 14

Common difference: The difference between two consecutive terms of an arithmetic sequence.   p. 444

Common ratio: The quotient of any term of a geometric sequence and its preceding term.   p. 445

Comparison Test (Direct, for improper integrals): For f and g continuous on $[a, \infty)$ with $0 \leq f(x) \leq g(x)$ for all $x \geq a$,

(1) $\int_a^\infty f(x)\, dx$ converges if $\int_a^\infty g(x)\, dx$ converges;

(2) $\int_a^\infty g(x)\, dx$ diverges if $\int_a^\infty f(x)\, dx$ diverges. p. 472

Comparison Test (Direct, for infinite series): Let $\sum a_n$ be a series with no negative terms. Then

(1) $\sum a_n$ converges if there is a convergent series $\sum c_n$ with $a_n \leq c_n$ for all $n > N$ for some integer N;

(2) $\sum a_n$ diverges if there is a divergent series $\sum d_n$ of nonnegative terms with $a_n \geq d_n$ for all $n > N$ for some integer N.   p. 515

Comparison Test (Limit, for infinite series): Suppose that $a_n > 0$ and $b_n > 0$ for all $n \geq N$, N an integer.

(1) If

$$\lim_{n \to \infty} \frac{a_n}{b_n} = c, \quad 0 < c < \infty$$

then $\sum a_n$ and $\sum b_n$ both converge or both diverge;

(2) if

$$\lim_{n \to \infty} \frac{a_n}{b_n} = 0$$

and $\sum b_n$ converges, then $\sum a_n$ converges;

(3) if

$$\lim_{n \to \infty} \frac{a_n}{b_n} = \infty$$

and $\sum b_n$ diverges, then $\sum a_n$ diverges.   p. 525

Complex number: An expression of the form $a + bi$ where a and b are real numbers and i is defined to be $\sqrt{-1}$.

Component form of a vector: If $\mathbf{v}$ is a vector in the plane equal to the vector with initial point $(0, 0)$ and terminal point (v_1, v_2), the component form of $\mathbf{v}$ is $\mathbf{v} = \langle v_1, v_2 \rangle$. The components are v_1 and v_2.   p. 550

Components of a vector: See *Component form of a vector.*

Composite function $f \circ g$: The function $(f \circ g)(x) = f(g(x))$.   p. 18

Compound interest formula: The value of an account in which initial principal P earns annual interest rate r compounded n times annually for t years is $P\left(1 + \dfrac{r}{n}\right)^{nt}$. p. 25

Concave down: The graph of a differentiable function $y = f(x)$ is concave down on an interval I if y' is decreasing on I. p. 213

Concave up: The graph of a differentiable function $y = f(x)$ is concave up on an interval I if y' is increasing on I. p. 213

Conditional convergence: An infinite series is conditionally convergent if it is convergent but not absolutely convergent. p. 528

Constant function: A function that assigns the same value to every element in its domain.

Continuity at an endpoint: A function $f(x)$ is continuous at a left endpoint a of its domain if $\lim_{x \to a^+} f(x) = f(a)$. The function is continuous at a right endpoint b of its domain if $\lim_{x \to b^-} f(x) = f(b)$. p. 79

Continuity at an interior point: A function $f(x)$ is continuous at an interior point c of its domain if $\lim_{x \to c} f(x) = f(c)$. p. 79

Continuity on an interval: A function is continuous on an interval if and only if it is continuous at each point of the interval. p. 81

Continuous extension of a function f: A function identical to f except that it is continuous at the points where f has removable discontinuities. p. 81

Continuous function: A function that is continuous at each point of its domain. p. 81

Continuously compounded interest formula: The value of an account in which initial principal P earns annual interest rate r compounded continuously for t years is Pe^{rt}. p. 360

Convergent improper integral: An improper integral whose related limit(s) is (are) finite. p. 467

Convergent sequence: A sequence converges if it has a limit. See *Limit at infinity*. p. 447

Convergent series: An infinite series converges if its sequence of partial sums has a finite limit. p. 482

Cosecant function: See *Basic trigonometric functions*.

Cosine function: See *Basic trigonometric functions*.

Cotangent function: See *Basic trigonometric functions*.

Critical point (value): A point (value) in the interior of the domain of a function f at which $f' = 0$ or f' does not exist. p. 196

Critical value: See *Critical point*.

Cross section area: The area of a cross section of a solid. p. 406

Decay models: See *Exponential growth and decay*.

Decreasing function: Let f be a function defined on an interval I. Then f decreases on I if, for any two points x_1 and x_2 in I,

$$x_1 < x_2 \Rightarrow f(x_1) > f(x_2).$$

p. 204

Decreasing on an interval: See *Decreasing function*.

Definite integral of f over an interval $[a, b]$: For any partition P of $[a, b]$, let a number c_k be chosen arbitrarily in each subinterval $[x_{k-1}, x_k]$, and let $\Delta x_k = x_k - x_{k-1}$. If there exists a number L such that

$$\lim_{\|P\| \to 0} \sum_{k=1}^{n} f(c_k)\Delta x_k = L$$

no matter how P and the c_k's are chosen, then L is the definite integral of f over $[a, b]$. p. 283

Delta notation (Δ): See *Increment*.

Derivative of a function f at a point a:

$$\lim_{h \to 0} \frac{f(a + h) - f(a)}{h},$$

provided the limit exists. Alternatively,

$$\lim_{x \to a} \frac{f(x) - f(a)}{x - a},$$

provided the limit exists. p. 101.

Derivative of a function f with respect to x: The function f', whose value at x is

$$\lim_{h \to 0} \frac{f(x + h) - f(x)}{h},$$

provided the limit exists. p. 101

Difference quotient of the function f at a:

$$\frac{f(a + h) - f(a)}{h}.$$

Alternatively,

$$\frac{f(x) - f(a)}{x - a}.$$

p. 90

Differentiability: If $f'(x)$ exists, the function f is differentiable at x. A function that is differentiable at every point of its domain is a differentiable function. p. 101

Differentiable curve: The graph of a differentiable function; also, a parametrized curve whose component functions are differentiable at every parameter value. pp. 101, 544

Differential: If $y = f(x)$ is a differentiable function, the differential dx is an independent variable and the differential dy is $dy = f'(x)\,dx$. p. 241

Differential calculus: The branch of mathematics that deals with derivatives. p. 101

Differential equation: An equation containing a derivative. p. 329

Differentiation: The process of taking a derivative. p. 101

Direction angle of a vector: The smallest nonnegative angle formed with the positive x-axis as the initial ray and the vector as the terminal ray. p. 551

Direction vector (also called Direction of motion): $\mathbf{v}/|\mathbf{v}|$, where $\mathbf{v}$ is the (nonzero) velocity vector of the motion. p. 554

Discontinuity: If a function f is not continuous at a point c, then c is a point of discontinuity of f. p. 80

Disk method: A method for finding the volume of a solid of revolution by evaluating $\int_a^b A(x)\,dx$, where $A(x)$ is the area of the disk cut by a cross section of the solid perpendicular to the axis of revolution at x. A special case of *Volume by slicing.*   p. 411

Distance traveled (from velocity): For *net distance,* the integral of the velocity over the time interval. For *total distance,* the integral of the absolute value of the velocity over the time interval.   p. 387

Divergent improper integral: An improper integral for which at least one of the defining limits does not exist.   p. 467

Divergent sequence: An infinite sequence that has no limit as $n \to \infty$.   p. 447

Divergent series: An infinite series whose sequence of partial sums diverges.   p. 482

Domain of a function: See *Function.*

Domination: A function f dominates a function g on a domain D if $f(x) \ge g(x)$ for all x in D. A sequence $\{a_n\}$ dominates a sequence $\{b_n\}$ if $a_n \ge b_n$ for all n. An infinite series $\sum a_n$ dominates an infinite series $\sum b_n$ if $a_n \ge b_n$ for all n.

Dot (inner) product: Of vectors $\mathbf{u} = \langle u_1, u_2 \rangle$ and $\mathbf{v} = \langle v_1, v_2 \rangle$, the number $\mathbf{u} \cdot \mathbf{v} = u_1 v_1 + u_2 v_2$.   p. 560

Dummy variable of integration: In $\int_a^b f(x)\,dx$, the variable x. It could be any other available letter without changing the value of the integral.   p. 284

$\dfrac{dy}{dx}$: The derivative of y with respect to x.   p. 185

e (the number): To 9 decimal places, $e = 2.718281828$. More formally,

$$e = \lim_{x \to \infty}\left(1 + \frac{1}{x}\right)^x.$$

p. 25

End behavior model: The function g is

(1) a right end behavior model for f if and only if

$$\lim_{x \to \infty} \frac{f(x)}{g(x)} = 1;\quad \text{p. 74}$$

(2) a left end behavior model for f if and only if

$$\lim_{x \to -\infty} \frac{f(x)}{g(x)} = 1;\quad \text{p. 74}$$

(3) an end behavior model for f if it is both a left end and a right end behavior model for f.   p. 74

Euler's method: A method using linearizations to approximate the solution of an initial value problem.   p. 333

Even function: A function f for which $f(-x) = f(x)$ for every x in the domain of f.   p. 16

Exponential change: See *Law of exponential change.*

Exponential function with base a: The function $f(x) = a^x$, $a > 0$ and $a \ne 1$.   p. 23

Exponential growth and decay: Growth and decay modeled by the functions $y = k \cdot a^x$, $k > 0$, with $a > 1$ for growth and $0 < a < 1$ for decay.   p. 25

Exponential growth (decay) constant: See *Law of exponential change.*

Extreme value: See *Extremum.*

Extremum: A maximum or minimum value (extreme value) of a function on a domain. See also *Absolute maximum; Absolute minimum; Local maximum; Local minimum.*   p. 193

Finite sequence: A sequence whose domain has a finite number of elements.   p. 443

First derivative test (for local extrema): For a continuous function f,

(1) if f' changes sign from positive to negative at a critical point c, then f has a local maximum value at c;

(2) if f' changes sign from negative to positive at a critical point c, then f has a local minimum value at c;

(3) if f' does not change sign at a critical point c, then f has no local extreme value at c;

(4) if $f' < 0\,(f' > 0)$ for $x > a$ where a is a left endpoint in the domain of f, then f has a local maximum (minimum) value at a;

(5) if $f' < 0\,(f' > 0)$ for $x < b$ where b is a right endpoint in the domain of f, then f has a local minimum (maximum) value at b.   p. 211

Floor function: The greatest integer less than or equal to x, sometimes denoted $[x]$, although $\lfloor x \rfloor$ is preferred. Also known as the greatest integer function and also written as int x.   p. 64

Free fall equation: When air resistance is absent or insignificant and the only force acting on a falling body is the force of gravity, we call the way the body falls *free fall*. In a free fall short enough for the acceleration of gravity to be assumed constant, call it g, the position of a body released to fall from position s_0 at time $t = 0$ with velocity v_0 is modeled by the equation $s(t) = (1/2)gt^2 + v_0 t + s_0$.   p. 132

Frequency of a periodic function: The reciprocal of the period of the function, or the number of cycles or periods per unit time. For example, the function $\sin x$, with x in seconds, has period 2π seconds and completes $1/2\pi$ cycles per second (has frequency $1/2\pi$).   p. 46

Function: A rule that assigns a unique element in a set R to each element in a set D. The set D is the *domain* of the function. The set of elements assigned from R is the *range* of the function.   p. 13

Fundamental Theorem of Calculus, Antiderivative Part: If f is continuous on $[a, b]$, then the function $F(x) = \int_a^x f(t)\,dt$ has a derivative with respect to x at every point in $[a, b]$ and

$$\frac{dF}{dx} = \frac{d}{dx}\int_a^x f(t)\,dt = f(x).$$

p. 302

Fundamental Theorem of Calculus, Evaluation Part: If f is continuous on $[a, b]$, and F is any antiderivative of f on $[a, b]$, then

$$\int_a^b f(x)\,dx = F(b) - F(a).$$

p. 307

Gaussian curve: See *Normal curve.*

General linear equation: $Ax + By = C$ (A and B not both 0). p. 6

Geometric sequence: A sequence of the form $a, ar, ar^2, \ldots,$ $ar^{n-1}, \ldots,$ in which each term after the first term is obtained by multiplying its preceding term by the same number r. The number r is the *common ratio* of the sequence.   p. 445

Geometric series: A series of the form

$$a + ar + ar^2 + \cdots + ar^{n-1} + \cdots = \sum_{n=1}^{\infty} ar^{n-1},$$

in which each term after the first term is obtained by multiplying its preceding term by the same number r. The number r is the *common ratio* of the series.   p. 483

Global maximum: See *Absolute maximum.*

Global minimum: See *Absolute minimum.*

Graph of a function: The set of points (x, y) in the coordinate plane whose coordinates are the input-output pairs of the function.   p. 14

Greatest integer function: See *Floor function.*

Growth models: See *Exponential growth and decay; Logistic growth.*

Half-life of a radioactive element: The time required for half of the radioactive nuclei present in a sample to decay. pp. 24, 360

Harmonic series: The divergent series

$$1 + \frac{1}{2} + \frac{1}{3} + \frac{1}{4} + \cdots + \frac{1}{n} + \cdots = \sum_{n=1}^{\infty} \frac{1}{n}.$$

p. 524

Hooke's Law: When a force is applied to stretch or compress a spring, the magnitude F of the force in the direction of motion is proportional to the distance x that the spring is stretched or compressed. In symbols, $F \sim x$ or $F = kx$, where k is the *constant of proportionality*. This relationship is *Hooke's Law.* If an elastic material is stretched too far, it becomes distorted and will not return to its original state. The distance beyond which distortion occurs is the material's *elastic limit.* Hooke's Law holds only as long as the material is not stretched past its elastic limit.   p. 391

Horizontal line: In the Cartesian coordinate plane, a line parallel to the x-axis.

Imaginary number: A complex number of the form $0 + bi$. See *Complex number.*

Implicit differentiation: A process for finding dy/dx when y is implicitly defined as a function of x by an equation of the form $f(x, y) = 0$.   p. 164

Improper integral: An integral on an infinite interval or on a finite interval containing one or more points of infinite discontinuity of the integrand. Its value is found as a limit or sum of limits.   p. 467

Increasing function: Let f be a function defined on an interval I. Then f increases on I if, for any two points x_1 and x_2 in I,

$$x_1 < x_2 \Rightarrow f(x_1) < f(x_2).$$

p. 204

Increasing on an interval: See *Increasing function.*

Increment: If coordinates change from (x_1, y_1) to (x_2, y_2), the increments in the coordinates are $\Delta x = x_2 - x_1$ and $\Delta y = y_2 - y_1$. The symbols Δx and Δy are read "delta x" and "delta y."   p. 3

Indefinite integral of a function f: The set of all antiderivatives of f, denoted by $\int f(x)\, dx$.   p. 340

Indeterminate form: A nonnumeric expression of the form $0/0, \infty/\infty, 0 \cdot \infty, \infty - \infty, 1^\infty, \infty^0,$ or 0^0 obtained when trying substitution to evaluate a limit. The expression reveals nothing about the limit, but does suggest how l'Hospital's Rule may be applied to help find the limit.   p. 452

Infinite discontinuity: A point of discontinuity where one or both of the one-sided limits are infinite.   p. 80

Infinite limit: If the values of a function $f(x)$ outgrow all positive bounds as x approaches a finite number a, we say

$$\lim_{x \to a} f(x) = \infty.$$

If the values of f become large and negative, exceeding all negative bounds as $x \to a$, we say

$$\lim_{x \to a} f(x) = -\infty.$$

p. 72

Infinite sequence: A sequence whose domain is an infinite subset of the positive integers.   p. 443

Infinite series: An expression of the form

$$a_1 + a_2 + a_3 + \cdots + a_n + \cdots = \sum_{k=1}^{\infty} a_k.$$

The numbers $a_1, a_2, \ldots$ are the *terms* of the series; a_n is the nth term. The *partial sums* of the series form a sequence

$$
\begin{aligned}
s_1 &= a_1 \\
s_2 &= a_1 + a_2 \\
s_3 &= a_1 + a_2 + a_3 \\
&\vdots \\
s_n &= a_1 + a_2 + a_3 + \cdots + a_n
\end{aligned}
$$

of numbers, each defined as a finite sum. If the sequence of partial sums has a limit S as $n \to \infty$, the series *converges* to the *sum S.* A series that fails to converge *diverges.*   p. 482

Inflection point: A point where the graph of a function has a tangent line and the concavity changes.   p. 214

Initial condition: See *Initial value problem.*

Initial value problem: For a first-order differential equation, the problem of finding the solution that has a particular value at a given point. The condition that the solution have this value at the point is called the *initial condition* of the problem.   p. 329

Inner product: See *Dot product.*

Instantaneous rate of change of f with respect to x at a: The derivative

$$f'(a) = \lim_{h \to 0} \frac{f(a + h) - f(a)}{h},$$

provided the limit exists.   pp. 91, 129

Instantaneous velocity: The derivative of a position function with respect to time.   p. 130

Integrable function on $[a, b]$: A function for which the definite integral over $[a, b]$ exists.   p. 283

Integral calculus: The branch of mathematics that deals with integrals.   p. 269

Integrand: $f(x)$ in $\int f(x)\, dx$ or in $\int_a^b f(x)\, dx$.   p. 284

Integration: The evaluation of a definite integral, an indefinite integral, or an improper integral.   p. 341

Integration by parts: See *Antidifferentiation by parts.*

Intermediate Value Theorem for Continuous Functions: A function $y = f(x)$ that is continuous on a closed interval $[a, b]$ takes on every y value between $f(a)$ and $f(b)$.   p. 83

Intermediate Value Theorem for Derivatives: If a and b are any two points in an interval on which f is differentiable, then f' takes on every value between $f'(a)$ and $f'(b)$.   p. 115

Interval: A subset of the number line formed by any of the following: (1) two points and the points in between; (2) only the points in between two points; (3) the points in between two points and one of the two points; (4) one point and the points to one side of it; (5) only the points to one side of a given point. The real line is also considered to be an interval.   p. 14

Interval of convergence: The interval of x-values for which a power series converges. See *Power series.*

Inverse function f^{-1}: The function obtained by reversing the ordered pairs of a one-to-one function f.   p. 37

Inverse function slope relationship: The slope of the function f^{-1} at the point (a, b) is the reciprocal of the slope of the function f at the point (b, a). Therefore,

$$\left.\frac{df^{-1}}{dx}\right|_{x=a} = \frac{1}{\left.\dfrac{df}{dx}\right|_{x=b}}.   \text{p. 173}$$

Jerk: The derivative of an acceleration function with respect to time.   p. 145

Jump discontinuity: A point of discontinuity where the one-sided limits exist but have different values. At such a point, the function jumps from one value to another.   p. 80

Lagrange error bound: A bound for truncation error obtained from the Lagrange form of the remainder for Taylor series.   p. 505

Lagrange form of the remainder: The formula

$$\frac{f^{(n+1)}(c)}{(n+1)!}(x - a)^{n+1}$$

for the remainder in Taylor's Theorem.   p. 505

Law of exponential change: If a quantity y changes at a rate proportional to the amount present $(dy/dt = ky)$ and $y = y_0$ when $t = 0$, then

$$y = y_0 e^{kt},$$

where $k > 0$ represents growth and $k < 0$ represents decay. The number k is the *exponential growth (decay) constant.*   p. 359

Left end behavior model: See *End behavior model.*

Left-hand derivative: The derivative defined as a left-hand limit.   p. 106

Left-hand limit: The limit of f as x approaches c from the left, or $\lim_{x \to c^-} f(x)$.   p. 63

Length (magnitude) of a vector: The length (magnitude) of $\mathbf{v} = \langle v_1, v_2 \rangle$ is $|\mathbf{v}| = \sqrt{v_1^2 + v_2^2}$.   p. 550

L'Hospital's Rule: Suppose that $f(a) = g(a) = 0$, that f and g are differentiable on an open interval I containing a, and that $g'(x) \neq 0$ on I if $x \neq a$. Then

$$\lim_{x \to a} \frac{f(x)}{g(x)} = \lim_{x \to a} \frac{f'(x)}{g'(x)},$$

provided the limit exists (or is $\pm\infty$). L'Hospital's Rule also applies to quotients that lead to ∞/∞. If $f(x)$ and $g(x)$ both approach ∞ as $x \to a$, then

$$\lim_{x \to a} \frac{f(x)}{g(x)} = \lim_{x \to a} \frac{f'(x)}{g'(x)},$$

provided the latter limit exists (or is $\pm\infty$). In this case, a may itself be either finite or infinite.   p. 452

Limit (formal definition): The function f has limit L as x approaches c if, given any positive number ε, there exists a positive number δ such that $|f(x) - L| < \varepsilon$ whenever $|x - c| < \delta$ and $x \neq c$. This is represented as $\lim_{x \to c} f(x) = L$.   p. 585

Limit (intuitive definition): The function f has limit L as x approaches c if we can force $f(x)$ to be as close to L as we wish simply by restricting the distance between x and c, but not allowing x to equal c. This is represented as $\lim_{x \to c} f(x) = L$.   p. 60

Limit at infinity (formal definition): The function f has limit L as x approaches ∞ if, given any positive number ε, there exists a positive number N such that for all $x > N$, $|f(x) - L| < \varepsilon$. This is represented as $\lim_{x \to \infty} f(x) = L$. The function f has limit L as x approaches $-\infty$ if, given any positive number ε, there is a negative number N such that for all x with $x < N$, $|f(x) - L| < \varepsilon$. This is represented as $\lim_{x \to -\infty} f(x) = L$. The sequence $f(n) = x_n$ has limit L, if $\lim_{n \to \infty} f(n) = L$.

Limit at infinity (intuitive definition): The function f has limit L as x approaches ∞ if we can force $f(x)$ to be as close to L as we wish simply by making x greater than some sufficiently large positive number. This is represented as $\lim_{x \to \infty} f(x) = L$. The function f has limit L as x approaches $-\infty$ if we can force $f(x)$ to be as close to L as we wish simply by making x less than some sufficiently large (in absolute value) negative number. This is represented as $\lim_{x \to -\infty} f(x) = L$.   p. 70

Limit of a sequence: See *Limit at infinity.*

Limits of integration: a and b in $\int_a^b f(x)\, dx$.   p. 284

Linear approximation (standard) of f at a: The approximation $f(x) \approx L(x)$, where $L(x)$ is the linearization of f at a.   p. 238

Linear equation: See *General linear equation.*

Linear function: A function that can be expressed in the form $f(x) = mx + b$.   p. 4

Linearization of f at a: The approximating function $L(x) = f(a) + f'(a)(x - a)$ when f is differentiable at $x = a$.*   p. 238

*Equivalently, the tangent line to the graph of f at $x = a$.

Local extrema: See *Local maximum; Local minimum.*

Local linearity: If a function $f(x)$ is differentiable at $x = a$, then, close to a, its graph resembles the tangent line at a. p. 112

Local linearization: See *Linearization of f at a.*

Local maximum: The function f has a local maximum value $f(c)$ at a point c in the interior of its domain if and only if $f(x) \le f(c)$ for all x in some open interval containing c. The function has a local maximum value at an endpoint c if the inequality holds for all x in some half-open domain interval containing c. p. 195

Local minimum: The function f has a local minimum value $f(c)$ at a point c in the interior of its domain if and only if $f(x) \ge f(c)$ for all x in some open interval containing c. The function has a local minimum value at an endpoint c if the inequality holds for all x in some half-open domain interval containing c. p. 195

Logarithm function with base a: The function $y = \log_a x$, which is the inverse of the exponential function $y = a^x, a > 0, a \ne 1$. p. 39

Logarithmic differentiation: The process of taking the natural logarithm of both sides of an equation, differentiating, and then solving for the desired derivative. p. 185

Logistic curve: A solution curve of the logistic differential equation. It describes population growth that begins slowly when the population is small, speeds up as the number of reproducing individuals increases and nutrients are still plentiful, and slows down again as the population reaches the carrying capacity of its environment. p. 372

Logistic differential equation:

$$\frac{dP}{dt} = kP(M - p),$$

where P is the current population, t is time, M is the carrying capacity of the environment, and k is a positive number called the logistic growth constant. p. 372

Logistic growth model: The solution

$$P = \frac{M}{1 + Ae^{-(MK)t}},$$

to the logistic differential equation, A an arbitrary constant. This model assumes that the relative growth rate of a population is positive, but decreases as the population increases due to environmental and economic factors. See *Logistic differential equation.* p. 374

Lower bound: See *Bounded.*

LRAM: Left-hand endpoint rectangular approximation method. The method of approximating a definite integral over an interval using the function values at the left-hand endpoints of the subintervals determined by a partition. p. 272

Maclaurin series: See *Taylor series.*

Magnitude: Of a number, its absolute value; of a vector, its length. p. 550

Maximum: See *Absolute maximum; Local maximum.*

Mean value: See *Average value of a continuous function on $[a, b]$.*

Mean Value Theorem for Definite Integrals: If f is continuous on $[a, b]$, then at some point c in $[a, b]$,

$$f(c) = \frac{1}{b - a} \int_a^b f(x) \, dx.$$

p. 296

Mean Value Theorem for Derivatives: If $y = f(x)$ is continuous at every point of the closed interval $[a, b]$ and differentiable at every point of its interior (a, b), then there is at least one point c in (a, b) at which

$$f'(c) = \frac{f(b) - f(a)}{b - a}.$$

p. 202

Minimum: See *Absolute minimum; Local minimum.*

Monotonic (monotone) function: A function that is always increasing on an interval or always decreasing on an interval. p. 204.

Monotonic sequence: See *Monotonic (monotone) function.*

MRAM: Midpoint rectangular approximation method. The method of approximating a definite integral over an interval, using the function values at the midpoints of the subintervals determined by a partition. p. 272

Natural logarithm: a is the natural logarithm of b if and only if $b = e^a$. The natural logarithm function $y = \ln x$ is the inverse of the exponential function $y = e^x$. p. 40

NDER$(f(x), a)$: The numerical derivative of f at $x = a$. p. 113

NINT$(f(x), x, a, b)$: The numerical integral of f with respect to x, from $x = a$ to $x = b$. p. 289

Nonremovable discontinuity: A discontinuity that is not removable. p. 80. See *Removable discontinuity.*

Norm of a partition: The longest subinterval length, denoted $\|P\|$, for a partition P. p. 282

Normal curve: The graph of a normal probability density function. p. 431

Normal line to a curve at a point: The line perpendicular to the tangent line at that point. p. 91

Normal probability density function: The normal probability density function for a population with *mean μ* and *standard deviation σ* is

$$f(x) = \frac{1}{\sigma \sqrt{2\pi}} e^{-(x-\mu)^2/(2\sigma^2)}.$$

The mean μ represents the average value of the variable x. The standard deviation σ measures the "scatter" around the mean. p. 431

Numerical derivative: An approximation of the derivative of a function using a numerical algorithm. p. 113

Numerical integration: Approximating the integral of a function using a numerical algorithm. p. 305

Numerical method: A method for generating a numerical solution of a problem. For example, a method for estimating the value of a definite integral, for estimating the zeros of a function or solutions of an equation, or for estimating values of the function that solves an initial value problem.

Numerical solution: Of an equation $f(x) = 0$, an estimate of one or more of its roots; of an initial value problem, a table of estimated values of the solution function. See *Euler's Method.*

Odd function: A function f for which $f(-x) = -f(x)$ for every x in the domain of f.   p. 16

One-sided limit: See *Left-hand limit; Right-hand limit.*

One-to-one function: A function f for which $f(a) \neq f(b)$ whenever $a \neq b$.   p. 36

Open interval (a, b): All numbers x with $a < x < b$.   p. 14

Optimization: In an application, maximizing or minimizing some aspect of the system being modeled.   p. 224

Order of a derivative: If y is a function of x, $y' = dy/dx$ is the first-order, or first, derivative of y with respect to x; $y'' = d^2y/dx^2$ is the second-order, or second, derivative of y; $y^{(n)} = d^ny/dx^n$ is the nth-order, or nth, derivative of y.   p. 124

Order of a differential equation: The order of the highest order derivative in the equation.   p. 329

Origin: The point $(0, 0)$ in the Cartesian coordinate plane.

Orthogonal curves: See *Perpendicular curves.*

Oscillating discontinuity: A point near which the function values oscillate without approaching a unique limit.   p. 80

Parallel curves: In the plane, curves that differ from one another by a vertical translation (shift).   p. 109

Parameter: See *Parametric equations.*

Parameter interval: See *Parametric equations.*

Parametric equations: If x and y are given as functions $x = f(t)$, $y = g(t)$, over an interval of t values, then the set of points $(x, y) = (f(t), g(t))$ defined by these equations is a *parametric curve*; the equations are *parametric equations* for the curve; the variable t is the *parameter* for the curve; and the interval of prescribed t values is the *parameter interval*. p. 29

Parametrization of a curve: The parametric equations and parameter interval describing a curve.   p. 29

Partial fractions: See *Antidifferentiation by partial fractions.*

Partial sum: See *Infinite series.*

Particular solution: The unique solution of a differential equation satisfying the given initial condition or conditions.   p. 329

Partition of an interval $[a, b]$: A set

$$\{a = x_0, x_1, x_2, \dots, x_n = b\}$$

of points in $[a, b]$ numbered in order from left to right.   p. 281

Percentage change: See *Absolute, relative, and percentage change.*

Percentage error:

$$\frac{|\text{approximate value} - \text{exact value}|}{|\text{exact value}|} \times 100. \quad \text{p. 338}$$

Perigee: The point in a satellite's orbit around the earth at which it is closest to the earth.   p. 561

Period of a periodic function f: The smallest positive number p for which $f(x + p) = f(x)$ for every value of x. See *Periodic function.*   p. 46

Periodic function: A function f for which there is a positive number p such that $f(x + p) = f(x)$ for every value of x.   p. 46

Perpendicular (orthogonal) curves: Two curves are said to be perpendicular (orthogonal) at a point of intersection if their tangents at that point are perpendicular.   p. 161

Piecewise-defined function: A function that is defined by applying different formulas to different parts of its domain.   p. 17

Point-slope equation of a line: The line with slope m that passes through the point (x_1, y_1) has equation $y - y_1 = m(x - x_1)$. Equivalently, $y = m(x - x_1) + y_1$. In calculus, the linearization of a differentiable function is best expressed in point-slope form.   p. 5

Polar coordinates: Each point P in the polar coordinate plane has polar coordinates (r, θ), where r gives the directed distance from the origin O to P and θ gives a directed angle from the initial ray to ray OP.   p. 562

Polar function: A function whose input is the angle from the initial ray out of the origin (usually the positive x-axis) and whose output is the directed distance from the origin.   p. 561

Pole: In the polar coordinate plane, the origin.   p. 562

Polynomial: An expression of the form

$$a_nx^n + a_{n-1}x^{n-1} + \cdots + a_1x + a_0. \quad \text{p. 62}$$

Position function: For linear motion, a function f that gives the position $f(t)$ of a body on a coordinate axis at time t.   p. 91

Position vector: The vector $\langle a, b \rangle$ is the position vector of the point (a, b).   p. 550

Power series: An expression of the form

$$c_0 + c_1x + c_2x^2 + \cdots + c_nx^n + \cdots = \sum_{n=0}^{\infty} c_nx^n$$

is a power series centered at $x = 0$. An expression of the form

$$c_0 + c_1(x - a) + c_2(x - a)^2 + \cdots$$
$$+ c_n(x - a)^n + \cdots = \sum_{n=0}^{\infty} c_n(x - a)^n$$

is a power series centered at $x = a$. The number a is the *center* of the series.   p. 484

Prime notation $(f'(x))$: If $y = f(x)$, then both y' and $f'(x)$ denote the derivative of the function with respect to x.   p. 103

Probability: See *Probability density function.*

Probability density function (pdf): A function $f(x)$ such that $f(x) \geq 0$ for all x and $\int_{-\infty}^{\infty} f(x)\, dx = 1$. The *probability* associated with the interval $[a, b]$ is $\int_a^b f(x)\, dx$.   p. 430

Product Rule: The product of two differentiable functions u and v is differentiable, and

$$\frac{d}{dx}(uv) = u\frac{dv}{dx} + v\frac{du}{dx}.$$

p. 121

p-series: A series of the form

$$\sum_{n=1}^{\infty} \frac{1}{n^p}, \quad p \text{ a nonzero constant.}$$

p. 524

Quotient Rule: At a point where $v \neq 0$, the quotient $y = u/v$ of two differentiable functions is differentiable, and

$$\frac{d}{dx}\left(\frac{u}{v}\right) = \frac{v\dfrac{du}{dx} - u\dfrac{dv}{dx}}{v^2}.$$

p. 122

Radian measure: If a central angle of a circle of radius r intercepts an arc of length s on the circle, the radian measure of the angle is s/r.   p. 45

Radius of convergence: In general, the positive number R for which the power series

$$\sum_{n=0}^{\infty} c_n(x - a)^n$$

converges when $|x - a| < R$ and diverges when $|x - a| > R$. If the series converges only for $x = a$, then $R = 0$. If the series converges for every x, then $R = \infty$.   p. 514

Range of a function: See *Function*.

Rate of change: See *Average rate of change of a quantity over a period of time; Instantaneous rate of change of f with respect to x at a.*

Ratio Test: Let $\sum a_n$ be a series with positive terms and with

$$\lim_{n \to \infty} \frac{a_{n+1}}{a_n} = L.$$

Then (1) the series converges if $L < 1$; (2) the series diverges if $L > 1$; (3) the test is inconclusive if $L = 1$.   p. 517

Rational function: A function that can be expressed as the quotient of two polynomial functions.

Regular partition: A partition in which consecutive points are equally spaced.   p. 283

Related rate equation: Given an equation that relates two or more variables, the equation that results from differentiating both sides of that equation with respect to time. This equation relates the rates at which the variables change with respect to time. p. 252

Relative change: See *Absolute, relative, and percentage change.*

Relative extrema: Same as *Local extrema*.

Relative maximum: Same as *Local maximum*.

Relative minimum: Same as *Local minimum*.

Remainder of order n: The remainder

$$R_n(x) = \frac{f^{(n+1)}(c)}{(n + 1)!}(x - a)^{n+1},$$

in Taylor's Theorem.   p. 505

Removable discontinuity: A discontinuity c of the function f for which $f(c)$ can be (re)defined so that $\lim_{x \to c} f(x) = f(c)$. p. 80

Resultant vector: The vector that results from adding or subtracting two vectors.   p. 552

Riemann sum: A sum of the form

$$\sum_{k=1}^{n} f(c_k) \cdot \Delta x_k,$$

where f is a continuous function on a closed interval $[a, b]$, c_k is some point in, and Δx_k is the length of, the kth subinterval in some partition of $[a, b]$.   p. 281

Right end behavior model: See *End behavior model*.

Right-hand derivative: The derivative defined as a right-hand limit.   p. 106

Right-hand limit: The limit of f as x approaches c from the right, or $\lim_{x \to c^+} f(x)$.   p. 63

Root of an equation: See *Zero of a function*.

Roundoff error: Error due to rounding numbers that are used in further computations.   p. 121

RRAM: Right-hand endpoint rectangular approximation method. The method of approximating a definite integral over an interval using the function values at the right-hand endpoints of the subintervals determined by a partition.   p. 272

Scalar: In the context of vectors, scalars are real numbers that behave like scaling factors.   p. 551

Scalar multiple of a vector: $k\mathbf{u} = \langle ku_1, ku_2 \rangle$, where k is a scalar (real number) and $\mathbf{u} = \langle u_1, u_2 \rangle$.   p. 552

Secant function: See *Basic trigonometric functions*.

Secant line to a curve: A line through two points on the curve.   p. 87

Second derivative: If y is a function of x and $y' = dy/dx$ is the first derivative of y with respect to x, then $y'' = dy'/dx = d^2y/dx^2$ is the second derivative of y with respect to x.   p. 124

Second derivative test (for local extrema): If $f'(c) = 0$ and $f''(c) < 0$, then f has a local maximum at $x = c$. If $f'(c) = 0$ and $f''(c) > 0$, then f has a local minimum at $x = c$. p. 217

Sensitivity: An interpretation of the derivative that describes how small changes in the input variable produce changes in the output variable.   p. 92

Separable differential equation: A differential equation $y' = f(x, y)$ in which f can be expressed as a product of a function of x and a function of y.   p. 358

Separating the variables: For a separable differential equation $y' = f(x, y)$, the process of combining all the y-terms multiplied by dy on one side of the equation and putting all the x-terms multiplied by dx on the other side.   p. 358

Sequence: A function whose domain is the set of positive integers.   p. 443

Sigma notation: Notation using the Greek letter capital sigma, Σ, for writing lengthy sums in compact form.   p. 281

Simple harmonic motion: Periodic motion, like the vertical motion of a weight bobbing up and down at the end of a spring, that can be modeled with a sinusoidal position function.   p. 145

Sine function: See *Basic trigonometric functions*.

Slope field: A slope field for the first-order differential equation $dy/dx = f(x, y)$ is a plot of short line segments with slopes $f(x, y)$ at a lattice of points (x, y) in the plane.   p. 331

Slope of a curve: The slope of a curve $y = f(x)$ at the point $(a, f(a))$ is $f'(a)$, provided f is differentiable at a.   p. 89

Smooth curve: The graph of a smooth function.   p. 421

Smooth function: A real-valued function $y = f(x)$ with a continuous first derivative.   p. 421

Solid of revolution: A solid generated by revolving a plane region about a line in the plane.   p. 407

Solution of a differential equation: Any function that together with its derivatives satisfies the equation. When we find all such functions, we have *solved* the differential equation.   p. 329

Speed: The absolute value, or magnitude, of velocity.   p. 131

Spiral of Archimedes: The spiral curve studied by Archimedes and given by a polar equation of the form $r = a + b\theta$.   p. 571

Standard position of a vector: The representative vector with initial point at the origin.   p. 550

Stationary point: A point in the interior of the domain of a function f at which $f' = 0$.   p. 196

Sum of a series: See *Infinite series*.

Sum of vectors:

$$\mathbf{v} + \mathbf{u} = \langle v_1, v_2 \rangle + \langle u_1, u_2 \rangle = \langle v_1 + u_1, v_2 + u_2 \rangle.$$

p. 552

Symmetric difference quotient: The quotient

$$\frac{f(a + h) - f(a - h)}{2h}$$

that a graphing calculator uses to calculate NDER$(f(x), a)$, the numerical derivative of f at $x = a$.   p. 113

Symmetry: For a curve to have

(1) symmetry about the x-axis, the point (x, y) must lie on the curve if and only if $(x, -y)$ lies on the curve;

(2) symmetry about the y-axis, (x, y) must lie on the curve if and only if $(-x, y)$ lies on the curve;

(3) symmetry about the origin, (x, y) must lie on the curve if and only if $(-x, -y)$ lies on the curve.   p. 16

Tabular integration: A time-saving way to organize the work of repeated integrations by parts.   p. 352

Tangent function: See *Basic trigonometric functions*.

Tangent line: To the graph of a function $y = f(x)$ at a point $x = a$ where f' exists, the line through $(a, f(a))$ with slope $f'(a)$.   p. 88

To a parametrized curve at a point P where $dx/dt \neq 0$, the line through P with slope equal to the value of $(dy/dt)/(dx/dt)$ at P.

The line $x = a$ is a vertical tangent line to a curve if the line $y = a$ is a horizontal tangent line to the curve defined by the inverse relation.   p. 88

Taylor polynomial: Let f be a function with derivatives through order n throughout some open interval containing 0. Then

$$P_n(x) = \sum_{k=0}^{n} \frac{f^{(k)}(0)}{k!} x^k$$

is the Taylor polynomial of order n for f at $x = 0$.   p. 493

If f is a function with derivatives through order n throughout some open interval containing the point $x = a$, then

$$P_n(x) = \sum_{k=0}^{n} \frac{f^{(k)}(a)}{k!} (x - a)^k$$

is the Taylor polynomial of order n for f at $x = a$.   p. 493

Taylor series: Let f be a function with derivatives of all orders throughout some open interval containing 0. Then

$$f(0) + f'(0)x + \frac{f''(0)}{2!} x^2 + \cdots + \frac{f^{(n)}(0)}{n!} x^n + \cdots = \sum_{k=0}^{\infty} \frac{f^{(k)}(0)}{k!} x^k$$

is the Taylor series generated by f at $x = 0$. This series is also called the *Maclaurin series* generated by f.   p. 495

If f is a function with derivatives of all orders throughout some open interval containing the point $x = a$, then

$$f(a) + f'(a)(x - a) + \frac{f''(a)}{2!} (x - a)^2 + \cdots$$
$$+ \frac{f^{(n)}(a)}{n!} (x - a)^n + \cdots,$$
$$\text{or} \quad \sum_{k=0}^{\infty} \frac{f^{(k)}(a)}{k!} (x - a)^k,$$

is the Taylor series generated by f at $x = a$.   p. 497

Term of a sequence or series: For the sequence

$$a_1, a_2, a_3, \ldots, a_n, \ldots,$$

or for the series

$$a_1 + a_2 + a_3 + \cdots + a_n + \cdots,$$

a_n is the nth term.   p. 482

Transcendental function: A function that is not algebraic. (See *Algebraic function*.) The six basic trigonometric functions are transcendental, as are the inverse trigonometric functions and the exponential and logarithmic functions studied in this book.

Trapezoidal Rule: To approximate $\int_a^b f(x)\, dx$, use

$$T = \frac{h}{2}(y_0 + 2y_1 + 2y_2 + \cdots + 2y_{n-1} + y_n),$$

where $[a, b]$ is partitioned into n subintervals of equal length $h = (b - a)/n$ and y_i is the value of f at each partition point x_i.   p. 315

Trigonometric function: See *Basic trigonometric functions*.

Truncation error: The error incurred in using a finite partial sum to estimate the sum of an infinite series.   p. 503

Two-sided limit: Limit at an interior point of a function's domain. See *Limit*.

Unit circle: The circle of radius 1 centered at the origin.

Unit vector: A vector with magnitude 1.   p. 552

Upper bound: See *Bounded*.

***u*-substitution:** See *Antidifferentiation by substitution*.

Value of an improper integral: See *Improper integral*.

Variable of integration: In $\int f(x)\, dx$ or $\int_a^b f(x)\, dx$, the variable x.   p. 284

Vector in the plane: A directed line segment in the plane, with the understanding that two such vectors are equal if they have the same length and direction.   p. 550

Velocity: The rate of change of position with respect to time. See also *Average velocity; Instantaneous velocity; Velocity vector.*   p. 130

Velocity vector: If $\langle x(t), y(t) \rangle$ is the position vector of a particle moving along a smooth curve in the plane, then at any time t, $\langle x'(t), y'(t) \rangle$ is the particle's velocity vector.   p. 554

Vertical line: In the Cartesian coordinate plane, a line parallel to the y-axis.

Viewing window: On a graphing calculator, the portion of the coordinate plane displayed on the screen.

Volume by slicing: A method for finding the volume of a solid by evaluating $\int_a^b A(x)\, dx$, where $A(x)$ (assumed integrable) is the solid cross section area at x.   p. 407

Work: For a constant force, force times displacement. For a varying force, the definite integral of force times the distance over which the force is applied.   p. 391

x-intercept: The x-coordinate of the point where a curve intersects the x-axis.

y-intercept: The y-coordinate of the point where a curve intersects the y-axis.   p. 6

Zero of a function: A solution of the equation $f(x) = 0$ is a zero of the function f or a *root* of the equation.

Zero vector: The vector $\langle 0, 0 \rangle$, which has zero length and no direction.   p. 550

Selected Answers

CHAPTER 1

Section 1.1

Quick Review 1.1

1. -2 **3.** -1 **5. (a)** Yes **(b)** No

7. $\sqrt{2}$ **9.** $y = \dfrac{4}{3}x - \dfrac{7}{3}$

Exercises 1.1

1. $\Delta x = -2, \Delta y = -3$ **3.** $\Delta x = -5, \Delta y = 0$

5. (a) and **(c)**, **(b)** 3 **7. (a)** and **(c)**, **(b)** 0

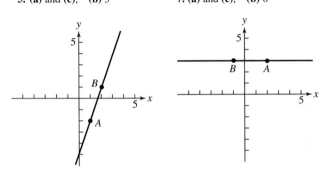

9. $y = 8$ **11.** $y = -4$ **13.** $d = 5.8$ km **15.** $d = 7.4$ km

17. $d = 0.4(t - 6) + 5$ **19.** $y = 1(x - 1) + 1$

21. $y = 2(x - 0) + 3$ **23.** $y = \dfrac{5}{2}x$

25. (a) $-\dfrac{3}{4}$ **(b)** 3 **27. (a)** $-\dfrac{4}{3}$ **(b)** 4

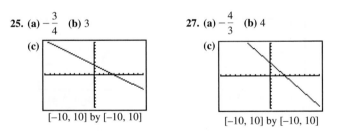

(c) $[-10, 10]$ by $[-10, 10]$ **(c)** $[-10, 10]$ by $[-10, 10]$

29. (a) $y = -x$ **(b)** $y = x$ **31. (a)** $x = -2$ **(b)** $y = 4$

33. $(3, -5)$ **35.** $(-1, 6)$ **37.** $(1/2, -2)$

39. A burger costs $4.28 and an order of fries costs $2.34.

41. (a) $k = 2$ **(b)** $k = -2$ **43.** 7:36 PM

45. False. A vertical line has no slope. **47.** A **49.** D

51. $y - 4 = -\dfrac{3}{4}(x - 3)$ (Notice that the radius has slope 4/3, and the tangent is perpendicular to the radius.)

53. (a) Both algebraic methods lead to solving an equation like $0 = 17$, which is impossible. The conclusion is that there is no pair (x, y) that satisfies both equations simultaneously.
(b) A graph shows the two lines to be parallel.
(c) Two linear equations that are dependent and inconsistent have parallel graphs that do not intersect. Therefore, there is no pair (x, y) that can satisfy both equations simultaneously.

55. The coordinates of the three missing vertices are $(5, 2)$, $(-1, 4)$ and $(-1, -2)$.

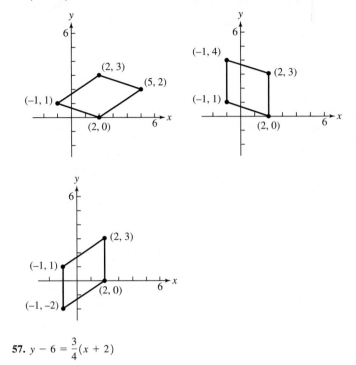

57. $y - 6 = \dfrac{3}{4}(x + 2)$

Section 1.2

Quick Review 1.2

1. $[-2, \infty)$ **3.** $[-1, 7]$ **5.** $(-4, 4)$

7. Translate the graph of f 2 units left and 3 units downward.

9. (a) $x = -3, 3$ **(b)** No real solution

11. (a) $x = 9$ **(b)** $x = -6$

Exercises 1.2

1. (a) $A(d) = \pi\left(\dfrac{d}{2}\right)^2$ **(b)** $A(4) = 4\pi$ in^2

3. (a) $S(e) = 6e^2$ **(b)** $S(5) = 150$ ft^2

5. (a) $(-\infty, \infty); (-\infty, 4]$ **7. (a)** $[1, \infty); [2, \infty)$

(b) **(b)**

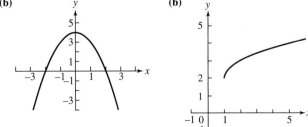

9. (a) $(-\infty, 2) \cup (2, \infty);$
$(-\infty, 0) \cup (0, \infty)$

(b)

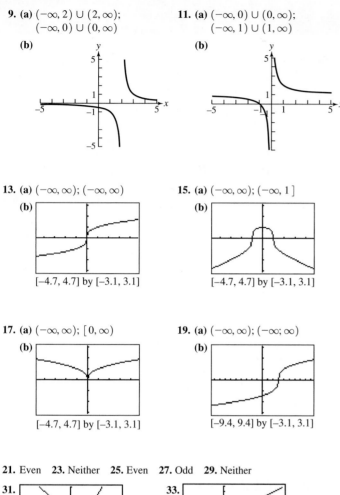

11. (a) $(-\infty, 0) \cup (0, \infty);$
$(-\infty, 1) \cup (1, \infty)$

(b)

13. (a) $(-\infty, \infty); (-\infty, \infty)$

(b)

$[-4.7, 4.7]$ by $[-3.1, 3.1]$

15. (a) $(-\infty, \infty); (-\infty, 1]$

(b)

$[-4.7, 4.7]$ by $[-3.1, 3.1]$

17. (a) $(-\infty, \infty); [0, \infty)$

(b)

$[-4.7, 4.7]$ by $[-3.1, 3.1]$

19. (a) $(-\infty, \infty); (-\infty; \infty)$

(b)

$[-9.4, 9.4]$ by $[-3.1, 3.1]$

21. Even **23.** Neither **25.** Even **27.** Odd **29.** Neither

31.

$[-4.7, 4.7]$ by $[-1, 6]$

33.

$[-3.7, 5.7]$ by $[-4, 9]$

35. Because if the vertical line test holds, then for each x-coordinate, there is at most one y-coordinate giving a point on the curve. This y-coordinate would correspond to the value assigned to the x-coordinate. Since there's only one y-coordinate, the assignment would be unique.

37. No **39.** Yes

41. $f(x) = \begin{cases} x, & 0 \le x \le 1 \\ 2 - x, & 1 < x \le 2 \end{cases}$

43. $f(x) = \begin{cases} 2 - x, & 0 < x \le 2 \\ \dfrac{5}{3} - \dfrac{x}{3}, & 2 < x \le 5 \end{cases}$

45. $f(x) = \begin{cases} -x, & -1 \le x < 0 \\ 1, & 0 < x \le 1 \\ \dfrac{3}{2} - \dfrac{x}{2}, & 1 < x < 3 \end{cases}$

47. $f(x) = \begin{cases} 0, & 0 \le x \le \dfrac{T}{2} \\ \dfrac{2}{T}x - 1, & \dfrac{T}{2} < x \le T \end{cases}$

49. (a)

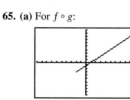

$[-9.4, 9.4]$ by $[-6.2, 6.2]$

(b) All reals **(c)** $(-\infty, 2]$

51. (a) $x^2 + 2$ **(b)** $x^2 + 10x + 22$ **(c)** 2 **(d)** 22 **(e)** -2 **(f)** $x + 10$

53. (a) $g(x) = x^2$ **(b)** $g(x) = \dfrac{1}{x - 1}$ **(c)** $f(x) = \dfrac{1}{x}$ **(d)** $f(x) = x^2$

55. (a) Because the circumference of the original circle was 8π and a piece of length x was removed.

(b) $r = \dfrac{8\pi - x}{2\pi} = 4 - \dfrac{x}{2\pi}$

(c) $h = \sqrt{16 - r^2} = \dfrac{\sqrt{16\pi x - x^2}}{2\pi}$

(d) $V = \dfrac{1}{3}\pi r^2 h = \dfrac{(8\pi - x)^2 \sqrt{16\pi x - x^2}}{24\pi^2}$

57. False. $f(-x) \ne f(x)$ **59.** B **61.** D

63. (a) For $f \circ g$:

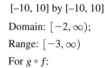

$[-10, 70]$ by $[-10, 3]$

Domain: $[0, \infty);$
Range: $[-7, \infty)$
For $g \circ f$:

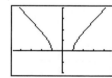

$[-3, 20]$ by $[-4, 4]$

Domain: $[7, \infty);$
Range: $[0, \infty)$

(b) $(f \circ g)(x) = \sqrt{x} - 7;$
$(g \circ f)(x) = \sqrt{x - 7}$

65. (a) For $f \circ g$:

$[-10, 10]$ by $[-10, 10]$

Domain: $[-2, \infty);$
Range: $[-3, \infty)$
For $g \circ f$:

$[-4.7, 4.7]$ by $[-2, 4]$

Domain: $(-\infty, -1] \cup [1, \infty);$
Range: $[0, \infty)$

(b) $(f \circ g)(x) = \left(\sqrt{x + 2}\right)^2 - 3$
$= x - 1, x \ge -2$
$(g \circ f)(x) = \sqrt{x^2 - 1}$

67. (a)

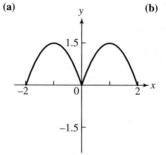

(b)

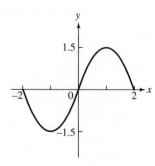

69. (a)   **(b)**

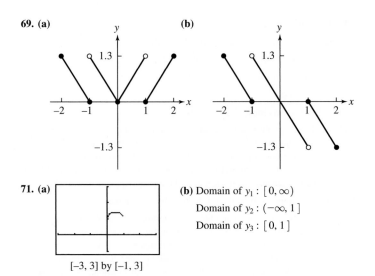

71. (a)

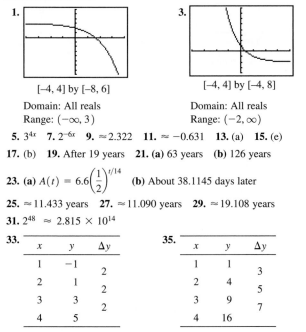

$[-3, 3]$ by $[-1, 3]$

(b) Domain of y_1 : $[0, \infty)$

Domain of y_2 : $(-\infty, 1]$

Domain of y_3 : $[0, 1]$

(c) The results for $y_1 - y_2$, $y_2 - y_1$, and $y_1 \cdot y_2$ are the same as for $y_1 + y_2$ above.

Domain of $\dfrac{y_1}{y_2}$: $[0, 1)$ Domain of $\dfrac{y_2}{y_1}$: $(0, 1]$

(d) The domain of a sum, difference, or product of two functions is the intersection of their domains.

The domain of a quotient of two functions is the intersection of their domains with any zeros of the denominator removed.

Section 1.3

Quick Review 1.3

1. 2.924   **3.** 0.192   **5.** 1.8882

7. \$630.58   **9.** $x^{-18}y^{-5} = \dfrac{1}{x^{18}y^5}$

Exercises 1.3

1.   **3.**

$[-4, 4]$ by $[-8, 6]$ $[-4, 4]$ by $[-4, 8]$

Domain: All reals   Domain: All reals

Range: $(-\infty, 3)$ Range: $(-2, \infty)$

5. 3^{4x} **7.** 2^{-6x} **9.** ≈ 2.322 **11.** ≈ -0.631 **13.** (a)   **15.** (e)

17. (b)   **19.** After 19 years   **21. (a)** 63 years   **(b)** 126 years

23. (a) $A(t) = 6.6\left(\dfrac{1}{2}\right)^{t/14}$ **(b)** About 38.1145 days later

25. ≈ 11.433 years   **27.** ≈ 11.090 years   **29.** ≈ 19.108 years

31. $2^{48} \approx 2.815 \times 10^{14}$

33.

x	y	Δy
1	-1	
		2
2	1	
		2
3	3	
		2
4	5	

35.

x	y	Δy
1	1	
		3
2	4	
		5
3	9	
		7
4	16	

37. Since $\Delta x = 1$, the corresponding value of Δy is equal to the slope of the line. If the changes in x are constant for a linear function, then the corresponding changes in y are constant as well.

39. $a = 4$ and $b = 3/2$ **41.** False. It is positive $1/9$

43. D   **45.** B

47. (a)

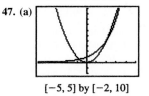

$[-5, 5]$ by $[-2, 10]$

In this window, it appears they cross twice, although a third crossing off-screen appears likely.

(b)

x	change in $Y1$	change in $Y2$
1		
	3	2
2		
	5	4
3		
	7	8
4		

(c) $x = -0.7667, x = 2, x = 4$ **(d)** $(-0.7667, 2) \cup (4, \infty)$

49. $a = 0.5, k = 3$

Quick Quiz (Sections 1.1–1.3)

1. C   **3.** E

Section 1.4

Quick Review 1.4

1. $y = -\dfrac{5}{3}x + \dfrac{29}{3}$ **3.** $x = 2$

5. x-intercepts: $x = -4$ and $x = 4$; y-intercepts: none

7. (a) Yes   **(b)** No   **(c)** Yes

9. (a) $t = \dfrac{-2x - 5}{3}$ **(b)** $t = \dfrac{3y + 1}{2}$

Exercises 1.4

1. Graph (c). Window: $[-4, 4]$ by $[-3, 3], 0 \le t \le 2\pi$

3. Graph (d). Window: $[-10, 10]$ by $[-10, 10], 0 \le t \le 2\pi$

5. (a)   **7. (a)**

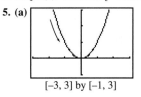   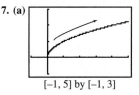

$[-3, 3]$ by $[-1, 3]$ $[-1, 5]$ by $[-1, 3]$

No initial or terminal point   Initial point: $(0, 0)$

Terminal point: None

(b) $y = x^2$; all   **(b)** $y = \sqrt{x}$; all (or $x = y^2$; upper half)

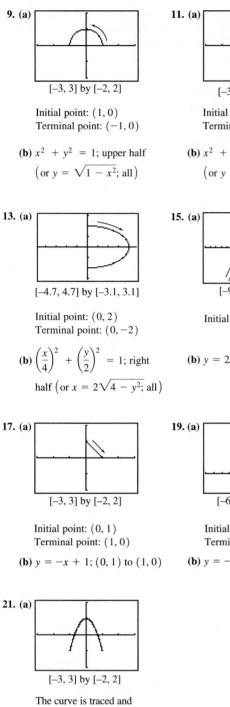

9. (a)

[−3, 3] by [−2, 2]

Initial point: $(1, 0)$
Terminal point: $(−1, 0)$

(b) $x^2 + y^2 = 1$; upper half
$\left(\text{or } y = \sqrt{1 − x^2}; \text{all}\right)$

11. (a)

[−3, 3] by [−2, 2]

Initial point: $(−1, 0)$
Terminal point: $(0, 1)$

(b) $x^2 + y^2 = 1$; upper half
$\left(\text{or } y = \sqrt{1 − x^2}; \text{all}\right)$

13. (a)

[−4.7, 4.7] by [−3.1, 3.1]

Initial point: $(0, 2)$
Terminal point: $(0, −2)$

(b) $\left(\dfrac{x}{4}\right)^2 + \left(\dfrac{y}{2}\right)^2 = 1$; right

half $\left(\text{or } x = 2\sqrt{4 − y^2}; \text{all}\right)$

15. (a)

[−9, 9] by [−6, 6]

Initial and terminal point: $(0, 5)$

(b) $y = 2x + 3$; all

17. (a)

[−3, 3] by [−2, 2]

Initial point: $(0, 1)$
Terminal point: $(1, 0)$

(b) $y = −x + 1$; $(0, 1)$ to $(1, 0)$

19. (a)

[−6, 6] by [−2, 6]

Initial point: $(4, 0)$
Terminal point: None

(b) $y = −x + 4$; $x \leq 4$

21. (a)

[−3, 3] by [−2, 2]

The curve is traced and
retraced in both directions,
and there is no initial or
terminal point.

(b) $y = −2x^2 + 1$; $−1 \leq x \leq 1$

23. Possible answer: $x = −1 + 5t, y = −3 + 4t, 0 \leq t \leq 1$
25. Possible answer: $x = t^2 + 1, y = t, t \leq 0$
27. Possible answer: $x = 2 − 3t, y = 3 − 4t, t \geq 0$
29. $1 < t < 3$ **31.** $−5 \leq t < −3$
33. Possible answer: $x = t, y = t^2 + 2t + 2, t > 0$

35. Possible answers:

(a) $x = a \cos t, y = −a \sin t, 0 \leq t \leq 2\pi$

(b) $x = a \cos t, y = a \sin t, 0 \leq t \leq 2\pi$

(c) $x = a \cos t, y = −a \sin t, 0 \leq t \leq 4\pi$

(d) $x = a \cos t, y = a \sin t, 0 \leq t \leq 4\pi$

37. False. It is an ellipse.   **39.** D   **41.** A

43. (a) The resulting graph appears to be the right half of a hyperbola in the
first and fourth quadrants. The parameter a determines the x-intercept.
The parameter b determines the shape of the hyperbola. If b is
smaller, the graph has less steep slopes and appears "sharper." If b is
larger, the slopes are steeper and the graph appears more "blunt."

(b) This appears to be the left half of the same hyperbola.

(c) The functions sec t and tan t both approach vertical asymptotes at
odd multiples of $\pi/2$, but the limits are $−\infty$ on one side and ∞ on
the other. This causes the graph to disappear off one corner of the
screen and reappear from the opposite corner, trailing the line in an
attempt to keep the graph "connected." For example, as t approaches
$\pi/2$ from the left, both sec t and tan t approach $+\infty$, so the graph
disappears in quadrant I (the upper-right corner). On the other side
of $\pi/2$, both limits are $−\infty$, so the graph reappears in quadrant III
(from the lower left corner).

(d) $\left(\dfrac{x}{a}\right)^2 − \left(\dfrac{y}{b}\right)^2 = (\sec t)^2 − (\tan t)^2 = 1$ by a standard trigonomet-

ric identity.

(e) This changes the orientation of the hyperbola. In this case, b determines the y-intercept of the hyperbola, and a determines the shape.

The parameter interval $\left(−\dfrac{\pi}{2}, \dfrac{\pi}{2}\right)$ gives the upper half of the hyper-

bola. The parameter interval $\left(\dfrac{\pi}{2}, \dfrac{3\pi}{2}\right)$ gives the lower half. The

same values of t cause discontinuities and may add extraneous lines
to the graph.

45. (a)

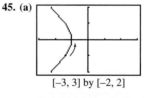

[−3, 3] by [−2, 2]

No initial or terminal point

(b) $x^2 − y^2 = 1$; left branch
$\left(\text{or } x = −\sqrt{y^2 + 1}; \text{all}\right)$

47. $x = 2 \cot t, y = 2 \sin^2 t, 0 < t < \pi$

Section 1.5

Quick Review 1.5

1. 1   **3.** $x^{2/3}$

5. Possible answer: $x = t, y = \dfrac{1}{t − 1}, t \geq 2$

7. $(4, 5)$ **9. (a)** $(1.58, 3)$ **(b)** No intersection

Exercises 1.5

1. No   **3.** Yes   **5.** Yes   **7.** Yes   **9.** No   **11.** No

13. $f^{-1}(x) = \dfrac{x − 3}{2}$ **15.** $f^{-1}(x) = (x + 1)^{1/3}$ or $\sqrt[3]{x + 1}$

17. $f^{-1}(x) = -x^{1/2}$ or $-\sqrt{x}$

19. $f^{-1}(x) = 2 - (-x)^{1/2}$ or $2 - \sqrt{-x}$

21. $f^{-1}(x) = \dfrac{1}{x^{1/2}}$ or $\dfrac{1}{\sqrt{x}}$ **23.** $f^{-1}(x) = \dfrac{1 - 3x}{x - 2}$

25.

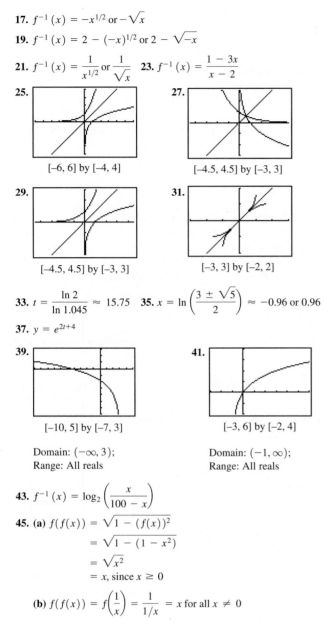

[–6, 6] by [–4, 4]

27.

[–4.5, 4.5] by [–3, 3]

29.

[–4.5, 4.5] by [–3, 3]

31.

[–3, 3] by [–2, 2]

33. $t = \dfrac{\ln 2}{\ln 1.045} \approx 15.75$ **35.** $x = \ln\left(\dfrac{3 \pm \sqrt{5}}{2}\right) \approx -0.96$ or 0.96

37. $y = e^{2t+4}$

39.

[–10, 5] by [–7, 3]

Domain: $(-\infty, 3)$;
Range: All reals

41.

[–3, 6] by [–2, 4]

Domain: $(-1, \infty)$;
Range: All reals

43. $f^{-1}(x) = \log_2\left(\dfrac{x}{100 - x}\right)$

45. (a) $f(f(x)) = \sqrt{1 - (f(x))^2}$
$= \sqrt{1 - (1 - x^2)}$
$= \sqrt{x^2}$
$= x$, since $x \geq 0$

(b) $f(f(x)) = f\left(\dfrac{1}{x}\right) = \dfrac{1}{1/x} = x$ for all $x \neq 0$

47. About 14.936 years. (If the interest is only paid annually, it will take 15 years.)

49. (a) All other values of t will make one of the expressions under the radicals negative.

(b) Every point of the form $\left(\sqrt{2 - t}, \sqrt{2 + t}\right)$ is at distance 4 from the origin.

(c) $(2, 0)$ at $t = -2$ and $(0, 2)$ at $t = 2$.

(d) Both radicals are positive.

(e) The curve is a quarter-circle of radius 4 centered at the origin.

51. (a) Suppose that $f(x_1) = f(x_2)$. Then $mx_1 + b = mx_2 + b$, which gives $x_1 = x_2$ since $m \neq 0$.

(b) $f^{-1}(x) = \dfrac{x - b}{m}$; the slopes are reciprocals.

(c) They are also parallel lines with nonzero slope.

(d) They are also perpendicular lines with nonzero slope.

53. False. Consider $f(x) = x^2$, $g(x) = \sqrt{x}$. Notice that $(f \circ g)(x) = x$ but f is not one-to-one.

55. A   **57.** B

59. If the graph of $f(x)$ passes the horizontal line test, so will the graph of $g(x) = -f(x)$, since it's the same graph reflected about the x-axis.

61. (a) Domain: All reals
Range: If $a > 0$, then (d, ∞)
If $a < 0$, then $(-\infty, d)$

(b) Domain: (c, ∞)
Range: All reals

Section 1.6

Quick Review 1.6

1. $60°$ **3.** $-\dfrac{2\pi}{9}$

5. $x \approx 0.6435$, $x \approx 2.4981$

7. $x \approx 0.7854\left(\text{or }\dfrac{\pi}{4}\right)$, $x \approx 3.9270\left(\text{or }\dfrac{5\pi}{4}\right)$

9. $f(-x) = (-x)^3 - 3(-x) = -x^3 + 3x$
$= -(x^3 - 3x) = -f(x)$
The graph is symmetric about the origin because if a point (a, b) is on the graph, then so is the point $(-a, -b)$.

Exercises 1.6

1. $\dfrac{5\pi}{4}$ **3.** $\dfrac{1}{2}$ radian or $\approx 28.65°$ **5.** Even   **7.** Odd

9. $\sin \theta = 8/17$, $\tan \theta = -8/15$, $\csc \theta = 17/8$,
$\sec \theta = -17/15$, $\cot \theta = -15/8$

11. (a) $\dfrac{2\pi}{3}$

(b) $x \neq \dfrac{k\pi}{3}$, for integers k

(c) $(-\infty, -5] \cup [1, \infty)$

(d)

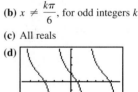

$\left[-\dfrac{2\pi}{3}, \dfrac{2\pi}{3}\right]$ by $[-8, 8]$

13. (a) $\dfrac{\pi}{3}$

(b) $x \neq \dfrac{k\pi}{6}$, for odd integers k

(c) All reals

(d)

$\left[-\dfrac{\pi}{2}, \dfrac{\pi}{2}\right]$ by $[-8, 8]$

15. Possible answers are:

(a) $[0, 4\pi]$ by $[-3, 3]$ (b) $[0, 4\pi]$ by $[-3, 3]$

(c) $[0, 2\pi]$ by $[-3, 3]$

17. (a) π (b) 1.5   (c) $[-2\pi, 2\pi]$ by $[-2, 2]$

19. (a) π (b) 3   (c) $[-2\pi, 2\pi]$ by $[-4, 4]$

21. (a) 6   (b) 4   (c) $[-3, 3]$ by $[-5, 5]$

23. (a) 330 Hz   (b) E

25. The portion of the curve $y = \cos x$ between $0 \leq x \leq \pi$ passes the horizontal line test, so it is one-to-one.

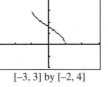

[–3, 3] by [–2, 4]

27. $\frac{\pi}{6}$ radian or 30°   **29.** ≈ -1.3734 radians or $-78.6901°$

31. $x \approx 1.190$ and $x \approx 4.332$

33. $x = \frac{\pi}{6}$ and $x = \frac{5\pi}{6}$

35. $x = \frac{7\pi}{6} + 2k\pi$ and $x = \frac{11\pi}{6} + 2k\pi$, k any integer

37. $\cos\theta = \frac{15}{17}$ $\sin\theta = \frac{8}{17}$ $\tan\theta = \frac{8}{15}$

$\sec\theta = \frac{17}{15}$ $\csc\theta = \frac{17}{8}$ $\cot\theta = \frac{15}{8}$

39. $\cos\theta = -\frac{3}{5}$ $\sin\theta = \frac{4}{5}$ $\tan\theta = -\frac{4}{3}$

$\sec\theta = -\frac{5}{3}$ $\csc\theta = \frac{5}{4}$ $\cot\theta = -\frac{3}{4}$

41. $\frac{\sqrt{72}}{11} \approx 0.771$ **43.** $A = -19.75$, $B = \pi/6$, and $C = 60.25$

45. (a) $\cot(-x) = \dfrac{\cos(-x)}{\sin(-x)} = \dfrac{\cos(x)}{-\sin(x)} = -\cot(x)$

(b) Assume that f is even and g is odd.

Then $\dfrac{f(-x)}{g(-x)} = \dfrac{f(x)}{-g(x)} = -\dfrac{f(x)}{g(x)}$ so $\dfrac{f}{g}$ is odd.

The situation is similar for $\dfrac{g}{f}$.

47. Assume that f is even and g is odd.
Then $f(-x)\,g(-x) = f(x)[-g(x)] = -f(x)g(x)$ so fg is odd.

49. (a) No, 2π **(b)** Yes, π

(c) $y = (\sin x)(\cos x) = \dfrac{1}{2}\sin 2x$

In general, a product of sinusoids is a sinusoid if they both have the same period.

51. False. The amplitude is $1/2$.

53. B   **55.** A

57. (a) $\sqrt{2}\sin\left(ax + \dfrac{\pi}{4}\right)$ **(b)** See part **(a)**.   **(c)** It works.

(d) $\sin\left(ax + \dfrac{\pi}{4}\right)$

$= \sin(ax) \cdot \dfrac{1}{\sqrt{2}} + \cos(ax) \cdot \dfrac{1}{\sqrt{2}}$

$= \dfrac{1}{\sqrt{2}}(\sin ax + \cos ax)$

So, $\sin(ax) + \cos(ax) = \sqrt{2}\sin\left(ax + \dfrac{\pi}{4}\right)$.

59. Since $\sin(x)$ has period 2π, $(\sin(x + 2\pi))^3 = (\sin(x))^3$.
This function has period 2π. A graph shows that no smaller number works for the period.

61. One possible graph:

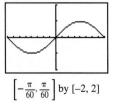

$\left[-\dfrac{\pi}{60}, \dfrac{\pi}{60}\right]$ by $[-2, 2]$

Quick Quiz (Sections 1.4–1.6)

1. C   **3.** E

Review Exercises

1. $y = 3x - 9$ **2.** $y = -\dfrac{1}{2}x + \dfrac{3}{2}$ **3.** $x = 0$ **4.** $y = -2x$

5. $y = 2$ **6.** $y = -\dfrac{2}{5}x + \dfrac{21}{5}$ **7.** $y = -3x + 3$ **8.** $y = 2x - 5$

9. $y = -\dfrac{4}{3}x - \dfrac{20}{3}$ **10.** $y = -\dfrac{5}{3}x - \dfrac{19}{3}$ **11.** $y = \dfrac{2}{3}x + \dfrac{8}{3}$

12. $y = \dfrac{5}{3}x - 5$ **13.** $y = -\dfrac{1}{2}x + 3$ **14.** $y = -\dfrac{2}{7}x - \dfrac{6}{7}$

15. Origin   **16.** y-axis   **17.** Neither   **18.** y-axis

19. Even   **20.** Odd   **21.** Even   **22.** Odd   **23.** Odd

24. Neither   **25.** Neither   **26.** Even

27. (a) Domain: All reals

(b) Range: $[-2, \infty)$

(c)

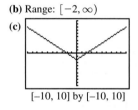

$[-10, 10]$ by $[-10, 10]$

28. (a) Domain: $(-\infty, 1]$

(b) Range $[-2, \infty)$

(c)

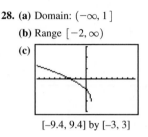

$[-9.4, 9.4]$ by $[-3, 3]$

29. (a) Domain: $[-4, 4]$

(b) Range: $[0, 4]$

(c)

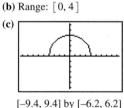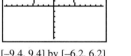

$[-9.4, 9.4]$ by $[-6.2, 6.2]$

30. (a) Domain: All reals

(b) Range: $(1, \infty)$

(c)

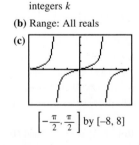

$[-6, 6]$ by $[-4, 20]$

31. (a) Domain: All reals

(b) Range: $(-3, \infty)$

(c)

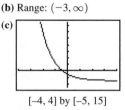

$[-4, 4]$ by $[-5, 15]$

32. (a) Domain: $x \neq \dfrac{k\pi}{4}$, for odd integers k

(b) Range: All reals

(c)

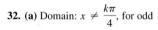

$\left[-\dfrac{\pi}{2}, \dfrac{\pi}{2}\right]$ by $[-8, 8]$

33. (a) Domain: All reals

(b) Range: $[-3, 1]$

(c)

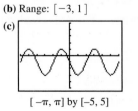

$[-\pi, \pi]$ by $[-5, 5]$

34. (a) Domain: All reals

(b) Range: $[0, \infty)$

(c)

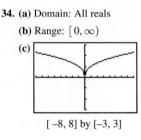

$[-8, 8]$ by $[-3, 3]$

35. (a) Domain: $(3, \infty)$
(b) Range: All reals
(c)

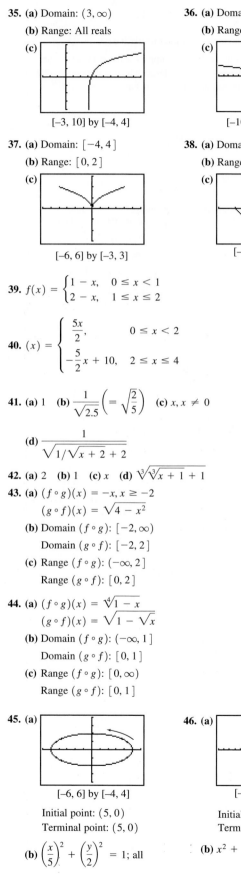

$[-3, 10]$ by $[-4, 4]$

36. (a) Domain: All reals
(b) Range: All reals
(c)

$[-10, 10]$ by $[-4, 4]$

37. (a) Domain: $[-4, 4]$
(b) Range: $[0, 2]$
(c)

$[-6, 6]$ by $[-3, 3]$

38. (a) Domain: $[-2, 2]$
(b) Range: $[-1, 1]$
(c)

$[-3, 3]$ by $[-2, 2]$

39. $f(x) = \begin{cases} 1 - x, & 0 \le x < 1 \\ 2 - x, & 1 \le x \le 2 \end{cases}$

40. $(x) = \begin{cases} \dfrac{5x}{2}, & 0 \le x < 2 \\ -\dfrac{5}{2}x + 10, & 2 \le x \le 4 \end{cases}$

41. (a) 1 **(b)** $\dfrac{1}{\sqrt{2.5}}\left(= \sqrt{\dfrac{2}{5}}\right)$ **(c)** $x, x \ne 0$

(d) $\dfrac{1}{\sqrt{1/\sqrt{x + 2} + 2}}$

42. (a) 2 **(b)** 1 **(c)** x **(d)** $\sqrt[3]{\sqrt[3]{\sqrt[3]{x + 1} + 1}}$

43. (a) $(f \circ g)(x) = -x, x \ge -2$
$(g \circ f)(x) = \sqrt{4 - x^2}$
(b) Domain $(f \circ g)$: $[-2, \infty)$
Domain $(g \circ f)$: $[-2, 2]$
(c) Range $(f \circ g)$: $(-\infty, 2]$
Range $(g \circ f)$: $[0, 2]$

44. (a) $(f \circ g)(x) = \sqrt[4]{1 - x}$
$(g \circ f)(x) = \sqrt{1 - \sqrt{x}}$
(b) Domain $(f \circ g)$: $(-\infty, 1]$
Domain $(g \circ f)$: $[0, 1]$
(c) Range $(f \circ g)$: $[0, \infty)$
Range $(g \circ f)$: $[0, 1]$

45. (a)

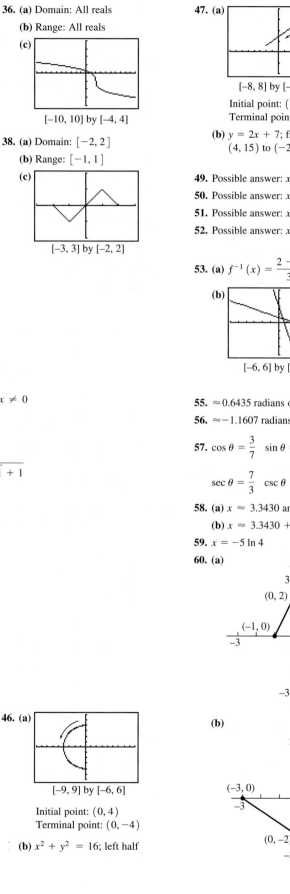

$[-6, 6]$ by $[-4, 4]$

Initial point: $(5, 0)$
Terminal point: $(5, 0)$

(b) $\left(\dfrac{x}{5}\right)^2 + \left(\dfrac{y}{2}\right)^2 = 1$; all

46. (a)

$[-9, 9]$ by $[-6, 6]$

Initial point: $(0, 4)$
Terminal point: $(0, -4)$

(b) $x^2 + y^2 = 16$; left half

47. (a)

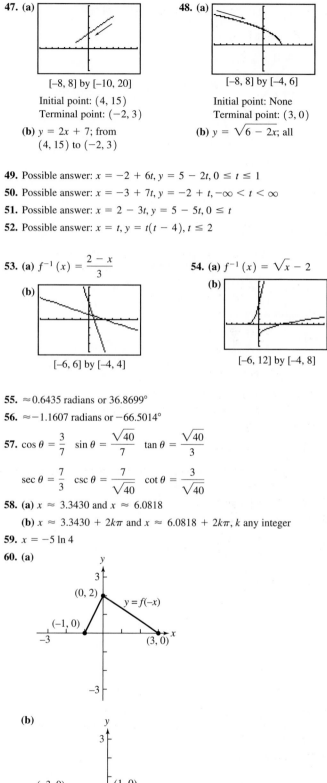

$[-8, 8]$ by $[-10, 20]$

Initial point: $(4, 15)$
Terminal point: $(-2, 3)$

(b) $y = 2x + 7$; from $(4, 15)$ to $(-2, 3)$

48. (a)

$[-8, 8]$ by $[-4, 6]$

Initial point: None
Terminal point: $(3, 0)$

(b) $y = \sqrt{6 - 2x}$; all

49. Possible answer: $x = -2 + 6t, y = 5 - 2t, 0 \le t \le 1$
50. Possible answer: $x = -3 + 7t, y = -2 + t, -\infty < t < \infty$
51. Possible answer: $x = 2 - 3t, y = 5 - 5t, 0 \le t$
52. Possible answer: $x = t, y = t(t - 4), t \le 2$

53. (a) $f^{-1}(x) = \dfrac{2 - x}{3}$
(b)

$[-6, 6]$ by $[-4, 4]$

54. (a) $f^{-1}(x) = \sqrt{x} - 2$
(b)

$[-6, 12]$ by $[-4, 8]$

55. ≈ 0.6435 radians or $36.8699°$
56. ≈ -1.1607 radians or $-66.5014°$

57. $\cos\theta = \dfrac{3}{7}$ $\sin\theta = \dfrac{\sqrt{40}}{7}$ $\tan\theta = \dfrac{\sqrt{40}}{3}$

$\sec\theta = \dfrac{7}{3}$ $\csc\theta = \dfrac{7}{\sqrt{40}}$ $\cot\theta = \dfrac{3}{\sqrt{40}}$

58. (a) $x \approx 3.3430$ and $x \approx 6.0818$
(b) $x \approx 3.3430 + 2k\pi$ and $x \approx 6.0818 + 2k\pi$, k any integer

59. $x = -5 \ln 4$

60. (a)

$(0, 2)$
$y = f(-x)$
$(-1, 0)$
-3
$(3, 0)$

(b)

$(-3, 0)$
$(1, 0)$
-3
3
$y = -f(x)$
$(0, -2)$
-3

(c)

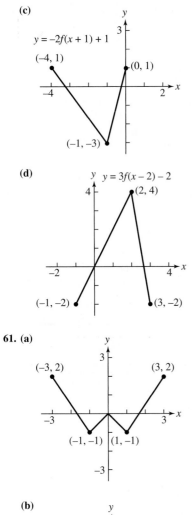

$y = -2f(x + 1) + 1$

(d)

$y \quad y = 3f(x - 2) - 2$

61. (a)

(b)

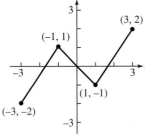

62. (a) $100{,}000 - 10{,}000x, \ 0 \le x \le 10$

(b) After 4.5 years

63. (a) 90 units

(b) $90 - 52 \ln 3 \approx 32.8722$ units

(c)

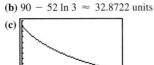

$[0, 4]$ by $[-20, 100]$

64. After $\dfrac{\ln (10/3)}{\ln 1.08} \approx 15.6439$ years

(If the bank pays interest only at the end of the year, it will take 16 years.)

65. (a) $N = 4 \cdot 2^t$ **(b)** 4 days: 64; 1 week: 512

(c) After $\dfrac{\ln 500}{\ln 2} \approx 8.9658$ days, or after nearly 9 days

(d) Because it suggests the number of guppies will continue to double indefinitely and become arbitrarily large, which is impossible due to the finite size of the tank and the oxygen supply in the water.

66. (a) $t = \dfrac{\ln 2}{r} \approx \dfrac{0.69}{r}$

(b) Note that $r = R/100$, so $t = \dfrac{\ln 2}{R/100} = \dfrac{100 \ln 2}{R} \approx \dfrac{69}{R}$

(c) Doubling time $t \approx \dfrac{69 + 1}{R} = \dfrac{70}{R}$

67. Since 72 is evenly divisible by so many integer factors, people find it easier to approximate the doubling time by using $72/R$ than by using $70/R$.

68. (a) $m = -1$ **(b)** $y = -x - 1$ **(c)** $y = x + 3$ **(d)** 2

69. (a) $(2, \infty)$ **(b)** $(-\infty, \infty)$ **(c)** $x = 2 + e \approx 4.718$

(d) $f^{-1}(x) = 2 + e^{1-x}$

(e) $(f \circ f^{-1})(x) = f(f^{-1}(x)) = f(2 + e^{1-x}) = 1 - \ln (2 + e^{1-x} - 2)$
$$= 1 - \ln (e^{1-x})$$
$$= 1 - (1 - x)$$
$$= x$$

$(f^{-1} \circ f)(x) = f^{-1}(f(x)) = f^{-1}(1 - \ln (x - 2)) = 2 + e^{1-(1-\ln (x-2))}$
$$= 2 + e^{\ln (x-2)}$$
$$= 2 + (x - 2)$$
$$= x$$

70. (a) $(-\infty, \infty)$ **(b)** $[-2, 4]$ **(c)** π **(d)** Even

(e) $x \approx 2.526$

CHAPTER 2

Section 2.1

Quick Review 2.1

1. 0 **3.** 0 **5.** $-4 < x < 4$ **7.** $-1 < x < 5$ **9.** $x - 6$

Exercises 2.1

1. 48 ft/sec **3.** 96 ft/sec

5. $2c^3 - 3c^2 + c - 1$ **7.** $-\dfrac{3}{2}$

9. -15 **11.** 0 **13.** 4

15. (a)

x	-0.1	-0.01	-0.001	-0.0001
$f(x)$	1.566667	1.959697	1.995997	1.999600

(b)

x	0.1	0.01	0.001	0.0001
$f(x)$	2.372727	2.039703	2.003997	2.000400

The limit appears to be 2.

17. (a)

x	-0.1	-0.01	-0.001	-0.0001
$f(x)$	-0.054402	-0.005064	-0.000827	-0.000031

(b)

x	0.1	0.01	0.001	0.0001
$f(x)$	-0.054402	-0.005064	-0.000827	-0.000031

The limit appears to be 0.

19. (a)

x	-0.1	-0.01	-0.001	-0.0001
$f(x)$	2.0567	2.2763	2.2999	2.3023

(b)

x	0.1	0.01	0.001	0.0001
$f(x)$	2.5893	2.3293	2.3052	2.3029

The limit appears to be approximately 2.3.

21. Expression not defined at $x = -2$. There is no limit.

23. Expression not defined at $x = 0$. There is no limit.

25. $\dfrac{1}{2}$ **27.** $-\dfrac{1}{2}$ **29.** 12   **31.** -1 **33.** 0

35. Answers will vary. One possible graph is given by the window $[-4.7, 4.7]$ by $[-15, 15]$ with Xscl = 1 and Yscl = 5.

37. 0   **39.** 0   **41.** 1

43. (a) True   **(b)** True   **(c)** False   **(d)** True   **(e)** True
(f) True   **(g)** False   **(h)** False   **(i)** False   **(j)** False

45. (a) 3   **(b)** -2 **(c)** No limit   **(d)** 1

47. (a) -4 **(b)** -4 **(c)** -4 **(d)** -4

49. (a) 4   **(b)** -3 **(c)** No limit   **(d)** 4

51. (c)   **53.** (d)

55. (a) 6   **(b)** 0   **(c)** 9   **(d)** -3

57. (a)

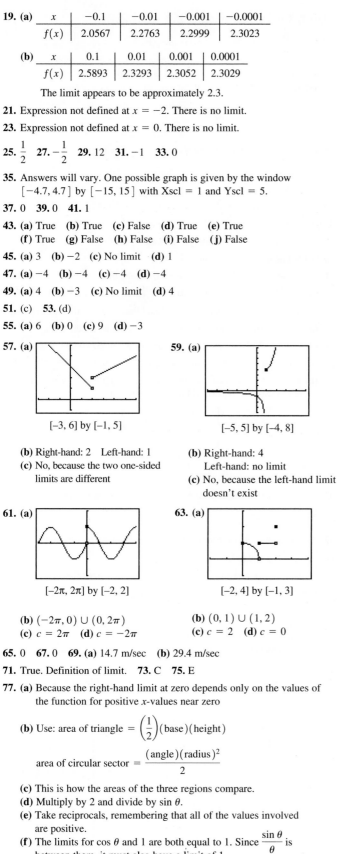

$[-3, 6]$ by $[-1, 5]$

59. (a)

$[-5, 5]$ by $[-4, 8]$

(b) Right-hand: 2   Left-hand: 1
(c) No, because the two one-sided limits are different

(b) Right-hand: 4
Left-hand: no limit
(c) No, because the left-hand limit doesn't exist

61. (a)

$[-2\pi, 2\pi]$ by $[-2, 2]$

63. (a)

$[-2, 4]$ by $[-1, 3]$

(b) $(-2\pi, 0) \cup (0, 2\pi)$
(c) $c = 2\pi$ **(d)** $c = -2\pi$

(b) $(0, 1) \cup (1, 2)$
(c) $c = 2$ **(d)** $c = 0$

65. 0   **67.** 0   **69. (a)** 14.7 m/sec   **(b)** 29.4 m/sec

71. True. Definition of limit.   **73.** C   **75.** E

77. (a) Because the right-hand limit at zero depends only on the values of the function for positive x-values near zero

(b) Use: area of triangle $= \left(\dfrac{1}{2}\right)(\text{base})(\text{height})$

area of circular sector $= \dfrac{(\text{angle})(\text{radius})^2}{2}$

(c) This is how the areas of the three regions compare.
(d) Multiply by 2 and divide by $\sin \theta$.
(e) Take reciprocals, remembering that all of the values involved are positive.
(f) The limits for $\cos \theta$ and 1 are both equal to 1. Since $\dfrac{\sin \theta}{\theta}$ is between them, it must also have a limit of 1.
(g) $\dfrac{\sin (-\theta)}{-\theta} = \dfrac{-\sin (\theta)}{-\theta} = \dfrac{\sin (\theta)}{\theta}$

(h) If the function is symmetric about the y-axis, and the right-hand limit at zero is 1, then the left-hand limit at zero must also be 1.
(i) The two one-sided limits both exist and are equal to 1.

79. (a) $f\left(\dfrac{\pi}{6}\right) = \dfrac{1}{2}$

(b) One possible answer: $a = 0.305, b = 0.775$
(c) One possible answer: $a = 0.513, b = 0.535$

Section 2.2

Quick Review 2.2

1. $f^{-1}(x) = \dfrac{x + 3}{2}$

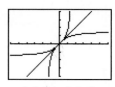

$[-12, 12]$ by $[-8, 8]$

3. $f^{-1}(x) = \tan (x), -\dfrac{\pi}{2} < x < \dfrac{\pi}{2}$

$[-6, 6]$ by $[-4, 4]$

5. $q(x) = \dfrac{2}{3}$

$r(x) = -3x^2 - \left(\dfrac{5}{3}\right)x + \dfrac{7}{3}$

7. (a) $f(-x) = \cos x$ **(b)** $f\left(\dfrac{1}{x}\right) = \cos \left(\dfrac{1}{x}\right)$

9. (a) $f(-x) = -\dfrac{\ln |x|}{x}$ **(b)** $f\left(\dfrac{1}{x}\right) = -x \ln |x|$

Exercises 2.2

1. (a) 1   **(b)** 1   **(c)** $y = 1$

3. (a) 0   **(b)** $-\infty$ **(c)** $y = 0$

5. (a) 3   **(b)** -3 **(c)** $y = 3, y = -3$

7. (a) 1   **(b)** -1 **(c)** $y = 1, y = -1$

9. 0   **11.** 0   **13.** ∞ **15.** $-\infty$

17. 0   **19.** ∞ **21.** Both are 1.   **23.** Both are 1.   **25.** Both are -2.

27. (a) $x = -2, x = 2$
(b) Left-hand limit at -2 is ∞.
Right-hand limit at -2 is $-\infty$.
Left-hand limit at 2 is $-\infty$.
Right-hand limit at 2 is ∞.

29. (a) $x = -1$
(b) Left-hand limit at -1 is $-\infty$.
Right-hand limit at -1 is ∞.

31. (a) $x = k\pi$, k any integer
(b) At each vertical asymptote:
Left-hand limit is $-\infty$.
Right-hand limit is ∞.

33. Vertical asymptotes at $a = (4k + 1)\dfrac{\pi}{2}$ and $b = (4k + 3)\dfrac{\pi}{2}$,

k any integer.

$\lim_{x \to a^-} f(x) = \infty, \lim_{x \to a^+} f(x) = -\infty, \lim_{x \to b^-} f(x) = -\infty,$
$\lim_{x \to b^+} f(x) = \infty$

35. (a) **37.** (d) **39.** (a) $3x^2$ **(b)** None

41. (a) $\dfrac{1}{2x}$ **(b)** $y = 0$ **43.** (a) $4x^2$ **(b)** None

45. (a) e^x **(b)** $-2x$ **47.** (a) x **(b)** x

49. At ∞: ∞ At $-\infty$: 0

51. At ∞: 0 At $-\infty$: 0

53. (a) 0 **(b)** -1 **(c)** $-\infty$ **(d)** -1

55. One possible answer:

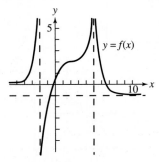

57. $\dfrac{f_1(x)/f_2(x)}{g_1(x)/g_2(x)} = \dfrac{f_1(x)/g_1(x)}{f_2(x)/g_2(x)}$. As x goes to infinity, $\dfrac{f_1}{g_1}$ and $\dfrac{f_2}{g_2}$

both approach 1. Therefore, using the above equation, $\dfrac{f_1/f_2}{g_1/g_2}$ must also

approach 1.

59. True. For example, $f(x) = \dfrac{x}{\sqrt{x^2 + 1}}$ has $y = \pm 1$ as horizontal

asymptotes.

61. A **63.** C

65. (a) $f \to -\infty$ as $x \to 0^-, f \to \infty$ as $x \to 0^-, g \to 0, fg \to 1$

(b) $f \to \infty$ as $x \to 0^-, f \to -\infty$ as $x \to 0^+, g \to 0, fg \to -8$

(c) $f \to -\infty$ as $x \to 2^-, f \to \infty$ as $x \to 2^+, g \to 0, fg \to 0$

(d) $x \to \infty, g \to 0, fg \to \infty$

(e) Nothing—you need more information to decide.

67. For $x > 0, 0 < e^{-x} < 1$, so $0 < \dfrac{e^{-x}}{x} < \dfrac{1}{x}$.

Since both 0 and $\dfrac{1}{x}$ approach zero as $x \to \infty$, the Squeeze

Theorem states that $\dfrac{e^{-x}}{x}$ must also approach zero.

69. Limit $= 2$, because $\dfrac{\ln x^2}{\ln x} = \dfrac{2 \ln x}{\ln x} = 2$.

71. Limit $= 1$. Since

$\ln (x + 1) = \ln x \left(1 + \dfrac{1}{x}\right) = \ln x + \ln \left(1 + \dfrac{1}{x}\right)$,

$\dfrac{\ln (x + 1)}{\ln x} = \dfrac{\ln x + \ln (1 + 1/x)}{\ln x} = 1 + \dfrac{\ln (1 + 1/x)}{\ln x}$.

But as $x \to \infty, 1 + \dfrac{1}{x}$ approaches 1, so $\ln \left(1 + \dfrac{1}{x}\right)$ approaches

$\ln (1) = 0$. Also, as $x \to \infty, \ln x$ approaches infinity. This means the
second term above approaches 0 and the limit is 1.

Section 2.3

Quick Review 2.3

1. 2 **3.** (a) 1 **(b)** 2 **(c)** No limit **(d)** 2

5. $g(x) = \sin x, x \geq 0$ $(f \circ g)(x) = \sin^2 x, x \geq 0$

7. $x = \dfrac{1}{2}, -5$ **9.** $x = 1$

Exercises 2.3

1. $x = -2$, infinite discontinuity **3.** None

5. All points not in the domain, i.e., all $x < -3/2$

7. $x = 0$, jump discontinuity **9.** $x = 0$, infinite discontinuity

11. (a) Yes **(b)** Yes **(c)** Yes **(d)** Yes **13.** (a) No **(b)** No **15.** 0

17. No, because the right-hand and left-hand limits are not the same at zero

19. (a) $x = 2$ **(b)** Not removable; the one-sided limits are different.

21. (a) $x = 1$ **(b)** Not removable; it's an infinite discontinuity.

23. (a) All points not in the domain along with $x = 0, 1$

(b) $x = 0$ is a removable discontinuity; assign $f(0) = 0, x = 1$ is not
removable; the two-sided limits are different.

25. $y = x - 3$ **27.** $y = \begin{cases} \dfrac{\sin x}{x}, & x \neq 0 \\ 1, & x = 0 \end{cases}$ **29.** $y = \sqrt{x} + 2$

31. The domain of f is all real numbers $x \neq 3$. f is continuous at all those
points, so f is a continuous function.

33. f is the composite of two continuous functions $g \circ h$ where $g(x) = \sqrt{x}$

and $h(x) = \dfrac{x}{x + 1}$.

35. f is the composite of three continuous functions $g \circ h \circ k$ where

$g(x) = \cos x, h(x) = \sqrt[3]{x}$, and $k(x) = 1 - x$.

37. Assume $y = x$, constant functions, and the square root function are
continuous.

Use the sum, composite, and quotient theorems.

Domain: $(-2, \infty)$

39. Assume $y = x$ and the absolute value function are continuous.

Use the product, constant multiple, difference, and composite theorems.

Domain: $(-\infty, \infty)$

41. One possible answer: **43.** One possible answer:

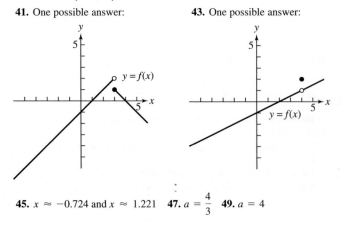

45. $x \approx -0.724$ and $x \approx 1.221$ **47.** $a = \dfrac{4}{3}$ **49.** $a = 4$

51. Consider $f(x) = x - e^{-x}$, f is continuous, $f(0) = -1$, and
$f(1) = 1 - \dfrac{1}{e} > 0.5$. By the Intermediate Value Theorem, for
some c in $(0, 1)$, $f(c) = 0$ and $e^{-c} = c$.

53. (a) $f(x) = \begin{cases} -1.10 \text{ int } (-x), & 0 \le x \le 6 \\ 7.25, & 6 < x \le 24 \end{cases}$

(b)

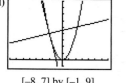

[0, 24] by [0, 9]

This is continuous at all values of x in the domain $[0, 24]$ except for
$x = 0, 1, 2, 3, 4, 5, 6$.

55. False. If f has a jump discontinuity at $x = a$, then
$\lim_{x \to a^-} f(x) \ne \lim_{x \to a} f(x)$ so f is not continuous at $x = a$.

57. E   **59.** E

61. This is because $\lim_{h \to 0} f(a + h) = \lim_{x \to a} f(x)$.

63. Since the absolute value function is continuous, this follows from the
theorem about continuity of composite functions.

Section 2.4

Quick Review 2.4

1. $\Delta x = 8$, $\Delta y = 3$ **3.** Slope $= -\dfrac{4}{7}$ **5.** $y = \dfrac{3}{2}x + 6$

7. $y = -\dfrac{3}{4}x + \dfrac{19}{4}$ **9.** $y = -\dfrac{2}{3}x + \dfrac{7}{3}$

Exercises 2.4

1. (a) 19   **(b)** 1

3. (a) $\dfrac{1 - e^{-2}}{2} \approx 0.432$ **(b)** $\dfrac{e^3 - e}{2} \approx 8.684$

5. (a) $-\dfrac{4}{\pi} \approx -1.273$ **(b)** $-\dfrac{3\sqrt{3}}{\pi} \approx -1.654$

7. Using $Q_1 = (10, 225)$, $Q_2 = (14, 375)$, $Q_3 = (16.5, 475)$,
$Q_4 = (18, 550)$, and $P = (20, 650)$

(a)

Secant	Slope
PQ_1	43
PQ_2	46
PQ_3	50
PQ_4	50

Units are meters/second.

(b) Approximately 50 m/sec

9. (a) -4 **(b)** $y = -4x - 4$ **(c)** $y = \dfrac{1}{4}x + \dfrac{9}{2}$

(d)

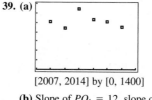

[−8, 7] by [−1, 9]

11. (a) -1 **(b)** $y = -x + 3$ **(c)** $y = x - 1$

(d)

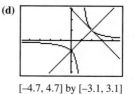

[−4.7, 4.7] by [−3.1, 3.1]

13. (a) 1   **(b)** -1

15. No. Slope from the left is -2; slope from the right is 2. The two-sided
limit of the difference quotient doesn't exist.

17. Yes. The slope is $-\dfrac{1}{4}$.

19. (a) $2a$

(b) The slope of the tangent steadily increases as a increases.

21. (a) $-\dfrac{1}{(a - 1)^2}$

(b) The slope of the tangent is always negative. The tangents are very steep
near $x = 1$ and nearly horizontal as a moves away from the origin.

23. 3 ft/sec   **25.** $-1/4$ ft/sec   **27.** 19.6 m/sec

29. 6π in²/in.   **31.** 3.72 m/sec   **33.** $(-2, -5)$

35. (a) At $x = 0$: $y = -x - 1$

At $x = 2$: $y = -x + 3$

(b) At $x = 0$: $y = x - 1$

At $x = 2$: $y = x - 1$

37. $-4/9$ degrees per mg. Additional dosage ΔD will drop temperature by
approximately $4/9 \, \Delta D$ degrees.

39. (a)

[2007, 2014] by [0, 1400]

(b) Slope of $PQ_1 = 12$, slope of $PQ_2 = -2$,
slope of $PQ_3 = -23$.

41. True. The normal line is perpendicular to the tangent line at the point.

43. D   **45.** C

47. (a) $\dfrac{e^{1+h} - e}{h}$ **(b)** Limit ≈ 2.718

(c) They're about the same.

(d) Yes, it has a tangent whose slope is about e.

49. No   **51.** Yes

53. This function has a tangent with slope zero at the origin. It is squeezed
between two functions, $y = x^2$ and $y = -x^2$, both of which have slope
zero at the origin.

Looking at the difference quotient, $-h \le \dfrac{f(0 + h) - f(0)}{h} \le h$,

so the Squeeze Theorem tells us that the limit is 0.

55. Slope ≈ 0.540

57. If $x = a + h$, then $x - a = h$. Replacing $f(a + h)$ by $f(x)$ and h by
$x - a$ turns the first expression given for the difference quotient into the
second expression.

Quick Quiz (Sections 2.3 and 2.4)

1. D   **3.** B

Review Exercises

1. -15 **2.** $\dfrac{5}{21}$ **3.** No limit **4.** No limit **5.** $-\dfrac{1}{4}$

6. $\dfrac{2}{5}$ **7.** $+\infty\,(\text{as } x \to +\infty), -\infty\,(\text{as } x \to -\infty)$ **8.** $\dfrac{1}{2}$

9. 2 **10.** 0 **11.** 6 **12.** 5 **13.** 0 **14.** 1 **15.** Limit exists

16. Limit exists **17.** Limit exists **18.** Doesn't exist

19. Limit exists **20.** Limit exists **21.** Yes **22.** No

23. No **24.** Yes

25. (a) 1 (b) 1.5 (c) No

  (d) g is discontinuous at $x = 3$ (and points not in domain).

  (e) Yes, can remove discontinuity at $x = 3$ by assigning the value 1 to $g(3)$.

26. (a) 1.5 (b) 0 (c) 0 (d) No

  (e) k is discontinuous at $x = 1$ (and points not in domain).

  (f) Discontinuity at $x = 1$ is not removable because the two one-sided limits are different.

27. (a) Vertical Asymp.: $x = -2$

  (b) Left-hand limit $= -\infty$

    Right-hand limit $= \infty$

28. (a) Vertical Asymp.: $x = 0$ and $x = -2$

  (b) At $x = 0$:

    Left-hand limit $= -\infty$

    Right-hand limit $= -\infty$

    At $x = -2$:

    Left-hand limit $= -\infty$

    Right-hand limit $= -\infty$

29. (a) At $x = -1$:

    Left-hand limit $= 1$

    Right-hand limit $= 1$

    At $x = 0$:

    Left-hand limit $= 0$

    Right-hand limit $= 0$

    At $x = 1$:

    Left-hand limit $= -1$

    Right-hand limit $= 1$

  (b) At $x = -1$:

    Yes, the limit is 1.

    At $x = 0$:

    Yes, the limit is 0.

    At $x = 1$:

    No, the limit doesn't exist because the two one-sided limits are different.

  (c) At $x = -1$:

    Continuous because $f(-1) =$ the limit.

    At $x = 0$:

    Discontinuous because $f(0) \neq$ the limit.

    At $x = 1$:

    Discontinuous because limit doesn't exist.

30. (a) Left-hand limit $= 3$ Right-hand limit $= -3$

  (b) No, because the two one-sided limits are different

  (c) Every place except for $x = 1$

  (d) At $x = 1$

31. $x = -2$ and $x = 2$

32. There are no points of discontinuity.

33. (a) $2/x$ (b) $y = 0$ (x-axis) **34.** (a) 2 (b) $y = 2$

35. (a) x^2 (b) None **36.** (a) x (b) None

37. (a) e^x (b) x **38.** (a) $\ln |x|$ (b) $\ln |x|$

39. $k = 8$ **40.** $k = \dfrac{1}{2}$

41. One possible answer: **42.** One possible answer:

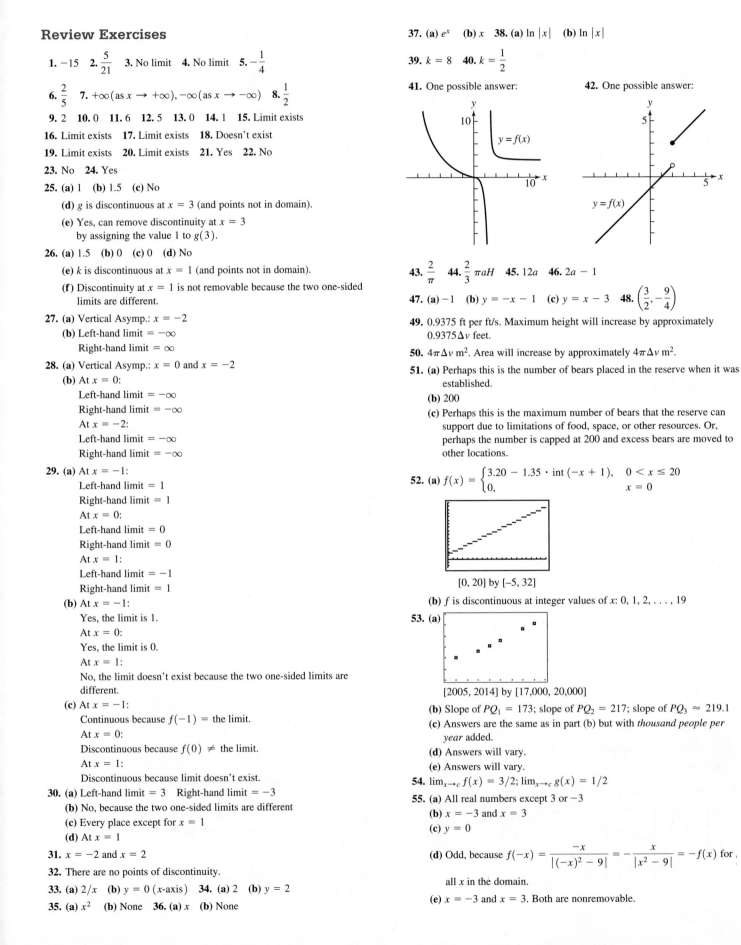

43. $\dfrac{2}{\pi}$ **44.** $\dfrac{2}{3}\pi aH$ **45.** $12a$ **46.** $2a - 1$

47. (a) -1 (b) $y = -x - 1$ (c) $y = x - 3$ **48.** $\left(\dfrac{3}{2}, -\dfrac{9}{4}\right)$

49. 0.9375 ft per ft/s. Maximum height will increase by approximately $0.9375\Delta v$ feet.

50. $4\pi\Delta v\ \text{m}^2$. Area will increase by approximately $4\pi\Delta v\ \text{m}^2$.

51. (a) Perhaps this is the number of bears placed in the reserve when it was established.

  (b) 200

  (c) Perhaps this is the maximum number of bears that the reserve can support due to limitations of food, space, or other resources. Or, perhaps the number is capped at 200 and excess bears are moved to other locations.

52. (a) $f(x) = \begin{cases} 3.20 - 1.35 \cdot \text{int}\,(-x + 1), & 0 < x \le 20 \\ 0, & x = 0 \end{cases}$

    [0, 20] by [–5, 32]

  (b) f is discontinuous at integer values of x: 0, 1, 2, ..., 19

53. (a)

    [2005, 2014] by [17,000, 20,000]

  (b) Slope of $PQ_1 = 173$; slope of $PQ_2 = 217$; slope of $PQ_3 \approx 219.1$

  (c) Answers are the same as in part (b) but with *thousand people per year* added.

  (d) Answers will vary.

  (e) Answers will vary.

54. $\lim_{x \to c} f(x) = 3/2$; $\lim_{x \to c} g(x) = 1/2$

55. (a) All real numbers except 3 or -3

  (b) $x = -3$ and $x = 3$

  (c) $y = 0$

  (d) Odd, because $f(-x) = \dfrac{-x}{|(-x)^2 - 9|} = -\dfrac{x}{|x^2 - 9|} = -f(x)$ for all x in the domain.

  (e) $x = -3$ and $x = 3$. Both are nonremovable.

56. (a) $\lim_{x \to 2^-} f(x) = \lim_{x \to 2^-} (x^2 - a^2 x) = 4 - 2a^2$.

(b) $\lim_{x \to 2^+} f(x) = \lim_{x \to 2^+} (4 - 2x^2) = -4$

(c) For $\lim_{x \to 2} f(x)$ to exist, we must have $4 - 2a^2 = -4$, so $a = \pm 2$. If $a = \pm 2$, then $\lim_{x \to 2^-} f(x) = \lim_{x \to 2^+} f(x) = f(2) = -4$, making f continuous at 2 by definition.

57. (a) The zeros of $f(x) = \dfrac{x^3 - 2x^2 + 1}{x^2 + 3}$ are the same as the zeros of the polynomial $x^3 - 2x^2 + 1$. By inspection, one such zero is $x = 1$. Divide $x^3 - 2x^2 + 1$ by $x - 1$ to get $x^2 - x - 1$, which has zeros $\dfrac{1 \pm \sqrt{5}}{2}$ by the quadratic formula. Thus, the zeros of f are 1, $\dfrac{1 + \sqrt{5}}{2}$, and $\dfrac{1 - \sqrt{5}}{2}$.

(b) $g(x) = x$

(c) $\lim_{x \to \infty} f(x) = +\infty$ and $\lim_{x \to \infty} \dfrac{f(x)}{g(x)} = \lim_{x \to \infty} \dfrac{x^3 - 2x^2 + 1}{x^3 + 3x} = 1$.

CHAPTER 3

Section 3.1

Quick Review 3.1

1. 4 **3.** -1 **5.** 0 **7.** $\lim_{x \to 1^+} f(x) = 0$; $\lim_{x \to 1^-} f(x) = 3$

9. No, the two one-sided limits are different.

Exercises 3.1

1. $-1/4$ **3.** 2 **5.** $-1/4$ **7.** $1/4$ **9.** $f'(x) = 3$ **11.** $2x$ **13.** (b)

15. (d) **17. (a)** $y = 5x - 7$ **(b)** $y = -\dfrac{1}{5}x + \dfrac{17}{5}$

19. (a) $y = 3x - 2$ **(b)** $y = -\dfrac{1}{3}x + \dfrac{4}{3}$

21. (a) Sometime around April 1. The rate then is approximately 1/6 hour per day.

(b) Yes. Jan. 1 and July 1

(c) Positive: Jan 1 through July 1 Negative: July 1 through Dec. 31

23. (a) 0, 0 **(b)** 120,000; 60,000 **(c)** 2 **25.** (iv)

27.

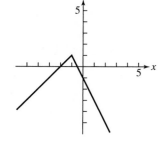

29. Graph of derivative:

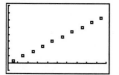

[0,10] by [−10,80]

(a) The speed of the skier

(b) Feet per second

(c) Approximately $D = 6.65t$

31. We show that the right-hand derivative at $x = 1$ does not exist:

$$\lim_{h \to 0^+} \frac{f(1 + h) - f(1)}{h} = \lim_{h \to 0^+} \frac{3(1 + h) - 2 - 2}{h}$$
$$= \lim_{h \to 0^+} \frac{3h - 1}{h} = -\infty$$

33.

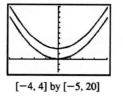

[−π, π] by [−1.5, 1.5]

Cosine could be the derivative of sine. The values of cosine are positive where sine is increasing, zero where sine has horizontal tangents, and negative where sine is decreasing.

35. Two parabolas are parallel if they have the same derivative at every value of x. This means their tangent lines are parallel at each value of x. Two such parabolas are given by $y = x^2$ and $y = x^2 + 4$. They are graphed below.

[−4, 4] by [−5, 20]

The parabolas are "everywhere equidistant," as long as the distance between them is always measured along a vertical line.

37. False. Let $f(x) = |x|$. The left-hand derivative at $x = 0$ is -1 and the right-hand derivative at $x = 0$ is 1. $f'(0)$ does not exist.

39. A **41.** C

43. (e) The y-intercept is $b - a$.

45. (a) 0.992 **(b)** 0.008

(c) If P is the answer to (b), then the probability of a shared birthday when there are four people is

$$1 - (1 - P)\frac{362}{365} \approx 0.016.$$

(d) No. Clearly, February 29th is a much less likely birth date. Furthermore, census data do not support the assumption that the other 365 birth dates are equally likely. However, this simplifying assumption may still give us some insight into this problem even if the calculated probabilities aren't completely accurate.

Section 3.2

Quick Review 3.2

1. Yes **3.** Yes **5.** No **7.** $[0, \infty)$ **9.** 3.2

Exercises 3.2

1. Left-hand derivative $= 0$
Right-hand derivative $= 1$

3. Left-hand derivative $= \dfrac{1}{2}$
Right-hand derivative $= 2$

5. (a) All points in $[-3, 2]$ **(b)** None **(c)** None

7. (a) All points in $[-3, 3]$ except $x = 0$ **(b)** None **(c)** $x = 0$

9. (a) All points in $[-1, 2]$ except $x = 0$ **(b)** $x = 0$ **(c)** None

11. Discontinuity   **13.** Corner   **15.** Corner   **17.** 4, yes   **19.** 2, yes

21. 8.000001, yes   **23.** 0, no   **25.** 0, no

27.
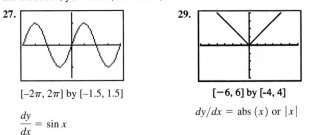

$[-2\pi, 2\pi]$ by $[-1.5, 1.5]$

$\dfrac{dy}{dx} = \sin x$

29.

$[-6, 6]$ by $[-4, 4]$

$dy/dx = $ abs (x) or $|x|$

31. All reals except $x = -1, 5$ **33.** All reals except $x = 0$

35. All reals except $x = 3$

37. The function $f(x)$ does not have the intermediate value property. Choose some a in $(-1, 0)$ and b in $(0, 1)$. Then $f(a) = 0$ and $f(b) = 1$, but f does not take on any value between 0 and 1.

39. **(a)** $a + b = 2$ **(b)** $a = -3$ and $b = 5$

41. False. The function $f(x) = |x|$ is continuous at $x = 0$ but is not differentiable at $x = 0$.

43. A   **45.** C

47. **(a)**
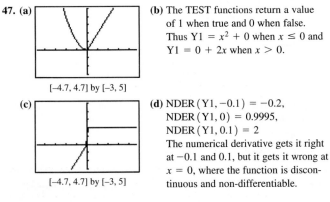

$[-4.7, 4.7]$ by $[-3, 5]$

(b) The TEST functions return a value of 1 when true and 0 when false. Thus Y1 $= x^2 + 0$ when $x \le 0$ and Y1 $= 0 + 2x$ when $x > 0$.

(c)

$[-4.7, 4.7]$ by $[-3, 5]$

(d) NDER $(Y1, -0.1) = -0.2$,
NDER $(Y1, 0) = 0.9995$,
NDER $(Y1, 0.1) = 2$
The numerical derivative gets it right at -0.1 and 0.1, but it gets it wrong at $x = 0$, where the function is discontinuous and non-differentiable.

Section 3.3

Quick Review 3.3

1. $x + x^2 - 2x^{-1} - 2$ **3.** $3x^2 - 2x^{-1} + 5x^{-2}$

5. $x^{-3} + x^{-1} + 2x^{-2} + 2$

7. Root: $x \approx 1.173, 500x^6 \approx 1305$
Root: $x \approx 2.394, 500x^6 \approx 94{,}212$

9. **(a)** 0   **(b)** 0   **(c)** 0

Exercises 3.3

1. $dy/dx = -2x$ **3.** $dy/dx = 2$ **5.** $dy/dx = x^2 + x + 1$

7. At $x = 1/3, 1$ **9.** At $x = 0, \pm\sqrt{2}$ **11.** At $x = -1, 0, 1$

13. **(a)** $3x^2 + 2x + 1$ **(b)** $3x^2 + 2x + 1$

15. $7x^6 + 10x^4 + 4x^3 + 6x^2 + 2x + 1$

17. $-\dfrac{19}{(3x - 2)^2}$ **19.** $\dfrac{3}{x^4}$ **21.** $\dfrac{x^4 + 2x}{(1 - x^3)^2}$

23. **(a)** 13   **(b)** -7 **(c)** $\dfrac{7}{25}$ **(d)** 20   **25.** (iii)

27. $y = \dfrac{1}{2}x + \dfrac{1}{2}$ **29.** $-8x^{-3} - 8$ **31.** $\dfrac{1}{\sqrt{x}(\sqrt{x} + 1)^2}$

33. $y' = 4x^3 + 3x^2 - 4x + 1, y'' = 12x^2 + 6x - 4,$
$y''' = 24x + 6, y^{(iv)} = 24$

35. $y' = -x^{-2} + 2x, y'' = 2x^{-3} + 2, y''' = -6x^{-4}, y^{(iv)} = 24x^{-5}$

37. $y = -\dfrac{1}{9}x + \dfrac{29}{9}$ **39.** $(-1, 27)$ and $(2, 0)$

41. At $(0, 0)$: $y = 4x$
At $(1, 2)$: $y = 2$

43. **(a)** Let $f(x) = x$,
$$\lim_{h \to 0} \frac{f(x + h) - f(x)}{h} = \lim_{h \to 0} \frac{(x + h) - x}{h}$$
$$= \lim_{h \to 0} \frac{h}{h} = \lim_{h \to 0} (1) = 1$$

(b) Note that $u = u(x)$ is a function of x,
$$\lim_{h \to 0} \frac{-u(x + h) - [-u(x)]}{h}$$
$$= \lim_{h \to 0} \left(-\frac{u(x + h) - u(x)}{h} \right)$$
$$= -\lim_{h \to 0} \frac{u(x + h) - u(x)}{h} = -\frac{du}{dx}$$

45. $-\dfrac{f'(x)}{[f(x)]^2}$ **47.** $\dfrac{ds}{dt} = 9.8t, \dfrac{d^2 s}{dt^2} = 9.8$

49. If the radius of a circle is changed by a very small amount Δr, the change in the area can be thought of as a very thin strip with length given by the circumference, $2\pi r$, and width Δr. Therefore, the change in the area can be thought of as $(2\pi r)(\Delta r)$, which means that the change in the area divided by the change in the radius is just $2\pi r$.

51. 390 bushels of annual production per year

53. False. π^3 is a constant so $d/dx\, (\pi^3) = 0$.

55. B   **57.** E

59. **(a)** It is insignificant in the limiting case and can be treated as zero (and removed from the expression).

(b) It was "rejected" because it is incomparably smaller than the other terms: $v\, du$ and $u\, dv$.

(c) The Product Rule given in the text.

(d) Because dx is "infinitely small," and this could be thought of as dividing by zero.

(e) $d\left(\dfrac{u}{v}\right) = \dfrac{u + du}{v + dv} - \dfrac{u}{v}$
$$= \frac{(u + du)v - u(v + dv)}{(v + dv)v}$$
$$= \frac{uv + vdu - uv - udv}{v^2 + vdv}$$
$$= \frac{vdu - udv}{v^2}$$

Quick Quiz (Sections 3.1–3.3)

1. D   **3.** C

Section 3.4

Quick Review 3.4

1. Downward   **3.** x-intercepts $= 2, 8$ **5.** $(5, 144)$ **7.** $x = \dfrac{15}{8}$ **9.** 64

Exercises 3.4

1. (a) $V = s^3$ **(b)** $\dfrac{dV}{ds} = 3s^2$ **(c)** 3, 75 **(d)** in³/in.

3. (a) $A = \dfrac{\sqrt{3}}{4}s^2$ **(b)** $\dfrac{dA}{ds} = \dfrac{\sqrt{3}}{2}s$ **(c)** $\sqrt{3}, 5\sqrt{3}$ **(d)** in²/in.

5. (a)

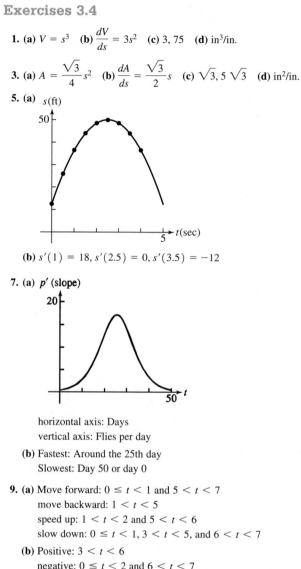

(b) $s'(1) = 18$, $s'(2.5) = 0$, $s'(3.5) = -12$

7. (a) p' (slope)

horizontal axis: Days
vertical axis: Flies per day

(b) Fastest: Around the 25th day
Slowest: Day 50 or day 0

9. (a) Move forward: $0 \le t < 1$ and $5 < t < 7$
move backward: $1 < t < 5$
speed up: $1 < t < 2$ and $5 < t < 6$
slow down: $0 \le t < 1$, $3 < t < 5$, and $6 < t < 7$

(b) Positive: $3 < t < 6$
negative: $0 \le t < 2$ and $6 < t < 7$
zero: $2 < t < 3$ and $7 < t \le 9$

(c) At $t = 0$ and $2 < t < 3$

(d) $7 < t \le 9$

11. (a) At $t = 2$ and $t = 7$

(b) Between $t = 3$ and $t = 6$

(c) Speed(m/sec)

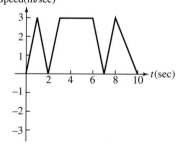

(d) Acceleration (m/sec²)

13. (a) vel$(t) = 24 - 1.6t$ m/sec, accel$(t) = -1.6$ m/sec²

(b) 15 seconds **(c)** 180 meters

(d) About 4.393 seconds **(e)** 30 seconds

15. About 29.388 meters

17. For the moon:
$$x_1(t) = 3(t < 160) + 3.1(t \ge 160)$$
$$y_1(t) = 832t - 2.6t^2$$
t-values: 0 to 320
window: $[0, 6]$ by $[-10{,}000, 70{,}000]$

For Earth:
$$x_1(t) = 3(t < 26) + 3.1(t \ge 26)$$
$$y_1(t) = 832t - 16t^2$$
t-values: 0 to 52
window: $[0, 6]$ by $[-1000, 11{,}000]$

19. (a) 10 m **(b)** 2 m/sec **(c)** 5 m/sec **(d)** 2 m/sec²

(e) At $t = \dfrac{3}{2}$ sec **(f)** At $s = -\dfrac{1}{4}$ m

21. (a) $v(t) = 3t^2 - 16t + 20 = (t - 2)(3t - 10)$

(b) $a(t) = 6t - 16$ **(c)** $t = 2, 10/3$

(d) The particle starts at the point $s = -16$ when $t = 0$ and moves right until it stops at $s = 0$ when $t = 2$, then it moves left to the point $s = -1.185$ when $t = 10/3$ where it stops again, and finally continues right from there on.

23. At $t = 1$: -6 m/sec²; at $t = 3$: 6 m/sec²

25. (a) $\dfrac{dy}{dt} = \dfrac{t}{12} - 1$ **(b)** Fastest: at $t = 0$
Slowest: at $t = 12$;

(c)

$[0, 12]$ by $[-2, 6]$

$\dfrac{dy}{dt} = -1$ at $t = 0$;

$\dfrac{dy}{dt} = 0$ at $t = 12$

y is decreasing and $\dfrac{dy}{dt}$ is negative over the entire interval.

y decreases more rapidly early in the interval, and the magnitude of $\dfrac{dy}{dt}$ is larger then. $\dfrac{dy}{dt}$ is 0 at $t = 12$, where y seems to have a horizontal tangent.

27. (a) $110 per machine **(b)** $80 per machine

(c) $79.90 for the 101ˢᵗ machine

29. (a)

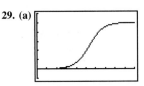

[0, 200] by [−2, 12]

(b) $x \geq 0$ (whole numbers)

(c)

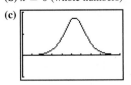

[0, 200] by [−0.1, 0.2]

P seems to be relatively sensitive to changes in x between approximately $x = 60$ and $x = 160$.

(d) The maximum occurs when $x \approx 106.44$. Since x must be an integer, $P(106) \approx 4.924$ thousand dollars or $4924.

(e) $13 per package sold, $165 per package sold, $118 per package sold, $31 per package sold, $6 per package sold, $P'(300) \approx 0$ (on the order of 10^{-6}, or $0.001 per package sold)

(f) The limit is 10. Maximum possible profit is $10,000 monthly.

(g) Yes. In order to sell more and more packages, the company might need to lower the price to a point where they won't make any additional profit.

31. Graph C is position, graph A is velocity, and graph B is acceleration. A is the derivative of C because it is positive, negative, and zero where C is increasing, decreasing, and has horizontal tangents, respectively. The relationship between B and A is similar.

33. Possible answer:

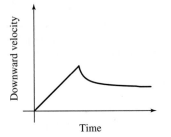

35. Exit velocity ≈ 348.712 ft/sec ≈ 237.758 mi/h

37. (a) It begins at the point $(-5, 2)$ moving in the positive direction. After a little more than one second, it has moved a bit past $(6, 2)$ and it turns back in the negative direction for approximately 2 seconds. At the end of that time, it is near $(-2, 2)$ and it turns back again in the positive direction. After that, it continues moving in the positive direction indefinitely, speeding up as it goes.

(b) Speeds up: $[1.153, 2.167]$ and $[3.180, \infty]$
Slows down: $[0, 1.153]$ and $[2.167, 3.180]$

(c) At $t \approx 1.153$ sec and $t \approx 3.180$ sec

(d) At $t \approx 1.153$ sec and $t \approx 3.180$ sec "instantaneously"

(e) The velocity starts out positive but decreasing, it becomes negative, then starts to increase, and becomes positive again and continues to increase. The speed is decreasing, reaches 0 at $t \approx 1.5$ sec, then increases until $t \approx 2.17$ sec, decreases until $t \approx 3.18$ sec when it is 0 again, then increases after that.

(f) At about 0.745 sec, 1.626 sec, 4.129 sec

39. Since profit = revenue − cost, using Rule 4 (the "difference rule"), and taking derivatives, we see that marginal profit = marginal revenue − marginal cost.

41. True. The acceleration is the first derivative of the velocity, which, in turn, is the first derivative of the position function.

43. D   **45.** C

47. (a) $g'(x) = h'(x) = t'(x) = 3x^2$

(b)

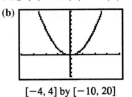

[−4, 4] by [−10, 20]

(c) $f(x)$ must be of the form $f(x) = x^3 + c$, where c is a constant.

(d) Yes. $f(x) = x^3$ **(e)** Yes. $f(x) = x^3 + 3$

49. (a) Assume that f is even. Then,

$$f'(-x) = \lim_{h \to 0} \frac{f(-x + h) - f(-x)}{h}$$

$$= \lim_{h \to 0} \frac{f(x - h) - f(x)}{h},$$

and substituting $k = -h$,

$$= \lim_{k \to 0} \frac{f(x + k) - f(x)}{-k}$$

$$= -\lim_{k \to 0} \frac{f(x + k) - f(x)}{k} = -f'(x)$$

So, f' is an odd function.

(b) Assume that f is odd. Then,

$$f'(-x) = \lim_{h \to 0} \frac{f(-x + h) - f(-x)}{h}$$

$$= \lim_{h \to 0} \frac{-f(x - h) + f(x)}{h}$$

and substituting $k = -h$,

$$= \lim_{k \to 0} \frac{-f(x + k) + f(x)}{-k}$$

$$= \lim_{k \to 0} \frac{f(x + k) - f(x)}{k} = f'(x)$$

So, f' is an even function.

Section 3.5

Quick Review 3.5

1. $3\pi/4 \approx 2.356$ **3.** $\sqrt{3}/2$

5. Domain: $x \neq k\dfrac{\pi}{2}$, where k is an odd integer; range: all reals

7. $\pm 1/\sqrt{2}$ **9.** $y = 12x - 35$

Exercises 3.5

1. $1 + \sin x$ **3.** $-\dfrac{1}{x^2} + 5 \cos x$ **5.** $-x^2 \cos x - 2x \sin x$

7. $4 \sec x \tan x$ **9.** $-\dfrac{\csc^2 x}{(1 + \cot x)^2} = -\dfrac{1}{(\sin x + \cos x)^2}$

11. $v = 5 \cos t$, $a = -5 \sin t$
The weight starts at 0, goes to 5, and then oscillates between 5 and −5. The period of the motion is 2π. The speed is greatest when $\cos t = \pm 1$ ($t = k\pi$), zero when $\cos t = 0$ ($t = k\pi/2$, k odd). The acceleration is greatest when $\sin t = \pm 1$ ($t = k\pi/2$, k odd), zero when $\sin t = 0$ ($t = k\pi$).

13. (a) $v = 3 \cos t$, speed $= |3 \cos t|$, $a = -3 \sin t$

(b) $v = 3\sqrt{2}/2$, speed $= 3\sqrt{2}/2$, $a = -3\sqrt{2}/2$

(c) The body starts at 2, goes up to 5, goes down to -1, and then oscillates between -1 and 5. The period of the motion is 2π.

15. (a) $v = 2 \cos t - 3 \sin t$,

speed $= |2\cos t - 3 \sin t|$, $a = -2 \sin t - 3 \cos t$

(b) $v = -\sqrt{2}/2$,

speed $= \sqrt{2}/2$, $a = -5\sqrt{2}/2$

(c) The body starts at 3, goes up to 3.606 $\left(\sqrt{13}\right)$, down to $-3.606\left(-\sqrt{13}\right)$, and then oscillates between -3.606 and 3.606. The period of the motion is 2π.

17. $2 \sin t$ **19.** $-\cos t - \sin t$

21. tangent: $y = -x + \pi + 3$, normal: $y = x - \pi + 3$

23. tangent: $y = -8.063x + 25.460$, normal: $y = 0.124x + 0.898$

25. (a) $\dfrac{d}{dx} \tan x = \dfrac{d}{dx} \dfrac{\sin x}{\cos x}$

$= \dfrac{(\cos x)(\cos x) - (\sin x)(-\sin x)}{(\cos x)^2}$

$= \dfrac{\cos^2 x + \sin^2 x}{\cos^2 x}$

$= \dfrac{1}{\cos^2 x} = \sec^2 x$

(b) $\dfrac{d}{dx} \sec x = \dfrac{d}{dx} \dfrac{1}{\cos x}$

$= \dfrac{(\cos x)(0) - (1)(-\sin x)}{(\cos x)^2}$

$= \dfrac{\sin x}{(\cos x)^2} = \sec x \tan x$

27. $d/dx \, (\sec x) = \sec x \tan x$, which is 0 at $x = 0$, so the slope of the tangent line is 0.
$d/dx \, (\cos x) = -\sin x$, which is 0 at $x = 0$, so the slope of the tangent line is 0.

29. Tangent: $y = -x + \dfrac{\pi}{4} + 1$

normal: $y = x + 1 - \dfrac{\pi}{4}$

31. (a) $y = -x + \dfrac{\pi}{2} + 2$ **(b)** $y = 4 - \sqrt{3}$

33. (a) Velocity: $-2 \cos t$ m/sec
Speed: $|2 \cos t|$ m/sec
Accel.: $2 \sin t$ m/sec^2
Jerk: $2 \cos t$ m/sec^3

(b) Velocity: $-\sqrt{2}$ m/sec
Speed: $\sqrt{2}$ m/sec
Accel.: $\sqrt{2}$ m/sec^2
Jerk: $\sqrt{2}$ m/sec^3

(c) The body starts at 2, goes to 0, and then oscillates between 0 and 4.
Speed: *Greatest* when $\cos t = \pm 1$ (or $t = k\pi$), at the center of the interval of motion.

Zero when $\cos t = 0$ $\left(\text{or } t = \dfrac{k\pi}{2}, k \text{ odd}\right)$, at the endpoints of the interval of motion.

Acceleration: *Greatest* (in magnitude) when

$\sin t = \pm 1$ $\left(\text{or } t = \dfrac{k\pi}{2}, k \text{ odd}\right)$

Zero when $\sin t = 0$ (or $t = k\pi$)

Jerk: *Greatest* (in magnitude) when $\cos t = \pm 1$ (or $t = k\pi$)

Zero when $\cos t = 0$ $\left(\text{or } t = \dfrac{k\pi}{2}, k \text{ odd}\right)$

35. $y'' = \csc^3 x + \csc x \cot^2 x$

37. Continuous if $b = 1$, because this makes the two one-sided limits equal. Differentiable: No, because for $b = 1$, the left-hand derivative is 1 and the right-hand derivative is 0. (The left-hand derivative does not exist for other values of b.)

39. $\cos x$

41. (a) 0.12

(b) $\sin (0.12) = 0.1197122073$ to 10 digits.

So 0.12 is only off by 0.00028779 from the computed actual value.

43. $\dfrac{d}{dx} \cos 2x = \dfrac{d}{dx} \left[(\cos x)(\cos x) - (\sin x)(\sin x)\right]$

$= \left[2(\cos x)(-\sin x) - 2(\sin x)(\cos x)\right]$

$= -4(\sin x)(\cos x) = -2(2 \sin x \cos x)$

$= -2 \sin 2x$

45. False. The velocity is negative and the speed is positive at $t = \pi/4$.

47. B   **49.** C

51. $\displaystyle\lim_{h \to 0} \dfrac{\cos h - 1}{h} = \lim_{h \to 0} \dfrac{(\cos h - 1)(\cos h + 1)}{h(\cos h + 1)}$

$= \displaystyle\lim_{h \to 0} \dfrac{\cos^2 h - 1}{h(\cos h + 1)}$

$= \displaystyle\lim_{h \to 0} \dfrac{-\sin^2 h}{h(\cos h + 1)}$

$= -\left(\displaystyle\lim_{h \to 0} \dfrac{\sin h}{h}\right)\left(\lim_{h \to 0} \dfrac{\sin h}{\cos h + 1}\right)$

$= -(1)\left(\dfrac{0}{2}\right) = 0$

Quick Quiz (Sections 3.4–3.5)

1. C   **3.** D

Review Exercises

1. $5x^4 - \dfrac{x}{4} + \dfrac{1}{4}$ **2.** $-21x^2 + 21x^6$ **3.** $-2 \cos^2 x + 2 \sin^2 x = 2 \cos 2x$

4. $-\dfrac{4}{(2x - 1)^2}$ **5.** $4t^3$ **6.** $\dfrac{4t}{(1 - t^2)^2}$ **7.** $\dfrac{1}{2\sqrt{x}} - \dfrac{1}{2x^{3/2}}$

8. $5x^4(3x^2 - x) + (6x - 1)(x^5 + 1)$ **9.** $10 \theta \sec \theta + 5\theta^2 \sec \theta \tan \theta$

10. $\dfrac{\sec^2 \theta(\theta^3 + \theta + 1) - \tan \theta(3\theta^2 + 1)}{(\theta^3 + \theta + 1)^2}$ **11.** $(x^2 + 1)\cos x + x \sin x$

12. $(x^2 - 1)\cos x + 3x \sin x$ **13.** $\dfrac{x \sec^2 x - 3 \tan x}{2x^4}$ **14.** $\sec^2 x + \csc^2 x$

15. $\dfrac{\sin x - \cos x}{(\sin x + \cos x)^2}$ **16.** $\sec x \tan x - \csc x \cot x$ **17.** $4\pi r^2 + 16\pi r$

18. $\left(\dfrac{\sqrt{3}}{2} + \dfrac{3\pi}{4}\right)s$ **19.** $\dfrac{\cos t(1 + \tan t) - \sec^2 t(1 + \sin t)}{(1 + \tan t)^2}$

20. $\dfrac{\cos t + \sin t + 1}{(1 + \cos t)^2}$ **21.** $2t + 1$ **22.** $\dfrac{12 - 2x \cos x - x^2 \sin x}{x^4}$

23. 0   **24.** 0   **25.** $6x^2 - 2$ **26.** $4 - 24x$ **27.** $\dfrac{2t}{\pi^3} + \dfrac{3\pi^2}{t^4}$

28. $\dfrac{3t^2}{\pi^2} + \dfrac{2\pi^3}{t^3}$ **29.** $\sec^2 x$ **30.** 0 **31.** For all $x \neq 0$ **32.** For all real x

33. For all $x \neq 2$ **34.** For all $x \neq \dfrac{7}{2}$ **35.** 0 **36.** 1 **37.** $\dfrac{1}{\pi^2}$

38. $\dfrac{1}{\pi}$ **39.** $\dfrac{\sin^2 x + 1}{\cos^3 x}$ **40.** $\dfrac{\cos^2 x + 1}{\sin^3 x}$

41. $2\cos x - x \sin x$ **42.** $x \cos x + 2 \sin x$

43. $y' = 2x^3 - 3x - 1$, $y'' = 6x^2 - 3$, $y''' = 12x$, $y^{(4)} = 12$, and the rest are all zero.

44. $y' = \dfrac{x^4}{24}$, $y'' = \dfrac{x^3}{6}$, $y''' = \dfrac{x^2}{2}$, $y^{(4)} = x$, $y^{(5)} = 1$, and the rest are all zero.

45. (a) $y - 2 = -2(x - 2)$ **(b)** $y - 2 = \dfrac{1}{2}(x - 2)$

46. (a) $y = -x + \dfrac{\pi}{2} + 2$ **(b)** $y = x - \dfrac{\pi}{2} + 2$

47. (a) $y = \sqrt{2}$ **(b)** $x = \dfrac{\pi}{4}$ **48. (a)** $y = 3$ **(b)** $x = 1$

49. $(1, 2)$ and $(-1, -2)$ **50.** $(3, 9/2)$ and $(-2, -14/3)$

51. $(0, 0)$ and $(-2, 12)$ **52.** None

53. (a)

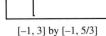

[-1, 3] by [-1, 5/3]

(b) Yes, because both of the one-sided limits as $x \to 1$ are equal to $f(1) = 1$.

(c) No, because the left-hand derivative at $x = 1$ is $+1$ and the right-hand derivative at $x = 1$ is -1.

54. (a) For all m, since $y = \sin 2x$ and $y = mx$ are both continuous on their domains, and they link up at the origin, where $\displaystyle\lim_{x \to 0^-} \sin 2x = \lim_{x \to 0^+} mx = 0$, regardless of the value of m.

(b) For $m = 2$ only, since the left-hand derivative at 0 (which is $2 \cos 0 = 2$) must match the right-hand derivative at 0 (which is m).

55. (a) For all $x \neq 0$ **(b)** At $x = 0$ **(c)** Nowhere

56. (a) For all $x \neq 0$ **(b)** At $x = 0$ **(c)** Nowhere

57. (a) $[-1, 0) \cup (0, 4]$ **(b)** At $x = 0$ **(c)** Nowhere in its domain

58. (a) $[-2, 0) \cup (0, 2]$ **(b)** Nowhere **(c)** Nowhere in its domain

59.

60.

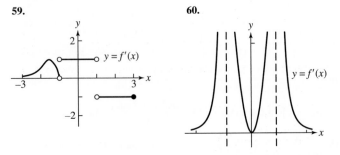

61. (a) iii **(b)** i **(c)** ii

62.

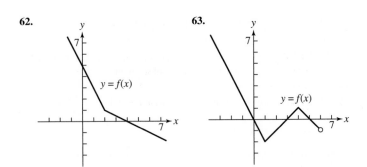

63.

64. Answer is **D: i** and **iii** only could be true.

65. (a)

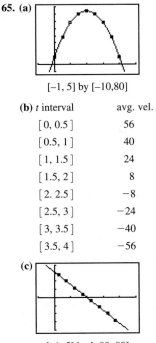

[-1, 5] by [-10, 80]

(b)

t interval	avg. vel.
$[0, 0.5]$	56
$[0.5, 1]$	40
$[1, 1.5]$	24
$[1.5, 2]$	8
$[2, 2.5]$	-8
$[2.5, 3]$	-24
$[3, 3.5]$	-40
$[3.5, 4]$	-56

(c)

[-1, 5] by [-80, 80]

(d) Average velocity is a good approximation to velocity.

66. $(x^n)' = nx^{n-1}$; $(x^n)'' = n(n-1)x^{n-2}$; $(x^n)''' = n(n-1)(n-2)x^{n-3}$; $\ldots$; and

$$\dfrac{d^n}{dx^n}(x^n) = n(n-1)(n-2)(n-3)\cdots 2 \cdot 1\, x^0 = n!$$

67. (a) 12 **(b)** 1 **(c)** -2 **(d)** 7 **(e)** -1 **(f)** -36

68. (a) 5 **(b)** 2 **(c)** -2 **(d)** $\dfrac{10}{9}$ **(e)** -2 **(f)** 6

69. Yes. The slope of $f + g$ at $x = 0$ is $(f + g)'(0) = f'(0) + g'(0)$. The sum of two positive numbers must also be positive.

70. No; it depends on the values of $f(0)$ and $g(0)$. For example, let $f(x) = x$ and $g(x) = x - 1$. Both lines have positive slope everywhere, but $(f \cdot g)(x) = x^2 - x$ has a negative slope at $x = 0$.

71. (a) $\dfrac{ds}{dt} = 64 - 32t$ $\dfrac{d^2 s}{dt^2} = -32$ **(b)** 2 sec **(c)** 64 ft/sec

(d) $\dfrac{64}{5.2} \approx 12.3$ sec; $s\left(\dfrac{64}{5.2}\right) \approx 393.8$ ft

72. (a) $\dfrac{4}{7}$ sec; 280 cm/sec **(b)** 560 cm/sec; 980 cm/sec^2

73. $\pi(20x - x^2)$

74. (a) $r(x) = \left(3 - \dfrac{x}{40}\right)^2 x = 9x - \dfrac{3}{20}x^2 + \dfrac{1}{1600}x^3$

   (b) 40 people; $4.00

   (c) One possible answer: Probably not, since the company charges less overall for 60 passengers than it does for 40 passengers.

75. (a) -0.6 km/sec   (b) $18/\pi \approx 5.73$ revolutions/min

76. (a) The derivative of y_1 is y_2.   (b) Let $y_2 = \dfrac{|\cos(x)|}{\cos(x)}$.

77. $a = \dfrac{3\sqrt[4]{2}}{8}$ **78.** $a = \sqrt{2}$

79. (a) $x \neq k\dfrac{\pi}{4}$, where k is an odd integer   (b) $(-\pi/2, \pi/2)$

   (c) Where it's not defined, at $x = k\dfrac{\pi}{4}$, k an odd integer

   (d) It has period $\pi/2$ and continues to repeat the pattern seen in this window.

80. $y'(r) = -\dfrac{1}{2r^2 l}\sqrt{\dfrac{T}{\pi d}}$, so increasing r decreases the frequency.

   $y'(l) = -\dfrac{1}{2rl^2}\sqrt{\dfrac{T}{\pi d}}$, so increasing l decreases the frequency.

   $y'(d) = -\dfrac{1}{4rl}\sqrt{\dfrac{T}{\pi d^3}}$, so increasing d decreases the frequency.

   $y'(T) = \dfrac{1}{4rl\sqrt{\pi Td}}$, so increasing T increases the frequency.

81. (a) $v(t) = x'(t) = 3t^2 - 12$ (b) $a(t) = v'(t) = 6t$

   (c) The particle is at rest when $3t^2 - 12 = 0$; that is, at $t = 2$.

   (d) $a(t) = 6t = 0$ when $t = 0$, at which point the speed is $|v(0)| = |-12| = 12$.

   (e) The position at $t = 3$ is $x(3) = -4$, and the velocity is $v(3) = 15$. Since the particle is to the left of the origin and moving to the right, it is moving toward the origin.

82. (a) $y - 3 = 5(x - 4)$

   (b) Yes. Since f is differentiable at $x = 3$, it is continuous at $x = 3$.

   (c) Yes. Since f is continuous on $[2, 4]$, it takes on all values between $f(2) = -1$ and $f(4) = 3$ (Intermediate Value Theorem).

   (d) $g'(2) = \dfrac{d}{dx}\left(\dfrac{f(x)}{f(x) - 3}\right)\Big|_{x=2}$

   $= \dfrac{f'(2)(f(2) - 3) - (f'(2) - 0)f(2)}{(f(2) - 3)^2} = -\dfrac{9}{16}$.

   (e) Since $f(4) - 3 = 0$, the function g is not defined at $x = 4$.

83. (a)

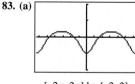

   $[-2\pi, 2\pi]$ by $[-2, 2]$

   (b) $f'(x) = \dfrac{2\sin x}{(\cos x - 2)^2}$ (c) $0, \pm\pi, \pm 2\pi$

   (d) The low turning points are $f(0) = f(\pm 2\pi) = \dfrac{1}{1 - 2} = -1$, and the high turning points are $f(\pm\pi) = \dfrac{-1}{-1 - 2} = \dfrac{1}{3}$. The range is the interval $\left[-1, \dfrac{1}{3}\right]$.

CHAPTER 4

Section 4.1

Quick Review 4.1

1. $\sin(x^2 + 1)$ **3.** $49x^2 + 1$

5. $\sin\dfrac{x^2 + 1}{7x}$ **7.** $g(h(f(x)))$ **9.** $f(h(h(x)))$

Exercises 4.1

1. $3\cos(3x + 1)$ **3.** $-\sqrt{3}\sin(\sqrt{3}x)$ **5.** $\dfrac{2\sin x}{(1 + \cos x)^2}$

7. $-\sin(\sin x)\cos x$ **9.** $3\sin\left(\dfrac{\pi}{2} - 3t\right)$

11. $\dfrac{4}{\pi}\cos 3t - \dfrac{4}{\pi}\sin 5t$ **13.** $-2\left(x + \sqrt{x}\right)^{-3}\left(1 + \dfrac{1}{2\sqrt{x}}\right)$

15. $-5\sin^{-6}x\cos x + 3\cos^2 x\sin x$

17. $4\sin^3 x\sec^2 4x + 3\sin^2 x\cos x\tan 4x$ **19.** $-3(2x + 1)^{-3/2}$

21. $6\sin(3x - 2)\cos(3x - 2) = 3\sin(6x - 4)$

23. $-42(1 + \cos^2 7x)^2\cos 7x\sin 7x$ **25.** $-\sec^2(2 - \theta)$

27. $\dfrac{\theta\cos\theta + \sin\theta}{2\sqrt{\theta\sin\theta}}$ **29.** $2\sec^2 x\tan x$

31. $18\csc^2(3x - 1)\cot(3x - 1)$ **33.** $5/2$ **35.** $-\pi/4$ **37.** 0

39. (a) $-6\sin(6x + 2)$ (b) $-6\sin(6x + 2)$

41. $y - \sqrt{2} = -1(x - \sqrt{2})$ **43.** $y + 1 = -1/2(x - 1)$

45. $y - 1/2 = 1(x - 1/4)$ **47.** $y - 1/2 = \sqrt{3}(x - \pi/3 + \sqrt{3}/2)$

49. (a) $\dfrac{\cos t}{2t + 1}$ (b) $\dfrac{d}{dt}\left(\dfrac{dy}{dx}\right) = -\dfrac{(2t + 1)(\sin t) + 2\cos t}{(2t + 1)^2}$

   (c) $\dfrac{d}{dx}\left(\dfrac{dy}{dx}\right) = -\dfrac{(2t + 1)(\sin t) + 2\cos t}{(2t + 1)^3}$ (d) part (c)

51. 5 **53.** $\dfrac{1}{2}$

55. Tangent: $y - 2 = \pi(x - 1)$; Normal: $y - 2 = (-1/\pi)(x - 1)$

57. $\dfrac{d}{dx}\cos(x°) = \dfrac{d}{dx}\cos\left(\dfrac{\pi x}{180}\right)$

   $= -\dfrac{\pi}{180}\sin\left(\dfrac{\pi x}{180}\right) = -\dfrac{\pi}{180}\sin(x°)$

59. The slope of $y = \sin(2x)$ at the origin is 2. The slope of $y = -\sin\dfrac{x}{2}$ at the origin is $-\dfrac{1}{2}$. So the lines tangent to the two curves at the origin are perpendicular.

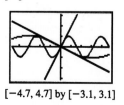

   $[-4.7, 4.7]$ by $[-3.1, 3.1]$

61. The amplitude of the velocity is doubled.
The amplitude of the acceleration is quadrupled.
The amplitude of the jerk is multiplied by 8.

63. Velocity $= \dfrac{2}{5}$ m/sec

acceleration $= -\dfrac{4}{125}$ m/sec^2

65. Given: $v = \dfrac{k}{\sqrt{s}}$

acceleration $= \dfrac{dv}{dt} = \dfrac{dv}{ds}\dfrac{ds}{dt} = \dfrac{dv}{ds}v$

$= \dfrac{-k}{2s^{3/2}}\dfrac{k}{\sqrt{s}} = -\dfrac{k^2}{2s^2}$

67. $\dfrac{dT}{du} = \dfrac{dT}{dL}\dfrac{dL}{du}$

$= \dfrac{\pi}{\sqrt{gL}}kL = k\pi\sqrt{\dfrac{L}{g}} = \dfrac{kT}{2}$

69. Yes. Either the graph of $y = g(x)$ must have a horizontal tangent at $x = 1$, or the graph of $y = f(u)$ must have a horizontal tangent at $u = g(1)$. This is because $\dfrac{d}{dx}f(g(x)) = f'(g(x))\,g'(x)$, so the slope of the tangent to the graph of $y = f(g(x))$ at $x = 1$ is given by $f'(g(1))\,g'(1)$. If this product is zero, then at least one of its factors must be zero.

71. False. It is $+1$.   **73.** C   **75.** B

77. As $h \to 0$, the second curve (the difference quotient) approaches the first ($y = -2x\sin(x^2)$). This is because $-2x\sin(x^2)$ is the derivative of $\cos(x^2)$, and the second curve is the difference quotient used to define the derivative of $\cos(x^2)$. As $h \to 0$, the difference quotient expression should be approaching the derivative.

79. $\dfrac{dG}{dx} = \dfrac{d}{dx}\sqrt{uv} = \dfrac{d}{dx}\sqrt{x^2 + cx} = \dfrac{2x + c}{2\sqrt{x^2 + cx}}$

$= \dfrac{x + \dfrac{c}{2}}{\sqrt{x^2 + cx}}$

$= \dfrac{A}{G}$, since $A = x + \dfrac{c}{2}$.

Section 4.2

Quick Review 4.2

1. $y_1 = \sqrt{x}, y_2 = -\sqrt{x}$

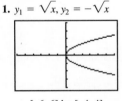

[−6, 6] by [−4, 4]

3. $y_1 = \dfrac{x}{2}, y_2 = -\dfrac{x}{2}$

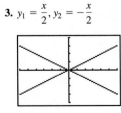

[−6, 6] by [−4, 4]

5. $y_1 = \sqrt{2x + 3 - x^2}, y_2 = -\sqrt{2x + 3 - x^2}$

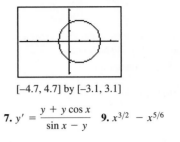

[−4.7, 4.7] by [−3.1, 3.1]

7. $y' = \dfrac{y + y\cos x}{\sin x - y}$ **9.** $x^{3/2} - x^{5/6}$

Exercises 4.2

1. $-\dfrac{2xy + y^2}{2xy + x^2}$ **3.** $\dfrac{1}{y(x + 1)^2}$ **5.** $\cos^2 y$ **7.** $-\dfrac{1}{x}\cos^2(xy) - \dfrac{y}{x}$

9. $\dfrac{dy}{dx} = -\dfrac{x}{y}, 2/3$ **11.** $\dfrac{dy}{dx} = -\dfrac{x - 1}{y - 1}, -2/3$

13. $\dfrac{dy}{dx} = \dfrac{2xy - y^2}{2xy - x^2}$, defined at every point except where $x = 0$ (which can not happen on this curve), or $y = x/2$

15. $\dfrac{dy}{dx} = \dfrac{3x^2 - y}{x - 3y^2}$, defined at every point except where $y^2 = x/3$

17. (a) $y - 3 = (7/4)(x - 2)$ (b) $y - 3 = (-4/7)(x - 2)$

19. (a) $y - 3 = 3(x + 1)$ (b) $y - 3 = (-1/3)(x + 1)$

21. (a) $y = (6/7)(x + 1)$ (b) $y = (-7/6)(x + 1)$

23. (a) $y - \pi/2 = (-\pi/2)(x - 1)$ (b) $y - \pi/2 = (2/\pi)(x - 1)$

25. (a) $y = 2\pi(x - 1)$ (b) $y = (-1/2\pi)(x - 1)$

27. $\dfrac{dy}{dx} = -\dfrac{x}{y}$

$\dfrac{d^2y}{dx^2} = -\dfrac{(x^2 + y^2)}{y^3} = -\dfrac{1}{y^3}$

29. $\dfrac{dy}{dx} = \dfrac{x + 1}{y}$

$\dfrac{d^2y}{dx^2} = -\dfrac{y^2 - (x + 1)^2}{y^3} = -\dfrac{1}{y^3}$

31. $(9/4)x^{5/4}$ **33.** $(1/3)x^{-2/3}$ **35.** $-(2x + 5)^{-3/2}$

37. $x^2(x^2 + 1)^{-1/2} + (x^2 + 1)^{1/2}$

39. $-\dfrac{1}{4}(1 - x^{1/2})^{-1/2}x^{-1/2}$ **41.** $-\dfrac{9}{2}(\csc x)^{3/2}\cot x$

43. (b), (c), and (d)

45. (a) At $\left(\dfrac{\sqrt{3}}{4}, \dfrac{\sqrt{3}}{2}\right)$: Slope $= -1$;

at $\left(\dfrac{\sqrt{3}}{4}, \dfrac{1}{2}\right)$: Slope $= \sqrt{3}$

(b)

[−1.8, 1.8] by [−1.2, 1.2]

Parameter interval:
$-1 \le t \le 1$

47. (a) $(-1)^3(1)^2 = \cos(\pi)$ is true, since both sides equal -1.

(b) The slope is $3/2$.

49. The points are $\left(\pm \sqrt{7}, 0 \right)$

$$\frac{dy}{dx} = -\frac{2x + y}{2y + x}$$

At both points, $\frac{dy}{dx} = -2$

51. First curve: $\frac{dy}{dx} = -\frac{2x}{3y}$

second curve: $\frac{dy}{dx} = \frac{3x^2}{2y}$

At $(1, 1)$, the slopes are $-\frac{2}{3}$ and $\frac{3}{2}$ respectively.

At $(1, -1)$, the slopes are $\frac{2}{3}$ and $-\frac{3}{2}$ respectively.

In both cases, the tangents are perpendicular.

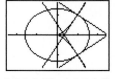

[–2.4, 2.4] by [–1.6, 1.6]

53. Acceleration $= \frac{dv}{dt} = 4(s - t)^{-1/2} (v - 1)$

$= 32$ ft/sec^2

55. (a) At $(4, 2)$: $\frac{5}{4}$; at $(2, 4)$: $\frac{4}{5}$

(b) At $\left(3\sqrt[3]{2}, 3\sqrt[3]{4} \right) \approx (3.780, 4.762)$

(c) At $\left(3\sqrt[3]{4}, 3\sqrt[3]{2} \right) \approx (4.762, 3.780)$

57. At $(-1, -1)$: $y = -2x - 3$; at $(3, -3)$: $y = -2x + 3$

59. False. It is equal to -2.

61. A   **63.** E

65. (a) $\frac{dy}{dx} = -\frac{b^2 x}{a^2 y}$

The tangent line is $y - y_1 = -\frac{b^2 x_1}{a^2 y_1} (x - x_1)$.

This gives: $a^2 y_1 y - a^2 y_1^2 = -b^2 x_1 x + b^2 x_1^2$,

$a^2 y_1 y + b^2 x_1 x = a^2 y_1^2 + b^2 x_1^2$.

But $a^2 y_1^2 + b^2 x_1^2 = a^2 b^2$ since (x_1, y_1) is on the ellipse.

Therefore, $a^2 y_1 y + b^2 x_1 x = a^2 b^2$, and dividing by $a^2 b^2$ gives

$\frac{x_1 x}{a^2} + \frac{y_1 y}{b^2} = 1$.   **(b)** $\frac{x_1 x}{a^2} - \frac{y_1 y}{b^2} = 1$.

Quick Quiz (Sections 4.1–4.2)

1. B   **3.** C

Section 4.3

Quick Review 4.3

1. Domain: $[-1, 1]$; Range: $[-\pi/2, \pi/2]$; At 1: $\pi/2$

3. Domain: all reals; Range: $(-\pi/2, \pi/2)$; At 1: $\pi/4$

5. Domain: all reals; Range: all reals; At 1: 1

7. $f^{-1}(x) = x^3 - 5$

9. $f^{-1}(x) = \dfrac{2}{3 - x}$

Exercises 4.3

1. $-\dfrac{2x}{\sqrt{1 - x^4}}$ **3.** $\dfrac{\sqrt{2}}{\sqrt{1 - 2t^2}}$ **5.** $-\dfrac{6}{t\sqrt{t^4 - 9}}$ **7.** $\sin^{-1} x$

9. $\sqrt{7}/7$ **11.** $1/5$ **13.** $\dfrac{1}{|2s + 1|\sqrt{s^2 + s}}$

15. $-\dfrac{2}{(x^2 + 1)\sqrt{x^2 + 2}}$ **17.** $-\dfrac{1}{\sqrt{1 - t^2}}$ **19.** $-\dfrac{1}{2t\sqrt{t - 1}}$

21. $0, x > 1$ **23.** $y = 0.289x + 0.470$ **25.** $y = 0.378x - 0.286$

27. (a) $y - 1 = 2(x - \pi/4)$ **(b)** $y - \pi/4 = 1/2(x - 1)$

29. (a) $f'(x) = 3 - \sin x$ and $f'(x) \neq 0$. So f has a differentiable inverse by Theorem 3.

(b) $f(0) = 1, f'(0) = 3$ **(c)** $f^{-1}(1) = 0, (f^{-1})'(1) = \dfrac{1}{3}$

31. (a) $v(t) = \dfrac{dx}{dt} = \dfrac{1}{1 + t^2}$, which is always positive.

(b) $a(t) = \dfrac{dv}{dt} = -\dfrac{2t}{(1 + t^2)^2}$, which is always negative.   **(c)** $\dfrac{\pi}{2}$

33. $\dfrac{d}{dx} \cot^{-1} x = \dfrac{d}{dx} \left(\dfrac{\pi}{2} - \tan^{-1} x \right)$

$= 0 - \dfrac{d}{dx} \tan^{-1} x$

$= -\dfrac{1}{1 + x^2}$

35. True. By definition of the function.   **37.** E   **39.** A

41. (a) $y = \pi/2$ **(b)** $y = -\pi/2$ **(c)** None

43. (a) $y = \pi/2$ **(b)** $y = \pi/2$ **(c)** None

45. (a) None   **(b)** None   **(c)** None

47. (a)

$\alpha = \cos^{-1} x, \beta = \sin^{-1} x$

So $\pi/2 = \alpha + \beta = \cos^{-1} x + \sin^{-1} x$.

(b)

$\alpha = \tan^{-1} x, \beta = \cot^{-1} x$

So $\pi/2 = \alpha + \beta = \tan^{-1} x + \cot^{-1} x$.

(c)

$\alpha = \sec^{-1} x, \beta = \csc^{-1} x$

So $\pi/2 = \alpha + \beta = \sec^{-1} x + \csc^{-1} x$.

49. Let s be the length of a side of the square, and let α, β, γ denote the angles labeled $\tan^{-1} 1, \tan^{-1} 2$, and $\tan^{-1} 3$, respectively.

$\tan \alpha = \dfrac{s}{s} = 1$, so $\alpha = \tan^{-1} 1$ and

$\tan \beta = \dfrac{s}{s/2} = 2$, so $\beta = \tan^{-1} 2$.

$\gamma = \pi - \alpha - \beta = \pi - \tan^{-1} 1 - \tan^{-1} 2$

$= \tan^{-1} 3$.

Section 4.4

Quick Review 4.4

1. $\dfrac{\ln 8}{\ln 5}$ **3.** $\tan x$ **5.** $3x - 15$ **7.** $\ln (4x^4)$

9. $t = \dfrac{\ln 18 - \ln (\ln 5)}{\ln 5} \approx 1.50$

Exercises 4.4

1. $2e^x$ **3.** $-e^{-x}$ **5.** $\dfrac{2}{3}e^{2x/3}$ **7.** $e^2 - e^x$ **9.** $e^{\sqrt{x}}/(2\sqrt{x})$

11. $8^x \ln 8$ **13.** $-3^{\csc x}(\ln 3)(\csc x \cot x)$ **15.** $\dfrac{2}{x}$ **17.** $-\dfrac{1}{x}, x > 0$

19. $\dfrac{1}{x \ln x}$ **21.** $\dfrac{2}{x \ln 4} = \dfrac{1}{x \ln 2}$ **23.** $-\dfrac{1}{x \ln 2}, x > 0$ **25.** $\dfrac{1}{x}, x > 0$

27. $\dfrac{1}{\ln 10}$ **29.** $\approx (1.379, 5.551)$ **31.** $2e^{-1}$ **33.** $\pi x^{\pi - 1}$

35. $-\sqrt{2}\,x^{-\sqrt{2}-1}$ **37.** $\dfrac{1}{x + 2}, x > -2$ **39.** $\dfrac{\sin x}{2 - \cos x}$, all reals

41. $\dfrac{3}{(3x + 1)\ln 2}, x > -1/3$ **43.** $(\sin x)^x\,[x \cot x + \ln (\sin x)]$

45. $\left(\dfrac{(x - 3)^4 (x^2 + 1)}{(2x + 5)^3}\right)^{1/5} \left(\dfrac{4}{5(x - 3)} + \dfrac{2x}{5(x^2 + 1)} - \dfrac{6}{5(2x + 5)}\right)$

47. $\dfrac{2x^{\ln x}\,(\ln x)}{x}$ **49.** $y = ex$

51. (a) 18   (b) 52 students per day
(c) After 4 days; 52 students per day

53. rate ≈ 0.098 grams/day

55. (a) $\ln 2$ (b) $f'(0) = \lim\limits_{h \to 0} \dfrac{2^h - 1}{h}$ (c) $\ln 2$ (d) $\ln 7$

57. False. It is $(\ln 2)2^x$.   **59.** B   **61.** A

63. (a) The graph of y_4 is a horizontal line at $y = a$.

(b) The graph of y_3 is a horizontal line at $y = \ln a$.

(c) $\dfrac{d}{dx}\,a^x = a^x$ if and only if $y_3 = \dfrac{y_2}{y_1} = 1$.

So if $y_3 = \ln a$, then $\dfrac{d}{dx}\,a^x$ will equal a^x if and only if $\ln a = 1$,

or $a = e$.

(d) $y_2 = \dfrac{d}{dx}\,a^x = a^x \ln a$. This will equal $y_1 = a^x$ if and only if

$\ln a = 1$, or $a = e$.

65. (a) $y = \dfrac{1}{e}x$

(b) Because the graph of $\ln x$ lies below the graph of the tangent line for all positive $x \neq e$.

(c) Multiplying by e, $e(\ln x) < x$, or $\ln x^e < x$.

(d) Exponentiate both sides of the inequality in part (c).

(e) Let $x = \pi$ to see that $\pi^e < e^\pi$.

Quick Quiz (Sections 4.3–4.4)

1. A   **3.** C

Review Exercises

1. $3e^{3x-7}$ **2.** $e^x \sec^2 (e^x)$ **3.** $3 \sin^2 x \cos x$ **4.** $-\cot x$

5. $2 \sin (1 - 2t)$ **6.** $\dfrac{2}{t^2} \csc^2 \dfrac{2}{t}$ **7.** $-\dfrac{\sin x}{2\sqrt{1 + \cos x}}$

8. $\dfrac{3x + 1}{\sqrt{2x + 1}}$ **9.** $3 \sec (1 + 3\theta) \tan (1 + 3\theta)$

10. $-4\theta \tan (3 - \theta^2) \sec^2 (3 - \theta^2)$ **11.** $-5x^2 \csc 5x \cot 5x + 2x \csc 5x$

12. $\dfrac{1}{2x}, x > 0$ **13.** $\dfrac{e^x}{1 + e^x}$ **14.** $-xe^{-x} + e^{-x}$ **15.** e

16. $\cot x$, where x is an interval of the form $(k\pi, (k + 1)\pi)$, k even

17. $-\dfrac{1}{\cos^{-1} x\sqrt{1 - x^2}}$ **18.** $\dfrac{2}{\theta \ln 2}$ **19.** $\dfrac{1}{(t - 7)\ln 5}, t > 7$

20. $-8^{-t} \ln 8$ **21.** $\dfrac{2(\ln x)x^{\ln x}}{x}$

22. $\dfrac{(2 \cdot 2^x)[x^3 \ln 2 + x \ln 2 + 1]}{(x^2 + 1)^{3/2}}$ or

$\dfrac{(2x)2^x}{\sqrt{x^2 + 1}}\left(\dfrac{1}{2} + \ln 2 - \dfrac{x}{x^2 + 1}\right)$

23. $\dfrac{e^{\tan^{-1} x}}{1 + x^2}$ **24.** $-\dfrac{u}{\sqrt{u^2 - u^4}} = -\dfrac{u}{|u|\sqrt{1 - u^2}}$

25. $\dfrac{t}{|t|\sqrt{t^2 - 1}} + \sec^{-1} t - \dfrac{1}{2t}$ **26.** $-\dfrac{2 + 2t^2}{1 + 4t^2} + 2t \cot^{-1} 2t$

27. $\cos^{-1} z$ **28.** $-\dfrac{1}{x} + \dfrac{\csc^{-1}\sqrt{x}}{\sqrt{x - 1}}$ **29.** -1

30. $2\left(\dfrac{1 + \sin \theta}{1 - \cos \theta}\right)\left(\dfrac{\cos \theta - \sin \theta - 1}{(1 - \cos \theta)^2}\right)$ **31.** For all $x \neq 0$

32. For all real x **33.** For all $x < 1$ **34.** For all $x \neq 0$ **35.** $-\dfrac{y + 2}{x + 3}$

36. $-\dfrac{1}{3}(xy)^{-1/5}$ **37.** $-\dfrac{y}{x}$ or $-\dfrac{1}{x^2}$ **38.** $\dfrac{1}{2y(x + 1)^2}$ **39.** $-\dfrac{2x}{y^5}$

40. $\dfrac{1 + 2xy^2}{x^4 y^3}$ **41.** $-2\dfrac{(3y^2 + 1)^2 \cos x + 12y \sin^2 x}{(3y^2 + 1)^3}$

42. $\dfrac{2}{3}x^{-4/3}y^{1/3} + \dfrac{2}{3}x^{-5/3}y^{2/3} = \dfrac{8}{3}x^{-5/3}y^{1/3}$

43. $32e^{x\sqrt[8]{2}}$ **44.** $y = 32 \sin (x\sqrt[8]{2})$

45. (a) $y - \sqrt{3} = (2/\sqrt{3})(x - 3)$

(b) $y - \sqrt{3} = (-\sqrt{3}/2)(x - 3)$

46. (a) $y + \sqrt{3} = 8\left(x - \dfrac{\pi}{3}\right)$ (b) $y + \sqrt{3} = -\dfrac{1}{8}\left(x - \dfrac{\pi}{3}\right)$

47. (a) $y - 2 = (-1/4)(x - 1)$ (b) $y - 2 = 4(x - 1)$

48. (a) $y - 1 = (-5/4)(x - 4)$ (b) $y - 1 = (4/5)(x - 4)$

49. $y + \sqrt{2} = x - \sqrt{2}$ **50.** $y - 2\sqrt{2} = (4/3)(x + 3\sqrt{2}/2)$

51. $y - 5/\sqrt{3} = (10/3)(x - 2\sqrt{3})$

52. $y + \pi/4 + \sqrt{2}/2 = (1 + \sqrt{2})(x - \sqrt{2}/2)$

53. (a) $\lim\limits_{x \to 0^-} f(x) = \lim\limits_{x \to 0^-} (\sin ax + b \cos x) = b$ and

$\lim\limits_{x \to 0^+} f(x) = \lim\limits_{x \to 0^+} (5x + 3) = 3$. Thus

$\lim\limits_{x \to 0} f(x) = f(0) = 3$ if and only if $b = 3$.

(b) $f'(x) = \begin{cases} a \cos ax - b \sin x, & x < 0 \\ 5, & x > 0 \end{cases}$. The slopes match at

$x = 0$ if and only if $a = 5$.

(c) No. Although the slopes match, the function is not continuous.

54. (a) The function is continuous for all values of m, because the right-hand limit as $x \to 0$ is equal to $f(0) = 0$ for any value of m.

(b) The left-hand derivative at $x = 0$ is 2, and the right-hand derivative at $x = 0$ is m, so in order for the function to be differentiable at $x = 0$, m must be 2.

55. (a) For all $x \neq 1$ **(b)** At $x = 1$ **(c)** Nowhere

56. (a) For all x **(b)** Nowhere **(c)** Nowhere

57. (a) $[-1, 1) \cup (1, 3]$ **(b)** At $x = 1$ **(c)** Nowhere

58. (a) $[-3, 0) \cup (0, 3]$ **(b)** Nowhere **(c)** At $x = 0$

59. (a) $-\cos x$ **(b)** $14x - 13$ **(c)** $2t - 3$ **(d)** $2t - 30t^5$

60. (a) $\dfrac{2}{2x + 7} - \dfrac{3}{3x + 2}$ **(b)** 1 **(c)** $-2t$ **(d)** $\dfrac{80}{3\sqrt[6]{t}}$

61. (a) $y - 4 = -\dfrac{1}{3}(x - 2)$ **(b)** $y - 2 = \dfrac{1}{3}(x - 4)$

(c) $y - 2 = \dfrac{1}{2}(x - 2)$

62. (a) $y - 3 = \dfrac{1}{2}(x - 1)$ **(b)** $y - 1 = -\dfrac{1}{2}(x - 3)$

(c) $y - 3 = -4(x - 1)$

63. $\dfrac{dy}{dx} = \dfrac{(x + 2)^5 (2x - 3)^4}{(x + 17)^2} \left(\dfrac{5}{x + 2} + \dfrac{8}{2x + 3} - \dfrac{2}{x + 17} \right)$

64. $\dfrac{dy}{dx} = (x^2 + 2)^{x+5} \left(\ln(x^2 + 2) + \dfrac{2x^2 + 10x}{x^2 + 2} \right)$

65. (a) $f(x) = \dfrac{x^2}{2}$ or $f(x) = \dfrac{x^2}{2} + C$

(b) $f(x) = e^x$ or $f(x) = Ce^x$

(c) $f(x) = e^{-x}$ or $f(x) = Ce^{-x}$

(d) $f(x) = e^x$ or $f(x) = e^{-x}$ or $f(x) = Ce^x + De^{-x}$

(e) $f(x) = \sin x$ or $f(x) = \cos x$ or $f(x) = C \sin x + D \cos x$

66. (a) $-13/10$ **(b)** $-1/3$ **(c)** $1/10$ **(d)** -1 **(e)** $-2/3$ **(f)** -12

67. (a) 5 **(b)** 0 **(c)** 8 **(d)** 2 **(e)** 4 **(f)** -1 **68.** $\sqrt{3}$ **69.** $-1/6$

70. (a) One possible answer:

$x(t) = 10 \cos\left(t + \dfrac{\pi}{4} \right)$

$y(t) = 0$

(b) $5\sqrt{2}$ **(c)** $s = -10$ and $s = 10$

(d) At $t = \pi/4$:

Velocity $= -10$

Speed $= 10$

Acceleration $= 0$

71. (a) $A(-1, 1); B(1, -1)$ **(b)** $C(-0.5, 2); D(0.5, -2)$

72. (a) $A\left(-\sqrt{2}, -2\sqrt{2}\right); B\left(\sqrt{2}, 2\sqrt{2}\right)$

(b) $C(-2, -2); D(2, 2)$

73. (a) $A(-2, -2)$ **(b)** $B(-1, -3)$

74. At y-intercept $\left(0, 2\sqrt{2}\right)$ the slope is $\dfrac{2 + \sqrt{2}}{2}$.

At y-intercept $\left(0, -2\sqrt{2}\right)$ the slope is $\dfrac{2 - \sqrt{2}}{2}$.

At x-intercept $\left(2 + 2\sqrt{3}, 0\right)$ the slope is $\dfrac{\sqrt{3}}{\sqrt{3} + 1}$.

At x-intercept $\left(2 - 2\sqrt{3}, 0\right)$ the slope is $\dfrac{\sqrt{3}}{\sqrt{3} - 1}$.

75. 6

76. Every sinusoid with amplitude A and period p is the graph of some equation of the form $y = A \sin\left(\dfrac{2\pi}{p} x + k \right) + D$. The slope at any x is $\dfrac{dy}{dx} = A \cdot \dfrac{2\pi}{p} \cos\left(\dfrac{2\pi}{p} x + k \right)$. Since the maximum value of cosine is 1, the maximum slope is $\dfrac{2\pi A}{p}$.

77. Yes

78. (a) $P(0) \approx 1.339$, so initially, one student was infected

(b) 200 **(c)** After 5 days, when the rate is 50 students/day

79. (a) $-\dfrac{2}{3}$ **(b)** $-\dfrac{5}{27}$ **80.** $-1/\left(3\sqrt{3}\right)$

81. (a) $g'(x) = k \cdot e^{kx} + f'(x)$, so $g'(0) = k + 3$.

$g''(x) = k^2 \cdot e^{kx} + f''(x)$, so $g''(0) = k^2 - 1$.

(b) $h'(x) = b \sin(bx) f(x) + f'(x) \cos(bx)$, so

$h'(0) = b \cdot \sin(0) + 3 \cdot \cos(0) = 3$. Note that

$h(0) = \cos(0) \cdot f(0) = 1 \cdot 2 = 2$, so the

tangent line has equation $y - 2 = 3(x - 0)$.

82. (a) $\dfrac{dy}{dx} = \dfrac{e^x - e^{-x}}{2}$ **(b)** $\dfrac{d^2 y}{dx^2} = \dfrac{e^x + e^{-x}}{2}$

(c) At $x = 1$, $\dfrac{dy}{dx} = \dfrac{e^1 - e^{-1}}{2} = 1.175$ and

$y = \dfrac{e^1 + e^{-1}}{2} = 1.543$. The tangent line has equation

$y - 1.543 = 1.175(x - 1)$.

(d) The normal line has equation $y - 1.543 = -0.851(x - 1)$.

(e) The tangent line is horizontal where $dy/dx = 0$; that is, where $e^x = e^{-x}$. This is true only at $x = 0$.

83. (a) The domain of f is the interval $(-1, 1)$.

(b) $f'(x) = \dfrac{-2x}{1 - x^2} = \dfrac{2x}{x^2 - 1}$ on the domain $(-1, 1)$.

(c) The domain of f' is the interval $(-1, 1)$.

(d) $f''(x) = \left(\dfrac{2x}{x^2 - 1} \right)' = \dfrac{2(x^2 - 1) - 2x(2x)}{(x^2 - 1)^2} = \dfrac{-2(x^2 + 1)}{(x^2 - 1)^2} < 0$

for all x in the domain of f, since $\dfrac{x^2 + 1}{(x^2 - 1)^2} > 0$ for all x between -1 and 1.

CHAPTER 5

Section 5.1

Quick Review 5.1

1. $\dfrac{-1}{2\sqrt{4 - x}}$ **3.** $\dfrac{-\sin(\ln x)}{x}$ **5.** (c)

7. (d) **9.** ∞ **11. (a)** 1 **(b)** 1 **(c)** Undefined

Exercises 5.1

1. Minima at $(-2, 0)$ and $(2, 0)$, maximum at $(0, 2)$

3. Maximum at $(0, 5)$

5. Maximum at $x = b$, minimum at $x = c_2$; Extreme Value Theorem applies, so both the max and min exist.

7. Maximum at $x = c$, no minimum; Extreme Value Theorem doesn't apply, since the function isn't defined on a closed interval.

9. Maximum at $x = c$, minimum at $x = a$; Extreme Value Theorem doesn't apply, since the function isn't continuous.

11. Maximum value is $\frac{1}{4} + \ln 4$ at $x = 4$; minimum value is 1 at $x = 1$;

local maximum at $\left(\frac{1}{2}, 2 - \ln 2\right)$

13. Maximum value is $\ln 4$ at $x = 3$; minimum value is 0 at $x = 0$.

15. Maximum value is 1 at $x = \frac{\pi}{4}$; minimum value is -1 at $x = \frac{5\pi}{4}$; local

minimum at $\left(0, \frac{1}{\sqrt{2}}\right)$; local maximum at $\left(\frac{7\pi}{4}, 0\right)$

17. Maximum value is $3^{2/5}$ at $x = -3$; minimum value is 0 at $x = 0$. $[(0, 0)$ is not a stationary point]

19. Min value 1 at $x = 2$

21. Local max at $(-2, 17)$: local min at $\left(\frac{4}{3}, -\frac{41}{27}\right)$

23. Min value 0 at $x = -1, 1$ **25.** Min value 1 at $x = 0$

27. Max value 2 at $x = 1$; min value 0 at $x = -1, 3$

29. Maximum value is $\frac{1}{2}$ at $x = 1$;

minimum value is $-\frac{1}{2}$ at $x = -1$.

31. Maximum value is 11 at $x = 5$;

minimum value is 5 on the interval $[-3, 2]$;

local maximum at $(-5, 9)$

33. Maximum value is 5 on the interval $[3, \infty)$;

minimum value is -5 on the interval $(-\infty, -2]$.

35.

crit. pt.	derivative	extremum	value
$x = -\frac{4}{5}$	0	local max	$\frac{12}{25}10^{1/3}$
$x = 0$	undefined	local min	0

$(0, 0)$ is not a stationary point.

37.

crit. pt.	derivative	extremum	value
$x = -2$	undefined	local max	0
$x = -\sqrt{2}$	0	minimum	-2
$x = \sqrt{2}$	0	maximum	2
$x = 2$	undefined	local min	0

$(-2, 0)$ and $(2, 0)$ are not stationary points.

39.

crit. pt.	derivative	extremum	value
$x = 1$	undefined	minimum	2

$(1, 2)$ is not a stationary point.

41.

crit. pt.	derivative	extremum	value
$x = -1$	0	maximum	5
$x = 1$	undefined	local min	1
$x = 3$	0	maximum	5

$(1, 1)$ is not a stationary point.

43. **(a)** Max value is 144 at $x = 2$.   **(b)** The largest volume of the box is 144 cubic units and it occurs when $x = 2$.

45. False. For example, the maximum could occur at a corner, where $f'(c)$ would not exist.

47. E   **49.** B

51. (a) No
   (b) The derivative is defined and nonzero for $x \neq 2$. Also, $f(2) = 0$, and $f(x) > 0$ for all $x \neq 2$.
   (c) No, because $(-\infty, \infty)$ is not a closed interval.
   (d) The answers are the same as (a) and (b) with 2 replaced by a.

53. (a) $f'(x) = 3ax^2 + 2bx + c$ is a quadratic, so it can have 0, 1, or 2 zeros, which would be the critical points of f. Examples:

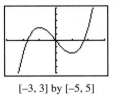

$[-3, 3]$ by $[-5, 5]$

The function $f(x) = x^3 - 3x$ has two critical points at $x = -1$ and $x = 1$.

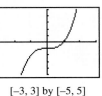

$[-3, 3]$ by $[-5, 5]$

The function $f(x) = x^3 - 1$ has one critical point at $x = 0$.

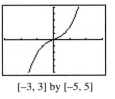

$[-3, 3]$ by $[-5, 5]$

The function $f(x) = x^3 + x$ has no critical points.

(b) Two or none.

55. (a)

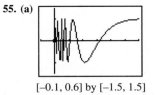

$f(0) = 0$ is not a local extreme value because in any open interval containing $x = 0$, there are infinitely many points where $f(x) = 1$ and where $f(x) = -1$.

$[-0.1, 0.6]$ by $[-1.5, 1.5]$

(b) One possible answer, on the interval $[0, 1]$:

$$f(x) = \begin{cases} (1 - x) \cos \dfrac{1}{1 - x}, & 0 \leq x < 1 \\ 0, & x = 1 \end{cases}$$

This function has no local extreme value at $x = 1$. Note that it is continuous on $[0, 1]$.

Section 5.2

Quick Review 5.2

1. $\left(-\sqrt{3}, \sqrt{3}\right)$ **3.** $[-2, 2]$ **5.** On $(-2, 2)$

7. For all x in its domain, or, for all $x \neq \pm 1$ **9.** $C = 3$

Exercises 5.2

1. (a) Yes.   **(b)** $2c + 2 = \dfrac{2 - (-1)}{1 - 0} = 3$, so $c = \dfrac{1}{2}$

3. No. There is a vertical tangent at $x = 0$.

5. (a) Yes.

(b) $\dfrac{1}{\sqrt{1 - c^2}} = \dfrac{(\pi/2) - (-\pi/2)}{1 - (-1)}$

$= \dfrac{\pi}{2}$, so $c = \sqrt{1 - 4/\pi^2} \approx 0.771$.

7. No. The split function is discontinuous at $x = \dfrac{\pi}{2}$.

9. (a) $y = \dfrac{5}{2}$ **(b)** $y = 2$

11. Because the trucker's average speed was 79.5 mph, and by the Mean Value Theorem, the trucker must have been going that speed at least once during the trip.

13. Because its average speed was approximately 7.667 knots, and by the Mean Value Theorem, it must have been going that speed at least once during the trip.

15. (a) Local maximum at $\left(\dfrac{5}{2}, \dfrac{25}{4}\right)$ **(b)** On $\left(-\infty, \dfrac{5}{2}\right]$ **(c)** On $\left[\dfrac{5}{2}, \infty\right)$

17. (a) None   **(b)** None   **(c)** On $(-\infty, 0)$ and $(0, \infty)$

19. (a) None   **(b)** On $(-\infty, \infty)$ **(c)** None

21. (a) Local maximum at $(-2, 4)$ **(b)** None   **(c)** On $[-2, \infty)$

23. (a) Local max at $\left(8/3, \dfrac{16\sqrt{3}}{9}\right)$; local min at $(4, 0)$

(b) On $(-\infty, 8/3]$ **(c)** On $[8/3, 4]$

25. (a) Local max at $(-2, 1/4)$;
local min at $(2, -1/4)$

(b) On $(-\infty, -2]$ and $[2, \infty)$ **(c)** On $[-2, 2]$

27. (a) Local maximum at $\approx (-1.126, -0.036)$;
local minimum at $\approx (0.559, -2.639)$

(b) On $(-\infty, -1.126]$ and $[0.559, \infty)$

(c) On $[-1.126, 0.559]$

29. $\dfrac{x^2}{2} + C$ **31.** $x^3 - x^2 + x + C$ **33.** $e^x + C$

35. $\dfrac{1}{x} + \dfrac{1}{2}, x > 0$ **37.** $\ln(x + 2) + 3$

39. Possible answers:

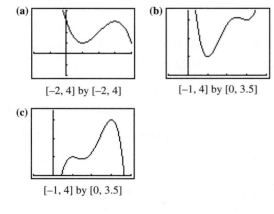

(a)   **(b)**

$[-2, 4]$ by $[-2, 4]$ $[-1, 4]$ by $[0, 3.5]$

(c)

$[-1, 4]$ by $[0, 3.5]$

41. One possible answer:

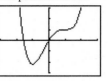

$[-3, 3]$ by $[-15, 15]$

43. (a) 48 m/sec
(b) 720 meters
(c) After about 27.604 seconds, and it will be going about 48.166 m/sec

45. Because the function is not continuous on $[0, 1]$

47. $f(x)$ must be zero at least once between a and b by the Intermediate Value Theorem.
Now suppose that $f(x)$ is zero twice between a and b. Then by the Mean Value Theorem, $f'(x)$ would have to be zero at least once between the two zeros of $f(x)$, but this can't be true, since we are given that $f'(x) \neq 0$ on this interval.
Therefore, $f(x)$ is zero once and only once between a and b.

49. Let $f(x) = x + \ln(x + 1)$. Then $f(x)$ is continuous and differentiable everywhere on $[0, 3]$. $f'(x) = 1 + \dfrac{1}{x + 1}$, which is never zero on $[0, 3]$. Now $f(0) = 0$, so $x = 0$ is one solution of the equation. If there were a second solution, $f(x)$ would be zero twice in $[0, 3]$, and by the Mean Value Theorem, $f'(x)$ would have to be zero somewhere between the two zeros of $f(x)$. But this can't happen, since $f'(x)$ is never zero on $[0, 3]$. Therefore, $f(x) = 0$ has exactly one solution in the interval $[0, 3]$.

51. False. For example, the function x^3 is increasing on $(-1, 1)$, but $f'(0) = 0$.

53. A   **55.** E

57. $\dfrac{f(b) - f(a)}{b - a} = \dfrac{\dfrac{1}{b} - \dfrac{1}{a}}{b - a} = -\dfrac{1}{ab}$

$f'(c) = -\dfrac{1}{c^2}$, so $-\dfrac{1}{c^2} = -\dfrac{1}{ab}$ and $c^2 = ab$.

Thus, $c = \sqrt{ab}$.

59. By the Mean Value Theorem, $\sin b - \sin a = (\cos c)(b - a)$ for some c between a and b. Taking the absolute value of both sides and using $|\cos c| \leq 1$ gives the result.

61. Let $f(x)$ be a monotonic function defined on an interval D. For any two values in D, we may let x_1 be the smaller value and let x_2 be the larger value, so $x_1 < x_2$. Then either $f(x_1) < f(x_2)$ (if f is increasing), or $f(x_1) > f(x_2)$ (if f is decreasing), which means $f(x_1) \neq f(x_2)$. Therefore, f is one-to-one.

63. (a) This is the point-slope form of the linear equation that passes through the point $(a, f(a))$ with slope $(f(b) - f(a))/(b - a)$.
(b) Since both f and the linear function are continuous and differentiable, their difference is both continuous and differentiable.

$$g(a) = f(a) - \dfrac{f(b) - f(a)}{b - a}(a - a) - f(a) = 0,$$

$$g(b) = f(b) - \dfrac{f(b) - f(a)}{b - a}(b - a) - f(a)$$

$$= f(b) - (f(b) - f(a)) - f(a) = 0$$

(c) Since g satisfies the conditions of Rolle's Theorem (Exercise 62), we know that there is at least one point c between a and b for which

$$0 = g'(c) = f'(c) - \dfrac{f(b) - f(a)}{b - a},$$

and therefore

$$f'(c) = \dfrac{f(b) - f(a)}{b - a}.$$

Section 5.3

Quick Review 5.3

1. $(-3, 3)$ **3.** f: all reals f': all reals   **5.** f: $x \neq 2$ f': $x \neq 2$

7. $y = 0$ **9.** $y = 0$ and $y = 200$

Exercises 5.3

1. Local minimum at $\left(\dfrac{1}{2}, -\dfrac{5}{4}\right)$; $-\dfrac{5}{4}$ is an absolute minimum.

3. Local maximum: $(0, 1)$; local minima: $(-1, -1)$ and $(1, -1)$; -1 is an absolute minimum.

5. Local maxima: $(-\sqrt{8}, 0)$ and $(2, 4)$; local minima: $(-2, -4)$ and $(\sqrt{8}, 0)$; 4 is an absolute maximum and -4 is an absolute minimum.

7. (a) $(-7/4, \infty)$ (b) $(-\infty, -7/4)$

9. (a) $(-\infty, 0)$ (b) $(0, \infty)$

11. (a) None   (b) $(1, \infty)$ **13.** $(-2, -2/e^2)$

15. $(0, 0)$ **17.** $(0, 0)$ and $(-2, 6\sqrt[3]{2})$ **19.** $(1, 1)$

21. (a) Zero: $x = \pm 1$; positive: $(-\infty, -1)$ and $(1, \infty)$; negative: $(-1, 1)$
(b) Zero: $x = 0$; positive: $(0, \infty)$; negative: $(-\infty, 0)$

23. (a) $(-\infty, -2]$ and $[0, 2]$ (b) $[-2, 0]$ and $[2, \infty)$
(c) Local maxima: $x = -2$ and $x = 2$; local minimum: $x = 0$

25. (a) $v(t) = 2t - 4$ (b) $a(t) = 2$
(c) It begins at position 3 moving in a negative direction. It moves to position -1 when $t = 2$, and then changes direction, moving in a positive direction thereafter.

27. (a) $v(t) = 3t^2 - 3$ (b) $a(t) = 6t$
(c) It begins at position 3 moving in a negative direction. It moves to position 1 when $t = 1$, and then changes direction, moving in a positive direction thereafter.

29. (a) $t = 2.2, 6, 9.8$ (b) $t = 4, 8, 11$

31. $y' = 3 - 3x^2$ and $y'' = -6x$.
$y' = 0$ at ± 1. $y''(-1) > 0$ and $y''(1) < 0$, so there is a local minimum at $(-1, 3)$ and a local maximum at $(1, 7)$.

33. $y' = 3x^2 + 6x$ and $y'' = 6x + 6$.
$y' = 0$ at -2 and 0. $y''(-2) < 0$ and $y''(0) > 0$, so there is a local maximum at $(-2, 2)$ and a local minimum at $(0, -2)$.

35. $y' = (x + 1)e^x$ and $y'' = (x + 2)e^x$.
$y' = 0$ at -1 and $y''(-1) > 0$, so there is a local minimum at $(-1, -1/e)$.

37. (a) None   (b) At $x = 2$ (c) At $x = 1$ and $x = \dfrac{5}{3}$

39.

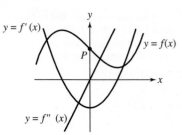

41. No. f must have a horizontal tangent line at that point, but it could be increasing (or decreasing) on both sides of the point, and there would be no local extremum.

43. One possible answer:

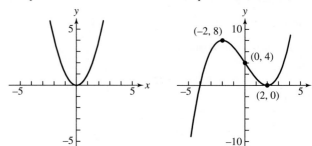

45. One possible answer:

47. (a) $[0, 1]$, $[3, 4]$, and $[5.5, 6]$ (b) $[1, 3]$ and $[4, 5.5]$
(c) Local maxima: $x = 1$, $x = 4$ (if f is continuous at $x = 4$), and $x = 6$; local minima: $x = 0$, $x = 3$, and $x = 5.5$

49. (a) Absolute maximum at $(1, 2)$; absolute minimum at $(3, -2)$
(b) None
(c) One possible answer:

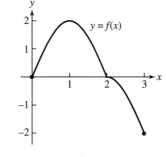

51.

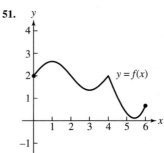

53. False. For example, consider $f(x) = x^4$ at $c = 0$.

55. A   **57.** C

59. (a) In Exercise 7, $a = 4$ and $b = 21$, so $-\dfrac{b}{3a} = -\dfrac{7}{4}$, which is the x value where the point of inflection occurs. The local extrema are at $x = -2$ and $x = -\dfrac{3}{2}$, which are symmetric about $x = -\dfrac{7}{4}$.

(b) In Exercise 2, $a = -2$ and $b = 6$, so $-\dfrac{b}{3a} = 1$, which is the x value where the point of inflection occurs. The local extrema are at $x = 0$ and $x = 2$, which are symmetric about $x = 1$.

(c) $f'(x) = 3ax^2 + 2bx + c$ and $f''(x) = 6ax + 2b$. The point of inflection will occur where $f''(x) = 0$, which is at $x = -\dfrac{b}{3a}$.
If there are local extrema, they will occur at the zeros of $f'(x)$. Since $f'(x)$ is quadratic, its graph is a parabola and any zeros will be symmetric about the vertex, which will also be where $f''(x) = 0$.

Quick Quiz (Sections 5.1–5.3)

1. C   **3.** B

Section 5.4

Quick Review 5.4

1. None   **3.** $\dfrac{200\pi}{3}$ cm^3

5. $-\sin\alpha$ **7.** $\sin\alpha$ **9.** $x = 1$ and $y = \sqrt{3}$

Exercises 5.4

1. (a) As large as possible: 0 and 20; as small as possible: 10 and 10

(b) As large as possible: $\dfrac{79}{4}$ and $\dfrac{1}{4}$; as small as possible: 0 and 20

3. Smallest perimeter $= 16$ in., dimensions are 4 in. by 4 in.

5. (a) $y = 1 - x$ **(b)** $A(x) = 2x(1 - x)$

(c) Largest area $= \dfrac{1}{2}$, dimensions are 1 by $\dfrac{1}{2}$

7. Largest volume is $\dfrac{2450}{27} \approx 90.74$ in^3; dimensions: $\dfrac{5}{3}$ in. by $\dfrac{14}{3}$ in. by $\dfrac{35}{3}$ in.

9. Largest area $= 80{,}000$ m^2; dimensions: 200 m (perpendicular to river) by 400 m (parallel to river)

11. (a) 10 ft by 10 ft by 5 ft
(b) Assume that the weight is minimized when the total area of the bottom and the 4 sides is minimized.

13. 18 in. high by 9 in. wide

15. $\theta = \dfrac{\pi}{2}$ **17.** $\dfrac{8}{\pi}$ to 1

19. (a) $V(x) = 2x(24 - 2x)(18 - 2x)$
(b) Domain: $(0, 9)$

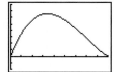

[0, 9] by [–400, 1600]

(c) Maximum volume ≈ 1309.95 in^3 when $x \approx 3.39$ in.
(d) $V'(x) = 24x^2 - 336x + 864$, so the critical point is at $x = 7 - \sqrt{13}$, which confirms the result in part (c).
(e) $x = 2$ in. or $x = 5$ in.
(f) The dimensions of the resulting box are $2x$ in., $(24 - 2x)$ in., and $(18 - 2x)$ in. Each of these measurements must be positive, so that gives the domain of $(0, 9)$.

21. Dimensions: width ≈ 3.44, height ≈ 2.61; maximum area ≈ 8.98

23. Set $r'(x) = c'(x)$: $4x^{-1/2} = 4x$. The only positive critical value is $x = 1$, so profit is maximized at a production level of 1000 units. Note that $(r - c)''(x) = -2(x)^{-3/2} - 4 < 0$ for all positive x, so the Second Derivative Test confirms the maximum.

25. Set $c'(x) = c(x)/x$: $3x^2 - 20x + 30 = x^2 - 10x + 30$. The only positive solution is $x = 5$, so average cost is minimized at a production level of 5000 units. Note that $\dfrac{d^2}{dx^2}\left(\dfrac{c(x)}{x}\right) = 2 > 0$ for all positive x, so the Second Derivative Test confirms the minimum.

27. 67 people

29. (a) $f'(x)$ is a quadratic polynomial, and as such it can have 0, 1, or 2 zeros. If it has 0 or 1 zeros, then its sign never changes, so $f(x)$ has no local extrema.

If $f'(x)$ has 2 zeros, then its sign changes twice, and $f(x)$ has 2 local extrema at those points.

(b) Possible answers:
No local extrema: $y = x^3$;
2 local extrema: $y = x^3 - 3x$

31. (a) $x = 12$ cm and $y = 6$ cm
(b) $x = 12$ cm and $y = 6$ cm

33. (a) $a = 16$ **(b)** $a = -1$

35. (a) $a = -3$ and $b = -9$ **(b)** $a = -3$ and $b = -24$

37. (a) $4\sqrt{3}$ in. wide by $4\sqrt{6}$ in. deep

(b)

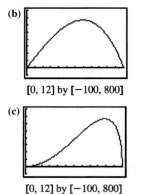

[0, 12] by [–100, 800]

(c)

[0, 12] by [–100, 800]

Changing the value of k changes the maximum strength, but not the dimensions of the strongest beam. The graphs for different values of k look the same except that the vertical scale is different.

39. (a) Maximum speed $= 10\pi$ cm/sec;

maximum speed is at $t = \dfrac{1}{2}, \dfrac{3}{2}, \dfrac{5}{2}, \dfrac{7}{2}$ seconds;

position at those times is $s = 0$ cm (rest position); acceleration at those times is 0 cm/sec^2.
(b) The magnitude of the acceleration is greatest when the cart is at positions $s = \pm 10$ cm; The speed of the cart is 0 cm/sec at those times.

41. The minimum distance is $\dfrac{\sqrt{5}}{2}$.

43. No. It has an absolute minimum at the point $\left(\dfrac{1}{2}, \dfrac{3}{4}\right)$.

45. (a) Whenever t is an integer multiple of π sec
(b) The greatest distance is $3\sqrt{3}/2$ m when $t = 2\pi/3$ and $4\pi/3$ sec.

47. $\theta = \dfrac{\pi}{6}$ **49.** $M = \dfrac{C}{2}$

51. True. This is guaranteed by the Extreme Value Theorem (Section 5.1).

53. D   **55.** B

57. Let P be the foot of the perpendicular from A to the mirror, and Q be the foot of the perpendicular from B to the mirror. Suppose the light strikes the mirror at point R on the way from A to B. Let:

$$a = \text{distance from } A \text{ to } P$$
$$b = \text{distance from } B \text{ to } Q$$
$$c = \text{distance from } P \text{ to } Q$$
$$x = \text{distance from } P \text{ to } R$$

To minimize the time is to minimize the total distance the light travels going from A to B. The total distance is

$$D(x) = (x^2 + a^2)^{1/2} + ((c - x)^2 + b^2)^{1/2}.$$

Then $D'(x) = 0$ and $D(x)$ has its minimum when

$$x = \frac{ac}{a + b}, \text{ or, } \frac{x}{a} = \frac{c}{a + b}.$$ It follows that

$$c - x = \frac{bc}{a + b}, \text{ or } \frac{c - x}{b} = \frac{c}{a + b}.$$ This means that the two triangles APR and BQR are similar, and the two angles must be equal.

59. (a) $\dfrac{dv}{dr} = cr(2r_0 - 3r)$ which is zero when $r = \dfrac{2}{3}r_0$.

(b)

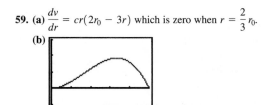

[0, 0.5] by [−0.01, 0.03]

61. $p(x) = 6x - (x^3 - 6x^2 + 15x),\ x \geq 0$. This function has its maximum value at the points $(0, 0)$ and $(3, 0)$.

63. (a) $y'(0) = 0$ **(b)** $y'(-L) = 0$
   (c) $y(0) = 0$, so $d = 0$. $y'(0) = 0$, so $c = 0$.
   Then $y(-L) = -aL^3 + bL^2 = H$ and
   $y'(-L) = 3aL^2 - 2bL = 0$.

   Solving, $a = 2\dfrac{H}{L^3}$ and $b = 3\dfrac{H}{L^2}$, which gives the equation shown.

65. (a) The x- and y-intercepts of the line through R and T are $x - \dfrac{a}{f'(x)}$
   and $a - xf'(x)$ respectively.

   The area of the triangle is the product of these two values.
   (b) Domain: $(0, 10)$

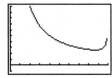

[0, 10] by [−100, 1000]

   The vertical asymptotes at $x = 0$ and $x = 10$ correspond to horizontal or vertical tangent lines, which do not form triangles.
   (c) Height $= 15$, which is 3 times the y-coordinate of the center of the ellipse.
   (d) Part (a) remains unchanged.
   The domain is $(0, C)$ and the graph is similar.

   The minimum area occurs when $x^2 = \dfrac{3C^2}{4}$. From this, it follows that

   the triangle has minimum area when its height is $3B$.

Section 5.5

Quick Review 5.5

1. $2x \cos (x^2 + 1)$ **3.** $x \approx -0.567$ **5.** $y = x + 1$

7. (a) $x = -1$ **(b)** $x = -\dfrac{e + 1}{2e} \approx -0.684$

9.

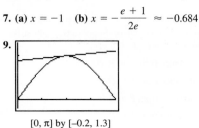

[0, π] by [−0.2, 1.3]

Exercises 5.5

1. (a) $L(x) = 10x - 13$
   (b) Differs from the true value in absolute value by less than 10^{-1}
3. (a) $L(x) = 2$
   (b) Differs from the true value in absolute value by less than 10^{-2}

5. (a) $L(x) = x - \pi$
   (b) Differs from the true value in absolute value by less than 10^{-3}
7. $f(0) = 1$. Also, $f'(x) = k(1 + x)^{k-1}$, so $f'(0) = k$. This means the linearization at $x = 0$ is $L(x) = 1 + kx$.

9. (a) $1 - 6x$ **(b)** $2 + 2x$ **(c)** $1 - \dfrac{x}{2}$

11. $y = 10 + 0.05(x - 10)$, so $y = 10.05$
13. $y = 10 + (1/300)(x - 1000)$, so $y = 10 - 1/150 = 9.99\overline{3}$
15. (a) $dy = (3x^2 - 3)\,dx$ **(b)** $dy = 0.45$ at the given values
17. (a) $dy = (2x \ln x + x)\,dx$ **(b)** $dy = 0.01$ at the given values
19. (a) $dy = (\cos x)\,e^{\sin x}\,dx$ **(b)** $dy = 0.1$ at the given values
21. (a) $dy = \dfrac{dx}{(x + 1)^2}$ **(b)** $dy = 0.01$ at the given values

23. $-\dfrac{x}{\sqrt{1 - x^2}}\,dx$ **25.** $\dfrac{4}{1 + 16x^2}\,dx$

27. (a) 0.21   **(b)** 0.2   **(c)** 0.01
29. (a) $-\dfrac{2}{11}$ **(b)** $-\dfrac{1}{5}$ **(c)** $\dfrac{1}{55}$

31. $\Delta V \approx 4\pi a^2\,\Delta r = 20\pi$ cm^3 **33.** $\Delta V \approx 3a^2\,\Delta x = 15$ cm^3
35. $\Delta V \approx 2\pi ah\,\Delta r = \pi h$ cm^3 **37.** $2\pi(10)(0.1) \approx 6.3$ in^2
39. $3(15)^2\,(0.2) \approx 135$ cm^3 **41. (a)** $x + 1$ **(b)** $f(0.1) \approx 1.1$

   (c) The actual value is less than 1.1, since the derivative is decreasing over the interval $[0, 0.1]$.

43. The diameter grew $\dfrac{2}{\pi} \approx 0.6366$ in. The cross-section area grew about 10 in^2.

45. The side should be measured to within 1%.

47. $V = \pi r^2 h$ (where h is constant), so $\dfrac{\Delta V}{V} \approx \dfrac{2\pi rh\Delta r}{\pi r^2 h} = 2\dfrac{\Delta r}{r} = 0.2\%$

49. Since $V = \dfrac{4}{3}\pi r^3$, we have $\Delta V = 4\pi r^2\,\Delta r = 4\pi r^2\left(\dfrac{1}{16\pi}\right) = \dfrac{r^2}{4}$.

   The volume error in each case is simply $\dfrac{r^2}{4}$ in^3.

Sphere Type	True Radius	Tape Error	Radius Error	Volume Error
Orange	2″	1/8″	$1/16\pi''$	1 in^3
Melon	4″	1/8″	$1/16\pi''$	4 in^3
Beach Ball	7″	1/8″	$1/16\pi''$	12.25 in^3

51. About 37.87 to 1   **53.** $x \approx 0.682328$ **55.** $x \approx 0.386237,\ 1.961569$
57. True. A look at the graph reveals the problem. The graph decreases after $x = 1$ toward a horizontal asymptote of $x = 0$, so the x-intercepts of the tangent lines keep getting bigger without approaching a zero.
59. B   **61.** D
63. If $f'(x_1) \neq 0$, then x_2 and all later approximations are equal to x_1.
65. $x_2 = -2,\ x_3 = 4,\ x_4 = -8$, and $x_5 = 16$;
   $|x_n| = 2^{n-1}$.

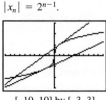

[−10, 10] by [−3, 3]

67. Finding a zero of $\sin x$ by Newton's method would use the recursive formula $x_{n+1} = x_n - \dfrac{\sin (x_n)}{\cos (x_n)} = x_n - \tan x_n$, and that is exactly what the calculator would be doing. Any zero of $\sin x$ would be a multiple of π.

69. $g(a) = c$, so if $E(a) = 0$, then $g(a) = f(a)$ and $c = f(a)$. Then $E(x) = f(x) - g(x) = f(x) - f(a) - m(x - a)$. Thus,

$$\frac{E(x)}{x - a} = \frac{f(x) - f(a)}{x - a} - m. \lim_{x \to a} \frac{f(x) - f(a)}{x - a} = f'(a), \text{ so if the limit}$$

of $\dfrac{E(x)}{x - a}$ is zero, then $m = f'(a)$ and $g(x) = L(x)$.

71. The equation for the tangent is $y - f(x_n) = f'(x_n)(x - x_n)$.

Set $y = 0$ and solve for x.

$$0 - f(x_n) = f'(x_n)(x - x_n)$$
$$-f(x_n) = f'(x_n) \cdot x - f'(x_n) \cdot x_n$$
$$f'(x_n) \cdot x = f'(x_n) \cdot x_n - f(x_n)$$
$$x = x_n - \frac{f(x_n)}{f'(x_n)} \quad (\text{If } f'(x_n) \neq 0)$$

The value of x is the next approximation x_{n+1}.

73. **(a)** $g(a) = (f(a) - f(a)) - f'(a)(a - a) = 0$,
$g'(x) = f'(x) - f'(a), \quad g'(a) = f'(a) - f'(a) = 0$,
$g''(x) = f''(x)$.

(b) By Theorem 1, page 194, $\frac{1}{2}g''(t)$ has a maximum and minimum value on the interval $[a, x]$, $A \leq \dfrac{g''(t)}{2} \leq B$. By the Intermediate Value Theorem, each value in the interval $[A, B]$ is equal to $\frac{1}{2}g''(t)$ for some value of t in $[a, x]$.

(c) The inequality $A \leq \frac{1}{2}g''(t)$ is equivalent to $g''(t) - 2A \geq 0$, and $\frac{1}{2}g''(t) \leq B$ is equivalent to $g''(t) - 2B \leq 0$.

(d) The derivative with respect to t of $g'(t) - 2A(t - a)$ is $g''(t) - 2A \geq 0$. By Corollary 1 on page 204. $g'(a) - 2A(a - a) = 0$ implies that $g'(t) - 2A(t - a) \geq 0$ for all t in $[a, x]$. Similarly, the derivative of $g'(t) - 2B(t - a)$ is $g''(t) - 2B \leq 0$ and $g'(a) - 2B(a - a) = 0$; therefore, $g'(t) - 2B(t - a) \leq 0$ for all t in $[a, x]$.

(e) The derivative with respect to t of $g(t) - A(t - a)^2$ is $g'(t) - 2A(t - a) \geq 0$ and $g(a) - A(a - a)^2 = 0$; therefore, $g(t) - A(t - a)^2 \geq 0$. Similarly, the derivative of $g(t) - B(t - a)^2$ is $g'(t) - 2B(t - a) \leq 0$ and $g(t) - B(t - a)^2 = 0$; therefore, $g(t) - B(t - a)^2 \leq 0$.

(f) The inequality $g(t) - A(t - a)^2 \geq 0$ is equivalent to $A \leq \dfrac{g(t)}{(t - a)^2}$,

and $g(t) - B(t - a)^2 \leq 0$ is equivalent to $\dfrac{g(t)}{(t - a)^2} \leq B$.

Therefore, $A \leq \dfrac{g(t)}{(t - a)^2} \leq B$ for all t in $(a, x]$ and, in particular,

$A \leq \dfrac{g(x)}{(x - a)^2} \leq B$. Therefore, $\dfrac{g(x)}{(x - a)^2} = \dfrac{g''(c)}{2}$ for some c in (a, x).

Section 5.6

Quick Review 5.6

1. $\sqrt{74}$ **3.** $\dfrac{1 - 2y}{2x + 2y - 1}$

5. $2x \cos^2 y$

7. One possible answer: $x = -2 + 6t, y = 1 - 4t, 0 \leq t \leq 1$.

9. One possible answer: $\pi/2 \leq t \leq 3\pi/2$

1. $\dfrac{dA}{dt} = 2\pi r \dfrac{dr}{dt}$

3. **(a)** $\dfrac{dV}{dt} = \pi r^2 \dfrac{dh}{dt}$ **(b)** $\dfrac{dV}{dt} = 2\pi rh \dfrac{dr}{dt}$ **(c)** $\dfrac{dV}{dt} = \pi r^2 \dfrac{dh}{dt} + 2\pi rh \dfrac{dr}{dt}$

5. $\dfrac{ds}{dt} = \dfrac{x \dfrac{dx}{dt} + y \dfrac{dy}{dt} + z \dfrac{dz}{dt}}{\sqrt{x^2 + y^2 + z^2}}$

7. **(a)** 1 volt/sec **(b)** $-\dfrac{1}{3}$ amp/sec **(c)** $\dfrac{dV}{dt} = I \dfrac{dR}{dt} + R \dfrac{dI}{dt}$

(d) $\dfrac{dR}{dt} = \dfrac{3}{2}$ ohms/sec. R is increasing since $\dfrac{dR}{dt}$ is positive.

9. **(a)** $\dfrac{dA}{dt} = 14$ cm^2/sec **(b)** $\dfrac{dP}{dt} = 0$ cm/sec **(c)** $\dfrac{dD}{dt} = -\dfrac{14}{13}$ cm/sec

(d) The area is increasing, because its derivative is positive. The perimeter is not changing, because its derivative is zero. The diagonal length is decreasing, because its derivative is negative.

11. **(a)** 1 ft/min **(b)** 40π ft^2/min

13. $\dfrac{dx}{dt} = \dfrac{3000}{\sqrt{51}}$ mph ≈ 420.084 mph **15.** $\dfrac{19\pi}{2500} \approx 0.0239$ in^3/min

17. **(a)** $\dfrac{32}{9\pi} \approx 1.13$ cm/min **(b)** $-\dfrac{80}{3\pi} \approx -8.49$ cm/min

19. **(a)** 12 ft/sec **(b)** $-\dfrac{119}{2}$ ft^2/sec **(c)** -1 radian/sec

21. **(a)** $\dfrac{5}{2}$ ft/sec **(b)** $-\dfrac{3}{20}$ radian/sec

23. **(a)** $\dfrac{24}{5}$ cm/sec **(b)** 0 cm/sec **(c)** $\dfrac{-1200}{160,801} \approx -0.00746$ cm/sec

25. 1 radian/sec **27.** 1.6 cm^2/min **29.** -3 ft/sec

31. In front: 2 radians/sec; Half second later: 1 radian/sec

33. 7.1 in./min **35.** 29.5 knots

37. **False.** Since $\dfrac{dA}{dt} = 2\pi r \dfrac{dr}{dt}$, the value of $\dfrac{dA}{dt}$ depends on r.

39. E **41.** B

43. **(a)** $\dfrac{dc}{dt} = 0.3, \quad \dfrac{dr}{dt} = 0.9, \quad \dfrac{dp}{dt} = 0.6$

(b) $\dfrac{dc}{dt} = -1.5625, \quad \dfrac{dr}{dt} = 3.5, \quad \dfrac{dp}{dt} = 5.0625$

45. **(a)** The point being plotted would correspond to a point on the edge of the wheel as the wheel turns.

(b) One possible answer:
$\theta = 16\pi t$, where t is in seconds.

(c) Assuming counterclockwise motion, the rates are as follows.

$\theta = \dfrac{\pi}{4}; \dfrac{dx}{dt} \approx -71.086$ ft/sec

$\dfrac{dy}{dt} \approx 71.086$ ft/sec

$\theta = \dfrac{\pi}{2}; \dfrac{dx}{dt} \approx -100.531$ ft/sec

$\dfrac{dy}{dt} = 0$ ft/sec

$\theta = \pi: \dfrac{dx}{dt} = 0$ ft/sec

$\dfrac{dy}{dt} \approx -100.531$ ft/sec

47. **(a)** 9% per year **(b)** Increasing at 1% per year

Quick Quiz (Sections 5.4–5.6)

1. B **3.** A

Review Exercises

1. Maximum: $\dfrac{4\sqrt{6}}{9}$ at $x = \dfrac{4}{3}$; minimum: -4 at $x = -2$

2. No global extrema

3. **(a)** $[-1, 0)$ and $[1, \infty)$ **(b)** $(-\infty, 1]$ and $(0, 1]$
   (c) $(-\infty, 0)$ and $(0, \infty)$ **(d)** None
   (e) Local minima at $(1, e)$ and $(-1, e)$ **(f)** None

4. **(a)** $[-\sqrt{2}, \sqrt{2}]$ **(b)** $[-2, -\sqrt{2}]$ and $[\sqrt{2}, 2]$
   (c) $(-2, 0)$ **(d)** $(0, 2)$
   (e) Local max: $(-2, 0)$ and $(\sqrt{2}, 2)$;
       local min: $(2, 0)$ and $(-\sqrt{2}, -2)$
   (f) $(0, 0)$

5. **(a)** Approximately $(-\infty, 0.385]$ **(b)** Approximately $[0.385, \infty)$
   (c) None **(d)** $(-\infty, \infty)$ **(e)** Local maximum at $\approx (0.385, 1.215)$
   (f) None

6. **(a)** $[1, \infty)$ **(b)** $(-\infty, 1]$ **(c)** $(-\infty, \infty)$ **(d)** None
   (e) Local minimum at $(1, 0)$ **(f)** None

7. **(a)** $[0, 1)$ **(b)** $(-1, 0]$ **(c)** $(-1, 1)$ **(d)** None
   (e) Local minimum at $(0, 1)$ **(f)** None

8. **(a)** $(-\infty, -2^{-1/3}] \approx (-\infty, -0.794]$
   (b) $[-2^{-1/3}, 1) \approx [-0.794, 1)$ and $(1, \infty)$
   (c) $(-\infty, -2^{1/3}) \approx (-\infty, -1.260)$ and $(1, \infty)$ **(d)** $(-1.260, 1)$
   (e) Local maximum at

$$\left(-2^{-1/3}, \frac{2}{3} \cdot 2^{-1/3}\right) \approx (-0.794, 0.529)$$

   (f) $\left(-2^{1/3}, \frac{1}{3} \cdot 2^{1/3}\right) \approx (-1.260, 0.420)$

9. **(a)** None **(b)** $[-1, 1]$ **(c)** $(-1, 0)$ **(d)** $(0, 1)$
   (e) Local maximum at $(-1, \pi)$; local minimum at $(1, 0)$ **(f)** $\left(0, \dfrac{\pi}{2}\right)$

10. **(a)** $[-\sqrt{3}, \sqrt{3}]$ **(b)** $(-\infty, -\sqrt{3}]$ and $[\sqrt{3}, \infty)$
   (c) Approximately $(-2.584, -0.706)$ and $(3.290, \infty)$
   (d) Approximately $(-\infty, -2.584)$ and $(-0.706, 3.290)$
   (e) Local maximum at

$$\left(\sqrt{3}, \frac{\sqrt{3}-1}{4}\right) \approx (1.732, 0.183);$$

       local minimum at

$$\left(-\sqrt{3}, \frac{-\sqrt{3}-1}{4}\right) \approx (-1.732, -0.683)$$

   (f) $\approx (-2.584, -0.573), (-0.706, -0.338),$ and $(3.290, 0.161)$

11. **(a)** $(0, 2]$ **(b)** $[-2, 0)$ **(c)** None **(d)** $(-2, 0)$ and $(0, 2)$
   (e) Local maxima at $(-2, \ln 2)$ and $(2, \ln 2)$ **(f)** None

12. **(a)** Approximately $[0, 0.176], \left[0.994, \dfrac{\pi}{2}\right],$
       $[2.148, 2.965], \left[3.834, \dfrac{3\pi}{2}\right],$ and $\left[5.591, 2\pi\right]$
   (b) Approximately $[0.176, 0.994], \left[\dfrac{\pi}{2}, 2.148\right],$
       $[2.965, 3.834],$ and $\left[\dfrac{3\pi}{2}, 5.591\right]$
   (c) Approximately $(0.542, 1.266), (1.876, 2.600), (3.425, 4.281),$ and
       $(5.144, 6.000)$

(d) Approximately $(0, 0.542), (1.266, 1.876), (2.600, 3.425),$
       $(4.281, 5.144),$ and $(6.000, 2\pi)$

(e) Local maxima at $\approx (0.176, 1.266), \left(\dfrac{\pi}{2}, 0\right)$

    and $(2.965, 1.266), \left(\dfrac{3\pi}{2}, 2\right),$ and $(2\pi, 1)$;

    local minima at $\approx (0, 1),$
       $(0.994, -0.513); (2.148, -0.513); (3.834, -1.806);$
       and $(5.591, -1.806)$
   Note that the local extrema at $x \approx 3.834,$

$$x = \frac{3\pi}{2}, \text{ and } x \approx 5.591 \text{ are also absolute extrema.}$$

(f) $\approx (0.542, 0.437), (1.266, -0.267), (1.876, -0.267),$
       $(2.600, 0.437), (3.425, -0.329), (4.281, 0.120), (5.144, 0.120),$
       and $(6.000, -0.329)$

13. **(a)** $\left(0, \dfrac{2}{\sqrt{3}}\right]$ **(b)** $(-\infty, 0]$ and $\left[\dfrac{2}{\sqrt{3}}, \infty\right)$ **(c)** $(-\infty, 0)$ **(d)** $(0, \infty)$
   (e) Local maximum at

$$\left(\frac{2}{\sqrt{3}}, \frac{16}{3\sqrt{3}}\right) \approx (1.155, 3.079)$$

   (f) None

14. **(a)** Approximately $[-0.578, 1.692]$
   (b) Approximately $(-\infty, -0.578]$ and $[1.692, \infty)$
   (c) Approximately $(-\infty, 1.079)$
   (d) Approximately $(1.079, \infty)$
   (e) Local maximum at $\approx (1.692, 20.517);$
       local minimum at $\approx (-0.578, 0.972)$
   (f) $\approx (1.079, 13.601)$

15. **(a)** $\left[0, \dfrac{8}{9}\right]$ **(b)** $(-\infty, 0]$ and $\left[\dfrac{8}{9}, \infty\right)$ **(c)** $\left(-\infty, -\dfrac{2}{9}\right)$
   (d) $\left(-\dfrac{2}{9}, 0\right)$ and $(0, \infty)$
   (e) Local maximum at $\approx (0.889, 1.011)$; local minimum at $(0, 0)$
   (f) $\approx \left(-\dfrac{2}{9}, 0.667\right)$

16. **(a)** Approximately $(-\infty, 0.215]$
   (b) Approximately $[0.215, 2)$ and $(2, \infty)$
   (c) Approximately $(2, 3.710)$
   (d) $(-\infty, 2)$ and approximately $(3.710, \infty)$
   (e) Local maximum at $\approx (0.215, -2.417)$
   (f) $\approx (3.710, -3.420)$

17. **(a)** None **(b)** At $x = -1$ **(c)** At $x = 0$ and $x = 2$

18. **(a)** At $x = -1$ **(b)** At $x = 2$ **(c)** At $x = \dfrac{1}{2}$

19. $f(x) = -\dfrac{1}{4}x^{-4} - e^{-x} + C$ **20.** $f(x) = \sec x + C$

21. $f(x) = 2\ln x + \dfrac{1}{3}x^3 + x + C$ **22.** $f(x) = \dfrac{2}{3}x^{3/2} + 2x^{1/2} + C$

23. $f(x) = -\cos x + \sin x + 2$ **24.** $f(x) = \dfrac{3}{4}x^{4/3} + \dfrac{x^3}{3} + \dfrac{x^2}{2} + x - \dfrac{31}{12}$

25. $s(t) = 4.9t^2 + 5t + 10$ **26.** $s(t) = 16t^2 + 20t + 5$

27. $L(x) = 2x + \dfrac{\pi}{2} - 1$ **28.** $L(x) = \sqrt{2}x - \dfrac{\pi\sqrt{2}}{4} + \sqrt{2}$

29. $L(x) = -x + 1$ **30.** $L(x) = 2x + 1$

31. Global minimum value of $\dfrac{1}{2}$ at $x = 2$ **32.** **(a)** T **(b)** P

33. (a) $(0, 2]$ **(b)** $[-3, 0)$ **(c)** Local maxima at $(-3, 1)$ and $(2, 3)$

34. The 24th day

35.

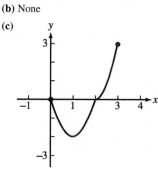

36. (a) Absolute minimum is -2 at $x = 1$;
absolute maximum is 3 at $x = 3$
(b) None
(c)

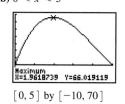

37. (a) $f(x)$ is continuous on $[0.5, 3]$ and differentiable on $(0.5, 3)$.
(b) $c \approx 1.579$ **(c)** $y \approx 1.457x - 1.075$ **(d)** $y \approx 1.457x - 1.579$

38. (a) $v(t) = -3t^2 - 6t + 4$ **(b)** $a(t) = -6t - 6$
(c) The particle starts at position 3 moving in the positive direction, but decelerating. At approximately $t = 0.528$, it reaches position 4.128 and changes direction, beginning to move in the negative direction. After that, it continues to accelerate while moving in the negative direction.

39. (a) $L(x) = -1$ **(b)** Using the linearization, $f(0, 1) \approx -1$
(c) Greater than the approximation in (b), since $f'(x)$ is actually positive over the interval $(0, 0.1)$ and the estimate is based on the derivative being 0.

40. (a) $dy = (2x - x^2)e^{-x}\, dx$ **(b)** $dy \approx 0.00368$ **41.** $x \approx 0.828361$

42. 1200 m/sec **43.** 1162.5 m **44.** $r = 25$ ft and $s = 50$ ft

45. 54 square units **46.** Base is 6 ft by 6 ft; height $= 3$ ft.

47. Base is 4 ft by 4 ft; height $= 2$ ft. **48.** Height $= 2$, radius $= \sqrt{2}$

49. $r = h = 4$ ft

50. (a) $V(x) = x(15 - 2x)(5 - x)$
(b) $0 < x < 5$

Maximum
X=1.9618739   Y=66.019119

$[0, 5]$ by $[-10, 70]$

(c) Maximum volume ≈ 66.019 in³ when $x \approx 1.962$ in.
(d) $V'(x) = 6x^2 - 50x + 75$, which is zero

at $x = \dfrac{25 - 5\sqrt{7}}{6} \approx 1.962$.

51. 29.925 square units

52. $x = \dfrac{48}{\sqrt{7}} \approx 18.142$ mi and $y = \dfrac{36}{\sqrt{7}} \approx 13.607$ mi

53. $x = 100$ m and $r = \dfrac{100}{\pi}$ m **54.** 276 grade A and 553 grade B tires

55. (a) 0.765 unit

(b) When $t = \dfrac{7\pi}{8} \approx 2.749$ (plus multiples of π if they keep going)

56. Dimensions: base is 6 in. by 12 in.,
height $= 2$ in.; maximum volume $= 144$ in³

57. -40 m²/sec **58.** 5 m/sec **59.** Increasing 1 cm/min

60. $\dfrac{dx}{dt} = 4$ units/second **61. (a)** $h = \dfrac{5r}{2}$ **(b)** $\dfrac{125}{144\pi} \approx 0.276$ ft/min

62. 5 radians/sec **63.** Not enough speed. Duck! **64.** $\Delta V \approx \dfrac{2\pi ah}{3} \Delta r$

65. (a) Within 1% **(b)** Within 3%

66. (a) Within 4% **(b)** Within 8% **(c)** Within 12%

67. Height $= 14$ feet, estimated error $= \pm\dfrac{2}{45}$ feet

68. $\dfrac{dy}{dx} = 2 \sin x \cos x - 3$.

Since $\sin x$ and $\cos x$ are both between 1 and -1,
$2 \sin x \cos x$ is never greater than 2, and therefore $\dfrac{dy}{dx} \leq 2 - 3 = -1$
for all values of x.

69. (a) The only x value for which f has a relative maximum is $x = -2$.
That is the only place where the derivative of f goes from positive to negative.
(b) The only x value for which f has a relative minimum is $x = 0$. That is the only place where the derivative of f goes from negative to positive.
(c) The graph of f is concave up on $(-1, 1)$ and on $(2, 3)$. Those are the intervals on which the derivative of f is increasing.
(d)

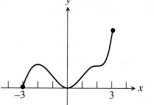

70. The volume V of a cone $\left(V = \frac{1}{3}\pi r^2 h\right)$ is increasing at the rate of 4π cubic inches per second. At the instant when the radius of the cone is 2 inches, its volume is 8π cubic inches and the radius is increasing at $1/3$ inch per second.

(a) $A = \pi r^2$, so $\dfrac{dA}{dt} = 2\pi r \dfrac{dr}{dt} = 2\pi(2)\left(\dfrac{1}{3}\right) = \dfrac{4\pi}{3}$ in²/sec.

(b) $V = \dfrac{1}{3}\pi r^2 h$, so $\dfrac{dV}{dt} = \dfrac{1}{3}\left(2\pi r \dfrac{dr}{dt} h + \pi r^2 \dfrac{dh}{dt}\right)$. Plugging in the

known values, we have $4\pi = \dfrac{1}{3}\left(2\pi \cdot 2 \cdot \dfrac{1}{3} \cdot 6 + \pi \cdot 2^2 \cdot \dfrac{dh}{dt}\right)$.

From this we get $\dfrac{dh}{dt} = 1$ in./sec.

(c) $\dfrac{dA}{dh} = \dfrac{dA/dt}{dh/dt} = \dfrac{4\pi/3}{1} = \dfrac{4\pi}{3}$ in²/in.

71. (a) $V = \pi\left(\dfrac{a}{2\pi}\right)^2 b$, and $b = \dfrac{60 - 2a}{4} = 15 - \dfrac{a}{2}$, so $V = \dfrac{30a^2 - a^3}{4\pi}$.

Thus $\dfrac{dV}{da} = \dfrac{1}{4\pi}(60a - 3a^2) = \dfrac{3}{4\pi} a(20 - a)$. The relevant domain for a in this problem is $(0, 30)$, so $a = 20$ is the only critical number. The cylinder of maximum volume is formed when $a = 20$ and $b = 5$.

(b) The sign graph for the derivative $\dfrac{dV}{da} = \dfrac{3}{4\pi} a(20 - a)$ on the interval $(0, 30)$ is as follows:

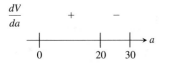

By the First Derivative Test, there is a maximum at $a = 20$.

CHAPTER 6

Section 6.1

Quick Review 6.1

1. 400 miles   **3.** 100 ft/sec $\approx$ 68.18 mph

5. 28 miles   **7.** $-3°$ **9.** 17,500 people

Exercises 6.1

1. Compute the area of the rectangle under the curve to find the particle is at $x = 20$.

3. 1095 cubic yards

5. Each rectangle has base 1. The area under the curve is approximately
$$1\left(\frac{5}{4} + \frac{13}{4} + \frac{29}{4} + \frac{53}{4}\right) = 25,$$ so the particle is close to $x = 25$.

7. (a)

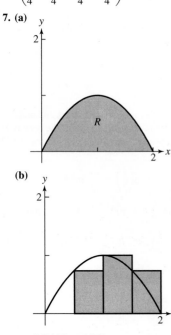

(b)

LRAM = 1.25

9.

n	LRAM$_n$	MRAM$_n$	RRAM$_n$
10	1.32	1.34	1.32
50	1.3328	1.3336	1.3328
100	1.3332	1.3334	1.3332
500	1.333328	1.333336	1.333328

11. 13.59   **13.** 0.868

15.

n	MRAM
10	526.21677
20	524.25327
40	523.76240
80	523.63968
160	523.60900

17. ≈ 44.8; ≈ 6.7 L/min   **19. (a)** 5220 m   **(b)** 4920 m

21. (a) 0.969 mi   **(b)** 0.006 h = 21.6 sec ; 116 mph

23. (a) $S_8 \approx 120.95132$ Underestimate   **(b)** 10%

25. (a) 15,465 ft^3 **(b)** 16,515 ft^3 **27.** 39.26991

29. (a) 240 ft/sec   **(b)** 1520 ft with RRAM and $n = 5$

31. (a) Upper: 60.9 tons; lower: 46.8 tons   **(b)** By the end of October

33. True. Because the graph rises from left to right, the left-hand rectangles will all lie under the curve.

35. E   **37.** C

39. (a) 2   **(b)** $2\sqrt{2} \approx 2.828$ **(c)** $8\sin\left(\dfrac{\pi}{8}\right) \approx 3.061$

(d) Each area is less than the area of the circle, π. As n increases, the polygon area approaches π.

41. RRAM$_n$ f = LRAM$_n f + f(x_n)\Delta x - f(x_0)\Delta x$

Since $f(a) = f(b)$, or $f(x_0) = f(x_n)$, we have

RRAM$_n$ f = LRAM$_n$ f.

Section 6.2

Quick Review 6.2

1. 55   **3.** 5500   **5.** $\displaystyle\sum_{k=0}^{25} 2k$ **7.** $\displaystyle\sum_{x=1}^{50}(2x^2 + 3x)$

9. $\displaystyle\sum_{k=0}^{n}(-1)^k = 0$ if n is odd.

Exercises 6.2

1. $\displaystyle\int_0^2 x^2\,dx$ **3.** $\displaystyle\int_1^4 \frac{1}{x}\,dx$ **5.** $\displaystyle\int_0^1 \sqrt{4 - x^2}\,dx$ **7.** 15   **9.** -480

11. 2.75   **13.** 21   **15.** $\dfrac{9\pi}{2}$ **17.** $\dfrac{5}{2}$ **19.** 3   **21.** $\dfrac{3\pi^2}{2}$ **23.** $\dfrac{1}{2}b^2$

25. $b^2 - a^2$ **27.** $\dfrac{3}{2}a^2$ **29.** $\displaystyle\int_8^{11} 87\,dt = 261$ miles

31. $\displaystyle\int_6^{7.5} 300\,dt = 450$ calories   **33.** $3(x - 2) = 3x - 6$

35. $x(4 - x) = 4x - x^2$ **37.** ≈ 0.9905 **39.** $\dfrac{32}{3}$

41. (a) 0   **(b)** 1   **43. (a)** -1 **(b)** $-\dfrac{7}{2}$

45. False. Consider the function in the graph below.

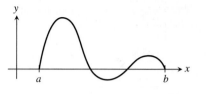

47. E **49.** C **51.** 0 **53.** $\dfrac{1}{4}$ **55.** $\dfrac{3}{4}$ **57.** $\dfrac{1}{2}$ **59.** $-\dfrac{3}{4}$

61. (a) $f \to +\infty$

(b) Using right endpoints we have

$$\int_0^1 \frac{1}{x^2}\,dx = \lim_{n\to\infty} \sum_{k=1}^n \frac{1}{n}\frac{n^2}{k^2}$$

$$= \lim_{n\to\infty} \sum_{k=1}^n \frac{n}{k^2} = \lim_{n\to\infty} n\left[1 + \frac{1}{2^2} + \cdots + \frac{1}{n^2}\right].$$

$$n\left(1 + \frac{1}{2^2} + \cdots + \frac{1}{n^2}\right) > n \text{ and } n \to \infty$$

$$\text{so } n\left(1 + \frac{1}{2^2} + \cdots + \frac{1}{n^2}\right) \to \infty.$$

Section 6.3

Quick Review 6.3

1. $\sin x$ **3.** $\tan x$ **5.** $\sec x$ **7.** x^n **9.** $xe^x + e^x$

Exercises 6.3

1. (a) 0 **(b)** -8 **(c)** -12 **(d)** 10 **(e)** -2 **(f)** 16

3. (a) 5 **(b)** $5\sqrt{3}$ **(c)** -5 **(d)** -5

5. (a) 4 **(b)** -4

7. $0 \le \displaystyle\int_0^1 \sin\left(x^2\right) dx \le \sin\left(1\right) < 1$

9. $0 \le (b - a) \min f(x) \le \displaystyle\int_a^b f(x)\,dx$ **11.** 0, at $x = 1$

13. -2, at $x = \dfrac{1}{\sqrt{3}}$ **15.** $\dfrac{3}{2}$ **17.** 0 **19.** $-\cos\left(2\pi\right) + \cos \pi = -2$

21. $e^1 - e^0 = e - 1$ **23.** $4^2 - 1^2 = 15$ **25.** $5(6) - 5(-2) = 40$

27. $\tan^{-1}\left(1\right) - \tan^{-1}\left(-1\right) = \pi/2$ **29.** $\ln e - \ln 1 = 1$ **31.** $2/\pi$

33. $4/\pi$ **35.** 4 **37.** $\dfrac{1}{2} \le \displaystyle\int_0^1 \frac{1}{1 + x^4}\,dx \le 1$

39. Yes; $av(f) = \dfrac{1}{b - a}\displaystyle\int_a^b f(x)\,dx$; therefore,

$$\int_a^b f(x)\,dx = av(f)(b - a) = \int_a^b av(f)\,dx.$$

41. Avg rate $= \dfrac{\text{total amount released}}{\text{total time}}$

$$= \frac{2000 \text{ m}^3}{100 \text{ min} + 50 \text{ min}} = 13\frac{1}{3} \text{ m}^3/\text{min}$$

43. $\dfrac{7}{6}$

45. False. For example, $\sin 0 = \sin \pi = 0$, but the average value of $\sin x$ on $[0, \pi]$ is greater than 0.

47. A **49.** B

51. (a) $A = \dfrac{1}{2}(b)(h) = \dfrac{1}{2}bh$ **(b)** $\dfrac{h}{2b}x^2 + C$

(c) $\displaystyle\int_0^b y(x)\,dx = \dfrac{h}{2b}x^2 \Big]_0^b = \dfrac{hb^2}{2b} = \dfrac{1}{2}bh$

53. $\displaystyle\int_a^b F'(x)\,dx = \int_a^b G'(x)\,dx \to F(b) - F(a) = G(b) - G(a)$

Quick Quiz (Sections 6.1–6.3)

1. D **3.** C

Section 6.4

Quick Review 6.4

1. $2x \cos x^2$ **3.** 0 **5.** $2^x \ln 2$

7. $\dfrac{-x \sin x - \cos x}{x^2}$ **9.** $\dfrac{y + 1}{2y - x}$

Exercises 6.4

1. $\sin^2 x$ **3.** $(x^3 - x)^5$ **5.** $\tan^3 x$ **7.** $\dfrac{1 + x}{1 + x^2}$ **9.** $2xe^{x^4}$

11. $\dfrac{\sqrt{1 + 25x^2}}{x}$ **13.** $-\ln\left(1 + x^2\right)$ **15.** $-\dfrac{3x^2 \cos x^3}{x^6 + 2}$

17. $\dfrac{dy}{dx} = \sin\left(x^2\right) - \dfrac{\sin x}{2\sqrt{x}}$ **19.** $3x^2 \cos\left(2x^3\right) - 2x \cos\left(2x^2\right)$

21. $y = \displaystyle\int_5^x \sin^3 t\,dt$ **23.** $y = \displaystyle\int_2^x \ln\left(\sin t + 5\right) dt + 3$

25. $y = \displaystyle\int_7^x \cos^2 5t\,dt - 2$ **27.** $5 - \ln 6 \approx 3.208$

29. 1 **31.** $\dfrac{5}{2}$ **33.** 2 **35.** $2\sqrt{3}$ **37.** 0 **39.** $\dfrac{8}{3}$ **41.** $\dfrac{5}{2}$ **43.** $\dfrac{1}{2}$ **45.** $\dfrac{5}{6}$

47. π **49.** ≈ 3.802 **51.** ≈ 8.886 **53.** $x \approx 0.699$ **55.** $-3/2$

57. (a) 0 **(b)** H is increasing on $[0, 6]$ where $H'(x) = f(x) > 0$.

(c) H is concave up on $(9, 12)$ where $H''(x) = f'(x) > 0$.

(d) $H(12) = \displaystyle\int_0^{12} f(t)\,dt > 0$ because there is more area above the x-axis than below for $y = f(x)$.

(e) $x = 6$, since $H'(6) = f(6) = 0$ and $H''(6) = f'(6) < 0$.

(f) $x = 0$, since $H(x) > 0$ on $(0, 12]$.

59. (a) $s'(3) = f(3) = 0$ **(b)** $s''(3) = f'(3) > 0$

(c) $s(3) = \displaystyle\int_0^3 f(x)\,dx = -\dfrac{1}{2}(3)(6) = -9$ units

(d) $s'(t) = 0$ at $t = 6$ sec because $\displaystyle\int_0^6 f(x)\,dx = 0$

(e) $s''(t) = f'(t) = 0$ at $t = 7$ sec

(f) $0 < t < 3$: $s < 0, s' < 0 \Rightarrow$ away
$3 < t < 6$: $s < 0, s' > 0 \Rightarrow$ toward
$t > 6$: $s > 0, s' > 0 \Rightarrow$ away

(g) The positive side

61. $L(x) = 2 + 10x$ **63.** $\displaystyle\int_0^{\pi/k} \sin kx\,dx = \dfrac{2}{k}$

65. True. The Fundamental Theorem of Calculus guarantees that F is differentiable on I, so it must be continuous on I.

67. D **69.** E

71. (a) $f(t)$ is even, so $\displaystyle\int_0^x f(t)\,dt = \int_{-x}^0 f(t)\,dt$,

$$\text{so} -\int_0^x f(t)\,dt = \int_{-x}^0 f(t)\,dt = \int_0^{-x} f(t)\,dt.$$

(b) 0   **(c)** $k\pi, k = \pm 1, \pm 2, \ldots$

(d)

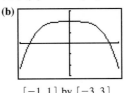

$[-20, 20]$ by $[-3, 3]$

73. $4500

75. (a) True, $h'(x) = f(x) \Rightarrow h''(x) = f'(x)$

(b) True, h and h' are both differentiable.

(c) $h'(1) = f(1) = 0$

(d) True, $h''(1) = f'(1) < 0$ and $h'(1) = 0$

(e) False, $h''(1) = f'(1) < 0$

(f) False, $h''(1) = f'(1) \neq 0$

(g) True, $\dfrac{dh}{dx} = f(x) = 0$ at $x = 1$ and $h'(x) = f(x)$ is a decreasing function.

77. Using area, $\displaystyle\int_0^x f(t)\,dt = \int_{-x}^0 f(t)\,dt = -\int_0^{-x} f(t)\,dt$

79. $x \approx 1.0648397$. $\displaystyle\lim_{t \to \infty} \dfrac{\sin t}{t} = 0$. Not enough area between x-axis

and $\dfrac{\sin x}{x}$ for $x > 1.0648397$ to get $\displaystyle\int_0^x \dfrac{\sin t}{t}\,dt$ back to 1.

or: $\text{Si}(x)$ doesn't decrease enough (for $x > 1.0648397$) to get back to 1.

Section 6.5

Quick Review 6.5

1. Concave down   **3.** Concave down   **5.** Concave up

7. Concave up   **9.** Concave down

Exercises 6.5

1. (a) 2   **(b)** Exact   **(c)** 2   **3. (a)** 4.25   **(b)** Over   **(c)** 4

5. (a) 5.146   **(b)** Under   **(c)** $\dfrac{16}{3}$

7. $\dfrac{1}{2}(12 + 2(10) + 2(9) + 2(11) + 2(13) + 2(16) + 18) = 74$

9. 15,990 ft³

11. $\dfrac{1}{60 \times 60}\left[1.8\left(\dfrac{0 + 30}{2}\right) + 1.3\left(\dfrac{30 + 40}{2}\right) + \cdots + 4.8\left(\dfrac{120 + 130}{2}\right)\right]$
≈ 0.6208 miles ≈ 3278 ft.

13. (a) $\left(\dfrac{1/2}{3}\right)\left(0 + 4\left(\dfrac{1}{2}\right) + 2(1) + 4\left(\dfrac{3}{2}\right) + 2\right) = 2$ **(b)** 2

15. (a) $\left(\dfrac{1/2}{3}\right)\left(0^3 + 4\left(\dfrac{1}{2}\right)^3 + 2(1)^3 + 4\left(\dfrac{3}{2}\right)^3 + 2^3\right) = 4$ **(b)** 4

17. (a) $\left(\dfrac{1}{3}\right)\left(\sqrt{0} + 4(\sqrt{1}) + 2(\sqrt{2}) + 4(\sqrt{3}) + (\sqrt{4})\right) \approx 5.2522$

(b) 16/3

19. (a) 12   **(b)** 12, $|E_S| = 0$

(c) $f^{(4)}(x) = 0$ for $f(x) = x^3 - 2x$, so $M_{f^{(4)}} = 0$.

(d) Simpson's Rule will always give the exact value for cubic polynomials.

21. (b) We are approximating the area under the temperature graph. Doubling the endpoints increases the error in the first and last trapezoids.

23. The exact value is π. $S_{50} \approx 3.1379$, $S_{100} \approx 3.14029$

25. $S_{50} \approx 1.37066$, $S_{100} = 1.37066$ using $a \approx 0.0001$ as lower limit
$S_{50} = 1.37076$, $S_{100} \approx 1.37076$ using
$a = 0.000000001$ as lower limit

27. (a) $T_{10} \approx 1.983523538$. $T_{100} \approx 1.999835504$
$T_{1000} \approx 1.999998355$

(b)

n	$|E_T|$
10	$0.016476462 = 1.6476462 \times 10^{-2}$
100	1.64496×10^{-4}
1000	1.645×10^{-6}

(c) $|E_{T_{10n}}| \approx 10^{-2} \times |E_{T_n}|$

(d) $|E_{T_n}| \leq \dfrac{\pi^3 M}{12n^2} \cdot |E_{T_{10n}}| \leq \dfrac{\pi^3 M}{12(10n)^2}$
$= \dfrac{\pi^3 M}{12n^2} \times 10^{-2}$

29. 466.67 in²

31. False. The Trapezoidal Rule will overestimate the integral if the curve is concave up.

33. A   **35.** C

37. (a) $f''(x) = 2\cos(x^2) - 4x^2\sin(x^2)$

(b)

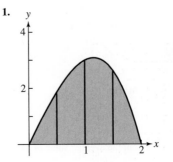

$[-1, 1]$ by $[-3, 3]$

(c) The graph shows that $-3 \leq f''(x) \leq 3$ for $-1 \leq x \leq 1$.

(d) $|E_T| \leq \dfrac{1 - (-1)}{12}(h^2)(3) = \dfrac{h^2}{2}$

(e) $|E_T| \leq \dfrac{h^2}{2} \leq \dfrac{0.1^2}{2} < 0.01$

(f) $n \geq 20$

39. Each quantity is equal to
$\dfrac{h}{2}(y_0 + 2y_1 + 2y_2 + \cdots + 2y_{n-1} + y_n)$.

Quick Quiz (Sections 6.4 and 6.5)

1. C   **3.** C

Review Exercises

1.

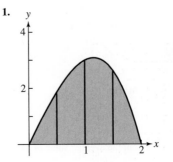

2. 3.75

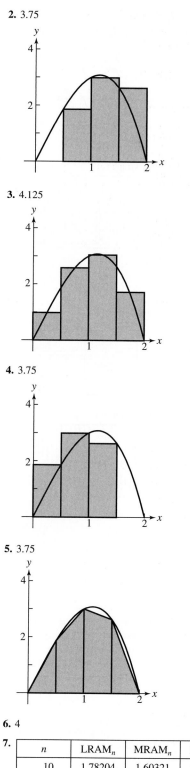

3. 4.125

4. 3.75

5. 3.75

6. 4

7.

n	LRAM$_n$	MRAM$_n$	RRAM$_n$
10	1.78204	1.60321	1.46204
20	1.69262	1.60785	1.53262
30	1.66419	1.60873	1.55752
50	1.64195	1.60918	1.57795
100	1.62557	1.60937	1.59357
1000	1.61104	1.60944	1.60784

8. $\ln 5$ **9. (a)** True   **(b)** True   **(c)** False

10. (a) $V = \lim\limits_{n \to \infty} \sum\limits_{i=1}^{n} \pi \sin^2 (m_i) \Delta x$ **(b)** $\int_0^{\pi} \pi \sin^2 x \, dx = 4.9348$

11. (a) 26.5 m

(b)

12. (a) $\int_0^{10} x^3 \, dx$ **(b)** $\int_0^{10} x \sin x \, dx$ **(c)** $\int_0^{10} x(3x - 2)^2 \, dx$

(d) $\int_0^{10} (1 + x^2)^{-1} \, dx$ **(e)** $\int_0^{10} \pi \left(9 - \sin^2 \dfrac{\pi x}{10} \right) dx$

13. 10   **14.** 2   **15.** 20   **16.** 42   **17.** $\dfrac{\sqrt{2}}{2}$ **18.** 16   **19.** 3   **20.** 2   **21.** 2

22. 1   **23.** $\sqrt{3}$ **24.** 1   **25.** 8   **26.** 2   **27.** -1 **28.** 0   **29.** $2 \ln 3$ **30.** π

31. 40   **32.** 64π **33. (a)** Upper = 4.392 L; lower = 4.008 L.   **(b)** 4.2 L

34. (a) Lower = 87.15 ft; upper = 103.05 ft   **(b)** 95.1 ft

35. One possible answer:
The dx is important because it corresponds to an actual physical quantity Δx in a Riemann sum.

36. $\dfrac{16}{3}$ **37.** $1 \le \sqrt{1 + \sin^2 x} \le \sqrt{2}$ **38. (a)** $\dfrac{4}{3}$ **(b)** $\dfrac{2}{3} a^{3/2}$

39. $\sqrt{2 + \cos^3 x}$ **40.** $14x \sqrt{2 + \cos^3 (7x^2)}$

41. $\dfrac{-6}{3 + x^4}$ **42.** $\dfrac{2}{4x^2 + 1} - \dfrac{1}{x^2 + 1}$ **43.** \$230

44. $av(I) = 4800$ cases; average holding cost = \$192 per day

45. $x \approx 1.63052$ or $x \approx -3.09131$

46. (a) True   **(b)** True   **(c)** True   **(d)** False   **(e)** True   **(f)** False   **(g)** True

47. $F(1) - F(0)$

48. $y = \int_5^x \dfrac{\sin t}{t} \, dt + 3$ **49.** Use the fact that $y' = 2x + \dfrac{1}{x}$.

50. (b); $\dfrac{dy}{dx} = 2x \to y = x^2 + c; y(1) = 4 \to c = 3$

51. (a) ≈ 2.42 gal   **(b)** ≈ 24.83 mpg   **52. (a)** 6144 ft   **(b)** 4296 ft   **(c)** B

53. (a) $h(y_1 + y_3) + 2(2hy_2) = h(y_1 + 4y_2 + y_3)$

(b) $\dfrac{1}{3} [h(y_0 + 4y_1 + y_2) + h(y_2 + 4y_3 + y_4)$
$+ \cdots + h(y_{2n-2} + 4y_{2n-1} + y_{2n})]$

54. (a) 0   **(b)** -1 **(c)** $-\pi$ **(d)** $x = 1$ **(e)** $y = 2x + 2 - \pi$
(f) $x = -1, x = 2$ **(g)** $[-2\pi, 0]$

55. (a) NINT $(e^{-x^2/2}, x, -10, 10) \approx 2.506628275$
NINT $(e^{-x^2/2}, x, -20, 20) \approx 2.506628275$
(b) The area is $\sqrt{2\pi}$.

56. ≈ 1500 yd^3

57. (a) $(V^2)_{av} = \dfrac{(V_{max})^2}{2}$, $V_{rms} = \dfrac{V_{max}}{\sqrt{2}}$
(b) ≈ 339 volts

58. (a) $\int_0^{24} R(t)\,dt \approx \dfrac{4}{2}(9.6 + 2(10.3) + 2(10.9) + 2(11.1) + 2(10.9) +$

$2(10.5) + 9.6) = 253.2$

This is the total number of gallons of water that flowed through the pipe during the 24-hour period.

(b) Yes. Because $R(0) = R(24)$, the Mean Value Theorem guarantees that there is a number c between 0 and 24 such that $R'(c) = 0$.

(c) Average rate $= \dfrac{1}{24 - 0}\int_0^{24} Q(t)\,dt = 10.58$ gallons per hour

59. Since $f'(x) = ax^2 + bx$, $f'(1) = a + b$. Also $f''(x) = 2ax + b$, so $f''(1) = 2a + b$. Applying property (ii), we have $a + b = -6$ and $2a + b = 6$. Solve these two equations simultaneously to get $a = 12$ and $b = -18$. Then

$f'(x) = 12x^2 - 18x$

$f(x) = 4x^3 - 9x^2 + C$ for some constant C

$\int_1^2 (4x^3 - 9x^2 + C)\,dx = x^4 - 3x^3 + Cx \Big|_1^2 =$

$16 - 24 + 2C - (1 - 3 + C) = -6 + C$

So $-6 + C = 14$, and $C = 20$. Putting it all together, $f(x) = 4x^3 - 9x^2 + 20$.

60. (a) Find these integrals using signed areas.

$g(4) = \int_1^4 f(t)\,dt = 1\left(\dfrac{3+1}{2}\right) + \dfrac{1}{2} + \left(-\dfrac{1}{2}\right) = 2$

$g(-2) = -\dfrac{1}{2}(3)(3) = -\dfrac{9}{2}$

(b) By the Fundamental Theorem of Calculus, $g'(2) = f(2) = 1$.

(c) Since $g'(x) = f(x)$ is positive on $(-2, 3)$ and negative on $(3, 4)$, the minimum value of g occurs at one of the two endpoints. Comparing the two values in part (a), we see that the minimum value is

$g(-2) = -\dfrac{9}{2}$.

(d) There is a point of inflection at $x = 1$ because $f = g'$ changes direction (from increasing to decreasing). There is no such change of direction at $x = 2$, so no point of inflection there.

CHAPTER 7

Section 7.1

Quick Review 7.1

1. Yes **3.** No **5.** No

7. Yes **9.** -5 **11.** 3

Exercises 7.1

1. $y = x^5 - \tan x + C$ **3.** $y = -\cos x + e^{-x} + 2x^4 + C$

5. $y = 5^x + \tan^{-1} x + C$ **7.** $y = \sin(t^3) + C$ **9.** $u = \tan(x^5) + C$

11. $y = -3\cos x + 5$ **13.** $u = x^7 - x^3 + 5x - 4$

15. $y = x^{-1} + x^{-3} + 12x - 11\ (x > 0)$ **17.** $y = \tan^{-1} t + 2^t + 2$

19. $v = 4\sec t + e^t + 3t^2\ (-\pi/2 < t < \pi/2)$ (Note that $C = 0$.)

21. $y = \int_1^x \sin(t^2)\,dt + 5$ **23.** $F(x) = \int_2^x e^{\cos t}\,dt + 9$

25. Graph (b) **27.** Graph (a)

29.

31.

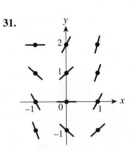

33.

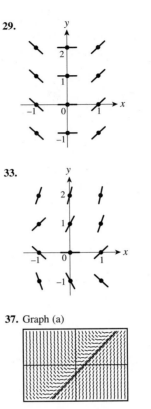

35. Graph (c)

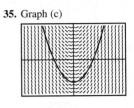

37. Graph (a)

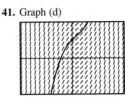

39. Graph (b)

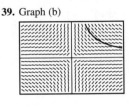

41. Graph (d)

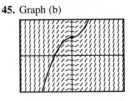

43. Graph (c)

45. Graph (b)

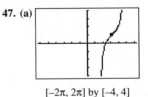

47. (a)

[-2π, 2π] by [-4, 4]

(b) The solution to the initial value problem includes only the continuous portion of the function $y = \tan x + 1$ that passes through the point $(\pi, 1)$.

49. The correct graph is (c), since $\dfrac{dy}{dx} = 2y + x = 0$ at the point $(-2, 1)$.

The line through $(2, 1)$ will have slope 4.

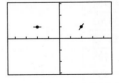

51. 2.03 **53.** 2.3 **55.** 0.97 **57.** 2.031

59. (a) Graph (b)

(b) The slope is always positive, so graphs (a) and (c) can be ruled out.

61. For one thing, there are positive slopes in the second quadrant of the slope field. The graph of $y = x^2$ has negative slopes in the second quadrant.

63. Euler's Method gives an estimate $f(1.4) \approx 4.32$. The solution to the initial value problem is $f(x) = x^2 + x + 1$, from which we get $f(1.4) = 4.36$. The percentage error is thus $(4.36 - 4.32)/4.36 = 0.9\%$.

65. At every point (x, y), $(e^{(x-y)/2})(-e^{(y-x)/2}) = -e^{(x-y)/2+(y-x)/2} = -e^0 = -1$, so the slopes are negative reciprocals. The slope lines are therefore perpendicular.

67. The perpendicular slope field would be produced by $dy/dx = -\sin x$, so $y = \cos x + C$ for any constant C.

69. True. They are all lines of the form $y = 5x + C$.

71. C   **73.** B

75. (a) $y = \dfrac{x^2}{2} + \dfrac{1}{x} + \dfrac{1}{2}, x > 0$ **(b)** $y = \dfrac{x^2}{2} + \dfrac{1}{x} + \dfrac{3}{2}, x < 0$

(c) $y' = \begin{cases} x - 1/x^2, & x < 0 \\ x - 1/x^2 & x > 0 \end{cases}$ **(d)** $C_1 = \dfrac{3}{2}, C_2 = \dfrac{1}{2}$

(e) $C_1 = \dfrac{1}{2}, C_2 = -\dfrac{7}{2}$

77. (a) $y = 2x^3 + 2x^2 + C_1x + C_2$ **(b)** $y = e^x - \sin x + C_1x + C_2$

(c) $y = \dfrac{x^5}{20} + \dfrac{x^{-1}}{2} + C_1x + C_2$

79. (a) $y = \dfrac{x^2}{2} + C$ **(b)** $y = -\dfrac{x^2}{2} + C$ **(c)** $y = Ce^x$

(d) $y = Ce^{-x}$ **(e)** $y = Ce^{x^2/2}$

Section 7.2

Quick Review 7.2

1. $32/5$ **3.** 3^x **5.** $4(x^3 - 2x^2 + 3)^3(3x^2 - 4x)$

7. $-\tan x$ **9.** $\sec x$

Exercises 7.2

1. $\sin x - x^3 + C$ **3.** $t^3/3 + t^{-1} + C$ **5.** $(3/5)x^5 + x^{-2} + \tan x + C$

7. $(-\cot u + C)' = -(-\csc^2 u) = \csc^2 u$

9. $\left(\dfrac{1}{2}e^{2x} + C\right)' = \dfrac{1}{2}e^{2x} \cdot 2 = e^{2x}$ **11.** $(\tan^{-1}u + C)' = \dfrac{1}{1 + u^2}$

13. $\displaystyle\int f(u) \, du = \int \sqrt{u} \, du = (2/3)u^{3/2} + C = (2/3)x^3 + C$

$\displaystyle\int f(u) \, dx = \int \sqrt{u} \, dx = \int \sqrt{x^2} \, dx = \int x \, dx = (1/2)x^2 + C$

15. $\displaystyle\int f(u) \, du = \int e^u \, du = e^u + C = e^{7x} + C$

$\displaystyle\int f(u) \, dx = \int e^u \, dx = \int e^{7x} \, dx = (1/7)e^{7x} + C$

17. $-\dfrac{1}{3}\cos 3x + C$ **19.** $\dfrac{1}{2}\sec 2x + C$ **21.** $(1/3)\tan^{-1}(x/3) + C$

23. $\dfrac{2}{3}\left(1 - \cos\dfrac{t}{2}\right)^3 + C$ **25.** $\dfrac{1}{1 - x} + C$ **27.** $\dfrac{2}{3}(\tan x)^{3/2} + C$

29. $-(1/4)\ln|\cos(4x + 2)| + C$ or $(1/4)\ln|\sec(4x + 2)| + C$

31. $\dfrac{1}{3}\sin(3z + 4) + C$ **33.** $\dfrac{1}{7}(\ln x)^7 + C$

35. $\dfrac{3}{4}\sin(s^{4/3} - 8) + C$ **37.** $(1/2)\sec(2t + 1) + C$

39. $\ln(\ln x) + C$ **41.** $(1/2)\ln(x^2 + 1) + C$

43. $\dfrac{1}{3}\ln|\sec(3x)| + C = -\dfrac{1}{3}\ln|\cos(3x)| + C$

45. $\ln|\sec x + \tan x| + C$ **47.** $\dfrac{\cos^3 2x}{6} - \dfrac{\cos 2x}{2} + C$

49. $x - \dfrac{\sin 2x}{2} + C$ **51.** $\dfrac{1}{3}\tan^3 x - \tan x + x + C$ **53.** $14/3$

55. $-1/2$ **57.** $10/3$ **59.** $2\sqrt{3}$ **61.** $\ln\left(\dfrac{9}{2}\right)$ **63.** $-\ln 2$ **65.** $\dfrac{1}{2}\ln 5$

67. (a) $\dfrac{1}{2}\sqrt{10} - \dfrac{3}{2}$ **(b)** $\dfrac{1}{2}\sqrt{10} - \dfrac{3}{2}$

69. Note that $dy/dx = \tan x$ and $y(3) = 5$.

71. False. The interval of integration should change from $[0, \pi/4]$ to $[0, 1]$, resulting in a different numerical answer.

73. D   **75.** B

77. (a) $\dfrac{d}{dx}\left(\dfrac{2}{3}(x + 1)^{3/2} + C\right) = \sqrt{x + 1}$

(b) Because $dy_1/dx = \sqrt{x + 1}$ and $dy_2/dx = \sqrt{x + 1}$ **(c)** $4\dfrac{2}{3}$

(d) $C = y_1 - y_2 = \displaystyle\int_0^x \sqrt{x + 1} \, dx - \int_3^x \sqrt{x + 1} \, dx$

$= \displaystyle\int_0^x \sqrt{x + 1} \, dx + \int_x^3 \sqrt{x + 1} \, dx = \int_0^3 \sqrt{x + 1} \, dx$

79. (a) $\displaystyle\int 2\sin x \cos x \, dx = \int 2u \, du = u^2 + C = \sin^2 x + C$

(b) $\displaystyle\int 2\sin x \cos x \, dx = -\int 2u \, du = -u^2 + C = -\cos^2 x + C$

(c) Since $\sin^2 x - (-\cos^2 x) = 1$, the two answers differ by a constant (accounted for in the constant of integration).

81. (a) $\displaystyle\int \dfrac{dx}{\sqrt{1 - x^2}} = \int \dfrac{\cos u \, du}{\sqrt{1 - \sin^2 u}} = \int \dfrac{\cos u \, du}{\sqrt{\cos^2 u}} = \int 1 \, du.$

(Note $\cos u > 0$, so $\sqrt{\cos^2 u} = |\cos u| = \cos u$.)

(b) $\displaystyle\int \dfrac{dx}{\sqrt{1 - x^2}} = \int 1 \, du = u + C = \sin^{-1}x + C$

83. (a) $\displaystyle\int_0^{1/2} \dfrac{\sqrt{x} \, dx}{\sqrt{1 - x}} = \int_{\sin^{-1}\sqrt{0}}^{\sin^{-1}\sqrt{1/2}} \dfrac{\sin y \cdot 2 \sin y \cos y \, dy}{\sqrt{1 - \sin^2 y}}$

$= \displaystyle\int_0^{\pi/4} \dfrac{2 \sin^2 y \cos y \, dy}{\cos y} = \int_0^{\pi/4} 2 \sin^2 y \, dy$

(b) $\displaystyle\int_0^{1/2} \dfrac{\sqrt{x} \, dx}{\sqrt{1 - x}} = \int_0^{\pi/4} 2 \sin^2 y \, dy$

$= \displaystyle\int_0^{\pi/4} (1 - \cos 2y) \, dy = \left[y - \dfrac{1}{2}\sin 2y\right]_0^{\pi/4}$

$= (\pi - 2)/4$

Section 7.3

Quick Review 7.3

1. $2x^3 \cos 2x + 3x^2 \sin 2x$ **3.** $\dfrac{2}{1 + 4x^2}$ **5.** $x = \dfrac{1}{3}\tan y$

7. $\dfrac{2}{\pi}$ **9.** $y = \dfrac{1}{2}x^2 - \cos x + 3$

Exercises 7.3

1. $-x \cos x + \sin x + C$ **3.** $\frac{3}{2} te^{2t} - \frac{3}{4} e^{2t} + C$

5. $x^2 \sin x + 2x \cos x - 2 \sin x + C$ **7.** $\frac{y^2}{2} \ln y - \frac{y^2}{4} + C$

9. $\frac{1}{\ln 2}(x \ln x - x) + C$

11. $-(x + 2) \cos x + \sin x + 4$ **13.** $u = x \tan x + \ln |\cos x| + 1$

[−4, 4] by [0, 10]   [−1.2, 1.2] by [0, 3]

15. $y = \frac{2x}{3}(x - 1)^{3/2} - \frac{4}{15}(x - 1)^{5/2} + 2$

[1, 5] by [0, 20]

17. $\frac{e^x}{2}(\sin x - \cos x) + C$ **19.** $\frac{e^x}{5}(2 \sin 2x + \cos 2x) + C$

21. $(-x^4 - 4x^3 - 12x^2 - 24x - 24)e^{-x} + C$

23. $\left(-\frac{x^3}{2} - \frac{3x^2}{4} - \frac{3x}{4} - \frac{3}{8}\right)e^{-2x} + C$ **25.** $\frac{\pi^2}{8} - \frac{1}{2} \approx 0.734$

27. $\frac{1}{13}\left[e^6(2 \cos 9 + 3 \sin 9) - e^{-4}(2 \cos 6 - 3 \sin 6)\right] \approx -18.186$

29. $y = \left(\frac{x^2}{4} - \frac{x}{8} + \frac{1}{32}\right)e^{4x} + C$ **31.** $y = \frac{\theta^2}{2} \sec^{-1} \theta - \frac{1}{2}\sqrt{\theta^2 - 1} + C$

33. (a) π (b) 3π (c) 4π **35.** $\frac{1 - e^{-2\pi}}{2\pi} \approx 0.159$

37. True. Use parts, letting $u = x^2$, $dv = g(x)\,dx$, and $v = f(x)$.

39. B **41.** C **43.** $-2\left(\sqrt{x} \cos \sqrt{x} - \sin \sqrt{x}\right) + C$

45. $\frac{(x^6 - 3x^4 + 6x^2 - 6)e^{x^2}}{2} + C$

47. $u = x^n, dv = \cos x\,dx$ **49.** $u = x^n, dv = e^{ax}\,dx$

51. (a) Let $y = f^{-1}(x)$. Then $x = f(y)$, so $dx = f'(y)\,dy$.
Substitute directly.
(b) $u = y, dv = f'(y)\,dy$

53. (a) $\int \sin^{-1} x\,dx = x \sin^{-1} x + \cos(\sin^{-1} x) + C$

(b) $\int \sin^{-1} x\,dx = x \sin^{-1} x + \sqrt{1 - x^2} + C$

(c) $\cos(\sin^{-1} x) = \sqrt{1 - x^2}$

55. (a) $\int \cos^{-1} x\,dx = x \cos^{-1} x - \sin(\cos^{-1} x) + C$

(b) $\int \cos^{-1} x\,dx = x \cos^{-1} x - \sqrt{1 - x^2} + C$

(c) $\sin(\cos^{-1} x) = \sqrt{1 - x^2}$

57. $\int \sec^3 x\,dx = \frac{1}{2}\left(\sec x \tan x + \ln |\sec x + \tan x|\right) + C$

1. E **3.** A

Section 7.4

Quick Review 7.4

1. $a = e^b$ **3.** $x = e^2 - 3$ **5.** $x = \frac{\ln 2.5}{\ln 0.85} \approx -5.638$

7. $t = \frac{\ln 10}{\ln 1.1} \approx 24.159$ **9.** $y = -1 + e^{2x-3}$

Exercises 7.4

1. $y = \sqrt{x^2 + 3}$, valid for all real numbers

3. $y = x$, valid on the interval $(0, \infty)$

5. $y = 6e^{x^2/2 + 2x} - 5$, valid for all real numbers

7. $y = -\ln(2 - e^{\sin x})$, valid for all real numbers

9. $y = (x^2 + 3)^{-1}$, valid for all real numbers

11. $y(t) = 100e^{1.5t}$ **13.** $y(t) = 50(2^{t/5}) = 50e^{(0.2 \ln 2)t}$

15. 8.06 yr doubling time; $13,197.14 in 30 yr

17. $600 initially; 13.2 yr doubling time

19. (a) 14.94 yr (b) 14.62 yr (c) 14.68 yr (d) 14.59 yr

21. 90 years

23. (a) 2.8×10^{14} bacteria

(b) The bacteria reproduce fast enough that even if many are destroyed, there are enough left to make the person sick.

25. 0.585 day **27.** $y \approx 2e^{0.4581t}$

29. $y = y_0 e^{-kt} = y_0 e^{-k(3/k)} = y_0 e^{-3} < 0.05y_0$

31. (a) 17.53 minutes longer (b) 13.26 minutes

33. (a) The bird gains weight faster at $B = 40$ than at $B = 70$, since $dB/dt = 0.2(100 - B)$ gives smaller values for larger values of B.

(b) $\frac{d^2B}{dt^2} = -0.2\frac{dB}{dt} = -0.04(100 - B) < 0$ for all B between 0 and 100. The graph of the function must be concave down throughout the interval shown, so it cannot resemble the given graph.

(c) $B(t) = 100 - 80e^{-0.2t}$

35. 6658 years **37.** 3.15 years **39.** 585.4 kg

41. (a) $p = 1013e^{-0.121h}$ (b) 2.383 millibars (c) 0.977 km

43. (a) $V = V_0 e^{-t/40}$ (b) 92.1 seconds

45. (a) $\frac{\ln 90}{100} \approx 0.045$ or 4.5% (b) $\frac{\ln 131}{100} \approx 0.049$ or 4.9%

47. False. The correct solution is $|y| = e^{kx+C}$, which can be written (with a new C) as $y = Ce^{kx}$.

49. D **51.** D

53. (a) Since acceleration is $\frac{dv}{dt}$, we have Force $= m\frac{dv}{dt} = -kv$.

(b) From $m\frac{dv}{dt} = -kv$, we get $\frac{dv}{dt} = -\frac{k}{m}v$, which is the differential equation for exponential growth modeled by $v = Ce^{-(k/m)t}$. Since $v = v_0$ at $t = 0$, it follows that $C = v_0$.

(c) In each case, we would solve $2 = e^{-(k/m)t}$. If k is constant, an increase in m would require an increase in t. The object of larger mass takes longer to slow down. Alternatively, one can consider the equation $\frac{dv}{dt} = -\frac{k}{m}v$ to see that v changes more slowly for larger values of m.

55. $s(t) = 1.32(1 - e^{-25t/33}) = 1.32(1 - e^{-0.758t})$

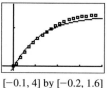

[−0.1, 4] by [−0.2, 1.6]

57. (b) $\sqrt{mg/k}$ **(c)** 179 ft/sec ≈ 122 mi/hr

Section 7.5

Quick Review 7.5

1. $x + 1 + \dfrac{1}{x - 1}$ **3.** $1 + \dfrac{3}{x^2 + x - 2}$

5. $(-\infty, \infty)$ **7.** 0 **9.** $y = 0, y = 60$

Exercises 7.5

1. $A = 3, B = -2$ **3.** $A = 2, B = -3$ **5.** $\ln\dfrac{|x|^3}{(x - 4)^2} + C$

7. $x^2 + \ln(x^2 - 4)^4 + C$ **9.** $2\tan^{-1} x + C$

11. $\ln\left|\dfrac{x - 3}{2x + 1}\right| + C$ **13.** $\ln(|x + 1|^3 \cdot |2x - 3|) + C$

15. $y = \ln\left|\dfrac{x^3}{x - 2}\right| + C$ **17.** $F(x) = \ln\dfrac{|x^2 - 1|}{x^2} + C$

19. $\ln|x^2 - 4| + C$ **21.** $x + \ln|x^2 - x| + C$

23. (a) 200 individuals **(b)** 100 individuals **(c)** 60 individuals per year

25. (a) 1200 individuals **(b)** 600 individuals **(c)** 72 individuals per year

27. $P = \dfrac{200}{1 + 24e^{-1.2t}}$

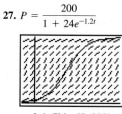

[−1, 7] by [0, 200]

29. $P = \dfrac{1200}{1 + 59e^{-0.24t}}$

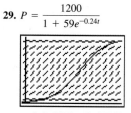

[−1, 30] by [0, 1200]

31. (a) $k = 0.0007; M = 1000$

(b) $P(0) \approx 8$; Initially there are 8 rabbits.

33. (a) $P(t) = \dfrac{150}{1 + 24e^{-0.225t}}$

(b) About 17.21 weeks; 21.28 weeks

35. Separate the variables and solve:

$$\frac{dP}{P(M - P)} = k\,dt$$

$$\frac{M\,dP}{P(M - P)} = Mk\,dt \qquad \text{Multiply by } M.$$

$$\left(\frac{1}{P} + \frac{1}{M - P}\right)dP = Mk\,dt \qquad \text{Partial fractions}$$

$$\left(\frac{1}{P - M} - \frac{1}{P}\right)dP = -Mk\,dt \qquad \text{Multiply by } -1.$$

$$\ln\left|\frac{P - M}{P}\right| = -Mk\,t + C$$

$$\left|1 - \frac{M}{P}\right| = e^{-Mk\,t} \cdot e^C$$

$$\frac{M}{P} = e^{-Mk\,t} \cdot A + 1 \qquad \text{Let } A = \pm e^C$$

$$\frac{P}{M} = \frac{1}{1 + Ae^{-Mk\,t}} \qquad \text{Reciprocate both sides.}$$

$$P = \frac{M}{1 + Ae^{-Mk\,t}}$$

37. Applying the general formula with $M = 216$ and $k = 0.0008$ gives

$W(t) = \dfrac{216}{1 + Ae^{-0.1728\,t}}$. The initial condition requires that $A = 8$.

Thus $W(t) = \dfrac{216}{1 + 8e^{-0.1728\,t}}$.

39. False. It does look exponential, but it resembles the solution to $dP/dt = kP(100 - 10) = (90k)P$

41. D **43.** D

45. (a) dP/dt has the same sign as $(M - P)(P - m)$.

(b) $P(t) = \dfrac{1200Ae^{11\,kt/12} + 100}{1 + Ae^{11\,kt/12}}$

(c) $P(t) = \dfrac{300(8e^{11\,kt/12} + 3)}{9 + 2e^{11\,kt/12}}$

(d)

[0, 75] by [0, 1500]

(e) $P(t) = \dfrac{AMe^{(M-m)kt/M} + m}{1 + Ae^{(M-m)kt/M}}$, where $A = \dfrac{P(0) - m}{M - P(0)}$

47. (a) $5\ln|x + 3| + \dfrac{15}{x + 3} + C$ **(b)** $-\dfrac{5}{x + 3} + \dfrac{15}{2(x + 3)^2} + C$

Quick Quiz (Sections 7.4 and 7.5)

1. C **3.** A

Review Exercises

1. $\sqrt{3}$ **2.** 2 **3.** 8 **4.** 0 **5.** 2 **6.** 147/8 **7.** $e - 1$ **8.** $\dfrac{2}{3}$

9. $\ln(64/9) - \ln(27/4) = \ln(256/243)$

10. $\ln (1/4) - \ln 16 = -6 \ln 2$ **11.** $-\ln |2 - \sin x| + C$

12. $\frac{1}{2}(3x + 4)^{2/3} + C$ **13.** $\frac{1}{2}\ln (t^2 + 5) + C$ **14.** $-\sec \frac{1}{\theta} + C$

15. $-\ln |\cos (\ln y)| + C$ **16.** $\ln |\sec (e^x) + \tan (e^x)| + C$

17. $\ln |\ln x| + C$ **18.** $-\frac{2}{\sqrt{t}} + C$

19. $x^3 \sin x + 3x^2 \cos x - 6x \sin x - 6 \cos x + C$

20. $\frac{x^5 \ln x}{5} - \frac{x^5}{25} + C$ **21.** $\left(\frac{3 \sin x}{10} - \frac{\cos x}{10}\right)e^{3x} + C$

22. $\left(-\frac{x^2}{3} - \frac{2x}{9} - \frac{2}{27}\right)e^{-3x} + C$ **23.** $\frac{5}{2}\ln \left|\frac{x - 5}{x + 5}\right| + C$

24. $\frac{1}{2}\ln |(2x - 1)^3(x + 1)^2| + C$ **25.** $y = \frac{x^3}{6} + \frac{x^2}{2} + x + 1$

26. $y = \frac{x^3}{3} + 2x - \frac{1}{x} - \frac{1}{3}$ **27.** $y = \ln (t + 4) + 2$

28. $y = -\frac{1}{2}\csc 2\theta + \frac{3}{2}$ **29.** $y = \frac{x^3}{3} + \ln x - x + \frac{2}{3}$

30. $r = \sin t - \frac{t^2}{2} - 2t - 1$ **31.** $y = 4e^x - 2$ **32.** $y = 2e^{x^2+x} - 1$

33. $y = \frac{1}{1 + 9e^{-t}}$ **34.** $y = \frac{100}{1 + 19e^{-0.1x}}$ **35.** $y = \int_4^x \sin^3 t \, dt + 5$

36. $y = \int_1^x \sqrt{1 + t^4} \, dt + 2$

37.

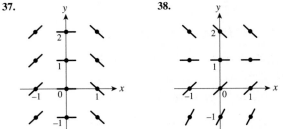

38.

39. Graph (b)   **40.** Graph (d)   **41.** Graph (c)   **42.** Graph (a)

43. 1.362   **44.** 2.362   **45.** Graph (b)   **46.** Graph (d)

47. iv. Since the given graph looks like $y = x^2$, which satisfies $dy/dx = 2x$ and $y(1) = 1$.

48. Yes, $y = x$ is a solution.   **49.** (a) $v = 2t + 3t^2 + 4$ (b) 6 m

50.

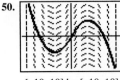

[−10, 10] by [−10, 10]

51. (a) $k \approx 0.262059$
(b) About 3.81593 years

52. About 92 minutes   **53.** −3°C   **54.** About 41.2 years

55. About 18,935 years old   **56.** About 5.3%   **57.** About 59.8 ft

58. (a) $y = c + (y_0 - c)e^{-(kA/V)t}$ (b) c

59. (a) $k = \frac{1}{150}$, carrying capacity = 150

(b) ≈ 2; Initially there were 2 infected students.

(c) About 6 days

60. Use the Fundamental Theorem of Calculus to obtain $y' = \sin (x^2) + 3x^2 + 1$. Then differentiate again and also verify the initial conditions.

61. $P = \dfrac{800}{1 + 15e^{-0.002t}}$

62. Method 1—Compare graph of $y_1 = x^2 \ln x$ with
$$y_2 = \text{NDER}\left(\frac{x^3 \ln x}{3} - \frac{x^3}{9}\right).$$
Method 2—Compare graph of $y_1 = \text{NINT}(x^2 \ln x)$ with
$$y_2 = \frac{x^3 \ln x}{3} - \frac{x^3}{9}.$$

63. (a) About 11.3 years   (b) About 11 years

64. (a) $\dfrac{d}{dx}\displaystyle\int_0^x u(t) \, dt = u(x)$

$\dfrac{d}{dx}\displaystyle\int_3^x u(t) \, dt = u(x)$

(b) $C = \displaystyle\int_0^3 u(t) \, dt$

65. (a)

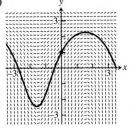

(b) The tangent line has equation $y = 2x + 1$. Thus $f(0.2) \approx 1.4$.

(c) $y = 3 - 2e^{-\sin x}$

66. (a) The tangent line has equation $y = -3(x - 1)$. Thus $f(1.2) \approx -0.6$.

(b) $y = -\ln (-x^3 + 3x^2 - 1)$

67. (a) 1/2

(b) Separate the variables to get $\dfrac{dy}{y(1 - y)} = 1.2 \, dt$. Solve the differential equation using the same steps as in Example 5 in Section 7.5 to obtain $y = \dfrac{1}{1 + 9e^{-1.2t}}$.

(c) Set $\dfrac{1}{2} = \dfrac{1}{1 + 9e^{-1.2t}}$ and solve for t to obtain $t = \dfrac{5 \ln 3}{3} \approx 1.83$ days.

68. (a) $dP/dt = k(600 - P)$. Separate the variables to obtain

$$\frac{dP}{600 - P} = k \, dt$$
$$\frac{dP}{P - 600} = -k \, dt$$
$$\ln |P - 600| = -kt + C_1$$
$$P - 600 = Ce^{-kt}$$
$$200 - 600 = Ce^0 \Rightarrow C = -400$$
$$P - 600 = -400e^{-kt}$$
$$P(t) = 600 - 400e^{-kt}$$

(b) $500 = 600 - 400e^{-k \cdot 2}$
$1/4 = e^{-2k}$
$k = \ln 2 \approx 0.693$

(c) $\displaystyle\lim_{t \to \infty} (600 - 400e^{-0.693t}) = 600$

69. (a) Separate the variables to obtain

$$\frac{dv}{v + 17} = -2dt$$

$$\ln |v + 17| = -2t + C_1$$

$$v + 17 = Ce^{-2t}$$

$$-47 + 17 = Ce^0 \Rightarrow C = -30$$

$$v + 17 = -30e^{-2t}$$

$$v = -30e^{-2t} - 17$$

(b) $\lim_{t \to \infty} (-30e^{-2t} - 17) = -17$ feet per second

(c) $-20 = -30e^{-2t} - 17$

$$t = \frac{\ln 10}{2} \approx 1.151 \text{ seconds}$$

CHAPTER 8

Section 8.1

Quick Review 8.1

1. Changes sign at $-\frac{\pi}{2}, 0, \frac{\pi}{2}$

3. Always positive

5. Changes sign at $\frac{\pi}{4}, \frac{3\pi}{4}, \frac{5\pi}{4}$

7. Changes sign at 0

9. Changes sign at $0.9633 + k\pi$
$2.1783 + k\pi$
where k is an integer

Exercises 8.1

1. (a) Right: $0 \le t < \pi/2, 3\pi/2 < t \le 2\pi$
Left: $\pi/2 < t < 3\pi/2$
Stopped: $t = \pi/2, 3\pi/2$
(b) 0; 3 **(c)** 20

3. (a) Right: $0 \le t < 5$
Left: $5 < t \le 10$
Stopped: $t = 5$
(b) 0; 3 **(c)** 245

5. (a) Right: $0 < t < \pi/2, 3\pi/2 < t < 2\pi$
Left: $\pi/2 < t < \pi, \pi < t < 3\pi/2$
Stopped: $t = 0, \pi/2, \pi, 3\pi/2, 2\pi$
(b) 0; 3 **(c)** 20/3

7. (a) Right: $0 \le t < \pi/2, 3\pi/2 < t \le 2\pi$
Left: $\pi/2 < t < 3\pi/2$
Stopped: $t = \pi/2, 3\pi/2$
(b) 0; 3 **(c)** $2e - (2/e) \approx 4.7$

9. (a) 63 mph **(b)** 344.52 feet

11. (a) -6 ft/sec **(b)** 5.625 sec **(c)** 0 **(d)** 253.125 feet

13. 33 cm **15.** $t = a$ **17. (a)** 6 **(b)** 4 meters **19. (a)** 5 **(b)** 7 meters

21. ≈ 332.965 billion barrels **23.** 161 light bulbs

25. $500 + 8000 - 7500 = 1000$ people **27.** 1156.5 cases

29. 1800 hot dogs **31.** ≈ 2.854 kg

33. (a) 2 miles **(b)** $2\pi r \, \Delta r$
(c) Population = population density $\times$ area **(d)** $\approx 83,776$ people

35. (a) 18 N **(b)** 81 N $\cdot$ cm

37. False. The displacement is the integral of the velocity from $t = 0$ to $t = 5$ and is positive.

39. C **41.** B **43.** 0.04875

45. For $0 \le T < 2$,

$$L(T) = 500 + \int_0^T (2000 - 250t - 1500)dt$$

$$= 500 + 500T - 125T^2, \quad L(2) = 1000.$$

From time $T = 2$ to $T = 3$,

$$L(T) = 1000 + \int_2^T (500 + 500t - 1500)dt$$

$$= 2000 - 1000T + 250T^2, \quad L(3) = 1250.$$

From time 3 to 4,

$$L(T) = 1250 + \int_3^T (5000 - 1000t - 1500)dt$$

$$= -4750 + 3500T - 500T^2, \quad L(4) = 1250.$$

From time 4 to 5,

$$L(T) = 1250 + \int_4^T (-1000 + 500t - 1500)dt$$

$$= 7250 - 2500T + 250T^2, \quad L(5) = 1000.$$

47. (a, b) Take $dm = \delta \, dA$ as m_k and let $dA \to 0, k \to \infty$ in the center of mass equations.

49. $\bar{x} = 4/3, \bar{y} = 0$

Section 8.2

Quick Review 8.2

1. 2 **3.** 2 **5.** $9\pi/2$ **7.** $(0, 1)$ **9.** $(-1, -1); (0, 0); (1, 1)$

Exercises 8.2

1. $\pi/2$ **3.** $1/12$ **5.** $128/15$ **7.** ≈ 1.670

9. $5/6$ **11.** ≈ 7.542 **13.** 16 **15.** $10\frac{2}{3}$ **17.** 4

19. $\frac{2}{3} a^3$ **21.** $21\frac{1}{3}$ **23.** $30\frac{3}{8}$ **25.** $8/3$ **27.** 8

29. $6\sqrt{3}$ **31.** $\frac{4 - \pi}{\pi} \approx 0.273$ **33.** $4 - \pi \approx 0.858$

35. ≈ 4.333 **37.** $1/2$ **39.** $\sqrt{2} - 1$

41. (a) $(-\sqrt{c}, c)$; $(\sqrt{c}, c)$

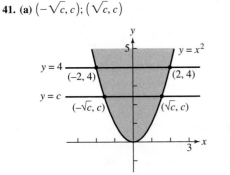

(b) $\int_0^c \sqrt{y}\, dy = \int_c^4 \sqrt{y}\, dy \Rightarrow c = 2^{4/3}$

(c) $\int_0^{\sqrt{c}} (c - x^2)\, dx = (4 - c)\sqrt{c} + \int_{\sqrt{c}}^2 (4 - x^2)\, dx \Rightarrow c = 2^{4/3}$

43. $3/4$　**45.** Neither; both are zero.

47. $\ln 4 - (1/2) \approx 0.886$　**49.** $k \approx 1.8269$

51. False. It is $\int_0^{0.739}(\cos x - x)\, dx$.　**53.** E　**55.** A

57. Since $f(x) - g(x)$ is the same for each region where $f(x)$ and $g(x)$ represent the upper and lower edges, area $= \int_a^b [f(x) - g(x)]\, dx$ will be the same for each.

Section 8.3

Quick Review 8.3

1. x^2　**3.** $\pi x^2/2$　**5.** $(\sqrt{3}/4)x^2$　**7.** $x^2/4$　**9.** $6x^2$

Exercises 8.3

1. (a) $\pi(1 - x^2)$　**(b)** $4(1 - x^2)$　**(c)** $2(1 - x^2)$　**(d)** $\sqrt{3}(1 - x^2)$

3. 16　**5.** $16/3$　**7.** $2\pi/3$　**9.** $4 - \pi$　**11.** $32\pi/5$　**13.** 36π

15. $2\pi/3$　**17.** $117\pi/5$　**19.** $\pi^2 - 2\pi$　**21.** $\int_0^4 \pi(2 - \sqrt{y})^2\, dy = \dfrac{8\pi}{3}$

23. 2.301　**25.** 2π　**27.** $4\pi/3$　**29.** 8π

31. (a) 8π　**(b)** $32\pi/5$　**(c)** $8\pi/3$　**(d)** $224\pi/15$

33. (a) $16\pi/15$　**(b)** $56\pi/15$　**(c)** $64\pi/15$

35. (a) $6\pi/5$　**(b)** $4\pi/5$　**(c)** 2π　**(d)** 2π

37. 8π　**39.** $128\pi/5$　**41. (a)** $2\sqrt{3}$　**(b)** 8　**43.** 8π

45. The volumes are equal by Cavalieri's Theorem.

47. (a) $512\pi/21$　**(b)** $832\pi/21$

49. (a) $11\pi/48$　**(b)** $11\pi/48$　**51. (a)** $36\pi/5$ cm³　**(b)** 192.3 g

53. (a) $32\pi/3$　**(b)** The answer is independent of r.

55. 5　**57.** ≈ 13.614　**59.** ≈ 16.110　**61.** ≈ 53.226

63. ≈ 6.283　**65.** True, by definition.　**67.** A　**69.** B

71. (a) $\dfrac{2}{\pi}, \dfrac{\pi^2 - 8}{2}$　**(b)** 0　**(c)** $V = \dfrac{\pi(2c^2\pi - 8c + \pi)}{2}$

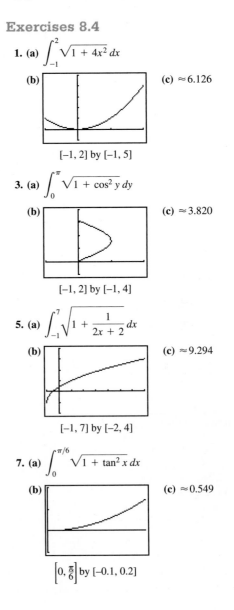

[0, 2] by [0, 6]

Volume $\to \infty$

73. Hemisphere cross-sectional area:
$$\pi\left(\sqrt{R^2 - h^2}\right)^2 = A_1$$
Right circular cylinder with cone removed cross-sectional area:
$$\pi R^2 - \pi h^2 = A_2$$
Since $A_1 = A_2$, the two volumes are equal by Cavalieri's theorem.
Thus, volume of hemisphere = volume of cylinder − volume of cone
$$= \pi R^3 - \frac{1}{3}\pi R^3 = \frac{2}{3}\pi R^3.$$

75. (a) $\pi h^2(3a - h)/3$　**(b)** $1/(120\pi)$ m/sec

Quick Quiz (Sections 8.1–8.3)

1. C　**3.** D

Section 8.4

Quick Review 8.4

1. $x + 1$　**3.** $\sec x$　**5.** $\sqrt{2}\cos x$　**7.** 0　**9.** 2

Exercises 8.4

1. (a) $\displaystyle\int_{-1}^2 \sqrt{1 + 4x^2}\, dx$

(b)

(c) ≈ 6.126

[−1, 2] by [−1, 5]

3. (a) $\displaystyle\int_0^\pi \sqrt{1 + \cos^2 y}\, dy$

(b)

(c) ≈ 3.820

[−1, 2] by [−1, 4]

5. (a) $\displaystyle\int_{-1}^7 \sqrt{1 + \dfrac{1}{2x + 2}}\, dx$

(b)

(c) ≈ 9.294

[−1, 7] by [−2, 4]

7. (a) $\displaystyle\int_0^{\pi/6} \sqrt{1 + \tan^2 x}\, dx$

(b)

(c) ≈ 0.549

$\left[0, \dfrac{\pi}{6}\right]$ by $[−0.1, 0.2]$

9. (a) $\displaystyle\int_{-\pi/3}^{\pi/3} \sqrt{1 + \sec^2 x \tan^2 x}\, dx$

(b) 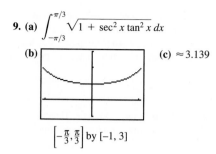   **(c)** ≈ 3.139

$\left[-\dfrac{\pi}{3}, \dfrac{\pi}{3}\right]$ by $[-1, 3]$

11. 12   **13.** $53/6$ **15.** $17/12$ **17.** 2

19. (a) $y = \sqrt{x}$

(b) Two. We know the absolute value of the derivative of the function and the value of the function at one value of x.

21. 1   **23.** ≈ 21.07 inches   **25.** ≈ 3.6142 **27.** ≈ 13.132 **29.** ≈ 16.647

31. No. Consider the curve $y = \dfrac{1}{3}\sin\left(\dfrac{1}{x}\right) + 0.5$ for $0 < x < 1$.

33. False. The derivative must be continuous on $[a, b]$.   **35.** C   **37.** A

39. (a) The fin is the hypotenuse of a right triangle with leg lengths Δx_k and

$$\left.\dfrac{df}{dx}\right|_{x=x_{k-1}} \Delta x_k = f'(x_{k-1})\Delta x_k.$$

(b) $\displaystyle\lim_{n\to\infty} \sum_{k=1}^{n} \sqrt{(\Delta x_k)^2 + (f'(x_{k-1})\Delta x_k)^2}$

$$= \lim_{n\to\infty} \sum_{k=1}^{n} \Delta x_k \sqrt{1 + (f'(x_{k-1}))^2}$$

$$= \int_{a}^{b} \sqrt{1 + (f'(x))^2}\, dx$$

Section 8.5

Quick Review 8.5

1. (a) $1 - (1/e)$ **(b)** ≈ 0.632

3. (a) $\dfrac{\sqrt{2}}{2}$ **(b)** ≈ 0.707 **5. (a)** $(1/3)\ln(9/2)$ **(b)** ≈ 0.501

7. $\displaystyle\int_{0}^{7} (1 - x^2)(2\pi x)\, dx$ **9.** $\displaystyle\int_{0}^{7} \pi(y/2)^2 (10 - y)\, dy$

Exercises 8.5

1. ≈ 4.4670 J   **3.** 9 J   **5.** 4900 J   **7.** 1944 ft-lb

9. (a) 7238 lb/in.   **(b)** ≈ 905 in.-lb and ≈ 2714 in.-lb   **11.** 780 J

13. (a) If y is the distance from the top, then the total force is approximately

$$\sum_{k=1}^{n} (62.4\, y_k)\left(2\sqrt{9 - y_k^2}\right)\Delta y.$$

(b) 1123.2 lb

15. (a) If y is the distance from the top, then the total force is approximately

$$\sum_{k=1}^{n} 62.4(y_k - 3)\left(\dfrac{3}{4}y_k\right)\Delta y.$$

(b) 3705 lb

17. (a) 1,497,600 ft-lb   **(b)** ≈ 100 min

(c) Work to empty half the tank $= \displaystyle\int_{0}^{10} 62.4(120\, y)\, dy = 374,400$ ft-lb,

and $37.400 + 250 = 1497.6$ sec $= 25$ min.

(d) 1,494,240 ft-lb, ≈ 100 min; 1,500,000 ft-lb, 100 min

19. Through valve: $\approx 84,687.3$ ft-lb; Over the rim: $\approx 98,801.8$ ft-lb; Through a hose attached to a valve in the bottom is less work.

21. $\approx 53,482.5$ ft-lb   **23.** $\approx 967,611$ ft-lb; yes

25. (a) ≈ 209.73 lb   **(b)** ≈ 838.93 lb; the fluid force doubles.

27. $1/3$ **29.** 68%

31. (a) $0.5\ (50\%)$ **(b)** $\approx 0.24\ (24\%)$ **(c)** $\approx 0.0036\ (0.36\%)$ **(d)** 0

33. The proportion of lightbulbs that last between 100 and 800 hours.

35. True. The force against each vertical side is 842.4 lb.   **37.** D   **39.** E

41. (a) 1.15×10^{-28} J   **(b)** $\approx 7.6667 \times 10^{-29}$ J

43. 72.5 J   **45.** ≈ 162.6 J   **47.** 152 J

Quick Quiz (Sections 8.4 and 8.5)

1. A   **3.** C

Review Exercises

1. ≈ 10.417 ft   **2.** ≈ 31.361 gal   **3.** ≈ 1464 **4.** 14 g   **5.** 14,400

6. 1   **7.** $\dfrac{9}{2}$ **8.** $1/6$ **9.** 18   **10.** 30.375   **11.** ≈ 0.0155 **12.** 4

13. ≈ 8.9023 **14.** ≈ 2.1043 **15.** $2\sqrt{3} - 2\pi/3 \approx 1.370$

16. $2\sqrt{3} + 4\pi/3 \approx 7.653$ **17.** ≈ 1.2956 **18.** ≈ 5.7312 **19.** 4π

20. 2π **21. (a)** $32\pi/3$ **(b)** $128\pi/15$ **(c)** $64\pi/5$ **(d)** $32\pi/3$

22. (a) 4π **(b)** πk^2 **(c)** $1/\pi$ **23.** $88\pi \approx 276$ in.^{3} **24.** $\pi^2/4$

25. $\pi(2 - \ln 3)$ **26.** $28\pi/3$ ft$^3 \approx 29.3215$ ft^3 **27.** ≈ 19.4942

28. ≈ 5.2454 **29.** 2.296 sec   **30. (a)** is true.   **31.** 39

32. (a) 4000 J   **(b)** 640 J   **(c)** 4640 J

33. 22,800,000 ft-lb   **34.** 12 J, ≈ 213.3 J

35. No, the work going uphill is positive, but the work going downhill is negative.

36. ≈ 113.097 in.-lb   **37.** ≈ 426.67 lb

38. base ≈ 6.6385 lb; front and back: 5.7726 lb; sides ≈ 9.4835 lb

39. 14.4   **40.** $\approx 0.2051\ (20.5\%)$ **41.** Answers will vary.

42. (a) $\approx 0.6827\ (68.27\%)$ **(b)** $0.9545\ (95.45\%)$; $0.9973\ (99.73\%)$

43. The probability that the variable has some value in the range of all possible values is 1.

44. π **45.** 3π **46.** $2\pi^2$ **47.** $16\pi/3$ **48.** ≈ 9.7717

49. (a) $y = 5 - \dfrac{5}{4}x^2$ **(b)** ≈ 335.1032 in.^{3}

50. $f(x) = \dfrac{x^2 - 2\ln x + 3}{4}$ **51.** ≈ 3.84 **52.** ≈ 5.02

53. (a) The two curves intersect at $x = 1.2237831$. Store this value as A.

Area $= \displaystyle\int_{0}^{A} (2 + \sin x - \sec x)\, dx = 1.366.$

(b) Volume $= \displaystyle\int_{0}^{A} \pi((2 + \sin x)^2 - (\sec x)^2)\, dx = 16.404.$

(c) Volume $= \displaystyle\int_{0}^{A} (2 + \sin x - \sec x)^2\, dx = 1.629.$

54. (a) Average temp $= \dfrac{1}{14 - 6}\displaystyle\int_{6}^{14}\left(80 - 10\cos\left(\dfrac{\pi t}{12}\right)\right) dt \approx 87°$F.

(b) $F(t) = 80 - 10\cos\left(\dfrac{\pi t}{12}\right) \geq 78$ for $5.2308694 \leq t \leq 18.766913$.

Store these two values as A and B.

(c) Cost $= 0.05\displaystyle\int_{A}^{B}\left(80 - 10\cos\left(\dfrac{\pi t}{12}\right) - 78\right) dt \approx 5.10$

The cost was about \$5.10.

55. (a) $\int_{9}^{17} \dfrac{15600}{(t^2 - 24t + 160)}\, dt \approx 6004$ people.

(b) $15\int_{9}^{17} \dfrac{15600}{(t^2 - 24t + 160)}\, dt + 11\int_{17}^{23} \dfrac{15600}{(t^2 - 24t + 160)}\, dt \approx$
104,048 dollars

(c) $H'(17) = E(17) - L(17) \approx -380$ people. $H(17)$ is the number of people in the park at 5:00, and $H'(17)$ is the rate at which the number of people in the park is changing at 5:00.

(d) When $H'(t) = E(t) - L(t) = 0$; that is, at $t = 15.795$.

CHAPTER 9

Section 9.1

Quick Review 9.1

1. 5/8   **3.** 1   **5.** 12   **7.** 0   **9.** 1

Exercises 9.1

1. $1/2, 2/3, 3/4, 4/5, 5/6, 6/7; 50/51$

3. $2, 9/4, 64/27, 625/256, 7776/3125 \approx 2.48832,$
$117649/46656 \approx 2.521626; (51/50)^{50} \approx 2.691588$

5. $3, 1, -1, -3; -11$ **7.** $2, 4, 8, 16; 256$ **9.** $1, 1, 2, 3; 21$

11. (a) 3   **(b)** 19   **(c)** $a_n = a_{n-1} + 3$ **(d)** $a_n = 3n - 5$

13. (a) $1/2$ **(b)** $9/2$ **(c)** $a_n = a_{n-1} + 1/2$ **(d)** $a_n = (n+1)/2$

15. (a) $1/2$ **(b)** $8(1/2)^8 = 0.03125$
(c) $a_n = (1/2)a_{n-1}$ **(d)** $a_n = 8(1/2)^{n-1} = 2^{4-n}$

17. (a) -3 **(b)** $(-3)^9 = -19{,}683$ **(c)** $a_n = (-3)a_{n-1}$
(d) $a_n = (-3)(-3)^{n-1} = (-3)^n$

19. $-5, a_n = a_{n-1} + 3$ for all $n \geq 2$

21. $a_1 = 3.01, r = 10.\ a_n = 3.01(10)^{n-1}, n \geq 1$

23.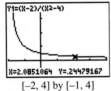
[0, 20] by [0, 1]

25.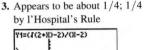
[0, 20] by [-5, 5]

27.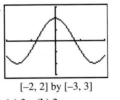
[0, 10] by [-25, 200]

29.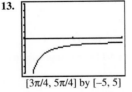
[0, 20] by [-1, 5]

31. converges, 3   **33.** converges, $2/5$ **35.** diverges

37. diverges   **39.** converges, 1   **41.** 0

43. $0\left(\text{Note: }\dfrac{1}{n!} \leq \dfrac{1}{n}\text{ for }n \geq 1\right)$

45. Graph (b)   **47.** Table (d)

49. False. Consider the sequence with nth term $a_n = -5 + 2(n-1)$.
Here $a_1 = -5, a_2 = -3, a_3 = -1,$ and $a_4 = 1$.

51. C   **53.** D

55. (a) Each polygon can be subdivided into $2n$ congruent right triangles with hypotenuse 1 and one vertex at the center O of the circle. The angle at O has measure $2\pi \div 2n = \pi/n$, so the opposite side has length $1 \cdot \sin(\pi/n)$. Since there are $2n$ such triangles, the perimeter of the polygon is $2n \sin\left(\dfrac{\pi}{n}\right)$.

(b) 2π

57. $a_n = ar^{n-1}$ implies that $\log a_n = \log a + (n-1)\log r$. Thus $\{\log a_n\}$ is an arithmetic sequence with first term $\log a$ and common difference $\log r$.

59. Given $\epsilon > 0$ choose $M = 1/\epsilon$. Then $\left|\dfrac{1}{n} - 0\right| < \epsilon$ if $n > M$.

Section 9.2

Quick Review 9.2

1. 1.1052   **3.** 1   **5.** 2   **7.** 3   **9.** $y = \dfrac{\sin h}{h}$

Exercises 9.2

1. Appears to be about $1/4$; $1/4$ by l'Hospital's Rule

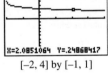
X=2.0851064 Y=.24479167
[-2, 4] by [-1, 4]

3. Appears to be about $1/4$; $1/4$ by l'Hospital's Rule

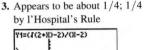
X=2.0851064 Y=.24868417
[-2, 4] by [-1, 1]

5. $1/2$ **7.** -1

9.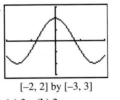
[-2, 2] by [-3, 3]
(a) 2   **(b)** 2

11.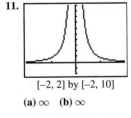
[-2, 2] by [-2, 10]
(a) ∞ **(b)** ∞

13.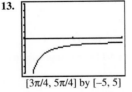
$[3\pi/4, 5\pi/4]$ by $[-5, 5]$
Left $(\infty)/(-\infty)$, right $(-\infty)/(\infty)$, limit $= -1$

15.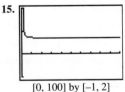
[0, 100] by [-1, 2]
$(\infty)/(\infty)$, limit $= \ln 2$

17. $\infty \cdot 0, 0$ **19.** $\infty - \infty, 1$ **21.** $1^{\infty}, e^2$ **23.** $0^0, 1$ **25.** $\infty^0, 1$

27. (a)

x	10	10^2	10^3	10^4	10^5
$f(x)$	1.1513	0.2303	0.0354	0.0046	0.00058

Estimated limit = 0

(b) Note $\ln x^5 = 5\ln x$.
$$\lim_{x\to\infty} \frac{5\ln x}{x} = \lim_{x\to\infty} \frac{5/x}{1} = \frac{0}{1} = 0$$

29. $3/4$ **31.** 1   **33.** 0   **35.** $\ln 3/\ln 2$ **37.** 1   **39.** ∞ **41.** 0

43. $e^{1/2}$ **45.** e **47.** e^{-1} **49.** $3/11$ **51.** $(\cos 1)/2$

53. (a) L'Hospital's Rule does not help because applying l'Hospital's Rule to this quotient essentially "inverts" the problem by interchanging the numerator and denominator. It is still essentially the same problem and one is no closer to a solution. Applying l'Hospital's Rule a second time returns to the original problem.

(b), (c) 3

55. $c = 27/10$, because this is the limit of $f(x)$ as x approaches 0.

57. (a) $\ln\left(1 + \dfrac{r}{k}\right)^{kt} = kt \ln\left(1 + \dfrac{r}{k}\right)$. And, as $k \to \infty$,

$$\lim_{k\to\infty} kt \ln\left(1 + \frac{r}{k}\right) = \lim_{k\to\infty} \frac{t\ln\left(1 + \dfrac{r}{k}\right)}{\dfrac{1}{k}}$$

$$= \lim_{k\to\infty} \frac{t\left(\dfrac{-r}{k^2}\right)\left(1 + \dfrac{r}{k}\right)^{-1}}{\dfrac{-1}{k^2}}.$$

$$= \lim_{k\to\infty} \frac{rt}{1 + \dfrac{r}{k}} = rt.$$

Hence, $\displaystyle\lim_{k\to\infty} A_0\left(1 + \frac{r}{k}\right)^{kt} = A_0 e^{rt}$.

(b) Part (a) shows that as the number of compoundings per year increases toward infinity, the limit of interest compounded k times per year is interest compounded continuously.

59. (a) 1 **(b)** $\pi/2$ **(c)** π

61. (a) $(-\infty, -1) \cup (0, \infty)$ **(b)** ∞ **(c)** e

63. False. The limit is 1. **65.** D **67.** E

69. Possible answers: **(a)** $f(x) = 3x + 1, g(x) = x$
(b) $f(x) = x + 1, g(x) = x^2$ **(c)** $f(x) = x^2, g(x) = x + 1$

71. (a) $c = 1/3$ **(b)** $c = \pi/4$

Quick Quiz (Sections 9.1 and 9.2)

1. C **3.** B

Section 9.3

Quick Review 9.3

1. 0 **3.** ∞ **5.** $-3x^4$

7. $\displaystyle\lim_{x\to\infty} \frac{f(x)}{g(x)} = \lim_{x\to\infty}\left(1 + \frac{1}{x}\right) = 1 + 0 = 1$

9. (a) Local minimum at $(0, 1)$ Local maximum at $\approx (2, 1.541)$
(b) $[0, 2]$ **(c)** $(-\infty, 0]$ and $[2, \infty)$

Exercises 9.3

1. $\displaystyle\lim_{x\to\infty} \frac{e^x}{x^3 - 3x + 1} = \infty$ **3.** $\displaystyle\lim_{x\to\infty} \frac{e^x}{e^{\cos x}} = \infty$

5. $\displaystyle\lim_{x\to\infty} \frac{\ln x}{x - \ln x} = 0$ **7.** $\displaystyle\lim_{x\to\infty} \frac{\ln x}{\sqrt[3]{x}} = 0$ **9.** $\displaystyle\lim_{x\to\infty} \frac{x^2 + 4x}{x^2} = 1$

11. $\displaystyle\lim_{x\to\infty} \frac{\sqrt[3]{x^6 + x^2}}{x^2} = 1$ **13.** $\displaystyle\lim_{x\to\infty} \frac{\log \sqrt{x}}{\ln x} = \frac{1}{2\ln 10}$

15. Slower **17.** Slower **19.** Slower **21.** Faster **23.** Slower

25. Same rate **27.** Same rate **29.** $e^{x/2}, e^x, (\ln x)^x, x^x$

31. $\displaystyle\lim_{x\to\infty} \frac{f_2(x)}{f_1(x)} = \sqrt{10}$ and $\displaystyle\lim_{x\to\infty} \frac{f_3(x)}{f_1(x)} = 1$, so f_2 and f_3 also grow at the same rate.

33. $\displaystyle\lim_{x\to\infty} \frac{f_2(x)}{f_1(x)} = 1$ and $\displaystyle\lim_{x\to\infty} \frac{f_3(x)}{f_1(x)} = 1$, so f_2 and f_3 also grow at the same rate.

35. f grows faster than g. **37.** f and g grow at the same rate.

39. (a) The nth derivative of x^n is $n!$, which is a constant. Therefore n applications of l'Hospital's Rule give

$$\lim_{x\to\infty} \frac{e^x}{x^n} = \cdots = \lim_{x\to\infty} \frac{e^x}{n!} = \infty.$$

(b) In this case, n applications of l'Hospital's Rule give

$$\lim_{x\to\infty} \frac{a^x}{x^n} = \cdots = \lim_{x\to\infty} \frac{a^x(\ln a)^n}{n!} = \infty$$

41. (a) $\displaystyle\lim_{x\to\infty} \frac{\ln x}{x^{1/n}} = \lim_{x\to\infty} \frac{1/x}{\left[\dfrac{x^{(1/n)-1}}{n}\right]} = \lim_{x\to\infty} \frac{n}{x^{1/n}} = 0$

(b) $\displaystyle\lim_{x\to\infty} \frac{\ln x}{x^a} = \lim_{x\to\infty} \frac{1/x}{ax^{a-1}} = \lim_{x\to\infty} \frac{1}{ax^a} = 0$

43. The one which is of order $\log_2 n$ is likely the most efficient, because of the three given functions, it grows the most slowly as $n \to \infty$.

45. (a) The limit will be the ratio of the leading coefficients of the polynomials.
(b) The limit will be the same as in part (a).

47. False. They grow at the same rate. **49.** E **51.** D

53. (a) and **(b)** both follow from the fact that if f and g are negative, then

$$\lim_{x\to\infty} \left|\frac{f(x)}{g(x)}\right| = \lim_{x\to\infty} \frac{-f(x)}{-g(x)} = \lim_{x\to\infty} \frac{f(x)}{g(x)}$$

Section 9.4

Quick Review 9.4

1. $\ln 2$ **3.** $\dfrac{1}{2}\tan^{-1}\dfrac{x}{2} + C$ **5.** $(-3, 3)$

7. Because $-1 \le \cos x \le 1$ for all x **9.** $\displaystyle\lim_{x\to\infty} \frac{4e^x - 5}{3e^x + 7} = \frac{4}{3}$

Exercises 9.4

1. (a) $\displaystyle\lim_{b\to\infty} \int_0^b \frac{2x}{x^2 + 1}\,dx$ **(b)** ∞, diverges

3. (a) $\displaystyle\lim_{b\to-\infty} \int_b^0 \frac{2x}{(x^2 + 1)^2}\,dx + \lim_{b\to\infty} \int_0^b \frac{2x}{(x^2 + 1)^2}\,dx$ **(b)** 0, converges

5. $1/3$ **7.** diverges **9.** 1 **11.** $\ln(3)$ **13.** $\ln(2)$

15. diverges **17.** $(3/4)\,e^{-2}$ **19.** diverges **21.** 2 **23.** $\pi/2$

25. (a) The integral has an infinite discontinuity at the interior point $x = 1$.
(b) diverges

27. (a) The integral has an infinite discontinuity at the endpoint $x = 0$.
(b) $\sqrt{3}$

29. (a) The integral has an infinite discontinuity at the endpoint $x = 0$.
(b) $-1/4$

31. $0 \le \dfrac{1}{1 + e^x} \le \dfrac{1}{e^x}$ on $[1, \infty)$, converges because $\displaystyle\int_1^\infty \frac{1}{e^x}\,dx$ converges

33. $0 \le \dfrac{1}{x} \le \dfrac{2 + \cos x}{x}$ on $[\pi, \infty)$, diverges because $\displaystyle\int_\pi^\infty \frac{1}{x}\,dx$ diverges

35. diverges **37.** π **39.** $2\pi^2$ **41.** diverges **43.** 1

45. (a) Since f is an even function, the substitution

$$u = -x \text{ gives } \int_{-\infty}^{0} f(x)\, dx = \int_{0}^{\infty} f(u)\, du.$$

(b) Since f is an odd function, the substitution

$$u = -x \text{ gives } \int_{-\infty}^{0} f(x)\, dx = -\int_{0}^{\infty} f(u)\, du.$$

47. 6 **49.** True. See Theorem 6. **51.** B **53.** C

55. (a) $A(x) = (\pi/4)\, e^{2x}$ **(b)** $V = \int_{-\infty}^{\ln 2} A(x)\, dx = \int_{-\infty}^{\ln 2} (\pi/4)\, e^{2x}\, dx$

(c) $\pi/2$

57. (a) For $x \geq 6$, $x^2 \geq 6x$, and therefore, $e^{-x^2} \leq e^{-6x}$. The inequality for the integrals follows. The value of the second integral is $e^{-36}/6$, which is less than 4×10^{-17}.

(b) The error in the estimate is the integral over the interval $[6, \infty)$, and we have shown that it is bounded by 4×10^{-17} in part (a).

(c) 0.13940279264 (This agrees with Figure 9.19.)

(d) $\int_{0}^{\infty} e^{-x^2}\, dx = \int_{0}^{3} e^{-x^2}\, dx + \int_{3}^{\infty} e^{-x^2}\, dx.$

The error in the approximation is

$$\int_{3}^{\infty} e^{-x^2}\, dx \leq \int_{3}^{\infty} e^{-3x}\, dx < 0.000042.$$

59. (a) $n = 0$: integral $= 1$

$n = 1$: integral $= 1$

$n = 2$: integral $= 2$

(b) Integration by parts gives

$$\int x^n e^{-x}\, dx = -x^n e^{-x} + n \int x^{n-1} e^{-x}\, dx + C.$$

Since the term $(-x^n e^{-x})$ has value 0 at $x = 0$ and has limit equal to 0 as $x \to \infty$, when the above equation is evaluated "from 0 to infinity," it gives $f(n + 1) = nf(n)$.

(c) This follows from the formula $f(n + 1) = nf(n)$ by an induction argument. In fact, it follows that $\int_{0}^{\infty} x^n e^{-x}\, dx = n!$.

61. (a) $\int_{-\infty}^{1} \dfrac{dx}{1 + x^2} = \dfrac{3\pi}{4}, \int_{1}^{\infty} \dfrac{dx}{1 + x^2} = \dfrac{\pi}{4}$

$$\int_{-\infty}^{\infty} \dfrac{dx}{1 + x^2} = \dfrac{3\pi}{4} + \dfrac{\pi}{4} = \pi$$

(b) $\int_{-\infty}^{c} f(x)\, dx = \int_{-\infty}^{0} f(x)\, dx + \int_{0}^{c} f(x)\, dx$

$$\int_{c}^{\infty} f(x)\, dx = \int_{c}^{0} f(x)\, dx + \int_{0}^{\infty} f(x)\, dx$$

Thus,

$$\int_{-\infty}^{c} f(x)\, dx + \int_{c}^{\infty} f(x)\, dx$$

$$= \int_{-\infty}^{0} f(x)\, dx + \int_{0}^{c} f(x)\, dx + \int_{c}^{0} f(x)\, dx + \int_{0}^{\infty} f(x)\, dx$$

$$= \int_{-\infty}^{0} f(x)\, dx + \int_{0}^{\infty} f(x)\, dx,$$

because

$$\int_{0}^{c} f(x)\, dx + \int_{c}^{0} f(x)\, dx = 0.$$

Quick Quiz (Sections 9.3 and 9.4)

1. E **3.** B

Review Exercises

1. $-1/2, 3/5, -2/3, 5/7; a_{40} = 41/43$

2. $-3, -6, -12, -24; a_{40} = -3(2^{39})$

3. (a) $3/2$ **(b)** $25/2$ **(c)** $a_n = \dfrac{3n - 5}{2}$

4. (a) -4 **(b)** 2048 **(c)** $a_n = (-1)^{n-1}(2^{2n-3})$

5.

[0, 20] by [−2, 4]

6.

[0, 20] by [−2, 2]

7. converges, $3/2$ **8.** diverges **9.** The limit doesn't exist.

10. $3/5$ **11.** 2 **12.** $1/e$ **13.** 1 **14.** e^3 **15.** 0 **16.** -1 **17.** $-1/2$

18. 1 **19.** 1 **20.** ∞ **21.** ∞ **22.** 0

23. Same rate, because $\lim\limits_{x \to \infty} \dfrac{f(x)}{g(x)} = \dfrac{1}{5}$

24. Same rate, because $\lim\limits_{x \to \infty} \dfrac{f(x)}{g(x)} = \dfrac{\ln 3}{\ln 2}$

25. Same rate, because $\lim\limits_{x \to \infty} \dfrac{f(x)}{g(x)} = 1$

26. Faster, because $\lim\limits_{x \to \infty} \dfrac{f(x)}{g(x)} = \infty$

27. Faster, because $\lim\limits_{x \to \infty} \dfrac{f(x)}{g(x)} = \infty$

28. Slower, because $\lim\limits_{x \to \infty} \dfrac{f(x)}{g(x)} = 0$

29. Same rate, because $\lim\limits_{x \to \infty} \dfrac{f(x)}{g(x)} = \dfrac{1}{2}$

30. Slower, because $\lim\limits_{x \to \infty} \dfrac{f(x)}{g(x)} = 0$

31. (a) $\lim\limits_{x \to 0} f(x) = 1/3$ **(b)** Define $f(0) = 1/3$

32. (a) $\lim\limits_{x \to 0} f(x) = 1$ **(b)** Define $f(0) = 1$

33. (a) $\lim\limits_{x \to 0} f(x) = -1$ **(b)** Define $f(0) = -1$

34. (a) $\lim\limits_{x \to 0} f(x) = 1$ **(b)** Define $f(0) = 1$

35. (a) $\lim\limits_{x \to 0} = \ln 2$ **(b)** Define $f(0) = \ln 2$.

36. (a) $\lim\limits_{x \to 0^+} f(x) = 0$ **(b)** Define $f(0) = 0$.

37. 2 **38.** $\ln (5/4)$ **39.** $-2 \ln (2)$ **40.** $\pi/2$ **41.** -1

42. 6 **43.** 0 **44.** $\ln (3)$ **45.** 2 **46.** $-1/9$ **47.** $\pi/2$

48. π **49.** diverges **50.** converges

51. (a) -6 **(b)** $1/2$ **(c)** $a_n = -3(2^{2-n})$

52. (a) 13 **(b)** -1.5 **(c)** $a_n = -1.5n + 14.5$

53. (a) $\lim\limits_{b \to -\infty} \int_{b}^{0} e^{2x}\, dx + \lim\limits_{b \to \infty} \int_{0}^{b} e^{-2x}\, dx$ **(b)** 1

54. 2π **55.** 1

56. (a) $\int_{0}^{\infty} x e^{-x/2}\, dx$ **(b)** $\lim\limits_{b \to \infty} \int_{0}^{b} x e^{-x/2}\, dx$

(c) Note that $\int xe^{-x/2}\, dx$ can be found by parts:

$$\int xe^{-x/2}\, dx = x(-2e^{-x/2}) - \int (-2e^{-x/2})dx = -2xe^{-x/2} - 4e^{-x/2} + C$$

Area =

$$\lim_{b\to\infty}\int_0^b xe^{-x/2}dx = \lim_{b\to\infty}\left[-2xe^{-x/2} - 4e^{-x/2}\right]_0^b$$

$$= \lim_{b\to\infty}(-2be^{-b/2} - 4e^{-b/2} + 0 + 4) = 4.$$

57. (a) $\displaystyle\int_0^\infty \pi x^2\, dy = \pi\int_0^\infty \frac{dy}{(y+1)^2}$

(b) $\displaystyle\lim_{b\to\infty} \pi\int_0^b \frac{dy}{(y+1)^2}$

(c) Volume $= \displaystyle\lim_{b\to\infty} \pi\int_0^b \frac{dy}{(y+1)^2} = \lim_{b\to\infty} \pi\left[-(y+1)^{-1}\right]_0^b$

$$= \lim_{b\to\infty} \pi\left(-\frac{1}{b+1} + 1\right) = \pi$$

58. Note that $\int xe^{-x}\, dx$ can be found by parts:

$$\int xe^{-x}\, dx = x(-e^{-x}) - \int (-e^{-x})\, dx = -xe^{-x} - e^{-x} + C$$

So,

$$\int_0^\infty xe^{-x}\, dx = \lim_{k\to\infty}\int_0^k xe^{-x}\, dx = \lim_{k\to\infty}\left[-xe^{-x} - e^{-x}\right]_0^k$$

$$= \lim_{k\to\infty}\left(-\frac{k}{e^k} - \frac{1}{e^k} + 1\right)$$

By l'Hospital's rule, $\displaystyle\lim_{k\to\infty}\left(-\frac{k}{e^k}\right) = \lim_{k\to\infty}\left(-\frac{1}{e^k}\right) = 0.$ Therefore,

$$\int_0^\infty xe^{-x}\, dx = \lim_{k\to\infty}\left(-\frac{k}{e^k} - \frac{1}{e^k} + 1\right) = 0 - 0 + 1 = 1.$$

The integral converges to 1.

CHAPTER 10

Section 10.1

Quick Review 10.1

1. $4/3, 1, 4/5, 2/3, 1/8$

3. (a) 3 **(b)** 39,366 **(c)** $a_n = 2(3^{n-1})$

5. (a)

[0, 23.5] by [−0.5, 0.5]

(b) 0

7. (a)

[0, 23.5] by [−2, 2]

(b) The limit does not exist.

9. (a)

[0, 23.5] by [−1, 3]

(b) 2

Exercises 10.1

1. (a) * $= n^2$ **(b)** * $= (n+1)^2$ **(c)** * $= 3$

3. Different **5.** Same **7.** Diverges **9.** Converges

11. Converges; sum $= 3$ **13.** Converges; sum $= 15/4$ **15.** Diverges

17. Converges; sum $= 2 - \sqrt{2}$ **19.** Converges; sum $= \dfrac{e}{\pi - e}$

21. Interval: $-\dfrac{1}{2} < x < \dfrac{1}{2}$; function: $f(x) = \dfrac{1}{1 - 2x}$

23. Interval: $1 < x < 5$; function: $f(x) = \dfrac{2}{x - 1}$

25. Converges for all values of x except odd integer multiples of $\dfrac{\pi}{2}$;

function: $f(x) = \dfrac{1}{1 - \sin x}$

27. $f'(x) = \dfrac{2}{(2x-1)^2} = \displaystyle\sum_{n=1}^\infty 2^n\, nx^{n-1}, -\dfrac{1}{2} < x < \dfrac{1}{2}$

29. $f'(x) = -\dfrac{2}{(x-1)^2} = \displaystyle\sum_{n=1}^\infty \left(-\dfrac{1}{2}\right)^n n(x-3)^{n-1}, 1 < x < 5$

31. $\displaystyle\int_0^x \dfrac{1}{1-2t}\, dt = -\dfrac{1}{2}\ln(|2x-1|) = \sum_{n=0}^\infty \dfrac{2^n}{n+1}x^{n+1}, -\dfrac{1}{2} < x < \dfrac{1}{2}$

33. $\displaystyle\int_3^x \dfrac{2}{t-1}\, dt = 2\ln\left(\dfrac{|x-1|}{2}\right) = \sum_{n=0}^\infty \left(-\dfrac{1}{2}\right)^n \dfrac{(x-3)^{n+1}}{n+1}, 1 < x < 5$

35. (a) The partial sums tend toward infinity.
(b) The partial sums are alternately 1 and 0.
(c) The partial sums alternate between positive and negative while their magnitude increases toward infinity.

37. $x = 19/20$ **39. (a)** $\displaystyle\sum_{n=1}^\infty 2\left(\dfrac{3}{5}\right)^{n-1}$ **(b)** $\displaystyle\sum_{n=1}^\infty \dfrac{13}{2}\left(-\dfrac{3}{10}\right)^{n-1}$

41. Let $a = 234/1000$ and $r = 1/1000$, giving
$(0.234) + (0.234)(0.001) + (0.234)(0.001)^2$
$+ (0.234)(0.001)^3 + \cdots$
The sum is $26/111$.

43. $d/9$ **45.** $157/111$ **47.** $22/7$ **49.** 7.113 seconds **51.** $\pi/2$

53. For $r \neq 1$, the result follows from:
If $|r| < 1$, $r^n \to 0$ as $n \to \infty$, and if $|r| > 1$ or $r = -1$, r^n has no finite limit as $n \to \infty$.
When $r = 1$, the nth partial sum is na, which goes to $\pm\infty$.

55. Series: $x + 2x^2 + 4x^3 + \cdots + 2^{n-1}x^n + \cdots$
Interval: $-1/2 < x < 1/2$

57. Series: $1 - (x-4) + (x-4)^2 - (x-4)^3 + \cdots$
$+ (-1)^n(x-4)^n + \cdots$
Interval: $3 < x < 5$

59. One possible series:
$1 + (x-1) + (x-1)^2 + \cdots + (x-1)^n + \cdots$
Interval: $0 < x < 2$

61. (a) 2 **(b)** $t > -1/2$ **(c)** $t > 9$

63. $(x-1) - \dfrac{(x-1)^2}{2} + \dfrac{(x-1)^3}{3} - \cdots + \dfrac{(-1)^{n-1}(x-1)^n}{n} + \cdots$

65. (a) No, because if you differentiate it again, you would have the original series for f, but by Theorem 1, that would have to converge for $-2 < x < 2$, which contradicts the assumption that the original series converges only for $-1 < x < 1$.
(b) No, because if you integrate it again, you would have the original series for f, but by Theorem 2, that would have to converge for $-2 < x < 2$, which contradicts the assumption that the original series converges only for $-1 < x < 1$.

67. False. It converges because it is a geometric series with ratio $1/2$ that is less than 1.

69. A **71.** D

73. Let $L = \lim\limits_{n\to\infty} a_n$. Then by definition of convergence, for $\dfrac{\epsilon}{2}$ there corresponds an N such that for all m and n, $n, m > N \Rightarrow |a_m - L| < \dfrac{\epsilon}{2}$ and $|a_n - L| < \dfrac{\epsilon}{2}$.

Now,
$$|a_m - a_n| = |a_m - L + L - a_n| \le |a_m - L| + |a_n - L|$$
$$< \frac{\epsilon}{2} + \frac{\epsilon}{2} = \epsilon \text{ whenever } m > N \text{ and } n > N.$$

75. Consider the two subsequences $a_{k(n)}$ and $a_{i(n)}$, where $\lim\limits_{n\to\infty} a_{k(n)} = L_1$, $\lim\limits_{n\to\infty} a_{i(n)} = L_2$, and $L_1 \ne L_2$. Given an $\epsilon > 0$ there corresponds an N_1 such that for $k(n) > N_1$, $|a_{k(n)} - L_1| < \epsilon$, and an N_2 such that for $i(n) > N_2$, $|a_{i(n)} - L_2| < \epsilon$. Assume a_n converges. Let $N = \max\{N_1, N_2\}$. Then for $n > N$, we have that $|a_n - L_1| < \epsilon$ and $|a_n - L_2| < \epsilon$ for infinitely many n. This implies that $\lim\limits_{n\to\infty} a_n = L_1$ and $\lim\limits_{n\to\infty} a_n = L_2$ where $L_1 \ne L_2$. Since the limit of a sequence is unique (by Exercise 74), a_n does not converge and hence diverges.

Section 10.2

Quick Review 10.2

1. $2^n e^{2x}$ **3.** $3^x (\ln 3)^n$ **5.** $n!$ **7.** $\dfrac{2n(x - a)^{n-1}}{(n - 1)!}$ **9.** $\dfrac{(x + a)^{2n-1}}{(2n - 1)!}$

Exercises 10.2

1. $P_4(x) = -\dfrac{1}{8}x^4 + \dfrac{1}{2}x^2 + 1$

3. $P_5(x) = -\dfrac{x^5}{2^6} + \dfrac{x^4}{2^5} - \dfrac{x^3}{2^4} + \dfrac{x^2}{2^3} - \dfrac{x}{2^2} + \dfrac{1}{2}, \sum\limits_{n=0}^{\infty} (-1)^n \dfrac{x^n}{2^{n+1}}$

5. $2x - \dfrac{4x^3}{3} + \dfrac{4x^5}{15} - \cdots + (-1)^n \dfrac{(2x)^{2n+1}}{(2n + 1)!} + \cdots$ converges for all real x

7. $x^2 - \dfrac{x^6}{3} + \dfrac{x^{10}}{5} - \cdots + (-1)^n \dfrac{x^{4n+2}}{2n + 1} + \cdots$ converges for $-1 \le x \le 1$

9. $1 - \dfrac{x^2}{2^2 2!} + \dfrac{x^4}{2^4 4!} - \dfrac{x^6}{2^6 6!} + \cdots + (-1)^n \dfrac{x^{2n}}{2^{2n}(2n)!} + \cdots$ The series converges for all real x.

11. $x + x^4 + x^7 + \cdots + x^{3n+1} + \cdots$ converges for $-1 < x < 1$

13. $\sum\limits_{n=0}^{\infty} (-1)^n \dfrac{(x - 2)^n}{3^{n+1}} = \dfrac{1}{3} - \dfrac{x - 2}{3^2} + \dfrac{(x - 2)^2}{3^3} - \dfrac{(x - 2)^3}{3^4} + \cdots$

15. (a) $4 - 2x + x^3$
   (b) $3 + (x - 1) + 3(x - 1)^2 + (x - 1)^3$

17. (a) 0
   (b) $1 + 4(x - 1) + 6(x - 1)^2 + 4(x - 1)^3$

19. $P_0(x) = \dfrac{\sqrt{2}}{2}$

$P_1(x) = \dfrac{\sqrt{2}}{2} + \left(\dfrac{\sqrt{2}}{2}\right)\left(x - \dfrac{\pi}{4}\right)$

$P_2(x) = \dfrac{\sqrt{2}}{2} + \left(\dfrac{\sqrt{2}}{2}\right)\left(x - \dfrac{\pi}{4}\right) - \left(\dfrac{\sqrt{2}}{4}\right)\left(x - \dfrac{\pi}{4}\right)^2$

$P_3(x) = \dfrac{\sqrt{2}}{2} + \left(\dfrac{\sqrt{2}}{2}\right)\left(x - \dfrac{\pi}{4}\right) - \left(\dfrac{\sqrt{2}}{4}\right)\left(x - \dfrac{\pi}{4}\right)^2$
$- \left(\dfrac{\sqrt{2}}{12}\right)\left(x - \dfrac{\pi}{4}\right)^3$

21. $P_0(x) = 2$

$P_1(x) = 2 + \dfrac{x - 4}{4}$

$P_2(x) = 2 + \dfrac{x - 4}{4} - \dfrac{(x - 4)^2}{64}$

$P_3(x) = 2 + \dfrac{x - 4}{4} - \dfrac{(x - 4)^2}{64} + \dfrac{(x - 4)^3}{512}$

23. (a) $P_3(x) = 4 - (x - 1) + \dfrac{3}{2}(x - 1)^2 + \dfrac{1}{3}(x - 1)^3$
   $f(1.2) \approx P_3(1.2) \approx 3.863$
   (b) For f', $P_2(x) = -1 + 3(x - 1) + (x - 1)^2$
   $f'(1.2) \approx P_2(1.2) = -0.36$

25. (a) $1 + \dfrac{x}{2} + \dfrac{x^2}{8} + \cdots + \dfrac{x^n}{2^n \cdot n!} + \cdots$
   (b) $1 + \dfrac{x}{2!} + \dfrac{x^2}{3!} + \cdots + \dfrac{x^n}{(n + 1)!} + \cdots$
   (c) $g'(1) = 1$ and from the series,
   $g'(1) = \dfrac{1}{2!} + \dfrac{2}{3!} + \dfrac{3}{4!} + \cdots + \dfrac{n}{(n + 1)!} + \cdots = \sum\limits_{n=1}^{\infty} \dfrac{n}{(n + 1)!}$

27. (a) $1 + \dfrac{x}{2} - \dfrac{x^2}{8} + \dfrac{x^3}{16}$ (b) $1 + \dfrac{x^2}{2} - \dfrac{x^4}{8} + \dfrac{x^6}{16}$ (c) $5 + x + \dfrac{x^3}{6} - \dfrac{x^5}{40}$

29. 27 terms (or, up to and including the 52nd-degree term)

31. (1) $\sin x$ is odd and $\cos x$ is even
   (2) $\sin 0 = 0$ and $\cos 0 = 1$

33. $1/24$

35. (a)
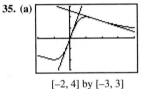
   [−2, 4] by [−3, 3]

   (b) $f''(a)$ must be 0 because of the inflection point, so the second-degree term in the Taylor series of f at $x = a$ is zero.

37. True. The constant term is $f(0)$. **39.** E **41.** C

43. (a) $1 - \dfrac{x^2}{3!} + \dfrac{x^4}{5!} - \cdots + \dfrac{(-1)^n x^{2n}}{(2n + 1)!} + \cdots$
   (b) Because f is undefined at $x = 0$
   (c) $k = 1$

45. (a) Differentiate 3 times.
   (b) Differentiate k times and let $x = 0$.
   (c) $\dfrac{m(m - 1)(m - 2) \cdots (m - k + 1)}{k!}$
   (d) $f(0) = 1, f'(0) = m$, and we're done by part (c).

Section 10.3

Quick Review 10.3

1. 2 **3.** 1 **5.** 7 **7.** No **9.** Yes

Exercises 10.3

1. $1 - 2x + \dfrac{4}{2}x^2 - \dfrac{8}{6}x^3 + \cdots + (-1)^n \dfrac{2^n}{n!}x^n + \cdots$

3. $-5x + \dfrac{5}{6}x^3 - \dfrac{5}{120}x^5 + \dfrac{5}{5040}x^7 - \cdots$
   $+ (-1)^{n+1} \dfrac{5}{(2n + 1)!}x^{2n+1} + \cdots$

5. $1 + 2x + 3x^2 + 4x^3 + \cdots + (n + 1)x^n + \cdots$

7. $x + x^2 + \dfrac{x^3}{2!} + \dfrac{x^4}{3!} + \cdots + \dfrac{x^{n+1}}{n!} + \cdots$

9. $x^2 - \dfrac{8x^4}{24} + \dfrac{32x^6}{720} - \dfrac{128x^8}{40320} + \cdots + (-1)^n \dfrac{2^{2n+1}x^{2n+2}}{(2n+2)!} + \cdots$

11. Degree 7 **13.** $\dfrac{(2|x|)^7}{1 - 2x}$

15. If $M = 1$ and $r = 1$, then $\left|\cos^{(n+1)}(t)\right| \le Mr^{n+1} = 1$ for all t, since all derivatives of the cosine function are sine or cosine functions bounded between -1 and 1.

17. If $M = 1$ and $r = 8$, then $\left|f^{(n+1)}(t)\right| \le Mr^{n+1} = 8^{n+1}$ for all t, since the $(n + 1)$st derivative of f is a sine or cosine function (bounded between -1 and 1), times 8^{n+1} (the result of $(n + 1)$ applications of the Chain Rule).

19. (a) $\dfrac{(0.5)^5}{5!} \approx 2.604 \times 10^{-4}$

(b) Since $P_3(x) = P_4(x)$, let $n = 4$. Then
$$error = \left|\cos(c)\right|\dfrac{(0.5)^5}{5!} < \dfrac{(0.5)^5}{5!} \approx 2.604 \times 10^{-4}$$

21. (a) $\dfrac{(0.5)^4}{4!} \approx 2.604 \times 10^{-3}$

(b) Since $P_2(x) = P_3(x)$, let $n = 3$. Then
$$error = \left|\cos(c)\right|\dfrac{(0.5)^4}{4!} < \dfrac{(0.5)^4}{4!} \approx 2.604 \times 10^{-3}$$
Since the next term of the series is the positive number $\dfrac{x^4}{4!}$, the partial sum $P_2(x)$ will be too small (except at 0, where $P_2(0) = \cos 0 = 1$).

23. A graph of the error $y = \left|\sqrt{1 + x} - (1 + x/2)\right|$ shows that $y < 1.26 \times 10^{-5}$.

25. All of the derivatives of $\cosh x$ are either $\cosh x$ or $\sinh x$. For any real x, $\cosh x$ and $\sinh x$ are both bounded by $e^{|x|}$. So for any real x, let $M = e^{|x|}$ and $r = 1$ in the Remainder Bounding Theorem. It follows that the series converges to $\cosh x$ for all real values of x.

27. (a) 0 **(b)** $-x^2/2$

29. (a) 1 **(b)** $1 + \dfrac{x^2}{2}$ **31. (a)** x **(b)** x

33. (a) The series is geometric, with first term $2x$ and ratio $= -x^2$. Therefore,
$$\dfrac{2x}{1 + x^2} = 2x - 2x^3 + 2x^5 - 2x^7 + \cdots + (-1)^n 2x^{2n+1} + \cdots$$

(b) No. The partial sums of the series form the sequence $2, 0, 2, 0, 2, 0, \ldots$, which does not converge.

(c) $\ln(1 + x^2) = \displaystyle\int_0^x \dfrac{2t}{1 + t^2}\,dt = \int_0^x (2t - 2t^3 + 2t^5 - 2t^7 + \cdots)\,dt$
$$= x^2 - \dfrac{1}{2}x^4 + \dfrac{1}{3}x^6 - \dfrac{1}{4}x^8 + \cdots$$

(d) Note that $\ln\left(\dfrac{5}{4}\right) = \ln\left(1 + \left(\dfrac{1}{2}\right)^2\right) = \left(\dfrac{1}{2}\right)^2 - \dfrac{1}{2}\left(\dfrac{1}{2}\right)^4 + \dfrac{1}{3}\left(\dfrac{1}{2}\right)^6$
$$- \dfrac{1}{4}\left(\dfrac{1}{2}\right)^8 + \cdots$$
The first term of this series that is less than $\dfrac{1}{100}$ is $\dfrac{1}{3}\left(\dfrac{1}{2}\right)^6$. Since the terms satisfy the three conditions for the alternating series bound, the truncated polynomial $P_2\left(\dfrac{1}{2}\right) = \left(\dfrac{1}{2}\right)^2 - \dfrac{1}{2}\left(\dfrac{1}{2}\right)^4 = \dfrac{7}{32}$ is within $\dfrac{1}{100}$ of $\ln\left(\dfrac{5}{4}\right)$. Let $A = \dfrac{7}{32}$.

35. (a) No

(b) Yes. $2 + x - \dfrac{x^3}{3} + \dfrac{x^5}{10} - \cdots + \dfrac{(-1)^{n+1}x^{2n-1}}{[(2n-1)(n-1)!]} + \cdots$

(c) For all real values of x. This is assured by Theorem 2 of Section 10.1, because the series for e^{-x^2} converges for all real values of x.

37. (a) $\tan x$ **(b)** $\sec x$

39. True. The coefficient of x is $f'(0)$.

41. E **43.** A

45. (a) It works.

(b) Let $P = \pi + x$ where x is the error in the original estimate. Then
$$P + \sin P = (\pi + x) + \sin(\pi + x)$$
$$= (\pi + x) - \sin x = \pi + (x - \sin x)$$
But by the alternating series error bound, $|x - \sin x| < \dfrac{|x|^3}{6}$.
Therefore, the difference between the new estimate $P + \sin P$ and π is less than $\dfrac{|x|^3}{6}$.

47. Note that $f(-1) = \dfrac{1}{2}$. The partial sums of the Maclaurin series $\displaystyle\sum_{n=0}^{\infty} (-1)^n$ are $1, 0, 1, 0, 1$, and so on, so the remainders are $-\dfrac{1}{2}, \dfrac{1}{2}, -\dfrac{1}{2}, \dfrac{1}{2}$, and so on. Thus
$$R_n(-1) = \dfrac{(-1)^{n+1}}{2}, \text{ and } \lim_{n\to\infty}\left(\dfrac{(-1)^{n+1}}{2}\right) \ne 0.$$

49. The derivative is $(ae^{ax})(\cos bx + i\sin bx) + (e^{ax})(-b\sin bx + ib\cos bx)$
$$= a[e^{ax}(\cos bx + i\sin bx)] + ib[e^{ax}(\cos bx + ib\sin bx)]$$
$$= (a + ib)e^{(a+ib)x}.$$

Quick Quiz (Sections 10.1 and 10.3)

1. D **3.** E

Section 10.4

Quick Review 10.4

1. $|x|$ **3.** 0 **5.** $\dfrac{|2x + 1|}{2}$ **7.** $a_n = 5^n, b_n = n^5, N = 6$

9. $a_n = \dfrac{1}{10^n}, b_n = \dfrac{1}{n!}, N = 25$

Exercises 10.4

1. $-6 < x < -4$; The graph of the function $y = \dfrac{-1}{x + 4}$ and $P_5(x)$ illustrates the support.

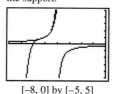

$[-8, 0]$ by $[-5, 5]$

3. $\dfrac{x^{4n}}{2n! + 1} \le \dfrac{x^{4n}}{n!} = \dfrac{(x^4)^n}{n!}$ and $\displaystyle\sum_{n=0}^{\infty} \dfrac{(x^4)^n}{n!}$ is the Taylor series for e^{x^4} which converges for all x.

5. $\left|\dfrac{(\cos x)^n}{n! + 1}\right| \le \left|\dfrac{(\cos x)^n}{n!}\right| \le \dfrac{1}{n!}$ and $\displaystyle\sum_{n=0}^{\infty} \dfrac{1}{n!}$ converges to e.

7. 1 **9.** 1/4 **11.** 10 **13.** 3 **15.** 5 **17.** 0 **19.** 1/2 **21.** 1

23. Interval: $-1 < x < 3$ Sum: $-\dfrac{4}{x^2 - 2x - 3}$

25. Interval: $0 < x < 16$ Sum: $\dfrac{2}{4 - \sqrt{x}}$

27. Interval: $-2 < x < 2$ Sum: $\dfrac{3}{4 - x^2}$

29. Diverges (nth-Term Test) **31.** Converges (Ratio Test)

33. Converges (Ratio Test, Direct Comparison Test)

35. Converges (Ratio Test) **37.** Converges (Ratio Test)

39. Converges (geometric series) **41.** Diverges (nth-Term Test, Ratio Test)

43. Converges (Ratio Test)

45. One possible answer:

$\sum \dfrac{1}{n}$ diverges (see Exploration 1 in this section) even though $\lim\limits_{n \to \infty} \dfrac{1}{n} = 0$.

47. Almost, but the Ratio Test won't determine whether there is convergence or divergence at the endpoints of the interval.

49. 3 **51.** 1 **53.** $-1/\ln 2$ **55.** True. See Theorem 8. **57.** B **59.** E

61. **(a)** For $k \le N$, it's obvious that

$$a_1 + \cdots + a_k \le a_1 + \cdots + a_N + \sum_{n=N+1}^{\infty} c_n$$

For all $k > N$,
$$a_1 + \cdots + a_k = a_1 + \cdots + a_N + a_{N+1} + \cdots + a_k$$
$$\le a_1 + \cdots + a_N + c_{N+1} + \cdots + c_k$$
$$\le a_1 + \cdots + a_N + \sum_{n=N+1}^{\infty} c_n$$

(b) Since all of the a_n are nonnegative, the partial sums of the series form a nondecreasing sequence of real numbers. Part (a) shows that the sequence is bounded above, so it must converge to a limit.

63. Answers will vary.

Section 10.5

Quick Review 10.5

1. Converges, $p > 1$

3. Diverges, comparison test with integral of $1/x$

5. Diverges, limit comparison test with integral of $1/\sqrt{x}$

7. Yes **9.** No

Exercises 10.5

1. Use $f(x) = 1/\sqrt[3]{x}$, diverges

3. $S_1 = 1, S_2 = 3/2, S_3 = 11/6, S_4 = 25/12, S_5 = 137/60, S_6 = 49/20$

5. Diverges, compare with $\sum_{n=1}^{\infty} (3/n)$ **7.** Diverges **9.** Diverges

11. Diverges **13.** Diverges **15.** Converges **17.** Diverges

19. Diverges **21.** Diverges **23.** Converges conditionally; 0.0101

25. Converges conditionally; ≈ 0.002 **27.** Diverges

29. Converges conditionally **31.** Converges conditionally

33. The positive terms $2 + \dfrac{4}{3^2} + \dfrac{6}{5^2} + \cdots + \dfrac{2n + 2}{(2n + 1)^2} + \cdots$ diverge

to ∞ and the negative term $-\dfrac{3}{2^2} - \dfrac{5}{4^2} - \dfrac{7}{6^2} - \cdots - \dfrac{2n + 1}{(2n)^2} - \cdots$

diverge to $-\infty$.
Answers will vary. Here is one possibility.
(a) Add positive terms until the partial sum is greater than 2. Then add negative terms until the partial sum is less than -2. Then add positive

terms until the partial sum is greater than 4. Then add negative terms until the partial sum is less than -4. Repeat this process so that the partial sums swing arbitrarily far in both directions.
(b) Add positive terms until the partial sum is greater than 4. Then add negative terms until the partial sum is less than 4. Continue in this manner indefinitely, always closing in on 4.

35. **(a)** $(-1, 1)$ **(b)** $(-1, 1)$ **(c)** None

37. **(a)** $(-1/2, 0)$ **(b)** $(-1/2, 0)$ **(c)** None

39. **(a)** $(-8, 12)$ **(b)** $(-8, 12)$ **(c)** None

41. **(a)** $[-3, 3]$ **(b)** $[-3, 3]$ **(c)** None

43. **(a)** $(-8, 2)$ **(b)** $(-8, 2)$ **(c)** None

45. **(a)** $(-3, 3)$ **(b)** $(-3, 3)$ **(c)** None

47. **(a)** $(1/2, 3/2)$ **(b)** $(1/2, 3/2)$ **(c)** None

49. **(a)** $[-\pi - 1, -\pi + 1)$ **(b)** $(-\pi - 1, -\pi + 1)$ **(c)** At $x = -\pi - 1$

51. $40.554 < \text{sum} < 41.555$

53.

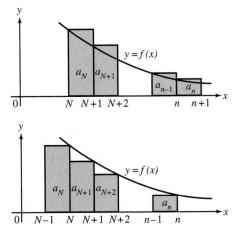

Comparing areas in the figures, we have for all $n \ge N$,
$$\int_{N}^{n+1} f(x)\, dx < a_N + \cdots + a_n < a_N + \int_{N}^{n} f(x)\, dx.$$

If the integral diverges, it must go to infinity, and the first inequality forces the partial sums of the series to go to infinity as well, so the series is divergent.

If the integral converges, then the second inequality puts an upper bound on the partial sums of the series, and since they are a nondecreasing sequence, they must converge to a finite sum for the series.

55. Radius of convergence is $\dfrac{3}{e}$ **57.** Possible answer: $\sum \dfrac{1}{n \ln n}$

This series diverges by the Integral Test, but its partial sums are roughly $\ln(\ln n)$, so they are much smaller than the partial sums for the harmonic series, which are about $\ln n$.

59. **(a)** Diverges

(b) $S = \sum_{n=1}^{\infty} \dfrac{3n}{3n^3 + n} = \sum_{n=1}^{\infty} \dfrac{3}{3n^2 + 1}$ which converges.

61. Convergent for $-1/2 \le x < 1/2$. Use the Ratio Test, Direct Comparison Test, and Alternating Series Test.

63. Use the Alternating Series Test.

65. **(a)** It fails to satisfy $u_n \ge u_{n+1}$ for all $n \ge N$. **(b)** The sum is $-1/2$.

67. True. The term $a_{101} = \dfrac{(-1)^{101}}{(101)^2}$ is negative.

69. A **71.** B **73.** **(a)** Converges **(b)** Converges **(c)** Converges

Quick Quiz (Sections 10.4 and 10.5)

1. E **3.** D

Review Exercises

1. (a) ∞ (b) All real numbers (c) All real numbers (d) None

2. (a) 3 (b) $[-7, -1)$ (c) $(-7, -1)$ (d) At $x = -7$

3. (a) $\dfrac{3}{2}$ (b) $(-1/2, 5/2)$ (c) $(-1/2, 5/2)$ (d) None

4. (a) ∞ (b) All real numbers (c) All real numbers (d) None

5. (a) $1/3$ (b) $[0, 2/3]$ (c) $[0, 2/3]$ (d) None

6. (a) 1 (b) $(-1, 1)$ (c) $(-1, 1)$ (d) None

7. (a) 1 (b) $(-3/2, 1/2)$ (c) $(-3/2, 1/2)$ (d) None

8. (a) ∞ (b) All real numbers (c) All real numbers (d) None

9. (a) 1 (b) $[-1, 1)$ (c) $(-1, 1)$ (d) At $x = -1$

10. (a) $1/e$ (b) $[-1/e, 1/e]$ (c) $[-1/e, 1/e]$ (d) None

11. (a) $\sqrt{3}$ (b) $\left(-\sqrt{3}, \sqrt{3}\right)$ (c) $\left(-\sqrt{3}, \sqrt{3}\right)$ (d) None

12. (a) 1 (b) $[0, 2]$ (c) $(0, 2)$ (d) At $x = 0$ and $x = 2$

13. (a) 0 (b) $x = 0$ only (c) $x = 0$ (d) None

14. (a) $1/10$ (b) $[-1/10, 1/10]$ (c) $(-1/10, 1/10)$ (d) At $x = -1/10$

15. (a) 0 (b) $x = 0$ only (c) $x = 0$ (d) None

16. (a) $\sqrt{3}$ (b) $\left(-\sqrt{3}, \sqrt{3}\right)$ (c) $\left(-\sqrt{3}, \sqrt{3}\right)$ (d) None

17. $f(x) = 1/(1 + x)$ evaluated at $x = 1/4$; Sum $= 4/5$

18. $f(x) = \ln(1 + x)$ evaluated at $x = 2/3$; Sum $= \ln(5/3)$.

19. $f(x) = \sin x$ evaluated at $x = \pi$; Sum $= 0$.

20. $f(x) = \cos x$ evaluated at $x = \pi/3$; Sum $x = 1/2$.

21. $f(x) = e^x$ evaluated at $x = \ln 2$; Sum $= 2$.

22. $f(x) = \tan^{-1} x$ evaluated at $x = 1/\sqrt{3}$; Sum $= \pi/6$.

23. $1 + 6x + 36x^2 + \cdots + (6x)^n + \cdots$

24. $1 - x^3 + x^6 - \cdots + (-1)^n x^{3n} + \cdots$ **25.** $1 - 2x^2 + x^9$

26. $4x + 4x^2 + 4x^3 + \cdots + 4x^{n+1} + \cdots$

27. $\pi x - \dfrac{(\pi x)^3}{3!} + \dfrac{(\pi x)^5}{5!} - \cdots + (-1)^n \dfrac{(\pi x)^{2n+1}}{(2n+1)!} + \cdots$

28. $\dfrac{-2x}{3} + \dfrac{4x^3}{81} - \dfrac{4x^5}{3645} + \cdots + \dfrac{(-1)^{n+1}}{(2n+1)!}\left(\dfrac{2x}{3}\right)^{2n+1} + \cdots$

29. $-\dfrac{x^3}{3!} + \dfrac{x^5}{5!} - \dfrac{x^7}{7!} + \cdots + (-1)^n \dfrac{x^{2n+1}}{(2n+1)!} + \cdots$

30. $1 + \dfrac{x^2}{2!} + \dfrac{x^4}{4!} + \cdots + \dfrac{x^{2n}}{(2n)!} + \cdots$

31. $1 - \dfrac{5x}{2!} + \dfrac{(5x)^2}{4!} - \cdots + (-1)^n \dfrac{(5x)^n}{(2n)!} + \cdots$

32. $1 + \dfrac{\pi x}{2} + \dfrac{\pi^2 x^2}{8} + \cdots + \dfrac{1}{n!}\left(\dfrac{\pi x}{2}\right)^n + \cdots$

33. $x - x^3 + \dfrac{x^5}{2!} - \dfrac{x^7}{3!} + \cdots + (-1)^n \dfrac{x^{2n+1}}{n!} + \cdots$

34. $3x - \dfrac{(3x)^3}{3} + \dfrac{(3x)^5}{5} - \cdots + (-1)^n \dfrac{(3x)^{2n+1}}{2n + 1} + \cdots$

35. $-2x - 2x^2 - \dfrac{8x^3}{3} - \cdots - \dfrac{(2x)^n}{n} - \cdots$

36. $-x^2 - \dfrac{x^3}{2} - \dfrac{x^4}{3} - \cdots - \dfrac{x^{n+1}}{n} - \cdots$

37. $1 + (x - 2) + (x - 2)^2 + (x - 2)^3 + \cdots + (x - 2)^n + \cdots$

38. $2 + 7(x + 1) - 5(x + 1)^2 + (x + 1)^3$
  (Finite. General term for $n \geq 4$ is 0.)

39. $\dfrac{1}{3} - \dfrac{x - 3}{9} + \dfrac{(x - 3)^2}{27} - \dfrac{(x - 3)^3}{81} + \cdots + (-1)^n \dfrac{(x - 3)^n}{3^{n+1}} + \cdots$

40. $-(x - \pi) + \dfrac{(x - \pi)^3}{3!} - \dfrac{(x - \pi)^5}{5!} + \dfrac{(x - \pi)^7}{7!} - \cdots$

$\qquad + (-1)^{n+1} \dfrac{(x - \pi)^{2n+1}}{(2n + 1)!} + \cdots$

41. Diverges. It is -5 times the harmonic series.

42. Converges conditionally. Alternating Series Test and $p = 1/2$.

43. Converges absolutely. Direct Comparison Test with $1/n^2$.

44. Converges absolutely. Ratio Test

45. Converges conditionally. Alternating Series Test and Direct Comparison Test with $1/n$.

46. Converges absolutely. Integral Test

47. Converges absolutely. Ratio Test

48. Converges absolutely. nth-Root Test or Ratio Test.

49. Diverges. nth-Term Test for Divergence

50. Converges absolutely. Direct Comparison Test with $1/n^{3/2}$.

51. Converges absolutely. Limit Comparison Test with $1/n^2$.

52. Diverges. nth-Term Test for Divergence **53.** $1/6$ **54.** -1

55. (a) $P_3(x) = 1 + 4(x - 3) + 3(x - 3)^2 + 2(x - 3)^3$
  $f(3.2) \approx P_3(3.2) = 1.936$
  (b) For f': $P_2(x) = 4 + 6(x - 3) + 6(x - 3)^2$
  $f'(2.7) \approx P_2(2.7) = 2.74$
  (c) It underestimates the values, since the graph of f is concave up near $x = 3$.

56. (a) $f(4) = 7$ and $f'''(4) = -12$
  (b) For f': $P_2(x) = -3 + 10(x - 4) - 6(x - 4)^2$
  $f'(4.3) \approx P_2(4.3) = -0.54$
  (c) $7(x - 4) - \dfrac{3}{2}(x - 4)^2 + \dfrac{5}{3}(x - 4)^3 - \dfrac{1}{2}(x - 4)^4$
  (d) No. One would need the entire Taylor series for $f(x)$, and it would have to converge to $f(x)$ at $x = 3$.

57. (a) $\dfrac{5x}{2} - \dfrac{5x^3}{48} + \dfrac{x^5}{768} - \cdots + (-1)^n \dfrac{5}{(2n + 1)!}\left(\dfrac{x}{2}\right)^{2n+1} + \cdots$
  (b) All real numbers. Use the Ratio Test.
  (c) Note that the absolute value of $f^{(n)}(x)$ is bounded by $5/2^n$ for all x and all $n = 1, 2, 3, \ldots$ So if $-2 < x < 2$, the truncation error using P_n is bounded by $\dfrac{5}{2^{n+1}} \cdot \dfrac{2^{n+1}}{(n + 1)!} = \dfrac{5}{(n + 1)!}$. To make this less than 0.1 requires $n \geq 4$. So, two nonzero terms (up through degree 4) are needed.

58. (a) $1 + 2x + 4x^2 + 8x^3 + \cdots + (2x)^n + \cdots$
  (b) $(-1/2, 1/2)$. The series for $1/(1 - t)$ is known to converge for $-1 < t < 1$, so by substituting $t = 2x$, we find the resulting series converges for $-1 < 2x < 1$.
  (c) Possible answer:
  $f(-1/4) = 2/3$, so one percent is approximately 0.0067. It takes 7 terms (up through degree 6). This can be found by trial and error.

59. (a) $1/e$ (b) $-5/18 \approx -0.278$
  (c) By the Alternating Series Bound Theorem, the error is bounded by the size of the next term, which is $32/243$, or about 0.132.

60. (a) $1 - (x - 3) + (x - 3)^2 - (x - 3)^3 + \cdots + (-1)^n(x - 3)^n + \cdots$
  (b) $(x - 3) - \dfrac{(x - 3)^2}{2} + \dfrac{(x - 3)^3}{3} - \dfrac{(x - 3)^4}{4} + \cdots$
  $\qquad + (-1)^n \dfrac{(x - 3)^{n+1}}{n + 1} + \cdots$

(c) Evaluate at $x = 3.5$. This is an alternating series. By the Alternating Series Bound Theorem, since the size of the third term is $1/24 < 0.05$, the first two terms will suffice. The estimate for $\ln(3/2)$ is 0.375.

61. (a) $1 - 2x^2 + 2x^4 - \dfrac{4x^6}{3} + \cdots + (-1)^n \dfrac{2^n x^{2n}}{n!} + \cdots$

(b) All real numbers. Use the Ratio Test.

(c) This is an alternating series. The difference will be bounded by the magnitude of the fifth term, which is $\dfrac{(2x^2)^4}{4!} = \dfrac{2x^8}{3}$.

Since $-0.6 \le x \le 0.6$, this term is less than $\dfrac{2(0.6)^8}{3}$ which is less than 0.02.

62. (a) $x^2 - x^3 + x^4 - x^5 + \cdots + (-1)^n x^{n+2} + \cdots$

(b) No. The partial sums form the sequence $1, 0, 1, 0, 1, 0, \ldots$ which has no limit.

63. (a) $\dfrac{x^3}{3} - \dfrac{x^7}{7(3!)} + \dfrac{x^{11}}{11(5!)} - \cdots + \dfrac{(-1)^n x^{4n+3}}{(4n+3)(2n+1)!} + \cdots$

(b) The first two nonzero terms suffice (through degree 7).

(c) 0.31026830

(d) Within 1.5×10^{-7}

64. (a) 0.88566

(b) $41/60 \approx 0.68333$

(c) Since f is concave up, the trapezoids used to estimate the area lie above the curve, and the estimate is too large.

(d) Since all the derivatives are positive (and $x > 0$), the remainder, $R_n(x)$, must be positive. This means that $P_n(x)$ is smaller than $f(x)$.

(e) $e - 2 \approx 0.71828$

65. (a) Because $[\,\$1000(1.08)^{-n}\,](1.08)^n = \$1000$ will be available after n years.

(b) Assume that the first payment goes to the charity at the end of the first year. Then, $1000(1.08)^{-1} + 1000(1.08)^{-2} + 1000(1.08)^{-3} + \cdots$

(c) This is a geometric series with sum equal to $\$12,500$. This represents the amount which must be invested today in order to completely fund the perpetuity forever.

66. $\$16,666.67$ [Again, assuming first payment at end of year.]

67. (a) $0\left(\dfrac{1}{2}\right) + 1\left(\dfrac{1}{2}\right)^2 + 2\left(\dfrac{1}{2}\right)^3 + 3\left(\dfrac{1}{2}\right)^4 + \cdots$

(b) $1 + 2x + 3x^2 + 4x^3 + \cdots$

(c) $x^2 + 2x^3 + 3x^4 + 4x^5 + \cdots$

(d) The expected payoff of the game is $1.

68. (a) $\dfrac{b^2\sqrt{3}}{4} + \dfrac{3b^2\sqrt{3}}{4^2} + \dfrac{3^2 b^2\sqrt{3}}{4^3} + \cdots$

(b) $b^2\sqrt{3}$. Note that this is the same as the area of the original triangle!

(c) No. For example, let $b = 1/2$ and set the base of the triangle along the x-axis from $(0,0)$ to $(1,0)$. The points removed by the construction are all of the form $(k/2^n, 0)$ so points of the form $(x, 0)$ with x irrational (among others) still remain. The same sort of thing is happening along the other two sides of the triangle (and, in fact, along any of the sides of any of the smaller blue triangles in the figure). While there are infinitely many points remaining throughout the triangle, they paradoxically take up zero area. (This figure, the Sierpinski triangle, is well known to students of fractal geometry.)

69. $\dfrac{1}{(1-x)^2} = 1 + 2x + 3x^2 + 4x^3 + 5x^4 + \cdots$; Substitute $x = 1/2$ to get the desired result.

70. (b) Solve $x = \dfrac{2x^2}{(x-1)^3}, x \approx 2.769$.

71. (a) Computing the coefficients,

$$f(1) = \frac{1}{2}$$

$$f'(x) = -(x+1)^{-2}, \text{ so } f'(1) = -\frac{1}{4}$$

$$f''(x) = 2(x+1)^{-3}, \text{ so } \frac{f''(1)}{2!} = \frac{1}{8}$$

$$f'''(x) = -6(x+1)^{-4}, \text{ so } \frac{f'''(1)}{3!} = -\frac{1}{16}$$

In general, $f^{(n)}(x) = \dfrac{(-1)^n n!}{(x+1)^{n+1}}$, so $\dfrac{f^{(n)}(1)}{n!} = \dfrac{(-1)^n}{2^{n+1}}$

So

$$f(x) = \frac{1}{2} - \frac{x-1}{4} + \frac{(x-1)^2}{8} - \cdots + (-1)^n \frac{(x-1)^n}{2^{n+1}} + \cdots$$

(b) Ratio Test for absolute convergence:

$$\lim_{n\to\infty} \frac{|x-1|^{n+1}}{2^{n+2}} \cdot \frac{2^{n+1}}{|x-1|^n} = \frac{|x-1|}{2}$$

$$\frac{|x-1|}{2} < 1 \Rightarrow -1 < x < 3. \text{ The series converges absolutely on}$$
$(-1, 3)$.

At $x = -1$, the series is $\displaystyle\sum_{n=0}^{\infty} \frac{1}{2}$, which diverges by the nth-Term Test.

At $x = 3$, the series is $\displaystyle\sum_{n=0}^{\infty} (-1)^n \frac{1}{2}$, which diverges by the nth-Term Test.

The interval of convergence is $(-1, 3)$.

(c) $P_3(x) = \dfrac{1}{2} - \dfrac{x-1}{4} + \dfrac{(x-1)^2}{8} - \dfrac{(x-1)^3}{16}$

$$P_3(0.5) = \frac{1}{2} - \frac{0.5-1}{4} + \frac{(0.5-1)^2}{8} - \frac{(0.5-1)^3}{16}$$

$$= 0.664025$$

72. (a) Ratio test for absolute convergence:

$$\lim_{n\to\infty} \frac{(n+1)|x|^{n+1}}{2^{n+1}} \cdot \frac{2^n}{n|x|^n} = \lim_{n\to\infty} \frac{n+1}{n} \cdot \frac{|x|}{2} = \frac{|x|}{2}$$

$$\frac{|x|}{2} < 1 \Rightarrow -2 < x < 2$$

The series converges absolutely on $(-2, 2)$.

The series diverges at both endpoints by the nth-Term Test, since $\lim_{n\to\infty} n \ne 0$ and $\lim_{n\to\infty} (-1)^n n \ne 0$.

The interval of convergence is $(-2, 2)$.

(b) The series converges at -1 and forms an alternating series:

$-\dfrac{1}{2} + \dfrac{2}{4} - \dfrac{3}{8} + \dfrac{4}{16} - \cdots (-1)^n \dfrac{n}{2^n} + \cdots$. The nth term of this series decreases in absolute value to 0, so the truncation error after 9 terms is less than the absolute value of the 10th term. Thus error

$$< \frac{10}{2^{10}} < 0.01.$$

73. (a) $P_1(x) = -1 + 2x$

(b) $P_2(x) = -1 + 2x - \dfrac{3}{2}x^2$

(c) $P_3(x) = -1 + 2x - \dfrac{3}{2}x^2 + \dfrac{2}{3}x^3$

(d) -0.106

CHAPTER 11

Section 11.1

Quick Review 11.1

1. $y = 2x + 1$ **3.** $x^2 + y^2 = 1$ **5.** $y^2 = 1 + x^2$
7. $y = 2x^2 - 1$ **9.** $y = \sqrt{1 - x^2}$

Exercises 11.1

1. Yes, y is a function of x.
$y = 2x - 9$

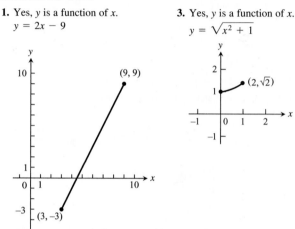

3. Yes, y is a function of x.
$y = \sqrt{x^2 + 1}$

5. Yes, y is a function of x.
$y = 1 - 2x^2$

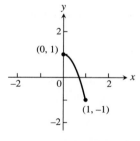

7. (a) $-\dfrac{1}{2} \tan t$ **(b)** $-\dfrac{1}{8} \sec^3 t$ **9. (a)** $-\sqrt{3 + \dfrac{3}{t}}$ **(b)** $-\dfrac{\sqrt{3}}{t^{3/2}}$

11. (a) $\dfrac{3t^2}{2t - 3}$ **(b)** $\dfrac{6t^2 - 18t}{(2t - 3)^3}$

13. (a) $\sin t$ **(b)** $\cos^3 t$ **15. (a)** 4 **(b)** 0

17. (a)

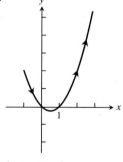

(b) $(0.5, -20.25)$
(c) We seek to minimize y as a function of t, so we compute
$dy/dt = 2t + 1$, which is negative for $-2 \le t < -0.5$ and positive
for $-0.5 < t \le 2$. There is a relative minimum at $t = -0.5$, where
$(x, y) = (0.5, -0.25)$.

19. (a)

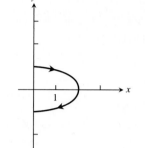

(b) $(2, 0)$
(c) We seek to maximize x as a function of t, so we compute
$dx/dt = 2 \cos t$, which is positive for $0 \le t < \pi/2$ and negative
for $\pi/2 < t \le \pi$. There is a relative maximum at $t = \pi/2$, where
$(x, y) = (2, 0)$.

21. (a)

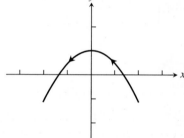

(b) $(0, 1)$
(c) We seek to maximize y as a function of t, so we compute
$dy/dt = -2 \sin (2t)$, which is positive for $1.5 \le t < \pi$ and negative for $\pi < t \le 4.5$. There is a relative maximum at $t = \pi$, where
$(x, y) = (0, 1)$.

23. (a) $(2, 0)$ and $(2, -2)$ **(b)** $(1, -1)$ and $(3, -1)$

25. (a) At $t = \pm\dfrac{2}{\sqrt{3}}$, or $\approx (0.845, -3.079)$ and $(3.155, 3.079)$

(b) Nowhere

27. 2π **29.** π^2 **31.** $21/2$

33. $\dfrac{2\sqrt{2} - 1}{3} \approx 0.609$ **35. (a)** π **(b)** π

37. Just substitute x for t and note that $dx/dx = 1$.

39. $3\pi a^2$

41. $x = at - b \sin t$ and $y = a - b \cos t$ $(0 < a < b)$

43. 21.010

45. False. Indeed, y may not even be a function of x. (See Example 1.)

47. B   **49.** C

51. (a) $x = \cos t + t \sin t, y = \sin t - t \cos t$ **(b)** $2\pi^2$

53. (a) ≈ 461.749 ft   **(b)** ≈ 41.125 ft

55. (a) ≈ 840.421 ft   **(b)** $16{,}875/64 \approx 263.672$ ft

57. $8\pi^2$ **59.** 178.561

Section 11.2

Quick Review 11.2

1. $\sqrt{17}$ **3.** $b = 5/2$ **5.** $a = 4$
7. $v(t) = \sin t + t \cos t; a(t) = 2 \cos t - t \sin t$
9. 32

Exercises 11.2

1. $\langle 2, 3 \rangle$ **3.** $\langle 1, -4 \rangle$ **5.** $\sqrt{8}, 45°$ **7.** 2, 30°   **9.** 5, 180°

11. $\langle -4, 0 \rangle$ **13.** $\langle -0.868, 4.924 \rangle$ **15.** $\langle 3, 3 \rangle$

17. (a) $\langle 9, -6 \rangle$ (b) $3\sqrt{13}$

19. (a) $\langle 1, 3 \rangle$ (b) $\sqrt{10}$

21. (a) $\langle 12, -19 \rangle$ (b) $\sqrt{505}$

23. (a) $\langle 1/5, 14/5 \rangle$ (b) $\sqrt{197}/5$

25. Speed ≈ 346.735 mph   direction $\approx 14.266°$ east of north

27. $\mathbf{v}(t) = \langle 6t, 6t^2 \rangle, \mathbf{a}(t) = \langle 6, 12t \rangle$

29. $\mathbf{v}(t) = \langle e^{-t} - te^{-t}, -e^{-t} \rangle, \mathbf{a}(t) = \langle -2e^{-t} + te^{-t}, e^{-t} \rangle$

31. $\mathbf{v}(t) = \langle 2t + 2\cos 2t, 2t + 2\sin 2t \rangle,$
$\mathbf{a}(t) = \langle 2 - 4\sin 2t, 2 + 4\cos 2t \rangle$

33. (a) $\langle 90\,t\cos 55°, 90t\sin 55° - 16t^2 \rangle$
(b) $\langle 90\cos 55°, 90\sin 55° - 32t \rangle$
(c) No, the ball hits the fence.

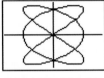

(d) About 4.456 seconds
(e) About 86.055 ft/sec

35. Velocity: $\langle -3\sin 3t, 2\cos 2t \rangle$; acceleration: $\langle -9\cos 3t, -4\sin 2t \rangle$

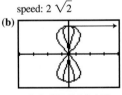

$[-1.6, 1.6]$ by $[-1.1, 1.1]$
$0 \le t \le 2\pi$

37. (a) Velocity: $\langle 4\cos 4t \cos t - \sin t \sin 4t, 2\cos 2t \rangle|_{t=5\pi/4} = \langle 2\sqrt{2}, 0 \rangle$;
speed: $2\sqrt{2}$
(b)

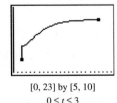

$[-4, 4]$ by $[-1.2, 1.2]$
$0 \le t \le 2\pi$

(c) To the right

39. (a) $(20, 9)$ (b) 19.343

41. (a) $(3 + \ln 4, -1.7)$ (b) 1.419

43. The parametric equations are $x = t^3 - t^2 + 2$ and
$y = t + \sin(\pi t)/\pi + 6$.

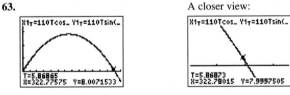

$[0, 23]$ by $[5, 10]$
$0 \le t \le 3$

45. (a) $\pi\sqrt{7/12} \approx 2.399$ (b) $\langle -5\pi^2/72, -\pi^2\sqrt{3}/24 \rangle$
(c) $\dfrac{x^2}{25} + \dfrac{y^2}{9} = 1$

47. (a) $\left\langle -\dfrac{4t}{(1 + t^2)^2}, \dfrac{2 - 2t^2}{(1 + t^2)^2} \right\rangle$
(b) No. The x-component of velocity is zero only if $t = 0$, while the y-component of velocity is zero only if $t = 1$. At no time will the velocity be $\langle 0, 0 \rangle$.
(c) $\displaystyle\lim_{t\to\infty} \left\langle \dfrac{1 - t^2}{1 + t^2}, \dfrac{2t}{1 + t^2} \right\rangle = \langle -1, 0 \rangle$

49. (a) $\left.\dfrac{e^t\cos t - e^t\sin t}{e^t\sin t + e^t\cos t}\right|_{t=\pi/2} = -1$ (b) 3.844   (c) 2.430

51. (a) $3 + \displaystyle\int_2^4 (2 + \sin(t^2))\, dt \approx 3.942$
(b) $y - 5 = \dfrac{-6}{2 + \sin 4}(x - 3)$
(c) $\sqrt{(2 + \sin 4)^2 + (-6)^2} \approx 6.127$
(d) $\langle 8\cos 16, 2(2 + \sin 16) + 7(8)\cos 16 \rangle \approx \langle -7.661, -50.205 \rangle$

53. False. For example, $\mathbf{u}$ and $-1(\mathbf{u})$ have opposite directions.

55. E   **57.** B

59. The velocity vector is $\langle -x, \sqrt{1 - x^2} \rangle$, which has slope $-\dfrac{\sqrt{1 - x^2}}{x}$.
The acceleration vector is $\left\langle \dfrac{d}{dt}(-x), \dfrac{d}{dt}\left(\sqrt{1 - x^2}\right) \right\rangle$
$= \left\langle -\dfrac{dx}{dt}, \dfrac{-x}{\sqrt{1 - x^2}}\dfrac{dx}{dt} \right\rangle$
$= \left\langle x, \dfrac{x^2}{\sqrt{1 - x^2}} \right\rangle$, which has slope $\dfrac{x}{\sqrt{1 - x^2}}$. Since the slopes are negative reciprocals of each other, the vectors are orthogonal.

61. (a) The particles collide when $t = 2$.
(b) First particle: $v_1(2) = \langle 1, -2 \rangle$, so the direction unit vector is $\langle 1/\sqrt{5}, -2/\sqrt{5} \rangle$.
Second particle: $v_2(t) = \langle 3/2, 3/2 \rangle$, so the direction unit vector is $\langle 1/\sqrt{2}, 1/\sqrt{2} \rangle$.

63.

A closer view:

65. (a) The diagram shows, by vector addition, that $\mathbf{v} + \mathbf{w} = \mathbf{u}$, so $\mathbf{w} = \mathbf{u} - \mathbf{v}$.
(b) This is just the Law of Cosines applied to the triangle, the sides of which are the magnitudes of the vectors.
(c) By the HMT Rule, $\mathbf{w} = \langle u_1 - v_1, u_2 - v_2 \rangle$. So
$|\mathbf{u}|^2 + |\mathbf{v}|^2 - |\mathbf{w}|^2 = (u_1^2 + u_2^2) + (v_1^2 + v_2^2)$
$\qquad - [(u_1 - v_1)^2 + (u_2 - v_2)^2]$
$= u_1^2 + u_2^2 + v_1^2 + v_2^2 - [u_1^2 - 2u_1v_1 + v_1^2$
$\qquad\qquad\qquad\qquad\qquad + u_2^2 - 2u_2v_2 + v_2^2]$
$= 2u_1v_1 + 2u_2v_2$
$= 2(u_1v_1 + u_2v_2)$
(d) From part (b), $|\mathbf{w}|^2 = |\mathbf{u}|^2 + |\mathbf{v}|^2 - 2|\mathbf{u}||\mathbf{v}|\cos\theta$, so
$|\mathbf{u}|^2 + |\mathbf{v}|^2 - |\mathbf{w}|^2 = 2|\mathbf{u}||\mathbf{v}|\cos\theta$.
From part (c), $|\mathbf{u}|^2 + |\mathbf{v}|^2 - |\mathbf{w}|^2 = 2(u_1v_1 + u_2v_2)$. Substituting, we get $2(u_1v_1 + u_2v_2) = 2|\mathbf{u}||\mathbf{v}|\cos\theta$, so $\mathbf{u} \cdot \mathbf{v} = u_1v_1 + u_2v_2 = |\mathbf{u}||\mathbf{v}|\cos\theta$.

Section 11.3

Quick Review 11.3

1. $\langle 2\sqrt{3}, 2 \rangle$ **3.** 4π

5. Graph $y = \left(\dfrac{4 - x^2}{3}\right)^{1/2}$ and $y = -\left(\dfrac{4 - x^2}{3}\right)^{1/2}$.

7. $-\dfrac{5}{3}\cot 2 \approx 0.763$ **9.** $(3, 0)$ and $(-3, 0)$

Exercises 11.3

1.

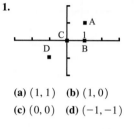

(a) $(1, 1)$ **(b)** $(1, 0)$
(c) $(0, 0)$ **(d)** $(-1, -1)$

3.

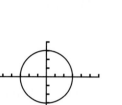

(a) $\left(\sqrt{2}, 3\pi/4\right)$ or $\left(\sqrt{2}, -5\pi/4\right)$
(b) $(2, -\pi/3)$ or $(-2, 2\pi/3)$
(c) $(3, \pi/2)$ or $(3, 5\pi/2)$
(d) $(1, \pi)$ or $(-1, 0)$

5.

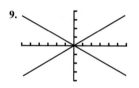

$0 \le \theta \le 2\pi$

7.

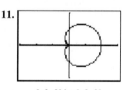

$0 \le \theta \le 2\pi$

9.

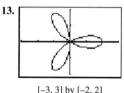

11.

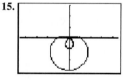

$[-3, 3]$ by $[-2, 2]$

$0 \le \theta \le 2\pi$

cardioid

13.

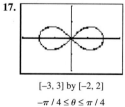

$[-3, 3]$ by $[-2, 2]$

$0 \le \theta \le \pi$

rose

15.

$[-4.5, 4.5]$ by $[-3, 3]$

$0 \le \theta \le 2\pi$

limaçon

17.

$[-3, 3]$ by $[-2, 2]$

$-\pi/4 \le \theta \le \pi/4$

lemniscate

19.

$[-6, 6]$ by $[-4, 4]$

$0 \le \theta \le \pi$

circle

21. $y = 4$, a horizontal line

23. $x + y = 1$, a line (slope $= -1$, y-intercept $= 1$)

25. $y - 2x = 5$, a line (slope $= 2$, y-intercept $= 5$)

27. $x^2 = y^2$, the union of two lines: $y = \pm x$

29. $x^2 + (y - 4)^2 = 16$, a circle (center $= (0, 4)$, radius $= 4$)

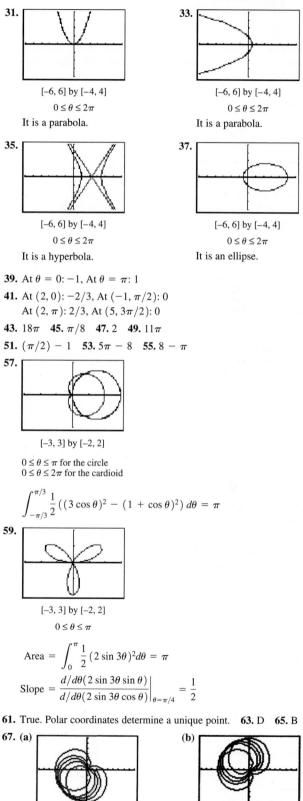

31.

$[-6, 6]$ by $[-4, 4]$

$0 \le \theta \le 2\pi$

It is a parabola.

33.

$[-6, 6]$ by $[-4, 4]$

$0 \le \theta \le 2\pi$

It is a parabola.

35.

$[-6, 6]$ by $[-4, 4]$

$0 \le \theta \le 2\pi$

It is a hyperbola.

37.

$[-6, 6]$ by $[-4, 4]$

$0 \le \theta \le 2\pi$

It is an ellipse.

39. At $\theta = 0$: -1, At $\theta = \pi$: 1

41. At $(2, 0)$: $-2/3$, At $(-1, \pi/2)$: 0
At $(2, \pi)$: $2/3$, At $(5, 3\pi/2)$: 0

43. 18π **45.** $\pi/8$ **47.** 2 **49.** 11π

51. $(\pi/2) - 1$ **53.** $5\pi - 8$ **55.** $8 - \pi$

57.

$[-3, 3]$ by $[-2, 2]$

$0 \le \theta \le \pi$ for the circle
$0 \le \theta \le 2\pi$ for the cardioid

$$\int_{-\pi/3}^{\pi/3} \frac{1}{2}\left((3\cos\theta)^2 - (1 + \cos\theta)^2\right) d\theta = \pi$$

59.

$[-3, 3]$ by $[-2, 2]$

$0 \le \theta \le \pi$

$$\text{Area} = \int_0^\pi \frac{1}{2}(2\sin 3\theta)^2 d\theta = \pi$$

$$\text{Slope} = \left.\frac{d/d\theta(2\sin 3\theta \sin\theta)}{d/d\theta(2\sin 3\theta \cos\theta)}\right|_{\theta = \pi/4} = \frac{1}{2}$$

61. True. Polar coordinates determine a unique point.   **63.** D   **65.** B

67. (a)

(b)

$[-9, 9]$ by $[-6, 6]$

$[-9, 9]$ by $[-6, 6]$

(c) The graph of r_2 is the graph of r_1 rotated counterclockwise about the origin by the angle α.

69. (a)

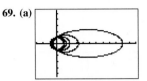

The graphs are ellipses that stretch out to the right. **(b)** The ellipse with eccentricity $-e$ is the reflection across the y-axis of the ellipse with eccentricity e.

71. (a)

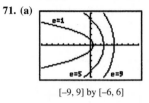

[−9, 9] by [−6, 6]

The graphs are parabolas.
(b) As $c \to 0^+$, the limit of the graph is the negative x-axis.

73. (a) a **(b)** a **(c)** $2a/\pi$

75. 8

77. $r^2 = x^2 + y^2 = (c - ex)^2 = c^2 - 2cex + e^2x^2$,

$(1 - e^2)x^2 + 2cex + y^2 = c^2$,

$(1 - e^2)\left(x^2 + \dfrac{2cex}{1 - e^2} + \dfrac{c^2e^2}{(1 - e^2)^2}\right) + y^2 = c^2 + \dfrac{c^2e^2}{1 - e^2} = \dfrac{c^2}{1 - e^2}$,

$\dfrac{(1 - e^2)^2}{c^2}\left(x + \dfrac{ce}{1 - e^2}\right)^2 + \dfrac{1 - e^2}{c^2}y^2 = 1$

79. The area swept out from time t_0 to time t is given by

$$A(t) = \int_{t_0}^{t_1} \frac{1}{2}r^2 \frac{d\theta}{dt}\, dt.$$

By the antiderivative part of the Fundamental Theorem of Calculus,

$$\frac{dA}{dt} = \frac{1}{2}r^2 \frac{d\theta}{dt}.$$

Quick Quiz (Sections 11.1–11.3)

1. A **3.** D

Review Exercises

1. (a) $\langle -17, 32 \rangle$ **(b)** $\sqrt{1313}$ **2. (a)** $\langle -1, -1 \rangle$ **(b)** $\sqrt{2}$
3. (a) $\langle 6, -8 \rangle$ **(b)** 10 **4. (a)** $\langle 10, -25 \rangle$ **(b)** $\sqrt{725} = 5\sqrt{29}$
5. $\langle -\sqrt{3}/2, -1/2 \rangle$ [assuming counterclockwise] **6.** $\langle \sqrt{3}/2, 1/2 \rangle$
7. $\langle 8/\sqrt{17}, -2/\sqrt{17} \rangle$ **8.** $\langle -3, -4 \rangle$
9. (a) $y = \dfrac{\sqrt{3}}{2}x + \dfrac{1}{4}$ **(b)** 1/4 **10. (a)** $y = -3x + \dfrac{13}{4}$ **(b)** 6
11. (a) $(0, 1/2)$ and $(0, -1/2)$ **(b)** Nowhere
12. (a) $(0, 2)$ and $(0, -2)$ **(b)** $(-2, 0)$ and $(2, 0)$
13. (a) $(0, 0)$ **(b)** Nowhere
14. (a) $(0, 9)$ and $(0, -9)$ **(b)** $(-4, 0)$ and $(4, 0)$

15.

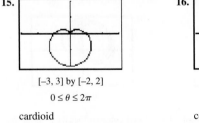

[−3, 3] by [−2, 2]

$0 \le \theta \le 2\pi$

cardioid

16.

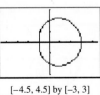

[−4.5, 4.5] by [−3, 3]

$0 \le \theta \le 2\pi$

convex limaçon

17.

[−1.5, 1.5] by [−1, 1]

$0 \le \theta \le 2\pi$

4-petaled rose

18.

[−3, 3] by [−2, 2]

$-\pi/2 \le \theta \le \pi/2$

vertical line

19.

[−1.5, 1.5] by [−1, 1]

$0 \le \theta \le \pi/2$

lemniscate

20.

[−1.5, 1.5] by [−1, 1]

$0 \le \theta \le \pi$

circle

21. 4.041 **22.** 0.346
23. Horizontal: $y = 0$, $y \approx \pm 0.443$, $y \approx \pm 1.739$
Vertical: $x = 2$, $x \approx 0.067$, $x \approx -1.104$
24. Horizontal: $y = 1/2$, $y = -4$
Vertical: $x = 0$, $x \approx \pm 2.598$
25. $y = \pm x + \sqrt{2}$ and $y = \pm x - \sqrt{2}$
26. $y = x - 1$ and $y = -x - 1$ **27.** $x = y$, a line
28. $x^2 + y^2 = 3x$, a circle $\left(\text{center} = \left(\dfrac{3}{2}, 0\right), \text{radius} = \dfrac{3}{2} \right)$
29. $x^2 = 4y$, a parabola **30.** $x - \sqrt{3}y = 4\sqrt{3}$ or $y = \dfrac{x}{\sqrt{3}} - 4$, a line
31. $r = -5 \sin \theta$ **32.** $r = 2 \sin \theta$
33. $r^2 \cos^2 \theta + 4r^2 \sin^2 \theta = 16$, or
$r^2 = \dfrac{16}{\cos^2 \theta + 4 \sin^2 \theta}$
34. $(r \cos \theta + 2)^2 + (r \sin \theta - 5)^2 = 16$ **35.** $9\pi/2$
36. $\pi/12$ **37.** $(\pi/4) + 2$ **38.** 5π
39. (a) $\mathbf{v}(t) = \langle -4 \sin t, \sqrt{2} \cos t \rangle$ and $\mathbf{a}(t) = \langle -4 \cos t, -\sqrt{2} \sin t \rangle$
(b) 3
40. (a) $\mathbf{v}(t) = \langle \sqrt{3} \sec t \tan t, \sqrt{3} \sec^2 t \rangle$ and
$\mathbf{a}(t) = \langle \sqrt{3}(\sec t \tan^2 t + \sec^3 t), 2\sqrt{3} \sec^2 t \tan t \rangle$
(b) $\sqrt{3}$
41. Speed $= |\mathbf{v}(t)| = \sqrt{\left(-\dfrac{t}{(1 + t^2)^{3/2}}\right)^2 + \left(\dfrac{1}{(1 + t^2)^{3/2}}\right)^2} = \dfrac{1}{1 + t^2}$
The maximum value of $\dfrac{1}{1 + t^2}$ is 1, when $t = 0$.
42. $\mathbf{r}(t) = \langle e^t \cos t, e^t \sin t \rangle$, with slope $\dfrac{e^t \sin t}{e^t \cos t} = \tan t$.
$\mathbf{v}(t) = \langle e^t \cos t - e^t \sin t, e^t \sin t + e^t \cos t \rangle$
$\mathbf{a}(t) = \langle -2e^t \sin t, 2e^t \cos t \rangle$, with slope $\dfrac{2e^t \cos t}{-2e^t \sin t} = -\dfrac{1}{\tan t}$
Since the slopes are negative reciprocals, the angle is always 90°.
43. $\mathbf{r}(t) = \langle \cos t - 1, \sin t + 1 \rangle$ **44.** $\mathbf{r}(t) = \langle \tan^{-1} t + 1, \sqrt{t^2 + 1} \rangle$
45. $\mathbf{r}(t) = \langle 1, t^2 \rangle$ **46.** $\mathbf{r}(t) = \langle -t^2 + 6t - 2, -t^2 + 2t + 2 \rangle$
47. (a) $\dfrac{\pi\sqrt{17}}{4} \approx 3.238$ **(b)** x-component: $\dfrac{3\pi^2}{16\sqrt{2}}$; y-component: $-\dfrac{5\pi^2}{16\sqrt{2}}$
(c) $\dfrac{x^2}{9} + \dfrac{y^2}{25} = 1$

48. (a) 1 **(b)** $e^3\sqrt{2}$ **(c)** $(e^3-1)\sqrt{2}$

49. (a) $104/5$ **(b)** $4144/135$ **(c)** $\dfrac{dy}{dx} = \dfrac{3}{5}\sqrt{x+2}$

50. Speed ≈ 591.982 mph; Direction $\approx 8.179°$ north of east

51. (a) $\mathbf{r}(t) = \langle t^2 + \pi, \cos(t^2 + \pi)\rangle$

(b) At this point $t^2 + \pi = 4$, so $t = \sqrt{4-\pi}$.

Speed $= \sqrt{(2t)^2 + (2t(-\sin(t^2+\pi))^2}\big|_{t=\sqrt{4-\pi}} = 2.324$

52. (a) $\mathbf{v}_A(t) = \langle 1, 2\rangle$ and $\mathbf{v}_B(t) = \langle 3/2, 3/2\rangle$

(b) $\displaystyle\int_0^3 \sqrt{1 + (2t-4)^2}\,dt = 6.126$

(c) Setting $x_A = x_B$, we find that $t = 4$. Plugging $t = 4$ into y_A and y_B, we find that both values are the same (4). Thus, the particles collide when $t = 4$. [*Note:* If you graph both paths, they will cross at $(-1, 1)$. However, the particles are there at different times.]

53. (a) Area $= \displaystyle\int_0^\pi \frac{1}{2}\left(\frac{4}{1+\sin\theta}\right)^2 d\theta = \frac{32}{3}$

(b) The polar equation is equivalent to $r + r\sin\theta = 4$. Thus,

$$r = 4 - r\sin\theta$$
$$r^2 = (4 - r\sin\theta)^2$$
$$x^2 + y^2 = (4-y)^2$$
$$x^2 + y^2 = 16 - 8y + y^2$$
$$8y = 16 - x^2$$

(c) Area $= \displaystyle\int_{-4}^4 \left(2 - \frac{x^2}{8}\right)dx$, which, indeed, is $\dfrac{32}{3}$.

APPENDIX

Section A2

1.

$\delta = 1/18$

3. $\delta = 0.39$ **5.** $(-2.01, -1.99);\ \delta = 0.01$

7. $(3, 15);\ \delta = 5$

9. (a) -4 **(b)** $\delta = 0.05$

11. (a) $\sin 1 \approx 0.841$ **(b)** $\delta = 0.018$

13. $\delta = \min\{1 - \sqrt{1-\epsilon},\ \sqrt{1+\epsilon} - 1\}$

15. (a) $I = (5, 5 + \epsilon^2)$ **(b)** $\displaystyle\lim_{x\to 5^+}\sqrt{x-5} = 0$

Section A4

1. $\cosh x = \dfrac{5}{4}$; $\tanh x = -\dfrac{3}{5}$; $\coth x = -\dfrac{5}{3}$; $\operatorname{sech} x = \dfrac{4}{5}$; $\operatorname{csch} x = -\dfrac{4}{3}$

3. $\sinh x = \dfrac{8}{15}$; $\tanh x = \dfrac{8}{17}$; $\coth x = \dfrac{17}{8}$; $\operatorname{sech} x = \dfrac{15}{17}$; $\operatorname{csch} x = \dfrac{15}{8}$

5. $x + \dfrac{1}{x}$ **7.** e^{5x} **9.** e^{4x} **13.** $\dfrac{dy}{dx} = 2\cosh\dfrac{x}{3}$

15. $\dfrac{dy}{dt} = \operatorname{sech}^2\sqrt{t} + \dfrac{\tanh\sqrt{t}}{\sqrt{t}}$ **17.** $\dfrac{dy}{dz} = \coth z$

19. $\dfrac{dy}{d\theta} = (\operatorname{sech}\theta\tanh\theta)(\ln\operatorname{sech}\theta)$

21. $\dfrac{dy}{dx} = \tanh^3 x$ **23.** $y = 2x;\ \dfrac{dy}{dx} = 2$ **25.** $\dfrac{dy}{dx} = \dfrac{1}{2\sqrt{x}(1+x)}$

27. $\dfrac{dy}{d\theta} = \dfrac{1}{1+\theta} - \tanh^{-1}\theta$ **29.** $\dfrac{dy}{dt} = \dfrac{1}{2\sqrt{t}} - \coth^{-1}\sqrt{t}$

31. $\dfrac{dy}{dx} = -\operatorname{sech}^{-1} x$ **33.** $\dfrac{dy}{d\theta} = \dfrac{\ln 2}{\sqrt{1 + \left(\dfrac{1}{2}\right)^{2\theta}}}$ **35.** $\dfrac{dy}{dx} = |\sec x|$

37. (a) $\dfrac{d}{dx}(\tan^{-1}(\sinh x) + C) = \operatorname{sech} x$

(b) $\dfrac{d}{dx}(\sin^{-1}(\tanh x) + C) = \operatorname{sech} x$

39. $\dfrac{d}{dx}\left(\dfrac{x^2-1}{2}\coth^{-1} x + \dfrac{x}{2} + C\right) = x\coth^{-1} x$

41. $\dfrac{\cosh 2x}{2} + C$ **43.** $12\sinh\left(\dfrac{x}{2} - \ln 3\right) + C$

45. $7\ln\left|\cosh\dfrac{x}{7}\right| + C$ **47.** $\tanh\left(x - \dfrac{1}{2}\right) + C$

49. $-2\operatorname{sech}\sqrt{t} + C$ **51.** $\ln(5/2) \approx 0.916$

53. $(3/32) + \ln 2 \approx 0.787$ **55.** $e - e^{-1} \approx 2.350$ **57.** $3/4$

59. $(3/8) + \ln\sqrt{2} \approx 0.722$ **61.** 2π

63. $\left(2\ln\dfrac{199}{100} - \dfrac{99}{100}\right)\pi \approx 1.214$

65. (a) If $g(x) = \dfrac{f(x) + f(-x)}{2}$, then

$$g(-x) = \dfrac{f(-x) + f(x)}{2} = g(x).\text{ Thus,}$$

$\dfrac{f(x) + f(-x)}{2}$ is even. If $h(x) = \dfrac{f(x) - f(-x)}{2}$,

then $h(-x) = \dfrac{f(-x) - f(x)}{2} = -\dfrac{f(x) - f(-x)}{2} = -h(x).$

Thus $\dfrac{f(x) - f(-x)}{2}$ is odd.

(b) Even part: $\dfrac{e^x + e^{-x}}{2} = \cosh x$ Odd part: $\dfrac{e^x + e^{-x}}{2} = \sinh x$

69. $y = \operatorname{sech}^{-1}(x) - \sqrt{1 - x^2}$

Applications Index

Note: Numbers in parenthesis refer to exercises on the page indicated.

Business, Economics, Industry, Labor

Average daily holding cost, 313(74)
Average daily inventory, 325(44)
Backpacks, selling, 235(50)
Box fabrication, 226, 232(18)
Burger prices, 10(39)
Can design, 226–227, 232(16–17)
Club fees, 10(18)
Depreciation of trucks, 55(62)
Factory electrical power consumption, 438(5)
Fence design, 231(9–10)
Finding profit, 140(29)
Fish pond, 320(10)
Fuel consumption, 394(28)
Great Molasses Flood, 429
Hot dog stand, 394(29)
Industrial costs, 21(56)
Industrial production, 261(47)
Marginal cost, 136, 140(27)
    cost from, 313(72)
Marginal revenue, 136, 140(28), 152(74)
    revenue from, 313(73)
Maximizing profit, 228–229, 232(23), 233(24)
Metal sheet fabrication, 424(23)
Milk carton filling, 394(27), 435(26)
Minimizing average cost, 229–230, 233(25–26)
Oil consumption
    of developing country, 419(3)
    on Pathfinder Island, 324(33)
    in U.S., 393(21)
Oil depletion, 366(40)
Oil refinery, 264(52)
Orchard farming, 127
Picnic pavilion rental, 127
Poster design, 232(13)
Potato consumption, 389
Printing costs, 325(43)
Production levels, 236(61–62)
Quickest routes, 232(20)
Rental charge *vs.* time, 37
Rice crops in Laos, 58
Salary negotiation, 86(29)
Shipping packages, 233(30)
Solid waste accumulation, 365(34)
Spinach boxes, 432
Stringing telephone cable, 265(62)
Suitcase design, 232(19)
Taxi fares, 98(52)
Time *vs.* rental charge, 37
Tire manufacturing, 264(54)
Tour services, 233(27)
Wheat exports, 95(39)
Wilson lot size formula, 236(60)

Computer Science, Geometry, Probability, Simulation, and Other Mathematics

Alternating harmonic series, 528
Approximation by rectangles, 272
Area formulas, 300(51)
Cartesian length formula, 548(37)
Cavalieri's theorem, 405(57), 412–413
Changing
    area, 264(57)
    cube, 264(59)
    rectangle, 257(9–10)
Changing voltage, 257(7)
Chaos theory, 328
Circles
    area of, 257(1), 280(39)
    expanding, 248(42)
    motion along, 261(45)
    radius of, 260(36–37)
Circumference, 473
Circumscribing ellipse, 237(65)
Cissoid of Diocles, 171(46)
Closing off first quadrant, 231(8)
Cone construction, 225, 233(32)
Controlling error, 265(65)
Cubic polynomial functions, 233(29)
Cubics, 222(59)
Cycloids, 545–546
    curtate, 548(41)
    prolate, 548(42)
Devil's Curve, 171(54)
Diagonals, 257(5)
Distance from point to line, 12(58)
Eight curve, 171(45)
Ellipse area, 405(56)
Fermat's principle in optics, 236(57)
Finding angles, 232(15), 235(47)
Finding area, 231(4)
Folium of Descartes, 171(55)
Fundamental Theorem
    application of, 303
    with Chain Rule, 304
    for initial value problems, 330
Generalized cone problem, 237(64)
Geometry, calculus and, 234(42)
Grapher failure, 83
Hyperbolic functions, 601(72)
Inscribing figures
    cones, 234(36), 264(49)
    cylinder, 264(48)
    rectangle, 224–225, 231(4), 232(21), 264(51)
John Napier's answer, 366(44)
Largest rectangle, 231(4)
Linearization, 250(69)
Maximizing area, 231(2)
Maximizing volume, 232(22)
Mean Value Theorem, 263(37), 460(71)
    proof of, 210(63)
Minimizing perimeter, 231(3)
Multiples of Pi, 250(67)

Net area, 286
Newton's method, 249(63), 263(41)
    formula for, 250(71)
Nicole Oresme's Theorem, 539(69)
Optical dimensions, 231(7)
Orthogonal curves, 171(51), 188(64)
Orthogonal vectors, 559(59–60)
Oscillation, 250(64)
Parameter values, 233(33), 234(34–35)
Percentage error, 248(44), 338(63–64)
Perimeter of ellipse, 548(36)
Probability
    of clock stopping, 430–431, 435(27–28)
    of shared birthdays, 105–106, 110(45)
Quadratic approximations, 250(66)
Quartic polynomial functions, 222(60)
Rectangular Approximation Methods, 280(40–41)
Rolle's Theorem, proof of, 210(62)
Rotational symmetry, 384
Search algorithms
    binary, 464, 466(44)
    efficient, 466(43)
    sequential, 464–465, 466(44)
Simpson's rule approximations, 319, 326(53)
Simulation of related motion, 255–256
Surface area, 247(32), 248(34), 248(36), 600(70)
    estimating, 248(50)
    of sphere, 257(2)
Tolerance, 248(45–46), 248(48)
Trapezoid rule approximations, 319
Triangle
    area of, 257(6)
    punching out, 539(68)
Twisted solids, 416(46)
Volume, 247(31), 248(33), 248(35)
    approximation by RAM, 274–275, 280(40–41)
    of bowl, 417(52)
    consistency of definitions, 418(76)
    of cube, 260(39)
    of cylinder, 257(3)
    by cylindrical shells, 410–411
    about each axis, 417(55)
    estimating, 248(49)
    of hemisphere, 418(73)
    of infinite solid, 474, 479(54)
    method comparison, 411–412
    of nose cone, 278(26)
    of reservoir, 278(24)
    of solid hemisphere, 278(22)
    of solids with rotational symmetry, 384
    of sphere, 274
    of swimming pool, 278(25), 320(9)
    of torus, 418(74)

Education

School projects, 394(30)
Test scores, 435(30)

Growth and Decay

Bacteria growth, 28(38), 141(46), 364(24)
Boys growing, 376(37)
Carbon-14 dating, 362, 381(55)
    Crater Lake, 365(35)
    measurement sensitivity, 365(36)
Cholera bacteria, 27(31), 364(23)
Cooling
    Newton's law of cooling, 362–363
    of pie, 380(52)
    silver, 365(32)
    soup, 365(31)
Depreciation of trucks, 55(62)
Exponential, 369
Girls growing, 377(38)
Growing
    raindrop, 257(12)
    rings on trees, 130
    sand piles, 258(16)
    trees, 248(43)
Half-life, 27(21), 27(22)
    Californium-252, 380(51)
    finding, 360–361
    of Np-240, 364(22)
    of Polonium-210, 364(26)
    of Radon-222, 364(25)
    of Sm-151, 364(21)
Logistic Growth Models, 374–375
Mean-life of radioactive nuclei, 364(29)
Money doubling, 27(25), 27(26), 27(27), 43(47)
Money tripling, 27(28), 27(29), 27(30)
Radioactive decay, 27(23), 360–361
    of plutonium, 187(53)
Savings account growth, 23
Transitivity of rates, 463

Home and Community

Air pollution, 279(31)
Automobile gas mileage, 192
Bathroom scale, 433(10)
Bundt cake, 440(49)
Catching rainwater, 231(12)
Filling a swamp, 326(56)
Flower vase, 418(72)
Home electricity use, 393(22)
Household electricity, 326(57)
Milk left on counter, 182
Storage bins, 263(46)
Water pollution, 279(30), 495(42)
Water tower, 435(22)

Interest, Investment, Financial Assistance

Appreciation of violin, 381(56)
Average value, 573(73)
Compounding interest continuously, 360, 367(56)
Cost, revenue, and profit, 260(43)
Depreciation of trucks, 55(62)
Expected payoffs, 539(67)
Finding times, 27(24)
Inflation, 396(44)

Maximizing profit, 228–229
Minimizing average cost, 229–230
Minting coins, 248(47)
Money doubling, 27(25), 27(26), 27(27), 43(47)
Money tripling, 27(28), 27(29), 27(30)
Perpetuities, 539
Rule of 70, 56(66), 366(46)
Rule of 72, 56(67), 366(46)
Savings account growth, 23

Life Science and Medicine

Angiography, 244
Angioplasty, 244
Avian development, 365(33)
Body's reaction to medicine, 127(48)
Cardiac output, 260(44), 275–276, 277(17)
Cell membrane transport, 381(58)
Cholera bacteria, 27(31)
Coughing, 236(59)
Disease elimination, 27(32)
Drug absorption, 55(63)
Effect of flight maneuvers on heart, 248(50)
First-order chemical reactions, 366(42)
Flu spreading, 185, 187(52)
Inversion of sugar, 366(39)
Motion sickness, 146
Patient temperature, 95(37)
Sensitivity to medicine, 92–93, 235(49)
Spread of measles, 376(32)
Unclogging arteries, 244–245

Linear Motion (acceleration, distance, height, position, time, velocity)

Acceleration, 554–556
    of car, 395(40)
    constant, 162(64)
    displacement and, 600(68)
    due to gravity, 209(43)
    effects of, 388
    particle, 162(66)
    of particles, 380(49)
    of projectiles, 393(11)
    from standstill, 93(7)
Coasting to a stop, 367(54–55)
Direction and magnitude, 551
Distance traveled
    displacement and, 556–557
    formulas, 573(72)
    modeling, 11(44)
    from point to line, 12(58)
    by projectile, 279(29)
    total, 387
    by toy car, 438(1)
    of train engine, 278(18)
    upstream, 278(19)
    when velocities varies, 271
    from velocity data, 278(21)
Finding height, 265(67)
Free fall
    100-m tower, 94(27)
    with air resistance, 279(28)

    of balls, 141(38)
    of bodies, 59
    constants on Earth, 132
    on Jupiter, 94(32), 138(14)
    on Mars, 94(31), 138(14)
    on moon, 209(43)
    from rest, 207
    of rocks, 92, 127(47)
    on small airless planet, 68(70)
    of two balls, 152(72)
    water balloon, 68(69)
Horizontal motion modeling, 133–134
Jerk, 145–146
Lunar projectile motion, 138(13)
Motion along line, 216, 235(46)
Particle motion
    acceleration, 380(49)
    of busy particles, 555
    on circle, 559(46–47)
    collisions, 560(61)
    on coordinate line, 138(9), 138(11), 162(63)
    along coordinate plane, 259(28)
    along curve, 264(60)
    force in, 436(36)
    along line, 139(19–23)
    on number line, 138(10), 141(37)
    along parabolas, 259(25–26)
    path of, 557
    in plane, 558(35–38), 559(48–49), 576(47–48)
    positions, 559(49)
    studying, 133–134
    velocity of, 395(38)
    along x-axis, 190(70), 220(25–28), 264(55)
Planar motion, 553–556
Projectile motion, 138
Speed, 554–556
    average, over short time intervals, 60
    finding, 139(24)
    ground, 553–554
    instantaneous, 60
    of triremes, 208(13)
Truck on highway, 140(26)
Velocity, 554–556
    ball, 95(37)
    downward, 207
    graphs, 131–132
    of race car, 131
    resistance proportional to, 367(53)
Vertical motion
    of hanging masses, 235(45)
    height of object in, 232(14)
    modeling, 132–133
    of paper clip, 152(71)
Weight on a spring, 145

Physical Science and Engineering

Aerodynamic drag, 321(29)
Airplane landing path, 237(63)
Airplane lift off, 100
Atmospheric pressure, 366(41)

Ball bearing, 437(48)
Balloon inflation, 141(34)
Boring a cylinder, 258(15)
Bouncing ball, 490(48)
Bullet speeds, 138(16)
Butterfly effect, 328
Car acceleration, 495(40)
Center of mass, 396(47)
Changing tires, 243–244
Classical bead problem, 417(53)
Cylinder construction, 233(31)
Cylinder pressure, 127(46)
Dam design, 429
Daylight hours in Fairbanks, Alaska,
    108(21)
Depth of well, 245
Diesel engine fuel consumption, 438(2)
Draining
    conical reservoir, 258(17)
    a hemispherical reservoir, 258(18)
    a tank, 138(8), 139(25)
    water, 264(61)
Earth's surface area, 244
Electrical current, 234(40)
Electrical power, 257(4)
Filling
    a bowl, 152(73), 418(75)
    a conical tank, 254
    a milk carton, 394(27), 435(26)
    a swamp, 326(56)
    a trough, 258(20)
Finding mass, 394(31)
Fish tank, 435(25)
Fluid force
    aquarium, 436(35)
    feeding trough, 440(37)
    fish tank, 435(25), 437(4)
    Great Molasses Flood, 429
    milk carton, 435(26)
    olive oil can, 440(38)
Forcing electrons together, 437(41)
Frequencies of musical notes, 48,
    51(23)
Frictionless cart, 234(39)
Fuel efficiency, 325(51)
Fundamental frequency of vibrating piano
    string, 153(80)
Gravity, 209(43)
    acceleration of, 249(52)
Growth
    raindrop, 257(12)
    rings on trees, 130
    sand piles, 258(16)
    trees, 248(43)
Harmonic notes on guitar, 524
Heating a plate, 257(8)
Hooke's law, 395(35–36)
Inflating balloons, 257(11)
Insulation, 10(42)
Jupiter, free fall on, 94(32), 138(14)
Kinetic energy, 437(42)
Leaky bucket, 433(5–6)
Leaky sand bag, 433(7)
Light bulbs, 393(23)
Lunar data, 94(8)

Lunar projectile motion, 138(13)
Mars
    free fall on, 94(31), 138(14)
    launching on, 263(43)
Melting ice, 259(27)
Meteorite falling, 162(65)
Newton's law of cooling, 362–363
Nose cone, 279(26)
Oil flow, 394(34)
Orbital mechanics, 573(79)
Pathfinder Island oil consumption, 324(33)
Plumb bob design, 417
Projectiles, 393(11)
Pumping rates, 390
Radiocarbon dating, 2
Rising balloons, 253, 258(22)
Rocket launch, 94(28), 139(18), 263(42)
Rubber-band-powered sled, 325(34)
Running machinery too fast, 162(61)
Satellite in orbit, 436(40), 560(62)
Scarpellone Panther I, 320(11)
Ship problem, 287
Sliding ladders, 256, 258(19)
Snowfall calculation, 270
Sojourner pathfinder, 442
Stiffness of a beam, 234(38)
Strength of a beam, 234(37)
Swimming pool, 278(25), 320(9)
Tank design, 231(11), 430
Temperature data
    averaging, 316
    changes in, 208(12)
    Chattanooga, 51(43)
    conversion, 8
    finding, 380(53)
    original temperature of beam, 365(30)
    pendulum period and, 162(67)
    Rocky Mountain, 51(44)
    St. Louis, 51(24)
    Tempe, 162(62)
Throwing dirt, 265(63)
Tin pest, 236(58)
Tractor trailers, 600(69)
Translunar injection, 542
Trireme speed, 208(13)
Tunnel construction, 424(24)
Vat design, 263(47)
Volcanic lava fountains, 141(35)
Washer cross sections, 408
Water in reservoir, 279(24)
Water tanks, 394(26)
Weight of air, 394(32)
Wind speeds, 268
Wing design, 321(30)
Work
    bathroom scale, 433(10)
    compressing gas, 433(12)
    drinking a milkshake, 434(20)
    emptying tanks, 434(18)
    by force, 427
    hauling rope, 433(11)
    hauling water, 439(33)
    leaky bucket, 433(5–6)
    leaky sandbag, 433(7), 436(37)
    lifting, 427–428

    pumping, 428–429, 434(17), 435(22),
        436(39)
    rolling a stone, 440(35)
    stretching a spring, 392, 433(8), 435(34),
        436(37), 440(34)
    subway car springs, 433(9)
    water tower, 435(22)

Population Modeling and Demographics

Bacterium populations, 141(46)
Bear population, 98(51), 372–373
Butterfly populations, 398
Extinct populations, 377(45)
Fruit fly population, 87, 137(7)
Gopher population, 391
Gorilla population, 376(34)
Guppy population, 55(65), 376(33)
Hare population, 108(23)
Height of females, 435(31)
Hornet population, 362
Lynx population, 108(23)
Moose population, 373–374
Population density, 394(33)
Population growth
    Florida, 99(53)
    Glenbrook, 43(48)
    Knoxville, 27(19)
    Silver Run, 27(20)
Rabbit population, 376(31)
Shared birthday probabilities, 105–106,
    110(45)
Yellow perch lengths, 440(40)

Sports

Athletic field design, 264(53)
Ball velocity, 95(38)
Baseball, 436(44), 558(33), 560(63)
Catching a fly ball, 554–555
Downhill skiing, 109(29)
Flying a kite, 258(14)
Football, 436(46), 439(23), 558(34)
Golf, 436(45)
Kelly Schmitzer skating data, 367(55)
Marathon running, 208(14)
Moving race car, 259(31)
Parachuting, 141(33)
Pole vaulting, 142(48)
Race car velocity, 131
Rock climbing, 439(32)
Running tracks, 425(38)
Skydiving, 326(52), 368(57), 600(67)
Softball, 436(47)
Tennis club fees, 10(18)
Tennis serves, 436(43)
Thoroughbred racing, 138(12)
Whitewater river kayaking, 109(30)

Miscellaneous

Air traffic control, 258(13)
Amusement parks, 389–390, 394(25)
Art forgery, 380(54)

Beauty bare, 494
Benjamin Franklin's will, 366(45)
Billboards, 438(3)
Bird feeder seed levels, 11(43)
Building's shadow, 259(33)
Dye concentration data, 275
Ferris wheel, 261(46)
Guitar, 524
Hanging cables, 601(71)

Hauling in a dinghy, 258(21)
Highway chase, 254
Length of road, 278(20)
Milk left on counter, 182
Moving shadows, 259(29–30)
Musical note frequencies, 48, 51(23)
National Defense Spending, 95(40)
Navigation, 558(25), 576(50)
Paper folding, 235(48)

Paperweights, 412
Rumor spreading, 187(51)
Searchlights, 152(75)
Speeding tickets, 208(11)
Speed trap, 259(32)
Telephone help line, 431, 435(29)
Traffic flow, 393(24)
Walkers, 260(34)
Working underwater, 381(57)

Subject Index

Note: Numbers in parenthesis refer to exercises on the page indicated.

A

Absolute change, 243–245
Absolute convergence, 516, 528–529
Absolute extrema, 193
  finding, 196
Absolute extreme values, 193–195
Absolute extremum, 195
Absolute maximum value, 193
Absolute minimum value, 193
Absolute value function, 18, 163(78), 341, 345
Absolute value theorem, 448
Acceleration, 555–556, 599(68)
  definition, 132
  modeling effects of, 388
  vector, 554
Accumulation
  general modeling strategy, 387–388
  net change and, 385–392
  problems as area, 269–272
Accumulator function
  definite integral as, 288
  definition, 288
Additivity Rule, 293
Aerodynamic drag, 321(29)
AGNESI, MARIA (1718–1799), 32
Algebra
  Binomial Theorem in, 577
  difference of like integer powers, 577
  formulas, 577–578
  fractions in, 577
  laws of exponents, 577
  Quadratic Formula, 578
  square, completing, 578
  zero in, 577
Algebraic combinations, 81–82
Algebraic mean, 163(79)
Alternating series, 527–528
  error bound, 504, 507
  test, 527
Antiderivatives, 206, 486
  area using, 308
  challenging, 356(57), 356(58)
  definite integral and, 293–298
  formula verification, 341
  in Fundamental Theorem of Calculus, 302–305
  graphical analysis of, 309
  Leibniz notation for, 342
Antidifferentiation, 206
  by parts, 349–354
  substitution, 340–346
Apogee, 561
Appreciation, 381(56)
Approximation error, 591
Arccosecant, 176–177
Arccosine, 176–177

Arccotangent
  derivatives of, 176–177
  tangent line to, 177
Archimedes area formula for parabolas, 312(64)
ARCHIMEDES OF SYRACUSE (287–212 B.C.E.), 571
Arc length, 45, 548(41)
  in parametric curves, 544–545
  tangent, 426(39)
Arcsecant, 175–176
Arcsine, 174–175
Arctangent, 175
Area, 257(1)
  accumulation problems as, 269–272
  antiderivatives for finding, 308
  of circles, 94(29)
  connection, 308–309
  under curve, 285
  between curves, 397–398
  definite integral and, 285–296
  differential, 567
  of ellipses, 405(56)
  finding, 231(4), 355(33), 355(34)
  formulas, 300(51)
  intersecting curves enclosing, 398–399
  maximizing, 231(2)
  under parabolic arc, 317
  in plane, 397–401
  polar coordinates, 567
  polar curve, 566–568
  signed, 286
  summing, 490(50), 490(51)
  surface, 248(50), 257(2), 413, 599(70)
  of triangle, 263(45)
Arithmetic mean, 210(58)
Arithmetic sequence, 445–446
  defining, 444
  explicit formulas for, 444
  recursive formulas for, 444
Astroid, length of, 424(22)
Asymptotes, 581
  limits and, 491(76)
Average cost minimization, 229
Average rates of changes, 87–88
Average speed, 59–60
Average value of function, 294–295
Average velocity, 130
Axis, rotation around, 409

B

Bacteria growth, 28(38)
Bead problem, 417(53)
Bell, 439(18)
BERNOULLI, JACOB (1654–1705), 570
Binary search, 464, 466(44)
Binomial powers, 240
Binomial series, 502(45)
Binomial Theorem, 502(46)
  in algebra, 577
BLACKWELL, DAVID H. (1919–2010), 105

BONNET, OSSIAN (1819–1892), 202
Boundary, 14
Bounded functions, 289
Bowl, volume of, 417(52)
Bow Tie, 439(17)
BROWNE, MARJORIE LEE (1914–1979), 87

C

Calculators
  conversion identities, 177
  identity conversion, 177
  integrals on, 289–290
  values, rounding, 121
Californium-252, 380(51)
Carbon-14 dating, 362, 365(36), 381(55)
Cardiac output, 275–276, 277(17)
Cardioid, length of, 573(75)
Cartesian length formula, 548(37)
CASSINI, GIOVANNI DOMENICO (1625–1712), 570
Cassini oval, 570
CAUCHY, AUGUSTIN-LOUIS (1789–1857), 303, 453
Cauchy's Mean Value Theorem, 460(71)
CAVALIERI, BONAVENTURA (1598–1647), 405(57), 412
Cavalieri's theorem, 405(57), 412–413
Center of mass, 396(47)
Chain Rule, 155–160, 162(68), 183
  applying, 156–157
  definition of, 156
  Fundamental Theorem of Calculus with, 304
  proof of, 591
  repeated use of, 157–158
Change
  absolute, 243–245
  average rate of, 87–88
  of base formula, 41
  differential estimate of, 242
  estimating, 265(64)
  instantaneous rate of, 91–92, 125, 129–130
  net, 385–392
  percentage, 243–245
  rates of, 59–60
  relative, 243–245
  sensitivity to, 135–136
Cholera, 27(31)
Circle-area function, 14
Circles, 581
  area of, 94(29)
  enlarging, 129
  formulas, 579
  graphing, 30
  motion along, 261
  parametrizing, 30, 34(35)
  in polar gallery, 569
Circular cross sections, 407–409
Circular orbit, 560(62)
Circular sector, 566

Circumference, improper integrals for, 473–474
Cissoid of Diocles, 171(46)
Classic mode, 113
Closed intervals, 14
Coasting, 367(54), 367(55)
Coming and going, 389–390
Common difference, 444
Common logarithm functions, 40
Companion integrals, 593
Comparison test, 472, 525–526
Component form, 550
Composite functions, 18–19
    continuous, 82
    derivative of, 155–157
Compound interest, 25
    continuous, 26, 359–360, 459(57)
Concavity
    definition, 213
    in parametric curves, 544
    test, 214
Conditional convergence, 528–529
Cones
    in cones, 264(49)
    constructing, 225, 233(32)
    draining, 258(17)
    formulas, 579
    generalized problem, 237(64)
    inscribing, 234(36)
    right circular, 579
    volume of, 279(26)
Conic sections, 581–582
Connectivity, 83
Constant-force formula, 391
Constant function
    derivative of, 118
    integrals of, 287
Constant Multiple Rule
    for definite integrals, 293
    for differentiation, 119
    of limits, 61, 71, 586
Consumption over time, 389
Continuity
    differentiability and, 115
    at points, 78–81
    properties of, 86(63)
Continuous extension, 81, 459(55), 459(56)
Continuous functions, 81, 85(47), 85(48), 85(49), 85(50)
    continuous, 82
    definite integral of, 283
    graphs of, 111
    Intermediate Value Theorem for, 83–84
    properties of, 82
Continuously compounded interest, 26, 359–360, 459(57)
Convergence
    absolute, 516, 528–529
    conditional, 528–529
    endpoint, 519–520, 523–533
    importance of, 513
    intervals of, 483, 491, 514, 529–531
    of Maclaurin series, 505–506
    procedure for determining, 532
    radius of, 513–520
    test for, 472–473

Convergence Theorem for Power Series, 514
Convergent sequences, 447
Convergent series, 482
    geometric, 490(53)
Corners, 422–423
Cosine function, 579
    derivative of, 144
Cos x, Taylor series for, 493–494
CRAMER, GABRIEL, 171
Critical point, 196
    without extreme values, 197
Cross sections, 406, 412–413
    circular, 407–409
    square, 407
    washer, 408
Cubes, 264(59)
Cubic functions, 201
    graphs of, 222(59)
Cubic polynomial functions, 233(29)
Curtate cycloid, 548(41)
Curve
    area under, 285
    intersecting, 398–399
    lemniscate, 570
    lengths of, 420–423
    limaçon, 564, 570
    normal to, 91
    orthogonal, 161, 171(51), 188(64)
    parametric, 29, 158, 543–547
    parametrization of, 29
    polar, 563–565, 573(74)
    rose, 569
    rotation of, 573(67)
    slope of, 89–90
    smooth, 421–422
    tangent to, 88–89
Cusps, 422–423
Cycloids
    curtate, 548(41)
    parametric curve, 545–547
    prolate, 548(42)
Cylinders
    boring, 258(15)
    inscribing, 264(48)
    with parallel bases, 579
    right circular, 579
Cylindrical shells, 409–412
    volume by, 410–411

D

Decay
    exponential, 24–25, 358–363
    radioactive, 24–25, 43(46), 187(53), 360
Decreasing function, 265(68)
    Mean Value Theorem and, 204–205
Definite integrals, 387, 388, 486. *See also* Integrals
    as accumulator function, 288
    Additivity Rule for, 293
    antiderivatives and, 293–298
    area and, 285–296
    Constant Multiple Rule for, 293

    of continuous functions, 283
    Difference Rule for, 293
    Domination Rule for, 293
    evaluation of, by substitution, 345
    existence of, 283
    as limit of Riemann sums, 283
    max-min Inequality for, 293
    Mean Value Theorem for, 295–296
    order of integration for, 293
    properties of, 293–294
    rules for, 293
    Sum Rule for, 293
    terminology and notation of, 283–285
    Zero Rule for, 293
Degrees, radians *vs.*, 149(50), 159–160
Delta, 3, 584–586
Density, 391
Dependent variables, 13
Depreciation, 55(62)
Derivatives
    of arccosecant, 176–177
    of arccosine, 176–177
    of arccotangent, 176–177
    of arcsecant, 175–176
    of arcsine, 174–175
    of arctangent, 175
    of composite functions, 155–157
    of constant function, 118
    of cos (x^2), 163(77)
    of cosine function, 144
    from data, 151(65)
    definition of, 101–102
    discontinuous, 219
    in economics, 135–136
    of e^x, 180
    of exponential functions, 180–186
    functions, learning about from, 218–219
    functions with same, 206
    graphing, 103–106
    graph reading, 215
    higher order, 124–125, 167
    of hyperbolic functions, 592–594
    of integrals, 297
    Intermediate Value Theorem for, 115
    inverse function, 173–174
    on inverse graph, 174
    of inverse hyperbolic functions, 595–597
    left-hand, 106
    of logarithmic functions, 180–186
    of $\log_a x$, 183–184
    Mean Value Theorem for, 202
    notation, 103
    nth, 124–125
    numerical, 113–115
    one-sided, 106
    at point, 102
    relating, 155–156
    right-hand, 106
    second, 124–125
    of sin $2x$, 163(76)
    of sine functions, 143–144
    of trigonometric functions, 143–147
    of a^x, 181–182

Derivative test
first, for local extrema, 211–213
second, for local extrema, 216–218
Devil's Curve, 171(54)
Diagonals, 257(5)
Difference
common, 444
of like integer powers, 577
quotient, 90
symmetric, quotient, 113
Difference Rule
for definite integrals, 293
for differentiation, 119
of limits, 61, 71, 586
Differentiability, 111, 554
continuity and, 115
local linearity and, 112
Differentiable function, 101–102
discrete phenomenon modeled with, 230
rational powers of, 167–170
Differential equations, 329–331, 381(66)
calculator mode, 332
logistic, 376(35)
nonexact, 332
potpourri, 339(79)
second-order, 339(77), 339(78)
separable, 358
slope fields matched with, 332–333
solving, 339(75), 339(76)
Differentials, 241, 263(40), 342
estimate of change, 242
formulas for, 250(68)
integrals and, 296–298
Differentiation, 491(64)
Constant Multiple Rule for, 119
Difference Rule for, 119
implicit, 164–170
logarithmic, 190(63), 190(64)
of negative integer powers of *x*, 123–124
parameteric, 544
of polynomials, 120
Power Rule for, 118
power series by, 485–486
Product Rule, 121
Quotient Rule for, 122–123
rules for, 118–125
Sum Rule for, 119
term-by-term, 486
Direct comparison test, 515
proof of, 522(61), 522(62)
Directed line segment, 550
Direction angle, 550
of vector, 551
Direction vector, 552, 554
Discontinuity
infinite, 80, 470–472
in initial value problem, 330
jump, 80
oscillating, 80
point of, 79
removable, 80
Discontinuous derivatives, 219
Discontinuous integrable functions, 290–291
Discontinuous integrand, 290
Discrete phenomenon, 230
Displacement, 130, 386, 556–557

Distance
formula, 573(72)
modeling, 11(44)
from point to line, 12
total, traveled, 387
traveled, 556–557
traveled by projectile, 279(29)
traveled upstream, 278(18), 278(19)
Distribution function, 476
Divergence
improper integral test for, 472–473
*n*th term test for, 514
Divergent sequences, 447
Divergent series, 482
Domain, 44(61)
of function, 13
identifying, 15, 16
implied, 14
relevant, 14
Domination Rule, 293
Dot product, 560(64), 560(65)
DREW, CHARLES RICHARD (1904–1950), 276
Drug absorption, 55(63)
Dummy variable, 284
DÜRER, ALBRECHT, (1471–1528), 570
Dye concentration data, 275

E

e (the number), 25–26
Eight curve, 171
Ellipses
area of, 405(56)
circumscribing, 237(65)
horizontal, 581
implicit, 191(72)
normal line to, 166
parametrizing, 31, 34(36)
perimeter of, 548(36)
reflection properties, 582
tangent to, 166
vertical, 581
End behavior models, 73, 77(57), 172(66)
finding, 74–75
left, 74
right, 74
Endpoint convergence, 519–520, 523–533
Epsilon, 584–586
Equivalence, 551
Error bounds, 319, 528
alternating series, 504, 507
Error term, 505
EULER, LEONHARD (1707–1783), 13
Euler's Formula, 508–509
Euler's Method, 329–334
application of, 333–334
definition, 333
grapher program using, 334
for initial value problem, 333
Even functions, 16–17, 22(72), 142(49)
Even-odd decompositions, 599(65)
Even trigonometric functions, 46–47
Existence theorems, 202
Explicitly defined sequences, 443

Exponential change, law of, 359
Exponential decay, 24, 358–363
definition, 25
Exponential formulas, 341
Exponential functions, 459(61)
with base *a*, 23
definition, 23
derivatives of, 180–186
polynomial functions and, 465(40)
power functions and, 465(39)
Exponential growth, 23–24, 358–363
definition, 25
modeling with other bases, 361–362
Exponents, laws of, 577
Extreme values of functions
absolute, 193–195
classifying, 195
critical points without, 197
finding, 195–199
graphical methods, 198–199
local, 195
Extreme Value Theorem, 194

F

FERMAT, PIERRE DE (1601–1665), 89
Fermat's principle, 236(57)
FIBONACCI. *See* PISANO, LEONARDO
Fibonacci sequence, 451(56)
Finite limits, 70–71
Finite sequences, 443
Finite sums, 269–276
First derivative test for local extrema, 211–213
Floor function, 64
Fluid force, 429–430, 440(37), 440(38)
Fluid pressure, 429–430
Folium of Descartes, 171(55)
Foot-pound, 391
Force
constant, 391
in work, 427
FOURIER, JOSEPH (1768–1830), 284
Fractions
in algebra, 577
partial, 377(47), 468
FRANKLIN, BENJAMIN (1706–1790), 366(45)
Free-fall, 132
Function. *See also* Continuous functions; Exponential functions; Logarithmic functions; Polynomial functions; Trigonometric functions
absolute value, 18, 163(78), 341, 345
accumulator, 288
approximating, 263(39)
average value of, 294–295
bounded, 289
circle-area, 14
common logarithm, 40
composing, 19
composite, 18–19, 82, 155–157
constant, 118
constructing, 305
cosine, 144, 579
cubic, 201, 222(59)
cubic polynomial, 233(29)

decreasing, 204–205, 265(68)
definition, 13
denoting, 119
dependent variable, 13
derivatives and learning about,
    218–219
differentiable, 101–102, 167–170, 230
discontinuous integrable, 290–291
distribution, 476
domain of, 13
even, 16–17, 22(72), 142(49)
even trigonometric, 46–47
exponential, 23, 180–186, 459(61),
    465(39), 465(40)
extreme values of, 193–199
floor, 64
graphs of, 13, 305–306
greatest integer, 77(66)
hyperbolic, 592–597, 600(72)
identity, 37
implicitly defined, 164–166
increasing, 204–205
independent variable, 13
inverse, 38–39, 43(51), 44(62), 173–174,
    176–177
inverse hyperbolic, 594–597
inverse logarithmic, 353–354
inverse trigonometric, 48–50, 353
linear, 3–8
natural logarithm, 40
nonintegrable, 290
nonnegative, 299(9)
nonpositive, 299(10)
notation, 13
odd, 16–17, 22(72), 142(49)
odd trigonometric, 46–47
one-to-one, 36–37, 44(59)
parametric, 543–547
periodic, 46
piecewise-defined, 17–18, 117
polar, 561–571
power, 15, 465(39), 465(41)
probability density, 430–431
quartic polynomial, 222(60)
range of, 13
rational, 62
with same derivative, 206
series for representation of, 484–485
sine, 96, 143–144, 579
sine integral, 313(71)
velocity, 385–386
Fundamental identities, 579–580
Fundamental Theorem of Calculus
    antiderivative part, 302–305
    application of, 303–304
    with Chain Rule, 304
    evaluation part, 307–308
    for initial value problem, 330
    variable lower limits of integration, 304

G

Gabriel's horn, 474
General conics, 582
General linear equation, 6
Geometric mean, 163(79), 210(57)

Geometric progression, finite, 490(52)
Geometric sequences, 445–446
Geometric series, 481–484
    analyzing, 483
    convergent, 490(53)
    error, 507
Geometry, 234(41), 234(42)
    formulas, 578–579
    sequences and, 450(55)
GIBBS, J. WILLARD (1839–1903), 550
Global maximum values, 193
Global minimum values, 193
Golden Ratio, 448
GRAHAM, FAN CHUNG (1949-), 241
Grapher failure, 15–16, 83
Grapher precision, 460
Greatest integer function, 64
GREGORY, JAMES (1638–1675), 496
Ground speed, 553
Growth rates. *See also* Exponential growth
    of bacteria, 28(38)
    comparing, 461–462
    faster, 461
    L'Hospital's Rule for, 461
    limited, equations, 376(36)
    logistic, 369–375
    population, 27(19), 27(20), 43(48)
    same-rate, 461, 466(45)
    savings account, 23
    slower, 461
    transitivity of, 463

H

Half-life, 24, 27(21), 27(22), 363(22), 364(21)
    definition, 360
Harmonic series, 524
HARRIS, BERNARD A., JR. (1956-), 443
AL-HAYTHAM, ABU ALI AL-HASAN IBN
    (965–1040), 409
Head Minus Tail (HMT) Rule, 551
HEAVISIDE, OLIVER (1850–1925), 550
Hemisphere, volume of, 278(22), 418(73)
Higher order derivative, 124–125, 167
Hooke's Law, 391, 395(35), 395(36)
HOPPER, GRACE MURRAY (1906–1992),
    461
Horizontal asymptote, 70
Horizontal components, 555
Horizontal line test, 36
Horizontal tangent, 94(33), 94(34), 166, 191(77)
    finding, 120
HUYGENS, CHRISTIAAN (1629–1695), 546
Huygen's clock, 546
Hyperbolas, 34(43)
    horizontal, 581
    implicit, 190(71)
    reflection properties, 582
    vertical, 581
Hyperbolic cosecant, 592
Hyperbolic cosine, 510(24), 592
Hyperbolic cotangent, 592, 594
Hyperbolic functions, 600(72)
    background, 592
    definitions, 592
    derivatives, 593, 594

identities for, 592, 594
    inverse, 594–597
Hyperbolic secant, 592
Hyperbolic sine, 510(24), 592
Hyperbolic tangent, 592

I

Identities, 179(47), 580
    calculator conversion, 177
    fundamental, 579–580
    for hyperbolic functions, 592, 594
    inverse cofunction, 176–177
    inverse function, 176–177
    for inverse hyperbolic functions, 595
    trigonometric, 344–345
Identity function, 37
Implicit differentiation, 164–170
Implicit ellipses, 191(72)
Implicit hyperbolas, 190(71)
Implicitly defined functions, 164–166
Implicit parabolas, 191(73)
Implied domain, 14
Improper integrals, 430, 467–474
    for circumference, 473–474
    convergent, 467
    divergent, 467
    with infinite discontinuities, 471
    with infinite integration limits, 467
    L'Hospital's Rule for, 469
    partial fractions with, 468
    test for convergence, 472–473
    test for divergence, 472–473
Increasing functions, 204–205
Increments
    definition, 3
    of linear functions, 3–5
    ratios of, 4
Indefinite integrals
    definition, 340
    exponential formulas, 341
    of indefinite integrals, 341
    logarithmic formulas, 341
    power formulas of, 341
    substitution in, 342–344
    trigonometric formulas of, 341
Independent variables, 13
Indeterminate form, 452–454
Infinite discontinuities, 80, 470–472
    at endpoint, 472
    at interior point, 471
Infinite integration limits, 467
Infinite limits, 72–73
Infinite sequences, 443
Infinite series, 482
Infinite solid, volume of, 474
Inflation rate, 396(44)
Inflection points, 214–216, 501(35)
Initial point, 551
Initial ray, 562
Initial value problem, 329
    discontinuity in, 330
    Euler's Method for, 333
    Fundamental Theorem of Calculus
        for, 330
    solving, 350–351

Instantaneous rate of change, 91–92, 125, 130
  definition, 129
Instantaneous speed, 59–60
Instantaneous velocity, 130
Integral Evaluation Theorem, 307
Integrals. *See also* Definite integral
  bounds for, 294
  on calculator, 289–290
  companion, 593
  of constant function, 287
  definition, 284, 486
  derivatives of, 297
  differentials and, 296–298
  estimating, 539(64)
  evaluating, 284, 388
  form, 349–351
  improper, 430, 467–474
  indefinite, 340–344
  inverse hyperbolic functions and, 596
  nonelementary, 539
  of nonnegative functions, 299(9)
  of nonpositive functions, 299(10)
  routes to, 347(67)
  sign, 284, 340
  sine, function, 313(71)
  solving for unknown, 351–352
  tables, 377(46), 601–603
  test, 523
  unknown, 351–352
  volume as, 406–407
Integrand, 284, 340
  discontinuous, 290
  with infinite discontinuity, 470–472
Integration
  constant of, 348(77)
  lower limit, 284
  by parts formula, 349
  power series by, 486–488
  with respect to *y*, 400–401
  tabular, 352–353
  term-by-term, 487
  terminology and notation, 283–285
  upper limit, 284
  variable lower limits of, 304
  variable of, 284, 340
Interest
  compound, 25
  continuously compounded, 26, 359–360, 459(57)
Interior, 14
Intermediate Value Theorem, 115
Intersecting curves, 398–399
Intervals
  closed, 14
  of convergence, 483, 491, 514, 529–531
  infinite, 14
  open, 14
  Riemann sums, 282
  subintervals, 282
Inverse cofunction identities, 176–177
Inverse function, 38–39, 43(51), 44(62)
  derivatives, 173–174
  identities, 176–177
  slope relationship, 173
Inverse hyperbolic functions, 594
  derivatives of, 595–597

identities for, 595
integrals and, 596
Inverse logarithmic functions, 353–354
Inverses, 36
  of *f*, 37
  finding, 37–38
  graphing parametrically, 39
Inverse trigonometric functions, 48–50, 353

J

JACKSON, SHIRLEY ANN (1946-), 80
Jerk, 145–146
JOULE, JAMES PRESCOTT (1818–1889), 391
Joules, 391
Jump discontinuity, 80

K

Kinetic energy, 436(42)
Kissing Fish, 439(19)
KOWA, SEKI (1642–1708), 514

L

LAGRANGE, JOSEPH LOUIS (1736–1813), 202
Lagrange error
  bounds, 505
  formula, 507
Lagrange form, 505
Left end behavior models, 74
Left-hand derivative, 106
Left-hand endpoint Rectangular Approximation Method (LRAM), 272
Left-hand limits, 589
LEIBNIZ, GOTTFRIED WILHELM (1646–1716), 121
  proof of Product Rule, 128
Leibniz notation, 342
Leibniz's Theorem, 527
Lemniscate curves, 570
Length
  of astroid, 424(22)
  of cardioid, 573(75)
  of curves, 420–423
  of polar curve, 573(74)
  of sine wave, 420
  of smooth curve, 421–422
Lenses, 166
L'HOSPITAL, GUILLAUME DE (1661–1704), 452
L'Hospital's Rule, 459(58)
  first form, 452
  graphical exploration of, 454
  for growth rates, 461
  for improper integrals, 469
  indeterminate form, 452–458
  with one-sided limits, 454
  stronger form, 453
L'Hospital's trap, 459(60)
Lifting, 427–428
Limaçon curves, 564
  discovery of, 570
  in polar gallery, 570

Limited growth equation, 376(36)
Limits
  asymptotes and, 491(76)
  Constant Multiple Rule, 61, 71, 586
  definition of, 60–61, 584
  Difference Rule, 61, 71, 586
  finite, 70–71
  formal definition of, 583–589
  geometry and, 69(80)
  infinite, 72–73
  infinite integration, 467
  left-hand, 589
  nonexistent, 63
  one-sided, 63–64, 454
  Power Rule, 61, 71, 586
  Product Rule, 61, 71, 586, 587
  properties of, 60–63, 77(65), 99(54), 447–448, 586
  Quotient Rule of, 61, 71, 586, 588
  right-hand, 589
  seeing, 75
  of sequences, 447–448
  Squeeze theorem and, 589
  subsequences of, 491(75)
  Sum Rule, 61, 71, 586
  theorems, 586–589
  two-sided, 63–64, 589
  uniqueness of, 491(74)
  variable lower, of integration, 304
Linear approximation, 239–240, 248(41)
  standard, 238
Linear equations
  general linear equation, 6
  modeling, 5
  slope-intercept equation, 6
  solving, simultaneously, 8–9, 11(53)
Linear functions
  additional values of, 5
  applications of, 7–8
  definition, 4
  increments, 3–5
  point-slope equation of, 5–6
Linearization, 238, 312
  at inflection points, 501(35)
Linear motion, 385–387
Lines
  distance from point to, 12
  graphing, 32
  motion along, 130–135, 216
  normal, 91, 166
  parallel, 6–7
  parametrizing, 32–33, 35(48)
  perpendicular, 6–7
LIPET, 349
Local extreme values, 195
  first derivative test for, 211–213
  second derivative test for, 216–218
Local linearity, 148(40), 238
  differentiability and, 112
Local maximum value, 195
Local minimum value, 195
Logarithmic differentiation, 190(63), 190(64)
Logarithmic formulas, 341

Logarithmic functions
  applications, 41–42
  base *a*, 39
  common, 40
  comparing, 463
  derivatives of, 180–186
  inverse, 353–354
  natural, 40
  polynomial functions and, 465(42)
  power functions and, 465(41)
  properties of, 40–41
$\log_a x$, 183–184
Logistic differential equation, 376(35)
Logistic equation, 381(59)
Logistic growth, 369–375
Lower limit of integration, 284
LRAM. *See* Left-hand endpoint Rectangular
  Approximation Method

M

MACLAURIN, COLIN (1698–1746), 496
Maclaurin series, 519, 533
  convergence of, 505–506
  table of, 498–499
  Taylor series and, 495–498
MADHAVA (1340–1425), p. 496
Magnitude, vector, 550
Marginal cost, 136, 140(27)
  cost from, 313(73)
Marginal revenue, 136, 140(28)
  revenue from, 313(73)
Mathprint, 113
Maximum profit, 228
Max-min Inequality, 293
Max-min problems, 418(71)
  strategies for, 224
Mean, 431
  algebraic, 163(79)
  arithmetic, 210(58)
  geometric, 163(79), 210(57)
Mean Value Theorem
  Cauchy's, 460(71)
  consequences of, 205–207
  decreasing functions and, 204–205
  for definite integrals, 295–296
  for derivatives, 202
  increasing functions and, 204–205
  physical interpretation of, 204
  proof of, 210(63)
MENDEL, GREGOR JOHANN (1822–1884),
  135
MERCATOR, NICHOLAS (1620–1687),
  p. 496
Midpoint Rectangular Approximation Method
  (MRAM), 272, 326(53)
Monotonic, 204, 210(61)
Motion
  along circle, 261
  linear, 385–387
  along lines, 130–135, 216
  particle, 91, 190(70), 576(47), 576(48),
    576(49)
  planar, 553–554
  related, simulation, 255–256
  simple harmonic, 145

MRAM. *See* Midpoint Rectangular
  Approximation Method
Multiple-choice challenges, 169–170
Musical note frequency, 48, 51(23)

N

NAPIER, JOHN (1550–1617), 366(44)
Natural logarithm functions, 40
NDER. *See* Numerical derivatives
Necklace, 438(15)
Negative integer powers of *x*
  differentiation of, 123–124
  Power Rule for, 123
Net change
  accumulation and, 385–392
  from data, 390
  in velocity as Riemann sums, 388
NEWTON, SIR ISAAC (1642–1727), 297
Newton's law of cooling, 362–363
Newton's method, 245–246
  formula for, 250(71)
Newton's serpentine, 126(41)
NINT *f*, 305–306
Nondecreasing sequencing, 522(61)
Nonelementary integrals, 539
Nonexact differential equation, 332
Nonexistent limits, 63
Nonintegrable function, 290
Nonnegative functions, 299(9)
Nonnegative series, 515–516
Nonpositive functions, 299(10)
Normal line, 166
  to curve, 91
  definition of, 91
  to ellipses, 166
Normal probabilities, 430–432
  density, 431
  distribution function, 476
Norms, 282
*n*th derivative, 124–125
*n*th terms, 443
  test, 491(62), 514
Numerical approximations, 113
Numerical derivatives (NDER), 115
  computing, 113–114
  of *f*, 113
  of *f* at *a*, 113
Numerical methods, 334
Numerical values, 161(56), 161(58), 190(67)

O

OCHOA, ELLEN (1958-), 165
Odd functions, 16–17, 22(72), 142(49)
Odd trigonometric functions, 46–47
One-sided derivatives, 106
One-sided limits, 63–64
  L'Hospital's Rule with, 454
One-to-one functions, 36–37, 44(59)
Open intervals, 14
Optimization
  business and industry examples, 226–227
  economics examples, 227–228
  examples from mathematics, 224–225
  strategies for, 224

Orbit, circular, 560(62)
Order of integration, 293
ORESME, NICOLE (1320–1382), 269
Oresme's Theorem, 539(69)
Orthogonal curves, 161, 171(51)
  families, 188(64)
Orthogonal vectors, 559(59), 559(60)
Oscillating discontinuity, 80
Outside-inside rule, 157

P

Parabolas
  Archimedes area formula for,
    312(64)
  horizontal, 582
  implicit, 191(73)
  reflection properties, 582
  vertical, 581
Parabolic arc, 317
Parallel lines, 6–7
Parallelogram
  formulas, 579
  representation, 552
Parallel tangents, 209(50)
Parameter internal, 29
Parameters, 29
Parametric curves
  arc length of, 544–545
  concavity of, 544
  cycloids, 545–547
  definition, 29
  reviewing, 543
  slope of, 158, 544
Parametric differentiation formulas, 544
Parametric equations
  definition, 29
  of polar curves, 565
  relations, 29
Parametric functions, 543–547
Parametric graphing, 138(17)
Parametrization
  of circles, 30, 34(35)
  of curves, 29
  of ellipses, 31, 34(36)
  of lines, 32–33, 35(48)
Partial fractions, 377(47)
  improper integrals with, 468
Partial sums, 482
Particle motion, 91, 190(70), 576(47), 576(48),
  576(49)
Parts
  antidifferentiation by, 349–354
  formula for integration by, 349
PASCAL, BLAISE (1623–1662), 570
PASCAL, ETIENNE (1588–1651), 570
pdf. *See* Probability density function
Percentage change, 243–245
Percentage error, 338(63), 338(64)
Perigee, 561
Periodic function, 46
Periodicity, 46
Perpendicular lines, 6–7
Perpetuities, 539(65)
Piecewise-defined functions, 17–18
  graphing, 117

PISANO, LEONARDO aka FIBONACCI
   (1170–1250), 448
Planar motion, 553–554
Plane
   area in, 397–401
   vectors in, 550–557
Point of discontinuity, 79
Point-slope equation, 5–6
Polar coordinates, 561–563
   area, 567
   graphing with, 563
Polar curves, 563–565
   area enclosed by, 566–568
   length of, 573(74)
   parametric equations of, 565
   slopes of, 566
Polar functions, 561–571
Polar graphing, 564
Polar-rectangular conversion formulas,
   565
Pole, 562
Polonium-210, 364(26)
Polynomial functions, 62
   cubic, 233(29)
   exponential functions and,
      465(40)
   logarithmic functions and,
      465(42)
   quartic, 222(60)
Polynomials, differentiating, 120
Position vector, 550, 554
Power Chain Rule, 158–159
Power formulas, 341
Power functions, 15
   exponential functions and, 465(39)
   logarithmic functions and, 465(41)
Power Rule, 49
   for arbitrary real powers, 184
   for differentiation, 118
   of limits, 61, 71, 586
   for negative integer powers of
      x, 123
   for rational powers, 168
Power series, 481–488, 529
   centered, 484
   Convergence Theorem for, 514
   definition of, 484
   by differentiation, 485–486
Precalculus mathematics, 577–582
Pretty Print, 113
Probabilities, normal, 430–432, 476
Probability density function (pdf),
   430
   normal, 431
Product Rule, 49
   for differentiation, 121
   extended, 142(50)
   in integral form, 349–351
   Leibniz's proof of, 128
   of limits, 61, 71, 586, 587
Projectiles, 393(11)
Prolate cycloid, 548(42)
p-series, 524
Pumping, 428–429
   rates, 390
Pythagorean Theorem, 578

Q
Quadratic approximations, 250(68),
   510(27)
Quadratic Formula, 578
Quartic polynomial functions, 222(60)
Quotient Rule, 44(58), 49
   for differentiation, 122–123
   of limits, 61, 71, 586, 588
Quotients of infinite small quantities, 296

R
Radian measure, 45, 145
Radian mode, 44–45
Radians *vs.* degrees, 149(50), 159–160
Radioactive decay, 24–25, 43(46), 187(53),
   360
Radioactivity, 360–361
Radiocarbon dating, 2, 362
Radius of convergence, 513–520
Radon-222, 364(25)
RAM. *See* Rectangular Approximation
   Method
RAMANUJAN, SRINIVASA (1887–1920),
   509
Range, 44(61)
   finding, 152(77), 153(78)
   of function, 13
   identifying, 15, 16
Rational functions, 62
Rational powers
   of differentiable function, 167–170
   Power Rule for, 168
Ratio test, 516–518
Rectangles, 231(6)
   approximation by, 272
   changing dimensions in, 257(9)
   dimensions, 257(9)
   inscribing, 224–225, 264(51)
Rectangular Approximation Method (RAM),
   273, 280(40)
   Left-hand endpoint, 272
   Midpoint, 272
   Right-hand endpoint, 272
Rectangular coordinates, 562
Recursively defined sequences, 443
Reference triangles, 580
Reflection properties, 582
Regular partitions, 283
Related rates
   equations, 252
   related motion simulation, 255–256
   solution strategy, 252–255
Relative change, 243–245
Relative extrema, 195
Relevant domain, 14
Remainder Bounding Theorem,
   506–507
Remainder of order n, 505
Removable discontinuities, 80
Repeated linear factors, 377(47), 3
   78(48)
Revolution, solids of, 407–408, 459(59)
RIEMANN, GEORG FRIEDRICH
   (1826–1866), 281, 283

Riemann sums, 281, 391
   definite integral as limit of, 283
   for f on interval $[a, b]$, 282
   net change in velocity as, 388
   terms of, 285
Right end behavior models, 74
Right-hand derivative, 106
Right-hand endpoint Rectangular
   Approximation Method (RRAM), 272
Right-hand limits, 589
ROBERVAL, GILLES-PERSONNE (1602–
   1675), 570
ROLLE, MICHEL (1652–1719), 202
Rolle's Theorem, 202
   proof of, 210(62)
Roots, approximating, 240
Rose curves, 569
Rotation
   around axis, 409
   of curves, 573(67)
Rounding calculator values, 121
RRAM. *See* Right-hand endpoint Rectangular
   Approximation Method
Rule of 70, 56(66), 366(46)
Rule of 72, 366(46)

S
Savings account growth, 23
Scalar multiplication, 551, 552
Search algorithms, 466(43)
Second derivative, 124–125
   finding, implicitly, 167
Second derivative test for local extrema,
   216–218
Second-order differential equations, 339(77),
   339(78)
Sensitivity, 4, 92–93, 95(37), 95(38), 98(49),
   98(50)
   analysis, 242–243
   to change, 135–136
   definition of, 242
Separable differential equations, 358
Sequences
   arithmetic, 444–446
   convergent, 447
   defining, 443–444
   divergent, 447
   explicitly defined, 443
   Fibonacci, 451(56)
   finite, 443
   geometric, 445–446
   geometry and, 450(55)
   graphing, 446
   infinite, 443
   limit of, 447–448
   nondecreasing, 522(61)
   recursively defined, 443
   Squeeze Theorem for, 448
   tail of, 491(73)
Sequential search, 464, 466(44)
Series. *See also* Maclaurin series; Taylor series
   alternating, 504, 507, 527–528
   binomial, 502(45)
   convergent, 482, 490(53)
   divergent, 482

functions represented by, 484–485
geometric, 481–484, 490(53), 507
harmonic, 524
identifying, 488
infinite, 482
nonnegative, 515–516
power, 481–488, 514, 529
p-series, 524
telescoping, 520
Sigma notation, 281
Signed areas, 286
Simple harmonic motion, 145
SIMPSON, THOMAS (1720–1761), 317
Simpson's Rule, 317, 326(53)
   approximations, 319
Simultaneous mode, 44–45
Sine functions, 96, 579
   derivatives of, 143–144
Sine integral function, 313(71)
Sine wave, length of, 420
Sinusoid, 47, 52(49)
   slope of, 191(75)
sin *x*, Taylor series for, 493–494
68-95-99.7 Rule for Normal Distribution, 431, 440(42)
Slope
   of curve, 89–90
   definition, 4
   inverse function and, 173
   in parametric curves, 158, 544
   of polar curves, 566
   seeing, 331
   of sinusoid, 191(75)
Slope fields, 329–334
   constructing, 331, 336(28)
   differential equations matched with, 332–333
   for nonexact differential equation, 332
   perpendicular, 338(65), 338(66)
   plowing through, 338(67), 338(68)
   solutions through, 381(65)
Slope-intercept equation, 6
Smooth curve, 421–422
Smoothness, 421
Solids
   infinite, 474
   of revolution, 407–408, 459(59)
   twisted, 416(46)
   volume of, 407
Speed, 554–556
   average, 59–60
   definition, 131
   finding, 139(24)
   ground, 553
   instantaneous, 59–60
   instantaneous rate of change, 91–92
Sphere
   formulas, 579
   volume of, 94(29), 274–275
Spiral of Archimedes, 571
Square, completing, 578
Square-based pyramid, 407
Square cross sections, 407
Squeeze Theorem, 64–65, 71, 77(67)
   limits and, 589
   for sequences, 448

Standard deviation, 431
Standard linear approximation, 238
Stationary point, 196
Subintervals, 282
Subsequences of limits, 491(75)
Substitution
   antidifferentiation by, 340–346
   definite integral evaluation, 345
   in indefinite integrals, 342–344
   trigonometric, 341(82), 341(83), 341(84), 348(81)
   with trigonometric identity, 344–345
Summing areas, 490(50), 490(51)
Sum Rule
   for definite integrals, 293
   for differentiation, 119
   of limits, 61, 71, 586
Surface area, 257(2), 413, 599(70)
   estimation of, 248(50)
Symmetric difference quotient, 113
Symmetry
   about origin, 16–17
   about *x*-axis, 20
   about *y*-axis, 16–17

T

Tabular integration, 352–353
Tail-to-head representation, 552
Tangent, 162(69), 166, 579
   arc length, 426(39)
   to curve, 88–89
   to ellipses, 166
   horizontal, 94(33), 94(34), 166, 191(77)
   hyperbolic, 592
   line, 177
   parallel, 209(50)
   vertical, 96(48), 111, 422–423
TAYLOR, BROOK (1685–1731), 496
Taylor polynomial, 493, 498, 503–504
Taylor series, 492–500
   combining, 498–499
   constructing, 492–493
   for cos *x*, 493–494
   Maclaurin series and, 495–498
   for sin *x*, 493–494
Taylor's formula, 505
Taylor's Theorem, 503–509
   remainder in, 504–505
Telescoping series, 520
Temperature data, 51(24)
   average, 52(43), 52(44)
   finding, 380(53)
Term-by-term differentiation, 486
Term-by-term integration, 487
Terminal point, 29, 551
Terms
   definition, 443
   error, 505
   *n*th, 443, 491(62), 514
   of Riemann sums, 285
Three-petaled rose, 566
Tic-tac-toe method, 352
Time
   consumption over, 389
   geometry formulas for saving, 401

Torus, volume of, 418(74)
TRACE, 386, 446, 473
Transformations, 18, 34(44)
   trigonometric graphs, 47–49
Trapezoid, 579
Trapezoidal approximations, 314–316, 319
Trapezoidal rule, 314–315
   algorithms, 316–317
   error analysis, 318–319
Triangle
   angles and sides of, 580
   area of, 263(45)
   formulas, 578
   reference, 580
Trigonometric formulas, 579–580
   of indefinite integrals, 341
Trigonometric functions
   derivatives of, 143–147
   even, 46–47
   graphs of, 45–46
   inverse, 48–50, 353
   odd, 46–47
Trigonometric graphs, 47–49
Trigonometric identity, 344–345
Trigonometric substitution, 341(82), 341(83), 341(84), 348(81)
Truncation error, 503
   analyzing, 507–508
Tunnel construction, 424(24)
Twelve-petaled rose, 564
Twisted solids, 416(46)
Two-dimensional vectors, 550–551
Two-sided limits, 63–64, 589

U

Unit vector, 552
Unknown integrals, 351–352
Upper limit of integration, 284

V

Vector
   acceleration, 554
   addition, 551, 552
   calculus of, 554
   direction, 552, 554
   direction angle of, 551
   magnitude of, 550
   orthogonal, 559(59), 559(60)
   parallelogram representation, 552
   in plane, 550–557
   position, 550
   properties of operations, 553
   tail-to-head representation, 552
   unit, 552
   of velocities, 553, 554
Velocity, 207, 555–556
   average, 130
   function, 385–386
   graphs, 131–132
   instantaneous, 130
   net change in, 388
   resistance proportional to, 367(53)
   varying, 271
   vectors representing, 553–554

Vertical asymptote, 72
Vertical line test, 20(35)
Vertical tangent, 96(48), 111, 422–423
Volume, 440(39)
    of bowls, 417(52)
    of cones, 279(26)
    consistency of definitions, 418
    by cylindrical shells, 410–411
    of hemisphere, 278(22), 418(73)
    of infinite solid, 474
    as integral, 406–407
    slicing method for finding, 407
    of solid, 407
    of sphere, 94(29), 274–275

    of torus, 418(74)
    of water, 279(24), 279(25), 320(9)

W

Washer cross sections, 408
Water, volume of, 279(24), 279(25), 320(9)
WILKINS, J. ERNEST, JR (1923-2011), 363
Witch of Agnesi, 32, 35(47)
Work, 391–392
    force, 427
    lifting, 427–428
    pumping, 428–429

X

x-intercepts, 10(40)

Y

y-intercepts, 10(40)

Z

Zero, 577
Zero Rule, 293

Credits

Photographs

Photo locators denoted as follows: Top (T), Center (C), Bottom (B), Left (L), Right (R), Background (Bkgd)

COVER Jule Berlin/Shutterstock.

Page 2, Andrey Burmakin/Shutterstock; **Page 58,** Pavel Ilyukhin/Shutterstock; **Page 78,** Yang yu/Fotolia; **Page 94,** Jet Propulson Labs/NASA; **Page 100,** Jag_cz/Shutterstock; **Page 141,** PSSC Education Development Center, Inc; **Page 162,** Jenny Thomas/Pearson Science; **Page 165,** JSC/NASA; **Page 192,** Mikael Damkier/Shutterstock; **Page 209,** Photodisc/Getty Images; **Page 249,** NASA; **Page 268,** Tony Moran/Shutterstock; **Page 297,** Georgios Kollidas/Shutterstock; **Page 321,** Marshall Henrichs/Pearson Education; **Page 328,** Zentilia/Shutterstock; **Page 352,** Moviestore collection Ltd/Alamy; **Page 362,** Photodisc/Getty Images; **Page 368,** Digital Vision/Getty Images; **Page 384,** SeanPavonePhoto/Fotolia; **Page 429,** Bettmann/Corbis; **Page 442,** JPL-Caltech/NASA; **Page 443,** NASA; **Page 461,** Navy Visual News Service; **Page 464,** George Doyle/Stockbyte/Getty Images; **Page 480,** JWS/Fotolia; **Page 490,** Terry Oakley/Alamy; **Page 524,** Photodisc/Getty Images; **Page 542,** NASA.

Text

Page 52, "*Rocky Mountain Highs Weatherbase*" from www.weatherbase.com. **Page 95,** Exercise 39, Table 2.2, U.S. Exported Wheat "*Economic Research Service, Wheat Data Table 21.*" Data from the US Department of Agriculture; **Page 95,** Exercise 40, Table 2.3 National Defense Spending, "*Budget Authority by Function and Subfunction, Outlay by Function and Subfunction, Table 492.*" Data from the US Office of Management and Budget; **Page 99,** Table 2.4 Exercise 53, Population of Florida 2012 "*Statistical Abstract of the United States US Census Bureau.*" Data from the US Census Bureau; **Page 127,** Exercise 48, "*The Body's Reaction to Medicine,*" *Some Mathematical Models in Biology, Revised Edition*; **Page 131,** Example 2, "*Finding the Velocity of a Race Car,*" *Road and Track.* **Page 366,** Exercise 45, "*Benjamin Franklin's Will.*" Data from constitution.org; **Page 367,** Table 7.1, Exercise 55, Coasting to a Stop, "*Kelly Schmitzer Skating Data.*" Sourced from St. Francis de Sales High School.

Illustrations

Page 13, Leonard Euler. Pearson Education, Inc.; **Page 32,** Maria Agnesi. Pearson Education, Inc.; **Page 80,** Shirley Ann Jackson. Pearson Education, Inc.; **Page 87,** Marjorie Lee Browne. Pearson Education, Inc.; **Page 89,** Pierre de Fermat. Pearson Education, Inc.; **Page 105,** David H. Blackwell. Pearson Education, Inc.; **Page 121,** Gottfried Wilhelm Leibniz. Pearson Education, Inc.; **Page 241,** Fan Chung Graham. Pearson Education, Inc.; **Page 269,** Nicole Oresme. Pearson Education, Inc.;